U0544551

中国人民大学食品安全治理协同创新中心丛书

欧洲人权法院
判例指南（上卷）

Case-law Guides
of the European Court of Human Rights

陆海娜 | 主编

图书在版编目（CIP）数据

欧洲人权法院判例指南：上卷、下卷／陆海娜主编．—北京：知识产权出版社，2019.12
ISBN 978-7-5130-6670-9

Ⅰ.①欧… Ⅱ.①陆… Ⅲ.①人权的国际保护—审判—案例—欧洲 Ⅳ.①D998.2

中国版本图书馆 CIP 数据核字（2019）第 274338 号

责任编辑：齐梓伊　　　　　　　　　　责任印制：刘译文
执行编辑：雷春丽　　　　　　　　　　封面设计：韩建文

欧洲人权法院判例指南（上卷、下卷）

陆海娜　主编

出版发行：知识产权出版社有限责任公司	网　　址：http://www.ipph.cn
社　　址：北京市海淀区气象路 50 号院	邮　　编：100081
责编电话：010-82000860 转 8176	责编邮箱：qiziyi2004@qq.com
发行电话：010-82000860 转 8101/8102	发行传真：010-82000893/82005070/82000270
印　　刷：北京嘉恒彩色印刷有限责任公司	经　　销：各大网上书店、新华书店及相关专业书店
开　　本：787mm×1092mm　1/16	印　　张：62
版　　次：2019 年 12 月第 1 版	印　　次：2019 年 12 月第 1 次印刷
字　　数：1065 千字	定　　价：280.00 元（上下卷）
ISBN 978-7-5130-6670-9	

出版权专有　侵权必究
如有印装质量问题，本社负责调换。

前言
Preface

本书的缘起要归功于一位中国人民大学法学院派往欧洲人权法院实习的学生。这名聪明好学的实习生从斯特拉斯堡联系我,带来了欧洲人权法院希望与中国人民大学进一步合作的消息,即将法院已经在其官方网站发布的判例指南(case-guide)翻译成中文在我国出版。这样的期望当然是基于早已开始的中国人民大学法学院和中国人民大学人权研究中心与欧洲人权法院的愉快的合作经历。

《欧洲人权法院判例指南》选择并收录了欧洲人权法院对《欧洲人权公约》中所保护的十项具体权利或原则的相关判例的指南。指南是欧洲人权法院以各项公约权利或原则为中心,对相关经典判例作出的回顾和总结,以及对相关权利或原则涉及的方方面面的法律问题作出的权威解释。指南对欧洲人权法院自身具有指导性的作用,也促进了《欧洲人权公约》中各项权利的法理学发展。

本书涉及以下权利或原则:禁止蓄奴和强迫劳动,人身自由和安全权,获得公正审判的权利(民事部分),获得公正审判的权利(刑事部分),法无明文规定不得处罚,思想、良心和宗教自由,紧急状态下的克减,受教育权,自由选举权以及禁止集体驱逐外国人。

指南对学习欧洲人权法院的经典案例有指导性作用,能够帮助读者快速了解各项具体权利或法律原则的主要内容以及欧洲人权法院的最新评判标准。本书由欧洲人权法院授权中国人民大学法学院和中国人民大学人权研究中心将指南的英文原版翻译成中文。为了避免重复,本书涉及的每一项权利或原则之后所附的相关案例索引没有在中文部分进行翻译,读者可在英文部分阅读。本书的部分中文文本已经被欧洲人权法院官方网站收录,成为各项指南的官方中文译本。作为世界上先进的国际人权保护机制的监督机构,欧洲人权法院的判例对各国都具有较强的参考价值。我们期望本书有助于我国读者加深对人权法的理解,并成为人权法或宪法等专业学者和学生的好用的工具书。

本书能顺利出版首先要感谢时任中国人民大学法学院院长韩大元教授以及现任院长王轶教授的大力支持和关心。其次要感谢参与此书翻译和校对的中国人民大学法学院学生团队,他们是:郝万媛、姚青、张志远、王茜雯、黎梦、刘连炻、詹鹤飞、刘念、应尔寅、詹尉珍同学。此外要特别感谢承担了很多审校以及出版联络工作的郝万媛和王陈平同学。还要感谢中国人民大学法学院洪荞博士和张永老师给予的行政支持。最后当然要感谢知识产权出版社的雷春丽编辑对本书注入的努力、心血和耐心。

当然,由于本人能力有限,此书可能难免出现各种错误或瑕疵,真诚希望各位读者批评指正,以帮助我们未来做得更好。

陆海娜

中国人民大学法学院副教授

中国人民大学人权研究中心秘书长

2019年2月26日

于中国人民大学明德法学楼

目 录
Contents

上 卷

第一章 《欧洲人权公约》第4条适用指南 禁止蓄奴和强迫劳动 / 1

读者须知 / 3

第一节 一般性规则 / 4

 一、第4条的结构 / 4

 二、解释的规则 / 5

 三、人口贩卖的特殊情况 / 5

第二节 禁止蓄奴和强迫劳动 / 6

 一、免予被蓄奴或奴役的自由 / 6

 二、免予强迫或强制劳动的自由 / 8

 三、范围限制 / 10

第三节 国家的积极义务 / 14

 一、建立适当的立法和行政体系的义务 / 14

 二、采取保护措施的义务 / 15

 三、进行调查的程序性义务 / 16

援引案例一览 / 18

Chapter I Guide on Article 4 of the European Convention on Human Rights Prohibition of Slavery and Forced Labour / 19

Note to readers / 21

Ⅰ. General principles / 22

    A. Structure of Article 4 / 22

    B. Principles of interpretation / 23

    C. Specific context of human trafficking / 24

Ⅱ. The prohibition of slavery and forced labour / 25

    A. Freedom from slavery or servitude / 25

    B. Freedom from forced or compulsory labour / 27

    C. Delimitations / 30

Ⅲ. Positive obligations / 35

    A. The positive obligation to put in place an appropriate legislative and administrative framework / 36

    B. The positive obligation to take operational measures / 37

    C. The procedural obligation to investigate / 38

List of cited cases / 40

第二章 《欧洲人权公约》第5条适用指南 人身自由和安全权 / 43

读者须知 / 45

第一节 适用范围 / 46

    一、剥夺人身自由 / 46

    二、适用标准 / 46

    三、监狱中采取的措施 / 47

    四、对乘飞机者进行安检 / 48

    五、正式逮捕或拘留之外剥夺人身自由 / 48

    六、剥夺他人自由的积极义务 / 48

第二节 第5条第1款下拘留的合法性 / 49

    一、第5条的目的 / 49

    二、符合国内法 / 49

    三、对遵循国内法的审查 / 49

    四、一般规则 / 50

五、法律确定性原则 / 50

六、禁止任意行为 / 51

七、法院指令 / 51

八、对决定的论证以及对非任意的要求 / 52

九、可接受的程序瑕疵 / 52

十、延迟执行释放指令 / 53

第三节　第5条第1款下授权剥夺人身自由的情形 / 53

一、定罪后监禁 / 53

二、不遵守法院指令或法律义务的拘留 / 55

三、还押候审 / 57

四、对未成年人的拘留 / 59

五、基于社会和医疗原因的拘留 / 60

六、拘留外国人 / 62

第四节　被剥夺人身自由的人应该得到的保障 / 65

一、拘留理由(第5条第2款) / 65

二、被立即送交法官的权利(第5条第3款) / 67

三、在合理的时间内得到审判或者在审判期间获得释放的权利(第5条第3款) / 71

四、要求法庭迅速审查拘留合法性的权利(第5条第4款) / 75

五、因非法拘留得到赔偿的权利(第5条第5款) / 80

援引案例一览 / 82

Chapter II Guide on Article 5 of the Convention Right to Liberty and Security / 83

Note to readers / 85

Ⅰ. Scope of application / 87

A. Deprivation of liberty / 87

B. Criteria to be applied / 88

C. Measures adopted within a prison / 89

D. Security checks of air travellers / 89

E. Deprivation of liberty outside formal arrest and detention / 90

F. Positive obligations with respect to deprivation of liberty / 90

Ⅱ. Lawfulness of the detention under Article 5 § 1 / 91

    A. Purpose of Article 5 / 91

    B. Compliance with national law / 91

    C. Review of compliance with national law / 92

    D. General principles / 92

    E. The principle of legal certainty / 92

    F. No arbitrariness / 94

    G. Court order / 95

    H. Reasoning of decisions and the requirement of non-arbitrariness / 95

    I. Some acceptable procedural flaws / 96

    J. Delay in executing order of release / 97

Ⅲ. Authorised deprivations of liberty under Article 5 § 1 / 97

    A. Detention after conviction / 97

    B. Detention for non-compliance with a court order or legal obligation / 100

    C. Detention on remand / 102

    D. Detention of a minor / 105

    E. Detention for medical or social reasons / 106

    F. Detention of a foreigner / 110

Ⅳ. Guarantees for persons deprived of liberty / 113

    A. Information on the reasons for arrest (Article 5 § 2) / 113

    B. Right to be brought promptly before a judge (Article 5 § 3) / 116

    C. Right to trial within a reasonable time or to be released pending trial (Article 5 § 3) / 121

    D. Right to have lawfulness of detention speedily examined by a court (Article 5 § 4) / 127

    E. Right to compensation for unlawful detention (Article 5 § 5) / 134

List of cited cases / 137

第三章 《欧洲人权公约》第6条适用指南 获得公正审判的权利（民事部分） / 151

读者须知 / 153

第一节　适用范围:"公民权利和义务"的概念 / 155
　　一、公约第 6 条第 1 款的一般适用条件 / 155
　　二、对其他争端形式的延伸适用 / 159
　　三、公约第 6 条对非主体诉讼程序的可适用性 / 161
　　四、被排除的争端事项 / 163
第二节　获得法院审判的权利 / 164
　　一、获得法院审判的权利 / 165
　　二、放弃权利 / 169
　　三、法律援助 / 170
第三节　制度要求 / 172
　　一、"审判机构"的概念 / 172
　　二、由法律所确立 / 179
　　三、独立和公正 / 180
第四节　程序要求 / 187
　　一、公平 / 187
　　二、公开审讯 / 204
　　三、诉讼期间 / 209
援引案例一览 / 215

Chapter Ⅲ　Guide on Article 6 of the European Convention on Human Rights Right to A Fair Trial(Civil Limb) / 217

Note to readers / 219
　Ⅰ. Scope:the concept of "civil rights and obligations" / 221
　　A. General requirements for applicability of Article 6 § 1 / 221
　　B. Extension to other types of dispute / 227
　　C. Applicability of Article 6 to proceedings other than main proceedings / 230
　　D. Excluded matters / 231
　Ⅱ. Right to acourt / 234
　　A. Right and access to a court / 234

B. Waiver / 240

C. Legal aid / 241

Ⅲ. Institutional requirements / 243

A. Concept of a "tribunal" / 243

B. Establishment by law / 254

C. Independence and impartiality / 256

Ⅳ. Procedural requirements / 266

A. Fairness / 266

B. Public hearing / 289

C. Length of proceedings / 295

List of cited cases / 304

第四章 《欧洲人权公约》第 6 条适用指南 获得公正审判的权利（刑事部分）/ 325

读者须知 / 327

第一节 适用范围："刑事指控"的概念 / 328

一、一般原则 / 329

二、一般原则的适用 / 330

第二节 向法院申诉的权利 / 334

一、限制 / 334

第三节 一般保障：制度要求 / 337

一、"审判机构"的概念 / 337

二、依法设立的审判机构 / 338

三、独立性和公正性 / 339

第四节 一般保障：程序要求 / 345

一、公正 / 345

二、公开审讯 / 356

三、合理的时间 / 359

第五节 具体保障 / 363

一、第 6 条第 2 款：无罪推定 / 363

二、第6条第3款：辩方的权利 / 368

第六节　第6条的域外效力 / 385

一、公然违背公正 / 386

二、"真实的风险"：审查标准和证明责任 / 387

援引案例一览 / 388

Chapter Ⅳ　Guide on Article 6 of the European Convention on Human Rights Right to A Fair Trial(Criminal Limb) / 389

Note to readers / 391

Ⅰ. Scope: the notion of "criminal charge" / 393

A. General principles / 393

B. Application of the general principles / 395

Ⅱ. Right of access to a court / 400

A. Limitations / 400

Ⅲ. General guarantees: institutional requirements / 404

A. The notion of a "tribunal" / 404

B. Tribunal established by law / 405

C. Independence and impartiality / 407

Ⅳ. General guarantees: procedural requirements / 415

A. Fairness / 415

B. Public hearing / 432

C. Reasonable time / 437

Ⅴ. Specific guarantees / 442

A. The presumption of innocence (Article 6 § 2) / 442

B. The rights of the defence (Article 6 § 3) / 449

Ⅵ. Extra-territorial effect of Article 6 / 474

A. Flagrant denial of justice / 474

B. The "real risk": standard and burden of proof / 476

List of cited cases / 477

下 卷

第五章　《欧洲人权公约》第 7 条适用指南　法无明文规定不得处罚：罪刑法定原则 / 497

读者须知 / 499

第一节　引言 / 500

第二节　范围 / 500

　一、"认定有罪"的概念 / 500

　二、"刑事犯罪"的概念 / 501

　三、"法律"的概念 / 501

　四、"刑罚"的概念 / 502

第三节　罪刑法定原则 / 506

　一、可获得性 / 508

　二、可预见性 / 508

第四节　刑法的法不溯及既往原则 / 513

　一、总体考量 / 513

　二、持续犯 / 515

　三、累犯 / 515

第五节　较轻刑罚的溯及原则 / 516

第六节　第 7 条第 2 款：文明国家所认可的一般法律原则 / 517

第七节　欧洲人权法院在违反公约第 7 条的案件中所指示的措施 / 518

援引案例一览 / 519

Chapter Ⅴ　Guide on Article 7 of the European Convention on Human Rights No Punishment Without Law: the Principle that Only the Law Can Define A Crime and Prescribe A Penalty / 521

Note to readers / 523

　Ⅰ. Introduction / 524

Ⅱ. Scope / 525

    A. The concept of "finding of guilt" / 525

    B. The concept of "criminal offence" / 525

    C. The concept of "law" / 526

    D. The concept of a "penalty" / 527

Ⅲ. Principle that only the law can define a crime and prescribe a penalty / 533

    A. Accessibility / 535

    B. Foreseeability / 535

Ⅳ. Principle of non-retroactivity of criminal law / 543

    A. General considerations / 543

    B. Continuing offences / 545

    C. Recidivism / 546

Ⅴ. Principe of the retroactivity of the lighter penalty / 547

Ⅵ. Article 7 § 2: the general principles of law recognised by civilised nations / 548

Ⅶ. Measures indicated by the Court in cases of violation of Article 7 of the Convention / 549

List of cited cases / 551

第六章 《欧洲人权公约》第 9 条适用指南 思想、良心和宗教自由 / 557

读者须知 / 559

第一节 引言 / 560

第二节 基本原则及其适用 / 562

    一、第 9 条在民主社会的重要性以及在宗教团体的法定地位 / 562

    二、第 9 条保护的信仰 / 562

    三、有信仰的权利以及表达信仰的权利 / 566

    四、国家的消极和积极义务 / 571

    五、第 9 条与公约其他条款规定的重叠之处 / 575

第三节 第 9 条保护的行为 / 577

一、消极方面 / 577

二、积极方面 / 582

三、宗教自由和迁徙自由 / 601

第四节 国家作为宗教自由保卫者的义务 / 604

一、消极义务：不妨碍宗教组织正常运作的义务 / 604

二、消极义务：尊重宗教组织的自治权 / 622

三、积极义务 / 633

援引案例一览 / 643

Chapter Ⅵ　Guide to Article 9 Freedom of Thought, Conscience and Religion / 645

Notice to readers / 647

Ⅰ. Introduction / 648

Ⅱ. General principles and applicability / 651

1. The importance of Article 9 of the convention in a democratic society and the locus standi of religious bodies / 651

2. Convictions protected under Article 9 / 652

3. The right to hold a belief and the right to manifest it / 656

4. Negative and positive obligations on the State / 663

5. Overlaps between the safeguards of Article 9 and the other convention provisions / 669

Ⅲ. Actions protected under article 9 / 672

1. Negative aspect / 672

2. Positive aspect / 680

3. Freedom of religion and immigration / 708

Ⅳ. The state's obligations as garantor of freedom of religion / 713

1. Negative obligations: obligation not to impede the normal functioning of religious organisations / 713

2. Negative obligations: respect for the autonomy of religious organisations / 740

3. Positive obligations / 758

Index of cited cases / 772

第七章 《欧洲人权公约》第 15 条适用指南 紧急状态下的克减 / 789

读者须知 / 791

第一节 基本原则 / 792

第二节 第 15 条第 1 款：缔约国何时能正当克减 / 793

  一、"战时或者其他威胁国家生存的公共紧急状态" / 793

  二、"情况的紧急性所严格要求的范围内" / 795

  三、"只要上述措施不与其根据国际法的规定所应当履行的其他义务相抵触" / 797

第三节 第 15 条第 2 款：不可克减的权利 / 798

第四节 第 15 条第 3 款：告知的要求 / 799

援引案例一览 / 801

Chapter Ⅶ Guide on Article 15 of the European Convention on Human Rights Derogation in Time of Emergency / 803

Note to readers / 805

Ⅰ. General principles / 806

Ⅱ. Article 15 § 1: when a State may validly derogate / 807

  A. "…war or other public emergency threatening the life of the nation…" / 808

  B. "…measures … strictly required by the exigencies of the situation…" / 810

  C. "… provided that such measures are not inconsistent with ［the High Contracting Party's］ other obligations under international law" / 812

Ⅲ. Article 15 § 2: non-derogable rights / 813

Ⅳ. Article 15 § 3: the notification requirements / 815

List of cited cases / 817

第八章 《欧洲人权公约》第一议定书第 2 条适用指南　受教育权 / 819

读者须知 / 821

第一节　基本原则 / 822

　　一、第一议定书第 2 条的结构 / 822

　　二、第一议定书第 2 条的含义和适用范围 / 822

　　三、解释的原则 / 823

第二节　受教育权 / 824

　　一、受教育权的原则 / 824

　　二、受教育权的限制 / 825

　　三、教育方面的歧视 / 828

第三节　尊重家长的权利 / 831

　　一、适用范围 / 831

　　二、免修课程的可能性 / 832

　　三、明显的宗教标志 / 833

援引案例一览 / 835

Chapter Ⅶ　Guide on Article 2 of Protocol No. 1 to the European Convention on Human Rights Right to Education / 837

Note to readers / 839

Ⅰ. General principles / 840

　　A. Structure of Article 2 of Protocol No. 1 / 840

　　B. Meaning and scope of Article 2 of Protocol No. 1 / 840

　　C. Principles of interpretation / 841

Ⅱ. Right to education / 842

　　A. Principle of the right to education / 842

　　B. Restrictions on access to education / 844

　　C. Discrimination in access to education / 848

Ⅲ. Respect for parental rights / 852

A. Scope / 852
　　　B. Possibility of exemption / 853
　　　C. Conspicuous religious symbols / 856
　List of cited cases / 858

第九章　《欧洲人权公约》第一议定书第 3 条适用指南　自由选举权 / 863

读者须知 / 865

第一节　基本原则 / 866

　一、含义和范围 / 866

　二、解释原则 / 867

第二节　积极方面:选举权 / 869

　一、公民权的丧失 / 869

　二、关于囚犯的特定案件 / 870

　三、居住与选举权的关系 / 872

第三节　消极方面:被选举权 / 875

　一、被选举权的剥夺和民主秩序 / 876

　二、历史环境的重要性 / 877

　三、组织选举 / 878

　四、其他的合法性目的 / 882

　五、"从竞选活动……" / 883

　六、"……到行使职权" / 885

第四节　选举争议 / 886

援引案例一览 / 889

Chapter Ⅸ　Guide on Article 3 of Protocol No. 1 to the European Convention on Human Rights Right to Free Elections / 891

Note to readers / 893

　Ⅰ. General principles / 894

      A. Meaning and scope ／ 894

      B. Principles of interpretation ／ 896

  Ⅱ. Active aspect: the right to vote ／ 898

      A. Loss of civil rights ／ 899

      B. Specific case of prisoners ／ 900

      C. Residence, condition of access to voting rights ／ 903

  Ⅲ. Passive aspect: the right to stand for election ／ 907

      A. Inability to stand for election and the democratic order ／ 909

      B. Importance of historical context ／ 910

      C. Organisation of elections ／ 912

      D. Other legitimate aims ／ 917

      E. From the election campaign... ／ 920

      F. ...to the exercise of office ／ 921

  Ⅳ. Electoral disputes ／ 924

List of cited cases ／ 928

第十章　《欧洲人权公约》第四议定书第4条适用指南　禁止集体驱逐外国人 ／ 935

读者须知 ／ 937

第一节　第4条的起源与宗旨 ／ 938

第二节　"集体驱逐"的定义 ／ 938

第三节　属人范围的适用："外国人"的定义 ／ 939

第四节　属地规则的适用及管辖问题 ／ 939

第五节　集体驱逐的案例 ／ 940

第六节　不属于集体驱逐的情况 ／ 942

第七节　与公约第13条的关系 ／ 943

援引案例一览 ／ 945

Chapter Ⅹ　Guide on Article 4 of Protocol No. 4 to the European Convention on Human Rights Prohibition of Collective Expulsions of Aliens / 947

　Note to readers / 949
　Ⅰ. Origins and purpose of the Article / 950
　Ⅱ. The definition of "collective expulsion" / 950
　Ⅲ. The personal scope of application: the definition of "aliens" / 952
　Ⅳ. Questions of territorial applicability and jurisdiction / 952
　Ⅴ. Examples of collective expulsions / 954
　Ⅵ. Examples of measures not amounting to collective expulsions / 956
　Ⅶ. Relationship with Article 13 of the Convention / 958
　List of cited cases / 960

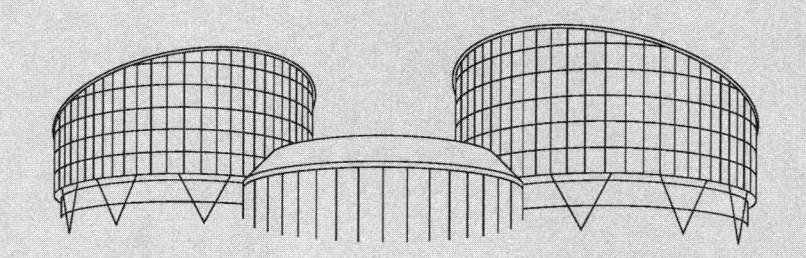

EUROPEAN COURT OF HUMAN RIGHTS
COUR EUROPÉENNE DES DROITS DE L'HOMME

第一章 《欧洲人权公约》第4条适用指南
禁止蓄奴和强迫劳动

读者须知

本指南是欧洲人权法院(以下简称"本法院""欧洲法院""斯特拉斯堡法院")出版的公约指南系列的一部分,旨在让执业律师了解斯特拉斯堡法院作出的基本判决。本指南分析和汇总了截至2014年6月30日的关于《欧洲人权公约》(以下简称《公约》《欧洲公约》)第4条的判例法。读者可以从中发现本领域的基本原则和相关判例。

援引的判例法从具有指导性的、重要的以及最新的判决中挑选得出。

本法院的判例不仅用于审判呈交至本法院的案件,而且从更为一般的意义上用于阐释、捍卫和发展《欧洲人权公约》创立的各项规则,并以此促使各缔约国对之加以遵守(Ireland v. the United Kingdom,1978年1月18日,§154,Series A no.25.)。因此,从普遍意义来说,《欧洲人权公约》确立的此机制的任务便是通过决定公共政策的各种问题来提升人权保护的标准,并在缔约国范围内推广人权法学(Konstantin Markin v. Russia [GC],30078/06,§89,ECHR 2012)。

第一节 一般性规则

> **第 4 条 禁止蓄奴和强迫劳动**
>
> "(1)不得将任何人蓄为奴隶或者是使其受到奴役。
>
> (2)不得要求任何人从事强制或者强迫劳动。
>
> (3)出于本条的目的考虑,本条的'强制或者强迫劳动'一词不应当包括:
>
> a. 在根据本公约第 5 条的规定而被监禁的正常程序中以及有条件地免除上述被监禁期间所必须完成的任何工作;
>
> b. 任何军事性质的劳役,或者是如果某些国家承认公民有出于良心拒绝服兵役的权利的,代替义务兵役的强制服务;
>
> c. 在紧急情况下或者是如果遇有威胁到社会生活或者安宁的灾祸时必须承担的服务;
>
> d. 作为普通公民义务的组成部分而承担的任何工作或者服务。"

一、第 4 条的结构

1. 公约第 4 条与第 2 条和第 3 条一起,规定了民主社会的基础性价值之神圣不可侵犯(*Siliadin v. France*,§112 and *Stummer v. Austria*[GC],§116)。

2. 第 4 条第 1 款要求不得将任何人蓄为奴隶或者是使其受到奴役。与公约中大部分实体性条款不同,第 4 条第 1 款不允许例外,也不允许削弱公约第 15 条第 2 款对于相关克减许可的规定,即便是处于威胁国家安全的紧急状态之中(*C. N. v. the United Kingdom*,§65;and *Stummer v. Austria*[GC],§116)。

3. 第 4 条第 2 款禁止强制或强迫性劳动(*Stummer v. Austria*,§116)。

4. 第 4 条第 3 款并不意味着限制第 2 款所确认的权利的行使,而是限制这项权利的内容,它与第 2 款构成了一个整体,说明了什么情况不包含在"强制或强迫性劳动"之中(*Stummer v. Austria*,§120)。在这种情况下,它就成为了解释第 2 款时的重要辅助条款。第 3 款中的 4 项内容,尽管涵盖了很多方面,但都是基于整体利益、社会稳定等这些很普遍的重要理念(*Van der Mussele v. Belgium*,§38;*Karlheinz Schmidt v. Germany*,§22;and *Zarb Adami v. Malta*,§44)。

二、解释的规则

5. 本法院从不将公约的条款视作在解释它所确立的权利和自由时的孤立参考体系。一直以来,公约条款适用中的一项主要原则就是不能在一个绝对封闭的内部体系中适用条款。作为一个国际条约,在对公约进行解释时,必须遵循1969年5月23日由《维也纳条约法公约》所确立的解释规则。在适用公约时,本法院应当查明这些词语在语境中的一般含义,并且依据它们所在条款的目标和目的进行解释。本法院必须考虑到,(公约)条款处在一个旨在有效保护个体人权的条约中,而且公约必须从一个整体角度去阅读和解释,以保持公约本身的连贯一致性以及不同条款间的协调。在解释时,还应当考虑适用于缔约方之间关系的相关规则和原则,同时也应当尽可能地与其他国际性法律规则保持协调。公约的目标和目的是作为一项保护个体人权的法律文件,这要求在解释和适用其条款时,要使公约的保障措施得以有效适用(*Rantsev v. Cyprus and Russia*,§§273-275)。

6. 在解释公约第 4 条时,本法院依据了诸如1926年《禁奴公约》(*Siliadin v. France*,§122)、《废止奴隶制、奴隶贩卖及类似奴隶制的制度与习俗补充公约》(*C. N. and V. v. France*,§90)、《国际劳工组织第 29 号公约》(《强迫劳动公约》)(*Van der Mussele v. Belgium*,§32)、《欧洲理事会反贩卖人口公约》和《联合国打击跨国有组织犯罪公约关于防止、禁止和惩治贩运人口特别是妇女和儿童行为议定书》(*Rantsev v. Cyprus and Russia*,§282)。

7. 公约的特征不容忽视,或者说,它作为一个正在使用中的法律文书,必然要求在对其进行解释时,参考当今的情况。保护人权及基本自由的标准不断提高,这也相应地且不可避免地要求对破坏民主社会基本价值的情况进行更严格的审查(*Siliadin v. France*,§121;and *Stummer v. Austria*,§118)。

三、人口贩卖的特殊情况

8. 第 4 条禁止"蓄奴""奴役"以及"强迫劳动",但并没有提到人口贩卖问题

(Rantsev v. Cyprus and Russia,§272)。

9. 从人口贩卖行为的性质以及它的剥削性而言,它是在进行与"所有权"相关的权力。它将人视为商品来买卖,强迫(被贩卖者)无偿或近乎无偿地在色情业或者其他行业劳动。它意味着受害者的行动是受约束的,他们的活动处于严密的监管之下,并通常包含了对在恶劣条件下生活和工作的受害者使用暴力和威胁的内容。人口贩卖在《反贩卖人口公约》附随解释报告中被描述为如同旧世界奴隶贸易的一种现代形式(*Rantsev v. Cyprus and Russia*,§281 and *M. and Others v. Italy and Bulgaria*,§151)。

10. 人口贩卖威胁到受害者作为人的尊严以及基本自由这一点是毫无疑问的。它与民主社会以及公约所阐述的价值是不相符的(*Rantsev v. Cyprus and Russia*,§282)。

11. 因此,本法院在解释公约时结合当今情况,认为有必要在特定情况下确认人口贩卖过程中是否存在构成对申请人进行"蓄奴""奴役"以及"强迫劳动"的行为(同上,§282)。本法院认为,加之《巴勒莫议定书》第3条以及《反贩卖人口公约》第4条a款的含义,人口贩卖本身应当属于公约第4条的适用范围(同上,and *M. and Others v. Italy and Bulgaria*,§151)。

第二节 禁止蓄奴和强迫劳动

一、免予被蓄奴或奴役的自由

> **第4条第1款**
> "不得将任何人蓄为奴隶或者是使其受到奴役。"

(一)奴隶

12. 在考虑第4条中"奴隶"一词的范围时,本法院参考了1926年《禁奴公约》中关于"奴隶"的经典定义:"奴隶是指被施加附属于所有权的任何或一切权力的人所处的状况或条件。"(*Siliadin v. France*,§122)

13. 在希莉亚丹诉法国案(Siliadin v. France)中,申诉人是一名18岁的多哥公民,她长达数年被迫当佣人,每天工作15个小时,而且没有休息日和薪水,法院认为她所遭受的这种对待虽然不属于奴隶,但依旧构成了奴役以及强迫和强制性劳动。虽然申诉人被剥夺了个人的人身自由,但她并没有被蓄为奴隶,因为针对她的行为并没有基于法律上所有权来降低她的人格使她成为一件物品。

14. 在最近的一件关于涉嫌贩卖年轻女孩的案件中,本法院也考虑到并没有充足的证据显示她被蓄为奴隶。即使假定申诉人的父亲从争议的婚姻中获得了一笔钱,但在本案中,这样的一笔钱并不能被认为构成了奴隶概念下所包含的所有权转移过程中的对价。在这一方面,本法院重申,婚姻根植于彼此不同的社会及文化内涵之中,因此这种支付金钱的行为有理由被作为一种在当今社会中很多不同文化中都存在的很普遍的行为,代表了一个家庭向另一个家庭的赠礼及接受(*M. and Others v. Italy and Bulgaria*,§161)。

(二)奴役

15. 从公约的目的考虑,"奴役"一词指因遭受胁迫而提供个人服务的一种义务,并与奴隶的概念有联系[*Siliadin v. France*,§124;and *Seguin v. France*(dec.)]。

16. 就奴役的概念而言,此处被禁止的是一种特别严重的对自由的否认。它包括了"除了为他人提供特定服务的义务之外,还有自己以他人的财产为生活依靠的义务以及改变所处条件的不可能性"(*Siliadin v. France*,§123)。

17. 本法院指出奴役是强迫或强制劳动的一种特别形式,换句话说,是加剧了的强迫或强制劳动。在本案中,依据第4条的含义将奴役与强迫或强制劳动区分的关键是受害人感受到他们的境遇不可能被改变以及没有改变的潜在可能性。本法院认为基于上述客观标准或自身境遇或生死由造成这种情形的人掌握的感觉就已经足够(来判断奴役的存在)(*C. N. and V. v. France*,§91)。

18. 家政奴役,不同于人口贩卖与剥削,是一种特殊的侵权行为。它包含了一种复杂的作用力,包括各种明显或者不明显的胁迫,以迫使(受害人)服从(*C. N. v. the United Kingdom*,§80)。

19. 在希莉亚丹诉法国案(*Siliadin v. France*)中,本法院认为申诉人处于一种被奴役的状态,是因为除了存在申诉人被要求提供强迫性劳力的事实之外,她是一个没有任何物力、财力、容易受到伤害的未成年人,并且与外界隔绝,除了她工作的那个使其备受宰割的家庭之外,她没有任何方法可以在其他地方生活,她完全地依附于雇主而没有任何活动自由以及自由时间(§§126-127)。也可参见 C. N. 和 V. 诉法国案(*C. N. and V. v. France*),本法院在此案中认为第一位申诉人被奴役而第二位申诉人没有被奴役(§§92-93)。

二、免予强迫或强制劳动的自由

> **第 4 条第 2 款**
> "不得要求任何人从事强制或者是强迫劳动。"

20. 公约第 4 条第 2 款禁止强迫或强制劳动(*Stummer v. Austria*,§116)。然而,第 4 条并没有定义什么是"强迫或强制劳动",而且,在众多的欧洲理事会与筹备公约工作相关的文件中,并没有发现关于这一点的任何指导性意见(*Van der Mussele v. Belgium*,§32)。

21. 在冯·德·穆塞尔案(*Van der Mussele v. Belgium*)中,本法院向《国际劳工组织第 29 号公约》(《强迫劳动公约》)寻求指导。出于公约的目的,"强迫或强制劳动"一词指以"惩罚相威胁,强使任何人从事其本人不曾表示自愿从事的所有工作和劳务"。本法院将这一定义作为解释公约第 4 条第 2 款的起点(*Van der Mussele v. Belgium*,§32;*Graziani-Weiss v. Austria*;*Stummer v. Austria*,§118)。

22. 英语的"劳动(labour)"一词确实常常以其狭义"体力劳动"来使用,但是它也承载了法语词汇"travail"的广泛含义,并且后一种在当前的语境下应当被采纳。本法院在包括第 29 号公约第 2 条第 1 款("*all work or service*""*tout travail ou service*")、《欧洲人权公约》第 4 条第 3 款 b 项("*any work or service*""*tout travail ou service*")以及活动并不仅仅局限于针对体力劳动范畴的国际劳工组织的名称(Organisation internationale du Travail)中都找到了佐证(*Van der Mussele v. Belgium*,§33)。

23. 为了阐明"劳动"一词在第 4 条第 2 款中的概念,本法院已经强调并非所有以"惩罚"相威胁而进行的劳动都必然地属于本条款所禁止的"强迫劳动"的范畴。工作的类型和工作量都是应该被考虑的因素。这些因素有助于区别"强迫劳动"与合理预期内为一起居住的人或家庭成员分担工作的助手工作。根据这些规则,本法院在冯·德·穆塞尔案(*Van der Mussele v. Belgium*)中使用了"不成比例的负担"的概念来决定法院指派律师免费进行辩护的行为是否属于强迫劳动(§39;同时参见 *C. N. and V. v.*

France, §74)。

24. 关于第一个形容词"强迫的(forced)",人们的第一反应是身体的或者精神的强迫。考虑到第二个形容词"强制的(compulsory)",它不应该仅仅指合法的强制或承担义务。例如,不能将依据自由协商拟定的合同来进行的工作划入第4条的范围之内,仅仅是因为合同一方与另一方着手工作、如果不信守合同承诺就会遭受惩罚(*Van der Mussele v. Belgium*,§34)。这里针对的是"以惩罚相威胁……强使"他人从事的工作,并且这种工作违背了当事人的意愿,当事人并非自愿来工作(同上)。

25. 本法院在一份于1999年国际劳工会议上发布的名为"强制的代价"的报告中注意到,"惩罚"这一概念是在广义范围内使用的,"任何惩罚"这一术语的使用可为其提供佐证。因此"惩罚"可能包含身体上的暴力或限制,但是也可能以更弱的形式进行,如心理上的惩罚,威胁将工作状态非法的受害人送去警察局或移民局(*C. N. and V. v. France*,§77)。

26. 关于首个标准,即"以任何惩罚相威胁"一词,本法院认为在冯·德·穆塞尔诉比利时案(*Van der Mussele v. Belgium*)中得到了体现。在本案中,申诉人是一名实习律师,他面临着律师协会将他的名字从实习名册中删除并且拒绝其律师注册申请的危险。同样的情形也出现在格拉亚-威斯诉奥地利案(*Graziani-Weiss v. Austria*)中。申诉人作为一名律师拒绝成为监护人,会面临纪律制裁;以及在 C. N. 和 V. 诉法国案(*C. N. and V. v. France*)中,当事人被威胁遣送回原国。

27. 在希莉亚丹诉法国案(*Siliadin v. France*)中,本法院考虑到虽然申诉人作为一名未成年人,并没有被"以惩罚相威胁",但基于她所感受到的作为一个孤身在异国的少女,非法进入法国领土所引发的威胁,以及可能被警察逮捕这一事实,可以认为她处在被强迫或强制劳动的状态中。她的恐惧不断滋生,而且她被促使相信她现在的状况会持续下去(§118)。

28. 关于第二个标准,即考虑申诉人是否自愿地进行工作(*Van der Mussele v. Belgium*,§36),本法院将考虑申诉人是否事先同意这份工作,但这并非决定性因素。

29. 鉴于公约第4条的目标,在考虑一项被要求实施的工作是否属于公约所禁止的"强迫或强制劳动"的范围时,本法院会考虑案件中的所有情形(*Van der Mussele v. Belgium*,§36;*Graziani-Weiss v. Austria*,§40)。在衡量特定职业工作者所负有的职责是否正常时,本法院所发展的标准中考虑了:这些工作是否在一般人所认为的正常职业活动范围之外；这些工作是否给付报酬或者是否包含了其他的补偿方式；这种义务是否是基于社会稳定性的要求；以及这种被施加的负担是否不成比例（*Graziani-Weiss v. Austria*，§38）。

30. 在雇员没有被给付报酬但工作是出于自愿并且关于报酬问题不存在争议[*Sokur v. Ukraine*（dec.）]，申诉人被调到一个报酬更少的工作岗位上[*Antonov v. Russia*（dec.）]，社会保障法令要求申诉人获取或接受任何劳动，而不论这种工作是否合适，是否会因她拒绝而引发她利益的减损[*Schuitemaker v. the Netherlands*（dec.）]，抑或申诉人作为一名公证员在为非盈利组织工作时被要求降低收费（*X v. Germany*, Commission decision of 13 December, 1979①）等案件中，本法院并没有发现违反公约第4条的情况。

三、范围限制

> **第 4 条第 3 款**
>
> "出于本条的目的考虑，本条的'强制或者强迫劳动'一词不应当包括：
>
> a. 在根据本公约第 5 条的规定而被监禁的正常程序中以及有条件地免除上述被监禁期间所必须完成的任何工作；
>
> b. 任何军事性质的劳役，或者是如果某些国家承认公民有对兵役良心拒绝的权力的，代替义务兵役的强制的服务；
>
> c. 在紧急情况下或者是如果遇有威胁到社会生活或者安宁的灾祸必须承担的服务；
>
> d. 作为普通公民义务的组成部分而承担的任何工作或者服务。"

31. 第 4 条第 3 款的作用是帮助解释第 2 款。第 3 款中的 4 个项虽然有所不同，但都服从于一般利益，社会团结以及什么是事务的正常状态这些主旨（*Van der Mussele v. Belgium*，§38；*Karlheinz Schmidt v. Germany*，§22；*Zarb Adami v. Malta*，§44）。

---

① 欧洲人权委员会（委员会），最初接受个人的诉请，在 1998 年 11 号议定书生效之后被废除。

（一）监禁及有条件释放期间的工作

32. 第 4 条第 3 款第 a 项表明，在一般的监禁过程中（Van Droogenbroeck v. Belgium，§59）或有条件释放期间完成的工作并不属于公约第 4 条第 3 款第 a 项中的"强迫或强制"劳动。

33. 在确定什么劳动可以被认为是"在一般的监禁过程中必须完成的工作"时，本法院参考了成员国践行的普遍标准（Stummer v. Austria［GC］，§128）。

34. 例如，当本法院在考虑一名累犯被要求工作，且对他进行有条件释放的前提是他通过工作赚到一定数量的钱时，虽然这一工作被认为是义务性的，但本法院认为因为本案中的情况符合第 4 条第 3 款的要求，所以并不违反公约第 4 条（Van Droogenbroeck v. Belgium，§59）。在本法院看来，这些工作并没有超出语境中"正常"的范围，因为这种工作是在帮助他改造自己重返社会，并且可以在欧洲理事会其他成员国中也找到相似的法律规定（Stummer v. Austria［GC］，§121；Van Droogenbroeck v. Belgium，§59；and De Wilde，Ooms and Versyp v. Belgium，§90）。

35. 关于囚犯的报酬及社会保障，委员会认为公约第 4 条并不涉及为囚犯给付工作报酬的问题。在这一方面，依据一贯的判例法，任何囚犯要求更高工作报酬的申诉都被视为不可受理而被拒绝（Stummer v. Austria［GC］，§122）。关于依据私人公司与监狱行政部门所订立的合同进行的工作，委员会认为第 4 条第 3 款是针对监狱劳动的问题，并不禁止国家订立这样的合同，或者包含表明囚犯的工作义务必须被限制在为监狱和国家工作的范围内的内容（Twenty-one detained persons v. Germany，Commission decision of 6 April，1968）。

36. 例如，在佛罗瑞诉罗马尼案（Floroiu v. Romania）中，本法院认为囚犯能够从事获得报酬的工作，如在监狱的日常运作中打下手，或者做一些没有报酬但可以使他们获得减刑的工作。在国内法下，囚犯在收到通知后能够在这两种工作之间进行选择。本法院意识到申诉人进行工作后为自己剩余的服刑期换来了很大的减刑期，因此他的工作并非完全无偿。因此他被要求进行的工作可以被视为"在一般监禁中所要求从事的工作"，符合公约第 4 条第 3 款第 a 项（§§35 – 37）的规定。

37. 最近，本法院被要求审查第 4 条是否要求国家将这些在进行工作的囚犯纳入社会保险的体系中，尤其是养老金的体系中。据显示，绝大部分缔约国已经通过某些方式将囚犯纳入社会保险的体系中并且为他们提供一些特殊的保险方案，但仅有略微过半的缔约国将囚犯纳入养老金的体系中。因此,奥地利法律反映出了欧洲法律在囚犯社会保障方面的发展,所有的囚犯都享有健康照料和意外护理,并且所有需要工作的囚犯都被纳入了失业保险的范围内,但是并没有被纳入养老金体系之内(*Stummer v. Austria*[GC],§131),因此可以认为在将从事工作的囚犯纳入养老金体系这个问题上并没有形成足够的统一。虽然《欧洲监狱规则》第26.17要求尽可能地要将从事工作的囚犯纳入国家社会保险系统中,这一条反映出了当前的发展趋势,但并不能被理解为公约第4条下的义务。所以,申诉人作为一名囚犯被要求进行义务性劳动且没有被纳入养老金体系之内,可以被视作公约第4条第3款第a项中的"在一般监禁的过程中所必须完成的工作"[同上,§132;*Floroiu v. Romania*(dec.),§32]。

(二)兵役及替代性服务

38. 第4条第3款将"任何军事性质的劳役,或者是如果某些国家承认公民有对兵役良心拒绝的权力的,代替义务兵役的强制的服务"排除在第4条第2款所禁止的"强迫或强制劳动"的范围之外(*Bayatyan v. Armenia*[GC],§100,*Johansen v. Norway*,Commission decision of 14 October,1985)。

39. 在W,X,Y和Z诉英国案(*W.,X.,Y. and Z. v. The United Kingdom*)中,申诉人在加入英国武装部队时还是未成年人,委员会认为申诉人所进行的劳役在第4条第3款限制条款的范围内,因此根据公约第4条第2款第b项的明文规定,任何关于此劳役构成"强迫或强制劳动"的申诉都因明显缺乏依据而被驳回(Commission decision of 19 July,1968)。

40. 委员会认为,虽然"奴役"和"强迫或强制劳动"在第4条中有所区分,但事实上它们一定会有重合之处,而不能被视为完全相等的,将军事性质的劳役排除在"强迫或强制劳动"的范围外,并不必然导致在任何情况下都将这些劳役排除在基于"蓄奴或奴役"禁止性规定的审查之外(*W.,X.,Y. and Z. v. The United Kingdom*,Commission decision of 19 July,1968)。委员会认为,一般来说,一名成年之后入伍的士兵所负有的遵守服役期、遵守随后对其自由和个人权利的限制规定的义务,并不构成"蓄奴或奴役"意义下的对权利的减损(同上)。申诉人在他们父母的同意下入伍,他们的不适龄并不能将"奴役"一词归结到正常的士兵身上(同上)。

41. 委员会的判例法在第9条和第4条第3款第b项之间建立了联系,认为第4条第3款将承认良心拒绝权利的选择留给了缔约国。因此,良心拒绝者被排除在了第9

条的保护范围之外,而第 9 条不能被解读为保证了当事人免予因拒绝服兵役而被起诉的自由(*Bayatyan v. Armenia*[GC],§99)。

42. 本法院认为,公约第 4 条第 3 款第 b 项既没有承认也没有排除良心拒绝权,因此并没有对第 9 条所保障的权利构成限制(同上,§100)。故而在这类案件中,第 9 条不应当再被解读为和第 4 条第 3 款第 b 项具有联系(同上,§109)。

(三)紧急状态或遇有灾祸时须承担的服务

43. 第 4 条第 3 款第 c 项将任何在紧急状态下或者是遇到威胁到社会生活或者安宁的灾祸时必须承担的服务排除在了强迫或强制劳动的范围之外。在这一方面,委员会认为一个狩猎权的享有者,作为抵御传染病行动的一部分,其承担积极参与向狐狸洞施放毒气活动的义务——即使这项义务在强制劳动的范围之内,也依旧满足了第 4 条第 3 款第 b 项,在紧急情况下或者是如果遇有威胁到社会生活或者安宁的灾祸必须承担的服务;或第 4 条第 3 款第 c 项,作为普通公民义务的组成部分而承担的任何工作或者服务(*S. v. the Federal Republic of Germany*,Commission decision of 4 October,1984)。在这一案件中,申诉人在挪威北部承担了一年的公共牙科服务,委员会中有两人认为这项服务是由于当事人处在威胁到社会安宁的紧急状态下而应承担的合理服务,并不是强迫或强制劳动(*Iversen v. Norway*,Commission decision of 17 December,1963)。

(四)普通公民义务

44. 第 4 条第 3 款第 d 项将作为普通公民义务的组成部分而承担的任何工作或者服务排除在强迫或强制劳动的范围之外(*Van der Mussele v. Belgium*,§38)。

45. 在冯·德·穆塞尔案(*Van der Mussele*)中,本法院接受了申诉人作为一名实习律师因缺少报酬和花费报销而遭受损失这一观点,但这种损失同时也给他带来了一些好处,并且并没有表明存在过分之处。有报酬的工作同样有可能会被认为构成强迫或强制劳动,所以在衡量什么是成比例的以及什么属于行业中常见处理方式时,缺少报酬及花费报销成为了需要考虑的相关因素。在本案中,申诉人并没有被施加过分的工作负担,并且他因本案所产生的花费相对很小,因此本法院认为,根据公约第 4 条第 2 款的目的,本案并不存在强制劳动的情形(*Van der Mussele v. Belgium*,§§34-41)。

46. 最近,本法院出于第 4 条第 2 款目的的考虑,确定医生参与紧急医疗服务的义务并不构成强制或强迫劳动,并且宣布申诉的其他相关部分明显缺乏依据,因此不予受理[*Steindel v. Germany*(dec.)]。在此案中,本法院认为以下因素特别相关:(1)这些工作是有偿的,并且没有超出一名医生正常职业活动的范围;(2)本案中的这种义务是基于其职业及社会稳定性的要求而进行,并且是为了应对紧急情况;(3)申诉人被施加的负担并非不成比例。

47. 委员会和本法院认为,"作为普通公民义务而承担的任何工作或者服务"包括:强制的陪审工作(*Zarb Adami v. Malta*);强制的消防服务或为服务工作付款(*Karlheinz Schmidt v. Germany*);免费开展医疗体检的义务(*Paul Reitmayr v. Austria*);参加紧急医疗救助的义务(*Steindel v. Germany*);公司为雇员计算、扣取税款及缴纳社保款项等义务(*Four companies v. Austria*, Commission decision of 27 September, 1976)。

48. 然而,以上对于强制劳动的限制包含了对工作的正常形式的考虑。正常的工作或者劳动也有可能因为群体或个体基于歧视性因素从事这些工作而变得不正常。因此在一些案件中,本法院基于第4条的目的考虑,认为并没有强迫或强制劳动的存在,但这并不意味着争议事实就完全不在第4条,以及由第4条引出的第14条的保护范围之内(*Van der Mussele v. Belgium*, §43; *Zarb Adami v. Malta*, §45)。例如,在施加公民义务时,任何男女间性别的歧视都会违反公约第4条和第14条(*Zarb Adami v. Malta*, §83; *Karlheinz Schmidt v. Germany*, §29)。

第三节 国家的积极义务

49. 在希莉亚丹诉法国案(*Siliadin v. France*)中,本法院指出,在公约的一些特定条文下,如第2条、第3条和第8条,国家仅仅克制自己不去侵犯这些条文所保障的权利已经不足以履行其在公约第1条下的义务(§77)。在这一方面,仅仅将符合公约要求的范围局限在国家的直接侵犯上,是与当前有关此问题的国际法律文书中的规定不符的,并且会使这一条规定变得无效(*Siliadin v. France*, §89)。因此,本法院认为国家在公约第4条之下负有积极的作为义务。

一、建立适当的立法和行政体系的义务

50. 第4条要求缔约国应当有效地处罚或者起诉任何将他人蓄为奴隶、奴役他人以及强迫或强制他人的行为(*C. N. v. the United Kingdom*, §66; *Siliadin v. France*, §112;

and *C. N. and V. v. France*,§105)。为了履行这一义务,缔约国应建立立法和行政体系,以禁止和惩处此类行为(*Rantsev v. Cyprus and Russia*,§285)。

51. 在人口贩卖这一特殊背景下,法院强调《巴勒莫议定书》和《反贩卖人口公约》指出有必要采取措施全面打击人口贩卖,例如,除了惩罚人口贩卖行为外,采取预防人口贩卖与保护受害人的措施。这两部文书的条款明确,且缔约国(基本包含了欧洲委员会的所有成员国)认为只有将这三个方面措施结合才能有效打击人口贩卖。因此,本法院强调起诉并惩罚人口贩卖行为人只是成员国履行打击人口贩卖义务的一个方面。第4条下的积极义务必须在更广的范围内被考量。

52. 在此情形下,本法院认为,一国立法中的系列保障措施必须为人口贩卖中受害人或潜在受害人的权利提供充分、实用且有效的保障。因此,除了刑法上惩罚人贩子的措施之外,第4条还要求缔约国规制经常掩护人口贩卖的商业活动。此外,一国移民法还必须应对那些鼓励、助长或容忍贩卖人口的情况(*Rantsev v. Cyprus and Russia*,§285)。同时,公约还要求国家为负责法律实施和移民的部门提供相关的培训(*Rantsev v. Cyprus and Russia*,§287)。

53. 在希莉亚丹诉法国案(*Siliadin v. France*,§148)、C. N. 和 V. 诉法国案(*C. N. and V. v. France*,§108)、C. N. 诉英国案(*C. N. v. the United Kingdom*)等案件中,本法院认为法国国内当时的立法并没有为申诉人针对公约第4条所禁止的遭遇提供实用且有效的保护(§76)。而在若瑟诉塞浦路斯和俄罗斯案(*Rantsev v. Cyprus and Russia*)中,基于此前的证据并且考虑到俄罗斯法院对本案这种特殊情况的管辖权限制,本法院认为俄罗斯在针对人口贩卖问题建立立法和行政体系方面并不存在不足之处(§§301-303)。在此案中,因为除了证实塞浦路斯境内人口贩卖活动的证据,以及一些报告中指出的其移民政策及立法缺陷鼓励了将妇女贩卖至塞浦路斯的情况外,塞浦路斯的演员签证制度也没有为若瑟女士提供实用且有效的保护(§§290-293)。

二、采取保护措施的义务

54. 在某些特定的情况下,公约第4条可能会要求国家采取一些具有操作性的措施保护违反第4条的行为侵害的受害者或者潜在受害者(*Rantsev v. Cyprus and Russia*,§286,*C. N. v. the United Kingdom*,§67)。为了在特定情形中履行这一义务、采取相关措施,有一点必须说明的是,基于可靠的怀疑,国家应该知道或者应当已经知道一个身份确认的人已经面临遭受违反公约第 4 条的行为的侵害的即刻现实风险。如果有关当局没有在他们的权力范围内将此人从这种境遇和危险中解救出来,那么就会构成对公约的违反(同上)。

55. 承担义务的同时还需要考虑维护现代社会治安中存在的困难,并考虑优先次序和所占用社会资源时必须做出的操作性选择。采取保护措施的义务必须被理解为,此项义务不为有关当局加诸不可能或不适当的负担(Rantsev v. Cyprus and Russia,§287)。

56. 在若瑟诉塞浦路斯和俄罗斯案(Rantsev v. Cyprus and Russia)中,警方的一系列失败行为,尤其是在调查若瑟女士是否被贩卖、决定将她交给 M. A(申诉人的哥哥)照管,以及在执行一系列国内法等方面的失败行为,让本法院认为塞浦路斯当局未能成功地采取措施保护申诉人的女儿约瑟女士。

57. 在 V. F. 诉法国案(V. F. v. France)中,考虑到贩卖尼日利亚妇女至法国的规模以及这些人所遭遇到的经历,如证明自身身份向当局寻求保护,本法院能够指出的是,在本案这种情况下,申诉人没有尝试联系有关当局告诉他们自己当前的情况。因此,可以得出这样的观点:申诉人提交的证据并不足以证明警方在决定驱逐她出境时知道或应当知道她是人口贩卖网络中的一名受害者。

三、进行调查的程序性义务

58. 公约第 4 条要求当存在可靠怀疑认为个人享有的权利被侵犯时,国家应该承担进行调查的程序性义务(C. N. v. the United Kingdom,§69 and Rantsev v. Cyprus and Russia,§288)。

59. 本法院强调,进行调查的要求并不是建立在受害者或其直系亲属的控诉之上,而是政府一旦注意到相关的情况就必须自己采取行动。本法院还确认,这项调查义务必须是有效的,必须与牵涉于相关事件中的人保持独立,并且必须足以去判断和惩罚责任人,这是一项对方式进行要求而非对结果进行要求的义务。另外,公约要求所有案件都受到立即且合理的处理。但当存在将个人从这种糟糕境遇中解救出来的可能性时,国家必须将相关调查作为一项紧急事务来进行。最后,国家必须将受害人或其近亲属置于保障其法律权益所必要的程序范围之内(Rantsev v. Cyprus and Russia,§288)。

60. 在人口贩卖的特殊背景下,除了对发生在领土上的此类事件展开调查的义务之外,缔约国在跨国人口贩卖的案件中还有责任对发生在其领土之外的人口贩卖活动与其他相关国家进行有效合作(*Rantsev v. Cyprus and Russia*,§289)。

61. 在若瑟诉塞浦路斯和俄罗斯案(*Rantsev v. Cyprus and Russia*)中,本法院认为,在调查涉嫌将若瑟小姐贩卖至塞浦路斯的个人或组织在俄罗斯境内运作的可能性时,俄罗斯政府的行动很失败(同上,§308)。而在M等人诉意大利和保加利亚案(*M. and Others v. Italy and Bulgaria*)中,本法院认为本案的情况不足以构成人口贩卖,并且不足以让保加利亚政府对发生在那里的任何人口贩卖活动承担责任(§169)。在本案中,本法院还认为,保加利亚政府对申诉人提供了帮助并且与意大利政府保持了联系(同上)。

援引案例一览

本指南援引的判例法涉及欧洲人权法院的判决或裁定以及欧洲人权委员会的决定或报告。

除非另行指明，所有参考皆是本法院审判庭依法做出的判决。缩写"（dec.）"是指该处援引为本法院裁定，"[GC]"是指该案件由大审判庭审判。

本指南电子版中援引案例的超链接直接跳转 HUDOC 数据库（http://hudoc.echr.coe.int）。该数据库提供本法院（包括大审判庭、审判庭和委员会的判决、裁定和相关案例、咨询意见以及案例法信息注解中的法律总结）、委员会（决定和报告）和部长委员会（决议）的判例法。

本法院以英语和/或法语这两种官方语言发布判决和裁定。HUDOC 也包含许多重要案例的近 30 种非官方言语的翻译，以及由第三方制作的大约 100 个在线案例汇总的链接。

（注：为了避免重复，本章所附的相关案例索引没有在中文部分进行翻译，读者可在对应的英文部分阅读。）

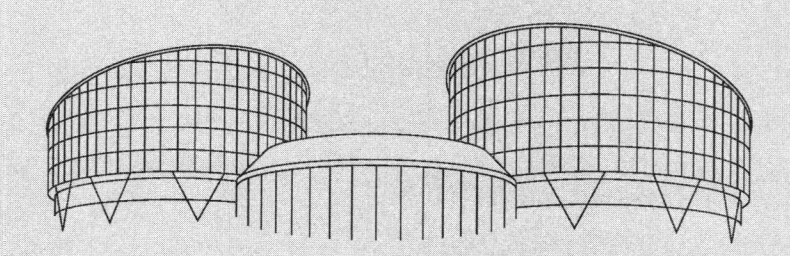

EUROPEAN COURT OF HUMAN RIGHTS
COUR EUROPÉENNE DES DROITS DE L'HOMME

Chapter I   Guide on Article 4 of the
European Convention on Human Rights
Prohibition of Slavery and Forced Labour

2nd edition–2014

COUNCIL OF EUROPE

CONSEIL DE L'EUROPE

Publishers or organisations wishing to reproduce this report (or a translation there of) in print or online are asked to contact publishing@echr.coe.int for further instructions.

This guide has been prepared by the Research and Library Division within the Directorate of the Jurisconsult and does not bind the Court. The first edition of this guide was published in December 2012. The manuscript for this second edition has been updated to 30 June 2014; it may be subject to editorial revision.

The document is available for downloading at ⟨www.echr.coe.int⟩ (Case-Law-Case-Law Analysis-Case-Law Guides).

For publication updates please follow the Court's Twitter account at ⟨https:/twitter.com/echrpublication⟩.

©Council of Europe/European Court of Human Rights, 2014

Note to readers

This guide is part of the series of Case-Law Guides published by the European Court of Human Rights(hereafter "the Court", "the European Court" or "the Strasbourg Court") to inform legal practitioners about the fundamental judgments delivered by the Strasbourg Court. This particular guide analyses and sums up the case-law on Article 4 of the European Convention on Human Rights(hereafter "the Convention" or "the European Convention") until 30 June 2014. Readers will find the key principles in this area and the relevant precedents.

The case-law cited has been selected among the leading, major, and/or recent judgments and decisions. *

The Court's judgments serve not only to decide those cases brought before the Court but, more generally, to elucidate, safeguard and develop the rules instituted by the Convention, thereby contributing to the observance by the States of the engagements undertaken by them as Contracting Parties(*Ireland v. the United Kingdom*, 18 January 1978, § 154, Series A no. 25.). The mission of the system set up by the Convention is thus to determine, in the general interest, issues of public policy, thereby raising the standards of protection of human rights and extending human rights jurisprudence throughout the community of the Convention States(*Konstantin Markin v. Russia* [GC], no. 30078/06, § 89, ECHR 2012).

---

* The case-law cited may be in either or both of the official languages(English and French) of the Court and the European Commission of Human Rights. Unless otherwise indicated, all references are to a judgment on the merits delivered by a Chamber of the Court. The abbreviation "(dec.)" indicates that the citation is of a decision of the Court and "[GC]" that the case was heard by the Grand Chamber.

I. General principles

> Article 4 of the Convention-Prohibition of slavery and forced labour
> "1. No one shall be held in slavery or servitude.
> 2. No one shall be required to perform forced or compulsory labour.
> 3. For the purpose of this article the term 'forced or compulsory labour' shall not include:
> (a) any work required to be done in the ordinary course of detention imposed according to the provisions of Article 5 of[the] Convention or during conditional release from such detention;
> (b) any service of a military character or, in case of conscientious objectors in countries where they are recognised, service exacted instead of compulsory military service;
> (c) any service exacted in case of an emergency or calamity threatening the life or well-being of the community;
> (d) any work or service which forms part of normal civic obligations."

A. Structure of Article 4

1. Article 4 of the Convention, together with Articles 2 and 3 of the Convention, enshrines one of the fundamental values of democratic societies(*Siliadin v. France*, § 112; *Stummer v. Austria*[GC], § 116).

2. Article 4 § 1 of the Convention requires that "no one shall be held in slavery or servitude". Unlike most of the substantive clauses of the Convention, Article 4 § 1 makes no provision for exceptions and no derogation from it is permissible under Article 15 § 2 even in the event of a public emergency threatening the life of the nation(*C. N. v. the United Kingdom*, § 65; *Stummer v. Austria*[GC], § 116).

3. Article 4 § 2 of the Convention prohibits forced or compulsory labour(ibid.).

4. Article 4 § 3 of the Convention is not intended to "limit" the exercise of the right guaranteed by paragraph 2, but to "delimit" the very content of that right, for it forms a whole with paragraph 2 and indicates what the term "forced or compulsory labour" is not to include(ibid., § 120).

B. Principles of interpretation

5. The Court has never considered the provisions of the Convention as the sole framework of reference for the interpretation of the rights and freedoms enshrined therein. It has long stated that one of the main principles of the application of the Convention provisions is that it does not apply them in a vacuum. As an international treaty, the Convention must be interpreted in the light of the rules of interpretation set out in the Vienna Convention of 23 May 1969 on the Law of Treaties. Under that Convention, the Court is required to ascertain the ordinary meaning to be given to the words in their context and in the light of the object and purpose of the provision from which they are drawn. The Court must have regard to the fact that the context of the provision is a treaty for the effective protection of individual human rights and that the Convention must be read as a whole, and interpreted in such a way as to promote internal consistency and harmony between its various provisions. Account must also be taken of any relevant rules and principles of international law applicable in relations between the Contracting Parties and the Convention should so far as possible be interpreted in harmony with other rules of international law of which it forms part. The object and purpose of the Convention, as an instrument for the protection of individual human beings, requires that its provisions be interpreted and applied so as to make its safeguards practical and effective (*Rantsev v. Cyprus and Russia*, §§ 273 – 275).

6. In interpreting the concepts under Article 4 of the Convention, the Court relies on international instruments such as the 1926 Slavery Convention(*Siliadin v. France*, § 122), Supplementary Convention on the Abolition of Slavery, the Slave Trade and Institutions and Practices Similar to Slavery(*C. N. and V. v. France*, § 90), ILO Convention No. 29(Forced Labour Convention)(*Van der Mussele v. Belgium*, § 32) and Council of Europe Convention

on Action against Trafficking in Human Beings and the Protocol to Prevent, Suppress and Punish Trafficking in Persons, especially Women and Children supplementing the United Nations Convention against Transnational Organised Crime, 2000 (*Rantsev v. Cyprus and Russia*, § 282).

7. Sight should not be lost of the Convention's special features or of the fact that it is a living instrument which must be interpreted in the light of present-day conditions, and that the increasingly high standard being required in the area of the protection of human rights and fundamental liberties correspondingly and inevitably requires greater firmness in assessing breaches of the fundamental values of democratic societies (*Siliadin v. France*, § 121; *Stummer v. Austria*[GC], § 118).

C. Specific context of human trafficking

8. Article 4 makes no mention of trafficking, proscribing "slavery", "servitude" and "forced and compulsory labour" (*Rantsev v. Cyprus and Russia*, § 272).

9. Trafficking in human beings, by its very nature and aim of exploitation, is based on the exercise of powers attaching to the right of ownership. It treats human beings as commodities to be bought and sold and put to forced labour, often for little or no payment, usually in the sex industry but also elsewhere. It implies close surveillance of the activities of victims, whose movements are often circumscribed. It involves the use of violence and threats against victims, who live and work under poor conditions. It is described in the explanatory report accompanying the Anti-Trafficking Convention as the modern form of the old worldwide slave trade (ibid., § 281; *M. and Others v. Italy and Bulgaria*, § 151).

10. There can be no doubt that trafficking threatens the human dignity and fundamental freedoms of its victims and cannot be considered compatible with a democratic society and the values expounded in the Convention (*Rantsev v. Cyprus and Russia*, § 282).

11. Thus, the Court, having regard to its obligation to interpret the Convention in light of present-day conditions, considers it unnecessary to identify, in the specific context of human trafficking, whether the treatment about which an applicant complains constitutes "slavery", "servitude" or "forced and compulsory labour" (ibid., § 282). It considers that

trafficking itself, within the meaning of Article 3 (a) of the Palermo Protocol and Article 4 (a) of the Anti-Trafficking Convention, falls within the scope of Article 4 of the Convention (ibid. ; *M. and Others v. Italy and Bulgaria*, § 151).

II. The prohibition of slavery and forced labour

A. Freedom from slavery or servitude

> **Article 4 § 1 of the Convention**
> "1. No one shall be held in slavery or servitude.
> ..."

1. Slavery

12. In considering the scope of "slavery" under Article 4, the Court refers to the classic definition of slavery contained in the 1926 Slavery Convention, which defines slavery as "the status or condition of a person over whom any or all of the powers attaching to the right of ownership are exercised" (*Siliadin v. France*, § 122).

13. In *Siliadin v. France*, where the applicant, an eighteen years old Togolese national, was made to work as a domestic servant fifteen hours a day without a day off or pay for several years, the Court found that the treatment suffered by her amounted to servitude and forced and compulsory labour, although it fell short of slavery. It held that, although the applicant was, cleary deprived of her personal autonomy, she was not held in slavery as there was no genuine right of legal ownership over her, thus reducing her to the status of an "object" (§ 122).

14. In a recent case concerning alleged trafficking of a minor girl, the Court also considered that there was not sufficient evidence indicating that she was held in slavery. It held that, even assuming that the applicant's father received a sum of money in respect of

the alleged marriage, in the circumstances of that case, such a monetary contribution could not be considered to amount to a price attached to the transfer of ownership, which would bring into play the concept of slavery. In this connection, the Court reiterated that marriage has deep-rooted social and cultural connotations which may differ largely from one society to another and that therefore this payment can reasonably be accepted as representing a gift from one family to another, a tradition common to many different cultures in today's society (*M. and Others v. Italy and Bulgaria*, § 161).

2. Servitude

15. For Convention purposes "servitude" means an obligation to provide one's services that is imposed by the use of coercion, and is to be linked with the concept of slavery (*Seguin v. France*(dec.); *Siliadin v. France*, § 124).

16. With regard to the concept of "servitude", what is prohibited is "particularly serious form of denial of freedom". It includes "in addition to the obligation to perform certain services for others…the obligation for the 'serf' to live on another person's property and the impossibility of altering his condition"(ibid., § 123).

17. The Court noted that servitude was a specific form of forced or compulsory labour, or, in other words, "aggravated" forced or compulsory labour. In fact, the fundamental distinguishing feature between servitude and forced or compulsory labour within the meaning of Article 4 of the Convention lies in the victims' feeling that their condition is permanent and that the situation is unlikely to change. The Court finds it sufficient that this feeling be based on the above-mentioned objective criteria or be brought about or kept alive by those responsible for the situation(*C. N. and V. v. France*, § 91).

18. In this connection, the Court underlined that domestic servitude is a specific offence, distinct from trafficking and exploitation and which involves a complex set of dynamics, involving both overt and more subtle forms of coercion, to force compliance(*C. N. v. the United Kingdom*, § 80).

19. In *Siliadin v. France* the Court considered that the applicant was held in servitude because, in addition to the fact that the applicant was required to perform forced labour, she was a minor with no resources, vulnerable and isolated with no means of living elsewhere

than the home where she worked at their mercy and completely depended on them with no freedom of movement and no free time(§§ 126 – 127). See also *C. N. and V. v. France*, where the Court found the first applicant to be held in servitude but not the second applicant (§§ 92 – 93).

B. Freedom from forced or compulsory labour

Article 4 § 2 of the Convention

" ...

2. No one shall be required to perform forced or compulsory labour.

... "

---

20. Article 4 § 2 of the Convention prohibits forced or compulsory labour(*Stummer v. Austria*[GC], § 117). However, Article 4 does not define what is meant by "forced or compulsory labour" and no guidance on this point is to be found in the various Council of Europe documents relating to the preparatory work of the European Convention(*Van der Mussele v. Belgium*, § 32).

21. In the case of *Van der Mussele v. Belgium* the Court had recourse to ILO Convention No. 29 concerning forced or compulsory labour. For the purposes of that Convention the term "forced or compulsory labour" means "all work or service which is exacted from any person under the menace of any penalty and for which the said person has not offered himself voluntarily". The Court has taken that definition as a starting point for its interpretation of Article 4 § 2 of the Convention (ibid. ; *Graziani-Weiss v. Austria*; *Stummer v. Austria*[GC], § 118).

22. It is true that the English word "labour" is often used in the narrow sense of manual work, but it also bears the broad meaning of the French word "*travail*" and it is the latter that should be adopted in the present context. The Court finds corroboration of this in the definition included in Article 2 § 1 of ILO Convention No. 29("all work or service", "*tout travail ou service*" in French), in Article 4 § 3(d) of the European Convention("any

work or service", "*tout travail ou service*" in French) and in the very name of the International Labour Organization(Organisation internationale du Travail), whose activities are in no way limited to the sphere of manual labour(*Van der Mussele v. Belgium*, § 33).

23. In order to clarify the notion of "labour" within the meaning of Article 4 § 2 of the Convention, the Court has underlined that not all work exacted from an individual under threat of a "penalty" is necessarily "forced or compulsory labour" prohibited by this provision. Factors that must be taken into account include the type and amount of work involved. These factors help distinguish between "forced labour" and a helping hand which can reasonably be expected of other family members or people sharing accommodation. Along these lines, in the case of *Van der Mussele v. Belgium* the Court made use of the notion of a "disproportionate burden" to determine whether a lawyer had been subjected to compulsory labour when required to defend clients free of charge as a court-appointed lawyer(§ 39;see also *C. N. and V. v. France*, § 74).

24. The first adjective "forced" brings to mind the idea of physical or mental constraint. As regards the second adjective "compulsory", it cannot refer just to any form of legal compulsion or obligation. For example, work to be carried out in pursuance of a freely negotiated contract cannot be regarded as falling within the scope of Article 4 on the sole ground that one of the parties has undertaken with the other to do that work and will be subject to sanctions if he does not honour his promise(*Van der Mussele v. Belgium*, § 34). What there has to be is work "exacted … under the menace of any penalty" and also performed against the will of the person concerned, that is work for which he "has not offered himself voluntarily"(ibid.).

25. The Court noted that in the global report "The cost of coercion" adopted by the International Labour Conference in 1999, the notion of "penalty" is used in the broad sense, as confirmed by the use of the term "any penalty". It therefore considered that the "penalty" may go as far as physical violence or restraint, but it can also take subtler forms, of a psychological nature, such as threats to denounce victims to the police or immigration authorities when their employment status is illegal(*C. N. and V. v. France*, § 77).

26. The Court has found the first criteria, namely "the menace of any penalty", fulfilled

in *Van der Mussele v. Belgium* where the applicant, a pupil advocate, ran the risk of having the Council of the *Ordre des avocats* strike his name off the roll of pupils or reject his application for entry on the register of advocates(§ 35); in *Graziani-Weiss v. Austria* where the refusal of the applicant, a lawyer, to act as a guardian gave rise to disciplinary sanctions (§ 39); in *C. N. and V. v. France* where the applicant was threatened to be sent back to her country of origin(§ 78).

27. In *Siliadin v. France* the Court considered that, although the applicant, a minor, was not threatened by a "penalty", the fact remained that she was in an equivalent situation in terms of the perceived seriousness of the threat as she was an adolescent girl in a foreign land, unlawfully present on French territory and in fear of arrest by the police. Her fear was nurtured and she was led to believe that her status would be regularised(§ 118).

28. As to the second criteria, namely whether the applicant offered himself voluntarily for the work in question(*Van der Mussele v. Belgium*, § 36), the Court takes into account but does not give decisive weight to the element of the applicant's prior consent to the tasks required(ibid.; *Graziani-Weiss v. Austria*, § 40).

29. Rather, the Court will have regard to all the circumstances of the case in the light of the underlying objectives of Article 4 when deciding whether a service required to be performed falls within the prohibition of "forced or compulsory labour" [ibid., § 37; *Bucha v. Slovakia*(dec.)]. The standards developed by the Court for evaluating what could be considered normal in respect of duties incumbent on members of a particular profession take into account whether the services rendered fall outside the ambit of the normal professional activities of the person concerned; whether the services are remunerated or not or whether the service includes another compensatory factor; whether the obligation is founded on a conception of social solidarity; and whether the burden imposed is disproportionate [*Graziani-Weiss v. Austria*, § 38; *Mihal v. Slovakia*(dec.), § 64].

30. No issue was found to arise under Article 4 in cases where an employee was not paid for work done but the work was performed voluntarily and entitlement to payment was not in dispute [*Sokur v. Ukraine*(dec.)], where the applicant was transferred to a less lucrative employment[*Antonov v. Russia*(dec.)], where the social assistance act required

the applicant to obtain and accept any kind of labour, irrespective of the question whether it would be suitable or not, by reducing her benefits if she refused to do so[*Schuitemaker v. the Netherlands*(dec.)] or where the applicant, a notary, was required to receive reduced fees when acting for non-profit making organisations (*X. v. Germany*, Commission decision).

C. Delimitations

> Article 4 § 3 of the Convention
>
> "...
>
> 3. For the purpose of this article the term 'forced or compulsory labour' shall not include:
>
> (a) any work required to be done in the ordinary course of detention imposed according to the provisions of Article 5 of[the] Convention or during conditional release from such detention;
>
> (b) any service of a military character or, in case of conscientious objectors in countries where they are recognised, service exacted instead of compulsory military service;
>
> (c) any service exacted in case of an emergency or calamity threatening the life or well-being of the community;
>
> (d) any work or service which forms part of normal civic obligations."

31. Paragraph 3 of Article 4 serves as an aid to the interpretation of paragraph 2. The four subparagraphs of paragraph 3, notwithstanding their diversity, are grounded on the governing ideas of general interest, social solidarity and what is normal in the ordinary course of affairs(*Van der Mussele v. Belgium*, §38; *Karlheinz Schmidt v. Germany*, §22; *Zarb Adami v. Malta*, §44).

1. Work during detention or conditional release

32. Article 4 §3(a) indicates that the term "forced or compulsory" labour does not

include "any work to be done in the ordinary course of detention" (*Stummer v. Austria* [GC], § 119) or during conditional release from such detention.

33. In establishing what is to be considered "work required to be done in the ordinary course of detention", the Court will have regard to the standards prevailing in member States (ibid., § 128).

34. For example, when the Court had to consider work a recidivist prisoner was required to perform, his release being conditional on accumulating a certain amount of savings, while accepting that the work at issue was obligatory, the Court found no violation of Article 4 of the Convention on the ground that the requirements of Article 4 § 3(a) were met (*Van Droogenbroeck v. Belgium*, § 59). In the Court's view the work required did not go beyond what is "ordinary" in this context since it was calculated to assist him in reintegrating himself into society and had as its legal basis provisions which find an equivalent in certain other member States of the Council of Europe (ibid.; *Stummer v. Austria* [GC], § 121; *De Wilde, Ooms and Versyp v. Belgium*, § 90).

35. Regarding prisoners' remuneration, the Commission has held that Article 4 does not contain any provision concerning the remuneration of prisoners for their work (*Twenty-one detained persons v. Germany*, Commission decision; *Stummer v. Austria* [GC], § 122). The Court has noted that there have been subsequent developments in attitudes to this issue, reflected in particular in the 1987 and 2006 European Prison Rules, which call for the equitable remuneration of the work of prisoners [*Zhelyazkov v. Bulgaria*, § 36; *Floroiu v. Romania* (dec.), § 34]. However, it has considered that the mere fact that a prisoner was not paid for the work he did, did not in itself prevent work of this kind from being regarded as "work required to be done in the ordinary course of detention" (ibid., § 33).

36. For example, in *Floroiu v. Romania*, the Court observed that prisoners were able to carry out either paid work or, in the case of tasks assisting the day-to-day running of the prison, work that does not give rise to remuneration but entitles them to a reduction in their sentence. Under domestic law prisoners were able to choose between the two types of work after being informed of the conditions applicable in each case. The Court, having regard to the fact that the applicant had been granted a significant reduction in the time remaining to

be served found that the work carried out by the applicant was not entirely unpaid and that therefore the work performed by the applicant can be regarded as "work required to be done in the ordinary course of detention" within the meaning of Article 4 § 3 (a) of the Convention(§ § 35 – 37).

37. Recently, the Grand Chamber was called upon to examine the question whether Article 4 requires the State to include working prisoners in the social security system, notably, as regards the old-age pension system. It noted that while an absolute majority of Contracting States affiliate prisoners in some way to the national social security system or provides them with some specific insurance scheme, only a small majority affiliate working prisoners to the old-age pension system. Thus Austrian law reflects the development of European law in that all prisoners are provided with health and accident care and working prisoners are affiliated to the unemployment insurance scheme but not to the old-age pension system(*Stummer v. Austria* [GC], § 131). It therefore considered that there was no sufficient consensus on the issue of the affiliation of working prisoners to the old-age pension system. It held that while Rule 26. 17 of the European Prison Rules, which provides that as far as possible, prisoners who work shall be included in national social security systems, reflects an evolving trend, it cannot be translated into an obligation under Article 4 of the Convention. Consequently, the obligatory work performed by the applicant as a prisoner without being affiliated to the old-age pension system had to be regarded as "work required to be done in the ordinary course of detention" within the meaning of Article 4 § 3 (a)[ibid. , § 132; *Floroiu v. Romania*(dec.), § 32].

2. Military service or substitute civilian service

38. Article 4 § 3 (b) excludes from the scope of "forced or compulsory labour" prohibited by Article 4 § 2 "any service of a military character or, in case of conscientious objectors in countries where they are recognised, service exacted instead of compulsory military service" (*Bayatyan v. Armenia* [GC], § 100; *Johansen v. Norway*, Commission decision).

39. In the case of *W. , X. , Y. and Z. v. the United Kingdom* (Commission decision), where the applicants were minors when they entered into the armed forces of the United

Kingdom, the Commission held that the service entered into by the applicants was subject to the limiting provision under Article 4 § 3, and therefore any complaint that such service constituted "forced or compulsory labour" had to be rejected as being manifestly ill-founded in view of the express provision of Article 4 § 2(b) of the Convention.

40. The Commission has held, however, that "servitude" and "forced or compulsory labour" are distinguished in Article 4 and, although they must in fact often overlap, they cannot be treated as equivalent, and that the clause excluding military service expressly from the scope of the term "forced or compulsory labour" does not forcibly exclude such service in all circumstances from an examination in the light of the prohibition directed against "slavery or servitude" (ibid.). The Commission held that generally the duty of a soldier who enlists after having attained the age of majority, to observe the terms of his engagement and the ensuing restriction of his freedom and personal rights does not amount to an impairment of rights which could come under the terms of "slavery or servitude" (ibid.). It found that the young age of the applicants who had entered into the services with their parents' consent cannot attribute the character "servitude" to the normal condition of a soldier (ibid.).

41. The Commission case-law drew a link between Article 9 and Article 4 § 3(b) of the Convention, finding that the latter left the choice of recognising a right to conscientious objection to the Contracting Parties. Consequently, conscientious objectors were excluded from the scope of protection of Article 9, which could not be read as guaranteeing freedom from prosecution for refusal to serve in the army (*Bayatyan v. Armenia* [GC], § 99).

42. The Court considered, however, that Article 4 § 3(b) neither recognises nor excludes a right to conscientious objection and should therefore not have a delimiting effect on the rights guaranteed by Article 9 (ibid., § 100). It has therefore held that Article 9 should no longer be read in conjunction with Article 4 § 3(b) in such cases (ibid., § 109).

3. Service required during an emergency or calamity

43. Article 4 § 3(c) excludes any service exacted in case of an emergency or calamity threatening the life or well-being of the community from the scope of forced or compulsory labour. In this connection, the Commission held that obligation of a holder of shooting rights

to actively participate in the gassing of fox-holes as part of a campaign against an epidemic-even if the above obligation fell within the notion of compulsory labour-was justified under Article 4 § 3 (c) which allows the exaction of services in case of an emergency or calamity threatening the life or well-being of the community, or under Article 4 § 3 (d) which allows service which forms part of normal civic obligations(*S. v. Germany*, Commission decision). In a case, which concerned a requirement that the applicant serve a year in the public dental service in northern Norway, two members of the Commission held the view that the service in question was service reasonably required of the applicant in an emergency threatening the well-being of the community and was not forced or compulsory labour (*I. v. Norway*, Commission decision).

4. Normal civic obligations

44. Article 4 § 3 (d) excludes any work or service which forms part of normal civil obligations from the scope of forced or compulsory labour(*Van der Mussele v. Belgium*, § 38).

45. In *Van der Mussele v. Belgium* the Court accepted that the applicant, a pupil-advocate, had suffered some prejudice by reason of the lack of remuneration and of reimbursement of expenses, but that prejudice went hand in hand with advantages and had not been shown to be excessive. It held that while remunerated work may also qualify as forced or compulsory labour, the lack of remuneration and of reimbursement of expenses constitutes a relevant factor when considering what is proportionate or in the normal course of business. Noting that the applicant had not had a disproportionate burden of work imposed on him and that the amount of expenses directly occasioned by the cases in question had been relatively small, the Court concluded that in that case there had been no compulsory labour for the purposes of Article 4 § 2 of the Convention(§ § 34 – 41).

46. More recently, the Court concluded that a physician's obligation to participate in emergency medical service did not amount to compulsory or forced labour for the purposes of Article 4 § 2 and declared the relevant part of the application inadmissible as being manifestly ill-founded [*Steindel v. Germany* (dec.)]. In that case the Court considered relevant, in particular, (i) that the services to be rendered were remunerated and did not fall

outside the ambit of a physician's normal professional activities; (ii) the obligation in issue was founded on a concept of professional and civil solidarity and was aimed at averting emergencies; and (iii) the burden imposed on the applicant was not disproportionate.

47. The Commission and the Court have also considered that "any work or service which forms part of normal civic obligations" includes: compulsory jury service (*Zarb Adami v. Malta*); compulsory fire service or financial contribution which is payable in lieu of service (*Karlheinz Schmidt v. Germany*); obligation to conduct free medical examinations (*Reitmayr v. Austria*); the obligation to participate in the medical emergency service (*Steindel v. Germany*); or the legal obligations imposed on companies in their quality of employers to calculate and withhold certain taxes, social security contributions etc. from the salaries and wages of their employers (*Four Companies v. Austria*, Commission decision).

48. However, the criteria which serve to delimit the concept of compulsory labour include the notion of what is in the normal course of business. Work or labour that is in itself normal may in fact be rendered abnormal if the choice of the groups or individuals bound to perform it is governed by discriminatory factors. Therefore in cases where the Court has found that there was no forced or compulsory labour for the purpose of Article 4, it does not follow that the facts in issue fall completely outside the ambit of Article 4 and, hence, of Article 14 (*Van der Mussele v. Belgium*, § 43; *Zarb Adami v. Malta*, § 45). For example, any unjustified discrimination between men and women in the imposition of a civic obligation is in breach of Article 14 in conjunction with Article 4 of the Convention (ibid., § 83; *Karlheinz Schmidt v. Germany*, § 29).

III. Positive obligations

49. In *Siliadin v. France* the Court noted that, with regard to certain Convention provisions, such as Articles 2, 3 and 8, the fact that a State refrains from infringing the guaranteed rights does not suffice to conclude that it has complied with its obligations under Article 1 of the Convention (§ 77). In this connection, it held that limiting compliance with

Article 4 of the Convention only to direct action by the State authorities would be inconsistent with the international instruments specifically concerned with this issue and would amount to rendering it ineffective (§89). It has therefore held that States have positive obligations under Article 4 of the Convention.

A. The positive obligation to put in place an appropriate legislative and administrative framework

50. Article 4 requires that member States penalise and prosecute effectively any act aimed at maintaining a person in a situation of slavery, servitude or forced or compulsory labour (*C. N. v. the United Kingdom*, §66; *Siliadin v. France*, §112; *C. N. and V. v. France*, §105). In order to comply with this obligation, member States are required to put in place a legislative and administrative framework to prohibit and punish such acts (*Rantsev v. Cyprus and Russia*, §285).

51. In the particular context of trafficking, the Court underlined that the Palermo Protocol and the Anti-Trafficking Convention refer to the need for a comprehensive approach to combat trafficking which includes measures to prevent trafficking and to protect victims, in addition to measures to punish traffickers. In its opinion, it was clear from the provisions of these two instruments that the Contracting States, including almost all of the member States of the Council of Europe, have formed the view that only a combination of measures addressing all three aspects can be effective in the fight against trafficking. Therefore, the Court emphasised that the duty to penalise and prosecute trafficking is only one aspect of member States' general undertaking to combat trafficking and that the extent of the positive obligations arising under Article 4 must be considered within this broader context (ibid.).

52. In this connection, the Court has held that the spectrum of safeguards set out in national legislation must be adequate to ensure the practical and effective protection of the rights of victims or potential victims of trafficking. It, accordingly, considered that, in addition to criminal law measures to punish traffickers, Article 4 requires member States to put in place adequate measures regulating businesses often used as a cover for human trafficking. Furthermore, a State's immigration rules must address relevant concerns relating to

encouragement, facilitation or tolerance of trafficking (ibid. , § 284). Moreover, States are required to provide relevant training for law enforcement and immigration officials (ibid. , § 287).

53. The Court found the legislation in force at the material time did not afford the applicants practical and effective protection against treatment failing within the scope of Article 4 of the Convention in *Siliadin v. France* (§ 148), in *C. N. and V. v. France* (§ 108), and in *C. N. v. the United Kingdom* (§ 76). Whereas in *Rantsev v. Cyprus and Russia*, on the basis of the evidence before it and bearing in mind the limits of Russian jurisdiction in the particular facts of the case, the Court found no such failure in the legislative and administrative framework in Russia with respect to trafficking [§ § 301 – 303; see also *V. F. v. France* (dec.) and *J. A. v. France* (dec.)]. In that case, Cyprus was found to be in violation of this obligation because, despite evidence of trafficking in Cyprus and the concerns expressed in various reports that Cypriot immigration policy and legislative shortcomings were encouraging the trafficking of women to Cyprus, its regime of artiste visas did not afford to Ms Rantseva practical and effective protection against trafficking and exploitation (§ § 290 – 293).

B. The positive obligation to take operational measures

54. Article 4 of the Convention may, in certain circumstances, require a State to take operational measures to protect victims, or potential victims, of treatment in breach of that Article (*Rantsev v. Cyprus and Russia*, § 286; *C. N. v. the United Kingdom*, § 67). In order for a positive obligation to take operational measures to arise in the circumstances of a particular case, it must be demonstrated that the State authorities were aware, or ought to have been aware, of circumstances giving rise to a credible suspicion that an identified individual had been, or was at real and immediate risk of being subjected to treatment in breach of Article 4 of the Convention. In the case of an answer in the affirmative, there will be a violation of that Article where the authorities fail to take appropriate measures within the scope of their powers to remove the individual from that situation or risk (ibid.).

55. However, bearing in mind the difficulties involved in policing modern societies and the operational choices which must be made in terms of priorities and resources, the

obligation to take operational measures must be interpreted in a way which does not impose an impossible or disproportionate burden on the authorities (ibid., § 68; *Rantsev v. Cyprus and Russia*, § 287).

56. In *Rantsev v. Cyprus and Russia* various failures of the police, notably, to inquire further into whether Ms Rantseva had been trafficked, the decision to confide her to the custody of M. A and their failure to comply with various domestic law provisions led the Court to find that the Cypriot authorities had failed to take measures to protect the applicant's daughter, Ms Rantseva from trafficking (§ 298).

57. In *V. F. v. France* the Court, while conscious of the scale of the phenomenon of trafficking of Nigerian women in France and the difficulties experienced by those persons in identifying themselves to the authorities in order to obtain protection, could only note, in the light of the circumstances of the case, that the applicant had not attempted to contact the authorities about her situation. It was therefore of the opinion that the evidence submitted by the applicant was not sufficient to demonstrate that the police authorities knew or ought to have known that the applicant was the victim of a human trafficking network when they decided to deport her.

C. The procedural obligation to investigate

58. Article 4 of the Convention entails a procedural obligation to investigate where there is a credible suspicion that an individual's rights under that Article have been violated (*C. N. v. the United Kingdom*, § 69; *Rantsev v. Cyprus and Russia*, § 288).

59. The Court underlines that the requirement to investigate does not depend on a complaint from the victim or next-of-kin but that the authorities must act of their own motion once the matter has come to their attention. It further affirms that for an investigation to be effective, it must be independent from those implicated in the events and that it must also be capable of leading to the identification and punishment of individuals responsible, an obligation not of result but of means. Moreover, a requirement of promptness and reasonable expedition is implicit in all cases but where the possibility of removing the individual from the harmful situation is available, the investigation must be undertaken as a matter of

urgency. Finally, the victim or the next-of-kin must be involved in the procedure to the extent necessary to safeguard their legitimate interests(ibid.).

60. In the particular context of human trafficking, in addition to the obligation to conduct a domestic investigation into events occurring on their own territories, member States are also subject to a duty in cross-border trafficking cases to cooperate effectively with the relevant authorities of other States concerned in the investigation of events which occurred outside their territories(ibid., § 289).

61. In *Rantsev v. Cyprus and Russia* the Court found that Russian authorities had failed to investigate the possibility that individual agents or networks operating in Russia were involved in trafficking Ms Rantseva to Cyprus (§ 308). In *M. and Others v. Italy and Bulgaria*, however, the Court has found that the circumstances of the case did not give rise to human trafficking, a situation which would have engaged the responsibility of the Bulgarian State, had any trafficking commenced there (§ 169). In that case, it has further held that the Bulgarian authorities assisted the applicants and maintained constant contact and co-operation with the Italian authorities(§ 169).

List of cited cases

The case-law cited in this Guide refers to judgments or decisions delivered by the Court and to decisions or reports of the European Commission of Human Rights ("the Commission").

Unless otherwise indicated, all references are to a judgment on the merits delivered by a Chamber of the Court. The abbreviation "(dec.)" indicates that the citation is of a decision of the Court and "[GC]" that the case was heard by the Grand Chamber.

The hyperlinks to the cases cited in the electronic version of the Guide are directed to the HUDOC database (〈http://hudoc.echr.coe.int〉) which provides access to the case-law of the Court (Grand Chamber, Chamber and Committee judgments and decisions, communicated cases, advisory opinions and legal summaries from the Case-Law Information Note) and of the Commission (decisions and reports), and to the resolutions of the Committee of Ministers.

The Court delivers its judgments and decisions in English and/or French, its two official languages. HUDOC also contains translations of many important cases into more than thirty non-official languages, and links to around one hundred online case-law collections produced by third parties.

— A —

Antonov v. Russia (dec.), no. 38020/03, 3 November 2005

— B —

Bayatyan v. Armenia [GC], no. 23459/03, ECHR 2011

Bucha v. Slovakia (dec.), no. 43259/07, 20 September 2011

— C —

C. N. v. the United Kingdom, no. 4239/08, 13 November 2012

C. N. and V. v. France, no. 67724/09, 11 October 2012

— D —

De Wilde, Ooms and Versyp v. Belgium, 18 June 1971, Series A no. 12

— F —

Floroiu v. Romania(dec.),no. 15303/10,12 March 2013

Four Companies v. Austria,no. 7427/76,Commission decision of 27 September 1976, Decisions and Reports 7

— G —

Graziani-Weiss v. Austria,no. 31950/06,18 October 2011

— I —

I. v. Norway,no. 1468/62,Commission decision of 17 December 1963

— J —

J. A. v. France(dec.),no. 45310/11,27 May 2014

Johansen v. Norway,no. 10600/83,Commission decision of 14 October 1985,Decisions and Reports 44

— K —

Karlheinz Schmidt v. Germany,18 July 1994,Series A no. 291 – B

— M —

M. and Others v. Italy and Bulgaria,no. 40020/03,31 July 2012

Mihal v. Slovakia(dec.),no. 31303/08,28 June 2011

— R —

Rantsev v. Cyprus and Russia,no. 25965/04,ECHR 2010(extracts)

Reitmayr v. Austria,no. 23866/94,Commission decision of 28 June 1995

— S —

S. v. Germany, no. 9686/82, Commission decision of 4 October 1984, Decisions and Reports 39

Schuitemaker v. the Netherlands(dec.),no. 15906/98,4 May 2010

Seguin v. France(dec.),no. 42400/98,7 March 2000

Siliadin v. France,no. 73316/01,ECHR 2005 – VII

Sokur v. Ukraine(dec.),no. 29439/02,26 November 2002

Steindel v. Germany(dec.),no. 29878/07,14 September 2010

Stummer v. Austria[GC],no. 37452/02,ECHR 2011

— T —

Twenty-one detained persons v. Germany, nos. 3134/67 and 20 others, Commission decision of 6 April 1968, Collection 27

— V —

V. F. v. France(dec.), no. 7196/10, 29 November 2011

Van derMussele v. Belgium, 23 November 1983, Series A no. 70

Van Droogenbroeck v. Belgium, 24 June 1982, Series A no. 50

— W —

W. , X. , Y. , and Z. v. the United Kingdom, nos. 3435/67 and 3 others, Commission decision of 19 July 1968, Collection 28

— X —

X. v. Germany, no. 8410/78, Commission decision of 13 December 1979, Decisions and Reports 18

— Z —

Zarb Adami v. Malta, no. 17209/02, ECHR 2006 – Ⅷ

Zhelyazkov v. Bulgaria, no. 11332/04, 9 October 2012

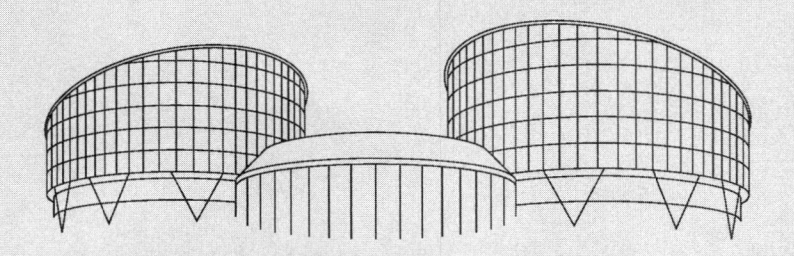

EUROPEAN COURT OF HUMAN RIGHTS
COUR EUROPÉENNE DES DROITS DE L'HOMME

第二章　《欧洲人权公约》第5条适用指南
人身自由和安全权

COUNCIL OF EUROPE
CONSEIL DE L'EUROPE

读者须知

本指南是欧洲人权法院(以下简称"本法院""欧洲法院""斯特拉斯堡法院")出版的公约指南系列的一部分,旨在让执业律师了解斯特拉斯堡法院作出的基本判决。本指南分析和汇总了《欧洲人权公约》(以下简称《公约》《欧洲公约》)第 5 条的判例法。读者可以从中发现本领域的基本原则和相关判例。

援引的判例法从具有指导性的、重要的以及最新的判决中挑选得出。

本法院的判例不仅用于审判呈交至本法院的案件,而且从更为一般的意义上用于阐释、捍卫和发展《公约》创立的各项规则,并以此促使各缔约国对之加以遵守(*Ireland v. the United Kingdom*, 1978 年 1 月 18 日, §154, Series A no. 25 和最近案例: *Jeronovičs v. Latvia* [GC], no. 44898/10, § 109, 2016 年 7 月 5 日)。因此,从普遍意义来说,《公约》确立的此机制的任务便是通过决定公共政策的各种问题来提升人权保护的标准,并在缔约国范围内推广人权法学(*Konstantin Markin v. Russia* [GC], 30078/06, § 89, ECHR 2012)。实际上法院强调过,《公约》的作用正如人权领域中的"欧洲公共秩序的宪法"(*Bosphorus Hava Yolları Turizm ve Ticaret Anonim Şirketi v. Ireland* [GC], no. 45036/98, § 156, ECHR 2005 – Ⅵ)。

这本案例指南包含了欧洲人权公约及其议定书的每一个条款的关键字索引。每一个案件的法律问题都直接从公约以及议定书中选取并被总结在关键字列表中。

本法院的 HUDOC 案例数据库能够通过关键字搜索案例。关键字搜索可以保证有相似法律内容的文件都能够被一起找到(法院对每个案例的推理和结论都通过关键字进行了总结)。点击 HUDOC 中案例详情标志可以找到个案关键字。更多关于 HUDOC 数据库以及关键字的内容请查阅 HUDOC 用户指南。

第一节 适用范围

> **第 5 条第 1 款人身自由和安全权**
> "任何人都享有人身自由和安全权。除了在下列情况下并遵循法律所规定的程序,任何人的人身自由不被剥夺……"

一、剥夺人身自由

1. 第 5 条捍卫自由权,维护的是个人的人身自由;其目的是为了保证任何人的人身自由不被任意剥夺。它并不仅仅关注第四议定书第 2 条中涉及的限制行动自由的内容(*Creangă v. Romania* [GC], §92;*Engel and Others v. the Netherlands*, §58)。

2. 严重限制行动自由而落入第 5 条第 1 款的范围和只受限于第四议定书第 2 条的单纯限制行动自由的区别在于它们的强度不同,并不是性质或实质上的不同(*Guzzardi v. Italy*, §93;*Rantsev v. Cyprus and Russia*, §314;*Stanev v. Bulgaria* [GC], §115)。

3. 剥夺人身自由不只限于典型的拘留和定罪后进行拘留的案件,也可能通过很多不同的形式发生(*Guzzardi v. Italy*, §95)。

二、适用标准

4. 法院认为其在是否存在剥夺人身自由这一问题上不受国内机构的法律推论的约束,法院自主评估案件的情况(*H. L. v. the United Kingdom*, §90;*H. M. v. Switzerland*, §§30 and 48;*Creangă v. Romania* [GC], §92)。

5. 为了决定是否存在第 5 条规定的"剥夺人身自由"的情形,分析的起点应该是涉案人的具体情况,应该考虑的因素包括涉案行为的类型,持续期间,影响和方式(*Guzzardi v. Italy*, §92;*Medvedyev and Others v. France* [GC], §73;*Creangă v. Romania* [GC], §91)。

6. 条文要求对所采取的限制性措施的"类型"以及"实施方式"进行考虑。这能够使法院考虑到与监禁之外的措施相关的特定背景与情况。事实上,由于很多情况发生在现代社会,民众们被要求为了公共利益而对限制自由迁徙或者限制自由的措施进行容忍,因此所采取的措施的背景是一项重要的考量因素。

7. 第5条第1款下"剥夺人身自由"这一概念的意义包括客观因素,即在一段不可忽视的时间内个人被控制在相对限制的空间内,还包括另一个主观因素,即上述个人并没有对此限制表示有效的同意(Storck v. Germany,§74;Stanev v. Bulgaria[GC],§117)。

8. 应考虑的客观因素包括:离开限制区域的可能性,监视和控制个人行动自由的程度,隔离的程度和社会交往的可能性(可参见,Guzzardi v. Italy,§95;H. M. v. Switzerland,§45;H. L. v. the United Kingdom,§91;and Storck v. Germany,§73)。

9. 当事实表明存在第5条第1款下剥夺人身自由的情形时,相对较短的拘留期间并不影响上述结论(Rantsev v. Cyprus and Russia,§317;Iskandarov v. Russia,§140)。

10. 即使行为持续时间较短,在警察行使搜查和限制的权力时存在"强迫"的因素即剥夺人身自由的表现(Foka v. Turkey,§78;Gillan and Quinton v. the United Kingdom,§57;Shimovolos v. Russia,§50;and Brega and Others v. Moldova,§43)。

11. 一个人没有被戴上手铐送入监狱或受到人身限制,并不构成存在剥夺人身自由的决定性因素(M. A. v. Cyprus,§193)。

12. 人身自由这一权利在民主社会中十分重要以至于不能仅基于一个简单理由就使个人丧失公约对这方面的保护的利益,即他可能愿意接受拘留,特别是当这个人从法律上讲无法做出同意或不同意的行为时(H. L. v. the United Kingdom,§90;Stanev v. Bulgaria[GC],§119)。

13. 一个人缺乏法定资格的事实并不一定意味着他或她不能明白或同意自己所处的情况(同上,§130,Shtukaturov v. Russia,§§107-109;Stanev v. Bulgaria[GC],§130;D. D. v. Lithuania,§150)。

三、监狱中采取的措施

14. 在监狱中采取的纪律措施对拘留的条件产生影响的,并不构成"剥夺人身自由"的情形。在正常情况下,该项措施应该被视为对合法的拘留条件进行了修改,并且不属于公约第5条第1款的范围内[Bollan v. the United Kingdom(dec.)]。

四、对乘飞机者进行安检

15. 在机场进行边境检查时,乘客被边检人员拦住,对自己的情况进行说明,拘留时间并未超过严格符合相关程序的时间时,并不产生适用《公约》第5条的问题。

五、正式逮捕或拘留之外剥夺人身自由

16. 在下列不同情况中均产生了第5条的适用问题:

- 将个人安置在精神或社会医疗机构(参见,在许多其他机构中,*De Wilde, Ooms and Versyp v. Belgium*; *Nielsen v. Denmark*; *H. M. v. Switzerland*; *H. L. v. the United Kingdom*; *Storck v. Germany*; *A. and Others v. Bulgaria*; *Stanev v. Bulgaria* [GC]);
- 在机场过境区的限制[*Amuur v. France*; *Shamsa v. Poland*; *Mogos and Others v. Romania*(dec.); *Mahdid and Haddar v. Austria*(dec.); and *Riad and Idiab v. Belgium*];
- 在警察局的询问(*I. I. v. Bulgaria*; *Osypenko v. Ukraine*; *Salayev v. Azerbaijan*; *Farhad Aliyev v. Azerbaijan*; and *Creangă v. Romania*[GC]);
- 被警方拦截并搜查(*Foka v. Turkey*, *Gillan and Quinton v. the United Kingdom*, and *Shimovolos v. Russia*);
- 因社会治安的原因警方采取措施控制人群(*Austin and Others v. the United Kingdom*[GC]);
- 软禁[*Mancini v. Italy*; *Lavents v. Latvia*; *Nikolova v. Bulgaria*(no. 2); and *Dacosta Silva v. Spain*]

六、剥夺他人自由的积极义务

17. 第5条第1款第1句,规定国家对保护公民的人身自由权承担积极义务。这不仅要求国家不积极侵犯相关权利,而且要求国家采取合理措施,禁止在其管辖范围内的任何人违法干预这些权利(*El-Masri v. the former Yugoslav Republic of Macedonia* [GC],§239)。

18. 国家因此应该采取有效措施保护弱势群体,包括相关国家机构在其知道或应该

知道上述情况时应该采取合理措施防止发生剥夺人身自由的情形(*Storck v. Germany*, §102)。

19. 国家应对其默许私人剥夺他人人身自由或者无法终止上述情形承担责任(*Riera Blume and Others v. Spain*; *Rantsev v. Cyprus and Russia*, §§319 – 321; *Medova v. Russia*, §§123 – 125)。

第二节　第5条第1款下拘留的合法性

一、第5条的目的

20. 第5条的主要目的是为了防止任意或不合法地剥夺个人人身自由(*McKay v. the United Kingdom* [GC], §30)。人身自由和安全权是在公约所指称的"民主社会"中最为重要的元素(*Medvedyev and Others v. France* [GC], §76; *Ladent v. Poland*, §45, 18 March, 2008)。

21. 法院因此认为未经许可拘留他人是对公约第5条中所重点保护的权利的绝对否认并且体现了严重违反该条规定的行为。缺乏关于拘留日期、时间、地点、被拘留人姓名、拘留原因和受拘留影响人的姓名的记录，是与公约第5条目的相违背的(参见 *Kurt v. Turkey*, §125)，这也和公约要求的合法性不符(*Anguelova v. Bulgaria*, §154)。

二、符合国内法

22. 为了满足合法性的要求，拘留必须"遵循法定程序"。这表示拘留必须和国内法中的相关实质和程序条款相符(或者相关的国际法，参见 *Medvedyev and Others v. France* [GC], §79; *Toniolo v. San Marino and Italy*, §46)。

23. 例如，法院认为当国家机关未在法定时间提出延长拘留的申请时便违反了公约第5条(*G. K. v. Poland*, §76)。相反，违反关于不同种罪行而应采取不同方式询问的通知，不会使之后的逮捕和拘留失去国内法依据(*Talat Tepe v. Turkey*, §62)。

三、对遵循国内法的审查

24. 虽然通常情况下首先由国家机构特别是法院，负责解释和适用国内法，但是当违反国内法的同时也违反了公约,那么情况会有所不同。当涉及可能违反第 5 条第 1 款的情况时,法院必须行使一定的权力来审查国内法是否被遵守(参见 *Creangă v. Romania* [GC], §101; *Baranowski v. Poland*, §50; *Benham v. the United Kingdom*, §41)。在这一过程中,法院必须考虑相关时间的法律情况(*Włoch v. Poland*, §114)。

四、一般规则

25. 合法性的要求并不仅意味着符合相关的国内法;国内法本身需要与《公约》相符,包括《公约》规定的一般原则或暗指的原则(*Plesó v. Hungary*, §59)。

《公约》暗指的原则在第 5 条第 1 款判例法下意味着法治原则,以及与其相关的法律的确定性,比例性原则以及公约宗旨所提倡的防止任意性的原则 [*Simons v. Belgium* (dec.), §32]。

五、法律确定性原则

26. 当涉及剥夺人身自由时,满足法律确定性的一般原则尤为重要。因此,国内法应明确界定剥夺人身自由的条件,而且相关规定应该在适用上具有可预见性,从而满足公约规定的"合法"标准,这个标准要求所有法律都应该足够明确,在必要时辅以适当的建议,从而使公民能在一定合理的程度内预见某一特定的行为在相关情况下会产生的后果(参见近期的案例,*Creangă v. Romania*, §120; and *Medvedyev and Others v. France* [GC], §80)。

27. 例如,在缺乏国内立法或判例法的特别规定的前提下就依据起诉书将某人拘留违反了公约第 5 条第 1 款(*Baranowski v. Poland*, §§50-58)。在缺乏明确的立法基础的前提下,自动重新开始审前拘留同样违反《公约》第 5 条第 1 款(*Svipsta v. Latvia*, §86)。对比而言,在没有下发正式的拘留令的前提下,依据公诉机构下达的指令,为了进行进一步调查而继续拘留某人并未表明违反了上述条款(*Laumont v. France*, §50)。

28. 国内机构关于某一法律条文不一致的,甚至出现互斥的解释和适用,同样不符合公约要求的"法律质量"的标准(*Nasrulloyev v. Russia*, §77; *Ječius v. Lithuania*, §§53-59)。但是,在缺乏判例法的时候,法院并不会对国内法进行解释。因此,也不愿认为国内法院违反法律规定的程序(参见 *Włoch v. Poland*, §§114-116; *Winterwerp v. the*

Netherlands, §§48-50)。

29. 尽管外交言论是国际法的一种渊源,在这种言论的基础上拘留相关人员在第5条第1款下是不合法的,只要它并不确切也没有足够的可预见性。尤其是在关于可能拘留和拘留相关人员问题上缺乏确切的规定时,将会触犯第5条第1款对法律确定性和可预见性的要求(*Medvedyev and Others v. France*[GC],§§96-100)。

六、禁止任意行为

30. 此外,任何对人身自由的剥夺都应该以坚持保护个人免于任意决断为目标(参见 *Witold Litwa v. Poland*,§78)。

31. 第5条第1款中"任意"的概念与国内法的规定存在出入,因此剥夺人身自由即便在国内法下是合法的,但也是任意的,这是与公约相违背的(*Creangă v. Romania*,§84;*A. and Others v. the United Kingdom*,§164)。

32. 根据拘留形式的不同,任意的概念也存在不同。本法院已经指出,当政府机构怀有恶意或欺骗之意时,任意就可能产生。在这种情况下拘留令以及执行拘留的指令违背了第5条第1款所述的限制性规定。拘留的地点和条件并不符合允许剥夺自由的情况。同时,拘留行为也不符合比例原则(主要原则的详细规定参见 *James, Wells and Lee v. the United Kingdom*,§§191-195;and *Saadi v. the United Kingdom*[GC],§§68-74)。

33. 一国法院替换已过期的或有缺陷的拘留令的速度,也是分析拘留决定是否是任意的另一个因素(*Mooren v. Germany*[GC],§80)。因此,法院认为在第5条第1款第3项的背景下,从最初的拘留令过期到上诉法院将案件发回下级法院重审后重新颁发新的、合理的拘留令中间少于一个月的,不能认为是对当事人的任意拘留(*Minjat v. Switzerland*,§§46 and 48)。相反,上诉法院将案件发回下级法院重审后超过一年时间的,在此期间当事人处于一种对于其还被关押候审情况感到不确定的状态,再加上下级法院重新审查其拘留没有一定的时间限制,这种拘留决定应被认为是任意的(*Khudoyorov v. Russia*,§§136-137)。

七、法院指令

34. 原则上,依据法院指令进行一段时间的拘留是"合法"的。国内法院可能认定一个依据后来被上级法院判定为不合法的指令而实施的拘留有效(*Bozano v. France*,

§55）。即使国内法院认为拘留的过程中存在一定的缺陷，但根据"法律规定的程序"，仍然可能会继续进行拘留（Erkalo v. the Netherlands, §§55-56）。因此，拘留令中存在的缺陷并不必然使得该拘留期间违反第5条第1款（Ječius v. Lithuania, §68; Benham v. the United Kingdom, §§42-47）。

35. 法院区分两种行为，一种是国内法院在其管辖权下的行为，而另一种是超越管辖权的行为（Benham v. the United Kingdom, §§43 et seq）。当利益相关人没有收到适当的开庭通知的情况下，拘留明显是不合法的（Khudoyorov v. Russia, §129）。国内法院没有按照国内立法的规定进行相关的询问（Lloyd and Others v. the United Kingdom, §§108 and 116），或者下级法院没有适当考虑可代替拘留的其他方法（参见以上，§113）。另一方面而言，当没有证据证明国内法院的行为达到"严重或明显的违反规则"的程度时，法院认为拘留是合法的（参见以上，§114）。

八、对决定的论证以及对非任意的要求

36. 缺乏对拘留令进行的论证或对其论证不充分是法院在第5条第1款下评估拘留合法性时会考虑的因素。因此，司法机关在授权延长拘留时间的决定中缺乏相应的依据和推理的，可能被视为与第5条第1款中保护免受任意的原则相冲突（Stašaitis v. Lithuania, §§66-67）。同样，一个极其简短的且未提及任何法律条款的拘留决定也无法为免受任意行为提供充足的保护（Khudoyorov v. Russia, §157）。

37. 然而，当国内法院认为对申诉人的拘留有足够的国内法依据时，即使在相关的拘留令中没有提及拘留的原因，本法院仍可能认为对申诉人的拘留符合国内法。（Minjat v. Switzerland, §43）。另外，国内法院撤销缺乏论证和原因说明的拘留令，但仍然认为对申诉人的拘留有一定的依据的情况下，这时拒绝释放被拘留人并且将拘留合法性的决定发回下级法院重审的，并不违反第5条第1款（Minjat v. Switzerland, §47）。

38. 公约要求拘留令应当具备具体的依据并且对拘留的时间限制进行明确规定（Meloni v. Switzerland, §53）。另外，相关机关应该考虑除拘留之外其他侵略性较弱的方法（Ambruszkiewicz v. Poland, §32）。

九、可接受的程序瑕疵

39. 下列程序瑕疵不会使对申诉人的拘留违法：

- 根据判例法,在个别情况下,如果有关机关真实地相信已经向申诉人下达了拘留令,那么在实际没有将拘留令正式地下达被告的情况下,并不构成"严重地或明显地违反规定"的行为[*Marturana v. Italy*,§79;但是在 *Voskuil v. the Netherlands* 案中,法院认为未能在法律规定的时间(3 天而不是 24 小时)内下达拘留令是违反公约的行为];
- 仅存在于逮捕令或拘留令上的文书错误,后来经过了司法机关修正的情况(*Nikolov v. Bulgaria*,§63;*Douiyeb v. the Netherlands*[GC],§52);
- 根据在法庭上披露的事实而对之前对申诉人做出拘留决定的依据进行更改的情况[*Gaidjurgis v. Lithuania*(dec.)],如果对更改依据的行为未能提供足够的理由,法院可能会认为更改依据的行为违反了第 5 条第 1 款(*Calmanovici v. Romania*,§65)。

十、延迟执行释放指令

40. 一个奉行法治的国家不能容忍法院已经下达释放指令但还有人的人身自由被剥夺(*Assanidze v. Georgia*[GC],§173)。但是法院认为延迟执行释放决定是可以理解的甚至经常是不可避免的。但是国内当局必须尽量降低延迟释放的时间(*Giulia Manzoni v. Italy*,§25)。延迟 11 个小时才执行对申诉人的释放指令违背了公约第 5 条第 1 款(*Quinn v. France*,§§39-43;*Giulia Manzoni v. Italy*,§25)。

第三节 第 5 条第 1 款下授权剥夺人身自由的情形

一、定罪后监禁

> **第 5 条第 1 款第 a 项**
>
> "任何人都享有人身自由和安全权。除了在下列情况下并遵循法律所规定的程序:
>
> a. 由具有管辖权的法院定罪后进行的合法拘留;"

(一)存在定罪

41. 第5条第1款适用于任何"定罪"后,由法院宣布剥夺人身自由,而且不区分当事人犯下的罪行应属于刑事犯罪还是一国内部法律中的纪律处分的情形(*Engel and Others v. the Netherlands*, §68; *Galstyan v. Armenia*, §46)。

42. 该术语意味着发现了罪行并通过惩罚或采取其他措施剥夺人身自由(*Del Río Prada v. Spain* [GC], §125; *James, Wells and Lee v. the United Kingdom*, §189; *M. v. Germany*, §87; *Van Droogenbroeck v. Belgium*, §35; *B. v. Austria*, §38)。

43. 该条文并不禁止缔约国执行由其领土外具有管辖权的法院作出的监禁决定(*X v. Federal Republic of Germany*, 1963年12月14日,委员会决定)。尽管缔约国并没有义务审核定罪程序是否符合公约第6条下的所有要求(*Drozd and Janousek v. France and Spain*, §110),但定罪不能公然违反正义(*Ilaşcu and Others v. Moldova and Russia* [GC], §461; *Stoichkov v. Bulgaria*, §51)。如果定罪的程序"明显地违背第6条的规定或者违背了其中的原则",那么根据第5条第1款的规定,剥夺人身自由的结果并不正当[*Willcox and Hurford v. the United Kingdom*(dec.), §95]。

(二)具有管辖权的法院

44. "法院"这一术语不仅是指那些具有独立于行政机关和案件当事人,并能保证遵循诉讼程序这样特征的机构(*De Wilde, Ooms and Versyp v. Belgium*, §78; *Weeks v. the United Kingdom*, §61)。每个需要法院介入的案子中的诉讼程序不需要都完全一样。为了确定某一诉讼程序是否提供了充足的保障,法院应该注意考虑该诉讼的具体情形的性质(同上)。

45. 另外,相关机构不应该只有提供建议的职能,而是必须有一定的职权来决定监禁的合法性并能在监禁不合法时作出释放决定(*X. v. the United Kingdom*, §61; *Weeks v. the United Kingdom*, §61)。

46. 如果某个法院并非依据"法律而建立",那么该法院就是不"具有职权的"(*Yefimenko v. Russia*, §§109–111)。

(三)监禁必须在定罪"之后"

47. "之后"一词并不仅仅意味着在时间上监禁必须在定罪之后。除此之外,监禁必须源于"定罪",随着并依附于"定罪"而发生。简而言之,定罪和剥夺人身自由之间要存在充分的因果关系(*James, Wells and Lee v. the United Kingdom*, §189; *Monnell and Morris v. the United Kingdom*, §40; *Del Río Prada v. Spain* [GC], §124)。

48. 然而,如果不予以释放并重新监禁的决定(包括延长预防性监禁)与立法目的以及法院目的无关,或者基于对这些目的的不合理分析而作出的,那么随着时间的推移,上述因果关系会逐渐变弱,也可能最后被切断。在这些情况下,一开始合法的拘留会成为任意剥夺人身自由,并违反第5条规定的行为(同上,§124; *H. W. v. Germany*, §102; *M. v. Germany*, §88,关于延续预防性监禁)。

49. 对"定罪以后"这一术语的解释不能限制解释为"最后的定罪"。因为这样会排除对那些在审判过程中依然享有自由的嫌疑人进行逮捕的情形。在上诉或审查过程中,根据第6条的要求,当事人的罪行已在审判中确立,这一点是不能忽视的(*Wemhoff v. Germany*, §9)。

50. 第5条第1款第一项适用于精神不健全的人一经定罪被拘禁于精神病院(*X. v. the United Kingdom*, §39)。但是,它并不适用于无罪释放后的情形(*Luberti v. Italy*, §25)。

(四)上诉程序的影响

51. 一定期间的拘留如果是根据法院指令来执行的,理论上来说是合法的。之后法院裁定在做出上述决定时出现法律适用或解释上的错误,并不必然追溯性地影响相应拘留的合法性。本法院拒绝支持被一审法院定罪但上诉法院裁定事实认定或法律适用有误的申诉人的申请(*Benham v. the United Kingdom*, §42)。但是,如果拘留没有国内法依据或是任意的,则该拘留是不合法的(*Tsirlis and Kouloumpas v. Greece*, §62)。

二、不遵守法院指令或法律义务的拘留

> **第5条第1款第b项**
> "b. 由于不遵守法院合法的命令或者为了保证履行法律所规定的任何义务而对某人予以合法拘留;"

(一)不遵守法院指令

52. 第5条第1款第b项中的用语意味着被逮捕或拘留的人有机会遵守法院的命令但他/她并没有这么做(*Beiere v. Latvia*, §49)。

53. 如果未经告知,个人不为不遵守法院指令负责(同上,§50)。

54. 具有管辖权的法院做出指令前,某人拒绝接受特定的措施或者拒绝遵守特定的前置程序的行为在判断是否符合法院指令时并不具有推断价值(*Petukhova v. Russia*,§59)。

55. 国内当局应对自由权的重要性和保证法院指令在民主社会被执行的重要性中做出衡量。应该衡量的因素包括法院指令的目的,遵守法院指令的可行性,拘留的时间长度。比例性原则的衡量保证了在整体中特定因素的重要性(*Gatt v. Malta*,§40)。

56. 法院已在一些案子中适用公约第5条第1款第b项,例如,未及时付清法院罚款的案子(*Airey v. Ireland*,Commission decision),拒绝进行精神健康检查的案子(*X v. Federal Republic of Germany*,Commission decision of 10 December 1975),或者拒绝进行法院指令的血液监测的案子(*X. v. Austria*,Commission decision),拒绝遵守居留限制的案子(*Freda v. Italy*,Commission decision),拒绝遵守法院做出的将孩子交还给父母的决定[*Paradis v. Germany*(dec.)],拒绝遵守签保令的案子(*Steel and Others v. the United Kingdom*),违反保释条款的案件(*Gatt v. Malta*)和在精神病院拘留的案子(*Beiere v. Latvia*,拘留决定被认为是"法院的合法命令")。

（二）履行法定义务

57. 第5条第1款第b项的第二个组成部分允许在保证履行法定义务时进行拘留。因此被拘留的人必须未履行特定义务,而且逮捕和拘留必须以保证义务履行为目的,而不是以惩罚为目的。只要相关义务已被履行,那基于第5条第1款第b项进行拘留的法律基础便不复存在(*Vasileva v. Denmark*,§36)。

58. 未履行的义务必须是特定的和具体的(*Ciulla v. Italy*,§36)。在这一点上的扩大解释会造成与法治不相符的后果(*Engel and Others v. the Netherlands*,§69;*Iliya Stefanov v. Bulgaria*,§72)。

59. 只有在犯罪行为迫近时,犯罪地点和时间以及潜在的受害人都十分特定时才能认为不进行刑事犯罪的义务是"特定且具体"的。不实行某事的义务与进行特定行为的义务之间存在很大的差别。在判定某人未能履行其义务之前,他/她有必要意识到特定的行为不应该被实行,并且其不愿意不去实行这一行为（*Ostendorf v. Germany*,§§93-94）。

60. 只有当"法律规定的义务"的履行无法以更温和的手段实现时,拘留才能为公约所接受(*Khodorkovskiy v. Russia*,§136)。比例性原则进一步要求在保证相关义务及时履行的重要性和自由权的重要性两者之中做出衡量(*Saadi v. the United Kingdom*[GC],§70)。

61. 在衡量过程中法院认为以下几点是相关的：相关法律规定的义务的性质，包括其背后的目的；被拘留的人和导致拘留的原因；还有拘留的时间长短(*Vasileva v. Denmark*,§38;*Epple v. Germany*,§37)。

62. 适用在第5条第1款第b项下的情形包括：进入一个国家时进行安全检查的义务[*McVeigh and Others v. United Kingdom*,(Commission report)]，公开个人身份的义务[*Vasileva v. Denmark*,*Novotka v. Slovakia*(dec.);*Sarigiannis v. Italy*]，进行精神检查的义务(*Nowicka v. Poland*)，离开特定区域的义务(*Epple v. Germany*)，到警察局接受盘问的义务(*Iliya Stefanov v. Bulgaria*;*Osypenko v. Ukraine*;and *Khodorkovskiy v. Russia*)以及坚守和平，不进行刑事犯罪行为,(*Ostendorf v. Germany*)。

三、还押候审

> **第5条第1款第c项**
>
> "c.如果有足够理由怀疑某人实施了犯罪行为或者如果合理地认为有必要防止某人犯罪或者是在某人犯罪后防止其逃脱，为了将其送交有关的法律当局而对其实施的合法的拘留或者拘留；"

（一）拘留或拘禁的目的

63. 在第5条第1款第c项中，"为了将其送交有关的法律当局"目的条件是逮捕或拘留的三种法律基础中必不可少的条件[*Lawless v. Ireland*(no.3),§§13 and 14;*Ireland v. the United Kingdom*,§196]。

64. 适用第5条第1款第c项，如果有理由怀疑个人实施了犯罪行为，其只能在刑事审判过程中被拘留，并以将其送交相关的合法当局为目的(*Ječius v. Lithuania*,§50;*Schwabe and M. G. v. Germany*,§72)。

65. 该条款的第二个可能性，即如果合理地认为有必要防止某人犯罪也适用于审前拘留，则并不适用于以预防为目的对于相关个人未被怀疑已经进行了刑事犯罪的拘留

(*Ostendorf v. Germany*)。

66. 将嫌疑犯送交法院的目的和达成这个目的,二者是相对独立的。第5条第1款第c项所规定的标准并不意味着在拘留或者拘留期间,警察必须有足够的证据起诉(*Erdagöz v. Turkey*,§51)。根据第5条第1款第c项,在拘留期间盘问的目的是通过确认或消除嫌疑而进行刑事侦查(*Brogan and Others v. the United Kingdom*,§§52-54;*Labita v. Italy*[GC],§155;*O'Hara v. the United Kingdom*,§36)。

67. 根据第5条第1款第c项采取的拘留必须要与目的之间符合比例原则(*Ladent v. Poland*,§§55-56)。

68. "有管辖权的法律当局"与第5条第3款中的"法官或其他由法律授权执行司法权威的官员"有相同的意思(*Schiesser v. Switzerland*,§29)。

(二)"合理怀疑"的含义

69. 关于实施了犯罪行为的"合理怀疑"意味着存在一定的事实或信息,会让一个客观公正的观察者认为某人实施了犯罪行为(*Erdagöz v. Turkey*,§51;*Fox, Campbell and Hartley v. the United Kingdom*,§32)。因此,有关当局没有对案件的基本情况进行实际调查从而判断相关控诉是否有根据的,违反了第5条第1款第c项(*Stepuleac v. Moldova*,§73;*Elci and Others v. Turkey*,§674)。

70. "合理"的标准取决于相关案件的事实(*Fox, Campbell and Hartley v. the United Kingdom*,§32)。

71. 在恐怖主义的背景下,虽然无法要求缔约方公开机密信息以建立嫌疑犯是恐怖分子的合理怀疑,法院认为打击恐怖犯罪的急迫性并不能成为扩大解释"合理性"使其损害第5条第1款第c项的借口(*O'Hara v. the United Kingdom*,§35)。

72. 匿名的线人提供的未经证实的证据不能建立对申请人涉及黑手党活动的"合理怀疑"(*Labita v. Italy*[GC],§§156 et seq)。相反被嫌疑人推翻的数年前的认罪陈述并不能移除对申请人和合理怀疑。另外,它并不影响拘留令的合法性(*Talat Tepe v. Turkey*,§61)。

(三)"违法行为"

73. "违法犯罪行为"一词与公约第6条中的"犯罪"有相同的意思。国内法中违法犯罪行为的分类是应该考虑的一个因素。但是,诉讼的性质和相关刑罚的严重性也是相关的(*Benham v. the United Kingdom*,§56)。

74. "违法行为"必须是特定的和具体的:依据国家的意志,由于某人的习性而认定其具有危险性并采取避免性拘留,这是不被允许的(*Guzzardi v. Italy*, §102;*Ciulla v. Italy*, §40;*M. v. Germany*, §89;*Shimovolos v. Russia*, §54)。

四、对未成年人的拘留

> **第5条第1款第d项**
>
> "d. 基于实行教育性监督的目的而根据合法命令拘留一个未成年人或者为了将其送交有关的法律当局而对其予以合法的拘留;"

(一)一般规定

75. 基于欧洲标准和欧洲理事会部长委员会通过的 CM(72)号决议(*X v. Switzerland*, Commission decision of 14 December 1979)。未成年人的概念包括年龄低于18岁的人[*Koniarska v. United Kingdom*(裁定)]。

76. 第 d 项不仅是有关允许拘留未成年人的条款。它包括一个具体的,但不穷尽的,未成年人可以被拘留的情况,那就是(1)实行教育性监督的目的,(2)为了将其送交有关的法律当局(*Mubilanzila Mayeka and Kaniki Mitunga v. Belgium*, §100)。

(二)教育性监督

77. 第5条第1款第d项授权根据法院或行政命令,以确保未成年人在教育机构的出勤率为目的所实施的拘留。

78. 在拘留未成年人的情况下,"教育监督"一词不应该僵硬地等同于课堂教学。这种监督包括很多方面,由有关当局实施的,以保证该未成年人的权益和保护(*Ichin and Others v. Ukraine*, §39;*D. G. v. Ireland*, §80)。

79. 第 d 项并没有排除监督教育机构采取初步的临时拘留措施,即使该措施本身没有涉及教育性监督。但是在这种情况下,应该在采取拘留措施之后尽快实施相关教育并提供足够的教育资源(*Bouamar v. Belgium*, §50)。

80. 如果一国选择了一种包括剥夺自由的教育监督系统,那么它应该投入适当的机构设施来满足教育和安全的目的,从而达到第5条第1款第d项的要求(*A. and Others*

v. Bulgaria, §69; D. G. v. Ireland, §79)。

81. 法院认为如果一个未成年人拘留机构中没有提供教育活动,那么该机构不能被定为实施"教育监督"(Ichin and Others v. Ukraine, §39)。

(三)有关法律当局

82. 第5条第1款第d项的第二个组成部分规定了以将相关未成年人送交法律当局为目的实施的合法拘留。根据条约缔结时的相关准备资料,该条文是为了涵盖在民事或行政诉讼之前拘留未成年人的情况,而第5条第1款第c项则涵盖与刑事诉讼相关的拘留。

83. 但是,在准备对该未成年人精神状况出具专家报告时对其进行拘留符合第d项的规定,即为了将其送交有关法律当局的目的[X. v. Switzerland,(裁定)cited above]。

五、基于社会和医疗原因的拘留

> **第5条第1款第e项**
> "e. 基于防止传染病蔓延的目的而对某人予以合法的拘留以及对精神失常者、酗酒者、吸毒者或者流氓予以合法的拘留;"

(一)一般规定

84. 公约第5条第1款第e项规定了多种不同类型的人,包括扩散传染病的人、精神失常者、酗酒者、吸毒者和流氓。在这些人中间存在一定的联系,即他们被剥夺自由是为了接受治疗或者为了社会公共政策的考量,又或者是二者兼有(Enhorn v. Sweden, §43)。

85. 公约允许剥夺这些不适应社会的人的自由,不仅仅因为他们对公共安全造成威胁,他们自身的利益也使得拘留对他们而言是有必要的(同上, Guzzardi v. Italy, §98)。

(二)预防传染病蔓延

86. 分析为了预防传染病蔓延而拘留某人的合法性时,一些重要的衡量因素包括:
- 该传染病蔓延是否对公共安全造成威胁,及
- 拘留受感染的人是否是为了防止传染病蔓延的最后方法,即考虑过其他较为不

严厉的方法而且这些方法不足以保障公共利益。

当不满足以上条件时,剥夺人身自由的法律基础停止存在(*Enhorn v. Sweden*,§44)。

(三)拘留精神失常者

87. 无论是在医学界还是在社会态度上"精神失常者"这一词语并没有精确的定义,因为精神病学一直在发展中。但是,这不意味着允许仅因为他或她的行为偏离既定的社会规范而将其拘留(*Rakevich v. Russia*,§26)。

88. 除非满足下列三个基本条件,否则不允许以"精神失常者"为理由剥夺他人的人身自由(*Stanev v. Bulgaria*[GC],§145;*D. D. v. Lithuania*,§156;*Kallweit v. Germany*,§45;*Shtukaturov v. Russia*,§114;and *Varbanov v. Bulgaria*,§45;*Winterwerp v. the Netherlands*,§39)。

- 一个人只能在有可靠客观的医学专家证明其精神失常的情况下才能被拘留,除非有紧急拘留的需要;
- 这个人的精神障碍必须属于需要强制拘留的类型。剥夺其自由必须是在特定情况上有必要的;
- 在整个拘留期间,被客观医学证据证实的精神障碍必须持续存在。

89. 在未向医学专家寻求意见的情况下,剥夺被认为精神失常的人的人身自由不符合公约第5条第1款e项的规定(*Ruiz Rivera v. Switzerland*,§59;*S. R. v. the Netherlands*(dec.),§31)。

精神状态必须达到特定的严重性才能被认为"真正的"精神失常(*Glien v. Germany*,§85)。

90. 关于以上第二个标准,需要拘留一个精神失常者不仅因为其需要治疗、药物或其他临床治疗来治愈或减轻病情,而且还因为其需要控制和监督,以防止其伤害自己或他人(*Hutchison Reid v. the United Kingdom*,§52)。

91. 在决定是否该将某人以"精神失常者"的理由拘留时,国家有关当局有一定的自由裁量权,因为在特定的案子中是相关当局首先分析提出的证据(*H. L. v. the United Kingdom*,§98)。

92. 在第5条第1款第e项的要求下,必须可靠地确定某人为精神失常者的时间应该是采取强制剥夺其人身自由权的措施的时间(*O. H. v. Germany*, §78)。

93. 当医学证据表明被拘留的精神失常者正在康复,有关当局需要一些时间来决定是否终止对其的强制措施(*Luberti v. Italy*, §28)。但是,单纯的行政理由不足以使继续拘留合法化(*R. L. and M. – J. D. v. France*, §129)。

94. 拘留精神失常者的机构必须是医院、诊所,或其经授权且合适拘留这些人的机构(*Ashingdane v. the United Kingdom*, §44;*O. H. v. Germany*, §79)。

95. 对比而言,在转移至合适的机构之前,某人可以被暂时置于不是专门拘留精神失常者的机构,但是等待转移的时间必须不能过长(参见 *Pankiewicz v. Poland*, §§44 – 45;*Morsink v. the Netherlands*, §§67 – 69;*Brand v. the Netherlands*, §§64 – 66)。

(四)拘留酗酒者和吸毒者

96. 公约第 5 条第 1 款第 e 项不应被解释为只允许拘留较有限的医学上定义的"酗酒者",因为该条文的规定并没有阻止国家为了限制酗酒的个人伤害自身或公众,或防止酒后危险行为,而针对酗酒的人采取措施(*Kharin v. Russia*, §34)。

97. 因此,一个在医学上并未被鉴定为"酗酒者"的人,其在酒精的影响下所做出的行动会对公共安全或其自身造成威胁的,基于公众或其自身的利益如个人健康或安全的目的,可以将其拘留(*Hilda Hafsteinsdóttir v. Iceland*, §42)。这并不意味着第 5 条第 1 款第 e 项允许仅仅因为其摄入酒精便拘留某人(*Witold Litwa v. Poland*, §§61 – 62)。

(五)流氓

98. 关于拘留"流氓"的案例非常少。该条文涉及范围包括居无定所、无法独立维持生计、没有正当职业的人。这三个条件,受比利时刑法的启发,应该是累积的:他们应该在同一个人身上同时满足(*De Wilde, Ooms and Versyp v. Belgium*, §68)。

六、拘留外国人

> **第 5 条第 1 款第 f 项**
>
> "f. 为防止某人未经许可进入国境或者为驱逐出境或者是引渡而对某人采取行动并予以合法的逮捕或者拘留。"

（一）为防止某人未经许可进入国境实施的拘留

99. 第 5 条第 1 款第 f 项允许国家在移民管制的背景下限制外国人的自由。虽然该条款的第一部分允许在国家许可入境前暂时拘留寻求庇护者和其他移民,但这种拘留必须符合第 5 条的目的,即保障自由并保证任何人都不会被任意剥夺人身自由(*Saadi v. the United Kingdom*[GC], §§64-66)。

100. 关于第 5 条第 1 款第 f 项的第一部分何时停止适用的问题,主要取决于国内法的规定,因为个人已被官方许可进入国境并居留(*Suso Musa v. Malta*, §97)。

101. 禁止任意拘留他人的原则适用于第 5 条第 1 款 f 项的第一部分,也同样适用于其第二部分(*Saadi v. the United Kingdom*[GC], §73)。

102. 第 5 条第 1 款第 f 项第一部分所规定的"禁止任意拘留"意味着必须善意执行拘留,必须与防止未经许可进入国境的目的紧密相关,并谨记这种措施并非针对罪犯,而是针对那些担心自己有生命危险而逃离自己国家的外国人,因此拘留的场所和条件应当适宜;拘留的时长不应超过条款目的合理要求的期间(*Saadi v. the United Kingdom*[GC], §74)。

103. 在审查拘留命令执行的方式时,本法院应该考虑那些可能成为移民的人的具体情况(*Kanagaratnam v. Belgium*, §80,申诉人和她的三个孩子被拘留在用于拘留成年人的密闭设施中;*Rahimi v. Greece*, §108,对没有他人陪伴的未成年人自动适用拘留)。

（二）为驱逐出境或引渡实施的拘留

104. 第 5 条第 1 款第 f 项并不要求拘留必须被合理地认为有必要进行,例如,防止其犯罪或逃跑。从这一点来说,第 5 条第 1 款第 f 项提供了不同于第 5 条第 1 款第 c 项的保护:第 f 项要求的是"所采取的行为是为了驱逐出境或引渡"。因此,在适用该条款时,相关的驱逐出境的决定是否符合国内法或公约,是无关紧要的(*Chahal v. the United Kingdom*, §112; *Čonka v. Belgium*, §38; *Nasrulloyev v. Russia*, §69; *Soldatenko v. Ukraine*, §109)。

105. 根据第 5 条第 1 款第 f 项的第二部分,拘留可因相关有权机关的询问而得以正当化——即使没有下发正式要求或引渡命令,因为"询问"可以被视为该条款规定中的"行动"(*X v. Switzerland*, Commission decision of 9 December 1980)。

106. 任何基于第 5 条第 1 款第 f 项的剥夺人身自由的行为只有在驱逐出境或引渡

程序正在进行的前提下才能得以正当化。如果上述程序没有得到尽职谨慎执行,那么第 5 条第 1 款第 f 项规定的剥夺人身自由的行为也将不被允许(*A. and Others v. the United Kingdom*[GC],§164;*Amie and Others v. Bulgaria*,§72)。

107. 要想避免被认为是任意拘留,根据第 5 条第 1 款第 f 项实施的拘留必须是善意执行的,必须与政府提出的理由紧密相关,拘留的场所和条件应该适宜,拘留的时长不应该超过该条款合理要求的期间(*Amie and Others v. Bulgaria*,§72;同时参见 *Yoh-Ekale Mwanje v. Belgium*,§§117–119)。

108. 出于驱逐目的而实施的拘留不应具有惩罚性质,而且应当采取恰当的保障措施(*Azimov v. Russia*,§172)。

109. 第 5 条第 1 款第 f 项或其他项并不允许在个人自由权利和国家保护其人民免受恐怖袭击的利益两者之间进行权衡(*A. and Others v. the United Kingdom*,§171)。

110. 公约并未规定在什么情况下许可引渡,也没有规定许可引渡前的程序,而且对逃犯进行逮捕的法律基础是逃犯所属国的国家当局发出的逮捕令,因此有关国家要进行合作,即使是非典型的引渡也不能认为是与公约相违背的(*Öcalan v. Turkey*[GC],§86;*Adamov v. Switzerland*,§57)。

111. 当涉及国家间的引渡约定时,如果其中一国是公约成员国而另一国不是,引渡条约所制定的规则,以及——在没有引渡条约时——国家间的合作,都是本法院在确定引起申诉的逮捕行为是否合法时需要考虑的有关因素。国家间合作引渡逃犯的行为本身并不会使得逮捕不合法,因此也不会引起有关公约第 5 条的问题(*Öcalan v. Turkey*[GC],§87)。

112. 成员国根据本法院的指示执行临时措施,即不将某人送回某一特定国家,这一临时措施本身与判断剥夺该个人的人身自由是否符合第 5 条第 1 款的问题并不相关(*Gebremedhin*[*Gaberamadhien*] *v. France*,§74)。拘留行为仍然应当合法且不任意(*Azimov v. Russia*,§169)。

适用该项临时措施阻止某人被驱逐出境,并不使得拘留行为不合法,只要相关的驱逐出境程序仍未完结,且继续拘留的时间合理[*S. P. v. Belgium*(dec.),and *Yoh-Ekale Mwanje v. Belgium*,§120]。

第四节　被剥夺人身自由的人应该得到的保障

一、拘留理由（第 5 条第 2 款）

> **第 5 条第 2 款**
> "应当以被逮捕的人所能理解的语言立即通知他被逮捕的理由以及被指控的罪名。"

（一）可适用性

113. 第 5 条第 2 款中所有的词语都应该灵活解释，特别是要与第 5 条保护所有人的人身自由不受任意剥夺的目的相一致。"逮捕"一词超出了刑事法律措施的范围，而"任何指控"也并非指适用条件，而是指一种可以考虑的可能性。第 5 条第 4 款并没有区分被逮捕人和被拘留人被剥夺人身自由的情况，因此也不应该将后者排除在第 5 条第 2 款的适用范围之外（*Van der Leer v. the Netherlands*, §§ 27 and 28）。因此第 5 条第 2 款可以适用于以引渡为目的的拘留（*Shamayev and Others v. Georgia and Russia*, §§ 414 and 415）和医学治疗的情况（*Van der Leer v. the Netherlands*, §§ 27 and 28; *X. v. the United Kingdom*, § 66），也适用于在假释后重新拘留某人的情况（*X v. Belgium*, Commission decision）。

（二）目的

114. 第 5 条第 2 款包含了最基本的保障，即被逮捕的人必须知道自己为什么被剥夺人身自由，这是第 5 条所提供的保护中必不可少的一部分。当一个人已得知被逮捕的原因，他就能——如果可行——根据第 5 条第 4 款的规定向法院申请质疑拘留的合法性（*Fox, Campbell and Hartley v. the United Kingdom*, § 40; *Čonka v. Belgium*, § 50）。

115. 任何有权提起诉讼、要求尽快确定拘留合法性的人，只有当他被及时恰当地告知剥夺其人身自由的原因时，才能有效利用这项权利（*Van der Leer v. the Netherlands*, § 28; *Shamayev and Others v. Georgia and Russia*, § 413）。

(三)应该向谁提供理由

116. 从第 5 条第 2 款的措辞可以看出,国家有义务向个人或其代理人提供具体信息(*Saadi v. the United Kingdom*,§53,由大审判庭于 2008 年确认)。如果申诉人无法理解这些信息,应该将相关细节提供给代表其利益的律师或监护人(*X v. the United Kingdom*,Commission Report,§106;*Z. H. v. Hungary*,§§42 – 43)。

(四)应该"及时"提供理由

117. 评估当局是否及时提供相关信息,应该根据不同案件的特殊情况来分析。但并不是说必须由实施逮捕的官员在逮捕的那一刻提供(*Fox,Campbell and Hartley v. the United Kingdom*,§40;*Murray v. the United Kingdom*,§72)。

118. 只要被逮捕的人在几个小时内被告知逮捕原因,那么就满足了及时性的要求[*Kerr v. the United Kingdom*(dec.);*Fox,Campbell and Hartley v. the United Kingdom*,§42]。

(五)提供理由的方式

119. 无须在许可逮捕的文件中写明理由,也不需要以书面方式或其他特殊方式告知[*X v. Germany*,Commission decision,1978 年 12 月 13 日;*Kane v. Cyprus*(dec.)]。

但是,如果在逮捕过程中没有对智力障碍人士的条件予以恰当的考虑——除非其律师或者其他被授权人已被告知该信息,就不能说已经向其提供了应有的信息,使其能够有效利用第 5 条第 4 款所保障的权利以质疑拘留的合法性(*Z. H. v. Hungary*,§41)。

120. 可以在逮捕后的讯问或询问阶段告知逮捕理由[*Fox,Campbell and Hartley v. the United Kingdom*,§41;*Murray v. the United Kingdom*,§77;*Kerr v. the United Kingdom*(dec.)]。

121. 如果被逮捕的人是在其实施故意犯罪行为后立即被逮捕的(*Dikme v. Turkey*,§54),或者是他们从之前的逮捕令或引渡请求中已经了解到所指控违法行为的细节[*Öcalan v. Turkey*(dec.)],就不能宣称不知道逮捕理由。

(六)需要提供的理由的范围

122. 关于当局所提供的信息内容是否充分,需要根据不同案件的特殊情况来审查(*Fox,Campbell and Hartley v. the United Kingdom*,§40)。但是,从第 5 条第 2 款的目的来看,单纯告知逮捕的法律依据,是不充分的(*Fox,Campbell and Hartley v. the United Kingdom*,§41;*Murray v. the United Kingdom*,§76;*Kortesis v. Greece*,§§61 – 62)。

123. 必须以一种简单的、被逮捕人能够理解的术语将逮捕理由告知被逮捕人,这样他们才能根据公约第 5 条第 4 款向法院申请质疑拘留的合法性(*Fox, Campbell and Hartley v. the United Kingdom*, §40;*Murray v. the United Kingdom*[GC], §72)。但是,第 5 条第 2 款并不要求所提供的信息包括被逮捕人被指控的全部罪行(*Bordovskiy v. Russia*, §56;*Nowak v. Ukraine*, §63;*Gasiņš v. Latvia*, §53)。

124. 出于引渡的目的而实施逮捕时,所提供的信息可以相对不那么完全(*Suso Musa v. Malta*, §§113 and 116;*Kaboulov v. Ukraine*, §144;*Bordovskiy v. Russia*, §56),因为基于这种目的进行逮捕不要求对指控罪行进行实质审查(*Bejaoui v. Greece*, Commission decision)。但是,这种情况下被逮捕的人也必须得知使他们能够根据公约第 5 条第 4 款向法院申请合法性审查的充分信息(*Shamayev and Others v. Georgia and Russia*, §427)。

(七)使用被逮捕人能够理解的语言

125. 如果逮捕令使用的是被逮捕人所不能理解的语言,就应该依据第 5 条第 2 款的要求,在之后的讯问阶段,以被逮捕人能理解的语言告知其逮捕原因(*Delcourt v. Belgium*, Commission decision)。

126. 但是,当出于这个目的而使用翻译人员时,当局有责任确保要求使用的翻译是谨慎且精确的(*Shamayev and Others v. Georgia and Russia*, §425)。

二、被立即送交法官的权利(第 5 条第 3 款)

> **第 5 条第 3 款**
> "根据本条第 1 款第 c 项的规定被逮捕或者拘留的任何人,应当立即送交法官或是其他经法律授权行使司法权的官员……"

(一)该条款的目的

127. 第 5 条第 3 款保障被怀疑实施犯罪行为而被逮捕或拘留的人免于被任意或不合理剥夺人身自由[*Aquilina v. Malta*[GC], §47;*Stephens v. Malta*(no. 2), §52]。

128. 对政府部门干预个人自由的行为加以司法控制是第 5 条第 3 款所提供保障的重要部分(*Brogan and Others v. the United Kingdom*, §58;*Pantea v. Romania*, §236;

Assenov and Others v. Bulgaria, §146)。司法控制是法治的应有之义,而法治是"公约前言明确提到的民主社会的一项基本原则",是"整个公约的精神源泉"(Brogan and Others v. the United Kingdom, §58)。

129. 司法控制是为了提供有效保障以防止虐待(虐待在拘留早期最可能发生),同时也为防止执法人员或其他有权机关滥用权力(Ladent v. Poland, §72)。

(二)及时自动进行司法控制

130. 第5条第3款的前半部分是为了保证对警察或者根据第1款第c项实施的行政拘留进行司法控制(De Jong, Baljet and Van den Brink v. the Netherlands, §51; Aquilina v. Malta[GC], §§48–49)。

131. 在被逮捕人第一次出庭时,司法控制最重要的就是要及时,从而有利于察觉虐待行为,也有利于保证对个人自由的不正当干预被控制在最低限度内。这一严格的时间要求只有很小的解释空间,否则就会减弱对个人的程序保障,同时可能会损害该权利的实质(McKay v. the United Kingdom[GC], §33)。

132. 第5条第3款并没有规定应将被逮捕人或被拘留人及时送交法官或其他司法官员这一要求的任何可能的例外,即使有预先的司法参与,也不例外(Bergmann v. Estonia, §45)。

133. 任何超过4天的期间,从表面上看,都属于过长的期间(Oral and Atabay v. Turkey, §43; McKay v. the United Kingdom[GC], §47; Nastase-Silivestru v. Romania, §32)。较短的时间也可能违反及时性的要求——如果不存在特别的困难或例外的情况阻止当局尽快将被逮捕人送交法官(Ipek and Others v. Turkey, §§36–37; and Kandzhov v. Bulgaria, §66)。

如果警方是在实际剥夺某人的自由一段时间之后拘留此人,那么及时性的要求就更为严格(Vassis and Others v. France, §60,将船员拘留在公海上)。

134. 将被逮捕人送交司法机关并不足以保证与第5条第3款的前半部分相符合(De Jong, Baljet and Van den Brink v. the Netherlands, §51; Pantea v. Romania, §231)。

135. 司法控制必须是自动适用的,而不能以被拘留人的预先申请为条件(McKay v. the United Kingdom[GC], §34; Varga v. Romania, §52; Viorel Burzo v. Romania, §107)。这种要求并不会改变第5条第3款所提供的保障的性质,这种保障不同于第5条第4款,后者所保障的是提起诉讼要求法院审查拘留合法性的权利。通过保证剥夺人身自由的行为受独立的司法监督,能有助于保证第5条第3款下保护个人免受任意拘留的目的(*Aquilina v. Malta*,§49;*Niedbala v. Poland*,§50)。

136. 要想实现该条款的目的,司法审查的自动适用性是必不可少的,因为一个受虐待的被拘留人可能无法提起要求法院审查其拘留合法性的申请;同样的情况也适用于其他弱势的被拘留人,例如,精神虚弱者或者那些不能理解司法人员所用语言的人(*McKay v. the United Kingdom*[GC],§34;*Ladent v. Poland*,§74)。

(三)恰当的司法人员的性质

137. 第5条第1款第c项中的"法官或其他经法律授权行使司法权的官员"与第5条第1款第c项中的"有关法律当局"有相同的意思(*Schiesser v. Switzerland*,§29)。

138. 行使"司法权力"并不局限于裁判法律纠纷。第5条第3款既包括检察院的官员,也包括法庭中的法官(*Schiesser v. Switzerland*,§28)。

139. 第三段中所指的"官员"必须能享有法律授予的恰当的"司法"权力(*Schiesser v. Switzerland*,§30)。

140. 就有权决定人身自由权事项的司法机关的身份认定而言,"法律"中规定的正式、明确的要求比实践标准更为重要(*Hood v. the United Kingdom*[GC],§60;*De Jong, Baljet and Van den Brink v. the Netherlands*,§48)。

141. "官员"与"法官"并不一样,但是应该具有后者的一些特性,那就是必须具备某些能为被逮捕人提供保障的条件(*Schiesser v. Switzerland*,§31)。

(四)独立性

142. 上述条件中独立性居首位,意指独立于执行机关和涉案当事人。这并不意味着该"官员"不可能在某种程度上从属于其他法官或者其他官员,只要他们自身享有相似的独立性便可(*Schiesser v. Switzerland*,§31)。

143. 一位有权决定拘留事项的司法官员有可能同时有其他的职责,如果该官员有权作为控方代表参与接下来的程序,那么就有理由对其独立性产生合理怀疑(*Huber v. Switzerland*,§43;*Brincat v. Italy*,§20)。

144. 就这一点而言,在对拘留问题做出决定的时候,公正十分重要:如果"由法律授权行使司法权力的官员"在之后代表控方参与刑事审判,其独立性和公正性将会受到质疑(*Brincat v. Italy*,§21;*Hood v. the United Kingdom*,§57;*Nikolova v. Bulgaria*[GC],§49;*Pantea v. Romania*,§236)。

(五) 程序要求

145. 程序上要求"官员"在做出任何恰当的决定前,有义务亲自听取个人证词(Schiesser v. Switzerland,§31;De Jong,Baljet and Van den Brink v. the Netherlands,§51;Nikolova v. Bulgaria[GC],§49;Aquilina v. Malta[GC],§50)。

146. 在审讯时,律师并不是必须在场(Schiesser v. Switzerland,§36)。但是,将律师排除在审讯程序之外有可能对申诉人陈述案件的能力造成负面影响(Lebedev v. Russia,§§83-91)。

(六) 实质要求

1. 审查拘留的实质内容

147. 实质上要求"官员"有义务审查各种支持或反对拘留的情况,并根据相关的法律标准,决定拘留是否有正当理由(Schiesser v. Switzerland,§31;Pantea v. Romania,§231)。换言之,第5条第3款要求司法官员审查有关拘留的实质内容(Aquilina v. Malta[GC],§47;Krejčíř v. the Czech Republic,§89)。

148. 对逮捕和拘留的最初自动审查必须审查合法性问题,并且审查是否能够合理怀疑被逮捕人实施了犯罪行为,换言之,就是拘留符合第5条第1款第c项规定的例外(McKay v. the United Kingdom[GC],§40;Oral and Atabay v. Turkey,§41)。

149. 司法官员必须审查的问题不仅仅是合法性问题。第5条第3款所要求的审查是为了确定剥夺个人人身自由的行为是否正当,需要考虑各种支持或反对拘留的情况(Aquilina v. Malta[GC],§52)。

150. 在具体案件的情况中,合法性审查的适用范围可能比第5条第4款更窄[Stephens v. Malta(no.2),§58]。

2. 释放权

151. 如果不存在正当的拘留理由,"官员"应当有权做出一项释放被拘留人的有效命令(Assenov and Others v. Bulgaria,§146;Nikolova v. Bulgaria[GC],§49;Niedbała v. Poland,§49;McKay v. the United Kingdom[GC],§40)。

152. 为了将延迟降到最低程度,强烈建议首次自动审查拘留合法性和拘留理由的司法官员同样有权决定保释问题。但这并非公约的要求,原则上来说,只要能在规定的时间内完成,这些问题也不是不能由两名不同的司法官员处理。因此,从解释的角度来看,不能要求对保释的审查在比首次自动审查更短的时间内完成,而法院已确定自动审查的最长时间为 4 天(*McKay v. the United Kingdom* [GC], §47)。

三、在合理的时间内得到审判或者在审判期间获得释放的权利(第 5 条第 3 款)

> **第 5 条第 3 款**
> "依照本条第 1 款第 c 项被逮捕或者拘留的任何人,有权在合理的时间内得到审判或者在审判期间得到释放。释放可以担保出庭为条件。"

(一)需要考虑的期限

153. 在确定公约第 5 条第 3 款所规定的审判期间的拘留期限时,需要考虑的期限从被告被拘留之日开始直到指控确定之日为止——即使只是由一审法院判决(*Solmaz v. Turkey*, §§23-24; *Kalashnikov v. Russia*, §110; *Wemhoff v. Germany*, §9)。

154. 鉴于公约第 5 条第 3 款与该条第 1 款第 c 项的紧密联系,一审被定罪的人不能被认为是后一项规定的出于"因对其实施犯罪的合理怀疑而将其移送至有管辖权的法院的目的"而被拘留的人,而是根据第 5 条第 1 款第 a 项规定而被拘留的人,该条款授权"在某人被有管辖权的法院定罪后"剥夺其人身自由(*Belevitskiy v. Russia*, §99; *Piotr Baranowski v. Poland*, §45; *Górski v. Poland*, §41)。

(二)一般原则

155. 第 5 条第 3 款的第二部分并非给予司法机关两个选择,即要么在合理的时间内审判被告的案件;要么在审判期间将被告临时释放。在被定罪之前,他必须被假定为无罪,该条款的目的主要是为了保证,当对他的继续拘留失去合理性时,就应该将其临时释放。

156. 只有当存在比公约第 5 条保护的个人人身自由更为重要的真正的公共利益需要时——尽管存在无罪的假定——继续拘留才是正当的。

157. 国内的司法机关负有首要责任,保证在具体案件中审前拘留的时间不超过合理时间。为了达到这个目的,他们必须考虑无罪假定这个原则,同时根据所有事实审查是否存在上述的公共利益可以使对第 5 条规定的违背得以正当化,并且将其记录于有关申请释放的决定中。本法院主要根据上述决定中给出的理由,以及申诉人出庭时陈述的已被确定的事实,来决定是否构成对公约第 5 条第 3 款的违反。

158. 能够持续合理怀疑被逮捕人实施了犯罪是继续拘留符合合法性的必要条件,但随着时间的推移,这个条件也不足以证明继续拘留的合法性,此时本法院就需要考虑司法机关给出的其他理由是否足以使剥夺个人人身自由的行为得以正当化。当存在"相关"且"充分"的理由时,国内法院还必须在审判过程中尽到"特殊注意"才能得到本法院的认可。

159. 总而言之,国内法院有义务审查审判期间的继续拘留行为,当情况不再足以使继续拘留得以正当化时,法院应该保证被告获得释放。在刚开始的阶段,合理怀疑可以使拘留得以正当化,但到某个阶段时,这个理由已经不够充分。至于拘留的期间是否合理,不能抽象审查,而是必须根据每个案件不同的情况来考虑,并不存在一个固定的时间标准(*McKay v. the United Kingdom*[GC],§§41－45;*Bykov v. Russia*[GC],§§61－64;*Idalov v. Russia*[GC],§§139－141;*Labita v. Italy*[GC],§§152－153;and *Kudła v. Poland*[GC],§§110－111)。

160. 支持或反对拘留的论据不能是"一般且抽象的"(*Boicenco v. Moldova*,§142;*Khudoyorov v. Russia*,§173),而必须根据具体的事实,以及能使拘留得以正当化的申诉人的具体情况(*Aleksanyan v. Russia*,§179)。

161. 准自动化地延长拘留时间违反了第 5 条第 3 款的规定(*Tase v. Romania*,§40)。

162. 在上述事项中,举证责任不能倒置,不能要求被拘留者证明存在释放自己的理由(*Bykov v. Russia*[GC],§64)。

163. 当可能存在相关事实可以使拘留得以正当化,但国内法院并未在决定中提及时,本法院没有义务确定这些事实,不需要代行国内法院的功能(*Bykov v. Russia*[GC],§66;*Giorgi Nikolaishvili v. Georgia*,§77)。只有通过给予一个合理的判决或决定,才有可能实现对司法机关运行的公众监督(*Tase v. Romania*,§41)。

(三)继续拘留的理由

164. 公约的案例法已经确定了 4 项拒绝保释的基本理由:(1)被告在应当出庭时缺席的风险;(2)一旦释放,被告会采取妨碍司法机关运行的行为,或(3)继续犯罪,或(4)扰乱公共秩序(*Tiron v. Romania*,§37;*Smirnova v. Russia*,§59;*Piruzyan v. Armenia*,§94)。

1. 潜逃的危险

165. 潜逃的危险并不应该仅从被告罪行的严重程度来考虑,还应该考虑其他的一些要么能够确定存在潜逃危险、要么使得审前拘留没有必要的因素(*Panchenko v. Russia*,§106)。

166. 审查潜逃危险大小时还应该考虑被告的性格、道德水平、住宅、职业、财产、家庭关系,还有与被告所在国的各种联系(*Becciev v. Moldova*,§58)。

167. 只是缺乏固定居住地并不一定引起潜逃的危险(*Sulaoja v. Estonia*,§64)。

168. 随着拘留时间的延长,潜逃危险必然会减小(*Neumeister v. Austria*,§10)。

169. 可能被判的刑罚严重程度是审查潜逃可能性大小的因素之一,但是指控的严重程度本身并不能使长期的审前拘留得以正当化(*Idalov v. Russia*[GC],§145;*Garycki v. Poland*,§47;*Chraidi v. Germany*,§40;*Ilijkov v. Bulgaria*,§§80-81)。

170. 虽然一般而言,"共犯"的供词可能是存在犯罪的主要表现,但是单凭该供词不足以使长时间的拘留得以正当化(*Dereci v. Turkey*,§38)。

2. 阻碍诉讼程序

171. 在判断被告是否有可能阻碍诉讼程序正常进行时,不应该只抽象地考虑,而需要用事实证据来证明(*Becciev v. Moldova*,§59)。

172. 在审判初期可以接受有可能对证人带来压力这个理由(*Jarzynski v. Poland*,§43)。

173. 但是长远而言,保证调查这个要求并不足以使拘留嫌疑人得以正当化:随着时间的推移,询问已经完成,陈述已经记录完毕,调查也已完成,上述风险会慢慢降低(*Clooth v. Belgium*,§44)。

3. 再次犯罪

174. 指控的严重性可能会使司法机关决定对嫌疑人还押拘留,以防止其再次犯罪。但是根据相关案件的情况,特别是以往的事实和被告的品格,这个风险必须是合理的,采取的措施也必须恰当(*Clooth v. Belgium*,§40)。

175. 以往的犯罪可以作为担心被告会再次犯罪的合理理由(*Selçuk v. Turkey*,§34;*Matznetter v. Austria*,§9)。

176. 不能从被告没有工作或家人这一事实推断出被告会再次犯罪(*Sulaoja v. Estonia*,§64)。

4. 保障公共秩序

177. 由于案件的严重性和公众的反应，某些犯罪有可能会造成社会秩序的混乱，从而使审前拘留至少在一段时间内得以正当化。在例外的情况下，本法院会根据公约的目的将这一因素纳入考虑范围，只要国内法律确认某一具体犯罪会导致公众秩序混乱。

178. 但是，只有当事实能够表明释放被告有可能会引起公共秩序混乱时，这一因素才会被认为是相关且充分的。另外，只有在公共秩序持续受到实际威胁时，继续拘留才是合法的，而且继续拘留也不代表被判处刑罚（Letellier v. France, §51; I. A. v. France, §104; Prencipe v. Monaco, §79; Tiron v. Romania, §§41–42）。

（四）特殊注意

179. 调查的复杂性和特殊性是在确定当局在诉讼程序中是否尽到了"特殊注意"时应该考虑的因素（Scott v. Spain, §74）。

180. 被拘留的被告要求其案件得到快速处理的权利不应该阻碍司法机关恰当地行使其职能（Shabani v. Switzerland, §65; Sadegül Özdemir v. Turkey, §44）。

（五）替代措施

181. 当决定是应该释放还是拘留某人时，当局应该考虑采取替代措施来保障其出庭（Idalov v. Russia [GC], §140）。该条规定不仅涉及"在合理时间内得到审判或是在审判期间得到释放"的权利，还涉及"如果能够保证被告出庭，就可以将其释放"（Khudoyorov v. Russia, §183; Lelièvre v. Belgium, §97; Shabani v. Switzerland, §62）。

（六）保释

182. 公约第5条第3款提供的保护不仅是为了保证损失得到赔偿，还为了保证被告能出庭。因此应该主要考虑"被告的财产以及担保人与被告的关系，换言之，就是考虑不出庭导致失去保释金或者有损于担保人的后果这一可能性足以使被告打消潜逃想法的程度"（Mangouras v. Spain [GC], §78; Neumeister v. Austria, §14）。

183. 只有当存在正当的拘留理由时，才会要求提供保释金（Musuc v. Moldova, §42; Aleksandr Makarov v. Russia, §139）。如果保释金或者其他保证能够避免潜逃的危险，那么被告就应该被释放，要注意，当有可能判处较轻刑罚时，被告潜逃的可能性会降低，应该将这一点纳入考虑范围（Vrenčev v. Serbia, §76）。当局在确定保释时应该考虑周全，要考虑是否必须继续拘留被告（Piotr Osuch v. Poland, §39; Bojilov v. Bulgaria,

§60;*Skrobol v. Poland*,§57)。

184. 另外,保释金的金额应该在确定保释的决定中解释清楚(*Georgieva v. Bulgaria*,§§15,30 and 31),而且必须考虑被告的收入(*Hristova v. Bulgaria*,§111)和他的支付能力(*Toshev v. Bulgaria*,§§69-73)。在某些特定情况中,也可以考虑应归咎于被告的损失(*Mangouras v. Spain*[GC],§§81 and 92)。

185. 在没有任何司法控制的情况下根据法律自动拒绝保释,这不符合第5条第3款的规定(*Piruzyan v. Armenia*,§105;*S. B. C. v. the United Kingdom*,§§23-24)。

(七)拘留期的合理性

186. 公约第5条第3款不能解释为,只要拘留不超过一定的最短时间段,就可以无条件允许审前拘留。任何长度的拘留期,无论多短,当局都应该表明其合法性(*Idalov v. Russia*[GC],§140;*Tase v. Romania*,§40;*Castravet v. Moldova*,§33;*Belchev v. Bulgaria*,§82)。

(八)对未成人的审前拘留

187. 对未成年人进行的审前拘留应该作为最后的不得已措施;拘留期间应该尽可能得短,而且,当拘留是严格必要时,未成年人应该与成年人分开关押(*Nart v. Turkey*,§31;*Güveç v. Turkey*,§109)。

四、要求法庭迅速审查拘留合法性的权利(第5条第4款)

> **第5条第4款**
> "每个因被逮捕或者被拘留而被剥夺自由的人都应该享有通过诉讼迅速确定其拘留的合法性以及当确定其拘留合法时得以释放的权利。"

(一)条款目的

188. 第5条第4款是公约中的人身保护规定,它为被拘留者提供了主动请求司法审查的权利(*Mooren v. Germany*[GC],§106;*Rakevich v. Russia*,§43)。

189. 本法院不认为违反公约第5条第1款,并不意味着可以免于对是否符合第5条第4款的审查。这两款规定是相互独立的,符合前者的要求并不意味着必然符合后者的要求(*Douiyeb v. the Netherlands*[GC],§57;*Kolompar v. Belgium*,§45)。

(二)所要求的审查的性质

190. 第5条第4款保障被逮捕人或被拘留人有权提起诉讼,请求法院审查剥夺其自由的程序性和实质性条件(从第5条第1款的意义上来说)的"合法性"(*Idalov v. Russia*[GC],§161;*Reinprecht v. Austria*,§31)。

第5条第4款中的"合法性"与第5条第1款中的含义相同,因此,被逮捕人或被拘留人不仅有权根据国内法的要求,还有权根据公约要求、公约的一般原则以及第5条第1款所允许的限制目的来要求审查对其拘留的"合法性"(*Suso Musa v. Malta*,§50)。

191. 符合第5条第4款的司法审查的形式在每个领域都可能有所差别,同时也取决于所涉及的剥夺自由的方式(*M. H. v. the United Kingdom*,§75)。

192. 并不排除法院对拘留合法性的定期自动审查机制可以保证符合第5条第4款的要求,但是,在建立起自动审查之后,应当在"合理时间间隔"做出关于拘留合法性的决定(*Abdulkhanov v. Russia*,§§209 and 212-214,总结概括了与第5条第1款第a、c、e和f项所规定的拘留情形有关的判例)。

193. 若根据公约第5条第1款第c项的规定拘留某人,"法院"必须被授权审查是否有足够证据合理怀疑他/她已犯罪,因为要想使得还押拘留在公约的意义上"合法",证明此种怀疑的存在就十分重要(*Nikolova v. Bulgaria*[GC],§58)。

194. 当某人被主管法庭定罪并剥夺自由时,第5条第4款所要求的监督就被包含在裁判程序最终的法庭判决中(*De Wilde, Ooms and Versyp v. Belgium*,§76),因此不需要进一步的审查。然而,如果判决并剥夺某人自由的依据容易随着时间的推移而改变,就要求保留对公约第5条第4款所规定的个体提出追索的可能性[*Kafkaris v. Cyprus*(dec.),§58]。

195. 根据第5条第4款,被拘留者有权依据在最初决定剥夺其人身自由之后出现的新因素,申请有管辖权的"法院"迅速确定对其自由的剥夺已变得"非法"(*Abdulkhanov v. Russia*,§208;*Azimov v. Russia*,§§151-152)。

196. 被长期强制监禁在精神治疗场所的精神不健全的人,有权"在合理的期间内"提起诉讼,质疑其监禁的合法性(*M. H. v. the United Kingdom*,§77,对可适用原则的最新总结)。仅依靠当局有权启动的定期审查机制是不够的(*X. v. Finland*,§170;*Raudevs v. Latvia*,§82)。

197. 第 5 条第 1 款第 e 项意义上的"合法拘留"的标准包括:在涉及精神疾病患者的继续拘留时,第 5 条第 4 款所保障的对合法性的审查应当以最新的医疗评估为证据,参考病人当时的健康状态(包括其危险性),而不是参考做出最初的拘留决定时的情况 [*Juncal v. the United Kingdom*(dec.), §30; *Ruiz Rivera v. Switzerland*, §60; *H. W. v. Germany*, §107]。

198. 被拘留者出于第 5 条第 4 款规定的目的而求助的"法院",并不必须是属于该国标准司法体系内的传统法院(*Weeks v. the United Kingdom*, §61)。但是它必须是一个能够提供一定程序保障、具有"裁判特征"的主体。因此该"法院"必须独立于行政机关和案件的双方[*Stephens v. Malta*(no. 1), §95]。

199. 要想满足公约的要求,国内法院所进行的审查必须符合国家司法的实体规则和程序规则,同时也要符合第 5 条的目的,即保护个人免受任意侵害(*Koendjbiharie v. the Netherlands*, §27)。

200. 尽管第 5 条第 4 款并不强制缔约国为审查拘留合法性建立第二层次的司法权,原则上来说,建立这种机制的国家必须在上诉程序中给予被拘留者与一审程序中相同的保障(*Kučera v. Slovakia*, §107; *Navarra v. France*, §28; *Toth v. Austria*, §84)。

201. 第 5 条第 4 款并不强制法院在审查对拘留的上诉时注重上诉人所提交的意见中所包含的每一项论据。然而,法院并不能忽视或忽略被拘留者所提供的、能引起对剥夺其自由的行为(在公约意义上的)"合法性"的质疑的具体事实(*Ilijkov v. Bulgaria*, §94)。

202. "法院"如果发现拘留不合法,必须具有下达释放命令的权力;仅仅拥有建议的权利是不够的(*Benjamin and Wilson v. the United Kingdom*, §§33-34)。

(三)程序保障

203. 第 5 条第 4 款中的程序公正要求并未规定适用于无关内容、事实和情形的固定不变的统一标准。尽管并不总是要求符合第 5 条第 4 款的程序必须具有和第 6 款中对刑事或民事诉讼所要求的相同的保障,但它也必须具有裁判特征,并为所涉及的剥夺自由的类型提供适当的保障(*A. and Others v. the United Kingdom*[GC], §203; *Idalov v. Russia*[GC], §161)。

204. 当对某人的拘留属于第 5 条第 1 款第 c 项所规定的情形时,必须开庭审理(*Nikolova v. Bulgaria*[GC], §58)。被拘留者本人或者通过其他形式的代理表达自己意见的机会是与剥夺自由有关的诉讼程序中最基本的保障之一(*Kampanis v. Greece*, §47)。

然而,第5条第4款并不要求每次在被拘留人提起反对延长其拘留的决定的上诉时都开庭审理,但是在合理的情况下,应该允许行使此项权利(*Çatal v. Turkey*, §33; *Altınok v. Turkey*, §45)。

205. 诉讼程序必须是对抗式的,并且必须允许双方之间的"平等手段原则" (*Reinprecht v. Austria*, §31; *A. and Others v. the United Kingdom*[GC], §204)。在还押候审的情况下,由于对被告实施了犯罪的合理怀疑是继续拘禁合法性的必要条件,就必须给予被拘留人有效质疑针对其指控的基础的机会。这可能要求法院听取证人与继续拘留的合法性有关的证言(*Ţurcan v. Moldova*, §§67 - 70)。

如果申诉人或其律师被拒绝获取调查档案里对于有效质疑拘留合法性来说十分重要的文件,那么平等手段原则就没有得到保障(*Ovsjannikov v. Estonia*, §72; *Fodale v. Italy*, §41; *Korneykova v. Ukraine*, §68)。同样重要的一点是,所涉及的个人不仅应当有机会被听取个人陈述,还应当有机会获得律师的有效帮助(*Cernák v. Slovakia*, §78)。

206. 对抗式程序以及平等手段的原则必须在上诉法庭的审理过程中得到同等的尊重(*Çatal v. Turkey*, §§33 - 34 以及其中引用的案例)。

(四)要求"迅速"

207. 第5条第4款不仅保障被拘留者有权提起诉讼质疑拘留的合法性,还保障其有权在提出诉讼之后就拘留的合法性得到迅速审判并在证明非法的情况下得到终止令 (*Idalov v. Russia*[GC], §154; *Baranowski v. Poland*, §68)。得到迅速审判的权利是否被尊重必须在不同案例中具体情况具体分析(*Rehbock v. Slovenia*, §84)。

208. 在某人被拘留之后,如果有必要,必须尽快提供法律审查的机会,并在之后的合理时间间隔内定期审查(*Molotchko v. Ukraine*, §148)。

209. 与第5条第3款的"及时"(马上)相比,"迅速"(在短时间内)的概念表示了较小的紧迫性(*E. v. Norway*, §64; *Brogan and Others v. the United Kingdom*, §59)。

然而,当非司法机关而不是法院决定拘留某人时,第5条第4款所要求的司法审查的"迅速"标准就接近于第5条第3款的"及时"标准了(*Shcherbina v. Russia*, §§65 - 70,对于公诉人向申诉人下达的拘留令的司法审查延迟了16天,本法院认为这一期限过长)。

210. 在上诉程序中,"迅速"标准就没有那么严格(*Abdulkhanov v. Russia*,§198)。如果最初的拘留令是由法院依据恰当程序做出的,那么本法院就会容忍二审法院在诉讼中适用较长的审查期限(*Shcherbina v. Russia*,§65)。

1. 需要考虑的期间

211. 本法院将提出释放申请或提起诉讼的时间作为起点。在对申诉人拘留的合法性做出最终决定时(包括任何上诉程序),相关的期间就随之结束(*Sanchez-Reisse v. Switzerland*,§54;*E. v. Norway*,§64)。

212. 如果在向法院提起诉讼之前必须先穷尽行政救济,那么期间就应该从行政当局着手处理时起算(*Sanchez-Reisse v. Switzerland*,§54)。

213. 如果在两个以上的审判层级进行了诉讼,就必须从总体上审查确定是否符合"迅速"这一要求(*Hutchison Reid v. the United Kingdom*,§78;*Navarra v. France*,§28)。

2. 评估速度需要考虑的相关因素

214. 不能抽象地定义"迅速"一词。就如同第5条第3款和第6条第1款中"合理的时间"一词一样,是否"迅速"也必须在不同的案例中具体情况具体分析(*R. M. D. v. Switzerland*,§42)。

215. 在审查第5条第4款所要求的迅速特征时,可以参照那些在审查公约第5条第3款和第6条第1款意义上的"合理时间"要求时发挥作用的因素,来考虑可以比较的因素,例如,当局表现出的勤勉程度,任何由被拘留人员造成的迟延以及其他不涉及国家责任的造成迟延的因素(*Mooren v. Germany*[GC],§106;*Kolompar v. Belgium*,§42)。

216. 在与第6条第1款有关的案例中,每一审级程序持续一年的做法或许可以作为惯例,但是第5条第4款是关于自由的问题,因此特别要求迅速(*Panchenko v. Russia*,§117)。在有关个人自由的问题上,本法院对于国家是否符合迅速审查拘留合法性的要求有着非常严格的标准(*Kadem v. Malta*,§§44-45,本法院认为,用17天来决定对申诉人的拘留是否合法,时间过长;*Mamedova v. Russia*,§96,上诉程序持续了26天,被认为是违反了"迅速"这一要求)。

217. 如果决定涉及复杂的问题——如被拘留人员的医疗状况,那么在确定多长时间属于第5条第4款所要求的"合理"时,应当考虑这些问题的复杂性。然而,即使在复杂情况下,仍然要求当局对某些因素进行极为迅速的审查,包括在审前拘留案件中的无罪推定(*Frasik v. Poland*,§63;*Jablonski v. Poland*,§§91－93)。

218. 在刑事案件中,对于还押候审的审查时间间隔应当很短(*Bezicheri v. Italy*,§21)。

219. 如果在做出决定前,时间长度初步看来就与迅速的概念不相符,本法院会要求国家解释迟延的原因,或者提出特别的理由来证明时间迟延的正当性(*Musiał v. Poland* [GC],§44;*Koendjbiharie v. the Netherlands*,§29)。

220. 无论是过重的工作负荷还是假期,都不能成为司法机关在一段时间内不作为的正当理由(*E. v. Norway*,§66;*Bezicheri v. Italy*,§25)。

五、因非法拘留得到赔偿的权利(第 5 条第 5 款)

> **第 5 条第 5 款**
> "违反本条规定被逮捕或者拘留的任何人都有权得到赔偿。"

(一)适用性

221. 第 5 款中规定的受赔偿权的前提是国内当局或者本法院已经确定拘留行为违反了第 5 条的其他任何一款规定(*N. C. v. Italy* [GC],§49;*Pantea v. Romania*,§262;*Vachev v. Bulgaria*,§78)。

222. 如果国内当局并不认为存在直接或实质违反第 5 条其他条款的情况,本法院必须自己首先确定存在上述的违反情况后,才能适用第 5 条第 5 款(*Nechiporuk and Yonkalo v. Ukraine*,§§227 and 229;*Yankov v. Bulgaria*,§§190－193)。

223. 第 5 条第 5 款的适用性并不取决于国内法院对行为违法的认定或者证明如果不是违反第 5 条的情况涉案人员本应该被释放的证据(*Blackstock v. the United Kingdom*,§51;*Waite v. the United Kingdom*,§73)。逮捕或拘留从国内法来看可能是合法的,但仍然违反了第 5 条,因此可以适用第 5 条第 5 款(*Harkmann v. Estonia*,§50)。

(二)司法救济

224. 第 5 条第 5 款规定了一项直接且可执行的在国内法院提起赔偿请求的权利(*A. and Others v. the United Kingdom* [GC],§229;*Storck v. Germany*,§122)。

（三）赔偿的可获得性

225. 遵守第5条第5款需要保证有可能就涉及剥夺人身自由的违反第5条第1、2、3、4款的行为要求赔偿（参见近期的案件，*Michalák v. Slovakia*，§204；*Lobanov v. Russia*，§54）。

226. 可执行的受赔偿权必须在本法院判决前或判决后是可获得的（*Stanev v. Bulgaria*[GC]，§§183－184；*Brogan and Others v. the United Kingdom*，§67）。

227. 有效地享有受赔偿权必须由足够的确定性来保证（*Ciulla v. Italy*，§44；*Sakık and Others v. Turkey*，§60）。赔偿必须在理论上（*Dubovik v. Ukraine*，§74）和实践上都具有可获得性（*Chitayev and Chitayev v. Russia*，§195）。

228. 在考虑赔偿的要求时，国内当局必须根据公约第5条的精神来解释和适用国内法，而不应过分形式主义（*Shulgin v. Ukraine*，§65；*Houtman and Meeus v. Belgium*，§46）。

（四）赔偿的性质

229. 受赔偿权主要指的是经济赔偿，它并不包括第5条第4款规定的保证被拘留人被释放的权利（*Bozano v. France*，Commission decision）。

230. 将审前拘留的时间计入刑罚时间并不属于第5条第5款规定的赔偿，因为它不是经济性的[*Włoch v. Poland*(no.2)，§32]。

（五）损害的存在

231. 第5条第5款并不禁止缔约国根据涉案当事人因违反公约的行为所受损害的程度来进行赔偿。如果不存在金钱上或精神上的损害，那就不存在"赔偿"的问题（*Wassink v. the Netherlands*，§38）。

232. 但是，过分形式主义地要求精神损害的证据，不符合受赔偿权的规定（*Danev v. Bulgaria*，§§34－35）。

（六）赔偿的数额

233. 公约第5条第5款并不赋予申诉人取得特定数额赔偿的权利（*Damian-Burueana and Damian v. Romania*，§89；*Çağdaş Şahin v. Turkey*，§34）。

234. 但是，可以忽视的或者与违反行为的严重性不相符的赔偿就不符合第5条第5款的规定，因为这会使得该条款保障的权利成为理论上的或虚幻的[*Cumber v. the United Kingdom*，Commission decision；*Attard v. Malta*(dec.)]。

235. 赔偿数额不能明显低于本法院在类似案件中判决的赔偿数额（*Ganea v. Moldova*，§30；*Cristina Boicenco v. Moldova*，§43）。

援引案例一览

本指南援引的判例法涉及欧洲人权法院的判决或裁定以及欧洲人权委员会的决定或报告。

除非另行指明,所有参考皆是本法院审判庭依法做出的判决。缩写"(dec.)"是指该处援引为本法院裁定,"[GC]"是指该案件由大审判庭审判。

本指南电子版中援引案例的超链接直接跳转 HUDOC 数据库(http://hudoc.echr.coe.int)。该数据库提供本法院(包括大审判庭、审判庭和委员会的判决、裁定和相关案例、咨询意见以及案例法信息注解中的法律总结)、委员会(决定和报告)和部长委员会(决议)的判例法。

本法院以英语和/或法语这两种官方语言发布判决和裁定。HUDOC 也包含许多重要案例的近 30 种非官方言语的翻译,以及由第三方制作的大约 100 个在线案例汇总的链接。

(注:为了避免重复,本章所附的相关案例索引没有在中文部分进行翻译,读者可在对应的英文部分阅读。)

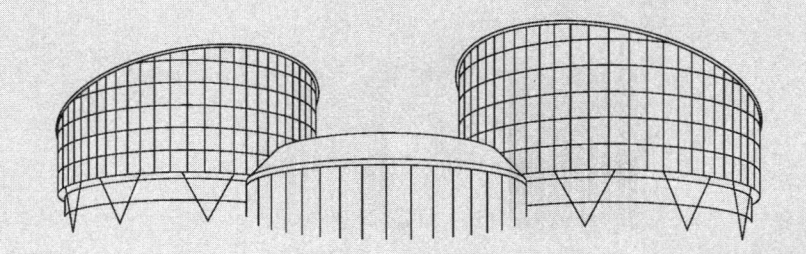

EUROPEAN COURT OF HUMAN RIGHTS
COUR EUROPÉENNE DES DROITS DE L'HOMME

Chapter Ⅱ Guide on Article 5 of the Convention Right to Liberty and Security

COUNCIL OF EUROPE
CONSEIL DE L'EUROPE

Publishers or organisations wishing to reproduce this report (or a translation thereof) in print or online are asked to contact publishing@echr.coe.int for further instructions.

© Council of Europe/European Court of Human Rights, 2014

This guide has been prepared by the Research Division and does not bind the Court. The first edition of the Guide was published in June 2012. The manuscript for this second edition has been updated to June 2014; it may be subject to editorial revision.

The document is available for downloading at www.echr.coe.int (Case-Law-Case-Law Analysis-Case-Law Guides).

Note to readers

This Guide is part of the series of Guides on the Convention published by the European Court of Human Rights (hereafter "the Court", "the European Court" or "the Strasbourg Court") to inform legal practitioners about the fundamental judgments and decisions delivered by the Strasbourg Court. This particular Guide analyses and sums up the case-law on Article 5 of the European Convention on Human Rights (hereafter "the Convention" or "the European Convention"). Readers will find herein the key principles in this area and the relevant precedents.

The case-law cited has been selected among the leading, major, and/or recent judgments and decisions.

The Court's judgments and decisions serve not only to decide those cases brought before it but, more generally, to elucidate, safeguard and develop the rules instituted by the Convention, thereby contributing to the observance by the States of the engagements undertaken by them as Contracting Parties (*Ireland v. the United Kingdom*, § 154, 18 January 1978, Series A no. 25, and, more recently, *Jeronovičs v. Latvia* [GC], no. 44898/10, § 109, 5 July 2016).

The mission of the system set up by the Convention is thus to determine issues of public policy in the general interest, thereby raising the standards of protection of human rights and extending human rights jurisprudence throughout the community of the Convention States (*Konstantin Markin v. Russia* [GC], § 89, no. 30078/06, ECHR 2012). Indeed, the Court has emphasised the Convention's role as a "constitutional instrument of European public order" in the field of human rights (*Bosphorus Hava Yolları Turizm ve Ticaret Anonim Şirketi v. Ireland* [GC], no. 45036/98, § 156, ECHR 2005-VI).

This Guide contains references to keywords for each cited Article of the Convention and its Additional Protocols. The legal issues dealt with in each case aresummarised in a List of keywords, chosen from a thesaurus of terms taken (in most cases) directly from the text of the Convention and its Protocols.

The HUDOC database of the Court's case-law enables searches to be made by keyword. Searching with these keywords enables a group of documents with similar legal content to be found (the Court's reasoning and conclusions in each case aresummarised through the keywords). Keywords for individual cases can be found by clicking on the Case Details tag in HUDOC. For further information about the HUDOC database and the keywords, please see the HUDOC user manual.

Ⅰ. Scope of application

> Article 5 § 1
>
> "1. Everyone has the right to liberty and security of person. No one shall be deprived of his liberty save in the following cases and in accordance with a procedure preschribed by law:..."

A. Deprivation of liberty

1. In proclaiming the "right to liberty", Article 5 contemplates the physical liberty of the person; its aim is to ensure that no one should be deprived of that liberty in an arbitrary fashion. It is not concerned with mere restrictions on liberty of movement, which are governed by Article 2 of Protocol No. 4 (*Creangă v. Romania* [GC]*, § 92; *Engel and Others v. the Netherlands*, § 58).

2. The difference between restrictions on movement serious enough to fall within the ambit of a deprivation of liberty under Article 5 § 1 and mere restrictions of liberty which are subject only to Article 2 of Protocol No. 4 is one of degree or intensity, and not one of nature or substance (*Guzzardi v. Italy*, § 93; *Rantsev v. Cyprus and Russia*, § 314; *Stanev v. Bulgaria* [GC], § 115).

3. A deprivation of liberty is not confined to the classic case of detention following arrest or conviction, but may take numerous other forms (*Guzzardi v. Italy*, § 95).

---

* The hyperlinks to the cases cited in the electronic version of the Guide refer to the original text in English or French (the two official languages of the Court) of the judgment or decision delivered by the Court and to the decisions or reports of the European Commission of Human Rights. Unless otherwise indicated, all references are to a judgment on the merits delivered by a Chamber of the Court. The abbreviation "(dec.)" indicates that the citation is of a decision of the Court and "[GC]" that the case was heard by the Grand Chamber.

B. Criteria to be applied

4. The Court does not consider itself bound by the legal conclusions of the domestic authorities as to whether or not there has been a deprivation of liberty, and undertakes an autonomous assessment of the situation (*H. L. v. the United Kingdom*, § 90; *H. M. v. Switzerland*, §§ 30 and 48; *Creangă v. Romania* [GC], § 92).

5. In order to determine whether someone has been "deprived of his liberty" within the meaning of Article 5, the starting point must be his concrete situation and account must be taken of a whole range of criteria such as the type, duration, effects and manner of implementation of the measure in question (*Guzzardi v. Italy*, § 92; *Medvedyev and Others v. France* [GC], § 73; *Creangă v. Romania* [GC], § 91).

6. The requirement to take account of the "type" and "manner of implementation" of the measure in question enables the Court to have regard to the specific context and circumstances surrounding types of restriction other than the paradigm of confinement in a cell. Indeed, the context in which the measure is taken is an important factor, since situations commonly occur in modern society where the public may be called on to endure restrictions on freedom of movement or liberty in the interests of the common good (*Nada v. Switzerland* [GC], § 226; *Austin and Others v. the United Kingdom* [GC], § 59).

7. The notion of deprivation of liberty within the meaning of Article 5 § 1 contains both an *objective element* of a person's confinement in a particular restricted space for a not negligible length of time, and an additional *subjective element* in that the person has not validly consented to the confinement in question (*Storck v. Germany*, § 74; *Stanev v. Bulgaria* [GC], § 117).

8. Relevant objective factors to be considered include the possibility to leave the restricted area, the degree of supervision and control over the person's movements, the extent of isolation and the availability of social contacts (see, for example, *Guzzardi v. Italy*, § 95; *H. M. v. Switzerland*, § 45; *H. L. v. the United Kingdom*, § 91; and *Storck v. Germany*, § 73).

9. Where the facts indicate a deprivation of liberty within the meaning of Article 5 § 1,

the relatively short duration of the detention does not affect this conclusion (*Rantsev v. Cyprus and Russia*, § 317; *Iskandarov v. Russia*, § 140).

10. An element of coercion in the exercise of police powers of stop and search is indicative of a deprivation of liberty, notwithstanding the short duration of the measure (*Krupko and Others v. Russia*, § 36; *Foka v. Turkey*, § 78; *Gillan and Quinton v. the United Kingdom*, § 57; *Shimovolos v. Russia*, § 50; and *Brega and Others v. Moldova*, § 43).

11. The fact that a person is not handcuffed, put in a cell or otherwise physically restrained does not constitute a decisive factor in establishing the existence of a deprivation of liberty (*M. A. v. Cyprus*, § 193).

12. The right to liberty is too important in a democratic society for a person to lose the benefit of Convention protection for the single reason that he may have given himself up to be taken into detention, especially when that person is legally incapable of consenting to, or disagreeing with, the proposed action (*H. L. v. the United Kingdom*, § 90; *Stanev v. Bulgaria* [GC], § 119).

13. The fact that a person lacks legal capacity does not necessarily mean that he is unable to understand and consent to situation (ibid., § 130; *Shtukaturov v. Russia*, §§ 107 – 109; *D. D. v. Lithuania*, § 150).

C. Measures adopted within a prison

14. Disciplinary steps imposed within a prison which have effects on conditions of detention cannot be considered as constituting deprivation of liberty. Such measures must be regarded in normal circumstances as modifications of the conditions of lawful detention and fall outside the scope of Article 5 § 1 of the Convention [*Bollan v. the United Kingdom* (dec.)].

D. Security checks of air travellers

15. Where a passenger has been stopped by border officials during border control in an airport in order to clarify his situation and where this detention has not exceeded the time strictly necessary to comply with relevant formalities, no issue arises under Article 5 of the

Convention [*Gahramanov v. Azerbaijan* (dec.), § 41].

E. Deprivation of liberty outside formal arrest and detention

16. The question of applicability of Article 5 has arisen in a variety of circumstances, including:

- the placement of individuals in psychiatric or social care institutions (see, among many other authorities, *De Wilde, Ooms and Versyp v. Belgium*; *Nielsen v. Denmark*; *H. M. v. Switzerland*; *H. L. v. the United Kingdom*; *Storck v. Germany*; *A. and Others v. Bulgaria*; *Stanev v. Bulgaria* [GC]);
- confinement in airport transit zones (*Amuur v. France*; *Shamsa v. Poland*; *Mogoş and Others v. Romania* (dec.); *Mahdid and Haddar v. Austria* (dec.); and *Riad and Idiab v. Belgium*);
- questioning in a police station (*I. I. v. Bulgaria*; *Osypenko v. Ukraine*; *Salayev v. Azerbaijan*; *Farhad Aliyev v. Azerbaijan*; and *Creangă v. Romania* [GC]);
- stops and searches by the police (*Foka v. Turkey*; *Gillan and Quinton v. the United Kingdom*; and *Shimovolos v. Russia*);
- crowd control measures adopted by the police on public order grounds (*Austin and Others v. the United Kingdom* [GC]);
- house arrest (*Mancini v. Italy*; *Lavents v. Latvia*; *Nikolova v. Bulgaria* (no. 2); and *Dacosta Silva v. Spain*).

F. Positive obligations with respect to deprivation of liberty

17. Article 5 § 1, first sentence, lays down a positive obligation on the State not only to refrain from active infringement of the rights in question, but also to take appropriate steps to provide protection against an unlawful interference with those rights to everyone within its jurisdiction (*El-Masri v. the former Yugoslav Republic of Macedonia* [GC], § 239).

18. The State is therefore obliged to take measures providing effective protection of vulnerable persons, including reasonable steps to prevent a deprivation of liberty of which

the authorities have or ought to have knowledge (*Storck v. Germany*, § 102).

19. The responsibility of a State is engaged if it acquiesces in a person's loss of liberty by private individuals or fails to put an end to the situation (*Riera Blume and Others v. Spain*; *Rantsev v. Cyprus and Russia*, §§ 319 – 321; *Medova v. Russia*, §§ 123 – 125).

II. Lawfulness of the detention under Article 5 § 1

A. Purpose of Article 5

20. The key purpose of Article 5 is to prevent arbitrary or unjustified deprivations of liberty (*McKay v. theUnited Kingdom* [GC], § 30). The right to liberty and security is of the highest importance in a "democratic society" within the meaning of the Convention (*Medvedyev and Others v. France* [GC], § 76; *Ladent v. Poland*, § 45, 18 March 2008).

21. The Court therefore considers that the unacknowledged detention of an individual is a complete negation of the fundamentally important guarantees contained in Article 5 of the Convention and discloses a most grave violation of that provision (*El-Masri v. the former Yugoslav Republic of Macedonia* [GC], § 233). The absence of a record of such matters as the date, time and location of detention, the name of the detainee, the reasons for the detention and the name of the person effecting it must be seen as incompatible, *inter alia*, with the very purpose of Article 5 of the Convention (*Kurt v. Turkey*, § 125). It is also incompatible with the requirement of lawfulness under the Convention (*Anguelova v. Bulgaria*, § 154).

B. Compliance with national law

22. In order to meet the requirement of lawfulness, detention must be "in accordance with a procedure prescribed by law". This means that detention must conform to the substantive and procedural rules of national law (*Del Río Prada v. Spain* [GC], § 125)

(or international law where appropriate (see, among many other authorities, *Medvedyev and Others v. France* [GC], § 79; *Toniolo v. San Marino and Italy*, § 46).

23. For example, the Court found that there had been a violation of Article 5 where the authorities had failed to lodge an application for extension of a detention order within the time-limit prescribed by law (*G. K. v. Poland*, § 76). By contrast, an alleged breach of a circular concerning the manner in which inquiries had to be conducted into certain types of offences did not invalidate the domestic legal basis for arrest and subsequent detention (*Talat Tepe v. Turkey*, § 62).

C. Review of compliance with national law

24. While it is normally in the first place for the national authorities, notably the courts, to interpret and apply domestic law, the position is different in relation to cases where failure to comply with such law entails a breach of the Convention. In cases where Article 5 § 1 of the Convention is at stake, the Court must exercise a certain power to review whether national law has been observed (see, among many other authorities, *Creangă v. Romania* [GC], § 101; *Baranowski v. Poland*, § 50; *Benham v. the United Kingdom*, § 41). In doing so, the Court must have regard to the legal situation as it stood at the material time (*Włoch v. Poland*, § 114).

D. General principles

25. The requirement of lawfulness is not satisfied merely by compliance with the relevant domestic law; domestic law must itself be in conformity with the Convention, including the general principles expressed or implied in it (*Plesó v. Hungary*, § 59).

The general principles implied by the Convention to which the Article 5 § 1 case-law refers are the principle of the rule of law and, connected to the latter, that of legal certainty, the principle of proportionality and the principle of protection against arbitrariness which is, moreover, the very aim of Article 5 [*Simons v. Belgium* (dec.), § 32].

E. The principle of legal certainty

26. Where deprivation of liberty is concerned it is particularly important that the general

principle of legal certainty be satisfied. It is therefore essential that the conditions for deprivation of liberty under domestic law be clearly defined and that the law itself be foreseeable in its application, so that it meets the standard of "lawfulness" set by the Convention, a standard which requires that all law be sufficiently precise to allow the person-if need be, with appropriate advice-to foresee, to a degree that is reasonable in the circumstances, the consequences which a given action may entail (see, among recent authorities, *Del Río Prada v. Spain* [GC], § 125; *Creangă v. Romania*, § 120; and *Medvedyev and Others v. France* [GC], § 80).

27. For example, the practice of keeping a person in detention under a bill of indictment without any specific basis in the national legislation or case-law is in breach of Article 5 § 1 (*Baranowski v. Poland*, §§ 50 – 58). Likewise, the practice of automatically renewing pre-trial detention without any precise legislative foundation is contrary to Article 5 § 1 (*Svipsta v. Latvia*, § 86). By contrast, the continued detention of a person on the basis of an order by the Indictment Chamber requiring further investigations, without issuing a formal detention order, did not disclose a violation of that Article (*Laumont v. France*, § 50).

28. Provisions which are interpreted in an inconsistent and mutually exclusive manner by the domestic authorities will, too, fall short of the "quality of law" standard required under the Convention (*Nasrulloyev v. Russia*, § 77; *Ječius v. Lithuania*, §§ 53 – 59). However, in the absence of any case-law, the Court is not called upon to give its own interpretation of national law. Therefore, it may be reluctant to conclude that the national courts have failed to act in accordance with a procedure prescribed by law (*Włoch v. Poland*, §§ 114 – 116; *Winterwerp v. the Netherlands*, §§ 48 – 50).

29. Although diplomatic notes are a source of international law, detention of crew on the basis of such notes is not lawful within the meaning of Article 5 § 1 of the Convention insofar as they are not sufficiently precise and foreseeable. In particular, the lack of specific reference to the potential arrest and detention of crew members will fall foul of the requirements of legal certainty and foreseeability under Article 5 § 1 of the Convention (*Medvedyev and Others v. France* [GC], §§ 96 – 100).

F. No arbitrariness

30. In addition, any deprivation of liberty should be in keeping with the purpose of protecting the individual from arbitrariness (see, among many other authorities, *Witold Litwa v. Poland*, § 78).

31. The notion of "arbitrariness" in Article 5 § 1 extends beyond lack of conformity with national law, so that a deprivation of liberty may be lawful in terms of domestic law but still arbitrary and thus contrary to the Convention (*Creangă v. Romania*, § 84; *A. and Others v. the United Kingdom* [GC], § 164).

32. The notion of arbitrariness varies to a certain extent depending on the type of detention involved. The Court has indicated that arbitrariness may arise where there has been an element of bad faith or deception on the part of the authorities; where the order to detain and the execution of the detention did not genuinely conform to the purpose of the restrictions permitted by the relevant sub-paragraph of Article 5 § 1; where there was no connection between the ground of permitted deprivation of liberty relied on and the place and conditions of detention; and where there was no relationship of proportionality between the ground of detention relied on and the detention in question (for a detailed overview of the key principles see *James, Wells and Lee v. the United Kingdom*, §§ 191–195; and *Saadi v. the United Kingdom* [GC], §§ 68–74).

33. The speed with which the domestic courts replace a detention order which has either expired or has been found to be defective is a further relevant element in assessing whether a person's detention must be considered arbitrary (*Mooren v. Germany* [GC], § 80). Thus, the Court considers in the context of sub-paragraph (c) that a period of less than a month between the expiry of the initial detention order and the issuing of a fresh, reasoned detention order following a remittal of the case from the appeal court to a lower court did not render the applicant's detention arbitrary (*Minjat v. Switzerland*, §§ 46 and 48). In contrast, a period of more than a year following a remittal from a court of appeal to a court of lower instance, in which the applicant remained in a state of uncertainty as to the grounds for his detention on remand, combined with the lack of a time-limit for the lower court to

re-examine his detention, was found to render the applicant's detention arbitrary (*Khudoyorov v. Russia*, §§ 136 – 137).

G. Court order

34. A period of detention is, in principle, "lawful" if it is based on a court order. Detention on the basis of an order later found to be unlawful by a superior court may still be valid under domestic law (*Bozano v. France*, § 55). Detention may remain in accordance with "a procedure prescribed by law" even though the domestic courts have admitted that there had been flaws in the detention proceedings but held the detention to be lawful nevertheless (*Erkalo v. the Netherlands*, §§ 55 – 56). Thus, even flaws in the detention order do not necessarily render the underlying period of detention unlawful within the meaning of Article 5 § 1 (*Yefimenko v. Russia*, §§ 102 – 108; *Ječius v. Lithuania*, § 68; *Benham v. the United Kingdom*, §§ 42 – 47).

35. The Court distinguishes between acts of domestic courts which are within their jurisdiction and those which are in excess of jurisdiction (ibid., §§ 43 et seq.). Detention orders have been found to be *ex facie* invalid in cases where the interested party did not have proper notice of the hearing (*Khudoyorov v. Russia*, § 129), the domestic courts had failed to conduct the means inquiry required by the national legislation (*Lloyd and Others v. the United Kingdom*, §§ 108 and 116), or the lower courts had failed properly to consider alternatives to imprisonment (ibid., § 113). On the other hand, where there was no evidence that the national courts' conduct amounted to a "gross or obvious irregularity", the Court held that the detention was lawful (ibid., § 114).

H. Reasoning of decisions and the requirement of non-arbitrariness

36. The absence or lack of reasoning in detention orders is one of the elements taken into account by the Court when assessing the lawfulness of detention under Article 5 § 1. Thus, the absence of *any* grounds given by the judicial authorities in their decisions authorising detention for a prolonged period of time may be incompatible with the principle of protection from arbitrariness enshrined in Article 5 § 1 (*Stašaitis v. Lithuania*, §§ 66 –

67). Likewise, a decision which is extremely laconic and makes no reference to any legal provision which would permit detention will fail to provide sufficient protection from arbitrariness (*Khudoyorov v. Russia*, § 157).

37. However, the Court may consider the applicant's detention to be in conformity with the domestic legislation despite the lack of reasons in the detention order where the national courts were satisfied that there had been some grounds for the applicant's detention on remand (*Minjat v. Switzerland*, § 43). Furthermore, where the domestic courts had quashed the detention order for lack of reasons but considered that there had been some grounds for the applicant's detention, the refusal to order release of the detainee and remittal of the case to the lower courts for determination of the lawfulness of detention did not amount to a violation of Article 5 § 1 (ibid., § 47).

38. What is required is a detention order based on concrete grounds and setting a specific time-limit (*Meloni v. Switzerland*, § 53). Moreover, authorities should consider less intrusive measures than detention (*Ambruszkiewicz v. Poland*, § 32).

I. Some acceptable procedural flaws

39. The following procedural flaws have been found not to render the applicant's detention unlawful:

—A failure to notify the detention order officially to the accused did not amount to a "gross or obvious irregularity" in the exceptional sense indicated by the case-law given that the authorities genuinely believed that the order had been notified to the applicant (*Marturana v. Italy*, § 79; but see *Voskuil v. the Netherlands*, in which the Court found a violation where there had been a failure to notify a detention order within the time-limit prescribed by law: three days instead of twenty-four hours);

—A mere clerical error in the arrest warrant or detention order which was later cured by a judicial authority (*Nikolov v. Bulgaria*, § 63; *Douiyeb v. the Netherlands* [GC], § 52);

—The replacement of the formal ground for an applicant's detention in view of the facts mentioned by the courts in support of their conclusions [*Gaidjurgis v. Lithuania* (dec.)]. A failure to give adequate reasons for such replacement however may lead the Court to conclude that there has been a breach of Article 5 § 1 (*Calmanovici v. Romania*, § 65).

J. Delay in executing order of release

40. It is inconceivable that in a State subject to the rule of law a person should continue to be deprived of his liberty despite the existence of a court order for his release (*Assanidze v. Georgia* [GC], § 173). The Court however recognises that some delay in carrying out a decision to release a detainee is understandable and often inevitable. Nevertheless, the national authorities must attempt to keep it to a minimum (*Giulia Manzoni v. Italy*, § 25). A delay of eleven hours in executing a decision to release the applicant "forthwith" was found to be incompatible with Article 5 § 1 of the Convention (ibid.; *Quinn v. France*, §§ 39–43).

III. Authorised deprivations of liberty under Article 5 § 1

A. Detention after conviction

> Article 5 § 1 (a)
> "1. ...No one shall be deprived of his liberty save in the following cases and in accordance with a procedure prescribed by law:
> (a) the lawful detention of a person after conviction by a competent court;"

1. Existence of a conviction

41. Article 5 § 1 (a) applies to any "conviction" occasioning deprivation of liberty pronounced by a court and makes no distinction based on the legal character of the offence of which a person has been found guilty whether classified as criminal or disciplinary by the

internal law of the State in question (*Engel and Others v. the Netherlands*, § 68; *Galstyan v. Armenia*, § 46).

42. The term signifies both a finding of guilt, and the imposition of a penalty or other measure involving the deprivation of liberty (*Del Río Prada v. Spain* [GC], § 125; *James, Wells and Lee v. the United Kingdom*, § 189; *M. v. Germany*, § 87; *Van Droogenbroeck v. Belgium*, § 35; *B. v. Austria*, § 38).

43. The provision does not prevent Contracting States from executing orders for detention imposed by competent courts outside their territory (*X. v. Germany*, Commission decision of 14 December 1963). Although Contracting States are not obliged to verify whether the proceedings resulting in the conviction were compatible with all the requirements of Article 6 (*Drozd and Janousek v. France and Spain*, § 110), a conviction can not be the result of a flagrant denial of justice (*Ilaşcu and Others v. Moldova and Russia* [GC], § 461; *Stoichkov v. Bulgaria*, § 51). If a conviction is the result of proceeedings which were "manifestly contrary to the provisions of Article 6 or the principles embodied therein", the resulting deprivation of liberty would not be justified under Article 5 § 1 (a) [*Willcox and Hurford v. the United Kingdom* (dec.), § 95].

2. Competent court

44. The term "court" denotes bodies which exhibit not only common fundamental features, of which the most important is independence of the executive and of the parties to the case, but also the guarantees of judicial procedure (*Weeks v. the United Kingdom*, § 61; *De Wilde, Ooms and Versyp v. Belgium*, § 78). The forms of the procedure need not, however, necessarily be identical in each of the cases where the intervention of a court is required. In order to determine whether a proceeding provides adequate guarantees, regard must be had to the particular nature of the circumstances in which such proceeding takes place (ibid.).

45. In addition, the body in question must not have merely advisory functions but must have the competence to decide the lawfulness of the detention and to order release if the detention is unlawful (*X. v. the United Kingdom*, § 61; *Weeks v. the United Kingdom*, § 61).

46. A court is not "competent" if its composition is not "established by law" (*Yefimenko v. Russia*, §§ 109 – 111).

3. Detention must follow "after" conviction

47. The term "after" does not simply mean that the detention must follow the conviction in point of time: in addition, the detention must result from, follow and depend upon or occur by virtue of the conviction. In short, there must be a sufficient causal connection between the conviction and the deprivation of liberty at issue (*Del Río Prada v. Spain* [GC], § 124; *James, Wells and Lee v. the United Kingdom*, § 189; *Monnell and Morris v. the United Kingdom*, § 40).

48. However, with the passage of time, the causal link gradually becomes less strong. and might eventually be broken if a position were reached in which a decision not to release, and to re-detain(including the prolonging of preventive detention), were based on grounds unconnected to the objectives of the legislature or the court or on an assessment that was unreasonable in terms of those objectives. In those circumstances, a detention that was lawful at the outset would be transformed into a deprivation of liberty that was arbitrary and, hence, incompatible with Article 5 (*Del Río Prada v. Spain* [GC], § 124; and *H. W. v. Germany*, § 102; *M. v. Germany*, § 88, for continued preventive detention).

49. The term "after conviction" cannot be interpreted as being restricted to the case of a final conviction, for this would exclude the arrest of convicted persons, who appeared for trial while still at liberty. It cannot be overlooked that the guilt of a person, detained during appeal or review proceedings, has been established in the course of a trial conducted in accordance with the requirements of Article 6 (*Wemhoff v. Germany*, § 9).

50. Article 5 § 1 (a) applies where persons of unsound mind are detained in psychiatric facilities after conviction (*Radu v. Germany*, § 97; *X. v. the United Kingdom*, § 39). However, it will not apply to such cases following an acquittal (*Luberti v. Italy*, § 25).

4. Impact of appellate proceedings

51. A period of detention will, in principle, be lawful if it is carried out pursuant to a court order. A subsequent finding that the court erred under domestic law in making the order will not necessarily retrospectively affect the validity of the intervening period of

detention. The Strasbourg organs have refused to uphold applications from persons convicted of criminal offences who complain that their convictions or sentences were found by domestic appellate courts to have been based on errors of fact or law (*Benham v. the United Kingdom*, § 42). However, detention following conviction is unlawful where it has no basis in domestic law or is arbitrary (*Tsirlis and Kouloumpas v. Greece*, § 62).

B. Detention for non-compliance with a court order or legal obligation

> Article 5 § 1 (b)
>
> "1. ...No one shall be deprived of his liberty save in the following cases and in accordance with a procedure prescribed by law:
>
> ...
>
> (b) the lawful arrest or detention of a person for non-compliance with the lawful order of a court or in order to secure the fulfilment of any obligation prescribed by law;"

1. Non-compliance with the order of a court

52. The choice of the language in the first limb of Article 5 § 1 (b) presumes that the person arrested or detained must have had an opportunity to comply with a court order and has failed to do so (*Beiere v. Latvia*, § 49).

53. Individuals cannot be held accountable for not complying with court orders if they have never been informed of them (ibid., § 50).

54. A refusal of a person to undergo certain measures or to follow a certain procedure prior to being ordered to do so by a competent court has no presumptive value in decisions concerning compliance with such a court order (*Petukhova v. Russia*, § 59).

55. The domestic authorities must strike a fair balance between the importance in a democratic society of securing compliance with a lawful order of a court, and the importance of the right to liberty. Factors to be taken into consideration include the purpose of the order, the feasibility of compliance with the order, and the duration of the detention. The issue of proportionality assumes particular significance in the overall scheme of things

(*Gatt v. Malta*, § 40).

56. The Convention organs have applied the first limb of Article 5 § 1 (b) to cases concerning, for example, a failure to pay a court fine (*Velinov v. the former Yugoslav Republic of Macedonia*; *Airey v. Ireland*, Commission decision), a refusal to undergo a medical examination concerning mental health (*X. v. Germany*, Commission decision of 10 December 1975), or a blood test ordered by a court (*X. v. Austria*, Commission decision), a failure to observe residence restrictions (*Freda v. Italy*, Commission decision), a failure to comply with a decision to hand over children to a parent [*Paradis v. Germany* (dec.)], a failure to observe binding-over orders (*Steel and Others v. the United Kingdom*), a breach of bail conditions (*Gatt v. Malta*) and a confinement in a psychiatric hospital (*Beiere v. Latvia*, where the detention decision was found not to be a "lawful order of a court").

2. Fulfilment of an obligation prescribed by law

57. The second limb of Article 5 § 1 (b) allows for detention only to "secure the fulfilment" of any obligation prescribed by law. There must therefore be an unfulfilled obligation incumbent on the person concerned and the arrest and detention must be for the purpose of securing its fulfilment and not punitive in character. As soon as the relevant obligation has been fulfilled, the basis for detention under Article 5 § 1 (b) ceases to exist (*Vasileva v. Denmark*, § 36).

58. The obligation must be of a specific and concrete nature (*Ciulla v. Italy*, § 36). A wide interpretation would entail consequences incompatible with the notion of the rule of law (*Engel and Others v. the Netherlands*, § 69; *Iliya Stefanov v. Bulgaria*, § 72).

59. The obligation not to commit a criminal offence can only be considered as "specific and concrete" if the place and time of the imminent commission of the offence and its potential victims have been sufficiently specified. In the context of a duty to refrain from doing something, as distinct from a duty to perform a specific act, it is necessary, prior to concluding that a person has failed to satisfy his obligation at issue, that the person concerned was made aware of the specific act which was to refrain from committing and that the person showed himself or herself not to be willing to refrain from so doing (*Ostendorf*

v. Germany, §§ 93 – 94).

60. An arrest will only be acceptable in Convention terms if "the obligation prescribed by law" cannot be fulfilled by milder means (*Khodorkovskiy v. Russia*, § 136). The principle of proportionality further dictates that a balance must be struck between the importance in a democratic society of securing the immediate fulfilment of the obligation in question, and the importance of the right to liberty (*Saadi v. the United Kingdom* [GC], § 70).

61. In this assessment the Court considers the following points relevant: the nature of the obligation arising from the relevant legislation including its underlying object and purpose; the person being detained and the particular circumstances leading to the detention; and the length of the detention (*Vasileva v. Denmark*, § 38; *Epple v. Germany*, § 37).

62. Situations examined under the second limb of Article 5 § 1 (b) include, for example, an obligation to submit to a security check when entering a country [*McVeigh and Others v. the United Kingdom*, (Commission report)], to disclose details of one's personal identity [*Vasileva v. Denmark*; *Novotka v. Slovakia* (dec.); *Sarigiannis v. Italy*], to undergo a psychiatric examination (*Nowicka v. Poland*), to leave a certain area (*Epple v. Germany*), to appear for questioning at a police station (*Iliya Stefanov v. Bulgaria*; *Osypenko v. Ukraine*; and *Khodorkovskiy v. Russia*) and to keep the peace by not committing a criminal offence (*Ostendorf v. Germany*).

C. Detention on remand

> Article 5 §1 (c)
>
> "1. ...No one shall be deprived of his liberty save in the following cases and in accordance with a procedure prescribed by law:
>
> ...
>
> (c) the lawful arrest or detention of a person effected for the purpose of bringing him before the competent legal authority on reasonable suspicion of having committed an offence or when it is reasonably considered necessary to prevent his committing an offence or fleeing after having done so;"

1. Purpose of arrest or detention

63. "Effected for the purpose of bringing him before the competent legal authority" qualifies all the three alternative bases for arrest or detention under Article 5 § 1 (c) [*Lawless v. Ireland* (no. 3), § § 13 – 14; *Ireland v. the United Kingdom*, § 196].

64. A person may be detained under Article 5 § 1 (c) only in the context of criminal proceedings, for the purpose of bringing him before the competent legal authority on suspicion of his having committed an offence (*Ječius v. Lithuania*, § 50; *Schwabe and M. G. v. Germany*, § 72).

65. The second alternative of that provision ("when it is reasonably considered necessary to prevent his committing an offence") also governs only pre-trial detention and not custody for preventive purposes without the person concerned being suspected of having already committed a criminal offence (*Ostendorf v. Germany*, § 82).

66. The existence of the purpose to bring a suspect before a court has to be considered independently of the achievement of that purpose. The standard imposed by Article 5 § 1 (c) does not presuppose that the police have sufficient evidence to bring charges at the time of arrest or while the applicant was in custody (*Petkov and Profirov v. Bulgaria*, § 52; *Erdagöz v. Turkey*, § 51). The object of questioning during detention under sub-paragraph (c) of Article 5 § 1 is to further the criminal investigation by way of confirming or dispelling the concrete suspicion grounding the arrest (*Brogan and Others v. the United Kingdom*, § § 52 – 54; *Labita v. Italy* [GC], § 155; *O'Hara v. the United Kingdom*, § 36).

67. Detention pursuant to Article 5 § 1 (c) must be a proportionate measure to achieve the stated aim (*Ladent v. Poland*, § § 55 – 56).

68. The expression "competent legal authority" has the same meaning as "judge or other officer authorised by law to exercise judicial power" in Article 5 § 3 (*Schiesser v. Switzerland*, § 29).

2. Meaning of "reasonable suspicion"

69. A "reasonable suspicion" that a criminal offence has been committed presupposes the existence of facts or information which would satisfy an objective observer that the person concerned may have committed an offence (*Ilgar Mammadov v. Azerbaijan*, § 88;

Erdagöz v. Turkey, §51; *Fox, Campbell and Hartley v. the United Kingdom*, §32). Therefore, a failure by the authorities to make a genuine inquiry into the basic facts of a case in order to verify whether a complaint was well-founded disclosed a violation of Article 5 §1 (c) (*Stepuleac v. Moldova*, §73; *Elçi and Others v. Turkey*, §674).

70. What may be regarded as "reasonable" will however depend upon all the circumstances of the cases (*Fox, Campbell and Hartley v. the United Kingdom*, §32).

71. In the context of terrorism, though Contracting States cannot be required to establish the reasonableness of the suspicion grounding the arrest of a suspected terrorist by disclosing confidential sources of information, the Court has held that the exigencies of dealing with terrorist crime cannot justify stretching the notion of "reasonableness" to the point where the safeguard secured by Article 5 §1 (c) is impaired (*O'Hara v. the United Kingdom*, §35).

72. Uncorroborated hearsay evidence of an anonymous informant was held not to be sufficient to found "reasonable suspicion" of the applicant being involved in mafia-related activities (*Labita v. Italy* [GC], §§156 et seq.). By contrast, incriminating statements dating back to a number of years and later withdrawn by the suspects did not remove the existence of a reasonable suspicion against the applicant. Furthermore, it did not have an effect on the lawfulness of the arrest warrant (*Talat Tepe v. Turkey*, §61).

3. The term "offence"

73. The term "offence" has an autonomous meaning, identical to that of "criminal offence" in Article 6. The classification of the offence under national law is one factor to be taken into account. However, the nature of the proceedings and the severity of the penalty at stake are also relevant (*Benham v. the United Kingdom*, §56).

74. The "offence" must be specific and concrete: preventive detention of individuals viewed by the State as presenting a danger on account of their continuing propensity to crime is not allowed (*Guzzardi v. Italy*, §102; *Ciulla v. Italy*, §40; *M. v. Germany*, §89; *Shimovolos v. Russia*, §54).

D. Detention of a minor

> Article 5 § 1 (d)
>
> "1. ...No one shall be deprived of his liberty save in the following cases and in accordance with a procedure prescribed by law:
>
> ...
>
> (d) the detention of a minor by lawful order for the purpose of educational supervision or his lawful detention for the purpose of bringing him before the competent legal authority;"

1. General

75. The notion of a minor encompasses persons under the age of 18 [*Koniarska v. the United Kingdom* (dec.)], in the light of European standards and Resolution CM (72) of the Committee of Ministers of the Council of Europe (*X. v. Switzerland*, Commission decision of 14 December 1979).

76. Sub-paragraph d) is not only a provision which permits the detention of a minor. It contains a specific, but not exhaustive, example of circumstances in which minors might be detained, namely for the purpose of (a) their educational supervision or (b) bringing them before the competent legal authority (*Mubilanzila Mayeka and Kaniki Mitunga v. Belgium*, § 100).

2. Educational supervision

77. The first limb of Article 5 § 1 (d) authorises detention pursuant to a court or administrative order for the purposes of securing a child's attendance at an educational establishment.

78. In the context of the detention of minors, the words "educational supervision" must not be equated rigidly with notions of classroom teaching. Such supervision must embrace many aspects of the exercise, by the authority, of parental rights for the benefit and protection of the person concerned (*P. and S. v. Poland*, § 147; *Ichin and Others v. Ukraine*, § 39; *D. G. v. Ireland*, § 80).

79. Sub-paragraph (d) does not preclude an interim custody measure being used as a

preliminary to a regime of supervised education, without itself involving any supervised education. In such circumstances, however, the imprisonment must be speedily followed by actual application of such a regime in a setting (open or closed) designed and with sufficient resources for the purpose (*Bouamar v. Belgium*, § 50).

80. If the State has chosen a system of educational supervision involving a deprivation of liberty, it is obliged to put in place appropriate institutional facilities which meet the security and educational demands of that system in order to satisfy the requirements of Article 5 § 1 d) (*A. and Others v. Bulgaria*, § 69; *D. G. v. Ireland*, § 79).

81. The Court does not consider that a juvenile holding facility itself constitutes "educational supervision", if no educational activities are provided (*Ichin and Others v. Ukraine*, § 39).

3. Competent legal authority

82. The second limb of Article 5 § 1 (d) governs the lawful detention of a minor for the purpose of bringing him or her before the competent legal authority. According to the *travaux préparatoires*, this provision was intended to cover detention of a minor prior to civil or administrative proceedings, while the detention in connection with criminal proceedings was intended to be covered by Article 5 § 1 (c).

83. However, the detention of a minor accused of a crime during the preparation of a psychiatric report necessary for the taking of a decision on his mental conditions has been considered to fall under sub-paragraph d), as being detention for the purpose of bringing a minor before the competent authority (*X. v. Switzerland*, Commission decision of 14 December 1979).

E. Detention for medical or social reasons

> Article 5 § 1 (e)
>
> "1. ...No one shall be deprived of his liberty save in the following cases and in accordance with a procedure prescribed by law:
>
> ...
>
> (e) the lawful detention of persons for the prevention of the spreading of infectious diseases, of persons of unsound mind, alcoholics or drug addicts or vagrants;"

1. General

84. Article 5 § 1 (e) of the Convention refers to several categories of individuals, namely persons spreading infectious diseases, persons of unsound mind, alcoholics, drug addicts and vagrants. There is a link between all those persons in that they may be deprived of their liberty either in order to be given medical treatment or because of considerations dictated by social policy, or on both medical and social grounds (*Enhorn v. Sweden*, § 43).

85. The reason why the Convention allows these individuals, all of whom are socially maladjusted, to be deprived of their liberty is not only that they may be a danger to public safety but also that their own interests may necessitate their detention (ibidem; *Guzzardi v. Italy*, § 98 *in fine*).

2. Prevention of the spreading of infectious diseases

86. The essential criteria when assessing the "lawfulness" of the detention of a person "for the prevention of the spreading of infectious diseases" are:

- whether the spreading of the infectious disease is dangerous to public health or safety; and
- whether detention of the person infected is the last resort in order to prevent the spreading of the disease, because less severe measures have been considered and found to be insufficient to safeguard the public interest.

When these criteria are no longer fulfilled, the basis for the deprivation of liberty ceases to exist (*Enhorn v. Sweden*, § 44).

3. Detention of persons of unsound mind

87. The term "a person of unsound mind" does not lend itself to precise definition since psychiatry is an evolving field, both medically and in social attitudes. However, it cannot be taken to permit the detention of someone simply because his or her views or behaviour deviate from established norms (*Rakevich v. Russia*, § 26).

88. An individual cannot be deprived of his liberty as being of "unsound mind" unless the following three minimum conditions are satisfied (*Stanev v. Bulgaria* [GC], § 145; *D. D. v. Lithuania*, § 156; *Kallweit v. Germany*, § 45; *Shtukaturov v. Russia*, § 114;

Varbanov v. Bulgaria, §45; and *Winterwerp v. the Netherlands*, §39):

- the individual must be reliably shown, by objective medical expertise, to be of unsound mind, unless emergency detention is required;
- the individual's mental disorder must be of a kind to warrant compulsory confinement. The deprivation of liberty must be shown to have been necessary in the circumstances;
- the mental disorder, verified by objective medical evidence, must persist throughout the period of detention.

89. No deprivation of liberty of a person considered to be of unsound mind may be deemed in conformity with Article 5 § 1 (e) of the Convention if it has been ordered without seeking the opinion of a medical expert [*Ruiz Rivera v. Switzerland*, § 59; *S. R. v. the Netherlands* (dec.), § 31].

90. As to the second of the above conditions, the detention of a mentally disordered person may be necessary not only where the person needs therapy, medication or other clinical treatment to cure or alleviate his condition, but also where the person needs control and supervision to prevent him, for example, causing harm to himself or other persons (*Hutchison Reid v. the United Kingdom*, § 52).

A mental condition must be of a certain gravity in order to be considered as a "true" mental disorder (*Glien v. Germany*, § 85).

91. In deciding whether an individual should be detained as a person "of unsound mind", the national authorities are to be recognised as having a certain discretion since it is in the first place for the national authorities to evaluate the evidence adduced before them in a particular case (*Plesó v. Hungary*, § 61; *H. L. v. the United Kingdom*, § 98).

92. The relevant time at which a person must be reliably established to be of unsound mind, for the requirements of sub-paragraph (e) of Article 5 § 1, is the date of the adoption of the measure depriving that person of his liberty as a result of that condition (*O. H. v. Germany*, § 78).

93. When the medical evidence points to recovery, the authorities may need some time to consider whether to terminate an applicant's confinement (*Luberti v. Italy*, § 28).

However, the continuation of deprivation of liberty for purely administrative reasons is not justified (*R. L. and M. -J. D. v. France*, § 129).

94. The detention of persons of unsound mind must be effected in a hospital, clinic, or other appropriate institution authorised for the detention of such persons (*L. B. v. Belgium*, § 93; *Ashingdane v. the United Kingdom*, § 44; *O. H. v. Germany*, § 79).

95. By contrast, a person can be placed temporarily in an establishment not specifically designed for the detention of mental health patients before being transferred to the appropriate institution, provided that the waiting period is not excessively long (*Pankiewicz v. Poland*, §§ 44 - 45; *Morsink v. the Netherlands*, §§ 67 - 69; *Brand v. the Netherlands*, §§ 64 - 66).

4. Detention of alcoholics and drug addicts

96. Article 5 § 1 (e) of the Convention should not be interpreted as only allowing the detention of "alcoholics" in the limited sense of persons in a clinical state of "alcoholism", because nothing in the text of this provision prevents that measure from being applied by the State to an individual abusing alcohol, in order to limit the harm caused by alcohol to himself and the public, or to prevent dangerous behaviour after drinking (*Kharin v. Russia*, § 34).

97. Therefore, persons who are not medically diagnosed as "alcoholics", but whose conduct and behaviour under the influence of alcohol pose a threat to public order or themselves, can be taken into custody for the protection of the public or their own interests, such as their health or personal safety (*Hilda Hafsteinsdóttir v. Iceland*, § 42). That does not mean however that Article 5 § 1 (e) permits the detention of an individual merely because of his alcohol intake (*Witold Litwa v. Poland*, §§ 61 - 62).

5. Vagrants

98. The case-law on "vagrants" is scarce. The scope of the provision encompasses persons who have no fixed abode, no means of subsistence and no regular trade or profession. These three conditions, inspired by the Belgian Criminal Code, are cumulative: they must be fulfilled at the same time with regard to the same person (*De Wilde, Ooms and Versyp v. Belgium*, § 68).

F. Detention of a foreigner

> Article 5 § 1 (f)
>
> "1. ...No one shall be deprived of his liberty save in the following cases and in accordance with a procedure prescribed by law:
>
> ...
>
> (f) the lawful arrest or detention of a person to prevent his effecting an unauthorised entry into the country or of a person against whom action is being taken with a view to deportation or extradition."

1. Detention to prevent unauthorised entry into country

99. Article 5 § 1 (f) allows States to control the liberty of aliens in an immigration context. While the first limb of that provision permits the detention of an asylum seeker or other immigrant prior to the State's grant of authorisation to enter, such detention must be compatible with the overall purpose of Article 5, which is to safeguard the right to liberty and ensure that no-one should be dispossessed of his or her liberty in an arbitrary fashion (*Saadi v. the United Kingdom* [GC], §§ 64 – 66).

100. The question as to when the first limb of Article 5 § 1 (f) ceases to apply, because the individual has been granted formal authorisation to enter or stay, is largely dependent on national law (*Suso Musa v. Malta*, § 97).

101. The principle that detention should not be arbitrary applies to the detention under the first limb of Article 5 § 1 (f) in the same manner as it applies to detention under the second limb (*Saadi v. the United Kingdom* [GC], § 73).

102. "Freedom from arbitrariness" in the context of the first limb of Article 5 § 1 (f) therefore means that such detention must be carried out in good faith; it must be closely connected to the purpose of preventing unauthorised entry of the person to the country; the place and conditions of detention should be appropriate, bearing in mind that the measure is applicable not to those who have committed criminal offences but to aliens who, often

fearing for their lives, have fled from their own country; and the length of the detention should not exceed that reasonably required for the purpose pursued (ibidem, § 74).

103. When reviewing the manner in which the detention order was implemented the Court must have regard to the particular situation of would-be immigrants (*Kanagaratnam v. Belgium*, § 80, where the applicant and her three children were kept in a closed facility designed for adults; *Rahimi v. Greece*, § 108, concerning the automatic application of detention to an unaccompanied minor).

2. Detention with a view to deportation or extradition

104. Article 5 § 1 (f) does not demand that detention be reasonably considered necessary, for example to prevent the individual from committing an offence or fleeing. In this respect, Article 5 § 1 (f) provides a different level of protection from Article 5 § 1 (c): all that is required under sub-paragraph (f) is that "action is being taken with a view to deportation or extradition". It is therefore immaterial, for the purposes of its application, whether the underlying decision to expel can be justified under national or Convention law (*Chahal v. the United Kingdom*, § 112; *Čonka v. Belgium*, § 38; *Nasrulloyev v. Russia*, § 69; *Soldatenko v. Ukraine*, § 109).

105. Detention may be justified for the purposes of the second limb of Article 5 § 1 (f) by enquiries from the competent authorities, even if a formal request or an order of extradition has not been issued, given that such enquires may be considered "actions" taken in the sense of the provision (*X. v. Switzerland*, Commission decision of 9 December 1980).

106. Any deprivation of liberty under the second limb of Article 5 § 1 (f) will be justified only for as long as deportation or extradition proceedings are in progress. If such proceedings are not prosecuted with due diligence, the detention will cease to be permissible under Article 5 § 1 (f) (*A. and Others v. the United Kingdom* [GC], § 164; *Amie and Others v. Bulgaria*, § 72).

107. To avoid being branded as arbitrary, detention under Article 5 § 1 (f) must be carried out in good faith; it must be closely connected to the ground of detention relied on by the government; the place and conditions of detention should be appropriate; and the

length of the detention should not exceed that reasonably required for the purpose pursued (ibidem; see also *Yoh-Ekale Mwanje v. Belgium*, §§117 – 119 with further references).

108. Detention with a view to expulsion should not be punitive in nature and should be accompanied by appropriate safeguards (*Azimov v. Russia*, §172).

109. Article 5 §1 (f) or other sub-paragraphs do not permit a balance to be struck between the individual's right to liberty and the State's interest in protecting its population from terrorist threat (*A. and Others v. the United Kingdom* [GC], §171).

110. The Convention contains no provisions concerning the circumstances in which extradition may be granted, or the procedure to be followed before extradition may be granted. Subject to it being the result of cooperation between the States concerned and provided that the legal basis for the order for the fugitive's arrest is an arrest warrant issued by the authorities of the fugitive's State of origin, even an atypical extradition cannot as such be regarded as being contrary to the Convention (*Öcalan v. Turkey* [GC], §86; *Adamov v. Switzerland*, §57).

111. As regards extradition arrangements between States when one is a party to the Convention and the other is not, the rules established by an extradition treaty or, in the absence of any such treaty, the cooperation between the States concerned are also relevant factors to be taken into account for determining whether the arrest that has led to the subsequent complaint to the Court was lawful. The fact that a fugitive has been handed over as a result of cooperation between States does not in itself make the arrest unlawful and does not therefore give rise to any problem under Article 5 (*Öcalan v. Turkey* [GC], §87).

112. The implementation of an interim measure following an indication by the Court to a State Party that it would be desirable not to return an individual to a particular country does not in itself have any bearing on whether the deprivation of liberty to which that individual may be subject complies with Article 5 §1 of the Convention (*Gebremedhin [Gaberamadhien] v. France*, §74). Detention should still be lawful and not arbitrary (*Azimov v. Russia*, §169).

The fact that the application of such a measure prevents the individual's deportation does not render his detention unlawful, provided that the expulsion proceedings are still pending and the duration of his continued detention is not unreasonable (*S. P. v. Belgium* (dec.), and *Yoh-Ekale Mwanje v. Belgium*, § 120).

IV. Guarantees for persons deprived of liberty

A. Information on the reasons for arrest (Article 5 §2)

> Article 5 §2
> "2. Everyone who is arrested shall be informed promptly, in a language which he understands, of the reasons for his arrest and of any charge against him."

1. Applicability

113. The words used in Article 5 § 2 should be interpreted autonomously and, in particular, in accordance with the aim and purpose of Article 5 which is to protect everyone from arbitrary deprivations of liberty. The term "arrest" extends beyond the realm of criminal law measures and the words "any charge" do not indicate a condition of applicability but an eventuality which is taken into account. Article 5 § 4 does not make any distinction between persons deprived of their liberty on the basis of whether they have been arrested or detained. Therefore, there are no grounds for excluding the latter from the scope of Article 5 § 2 (*Van der Leer v. the Netherlands*, §§ 27 – 28) which extends to detention for the purposes of extradition (*Shamayev and Others v. Georgia and Russia*, §§ 414 – 415) and medical treatment (*Van der Leer v. the Netherlands*, §§ 27 – 28; *X. v. the United Kingdom*, § 66) and also applies where persons have been recalled to places of detention following a period of conditional release (*ibid.*; *X v. Belgium*, Commission decision).

2. Purpose

114. Article 5 § 2 contains the elementary safeguard that any person arrested should

know why he is being deprived of his liberty and is an integral part of the scheme of protection afforded by Article 5. Where a person has been informed of the reasons for his arrest or detention, he may, if he sees fit, apply to a court to challenge the lawfulness of his detention in accordance with Article 5 § 4 (*Fox, Campbell and Hartley v. the United Kingdom*, § 40; *Čonka v. Belgium*, § 50).

115. Any person who is entitled to take proceedings to have the lawfulness of his detention decided speedily cannot make effective use of that right unless he is promptly and adequately informed of the reasons why he has been deprived of his liberty (*Van der Leer v. the Netherlands*, § 28; *Shamayev and Others v. Georgia and Russia*, § 413).

3. Person to whom the reasons must be provided

116. It is plain from the wording of Article 5 § 2 that the duty on States is to furnish specific information to the individual or his representative (*Saadi v. the United Kingdom*, § 53, confirmed by the Grand Chamber in 2008). If the applicant is incapable of receiving the information, the relevant details must be given to those persons who represent his interests such as a lawyer or guardian (*X. v. the United Kingdom*, Commission Report, § 106; *Z. H. v. Hungary*, §§ 42 – 43).

4. Reasons must be provided "promptly"

117. Whether the promptness of the information conveyed is sufficient must be assessed in each case according to its special features. However, the reasons need not be related in their entirety by the arresting officer at the very moment of the arrest (*Fox, Campbell and Hartley v. the United Kingdom*, § 40; *Murray v. the United Kingdom* [GC], § 72).

118. The constraints of time imposed by the notion of promptness will be satisfied where the arrested person is informed of the reasons for his arrest within a few hours (*Kerr v. the United Kingdom* (dec.); *Fox, Campbell and Hartley v. the United Kingdom*, § 42).

5. Manner in which the reasons are provided

119. The reasons do not have to be set out in the text of any decision authorising detention and do not have to be in writing or in any special form [*X. v. Germany*,

Commission decision of 13 December 1978; *Kane v. Cyprus* (dec.)].

However, if the condition of a person with intellectual disability is not given due consideration in this process, it cannot be said that he was provided with the requisite information enabling him to make effective and intelligent use of the right ensured by Article 5 § 4 to challenge the lawfulness of detention unless a lawyer or another authorised person was informed in his stead (*Z. H. v. Hungary*, § 41).

120. The reasons for the arrest may be provided or become apparent in the course of post-arrest interrogations or questioning [*Fox, Campbell and Hartley v. the United Kingdom*, § 41; *Murray v. the United Kingdom* [GC], § 77; *Kerr v. the United Kingdom* (dec.)].

121. Arrested persons may not claim a failure to understand the reasons for their arrest in circumstances where they were arrested immediately after the commission of a criminal and intentional act (*Dikme v. Turkey*, § 54) or where they were aware of the details of alleged offences contained within previous arrest warrants and extradition requests [*Öcalan v. Turkey* (dec)].

6. Extent of the reasons required

122. Whether the content of the information conveyed is sufficient must be assessed in each case according to its special features (*Fox, Campbell and Hartley v. the United Kingdom*, § 40). However, a bare indication of the legal basis for the arrest, taken on its own, is insufficient for the purposes of Article 5 § 2 (ibidem, § 41; *Murray v. the United Kingdom* [GC], § 76; *Kortesis v. Greece*, §§ 61 – 62).

123. Arrested persons must be told, in simple, non-technical language that they can understand, the essential legal and factual grounds for the arrest, so as to be able, if they see fit, to apply to a court to challenge its lawfulness in accordance with Article 5 § 4 (*Fox, Campbell and Hartley v. the United Kingdom*, § 40; *Murray v. the United Kingdom* [GC], § 72). However, Article 5 § 2 does not require that the information consist of a complete list of the charges held against the arrested person (*Bordovskiy v. Russia*, § 56; *Nowak v. Ukraine*, § 63; *Gasiņš v. Latvia*, § 53).

124. Where persons are arrested for the purposes of extradition, the information given

may be even less complete (*Suso Musa v. Malta*, §§ 113 and 116; *Kaboulov v. Ukraine*, § 144; *Bordovskiy v. Russia*, § 56) as arrest for such purposes does not require a decision on the merits of any charge (*Bejaoui v. Greece*, Commission decision). However, such persons must nonetheless receive sufficient information so as to be able to apply to a court for the review of lawfulness provided for in Article 5 § 4 (*Shamayev and Others v. Georgia and Russia*, § 427).

7. In a language which he understands

125. Where the warrant of arrest, if any, is written in a language which the arrested person does not understand, Article 5 § 2 will be complied with where the applicant is subsequently interrogated, and thus made aware of the reasons for his arrest, in a language which he understands (*Delcourt v. Belgium*, Commission decision).

126. However, where translators are used for this purpose, it is incumbent on the authorities to ensure that requests for translation are formulated with meticulousness and precision (*Shamayev and Others v. Georgia and Russia*, § 425).

B. Right to be brought promptly before a judge (Article 5 § 3)

> Article 5 § 3
> "3. Everyone arrested or detained in accordance with the provision of paragraph 1 (c) of this Article shall be brought promptly before a judge or other officer authorised by law to exercise judicial power…"

1. Aim of the provision

127. Article 5 § 3 of the Convention provides persons arrested or detained on suspicion of having committed a criminal offence with a guarantee against any arbitrary or unjustified deprivation of liberty [*Aquilina v. Malta* [GC], § 47; *Stephens v. Malta*(no. 2), § 52].

128. Judicial control of interferences by the executive with the individual's right to liberty is an essential feature of the guarantee embodied in Article 5 § 3 (*Brogan and Others v. the United Kingdom*, § 58; *Pantea v. Romania*, § 236; *Assenov and Others v.*

Bulgaria, § 146). Judicial control is implied by the rule of law, "one of the fundamental principles of a democratic society…, which is expressly referred to in the Preamble to the Convention" and "from which the whole Convention draws its inspiration" (*Brogan and Others v. the United Kingdom*, § 58).

129. Judicial control serves to provide effective safeguards against the risk of ill-treatment, which is at its greatest in this early stage of detention, and against the abuse of powers bestowed on law enforcement officers or other authorities for what should be narrowly restricted purposes and exercisable strictly in accordance with prescribed procedures (*Ladent v. Poland*, § 72).

2. Prompt and automatic judicial control

130. The opening part of Article 5 § 3 is aimed at ensuring prompt and automatic judicial control of police or administrative detention ordered in accordance with the provisions of paragraph 1 (c) (*De Jong, Baljet and Van den Brink v. the Netherlands*, § 51; *Aquilina v. Malta* [GC], §§ 48–49).

131. Judicial control on the first appearance of an arrested individual must above all be prompt, to allow detection of any ill-treatment and to keep to a minimum any unjustified interference with individual liberty. The strict time constraint imposed by this requirement leaves little flexibility in interpretation, otherwise there would be a serious weakening of a procedural guarantee to the detriment of the individual and the risk of impairing the very essence of the right protected by this provision (*McKay v. the United Kingdom* [GC], § 33).

132. Article 5 § 3 does not provide for any possible exceptions from the requirement that a person be brought promptly before a judge or other judicial officer after his or her arrest or detention, not even on grounds of prior judicial involvement (*Bergmann v. Estonia*, § 45).

133. Any period in excess of four days is *prima facie* too long (*Oral and Atabay v. Turkey*, § 43; *McKay v. the United Kingdom* [GC], § 47; *Năstase-Silivestru v. Romania*, § 32). Shorter periods can also breach the promptness requirement if there are no special difficulties or exceptional circumstances preventing the authorities from bringing the arrested person before a judge sooner (*Gutsanovi v. Bulgaria*, §§ 154–159; *İpek and Others v.*

Turkey, §§ 36 – 37; and *Kandzhov v. Bulgaria*, § 66).

The requirement of promptness is even stricter in a situation where the placement in police custody follows on from a period of actual deprivation of liberty (*Vassis and Others v. France*, § 60, concerning the detention of a crew on the high seas).

134. The fact that an arrested person had access to a judicial authority is not sufficient to constitute compliance with the opening part of Article 5 § 3 (*De Jong, Baljet and Van den Brink v. the Netherlands*, § 51; *Pantea v. Romania*, § 231).

135. Judicial control of detention must be automatic and cannot be made to depend on a previous application by the detained person (*McKay v. the United Kingdom* [GC], § 34; *Varga v. Romania*, § 52; *Viorel Burzo v. Romania*, § 107). Such a requirement would not only change the nature of the safeguard provided for under Article 5 § 3, a safeguard distinct from that in Article 5 § 4, which guarantees the right to institute proceedings to have the lawfulness of detention reviewed by a court. It might even defeat the purpose of the safeguard under Article 5 § 3 which is to protect the individual from arbitrary detention by ensuring that the act of deprivation of liberty is subject to independent judicial scrutiny (*Aquilina v. Malta* [GC], § 49; *Niedbała v. Poland*, § 50).

136. The automatic nature of the review is necessary to fulfil the purpose of the paragraph, as a person subjected to ill-treatment might be incapable of lodging an application asking for a judge to review their detention; the same might also be true of other vulnerable categories of arrested person, such as the mentally frail or those ignorant of the language of the judicial officer (*McKay v. the United Kingdom* [GC], § 34; *Ladent v. Poland*, § 74).

3. The nature of the appropriate judicial officer

137. The expression "judge or other officer authorised by law to exercise judicial power" is a synonym for "competent legal authority" in Article 5 § 1 (c) (*Schiesser v. Switzerland*, § 29).

138. The exercise of "judicial power" is not necessarily confined to adjudicating on legal disputes. Article 5 § 3 includes officials in public prosecutors' departments as well as

judges sitting in court (ibidem, § 28).

139. The "officer" referred to in paragraph 3 must offer guarantees befitting the "judicial" power conferred on him by law (ibidem, § 30).

140. Formal, visible requirements stated in the "law" as opposed to standard practices are especially important for the identification of the judicial authority empowered to decide on the liberty of an individual (*Hood v. the United Kingdom* [GC], § 60; *De Jong, Baljet and Van den Brink v. the Netherlands*, § 48).

141. The "officer" is not identical with the "judge" but must nevertheless have some of the latter's attributes, that is to say he must satisfy certain conditions each of which constitutes a guarantee for the person arrested (*Schiesser v. Switzerland*, § 31).

4. Independence

142. The first of such conditions is independence of the executive and of the parties. This does not mean that the "officer" may not be to some extent subordinate to other judges or officers provided that they themselves enjoy similar independence (ibid).

143. A judicial officer who is competent to decide on detention may also carry out other duties, but there is a risk that his impartiality may arouse legitimate doubt on the part of those subject to his decisions if he is entitled to intervene in the subsequent proceedings as a representative of the prosecuting authority (*Huber v. Switzerland*, § 43; *Brincat v. Italy*, § 20).

144. In this respect, objective appearances at the time of the decision on detention are material: if it then appears that the "officer authorised by law to exercise judicial power" may later intervene in subsequent criminal proceedings on behalf of the prosecuting authority, his independence and impartiality may be open to doubt (ibid., § 21; *Hood v. the United Kingdom*, § 57; *Nikolova v. Bulgaria* [GC], § 49; *Pantea v. Romania*, § 236).

5. Procedural requirement

145. The procedural requirement places the "officer" under the obligation of hearing the individual brought before him or her in person before taking the appropriate decision (*Schiesser v. Switzerland*, § 31; *De Jong, Baljet and Van den Brink v. the Netherlands*,

§ 51; *Nikolova v. Bulgaria* [GC], § 49; *Aquilina v. Malta* [GC], § 50).

146. A lawyer's presence at the hearing is not obligatory (*Schiesser v. Switzerland*, § 36). However, the exclusion of a lawyer from a hearing may adversely affect the applicant's ability to present his case (*Lebedev v. Russia*, §§ 83 – 91).

6. Substantive requirement

a. Review of the merits of detention

147. The substantive requirement imposes on the "officer" the obligations of reviewing the circumstances militating for or against detention and of deciding, by reference to legal criteria, whether there are reasons to justify detention (*Schiesser v. Switzerland*, § 31; *Pantea v. Romania*, § 231). In other words, Article 5 § 3 requires the judicial officer to consider the merits of the detention (*Aquilina v. Malta* [GC], § 47; *Krejčíř v. the Czech Republic*, § 89).

148. The initial automatic review of arrest and detention must be capable of examining lawfulness issues and whether or not there is a reasonable suspicion that the arrested person had committed an offence, in other words, that detention falls within the permitted exception set out in Article 5 § 1 (c) (*McKay v. the United Kingdom* [GC], § 40; *Oral and Atabay v. Turkey*, § 41).

149. The matters which the judicial officer must examine go beyond the question of lawfulness. The review required under Article 5 § 3, being intended to establish whether the deprivation of the individual's liberty is justified, must be sufficiently wide to encompass the various circumstances militating for or against detention (*Aquilina v. Malta* [GC], § 52).

150. The examination of lawfulness may be more limited in scope in the particular circumstances of a given case than under Article 5 § 4 (*Stephens v. Malta* (no. 2), § 58).

b. Power of release

151. If there are no reasons to justify detention, the "officer" must have the power to make a binding order for the detainee's release (*Assenov and Others v. Bulgaria*, § 146; *Nikolova v. Bulgaria* [GC], § 49; *Niedbała v. Poland*, § 49; *McKay v. the United Kingdom* [GC], § 40).

152. It is highly desirable in order to minimise delay, that the judicial officer who conducts the first automatic review of lawfulness and the existence of a ground for detention, also has the competence to consider release on bail. It is not however a requirement of the Convention and there is no reason in principle why the issues cannot be dealt with by two judicial officers, within the requisite time frame. In any event, as a matter of interpretation, it cannot be required that the examination of bail take place with any more speed than is demanded of the first automatic review, which the Court has identified as being a maximum four days (ibidem, § 47).

C. Right to trial within a reasonable time or to be released pending trial (Article 5 §3)

> Article 5 §3
> "3. Everyone arrested or detained in accordance with the provisions of paragraph 1 (c) of this Article... shall be entitled to trial within a reasonable time or to release pending trial. Release may be conditioned by guarantees to appear for trial."

1. Period to be taken into consideration

153. In determining the length of detention pending trial under Article 5 §3 of the Convention, the period to be taken into consideration begins on the day the accused is taken into custody and ends on the day when the charge is determined, even if only by a court of first instance (see, for example, *Solmaz v. Turkey*, §§ 23 – 24; *Kalashnikov v. Russia*, § 110; *Wemhoff v. Germany*, § 9).

154. In view of the essential link between Article 5 §3 of the Convention and paragraph 1 (c) of that Article, a person convicted at first instance cannot be regarded as being detained "for the purpose of bringing him before the competent legal authority on reasonable suspicion of having committed an offence", as specified in the latter provision, but is in the position provided for by Article 5 §1 (a), which authorises deprivation of liberty "after conviction by a competent court" (see, among numerous authorities,

Belevitskiy v. Russia, §99; *Piotr Baranowski v. Poland*, §45; *Górski v. Poland*, §41).

2. General principles

155. The second limb of Article 5 §3 does not give judicial authorities a choice between either bringing an accused to trial within a reasonable time or granting him provisional release pending trial. Until conviction, he must be presumed innocent, and the purpose of the provision under consideration is essentially to require his provisional release once his continuing detention ceases to be reasonable.

156. Continued detention therefore can be justified in a given case only if there are specific indications of a genuine requirement of public interest which, notwithstanding the presumption of innocence, outweighs the rule of respect for individual liberty laid down in Article 5 of the Convention.

157. The responsibility falls in the first place to the national judicial authorities to ensure that, in a given case, the pre-trial detention of an accused person does not exceed a reasonable time. To this end they must, paying due regard to the principle of the presumption of innocence, examine all the facts arguing for or against the existence of the above-mentioned demand of public interest justifying a departure from the rule in Article 5 and must set them out in their decisions on the applications for release. It is essentially on the basis of the reasons given in these decisions and of the established facts stated by the applicant in his appeals that the Court is called upon to decide whether or not there has been a violation of Article 5 §3.

158. The persistence of reasonable suspicion that the person arrested has committed an offence is a condition *sine qua non* for the lawfulness of the continued detention, but with the lapse of time this no longer suffices and the Court must then establish whether the other grounds given by the judicial authorities continued to justify the deprivation of liberty. Where such grounds were "relevant" and "sufficient", the Court must also be satisfied that the national authorities displayed "special diligence" in the conduct of the proceedings.

159. In sum, domestic courts are under an obligation to review the continued detention of persons pending trial with a view to ensuring release when circumstances no longer justify continued deprivation of liberty. For at least an initial period, the existence of reasonable

suspicion may justify detention but there comes a moment when this is no longer enough. As the question whether or not a period of detention is reasonable cannot be assessed in the abstract but must be assessed in each case according to its special features, there is no fixed time-frame applicable to each case (*McKay v. the United Kingdom* [GC], §§ 41 – 45; *Bykov v. Russia* [GC], §§ 61 – 64; *Idalov v. Russia* [GC], §§ 139 – 141; see also *Labita v. Italy* [GC], §§ 152 – 153; and *Kudła v. Poland* [GC], §§ 110 – 111).

160. The arguments for and against release must not be "general and abstract" (*Boicenco v. Moldova*, § 142; *Khudoyorov v. Russia*, § 173), but contain references to the specific facts and the applicant's personal circumstances justifying his detention (*Aleksanyan v. Russia*, § 179).

161. Quasi-automatic prolongation of detention contravenes the guarantees set forth in Article 5 § 3 (*Tase v. Romania*, § 40).

162. The burden of proof in these matters should not be reversed by making it incumbent on the detained person to demonstrate the existence of reasons warranting his release (*Bykov v. Russia* [GC], § 64).

163. Where circumstances that could have warranted a person's detention may have existed but were not mentioned in the domestic decisions it is not the Court's task to establish them and to take the place of the national authorities which ruled on the applicant's detention (*ibid.*, § 66; *Giorgi Nikolaishvili v. Georgia*, § 77). It is only by giving a reasoned decision that there can be public scrutiny of the administration of justice (*Tase v. Romania*, § 41).

3. Grounds for continued detention

164. The Convention case-law has developed four basic acceptable reasons for refusing bail: (a) the risk that the accused will fail to appear for trial; (b) the risk that the accused, if released, would take action to prejudice the administration of justice, or (c) commit further offences, or (d) cause public disorder (*Tiron v. Romania*, § 37; *Smirnova v. Russia*, § 59; *Piruzyan v. Armenia*, § 94).

a. Danger of absconding

165. The danger of absconding cannot be gauged solely on the basis of the severity of

the sentence risked. It must be assessed with reference to a number of other relevant factors which may either confirm the existence of a danger of absconding or make it appear so slight that it cannot justify pre-trial detention (*Panchenko v. Russia*, § 106).

166. The risk of absconding has to be assessed in light of the factors relating to the person's character, his morals, home, occupation, assets, family ties and all kinds of links with the country in which he is being prosecuted (*Becciev v. Moldova*, § 58).

167. The mere absence of a fixed residence does not give rise to a danger of flight (*Sulaoja v. Estonia*, § 64).

168. The danger of flight necessarily decreases with the passages of time spent in detention (*Neumeister v. Austria*, § 10).

169. While the severity of the sentence faced is a relevant element in the assessment of the risk that an accused might abscond, the gravity of the charges cannot by itself serve to justify long periods of detention on remand (*Idalov v. Russia* [GC], § 145; *Garycki v. Poland*, § 47; *Chraidi v. Germany*, § 40; *Ilijkov v. Bulgaria*, §§ 80 – 81).

170. Although, in general, the expression "the state of evidence" may be a relevant factor for the existence and persistence of serious indications of guilt, it alone cannot justify lengthy detention (*Dereci v. Turkey*, § 38).

b. Obstruction of the proceedings

171. The danger of the accused's hindering the proper conduct of the proceedings cannot be relied upon *in abstracto*, it has to be supported by factual evidence (*Becciev v. Moldova*, § 59).

172. The risk of pressure being brought to bear on witnesses can be accepted at the initial stages of the proceedings (*Jarzynski v. Poland*, § 43).

173. In the long term, however, the requirements of the investigation do not suffice to justify the detention of a suspect: in the normal course of events the risks alleged diminish with the passing of time as the inquiries are effected, statements taken and verifications carried out (*Clooth v. Belgium*, § 44).

c. Repetition of offences

174. The seriousness of a charge may lead the judicial authorities to place and leave a

suspect in detention on remand in order to prevent any attempts to commit further offences. It is however necessary that the danger be a plausible one and the measure appropriate, in the light of the circumstances of the case and in particular the past history and the personality of the person concerned (*ibid.*, § 40).

175. Previous convictions could give a ground for a reasonable fear that the accused might commit a new offence (*Selçuk v. Turkey*, § 34; *Matznetter v. Austria*, § 9).

176. It cannot be concluded from the lack of a job or a family that a person is inclined to commit new offences (*Sulaoja v. Estonia*, § 64).

d. Preservation of public order

177. It is accepted that, by reason of their particular gravity and public reaction to them, certain offences may give rise to a social disturbance capable of justifying pre-trial detention, at least for a time. In exceptional circumstances this factor may therefore be taken into account for the purposes of the Convention, in any event in so far as domestic law recognises the notion of disturbance to public order caused by an offence.

178. However, this ground can be regarded as relevant and sufficient only provided that it is based on facts capable of showing that the accused's release would actually disturb public order. In addition, detention will continue to be legitimate only if public order remains actually threatened; its continuation cannot be used to anticipate a custodial sentence (*Letellier v. France*, § 51; *I. A. v. France*, § 104; *Prencipe v. Monaco*, § 79; *Tiron v. Romania*, § § 41 – 42).

4. Special diligence

179. The complexity and special characteristics of the investigation are factors to be considered in ascertaining whether the authorities displayed "special diligence" in the proceedings (*Scott v. Spain*, § 74).

180. The right of an accused in detention to have his case examined with particular expedition must not unduly hinder the efforts of the judicial authorities to carry out their tasks with proper care (*Shabani v. Switzerland*, § 65; *Sadegül Özdemir v. Turkey*, § 44).

5. Alternative measures

181. When deciding whether a person should be released or detained, the authorities

are obliged to consider alternative measures of ensuring his appearance at trial (*Idalov v. Russia* [GC], § 140). That provision proclaims not only the right to "trial within a reasonable time or to release pending trial" but also lays down that "release may be conditioned by guarantees to appear for trial" (*Khudoyorov v. Russia*, § 183; *Lelièvre v. Belgium*, § 97; *Shabani v. Switzerland*, § 62).

6. Bail

182. The guarantee provided for by Article 5 § 3 of the Convention is designed to ensure not the reparation of loss but, in particular, the appearance of the accused at the hearing. Its amount must therefore be assessed principally "by reference to [the accused], his assets and his relationship with the persons who are to provide the security, in other words to the degree of confidence that is possible that the prospect of loss of the security or of action against the guarantors in case of his non-appearance at the trial will act as a sufficient deterrent to dispel any wish on his part to abscond" (*Mangouras v. Spain* [GC], § 78; *Neumeister v. Austria*, § 14).

183. Bail may only be required as long as reasons justifying detention prevail (*Muşuc v. Moldova*, § 42; *Aleksandr Makarov v. Russia*, § 139). If the risk of absconding can be avoided by bail or other guarantees, the accused must be released, bearing in mind that where a lighter sentence could be anticipated, the reduced incentive for the accused to abscond should be taken into account (*Vrenčev v. Serbia*, § 76). The authorities must take as much care in fixing appropriate bail as in deciding whether or not the accused's continued detention is indispensable (see, among other authorities, *Piotr Osuch v. Poland*, § 39; *Bojilov v. Bulgaria*, § 60; *Skrobol v. Poland*, § 57).

184. Furthermore, the amount set for bail must be duly justified in the decision fixing bail (*Georgieva v. Bulgaria*, §§ 15 and 30 – 31) and must take into account the accused's means (*Hristova v. Bulgaria*, § 111) and his capacity to pay (*Toshev v. Bulgaria*, §§ 69 – 73). In certain circumstances it may not be unreasonable to take into account also the amount of the loss imputed to him (*Mangouras v. Spain* [GC], §§ 81 and 92).

185. Automatic refusal of bail by virtue of the law, devoid of any judicial control, is incompatible with the guarantees of Article 5 § 3 (*Piruzyan v. Armenia*, § 105; *S. B. C. v.*

the United Kingdom, §§ 23 – 24).

7. Justification for any period of detention

186. Article 5 § 3 of the Convention cannot be seen as authorising pre-trial detention unconditionally provided that it lasts no longer than a certain minimum period. Justification for any period of detention, no matter how short, must be convincingly demonstrated by the authorities (*Idalov v. Russia* [GC], § 140; *Tase v. Romania*, § 40; *Castravet v. Moldova*, § 33; *Belchev v. Bulgaria*, § 82).

8. Pre-trial detention of minors

187. The pre-trial detention of minors should be used only as a measure of last resort; it should be as short as possible and, where detention is strictly necessary, minors should be kept apart from adults (*Nart v. Turkey*, § 31; *Güveç v. Turkey*, § 109).

D. Right to have lawfulness of detention speedily examined by a court (Article 5 §4)

> Article 5 §4
> "4. Everyone who is deprived of his liberty by arrest or detention shall be entitled to take proceedings by which the lawfulness of his detention shall be decided speedily by a court and his release ordered if the detention is not lawful. "

1. Aim of the provision

188. Article 5 § 4 is the *habeas corpus* provision of the Convention. It provides detained persons with the right to actively seek a judicial review of their detention (*Mooren v. Germany* [GC], § 106; *Rakevich v. Russia*, § 43).

189. The fact that the Court has found no breach of the requirements of Article 5 § 1 of the Convention does not mean that it is dispensed from carrying out a review of compliance with Article 5 § 4. The two paragraphs are separate provisions and observance of the former does not necessarily entail observance of the latter (*Douiyeb v. the Netherlands* [GC], § 57; *Kolompar v. Belgium*, § 45).

2. The nature of the review required

190. Article 5 § 4 entitles an arrested or detained person is entitled to bring proceedings for review by a court of the procedural and substantive conditions which are essential for the "lawfulness", in the sense of Article 5 § 1, of his or her deprivation of liberty (see, among many authorities, *Idalov v. Russia* [GC], § 161; *Reinprecht v. Austria*, § 31).

The notion of "lawfulness" under Article 5 § 4 has the same meaning as in Article 5 § 1, so that the arrested or detained person is entitled to a review of the "lawfulness" of his detention in the light not only of the requirements of domestic law but also of the Convention, the general principles embodied therein and the aim of the restrictions permitted by Article 5 § 1 (*Suso Musa v. Malta*, § 50).

191. The forms of judicial review satisfying the requirements of Article 5 § 4 may vary from one domain to another, and will depend on the type of deprivation of liberty in issue (*M. H. v. the United Kingdom*, § 75).

192. It is not excluded that a system of automatic periodic review of the lawfulness of detention by a court may ensure compliance with the requirements of Article 5 § 4. However, where automatic review has been instituted, the decisions on the lawfulness of detention must follow at "reasonable intervals" (*Abdulkhanov v. Russia*, §§ 209 and 212 – 214, for a summary of the case-law in the context of detention under sub-paragprahs (a), (c), (e) and (f) of Article 5 § 1).

193. If a person is detained under Article 5 § 1 (c) of the Convention, the "court" must be empowered to examine whether or not there is sufficient evidence to give rise to a reasonable suspicion that he or she has committed an offence, because the existence of such a suspicion is essential if detention on remand is to be "lawful" under the Convention (*Nikolova v. Bulgaria* [GC], § 58).

194. Where a person is deprived of his liberty pursuant to a conviction by a competent court, the supervision required by Article 5 § 4 is incorporated in the decision by the court at the close of judicial proceedings (*De Wilde, Ooms and Versyp v. Belgium*, § 76) and no further review is therefore required. However, in cases where the grounds justifying the person's deprivation of liberty are susceptible to change with the passage of time, the

possibility of recourse to a body satisfying the requirements of Article 5 § 4 of the Convention is required [*Kafkaris v. Cyprus* (no. 2) (dec.), § 58].

195. By virtue of Article 5 § 4, a detainee is entitled to apply to a "court" having jurisdiction to decide "speedily" whether or not his deprivation of liberty has become "unlawful" in the light of new factors which have emerged subsequently to the initial decision depriving a person of his liberty (*Abdulkhanov v. Russia*, § 208; *Azimov v. Russia*, §§ 151 – 152).

196. A person of unsound mind who is compulsorily confined in a psychiatric institution for a lengthy period is entitled to take proceedings "at reasonable intervals" to put in issue the lawfulness of his detention (*M. H. v. the United Kingdom*, § 77, for a recent summary of the applicable principles). A system of periodic review in which the initiative lies solely with the authorities is not sufficient on its own (*X. v. Finland*, § 170; *Raudevs v. Latvia*, § 82).

197. The criteria for "lawful detention" under Article 5 § 1 (e) entail that the review of lawfulness guaranteed by Article 5 § 4 in relation to the continuing detention of a mental health patient should be made by reference to the patient's contemporaneous state of health, including his or her dangerousness, as evidenced by up-to-date medical assessments, and not by reference to past events at the origin of the initial decision to detain (*Juncal v. the United Kingdom* (dec.), § 30; *Ruiz Rivera v. Switzerland*, § 60; *H. W. v. Germany*, § 107).

198. The "court" to which the detained person has access for the purposes of Article 5 § 4 does not have to be a court of law of the classical kind integrated within the standard judicial machinery of the country (*Weeks v. the United Kingdom*, § 61). It must however be a body of "judicial character" offering certain procedural guarantees. Thus the "court" must be independent both of the executive and of the parties to the case (*Stephens v. Malta* (no. 1), § 95).

199. To satisfy the requirements of the Convention the review of the national court should comply with both the substantial and procedural rules of the national legislation and be conducted in conformity with the aim of Article 5, the protection of the individual

against arbitrariness (*Koendjbiharie v. the Netherlands*, §27).

200. Although Article 5 §4 does not compel the Contracting States to set up a second level of jurisdiction for the examination of the lawfulness of detention, a State which institutes such a system must in principle accord to the detainees the same guarantees on appeal as at first instance (*Kučera v. Slovakia*, §107; *Navarra v. France*, §28; *Toth v. Austria*, §84).

201. Article 5 §4 does not impose an obligation on a court examining an appeal against detention to address every argument contained in the appellant's submissions. However, the court cannot treat as irrelevant, or disregard, concrete facts invoked by the detainee and capable of putting into doubt the existence of the conditions essential for the "lawfulness", in the sense of the Convention, of the deprivation of liberty (*Ilijkov v. Bulgaria*, §94).

202. The "court" must have the power to order release if it finds that the detention is unlawful; a mere power of recommendation is insufficient (*Benjamin and Wilson v. the United Kingdom*, §§33–34).

3. Procedural guarantees

203. The requirement of procedural fairness under Article 5 §4 does not impose a uniform, unvarying standard to be applied irrespective of the context, facts and circumstances. Although it is not always necessary that an Article 5 §4 procedure be attended by the same guarantees as those required under Article 6 for criminal or civil litigation, it must have a judicial character and provide guarantees appropriate to the type of deprivation of liberty in question (*A. and Others v. the United Kingdom* [GC], §203; *Idalov v. Russia* [GC], §161).

204. In the case of a person whose detention falls within the ambit of Article 5 §1 (c), a hearing is required (*Nikolova v. Bulgaria* [GC], §58). The opportunity for a detainee to be heard either in person or through some form of representation features among the fundamental guarantees of procedure applied in matters of deprivation of liberty (*Kampanis v. Greece*, §47).

However, Article 5 §4 does not require that a detained person be heard every time he lodges an appeal against a decision extending his detention, but that it should be possible to exercise the right to be heard at reasonable intervals (*Çatal v. Turkey*, § 33; *Altınok v. Turkey*, § 45).

205. The proceedings must be adversarial and must always ensure "equality of arms" between the parties (*Reinprecht v. Austria*, § 31; *A. and Others v. the United Kingdom* [GC], § 204). In remand cases, since the persistence of a reasonable suspicion that the accused person has committed an offence is a condition *sine qua non* for the lawfulness of the continued detention, the detainee must be given an opportunity effectively to challenge the basis of the allegations against him. This may require the court to hear witnesses whose testimony appears to have a bearing on the continuing lawfulness of the detention (*Turcan v. Moldova*, §§ 67 – 70).

Equality of arms is not ensured if the applicant, or his counsel, is denied access to those documents in the investigation file which are essential in order effectively to challenge the lawfulness of his detention (*Ovsjannikov v. Estonia*, § 72; *Fodale v. Italy*, § 41; *Korneykova v. Ukraine*, § 68). It may also be essential that the individual concerned should not only have the opportunity to be heard in person but that he should also have the effective assistance of his lawyer (*Cernák v. Slovakia*, § 78).

206. The principle of adversarial proceedings and equality of arms must equally be respected in the proceedings before the appeal court (*Çatal v. Turkey*, §§ 33 – 34 and the cases referred to therein).

4. The "speediness" requirement

207. Article 5 § 4, in guaranteeing to detained persons a right to institute proceedings to challenge the lawfulness of their detention, also proclaims their right, following the institution of such proceedings, to a speedy judicial decision concerning the lawfulness of detention and the ordering of its termination if it proves unlawful (*Idalov v. Russia* [GC], § 154; *Baranowski v. Poland*, § 68). The question whether the right to a speedy decision has been respected must be determined in the light of the circumstances of each case (*Rehbock v. Slovenia*, § 84).

208. The opportunity for legal review must be provided soon after the person is taken into detention and thereafter at reasonable intervals if necessary (*Molotchko v. Ukraine*,

§ 148).

209. The notion of "speedily" (*à bref délai*) indicates a lesser urgency than that of "promptly" (*aussitôt*) in Article 5 § 3 (*E. v. Norway*, § 64; *Brogan and Others v. the United Kingdom*, § 59).

However, where a decision to detain a person has been taken by a non-judicial authority rather than a court, the standard of "speediness" of judicial review under Article 5 § 4 comes closer to the standard of "promptness" under Article 5 § 3 (*Shcherbina v. Russia*, § § 65 – 70, where a delay of sixteen days in the judicial review of the applicant's detention order issued by the prosecutor was found to be excessive).

210. The standard of "speediness" is less stringent when it comes to proceedings before a court of appeal (*Abdulkhanov v. Russia*, § 198). Where the original detention order was imposed by a court in a procedure offering appropriate guarantees of due process, the Court is prepared to tolerate longer periods of review in the proceedings before the second instance court (*Shcherbina v. Russia*, § 65).

a. The period to be taken into consideration

211. The Court has taken as a starting point the moment that the application for release was made/proceedings were instituted. The relevant period comes to an end with the final determination of the legality of the applicant's detention, including any appeal (*Sanchez-Reisse v. Switzerland*, § 54; *E. v. Norway*, § 64).

212. If an administrative remedy has to be exhausted before recourse can be had to a court, time begins to run when the administrative authority is seised of the matter (*Sanchez-Reisse v. Switzerland*, § 54).

213. If the proceedings have been conducted over two levels of jurisdiction, an overall assessment must be made in order to determine whether the requirement of "speedily" has been complied with (*Hutchison Reid v. the United Kingdom*, § 78; *Navarra v. France*, § 28).

b. Relevant factors to be taken into consideration when assessing speediness

214. The term "speedily" cannot be defined in the abstract. As with the "reasonable

time" stipulations in Article 5 § 3 and Article 6 § 1 it must be determined in the light of the circumstances of the individual case (*R. M. D. v. Switzerland*, § 42).

215. In assessing the speedy character required by Article 5 § 4, comparable factors may be taken into consideration as those which play a role with respect to the requirement of trial within a reasonable time under Article 5 § 3 and Article 6 § 1 of the Convention such as, the diligence shown by the authorities, any delay caused by the detained person and any other factors causing delay that do not engage the state's responsibility (*Mooren v. Germany* [GC], § 106; *Kolompar v. Belgium*, § 42).

216. Where one year per instance may be a rough rule of thumb in Article 6 § 1 cases, Article 5 § 4, concerning issues of liberty, requires particular expedition (*Panchenko v. Russia*, § 117). Where an individual's personal liberty is at stake, the Court has very strict standards concerning the State's compliance with the requirement of speedy review of the lawfulness of detention (see, for example, *Kadem v. Malta*, § § 44 – 45, where the Court considered a time-period of seventeen days in deciding on the lawfulness of the applicant's detention to be excessive, and *Mamedova v. Russia*, § 96, where the length of appeal proceedings lasting, *inter alia*, twenty-six days, was found to be in breach of the "speediness" requirement).

217. Where the determination involves complex issues-such as the detained person's medical condition-this may be taken into account when considering how long is "reasonable" under Article 5 § 4. However, even in complex cases, there are factors which require the authorities to carry out a particularly speedy review, including the presumption of innocence in the case of pre-trial detention (*Frasik v. Poland*, § 63; *Jablonski v. Poland*, § § 91 – 93).

218. Detention on remand in criminal cases calls for short intervals between reviews (*Bezicheri v. Italy*, § 21).

219. If the length of time before a decision is taken is *prima facie* incompatible with the notion of speediness, the Court will look to the State to explain the reason for the delay or to put forward exceptional grounds to justify the lapse of time in question (*Musiał v.*

Poland [GC], § 44; *Koendjbiharie v. the Netherlands*, § 29).

220. Neither an excessive workload nor a vacation period can justify a period of inactivity on the part of the judicial authorities (*E. v. Norway*, § 66; *Bezicheri v. Italy*, § 25).

E. Right to compensation for unlawful detention (Article 5 §5)

> Article 5 §5
>
> "5. Everyone who has been the victim of arrest or detention in contravention of the provisions of this Article shall have an enforceable right to compensation."

1. Applicability

221. The right to compensation set forth in paragraph 5 presupposes that a violation of one of the other paragraphs has been established, either by a domestic authority or by the Court (see, among many other authorities, *N. C. v. Italy* [GC], § 49; *Pantea v. Romania*, § 262; *Vachev v. Bulgaria*, § 78).

222. In the absence of a finding by a domestic authority of a breach of any of the other provisions of Article 5, either directly or in substance, the Court itself must first establish the existence of such a breach for Article 5 § 5 to apply (see, for example, *Nechiporuk and Yonkalo v. Ukraine*, §§ 227 and 229; *Yankov v. Bulgaria*, §§ 190 – 193).

223. The applicability of Article 5 § 5 is not dependant on a domestic finding of unlawfulness or proof that but for the breach the person would have been released (*Blackstock v. the United Kingdom*, § 51; *Waite v. the United Kingdom*, § 73). The arrest or detention may be lawful under domestic law, but still in breach of Article 5, which makes Article 5 § 5 applicable (*Harkmann v. Estonia*, § 50).

2. Judicial remedy

224. Article 5 § 5 creates a direct and enforceable right to compensation before the national courts (see *A. and Others v. the United Kingdom* [GC], § 229; *Storck v. Germany*, § 122).

3. Availability of compensation

225. Article 5 § 5 is complied with where it is possible to apply for compensation in respect of a deprivation of liberty effected in conditions contrary to paragraphs 1, 2, 3 or 4 (see, as more recent authorities, *Michalák v. Slovakia*, § 204; *Lobanov v. Russia*, § 54).

226. An enforceable right to compensation must be available either before or after the Court's judgment (*Stanev v. Bulgaria* [GC], §§ 183 – 184; *Brogan and Others v. the United Kingdom*, § 67).

227. The effective enjoyment of the right to compensation must be ensured with a sufficient degree of certainty (see, for example, *Ciulla v. Italy*, § 44; *Sakık and Others v. Turkey*, § 60). Compensation must be available both in theory (*Dubovik v. Ukraine*, § 74) and practice (*Chitayev and Chitayev v. Russia*, § 195).

228. In considering compensation claims, the domestic authorities are required to interpret and apply domestic law in the spirit of Article 5, without excessive formalism (*Shulgin v. Ukraine*, § 65; *Houtman and Meeus v. Belgium*, § 46).

4. Nature of compensation

229. The right to compensation relates primarily to financial compensation. It does not confer a right to secure the detained person's release, which is covered by Article 5 § 4 of the Convention (*Bozano v. France*, Commission decision).

230. Crediting a period of pre-trial detention towards a penalty does not amount to compensation required by Article 5 § 5, because of its non-financial character [*Włoch v. Poland* (no. 2), § 32].

5. Existence of damage

231. Article 5 § 5 does not prohibit the Contracting States from making the award of compensation dependent upon the ability of the person concerned to show damage resulting from the breach. There can be no question of "compensation" where there is no pecuniary or non-pecuniary damage to compensate (*Wassink v. the Netherlands*, § 38).

232. However, excessive formalism in requiring proof of non-pecuniary damage resulting from unlawful detention is not compliant with the right to compensation (*Danev v.*

Bulgaria, §§ 34 – 35).

6. Amount of compensation

233. Article 5 § 5 of the Convention does not entitle the applicant to a particular amount of compensation (*Damian-Burueana and Damian v. Romania*, § 89; *Şahin Çağdaş v. Turkey*, § 34).

234. However, compensation which is negligible or disproportionate to the seriousness of the violation would not comply with the requirements of Article 5 § 5 as this would render the right guaranteed by that provision theoretical and illusory [*Cumber v. the United Kingdom*, Commission decision; *Attard v. Malta* (dec.)].

235. An award cannot be considerably lower than that awarded by the Court in similar cases (*Ganea v. Moldova*, § 30; *Cristina Boicenco v. Moldova*, § 43).

List of cited cases

The case-law cited in this Guide refers to judgments or decisions delivered by the European Court of Human Rights and to decisions or reports of the European Commission of Human Rights.

Unless otherwise indicated, all references are to a judgment on the merits delivered by a Chamber of the Court. The abbreviation "(dec.)" indicates that the citation is of a decision of the Court and "[GC]" that the case was heard by the Grand Chamber.

The hyperlinks to the cases cited in the electronic version of the Guide are directed to the HUDOC database (http://hudoc.echr.coe.int) which provides access to the case-law of the Court (Grand Chamber, Chamber and Committee judgments, decisions, communicated cases, advisory opinions and legal summaries from the Case-Law Information Note), the Commission (decisions and reports) and the Committee of Ministers (resolutions).

The Court delivers its judgments and decisions in English and/or French, its two official languages. HUDOC also contains translations of many important cases into nearly thirty non-official languages, and links to around one hundred online case-law collections produced by third parties.

— A —

A. and Others v. Bulgaria, no. 51776/08, 29 November 2011

A. and Others v. the United Kingdom [GC], no. 3455/05, ECHR 2009

Abdulkhanov v. Russia, no. 14743/11, 2 October 2012

Adamov v. Switzerland, no. 3052/06, 21 June 2011

Airey v. Ireland, no. 6289/73, Commission decision of 7 July 1977, Decisions and Reports (DR) 8

Aleksandr Makarov v. Russia, no. 15217/07, 12 March 2009

Aleksanyan v. Russia, no. 46468/06, 22 December 2008

Altınok v. Turkey, no. 31610/08, 29 November 2011

Ambruszkiewicz v. Poland, no. 38797/03, 4 May 2006

Amie and Others v. Bulgaria, no. 58149/08, 12 February 2013

Amuur v. France, 25 June 1996, *Reports of Judgments and Decisions* 1996 – III

Anguelova v. Bulgaria, no. 38361/97, ECHR 2002 – IV

Aquilina v. Malta [GC], no. 25642/94, ECHR 1999 – III

Ashingdane v. the United Kingdom, 28 May 1985, Series A no. 93

Assanidze v. Georgia [GC], no. 71503/01, ECHR 2004 – II

Assenov and Others v. Bulgaria, 28 October 1998, *Reports* 1998 – VIII

Attard v. Malta (dec.), no. 46750/99, 28 September 2000

Austin and Others v. the United Kingdom [GC], nos. 39692/09, 40713/09 and 41008/09, 15 March 2012

Azimov v. Russia, no. 67474/11, 18 April 2013

— B —

B. v. Austria, 28 March 1990, Series A no. 175

Baranowski v. Poland, no. 28358/95, ECHR 2000 – III

Becciev v. Moldova, no. 9190/03, 4 October 2005

Beiere v. Latvia, no. 30954/05, 29 November 2011

Bejaoui v. Greece, no. 23916/94, Commission decision of 6 April 1995

Belchev v. Bulgaria, no. 39270/98, 8 April 2004

Belevitskiy v. Russia, no. 72967/01, 1 March 2007

Benham v. the United Kingdom, 10 June 1996, *Reports* 1996 – III

Benjamin and Wilson v. the United Kingdom, no. 28212/95, 26 September 2002

Bergmann v. Estonia, no. 38241/04, 29 May 2008

Bezicheri v. Italy, 25 October 1989, Series A no. 164

Blackstock v. the United Kingdom, no. 59512/00, 21 June 2005

Boicenco v. Moldova, no. 41088/05, 11 July 2006

Bojilov v. Bulgaria, no. 45114/98, 22 December 2004

Bollan v. the United Kingdom (dec.), no. 42117/98, ECHR 2000 – V

Bordovskiy v. Russia, no. 49491/99, 8 February 2005

Bouamar v. Belgium, 29 February 1988, Series A no. 129

Bozano v. France, no. 9990/82, Commission decision of 15 May 1984, DR 39

Bozano v. France, 18 December 1986, Series A no. 111

Brand v. the Netherlands, no. 49902/99, 11 May 2004

Brega and Others v. Moldova, no. 61485/08, 24 January 2012

Brincat v. Italy, 26 November 1992, Series A no. 249 – A

Brogan and Others v. the United Kingdom, 29 November 1988, Series A no. 145 – B

Bykov v. Russia [GC], no. 4378/02, 10 March 2009

— C —

Calmanovici v. Romania, no. 42250/02, 1 July 2008

Castravet v. Moldova, no. 23393/05, 13 March 2007

Çatal v. Turkey, no. 26808/08, 17 April 2012

Chahal v. the United Kingdom, 15 November 1996, *Reports* 1996 – V

Chitayev and Chitayev v. Russia, no. 59334/00, 18 January 2007

Chraidi v. Germany, no. 65655/01, ECHR 2006 – XII

Cernák v. Slovakia, no. 36997/08, 17 December 2013

Ciulla v. Italy, 22 February 1989, Series A no. 148

Clooth v. Belgium, 12 December 1991, Series A no. 225

Čonka v. Belgium, no. 51564/99, ECHR 2002 – I

Creangă v. Romania [GC], no. 29226/03, 23 February 2012

Cristina Boicenco v. Moldova, no. 25688/09, 27 September 2011

Cumber v. the United Kingdom, no. 28779/95, Commission decision of 27 November 1996

— D —

D. D. v. Lithuania, no. 13469/06, 14 February 2012

D. G. v. Ireland, no. 39474/98, ECHR 2002 – III

Dacosta Silva v. Spain, no. 69966/01, ECHR 2006 – XIII

Damian-Burueana and Damian v. Romania, no. 6773/02, 26 May 2009

Danev v. Bulgaria, no. 9411/05, 2 September 2010

De Jong, Baljet and Van den Brink v. the Netherlands, 22 May 1984, Series A no. 77

Delcourt v. Belgium, no. 2689/65, Commission decision of 7 February 1967 referred to in the Commission's report of 1 October 1968

Del Río Prada v. Spain [GC], no. 42750/09, ECHR 2013

Dereci v. Turkey, no. 77845/01, 24 May 2005

De Wilde, Ooms and Versyp v. Belgium, 18 June 1971, Series A no. 12 [link changed]

Dikme v. Turkey, no. 20869/92, ECHR 2000 – VIII

Douiyeb v. the Netherlands [GC], no. 31464/96, 4 August 1999

Drozd and Janousek v. France and Spain, 26 June 1992, Series A no. 240

Dubovik v. Ukraine, nos. 33210/07 and 41866/08, 15 October 2009

— E —

E. v. Norway, 29 August 1990, Series A no. 181 – A

El-Masri v. the former Yugoslav Republic of Macedonia [GC], no. 39630/09, ECHR 2012

Elçi and Others v. Turkey, nos. 23145/93 and 25091/94, 13 November 2003

Engel and Others v. the Netherlands, 8 June 1976, Series A no. 22

Enhorn v. Sweden, no. 56529/00, ECHR 2005 – I

Epple v. Germany, no. 77909/01, 24 March 2005

Erdagöz v. Turkey, no. 21890/93, 22 October 1997, *Reports* 1997 – VI

Erkalo v. the Netherlands, 2 September 1998, *Reports* 1998 – VI

— F —

Farhad Aliyev v. Azerbaijan, no. 37138/06, 9 November 2010

Fodale v. Italy, no. 70148/01, ECHR 2006 – VII

Foka v. Turkey, no. 28940/95, 24 June 2008

Fox, Campbell and Hartley v. the United Kingdom, 30 August 1990, Series A no. 182

Frasik v. Poland, no. 22933/02, ECHR 2010

Freda v Italy, no. 8916/80, Commission decision of 7 October 1980, DR 21

— G —

Gahramanov v. Azerbaijan (dec.), no. 26291/06, 15 October 2013

Ganea v. Moldova, no. 2474/06, 17 May 2011

G. K. v. Poland, no. 38816/97, 20 January 2004

Gaidjurgis v. Lithuania (dec.), no. 49098/99, 16 June 2001

Galstyan v. Armenia, no. 26986/03, 15 November 2007

Garycki v. Poland, no. 14348/02, 6 February 2007

Gasiņš v. Latvia, no. 69458/01, 19 April 2011

Gatt v. Malta, no. 28221/08, ECHR 2010

Gebremedhin [Gaberamadhien] v. France, no. 25389/05, ECHR 2007 – II

Georgieva v. Bulgaria, no. 16085/02, 3 July 2008

Gillan and Quinton v. the United Kingdom, no. 4158/05, ECHR 2010

Giorgi Nikolaishvili v. Georgia, no. 37048/04, 13 January 2009

Giulia Manzoni v. Italy, 1 July 1997, *Reports* 1997 – IV

Glien v. Germany, no. 7345/12, 28 November 2013

Górski v. Poland, no. 28904/02, 4 October 2005

Gutsanovi v. Bulgaria, no. 34529/10, ECHR 2013

Güveç v. Turkey, no. 70337/01, ECHR 2009

Guzzardi v. Italy, 6 November 1980, Series A no. 39

— H —

H. L. v. the United Kingdom, no. 45508/99, ECHR 2004 – IX

H. M. v. Switzerland, no. 39187/98, ECHR 2002 – II

H. W. v. Germany, no. 17167/11, 19 September 2013

Harkmann v. Estonia, no. 2192/03, 11 July 2006

Hilda Hafsteinsdóttir v. Iceland, no. 40905/98, 8 June 2004

Hood v. the United Kingdom [GC], no. 27267/95, ECHR 1999 – I

Houtman and Meeus v. Belgium, no. 22945/07, 17 March 2009

Hristova v. Bulgaria, no. 60859/00, 7 December 2006

Huber v. Switzerland, 23 October 1990, Series A no. 188

Hutchison Reid v. the United Kingdom, no. 50272/99, ECHR 2003 – Ⅳ

— I —

I. A. v. France, 23 September 1998, *Reports* 1998 – Ⅶ

I. I. v. Bulgaria, no. 44082/98, 9 June 2005

Ichin and Others v. Ukraine, nos. 28189/04 and 28192/04, 21 December 2010

Idalov v. Russia [GC], no. 5826/03, 22 May 2012

Ilaşcu and Others v. Moldova and Russia [GC], no. 48787/99, ECHR 2004 – Ⅶ

Ilgar Mammadov v. Azerbaijan, no. 15172/13, 22 May 2014

Ilijkov v. Bulgaria, no. 33977/96, 26 July 2001

Iliya Stefanov v. Bulgaria, no. 65755/01, 22 May 2008

İpek and Others v. Turkey, nos. 17019/02 and 30070/02, 3 February 2009

Ireland v. the United Kingdom, 18 January 1978, Series A no. 25

Iskandarov v. Russia, no. 17185/05, 23 September 2010

— J —

Jablonski v. Poland, no. 33492/96, 21 December 2000

James, Wells and Lee v. the United Kingdom, nos. 25119/09, 57715/09 and 57877/09, 18 September 2012

Jarzyński v. Poland, no. 15479/02, 4 October 2005

Ječius v. Lithuania, no. 34578/97, ECHR 2000 – Ⅸ

Juncal v. the United Kingdom (dec.), no. 32357/09, 17 September 2013

— K —

Kerr v. the United Kingdom (dec.), no. 40451/98, 7 December 1999

Kaboulov v. Ukraine, no. 41015/04, 19 November 2009

Kadem v. Malta, no. 55263/00, 9 January 2003

Kafkaris v. Cyprus (no. 2)(dec.), no. 9644/09, 21 June 2011

Kalashnikov v. Russia, no. 47095/99, ECHR 2002 – Ⅵ

Kallweit v. Germany, no. 17792/07, 13 January 2011

Kampanis v. Greece, no. 17977/91, 13 July 1995

Kanagaratnam v. Belgium, no. 15297/09, 13 December 2011

Kandzhov v. Bulgaria, no. 68294/01, 6 November 2008

Kane v. Cyprus (dec.), no. 33655/06, 13 September 2011

Kharin v. Russia, no. 37345/03, 3 February 2011

Khodorkovskiy v. Russia, no. 5829/04, 31 May 2011

Khudoyorov v. Russia, no. 6847/02, ECHR 2005 – X

Koendjbiharie v. the Netherlands, 25 October 1990, Series A no. 185 – B

Kolompar v. Belgium, 24 September 1992, Series A no. 235 – C

Koniarska v. United Kingdom, no. 33670/96, (dec.) 12 October 2000

Korneykova v. Ukraine, no. 39884/05, 19 January 2012

Kortesis v. Greece, no. 60593/10, 12 June 2012

Krejčíř v. the Czech Republic, nos. 39298/04 and 8723/05, 26 March 2009

Krupko and Others v. Russia, no. 26587/07, 26 June 2014

Kučera v. Slovakia, no. 48666/99, 17 July 2007

Kudła v. Poland [GC], no. 30210/96, ECHR 2000 – XI

Kurt v. Turkey, 25 May 1998, *Reports* 1998 – III

— L —

L. B. v. Belgium, no. 22831/08, 2 October 2012

Labita v. Italy [GC], no. 26772/95, ECHR 2000 – IV

Ladent v. Poland, no. 11036/03, 18 March 2008

Laumont v. France, no. 43626/98, ECHR 2001 – XI

Lavents v. Latvia, no. 58442/00, 28 November 2002

Lawless v. Ireland (no. 3), 1 July 1961, Series A no. 3

Lebedev v. Russia, no. 4493/04, 25 October 2007

Lelièvre v. Belgium, no. 11287/03, 8 November 2007

Letellier v. France, 26 June 1991, Series A no. 207

Lloyd and Others v. the United Kingdom, nos. 29798/96 et al., 1 March 2005

Lobanov v. Russia, no. 16159/03, 16 October 2008

Luberti v. Italy, 23 February 1984, Series A no. 75

— M —

M. v. Germany, no. 19359/04, ECHR 2009

M. A. v. Cyprus, no. 41872/10, ECHR 2013

Mahdid and Haddar v. Austria (dec.), no. 74762/01, ECHR 2005 - XIII

Mamedova v. Russia, no. 7064/05, 1 June 2006

Mancini v. Italy, no. 44955/98, ECHR 2001 - IX

Mangouras v. Spain [GC], no. 12050/04, ECHR 2010

Marturana v. Italy, no. 63154/00, 4 March 2008

Matznetter v. Austria, 10 November 1969, Series A no. 10

McKay v. the United Kingdom [GC], no. 543/03, ECHR 2006 - X

McVeigh and Others v. United Kingdom, nos. 8022/77, 8025/77, 8027/77, Commission report of 18 March 1981

Medova v. Russia, no. 25385/04, 15 January 2009

Medvedyev and Others v. France [GC], no. 3394/03, ECHR 2010

Meloni v. Switzerland, no. 61697/00, 10 April 2008

M. H. v. the United Kingdom, no. 11577/06, 22 October 2013

Michalák v. Slovakia, no. 30157/03, 8 February 2011

Minjat v. Switzerland, no. 38223/97, 28 October 2003

Mogoş and Others v. Romania (dec.), no. 20420/02, 6 May 2004

Molotchko v. Ukraine, no. 12275/10, 26 April 2012

Monnell and Morris v. the United Kingdom, 2 March 1987, Series A no. 115

Mooren v. Germany [GC], no. 11364/03, 9 July 2009

Morsink v. the Netherlands, no. 48865/99, 11 May 2004

Mubilanzila Mayeka and Kaniki Mitunga v. Belgium, no. 13178/03, ECHR 2006 - XI

Murray v. the United Kingdom [GC], 28 October 1994, Series A no. 300 - A

Musiał v. Poland [GC], no. 24557/94, ECHR 1999 - II

Muşuc v. Moldova, no. 42440/06, 6 November 2007

— N —

N. C. v. Italy [GC], no. 24952/94, ECHR 2002 - X

Nada v. Switzerland [GC], no. 10593/08, ECHR 2012

Nart v. Turkey, no. 20817/04, 6 May 2008

Nasrulloyev v. Russia, no. 656/06, 11 October 2007

Năstase-Silivestru v. Romania, no. 74785/01, 4 October 2007

Navarra v. France, 23 November 1993, Series A no. 273 – B

Nechiporuk and Yonkalo v. Ukraine, no. 42310/04, 21 April 2011

Neumeister v. Austria, 27 June 1968, Series A no. 8

Niedbała v. Poland, no. 27915/95, 4 July 2000

Nielsen v. Denmark, 28 November 1988, Series A no. 144

Nikolov v. Bulgaria, no. 38884/97, 30 January 2003

Nikolova v. Bulgaria [GC], no. 31195/96, ECHR 1999 – II

Nikolova v. Bulgaria (no. 2), no. 40896/98, 30 September 2004

Novotka v. Slovakia (dec.), no. 47244/99, 4 November 2003

Nowak v. Ukraine, no. 60846/10, 31 March 2011

Nowicka v. Poland, no. 30218/96, 3 December 2002

— O —

O. H. v. Germany, no. 4646/08, 24 November 2011

O'Hara v. the United Kingdom, no. 37555/97, ECHR 2001 – X

Ostendorf v. Germany, no. 15598/08, 7 March 2013

Osypenko v. Ukraine, no. 4634/04, 9 November 2010

Öcalan v. Turkey (dec.), no. 46221/99, 14 December 2000

Öcalan v. Turkey [GC], no. 46221/99, ECHR 2005 – IV

Oral and Atabay v. Turkey, no. 39686/02, 23 June 2009

Ovsjannikov v. Estonia, no. 1346/12, 20 February 2014

— P —

P. and S. v. Poland, no. 57375/08, 30 October 2012

Panchenko v. Russia, no. 45100/98, 8 February 2005

Pankiewicz v. Poland, no. 34151/04, 12 February 2008

Pantea v. Romania, no. 33343/96, ECHR 2003 – VI

Paradis v. Germany (dec.), no. 4065/04, 4 September 2007

Petkov and Profirov v. Bulgaria, nos. 50027/08 and 50781/09, 24 June 2014

Petukhova v. Russia, no. 28796/07, 2 May 2013

Piotr Baranowski v. Poland, no. 39742/05, 2 October 2007

Piotr Osuch v. Poland, no. 30028/06, 3 November 2009

Piruzyan v. Armenia, no. 33376/07, 26 June 2012

Plesó v. Hungary, no. 41242/08, 2 October 2012

Prencipe v. Monaco, no. 43376/06, 16 July 2009

— Q —

Quinn v. France, 22 March 1995, Series A no. 311

— R —

R. L. and M. -J. D. v. France, no. 44568/98, 19 May 2004

R. M. D. v. Switzerland, 26 September 1997, *Reports* 1997 – VI

Radu v. Germany, no. 20084/07, 16 May 2013

Rahimi v. Greece, no. 8687/08, 5 April 2011

Rakevich v. Russia, no. 58973/00, 28 October 2003

Rantsev v. Cyprus and Russia, no. 25965/04, ECHR 2010

Raudevs v. Latvia, no. 24086/03, 17 December 2013

Rehbock v. Slovenia, no. 29462/95, ECHR 2000 – XII

Reinprecht v. Austria, no. 67175/01, ECHR 2005 – XII

Riad and Idiab v. Belgium, nos. 29787/03 and 29810/03, 24 January 2008

Riera Blume and Others v. Spain, no. 37680/97, ECHR 1999 – VII

Ruiz Rivera v. Switzerland, no. 8300/06, 18 February 2014

— S —

S. B. C. v. the United Kingdom, no. 39360/98, 19 June 2001

S. P. v. Belgium (dec.), no. 12572/08, 14 June 2011

S. R. v. the Netherlands (dec.), no. 13837/07, 18 September 2012

Saadi v. the United Kingdom, no. 13229/03, 11 July 2006

Saadi v. the United Kingdom [GC], no. 13229/03, ECHR 2008

Sadegül Özdemir v. Turkey, no. 61441/00, 2 August 2005

Şahin Çağdaş v. Turkey, no. 28137/02, 11 April 2006

Sakık and Others v. Turkey, 26 November 1997, *Reports* 1997 – Ⅶ

Salayev v. Azerbaijan, no. 40900/05, 9 November 2010

Sanchez-Reisse v. Switzerland, 21 October 1986, Series A no. 107

Sarigiannis v. Italy, no. 14569/05, 5 April 2011

Schiesser v. Switzerland, 4 December 1979, Series A no. 34

Schwabe and M. G. v. Germany, no. 8080/08, 1 December 2011

Scott v. Spain, 18 December 1996, *Reports* 1996 – Ⅵ

Selçuk v. Turkey, no. 21768/02, 10 January 2006

Shabani v. Switzerland, no. 29044/06, 5 November 2009

Shamayev and Others v. Georgia and Russia, no. 36378/02, ECHR 2005 – Ⅲ

Shamsa v. Poland, nos. 45355/99 and 45357/99, 27 November 2003

Shcherbina v. Russia, no. 41970/11, 26 June 2014

Shimovolos v. Russia, no. 30194/09, 21 June 2011

Shtukaturov v. Russia, no. 44009/05, ECHR 2008

Shulgin v. Ukraine, no. 29912/05, 8 December 2011

Simons v. Belgium (dec.), no. 71407/10, 28 August 2012

Skrobol v. Poland, no. 44165/98, 13 September 2005

Smirnova v. Russia, nos. 46133/99 and 48183/99, ECHR 2003 – Ⅸ

Soldatenko v. Ukraine, no. 2440/07, 23 October 2008

Solmaz v. Turkey, no. 27561/02, 16 January 2007

Stanev v. Bulgaria [GC], no. 36760/06, 17 January 2012

Stašaitis v. Lithuania, no. 47679/99, 21 March 2002

Steel and Others v. the United Kingdom, 23 September 1998, *Reports* 1998 – Ⅶ

Stephens v. Malta (no. 1), no. 11956/07, 21 April 2009

Stephens v. Malta (no. 2), no. 33740/06, 21 April 2009

Stepuleac v. Moldova, no. 8207/06, 6 November 2007

Stoichkov v. Bulgaria, no. 9808/02, 24 March 2005

Storck v. Germany, no. 61603/00, ECHR 2005 V

Sulaoja v. Estonia, no. 55939/00, 15 February 2005

Suso Musa v. Malta, no. 42337/12, 23 July 2013

Svipsta v. Latvia, no. 66820/01, ECHR 2006 – III

— T —

Talat Tepe v. Turkey, no. 31247/96, 21 December 2004

Tepe v. Turkey, no. 31247/96, 21 December 2004

Tase v. Romania, no. 29761/02, 10 June 2008

Tiron v. Romania, no. 17689/03, 7 April 2009

Toniolo v. San Marino and Italy, no. 44853/10, 26 June 2012

Toshev v. Bulgaria, no. 56308/00, 10 August 2006

Toth v. Austria, 12 December 1991, Series A no. 224

Tsirlis and Kouloumpas v. Greece, 29 May 1997, Reports 1997 – III

Ţurcan v. Moldova, no. 39835/05, 23 October 2007

— V —

Vachev v. Bulgaria, no. 42987/98, ECHR 2004 – VIII

Van der Leer v. the Netherlands, 21 February 1990, Series A no. 170 – A

Van Droogenbroeck v. Belgium, 24 June 1982, Series A no. 50

Varbanov v. Bulgaria, no. 31365/96, ECHR 2000 – X

Varga v. Romani, no. 73957/01, 1 April 2008

Vasileva v. Denmark, no. 52792/99, 25 September 2003

Vassis and Others v. France, no. 62736/09, 27 June 2013

Velinov v. theformer Yugoslav Republic of Macedonia, no. 16880/08, 19 September 2013

Viorel Burzo v. Romania, nos. 75109/01 and 12639/02, 30 June 2009

Voskuil v. the Netherlands, no. 64752/01, 22 November 2007

Vrenčev v. Serbia, no. 2361/05, 23 September 2008

— W —

Waite v. the United Kingdom, no. 53236/99, 10 December 2002

Wassink v. the Netherlands, 27 September 1990, Series A no. 185 – A

Weeks v. the United Kingdom, 2 March 1987, Series A no. 114

Wemhoff v. Germany, 27 June 1968, Series A no. 7

Willcox and Hurford v. the United Kingdom (dec.). nos. 43759/10 and 43771/12, 8 January 2013

Winterwerp v. the Netherlands, 24 October 1979, Series A no. 33

Witold Litwa v. Poland, no. 26629/95, ECHR 2000 – III

Włoch v. Poland, no. 27785/95, ECHR 2000 – XI

Włoch v. Poland (no. 2), no. 33475/08, 10 May 2011

— X —

X. v. Austria, no. 8278/78, Commission decision of 13 December 1979, DR 18

X. v. Belgium, no. 4741/71, Commission decision of 2 April 1973

X. v. Finland, no. 34806/04, ECHR 2012

X. v. Germany, no. 1322/62, Commission decision of 14 December 1963

X. v. Germany, no. 6659/74, Commission decision of 10 December 1975

X. v. Germany, no. 8098/77, Commission decision of 13 December 1978, DR 16

X. v. Switzerland, no. 8500/79, Commission decision of 14 December 1979, DR 18

X. v. Switzerland, no. 9012/80, Commission decision of 9 December 1980, DR 25

X. v. the United Kingdom, no. 6998/75, Commission report of 16 July 1980

X v. the United Kingdom, 5 November 1981, Series A no. 46

— Y — Z —

Yankov v. Bulgaria, no. 39084/97, ECHR 2003 – XII

Yefimenko v. Russia, no. 152/04, 12 February 2013

Yoh-Ekale Mwanje v. Belgium, no. 10486/10, 20 December 2011

Z. H. v. Hungary, no. 28973/11, 8 November 2012

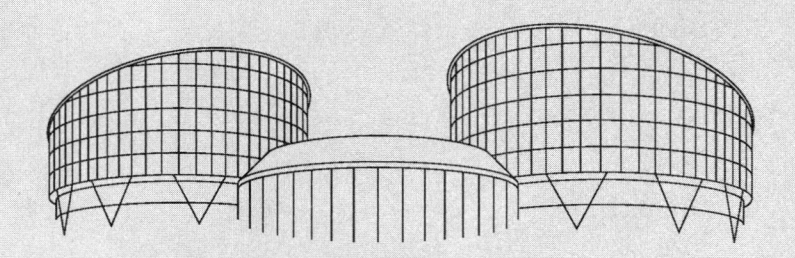

EUROPEAN COURT OF HUMAN RIGHTS
COUR EUROPÉENNE DES DROITS DE L'HOMME

第三章 《欧洲人权公约》第6条适用指南

获得公正审判的权利

（民事部分）

COUNCIL OF EUROPE
CONSEIL DE L'EUROPE

读者须知

本报告旨在为法律工作者们提供欧洲人权法院成立至今所发布的最为重要的判决中所涉及的重要主题相关的信息①。因此,本报告展现了由本院判例法以及相关的先例所发展出的诸多重要原则②。本报告中所援引的判例是经过选择的:它们都是最为典型的、重要的且为最新的判决和裁定。

本法院所做出的判决在事实上并不仅作用于本法院所受理的案件,而是在更宽泛意义上用于阐明、保障和发展欧洲人权公约中所设立的规则,从而让缔约国得以更好的遵守(*Ireland v. the United Kingdom*, §154)。因此,欧洲人权公约体系的使命是为了共同的利益对公共政策层面的事项做出决定,从而提高人权保护的整体水平并在整个公约缔约国集团内扩展人权的司法保障体系(*Konstantin Markin v. Russia*[GC], §89)。

---

① 判例法参考已更新至 2013 年 5 月 1 日。
② 文中所引判决和决定的超级链接将连接到该文件的原始英文或法文文本(本法院的两种官方语言)。读者可访问本法院的 HUDOC 判例法数据库来获取这些判决和决定的英文或法文文本,以及其他语种的译本。

第 6 条　获得公正审判的权利

"(1)在决定某人的公民权利和义务或者在决定对某人确定任何刑事罪名时,任何人有权在合理的时间内受到依法设立的独立而公正的审判机构的公平且公开的审讯。判决应当公开宣布。但是,基于对民主社会中的道德、公共秩序或者国家安全的利益,以及对民主社会中的少年的利益或者是保护当事人的私生活权利的考虑,或者是法院认为,在特殊情况下,如果公开审讯将损害公平利益的话,可以拒绝记者和公众参与旁听全部或者部分审讯。

(2)凡受刑事罪指控者在未经依法证明为有罪之前,应当推定为无罪。

(3)凡受刑事罪指控者具有下列最低限度的权利:

a. 以他所了解的语言立即详细地通知他被指控罪名的性质以及被指控的原因;

b. 应当有适当的时间和便利条件为辩护作准备;

c. 由他本人或者由他自己选择的律师协助自己辩护,或者如果他无力支付法律协助费用的,则基于公平利益的考虑,应当免除他的有关费用;

d. 询问不利于他的证人,并在与不利于他的证人具有相同的条件下,让有利于他的证人出庭接受询问;

e. 如果他不懂或者不会讲法院所使用的工作语言,可以请求免费的译员协助翻译。"

第一节 适用范围:"公民权利和义务"的概念[①]

> **公约第 6 条第 1 款**
>
> "在决定某人的公民权利和义务……时,任何人有权……受到审判机构……的审讯……"

一、公约第 6 条第 1 款的一般适用条件

1. "公民权利和义务"的概念不能单独依被申诉国国内法进行解释;它是公约引申出来的"自治概念"。公约第 6 条第 1 款的适用不受案件双方的状态、争议事项相关立法的特点、对争议事项有管辖权的有权机关的特点所制约(参见 *Georgiadis v. Greece* 案,§34)。

2. 然而,公约中规定的自治概念原则必须根据现今情势进行解释,法院无权在解释公约第 6 条第 1 款时忽略"公民(civil)"这一形容词,因为"公民"一词限定了本条中"权利和义务"的属性,尽管其并未出现在文本之中(*Ferrazzini v. Italy*[GC], §30)。

3. 公约第 6 条第 1 款在公民事项中的适用首先基于争议的存在。其次,该争议必须与至少可被相关国内法承认的"权利和义务"有关。最后,这些"权利和义务"必须在公约下被认定为具有"公民"(civil)属性,尽管第 6 条未给这些"权利和义务"在缔约国法律体系内规定任何特定内容(*James and others v. United Kingdom*, §81)。

(一)"争端(dispute)"的概念

4. "争端"一词(法文"*contestation*")必须被赋予实际意义而不仅是形式意义(*Le Compte, Van Leuven and De Meyere v. Belgium*, §45)。因此有必要透过语言的表面解读将注意力集中在每个案件的不同事实情况上(参见 *Gorou v. Greece*(no.2)[GC], §29;以及 *Boulois v. Luxembourg*[GC], §92)。第 6 条并不适用于无争议且单边的程

---

① 本部分是在本法院《受理标准实践指南》的相关部分基础上的修订和更新。

序,这些程序没有对立的当事人,且只有当事人对权利没有争议时才可适用[*Alaverdyan v. Armenia*,(dec.),§35]。

5. 该"争端"必须真实且程度严重(*Sporrong and Lönnroth v. Sweden*,§81)。这就可以排除,如仅因监狱中有 HIV 感染者便向监狱管理机关提出民事诉讼的情形[*Skorobogatykh v. Russia*(dec.)]。例如,欧洲人权法院将涉及向检察官基于法律层面问题提出的上诉请求认定为真实的"争端",因为其构成了该申诉人以公民一方的身份参加诉讼以意图获得赔偿的整个诉讼过程的不可分割的一部分[*Gorou v. Greece*(no. 2)[GC],§35]。

6. 此处的争端不仅关系着某权利的实际存在,而且与该权利行使的范围和方式也有关(*Benthem v. the Netherlands*,§32)。该争端还可能与事实问题有关。

7. 诉讼结果必须与所争议问题直接相关[例如,*Ulyanov v. Ukraine*(dec.)]。也就是说,一个模糊的关联或较远的结果不足以适用公约第 6 条第 1 款(*Boulois v. Luxembourg*[GC],§90)。例如,法院认为对延续某核电站执业执照决定合法性提起的诉讼不符合公约第 6 条第 1 款的范围,因为延续执照的决定与保护生命、身体完整和财产的权利间的联系过于"模糊和遥远",申诉人未能证明他们本身已处于具体且迫近的危险中(*Balmer-Schafroth and Others v. Switzerland*,§40;*Athanassoglou and Others v. Switzerland*[GC],§§46 - 55);参见最新案例,*Sdruzeni Jihoceske Matky v. the Czech Republic*(dec.);涉及工厂产生有限噪音污染的案件,参见 *Zapletal v. the Czech Republic*(dec.);或者假想煤矿废物处理对植物的环境影响,参见 *Ivan Atanasov v. Bulgaria*,§§90 - 95。类似案例还有:两名公务人员因他们另一名同事被任命为某职位而提出的申诉与他们实际公民权利的关系过于遥远[具体而言涉及他们自己被任命的权利,参见 *Revel and Mora v. France*(dec.)]。

8. 相反,本法院认为公约第 6 条第 1 款适用于关于修建大坝会导致申诉人的村庄遭受水灾的案件(*Gorraiz Lizarraga and Others v. Spain*,§46)和涉及在申诉人村庄附近使用氰化浸出法开采金矿的许可决定的案件(*Taşkın and Others v. Turkey*,§133;同时参见 *Zander v. Sweden*,§§24 - 25)。较新的案件包括,当地某环境保护协会上诉要求复审某计划的决定,欧洲人权法院认为该争端与该协会主张的权利间存在充分的联系,尤其是考虑到该协会的地位和其创始人,及其在空间和物质上有限的目标(*L'Erablière*

A. S. B. L. v. Belgium，§§28 – 30）。进一步而言,针对个人法律权利能力恢复的诉讼程序对于其公民权利和义务是具有直接的决定意义的(*Stanev v. Bulgaria*［GC］,§233)。

（二）国内法中存在争议的相关权利

9. 申请人必须能够声明享有一项由本国法所承认的权利(*Masson and Van Zon v. the Netherlands*，§48；*Gutfreund v. France*，§41；和 *Boulois v. Luxembourg*［GC］,§§90 – 94)。公约第6条本身并未对缔约国国内法中的权利赋予任何具体内容,且原则上本法院必须参考国内法才可判定权利是否存在。缔约国权力机关享有自由裁量权,在做出决定时,可能考虑是否授予特定申请人所申请的措施,也可能直接决定。尽管如此,仅仅在某法律规范文本中提到存在此种裁量权并不足以否定存在某项权利。本院还可以考虑的其他标准,包括本国法院在类似情况承认过存在该项权利,或者国内法院审查了申请者所请求的实质内容等(*Boulois v. Luxembourg*［GC］,§§91 – 101)。

10. 本法院可以判定国内法承认诸如生命权、健康权、环境权和财产权等权利(*Athanassoglou and Others v. Switzerland*［GC］,§44)。

11. 所争议的权利必须在国内法中具有法律基础(*Szücs v. Austria*,§33)。

12. 然而个人的诉求在国内是否可诉,不仅可以依据被国内法所承认的相关公民权利,而且还可依据其向国内法院起诉的可能性、在程序上遭受阻碍或限制的事实。对于程序障碍可适用公约第6条第1款,参见(*Al-Adsani v. the United Kingdom*［GC］,§§47；*McElhinney v. Ireland*［GC］,§25)。尽管原则上公约第6条不能适用于对国内法已有权利的实质性限制(*Roche v. the United Kingdom*［GC］,§119),公约机构不得通过解释第6条第1款来创造一项在国内法上没有法律基础的民事实体权利(出处同上,§117)。

13. 在确定是否存在某项公民权利以及对某权利的限制是实体性还是程序性时,必须首先考虑国内法的相关条文及国内法院对该条文的解释(*Masson and Van Zon v. the Netherlands*,§49)。对条文的解读不能停留于表面,而需要深入研究国内法是如何对特定限制进行分类的,且要注意与现实结合(*Van Droogenbroeck v. Belgium*,§38)。最后要明确的是,终决法院的裁决并不绝对地剥夺申诉人诉求的可争议性(*Le Calvez v. France*,§56)。例如,对由外国政策引导下的行为(北约空袭塞尔维亚)进行司法审查的范围是有限的,但这并不会使申诉人的申诉丧失可争议性,因为这其实是国内法院第一次被要求审理相关事项(*Markovic and Others v. Italy*［GC］,§§100 – 102)。

14. 上述标准适用于实体方面和程序方面的限制有所区别,欧洲人权法院确认了对警方失职提出的民事诉讼(参见 Osman v. the United Kingdom)或对当地政府机关的民事诉讼(参见 Z and Others v. the United Kingdom[GC])适用公约第 6 条第 1 款,并且考虑到了特定的限制(诉讼豁免或免除责任)是否符合公约第 6 条第 1 款的出发点。另一方面,法院承认官方对军方人员从实体限制方面衍生出的豁免,且其国内法不承认该种豁免为公约第 6 条第 1 款下的"权利"[Roche v. the United Kingdom[GC],§124;同时参见 Hotter v. Austria(dec.),and Andronikashvili v. Georgia(dec.)]。

15. 欧洲人权法院认为如果是为了其成员的特定权利和利益(Gorraiz Lizarraga and Others v. Spain,§45),协会、组织等也可以成为公约第 6 条第 1 款的适格主体,或者甚至是为了基于其法人身份而享有的特定权利[如公众知情权和参与环境决策权,参见 Collectif national d'information et d'opposition à l'usine Melox-Collectif Stop Melox et Mox v. France(dec.)],或者当该协会的诉讼未能被看作为公益之诉(actio popularis)(参见 L'Erablière A. S. B. L. v. Belgium)。

16. 当立法对从事相关职业或专业人士设定了特别条件时,个人必须满足该条件才能被准许从事相应职业或专业(De Moor v. Belgium,§43)。例如,申诉人在其诉求中认为其已经符合法律对医生职业注册的要求,则此时公约第 6 条便可适用[Chevrol v. France,§55;反例参见,Bouilloc v. France(dec.)]。在任何情况下,如果涉及某公民权利的诉讼之合法性因申诉人已使用了相关的司法救济而遭到质疑,尽管最终也许发现申诉人并不满足法律上的要求(申诉人要求继续其在外国从事的医药职业的权利,参见 Kök v. Turkey,§37),也可以得出存在有"公民权利"的"争议"的结论。

(三)权利的"公民"本质

17. 某权利是否在公约下被视为具有公民本质,必须根据所涉缔约国国内法规定的该权利的实体内容和效果判断,而不是依据该权利的法律分类确定。为了行使法院的监督权,法院同时应考虑公约的目标和宗旨以及其他缔约国的国内法律体系(König v. Germany,§89)。

18. 原则上,对国内法上所认为的私人主体间的公民争端在向欧洲人权法院提起时是默认可适用公约第 6 条第 1 款的(有关一个司法分离的案件,参见 Airey v. Ireland,§21)。

(四)权利的私人属性:以金钱的视角审视

19. 法院认为在国内法上属于"公法"范围且其结果对私人权利和义务的确定有决定性影响的诉讼符合公约第 6 条第 1 款的范围要求。相关的诉讼参见出卖土地许可(参见 *Ringeisen v. Austria*,§94),开办私人诊所(参见 *König v. Germany*,§§94 – 95),建筑许可(尤其参见 *Sporrong and Lönnroth v. Sweden*,§79),宗教建筑的所有权和使用权(参见 *Sâmbata Bihor Greco-Catholic Parish v. Romania*,§65),从业要求行政许可(*Benthem v. the Netherlands*,§36),销售酒精饮料许可(参见 *Tre Traktörer Aktiebolag v. Sweden*,§43)或涉及与工作相关的疾病或事故的赔偿争议支付(*Chaudet v. France*,§30)。

20. 同样,第 6 条也适用于特定职业机构内部的有关行使职业权利的纪律处罚程序[参见 *Le Compte*,*Van Leuven and De Meyere v. Belgium*;*Philis v. Greece*(no.2)],对国家提出的失职诉讼(参见 *X. v. France*),因行政决定的撤销危及申诉人的权利而提起的诉讼(参见 *De Geouffre de la Pradelle v. France*),禁止在属于申诉人的水域捕鱼的行政诉讼(参见 *Alatulkkila and Others v. Finland*,§49)以及就某项公民权利提出的赔偿诉讼——如在为某公共项目投标时,不因个人宗教信仰或政治观点而被歧视的权利[参见 *Tinnelly &Sons Ltd and Others and McElduff and Others v. the United Kingdom*,§61;反例参见 *I. T. C. Ltd v. Malta*(dec.)]。

21. 公约第 6 条第 1 款也适用于刑事程序中的民事赔偿诉求(参见 *Perez v. France*[GC],§§70 – 71),除非该民事诉讼仅是为了达到个人报复或惩罚的目的[参见 *Sigalas v. Greece*,§29;*Mihova v. Italy*(dec.)]。公约并不包含任何可使第三方被指控或获罪的权利。符合公约范围的权利必须与受害人在国内法上提出民事诉讼权利的行使不可分离,即使该权利只是为了确保表面上的赔偿,或保护诸如"良好名誉"之类的公民权利(参见 *Perez v. France*[GC],§70;同时参见,关于象征性奖励的案件,*Gorou v. Greece*(no.2)[GC],§24)。因此自申诉人成为公民一方开始,公约第 6 条可以适用于其所涉诉讼,除非申诉人清楚明白地放弃其赔偿权。

22. 公约第 6 条第 1 款还可以适用于因国家机关工作人员的不合理对待而寻求赔偿的民事诉讼(参见 *Aksoy v. Turkey*,§92)案件。

二、对其他争端形式的延伸适用

23. 欧洲人权法院主张公约第 6 条第 1 款适用于社会事务,包括有关雇员被私人公司解雇的诉讼（参见 *Buchholz v. Germany*），发放社会保险福利的诉讼（参见 *Feldbrugge v. the Netherlands*）或关于福利援助金的诉讼，即使属于不必摊付公积金的情况（参见 *Salesi v. Italy*），还包括有关强制社会保障缴款的诉讼（参见 *Schouten and Meldrum v. the Netherlands*）。在上述案件中，本法院认为私法方面考量优先于公法方面的考量。此外本法院还认为获得福利津贴和获得因纳粹迫害而在私法上给予的赔偿金有一定相似之处（参见 *Woś v. Poland*，§76）。

24. 公职人员提起的争端在原则上属于公约第 6 条第 1 款的范围。在帕乐归（*Pellegrin*）案的判决中（参见 *Pellegrin v. France*［GC］，§§64 – 71），法院采用了一种"功能性"标准。法院在艾斯克林（*Eskelinen*）判决中决定使用一种新的方法（参见 *Vilho Eskelinen and Others v. Finland*［GC］，§§50 – 62）。该原则首先推定公约第 6 条适用，然后需要由被申诉国政府来证明，第一，提起民事诉讼的公职人员在国内法上不享有获得法院救济权；第二，排除公职人员享有公约第 6 条的权利是合理的。若申诉人在国内法院享有了救济权，则公约第 6 条可以适用（甚至适用于现役部队军官及其向军事法院提出的诉求，参见 *Pridatchenko and Others v. Russia*，§47）。如果一个非司法机构十分清楚地履行着司法职能，那么就实质意义而言，它有可能在国内法上具有"法院"的资格（*Oleksandr Volkov v. Vkiaine*，§§88 – 91）。考虑到上述第二条标准，对公职人员权利的排除需要在"国家利益的客观基础"上加以合法性阐释，从而要求国家去证明该争议的主体事由与国家权力的行使有关或者会动摇国家与其公职人员的特殊联系。因此在原则上对于普通劳动争议案件，如有关薪水、津贴或类似补贴，排除第 6 条权利的适用上是没有正当性理由的，这是考虑到特定公职人员与国家间的特殊关系（如有关警察人员特殊津贴的争议，参见 *Vilho Eskelinen and Others v. Finland*［GC］）。最近的艾斯克林判决确立了新的标准，法院宣布公约第 6 条第 1 款适用于有关不公平地开除使馆工作人员案件（波兰使馆的秘书兼接线员的诉讼，参见 *Cudak v. Lithuania*［GC］，§§44 – 47），一个高级警察官员（*Šikić v. Croatia*，§§18 – 20）或者一个军事法庭中的军事官员［*Vasilchenko v. Russia*(dec.)案件，§§34 – 36］，还适用于有关议会助理职位获取的诉讼（*Savino and Others v. Italy*）和对一名法官提起的纪律处罚诉讼（参见 *Olujić v. Croatia*），检察官提起的对于其转任的总统法令的上诉［参见 *Zalli v. Albania*(dec.)，以及其中引用的其他参考资源］，涉及海关官员的职业生涯的程序（申请获得内部升职的权利：*Fiume v. Italy*，§§33 – 36）。

25. 宪法性争端也可以属于公约第 6 条的范围,前提是该宪法性程序对于普通法院进行的公民权利争端的结果有着决定性的影响(参见 *Ruiz-Mateos v. Spain*)。这并不适用于涉及作为特例授予个人公民身份的总统法令的纠纷,或者决定总统是否违反了宪法宣誓的问题,因为这些程序并不涉及公民权利和义务(*Paksas v. Lithuania*[GC],§§65 – 66)。第 6 条第 1 款适用于临时措施的标准延伸至宪法法院(*Kübler v. Germany*,§§47 – 48)。

26. 最后一点,公约第 6 条同时也适用于其他非严格意义上的金钱性事项,如环境问题,其争议事项可能会涉及生命权、健康权或环境健康权(参见 *Taşkın and Others v. Turkey*);收养儿童问题(参见 *McMichael v. the United Kingdom*);儿童的上学安排(*Ellès and Others v. Switzerland*,§§21 – 23);建立亲子关系的权利(*Alaverdyan v. Armenia*(裁定),§33);自由权[参见 *Laidin v. France*(no. 2)];囚犯的羁押安排(例如,有关囚犯在何种限制条件下会被安排到高安全级别的囚房,参见 *Enea v. Italy*[GC],§§97 – 107 或者到高级安全室(*Stegarescu and Bahrin v. Portugal*)的问题,或者根据监狱纪律处罚程序导致限制了其家人探视的权利(*Gülmez v. Turkey*,§30);良好名誉权(参见 *Helmers v. Sweden*,§27);获得行政文件的权利[参见 *Loiseau v. France*(dec.)];或者反对他人获取将影响名誉权的警察文档的上诉,获得保护财产以及就业因而能够生存的权利(*Pocius v. Lithuania* 案,§§38 – 46,以及 *Užukauskas v. Lithuania*,§§32 – 40);成为社团成员的权利[*Sakellaropoulos v. Greece*(dec.)同样地,第 6 条也适用于关系到社团的民事权利的,即使在国内法下结社自由是在公法领域内的问题:参见 *APEH Üldözötteinek Szövetsége and Others v. Hungary*,§§34 – 35];以及继续高等教育的权利(参见 *Emine Araç v. Turkey*,§§18 – 25)在基础教育背景下更为适用的立场(*Oršuš and Others v. Croatia*[GC],§104)。因此,公约第 6 条扩展至那些毫无疑问可能对非个人私生活产生直接且重要影响的诉讼程序(*Alexandre v. Portugal*,§§51 and 54)。

三、公约第 6 条对非主体诉讼程序的可适用性

27. 初步程序(如有关采取临时措施如禁令)通常不被认为可以"决定"公民权利和义务,从而一般不属于第 6 条的保护范围[尤其参见 *Verlagsgruppe News GmbH v. Austria*(dec.)和 *Libert v. Belgium*(dec.)]。然而,欧洲人权法院近来背离了其之前的判例法而采纳了一种新的路径。

28. 在米卡莱夫诉马耳他案（Micallef v. Malta[GC]，§§83-86）中，欧洲人权法院确定了可采取临时措施适用公约第6条需满足的若干条件。首先，同时存在于主体和临时禁令程序中的争议权利需要在公约的意义下属于"公民"的范畴。其次，该临时措施的本质、目标、宗旨及效果应当被仔细审查。只要是能有效确定争议中的权利或义务的临时措施，不论其生效时间有多久，都可以适用公约第6条。

29. 诉讼中的判决可被视为临时或过渡性的手段和程序，因此判定第6条在民事案件中是否适用时采取的是同样的标准（Mercieca and Others v. Malta，§35）。

30. 同样依据米卡莱夫诉马耳他案（Micallef v. Malta）中所确立的原则，公约第6条可以在符合以上标准的前提下适用于延缓执行判决程序[Central Mediterranean Development Corporation Limited v. Malta（no.2），§§21-23]。

31. 第6条可以适用于与待进行的主要程序追求同样目的的临时程序，前提是该临时禁令是立即生效的并且是针对同一权利而做出（RTBF v. Belgium，§§64-65）。

32. 有关连续的刑事和民事诉讼。如果某缔约国国内法规定了诉讼分为两阶段——法院在第一阶段确定是否需要给予原告赔偿，而在第二阶段确定赔偿的具体金额——这样在公约第6条的目的下看是合理的，因为公民权利只有在准确金额决定后才真正得以确定：确定权利的判决不仅包括该权利的存在与否，其行使范围和方式，当然还包括对赔偿的确定（Torri v. Italy，§19）。

33. 关于法院裁决的执行，公约第6条第1款适用于"确定……公民权利和义务"的法律诉讼程序的全部阶段，故也包括实体判决的后续阶段。所以在公约第6条的意义下，判决的执行就自然被看作"审判"程序不可分割的一部分（参见 Hornsby v. Greece，§40；Romańczyk v. France，§53，涉及授予赡养费债务的恢复的判决的执行）。不用考虑公约第6条对之前的诉讼程序是否适用，实施确定公民权利的执行程序不需要之前的诉讼也可适用公约第6条（参见 Buj v. Croatia，§19）。对本国承认的外国法院没收决定的裁定，只有当所涉权利为公民权利时，才可以适用公约第6条[参见 Saccoccia v. Austria（dec.）]。

34. 有关欲重启国内诉讼程序的申诉，公约第6条不适用于欲重启已在国内得到终决裁决的民事诉讼的申诉程序（Sablon v. Belgium，§86）。该结论同样适用于在欧洲人权法院已做出确定违反公约权利的判决后要求重启国内诉讼的情形[Verein gegen Tierfabriken Schweiz（VgT）v. Switzerland（no.2）§24]。然而，依然存在非常例外的情形,在国内法律体系下申请重启程序是寻求民事权利请求救济的唯一的法律手段,因此其结果也就对申诉人的"公民权利和义务"是决定性的(*Melis v. Greece*,§§19 – 20)。

35. 公约第6条也被声明可适用于对申请人公民权利义务有直接影响的第三方上诉(*Kakamoukas and Others v. Greece*[GC],§32)。

四、被排除的争端事项

36. 某争端的本质仅仅体现出金钱性并不足以使其适用公约第 6 条第 1 款(*Ferrazzini v. Italy*[GC],§25)。

37. 涉税事项不属于公约第 6 条的适用范围:涉税事项属于国家公权力的核心内容,纳税人和国家间的关系仍然是以公权力性质为主导(*Ferrazzini v. Italy*,§29)。类似事项还包括涉及海关关税或费用的简易强制程序[*Emesa Sugar N. V. v. the Netherlands*(dec.)]。

38. 上述规则同样适用于移民领域与被授予政治庇护或驱逐出境的诉讼相关的外国人入境、居留和驱逐等问题[为推翻某驱逐令提出的申诉:参见:*Maaouia v. France*[GC]§38;引渡案件,参见 *Peñafiel Salgado v. Spain*(dec.)及 *Mamatkulov and Askarov v. Turkey*[GC],§§81 – 83;由未获得政治庇护的寻求庇护者提起的赔偿诉讼,参见 *Panjeheighalehei v. Denmark*(dec.)],而不考虑其中对私人或家庭生活或就业方面的潜在严重影响。这一不可适用性扩展至申根信息系统接纳外国人的事宜[*Dalea v. France*(dec.)]。持有护照的权利和享有国籍权不是公约第 6 条保护的公民权利[*Smirnov v. Russia*(dec.)]。然而外国人申请工作许可的权利或许可以适用公约第 6 条,不论涉及该雇员还是其雇主,而且即使由于所涉事项仅为程序性限制而非实体权利使得该雇员在国内法上并不拥有适格的诉讼地位,该条也可适用(*Jurisic and Collegium Mehrerau v. Austria*,§§54 – 62)。

39. 根据威虎等人诉芬兰案(*Vilho Eskelinen and Others v. Finland*[GC]),当满足以下两项标准时,涉及国家公职人员的争端不适用公约第 6 条:国家在其国内法中必须明确排除所涉及的职位或人员类别向国内法院提起诉讼的权利,同时该项排除行为必须能够基于国家利益这一客观理由而得到合理解释(§62)。例如,因纪律惩罚的原因被开除的士兵无法向审判庭起诉该决定,因为这涉及该申诉人与国家间的特殊关系[参见 *Suküt v. Turkey*(dec.)]。借用法院在帕乐归案(pellegrin)中的用词,为了使此种例外具有合理性,仅仅由国家确立案件所涉公务人员参与了公权力的行使是不够的,在公务人员和作为雇主的国家之间存在特殊的信任和忠诚关系的结合。国家还需要表明争议的事项必须与国家权力的行使相关,或者它对这种"结合"提出了疑问。原则上,基于涉案的特定公务人员和国家之间关系的特殊性,对于一般的劳动争议——比如与薪资、补助或者类似权利相关的争议而言,对第6条的保障进行排除并无正当理由[*Vilho Eskelinen and Others v. Finland*[GC],§62)]。

40. 最后,政治权利不能像公民权利一样受到公约第6条第1款的保护。相关案件包括:参加竞选并保留其席位的权利(竞选纠纷,参见 *Pierre-Bloch v. France*,§50);有关前议成员获得退休金的权利[参见 *Papon v. France*(dec.)];有关某政党进行其政治活动的权利:[关于政党的解散,参见 *Refah Partisi*(*The Welfare Party*)*and Others v. Turkey*(dec.)]。类似地,对议会选举进行观察的某非政府组织因获取内容与己无关的相关文件的要求被拒绝而提出的申诉也不属于公约第6条第1款的范围内[参见 *Geraguyn Khorhurd Patgamavorakan Akumb v. Armenia*(dec.)]。

41. 同时,本法院最近再次确认,在某个公开法庭中陈述的事项的报告,不是民事权利(*Mackay and BBC Scotland v. the United Kingdom*,§§20-22)。

42. 结论:当存在以上标准所定义的与"公民权利义务"相关的"争议"时,公约第6条第1款赋予相关法院或审判庭就其公民权利和义务提出任何诉请的权利。因此,这一条包含了"获得法院审判的权利",其中又包含了诉权,即就民事事项向法院提起诉讼的权利。公约第6条第1款对此权利在法院的机构和组成以及程序的操作上都给予了保障。总之,这一整体构成了获得公正审判的权利(*Golder v. the United Kingdom*,§36)。

第二节 获得法院审判的权利

> **第6条第1款**
>
> "在决定某人的公民权利和义务……时,任何人有权在合理的时间内受到依法设立的独立而公正的审判机构的公平且公开的审讯。……"

一、获得法院审判的权利

43. 公约第 6 条第 1 款所保障的获得公正审判的权利必须根据法治理念来解释,这要求诉讼当事人应当享有有效的司法救济手段来保护其公民权利(*Beles and others v. the Czech Republic*,§49)。

任何人都享有向法院或审判机构提出与其公民权利和义务相关的主张。因此公约第 6 条第 1 款包含了"获得法院审判的权利",其中又包含了诉权,即就民事事项向法院提起诉讼的权利(*Golder v. the United Kingdom*,§36)。"进入法院"的权利以及向法院申诉的权利并非绝对,而可能受到诸多约束,但是这些约束不得限制或减少留给个体在其权利的核心被损害时向法院提起诉讼的权利(*Philis v. Greece*,§59;*De Geouffre de la Pradelle v. France*,§28,and *Stanev v. Bulgaria*[GC],§229)。①

(一)现实且有效的权利

44. 向法院提起诉讼的权利必须是"现实且有效"的(*Bellet v. France*,§38)。为保证诉权是有效的,个人必须拥有清楚、可行的机会来挑战对其权利构成干涉的行为[*Bellet v. France*,§36;*Nunes Dias v. Portugal*(dec.),关于出庭通知的规则]。规范提起上诉或申请复审的正式步骤以及时间限制的规则旨在确保司法公正,特别是要符合法律的确定性原则(*Cañete de Goñi v. Spain*,§36)。因此,有争议的规则或其应用不得阻碍当事人寻求有效的救济手段(*Miragall Escolano v. Spain*;*Zvolsky and Zvolska v. the Czech Republic*,§51)。

45. 在某些情形下,此项权利的现实性和有效性可能受到损害,如以下几种情形。

(1)鉴于个体的经济状况,司法程序的成本过高:

- 作为民事主体申请加入刑事诉讼程序的保证成本过高(*Aït-Mouhoub v. France*,§§57 – 58;同时参考 *Garcia Manibardo v. Spain*,§§38 – 45);
- 过高的庭审费用[*Kreuz v. Poland*(no. 1),§§60 – 67);*Podbielski and PPU PolPure v. Poland*,§§65 – 66;*Weissman and others v. Romania*,§42;反例可参见,*Reuther v. Germany*(dec.)];

(2)与时间限制相关的事项:

---

① 同时参见"公平"部分。

- 上诉聆讯的时间导致该上诉被宣告不予接受(Melnyk v. Ukraine, §26);
- 申请人在诉讼程序的后期才被告知他们一直以来善意且勤勉实施的请求已逾时效,他们维护权利的可能性则被永远剥夺了(Yagtzilar and Others v. Greece, §27);

(3)程序上禁令的存在阻止或限制了向法院提出申请的可能性:

- 本国法院对于程序规则极其严格的解释可能剥夺申请人获得审判的权利(Perez de Rada Cavanilles v. Spain, §49; Miragall Escolano v. Spain, §38; Société anonyme Sotiris and Nikos Koutras ATTEE v. Greece, §20; Beles and others v. Czech Republic, §50; RTBF v. Belgium, §§71,72,74);
- 与执行较早裁决的相关的要求可能损害获得审判的权利,例如,申请人资金的缺乏导致其根本不可能履行之前的判决[Annoni di Gussola and Others v. France, §56;与之相较,可参见 Arvanitakis v. France(dec)]。
- 程序规则禁止特定法律主体进入法院审判程序[The Holy Monasteries v. Greece §83; Philis v. Greece, §65;同时参见 Lupas and others v. Romania(no.1), §§64-67;以及具有能力缺陷的少数群体相关案件,可参见:Stanev v. Bulgaria[GC], §§241-245]。①

尽管如此,从形式主义的角度看,上诉的受理条件可以依法严于普通上诉的受理条件。考虑到上诉法院角色的特殊性,案件经其受理之后的程序可以更加正式,尤其是当在其受理案件之前本案已经由具有管辖权的初审法院和上诉法院审理过时(Levages Prestations Services v. France, §§44-48; Brualla Gomez de la Torre v. Spain, §§34-39)。

46.进一步而言,进入法院的权利不仅包括开始诉讼程序的权利,还包括获得法院对此争议的判决的权利(Kutic v. Croatia, §25 and 32,涉及诉讼程序的停滞;Acimovic v. Croatia, §41; Beneficio Cappella Paolini v. San Marino, §29,涉及违背司法公正)。若法院未按照法定的时间期限审理以一系列仅存在于有限期间内的决定为对象的上诉时,或在缺乏判决的情况下(Ganci v. Italy, §31),其获得法院审判的权利也可能被侵害(Musumeci v. Italy, §§41-43)。"获得法院审判的权利"也包括判决的执行。②

---

① 同时参见"法律援助"部分。
② 同时参见"执行"部分。

(二) 限制

47. 获得法院审判的权利并非绝对,而是受到诸多潜在因素的限制(Golder v. the United Kingdom, §38; Stanev v. Bulgaria[GC], §§230)。这尤其适用于关乎上诉申请的受理条件的情形,因为本质上其要求享有一定裁量空间的国家来予以规范。(Luordo v. Italy, §85)

48. 尽管如此,这些约束的适用不得限制或减少个人在权利被侵犯时所享有的解除权。进一步而言,一项约束若不具备合法的目的或者在手段和目的之间没有合理适当的联系,便不符合第6条第1款的要求(Ashingdane v. the United Kingdom, §57; Fayed v. the United Kingdom, §65; Markovic and Others v. Italy[GC], §99)。

49. 获得法院审判的权利在特定情形下也可能受到一系列合法限制的约束,例如,法定的时效(Stubbings and Others v. the United Kingdom, §§51 – 52),诉讼费用担保令(Tolstoy Miloslavsky v. the United Kingdom, §§62 – 67)或者法律陈述的要件(R. P. and Others v. the United Kingdom, §§63 – 67)。

50. 获得法院审判的权利在法律上或实践中被限制的,本法院审查该限制是否影响到权利的实质,具体而言,该限制是否具备合法的目的或者在手段和目的之间是否具有合理适当的联系:如安塞丹诉联合王国案(Ashingdane v. the United Kingdom, §57)。若该限制与本法院所确立的原则相符,则并不存在违反第6条第1款的情形。

51. 国际组织对国内司法管辖的豁免:这一以条约为基础的规则——旨在追求合法目的——(Waite and Kennedy v. Germany[GC], §63)只要与其衍生的限制是相称的,则被第6条第1款所允许。因此,若相关当事人拥有合理的替代性手段来有效保护其公约权利,则这种豁免是与第6条第1款的规定相符的(Waite and Kennedy v. Germany[GC], §§68 – 74; Prince Hans-Adam II of Liechtenstein v. Germany[GC] §48; Chapman v. Belgium(dec.), §§51 – 56)。

52. 国家豁免:国家豁免理论被各国广泛接受。成员国所采取的支持国际公法上国家豁免的措施并不必然构成对接触法院权的不适当限制(Fogarty v. the United Kingdom[GC], §36; McElhinney v. Ireland [GC], §37; Sabeh El Leil v. France [GC], §49)。

- 国家管辖豁免:在国家司法管辖豁免原则的适用限制了获得法院审判权的案件中,必须确定案件的情形是否能证明该限制的正当性。该限制必须具有合法目的且与该目的相称（*Cudak v. Lithuania*［GC］，§59；*Sabeh El Leil v. France*［GC］，§§51-54）。在民事诉讼中授予国家主权豁免追求的是符合国际法规定、旨在促进睦邻友好关系的合法目的［*Fogarty v. the United Kingdom*［GC］，§34，and *Al-Adsani v. the United Kingdom*［GC］，§54；*Treska v. Albania and Italy*，(dec.)］。关于采取的措施是否合适，其在部分案件中损害了个人获得法院审判权的核心（*Cudak v. Lithuania*［GC］，§74；*Sabeh El Leil v. France*［GC］，§49），但在其他案件中却并不构成损害（*Al-Adsani v. the United Kingdom*［GC］，§67；*Fogarty v. the United Kingdom*［GC］，§39；*McElhinney v. Ireland*［GC］，§38）。

国家司法管辖豁免受到国际习惯法的发展限制，例如，除仅有的几种情形外，豁免规则对国家与其在国外执行外交使命的雇员之间的雇佣合同并不适用（*Sabeh El Leil v. France*［GC］，§§53-54 and §§57-58）。对豁免的限制手段也可能被施加于国家和外国私主体之间的商务交易之间。（*Oleynikov v. Russia*，§§61 and 66）。另一方面，本法院注意到在2001年，对于在法院所在国实施的行为或疏忽造成个人伤害的情形，尽管在国际法和比较法上呈现出对国家豁免予以限制的趋势，但这种实践却并非普遍（*McElhinney v. Ireland*［GC］，§38）。

- 国家执行豁免本身并不构成对第6条第1款的违背。本法院注意到在2005年所有管理国家豁免的国际法律机构都设立了一项一般性原则，即除了严格界定的特定例外之外，外国享有在法院所在国的执行豁免权［*Manoilescu and Dobrescu v. Romania and Russia*(dec.)，§73］。通过例证，本法院在2002年认为尽管希腊法庭决定由德国政府向申请者予以赔偿，这并不必然要求希腊政府确保申请者能够通过希腊的执行程序得到补偿［*Kalogeropoulou and Others v. Greece and Germany*(dec.)］。这些决定对当时国际法上的缔约国有效，但并不预先排除法律在未来的变化。

53. 议员免责权：为了保障人民代表的自由发言并且防止党派争论干涉议会的运作，国家授予议会成员不同程度的豁免权已成为一项长期的实践［*C. G. I. L. and Cofferati*(no.2)*v. Italy*，§44］。因此，在满足以下条件时，议员豁免权是与公约第6条相符的：

(1)追求合法目的:保护议会中的言论自由,维护立法和司法权力的相互独立(*A. v. the United Kingdom*,§§75-77 and §79);

(2)与力图实现的目的相称(如果相关当事人有合理的替代性手段来有效保护其权利)(*A. v. the United Kingdom*,§86),且该豁免权仅限于议会职能的行使。[*A. v. the United Kingdom*,§84;*Zollmann v. the United Kingdom*(dec.)]若欠缺与议会行为的明确联系,则要求对手段与目的之间"相称性"进行限制解释[*Cordova v. Italy*(no. 2),§64;*Syngelidis v. Greece*,§44]。无论议会成员何时做出抨击性言论,个人获得法院审判权不得被与第6条第1款不符的手段予以限制[*Cordova v. Italy*(no. 1),§63;*C. G. I. L. and Cofferati*(no. 2)*v. Italy*,§§46-50,此案中受害者无任何保护其权利的替代性方法]。

54. 法官的司法管辖免除同样符合第6条第1款的精神,前提是其须追求合法的目的,即正当行使司法权(*Ernst and Others v. Belgium*,§50),且遵守比例原则——申请者有合理的替代性手段来有效保护其公约下的权利(*Ernst and Others v. Belgium*,§§53-55)。

55. 公务员豁免权:对个人所享有的针对公务员的言论和调查结果提起损害公务员声誉的法律诉讼的能力所施加的限制可能是追求基于公共利益的合法目的(*Fayed v. the United Kingdom*,§70);尽管如此,在所采取的手段和合法目的之间必须有相称的联系(*Fayed v. the United Kingdom*,§§75-82)。

56. 豁免的限制:如果一个不受公约执行机构制约或控制的国家能够将整个民事申诉从法院的管辖中剥离或者将豁免权授予大规模或多类别的人群,便不符合民主社会中的法治原则或第6条第1款的基本原则——即民事申诉必须能够被提交给法官予以裁判(*Fayed v. the United Kingdom*,§65;*McElhinney v. Ireland*[GC],§§23-26;*Sabeh El Leil v. France*[GC],§50)。

二、放弃权利

(一)原则

57. 在缔约国国内法律制度中,个人对其案件被法院或审判机构审理的权利的放弃在民事案件中经常发生,特别是以合同中仲裁条款的形式。放弃权利,无疑对相关个人以及司法都具有好处,在原则上并不与公约相违背(*Deweer v. Belgium*,§49)。

（二）条件

58. 当事人可以赞成仲裁而放弃获得法院审判，前提是规则允许进行这种放弃，并是在自由状态下明确做出放弃（*Suda v. the Czech Republic*，§§48－49）。在民主社会中，接触法院权十分重要，不能仅由于个人作为参与者在除法庭程序之外的辅助性程序中形成了解决方法便放弃接触法院权带来的利益（同上）。①

三、法律援助

（一）法律援助的授予

59. 第6条第1款并未暗示政府必须对所有与"公民权利"相关的争议提供免费的法律援助（*Airey v. Ireland*，§26）。旨在保障特定情形下在刑事诉讼中享有免费法律援助的权利的第6条第3款第c项和并未提及法律援助的第6条第1款之间有明显的区别（*Essaadi v. France*，§30）。

60. 尽管如此，公约仍试图保障现实有效的权利，特别是获得法院审判权。因此，第6条第1款有时仍可督促政府提供律师的援助，前提是这种援助被证明是对有效的获得法院审判权必不可少的（*Airey v. Ireland*，§26）。

61. 公约第6条是否要求诉讼当事人必须有法定代理人这一问题应依据案件特定情形来判断（*Airey v. Ireland*，§26；*McVicar v. the United Kingdom*，§48；*Steel and Morris v. the United Kingdom*，§61）。在所有情形中都必须被确认的是，法律援助的缺乏是否剥夺了申请人被公正审理的权利（*McVicar v. the United Kingdom*，§51）。

62. 第6条是否暗示提供法律援助的要求取决于：

- 申请者面临危害的权利的重要性（*Steel and Morris v. the United Kingdom*，§61）；
- 相关法律或程序的复杂性（*Airey v. Ireland*，§24）；
- 申请者有效代表其自身的能力（*McVicar v. the United Kingdom*，§§48－62；*Steel and Morris v. the United Kingdom*，§61；*P., C. and S. v. the United Kingdom*，§100）；
- 法律规定必须有法律代表（*Airey v. Ireland*，§26；*Gnahoré v. France*，§41）。

---

① 同时参见"公开审讯"部分。

63. 但这项权利并非绝对，因此，除了前文所列举的情形，允许基于以下考虑对授予法律援助规定约束性条件：

- 诉讼当事人的经济状况（*Steel and Morris v. the United Kingdom*，§62）；
- 其胜诉可能性（*Steel and Morris v. the United Kingdom*，§62）。

因此，可以存在一个筛选符合条件的案件的法律援助系统（*Gnahoré v. France*，§41；*Essaadi v. France*，§36；*Del Sol v. France*，§26；*Bakan v. Turkey*，*Aerts v. Belgium*）。然而，对一国内的法律援助机制的质量予以必要的考量（*Essaadi v. France*，§35）并核实国家机关所选择的方法是否与公约相符是很重要的（*Santambrogio v. Italy*，§52；*Bakan v. Turkey*，§§74-78；*Pedro Ramos v. Switzerland*，§§41-45）。

64. 法院给出拒绝法律援助的理由并勤勉审查法律援助申请是非常重要的（*Tabor v. Poland*，§§45-46；*Saoud v. France*，§§133-136）。

65. 不仅如此，拒绝向外国人提供法律援助并不违背第6条的精神（*Granos Organicos Nacionales S. A. v. Germany*，§§48-53）。

（二）授予的法律援助的有效性

66. 国家对正式任命的律师的行为不负责任。这是法律职业者独立于国家的应有之意（*Staroszczyk v. Poland*，§133），辩护的行为根本上是被告和其律师之间的事务，无论这个律师是被法律援助机制任命或者是个人雇佣的。这种辩护，除特定情形外，不能导致国家在公约下的责任[*Tuziński v. Poland*(*dec.*)]。

67. 然而指派律师代表一方当事人本身并不能保证有效的协助（*Siałkowska v. Poland*，§§110 and 116）。被指派进行法律援助的律师可能在被延长的期限内被禁止履行或逃避其职责。有权机关在被告知此种情形时，必须替换该律师，否则尽管有免费法律援助的规定，在实践中诉讼当事人仍会无法获得有效协助（*Bertuzzi v. France*，§30）。

68. 政府有责任保证有效享有获得法院审判的权利与法律职业独立性之间的必要平衡。本法院已经明确强调过，若承担法律援助义务的律师要拒绝进行援助，则其必须满足一定的要求。若法律援助体系剥夺了个人应当享有的"现实且有效"获得法院审判的权利，则这些要求便未得到满足（*Staroszczyk v. Poland*，§135；*Siałkowska v. Poland*，§114 violation）。

第三节　制度要求

> **第 6 条第 1 款**
> "在决定某人的公民权利和义务……时,任何人有理由……受到依法设立的独立而公正的审判机构的……审讯……"

一、"审判机构"的概念

（一）自治概念

69. 从第 6 条第 1 款的目的出发,未被纳入国家法院体系的机构也可以被认为是实质意义上的"审判机构"（*Sramek v. Austria*,§36）。

70. 法院或审判机构是基于其司法功能而言的实质意义上的概念,该司法功能是指,在法治基础上的管辖权内且采取事先规定的程序之后,对事项做出决定（*Sramek v. Austria*,§36; *Cyprus v. Turkey*［GC］,§233）。

71. 做决定的权力是"审判机构"这一概念的固有内涵。根据第 6 条第 1 款的要求,诉讼程序必须提供法庭就争议事项所做出的决定（*Benthem v. the Netherlands*,§40）。

72. 因此,仅给出具有参考性但无约束力的意见是不够的,即使这些意见被绝大多数案件所遵从（参考前案）。

73. 从第 6 条第 1 款的目的出发,"审判机构"并不必须是相关国家标准司法机制内的法院。它可以基于处理在一般的法院系统之外由于适当管理的特定事项的目的被设立。对确保符合第 6 条第 1 款的规定重要的是保证,包括适当的实体和程序保证（*Rolf Gustafson v. Sweden*,§45）。

74. 因此,"审判机构"可以包含被设立用于决定有限数量特定事项的机构,前提是它必须一直提供适当的保证（*Lithgow and Others v. the United Kingdom*,§201,在有仲裁庭的情形下）。

75. 一个机构拥有多种职能（行政、规范、仲裁、建议和纪律等）的事实本身并不将其排除在"审判机构"的范畴之外(*H. v. Belgium*,§50)。

76. 做出一项不可被非司法机构朝着不利于独立主体的方向更改的有约束力的决定的权力,是"审判机构"的固有内涵(*Van de Hurk v. the Netherlands*,§45)。法治的一个基本要素是司法稳定,这尤其要求若法院最终对事项做出了决定,则其裁决不应被质疑(这同样适用于上诉申请[GC],§61)。①

77. "审判机构"必须满足一系列进一步的要求——独立,尤其是在执行上;公正;成员有限任职期限;程序所提供的保证——这其中的部分出现在第6条第1款的文本上(*Le Compte, Van Leuven and De Meyere v. Belgium*,§55;*Cyprus v. Turkey*[GC],§233)。事实上,独立和公正是"审判机构"概念的关键组成。②

78. 符合公约第6条第1款下的"审判机构"概念的机构举例如下:

(1)地区性不动产交易机构:拉梅克诉奥地利案(*Sramek v. Austria*,§36);

(2)刑事损害补偿董事会:罗尔夫·古斯塔夫森诉瑞典案,(*Rolf Gustafson v. Sweden*,§48);

(3)森林争端解决委员会:阿吉鲁及其他人诉希腊案(*Argyrou and Others v. Greece*,§27)。

(二)管辖权级别

79. 尽管第6条第1款并不强制成员国设立上诉或最高法院,但是设立此类法院的国家必须确保服从于法律的人必须在法院面前享有第6条第1款包含的基本保证(*Platakou v. Greece*,§38):

- 具体性审查:第6条第1款适用于上诉法院或终审法院的方式取决于相关程序的特征。就法律条文所提起的上诉的受理条件可以比普通上诉的要求更严格(*Levages Prestations Services v. France*,§45);
- 整体性审查:本国法律体系中所采取的诉讼程序的整体都必须被纳入考量(*Levages Prestations Services v. France*,§§44-45)。因此,上级或最高法院在某些情形下可以对违反公约规范之一的行为做出赔偿(*De Haan v. the Netherlands*,§54)。

---

① 同时参见本报告"判决执行"部分。
② 参见"独立和公正"部分。

80. 对灵活性和效率的要求与保护人权完全不矛盾,可能使得行政性或职业性机构的干涉具备合理性,更不必说使得不符合公约第 6 条要求的司法机构等的事先干涉成为合法。(Le Compte, Van Leuven and De Meyere v. Belgium, §51)。如果这些机构的程序"受到后来的具有完全管辖权的司法机构的控制"且提供了第 6 条要求的保障,则并不违反公约(Zumtobel v. Austria, §§29 – 32; Bryan v. the United Kingdom, §40)。

81. 同理,将裁决义务赋予惩戒机构本身也并不构成对公约的侵害。尽管如此,在这些情形下,公约要求以下两种系统中应至少存在一种:要么该职业惩戒机构自身符合公约的要求,要么尽管其不符合要求,但是受到"具有完全管辖权的司法机构"的事后审查并提供第 6 条第 1 款要求的保证(Albert and Le Compte v. Belgium, §29; Gautrin and Others v. France, §57)。

82. 本法院反复声明在第 6 条第 1 款下,本身并不满足本条要求的行政机关所做出的决定必须受到"有完全管辖权的司法机构"的事后控制(Ortenberg v. Austria, §31)。①

(三)具有完全管辖权的法院的审查

83. 只有具有完全管辖权的机构才可被称作第 6 条第 1 款中的"审判机构"(Beaumartin v. France, §38)。第 6 条第 1 款要求法院做出有效的司法审查(Obermeier v. Austria, §70)。法院应当行使完全管辖权的原则要求它不得废弃其司法功能中的任何部分(Chevrol v. France, §63)。

84. 所涉及的"审判机构"必须具有完全管辖权来审查与其所受理的争议相关的所有事实和法律问题(Terra Woningen B. V. v. the Netherlands, §52)。

85. 尽管如此,在数种专门法律领域(如城乡规划领域)中法院对于事实方面仅享有有限的管辖权,但若行政机关的决定是基于被推翻或不合理的事实,则法院可以推翻该决定(Bryan v. the United Kingdom, §§44 – 47; Crompton v. the United Kingdom, §§70 – 73)。

86. 判例法确立了衡量审查的诸多标准是否是由享有完全管辖权的机关在保障公约实施的目的下做出的(Sigma Radio Television Ltd v. Cyprus, §§151 – 157)。因此,为了确定司法机构是否做出了足够的审查,下述三项原则必须被统一考虑:

(1)上诉申请针对的决定的主要事项:

---

① 同时参见"公正"部分。

- 如果行政决定关乎一项简单的事实问题,相对于关乎需要技术知识的专业领域的决定而言,法院的审查需要更严格;
- 欧洲现存的体系经常限制法院审查事实问题的权力,但不阻止其在不同层面推翻之前的决定。这在判例法下并不存在问题。

(2)决定做出的方式:在行政机关关注之前存在何种程序性保障?

在前置的行政程序中,如果申诉享有诸多符合第6条规定的程序保障,这就使得之后的司法控制可以采取更轻的形式[*Bryan v. the United Kingdom*,§§46-47;*Holding and Barnes plc v. the United Kingdom*(dec.)]。

(3)争议的内容,包括上诉的期望和现实层面(*Bryan v. the United Kingdom*,§45):

判决必须能够逐点审查申诉者的所有意见,不得拒绝审查其中任何内容,并给出驳回的明确原因。针对事实,法院必须被授权复审申诉案件的核心内容。因此,如果申诉者仅提出程序性意见,其并不得因此批评法院未对事实问题予以审查(*Potocka and Others v. Poland*,§57)。

87. 例如,法院拒绝对特定的对于解决争议十分重要的事实问题独立做出可能违反第6条第1款的决定(*Terra Woningen B. V. v. the Netherlands*,§§53-55)。这同样适用于法院不具有对争议的核心问题做出决定的管辖权的情形(*Tsfayo v. the United Kingdom* §48)。在此类案件中对案件结果具有决定性作用的事项没有受到独立的司法审查。

88. 如果上诉的一个方面得到了支持,审查法院必须有权撤销被质疑的决定,并做出新的决定或将案件发回原机关或其他机关重新做出决定(*Kingsley v. the United Kingdom*[GC],§§32,34)。

89. 若事实已经在满足第6条第1款的诸多要求的准司法程序中被行政机关确立,且对于被行政机关确立的事实或其做出的援引并无争议,同时法院对诉讼当事人上诉的其他方面也逐点进行了审查,则上诉法院所做出的审查的范围就被认为符合第6条第1款的规定(*Bryan v. the United Kingdom*,§§44-47)。

90. 不被认为具有"完全管辖权"的司法机构列举如下:
- 仅有权决定行政机关是否在符合法律规定的前提下行使其裁量权的行政法院(*Obermeier v. Austria*,§70);
- 审理针对职业协会的纪律机关所做出决定的法律适用部分所提起的上诉,却并无权判断处罚是否与行为相称的法院(*Diennet v. France*, §34,涉及医疗协会, *Merigaud v. France*, §69,涉及勘测员协会);
- 仅有权从合宪性角度调查反驳程序却不能审查所有相关事实的宪法法院(*Zumtobel v. Austria*, §§29-30);
- 法国最高行政法院,基于其判例法,在案件涉及公约的适用之前处理案件时,有义务遵循机关对外代表(部长)的意见,而不必将该意见置于当事方的任何批评和讨论之下(*Chevrol v. France*, §§81-82)。

91. 相反地,
- 肖代诉法国案(*Chaudet v. France*):最高行政法院仅做出过一次对申请进行司法审查的决定。在此案中最高行政法院不具有完全管辖权,这本应当造成其决定被民航医疗董事会所替代的结果。但是从案件材料上可以清楚地发现,最高行政法院在事实和法律两方面处理了申请者的所有意见,评估了医疗文件中的所有证据,考虑了各方在庭上对所有医疗报告的讨论结果。本法院因此认为申请者的案件以符合第6条第1款的要求的方式得到了审查(§§37-38);
- 奥德堡诉奥地利案(*Zumtobel v. Austria*):本法院认为奥地利行政法院满足了第6条第1款对不仅限于行政机构裁量权的事项的要求,并且其逐点考量了实体上的意见,同时并未拒绝履行对申请者做出答复或者查明各种事实等管辖职能(§§31-32——同时参见 *Ortenberg v. Austria*, §§33-34; *Fischer v. Austria*, §34)。
- 麦克迈克尔诉联合王国案(*McMichael v. the United Kingdom*):在此案中,治安法庭允许某儿童被自由收养的命令被上诉到最高民事法院,后者对此享有完全管辖权。最高民事法院一般而言会就治安法庭发现的事实开展诉讼,但这并非必要,其可以在适当情形下自行获取证据,或者将案件发回治安法庭并告知其应当如何继续进行审理(§66)。进一步而言,治安法庭在审理针对儿童案件的上诉时,也享有完全管辖权,并被授权审查实体和程序上的不合规事项(§82);
- 波托茨卡及其他人诉波兰案(*Potocka and Others v. Poland*):行政诉讼法规定最高行政法院的管辖权范围限制于评定受争议的行政决定的合法性方面。如果发现法院作出决定的过程中程序公正的要求未得到满足,该法院也被授权部分或全部废止该项决定。最高行政法院的论证过程表明事实上其审查了该案件的适当性。尽管该法院本可以基于申请人所提出的申请中存在的程序和实体错误,对其法律分析进行限制,继续维持具有争议的决定,但法院仍然详细考虑了申请人所提交的所有意见的实质内容,从来没有在对他们做出答复或查明相关事实时拒绝管辖权。该法院已经发布了一项经过认真论证的判决,且仔细处理了申请人提出的与案件结果相关的论点。因此,最高行政法院的审查范围符合公约第6条第1款(§§56-59)。

(四)判决的执行

1. 迅速落实终局性且具有约束力的司法决定的权利

92. 公约第6条第1款保护终局性且具有约束力的司法决定的执行(与可能受到上级法院审查的决定的执行相区别)(*Ouzounis and Others v. Greece*,§21)。

93. 无论由何种法院进行判决,判决被执行的权利都是获得法院审判权的必要组成部分(*Hornsby v. Greece*,§40;*Scordino v. Italy*(no.1)[GC],§196)。否则第6条第1款的规定将无任何作用(*Burdov v. Russia*,§§34 and 37)。

94. 通过向最高行政法院提起司法审查申请,诉讼当事人所寻求的不仅是废除受到质疑的决定,而更重要的是消除其影响。

95. 上述内容在行政程序中更加重要。对当事人的有效保护以及对合法性的恢复为行政机关预先假定了服从判决的义务(*Hornsby v. Greece*,§41;*Kyrtatos v. Greece*,§§31-32)。

96. 因此,尽管在特定情形下判决的延迟执行也具有正当性,这种延迟不得损害诉讼当事人要求判决被强制执行的权利(*Burdov v. Russia*,§§35-37)。

97. 以这种方式进行理解,判决必须被完整且圆满地执行(*Matheus v. France*,§58;*Sabin Popescu v. Romania*,§§68-76),且不得被阻碍、作废或不正当地延迟(*Immobiliare Saffi v. Italy*[GC],§74)。

98. 权力机关拒绝采纳上级法院的决定也是与第6条第1款相违背的(*Turczanik v. Poland*,§§49-51),将潜在导致相同诉讼程序中的一系列判决,弃已有判决于不顾。

99. 对生效判决不合理地长期延迟可构成对公约的违反。延迟执行是否合理需要具体考虑执行程序的复杂性,申请者自身以及相对机关的行为,以及执行内容的数量和特征(*Raylyan v. Russia*,§31)。

100. 例如,本法院曾判决国家机关持续五年以上抵触采取必要措施来执行一项最终可执行的司法决定的行为剥夺了第 6 条第 1 款的所有作用(*Hornsby v. Greece*, §45)。

101. 在另一案件中,在其特定情形下,国家机关耗费总计 9 个月时间去执行一项判决被认为是合理的(*Moroko v. Russia*, §§43 – 45)。

102. 本法院发现,权力机关在超过 4 年时间里拒绝利用警察的协助来执行一项针对承租人所有权的命令的行为(*Lunari v. Italy*, §§38 – 42),以及由于立法机关质疑法院将承租人驱逐的命令而搁置执行达 6 年时间的行为,完全剥夺了第 6 条第 1 款的规定,因此损害了第 6 条第 1 款中的获得法院审判权(*Immobiliare Saffi v. Italy* [GC], §§70 and 74)。

103. 个人在诉讼程序末期得到一项针对国家的判决可不提起单独的执行程序[*Burdov v. Russia* (no.2), §68]。国家机关自判决具有约束力和执行力时起[*Burdov v. Russia* (no.2), §69]负有确保该判决执行的义务(*Yavorivskaya v. Russia*, §25)。

104. 为了同意或加速判决的执行,胜诉方可以被要求采取一定的程序措施。尽管如此,要求债权人进行合作的程度不得超过严格的必要性且不得减轻权利机关的义务[*Burdov v. Russia* (no.2), §69]。

105. 执行程序之后对申请人的延迟支付不能免除国家机关长期不服从判决的责任,且不能构成足够的救济(*Scordino v. Italy* (no.1) [GC], §198)。

106. 本法院也认为权力机关不考虑申请者的经济状况,坚持申请者应当承担启动对其有利的生效判决的执行的立场,给申请者造成了过多的负担且限制了其获得法院审判的权利以至于侵害了该权利的核心(*Apostol v. Georgia*, §65)。

107. 诉讼当事人在合理期限内不得被剥夺生效判决所赋予其的损害赔偿(*Burdov v. Russia*, §35)或房屋中的利益(*Teteriny v. Russia*, §§41 – 42),不论本国判决执行程序的复杂程度或国家财政预算状况如何。国家机关不得以基金或其他资源不足为借口不支付司法债务(*Burdov v. Russia*, §35; *Amat-G Ltd and Mebaghishvili v. Georgia*, §47; *Scordino v. Italy* (no.1) [GC], §199)。企业不得以欠缺替代性住房为借口不执行判决(*Prodan v. Moldova*, §53)。

108. 国家负债[*Burdov v. Russia* (no.2), §§68 and 69 and §72 et seq.]和个人负债必须加以区分:国家的责任不能因"个体"债权人破产而导致其被免除[*Sanglier v. France*, §39; *Ciprova v. the Czech Republic* (dec.); *Cubănit v. Romania* (dec.)]。尽管如此,国家具有积极义务组织一个在法律上和实践中都能有效执行处理私主体之间争

议的最终决定的系统(*Fuklev v. Ukraine*, §84)。如果执行程序中包含的公共机关未尽到必要职责甚至阻碍执行,则国家的责任可以因此得到免除(*Fuklev v. Ukraine*, §67)。鉴于其在执行中的责任,由于国家机关是行使公共权力的主体,因此其用以确保判决执行的方式必须足够实现其目的(*Ruianu v. Romania*, §66)(同上, §§72 – 73)。

109. 因此,如本法院认定国家机关拒绝对未有效配合判决执行的第三方(个人)主体施加惩罚的行为剥夺了第 6 条第 1 款的所有作用(*Pini and Others v. Romania*, §§186 – 188;在此案中,两个儿童生活的私人机构在超过三年时间里阻碍关于小孩收养命令的执行)。

110. 尽管如此,国家已经采取所有法律规定的的步骤来确保私主体服从一项决定,其不应对债权人拒绝履行义务承担责任(*Fociac v. Romania*, §§74 and 78)。

111. 最后,获得法院审判同样保障进入执行程序的权利,即启动执行程序的权利(*Apostol v. Georgia*, §56)。

2. 使最终司法决定不受异议的权利

112. 进一步而言,获得公正审理的权利必须在法治体系下予以解释。法治最基本的方面之一是司法稳定原则(*Okyay and others v. Turkey*, §73),这尤其要求法院就事项做出最终决定后,其决定不应再受到异议(*Brumarescu v. Romania* [GC], §61; *Agrokompleks v. Ukraine*, §148)。

113. 若司法系统中,最终判决要受到不明确的审查且具有被反复废止的危险,则此系统违反了第 6 条第 1 款的规定(*Sovtransavto Holding v. Ukraine*, §§74, 77 and 82:此案涉及反对程序,最高仲裁庭的主席、检察长及其副手享有在审判监督程序中通过提起反对来挑战终审判决的裁量权力)。

114. 通过这种方法对决定提出异议是不能被接受的,无论是由法官或执行机构的成员(*Tregubenko v. Ukraine*, §36)或由非司法机关所提起(*Agrokompleks v. Ukraine*, §§150 – 151)。

115. 除非具有诸如司法错误等具有实质性且十分重要的情形,最终判决不得被提起异议(*Ryabykh v. Russia*, §52)。

二、由法律所确立

116. 在法治原则下,也是公约体系所固有的,本法院认为"审判机构"必须是由法律确立的,否则其审理个人案件时便缺乏民主社会中所要求的合法性(Lavents v. Latvia, §81)。

117. "由法律确立"不仅指"法庭"的存在具有法律基础,也指法庭必须符合对其加以规范的规则(Sokurenko and Strygun v. Ukraine, §24)。法院或法庭的合法性必须包括其组成部分[Buscarini v. San Marino(dec.)]。法官合法任期到期后默示延长其任期且搁置其重新任命的实践被认为是与"法庭由法律确立"的原则相违背(Oleksandr Volkov v. Ukraine, §151)。规范法官任命的程序不能被降为内部操作(参考前案,§§154-156)。

118. 第6条第1款中的"法律"不仅包含设立司法机构并赋予管辖权的立法,也包含其他在其被违反后会导致一个或多个法官对不合法事项进行审查的本国规范(DMD Group, A. S. v. Slovakia, §59)。这具体包括有关法庭成员独立,任职期限,公正,程序保障的规定(Gurov v. Moldova, §36)。

119. 原则上,法院违反本国法律规范的行为构成对第6条第1款的违背(DMD Group, A. S. v. Slovakia, §61)。本法院可因此审查本国法律是否被遵守。尽管如此,考虑到原则上首先是由本国法院自身来解释本国法,本法院认为除非有明显违法行为存在,否则不得质疑国内法院对法律的解释(DMD Group, A. S. v. Slovakia, §61)。在诉讼程序中,无正当解释故意非法逾越其司法管辖权范围的法院不是"由法律设立的法庭"(Sokurenko and Strygun v. Ukraine, §§27-28)。

120. 公约第6条第1款规定"由法律设立"的目的是确保司法体系的组成不依赖于执行机关的自由裁量,而是由议会发布的法律所规范的(Savino and Others v. Italy, §94)。

121. 在法典主义的国家,司法体系的组成也不得由司法机关自由裁量,尽管这并不意味着本国法院不享有解释相关本国法律的自由(Savino and Others v. Italy, §94)。

122. 进一步而言,在关于司法体系组成的事项中进行授权是被允许的,前提是包括宪法在内的国内法存在对这种可能性进行规定的条款(同上)。

三、独立和公正

(一)一般性考虑因素

123. 第6条第1款下被公正审判的权利要求案件由"独立且公正的法庭"予以审

理。"独立"和"公正"这两者的保证之间具有紧密的内在联系。基于此原因,本法院通常同时考察这两项要求(*Kleyn and Others v. the Netherlands*[GC],§192)。

124. 非专业性法官参与案件并不违反第 6 条第 1 款。由法官主导、公务员和利益相关方列席的审判小组并不当然导致偏见(*Le Compte, Van Leuven and De Meyere v. Belgium*,§§57 and 58),让非专业性法官参与判决的形成,这本身也并无异议(*Pabla Ky v. Finland*,§32)。

125. 判例法中确立的关乎公正的原则对非专业性法官和专业法官平等适用(*Langborger v. Sweden*,§§34 – 35;*Cooper v. the United Kingdom*[GC],§123)。

126. 原则上,如果判决受到后续的具有完全管辖权的司法机构的控制且通过弥补缺陷而确保了相关的保障,则不得基于做出审判的法庭欠缺独立性或公正性,或者法庭违反了根本的程序保障而得出其违反了第 6 条第 1 款的结论(*De Haan v. the Netherlands*,§§52 – 55)。①

127. 本法院一直强调国家确保案件由公约第 6 条第 1 款规定的独立公正的法庭所审理的责任不仅限于由司法机关来承担。该条款为执行机关、立法机关及其他国家机关规定了尊重并维护法院的判决和决定的义务,无论该机关的级别如何,无论其是否赞同判决和决定。因此,国家尊重法庭的权威是大众取信于法庭的前提,广义而言即对法治的信念。在这种情况下,宪法保障司法独立与公正仍不足,而应该在日常行政事务的处理态度中有所体现(*Agrokompleks v. Ukraine*,§136)。

(二)独立的法庭

128. "独立"是指独立于其他权力机关(执行机关和议会)(*Beaumartin v. France*,§38)以及诉讼参与方(*Sramek v. Austria*,§42)。

129. 尽管政府的政治机构和司法机构之间的"权力分离"在本法院的判例法中越来越重要,第 6 条或公约的其他规定均未要求国家服从这一可能限制权力间互动的宪法理论概念(*Kleyn and Others v. the Netherlands*[GC],§193)。事实上,法庭的独立性要求存在程序保障将司法权与其他权力相分离。

1. 独立于执行机关

130. 若执行机关在案件审理中干涉审判结果的形成,则法官的独立性遭到了破坏

---

① 同时参见"具有完整管辖权的法院的审查"及"公平"两章节。

(*Sovtransavto Holding v. Ukraine*，§80；*Mosteanu and Others v. Romania*，§42)。

131. 法官由执行机关任命且可能被解职这一事实本身并不足以构成对第6条第1款的违反[*Clarke v. the United Kingdom*(dec.)]。由执行机关任命法官是被允许的,前提是该任命的形成未受到非法的影响或压力[*Flux v. Moldova*(no.2),§27]。

132. 最高法院的主席由执行机关任命的事实本身并未危害其独立性,前提是一旦被任命,他便不再受到来自执行机关的压力或指示,完全独立地行使其职权(*Zolotas v. Greece*,§24)。

133. 同理,行政理事会的法官由地区行政机关任命的事实本身也不能对法官的独立性或公正性构成质疑,前提是一旦被任命,他便不再受到来自执行机关的压力或指示,完全独立地行使其职权[*Majorana v. Italy*,(dec.)]。

2. 独立于议会

134. 法官由议会任命的事实本身并不会导致法官附属于议会机关,只要他们一旦被任命,其司法职能的履行便不受到压力或指示(*Sacilor-Lormines v. France*,§67)。进一步而言,若上诉法院的成员(主要是职业法官)之一也是议会的成员,这本身也不违背使案件被独立且公正的法庭审判的权利(*Pabla Ky v. Finland*,§§31-35)。

3. 独立于案件参与方

135. 若法庭成员中有人基于其职责和业务的组织而附属于案件当事方,诉讼当事人可对其独立性提出合法的怀疑。这种情形严重影响了在民主社会中对法院的必须的信任(*Sramek v. Austria*,§42)。

4. 评估独立性的准则

136. 为了确定某机构是否"独立",本法院认为需要格外关注以下准则(*Langborger v. Sweden*,§32；*Kleyn and Others v. the Netherlands*[GC],§190):

①机构成员任命的方式；

②机构成员任命的期限；

③抵御外部压力的保障；

④该机构是否表现出独立性。

(1)机构成员任命的方式:

137. 司法部长对裁判组成员的任命和解职的干涉受到了质疑[*Sramek v. Austria*,§38；*Brudnicka and Others v. Poland*,§41；*Clarke v. United Kingdom*(dec.)]。

138. 尽管在这种事件中,将案件指派给特定的法官或法院属于国家的裁量权范围,但是必须使本法院相信其符合第 6 条第 1 款的规定,具体而言,符合独立性和公正性的要求(*Bochan v. Ukraine*,§71)。

(2)机构成员被任命的期限:

139. 本法院并未对做出判决的机关的成员任期做出任何具体规定,但是无限的任期必然被认为是对其独立性的威胁。尽管如此,法律中未规定此种不可解职的正式任命并不当然意味欠缺独立性,前提是事实上其是被认可且具备其他必要的保障(*SacilorLormines v. France*,§67;*Luka v. Romania*,§44)。

(3)反抗外部压力的保障:

140. 司法独立要求法官个人不受司法程序内外的不正当影响。内部的司法独立要求其免受其他法官或诸如法院院长或法院部门主任等对法院负有行政责任的人的指导或压迫。独立性的措施在司法部门内欠缺保障法官,尤其是针对其司法长官,可能导致本法院认为申请人关于法院独立性和公正性的怀疑是客观正确的(*Parlov-Tkalčić v. Croatia*,§86;*Agrokompleks v. Ukraine*,§137)。

141. 郡法院法官被认为独立于该法院的院长,原因在于法院院长仅履行行政(管理和组织)职能,这些职能与司法职能相分离。司法体系提供了足够的保障用于反对法院院长向法官指派案件的任意妄为(*Parlov-Tkalčić v. Croatia*,§§88–95)。

(4)独立性外观:

142. 在确定某法院是否符合第 6 条第 1 款规定的独立性标准时,出庭十分重要(*Sramek v. Austria*,§42)。对于独立出庭而言,出庭方的立场十分重要但并非决定性的;具有决定性意义的是相关方的恐惧是否是"客观正当"的(*Sacilor-Lormines v. France*,§63)。因此,如果本法院认为一个"客观观察者"在案件的情形中也不能看出任何值得怀疑之处,则此案便不涉及关乎独立性的问题[*Clarke v. United Kingdom*(dec.)]。

(三)公正的法庭

143. 第 6 条第 1 款要求其规定范围内的法庭是公正的。公正性一般表示不存在偏见,或法庭的存在能经得起不同方式的检验(*Wettstein v. Switzerland*,§43;*Micallef v. Malta*[GC],§93)。独立性和公正性的内涵式紧密联系的,根据具体情形,可能需要统一审查(*Sacilor-Lormines v. France* §62；*Oleksandr Volkov v. Ukraine*, §107)。

1. 评估公正性的标准

144. 公正性必须从以下方面进行判断(*Micallef v. Malta* [GC], §§93)：

- 主观检查，即特定法官的个人确信和行为必须被考察，具体而言，该法官是否对案件具有任何偏见；
- 客观检查，即通过确认法庭本身和其组成是否提供了足够的保障来排除对其公正性的合法质疑。

145. 主观公正和客观公正之间并无绝对的区分，原因在于法官的行为不仅可能在外部观察者看来不足以提供足够的排除合法怀疑的保障(客观检查)，也可能受到其自身确信的影响(主观检查)。

146. 因此，在难以举证反驳法官的主观公正性的案件中，客观公正性的要求提供了更重要的保障(*Micallef v. Malta* [GC], §§95 and 101)。

(1) 主观途径：

147. 进行主观检查时，本法院一致认为除非有相反证据，应当推定法官是公正的(*Le Compte, Van Leuven and De Meyere v. Belgium*, §58；*Micallef v. Malta* [GC], §94)。关于所需证据的形式，本法院曾经尝试确认法官是否表现出了敌意(*Buscemi v. Italy*, §§67-68)。法官在参与了在先的民事诉讼之后并未回避处理与之相关民事上诉案件这一事实本身并不构成足以反驳公正性推定所需的证据(*Golubović v. Croatia*, §52)。

148. 法庭被假定未收到个人偏见或不公的影响这一原则在本法院的判例法中确立已久(*Le Compte, Van Leuven and De Meyere v. Belgium*, §58；*Driza v. Albania*, §75)。

(2) 客观途径：

149. 除了法官的行为，必须确定是否存在可以质疑法官公正性的确定的事实。当适用于审判机构时，这意味着，除了该机构成员的个人行为之外，应确定是否存在足以质疑该机构公正性的确切事实。这意味着在特定案件中，在确定是否存在合法原因来怀疑某法官(*Morel v. France*, §§45-50；*Pescador Valero v. Spain*, §23)或审判机构(*Luka v. Romania*, §40)缺乏公正性时，个人的立场十分重要但不具有决定性。具有决定性的是这样的担忧能否符合客观合理性(*Wettstein v. Switzerland*, §44；*Pabla Ky v. Finland*, §30；*Micallef v. Malta* [GC], §96)。

150. 客观检查主要涉及法官和其他诉讼参与人之间的级别或其他联系(参见与法官

正当角色相关的案件,例如 *Mežnarić v. Croatia*,§36;*Wettstein v. Switzerland*,§47),若该联系客观上使对法庭公正性的质疑成为正当行为,便不符合在客观检查下的公约标准。

151. 因此,在个案中必须确定该联系在质和量两方面是否足以表明法庭欠缺公正性(*Micallef v. Malta*,[GC],§§97 and 102)。

152. 在这一方面,出庭也可以具有一定重要性,换句话说,"司法不仅要公正,还必须让人看到其公正"。法院在民主社会中必须被赋予民众的信任正面临危险。因此,任何公正性受到合法质疑的法官都必须被免职(*Micallef v. Malta*[GC],§98)。

153. 为了使法院获得不可或缺的来自公众的信任,内部组织的问题也必须被考虑。存在规范法官罢免事项的规定是表明国内存在确保公正程序的一个相关因素(参见质疑法官的特定规范,*Micallef v. Malta*[GC],§§99-100)。这些规定体现了国家立法者排除对法官或法院的公正性的所有合理怀疑的忧虑,也构成一种通过消除这些忧虑产生的原因来确保公正性的尝试。除了确保避免事实上的偏见,它们也被用来消除任何不公正的表现,以促进民主社会中公众对法院的信任(*Mežnarić v. Croatia*,§27)。

2. 可能缺乏公正性的情形

154. 以下两种情形下可能存在缺乏公正性的问题:

①首先是职能性质,例如,同一个人在司法程序中行使不同职能,或者与程序中的其他参与人具有上下级或其他联系。

②第二种情形是个人品质,源于法官在给定案件中的行为。

(1)职能性质的情形:

①在相同案件中同时履行建议和司法职能。

155. 在一个机构中连续行使建议和司法职能,在特定情形下,可能从客观角度上引起第6条第1款下的公正性问题(*Procola v. Luxembourg*,§45——判定违反公约)。

156. 这个问题在于是否在"同一案件""同一决定"或"类似事件"中同时行使了司法和建议职能(*Kleyn and Others v. the Netherlands*[GC],§200;*Sacilor-Lormines v. France*,§74——判定并未违反)。

②同一案件中同时行使司法职能和超司法职能。

157. 衡量申请者的担忧的客观公正性时,例如,关于法官在诉讼中的正当角色,其参与其中以及参与的不同程度之间相隔的时间等因素都可以被考虑在内(*McGonnell v. the United Kingdom*,§§52-57)。

158. 任何与法律或行政规则的出台有直接牵连的情况,都可能足以使人就立法以及规则中的用语变化纠纷是否存在合理理由而对司法公正产生怀疑(参见 *McGonnell v. the United Kingdom*, §§55 – 58,本法院认为法官直接参与到发展计划的出台中违反了第 6 条第 1 款,与之相较 *Pabla Ky v. Finland*, §34——并未违反)。

159. 若同一个人在两个并行的诉讼中分别担任法官和对立方的代表人,申请人可以有合理原因怀疑该法官将继续将其视为对立方(*Wettstein v. Switzerland*, §§44 – 47)。

160. 一名法官曾经在诉讼初期作为申请人对立方律师,在审理对此提起的宪法争议后,本法院认为存在对第 6 条第 1 款的违反(*Mežnarić v. Croatia*, §36)。关于曾在民事诉讼之初担任申请人对立方的法律顾问的宪法法院法官的公正性问题(参见 *Švarc and Kavnik v. Slovenia*, §44)。

③履行不同司法职能。

161. 衡量同一法官参与民事案件的不同阶段是否符合第 6 条第 1 款规定的公正性要求时,应当逐案分别处理,且要考虑不同案件个别的情况。

162. 法官已经做出诉前决定这一事实本身不足以被认定为对公正性的正当怀疑。重要的是该法官在诉前所采取措施的性质和范围。同理,法官对案件材料有详细了解也并不表明其在做出决定时存在偏见。对可知信息的前期分析也不表明最终的分析是偏颇的。重要的是,判决发布时要同时公布其分析,且该分析是基于在审理过程中被采纳的证据和意见而做出的(*Morel v. France*, §45)。

163. 有必要考虑诉讼不同阶段所确定的实体事项是否足以对参与这些阶段的法官的公正性构成质疑(*Toziczka v. Poland*, §36)。

例如,

- 保持公正的义务并未形成一般性原则要求废除行政或司法决议的最高法院必须将案件发回不同的司法机关或发回该机关的不同组成部门(*Ringeisen v. Austria*, §97);
- 如果法官参与两个与相同事实相关的不同诉讼,则可能导致对其公正性的疑问(*Indra v. Slovakia*, §§51 – 53);
- 由两名非专业性法官协助的上诉法庭的主审法官不应审理关于他之前已做出判决的上诉(*De Haan v. the Netherlands*, §51);
- 上诉法院的法官被要求对在之前做出的决定中是否存在法律解释或适用上的错

误进行判断,可能引起对公正性的质疑(*San Leonard Band Club v. Malta*,§64);
- 同一法官参与了关于一个案件实体内容的决定,又参与了审查就该决定所提起的上诉申请的审查,这并非与公正性要求明确不符(*Warsicka v. Poland*,§§38－47);
- 拥有双重身份的法官,在前一个诉讼中担任申请人对立方的律师,在后一诉讼中担任上诉法院的法官:具体考虑到其相隔的时间以及两个案件的差异,且行使律师职责和行使法官职能并未在时间上重叠,本法院认为申请人对法官的公正性不具有客观合理的怀疑(*Puolitaival and Pirttiaho v. Finland*,§§46－54);
- 在一个案件中,若干已经就案件做出决定的法官被要求判断他们是否在该决定中存在失误,且其他三个法官已经在该案件中表达了自己的观点,本法院认为这构成对公正性原则的违背(*Driza v. Albania*,§§78－83——判定违反公约);
- 其中一位法官参与了关于法律本身的上诉程序,其在此前作为中级法院的法官参与了该案件(*Peruš v. Slovenia*,§§38－39)。

(2)有关个人性质的情形。

164. 若法官对案件存在个人利益,则公正性原则也会被侵害(*Langborger v. Sweden*,§35;*Gautrin and Others v. France*,§59)。

165. 法官和案件当事一方或其代理人之间存在职业或个人牵连,也可能引起对公正性的质疑(*Pescador Valero v. Spain*,§27;*Tocono and Profesorii Prometeişti v. Moldova*,§31;*Micallef v. Malta*[GC],§102)。间接因素也可能被考虑在内(*Pétur Thór Sigurðn v. Iceland*,§45)。

第四节　程序要求

一、公平

> **第6条第1款**
>
> "在决定某人的公民权利和义务……时,任何人有理由受到……审判机构……的公平审讯。……"

(一)一般性原则

166. 显著地位:本法院一直强调受到公平审理的权利在民主社会中的显著地位(*Airey v. Ireland*,§24;*Stanev v. Bulgaria*[GC],§231)。这项保障是公约意义下的民主社会的一项基本原则(*Pretto and Others v. Italy*,§21)。因此不得对公约第6条第1款做限制解释(*Moreira de Azevedo v. Portugal*,§66)。公平性要求适用于诉讼程序全程,并不限于当事人间的审理(*Stran Greek Refineries and Stratis Andreadis v. Greece*,§49)。

167. 内容:民事诉请必须能够被提交给法官(*Fayed v. the United Kingdom*,§65;*Sabeh El Leil v. France*[GC],§46)。第6条第1款详细描述了民事诉讼中当事人被赋予的程序保障,其旨在确保当事方的利益以及司法权的正当行使(*Nideröst-Huber v. Switzerland*,§30)。因此诉讼当事人必须能够在其案件中做出有效辩论(*H. v. Belgium*,§53)。

168. 国家机关的角色:本法院一直表明国家机关必须在个案中确保公约意义下的公平审理的要求得到满足(*Dombo Beheer B. V. v. the Netherlands*,§33)。

169. 诉讼当事人的主张:在确定斯特拉斯堡法院①判例法所定义的"公民权利和义务"时,原则上,每个人都应受到法庭公平审理。第6条第1款为此增添了关于法院组成及组织机构以及诉讼程序的进行等方面的保障。总之,以上所有共同构成被公平审判的权利(*Golder v. the United Kingdom*,§36)。

170. 法律解释的原则:

(1)民事诉请必须能够被提交给法官的原则是一项被普遍承认的基本法律原则;国际法上禁止司法拒绝的原则也是如此。第6条第1款必须在这些原则下被解读(*Golder v. the United Kingdom*,§35);

(2)第6条第1款保障被法院公平审理的权利必须结合公约的前言予以解释,前言中申明了法治是缔约国的一项共同财富(*Brumarescu v. Romania*,§61;*Nejdet Şahin and Perihan Şahin v. Turkey*[GC],§57);

(3)司法确定原则是法治的重要组成之一[*Beian v. Romania*(no.1),§39];

(4)在公约语境下,在民主社会享受公平司法的权利享有突出地位,因此对第6条第1款的任何限制解释都不符合该规定的宗旨(*Ryakib Biryoukov v. Russia*,§37);

---

① 参见"范围"一节。

(5) 同时,公约不保障任何理论性或虚幻的权利,只保障现实和有效的权利(*Airey v. Ireland*, §24)。

171. 国家在民事案件中享有更大的裁量空间:本法院承认"公平审理"概念所包含的要求在民事案件和刑事案件中并不必须相同:"缔约国在处理关乎公民权利义务的民事案件时比其处理刑事案件享有更大的裁量空间"(*Dombo Beheer B. V. v. the Netherlands*, §32; *Levages Prestations Services v. France*, §46)。第6条第1款对民事案件的要求比对刑事指控案件的要求更宽松(*König v. Germany*, §96)。

(二) 范围

172. 有效的权利:诉讼参与方有权将其认为相关的评论提交给法庭。只有这些评论被真实地听取,即被受理法院合法地考量之后,该权利才能被认为有效(*Kraska v. Switzerland*, §30; *Van de Hurk v. the Netherlands*, §59; *Perez v. France*, §80)。为使本条所保障的权利切实有效,国家机关必须尽职:关于无律师代表的上诉人,参见 *Kerojärvi v. Finland*, §42 以及 *Fretté v. France*, §49;关于有律师代表的上诉人,参见 *Göç v. Turkey*[GC], §57。

173. 上诉人正当参与诉讼程序,要求法院主动与上诉人就案件材料进行沟通。因此,申请人对未经沟通的相关材料无异议或者率先查看案件材料等情形并不重要(*Kerojärvi v. Finland*, §42)。上诉人仅具有查询案件材料且获得复印件的可能性本身还不足以构成充分保障(*Göç v. Turkey*[GC], §57)。

174. 行政机关所负义务:上诉人必须有权查看行政机关占有的相关材料,必要时可通过文件公示程序(*McGinley and Egan v. the United Kingdom*, §§86 and 90)。如果被告国家无正当理由阻止上诉人查看其占有的有利于被告方的材料,或者不实地否认其存在,将构成否认上诉人公平审理权,从而违反第6条第1款的规定(同上)。

175. 对诉讼程序进行整体审查:诉讼程序是否公平是基于对其整体的审查而判断的(*Ankerl v. Switzerland*, §38; *Centro Europa 7 S. R. L. and di Stefano v. Italy* [GC], §197)。

176. 因此,诉讼程序公平性的任何瑕疵,在特定情形下,可能会在之后的阶段被弥补,无论是在同一级别(*Helle v. Finland*, §54)或者来自上级法院(*Schuler-Zgraggen v. Switzerland*, §52; 反例参见 *Albert and Le Compte v. Belgium*, §36; *Feldbrugge v. the Netherlands*, §§45-46)。

177. 在任何情况下,若最高司法机关层面存在瑕疵——如不存在对提交给该机关的决定做出回应的可能性——则构成对公平审判权的侵害(Ruiz-Mateos v. Spain, §§65-67)。

178. 仅当受争议的决定受到具有完全管辖权且提供了满足公约第6条第1款要求的各种保障的独立司法机构的审查时,做出该决定的程序瑕疵才能被弥补。重要的是上诉法院司法审查权的范围,以及是基于案件具体情形做出的审查(Obermeier v. Austria, §70)。①

179. 未提供公平审理保障的初步决定:在这类案件中,若上诉人享有具有完全管辖权且能提供公约要求的保障手段的独立司法机构所提供的救济手段,则并不会产生有关公平性的问题(Oerlemans v. the Netherlands, §§53-58; British-American Tobacco Company Ltd v. the Netherlands, §78)。重要的是存在这种提供足够保障的救济手段(Air Canada v. the United Kingdom, §62)。

180. 在上诉法院面前:第6条第1款并未强迫缔约国设立上诉法院或最高法院,但是存在此类法院的国家必须确保诉讼当事人享有第6条第1款规定的基本保障。尽管如此,该条款对上诉程序适用的方法要基于相关诉讼程序的特征;且必须整体考虑民主法律秩序中该程序的整体以及上诉法院(Helmers v. Sweden, §31)或最高法院所扮演的角色(Levages Prestations Services v. France, §§44-45; K. D. B. v. the Netherlands, §41)。

181. 考虑到最高法院的特殊作用,即其被限制在审查法律是否被正确适用上,其诉讼程序可以更加形式化(Levages Prestations Services v. France, §48)。最高法院审理时要求当事人有专业律师作为代表并未违背第6条的规定[G. L. and S. L. v. France (dec.); Tabor v. Poland, §42]。

182. 限制:作为一项一般规则,案件事实由国内法院审查:本法院不对案件事实做出审查(Dombo Beheer B. V. v. the Netherlands, §31)。② 进一步而言,尽管上诉人享有将其认为相关的评论提交法庭的权利,第6条第1款并不保障该当事人获得一个良好的结果(Andronicou and Constantinou v. Cyprus, §201)。

183. 出庭理论:本法院强调过出庭在司法行政中的重要性;确保诉讼公正十分重要。尽管如此,本法院明确表示相关个人的立场并非决定性的,诉讼个人对诉讼公平性

---

① 同时参见"具有完整管辖权的法院的审查"一章。
② 参见"第四种情形"一节。

的怀疑必须是客观公正的(*Kraska v. Switzerland*,§32)。因此有必要审查法院是如何处理案件的。

184. 在其他终审案件中,本法院曾指出公众对司法公正越来越高的敏感度使得司法出庭的重要性越来越高(*Kress v. France*[GC],§82;*Martinie v. France*[GC],§53;*Menchinskaya v. Russia*,§32)。本法院在这些案件中赋予出庭以重要性(同时参见*Vermeulen v. Belgium*,§34;*Lobo Machado v. Portugal*,§32)。

185. 司法实践:为了考虑本国司法制度的现状,本法院在审查本国法是否符合第6条第1款时,一直对本国司法实践予以重视[*Kerojärvi v. Finland*,§42;*Gorou v. Greece*(no.2)[GC]§32]。事实上,在审查诉讼当事人是否被公平审理时,不得忽视案件的一般性事实和法律背景(*Stankiewicz v. Poland*,§70)。

186. 国家机关不能摒弃法院在国家安全和反恐领域的有效控制:可使用技术手段使对安全性的合法担忧与个人的程序权利相适应(*Dağtekin and Others v. Turkey*,§34)。

187. 独立于结果和过程的原则:第6条第1款的程序保障适用于所有诉讼当事人,不仅是那些在国内法院未胜诉的当事人[*Philis v. Greece*(no.2),§45]。

示例:

188. 判例法包含了以下多种情形。

189. 法院提交给上诉法院的评论明显意在影响判决:当事各方必须能够对该评论做出点评,无论其对法院的实际影响如何。即使这些评论并未出现在上诉法院(*Nideröst-Huber v. Switzerland*,§§26-32)或本院审理的被诉国政府的决定中(*APEH Üldözötteinek Szövetsége and Others v. Hungary*,§42)。

190. 预备性问题:国内存在预备性参考机制,本国法院拒绝授权申请该机制的,在特定情形下,可构成对程序公正的侵害(*Ullens de Schooten and Rezabek v. Belgium*,§§57-67,with further references)。当该拒绝行为被认定具有任意性时,则构成侵害:

- 相关规则不允许任何对预备性参考的例外或替代性措施,但仍然拒绝的;
- 基于法律规定之外的原因做出拒绝决定的;
- 或者该拒绝行为未依据相关规定被适当地论证。

191. 因此,第6条第1款并不保障由本国法院将案件提交至欧盟法院的任何权利[*Dotta v. Italy*(dec.)]。通过适用上述被引用的判例法,本法院审查该拒绝行为是否呈现任意性[*Canela Santiago v. Spain*(dec.)]。

192. 本国判例法的变化:法律稳定和保护合法期待的要求并不包含确立的法律体系的权利(*Unédic v. France*,§74)。判例法的发展本身并不与正当司法相矛盾,原因在于若法律不能保持动态且发展,则改革和进步便会受到阻碍(*Atanasovski v. "The former Yugoslav Republic of Macedonia"*,§38)。在该判决中,本法院认为良好的法律体系的存在给最高法院施加了对其与判例法的分歧做出更加实质性解释的义务,否则个人享有的获得经合理论证的决定的权利便会受到损害。在一些案件中,本国法理的变化对待审的民事诉讼产生影响,因而违反公约的规定(*Petko Petkov v. Bulgaria*,§§32-34)。

193. 关于判例法中存在的分歧,本法院曾经强调设立适当的机制从而保障法院实践的连续性以及判例法的统一性[*Frimu and Others v. Romania*(dec.),§§43-44]的重要性。尽管如此,要实现法律的连续性可能要耗费一定的时间,因此未破坏法律稳定的判例法之间的冲突可以被容忍(*Nejdet Şahin and Perihan Şahin v. Turkey*[GC],§83;*Albu and Others v. Romania*,§§36 and 40-43)。①

194. 一项法律在国家作为当事方所涉案件仍在进行时生效:本法院特别关注溯及既往的法律的危险性,它对国家所涉案件争议的司法判决产生的影响,具有使待定案件丧失可胜诉能力的作用。任何使这样的措施合理化的理由都必须经过严密的审查(*National & Provincial Building Society, Leeds Permanent Building Society and Yorkshire Building Society v. the United Kingdom*,§112)。原则上,在民事案件中,立法机关并未被阻止出台新的溯及既往的条款以便对现有法律框架下的权利进行规制。但是,第6条排除了立法机关对司法机关施加的旨在影响其对争议做出司法决定的干涉,除非其具有广泛关注的令人信服的理由(*Zielinski and Pradal and Gonzalez and Others v. France*[GC],§57;*Scordino v. Italy*(no.1)[GC],§126)。

举例而言,本法院发现在下述方面存在对公约的违反:

- 立法机关进行干涉,使得案件结果朝着有利于国家的方向发展:当国家所涉案件待审时间达9年,且申请者获得一项最终可执行的判决时(*Stran Greek Refineries and Stratis Andreadis v. Greece*,§§49-50);
- 一部对即将出现的案件结果具有有利于国家一方的决定性影响的法律

---

① 同时参见"第四审"部分。

(*Zielinski and Pradal and Gonzalez and Others v. France*,[GC],§59);

- 在终审程序的关键时期,出台了一部法律使得争议被解决且诉讼程序的进行变得毫无必要性(*Papageorgiou v. Greece*);
- 上诉法院所做出的判决基于,甚至依附于在诉讼过程中已经生效的法律且影响诉讼结果(*Anagnostopoulos and Others v. Greece*,§§20-21)。

然而第6条第1款不得被解释为阻止权力机关对其所涉待审司法程序进行的任何干涉。在其他案件中,本法院认为被告国家的考量依据的是强制的公共利益动机,从而赋予法律溯及力的正当性[*National & Provincial Building Society*, *Leeds Permanent Building Society and Yorkshire Building Society v. the United Kingdom*, §112; *Forrer-Niedenthal v. Germany*, §64; *OGIS-Institut Stanislas*, *OGEC Saint-Pie X and Blanche de Castille and Others v. France*, §§71-72; *EEG-Slachthuis Verbist Izegem v. Belgium*(dec.)]。

195. 本判例法也适用于国家虽不是当事方但通过立法权力破坏诉讼程序的案件(*Ducret v. France*,§§33-42)。

196. 其他类型的立法干涉:

- 法律可以在诉讼开始前[*Organisation nationale des syndicats d'infirmiers libéraux*(*O. N. S. I. L.*)*v. France*(dec.)]或诉讼结束后[*Preda and Dardari v. Italy*(dec.)]被颁布而不会引起关于公约第6条的争议;
- 一般性法律的颁布即使没有现实地指向待定的司法程序或借此规避法治的原则,也可能被证明是对诉讼当事人不利的(*Gorraiz Lizarraga and Others v. Spain*,§72);
- 在诉讼程序进行中,一部法律可以被宣布违宪,只要该行为并无影响该诉讼的目的[*Dolca v. Romania*(dec.)]。

197. 在最高法院的审判前,未与诉讼当事人就国家法律服务机构的独立成员的意见进行沟通(公共检察部的成员):维穆伦诉比利时案(*Vermeulen v. Belgium*),范·奥修文诉比利时案(*Van Orshoven v. Belgium*);K. D. B 诉尼德兰案(*K. D. B. v. the Netherlands*)主要的公共检察官/总检察长:高奇诉土耳其案(*Göç v. Turkey*[GC]);洛沃·马沙多诉葡萄牙案(*Lobo Machado v. Portugal*);政府委员:克雷斯诉法官案(*Kress v. France*[GC]);没有回应这些评论的机会:很多被告国家辩称国家法律服务中的这类人员既不是诉讼参与方也不是任何一方的同盟或敌对者,但是本法院发现对这些相关人员在诉讼中起到的现实作用必须予以考虑,更确切的是,考虑其观点的内容和影响(*Vermeulen v. Belgium*,§31;*Kress v. France*[GC],§71)。

198. 本法院强调过,在民事案件中,若国家法律服务机构的独立成员提交的意见未提前交予当事各方讨论,则剥夺了其做出回应的机会,在此类案件中,对抗性的程序显得尤为重要(*Vermeulen v. Belgium*,§33;*Lobo Machado v. Portugal*,§31;*Van Orshoven v. Belgium*,§41;*Göç v. Turkey*[GC],§§55-56;*Kress v. France*,§76;*Immeubles Groupe Kosser v. France*,§26)。

199. 上述提及的从事国内法律服务的人员,无论主动亦或被动公开对案件发表观点,之后参与或出席审议的行为已经受到指责(*Vermeulen v. Belgium*,§34;*Lobo Machado v. Portugal*,§32;*Kress v. France*,§87)。这项判例法主要是基于出庭理论[①](*Martinie v. France*[GC],§53)。

200. 因此,为了确定问题是否应归结于诉讼当事人的行为或国家的态度或可适用的法律(*Fretté v. France*,§§49-51),诉讼发生的状况必须被审查,更具体而言,该诉讼程序是否是对抗性的,且是否满足双方力量对等的原则(比较 *Kress v. France*,§76,和 *Göç v. Turkey* §§55-57)。

关于欧盟法院的案件[②]:*Cooperatieve Producentenorganisatie van de Nederlandse Kokkelvisserij U. A. v. the Netherlands*(dec.)。

201. 限制:

- 力量对等并不表示,在审理前未向对方或法官披露己方观点的当事方享有要求对方向其披露观点的权利(*Kress v. France*,§73);
- 承认一项并不具备实际范围或实质性的权利是毫无意义的:这种情形是指,由于所采取的手段在法律上是不容置疑的,所依据的公约下的权利在该案件的结果中根本不可能发生(*Stepinska v. France*,§18)。

(三)第四审诉求[③]

1. 一般性原则

202. "第四审"诉求是提交到法院的一类特殊诉求类型。"第四审"这个词本身并

---

① 见上文。
② Court of Justice of the European Communities/Court of Justice of the European Union.
③ 本部分内容参考了《受理标准实践指南》的相关内容。

没有出现在公约里而是来自公约机构确立的判例法[*Kemmache v. France* (no. 3) , §44]——矛盾的是这类诉求混淆了法院的真正作用:其不是一个上诉法院或者推翻缔约国国内法院判决的法院或者可以再审缔约国国内法院已审案件的法院,又或者可以像最高法院一样重审案件的法院。第四审申诉是由于两个层面的长期误解而产生的。

203. 首先,申诉人一方对欧洲人权公约确立的欧洲人权法院这一司法机构的身份和性质有一个普遍的误解。本法院不可替代本国法院的角色;法院的权力应限定在确认缔约国是否遵守其在加入公约及其议定书时做出的人权承诺。此外,除了不能直接干预缔约国的法律体系外,法院还要尊重国内法律系统的自治性。这意味着法院不可处理缔约国国内法院在事实或法律方面的错误,除非其已经侵害到了公约所保护的权利和自由。法院不能因为国内法院根据某案件事实为何采纳某个决定而非其他决定,而自己就案件事实做出评判,否则其即事实上扮演了第三审或第四审法院的角色,超越了其自身的权限(*García Ruiz v. Spain* [GC], §28)。

204. 其次,公约第6条第1款中的"公正"的确切含义也经常被误解。即公约第6条第1款所规定的"公正"不是指"实体"公正(该概念是部分法律、部分伦理的,只能由审判法官来具体评判),而是"程序"公正。具体说即在对抗制诉讼程序中要听取双方的意见且双方应被平等对待[*Star Cate Epilekta Gevmata and Others v. Greece* (dec.)]。程序公正总是在整体上被衡量的,因此孤立的违法行为可能并不足以否定整个诉讼的公正性(*Miroļubovs and Others v. Latvia* , §103)。

205. 进一步而言,本法院尊重欧洲立法和司法体系的多样性,并且本法院并不承担使其标准化的任务。正如若没有证据证明存在任意性行为时,本法院不就国内法院做出判决的智慧进行审查(*Nejdet Şahin and Perihan Şahin v. Turkey* [GC], §§68, 89 and 94)。

2. 本法院监督的范围和限制

206. 本法院一直表示不处理缔约国国内法院在事实和法律上的错误,除非该错误十分明显且已经侵害了公约所保护的权利和自由[*García Ruiz v. Spain* [GC], §28; *Perez v. France* [GC], §82;在 *Dulaurans v. France* (§38)案中,本法院基于"判决中的明显错误"认定了对第6条第1款的违反,反例可参见 *Société anonyme d'habitations à loyers modérés terre et famille v. France* (dec.)]。

207. 这意味着作为一般规则,本法院不对下列本国法院的发现和结论提出质疑:

- 案件事实的确定:本法院不得质疑国内法院的发现,除非其具有恶劣且明显的武断行为(*García Ruiz v. Spain*[GC],§§28-29)。
- 国内法的解释和适用:优先由国内法院解决该国法律的解释问题(*Perez v. France*[GC],§82),而不是由本法院解决,因为本法院的职责在于核实其解释是否符合公约的要求(*Nejdet Şahin and Perihan Şahin v. Turkey*[GC],§49)。在一些例外的案件中,若国内法院在解释本国法律时是明显武断的或错误的,本法院可以就法律的解释做出适当的结论[*Barać and Others v. Montenegro*,§§32-34,包括进一步参考;*Anđelković v. Serbia*,§§24-27(司法拒绝);同时参考 *Laskowska v. Poland*,§61],但这经常发生在公约其他条款下,而并非第6条第1款(*Kushoglu v. Bulgaria*,§50;*Işyar v. Bulgaria*,§48;*Fabris v. France*[GC],§60)。
- 证据能力和证明力①:第6条第1款提供的保障仅限于诉讼阶段对证据的处理。证据能力以及证据被审核的方法主要是国内法院处理的事项,因为国内法院负有衡量其收到的证据的任务[*García Ruiz v. Spain*[GC],*Farange S. A. v. France* §28;(dec.)]。

208. 因此第6条第1款并不允许本法院质疑一项民事纠纷结果的实体公正性,在此类纠纷中,时常是参与方一方胜诉,其他参与方败诉。

209. 如果申请者在对抗性诉讼中享有利益;其能够在诉讼不同阶段援引其认为与案件相关的论点和证据;其有机会有效挑战对方援引的论点和证据;其被客观审查过的与案件处理结果所有相关论点均被法院按照规定予以听取和审查;被审理的决定的所有事实和法律缘由最终被披露;以及诉讼程序因此在整体上是公正的,则本法院会拒绝基于公约第6条第1款提出的第四审申诉(*García Ruiz v. Spain*[GC],§29)。大部分第四审申请被独任法官或三人委员会宣布不予受理(公约第27及28条)。反例可参见 *Donadzé v. Georgia*,§35。

3. 国内判例法的连续性

210. 第6条第1款并未赋予要求判例法保持稳定性的权利。判例法的发展本身并不与司法公正相矛盾,因为其若不保持动态和发展的状态,则会有危害改革和进步的风

---

① 同时参见证据审查部分。

险(Nejdet Şahin and Perihan Şahin v. Turkey[GC],§58)。

211. 原则上,即使是在明显具有可比性和关联性的案件中,本法院也不对独立性应得到尊重的国内法院发布的不同决定进行比较。判例法的"分歧可能性"是任何建立在由在其管辖领域内享有权力的初审法院和上诉法院组成的网络上的司法体系的内在必然特征。这种分歧甚至可能在同一法院内部产生。就其本身而言并不能认为与公约相悖(Santos Pinto v. Portugal,§41)。进一步而言,若诸案件的现实情形在客观上完全不同,则没有必要谈"分歧"[Uçar v. Turkey(dec.)]。

212. 因此,可能存在由于判例法的分歧而导致被认定违反第6条第1款的案件。基于该分歧存在于法院的同一机构或相互独立的不同机构之间,本法院衡量的要求有所不同。

213. 第一种情形,具有分歧的诸决定是由一个单一的国内最高法院发布,或由法律体系同一分支中负责终审程序的不同法院发布。在此类案件中,相互冲突的诸判决的持续性造成了可能有损司法公信力的法律不稳定的状态,这种公信力是法治国家最根本的组成部分。本法院基于三个主要标准来逐案审查这些不稳定性:

- 判例法的分歧是否持续且具有深远意义;
- 本国法是否提供了足以解决这种不一致性的机制;以及
- 这些机制是否被适用,在何种程度上被适用。缔约国有义务规划其司法体系,以避免发布此类具有分歧的判决,同时通过适当的程序手段解决任何严重的矛盾[Beian v. Romania(no. 1),§§37 et 39;Nejdet Şahin and Perihan Şahin v. Turkey[GC],§§56 – 57 and 80]。

本法院考虑的一项额外标准是,此种不一致是否仅限于一个孤立案件,或是影响了数量众多的人(Albu and Others v. Romania,§38)。

214. 第二种假设是,相冲突的诸决定分别是在终审程序中,由归属于司法体系不同分支的法院发布,这其中的每个法院均是其独立体系中的最高法院。在此第6条第1款并未要求设立纵向的审查机制或一般性的规范机构(如司法争议法院)。在具有多个法院的司法体系中并存多个最高法院且均被要求对法律做出解释,此时要获得判例法的稳定性需要花费较长时间,因此不足以破坏法律稳定性的相冲突的判例法在一段时间内将会被容忍。因此,拥有各自管辖区域的两个法院,在审查不同的案件时,针对由相似的事实情况所引起的同一法律问题,很有可能会得出不同但是却符合理性且合理的结论,这并不违反第 6 条第 1 款(*Nejdet Şahin and Perihan Şahin v. Turkey* [GC], §§ 81 – 83 and 86)。

(四)对抗性诉讼程序

215. 对抗原则:公正审判的概念包含了享有对抗性诉讼程序的基本权利。

216. 享有对抗性诉讼程序的权利所延伸出的要求在民事和刑事案件中基本相同(*Werner v. Austria*, § 66)。

217. 不得基于节省时间及加快诉讼进程的目的而忽视获得对抗性诉讼程序的权利这一基本原则(*Nideröst-Huber v. Switzerland*, § 30)。

218. 内容:享有对抗性诉讼程序的权利主要意味着刑事或民事案件的参与方有机会对所有旨在影响法院判决的被采纳的证据或被提交的答辩进行了解并做出评论,即使是国家法律服务体系的独立成员采纳的证据或提交的答辩也不例外(*Ruiz-Mateos v. Spain*, § 63; *McMichael v. the United Kingdom*, § 80; *Vermeulen v. Belgium*, § 33; *Lobo Machado v. Portugal*, § 31; *Kress v. France* [GC], § 74)。这项要求可以适用于宪法法院审理的案件(*Milatova v. the Czech Republic*, §§ 63 – 66; *Gaspari v. Slovenia*, § 53)。

- 法院判决的实际效果并无太大意义(*Nideröst-Huber v. Switzerland*, § 27; *Ziegler v. Switzerland*, § 38);
- 享有对抗性诉讼程序的权利必须能够在令人满意的条件下被行使:诉讼参与一方必须有熟知法院收到的证据的可能性,以及在适当时间内通过适当形式对证据的存在、内容以及可信度予以评价的可能性(*Krčmář and Others v. the Czech Republic*, § 42; *Immeubles Groupe Kosser v. France*, § 26),必要时可延期行使(*Yvon v. France* § 39);
- 诉讼参与双方应当有机会为了胜诉而将任何证据予以公开(*Clinique des Acacias and Others v. France*, § 37);
- 法院本身必须尊重对抗性原则,例如,其判定对法律要点提出上诉的权利已经由于申诉不应被受理而丧失时[*Clinique des Acacias and Others v. France*, § 38;比较 *Andret and Others v. France* (dec.),不受理:在最后这个案件中,最高法院告知各方新的论点被提出,各方享有在最高法院发布判决前做出回应的机会];
- 由争议的当事方单独决定是否对另一方提供的文件或目击者提供的证据做出评论。诉讼当事人对司法运作的信任是基于他们有机会对任何文件表达观点这一认知(也包括法院自己获得的文件:*K. S. v. Finland*,§22)(*Nideröst-Huber v. Switzerland*,§29;*Pellegrini v. Italy*,§45)。

219. 未披露以下文件或证据而侵害对抗性诉讼的权利:

- 在一项关于安置儿童的诉讼中,未披露社会福利部门提供的包含有该儿童信息和案件背景详情且提出建议的报告——即使在审判过程中将其中的内容告知了其父母(*McMichael v. the United Kingdom*,§80);
- 未披露检察官提交的证据,无论其是否被视为案件"当事方",因为其旨在基于所负职责对法院的判决施加可能不利于相关当事人的影响[*Ferreira Alves v. Portugal*(no. 3),§§36 – 39];
- 未披露由下级法院提交给上诉法院旨在影响后者判决的提示,即使该提示未呈现任何新的事实或理由[*Ferreira Alves v. Portugal*(no. 3),§41];
- 未披露法官直接占有的、包含有关案件实体内容的合理意见的文件(*K. S. v. Finland*,§§23 – 24)。

220. 限制:对抗性诉讼的权利并非绝对,而且根据案件的特定情形,其范围也会有所不同(*Hudakova and others v. Slovakia*,§§26 – 27)。对抗性原则不要求各方必须向对方递交尚未提交给法庭的文件(*Yvon v. France*,§38),也不要求制作不足以影响案件结果的备忘录[*Asnar v. France*(no. 2),§26]。

(五)平等手段

221. "平等手段"原则是广义的公正审判概念的应有之义。从诉讼各方"适当平衡"的意义上讲,"平等手段"的要求同时适用于民事和刑事案件(*Feldbrugge v. the Netherlands*,§44)。

222. 内容:保持诉讼各方"适当平衡"。平等手段原则意味着诉讼各方必须享有合理机会呈现其案件——包括其证据,且不得因此而被置于相对于其他当事方来说实质上不利的境地(*Dombo Beheer B. V. v. the Netherlands*,§33)。

- 不允许一方向法院提交意见却未告知对方而导致对方丧失答复的机会。应当由当事各方决定是否有必要向某一意见做出回应(*APEH Üldözötteinek Szövetsége and Others v. Hungary*,§42);
- 尽管如此,向法院提交的答辩未告知另外一方,这并不违反平等手段原则,但违反了广义的程序公正(*Nideröst-Huber v. Switzerland*,§§23 – 24;*Clinique des Acacias and Others v. France*,§§36 – 37)。

223. 不符合平等手段原则的例子：在下列案件中，由于其中一方处于明显不利地位，因此违反了这一原则：

- 一方的上诉未送达或告知对方，对方因此丧失回应的可能性（Beer v. Austria, §19）；
- 期间仅对一方当事人停止，使另一方处于实质上不利地位（Platakou v. Greece, §48; Wynen v. Belgium, §32）；
- 两个关键证人中仅有一位被准许出庭作证（Dombo Beheer B. V. v. the Netherlands, §§34 – 35）；
- 对立方享有获取相关信息的重要优势，在诉讼中占据支配性地位且对法院的判断施加了重大影响（Yvon v. France, §37）；
- 一方享有可将其置于优势的地位或职能，而且法院不允许另一方援引相关文件或提供认证，从而其很难对优势方提出质疑（De Haes and Gijsels v. Belgium, §§54 and 58）；
- 在行政诉讼中，行政机关给出的原因太过概要和泛化，以至于上诉人无法对其审查提出合理质疑；并且审查事实的法庭不允许申诉人提交支持其诉讼请求的意见（Hentrich v. France, §56）；
- 拒绝向诉讼一方提供法律援助，使得他们在面对一个富有的对手时无法有效地参与诉讼（Steel and Morris v. the United Kingdom, §72）；
- 在马蒂尼诉法国案（Martinie v. France [GC], §50）的判决中，本法院认为，政府律师不同于其他参与方，其在庭审中列席，被提前告知了进行报告的法官的观点，而且在庭审中听取报告法官的意见，全程参与诉讼程序且能在不受其他方反驳的情况下口头表达其观点。因此，考虑到政府律师在审计法院的诉讼中的这一地位，存在着对诉讼当事人不利的不均衡情形，而审判未被公开的事实则加重了这种不平衡的程度；
- 检察官介入并支持了申诉人对立方的观点（Menchinskaya v. Russia, §§35 – 39）。

224. 然而，本法院认为，庭审中对双方证人进行差别对待（一方的言词证据是经宣誓后陈述但另一方没有），并未实际影响审判的最终结果，因此符合第 6 条第 1 款的规定（Ankerl v. Switzerland, §38）。

225. 公民个人提起的特定案件：本法院区分了公民个人提起的诉讼和公共检察官

提起的诉讼,后者享有公共权力且有责任保障公共利益[*Guigue and SGENCFDT v. France*(*dec.*)]。因此,提起上诉的形式要件和期限(个人提起上诉的期限更短)的不同并不违背平等手段原则,前提是这种救济手段能够起到有意义的作用(如相关体系的特殊性质)。

226. 本法院还认为,如果一项法律规定仅限制公民的上诉可能性却并未限制公共检察官的上诉可能性,并不违反平等手段原则,因为公民和检察官的角色和目的是明显不同的(*Berger v. France*,§38)。

227. 对于检察机关和私人主体之间的案件,检察机关可以基于保护法律秩序的目的享有特权地位。但是,这不得导致民事诉讼的一方相对于检察机关而言具有不合理的劣势(*Stankiewicz v. Poland*,§68)。

(六)证据审查

228. 一般原则[①]:公约并未就证据制定规则(*Mantovanelli v. France*,§34)。证据可否被采用以及证据审查的方式主要由国内法和国内法院处理(*García Ruiz v. Spain*[GC],§28)。这同样适用于证明力和举证责任问题[*Tiemann v. France and Germany*(*dec.*)]。国内法院同样要审查所提交证据的相关性(*Centro Europa 7 S. r. l. and Di Stefano v. Italy*[GC],§198)。

尽管如此,公约赋予本法院的任务是确定诉讼整体是否公正,包括证据被采纳的方式(*Elsholz v. Germany*[GC],§66)。因此必须确定证据是否通过旨在保障审判公正的方式被呈现(*Blucher v. the Czech Republic*,§65)。

国内法院有义务对各方提交的意见、论据和证据进行适当的审查(*Van de Hurk v. the Netherlands*,§59)。

1. 人证

229. 第6条第1款并未明确保障要求证人出庭的权利,并且人证的证据能力原则上是由国内法院处理的事项。尽管如此,诉讼程序的整体,包括证据被采纳的方式,必须符合第6条第1款意义上的"公正"要求(*Dombo Beheer B. V. v. the Netherlands*,§31)。

- 若国内法院驳回了让证人出庭的请求,它们必须给出足够的理由并且驳回的决

[①] 同时参见"第四审"一节。

定不能是任意的：不得给诉讼当事人提出支持其自身立场的论据的能力造成不合理的限制(Wierzbicki v. Poland, §45)；

- 在庭审中对双方证人的区别对待可能会违反"平等手段原则"[Ankerl v. Switzerland, §38, 在此案中，本法院认为区别对待并未将申诉人置于相对于对方而言实质性的不利地位；相反地，参见 Dombo Beheer B. V. v. the Netherlands, §35, 在此案中，事件亲历者两人中只有一人被允许作证(违反了该原则)]。

2. 专家意见

230. 拒绝寻求专家意见：

- 国内法院拒绝寻求专家意见本身并非不公正；本法院必须确定诉讼程序在整体上是否公正(H. v. France, §61 and 70)。拒绝的原因必须合理；
- 在一个有关儿童监护和探视的案件中，必须根据案件的特殊情况，对拒绝命令专家做出心理报告的做法进行审查(Elsholz v. Germany [GC], §66, 加之必要的变更 Sommerfeld v. Germany, [GC], §71)；
- 在一个诱拐儿童的案件中[Tiemann v. France and Germany(dec.)]，本法院审查了上诉法院是否就其拒绝申诉人寻求另一专家意见的请求给出了充分的原因，从而确定该拒绝决定是否合理。

231. 专家的任命：正如同遵守第6条第1款规定的其他程序保障一样，遵守对抗性原则与"法庭"内的诉讼程序相关；这一规定并未一般性、原则性地要求在国内法院任命专家后，诉讼各方在各种情况下都能参与专家主持的面谈或查阅所有专家已经考量过的文件。

232. 重要的是诉讼双方应当能够恰当参与诉讼程序(Mantovanelli v. France, §33)。

233. 专家欠缺中立性，连同其在诉讼程序中的地位和角色，都会使诉讼中的天平向一方倾斜而对另一方不利，这便违背了平等手段原则(Sara Lind Eggertsdottir v. Iceland, §53)；此外，专家可在诉讼程序中享有优势地位，并对国内法院的审查产生重大影响(Yvon v. France, §37)。

234. 一份关于超出法官知识的技术领域的医学专家报告，很可能对法官审查事实产生重大的影响；这是一项关键证据，诉讼双方必须能够有效地对之做出评论(Mantovanelli v. France, §36; Storck v. Germany, §135)。

- 在芒多瓦内里诉法国案(*Mantovanelli v. France*)中,申诉人不能对作为主要证据的专家报告的结果做出有效评论,这违反了第6条第1款;
- 在奥古斯托诉法国案(*Augusto v. France*)中,国内法院未披露被委任的医生做出的关于申诉人是否符合享受福利待遇的医学标准的意见——其很可能是对判决具有决定性作用的证据,尽管该意见在法律上对法官并无约束力,但这仍然违反了第6条第1款。

235. 诉讼双方关于专家的权利:比较菲尔德布鲁日诉荷兰案[*Feldbrugge v. the Netherlands*,§44(违反)]和奥尔森诉瑞典案[*Olsson v. Sweden*(no.1),§§89-91(未违反)]。关于要求披露一份不利的报告的案件,参见 *L. v. United Kingdom*(dec.)。

(七)司法决定的论证

236. 第6条第1款规定的保障包括国内法院有义务对其做出的决定给予充分的理由(*H. v. Belgium*,§53)。一个被充分论证的决定能够向诉讼双方表明其案件受到了切实地审理。

237. 尽管国内法院在选取论据和采纳证据时享有一定的自由裁量权,但其有义务通过出具判决理由而使其决定具有正当性(*Suominen v. Finland*,§36)。

238. 出具的理由必须能确保双方有效利用其现有的上诉权(*Hirvisaari v. Finland*,§30最后)。

239. 第6条第1款要求法院为其决定出具理由,但不可被理解为要求法院对所有论据都做出详细回答[*Van de Hurk v. the Netherlands*,§61;*Garcia Ruiz v. Spain*[GC],§26;*Jahnke and Lenoble v. France*(dec.);*Perez v. France*[GC],§81]。

240. 国内法院给出理由的义务,因该决定的性质不同而在程度上有所差异(*Ruiz Torija v. Spain*,§29;*Hiro Balani v. Spain*,§27),具体的程度只能根据案件具体情形来判定:特别有必要考虑的是诉讼当事人在庭上可能提出的观点的多样性以及各缔约国在法律规定、习惯规则、法律意见以及判决的陈述和起草上存在的差异(*Ruiz Torija v. Spain*,§29;*Hiro Balani v. Spain*,§27)。

241. 尽管如此,如果一方提交的意见对诉讼结果具有决定意义,则要求对其有具体和明确的答复(*Ruiz Torija v. Spain*,§30;*Hiro Balani v. Spain*,§28)。

242. 因此,国内法院需要审查:
- 诉讼当事人的主要论据(*Buzescu v. Romania*,§67;*Donadze v. Georgia* §35);
- 与公约及其议定书所保障的权利和自由相关的抗辩:国内法院必须对此进行严

格细致的审查(*Wagner and J. M. W. L. v. Luxembourg*, §96)。

243. 上诉法院仅通过直接适用特定法律规范驳回就法律要点提出的毫无胜诉希望的上诉请求,未做出进一步解释的,第 6 条第 1 款并不要求其提供更多的详细论证(*Gorou v. Greece*(no. 2)[GC], §41)。

244. 类似地,在有关申请上诉许可(这种许可是上级法院审理该案件及做出最终判决的前提条件)的案件中,第 6 条第 1 款不得被理解为若拒绝许可则必须给出详细的理由[*Kukkonen v. Finland* no. 2, §24; *Bufferne v. France*(dec.)]。

245. 进一步而言,上诉法院驳回请求时,原则上可以仅直接赞同下级法院判决中的理由(*Garcia Ruiz v. Spain*[GC], §26;反例 *Tatishvili v. Russia*, §62)。但是,如果国内法院对其决定给出了很少的理由,那么程序公正的理念要求它必须在事实上处理了提交给其处理的核心事项——无论是通过合并下级法院理由的方式或是通过其他方式,且没有未经进一步判断便草率认同下级法院提交的意见(*Helle v. Finland*, §60)。当诉讼当事人在国内诉讼中不能在审判中进行口头陈述时,上述要求显得更为重要(*Helle v. Finland*)。

二、公开审讯

> **第 6 条第 1 款**
> "在决定某人的公民权利和义务或者在决定对某人确定任何刑事罪名时,任何人有权在合理的时间内受到依法设立的独立而公正的审判机构的公平且公开的审讯。判决应当公开宣布。但是,基于对民主社会中的道德、公共秩序或者国家安全的利益,以及对民主社会中的少年的利益或者是保护当事人的私生活权利的考虑,或者是法院认为,在特殊情况下,如果公开审讯将损害公平利益的话,可以拒绝记者和公众参与旁听全部或者部分审讯。"

(一)审讯

246. 一般原则:原则上,若不存在第 6 条第 1 款中规定的例外情形(见前文,进一步的分析见下文),诉讼当事人应当有权受到公开审讯。公开审讯保护诉讼当事人免于遭受未经公众监督的秘密司法。司法透明有利于第 6 条第 1 款目的的实现,即公正审判

(*Diennet v. France*, §33; *Martinie v. France* [GC], §39)。

247. 要确定审判是否符合公开性要求,需要对诉讼程序进行整体考察(*Axen v. Germany*, §28)。

248. 在一审程序中,第6条第1款规定的"公开的审讯"要求必须进行"口头审讯"[*Fredin v. Sweden*(no.2), §§21-22; *Allan Jacobsson v. Sweden*(no.2), §46; *Göç v. Turkey*[GC], §47],除非具有可以不公开审讯的特殊情形[*Hesse-Anger v. Germany*, (dec.)]。

249. 在例外的情形下,省略口头审讯可能合理,这与有资质的国内法院判决所涉及的问题的实质相关,而与这些情形发生的频率无关(*Miller v. Sweden*, §29; *Martinie v. France* [GC], §41)。

250. 基于相关诉讼程序的特殊性,在二审或三审中可以不进行审讯,前提是一审中已经进行过审讯(*Helmers v. Sweden*, §36,相反见§§38-39)。因此,请求准许上诉的程序以及仅涉及法律问题的程序中,即使上诉法院或最高法院未给予上诉人被审讯的机会,也可能不违反第6条的规定(*Miller v. Sweden*, §30)。

251. 相应地,除非有法定的特殊情形,第6条第1款规定的公开审讯权要求在各级审判中至少有一次口头审讯(*Fischer v. Austria*, §44; *Salomonsson v. Sweden*, §36)。

252. 根据一般且绝对的原则,在非公开状态下进行的关于案件实体的民事诉讼,如果诉讼当事人基于其案件特殊性不能要求进行公开审讯,这类诉讼不得在原则上被认为符合第6条第1款;除了在完全例外情形中,诉讼当事人必须至少有要求公开审讯的机会,即使法院可以基于案件情形和恰当的原因予以拒绝(*Martinie v. France* [GC], §42)。

253. 最后,诉讼关键阶段审讯的欠缺能或者不能在后续阶段得到有效救济(*Le Compte, Van Leuven and De Meyere v. Belgium*, §§60-61; *Malhous v. the Czech Republic*[GC], §62)。

254. 具体应用:

- 若不存在有必要进行审讯的与可信度相关的事项或存疑的证据,且法院能够公平合理地基于诉讼双方的意见和其他材料对案件作出决定的,审讯可以不必进行(*Döry v. Sweden*, §37; *Saccoccia v. Austria*, §73);
- 本法院还接受,在仅涉及较少或简单的法律本身的争议的案件中,也可以不进行审讯(*Allan Jacobsson v. Sweden*(no. 2),§§48 – 49; *Valová and Others v. Slovakia*,§§65 – 68)[*Varela Assalino v. Portugal*(dec.); *Speil v. Austria*(dec.)];

- 这也适用于技术含量较高的问题。本法院曾处理过有关社会安全利益的争议的技术问题,相较于口头辩论,用书面方式处理这些问题更有效。本法院多次表示,出于效率和经济的考虑,国家机关可以避免在这个领域采用公开审讯的方式,原因在于机械地采用审讯的方式可能对有关社会安全的诉讼所要求的特定注意事项构成妨碍(*Schuler-Zgraggen v. Switzerland*,§58; *Döry v. Sweden*,§41;反例参见 *Salomonsson v. Sweden*,§§39 – 40)。

255. 相反,在下列情形中,进行口头审讯被认为是必要的:当法院的管辖权延伸至法律争议以及重要的事实争议(*Fischer v. Austria*,§44),或关于审查权力机关是否正确确认事实(*Malhous v. the Czech Republic*[GC],§60),在要求法院获取对申诉人的个人印象从而给予申诉人个人或通过代表阐述其个人状况的权利(*Miller v. Sweden*,§34 最后;*Andersson v. Sweden*,§57)——如必须听取申诉人与赔偿级别相关的个人遭遇时(*Göç v. Turkey*[GC],§51; *Lorenzetti v. Italy*,§33),或通过此种方法使得法院能够对部分争议点予以澄清时[*Fredin v. Sweden*(no. 2),§22; *Lundevall v. Sweden*,§39]。

256. 媒体和公众的出席:获得公开审讯的权利原则上要求在相关法院进行公开审讯。但第6条第1款并不禁止法院基于案件特殊情形而决定排除适用该原则(*Martinie v. France*[GC],§40)。第6条第1款文本中包含了若干例外情形。

257. "可以拒绝媒体和公众参与旁听全部或部分审讯":

- "出于对民主社会中的道德、公共秩序或者国家安全利益的考虑"(*Zagorodnikov v. Russia*,§26;*B. and P. v. the United Kingdom*,§39);
- "出于对未成人年利益或当事人私生活的保护":在有关未成年人在父母分居后的住所问题或者家庭成员之间的矛盾的案件中,会涉及到对未成年人利益或诉讼方私生活的保护(*B. and P. v. the United Kingdom*,§38);但是,在涉及将儿童移交公共机构的案件中,必须对将案件排除在公众监督之外的原因进行仔细审查(*Moser v. Austria*,§97)。至于针对医生的纪律程序,尽管对职业秘密和患者私生活的保护可以作为不公开审讯的正当理由,但这必须要限制在极其严格的条件下(*Diennet v. France*,§34;以及在一个针对律师的诉讼中,*Hurter v.*

Switzerland,§§30－32)。

- "再或者是,在特殊情况下,法院认为公开审讯会损害公正利益":通过限制诉讼的公开性来保护目击者的安全和隐私或者为追求正义而促进信息和意见的交流是可行的(B. and P. v. the United Kingdom,§38;Osinger v. Austria,§45)。

258. 对公开审讯权的放弃:无论是从文本还是精神来看,第6条第1款都未禁止个人自愿明示或默示放弃公开审讯权,但这种放弃必须以明确方式做出,且不得违背任何重要的公共利益(Le Compte,Van Leuven and De Meyere v. Belgium,§59;Håkansson and Sturesson v. Sweden,§66;Exel v. the Czech Republic,§46)。出庭传票必须被及时接收(Yakovlev v. Russia,§§20－22)。

259. 放弃权利的条件:当事人必须基于其自由意志(Albert and Le Compte v. Belgium,§35)做出同意(Le Compte,Van Leuven and De Meyere v. Belgium,§59)的决定。权利放弃可以明示或默示的方式做出(Le Compte,Van Leuven and De Meyere v. Belgium,§59),但必须采取明确的方式(Albert and Le Compte v. Belgium,§35;Håkansson and Sturesson v. Sweden,§67),且不得违背任何重要的公共利益(Håkansson and Sturesson v. Sweden,§66)。

260. 请求进行公开审讯失败并不必然意味着当事人已经放弃了该项权利,必须结合相关国内法予以考察(Exel v. the Czech Republic,§47;Göç v. Turkey[GC],§48)。如果可适用的国内法明确排除了公开审讯的可能性,那么申诉人是否请求进行公开审讯就不具有相关性(Eisenstecken v. Austria,§33)。

261. 例如,在纪律程序中放弃公开审讯的权利:Le Compte,Van Leuven and De Meyere v. Belgium,§59;H. v. Belgium,§54。明确表示放弃公开审讯权:Schuler-Zgraggen v. Switzerland,§58;反例参见 Exel v. the Czech Republic,§§48－53。

(二)宣判

262. 诉讼程序的公开性保护诉讼当事人免于遭受未经公共监督的秘密司法(Fazliyski v. Bulgaria,§69,关于被保密的案件——违反公约)。这也是保持司法公信力的方式(Pretto and Others v. Italy,§21)。

263. 第6条第1款规定"判决应当公开宣布",这表明判决需要在公开的法庭中被宣读。但本法院认为"其他宣布判决的方式"也可能符合第6条第1款的要求(Moser

v. Austria，§101）。

264. 要确定国内法规定的公开形式是否符合第6条第1款对公开宣判的要求，"必须基于该诉讼程序的特点以及第6条第1款的立法目的，在国内法下对各案件中判决的公开形式做出审查"（Pretto and Others v. Italy，§26，Axen v. Germany，§31）。第6条第1款追求的目标，也就是确保公众对司法的监督从而保障获得公正审判的权利，必须在诉讼过程的整体上得以实现（Axen v. Germany，§32）。

265. 判决未被公开宣布的，必须确定其是否通过其他方式满足了必要的公开性。

266. 在下列案件中，通过公开宣布之外的其他方式实现了足够的公开性。

- 上级法院未公开发布驳回基于法律提出的上诉的决定：要确定上诉法院做出判决的方法是否符合第6条第1款的规定，必须考虑国内法律体系中实行的该诉讼程序的整体以及该法院所扮演的角色（Pretto and Others v. Italy，§27）。在认定没有违反第6条第1款时，本法院格外注意了诉讼的级别和这些法院受到的监督——仅限于法律层面，以及他们发布的完全支持下级法院决定、对针对申诉人的结果不做出任何改变的判决。基于这些考虑，本法院认为，国内法院通过将判决放置于法院书记处，使判决全文为公众所知，因此符合公开宣判的要求（Pretto and Others v. Italy，§§27-28），这同样适用于上级法院未经审讯而决定维持下级法院已经公开宣布过的判决的情形（Axen v. Germany，§32）；

- 初审法院：初审法院通过审讯而做出判决但并未向公众发布，而上诉法院公开发布了一项概括并支持该初审法院决定的判决，此案中本法院认为不存在违反公约的行为（Lamanna v. Austria，§§33-34）；

- 有关儿童安置问题的案件：国内当局为了保护儿童和诉讼方的隐私以及避免损害公正利益，而在法官办公室进行审理程序的做法，是具有正当性的，如果公开宣读判决，就会在很大程度上阻碍这些目的的实现。如果任何利害相关人都可以查询或复印决定全文，对涉及特殊利益的内容进行常规公布，从而使得公众能够研究国内法院处理这些案件的方式以及所适用的原则，那么就能满足第6条第1款对于公开宣判的要求（B. and P. v. the United Kingdom，§47）。

267. 在下列案件中，未公布判决内容，违反了公约规定。

- 在某儿童的亲属和公共机构之间就有关儿童安置问题的案件中：赋予在本案中具有诉讼利益的当事人接触文件的权利，并且公布涉及特殊利益的决定（大多是由上诉法院或最高法院做出),不满足第6条第1款对公开性的要求(*Moser v. Austria*,§§102 – 103);
- 一审或者二审法院在法官办公室审理拘留赔偿请求,未公开发布也未以其他方式公开其决定(*Werner v. Austria*,§§56 – 60)。

268. 仅判决的重要部分被公开宣读:必须确定公众是否能通过其他方式了解未经宣读的判决,必须审查公开的方式是否足以将判决置于公众的监督之下(*Ryakib Biryukov v. Russia*,§§38 – 46,所引用的参考见§§33 – 36)。公众无法得知申诉人的诉请被拒绝的原因,因此第6条第1款所追求的目的未得到实现(*Ryakib Biryukov v. Russia*,§45)。

三、诉讼期间

> **第6条第1款**
> "在决定某人的民事权利和义务……时,任何人有权在合理的时间内受到……审判机构的审讯……"

269. 公约通过要求在"合理时间"内审理案件,强调了及时司法的重要性,延迟审理可能会损害司法的效率和信用(*H. v. France*,§58;*Katte Klitsche de la Grange v. Italy*,§61)。第6条第1款要求缔约国通过其司法体系来确保国内法院符合公约的各项要求。

270. 本法院多次强调及时司法的重要性(*Scordino v. Italy*(no. 1)[GC],§224)。国家多次违反此要求会构成对公约的违反(*Bottazzi v. Italy*[GC],§22)。

(一)诉讼期间的确定

271. 关于相关时间段的起始点,一般而言,期间从案件提交到国内法院时起算(*Poiss v. Austria*,§50;*Bock v. Germany*,§35),除非在法院程序开始前必须向行政机关提出前置性申请,这种情况下诉讼期间可包括强制的前置性行政程序的时间(*König v. Germany*,§98;*X. v. France*,§31;*Kress v. France*[GC],§90)。

272. 因此,在某些情形中,在受诉法院发布令状之前,诉讼期间便开始计算(*Golder v. the United Kingdom*,§32;*Erkner and Hofauer v. Austria*,§64;*Vilho Eskelinen and Others v. Finland*[GC],§65)。但是,这是例外情形,而且只有当特定前置步骤对诉讼

程序必不可少时方可适用(*Blake v. the United Kingdom*,§40)。

273. 第6条第1款也适用于非完全司法性但与司法机构的监督密切相关的程序。例如,由两名公证员操作的非讼性的、但需法院命令和同意的财产分割程序(*Siegel v. France*,§§33-38)。因此,公证程序持续的时间也被纳入合理诉讼期间。

274. 至于期间的终止,一般而言包含整个诉讼持续的期间,包括上诉程序(*König v. Germany*,§98),并持续至最终决定做出之时(*Poiss v. Austria*,§50)。因此,合理时间要求适用于旨在解决纠纷的诉讼的各个阶段,包括判决做出之后的阶段(*Robins v. the United Kingdom*,§§28-29)。

275. 在计算诉讼持续期间时,任何法院做出的判决的执行也被认为是诉讼程序的一部分(*Martins Moreira v. Portugal*,§44;*Silva Pontes v. Portugal*,§33;*Di Pede v. Italy*,§24)。直到诉讼中确认的权利得以实现时,诉讼持续期间方停止计算(*Estima Jorge v. Portugal*,§§36-38)。

276. 若宪法法院的决定能够影响普通法院处理争议的结果,即使其对实体内容不具有管辖权,其审理的诉讼程序也应纳入考虑范围(*Deumeland v. Germany*,§77;*Pammel v. Germany*,§§51-57;*Süßmann v. Germany*[GC],§39)。但是,对普通法院而言,不得用此种方法解释在合理时间内审理案件的义务(*Süßmann v. Germany*[GC],§56;*Oršuš and Others v. Croatia*[GC],§109)。

277. 最后,关于民事诉讼中第三方的干预,需注意如下区别:若申诉人代表本人对国内诉讼程序进行干预,则应当考量的时间从干预发生之日起算,若申诉人声明了其作为继承人继续进行诉讼的意愿,则其可对诉讼全过程提出抗议[*Scordino v. Italy*(no.1),§220]。

(二)对合理时间要求的审查

1. 原则

278. 在特定案件中进行审查:第6条第1款意义上的诉讼时间的合理性必须在个案中基于具体情形予以审查(*Frydlender v. France*[GC],§43),这也可能需要整体性衡量(*Obermeier v. Austria*,§72;*Comingersoll S. A. v. Portugal*[GC],§23)。

279. 必须考量整个诉讼过程(*König v. Germany*,§98)。

- 尽管不同的延迟本身可能并不导致任何问题,但当对这些延迟累加起来考量时,就有可能超过了合理时间(*Deumeland v. Germany*,§90)。

- 在诉讼特定阶段的延迟是可以被允许的,前提是诉讼期间整体上未超过合理范围(*Pretto and Others v. Italy*,§37)。
- 本法院不接受"诉讼长期停滞且……"无任何解释的情形(*Beaumartin v. France*,§33)。

280. 第6条第1款是否可适用于诉前程序取决于是否满足特定条件(*Micallef v. Malta*[GC],§§83 – 86)。①

281. 将问题转交欧洲共同体/欧盟法院进行先行裁决的程序的时间不纳入考虑范围(*Pafitis and Others v. Greece*,§95)。

2. 标准

282. 诉讼期间的合理性必须根据本法院判例法中确立的如下标准进行审查:案件复杂性、申诉人和有关当局的行为,以及申诉人在争议中受到损害的权利(*Comingersoll S. A. v. Portugal*[GC];[GC],§43;*Sürmeli v. Germany*[GC],§128)。

(1)案件复杂性。

283. 案件的复杂性包含事实层面和法律层面(*Katte Klitsche de la Grange v. Italy*,§55;*Papachelas v. Greece*[GC]§39)。例如,案件由多方参与(*H. v. the United Kingdom*,§72),或者需要获取多项证据(*Humen v. Poland*[GC]§63)。

284. 国内诉讼程序的复杂性可能解释其诉讼期间(*Tierce v. San Marino*,§31)。

(2)申诉人的行为。

285. 第6条第1款并未要求申诉人积极配合司法机关,也不得因申诉人未充分利用国内可行的救济手段而对其进行责难(*Erkner and Hofauer v. Austria*,§68)。

286. 相关当事人仅被要求在与其相关的诉讼阶段尽到勤勉职责,不得使用拖延战术,并利用国内法提供的手段来缩短诉讼时间(*Unión Alimentaria Sanders S. A. v. Spain*,§35)。

287. 申诉人的行为属于不可归咎于应诉国的客观事实,在确定是否超过第6条第1款规定的合理时间时,必须将该行为纳入考虑范围(*Poiss v. Austria*,§57;*Wiesinger v. Austria*,§57;*Humen v. Poland*[GC],§66)。申诉人的行为本身不得作为诉讼进展缓慢的理由。

---

① 参见"范围"部分。

288. 与申诉人行为有关的例子包括如下几种情形。

- 当事方提交意见时行动迟缓，构成诉讼进程缓慢的关键原因（*Vernillo v. France*，§34）；
- 频繁/重复更换律师（*König v. Germany*，§103）；
- 影响诉讼进行的请求或疏漏（*Acquaviva v. France*，§61）；
- 试图达成友好和解（*Pizzetti v. Italy* §18；*Laino v. Italy* [GC]§22）；
- 错误地将案件提交至缺乏管辖权的法院进行诉讼（*Beaumartin v. France*，§33）。

289. 尽管国内当局不应对被告的行为负责，但诉讼一方所使用的拖延战术并不能免除当局确保诉讼在合理时间内进行的义务（*Mincheva v. Bulgaria*，§68）。

（3）有关当局的行为。

290. 仅当迟延可归责于国家时，此迟延所构成的对"合理时间"要求的违反才具有正当性（*Buchholz v. Germany*，§49；*Papageorgiou v. Greece*，§40；*Humen v. Poland* [GC]，§66）。国家对其所有机构负责：不仅是司法机关，还包括所有公共机构（*Martins Moreira v. Portugal*，§60）。

291. 即使在实行由诉讼当事方启动诉讼这一原则的法律体系中，当事方的态度也不能免除第6条第1款所要求的法院确保诉讼迅速而有效进行的义务（*Pafitis and Others v. Greece*，§93；*Tierce v. San Marino*，§31；*Sürmeli v. Germany* [GC]，§129）。

292. 这也适用于诉讼中需要专家配合的情形：法官有责任对案件进行准备并使审判快速进行（*Capuano v. Italy*，§§30–31；*Versini v. France*，§29；*Sürmeli v. Germany* [GC]，§129）。

293. 由缔约国建立其自身的法律体系，从而使其国内法院能够保障所有人在合理时间内获得关于民事权利义务争议的最终决定（*Sürmeli v. Germany* [GC]；*Scordino v. Italy*（no.1）[GC]，§183）。

294. 尽管这项义务也适用于宪法法院，但适用方式不同于普通法院。宪法法院所具有的宪法卫士的角色使得其尤其有必要考虑除案件被提交的时间顺序之外的其他因素，如案件性质以及案件的政治和社会重要性（比较 *Süßmann v. Germany* [GC]，§§56–58；*Voggenreiter v. Germany*，§§51–52；*Oršuš and Others v. Croatia* [GC]，§109）。进一步而言，尽管第6条第1款要求司法程序快速且有效进行，但其也强调司法公正这一基本原则(*Von Maltzan and Others v. Germany*(dec.)[GC],§132)。但是,长期的超负荷也不能赋予诉讼超时以正当性(*Probstmeier v. Germany*,§64)。

295. 由于是由成员国建立其自身的法律体系从而保障在合理时间内获得司法判决的权利,因此超额的工作量不得作为考虑因素(*Vocaturo v. Italy*,§17;*Cappello v. Italy*,§17)。但是,临时的业务积压并不导致国家的责任,前提是国家已采取合理及时的补救措施处理此类特殊情形(*Buchholz v. Germany*,§51)。可被视为临时性权宜手段的方式,包括采用特定顺序处理案件——不仅考虑案件提交的日期,还考虑案件的紧急和重要程度,以及当事人受损害的权利。但是,如果此类事项的处理被延长且变成了结构组织问题,上述方式便不再满足要求,国家必须确保采取有效应对措施(*Zimmermann and Steiner v. Switzerland*,§29;*Guincho v. Portugal*,§40)。这种积压成为普遍情形的事实也不能使诉讼超时具备正当性(*Unión Alimentaria Sanders S. A. v. Spain*,§40)。

296. 进一步而言,旨在加快案件审查的改革也不能使迟延具备正当性,因为国家有义务通过能避免延长未决案件审查时间的方式,来保障这些措施的生效和实施(*Fisanotti v. Italy*,§22)。在这一点上,要衡量成员国为了避免或解决超时诉讼而采用的救济手段是否适当,必须结合本法院所确立的各项原则进行审查(*Scordino v. Italy*(no.1)[GC],§178及之后以及§223)。

297. 在某案件中,司法活动过度关注申诉人的精神状态,国家对违反合理时间的要求负责。此案中,尽管已有五份报告表明申诉人意识正常,且其对两份监护申请不予理睬,国内法院仍对申诉人的精神状况抱有怀疑;而且,这项诉讼持续时间超过9年(*Bock v. Germany*,§47)。

298. 法庭成员的罢工并不免除缔约国遵守合理时间要求的义务;但是,在确定缔约国是否遵守此要求时,应当考虑国家所做出的旨在减少迟延的努力(*Papageorgiou v. Greece*,§47)。

299. 频繁更换法官而减缓诉讼进程的——因为每一名法官都要重新熟悉案件情况,国家要对违反合理时间要求负责,因为国家有义务合理组织其司法行政机构的活动(*Lechner and Hess v. Austria*,§58)。

(4)争议中受到损害的权利。

300. 基于其自身性质而要求得到快速有效审理的案件类型示例如下:

- 有关民事地位和民事能力的案件要求特别勤勉(*Bock v. Germany*,§49;*Laino*

v. Italy[GC], §18; *Mikulić v. Croatia*, §44);

- 儿童监护案件必须快速处理(*Hokkanen v. Finland*, §72; *Niederböster v. Germany*, §39),尤其是当时间流逝会对亲子关系造成不可恢复的影响时(*Tsikakis v. Germany*, §§64 & 68),与此相类似,关于家长责任和合同权利的案件也需要特别快速审理(*Paulsen-Medalen and Svensson v. Sweden*, §39; *Laino v. Italy*[GC], §22);

- 职业纠纷基于其性质而要求快速审理(*Vocaturo v. Italy*, §17),无论争议事项是自由职业(*Thlimmenos v. Greece*[GC], §§60 & 62)、申诉人的全部职业生计(*König v. Germany*, §111)、申诉人职业的持续性(*Garcia v. France*, §14)、对解雇的上诉(*Buchholz v. Germany*, §52; *Frydlender v. France*[GC], §45)、申诉人被停职(*Obermeier v. Austria*, §72)、调任(*Sartory v. France*, §34)或复职(*Ruotolo v. Italy*, §117),或者是主张的数量对申诉人具有突出重要性(*Doustaly v. France*, §48)。这一类型中也包括养老金争议(*Borgese v. Italy*, §18);

- 在申诉人遭受"绝症"并且"寿命缩短"的案件中,当局必须极其勤勉(*X. v. France*, §47; *A. and Others v. Denmark*, §§78–81)。

301. 其他案例

- 在审查个人声称其遭受警察暴力迫害的控诉时,相关司法机关必须尤其尽职和勤勉(*Caloc v. France*, §120);

- 在申诉人以残疾保障金作为主要生活来源的案件中,申诉人由于健康状况恶化而要求增加保障金的诉讼程序对其而言具有相当的重要性,因此国内机构必须在此案中表现出特殊的勤勉(*Mocié v. France*, §22);

- 一名65岁的申诉人遭受了人身伤害,作为民事主体提起赔偿之诉,针对申诉人受损害的权利要求国内机构表现出特殊的勤勉(*Codarcea v. Romania*, §89)。

- 申诉人受损害的权利也可以是受教育权(*Oršuš and Others v. Croatia*[GC], §109)。

援引案例一览

本指南援引的判例法涉及欧洲人权法院的判决或裁定以及欧洲人权委员会的决定或报告。

除非另行指明,所有参考皆是本法院审判庭依法做出的判决。缩写"(dec.)"是指该处援引为本法院裁定,"[GC]"是指该案件由大审判庭审判。

本指南电子版中援引案例的超链接直接跳转 HUDOC 数据库〈http://hudoc.echr.coe.int〉。该数据库提供本法院(包括大审判庭、审判庭和委员会的判决、裁定和相关案例、咨询意见以及案例法信息注解中的法律总结)、委员会(决定和报告)和部长委员会(决议)的判例法。本法院以英语和/或法语这两种官方语言发布判决和裁定。HUDOC 也包含许多重要案例的近 30 种非官方语言的翻译,以及由第三方制作的大约 100 个在线案例汇总的链接。

(注:为了避免重复,本章所附的相关案例索引没有在中文部分进行翻译,读者可在对应的英文部分阅读。)

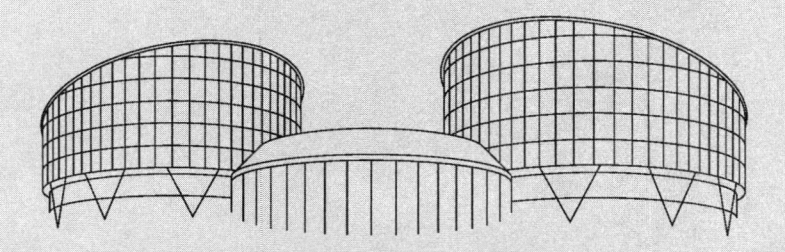

EUROPEAN COURT OF HUMAN RIGHTS
COUR EUROPÉENNE DES DROITS DE L'HOMME

Chapter Ⅲ   Guide on Article 6 of the European Convention on Human Rights Right to A Fair Trial

(Civil Limb)

COUNCIL OF EUROPE
CONSEIL DE L'EUROPE

Publishers or organisations wishing to reproduce this report (or a translation thereof) in print or online are asked to contactpublishing@echr.coe.int for further instructions.

This Guide has been prepared by the Research and Library Division, within the Directorate of the Jurisconsult, and does not bind the Court. The text was finalised on 30 April 2013; it may be subject to editorial revision.

The document is available for downloading at < www.echr.coe.int > (Case-Law-Case-Law Analysis-Case-Law Guides).

For publication updates please follow the Court's Twitter account at < https:/twitter.com/echrpublication >.

©Council of Europe/European Court of Human Rights, 2013

Note to readers

This Guide is part of the series of Case-Law Guides published by the European Court of Human Rights (hereafter "the Court", "the European Court" or "the Strasbourg Court") to inform legal practitioners about the fundamental judgments delivered by the Strasbourg Court. This particular Guide analyses and sums up the case-law under Article 6 (civil limb) of the European Convention on Human Rights (hereafter "the Convention" or "the European Convention") until 30 April 2013. Readers will find the key principles in this area and the relevant precedents.

The case-law cited has been selected among the leading, major, and/or recent judgments and decisions. *

The Court's judgments serve not only to decide those cases brought before the Court but, more generally, to elucidate, safeguard and develop the rules instituted by the Convention, thereby contributing to the observance by the States of the engagements undertaken by them as Contracting Parties (*Ireland v. the United Kingdom*, § 154, 18 January 1978, Series A no. 25.). The mission of the system set up by the Convention is thus to determine, in the general interest, issues of public policy, thereby raising the standards of protection of human rights and extending human rights jurisprudence throughout the community of the Convention States (*Konstantin Markin v. Russia* [GC], § 89, no. 30078/06, ECHR 2012).

---

* The case-law cited may be in either or both of the official languages (English and French) of the Court and the European Commission of Human Rights. Unless otherwise indicated, all references are to a judgment on the merits delivered by a Chamber of the Court. The abbreviation "(dec.)" indicates that the citation is of a decision of the Court and "[GC]" that the case was heard by the Grand Chamber.

Article 6 of the Convention-Right to a fair trial

"1. In the determination of his civil rights and obligations or of any criminal charge against him, everyone is entitled to a fair and public hearing within a reasonable time by an independent and impartial tribunal established by law. Judgment shall be pronounced publicly but the press and public may be excluded from all or part of the trial in the interests of morals, public order or national security in a democratic society, where the interests of juveniles or the protection of the private life of the parties so require, or to the extent strictly necessary in the opinion of the court in special circumstances where publicity would prejudice the interests of justice.

2. Everyone charged with a criminal offence shall be presumed innocent until proved guilty according to law.

3. Everyone charged with a criminal offence has the following minimum rights:

(a) to be informed promptly, in a language which he understands and in detail, of the nature and cause of the accusation against him;

(b) to have adequate time and facilities for the preparation of his defence;

(c) to defend himself in person or through legal assistance of his own choosing or, if he has not sufficient means to pay for legal assistance, to be given it free when the interests of justice so require;

(d) to examine or have examined witnesses against him and to obtain the attendance and examination of witnesses on his behalf under the same conditions as witnesses against him;

(e) to have the free assistance of an interpreter if he cannot understand or speak the language used in court."

I. Scope: the concept of "civil rights and obligations"

> Article 6 § 1 of the Convention
> "1. In the determination of his civil rights and obligations..., everyone is entitled to a...hearing...by [a] tribunal..."

A. General requirements for applicability of Article 6 § 1

1. The concept of "civil rights and obligations" cannot be interpreted solely by reference to the respondent State's domestic law; it is an "autonomous" concept deriving from the Convention. Article 6 § 1 of the Convention applies irrespective of the parties' status, the character of the legislation which governs how the "dispute" is to be determined, and the character of the authority which has jurisdiction in the matter (*Georgiadis v. Greece*, § 34).

2. However, the principle that the autonomous concepts contained in the Convention must be interpreted in the light of present-day conditions does not give the Court power to interpret Article 6 § 1 as though the adjective "civil" (with the restrictions which the adjective necessarily places on the category of "rights and obligations" to which that Article applies) were not present in the text (*Ferrazzini v. Italy* [GC], § 30).

3. The applicability of Article 6 § 1 in civil matters firstly depends on the existence of a "dispute" (in French, "*contestation*"). Secondly the dispute must relate to "rights and obligations" which, arguably at least, can be said to be recognised under domestic law. Lastly these "rights and obligations" must be "civil" ones within the meaning of the Convention, although Article 6 does not itself assign any specific content to them in the Contracting States' legal systems (*James and Others v. the United Kingdom*, § 81).

1. The term "dispute"

4. The word "dispute" must be given a substantive meaning rather than a formal one

(*Le Compte, Van Leuven and De Meyere v. Belgium*, § 45). It is necessary to look beyond the appearances and the language used and concentrate on the realities of the situation according to the circumstances of each case (*Gorou v. Greece* (no. 2) [GC], § 29; *Boulois v. Luxembourg* [GC], § 92). Article 6 does not apply to a non-contentious and unilateral procedure which does not involve opposing parties and which is available only where there is no dispute over rights [*Alaverdyan v. Armenia* (dec.), § 35].

5. The "dispute" must be genuine and of a serious nature (*Sporrong and Lönnroth v. Sweden*, § 81). This rules out, for example, civil proceedings taken against prison authorities on account of the mere presence in the prison of HIV-infected prisoners [*Skorobogatykh v. Russia* (dec.)]. For example, the Court held a "dispute" to be real in a case concerning a request to the public prosecutor to lodge an appeal on points of law, as it formed an integral part of the whole of the proceedings that the applicant had joined as a civil party with a view to obtaining compensation (*Gorou v. Greece* (no. 2) [GC], § 35).

6. The dispute may relate not only to the actual existence of a right but also to its scope or the manner in which it is to be exercised (*Benthem v. the Netherlands*, § 32). It may also concern matters of fact.

7. The result of the proceedings must be directly decisive for the right in question [*Ulyanov v. Ukraine* (dec.)]. Consequently, a tenuous connection or remote consequences are not enough to bring Article 6 § 1 into play (*Boulois v. Luxembourg* [GC], § 90). For example, the Court found that proceedings challenging the legality of extending a nuclear power station's operating licence did not fall within the scope of Article 6 § 1 because the connection between the extension decision and the right to protection of life, physical integrity and property was "too tenuous and remote", the applicants having failed to show that they personally were exposed to a danger that was not only specific but above all imminent (*Balmer-Schafroth and Others v. Switzerland*, § 40; *Athanassoglou and Others v. Switzerland* [GC], §§ 46 – 55; *Sdružení Jihočeské Matky v. the Czech Republic* (dec.). For a case concerning limited noise pollution at a factory, see *Zapletal v. the Czech Republic* (dec.). For the hypothetical environmental impact of a plant for treatment of mining waste, see *Ivan Atanasov v. Bulgaria*, §§ 90 – 95. Similarly, proceedings which

two public-sector employees brought to challenge one of their colleagues' appointment to a post could have only remote effects on their civil rights, specifically, their own right to appointment [*Revel and Mora v. France* (dec.)].

8. In contrast, the Court found Article 6 § 1 to be applicable to a case concerning the building of a dam which would have flooded the applicants' village (*Gorraiz Lizarraga and Others v. Spain*, § 46) and to a case about the operating permit for a gold mine using cyanidation leaching near the applicants' villages (*Taşkın and Others v. Turkey*, § 133; see also *Zander v. Sweden*, §§ 24 – 25). More recently, in a case regarding the appeal submitted by a local environmental-protection association for judicial review of a planning permission, the Court found that there was a sufficient link between the dispute and the right claimed by the legal entity, in particular in view of the status of the association and its founders, and the fact that the aim it pursued was limited in space and in substance (*L'Érablière A. S. B. L. v. Belgium*, §§ 28 – 30). Furthermore, proceedings for the restoration of a person's legal capacity are directly decisive for his or her civil rights and obligations (*Stanev v. Bulgaria* [GC], § 233).

2. Existence of an arguable right in domestic law

9. The applicant must be able to claim, on arguable grounds, a right recognised in domestic law (*Masson and Van Zon v. the Netherlands*, § 48; *Gutfreund v. France*, § 41; *Boulois v. Luxembourg* [GC], §§ 90 – 94). Article 6 does not lay down any specific content for a "right" in Contracting States' domestic law, and in principle the Court must refer to domestic law in determining whether a right exists. Whether or not the authorities enjoyed discretion in deciding whether to grant the measure requested by a particular applicant may be taken into consideration and may even be decisive. Nevertheless, the mere fact that the wording of a legal provision affords an element of discretion does not in itself rule out the existence of a right. Other criteria which may be taken into consideration by the Court include the recognition of the alleged right in similar circumstances by the domestic courts or the fact that the latter examined the merits of the applicant's request (ibid., §§ 91 – 101).

10. The Court may decide that rights such as the right to life, to health, to a healthy

environment and to respect for property are recognised in domestic law (*Athanassoglou and Others v. Switzerland* [GC], § 44).

11. The right in question has to have a legal basis in domestic law (*Szücs v. Austria*, § 33).

12. However, it is important to point out that whether a person has an actionable domestic claim may depend not only on the content, properly speaking, of the relevant civil right as defined in national law but also on the existence of procedural bars preventing or limiting the possibilities of bringing potential claims to court. In the latter category of cases, Article 6 § 1 of the Convention may apply (*Al-Adsani v. the United Kingdom* [GC], §§ 47; *McElhinney v. Ireland* [GC], § 25). In principle, though, it cannot have any application to substantive limitations on a right existing under domestic law (*Roche v. the United Kingdom* [GC], § 119). The Convention institutions may not create through the interpretation of Article 6 § 1 a substantive civil right which has no legal basis in the State concerned (ibid., § 117).

13. In deciding whether there is a civil "right" and whether to classify a restriction as substantive or procedural, regard must first be had to the relevant provisions of national law and how the domestic courts interpret them (*Masson and Van Zon v. the Netherlands*, § 49). It is necessary to look beyond the appearances, examine how domestic law classifies the particular restriction and concentrate on the realities (*Van Droogenbroeck v. Belgium*, § 38). Lastly, a final court decision does not necessarily retrospectively deprive applicants' complaints of their arguability (*Le Calvez v. France*, § 56). For instance, the limited scope of the judicial review of an act of foreign policy (NATO air strikes on Serbia) cannot make the applicants' claims against the State retrospectively unarguable, since the domestic courts were called upon to decide for the first time on this issue (*Markovic and Others v. Italy* [GC], §§ 100 – 102).

14. Applying the distinction between substantive limitations and procedural bars in the light of these criteria, the Court has, for example, recognised as falling under Article 6 § 1 civil actions for negligence against the police (*Osman v. the United Kingdom*) or against local authorities (*Z and Others v. the United Kingdom* [GC]) and has considered whether a

particular limitation (exemption from prosecution or non-liability) was proportionate from the standpoint of Article 6 § 1. On the other hand it held that the Crown's exemption from civil liability *vis-à-vis* members of the armed forces derived from a substantive restriction and that domestic law consequently did not recognise a "right" within the meaning of Article 6 § 1 of the Convention (*Roche v. the United Kingdom* [GC], § 124; see also *Hotter v. Austria* (dec.) and *Andronikashvili v. Georgia* (dec.)).

15. The Court has accepted that associations also qualify for protection under Article 6 § 1 if they seek recognition of specific rights and interests of their members (*Gorraiz Lizarraga and Others v. Spain*, § 45) or even of particular rights to which they have a claim as legal persons (such as the right of the "public" to information and to take part in decisions regarding the environment [*Collectif national d'information et d'opposition à l'usine Melox-Collectif Stop Melox and Mox v. France* (dec.)], or when the association's action cannot be regarded as an *actio popularis* (*L'Érablière A. S. B. L. v. Belgium*).

16. Where legislation lays down conditions for admission to an occupation or profession, a candidate who satisfies them has a right to be admitted to the occupation or profession (*De Moor v. Belgium*, § 43). For example, if the applicant has an arguable case that he or she meets the legal requirements for registration as a doctor, Article 6 applies [*Chevrol v. France*, § 55; see, conversely, *Bouilloc v. France* (dec.)]. At all events, when the legality of proceedings concerning a civil right is challengeable by a judicial remedy of which the applicant has made use, it has to be concluded that there was a "dispute" concerning a "civil right" even if the eventual finding was that the applicant did not meet the legal requirements (right to continue practising the medical specialisation which the applicant had taken up abroad; see *Kök v. Turkey*, § 37).

3. "Civil" nature of the right

17. Whether or not a right is to be regarded as civil in the light of the Convention must be determined by reference to the substantive content and effects of the right-and not its legal classification-under the domestic law of the State concerned. In the exercise of its supervisory functions, the Court must also take into account the Convention's object and purpose and the national legal systems of the other Contracting States (*König v. Germany*, § 89).

18. In principle the applicability of Article 6 § 1 to disputes between private individuals which are classified as civil in domestic law is uncontested before the Court (for a judicial separation case, see *Airey v. Ireland*, § 21).

4. Private rights: the pecuniary dimension

19. The Court regards as falling within the scope of Article 6 § 1 proceedings which, in domestic law, come under "public law" and whose result is decisive for private rights and obligations. Such proceedings may, *inter alia*, have to do with permission to sell land (*Ringeisen v. Austria*, § 94), running a private clinic (*König v. Germany*, §§ 94 – 95), building permission (see, *inter alia*, *Sporrong and Lönnroth v. Sweden*, § 79), the ownership and use of a religious building (*Sâmbata Bihor Greco-Catholic Parish v. Romania*, § 65), administrative permission in connection with requirements for carrying on an occupation (*Benthem v. the Netherlands*, § 36), a licence for serving alcoholic beverages (*Tre Traktörer Aktiebolag v. Sweden*, § 43), or a dispute concerning the payment of compensation for a work-related illness or accident (*Chaudet v. France*, § 30).

20. On the same basis Article 6 is applicable to disciplinary proceedings before professional bodies where the right to practise the profession is at stake (*Le Compte, Van Leuven and De Meyere v. Belgium*; *Philis v. Greece* (no. 2), § 45), a negligence claim against the State (*X v. France*), an action for cancellation of an administrative decision harming the applicant's rights (*De Geouffre de la Pradelle v. France*), administrative proceedings concerning a ban on fishing in the applicants' waters (*Alatulkkila and Others v. Finland*, § 49) and proceedings for awarding a tender in which a civil right—such as the right not to be discriminated against on grounds of religious belief or political opinion when bidding for public-works contracts-is at stake [*Tinnelly & Sons Ltd and Others and McElduff and Others v. the United Kingdom*, § 61; contrast *I. T. C. Ltd v. Malta* (dec.)].

21. Article 6 § 1 is applicable to a civil-party complaint in criminal proceedings (*Perez v. France* [GC], §§ 70 – 71), except in the case of a civil action brought purely to obtain private vengeance or for punitive purposes [*Sigalas v. Greece*, § 29; *Mihova v. Italy* (dec.)]. The Convention does not confer any right, as such, to have third parties prosecuted or sentenced for a criminal offence. To fall within the scope of the Convention,

such right must be indissociable from the victim's exercise of a right to bring civil proceedings in domestic law, even if only to secure symbolic reparation or to protect a civil right such as the right to a "good reputation" (*Perez v. France* [GC], § 70; see also, regarding a symbolic award, *Gorou v. Greece* (no. 2) [GC], § 24). Therefore, Article 6 applies to proceedings involving civil-party complaints from the moment the complainant is joined as a civil party, unless he or she has waived the right to reparation in an unequivocal manner.

22. Article 6 § 1 is also applicable to a civil action seeking compensation for ill-treatment allegedly committed by agents of the State (*Aksoy v. Turkey*, § 92).

B. Extension to other types of dispute

23. The Court has held that Article 6 § 1 is applicable to disputes concerning social matters, including proceedings relating to an employee's dismissal by a private firm (*Buchholz v. Germany*), proceedings concerning social-security benefits (*Feldbrugge v. the Netherlands*), even on a non-contributory basis (*Salesi v. Italy*), and also proceedings concerning compulsory social-security contributions (*Schouten and Meldrum v. the Netherlands*). (For the challenging by an employer of the finding that an employee's illness was occupation-related, see *Eternit v. France* (dec.), § 32). In these cases the Court took the view that the private-law aspects predominated over the public-law ones. In addition, it has held that there were similarities between entitlement to a welfare allowance and entitlement to receive compensation for Nazi persecution from a private-law foundation (*Woś v. Poland*, § 76).

24. Disputes concerning public servants fall in principle within the scope of Article 6 § 1. In *Pellegrin v. France* [GC] (§§ 64 – 71), the Court had adopted a "functional" criterion. In its judgment in *Vilho Eskelinen and Others v. Finland* [GC], §§ 50 – 62, it decided to adopt a new approach. The principle is now that there will be a presumption that Article 6 applies, and it will be for the respondent government to demonstrate, firstly, that a civil-servant applicant does not have a right of access to a court under national law and, secondly, that the exclusion of the rights under Article 6 for the civil servant is justified

(§ 62 in particular). If the applicant had access to a court under national law, Article 6 applies (even to active army officers and their claims before the military courts: see *Pridatchenko and Others v. Russia*, § 47). A non-judicial body under domestic law may be qualified as a "court", in the substantive sense of the term, if it quite clearly performs judicial functions (*Oleksandr Volkov v. Ukraine*, §§ 88 – 91). With regard to the second criterion, the exclusion must be justified on "objective grounds in the State's interest"; this obliges the State to show that the subject matter of the dispute in issue is related to the exercise of State power or that it has called into question the special bond between the civil servant and the State. Thus, there can in principle be no justification for the exclusion from the guarantees of Article 6 of ordinary labour disputes, such as those relating to salaries, allowances or similar entitlements, on the basis of the special nature of the relationship between the particular civil servant and the State in question (see, for instance, a dispute regarding police personnel's entitlement to a special allowance in *Vilho Eskelinen and Others v. Finland* [GC]). In the light of the criteria laid down in the *Vilho Eskelinen and Others* judgment, the Court declared Article 6 § 1 to be applicable to proceedings for unfair dismissal instituted by an embassy employee (a secretary and switchboard operator in the Polish embassy: *Cudak v. Lithuania* [GC], §§ 44 – 47; and, to similar effect, a head accountant: *Sabeh El Leil v. France* [GC], § 39), a senior police officer (*Šikić v. Croatia*, §§ 18 – 20) or an army officer in the military courts (*Vasilchenko v. Russia*, §§ 34 – 36), to proceedings regarding the right to obtain the post of parliamentary assistant (*Savino and Others v. Italy*), to disciplinary proceedings against a judge (*Olujić v. Croatia*), to an appeal by a prosecutor against a presidential decree ordering his transfer (*Zalli v. Albania* (dec.) and the other references cited therein), and to proceedings concerning the professional career of a customs officer (right to apply for an internal promotion: *Fiume v. Italy*, §§ 33 – 36).

25. Constitutional disputes may also come within the ambit of Article 6 if the constitutional proceedings have a decisive bearing on the outcome of the dispute (about a "civil" right) in the ordinary courts (*Ruiz-Mateos v. Spain*). This does not apply in the case of disputes relating to a presidential decree granting citizenship to an individual as an

exceptional measure, or to the determination of whether the President has breached his constitutional oath (*Paksas v. Lithuania* [GC], §§ 65 – 66). The criteria governing the application of Article 6 § 1 to an interim measure extend to the Constitutional Court (*Kübler v. Germany*, §§ 47 – 48).

26. Lastly, Article 6 is also applicable to other not strictly pecuniary matters such as the environment, where disputes may arise involving the right to life, to health or to a healthy environment (*Taşkın and Others v. Turkey*); the fostering of children (*McMichael v. the United Kingdom*); children's schooling arrangements (*Ellès and Others v. Switzerland*, §§ 21 – 23); the right to have paternity established (*Alaverdyan v. Armenia* (dec.), § 33); the right to liberty [*Laidin v. France* (no. 2)]; prisoners' detention arrangements (for instance, disputes concerning the restrictions to which prisoners are subjected as a result of being placed in a high-security unit [*Enea v. Italy* [GC], §§ 97 – 107) or in a high-security cell (*Stegarescu and Bahrin v. Portugal*)], or disciplinary proceedings resulting in restrictions on family visits to prison (*Gülmez v. Turkey*, § 30) or other similar restrictions (*Ganci v. Italy*, § 25); the right to a good reputation (*Helmers v. Sweden*); the right of access to administrative documents [*Loiseau v. France* (dec.)], or an appeal against an entry in a police file affecting the right to a reputation, the right to protection of property and the possibility of finding employment and hence earning a living (*Pocius v. Lithuania*, §§ 38 – 46; *Užukauskas v. Lithuania*, §§ 32 – 40); the right to be a member of an association (*Sakellaropoulos v. Greece* (dec.)-similarly, proceedings concerning the lawful existence of an association concern the association's civil rights, even if under domestic legislation the question of freedom of association belongs to the field of public law: see *APEH Üldözötteinek Szövetsége and Others v. Hungary*, §§ 34 – 35); and, lastly, the right to continue higher education studies (*Emine Araç v. Turkey*, §§ 18 – 25), a position which applies *a fortiori* in the context of primary education (*Oršuš and Others v. Croatia* [GC], § 104). Thus, Article 6 extends to proceedings which may unquestionably have a direct and significant impact on the individual's private life (*Alexandre v. Portugal*, §§ 51 and 54).

C. Applicability of Article 6 to proceedings other than main proceedings

27. Preliminary proceedings, like those concerned with the grant of an interim measure such as an injunction, were not normally considered to "determine" civil rights and obligations and did not therefore normally fall within the protection of Article 6 [see, *inter alia*, *Verlagsgruppe News GmbH v. Austria* (dec.) and *Libert v. Belgium* (dec.)]. However, the Court has recently departed from its previous case-law and taken a new approach.

28. In *Micallef v. Malta* ([GC], §§83 – 86), the Court established that the applicability of Article 6 to interim measures will depend on whether certain conditions are fulfilled. Firstly, the right at stake in both the main and the injunction proceedings should be "civil" within the meaning of the Convention. Secondly, the nature of the interim measure, its object and purpose as well as its effects on the right in question should be scrutinised. Whenever an interim measure can be considered effectively to determine the civil right or obligation at stake, notwithstanding the length of time it is in force, Article 6 will be applicable.

29. An interlocutory judgment can be equated to interim or provisional measures and proceedings, and the same criteria are thus relevant to determine whether Article 6 is applicable under its civil head (*Mercieca and Others v. Malta*, §35).

30. Again with reference to the principles established in *Micallef v. Malta* [GC], Article 6 may apply to the stay of execution proceedings in accordance with the above-mentioned criteria (*Central Mediterranean Development Corporation Limited v. Malta* (no. 2), §§21 – 23).

31. Article 6 is applicable to interim proceedings which pursue the same purpose as the pending main proceedings, where the interim injunction is immediately enforceable and entails a ruling on the same right (*RTBF v. Belgium*, §§64 – 65).

32. As regards consecutive criminal and civil proceedings, if a State's domestic law provides for proceedings consisting of two stages-the first where the court rules on whether there is entitlement to damages and the second where it fixes the amount-it is reasonable,

for the purposes of Article 6 § 1, to regard the civil right as not having been "determined" until the precise amount has been decided: determining a right entails ruling not only on the right's existence, but also on its scope or the manner in which it may be exercised, which of course includes assessing the damages (*Torri v. Italy*, § 19).

33. With regard to the execution of court decisions, Article 6 § 1 applies to all stages of legal proceedings for the "determination of…civil rights and obligations", not excluding stages subsequent to judgment on the merits. Execution of a judgment given by any court must therefore be regarded as an integral part of the "trial" for the purposes of Article 6 (*Hornsby v. Greece*, § 40; *Romańczyk v. France*, § 53, concerning the execution of a judgment authorising the recovery of maintenance debts). Regardless of whether Article 6 is applicable to the initial proceedings, an enforcement title determining civil rights does not necessarily have to result from proceedings to which Article 6 is applicable (*Buj v. Croatia*, § 19). The *exequatur* of a foreign court's forfeiture order falls within the ambit of Article 6, under its civil head only [*Saccoccia v. Austria* (dec.)]

34. Applications to have proceedings reopened: Article 6 is not applicable to proceedings concerning an application for the reopening of civil proceedings which have been terminated by a final decision (*Sablon v. Belgium*, § 86). This reasoning also applies to an application to reopen proceedings after the Court has found a violation of the Convention (*Verein gegen Tierfabriken Schweiz (VgT) v. Switzerland* (no. 2), § 24). There was one highly exceptional case, however, in which a procedure denoted in the domestic legal system as an application for the reopening of proceedings was the only legal means of seeking redress in respect of civil claims, and its outcome was thus held to be decisive for the applicant's "civil rights and obligations" (*Melis v. Greece*, §§ 19 – 20).

35. Article 6 has also been declared applicable to a third-party appeal which had a direct impact on the applicants' civil rights and obligations (*Kakamoukas and Others v. Greece* [GC], § 32).

D. Excluded matters

36. Merely showing that a dispute is "pecuniary" in nature is not in itself sufficient to

attract the applicability of Article 6 § 1 under its civil head (*Ferrazzini v. Italy* [GC], § 25).

37. Matters outside the scope of Article 6 include tax proceedings: tax matters still form part of the hard core of public-authority prerogatives, with the public nature of the relationship between the taxpayer and the community remaining predominant (ibid., § 29). Similarly excluded are summary injunction proceedings concerning customs duties or charges [*Emesa Sugar N. V. v. the Netherlands* (dec.)].

38. The same applies, in the immigration field, to the entry, residence and removal of aliens, in relation to proceedings concerning the granting of political asylum or deportation (application for an order quashing a deportation order: see *Maaouia v. France* [GC], § 38; extradition: see *Peñafiel Salgado v. Spain* (dec.); *Mamatkulov and Askarov v. Turkey* [GC], §§ 81 – 83; and an action in damages by an asylum-seeker on account of the refusal to grant asylum: see *Panjeheighalehei v. Denmark* (dec.)), despite the possibly serious implications for private or family life or employment prospects. This inapplicability extends to the inclusion of an alien in the Schengen Information System [*Dalea v. France* (dec.)]. The right to hold a passport and the right to nationality are not civil rights for the purposes of Article 6 [*Smirnov v. Russia* (dec.)]. However, a foreigner's right to apply for a work permit may come under Article 6, both for the employer and the employee, even if, under domestic law, the employee has no *locus standi* to apply for it, provided that what is involved is simply a procedural bar that does not affect the substance of the right (*Jurisic and Collegium Mehrerau v. Austria*, §§ 54 – 62).

39. According to *Vilho Eskelinen and Others v. Finland* [GC], disputes relating to public servants do not fall within the scope of Article 6 when two criteria are met: the State in its national law must have expressly excluded access to a court for the post or category of staff in question, and the exclusion must be justified on objective grounds in the State's interest (§ 62). That was the case of a soldier discharged from the army for breaches of discipline who was unable to challenge his discharge before the courts and whose "special bond of trust and loyalty" with the State had been called into question [*Suküt v. Turkey* (dec.)]. In order for the exclusion to be justified, it is not enough for the State to establish

that the civil servant in question participates in the exercise of public power or that there exists, to use the words of the Court in *Pellegrin*, a "special bond of trust and loyalty" between the civil servant and the State, as employer. It is also for the State to show that the subject matter of the dispute in issue is related to the exercise of State power or that it has called into question the special bond. There can in principle be no justification for the exclusion from the guarantees of Article 6 of ordinary labour disputes, such as those relating to salaries, allowances or similar entitlements, on the basis of the special nature of the relationship between the particular civil servant and the State in question (*Vilho Eskelinen and Others v. Finland* [GC], § 62).

40. Lastly, political rights such as the right to stand for election and retain one's seat (electoral dispute: see *Pierre-Bloch v. France*, § 50), the right to a pension as a former member of Parliament [*Papon v. France* (dec.)], or a political party's right to carry on its political activities [for a case concerning the dissolution of a party, see *Refah Partisi (The Welfare Party) and Others v. Turkey* (dec.)] cannot be regarded as civil rights within the meaning of Article 6 § 1. Similarly, proceedings in which a non-governmental organisation conducting parliamentary-election observations was refused access to documents not containing information relating to the applicant itself fell outside the scope of Article 6 § 1 [*Geraguyn Khorhurd Patgamavorakan Akumb v. Armenia* (dec.)].

41. In addition, the Court recently reaffirmed that the right to report matters stated in open court is not a civil right (*Mackay and BBC Scotland v. the United Kingdom*, §§ 20–22).

42. Conclusion: Where there exists a "dispute" concerning "civil rights and obligations", as defined according to the above-mentioned criteria, Article 6 § 1 secures to the person concerned the right to have any claim relating to his civil rights and obligations brought before a court or tribunal. In this way the Article embodies the "right to a court", of which the right of access, that is the right to institute proceedings before courts in civil matters, constitutes one aspect. To this are added the guarantees laid down by Article 6 § 1 as regards both the organisation and composition of the court and the conduct of the proceedings. In sum, the whole makes up the right to a "fair hearing" (*Golder v. the United Kingdom*, § 36).

II. Right to acourt

> **Article 6 § 1 of the Convention**
> "1. In the determination of his civil rights and obligations..., everyone is entitled to a fair and public hearing within a reasonable time by an independent and impartial tribunal established by law...."

A. Right and access to a court

43. The right to a fair trial, as guaranteed by Article 6 § 1, must be construed in the light of the rule of law, which requires that litigants should have an effective judicial remedy enabling them to assert their civil rights (*Běleš and Others v. the Czech Republic*, § 49).

Everyone has the right to have any claim relating to his "civil rights and obligations" brought before a court or tribunal. In this way Article 6 § 1 embodies the "right to a court", of which the right of access, that is, the right to institute proceedings before courts in civil matters, constitutes one aspect (*Golder v. the United Kingdom*, § 36). The "right to a court" and the right of access are not absolute. They may be subject to limitations, but these must not restrict or reduce the access left to the individual in such a way or to such an extent that the very essence of the right is impaired (*Philis v. Greece* (no. 1), § 59; *De Geouffre de la Pradelle v. France*, § 28; *Stanev v. Bulgaria* [GC], § 229). ①

1. A right that is practical and effective

44. The right of access to a court must be "practical and effective" (*Bellet v. France*, § 38). For the right of access to be effective, an individual must "have a clear, practical

---

① See also the section on "Fairness".

opportunity to challenge an act that is an interference with his rights" (ibid., § 36; *Nunes Dias v. Portugal* (dec.) regarding the rules governing notice to appear). The rules governing the formal steps to be taken and the time-limits to be complied with in lodging an appeal or an application for judicial review are aimed at ensuring a proper administration of justice and compliance, in particular, with the principle of legal certainty (*Cañete de Goñi v. Spain*, § 36). That being so, the rules in question, or their application, should not prevent litigants from using an available remedy (*Miragall Escolano v. Spain*; *Zvolsky and Zvolská v. the Czech Republic*, § 51).

45. In the specific circumstances of a case, the practical and effective nature of this right may be impaired, for instance:

- by the prohibitive cost of the proceedings in view of the individual's financial capacity:
    - the excessive amount of security for costs in the context of an application to join criminal proceedings as a civil party (*Aït-Mouhoub v. France*, §§ 57 – 58; *García Manibardo v. Spain*, §§ 38 – 45);
    - excessive court fees (*Kreuz v. Poland*, §§ 60 – 67); *Podbielski and PPU Polpure v. Poland*, §§ 65 – 66; *Weissman and Others v. Romania*, § 42; and, conversely, *Reuther v. Germany* (dec.);
- by issues relating to time-limits:
    - the time taken to hear an appeal leading to its being declared inadmissible (*Melnyk v. Ukraine*, § 26);
    - where "the fact that the applicants were told that their action was statute-barred at such a late stage of the proceedings, which they had been conducting in good faith and with sufficient diligence, deprived them once and for all of any possibility of asserting their right" (*Yagtzilar and Others v. Greece*, § 27);
- by the existence of procedural bars preventing or limiting the possibilities of applying to a court:
    - a particularly strict interpretation by the domestic courts of a procedural rule (excessive formalism) may deprive applicants of their right of access to a court

(*Pérez de Rada Cavanilles v. Spain*, § 49; *Miragall Escolano v. Spain*, § 38; *Sotiris and Nikos Koutras ATTEE v. Greece*, § 20; *Běleš and Others v. the Czech Republic*, § 50; *RTBF v. Belgium*, § § 71 – 72 and 74);

- the requirements linked to execution of an earlier ruling may impair the right of access to a court, for instance where the applicant's lack of funds makes it impossible for him even to begin to comply with the earlier judgment [*Annoni di Gussola and Others v. France*, § 56; compare with *Arvanitakis v. France* (dec.)];
- procedural rules barring certain subjects of law from taking court proceedings (*The Holy Monasteries v. Greece*, § 83; *Philis v. Greece* (no. 1), § 65; *Lupaş and Others v. Romania*, § § 64 – 67; and, regarding minors lacking capacity, *Stanev v. Bulgaria* [GC], § § 241 – 245). ①

However, again on the subject of formalism, the conditions of admissibility of an appeal on points of law may quite legitimately be stricter than for an ordinary appeal. Given the special nature of the Court of Cassation's role, the procedure followed in the Court of Cassation may be more formal, especially where the proceedings before it follow the hearing of the case by a first-instance court and then a court of appeal, each with full jurisdiction (*Levages Prestations Services v. France*, § § 44 – 48; *Brualla Gómez de la Torre v. Spain*, § § 34 – 39).

46. Furthermore, the right to a court includes not only the right to institute proceedings but also the right to obtain a determination of the dispute by a court (*Kutić v. Croatia*, § § 25 and 32 regarding the staying of proceedings; *Aćimović v. Croatia*, § 41; *Beneficio Cappella Paolini v. San Marino*, § 29 concerning a denial of justice). The right to a court may also be infringed where a court fails to comply with the statutory time-limit in ruling on appeals against a series of decisions of limited duration (*Musumeci v. Italy*, § § 41 – 43) or in the absence of a decision (*Ganci v. Italy*, § 31). The "right to a court" also encompasses the execution of judgments. ②

---

① See also the section on "Legal aid".
② See the section on "Execution".

2. Limitations

47. The right of access to the courts is not absolute but may be subject to limitations permitted by implication (*Golder v. the United Kingdom*, § 38; *Stanev v. Bulgaria* [GC], § 230). This applies in particular where the conditions of admissibility of an appeal are concerned, since by its very nature it calls for regulation by the State, which enjoys a certain margin of appreciation in this regard (*Luordo v. Italy*, § 85).

48. Nonetheless, the limitations applied must not restrict or reduce the access left to the individual in such a way or to such an extent that the very essence of the right is impaired. Furthermore, a limitation will not be compatible with Article 6 § 1 if it does not pursue a "legitimate aim" and if there is not a "reasonable relationship of proportionality between the means employed and the aim sought to be achieved" (*Ashingdane v. the United Kingdom*, § 57; *Fayed v. the United Kingdom*, § 65; *Markovic and Others v. Italy* [GC], § 99).

49. The right of access to a court may also be subject, in certain circumstances, to legitimate restrictions, such as statutory limitation periods (*Stubbings and Others v. the United Kingdom*, § § 51 – 52), security for costs orders (*Tolstoy Miloslavsky v. the United Kingdom*, § § 62 – 67) or a legal representation requirement (*R. P. and Others v. the United Kingdom*, § § 63 – 67).

50. Where access to a court is restricted by law or in practice, the Court examines whether the restriction affects the substance of the right and, in particular, whether it pursues a legitimate aim and whether there is a reasonable relationship of proportionality between the means employed and the aim sought to be achieved; *Ashingdane v. the United Kingdom*, § 57. No violation of Article 6 § 1 can be found if the restriction is compatible with the principles established by the Court.

51. International organisations' immunity from national jurisdiction: this treaty-based rule-which pursues a legitimate aim (*Waite and Kennedy v. Germany* [GC], § 63)-is permissible from the standpoint of Article 6 § 1 only if the restriction stemming from it is not disproportionate. Hence, it will be compatible with Article 6 § 1 if the persons concerned have available to them reasonable alternative means to protect effectively their

rights under the Convention (ibid., §§ 68 – 74; *Prince Hans-Adam II of Liechtenstein v. Germany* [GC], § 48; *Chapman v. Belgium* (dec.), §§ 51 – 56).

52. State immunity: the doctrine of State immunity is generally accepted by the community of nations. Measures taken by a member State which reflect generally recognised rules of public international law on State immunity do not automatically constitute a disproportionate restriction on the right of access to court (*Fogarty v. the United Kingdom* [GC], § 36; *McElhinney v. Ireland* [GC], § 37; *Sabeh El Leil v. France* [GC], § 49).

- State immunity from jurisdiction: In cases where the application of the principle of State immunity from jurisdiction restricts the exercise of the right of access to a court, it must be ascertained whether the circumstances of the case justify such restriction. The restriction must pursue a legitimate aim and be proportionate to that aim (ibid., §§ 51 – 54; *Cudak v. Lithuania* [GC], § 59). The grant of sovereign immunity to a State in civil proceedings pursues the "legitimate aim" of complying with international law to promote comity and good relations between States [*Fogarty v. the United Kingdom* [GC], § 34; *Al-Adsani v. the United Kingdom* [GC], § 54; *Treska v. Albania and Italy* (dec.)]. As to whether the measure taken is proportionate, it may in some cases impair the very essence of the individual's right of access to a court (*Cudak v. Lithuania* [GC], § 74; *Sabeh El Leil v. France* [GC], § 49) while in other cases it may not (*Al-Adsani v. the United Kingdom* [GC], § 67; *Fogarty v. the United Kingdom* [GC], § 39; *McElhinney v. Ireland* [GC], § 38).

State immunity from jurisdiction has been circumscribed by developments in customary international law: for instance, the immunity rule does not apply to a State's employment contracts with the staff of its diplomatic missions abroad, except in situations that are exhaustively enumerated (*Sabeh El Leil v. France* [GC], §§ 53 – 54 and 57 – 58). A restrictive approach to immunity may also be taken in relation to commercial transactions between the State and foreign private individuals (*Oleynikov v. Russia*, §§ 61 and 66). On the other hand, the Court noted in 2001 that, while there appeared to be a trend in international and comparative law towards limiting State immunity in respect of personal injury caused by an act or omission within the forum State, that practice was by no means universal (*McElhinney v. Ireland* [GC], § 38).

- State immunity from execution is not in itself contrary to Article 6 § 1. The Court noted in 2005 that all the international legal instruments governing State immunity set forth the general principle that, subject to certain strictly delimited exceptions, foreign States enjoyed immunity from execution in the territory of the forum State (*Manoilescu and Dobrescu v. Romania and Russia* (dec.), § 73). By way of illustration, the Court held in 2002 that "although the Greek courts ordered the German State to pay damages to the applicants, this did not necessarily oblige the Greek State to ensure that the applicants could recover their debt through enforcement proceedings in Greece" [*Kalogeropoulou and Others v. Greece and Germany* (dec.)]. These decisions are valid in relation to the state of international law at the relevant time and do not preclude future developments in that law.

53. Parliamentary immunity: it is a long-standing practice for States generally to confer varying degrees of immunity on parliamentarians, with the aim of allowing free speech for representatives of the people and preventing partisan complaints from interfering with parliamentary functions (*C. G. I. L. and Cofferati v. Italy* (no. 2), § 44). Hence, parliamentary immunity may be compatible with Article 6, provided that it:

- pursues legitimate aims: protecting free speech in Parliament and maintaining the separation of powers between the legislature and the judiciary (*A. v. the United Kingdom*, §§ 75 – 77 and 79);
- is not disproportionate to the aims sought to be achieved [if the person concerned has reasonable alternative means to protect effectively his or her rights (ibid., § 86) and immunity attaches only to the exercise of parliamentary functions (ibid., § 84); *Zollmann v. the United Kingdom* (dec.)]. A lack of any clear connection with parliamentary activity calls for a narrow interpretation of the concept of proportionality between the aim sought to be achieved and the means employed [*Cordova v. Italy* (no. 2), § 64; *Syngelidis v. Greece*, § 44]. Individuals' right of

access to a court cannot be restricted in a manner incompatible with Article 6 § 1 whenever the impugned remarks were made by a member of Parliament [*Cordova v. Italy* (no. 1), § 63; *C. G. I. L. and Cofferati v. Italy* (no. 2), § § 46 – 50, where, in addition, the victims did not have any reasonable alternative means to protect their rights].

54. Judges' exemption from jurisdiction is likewise not incompatible with Article 6 § 1 if it pursues a legitimate aim, namely the proper administration of justice (*Ernst and Others v. Belgium*, § 50), and observes the principle of proportionality in the sense that the applicants have reasonable alternative means to protect effectively their rights under the Convention (*Ernst and Others v. Belgium*, § 53 – 55).

55. Immunities enjoyed by civil servants: limitations on the ability of individuals to take legal proceedings to challenge statements and findings made by civil servants which damage their reputation may pursue a legitimate aim in the public interest (*Fayed v. the United Kingdom*, § 70); however, there must be a relationship of proportionality between the means employed and that legitimate aim (ibid. , § § 75 – 82).

56. Limits to immunity: it would not be consistent with the rule of law in a democratic society or with the basic principle underlying Article 6 § 1 – namely that civil claims must be capable of being submitted to a judge for adjudication-if a State could, without restraint or control by the Convention enforcement bodies, remove from the jurisdiction of the courts a whole range of civil claims or confer immunities from civil liability on large groups or categories of persons (ibid. , § 65; *McElhinney v. Ireland* [GC], § § 23 – 26; *Sabeh El Leil v. France* [GC], § 50).

B. Waiver

1. Principle

57. In the Contracting States' domestic legal systems a waiver of a person's right to have his or case heard by a court or tribunal is frequently encountered in civil matters, notably in the shape of arbitration clauses in contracts. The waiver, which has undeniable advantages for the individual concerned as well as for the administration of justice, does not in principle offend against the Convention (*Deweer v. Belgium*, § 49).

2. Conditions

58. Persons may waive their right to a court in favour of arbitration, provided that such waiver is permissible and is established freely and unequivocally (*Suda v. the Czech Republic*, §§ 48 – 49). In a democratic society too great an importance attaches to the right to a court for its benefit to be forfeited solely by reason of the fact that an individual is a party to a settlement reached in the course of a procedure ancillary to court proceedings (ibid.)[①].

C. Legal aid

1. Granting of legal aid

59. Article 6 § 1 does not imply that the State must provide free legal aid for every dispute relating to a "civil right" (*Airey v. Ireland*, § 26). There is a clear distinction between Article 6 § 3 (c)-which guarantees the right to free legal aid in criminal proceedings subject to certain conditions-and Article 6 § 1, which makes no reference to legal aid (*Essaadi v. France*, § 30).

60. However, the Convention is intended to safeguard rights which are practical and effective, in particular the right of access to a court. Hence, Article 6 § 1 may sometimes compel the State to provide for the assistance of a lawyer when such assistance proves indispensable for an effective access to court (*Airey v. Ireland*, § 26).

61. The question whether or not Article 6 requires the provision of legal representation to an individual litigant will depend upon the specific circumstances of the case (ibid.; *Steel and Morris v. the United Kingdom*, § 61; *McVicar v. the United Kingdom*, § 48). What has to be ascertained is whether, in the light of all the circumstances, the lack of legal aid would deprive the applicant of a fair hearing (ibid., § 51).

62. The question whether Article 6 implies a requirement to provide legal aid will depend, among other factors, on:
- the importance of what is at stake for the applicant (*Steel and Morris v. the United Kingdom*, § 61; *P., C. and S. v. the United Kingdom*, § 100);

---

① See also the section on "Public hearing".

- the complexity of the relevant law or procedure (*Airey v. Ireland*, § 24);
- the applicant's capacity to represent him or herself effectively (*McVicar v. the United Kingdom*, § § 48 – 62; *Steel and Morris v. the United Kingdom*, § 61);
- the existence of a statutory requirement to have legal representation (*Airey v. Ireland*, § 26; *Gnahoré v. France*, § 41 *in fine*).

63. However, the right in question is not absolute and it may therefore be permissible to impose conditions on the grant of legal aid based in particular on the following considerations, in addition to those cited in the preceding paragraph:

- the financial situation of the litigant (*Steel and Morris v. the United Kingdom*, § 62);
- his or her prospects of success in the proceedings (ibid).

Hence, a legal aid system may exist which selects the cases which qualify for it. However, the system established by the legislature must offer individuals substantial guarantees to protect them from arbitrariness (*Gnahoré v. France*, § 41; *Essaadi v. France*, § 36; *Del Sol v. France*, § 26; *Bakan v. Turkey*, § § 75 – 76 with a reference to the judgment in *Aerts v. Belgium* concerning an impairment of the very essence of the right to a court). It is therefore important to have due regard to the quality of a legal aid scheme within a State (*Essaadi v. France*, § 35) and to verify whether the method chosen by the authorities is compatible with the Convention (*Santambrogio v. Italy*, § 52; *Bakan v. Turkey*, § § 74 – 78; *Pedro Ramos v. Switzerland*, § § 41 – 45).

64. It is essential for the court to give reasons for refusing legal aid and to handle requests for legal aid with diligence (*Tabor v. Poland*, § § 45 – 46; *Saoud v. France*, § § 133 – 136).

65. Furthermore, the refusal of legal aid to foreign legal persons is not contrary to Article 6 (*Granos Organicos Nacionales S. A. v. Germany*, § § 48 – 53).

2. Effectiveness of the legal aid granted

66. The State is not accountable for the actions of an officially appointed lawyer. It follows from the independence of the legal profession from the State (*Staroszczyk v. Poland*, § 133), that the conduct of the defence is essentially a matter between the

defendant and his counsel, whether counsel is appointed under a legal aid scheme or is privately financed. The conduct of the defence as such cannot, other than in special circumstances, incur the State's liability under the Convention [*Tuziński v. Poland* (dec.)].

67. However, assigning a lawyer to represent a party does not in itself guarantee effective assistance (*Siałkowska v. Poland*, §§ 110 and 116). The lawyer appointed for legal aid purposes may be prevented for a protracted period from acting or may shirk his duties. If they are notified of the situation, the competent national authorities must replace him; should they fail to do so, the litigant would be deprived of effective assistance in practice despite the provision of free legal aid (*Bertuzzi v. France*, § 30).

68. It is above all the responsibility of the State to ensure the requisite balance between the effective enjoyment of access to justice on the one hand and the independence of the legal profession on the other. The Court has clearly stressed that any refusal by a legal aid lawyer to act must meet certain quality requirements. Those requirements will not be met where the shortcomings in the legal aid system deprive individuals of the "practical and effective" access to a court to which they are entitled (*Staroszczyk v. Poland*, § 135; *Siałkowska v. Poland*, § 114 violation).

III. Institutional requirements

Article 6 § 1 of the Convention

"1. In the determination of his civil rights and obligations…, everyone is entitled to a…hearing…by an independent and impartial tribunal established by law…."

A. Concept of a "tribunal"

1. Autonomous concept

69. An authority not classified as one of the courts of a State may nonetheless, for the

purposes of Article 6 § 1, come within the concept of a "tribunal" in the substantive sense of the term (*Sramek v. Austria*, § 36).

70. A court or tribunal is characterised in the substantive sense of the term by its judicial function, that is to say determining matters within its competence on the basis of rules of law and after proceedings conducted in a prescribed manner (ibid., § 36; *Cyprus v. Turkey* [GC], § 233).

71. A power of decision is inherent in the very notion of "tribunal". The proceedings must provide the "determination by a tribunal of the matters in dispute" which is required by Article 6 § 1 (*Benthem v. the Netherlands*, § 40).

72. The power simply to issue advisory opinions without binding force is therefore not sufficient, even if those opinions are followed in the great majority of cases (ibid.).

73. For the purposes of Article 6 § 1 a "tribunal" need not be a court of law integrated within the standard judicial machinery of the country concerned. It may be set up to deal with a specific subject matter which can be appropriately administered outside the ordinary court system. What is important to ensure compliance with Article 6 § 1 are the guarantees, both substantive and procedural, which are in place (*Rolf Gustafson v. Sweden*, § 45).

74. Hence, a "tribunal" may comprise a body set up to determine a limited number of specific issues, provided always that it offers the appropriate guarantees (*Lithgow and Others v. the United Kingdom*, § 201, in the context of an arbitration tribunal).

75. The fact that it performs many functions (administrative, regulatory, adjudicative, advisory and disciplinary) cannot *in itself* preclude an institution from being a "tribunal" (*H. v. Belgium*, § 50).

76. The power to give a binding decision which may not be altered by a non-judicial authority to the detriment of an individual party is inherent in the very notion of a "tribunal" (*Van de Hurk v. the Netherlands*, § 45). One of the fundamental aspects of the rule of law is the principle of legal certainty, which requires, *inter alia*, that where the courts have finally determined an issue their ruling should not be called into question

(similarly, in the case of applications for leave to appeal: *Brumărescu v. Romania* [GC], § 61). ①

77. A "tribunal" must also satisfy a series of further requirements-independence, in particular of the executive; impartiality; duration of its members' terms of office; guarantees afforded by its procedure-several of which appear in the text of Article 6 § 1 (*Le Compte, Van Leuven and De Meyere v. Belgium*, § 55; *Cyprus v. Turkey* [GC], § 233). Indeed, both independence and impartiality are key components of the concept of a "tribunal". ②

78. Examples of bodies recognised as having the status of a "tribunal" within the meaning of Article 6 § 1 of the Convention include:

- a regional real-property transactions authority (*Sramek v. Austria*, § 36);
- a criminal damage compensation board (*Rolf Gustafson v. Sweden*, § 48);
- a forestry disputes resolution committee (*Argyrou and Others v. Greece*, § 27).

2. Level of jurisdiction

79. While Article 6 § 1 does not compel the Contracting States to set up courts of appeal or of cassation, a State which does institute such courts is required to ensure that persons amenable to the law shall enjoy before these courts the fundamental guarantees contained in Article 6 § 1 (*Platakou v. Greece*, § 38):

- Assessment *in concreto*: The manner in which Article 6 § 1 applies to courts of appeal or of cassation will, however, depend on the special features of the proceedings concerned. The conditions of admissibility of an appeal on points of law may be stricter than for an ordinary appeal (*Levages Prestations Services v. France*, § 45).
- Assessment *in globo*: Account must be taken of the entirety of the proceedings conducted in the domestic legal order (ibid.). Consequently, a higher or the highest court may, in some circumstances, make reparation for an initial violation of one of the Convention's provisions (*De Haan v. the Netherlands*, § 54).

---

① See also the section on "Execution of judgments".
② See the section on "Independence and impartiality".

80. Demands of flexibility and efficiency, which are fully compatible with the protection of human rights, may justify the prior intervention of administrative or professional bodies and, *a fortiori*, of judicial bodies which do not satisfy the requirements of Article 6 in every respect (*Le Compte, Van Leuven and De Meyere v. Belgium*, § 51). No violation of the Convention can be found if the proceedings before those bodies are "subject to subsequent control by a judicial body that has full jurisdiction" and does provide the guarantees of Article 6 (*Zumtobel v. Austria*, §§ 29 – 32; *Bryan v. the United Kingdom*, § 40).

81. Likewise, the fact that the duty of adjudicating is conferred on professional disciplinary bodies does not in itself infringe the Convention. Nonetheless, in such circumstances the Convention calls for at least one of the following two systems: either the professional disciplinary bodies themselves comply with the requirements of that Article, or they do not so comply but are subject to subsequent review by "a judicial body that has full jurisdiction" and does provide the guarantees of Article 6 § 1 (*Albert and Le Compte v. Belgium*, § 29; *Gautrin and Others v. France*, § 57).

82. Accordingly, the Court has consistently reiterated that under Article 6 § 1 it is necessary that the decisions of administrative authorities which do not themselves satisfy the requirements of that Article should be subject to subsequent control by "a judicial body that has full jurisdiction" (*Ortenberg v. Austria*, § 31). ①

3. Review by a court having full jurisdiction

83. Only an institution that has full jurisdiction merits the designation "tribunal" within the meaning of Article 6 § 1 (*Beaumartin v. France*, § 38). Article 6 § 1 requires the courts to carry out an effective judicial review (*Obermeier v. Austria*, § 70). The principle that a court should exercise full jurisdiction requires it not to abandon any of the elements of its judicial function (*Chevrol v. France*, § 63).

84. The "tribunal" in question must have jurisdiction to examine all questions of fact and law relevant to the dispute before it (*Terra Woningen B. V. v. the Netherlands*, § 52).

---

① See also the section on "Fairness".

85. However, there are some specialised areas of the law (for instance, in the sphere of town and country planning) where the courts have limited jurisdiction as to the facts, but may overturn the administrative authorities' decision if it was based on an inference from facts which was perverse or irrational. More generally, this raises the issue of the scope of review of administrative decisions (*Bryan v. the United Kingdom*, §§ 44 – 47; *Crompton v. the United Kingdom*, §§ 70 – 73).

86. The case-law has established certain criteria for assessing whether the review was conducted by a body with "full jurisdiction" for the purposes of the Convention (*Sigma Radio Television Ltd v. Cyprus*, §§ 151 – 157). Thus, in order to determine whether the judicial body in question provided a sufficient review, the following three criteria must be considered in combination:

- The subject matter of the decision appealed against:
  - if the administrative decision concerned a simple question of fact the court's scrutiny will need to be more intense than if it concerned a specialised field requiring specific technical knowledge;
  - the systems existing in Europe usually limit the courts' power to review factual issues, while not preventing them from overturning the decision on various grounds. This is not called into question by the case-law.
- The manner in which that decision was arrived at: what procedural safeguards were in place before the administrative authority concerned?
  - If the complainant enjoyed procedural safeguards satisfying many of the requirements of Article 6 during the prior administrative procedure, this may justify a lighter form of subsequent judicial control (*Bryan v. the United Kingdom*, §§ 46 – 47; *Holding and Barnes PLC v. the United Kingdom* (dec.)).
- The content of the dispute, including the desired and actual grounds of appeal (*Bryan v. the United Kingdom*, § 45):
  - the judgment must be able to examine all the complainant's submissions on their merits, point by point, without declining to examine any of them, and to give clear reasons for rejecting them. As to the facts, the court must be empowered to re-

examine those which are central to the complainant's case. Hence, if the complainant makes only procedural submissions, he or she cannot subsequently criticise the court for not having ruled on the facts (*Potocka and Others v. Poland*, § 57).

87. For example, the refusal of a court to rule independently on certain issues of fact which are crucial to the settlement of the dispute before it may amount to a violation of Article 6 § 1 (*Terra Woningen B. V. v. the Netherlands*, § § 53 – 55). The same applies if the court does not have jurisdiction to determine the central issue in the dispute (*Tsfayo v. the United Kingdom*, § 48). In such cases the matter which is decisive for the outcome of the case is not subjected to independent judicial scrutiny.

88. If a ground of appeal is upheld, the reviewing court must have the power to quash the impugned decision and to either take a fresh decision itself or remit the case for decision by the same or a different body (*Kingsley v. the United Kingdom* [GC], § § 32 and 34).

89. Where the facts have already been established by the administrative authority in the course of a quasi-judicial procedure satisfying many of the requirements laid down by Article 6 § 1, where there is no dispute as to the facts thus established or the inferences drawn from them by the administrative authority, and where the court has dealt point by point with the litigant's other grounds of appeal, the scope of the review conducted by the appellate court will be held to be sufficient to comply with Article 6 § 1 (*Bryan v. the United Kingdom*, § § 44 – 47).

90. Below are some examples of judicial bodies that have not been considered to have "full jurisdiction":

- an administrative court which was empowered only to determine whether the discretion enjoyed by the administrative authorities was used in a manner compatible with the object and purpose of the law (*Obermeier v. Austria*, § 70);
- a court which heard appeals on points of law from decisions of the disciplinary sections of professional associations, without having the power to assess whether the penalty was proportionate to the misconduct (*Diennet v. France*, § 34, in the context of a medical association; *Mérigaud v. France*, § 69, in the context of an association of surveyors);

- a Constitutional Court which could inquire into the contested proceedings solely from the point of view of their conformity with the Constitution, thus preventing it from examining all the relevant facts (*Zumtobel v. Austria*, §§ 29 – 30);

- the*Conseil d'État* which, in accordance with its own case-law, was obliged, in resolving the issue before it concerning the applicability of treaties, to abide by the opinion of the minister-an external authority who was also a representative of the executive-without subjecting that opinion to any criticism or discussion by the parties. The minister's involvement, which was decisive for the outcome of the legal proceedings, was not open to challenge by the applicant, who was, moreover, not afforded any opportunity to have the basis of her own reply to the minister examined (*Chevrol v. France*, §§ 81 – 82).

91. By contrast:

- *Chaudet v. France*: the *Conseil d'État* determined an application for judicial review as the court of first and last instance. In this case the *Conseil d'État* did not have "full jurisdiction", which would have had the effect of substituting its decision for that of the civil aviation medical board. However, it was clear from the case file that it had nonetheless addressed all of the submissions made by the applicant, on factual and legal grounds, and assessed all of the evidence in the medical file, having regard to the conclusions of all the medical reports discussed before it by the parties. The Court therefore held that the applicant's case had been examined in compliance with the requirements of Article 6 § 1 (§§ 37 – 38).

- *Zumtobel v. Austria*: the Court held that the Austrian Administrative Court had met the requirements of Article 6 § 1 in relation to matters not exclusively within the discretion of the administrative authorities, and that it had considered the submissions on their merits, point by point, without ever having to decline jurisdiction in replying to them or in ascertaining various facts (§§ 31 – 32 – also *Ortenberg v. Austria*, §§ 33 – 34; *Fischer v. Austria*, § 34).

- *McMichael v. the United Kingdom*: in this case, an order of the *Sheriff Court* freeing a child for adoption was subject to appeal to the Court of Session. The latter had full jurisdiction in that regard; it normally proceeded on the basis of the Sheriff's findings of fact but was not obliged to do so. It could, where appropriate, take evidence itself or remit the case to the Sheriff with instructions as to how he should proceed (§66). Furthermore, the Sheriff Court, in determining appeals against the decisions of children's hearings, also had full jurisdiction, being empowered to examine both the merits and alleged procedural irregularities (§82).

- *Potocka and Others v. Poland*: the scope of the Supreme Administrative Court's jurisdiction as determined by the Code of Administrative Procedure was limited to the assessment of the lawfulness of contested administrative decisions. However, the court was also empowered to set aside a decision wholly or in part if it was established that procedural requirements of fairness had not been met in the proceedings which had led to its adoption. The reasoning of the Supreme Administrative Court showed that in fact it had examined the expediency aspect of the case. Even though the court could have limited its analysis to finding that the contested decisions had to be upheld in the light of the procedural and substantive flaws in the applicants' application, it had considered all their submissions on their merits, point by point, without ever having to decline jurisdiction in replying to them or in ascertaining the relevant facts. It had delivered a judgment which was carefully reasoned, and the applicants' arguments relevant to the outcome of the case had been dealt with thoroughly. Accordingly, the scope of review of the Supreme Administrative Court had been sufficient to comply with Article 6 §1 (§§56 – 59).

4. Execution of judgments

a. Right to prompt implementation of a final and binding judicial decision

92. Article 6 §1 protects the implementation of final, binding judicial decisions (as distinct from the implementation of decisions which may be subject to review by a higher court) (*Ouzounis and Others v. Greece*, §21).

93. The right to execution of such decisions, given by any court, is an integral part of the "right to a court" (*Hornsby v. Greece*, §40; *Scordino v. Italy* (no. 1) [GC], §196).

Otherwise, the provisions of Article 6 § 1 would be deprived of all useful effect (*Burdov v. Russia*, §§ 34 and 37).

94. This is of even greater importance in the context of administrative proceedings. By lodging an application for judicial review with the State's highest administrative court, the litigant seeks not only annulment of the impugned decision but also and above all the removal of its effects.

95. The effective protection of the litigant and the restoration of legality therefore presuppose an obligation on the administrative authorities' part to comply with the judgment (*Hornsby v. Greece*, § 41; *Kyrtatos v. Greece*, §§ 31 – 32).

96. Thus, while some delay in the execution of a judgment may be justified in particular circumstances, the delay may not be such as to impair the litigant's right to enforcement of the judgment (*Burdov v. Russia*, §§ 35 – 37).

97. Understood in this way, execution must be full and exhaustive and not just partial (*Matheus v. France*, § 58; *Sabin Popescu v. Romania*, §§ 68 – 76), and may not be prevented, invalidated or unduly delayed (*Immobiliare Saffi v. Italy* [GC], § 74).

98. The refusal of an authority to take account of a ruling given by a higher court- leading potentially to a series of judgments in the context of the same set of proceedings, repeatedly setting aside the decisions given-is also contrary to Article 6 § 1 (*Turczanik v. Poland*, §§ 49 – 51).

99. An unreasonably long delay in enforcement of a binding judgment may breach the Convention. The reasonableness of such delay is to be determined having regard in particular to the complexity of the enforcement proceedings, the applicant's own behaviour and that of the competent authorities, and the amount and nature of the court award (*Raylyan v. Russia*, § 31).

100. For example, the Court held that by refraining for more than five years from taking the necessary measures to comply with a final, enforceable judicial decision the national authorities had deprived the provisions of Article 6 § 1 of all useful effect (*Hornsby v. Greece*, § 45).

101. In another case, the overall period of nine months taken by the authorities to

enforce a judgment was found not to be unreasonable in view of the circumstances (*Moroko v. Russia*, §§43 –45).

102. The Court has found the right to a court under Article 6 § 1 to have been breached on account of the authorities' refusal, over a period of approximately four years, to use police assistance to enforce an order for possession against a tenant (*Lunari v. Italy*, §§38 –42), and on account of a stay of execution-for over six years-resulting from the intervention of the legislature calling into question a court order for a tenant's eviction, which was accordingly deprived of all useful effect by the impugned legislative provisions (*Immobiliare Saffi v. Italy* [GC], §§70 and 74).

103. A person who has obtained judgment against the State at the end of legal proceedings may not be expected to bring separate enforcement proceedings (*Burdov v. Russia* (no. 2), § 68). The burden to ensure compliance with a judgment against the State lies with the State authorities (*Yavorivskaya v. Russia*, § 25), starting from the date on which the judgment becomes binding and enforceable (*Burdov v. Russia* (no. 2), § 69).

104. A successful litigant may be required to undertake certain procedural steps in order to allow or speed up the execution of a judgment. The requirement of the creditor's cooperation must not, however, go beyond what is strictly necessary and does not relieve the authorities of their obligations (ibid.).

105. It follows that the late payment, following enforcement proceedings, of amounts owing to the applicant cannot cure the national authorities' long-standing failure to comply with a judgment and does not afford adequate redress (*Scordino v. Italy* (no. 1) [GC], § 198).

106. The Court has also held that the authorities' stance of holding the applicant responsible for the initiation of execution proceedings in respect of an enforceable decision in his favour, coupled with the disregard for his financial situation, constituted an excessive burden and restricted his right of access to a court to the extent of impairing the very essence of that right (*Apostol v. Georgia*, § 65).

107. A litigant may not be deprived of the benefit, within a reasonable time, of a final decision awarding him compensation for damage (*Burdov v. Russia*, § 35), or housing

(*Teteriny v. Russia*, §§ 41 – 42), regardless of the complexity of the domestic enforcement procedure or of the State budgetary system. It is not open to a State authority to cite lack of funds or other resources as an excuse for not honouring a judgment debt (*Burdov v. Russia*, § 35; *Amat-G Ltd and Mebaghishvili v. Georgia*, § 47; *Scordino v. Italy* (no. 1) [GC], § 199). Nor may it cite a lack of alternative accommodation as an excuse for not honouring a judgment (*Prodan v. Moldova*, § 53).

108. A distinction has to be made between debts *owed by the State* (*Burdov v. Russia* (no. 2), §§ 68 – 69, 72 et seq.) and those *owed by an individual*: the responsibility of the State cannot be engaged on account of non-payment of an enforceable debt as a result of the insolvency of a "private" debtor [*Sanglier v. France*, § 39; *Ciprová v. the Czech Republic* (dec.); *Cubanit v. Romania* (dec.)]. Nevertheless, the State has a positive obligation to organise a system for enforcement of final decisions in disputes between private persons that is effective both in law and in practice (*Fuklev v. Ukraine*, § 84). The State's responsibility may therefore be engaged if the public authorities involved in enforcement proceedings fail to display the necessary diligence, or even prevent enforcement (ibid., § 67). The measures taken by the national authorities to secure enforcement must be adequate and sufficient for that purpose (*Ruianu v. Romania*, § 66), in view of their obligations in the matter of execution, since it is they who exercise public authority (ibid., §§ 72 – 73).

109. Thus, for example, the Court held that, by refraining from taking sanctions in respect of the failure of a (private) third party to cooperate with the authorities empowered to enforce final enforceable decisions, the national authorities deprived the provisions of Article 6 § 1 of all useful effect (*Pini and Others v. Romania*, §§ 186 – 188, where the private institution where two children were living had prevented the execution for over three years of the orders for the children's adoption).

110. Nevertheless, where the State has taken all the steps envisaged by the law to ensure that a private individual complies with a decision, the State cannot be held responsible for the debtor's refusal to comply with his obligations (*Fociac v. Romania*, §§ 74 and 78).

111. Lastly, the right to a court likewise protects the right of access to enforcement

proceedings, that is, the right to have enforcement proceedings initiated (*Apostol v. Georgia*, § 56).

b. Right not to have a final judicial decision called into question

112. Furthermore, the right to a fair hearing must be interpreted in the light of the rule of law. One of the fundamental aspects of the rule of law is the principle of legal certainty (*Okyay and Others v. Turkey*, § 73), which requires, *inter alia*, that where the courts have finally determined an issue their ruling should not be called into question (*Brumărescu v. Romania* [GC], § 61; *Agrokompleks v. Ukraine*, § 148).

113. Judicial systems characterised by final judgments that are liable to review indefinitely and at risk of being set aside repeatedly are in breach of Article 6 § 1 (*Sovtransavto Holding v. Ukraine*, §§ 74, 77 and 82, concerning the protest procedure whereby the President of the Supreme Arbitration Tribunal, the Attorney-General and their deputies had discretionary power to challenge final judgments under the supervisory review procedure by lodging an objection).

114. The calling into question of decisions in this manner is not acceptable, whether it be by judges and members of the executive (*Tregubenko v. Ukraine*, § 36) or by non-judicial authorities (*Agrokompleks v. Ukraine*, §§ 150 – 151).

115. A final decision may be called into question only when this is made necessary by circumstances of a substantial and compelling character such as a judicial error (*Ryabykh v. Russia*, § 52).

B. Establishment by law

116. In the light of the principle of the rule of law, inherent in the Convention system, the Court considers that a "tribunal" must always be "established by law", as it would otherwise lack the legitimacy required in a democratic society to hear individual cases (*Lavents v. Latvia*, § 81).

117. The phrase "established by law" covers not only the legal basis for the very existence of a "tribunal", but also compliance by the tribunal with the particular rules that govern it (*Sokurenko and Strygun v. Ukraine*, § 24). The lawfulness of a court or tribunal

must by definition also encompass its composition [*Buscarini v. San Marino* (dec.)]. The practice of tacitly renewing judges' terms of office for an indefinite period after their statutory term of office had expired and pending their reappointment was held to be contrary to the principle of a "tribunal established by law" (*Oleksandr Volkov v. Ukraine*, § 151). The procedures governing the appointment of judges could not be relegated to the status of internal practice (ibid., §§ 154–156).

118. "Law", within the meaning of Article 6 § 1, thus comprises not only legislation providing for the establishment and competence of judicial organs, but also any other provision of domestic law which, if breached, would render the participation of one or more judges in the examination of a case irregular (*DMD Group, A. S., v. Slovakia*, § 59). This includes, in particular, provisions concerning the independence of the members of a "tribunal", the length of their term of office, impartiality and the existence of procedural safeguards (*Gurov v. Moldova*, § 36).

119. In principle, a breach by a court of these domestic legal provisions gives rise to a violation of Article 6 § 1 (*DMD Group, A. S., v. Slovakia*, § 61). The Court may therefore examine whether the domestic law has been complied with in this respect. However, having regard to the general principle that it is, in the first place, for the national courts themselves to interpret the provisions of domestic law, the Court finds that it may not question their interpretation unless there has been a flagrant violation of the legislation (ibid.). A court which, without any explanation, oversteps the usual limits of its jurisdiction in deliberate breach of the law is not a "tribunal established by law" in the proceedings in question (*Sokurenko and Strygun v. Ukraine*, §§ 27–28).

120. The object of the term "established by law" in Article 6 § 1 is to ensure that the organisation of the judicial system does not depend on the discretion of the executive but is regulated by law emanating from Parliament (*Savino and Others v. Italy*, § 94).

121. Nor, in countries where the law is codified, can organisation of the judicial system be left to the discretion of the judicial authorities, although this does not mean that the courts do not have some latitude to interpret the relevant national legislation (ibid.).

122. Furthermore, delegating powers in matters concerning the organisation of the

judicial system is permissible provided that this possibility is enshrined in the domestic law of the State, including the relevant provisions of the Constitution (ibid.).

C. Independence and impartiality

1. General considerations

123. The right to a fair hearing under Article 6 § 1 requires that a case be heard by an "independent and impartial tribunal". There is a close inter-relationship between the guarantees of an "independent" and an "impartial" tribunal. For this reason the Court commonly considers the two requirements together (*Kleyn and Others v. the Netherlands* [GC], § 192).

124. The participation of lay judges in a case is not, as such, contrary to Article 6 § 1. The existence of a panel with mixed membership comprising, under the presidency of a judge, civil servants and representatives of interested bodies does not in itself constitute evidence of bias (*Le Compte, Van Leuven and De Meyere v. Belgium*, §§ 57–58), nor is there any objection *per se* to expert lay members participating in the decision-making in a court (*Pabla Ky v. Finland*, § 32).

125. The principles established in the case-law concerning impartiality apply to lay judges as to professional judges (*Langborger v. Sweden*, §§ 34–35; *Cooper v. the United Kingdom* [GC], § 123).

126. As a matter of principle, a violation of Article 6 § 1 cannot be grounded on the lack of independence or impartiality of a decision-making tribunal or the breach of an essential procedural guarantee by that tribunal, if the decision taken was subject to subsequent control by a judicial body that has "full jurisdiction" and ensures respect for the relevant guarantees by curing the failing in question (*De Haan v. the Netherlands*, §§ 52–55).①

127. The Court has consistently stressed that the scope of the State's obligation to ensure a trial by an "independent and impartial tribunal" under Article 6 § 1 of the

---

① See also the sections on "Review by a court having full jurisdiction" and "Fairness".

Convention is not limited to the judiciary. It also implies obligations on the executive, the legislature and any other State authority, regardless of its level, to respect and abide by the judgments and decisions of the courts, even when they do not agree with them. Thus, the State's respecting the authority of the courts is an indispensable precondition for public confidence in the courts and, more broadly, for the rule of law. For this to be the case, the constitutional safeguards of the independence and impartiality of the judiciary do not suffice. They must be effectively incorporated into everyday administrative attitudes and practices (*Agrokompleks v. Ukraine*, § 136).

2. An independent tribunal

128. The term "independent" refers to independence *vis-à-visthe other powers* (the executive and the Parliament) (*Beaumartin v. France*, § 38) and also *vis-à-visthe parties* (*Sramek v. Austria*, § 42).

129. Although the notion of the separation of powers between the political organs of government and the judiciary has assumed growing importance in the Court's case-law, neither Article 6 nor any other provision of the Convention requires States to comply with any theoretical constitutional concepts regarding the permissible limits of the powers' interaction. The question is always whether, in a given case, the requirements of the Convention are met (*Kleyn and Others v. the Netherlands* [GC], § 193). Indeed, the notion of independence of a tribunal entails the existence of procedural safeguards to separate the judiciary from other powers.

a. Independence *vis-à-vis* the executive

130. The independence of judges will be undermined where the executive intervenes in a case pending before the courts with a view to influencing the outcome (*Sovtransavto Holding v. Ukraine*, § 80; *Mosteanu and Others v. Romania*, § 42).

131. The fact that judges are appointed by the executive and are removable does not *per se* amount to a violation of Article 6 § 1 [*Clarke v. the United Kingdom* (dec.)]. The appointment of judges by the executive is permissible provided that the appointees are free from influence or pressure when carrying out their adjudicatory role (*Flux v. Moldova* (no. 2), § 27).

132. The fact that the President of the Court of Cassation is appointed by the executive does not in itself undermine his independence provided that, once appointed, he is not subject to any pressure, does not receive any instructions and performs his duties with complete independence (*Zolotas v. Greece*, § 24).

133. Likewise, the mere fact that judges of the Council of Administrative Law are appointed by the regional administrative authority is not capable of casting doubt on their independence or impartiality provided that, once appointed, they are not subject to any pressure, do not receive any instructions and exercise their judicial activity with complete independence [*Majorana v. Italy* (dec.)].

b. Independence *vis-à-vis* Parliament

134. The fact that judges are appointed by Parliament does not by itself render them subordinate to the authorities if, once appointed, they receive no pressure or instructions in the performance of their judicial duties (*Sacilor-Lormines v. France*, § 67). Furthermore, the fact that one of the expert members of the Court of Appeal, comprising mainly professional judges, was also a member of Parliament did not *per se* breach the right to an independent and impartial tribunal (*Pabla Ky v. Finland*, §§ 31 – 35).

c. Independence *vis-à-vis* the parties

135. Where a tribunal's members include a person who is in a subordinate position, in terms of his duties and the organisation of his service, *vis-à-vis* one of the parties, litigants may entertain a legitimate doubt about that person's independence. Such a situation seriously affects the confidence which the courts must inspire in a democratic society (*Sramek v. Austria*, § 42).

d. Criteria for assessing independence

136. In determining whether a body can be considered to be "independent", the Court has had regard, *inter alia*, to the following criteria (*Langborger v. Sweden*, § 32; *Kleyn and Others v. the Netherlands* [GC], § 190):

i. the manner of appointment of its members and

ii. the duration of their term of office;

iii. the existence of guarantees against outside pressures; and

iv. whether the body presents an appearance of independence.

i. Manner of appointment of a body's members

137. Questions have been raised as to the intervention of the Minister of Justice in the appointment and/or removal from office of members of a decision-making body [*Sramek v. Austria*, § 38; *Brudnicka and Others v. Poland*, § 41; *Clarke v. the United Kingdom* (dec.)].

138. Although the assignment of a case to a particular judge or court falls within the margin of appreciation enjoyed by the domestic authorities in such matters, the Court must be satisfied that it was compatible with Article 6 § 1, and, in particular, with the requirements of independence and impartiality (*Bochan v. Ukraine*, § 71).

ii. Duration of appointment of a body's members

139. The Court has not specified any particular term of office for the members of a decision-making body, although their irremovability during their term of office must in general be considered as a corollary of their independence. However, the absence of a formal recognition of this irremovability in the law does not in itself imply lack of independence provided that it is recognised in fact and that other necessary guarantees are present (*Sacilor-Lormines v. France*, § 67; *Luka v. Romania*, § 44).

iii. Guarantees against outside pressure

140. Judicial independence demands that individual judges be free from undue influence outside the judiciary, and from within. Internal judicial independence requires that they be free from directives or pressures from fellow judges or those who have administrative responsibilities in the court such as the president of the court or the president of a division in the court. The absence of sufficient safeguards securing the independence of judges within the judiciary and, in particular, *vis-à-vis* their judicial superiors, may lead the Court to conclude that an applicant's doubts as to the independence and impartiality of a court can be said to have been objectively justified (*Agrokompleks v. Ukraine*, § 137; *Parlov-Tkalčić v. Croatia*, § 86).

141. The judges of a County Court were found to be sufficiently independent of that court's president since court presidents performed only administrative (managerial and

organisational) functions, which were strictly separated from the judicial function. The legal system provided for adequate safeguards against the arbitrary exercise of court presidents' duty to (re)assign cases to judges (ibid., §§88 – 95).

iv. Appearence of independence

142. In order to determine whether a tribunal can be considered to be independent as required by Article 6 §1, appearances may also be of importance (*Sramek v. Austria*, §42). As to the appearance of independence, the standpoint of a party is important but not decisive; what is decisive is whether the fear of the party concerned can be held to be "objectively justified" (*Sacilor-Lormines v. France*, §63). Therefore, no problem arises as regards independence when the Court is of the view that an "objective observer" would see no cause for concern about it in the circumstances of the case at hand [*Clarke v. the United Kingdom* (dec.)].

3. An impartial tribunal

143. Article 6 § 1 requires a tribunal falling within its scope to be impartial. Impartiality normally denotes the absence of prejudice or bias and its existence or otherwise can be tested in various ways (*Wettstein v. Switzerland*, §43; *Micallef v. Malta* [GC], §93). The concepts of independence and impartiality are closely linked and, depending on the circumstances, may require joint examination (*Sacilor-Lormines v. France*, §62; *Oleksandr Volkov v. Ukraine*, §107).

a. Criteria for assessing impartiality

144. The existence of impartiality must be determined on the basis of the following (*Micallef v. Malta* [GC], §93):

i. a *subjective test*, where regard must be had to the personal conviction and behaviour of a particular judge, that is, whether the judge held any personal prejudice or bias in a given case; and also

ii. an *objective test*, that is to say by ascertaining whether the tribunal itself and, among other aspects, its composition, offered sufficient guarantees to exclude any legitimate doubt in respect of its impartiality.

145. However, there is no watertight division between subjective and objective

impartiality since the conduct of a judge may not only prompt objectively held misgivings as to impartiality from the point of view of the external observer (objective test) but may also go to the issue of his or her personal conviction (subjective test).

146. Thus, in some cases where it may be difficult to procure evidence with which to rebut the presumption of the judge's subjective impartiality, the requirement of objective impartiality provides a further important guarantee (ibid., §§ 95 and 101).

i. Subjective approach

147. In applying the subjective test, the Court has consistently held that "the personal impartiality of a judge must be presumed until there is proof to the contrary" (*Le Compte, Van Leuven and De Meyere v. Belgium*, § 58 *in fine*; *Micallef v. Malta* [GC], § 94). As regards the type of proof required, the Court has, for example, sought to ascertain whether a judge has displayed hostility (*Buscemi v. Italy*, §§ 67-68). The fact that a judge did not withdraw from dealing with a civil action on appeal following his earlier participation in another related set of civil proceedings did not constitute the required proof to rebut the presumption (*Golubović v. Croatia*, § 52).

148. The principle that a tribunal shall be presumed to be free of personal prejudice or partiality is long-established in the case-law of the Court (*Le Compte, Van Leuven and De Meyere v. Belgium*, § 58; *Driza v. Albania*, § 75).

ii. Objective approach

149. It must be determined whether, quite apart from the judge's conduct, there are ascertainable facts which may raise doubts as to his impartiality. When applied to a body sitting as a bench, it means determining whether, quite apart from the personal conduct of any of the members of that body, there are ascertainable facts which may raise doubts as to the impartiality of the body itself. This implies that, in deciding whether in a given case there is a legitimate reason to fear that a particular judge (*Morel v. France*, §§ 45-50; *Pescador Valero v. Spain*, § 23) or a body sitting as a bench (*Luka v. Romania*, § 40) lacks impartiality, the standpoint of the person concerned is important but not decisive. What is decisive is whether this fear can be held to be objectively justified (*Wettstein v. Switzerland*, § 44; *Pabla Ky v. Finland*, § 30; *Micallef v. Malta* [GC], § 96).

150. The objective test mostly concerns hierarchical or other links between the judge and other actors in the proceedings (see cases regarding the dual role of a judge, for example *Mežnarić v. Croatia*, § 36; and *Wettstein v. Switzerland*, § 47, where the lawyer representing the applicant's opponents subsequently judged the applicant in a single set of proceedings and overlapping proceedings respectively) which objectively justify misgivings as to the impartiality of the tribunal, and thus fail to meet the Convention standard under the objective test.

151. Therefore, it must be decided in each individual case whether the relationship in question is of such a nature and degree as to indicate a lack of impartiality on the part of the tribunal (*Micallef v. Malta* [GC], §§ 97 and 102).

152. In this respect even appearances may be of a certain importance or, in other words, "justice must not only be done, it must also be seen to be done". What is at stake is the confidence which the courts in a democratic society must inspire in the public. Thus, any judge in respect of whom there is a legitimate reason to fear a lack of impartiality must withdraw (ibid., § 98).

153. In order that the courts may inspire in the public the confidence which is indispensable, account must also be taken of questions of internal organisation. The existence of national procedures for ensuring impartiality, namely rules regulating the withdrawal of judges, is a relevant factor (see the specific provisions regarding the challenging of judges, *Micallef v. Malta* [GC], §§ 99 – 100). Such rules manifest the national legislature's concern to remove all reasonable doubts as to the impartiality of the judge or court concerned and constitute an attempt to ensure impartiality by eliminating the causes of such concerns. In addition to ensuring the absence of actual bias, they are directed at removing any appearance of partiality and so serve to promote the confidence which the courts in a democratic society must inspire in the public (*Mežnarić v. Croatia*, § 27).

b. Situations in which the question of a lack of judicial impartiality may arise

154. There are two possible situations in which the question of a lack of judicial impartiality may arise:

i. The first is *functional in nature* and concerns, for instance, the exercise of different functions within the judicial process by the same person, or hierarchical or other links with another actor in the proceedings.

ii. The second is *of a personal character* and derives from the conduct of the judges in a given case.

i. Situations of a functional nature

α. *The exercise of both advisory and judicial functions in the same case*

155. The consecutive exercise of advisory and judicial functions within one body may, in certain circumstances, raise an issue under Article 6 § 1 as regards the impartiality of the body seen from the objective viewpoint (*Procola v. Luxembourg*, § 45 – violation).

156. The issue is whether there has been an exercise of judicial and advisory functions concerning "the same case", "the same decision" or "analogous issues" (*Kleyn and Others v. the Netherlands* [GC], § 200; *Sacilor-Lormines v. France*, § 74 – no violation).

β. *The exercise of both judicial and extra-judicial functions in the same case*

157. When determining the objective justification for the applicant's fear, such factors as the judge's dual role in the proceedings, the time which elapsed between the two occasions on which he participated and the extent to which he was involved in the proceedings may be taken into consideration (*McGonnell v. the United Kingdom*, §§ 52 – 57).

158. Any direct involvement in the passage of legislation, or of executive rules, is likely to be sufficient to cast doubt on the judicial impartiality of a person subsequently called on to determine a dispute over whether reasons exist to permit a variation from the wording of the legislation or rules at issue (ibid., §§ 55 – 58, where the Court found a violation of Article 6 § 1 on account of the direct involvement of a judge in the adoption of the development plan at issue in the proceedings; compare with *Pabla Ky v. Finland*, § 34 – no violation).

159. When there are two parallel sets of proceedings with the same person in the dual role of judge on the one hand and legal representative of the opposing party on the other, an applicant could have reason for concern that the judge would continue to regard him as the opposing party (*Wettstein v. Switzerland*, §§ 44 – 47).

160. The hearing of a constitutional complaint by a judge who had acted as counsel for

the applicant's opponent at the start of the proceedings led to a finding of a violation of Article 6 § 1 (*Mežnarić v. Croatia*, § 36). As to the impartiality of a Constitutional Court judge who had acted as legal expert for the applicant's opponent in the civil proceedings at first instance, see *Švarc and Kavnik v. Slovenia*, § 44.

χ. *The exercise of different judicial functions*

161. The assessment of whether the participation of the same judge in different stages of a civil case complies with the requirement of impartiality laid down by Article 6 § 1 is to be made on a case-by-case basis, regard being had to the circumstances of the individual case.

162. The mere fact that a judge has already taken pre-trial decisions cannot by itself be regarded as justifying concerns about his impartiality. What matters is the scope and nature of the measures taken by the judge before the trial. Likewise, the fact that the judge has detailed knowledge of the case file does not entail any prejudice on his part that would prevent his being regarded as impartial when the decision on the merits is taken. Nor does a preliminary analysis of the available information mean that the final analysis has been prejudged. What is important is for that analysis to be carried out when judgment is delivered and to be based on the evidence produced and argument heard at the hearing (*Morel v. France*, § 45).

163. It is necessary to consider whether the link between substantive issues determined at various stages of the proceedings is so close as to cast doubt on the impartiality of the judge participating in the decision-making at these stages (*Toziczka v. Poland*, § 36).

For example:

- It cannot be stated as a general rule resulting from the obligation to be impartial, that a superior court which sets aside an administrative or judicial decision is bound to send the case back to a different jurisdictional authority or to a differently composed branch of that authority (*Ringeisen v. Austria*, § 97 *in fine*).
- An issue may arise if a judge takes part in two sets of proceedings relating to the same sets of facts (*Indra v. Slovakia*, §§ 51 – 53).
- A judge who is the presiding judge of an appeals tribunal assisted by two lay judges

should not hear an appeal from his own decision (*De Haan v. the Netherlands*, § 51).

- A Court of Appeal in which the trial judges are called upon to ascertain whether or not they themselves committed an error of legal interpretation or application in their previous decision can raise doubts as to impartiality (*San Leonard Band Club v. Malta*, § 64).
- It is not prima facie incompatible with the requirements of impartiality if the same judge is involved, first, in a decision on the merits of a case and, subsequently, in proceedings in which the admissibility of an appeal against that decision is examined (*Warsicka v. Poland*, §§ 38 – 47).
- A judge having a dual role, as counsel representing the party opposing the applicants' company in the first set of proceedings and as a Court of Appeal judge in the second set of proceedings; having regard in particular to the remoteness in time and the different subject matter of the first set of proceedings in relation to the second set and to the fact that the functions as counsel and judge did not overlap in time, the Court found that the applicants could not have entertained any objectively justified doubts as to the judge's impartiality (*Puolitaival and Pirttiaho v. Finland*, §§ 46 – 54).
- The Court found a violation of the principle of impartiality in a case where some judges who had already ruled on the case were required to decide whether or not they had erred in their earlier decision and where another three judges had already expressed their opinions on the matter (*Driza v. Albania*, §§ 78 – 83 – violation).
- One of the judges involved in the proceedings concerning an appeal on points of law had prior involvement in the case as a judge of the Higher Court (*Peruš v. Slovenia*, §§ 38 – 39).

ii. Situations of a personal nature

164. The principle of impartiality will also be infringed where the judge has a personal interest in the case (*Langborger v. Sweden*, § 35; *Gautrin and Others v. France*, § 59).

165. Professional or personal links between a judge and a party to a case, or the party's

advocate, may also raise questions of impartiality (*Pescador Valero v. Spain*, § 27; *Tocono and Profesorii Prometeişti v. Moldova*, § 31; *Micallef v. Malta* [GC], § 102). Even indirect factors may be taken into account (*Pétur Thór Sigurðsson v. Iceland*, § 45).

Ⅳ. Procedural requirements

A. Fairness

> Article 6 § 1 of the Convention
> "1. In the determination of his civil rights and obligations…, everyone is entitled to a fair…hearing by [a] tribunal…"

1. General principles

166. A prominent place: the Court has always emphasised the prominent place held in a democratic society by the right to a fair trial (*Airey v. Ireland*, § 24; *Stanev v. Bulgaria* [GC], § 231). This guarantee "is one of the fundamental principles of any democratic society, within the meaning of the Convention" (*Pretto and Others v. Italy*, § 21). There can therefore be no justification for interpreting Article 6 § 1 restrictively (*Moreira de Azevedo v. Portugal*, § 66). The requirement of fairness applies to proceedings in their entirety; it is not confined to hearings *inter partes* (*Stran Greek Refineries and Stratis Andreadis v. Greece*, § 49).

167. Content: civil claims must be capable of being submitted to a judge (*Fayed v. the United Kingdom*, § 65; *Sabeh El Leil v. France* [GC], § 46). Article 6 § 1 describes in detail the procedural guarantees afforded to parties in civil proceedings. It is intended above all to secure the interests of the parties and those of the proper administration of justice (*Nideröst-Huber v. Switzerland*, § 30). Litigants must therefore be able to argue their case with the requisite effectiveness (*H. v. Belgium*, § 53).

168. Role of the national authorities: the Court has always said that the national

authorities must ensure in each individual case that the requirements of a "fair hearing" within the meaning of the Convention are met (*Dombo Beheer B. V. v. the Netherlands*, § 33 *in fine*).

169. The litigant's claims: it is a matter of principle that in the determination of his "civil rights and obligations"-as defined in the case-law of the Strasbourg Court[①]-everyone is entitled to a fair hearing by a tribunal. To this are added the guarantees laid down by Article 6 § 1 as regards both the organisation and the composition of the court, and the conduct of the proceedings. In sum, the whole makes up the right to a fair hearing (*Golder v. the United Kingdom*, § 36).

170. Principles of interpretation:

- The principle whereby a civil claim must be capable of being submitted to a judge ranks as one of the universally recognised fundamental principles of law; the same is true of the principle of international law which forbids the denial of justice. Article 6 § 1 must be read in the light of these principles (ibid., § 35).

- The right to a fair hearing before a tribunal as guaranteed by Article 6 § 1 must be interpreted in the light of the Preamble to the Convention, which declares the rule of law to be part of the common heritage of the Contracting States (*Brumărescu v. Romania*, § 61; *Nejdet Şahin and Perihan Şahin v. Turkey* [GC], § 57).

- The principle of legal certainty constitutes one of the basic elements of the rule of law (*Beian v. Romania* (no. 1), § 39).

- In a democratic society within the meaning of the Convention, the right to a fair administration of justice holds such a prominent place that a restrictive interpretation of Article 6 § 1 would not correspond to the aim and the purpose of that provision (*Ryakib Biryukov v. Russia*, § 37).

- In addition, the Convention is intended to guarantee not rights that are theoretical or illusory but rights that are practical and effective (*Airey v. Ireland*, § 24).

171. States have greater latitude in civil matters: the Court has acknowledged that the

---

① See next section "Scope".

requirements inherent in the concept of a "fair hearing" are not necessarily the same in cases concerning the determination of civil rights and obligations as they are in cases concerning the determination of a criminal charge: "the Contracting States have greater latitude when dealing with civil cases concerning civil rights and obligations than they have when dealing with criminal cases" (*Dombo Beheer B. V. v. the Netherlands*, § 32; *Levages Prestations Services v. France*, § 46). The requirements of Article 6 § 1 as regards cases concerning civil rights are less onerous than they are for criminal charges (*König v. Germany*, § 96).

2. Scope

172. An effective right: the parties to the proceedings have the right to present the observations which they regard as relevant to their case. This right can only be seen to be effective if the observations are actually "heard", that is to say duly considered by the trial court. In other words, the "tribunal" has a duty to conduct a proper examination of the submissions, arguments and evidence adduced by the parties (*Kraska v. Switzerland*, § 30; *Van de Hurk v. the Netherlands*, § 59; *Perez v. France* [GC], § 80). In order for the right guaranteed by this Article to be effective, the authorities must exercise "diligence": for an appellant not represented by a lawyer, see *Kerojärvi v. Finland*, § 42; *Fretté v. France*, § 49; for an appellant represented by a lawyer, see *Göç v. Turkey* [GC], § 57.

173. Proper participation of the appellant party in the proceedings requires the court, of its own motion, to communicate the documents at its disposal. It is not material, therefore, that the applicant did not complain about the non-communication of the relevant documents or took the initiative to access the case file (*Kerojärvi v. Finland*, § 42). The mere possibility for the appellant to consult the case file and obtain a copy of it is not, of itself, a sufficient safeguard (*Göç v. Turkey* [GC], § 57).

174. Obligation incumbent on the administrative authorities: the appellant must have access to the relevant documents in the possession of the administrative authorities, if necessary via a procedure for the disclosure of documents (*McGinley and Egan v. the United Kingdom*, §§ 86 and 90). Were the respondent State, without good cause, to prevent appellants from gaining access to documents in its possession which would have

assisted them in defending their case, or to falsely deny their existence, this would have the effect of denying them a fair hearing, in violation of Article 6 § 1 (ibid.).

175. Assessment of the proceedings as a whole: whether or not proceedings are fair is determined by examining them in their entirety (*Ankerl v. Switzerland*, § 38; *Centro Europa 7 S. r. l. and Di Stefano v. Italy* [GC], § 197).

176. That being so, any shortcoming in the fairness of the proceedings may, under certain conditions, be remedied at a later stage, either at the same level (*Helle v. Finland*, § 54) or by a higher court (*Schuler-Zgraggen v. Switzerland*, § 52; contrast *Albert and Le Compte v. Belgium*, § 36; *Feldbrugge v. the Netherlands*, § § 45 – 46).

177. In any event, if the defect lies at the level of the highest judicial body-for example because there is no possibility of replying to conclusions submitted to that body-there is an infringement of the right to a fair hearing (*Ruiz-Mateos v. Spain*, § § 65 – 67).

178. A procedural flaw can be remedied only if the decision in issue is subject to review by an independent judicial body that has full jurisdiction and itself offers the guarantees required by Article 6 § 1. It is the scope of the appeal court's power of review that matters, and this is examined in the light of the circumstances of the case (*Obermeier v. Austria*, § 70). ①

179. Previous decisions which do not offer the guarantees of a fair hearing: in such cases no question arises if a remedy was available to the appellant before an independent judicial body which had full jurisdiction and itself provided the safeguards required by Article 6 § 1 (*Oerlemans v. the Netherlands*, § § 53 – 58; *British-American Tobacco Company Ltd v. the Netherlands*, § 78). What counts is that such a remedy offering sufficient guarantees exists (*Air Canada v. the United Kingdom*, § 62).

180. Before the appellate courts: Article 6 § 1 does not compel the Contracting States to set up courts of appeal or of cassation, but where such courts do exist the State is required to ensure that litigants before these courts enjoy the fundamental guarantees contained in Article 6 § 1 (*Andrejeva v. Latvia* [GC], § 97). However, the manner of application of

---

① See also the section on "Review by a court having full jurisdiction".

Article 6 § 1 to proceedings before courts of appeal depends on the special features of the proceedings involved; account must be taken of the entirety of the proceedings in the domestic legal order and of the role played therein by the appellate court (*Helmers v. Sweden*, § 31) or the court of cassation (*K. D. B. v. the Netherlands*, § 41; *Levages Prestations Services v. France*, § § 44 – 45).

181. Given the special nature of the Court of Cassation's role, which is limited to reviewing whether the law has been correctly applied, the procedure followed may be more formal (ibid., § 48). The requirement to be represented by a specialist lawyer before the Court of Cassation is not in itself contrary to Article 6 (*G. L. and S. L. v. France* (dec.); *Tabor v. Poland*, § 42).

182. Limits: as a general rule it is for the national courts to assess the facts: is not the Court's role to substitute its own assessment of the facts for that of the national courts (*Dombo Beheer B. V. v. the Netherlands*, § 31).① Furthermore, while appellants have the right to present the observations which they regard as relevant to their case, Article 6 § 1 does not guarantee a litigant a favourable outcome (*Andronicou and Constantinou v. Cyprus*, § 201).

183. The theory of appearances: the Court has stressed the importance of appearances in the administration of justice; it is important to make sure the fairness of the proceedings is apparent. The Court has also made it clear, however, that the standpoint of the persons concerned is not in itself decisive; the misgivings of the individuals before the courts with regard to the fairness of the proceedings must in addition be capable of being held to be objectively justified (*Kraska v. Switzerland*, § 32). It is therefore necessary to examine how the courts handled the case.

184. In other cases, before Supreme Courts, the Court has pointed out that the public's increased sensitivity to the fair administration of justice justified the growing importance attached to appearances (*Kress v. France* [GC], § 82; *Martinie v. France* [GC], § 53; *Menchinskaya v. Russia*, § 32). The Court attached importance to appearances in these

---

① See the section on "Fourth instance".

cases (see also *Vermeulen v. Belgium*, § 34; *Lobo Machado v. Portugal*, § 32).

185. Judicial practice: in order to take the reality of the domestic legal order into account, the Court has always attached a certain importance to judicial practice in examining the compatibility of domestic law with Article 6 § 1 (*Kerojärvi v. Finland*, § 42; *Gorou v. Greece* (no. 2) [GC], § 32). Indeed, the general factual and legal background to the case should not be overlooked in the assessment of whether the litigants had a fair hearing (*Stankiewicz v. Poland*, § 70).

186. The State authorities cannot dispense with effective control by the courts on grounds of national security or terrorism: there are techniques that can be employed which accommodate both legitimate security concerns and the individual's procedural rights (*Dağtekin and Others v. Turkey*, § 34).

187. A principle independent of the outcome of the proceedings: the procedural guarantees of Article 6 § 1 apply to all litigants, not just those who have not won their cases in the national courts (*Philis v. Greece* (no. 2), § 45).

Examples

188. The case-law has covered numerous situations, including:

189. Observations submitted by the court to the appellate court manifestly aimed at influencing its decision: the parties must be able to comment on the observations, irrespective of their actual effect on the court, and even if the observations do not present any fact or argument which has not already appeared in the impugned decision in the opinion of the appellate court (*Nideröst-Huber v. Switzerland*, §§ 26 – 32) or of the respondent Government before the Strasbourg Court (*APEH Üldözötteinek Szövetsége and Others v. Hungary*, § 42).

190. Preliminary questions: where a preliminary reference mechanism exists, refusal by a domestic court to grant a request for such a referral may, in certain circumstances, infringe the fairness of proceedings (*Ullens de Schooten and Rezabek v. Belgium*, §§ 57 – 67, with further references). This is so where the refusal proves arbitrary:

- where there has been a refusal even though the applicable rules allow no exception to

- the principle of preliminary reference or no alternative thereto;
- where the refusal is based on reasons other than those provided for by the rules;
- or where the refusal has not been duly reasoned in accordance with those rules.

191. Article 6 § 1 does not, therefore, guarantee any right to have a case referred by a domestic court to the Court of Justice of the European Union [*Dotta v. Italy* (dec.)]. Applying the case-law cited above, the Court examines whether the refusal appears arbitrary [*Canela Santiago v. Spain* (dec.)].

192. Changes in domestic case-law: the requirement of legal certainty and the protection of legitimate expectations do not involve the right to an established jurisprudence (*Unédic v. France*, § 74). Case-law development is not, in itself, contrary to the proper administration of justice since a failure to maintain a dynamic and evolutive approach would prevent any reform or improvement (*Atanasovski v. the former Yugoslav Republic of Macedonia*, § 38). In that judgment the Court held that the existence of well-established jurisprudence imposed a duty on the Supreme Court to make a more substantial statement of reasons justifying its departure from the case-law, failing which the individual's right to a duly reasoned decision would be violated. In some cases changes in domestic jurisprudence which affect pending civil proceedings may violate the Convention (*Petko Petkov v. Bulgaria*, §§ 32 – 34).

193. On the subject of divergences in case-law, the Court has stressed the importance of setting mechanisms in place to ensure consistency in the practice of the courts and uniformity of case-law (*Frimu and Others v. Romania* (dec.), §§ 43 – 44). However, achieving consistency of the law may take time, and periods of conflicting case-law may therefore be tolerated without undermining legal certainty (*Nejdet Şahin and Perihan Şahin v. Turkey* [GC], § 83; *Albu and Others v. Romania*, §§ 36 and 40 – 43).①

194. Entry into force of a law when a case to which the State is a party is still pending: the Court is especially mindful of the dangers inherent in the use of retrospective legislation which has the effect of influencing the judicial determination of a dispute to which the State

---

① See also the section on "Fourth instance".

is a party, including where the effect is to make pending litigation unwinnable. Any reasons adduced to justify such measures must be closely examined (*National & Provincial Building Society, Leeds Permanent Building Society and Yorkshire Building Society v. the United Kingdom*, § 112). In principle the legislature is not precluded in civil matters from adopting new retrospective provisions to regulate rights arising under existing laws. Article 6 does, however preclude any interference by the legislature with the administration of justice designed to influence the judicial determination of a dispute-except on "compelling grounds of the general interest" (*Zielinski, Pradal, Gonzalez and Others v. France* [GC], § 57; *Scordino v. Italy* (no. 1) [GC], § 126).

The Court found violations, for example, in respect of:

- intervention by the legislature-at a time when proceedings to which the State was party had been pending for nine years and the applicants had a final, enforceable judgment against the State-to influence the imminent outcome of the case in the State's favour (*Stran Greek Refineries and Stratis Andreadis v. Greece*, §§ 49 – 50);
- a law which decisively influenced the imminent outcome of a case favour of the State (*Zielinski, Pradal, Gonzalez and Others v. France* [GC], § 59);
- the enactment, at a crucial point in proceedings before the Court of Cassation, of a law which for practical purposes resolved substantive issues and made carrying on with the litigation pointless (*Papageorgiou v. Greece*);
- a decision of an appellate court based, even subsidiarily, on a law enacted in the course of proceedings and which affected the outcome of the proceedings (*Anagnostopoulos and Others v. Greece*, §§ 20 – 21).

However, Article 6 § 1 cannot be interpreted as preventing any interference by the authorities with pending legal proceedings to which they are party. In other cases the Court has held that the considerations relied on by the respondent State were based on the compelling public-interest motives required to justify the retroactive effect of the law [*National & Provincial Building Society, Leeds Permanent Building Society and Yorkshire Building Society v. the United Kingdom*, § 112; *Forrer-Niedenthal v. Germany*, § 64;

OGIS-Institut Stanislas, *OGEC Saint-Pie X and Blanche de Castille and Others v. France*, §§ 71 – 72; *EEG-Slachthuis Verbist Izegem v. Belgium* (dec.)].

195. This case-law also applies to cases where the State, although not a party, vitiates the proceedings through its legislative powers (*Ducret v. France*, §§ 33 – 42).

196. Other types of legislative intervention:

- Laws may be enacted before the start of proceedings [*Organisation nationale des syndicats d'infirmiers libéraux* (*ONSIL*) *v. France* (dec.)] or once they have ended [*Preda and Dardari v. Italy* (dec.)] without raising an issue under Article 6.
- The enactment of general legislation may prove unfavourable to litigants without actually targeting pending judicial proceedings and thereby circumventing the principle of the rule of law (*Gorraiz Lizarraga and Others v. Spain*, § 72).
- A law may be declared unconstitutional while proceedings are pending without there being any intention of influencing those proceedings [*Dolca and Others v. Romania* (dec.)].

197. Failure to communicate the observations of an "independent member of the national legal service" to litigants before a Supreme Court (members of the public prosecutor's department: *Vermeulen v. Belgium*, *Van Orshoven v. Belgium*, *K. D. B. v. the Netherlands*; Principal Public Prosecutor/Attorney General: *Göç v. Turkey* [GC], *Lobo Machado v. Portugal*; Government Commissioner: *Kress v. France* [GC], *Martinie v. France* [GC]) and no opportunity to reply to such observations: many respondent States have argued that this category of members of the national legal service was neither party to the proceedings nor the ally or adversary of any party, but the Court has found that regard must be had to the part actually played in the proceedings by the official concerned, and more particularly to the content and effects of his submissions (*Vermeulen v. Belgium*, § 31; *Kress v. France* [GC], § 71 *in fine*).

198. The Court has stressed the importance of adversarial proceedings in cases where the submissions of an independent member of the national legal service in a civil case were not communicated in advance to the parties, depriving them of an opportunity to reply to them (ibid., § 76; *Lobo Machado v. Portugal*, § 31; *Van Orshoven v. Belgium*, § 41;

Göç v. Turkey [GC], §§ 55 – 56; *Immeubles Groupe Kosser v. France*, § 26; *Vermeulen v. Belgium*, § 33).

199. Participation by and even the mere presence of these members of the national legal service in the deliberations, be it "active" or "passive", after they have publicly expressed their views on the case has been condemned (ibid., § 34; *Lobo Machado v. Portugal*, § 32; *Kress v. France* [GC], § 87). This case-law is largely based on the theory of appearances①(*Martinie v. France* [GC], § 53).

200. The conditions in which the proceedings took place must therefore be examined, and in particular whether the proceedings were adversarial and complied with the equality of arms principle (compare *Kress v. France* [GC], § 76; *Göç v. Turkey* [GC], §§ 55 – 57), in order to determine whether the problem was attributable to the litigant's conduct or to the attitude of the State or the applicable legislation (*Fretté v. France*, §§ 49 – 51).

For the procedure before the Court of Justice of the European Communities/of the European Union: *Cooperatieve Producentenorganisatie van de Nederlandse Kokkelvisserij U. A. v. the Netherlands* (dec.).

201. Limits:

- Equality of arms does not entail a party's right to have disclosed to him or her, before the hearing, submissions which have not been disclosed to the other party to the proceedings or to the reporting judge or the judges of the trial bench (*Kress v. France* [GC], § 73).

- There is no point in recognising a right that has no real reach or substance: that would be the case if the right relied on under the Convention would have had no incidence on the outcome of the case because the legal solution adopted was legally unobjectionable (*Stepinska v. France*, § 18).

3. Fourth instance

a. General principles

202. One particular category of complaints submitted to the Court comprises what are

---

① See above.

commonly referred to as "fourth-instance" complaints. This term-which does not feature in the text of the Convention and has become established through the case-law of the Convention institutions (*Kemmache v. France* (no. 3), § 44)-is somewhat paradoxical, as it places the emphasis on what the Court is not: it is not a court of appeal or a court which can quash rulings given by the courts in the States Parties to the Convention or retry cases heard by them, nor can it re-examine cases in the same way as a Supreme Court. Fourth-instance applications therefore stem from a frequent misapprehension on two levels.

203. Firstly, there is often a widespread misconception on the part of the applicants as to the Court's role and the nature of the judicial machinery established by the Convention. It is not the Court's role to substitute itself for the domestic courts; its powers are limited to verifying the Contracting States' compliance with the human rights engagements they undertook in acceding to the Convention. Furthermore, in the absence of powers to intervene directly in the legal systems of the Contracting States, the Court must respect the autonomy of those legal systems. That means that it is not its task to deal with errors of fact or law allegedly committed by a national court unless and in so far as such errors may have infringed rights and freedoms protected by the Convention. It may not itself assess the facts which have led a national court to adopt one decision rather than another. If it were otherwise, the Court would be acting as a court of third or fourth instance, which would be to disregard the limits imposed on its action (*García Ruiz v. Spain* [GC], § 28).

204. Secondly, there is often misunderstanding as to the exact meaning of the term "fair" in Article 6 § 1 of the Convention. The "fairness" required by Article 6 § 1 is not "substantive" fairness (a concept which is part-legal, part-ethical and can only be applied by the trial court), but "procedural" fairness. Article 6 § 1 only guarantees "procedural" fairness, which translates in practical terms into adversarial proceedings in which submissions are heard from the parties and they are placed on an equal footing before the court [*Star Cate Epilekta Gevmata and Others v. Greece* (dec.)]. The fairness of proceedings is always assessed by examining them in their entirety, so that an isolated irregularity may not be sufficient to render the proceedings as a whole unfair (*Miroļubovs and Others v. Latvia*, § 103).

205. Furthermore, the Court respects the diversity of Europe's legal and judicial systems, and it is not the Court's task to standardise them. Just as it is not its task to examine the wisdom of the domestic courts' decisions where there is no evidence of arbitrariness (*Nejdet Şahin and Perihan Şahin v. Turkey* [GC], §§ 68, 89 and 94).

b. Scope and limits of the Court's supervision

206. The Court has always said that it is generally not its task to deal with errors of fact or law allegedly committed by a national court unless and in so far as such errors are manifest and infringed rights and freedoms protected by the Convention [*García Ruiz v. Spain* [GC], § 28; *Perez v. France* [GC], § 82; in *Dulaurans v. France* (§ 38) the Court found a violation of Article 6 § 1 because of a "manifest error of judgment"; but contrast *Société anonyme d'habitations à loyers modérés Terre et Famille v. France* (dec.)].

207. This means that the Court may not, as a general rule, question the findings and conclusions of the domestic courts as regards:

- The establishment of the facts of the case: the Court cannot challenge the findings of the domestic courts, save where they are flagrantly and manifestly arbitrary (*García Ruiz v. Spain* [GC], §§ 28 – 29).

- The interpretation and application of domestic law: it is primarily for the domestic courts to resolve problems of interpretation of national legislation (*Perez v. France* [GC], § 82), not for the Strasbourg Court, whose role is to verify whether the effects of such interpretation are compatible with the Convention (*Nejdet Şahin and Perihan Şahin v. Turkey* [GC], § 49). In exceptional cases the Court may draw the appropriate conclusions where a Contracting State's domestic courts have interpreted a domestic law in a manifestly arbitrary or erroneous manner (*Barać and Others v. Montenegro*, §§ 32 – 34, with further references; *Anđelković v. Serbia*, §§ 24 – 27 (denial of justice); *Laskowska v. Poland*, § 61), but it generally does so under other provisions of the Convention rather than under Article 6 § 1 (*Kushoglu v. Bulgaria*, § 50; *Işyar v. Bulgaria*, § 48; *Fabris v. France* [GC], § 60).

- The admissibility and assessment of evidence: ① the guarantees under Article 6 § 1 only cover the administration of evidence at the procedural level. The admissibility of evidence or the way it should be assessed on the merits are primarily matters for the national courts, whose task it is to weigh the evidence before them [*García Ruiz v. Spain* [GC], § 28; *Farange S. A. v. France* (dec.)].

208. So Article 6 § 1 does not allow the Court to question the substantive fairness of the outcome of a civil dispute, where more often than not one of the parties wins and the other loses.

209. A fourth-instance complaint under Article 6 § 1 of the Convention will be rejected by the Court on the grounds that the applicant had the benefit of adversarial proceedings; that he was able, at the various stages of those proceedings, to adduce the arguments and evidence he considered relevant to his case; that he had the opportunity of challenging effectively the arguments and evidence adduced by the opposing party; that all his arguments which, viewed objectively, were relevant to the resolution of the case were duly heard and examined by the courts; that the factual and legal reasons for the impugned decision were set out at length; and that, accordingly, the proceedings taken as a whole were fair (*García Ruiz v. Spain* [GC], § 29). The majority of fourth-instance applications are declared inadmissible de plano by a single judge or a three-judge Committee (Articles 27 and 28 of the Convention). By contrast, see, for example, *Donadzé v. Georgia*, § 35.

c. Consistency of domestic case-law

210. Article 6 § 1 does not confer an acquired right to consistency of case-law. Case-law development is not, in itself, contrary to the proper administration of justice since a failure to maintain a dynamic and evolutive approach would risk hindering reform or improvement (*Nejdet Şahin and Perihan Şahin v. Turkey* [GC], § 58).

211. In principle it is not the Court's role, even in cases which at first sight appear comparable or connected, to compare the various decisions pronounced by the domestic courts, whose independence it must respect. The possibility of divergences in case-law is an

---

① See also the section on "Administration of evidence".

inherent consequence of any judicial system which is based on a network of trial and appeal courts with authority over the area of their territorial jurisdiction. Such divergences may even arise within the same court. That in itself cannot be considered contrary to the Convention (*Santos Pinto v. Portugal*, § 41). Furthermore, there can be no "divergence" where the factual situations in issue are objectively different [*Uçar v. Turkey* (dec.)].

212. There may, however, be cases where divergences in case-law lead to a finding of a violation of Article 6 § 1. Here the Court's approach differs depending on whether the divergences exist within the same branch of courts or between two different branches of court which are completely independent from one another.

213. In the first case the divergent decisions are pronounced by a single domestic Supreme Court, or by various courts in the same branch of the legal system ruling in the last instance. In such cases the persistence of conflicting judgments can create a state of legal uncertainty likely to reduce public confidence in the judicial system, whereas such confidence is clearly one of the essential components of a State based on the rule of law. The Court determines whether such uncertainty exists case by case, based on three main criteria:

- whether the divergences in the case-law are profound and lasting;
- whether the domestic law provides for mechanisms capable of resolving such inconsistencies; and
- whether those mechanisms were applied and to what effect. The Contracting States have an obligation to organise their legal systems in such a way as to avoid the adoption of divergent judgments and resolve any serious contradictions by appropriate procedural means (*Beian v. Romania* (no. 1), §§ 37 and 39; *Nejdet Şahin and Perihan Şahin v. Turkey* [GC], §§ 56 – 57 and 80).

An additional criterion the Court takes into account is whether the inconsistency is an isolated case or affects large numbers of people (*Albu and Others v. Romania*, § 38).

214. In the second hypothesis the conflicting decisions are pronounced at last instance by courts in two different branches of the legal system, each with its own, independent Supreme Court not subject to any common judicial hierarchy. Here Article 6 § 1 does not go

as far as to demand the implementation of a vertical review mechanism or a common regulatory authority (such as a jurisdiction disputes court). In a judicial system with several different branches of courts, and where several Supreme Courts exist side by side and are required to give interpretations of the law at the same time and in parallel, achieving consistency of case-law may take time, and periods of conflicting case-law may therefore be tolerated without undermining legal certainty. So two courts, each with its own area of jurisdiction, examining different cases may very well arrive at divergent but nevertheless rational and reasoned conclusions regarding the same legal issue raised by similar factual circumstances without violating Article 6 § 1 (*Nejdet Şahin and Perihan Şahin v. Turkey* [GC], §§ 81 – 83 and 86).

4. Adversarial proceedings

215. The adversarial principle: the concept of a fair trial comprises the fundamental right to adversarial proceedings.

216. The requirements resulting from the right to adversarial proceedings are in principle the same in both civil and criminal cases (*Werner v. Austria*, § 66).

217. The desire to save time and expedite the proceedings does not justify disregarding such a fundamental principle as the right to adversarial proceedings (*Nideröst-Huber v. Switzerland*, § 30).

218. Content: the right to adversarial proceedings means in principle the opportunity for the parties to a criminal or civil trial to have knowledge of and comment on all evidence adduced or observations filed, even by an independent member of the national legal service, with a view to influencing the court's decision (*Ruiz-Mateos v. Spain*, § 63; *McMichael v. the United Kingdom*, § 80; *Vermeulen v. Belgium*, § 33; *Lobo Machado v. Portugal*, § 31; *Kress v. France* [GC], § 74). This requirement may also apply before a Constitutional Court (*Milatová and Others v. the Czech Republic*, §§ 63 – 66; *Gaspari v. Slovenia*, § 53).

- The actual effect on the court's decision is of little consequence (*Nideröst-Huber v. Switzerland*, § 27; *Ziegler v. Switzerland*, § 38).
- The right to adversarial proceedings must be capable of being exercised in

satisfactory conditions: a party to the proceedings must have the possibility to familiarise itself with the evidence before the court, as well as the possibility to comment on its existence, contents and authenticity in an appropriate form and within an appropriate time (*Krčmář and Others v. the Czech Republic*, § 42; *Immeubles Groupe Kosser v. France*, § 26), if necessary by obtaining an adjournment (*Yvon v. France*, § 39).

- The parties should have the opportunity to make known any evidence needed for their claims to succeed (*Clinique des Acacias and Others v. France*, § 37).

- The court itself must respect the adversarial principle, for example if it rules that the right to appeal on points of law has been forfeited on grounds of inadmissibility which it advances of its own motion (ibid., § 38; compare *Andret and Others v. France* (dec.), inadmissible: in this last case the Court of Cassation had informed the parties that new arguments were envisaged and the applicants had had an opportunity to reply before the Court of Cassation pronounced judgment).

- It is for the parties to a dispute alone to decide whether a document produced by the other party or evidence given by witnesses calls for their comments. Litigants' confidence in the workings of justice is based on the knowledge that they have had the opportunity to express their views on every document in the file (including documents obtained by the court of its own motion: *K. S. v. Finland*, § 22) (*Nideröst-Huber v. Switzerland*, § 29; *Pellegrini v. Italy*, § 45).

219. Examples of infringement of the right to adversarial proceedings as a result of non-disclosure of the following documents or evidence:

- in proceedings concerning the placement of a child, of reports by the social services containing information about the child and details of the background to the case and making recommendations, even though the parents were informed of their content at the hearing (*McMichael v. the United Kingdom*, § 80);

- evidence adduced by the public prosecutor, irrespective of whether he was or was not regarded as a "party", since he was in a position, above all by virtue of the authority conferred on him by his functions, to influence the court's decision in a manner that might be unfavourable to the person concerned (*Ferreira Alves v. Portugal* (no. 3), §§ 36 – 39);

- a note from the lower court to the appellate court aimed at influencing the latter court's decision, even though the note did not set out any new facts or arguments (ibid., § 41);

- documents obtained directly by the judges, containing reasoned opinions on the merits of the case (*K. S. v. Finland*, §§ 23 – 24).

220. Limit: the right to adversarial proceedings is not absolute and its scope may vary depending on the specific features of the case in question (*Hudáková and Others v. Slovakia*, §§ 26 – 27). The adversarial principle does not require that each party must transmit to its opponent documents which have not been presented to the court either (*Yvon v. France*, § 38). Nor does it require production of a memorial not capable of affecting the outcome of the case (*Asnar v. France* (no. 2), § 26).

5. Equality of arms

221. The principle of "equality of arms" is inherent in the broader concept of a fair trial. The requirement of "equality of arms", in the sense of a "fair balance" between the parties, applies in principle to civil as well as to criminal cases (*Feldbrugge v. the Netherlands*, § 44).

222. Content: maintaining a "fair balance" between the parties. Equality of arms implies that each party must be afforded a reasonable opportunity to present his case-including his evidence-under conditions that do not place him at a substantial disadvantage vis-à-vis the other party (*Dombo Beheer B. V. v. the Netherlands*, § 33).

- It is inadmissible for one party to make submissions to a court without the knowledge of the other and on which the latter has no opportunity to comment. It is a matter for the parties alone to assess whether a submission deserves a reaction (*APEH Üldözötteinek Szövetsége and Others v. Hungary*, § 42).

- However, if observations submitted to the court are not communicated to either of the parties there will be no infringement of equality of arms as such, but rather of the broader fairness of the proceedings (*Nideröst-Huber v. Switzerland*, §§ 23 – 24; *Clinique des Acacias and Others v. France*, §§ 36 – 37).

223. Examples of failure to observe the equality of arms principle: this principle was found to have been breached in the following cases because one of the parties had been placed at a clear disadvantage:

- A party's appeal was not served on the other party, who therefore had no possibility to respond (*Beer v. Austria*, § 19).
- Time had ceased to run against one of the parties only, placing the other at a substantial disadvantage (*Platakou v. Greece*, § 48; *Wynen and Centre hospitalier interrégional Edith-Cavell v. Belgium*, § 32).
- Only one of the two key witnesses was permitted to be heard (*Dombo Beheer B. V. v. the Netherlands*, §§ 34 – 35).
- The opposing party enjoyed significant advantages as regards access to relevant information, occupied a dominant position in the proceedings and wielded considerable influence with regard to the court's assessment (*Yvon v. France*, § 37).
- The opposing party held positions or functions which put them at an advantage and the court made it difficult for the other party to challenge them seriously by not allowing it to adduce relevant documentary or witness evidence (*De Haes and Gijsels v. Belgium*, §§ 54 and 58).
- In administrative proceedings the reasons given by the administrative authority were too summary and general to enable the appellant to mount a reasoned challenge to their assessment; and the tribunals of fact declined to allow the applicant to submit arguments in support of his case (*Hentrich v. France*, § 56).
- The denial of legal aid to one of the parties deprived them of the opportunity to present their case effectively before the court in the face of a far wealthier opponent (*Steel and Morris v. the United Kingdom*, § 72).
- In its *Martinie v. France* judgment ([GC], § 50) the Court considered that there was an imbalance detrimental to litigants on account of State Counsel's position in

the proceedings before the Court of Audit: unlike the other party, he was present at the hearing, was informed beforehand of the reporting judge's point of view, heard the latter's submissions at the hearing, fully participated in the proceedings and could express his own point of view orally without being contradicted by the other party, and that imbalance was accentuated by the fact that the hearing was not public.

- The prosecutor intervened in support of the arguments of the applicant's opponent (*Menchinskaya v. Russia*, §§ 35 – 39).

224. However, the Court found compatible with Article 6 § 1 a difference of treatment in respect of the hearing of the parties' witnesses (evidence given under oath for one party and not for the other), as it had not, in practice, influenced the outcome of the proceedings (*Ankerl v. Switzerland*, § 38).

225. Specific case of a civil-party action: the Court has distinguished between the system of a complaint accompanied by a civil-party action and an action brought by the public prosecutor, who is vested with public authority and responsible for defending the general interest [*Guigue and SGEN-CFDT v. France* (dec.)]. As a result, different formal conditions and time-limits for lodging an appeal (a shorter time-limit for the private party) did not breach the "equality of arms" principle, provided that meaningful use could be made of that remedy (cf. the special nature of the system concerned).

226. The Court has also found it compatible with the principle of equality of arms for a provision to limit the civil party's possibilities of appeal without limiting those of the public prosecutor-as their roles and objectives are clearly different (*Berger v. France*, § 38).

227. As regards cases opposing the prosecuting authorities and a private individual, the prosecuting authorities may enjoy a privileged position justified for the protection of the legal order. However, this should not result in a party to civil proceedings being put at an undue disadvantage *vis-à-vis* the prosecuting authorities (*Stankiewicz v. Poland*, § 68).

6. Administration of evidence

228. General principles:[1] the Convention does not lay down rules on evidence as such

---

[1] See also the section on "Fourth instance".

(*Mantovanelli v. France*, § 34). The admissibility of evidence and the way it should be assessed are primarily matters for regulation by national law and the national courts (*García Ruiz v. Spain* [GC], § 28). The same applies to the probative value of evidence and the burden of proof [*Tiemann v. France and Germany* (dec.)]. It is also for the national courts to assess the relevance of proposed evidence (*Centro Europa 7 S. r. l. and Di Stefano v. Italy* [GC], § 198).

However, the Court's task under the Convention is to ascertain whether the proceedings as a whole were fair, including the way in which evidence was taken (*Elsholz v. Germany* [GC], § 66). It must therefore establish whether the evidence was presented in such a way as to guarantee a fair trial (*Blücher v. the Czech Republic*, § 65).

It is the duty of the national courts to conduct a proper examination of the submissions, arguments and evidence adduced by the parties (*Van de Hurk v. the Netherlands*, § 59).

a. Witness evidence

229. Article 6 § 1 does not explicitly guarantee the right to have witnesses called, and the admissibility of witness evidence is in principle a matter of domestic law. However, the proceedings in their entirety, including the way in which evidence was permitted, must be "fair" within the meaning of Article 6 § 1 (*Dombo Beheer B. V. v. the Netherlands*, § 31).

- Where courts refuse requests to have witnesses called, they must give sufficient reasons and the refusal must not be tainted by arbitrariness: it must not amount to a disproportionate restriction of the litigant's ability to present arguments in support of his case (*Wierzbicki v. Poland*, § 45).

- A difference of treatment in respect of the hearing of the parties' witnesses may be such as to infringe the "equality of arms" principle [*Ankerl v. Switzerland*, § 38, where the Court found that the difference of treatment had not placed the applicant at a substantial disadvantage *vis-à-vis* his opponent; contrast *Dombo Beheer B. V. v. the Netherlands*, § 35, where only one of the two participants in the events in issue was allowed to give evidence (violation)].

b. Expert opinions

230. Refusal to order an expert opinion:

- Refusal to order an expert opinion is not, in itself, unfair; the Court must ascertain whether the proceedings as a whole were fair (*H. v. France*, § 61 and 70). The reasons given for the refusal must be reasonable.

- Refusal to order a psychological report in a case concerning child custody and access must also be examined in the light of the particular circumstances of the case (*Elsholz v. Germany* [GC], § 66, and *mutatis mutandis Sommerfeld v. Germany* [GC], § 71).

- In a child abduction case [*Tiemann v. France and Germany* (dec.)] the Court examined whether a Court of Appeal had given sufficient grounds for its refusal to allow the applicant's request for a second expert opinion, in order to ascertain whether the refusal had been reasonable.

231. Appointment of an expert: just like observance of the other procedural safeguards enshrined in Article 6 § 1, compliance with the adversarial principle relates to proceedings in a "tribunal"; no general, abstract principle may therefore be inferred from this provision that, where an expert has been appointed by a court, the parties must in all instances be able to attend the interviews held by him or be shown the documents he has taken into account.

232. What is essential is that the parties should be able to participate properly in the proceedings (*Mantovanelli v. France*, § 33).

233. Lack of neutrality on the part of an expert, together with his position and role in the proceedings, can tip the balance of the proceedings in favour of one party to the detriment of the other, in violation of the equality of arms principle (*Sara Lind Eggertsdóttir v. Iceland*, § 53); likewise, the expert may occupy a preponderant position in the proceedings and exert considerable influence on the court's assessment (*Yvon v. France*, § 37).

234. A medical expert report pertaining to a technical field that is not within the judges' knowledge is likely to have a preponderant influence on their assessment of the facts; it is an essential piece of evidence and the parties must be able to comment effectively on it (*Mantovanelli v. France*, § 36; *Storck v. Germany*, § 135).

- In the *Mantovanelli v. France* case the fact that the applicants were not able to comment effectively on the findings of the expert report, which was the main piece of evidence, violated Article 6 § 1.

- In the *Augusto v. France* case the failure to disclose the opinion of an accredited doctor as to whether the applicant met the medical requirements for entitlement to a welfare benefit, which was likely to have a decisive influence on the judgment, violated Article 6 § 1 even though that opinion was not binding on the judge by law.

235. Concerning the parties' rights *vis-à-vis* the expert: compare *Feldbrugge v. the Netherlands*, § 44 (violation), with *Olsson v. Sweden* (no. 1), § § 89 – 91 (no violation). As regards the requirement to disclose an adverse report, see *L. v. the United Kingdom* (dec.).

7. Reasoning of judicial decisions

236. The guarantees enshrined in Article 6 § 1 include the obligation for courts to give sufficient reasons for their decisions (*H. v. Belgium*, § 53). A reasoned decision shows the parties that their case has truly been heard.

237. Although a domestic court has a certain margin of appreciation when choosing arguments and admitting evidence, it is obliged to justify its activities by giving reasons for its decisions (*Suominen v. Finland*, § 36).

238. The reasons given must be such as to enable the parties to make effective use of any existing right of appeal (*Hirvisaari v. Finland*, § 30 *in fine*).

239. Article 6 § 1 obliges courts to give reasons for their decisions, but cannot be understood as requiring a detailed answer to every argument (*Van de Hurk v. the Netherlands*, § 61; *García Ruiz v. Spain* [GC], § 26 ; *Jahnke and Lenoble v. France* (déc.); *Perez v. France* [GC], § 81).

240. The extent to which this duty to give reasons applies may vary according to the nature of the decision (*Ruiz Torija v. Spain*, § 29; *Hiro Balani v. Spain*, § 27) and can only be determined in the light of the circumstances of the case: it is necessary to take into account, *inter alia*, the diversity of the submissions that a litigant may bring before the courts and the differences existing in the Contracting States with regard to statutory

provisions, customary rules, legal opinion and the presentation and drafting of judgments (*Ruiz Torija v. Spain*, § 29; *Hiro Balani v. Spain*, § 27).

241. However, where a party's submission is decisive for the outcome of the proceedings, it requires a specific and express reply (*Ruiz Torija v. Spain*, § 30; *Hiro Balani v. Spain*, § 28).

242. The courts are therefore required to examine:

- the litigants' main arguments (*Buzescu v. Romania*, § 67; *Donadzé v. Georgia*, § 35);

- pleas concerning the rights and freedoms guaranteed by the Convention and its Protocols: the national courts are required to examine these with particular rigour and care (*Wagner and J. M. W. L. v. Luxembourg*, § 96).

243. Article 6 § 1 does not require an appellate court to give more detailed reasoning when it simply applies a specific legal provision to dismiss an appeal on points of law as having no prospects of success, without further explanation (*Burg and Others v. France* (dec.); *Gorou v. Greece* (no. 2) [GC], § 41).

244. Similarly, in the case of an application for leave to appeal, which is the precondition for a hearing of the claims by the superior court and the eventual issuing of a judgment, Article 6 § 1 cannot be interpreted as requiring that the rejection of leave be itself subject to a requirement to give detailed reasons [*Kukkonen v. Finland* (no. 2), § 24; *Bufferne v. France* (dec.)]

245. Furthermore, in dismissing an appeal, an appellate court may, in principle, simply endorse the reasons for the lower court's decision (*García Ruiz v. Spain* [GC], § 26; contrast *Tatishvili v. Russia*, § 62). However, the notion of a fair procedure requires that a national court which has given sparse reasons for its decisions, whether by incorporating the reasons of a lower court or otherwise, did in fact address the essential issues which were submitted to its jurisdiction and did not merely endorse without further ado the findings reached by a lower court (*Helle v. Finland*, § 60). This requirement is all the more important where a litigant has not been able to present his case orally in the domestic proceedings (ibid.).

B. Public hearing

> **Article 6 § 1 of the Convention**
>
> "1. In the determination of his civil rights and obligations..., everyone is entitled to a fair and public hearing by [a] tribunal established by law. Judgment shall be pronounced publicly but the press and public may be excluded from all or part of the trial in the interests of morals, public order or national security in a democratic society, where the interests of juveniles or the protection of the private life of the parties so require, or to the extent strictly necessary in the opinion of the court in special circumstances where publicity would prejudice the interests of justice."

1. Hearing

246. General principles: in principle litigants have a right to a public hearing when none of the possible exceptions outlined in the second sentence of Article 6 § 1 applies (see above, and further explanations below). The public hearing protects litigants against the administration of justice in secret with no public scrutiny. Rendering the administration of justice visible contributes to the achievement of the aim of Article 6 § 1, namely a fair trial (*Diennet v. France*, § 33; *Martinie v. France* [GC], § 39).

247. To establish whether a trial complies with the requirement of publicity, it is necessary to consider the proceedings as a whole (*Axen v. Germany*, § 28).

248. In proceedings before a court of first and only instance the right to a "public hearing" under Article 6 § 1 entails an entitlement to an "oral hearing" (*Fredin v. Sweden* (no. 2), §§ 21 – 22; *Allan Jacobsson v. Sweden* (no. 2), § 46; *Göç v. Turkey* [GC], § 47) unless there are exceptional circumstances that justify dispensing with such a hearing [*Hesse-Anger and Hanger v. Germany* (dec.)].

249. The exceptional character of the circumstances that may justify dispensing with an oral hearing essentially comes down to the nature of the issues to be decided by the competent national court, not to the frequency of such situations (*Miller v. Sweden*, § 29; *Martinie v. France* [GC], § 41).

250. The absence of a hearing before a second or third instance may be justified by the special features of the proceedings concerned, provided a hearing has been held at first instance (*Helmers v. Sweden*, §36, but contrast §§38 – 39). Thus, leave-to-appeal proceedings and proceedings involving only questions of law, as opposed to questions of fact, may comply with the requirements of Article 6 even though the appellant was not given an opportunity of being heard in person by the appeal or cassation court (*Miller v. Sweden*, §30).

251. Accordingly, unless there are exceptional circumstances that justify dispensing with a hearing, the right to a public hearing under Article 6 §1 implies a right to an oral hearing at least before one instance (*Fischer v. Austria*, §44; *Salomonsson v. Sweden*, §36).

252. Civil proceedings on the merits which are conducted in private in accordance with a general and absolute principle, without the litigant being able to request a public hearing on the ground that his case presents special features, cannot in principle be regarded as compatible with Article 6 §1 of the Convention; other than in wholly exceptional circumstances, litigants must at least have the opportunity of requesting a public hearing, though the court may refuse the request and hold the hearing in private on account of the circumstances of the case and for pertinent reasons (*Martinie v. France* [GC], §42).

253. Lastly, the lack of a hearing at the decisive stage of the proceedings may or may not be sufficiently remedied at a later stage in the proceedings (*Le Compte, Van Leuven and De Meyere v. Belgium*, §§60 – 61; *Malhous v. the Czech Republic* [GC], §62).

254. Specific applications:

- A hearing may not be required where there are no issues of credibility or contested facts which necessitate a hearing and the courts may fairly and reasonably decide the case on the basis of the parties' submissions and other written materials (*Döry v. Sweden*, §37; *Saccoccia v. Austria*, §73).
- The Court has also accepted that forgoing a hearing may be justified in cases raising merely legal issues of a limited nature (*Allan Jacobsson v. Sweden* (no. 2), §49;

Valová, Slezák and Slezák v. Slovakia, §§ 65 – 68) or which present no particular complexity [*Varela Assalino v. Portugal* (dec.); *Speil v. Austria* (dec.)].

- The same also applies to highly technical questions. The Court has had regard to the technical nature of disputes over social-security benefits, which are better dealt with in writing than by means of oral argument. It has repeatedly held that in this sphere the national authorities, having regard to the demands of efficiency and economy, could abstain from holding a hearing since systematically holding hearings could be an obstacle to the particular diligence required in social-security proceedings (*Schuler-Zgraggen v. Switzerland*, § 58; *Döry v. Sweden*, § 41; and contrast *Salomonsson v. Sweden*, §§ 39 – 40).

255. By contrast, holding an oral hearing will be deemed necessary, for example, when the court's jurisdiction extends to issues of law and important factual questions (*Fischer v. Austria*, § 44), or to the assessment of whether the facts were correctly established by the authorities (*Malhous v. the Czech Republic* [GC], § 60), in circumstances which would require the courts to gain a personal impression of the applicants to afford the applicant the right to explain his personal situation, in person or through his representative (*Miller v. Sweden*, § 34 *in fine*; *Andersson v. Sweden*, § 57)-for example when the applicant should be heard on elements of personal suffering relevant to levels of compensation (*Göç v. Turkey* [GC], § 51; *Lorenzetti v. Italy*, § 33)-or to enable the court to obtain clarifications on certain points, *inter alia* by this means (*Fredin v. Sweden* (no. 2]), § 22; *Lundevall v. Sweden*, § 39).

256. Presence of press and public: The right to a public hearing implies, in principle, a public hearing before the relevant court. Article 6 § 1 does not, however, prohibit courts from deciding, in the light of the special features of the case, to derogate from this principle (*Martinie v. France* [GC], § 40). The wording of Article 6 § 1 provides for several exceptions to this rule.

257. "The press and public may be excluded from all or part of the trial":

- "in the interests of morals, public order or national security in a democratic society" (*Zagorodnikov v. Russia*, § 26; *B. and P. v. the United Kingdom*, § 39);

- "where the interests of juveniles or the protection of the private life of the parties so require": the interests of juveniles or the protection of the private life of the parties are in issue, for example, in proceedings concerning the residence of minors following their parents' separation, or disputes between members of the same family (ibid. , § 38); however, in cases involving the transfer of a child to a public institution the reasons for excluding a case from public scrunity must be subject to careful examination (*Moser v. Austria*, § 97). As for disciplinary proceedings against a doctor, while the need to protect professional confidentiality and the private lives of patients may justify holding proceedings in private, such an occurrence must be strictly required by the circumstances (*Diennet v. France*, § 34; and for an example of proceedings against a lawyer: *Hurter v. Switzerland*, § § 30 – 32);

- " or to the extent strictly necessary in the opinion of the court in special circumstances where publicity would prejudice the interests of justice ": it is possible to limit the open and public nature of proceedings in order to protect the safety and privacy of witnesses, or to promote the free exchange of information and opinion in the pursuit of justice (*B. and P. v. the United Kingdom*, § 38; *Osinger v. Austria*, § 45).

258. Waiver of the right to a public hearing: neither the letter nor the spirit of Article 6 § 1 prevents an individual from waiving his right to a public hearing of his own free will, whether expressly or tacitly, but such a waiver must be made in an unequivocal manner and must not run counter to any important public interest (*Le Compte, Van Leuven and De Meyere v. Belgium*, § 59; *Håkansson and Sturesson v. Sweden*, § 66; *Exel v. the Czech Republic*, § 46). The summons to appear must also have been received in good time (*Yakovlev v. Russia*, § § 20 – 22).

259. Conditions governing waiver of the right to a public hearing: the person concerned must consent (*Le Compte, Van Leuven and De Meyere v. Belgium*, § 59), of his own free will (*Albert and Le Compte v. Belgium*, § 35). The right may be waived expressly or tacitly (*Le Compte, Van Leuven and De Meyere v. Belgium*, § 59). But it must be done in an

unequivocal manner (*Albert and Le Compte v. Belgium*, § 35; *Håkansson and Sturesson v. Sweden*, § 67) and it must not run counter to any important public interest (ibid., § 66).

260. Failure to request a public hearing does not necessarily mean the person concerned has waived the right to have one held; regard must be had to the relevant domestic law (*Exel v. the Czech Republic*, § 47; *Göç v. Turkey* [GC], § 48 *in fine*). Whether or not the applicant requested a public hearing is irrelevant if the applicable domestic law expressly excludes that possibility (*Eisenstecken v. Austria*, § 33).

261. Examples: waiver of the right to a public hearing in disciplinary proceedings: *Le Compte, Van Leuven and De Meyere v. Belgium*, § 59; *H. v. Belgium*, § 54. Unequivocal waiver of the right to a public hearing: *Schuler-Zgraggen v. Switzerland*, § 58; and contrast *Exel v. the Czech Republic*, §§ 48 – 53.

2. Delivery

262. The public character of proceedings before judicial bodies protects litigants against the administration of justice in secret with no public scrutiny (*Fazliyski v. Bulgaria*, § 69, concerning a case classified secret-violation). It is also a means of maintaining confidence in the courts (*Pretto and Others v. Italy*, § 21).

263. Article 6 § 1 states "Judgment shall be pronounced publicly", which would seem to suggest that reading out in open court is required. The Court has found, however, that "other means of rendering a judgment public" may also be compatible with Article 6 § 1 (*Moser v. Austria*, § 101).

264. In order to determine whether the forms of publicity provided for under domestic law are compatible with the requirement for judgments to be pronounced publicly within the meaning of Article 6 § 1, "in each case the form of publicity to be given to the judgment under the domestic law ... must be assessed in the light of the special features of the proceedings in question and by reference to the object and purpose of Article 6 § 1" (*Pretto and Others v. Italy*, § 26; *Axen v. Germany*, § 31). The object pursued by Article 6 § 1 in this context-namely, to ensure scrutiny of the judiciary by the public with a view to safeguarding the right to a fair trial-must have been achieved during the course of the proceedings, which must be taken as a whole (ibid., § 32).

265. Where judgment is not pronounced publicly it must be ascertained whether sufficient publicity was achieved by other means.

266. In the following examples sufficient publicity was achieved by means other than public pronouncement:

- Higher courts which did not publicly pronounce decisions rejecting appeals on points of law: in order to determine whether the manner in which a Court of Cassation delivered its judgment met the requirements of Article 6 § 1, account must be taken of the entirety of the proceedings conducted in the domestic legal order and of the role of that court therein (*Pretto and Others v. Italy*, § 27).

  In finding no violation of Article 6 § 1 the Court paid particular attention to the stage of the procedure and to the scrutiny effected by these courts-which was limited to points of law-and to the judgments they delivered, upholding the decisions of the lower courts without any change to the consequences for the applicants. In the light of these considerations it found that the requirement for public pronouncement had been complied with where, by being deposited in the court registry, the full text of the judgment had been made available to everyone (ibid., §§ 27 – 28), or where a judgment upholding that of a lower court which itself had been pronounced publicly had been given without a hearing (*Axen v. Germany*, § 32).

- Trial court: the Court found no violation in a case where an appellate court publicly delivered a judgment summarising and upholding the decision of a first-instance court which had held a hearing but had not delivered its judgment in public (*Lamanna v. Austria*, §§ 33 – 34).

- Cases concerning the residence of children: while the domestic authorities are justified in conducting these proceedings in chambers in order to protect the privacy of the children and the parties and to avoid prejudicing the interests of justice, and to pronounce the judgment in public would, to a large extent, frustrate these aims, the requirement under Article 6 § 1 concerning the public pronouncement of judgments is satisfied where anyone who can establish an interest may consult or obtain a copy of the full text of the decisions, those of special interest being routinely published, thereby enabling the public to study the manner in which the courts generally approach such cases and the principles applied in deciding them (*B. and P. v. the United Kingdom*, § 47).

267. In the following cases, failure to pronounce the judgment publicly led to the finding of a violation:

- In a child residence case between a parent and a public institution: giving persons who established a legal interest in the case access to the file and publishing decisions of special interest (mostly of the appellate courts or the Supreme Court) did not suffice to comply with the requirements of Article 6 § 1 concerning publicity (*Moser v. Austria*, §§ 102 – 103).

- When courts of first and second instance examined in chambers a request for compensation for detention without their decisions being pronounced publicly or publicity being sufficiently ensured by other means (*Werner v. Austria*, §§ 56 – 60).

268. Where only the operative part of the judgment is read out in public: it must be ascertained whether the public had access by other means to the reasoned judgment which was not read out and, if so, the forms of publicity used must be examined in order to subject the judgment to public scrutiny (*Ryakib Biryukov v. Russia*, §§ 38 – 46 and references cited in §§ 33 – 36). As the reasons which would have made it possible to understand why the applicant's claims had been rejected were inaccessible to the public, the object pursued by Article 6 § 1 was not achieved (ibid., § 45).

C. Length of proceedings

Article 6 § 1 of the Convention

"1. In the determination of his civil rights and obligations…, everyone is entitled to a…hearing within a reasonable time by [a] tribunal…"

269. In requiring cases to be heard within a "reasonable time", the Convention underlines the importance of administering justice without delays which might jeopardise its

effectiveness and credibility (*H. v. France*, §58; *Katte Klitsche de la Grange v. Italy*, §61). Article 6 § 1 obliges the Contracting States to organise their legal systems so as to enable the courts to comply with its various requirements.

270. The Court has repeatedly stressed the importance of administering justice without delays which might jeopardise its effectiveness and credibility (*Scordino v. Italy* (no. 1) [GC], §224). An accumulation of breaches by the State constitutes a practice that is incompatible with the Convention (*Bottazzi v. Italy* [GC], §22).

1. Determination of the length of the proceedings

271. As regards the starting-point of the relevant period, time normally begins to run from the moment the action was instituted before the competent court (*Poiss v. Austria*, §50; *Bock v. Germany*, §35), unless an application to an administrative authority is a prerequisite for bringing court proceedings, in which case the period may include the mandatory preliminary administrative procedure (*König v. Germany*, §98; *X v. France*, §31; *Kress v. France* [GC], §90).

272. Thus, in some circumstances, the reasonable time may begin to run even before the issue of the writ commencing proceedings before the court to which the claimant submits the dispute (*Golder v. the United Kingdom*, §32 *in fine*; *Erkner and Hofauer v. Austria*, §64; *Vilho Eskelinen and Others v. Finland* [GC], §65). However, this is exceptional and has been accepted where, for example, certain preliminary steps were a necessary preamble to the proceedings (*Blake v. the United Kingdom*, §40).

273. Article 6 § 1 may also apply to proceedings which, although not wholly judicial in nature, are nonetheless closely linked to supervision by a judicial body. This was the case, for example, with a procedure for the partition of an estate which was conducted on a non-contentious basis before two notaries, but was ordered and approved by a court (*Siegel v. France*, §§33–38). The duration of the procedure before the notaries was therefore taken into account in calculating the reasonable time.

274. As to when the period ends, it normally covers the whole of the proceedings in question, including appeal proceedings (*König v. Germany*, §98 in fine) and extends right up to the decision which disposes of the dispute (*Poiss v. Austria*, §50). Hence, the

reasonable-time requirement applies to all stages of the legal proceedings aimed at settling the dispute, not excluding stages subsequent to judgment on the merits (*Robins v. the United Kingdom*, §§ 28-29).

275. The execution of a judgment, given by any court, is therefore to be considered as an integral part of the proceedings for the purposes of calculating the relevant period (*Martins Moreira v. Portugal*, § 44; *Silva Pontes v. Portugal*, § 33; *Di Pede v. Italy*, § 24). Time does not stop running until the right asserted in the proceedings actually becomes effective (*Estima Jorge v. Portugal*, §§ 36-38).

276. Proceedings before a Constitutional Court are taken into consideration where, although the court has no jurisdiction to rule on the merits, its decision is capable of affecting the outcome of the dispute before the ordinary courts (*Deumeland v. Germany*, § 77; *Pammel v. Germany*, §§ 51-57; *Süßmann v. Germany* [GC], § 39). Nevertheless, the obligation to hear cases within a reasonable time cannot be construed in the same way as for an ordinary court (ibid., § 56; *Oršuš and Others v. Croatia* [GC], § 109).

277. Lastly, as regards the intervention of third parties in civil proceedings, the following distinction should be made: where the applicant has intervened in domestic proceedings only on his or her own behalf the period to be taken into consideration begins to run from that date, whereas if the applicant has declared his or her intention to continue the proceedings as heir he or she can complain of the entire length of the proceedings (*Scordino v. Italy* (no. 1) [GC], § 220).

2. Assessment of the reasonable-time requirement

a. Principles

278. Assessment in the specific case: The reasonableness of the length of proceedings coming within the scope of Article 6 § 1 must be assessed in each case according to the particular circumstances (*Frydlender v. France* [GC], § 43), which may call for a global assessment (*Obermeier v. Austria*, § 72; *Comingersoll S. A. v. Portugal* [GC], § 23).

279. The whole of the proceedings must be taken into account (*König v. Germany*, § 98 *in fine*).

- While different delays may not in themselves give rise to any issue, they may, when

- viewed together and cumulatively, result in a reasonable time being exceeded (*Deumeland v. Germany*, § 90).
- A delay during a particular phase of the proceedings may be permissible provided that the total duration of the proceedings is not excessive (*Pretto and Others v. Italy*, § 37).
- "Long periods during which the proceedings… stagnate…" without any explanations being forthcoming are not acceptable (*Beaumartin v. France*, § 33).

280. The applicability of Article 6 § 1 to preliminary proceedings will depend on whether certain conditions are fulfilled (*Micallef v. Malta* [GC], §§ 83–86).①

281. Proceedings concerning the referral of a question to the Court of Justice of the European Communities/of the European Union for a preliminary ruling are not taken into consideration (*Pafitis and Others v. Greece*, § 95).

b. Criteria

282. The reasonableness of the length of proceedings must be assessed in the light of the following criteria established by the Court's case-law: the complexity of the case, the conduct of the applicant and of the relevant authorities and what was at stake for the applicant in the dispute (*Comingersoll S. A. v. Portugal* [GC]; *Frydlender v. France* [GC], § 43; *Sürmeli v. Germany* [GC], § 128).

i. Complexity of the case

283. The complexity of a case may relate both to the facts and to the law (*Katte Klitsche de la Grange v. Italy*, § 55; *Papachelas v. Greece* [GC], § 39). It may relate, for instance, to the involvement of several parties in the case (*H. v. the United Kingdom*, § 72) or to the various items of evidence that have to be obtained (*Humen v. Poland* [GC], § 63).

284. The complexity of the domestic proceedings may explain their length (*Tierce v. San Marino*, § 31).

ii. The applicant's conduct

285. Article 6 § 1 does not require applicants actively to cooperate with the judicial

---

① See the section on "Scope".

authorities, nor can they be blamed for making full use of the remedies available to them under domestic law (*Erkner and Hofauer v. Austria*, § 68).

286. The person concerned is required only to show diligence in carrying out the procedural steps relating to him, to refrain from using delaying tactics and to avail himself of the scope afforded by domestic law for shortening the proceedings (*Unión Alimentaria Sanders S. A. v. Spain*, § 35).

287. Applicants' behaviour constitutes an objective fact which cannot be attributed to the respondent State and which must be taken into account for the purpose of determining whether or not the reasonable time referred to in Article 6 § 1 has been exceeded (*Poiss v. Austria*, § 57; *Wiesinger v. Austria*, § 57; *Humen v. Poland* [GC], § 66). An applicant's conduct cannot by itself be used to justify periods of inactivity.

288. Some examples concerning the applicant's conduct:

- a lack of alacrity by the parties in filing their submissions may contribute decisively to the slowing-down of the proceedings (*Vernillo v. France*, § 34);
- frequent/repeated changes of counsel (*König v. Germany*, § 103);
- requests or omissions which have an impact on the conduct of the proceedings (*Acquaviva v. France*, § 61);
- an attempt to secure a friendly settlement (*Pizzetti v. Italy*, § 18; *Laino v. Italy* [GC], § 22);
- proceedings brought erroneously before a court lacking jurisdiction (*Beaumartin v. France*, § 33).

289. Although the domestic authorities cannot be held responsible for the conduct of a defendant, the delaying tactics used by one of the parties do not absolve the authorities from their duty to ensure that the proceedings are conducted within a reasonable time (*Mincheva v. Bulgaria*, § 68).

iii. Conduct of the competent authorities

290. Only delays attributable to the State may justify a finding of failure to comply with the "reasonable time" requirement (*Buchholz v. Germany*, § 49; *Papageorgiou v. Greece*, § 40; *Humen v. Poland* [GC], § 66). The State is responsible for all its authorities: not

just the judicial organs, but all public institutions (*Martins Moreira v. Portugal*, § 60).

291. Even in legal systems applying the principle that the procedural initiative lies with the parties, the latter's attitude does not absolve the courts from the obligation to ensure the expeditious trial required by Article 6 § 1 (*Pafitis and Others v. Greece*, § 93; *Tierce v. San Marino*, § 31; *Sürmeli v. Germany* [GC], § 129).

292. The same applies where the cooperation of an expert is necessary during the proceedings: responsibility for the preparation of the case and the speedy conduct of the trial lies with the judge (*Capuano v. Italy*, §§ 30 – 31; *Versini v. France*, § 29; *Sürmeli v. Germany* [GC], § 129).

293. It is for the Contracting States to organise their legal systems in such a way that their courts can guarantee the right of everyone to obtain a final decision on disputes relating to civil rights and obligations within a reasonable time (ibid.; *Scordino v. Italy* (no. 1) [GC], § 183).

294. Although this obligation applies also to a Constitutional Court, when so applied it cannot be construed in the same way as for an ordinary court. Its role as guardian of the Constitution makes it particularly necessary for a Constitutional Court sometimes to take into account other considerations than the mere chronological order in which cases are entered on the list, such as the nature of a case and its importance in political and social terms (compare *Süßmann v. Germany* [GC], §§ 56 – 58; *Voggenreiter v. Germany*, §§ 51 – 52; *Oršuš and Others v. Croatia* [GC], § 109). Furthermore, while Article 6 requires that judicial proceedings be expeditious, it also lays emphasis on the more general principle of the proper administration of justice (*Von Maltzan and Others v. Germany* (dec.) [GC], § 132). Nevertheless, a chronic overload cannot justify excessive length of proceedings (*Probstmeier v. Germany*, § 64).

295. Since it is for the member States to organise their legal systems in such a way as to guarantee the right to obtain a judicial decision within a reasonable time, an excessive workload cannot be taken into consideration (*Vocaturo v. Italy*, § 17; *Cappello v. Italy*, § 17). Nonetheless, a temporary backlog of business does not involve liability on the part of the State provided the latter has taken reasonably prompt remedial action to deal with an

exceptional situation of this kind (*Buchholz v. Germany*, § 51). Methods which may be considered, as a provisional expedient, include choosing to deal with cases in a particular order, based not just on the date when they were brought but on their degree of urgency and importance and, in particular, on what is at stake for the persons concerned. However, if a state of affairs of this kind is prolonged and becomes a matter of structural organisation, such methods are no longer sufficient and the State must ensure the adoption of effective measures (*Zimmermann and Steiner v. Switzerland*, § 29; *Guincho v. Portugal*, § 40). The fact that such backlog situations have become commonplace does not justify the excessive length of proceedings (*Unión Alimentaria Sanders S. A. v. Spain*, § 40).

296. Furthermore, the introduction of a reform designed to speed up the examination of cases cannot justify delays since States are under a duty to organise the entry into force and implementation of such measures in a way that avoids prolonging the examination of pending cases (*Fisanotti v. Italy*, § 22). In that connection, the adequacy or otherwise of the domestic remedies introduced by a member State in order to prevent or provide redress for the problem of excessively long proceedings must be assessed in the light of the principles established by the Court (*Scordino v. Italy* (no. 1) [GC], §§ 178 et seq. and 223).

297. The State was also held to be responsible for the failure to comply with the reasonable-time requirement in a case where there was an excessive amount of judicial activity focusing on the applicant's mental state. The domestic courts continued to have doubts in that regard despite the existence of five reports attesting the applicant's soundness of mind and the dismissal of two guardianship applications; moreover, the litigation lasted for over nine years (*Bock v. Germany*, § 47).

298. A strike by members of the Bar cannot by itself render a Contracting State liable with respect to the "reasonable time" requirement; however, the efforts made by the State to reduce any resultant delay are to be taken into account for the purposes of determining whether the requirement has been complied with (*Papageorgiou v. Greece*, § 47).

299. Where repeated changes of judge slow down the proceedings because each of the judges has to begin by acquainting himself with the case, this cannot absolve the State from

its obligations regarding the reasonable-time requirement, since it is the State's task to ensure that the administration of justice is properly organised (*Lechner and Hess v. Austria*, § 58).

iv. What is at stake in the dispute

300. Examples of categories of cases which by their nature call for particular expedition:

- Particular diligence is required in cases concerning civil status and capacity (*Bock v. Germany*, § 49; *Laino v. Italy* [GC], § 18; *Mikulić v. Croatia*, § 44).
- Child custody cases must be dealt with speedily (*Hokkanen v. Finland*, § 72; *Niederböster v. Germany*, § 39), all the more so where the passage of time may have irreversible consequences for the parent-child relationship (*Tsikakis v. Germany*, § § 64 and 68)-likewise, cases concerning parental responsibility and contact rights call for particular expedition (*Paulsen-Medalen and Svensson v. Sweden*, § 39; *Laino v. Italy* [GC], § 22).
- Employment disputes by their nature call for expeditious decision (*Vocaturo v. Italy*, § 17)-whether the issue at stake is access to a liberal profession (*Thlimmenos v. Greece* [GC], § § 60 and 62), the applicant's whole professional livelihood (*König v. Germany*, § 111), the continuation of the applicant's occupation (*Garcia v. France*, § 14), an appeal against dismissal (*Buchholz v. Germany*, § 52; *Frydlender v. France* [GC], § 45), the applicant's suspension (*Obermeier v. Austria*, § 72), his transfer (*Sartory v. France*, § 34) or his reinstatement (*Ruotolo v. Italy*, § 117), or where an amount claimed is of vital significance to the applicant (*Doustaly v. France*, § 48). This category includes pensions disputes (*Borgese v. Italy*, § 18).
- Exceptional diligence is required from the authorities in the case of an applicant who suffers from an "incurable disease" and has "reduced life expectancy" (*X v. France*, § 47; *A. and Others v. Denmark*, § § 78 – 81).

301. Other precedents

- Special diligence was required of the relevant judicial authorities in investigating a complaint lodged by an individual alleging that he had been subjected to violence by police officers (*Caloc v. France*, § 120).

- In a case where the applicant's disability pension made up the bulk of his resources, the proceedings by which he sought to have that pension increased in view of the deterioration of his health were of particular significance for him, justifying special diligence on the part of the domestic authorities (*Mocié v. France*, § 22).

- In a case concerning an action for damages brought by an applicant who had suffered physical harm and was aged 65 when she applied to join the proceedings as a civil party, the issue at stake called for particular diligence from the domestic authorities (*Codarcea v. Romania*, § 89).

- The issue at stake for the applicant may also be the right to education (*Oršuš and Others v. Croatia* [GC], § 109).

List of cited cases

The case-law cited in this Guide refers to judgments or decisions delivered by the Court and to decisions or reports of the European Commission of Human Rights ("the Commission").

Unless otherwise indicated, all references are to a judgment on the merits delivered by a Chamber of the Court. The abbreviation "(dec.)" indicates that the citation is of a decision of the Court and "[GC]" that the case was heard by the Grand Chamber.

The hyperlinks to the cases cited in the electronic version of the Guide are directed to the HUDOC database ⟨http://hudoc.echr.coe.int⟩ which provides access to the case-law of the Court (Grand Chamber, Chamber and Committee judgments and decisions, communicated cases, advisory opinions and legal summaries from the Case-Law Information Note) and of the Commission (decisions and reports), and to the resolutions of the Committee of Ministers.

The Court delivers its judgments and decisions in English and/or French, its two official languages. HUDOC also contains translations of many important cases intomore than thirty non-official languages, and links to around one hundred online case-law collections produced by third parties.

— A —

A. v. the United Kingdom, no. 35373/97, ECHR 2002 – X

A. and Others v. Denmark, 8 February 1996, Reports of Judgments and Decisions 1996 – I

Aćimović v. Croatia, no. 61237/00, ECHR 2003 – XI

Acquaviva v. France, 21 November 1995, Series A no. 333 – A

Aerts v. Belgium, 30 July 1998, Reports of Judgments and Decisions 1998 – V

Agrokompleks v. Ukraine, no. 23465/03, 6 October 2011

Air Canada v. the United Kingdom, 5 May 1995, Series A no. 316 – A

Airey v. Ireland, 9 October 1979, Series A no. 32

Aït-Mouhoub v. France, 28 October 1998, Reports of Judgments and Decisions 1998 – VIII

Aksoy v. Turkey, 18 December 1996, Reports of Judgments and Decisions 1996 – VI

Alaverdyan v. Armenia (dec.), no. 4523/04, 24 August 2010

Al-Adsani v. the United Kingdom [GC], no. 35763/97, ECHR 2001 – XI

Alatulkkila and Others v. Finland, no. 33538/96, 28 July 2005

Albert and Le Compte v. Belgium, 10 February 1983, Series A no. 58

Albu and Others v. Romania, nos. 34796/09 and 63 others, 10 May 2012

Alexandre v. Portugal, no. 33197/09, 20 November 2012

Allan Jacobsson v. Sweden (no. 2), 19 February 1998, Reports of Judgments and Decisions 1998 – I

Amat-G Ltd and Mebaghishvili v. Georgia, no. 2507/03, ECHR 2005 – VIII

Anagnostopoulos and Others v. Greece, no. 39374/98, ECHR 2000 – XI

Anđelković v. Serbia, no. 1401/08, 9 April 2013

Andersson v. Sweden, no. 17202/04, 7 December 2010

Andrejeva v. Latvia [GC], no. 55707/00, ECHR 2009

Andret and Others v. France (dec.), no. 1956/02, 25 May 2004

Andronicou and Constantinou v. Cyprus, 9 October 1997, Reports of Judgments and Decisions 1997 – VI

Andronikashvili v. Georgia (dec.), no. 9297/08, 22 June 2010

Ankerl v. Switzerland, 23 October 1996, Reports of Judgments and Decisions 1996 – V

Annoni di Gussola and Others v. France, nos. 31819/96 and 33293/96, ECHR 2000 – XI

APEH Üldözötteinek Szövetsége and Others v. Hungary, no. 32367/96, ECHR 2000 – X

Apostol v. Georgia, no. 40765/02, ECHR 2006 – XIV

Argyrou and Others v. Greece, no. 10468/04, 15 January 2009

Arvanitakis v. France (dec.), no. 46275/99, ECHR 2000 – XII

Ashingdane v. the United Kingdom, 28 May 1985, Series A no. 93

Asnar v. France (no. 2), no. 12316/04, 18 October 2007

Atanasovski v. theformer Yugoslav Republic of Macedonia, no. 36815/03, 14 January 2010

Athanassoglou and Others v. Switzerland [GC], no. 27644/95, ECHR 2000 – IV

Augusto v. France, no. 71665/01, 11 January 2007

Axen v. Germany, 8 December 1983, Series A no. 72

— B —

B. and P. v. the United Kingdom, nos. 36337/97 and 35974/97, ECHR 2001 – III

Bakan v. Turkey, no. 50939/99, 12 June 2007

Balmer-Schafroth and Others v. Switzerland, 26 August 1997, Reports of Judgments and Decisions 1997 – IV

Barać and Others v. Montenegro, no. 47974/06, 13 December 2011

Beaumartin v. France, 24 November 1994, Series A no. 296 – B

Beer v. Austria, no. 30428/96, 6 February 2001

Beian v. Romania (no. 1), no. 30658/05, ECHR 2007 – V (extracts)

Běleš and Others v. the Czech Republic, no. 47273/99, ECHR 2002 – IX

Bellet v. France, 4 December 1995, Series A no. 333 – B

Beneficio Cappella Paolini v. San Marino, no. 40786/98, ECHR 2004 – VIII (extracts)

Benthem v. the Netherlands, 23 October 1985, Series A no. 97

Berger v. France, no. 48221/99, ECHR 2002 – X (extracts)

Bertuzzi v. France, no. 36378/97, ECHR 2003 – III

Blake v. the United Kingdom, no. 68890/01, 26 September 2006

Blücher v. the Czech Republic, no. 58580/00, 11 January 2005

Bochan v. Ukraine, no. 7577/02, 3 May 2007

Bock v. Germany, 29 March 1989, Series A no. 150

Borgese v. Italy, 26 February 1992, Series A no. 228 – B

Bottazzi v. Italy [GC], no. 34884/97, ECHR 1999 – V

Bouilloc v. France (dec.), no. 34489/03, 28 November 2006

Boulois v. Luxembourg [GC], no. 37575/04, ECHR 2012

British-American Tobacco Company Ltd v. the Netherlands, 20 November 1995, Series A no. 331

Brualla Gómez de la Torre v. Spain, 19 December 1997, Reports of Judgments and Decisions 1997 – VIII

Brudnicka and Others v. Poland, no. 54723/00, ECHR 2005 – II

Brumărescu v. Romania [GC], no. 28342/95, ECHR 1999 – VII

Bryan v. the United Kingdom, 22 November 1995, Series A no. 335 – A

Buchholz v. Germany, 6 May 1981, Series A no. 42

Bufferne v. France (dec.), no. 54367/00, ECHR 2002 – III (extracts)

Buj v. Croatia, no. 24661/02, 1 June 2006

Burdov v. Russia, no. 59498/00, ECHR 2002 – III

Burdov v. Russia (no. 2), no. 33509/04, ECHR 2009

Burg andOthers v. France (dec.), no. 34763/02, ECHR 2003 – II

Buscarini v. San Marino (dec.), no. 31657/96, 4 May 2000

Buscemi v. Italy, no. 29569/95, ECHR 1999 – VI

Buzescu v. Romania, no. 61302/00, 24 May 2005

— C —

C. G. I. L. and Cofferati v. Italy (no. 2), no. 2/08, 6 April 2010

Caloc v. France, no. 33951/96, ECHR 2000 – IX

Canela Santiago v. Spain (dec.), no. 60350/00, 4 October 2001

Cañete de Goñi v. Spain, no. 55782/00, ECHR 2002 – VIII

Cappello v. Italy, 27 February 1992, Series A no. 230 – F

Capuano v. Italy, 25 June 1987, Series A no. 119

Central Mediterranean Development Corporation Limited v. Malta (no. 2), no. 18544/08, 22 November 2011

Centro Europa 7 S. r. l. and Di Stefano v. Italy [GC], no. 38433/09, ECHR 2012

Chapman v. Belgium (dec.), no. 39619/06, 5 March 2013

Chaudet v. France, no. 49037/06, 29 October 2009

Chevrol v. France, no. 49636/99, ECHR 2003 – III

Ciprová v. the Czech Republic（dec.），no. 33273/03，22 March 2005

Clarke v. the United Kingdom（dec.），no. 23695/02，ECHR 2005 – X（extracts）

Clinique des Acacias and Others v. France, nos. 65399/01 and 3 others，13 October 2005

Codarcea v. Romania, no. 31675/04，2 June 2009

Collectif national d'information et d'opposition à l'usine Melox-Collectif Stop Melox and Mox v. France（dec.），no. 75218/01，28 March 2006

Comingersoll S. A. v. Portugal [GC]，no. 35382/97，ECHR 2000 – IV

Cooper v. the United Kingdom [GC]，no. 48843/99，ECHR 2003 – XII

Cooperatieve Producentenorganisatie van de Nederlandse Kokkelvisserij U. A. v. Netherlands（dec.），no. 13645/05，ECHR 2009

Cordova v. Italy（no. 1），no. 40877/98，ECHR 2003 – I

Cordova v. Italy（no. 2），no. 45649/99，ECHR 2003 – I（extracts）

Crompton v. the United Kingdom, no. 42509/05，27 October 2009

Cubanit v. Romania（dec.），no. 31510/02，4 January 2007

Cudak v. Lithuania [GC]，no. 15869/02，ECHR 2010

Cyprus v. Turkey [GC]，no. 25781/94，ECHR 2001 – IV

— D —

Dağtekin and Others v. Turkey, no. 70516/01，13 December 2007

Dalea v. France（dec.），no. 964/07，2 February 2010

De Geouffre de la Pradelle v. France, 16 December 1992，Series A no. 253 – B

De Haan v. the Netherlands, 26 August 1997，Reports of Judgments and Decisions 1997 – IV

De Haes and Gijsels v. Belgium, 24 February 1997，Reports of Judgments and Decisions 1997 – I

De Moor v. Belgium, 23 June 1994，Series A no. 292 – A

Del Sol v. France, no. 46800/99，ECHR 2002 – II

Deumeland v. Germany, 29 May 1986，Series A no. 100

Deweer v. Belgium, 27 February 1980，Series A no. 35

Di Pede v. Italy, 26 September 1996, Reports of Judgments and Decisions 1996 – IV

Diennet v. France, 26 September 1995, Series A no. 325 – A

DMD Group, A. S., v. Slovakia, no. 19334/03, 5 October 2010

Dolca and Others v. Romania (dec.), nos. 59282/11 and 2 others, 4 September 2012

Dombo Beheer B. V. v. the Netherlands, 27 October 1993, Series A no. 274

Donadzé v. Georgia, no. 74644/01, 7 March 2006

Döry v. Sweden, no. 28394/95, 12 November 2002

Dotta v. Italy (dec.), no. 38399/97, 7 September 1999

Doustaly v. France, 23 April 1998, Reports of Judgments and Decisions 1998 – II

Driza v. Albania, no. 33771/02, ECHR 2007 – V (extracts)

Ducret v. France, no. 40191/02, 12 June 2007

Dulaurans v. France, no. 34553/97, 21 March 2000

— E —

EEG-Slachthuis Verbist Izegem v. Belgium (dec.), no. 60559/00, ECHR 2005 – XII

Eisenstecken v. Austria, no. 29477/95, ECHR 2000 – X

Elsholz v. Germany [GC], no. 25735/94, ECHR 2000 – VIII

Ellès and Others v. Switzerland, no. 12573/06, 16 December 2010

Emesa Sugar N. V. v. the Netherlands (dec.), no. 62023/00, 13 January 2005

Emine Araç v. Turkey, no. 9907/02, ECHR 2008

Enea v. Italy [GC], no. 74912/01, ECHR 2009

Erkner and Hofauer v. Austria, 23 April 1987, Series A no. 117

Ernst and Others v. Belgium, no. 33400/96, 15 July 2003

Essaadi v. France, no. 49384/99, 26 February 2002

Estima Jorge v. Portugal, 21 April 1998, Reports of Judgments and Decisions 1998 – II

Eternit v. France (dec.), no. 20041/10, 27 March 2012

Exel v. the Czech Republic, no. 48962/99, 5 July 2005

— F —

Fabris v. France [GC], no. 16574/08, ECHR 2013 (extracts)

Farange S. A. v. France (dec.), no. 77575/01, 14 September 2004

Fayed v. the United Kingdom, 21 September 1994, Series A no. 294 – B

Fazliyski v. Bulgaria, no. 40908/05, 16 April 2013

Feldbrugge v. the Netherlands, 29 May 1986, Series A no. 99

Ferrazzini v. Italy [GC], no. 44759/98, ECHR 2001 – VII

Ferreira Alves v. Portugal (no. 3), no. 25053/05, 21 June 2007

Fisanotti v. Italy, 23 April 1998, Reports of Judgments and Decisions 1998 – II

Fischer v. Austria, 26 April 1995, Series A no. 312

Fiume v. Italy, no. 20774/05, 30 June 2009

Flux v. Moldova (no. 2), no. 31001/03, 3 July 2007

Fociac v. Romania, no. 2577/02, 3 February 2005

Fogarty v. the United Kingdom [GC], no. 37112/97, ECHR 2001 – XI (extracts)

Forrer-Niedenthal v. Germany, no. 47316/99, 20 February 2003

Fredin v. Sweden (no. 2), 23 February 1994, Series A no. 283 – A

Fretté v. France, no. 36515/97, ECHR 2002 – I

Frimu and Others v. Romania (dec.), nos. 45312/11 and 2 others, 13 November 2012

Frydlender v. France [GC], no. 30979/96, ECHR 2000 – VII

Fuklev v. Ukraine, no. 71186/01, 7 June 2005

— G —

G. L. and S. L. v. France (dec.), no. 58811/00, ECHR 2003 – III (extracts)

Ganci v. Italy, no. 41576/98, ECHR 2003 – XI

Garcia v. France, no. 41001/98, 26 September 2000

García Manibardo v. Spain, no. 38695/97, ECHR 2000 – II

García Ruiz v. Spain [GC], no. 30544/96, ECHR 1999 – I

Gaspari v. Slovenia, no. 21055/03, 21 July 2009

Gautrin and Others v. France, 20 May 1998, Reports of Judgments and Decisions 1998 – III

Georgiadis v. Greece, 29 May 1997, Reports of Judgments and Decisions 1997 – III

Geraguyn Khorhurd Patgamavorakan Akumb v. Armenia (dec.), no. 11721/04, 14

April 2009

 Gnahoré v. France, no. 40031/98, ECHR 2000 – IX

 Göç v. Turkey [GC], no. 36590/97, ECHR-2002 – V

 Golder v. the United Kingdom, 21 February 1975, Series A no. 18

 Golubović v. Croatia, no. 43947/10, 27 November 2012

 Gorou v. Greece (no. 2) [GC], no. 12686/03, 20 March 2009

 Gorraiz Lizarraga and Others v. Spain, no. 62543/00, ECHR 2004 – III

 Granos Organicos Nacionales S. A. v. Germany, no. 19508/07, 22 March 2012

 Gülmez v. Turkey, no. 16330/02, 20 May 2008

 Guigue and SGEN-CFDT v. France (dec.), no. 59821/00, ECHR 2004 – I

 Guincho v. Portugal, 10 July 1984, Series A no. 81

 Gurov v. Moldova, no. 36455/02, 11 July 2006

 Gutfreund v. France, no. 45681/99, ECHR 2003 – VII

— H —

 H. v. Belgium, 30 November 1987, Series A no. 127 – B

 H. v. France, 24 October 1989, Series A no. 162 – A

 H. v. the United Kingdom, 8 July 1987, Series A no. 120

 Håkansson and Sturesson v. Sweden, 21 February 1990, Series A no. 171 – A

 Helle v. Finland, 19 December 1997, Reports of Judgments and Decisions 1997 – VIII

 Helmers v. Sweden, 29 October 1991, Series A no 212 – A

 Hentrich v. France, 22 September 1994, Series A no. 296 – A

 Hesse-Anger and Hanger v. Germany (dec.), no. 45835/99, ECHR 2001 – VI

 Hiro Balani v. Spain, 9 December 1994, Series A no. 303 – B

 Hirvisaari v. Finland, no. 49684/99, 27 September 2001

 Hokkanen v. Finland, 23 September 1994, Series A no. 299 – A

 Holding and Barnes PLC v. the United Kingdom (dec.), no. 2352/02, ECHR 2002 – IV

 Hornsby v. Greece, 19 March 1997, Reports of Judgments and Decisions 1997 – II

 Hotter v. Austria (dec.), no. 18206/06, 7 October 2010

 Hudáková and Others v. Slovakia, no. 23083/05, 27 April 2010

Humen v. Poland [GC], no. 26614/95, 15 October 1999

Hurter v. Switzerland, no. 53146/99, 15 December 2005

— I —

I. T. C. Ltd v. Malta (dec.), no. 2629/06, 11 December 2007

Immeubles Groupe Kosser v. France, no. 38748/97, 21 March 2002

Immobiliare Saffi v. Italy [GC], no. 22774/93, ECHR 1999 – V

Indra v. Slovakia, no. 46845/99, 1 February 2005

Işyar v. Bulgaria, no. 391/03, 20 November 2008

Ivan Atanasov v. Bulgaria, no. 12853/03, 2 December 2010

— J —

Jahnke and Lenoble v. France (dec.), no. 40490/98, ECHR 2000 – IX

James and Others v. the United Kingdom, 21 February 1986, Series A no. 98

Jurisic and Collegium Mehrerau v. Austria, no. 62539/00, 27 July 2006

— K —

K. D. B. v. the Netherlands, 27 March 1998, Reports of Judgments and Decisions 1998 – II

K. S. v. Finland, no. 29346/95, 31 May 2001

Kakamoukas and Others v. Greece [GC], no. 38311/02, 15 February 2008

Kalogeropoulou and Others v. Greece and Germany (dec.), no. 59021/00, ECHR 2002 – X

Katte Klitsche de la Grange v. Italy, 27 October 1994, Series A no. 293 – B

Kemmache v. France (no. 3), 24 November 1994, Series A no. 296 – C

Kerojärvi v. Finland, 19 July 1995, Series A no. 322

Kingsley v. the United Kingdom [GC], no. 35605/97, ECHR 2002 – IV

Kleyn and Others v. the Netherlands [GC], nos. 39343/98 and 3 others, ECHR 2003 – VI

Kök v. Turkey, no. 1855/02, 19 October 2006

König v. Germany, 28 June 1978, Series A no. 27

Kraska v. Switzerland, 19 April 1993, Series A no. 254 – B

Krčmář and Others v. the Czech Republic, no. 35376/97, 3 March 2000

Kress v. France [GC], no. 39594/98, ECHR 2001 – VI

Kreuz v. Poland, no. 28249/95, ECHR 2001 – VI

Kübler v. Germany, no. 32715/06, 13 January 2011

Kukkonen v. Finland (no. 2), no. 47628/06, 13 January 2009

Kushoglu v. Bulgaria, no. 48191/99, 10 May 2007

Kutić v. Croatia, no. 48778/99, ECHR 2002 – II

Kyrtatos v. Greece, no. 41666/98, ECHR 2003 – VI (extracts)

— L —

L. v. the United Kingdom (dec.), no. 34222/96, ECHR 1999 – VI

L'Érablière A. S. B. L. v. Belgium, no. 49230/07, ECHR 2009

Laidin v. France (no. 2), no. 39282/98, 7 January 2003

Laino v. Italy [GC], no. 33158/96, ECHR 1999 – I

Lamanna v. Austria, no. 28923/95, 10 July 2001

Langborger v. Sweden, 22 June 1989, Series A no. 155

Laskowska v. Poland, no. 77765/01, 13 March 2007

Lavents v. Latvia, no. 58442/00, 28 November 2002

Le Calvez v. France, 29 July 1998, Reports of Judgments and Decisions 1998 – V

Le Compte, Van Leuven and De Meyere v. Belgium, 23 June 1981, Series A no. 43

Lechner and Hess v. Austria, 23 April 1987, Series A no. 118

Levages Prestations Services v. France, 23 October 1996, Reports of Judgments and Decisions 1996 – V

Libert v. Belgium (dec.), no. 44734/98, 8 July 2004

Lithgow and Others v. the United Kingdom, 8 July 1986, Series A no. 102

Lobo Machado v. Portugal, 20 February 1996, Reports of Judgments and Decisions 1996 – I

Loiseau v. France (dec.), no. 46809/99, ECHR 2003 – XII

Lorenzetti v. Italy, no. 32075/09, 10 April 2012

Luka v. Romania, no. 34197/02, 21 July 2009

Lunari v. Italy, no. 21463/93, 11 January 2001

Lundevall v. Sweden, no. 38629/97, 12 November 2002

Luordo v. Italy, no. 32190/96, ECHR 2003 – IX

Lupaş and Others v. Romania, nos. 1434/02 and 2 others, ECHR 2006 – XV (extracts)

— M —

Maaouia v. France [GC], no. 39652/98, ECHR 2000 – X

Mackay and BBC Scotland v. the United Kingdom, no. 10734/05, 7 December 2010

Majorana v. Italy (dec.), no. 75117/01, 26 May 2005

Malhous v. the Czech Republic [GC], no. 33071/96, 12 July 2001

Mamatkulov and Askarov v. Turkey [GC], nos. 46827/99 and 46951/99, ECHR 2005 – I

Manoilescu and Dobrescu v. Romania and Russia (dec.), no. 60861/00, ECHR 2005 VI

Mantovanelli v. France, 18 mars 1997, Reports of Judgments and Decisions 1997 – II

Markovic and Others v. Italy [GC], no. 1398/03, ECHR 2006 – XIV

Martinie v. France [GC], no. 58675/00, ECHR 2006 – VI

Martins Moreira v. Portugal, 26 October 1988, Series A no. 143,

Masson and Van Zon v. the Netherlands, 28 September 1995, Series A no. 327 – A

Matheus v. France, no. 62740/00, 31 March 2005

McElhinney v. Ireland [GC], no. 31253/96, ECHR 2001 – XI (extracts)

McGinley and Egan v. the United Kingdom, 9 June 1998, Reports of Judgments and Decisions 1998 – III

McGonnell v. the United Kingdom, no. 28488/95, ECHR 2000 – II

McMichael v. the United Kingdom, 24 February 1995, Series A no. 307 – B

McVicar v. the United Kingdom, no. 46311/99, ECHR 2002 – III

Melis v. Greece, no. 30604/07, 22 July 2010

Melnyk v. Ukraine, no. 23436/03, 28 March 2006

Menchinskaya v. Russia, no. 42454/02, 15 January 2009

Mercieca and Others v. Malta, no. 21974/07, 14 June 2011

Mérigaud v. France, no. 32976/04, 24 September 2009

Mežnarić v. Croatia, no. 71615/01, 15 July 2005

Micallef v. Malta [GC], no. 17056/06, ECHR 2009

Mihova v. Italy (dec.), no. 25000/07, 30 March 2010

Mikulić v. Croatia, no. 53176/99, ECHR 2002 – I

Milatová and Others v. the Czech Republic, no. 61811/00, ECHR 2005 – V

Miller v. Sweden, no. 55853/00, 8 February 2005

Mincheva v. Bulgaria, no. 21558/03, 2 September 2010

Miragall Escolano v. Spain, nos. 38366/97 and 9 others, ECHR 2000 – I

Miroļubovs and Others v. Latvia, no. 798/05, 15 September 2009

Mocié v. France, no. 46096/99, 8 April 2003

Moreira de Azevedo v. Portugal, 23 October 1990, Series A no. 189

Morel v. France, no. 34130/96, ECHR 2000 – VI

Moroko v. Russia, no. 20937/07, 12 June 2008

Moser v. Austria, no. 12643/02, 21 September 2006

Mosteanu and Others v. Romania, no. 33176/96, 26 November 2002

Musumeci v. Italy, no. 33695/96, 11 January 2005

— N —

National & Provincial Building Society, Leeds Permanent Building Society and Yorkshire Building Society v. the United Kingdom, 23 October 1997, Reports of Judgments and Decisions 1997 – VII

Nejdet Şahin and Perihan Şahin v. Turkey [GC], no. 13279/05, 20 October 2011

Nideröst-Huber v. Switzerland, 18 February 1997, Reports of Judgments and Decisions 1997 – I

Niederböster v. Germany, no. 39547/98, ECHR 2003 – IV (extracts)

Nunes Dias v. Portugal (dec.), nos. 2672/03 and 69829/01, ECHR 200 – 3 IV

— O —

Obermeier v. Austria, 28 June 1990, Series A no. 179

Oerlemans v. the Netherlands, 27 November 1991, Series A no. 219

OGIS-Institut Stanislas, OGEC Saint-Pie X and Blanche de Castille and Others v.

France, nos. 42219/98 and 54563/00, 27 May 2004

Okyay andOthers v. Turkey, no. 36220/97, ECHR 2005 – Ⅶ

Oleksandr Volkov v. Ukraine, no. 21722/11, ECHR 2013

Oleynikov v. Russia, no. 36703/04, 14 March 2013

Olsson v. Sweden (no. 1), 24 March 1988, Series A no. 130

Olujić v. Croatia, no. 22330/05, 5 February 2009

Organisation nationale des syndicats d'infirmiers libéraux (ONSIL) v. France (dec.), no. 39971/98, ECHR 2000 – Ⅸ

Oršuš and Others v. Croatia [GC], no. 15766/03, ECHR 2010

Ortenberg v. Austria, 25 November 1994, Series A no. 295 – B

Osinger v. Austria, no. 54645/00, 24 March 2005

Osman v. the United Kingdom 28 October 1998, Reports of Judgments and Decisions 1998 – Ⅷ

Ouzounis and Others v. Greece, no. 49144/99, 18 April 2002

— P —

P., C. and S. v. the United Kingdom, no. 56547/00, ECHR 2002 – Ⅵ

Pabla Ky v. Finland, no. 47221/99, ECHR 2004 – Ⅴ

Pafitis and Others v. Greece, 26 February 1998, Reports of Judgments and Decisions 1998 – Ⅰ

Paksas v. Lithuania [GC], no. 34932/04, ECHR 2011

Pammel v. Germany, 1 July 1997, Reports of Judgments and Decisions 1997 – Ⅳ

Panjeheighalehei v. Denmark (dec.), no. 11230/07, 13 October 2009

Papachelas v. Greece [GC], no. 31423/96, ECHR 1999 – Ⅱ

Papageorgiou v. Greece, 22 October 1997, Reports of Judgments and Decisions 1997 – Ⅵ

Papon v. France (dec.), no. 344/04, ECHR 2005 – Ⅺ

Parlov-Tkalčić v. Croatia, no. 24810/06, 22 December 2009

Paulsen-Medalen and Svensson v. Sweden, 19 February 1998, Reports of Judgments and Decisions 1998 – Ⅰ

Pedro Ramos v. Switzerland, no. 10111/06, 14 October 2010

Pellegrin v. France [GC], no. 28541/95, ECHR 1999 – VIII

Pellegrini v. Italy, no. 30882/96, ECHR 2001 – VIII

Peñafiel Salgado v. Spain (dec.), no. 65964/01, 16 April 2002

Perez v. France [GC], no. 47287/99, ECHR 2004 – I

Pérez de Rada Cavanilles v. Spain, 28 October 1998, Reports of Judgments and Decisions 1998 – VIII

Peruš v. Slovenia, no. 35016/05, 27 September 2012

Pescador Valero v. Spain, no. 62435/00, ECHR 2003 – VII

Petko Petkov v. Bulgaria, no. 2834/06, 19 February 2013

Pétur Thór Sigurðsson v. Iceland, no. 39731/98, ECHR 2003 – IV

Philis v. Greece (no. 1), 27 August 1991, Series A no. 209

Philis v. Greece (no. 2), 27 June 1997, Reports of Judgments and Decisions 1997 – IV

Pierre-Bloch v. France, 21 October 1997, Reports of Judgments and Decisions 1997 – VI

Pini and Others v. Romania, nos. 78028/01 and 78030/01, ECHR 2004 – V (extracts)

Pizzetti v. Italy, 26 February 1993, Series A no. 257 – C

Platakou v. Greece, no. 38460/97, ECHR 2001 – I

Pocius v. Lithuania, no. 35601/04, 6 July 2010

Podbielski and PPU Polpure v. Poland, no. 39199/98, 26 July 2005

Poiss v. Austria, 23 April 1987, Series A no. 117

Potocka and Others v. Poland, no. 33776/96, ECHR 2001 – X

Preda and Dardari v. Italy (dec.), nos. 28160/95 and 28382/95, ECHR 1999 – III

Pretto and Others v. Italy, 8 December 1983, Series A no. 71

Pridatchenko and Others v. Russia, nos. 2191/03 and 3 others, 21 June 2007

Prince Hans-Adam II of Liechtenstein v. Germany [GC], no. 42527/98, ECHR 2001 – VIII

Probstmeier v. Germany, 1 July 1997, Reports of Judgments and Decisions 1997 – Ⅳ

Procola v. Luxembourg, 28 September 1995, Series A no. 326

Prodan v. Moldova, no. 49806/99, ECHR 2004 – Ⅲ (extracts)

Puolitaival and Pirttiaho v. Finland, no. 54857/00, 23 November 2004

— R —

R. P. and Others v. the United Kingdom, no. 38245/08, 9 October 2012

Raylyan v. Russia, no. 22000/03, 15 February 2007

Refah Partisi (The Welfare Party) and Others v. Turkey (dec.), nos. 41340/98 and 3 others, 3 October 2000

Reuther v. Germany (dec.), no. 74789/01, ECHR 2003 – Ⅸ

Revel and Mora v. France (dec.), no. 171/03, 15 November 2005

Ringeisen v. Austria, 16 July 1971, Series A no. 13

Robins v. the United Kingdom, 23 September 1997, Reports of Judgments and Decisions 1997 – Ⅴ

Roche v. the United Kingdom [GC], 32555/96, ECHR 2005 – Ⅹ

Rolf Gustafson v. Sweden, 1 July 1997, Reports of Judgments and Decisions 1997 – Ⅳ

Romańczyk v. France, no. 7618/05, 18 November 2010

RTBF v. Belgium, no. 50084/06, ECHR 2011

Ruianu v. Romania, no. 34647/97, 17 June 2003

Ruiz-Mateos v. Spain, 23 June 1993, Series A no. 262

Ruiz Torija v. Spain, 9 December 1994, Series A no. 303 – A

Ruotolo v. Italy, 27 February 1992, Series A no. 230 – D

Ryabykh v. Russia, no. 52854/99, ECHR 2003 – Ⅸ

Ryakib Biryukov v. Russia, no. 14810/02, ECHR 2008

— S —

Sabeh El Leil v. France [GC], no. 34869/05, 29 June 2011

Sabin Popescu v. Romania, no. 48102/99, 2 March 2004

Sablon v. Belgium, no. 36445/97, 10 April 2001

Saccoccia v. Austria (dec.), no. 69917/01, 5 July 2007

Saccoccia v. Austria, no. 69917/01, 18 December 2008

Sacilor-Lormines v. France, no. 65411/01, ECHR 2006 – XIII

Sakellaropoulos v. Greece (dec), no. 38110/08, 6 January 2011

Salesi v. Italy, no. 26 February 1993, Series A no. 257 – E

Salomonsson v. Sweden, no. 38978/97, 12 November 2002

Sâmbata Bihor Greco-Catholic Parish v. Romania, no. 48107/99, 12 January 2010

San Leonard Band Club v. Malta, no. 77562/01, ECHR 2004 – IX

Sanglier v. France, no. 50342/99, 27 May 2003

Santambrogio v. Italy, no. 61945/00, 21 September 2004

Santos Pinto v. Portugal, no. 39005/04, 20 May 2008

Saoud v. France, no. 9375/02, 9 October 2007

Sara Lind Eggertsdóttir v. Iceland, no. 31930/04, 5 July 2007

Sartory v. France, no. 40589/07, 24 September 2009

Savino and Others v. Italy, nos. 17214/05 and 2 others, 28 April 2009

Schouten and Meldrum v. the Netherlands, 9 December 1994, Series A no. 304

Schuler-Zgraggen v. Switzerland, 24 June 1993, Series A no. 263

Scordino v. Italy (no. 1) [GC], no. 36813/97, ECHR 2006 – V

Sdružení Jihočeské Matky v. the Czech Republic (dec.), no. 19101/03, 10 July 2006

Siałkowska v. Poland, no. 8932/05, 22 March 2007

Siegel v. France, no. 36350/97, ECHR 2000 – XII

Sigalas v. Greece, no. 19754/02, 22 September 2005

Sigma Radio Television Ltd v. Cyprus, nos. 32181/04 and 35122/05, 21 July 2011

Šikić v. Croatia, no. 9143/08, 15 July 2010

Silva Pontes v. Portugal, 23 March 1994, series A n° 286 – A

Skorobogatykh v. Russia (dec.), no. 37966/02, 8 June 2006

Smirnov v. Russia (dec.), no. 14085/04, 6 July 2006

Société anonyme d'habitations à loyers modérés Terre et Famille v. France (dec.), no. 62033/00, 17 February 2004

Sokurenko and Strygun v. Ukraine, nos. 29458/04 and 29465/04, 20 July 2006

Sommerfeld v. Germany [GC], no. 31871/96, ECHR 2003 – VIII (extracts)

Sotiris and Nikos Koutras ATTEE v. Greece, no. 39442/98, ECHR 2000 – XII

Sovtransavto Holding v. Ukraine, no. 48553/99, ECHR 2002 – VII

Speil v. Austria (dec.), no. 42057/98, 5 September 2002

Sporrong and Lönnroth v. Sweden, 23 September 1982, Series A no. 52

Sramek v. Austria, 22 October 1984, Series A no. 84

Stanev v. Bulgaria [GC], no. 36760/06, ECHR 2012

Stankiewicz v. Poland, no. 46917/99, ECHR 2006 – VI

Star Cate Epilekta Gevmata and Others v. Greece (dec.), no. 54111/07, 6 July 2010

Staroszczyk v. Poland, no. 59519/00, 22 March 2007

Steel and Morris v. the United Kingdom, no. 68416/01, ECHR 2005 – II

Stegarescu and Bahrin v. Portugal, no. 46194/06, 6 April 2010

Stepinska v. France, no. 1814/02, 15 June 2004

Storck v. Germany, no. 61603/00, ECHR 2005 – V

Stran Greek Refineries and Stratis Andreadis v. Greece, 9 December 1994, Series A no. 301 – B

Stubbings and Others v. the United Kingdom, 22 October 1996, Reports of Judgments and Decisions 1996 – IV

Suda v. the Czech Republic, no. 1643/06, 28 October 2010

Sukut v. Turkey (dec.), no. 59773/00, 11 September 2007

Suominen v. Finland, no. 37801/97, 1 July 2003

Sürmeli v. Germany [GC], no. 75529/01, ECHR 2006 – VII

Süßmann v. Germany [GC], 16 September 1996, Reports of Judgments and Decisions 1996 – IV

Švarc and Kavnik v. Slovenia, no. 75617/01, 8 February 2007

Syngelidis v. Greece, no. 24895/07, 11 February 2010

Szücs v. Austria, 24 November 1997, Reports of Judgments and Decisions 1997 – VII

— T —

Tabor v. Poland, no. 12825/02, 27 June 2006

Taşkın and Others v. Turkey, no. 46117/99, ECHR 2004 – X

Tatishvili v. Russia, no. 1509/02, ECHR 2007 – I

Terra Woningen B. V. v. the Netherlands, 17 December 1996, Reports of Judgments and Decisions 1996 – VI

Teteriny v. Russia, no. 11931/03, 30 June 2005

The Holy Monasteries v. Greece, 9 December 1994, Series A no. 301 – A

Thlimmenos v. Greece[GC], no. 34369/97, ECHR 2000 – IV

Tiemann v. France and Germany (dec.), nos. 47457/99 and 47458/99, ECHR 2000 – IV

Tierce v. San Marino, no. 69700/01, ECHR 2003 – VII

Tinnelly & Sons Ltd and Others and McElduff and Others v. the United Kingdom, 10 July 1998, Reports of Judgments and Decisions 1998 – IV

Tocono and Profesorii Prometeişti v. Moldova, no. 32263/03, 26 June 2007

Tolstoy Miloslavsky v. the United Kingdom, 13 July 1995, Series A no. 316 – B

Torri v. Italy, 1 July 1997, Reports of Judgments and Decisions 1997 – IV

Toziczka v. Poland, no. 29995/08, 24 July 2012

Tre Traktörer Aktiebolag v. Sweden, 7 July 1989, Series A no. 159

Tregubenko v. Ukraine, no. 61333/00, 2 November 2004

Treska v. Albania and Italy (dec.), no. 26937/04, ECHR 2006 – XI (extracts)

Tsfayo v. the United Kingdom, no. 60860/00, 14 November 2006

Tsikakis v. Germany, no. 1521/06, 10 February 2011

Turczanik v. Poland, no. 38064/97, ECHR 2005 – VI

Tuziński v. Poland (dec), no. 40140/98, 30 March 1999

— U —

Uçar v. Turkey (dec.), no. 12960/05, 29 September 2009

Ullens de Schooten and Rezabek v. Belgium, nos. 3989/07 and 38353/07, 20 September 2011

Ulyanov v. Ukraine (dec.), no. 16472/04, 5 October 2010

Unédic v. France, no. 20153/04, 18 December 2008

Unión Alimentaria Sanders S. A. v. Spain, 7 July 1989, Series A no. 157

Užukauskas v. Lithuania, no. 16965/04, 6 July 2010

— V —

Valová, Slezák and Slezák v. Slovakia, no. 44925/98, 1 June 2004

Van de Hurk v. the Netherlands, 19 April 1994, Series A no. 288

Van Droogenbroeck v. Belgium, 24 June 1982, Series A no. 50

Van Orshoven v. Belgium, 25 June 1997, Reports of Judgments and Decisions 1997 – Ⅲ

Varela Assalino v. Portugal (dec.), no. 64336/01, 25 April 2002

Vasilchenko v. Russia, no. 34784/02, 23 September 2010

Verein gegen Tierfabriken Schweiz (VgT) v. Switzerland (no. 2), no. 32772/02, 4 October 2007

Verlagsgruppe News GmbH v. Austria (dec.), no. 62763/00, 16 January 2003

Vermeulen v. Belgium, 20 February 1996, Reports of Judgments and Decisions 1996 – Ⅰ

Vernillo v. France, 20 February 1991, Series A no. 198

Versini v. France, no. 40096/98, 10 July 2001

Vilho Eskelinen and Others v. Finland [GC], no. 63235/00, ECHR 2007 – Ⅱ

Vocaturo v. Italy, 24 May 1991, Series A no. 206 – C

Voggenreiter v. Germany, no. 47169/99, ECHR 2004 – Ⅰ (extracts)

Von Maltzan and Others v. Germany (dec.) [GC], nos. 71916/01 and 2 others, ECHR 2005 – Ⅴ

— W —

Wagner and J. M. W. L. v. Luxembourg, no. 76240/01, 28 June 2007

Waite and Kennedy v. Germany [GC], no. 26083/94, ECHR 1999 – Ⅰ

Warsicka v. Poland, no. 2065/03, 16 January 2007

Weissman andOthers v. Romania, no. 63945/00, ECHR 2006 – Ⅶ (extracts)

Werner v. Austria, 24 November 1997, Reports of Judgments and Decisions 1997 – Ⅶ

Wettstein v. Switzerland, no. 33958/96, ECHR 2000 – Ⅻ

Wierzbicki v. Poland, no. 24541/94, 18 June 2002

Wiesinger v. Austria, 30 October 1991, Series A no. 213

Woś v. Poland, no. 22860/02, ECHR 2006 – VII

Wynen and Centre hospitalier interrégional Edith-Cavell v. Belgium, no. 32576/96, ECHR 2002 – VIII

— X —

X v. France, 31 March 1992, Series A no. 234 – C

— Y —

Yagtzilar and Others v. Greece, no. 41727/98, ECHR 2001 – XII

Yakovlev v. Russia, no. 72701/01, 15 March 2005

Yavorivskaya v. Russia, no. 34687/02, 21 July 2005

Yvon v. France, no. 44962/98, ECHR 2003 – V

— Z —

Z and Others v. the United Kingdom [GC], no. 29392/95, ECHR 2001 – V

Zagorodnikov v. Russia, no. 66941/01, 7 June 2007

Zalli v. Albania (dec.), no. 52531/07, 8 February 2011

Zander v. Sweden, 25 November 1993, Series A no. 279 – B

Zapletal v. the Czech Republic (dec.), no. 12720/06, 30 November 2010

Ziegler v. Switzerland, no. 33499/96, 21 February 2002

Zielinski, Pradal, Gonzalez and Others v. France [GC], nos. 24846/94 and 9 others, ECHR 1999 – VII

Zimmermann and Steiner v. Switzerland, 13 July 1983, Series A no. 66

Zollmann v. the United Kingdom (dec.), no. 62902/00, ECHR 2003 – XII

Zolotas v. Greece, no. 38240/02, 2 June 2005

Zumtobel v. Austria, 21 September 1993, Series A no. 268 – A

Zvolsky and Zvolská v. the Czech Republic, no. 46129/99, ECHR 2002 – IX

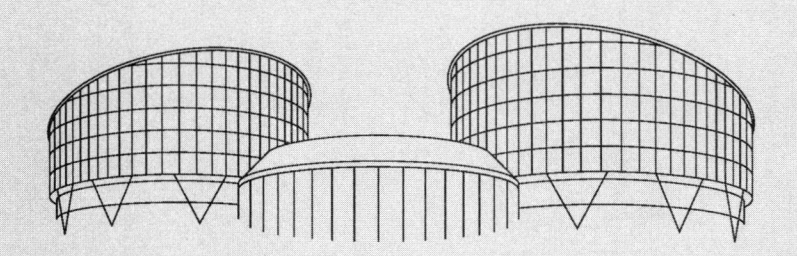

EUROPEAN COURT OF HUMAN RIGHTS
COUR EUROPÉENNE DES DROITS DE L'HOMME

第四章 《欧洲人权公约》第6条适用指南
获得公正审判的权利

（刑事部分）

COUNCIL OF EUROPE
CONSEIL DE L'EUROPE

读者须知

本指南是欧洲人权法院(以下简称本法院、欧洲法院、斯特拉斯堡法院)出版的公约指南系列的一部分,旨在让执业律师了解斯特拉斯堡法院做出的基本判决。本指南分析和汇总了截至 2015 年 12 月 31 日的关于《欧洲人权公约》(以下简称公约、欧洲公约)第 1 号议定书第 2 条的判例法。读者可以从中发现本领域的基本原则和相关判例。

援引的判例法选取了具有指导性的、重要的以及最新的判决。

本法院的判例不仅用于审判呈交至本法院的案件,而且从更为一般的意义上用于阐释、捍卫和发展"公约"创立的各项规则,并以此促使各缔约国对之加以遵守(*Irelandv. the United Kingdom*, 1978 年 1 月 18 日, §154, Series A no.25.)。因此,从普遍意义来说,公约确立的此机制的任务便是通过决定公共政策的各种问题来提升人权保护的标准,并在缔约国范围内推广人权法学(*Konstantin Markin v. Russia*[GC], 30078/06, §89, ECHR 2012)。

第6条　获得公正审判的权利

"(1)在决定某人的公民权利和义务或者在决定对某人确定任何刑事罪名时,任何人有权在合理的时间内受到依法设立的独立而公正的审判机构的公平且公开的审讯。判决应当公开宣布。但是,基于对民主社会中的道德、公共秩序或者国家安全的利益,以及对民主社会中的少年的利益或者是保护当事人的私生活权利的考虑,或者是法院认为,在特殊情况下,如果公开审讯将损害公平利益的话,可以拒绝记者和公众参与旁听全部或者部分审讯。

(2)凡受刑事罪指控者在未经依法证明为有罪之前,应当推定为无罪。

(3)凡受刑事罪指控者具有下列最低限度的权利:

a. 以他所了解的语言立即详细地通知他被指控罪名的性质以及被指控的原因;

b. 应当有适当的时间和便利条件为辩护作准备;

c. 由他本人或者由他自己选择的律师协助自己辩护,或者如果他无力支付法律协助费用的,则基于公平利益的考虑,应当免除他的有关费用;

d. 询问不利于他的证人,并在与不利于他的证人具有相同的条件下,让有利于他的证人出庭接受询问;

e. 如果他不懂或者不会讲法院所使用的工作语言,可以请求免费的译员协助翻译。"

第一节　适用范围:"刑事指控"的概念

第6条第1款

"在决定……对某人确定任何刑事罪名时,任何人有权……受到……审判机构的公平……的审讯。……"

一、一般原则

1. "刑事指控"的概念有着一定的"自治"意义,独立于各成员国国内法律体系中所规定的分类(*Adolf v. Austria*, § 30)。

2. 必须在公约的范畴内来理解"指控"的概念。因此,可以将其定义为"由当局针对个人做出的、声明其已犯下刑事罪行的官方通知"。这个定义同样呼应了判定"犯罪嫌疑人的状况是否受到了实质影响"的测试(*Deweer v. Belgium*, §§ 42 and 46; *Eckle v. Germany*, § 73)。本法院也认为,受警方看管并被要求作为证人在受询问前宣誓的人,也已经是"刑事指控"的对象,并有权保持沉默(*Brusco v. France*, §§ 46-50)。

3. 从"刑事"的自治意义来说,公约并不反对各缔约国所采取的"去刑事化"行动。去刑事化之后的行为在缔约国可能已不构成刑事犯罪,但是仍然可能属于公约所定义的"犯罪"的范畴。因此,如果让各缔约国自由裁量排除这些罪行,可能导致违背公约意旨的结果(见 *Öztürk v. Germany*, § 49)。

4. 从以下标准出发,判断是否可以适用公约第6条刑事部分——这些标准在恩格尔等人诉荷兰案(*Engel and Others v. the Netherlands*, §§ 82-83)中得以确立:

(1)国内法的分类;

(2)犯罪的性质;

(3)相关人员可能受到的刑罚的严重程度。

5. 作为起点,第1条标准的重要性是相对的。若国内法把一项犯罪规定为刑事犯罪,那么可以适用公约第6条的刑事部分。反之,法院将根据国内法的分类,查明所涉程序的实体内容。

6. 第2条标准较之第1条更为重要(*Jussila v. Finland* [GC], § 38),在适用时,将考虑以下因素:

- 所涉的法律规则是仅仅针对一个特定群体,还是具有普适性(*Bendenoun v. France*, § 47);
- 诉讼是否由具有规制性执法权的公共机构提起(*Benham v. the United Kingdom*, § 56);
- 该法律规则是否具有惩罚性或威慑性目的(*Öztürk v. Germany*, § 53; *Bendenoun v. France*, § 47);

- 是否必须在定罪的前提下才能施加刑罚(Benham v. the United Kingdom, § 56);
- 在欧洲委员会其他成员国中相应的程序是如何归类的(Öztürk v. Germany, § 53)。

7. 第 3 条标准是由相关法律中的最高法定刑来决定的(Campbell and Fell v. the United Kingdom, § 72; Demicoli v. Malta, § 34)。

8. 在恩格尔等人诉荷兰(Engel and Others v. the Netherlands, § 85)案中确立的第 2、3 条标准不需要同时满足,只需满足其一即可;若要适用公约第 6 条,可以是所涉罪行在本质上属于公约意义上的"刑事"罪行,也可以是行为人因该罪行所受的惩罚从本质上和严重程度来说属于普遍意义上的"刑事"范畴(Lutz v. Germany, § 55; Öztürk v. Germany, § 54)。即使一项罪行不会被判处监禁刑,其仍可能成为一项刑事罪行,不能因刑罚较轻而否定其刑事性质(Öztürk v. Germany, § 53; Nicoleta Gheorghe v. Romania, § 26)。

然而,如果单独分析某一标准无法明确判断是否构成刑事指控时,可以同时参考这两项标准(Bendenoun v. France, § 47)。

9. 在用到术语"刑事指控"(criminal charge)以及"被指控刑事犯罪"(charged with a criminal offence)时,第 6 条的三项表达的是完全相同的情形。因此,第 6 条刑事部分的适用性对于这三项而言是完全一致的。

二、一般原则的适用

(一)纪律处分程序

10. 由于违反军纪而被纪律部门监禁数月的情形,可适用公约第 6 条刑事部分的规定(Engel and Others v. the Netherlands, § 85)。另外,本法院认为,两天的逮捕期间太短,不属于"刑事法律"范畴(同前注)。

11. 对于职业纪律处分程序是否适用刑事部分的问题并没有定论,因为本法院认为这种程序是民事性质的,而无须做出刑事判决(Albert and Le Compte v. Belgium, § 30)。在这一案件中,当事人受到了强制退休的纪律处分,本法院认为,只要国内当局确保其决定只在纯粹的行政范畴之内,这种程序就不属于第 6 条所定义的"刑事"范畴[Moullet v. France(dec.)]。本法院还认为,军队长官因触犯纪律而被开除引起的纠纷不适用第 6 条刑事部分[*Suküt v. Turkey*(dec.)]。

12. "适当考虑"到监狱环境以及特殊的监狱纪律制度,公约第 6 条也可以适用于违反监狱纪律的罪行,这取决于指控的性质以及处罚的性质和严重程度[在厄泽和康纳斯诉英国案(*Ezeh and Connors v. the United Kingdom*[GC],§ 82)中,两名申诉人分别被判处了额外的 40 天和 7 天的监禁;相反参见 *Štitić v. Croatia*,§§ 51 - 63)]。但是,原则上,涉及监狱系统的处分程序本身并不直接适用于公约第 6 条刑事部分(*Boulois v. Luxembourg*[GC],§ 85)。因此,将囚犯置于高度监管单位之类的行为并不涉及刑事指控;法院应该根据公约第 6 条第 1 款民事部分的规定,处理针对此种手段及附加限制的申诉。(*Enea v. Italy*[GC],§ 98)。

13. 一般认为,本法院根据扰乱庭审秩序(蔑视法庭)的相关规则下达的措施,不属于公约第 6 条的范畴,因为这与行使纪律权力相类似(*Ravnsborg v. Sweden*,§ 34;*Putz v. Austria*,§§ 33 - 37)。然而,若国内法将蔑视法庭规定为刑事犯罪,考虑到惩罚的性质和严重程度,可能会适用第 6 条加以定罪(*Kyprianou v. Cyprus*[GC],§§ 61 - 64,关于一项监禁 5 天的刑罚)。

14. 对于蔑视议会,本法院区分以下两方面:一方面,立法机构规制其内部侵犯议员特权的行为;另一方面,立法机构的管辖权得以延伸,可以惩罚来自非议员的外部行为。从性质上而言,前者被认为是纪律处分性的,而对于后者,考虑到普适性以及可能施加的惩罚的严重程度,本法院将其认定为刑罚(在 *Demicoli v. Malta*,§ 32 一案中,判处了长达 60 天的监禁,并处罚金)。

(二)行政、税收、海关、金融以及竞争法诉讼

15. 以下行政违法行为可能适用第 6 条刑事部分的规定:

- 某些道路交通违法行为可能被处以罚金或被限制驾驶的,如处罚扣分或剥夺驾驶资格(*Lutz v. Germany*,§ 182;*Schmautzer v. Austria*;*Malige v. France*);
- 构成妨害或扰乱治安的轻微违法(*Lauko v. Slovakia*;*Nicoleta Gheorghe v. Romania*,§§ 25 - 26);
- 触犯社会保障法的违法行为(*Hüseyin Turan v. Turkey*,§§ 18 - 21,此案中处罚的是没有申报就业的情况,不过罚金不高);
- 宣扬并传播煽动种族仇恨的行政违法行为,可受行政警告以及被没收涉案出版物的(*Balsytė-Lideikienė v. Lithuania*,§ 61)。

16. 基于以下的要素，第6条曾适用于税收滞纳金诉讼中：
- 规定处罚的法律适用于所有作为纳税人的公民；
- 税收滞纳金的目的并不在于补偿经济损失，而是主要作为一种惩罚来防止行为人再犯；
- 罚以税收滞纳金的依据是一项兼有威慑性和惩罚性目的的一般规则；
- 税收滞纳金数额巨大 [Bendenoun v. France；相反地，参见 Mieg de Boofzheim v. France(dec.)一案中迟缴的利率]。

虽然一些税收滞纳金很低（在 Jussila v. Finland [GC]，§38一案中，滞纳金仅为重新评估后应缴税款的10%），但其刑事本质可能使其足以适用第6条。

17. 第6条刑事部分曾适用于海关法（Salabiaku v. France），适用于拥有预算和金融问题管辖权的法院判处的处罚（Guisset v. France），以及适用于某些有权处理经济、金融和竞争法领域问题的行政机关 [Lilly France S. A. v. France(dec.)；Dubus S. A. v. France；A. Menarini Diagnostics S. r. l. v. Italy]。

（三）政治问题

18. 第6条刑事部分不适用于涉及选举制裁的诉讼（Pierre-Bloch v. France，§§53-60）；政党的解散 [Refah Partisi (the Welfare Party) and Others v. Turkey (dec.)]；议会委员会的调查 [Montera v. Italy(dec.)]；以及针对一国总统明显触犯宪法行为的弹劾程序（Paksas v. Lithuania [GC]，§§66-67）。

19. 对于肃清程序，本法院认为其具有强烈的刑事含义（违法行为的性质—不真实的肃清宣告—处罚的性质和严重程度—长时间禁止从事特定职业），因此可以适用第6条刑事部分 [Matyjek v. Poland(dec.)；相反的情形，参见 Sidabras and Džiautas v. Lithuania(dec.)]。

（四）驱逐和引渡

20. 虽然在刑事诉讼中可能涉及对外国人的驱逐程序，但是这一程序并不适用于第6条刑事部分（Maaouia v. France [GC]，§39）。引渡程序 [Peñafiel Salgado v. Spain (dec.)] 及欧洲逮捕令的相关程序 [Monedero Angora v. Spain(dec.)] 均同样排除适用第6条刑事部分。

21. 与此相反，将徒刑变更为驱除出国境10年，可以基于与最初定罪时相同的原因而被认定为一种处罚（Gurguchiani v. Spain，§§40 and 47-48）。

(五)刑事诉讼、辅助程序以及后续救济的不同阶段

22. 为了预防混乱或犯罪而采取的措施不适用公约第 6 条[警察的特别监督：*Raimondo v. Italy*，§ 43；一个青年人非礼同校女生，警察对其警告：*R. v. the United Kingdom*(dec.)]。

23. 在庭审前(询问、调查)的阶段,本法院将刑事诉讼视作一个整体。因此,倘若违背第 6 条的相关要求有可能严重影响公正审判的话,这些要求如合理期限或者辩护权的行使就可能也需要在这些阶段予以考虑(*Imbrioscia v. Switzerland*，§ 36)。虽然预审法官并不决定一项"刑事指控",但其所采取的步骤对接下来包括实际庭审在内的诉讼程序的进行和公正性有直接影响。因此,预审法官可能在调查阶段适用第 6 条第 1 款,虽然该款的某些程序性保障可能无法适用(*Vera Fernández-Huidobro v. Spain*，§§ 108 - 114)。

24. 第 6 条第 1 款适用于"刑事指控"诉讼程序的整个过程,包括量刑程序(例如,让国内法院评估没收数额的没收程序：*Phillips v. the United Kingdom*，§ 39)。第 6 条刑事部分同样可以适用于拆除无规划许可的房屋引发的诉讼程序,因为这种拆除可以被视作一种"处罚"(*Hamer v. Belgium*，§ 60)。然而,其不适用于请求根据新的更有利于行为人的刑法条文重新确定刑罚的诉讼(*Nurmagomedov v. Russia*，§ 50)。

25. 涉及刑罚执行的程序——例如执行大赦的程序[*Montcornet de Caumont v. France*(dec.)]、假释程序[*A. v. Austria*(dec.)],基于《被判刑人移管公约》的移管程序[*Szabó v. Sweden*(dec.)](但是也有相反的判决——参见 *Buijen v. Germany*，§§ 40 - 45),以及涉及执行外国法院下达的没收令的执行令程序[*Saccoccia v. Austria*(dec.)]不适用第 6 条刑事部分。

26. 原则上,对于第三方财产权有消极影响的没收措施,在没有受到任何刑事诉讼威胁时,并不属于"确定一项刑事指控"(如对飞行器的控制：*Air Canada v. the United Kingdom*，§ 54；对金币的没收：*AGOSI v. the United Kingdom*，§§ 65 - 66)。这些措施应适用第 6 条民事部分(*Silickienė v. Lithuania*，§§ 45 - 46)。

27. 对于基于法律条文的申诉(*Meftah and Others v. France*[GC]，§ 40),以及宪法诉讼[*Gast and Popp v. Germany*，§§ 65 - 66；*Caldas Ramírez de Arellano v. Spain*(dec.)],当这些诉讼是相关刑事诉讼的后续阶段,且其结果对被定罪之人具有决定性作用时,原则上可以适用第 6 条。

28. 最后,第 6 条不适用于案件的重审程序,因为从该条的意义上来说,一个已被定刑且要求重审案件的人并没有"受到刑事指控"[*Fischer v. Austria*(dec.)]。只有在重审案件的请求被通过后,新的诉讼程序才能被认定为一项刑事指控(*Löffler v. Austria*, §§ 18 – 19)。类似地,第 6 条并不适用于在本法院判定侵犯公约权利后重审的刑事诉讼[*Öcalan v. Turkey*(dec.)]。然而,监管审查程序所导致的判决修改适用于公约第 6 条刑事部分(*Vanyan v. Russia*, § 58)。

第二节　向法院申诉的权利

> **第 6 条第 1 款**
> "在决定……对某人确定任何刑事罪名时,任何人有权……受到……审判机构的公平……的审讯。……"

29. "向法院申诉的权利"在刑事案件中并不比在民事案件中更绝对。它受到暗含的限制(*Deweer v. Belgium*, § 49;*Kart v. Turkey*[GC], § 67)。

30. 然而,这些限制的方式和程度不能损害该权利的核心。做出限制的目的必须是合法的,且在手段和目的之间必须有合理的比例(*Guérin v. France*[GC], § 37;*Omar v. France*[GC], § 34,参考民事案件)。

一、限制

31. 对于向法院申诉的权利的限制可能来自以下几方面。

(一)议员豁免权

32. 议员豁免权的两种类型(无责任和不可侵犯)提供的保障出于同种目的——保证议会在执行任务时的独立性。毫无疑问,不可侵犯性通过防止任何出于政治目的提起刑事诉讼的可能性,帮助实现议会的完全独立性,并保障反对派不受多数派的压力或权力滥用(*Kart v. Turkey*[GC], § 90,引用民事案件)。另外,对议员提起诉讼可能会影响其所在议会的运作,并妨碍议会的工作。这种作为一般法律特例的免责体系可以被认为是追求合法目的(同上,§91)。

33. 然而,在没有考虑案件具体情形时,无法就该议员豁免权是否符合公约内涵做出结论。必须明确的是,议员豁免权这一限制对申诉权是否构成根本性损害。审查这一措施的合比例性意味着需要考虑均衡以下两方面的利益:一方面是保障议会独立性带来的普遍利益,另一方面则是申诉人的个人利益,即通过排除议员豁免权,申诉人得以在法庭上对刑事指控进行答辩。在检验这一合比例性问题时,法院必须特别注意案件的免责范围(同上,§§92-93)。保护议会独立性的措施越少,则越需要更充分的正当性理由(同上,§95)。因此,例如,本法院认为,议员不放弃其豁免权,并不影响其向本法院申诉的权利,因为这项免责仅仅是刑事诉讼的临时程序性障碍——但被限定只能在该议员任期内行使(同上,§§111-113)。

(二)程序性规则

34. 程序性规则即对一项申诉的可受理性要求。

35. 虽然申诉权会受到法定要求限制,但是在适用程序性规则时,各法院必须避免过度的形式主义,以免侵犯诉讼的公正性(*Walchli v. France*, §29)。有时,过于严苛地适用一项程序性规则,可能会削弱申诉权(*Labergère v. France*, §23),尤其考虑到申诉的重要性以及被判处长期徒刑的申诉人在诉讼中的利益(*Labergère v. France*, §20)。

36. 程序不当也会根本性地削弱申诉权,如这种情况:负责审查针对罚金或免责申请提起的申诉是否可受理的检察官,越权对申诉的实质部分进行了判决,从而使得申诉人丧失了本可以得到社区法官判决的机会(*Josseaume v. France*, §32)。

37. 这也适用下列情况:一项基于错误理由宣布申诉不可受理的决定导致扣留了与标准罚金等额的保证金,因此被认为已支付罚金,且公诉已中止,这就使得申诉人一旦赔偿了罚金后就不可能向法院对其受到的道路交通违法指控提出质疑(*Célice v. France*, §34)。

38. 另一个例子是过分限制申诉人向法院提请申诉的权利:申诉人针对法律条文申诉,因未在法定时限内提出而被宣布不可受理,但之所以未在时限内申诉,是因为当局未能恰当履行下级法院判决施加给申诉人的义务,使得当时申诉人仍处于拘留中(*Davran v. Turkey*, §§40-47)。

(三)实施先前判决的要求

39. 已发出针对申诉人的逮捕令,而申诉人不服从逮捕,其针对法律条文提出的申诉被自动判为不可受理:

- 一项针对法律条文的申诉因申诉人潜逃而被宣告不可受理:考虑到辩护权的重要意义以及民主社会的法治原则,这会构成一项不合比例的惩罚(*Poitrimol v. France*, § 38; *Guérin v. France*, § 45; *Omar v. France*, § 42);

- 一项针对法律条文的申诉仅仅因为申诉人拒绝接受逮捕而被宣告不可受理:该逮捕令是由被申诉的决定下达的,虽然在申诉判决下达后或申诉期限届满前,这项决定并不具有终局性,但这项决定使得申诉人提前被剥夺人身自由。这对申诉人施加了不合理的负担,因而打破了保证司法决定被执行的合法考虑与向上诉法院的申诉权及辩护权之间的平衡(*Omar v. France*, §§ 40-41; *Guérin v. France*, § 43)。

40. 这同样适用于因不接受逮捕而丧失针对法律条文的申诉权的情况[*Khalfaoui v. France*, § 46; *Papon v. France* (no.2), § 100]。

41. 然而,出于道路交通违法范围内防止拖延或无理申诉的目的,在超速罚款申诉前提交押金的要求可以被认为是一项合法且合比例的对申诉权的限制[*Schneider v. France*(dec.)]。

(四)其他侵犯了申诉权的限制情形

42. 如当局虚假承诺削减一审法院对申诉人判处的刑罚,从而说服其撤诉(*Marpa Zeeland B. V. and Metal Welding B. V. v. the Netherlands*, §§ 46-51);或者在申诉人正式指派的律师拒绝帮助他之后,申诉法院没有告知申诉人针对法律条文申诉的新的时限(*Kulikowski v. Poland*, § 70)。

第三节 一般保障：制度要求

> **第 6 条第 1 款**
> "在决定……对某人确定任何刑事罪名时，任何人有权……受到……审判机构的公平……的审讯。……"

一、"审判机构"的概念

43. 一个纪律性或行政性的机构，即使不被国内法律体系称为"审判机构"或者"法院"，也可能具备第 6 条自治意义下"审判机构"的特点。在本法院的判例法中，一个审判机构的特征在于其实质意义上的司法职能，也就是依据法治原则以及法定程序对问题进行判决。审判机构同时还必须满足其他一系列进一步的要求：独立性，特别是独立于行政机构；公正性；其成员有一定任期；程序性保障——其中一些要求在第 6 条第 1 款中有所体现（*Belilos v. Switzerland*，§ 64；*Coëme and Others v. Belgium*，§ 99；*Richert v. Poland*，§ 43）。

44. 如果所涉当事人可以针对决定向符合第 6 条规定的审判机构申诉，那么将轻微的"刑事"犯罪起诉和惩罚交由行政机关进行不违反公约（*Öztürk v. Germany*，§ 56；*A. Menarini Diagnostics S. R. L. v.* Italy）。因此，行政机构所做的决定本身不符合《公约》第 6 条第 1 款要求的，之后会由"拥有完全管辖权的司法机构"对该决定进行审查。这种司法机构的决定性特征包括有权撤销以下机构针对事实或法律问题的所有决定（*Schmautzer v. Austria*，§ 36；*Gradinger v. Austria*，§ 44；*A. Menarini Diagnostics S. R. L. v. Italy*，§ 59）：例如，行政法院进行一项超越合法性"形式"审查的司法审查，并包括了对行政机关所处惩罚的合理性及合比例性的详尽分析（*A. Menarini Diagnostics S. R. L. v. Italy*，§§ 63–67，一项由独立规制机构针对竞争处以的罚款）。即便是法律本身决定了与违法行为严重性相当的惩戒，司法审查仍可能满足第 6 条的要求（*Malige v. France*，§§ 46–51，关于对驾照的扣分）。

45. 有权做出不可被非司法机构改判的具有强制力的决定,本身就属于"审判机构"一词的应有之意(*Findlay v. the United Kingdom*, § 77)。

二、依法设立的审判机构

46. 根据公约第 6 条第 1 款,一个审判机构必须"依法设立"。这种表述反映了法治原则,该原则是公约及其议定书所建立的保障体系的固有组成部分(*Jorgic v. Germany*, § 64; *Richert v. Poland*, § 41)。在民主社会中,非依法设立的机构的确不具备听取个体诉求的合法性(*Lavents v. Latvia*, § 114; *Gorgiladze v. Georgia*, § 67; *Kontalexis v. Greece*, § 38)。

47. 第 6 条第 1 款所指的"法律",特别包括了规定司法机关成立以及相应权限的法律(*Lavents v. Latvia*, § 114; *Richert v. Poland*, § 41, *Jorgic v. Germany*, § 64),也包括其他的一些国内法,一旦违反,将使得一名或多名法官对于案件的审查不再合法(*Gorgiladze v. Georgia*, § 68; *Pandjikidze and Others v. Georgia*, § 104)。"依法设立"这个词汇不仅仅指审判机构存在的法律基础,也指规制审判机构的法律的合规性(*Gorgiladze v. Georgia*, § 68),以及每个案件中法官组成的合法性(*Posokhov v. Russia*, § 39; *Fatullayev v. Azerbaijan*, § 144; *Kontalexis v. Greece*, § 42)。

48. 如果依据国内法律审判庭无权起诉被告,就不属于第 6 条第 1 款规定的"依法设立"(*Richert v. Poland*, § 41; *Jorgic v. Germany*, § 64)。

49. 第 6 条"依法设立"的目标是"保证民主社会司法机关不依据执行机关的自由裁量而设立,而是依据议会制定的法律而设立"(*Coëme and Others v. Belgium*, § 98; *Richert v. Poland*, § 42)。在法典化国家,司法机构对司法系统的组成也没有自由裁量权,但这并不意味着法院无权解释相关的国内法(*Coëme and Others v. Belgium*, § 98, *Gorgiladze v. Georgia*, § 69)。

50. 原则上,违反有关国内司法机关的组成和职权的法律也违反了第 6 条第 1 款。本法院因此有权审核国内法律在此是否适用。然而,考虑到一般首先是由国内法院解释其国内法,因此,除非它们的解释明显与国内法冲突,否则本法院不会提出质疑(例如,比照以下两个案件,*Coëme and Others v. Belgium*, § 98 最后; *Lavents v. Latvia*, § 114)。因此本法院的职责仅限于审查司法机关的设立是否有合理依据(例如,*Jorgic v. Germany*, § 65)。

51. 在下列案件中,本法院认为这些机构不是"依法设立的审判机构":

- 上诉法院对共同被告中除了被诉官员以外的、与被诉官员受审案件有关联的人进行了审判,然而法律没有规定这样的连带规则(Coëme and Others v. Belgium, §§ 107 – 108);
- 在一起违反了抽签规则以及每年最多提供两周社区服务的规定的案件中,由两名非职业法官组成的法庭进行审判(Posokhov v. Russia, § 43);
- 由非职业法官组成的法庭决定依据已有的旧法继续审理案件,尽管旧法被申诉而新法还未制定(Pandjikidze and Others v. Georgia, §§ 108 – 111);
- 法庭的组成不符合法律规定,因为其中两名法官依据法律不具备审理该案件的资格(Lavents v. Latvia, § 115)。

52. 在下列案件中,本法院认为审判机构是"依法设立的":

- 德国一法院对行为人在波斯尼亚犯下的种族灭绝罪进行审判(Jorgic v. Germany, §§ 66 – 71);
- 为审理贪污和有组织犯罪而设立的特别法庭(Fruni v. Slovakia, § 140)。

三、独立性和公正性

53. 第6条第1款规定的获得公正审判的权利要求案件由依法设立的"独立公正的审判机构"审理。独立和客观公正这两个概念间有紧密的联系,因此本法院通常会将这两个要求结合起来考虑(Findlay v. the United Kingdom, § 73)。

当判断某个审判庭是否"独立公正"时,所适用的原则同样适用于职业法官、非职业法官以及陪审员(Holm v. Sweden, § 30)。

(一)独立的审判庭

1. 一般原则

54. 公约第6条第1款要求审判庭保持独立,不受执法机关、立法机关和党派的干涉[Ninn-Hansen v. Denmark(dec.)]。

55. 尽管在本法院的判例法中,行政机关和司法部门之间分权的概念越来越重要,但不管是公约第6条还是其他条款都没有要求国家遵守任何理论上的宪法概念,这些概念涉及的是权力相互作用可允许的最大限度。问题始终在于,所涉及的特定案件中是否满足了公约的要求(Henryk Urban and Ryszard Urban v. Poland, § 46)。

2. 独立性的审查标准

56. 法院在判断机构是否"独立"时,遵循下列标准(Findlay v. the United Kingdom,§ 73):(1)其成员的任命方式;(2)其成员的任期;(3)是否存在针对外界压力的保障;(4)该机构形式上是否独立。

(1)机构成员的任命方式。

57. 不能因为法官仅由议会直接任命就对其独立性产生质疑[Filippini v. San Marino(dec.);Ninn-Hansen v. Denmark(dec.)]。

58. 同样,如果行政机关任命的法官在审判时能够不受影响或压力,这样的任命方式也是允许的(Henryk Urban and Ryszard Urban v. Poland,§ 49;Campbell and Fell v. the United Kingdom,§ 79)。

59. 尽管国内当局对某一案件的法官或法院的安排享有自由裁量权,该安排也必须符合第6条第1款,特别是符合关于独立性和公正性的要求(Moiseyev v. Russia,§ 176)。

(2)机构成员的任职期限。

60. 任职期限没有规定最低年限。通常来说,法官在任期内的不可撤职性是独立性的必要条件。但是,没有在法律上正式承认这一点,不意味着缺乏独立性。假如事实上这一点得到了确认,并且也得到了其他必要保证,那就说明具有独立性(Campbell and Fell v. the United Kingdom,§ 80)。

(3)针对外界压力的保障。

61. 司法公正要求每一个法官都不受司法机关内部或外部不合理的压力。内部司法独立性要求法官不受其他法官的压力或指令,也不受法院内承担行政职责的人员,如院长或部门领导的压力或指令。如果对法官的独立性缺乏足够的保障,特别是针对上级压力的保障,那么本法院很有可能认为申诉人对该国内法院的独立性和公正性的质疑是合理的(Parlov-Tkalcic v. Croatia,§ 86;Daktaras v. Lithuania,§ 36;Moiseyev v. Russia,§ 184)。

(4)形式上的独立性。

62. 为了判断一个审判机构是否符合第6条第1款规定的"独立"要求,形式标准也非常重要。就刑事程序而言,民主社会中法院必须具有公信力,这一点非常重要(Şahiner v. Turkey,§ 44)。

63. 在确认是否有合法的理由质疑某一法院的独立性或公正性时,被告的立场很重要,但不起决定作用。真正起决定性作用的是该质疑能否被客观证明。如果本法院认为在所涉案件中,作为一个"客观的观察者"没有理由担心,那么独立性就不存在问题[Clarke v. the United Kingdom(dec.)]。

64. 当审判庭中的某一成员就其职责和服务而言,相对于团队中的其他人处于下属地位时,被告有合理的理由怀疑该审判机构的独立性(Şahiner v. Turkey,§45)。

(二)公正的审判庭

65. 公约第6条第1款要求审判庭保持"公正"。公正通常表示没有偏见,而且经得起各种方式的考验(Kyprianou v. Cyprus[GC],§118;Micallef v. Malta[GC],§93)。

1. 公正的审查标准

66. 法院区分了下列两种方法:

(1)主观方法,即确认特定案件中特定法官的个人信仰或利益;

(2)客观方法,判断法官是否有足够的依据排除任何合法的质疑(Kyprianou v. Cyprus[GC],§118;Piersack v. Belgium,§30;Grieves v. the United Kingdom[GC],§69)。

67. 然而,这两种概念并没有明确的区分,因为法官的行为不仅从外人看来在公正方面存疑(客观检验),也有关乎个人信仰的因素(主观检验)。因此,一个案子适用何种方法,或是两者都适用,取决于被检验行为的事实(Kyprianou v. Cyprus[GC],§119和121)。

(1)主观方法。

68. 在采用主观方法时,本法院始终假定法官是公正的,除非有相反的证明(Kyprianou v. Cyprus[GC],§119;Hauschildt v. Denmark,§47)。

69. 关于这类证明的要求,本法院会确认法官是否表现出了敌意或恶意,或是因为私人的原因而指派本人得到这个案子(De Cubber v. Belgium,§25)。

70. 但是在某些案件中难以获取推翻法官主观公正假设的证据,此时客观公正的要求就提供了进一步的保证。本法院确实认识到依靠主观方法难以证明违反第6条,因此大量案件侧重于采用客观方法(Kyprianou v. Cyprus[GC],§119)。

(2)客观方法。

71. 在对审判机构采用客观方法检验时,除了成员的私人行为外,必须确认是否可依据确定事实对其公正性提出合理的质疑(Castillo Algar v. Spain, § 45)。

72. 在决定某一案件中是否有合法理由质疑审判庭缺乏公正性时,质疑方的立场很重要,但并不起决定性作用。真正起决定性作用的是质疑能否被客观证明(Ferrantelli and Santangelo v. Italy, § 58;Padovani v. Italy, § 27)。

73. 客观方法主要关注案件中法官和其他人之间的等级关系或其他关系,这可以支持对于审判机构公正性的质疑,从而证明没有达到公约的公正性标准(Micallef v. Malta [GC], § 97)。因此每一个案件中受到质疑的关系必须达到足以证明审判庭缺乏公正性的程度(Pullar v. the United Kingdom, § 38)。

74. 在这方面,甚至连形式也有一定的重要性。有一点非常重要,民主社会中法院必须具有公信力,也包括赢取被告的信任。因此,一旦有合法的理由质疑任何一位法官的公正性,该法官必须回避(Castillo Algar v. Spain, § 45)。

75. 国内机关的问题也必须考虑到。各国内保证公正的程序,即规制法官撤职的规则也是一个相关因素。这些规则体现了各国立法机关对排除关于法官公正性的合理怀疑十分关注,也体现了其试图排除造成怀疑的原因来保证公正。除了减少事实上的偏见,他们也致力于减少形式上的不公正来提高法院的公信力[Piersack v. Belgium, § 30 (d)](Micallef v. Malta[GC], § 99;Meznaric v. Croatia, § 27;Harabin v. Slovakia, § 132)。本法院在评估一个审判庭是否公正时,特别是申请者的质疑能否被客观证明时,会考虑上述规则(Pfeifer and Plankl v. Austria, § 6;Oberschlick v. Austria(no. 2), § 50; Pescador Valero v. Spain, §§ 24 - 29)。

2. 质疑公正性的两种情形

76. 有两种情形可能产生对公正性的质疑(Kyprianou v. Cyprus[GC], § 121):

(1)第一种与职能相关,例如,司法过程中同一个人行使了多项职能,或者和此过程中的其他人有等级或其他方面的联系;

(2)第二种与个人品格相关,源于某一特定案件中法官的行为。

(1)与职能相关的情况。

①不同司法职能的执行。

77. 如果一名负责刑事审判的法官同时已在预审阶段做出包括还押拘留在内的决定,不能仅凭该事实本身认为他不公正,还应该考察这些决定的程度和性质(Fey v. Austria, § 30;Sainte-Marie v. France, § 32;Nortier v. the Netherlands, § 33)。如果还押拘留的决定需要以"有极大可能性"定罪为前提,本法院认为审判庭的公正性值得质疑,申诉人的质疑是可以从客观上证明合法的(*Hauschildt v. Denmark*, §§ 49－52)。

78. 法官曾是检察部门的一员这一事实不可以成为怀疑其公正性的理由。不过,如果某人在检察部门工作时曾处理过相关案件,而后又以法官的身份处理同一案件,那么公众有权担心其公正性得不到保证[*Piersack v. Belgium*, § 30(b) and (d)]。

79. 同一案件中,如果法官既调查又审判,本法院认为申诉人有理由怀疑该法官的公正性(*De Cubber v. Belgium*, §§ 27－30)。

然而,如果审判法官在调查中参与的时间有限,仅仅质询了两名证人,并没有对证据做任何的审核或被要求得出结论,本法院认为申诉人在客观上没有理由怀疑国内法院的公正性(*Bulut v. Austria*, §§ 33－34)。

80. 在诉讼的其他阶段,如果法官做出的纯粹是形式上或程序上的决定,那么就不存在缺乏司法公正性的问题。然而,如果在诉讼的其他阶段,法官表达过对被告罪行的观点,这可能会产生不公正的问题(*Gómez de Liaño y Botella v. Spain*, §§ 67－72)。

81. 法官曾对相似但没有联系的案件做出过判决,或是在彼此独立的刑事程序中对同一被告做出过判决,这一事实本身不足以构成对其公正性的合理怀疑[*Kriegisch v. Germany*(dec.);*Khodorkovskiy and Lebedev v. Russia*, § 544]。但如果前述判决所含的事实会对下一判决的被告造成预判,那么另当别论(*Poppe v. the Netherlands*, § 26;*Schwarzenberger v. Germany*, § 42;*Ferrantelli and Santangelo v. Italy*, § 59)。

82. 保持公正的义务不能被解释为上级法院具有将行政或司法决定置之一旁,而将案件送至另一个司法机关或本司法机关的另一分支机构的义务[*Thomann v. Switzerland*, § 33;*Stow and Gai v. Portugal*(dec.)]。

②案件进程中和其他参与人在等级或其他方面的关系。

• 等级关系

83. 原则上而言,军事法庭对军职人员提起刑事诉讼的决定和公约第6条并不冲突(*Cooper v. the United Kingdom*[GC], § 110)。然而,当军事法院的所有成员都是召集人的下级并听从其指挥时,可以认为申诉人有客观理由质疑该审判庭的独立性和公正性(*Findlay v. the United Kingdom*, § 76;*Miller and Others v. the United Kingdom*, §§ 30－31)。

84. 成员中有军方人士的法庭对平民的审判,可以引起人们的合法怀疑,认为法院可能会被偏见影响(*Incal v. Turkey*, §72; *Iprahim Ülger v. Turkey*, §26)。即使一名军事法官在起诉公民的过程中仅仅参与做出了一个中间的但持续有效的决定,整个诉讼都将被认为不是由独立公正的法院进行的(*Öcalan v. Turkey*[GC], §115)。

85. 在军事法院做出有关公民起诉军队的判决的情形中,对该法院的客观公正可能产生合理的质疑。一个司法系统中,如果军事法院有权对非军事系统的公民审判,那么即使有足够的安全措施保障法院的独立,也很容易会导致本应存在于法院和刑事诉讼当事人之间的距离消失[*Ergin v. Turkey*(no.6), §49]。

86. 只有在极特殊情况下,军事法院对平民的刑事指控决定才符合第6条的规定(*Martin v. the United Kingdom*, §44)。

● 其他关系

87. 当案件调查组组长是申诉人的丈夫时,质疑该审判庭的公正性是客观合法的(*Dorozhko and Pozharskiy v. Estonia*, §§56-58)。

88. 审判庭的某一成员与案件中的某一证人私下认识时,这不必然意味着他会偏向于采信该证人的证词。每一起案件中都必须判断此种联系是否足以导致缺乏公正性(*Pullar v. the United Kingdom*, §38,陪审团的一名成员是两名关键的控方证人之一的员工;*Hanif and Khan v. the United Kingdom*, §141,陪审团一名成员为警察)。

(2)与个人品格相关的情况。

89. 在审理案件时,为了体现法官公正无私的一面,司法机关被要求行使最高限度的自由裁量权。此种权力要求他们即使是受到挑衅也不利用媒体。这项义务是对司法的更高要求,也体现了司法机关的庄严性(*Lavents v. Latvia*, §118; *Buscemi v. Italy*, §67)。因此,如果法院院长在主持法院判决之前公开表示对申诉人不利的观点,可以认为有客观理由怀疑他的公正性(*Buscemi v. Italy*, §68;也可见 *Lavents v. Latvia*, §119,一名法官参与了对辩方的公开批评,并对该被告辩护无罪的情况公开表示惊讶)。

90. 国家法律职业的从业人员以及国家法官、检察官联盟在媒体上发表声明或文章,批判了审判时的政治环境、政府的立法改革措施和辩方策略,但没有对申诉人的罪过做声明,这种情况不被视为违反了第6条。另外,听审申诉人案子的法官,全部是富有经验、接受过训练的职业法官,这使得他们能够不受外界的影响[*Previti v. Italy*(dec.), §253]。

第四节　一般保障：程序要求

一、公正

> **第 6 条第 1 款**
> "在决定……对某人确定任何刑事罪名时,任何人有权……受到……审判机构的公平的……的审讯。……"

(一)平等手段原则和对抗程序

91. 平等手段原则是公正审判的内在特征。该原则要求双方都有合理的机会陈述案情,以使自己不处于下风(*Foucher v. France*,§ 34;*Bulut v. Austria*;*Bobek v. Poland*,§ 56;*Klimentyev v. Russia*,§ 95)。平等手段原则要求各方保持平衡,并且同等适用于刑事案件和民事案件。

92. 参与对抗式庭审的权利意味着原则上各方对引证证据或影响法院判决的观点都有知悉、评论的机会。参与对抗式庭审的权利与平等手段原则紧密相关,而且,实际上,在某些案件中,法院会同时依据这两个概念判定行为违反第 6 条第 1 款的规定。

93. 本法院的判例法有非常大的进步,特别是越来越重视程序形式,公众对司法公正的关注也越来越多(*Borgers v. Belgium*,§ 24)。

94. 刑事案件中,第 6 条第 1 款和第 3 款的特别保证重合,尽管第 3 款不仅限于第 1 款规定的最低权利。事实上,第 6 条第 3 款的保证是组合概念,包含了第 1 款列举的公正审判的概念。

1. 平等手段原则

95. 博格斯诉比利时案(*Borgers v. Belgium*)中,法院限制了申诉人的权利,禁止申诉人对检察官提交给上诉法院的意见进行答辩,申诉人也无法获得副本。在法庭的审理下,检察官作为顾问的身份参与其中加剧了这种不平等。

96. 法院发现下列刑事诉讼中的情况既违反了第6条第1款,又违反了第3款:辩方律师必须等待15个小时,直到次日清晨才得以有机会辩护(*Makhfi v. France*)。同样地,本法院在某最高法院审查一起刑事案件中也发现了违反平等手段原则的情形,申诉人在上诉中被判定有罪,但其出席一场秘密预审听证会的请求被拒绝(*Zhuk v. Ukraine*,§ 35)。

97. 相反,由于没有充分的理由,一项关于平等手段原则的请求被宣布不予受理。申诉人提出公诉人与涉诉方相关,但从辩护其自身利益的角度来看,被告并没有处于不利位置(*Diriöz v. Turkey*,§ 25)。

98. 未能制定关于刑事程序的法律也有可能会违反平等手段原则,因为该法律的目的是为了保护被告不受权力滥用的侵害,而这类法律的缺失或不明晰最容易导致被告方受侵害(*Coëme and Others v. Belgium*,§ 102)。

99. 控方和辩方的证人必须得到平等对待;然而,是否违反了该原则取决于证人是否实际享有特权(*Bonisch v. Austria*,§ 32;相反地,参见 *Brandstetter v. Austria*,§ 45)。

100. 不向辩方披露证据会违反平等手段原则(以及参与对抗式庭审的权利)(*Kuopila v. Finland*,§ 38,辩方无法对警方补充报告发表评论)。

101. 以维护公共利益为理由,限制被告获取个人材料文件的权利,这也违反了平等手段原则(*Matyjek v. Poland*,§ 65)。

2. 对抗式庭审

102. 在获得公正审判的权利中,基本点是在刑事诉讼中,也包括任何诉讼中的刑事部分程序,都应当是对抗制的,辩方和控方享有平等权利。参与对抗式庭审的权利意味着在一起刑事案件中,控辩双方都有机会了解评论另一方上交的报告和提出的证据。另外,第6条第1款要求控方必须向辩方提供其掌握的所有有利或不利于辩方的物证(*Rowe and Davis v. the United Kingdom*[GC],§ 60)。

103. 在刑事审判中,第6条第1款经常和第6条第3款的辩方权利重合,如询问证人的权利。

104. 基于公共利益的理由不向辩方披露证据时,本法院不会审查该命令。相反,本法院会尽可能地审查做出该命令的程序是否符合对抗制程序、平等手段原则的要求,以及是否有充分的保障措施保护被告的利益。

105. 在罗、戴维斯诉英国案(*Rowe and Davis v. the United Kingdom*[GC])中,本

法院认为有违反第 6 条第 1 款的情形,控方未能向主审法官提供相关证据,使得法官无法对披露问题做出判决,因此剥夺了申诉人获得公正审判的权利。然而,在贾斯珀诉英国案(*Jasper v. the United Kingdom*[GC],§ 58)中,本法院认为未披露的材料不属于诉讼案件的一部分,无须向陪审团提交,因此判定没有违反第 6 条第 1 款的情形。

106. 然而,披露相关证据的权利并不是绝对的。刑事诉讼中可能存在相互冲突的利益,如国家安全、保护证人不受报复以及对警方调查案件的手段保密,这些必须和被告的权利进行权衡。在某些案件中,为了保护其他人的基本权利或是重要的公众利益,有必要不向辩方披露特定的证据。然而,只有在确实需要时,第 6 条第 1 款才允许对辩方权利进行限制(*Van Mechelen and Others v. the Netherlands*,§ 58)。另外,为了保证被告能得到公正的审判,任何造成辩方行使权利的困难都必须在之后的程序中经过司法机关的充分衡量(*Doorson v. the Netherlands*,§ 72;*Van Mechelen and Others v. the Netherlands*,§ 54)。

107. 在爱德华兹、路易斯诉英国案(*Edwards and Lewis v. the United Kingdom*[GC])中,申诉人无法接触证据,因此其代理人无法在法官面前辩称这个案子完全是诱捕。因此,本法院认为这违反了第 6 条第 1 款,因为决定披露证据的程序以及诱捕手段违反了对抗式诉讼和平等手段原则的要求,也无法充分保护被告利益。

108. 下面这种情形也被认为侵犯了获得对抗式庭审的权利:申诉人没有在听证会前收到负责撰写报告的法官的报告,然而检察官却收到了报告,这就使得申诉人没有机会对检察官提交的意见进行答辩(*Reinhardt and Slimane-Kaïd v. France*,§§ 105–106)。

(二)司法判决理由

109. 已有的判例法体现了一条原则,即正当的司法行政,法院和审判机构的判决应当充分说明其所依据的理由[*Papon v. France*(dec.)]。

110. 具备充分理由的判决说明法院和审判机构听取了各方意见,因此更容易被接受。另外,这促使法官依据客观论据做出推论,也保护了辩方的权利。然而,判决的性质和客观情况不同,要求提供理由的程度也有所不同(*Ruiz Torija v. Spain*,§ 29)。

111. 尽管法院没有义务对每一个主张都给出详细的回答(*Van de Hurk v. the Netherlands*,§ 61),但案件关键的争议点必须解释清楚(*Boldea v. Romania*,§ 30)。

112. 国内法院应该解释清楚判决的依据,以便当事人充分行使申诉权

(*Hadjianastassiou v. Greece*；*Boldea v. Romania*)。

陪审团判决理由如下：

113. 刑事案件的陪审团很少详细论述判决的理由，但在很多案件中，是否详细论述判决理由与是否公正有关。这其中的相关性首先由欧盟委员会认定，之后由本法院判定。

114. 公约不要求陪审员为判决提供理由，根据第6条，即使陪审团没有给出判决理由，也不能排除由陪审团审判[*Saric v. Denmark*(dec.)]。不过，为了符合公正审判的要求，被告和公众必须能够理解判决，这是防止任意裁判的重要措施(*Taxquet v. Belgium*[GC]，§92；*Legillon v. France*，§53)。

115. 当巡回法庭与陪审团审判时，必须允许采用程序上的特别要求，因为陪审员不被要求或是不被允许解释他们个人的观点。在这些情况下，第6条要求审查保护措施是否足以防止任意专断并且帮助被告理解定罪理由。这些程序上的保护措施包括主审法官向陪审员提供关于法律问题的指令或指导，或者法官向陪审团展示证据和提出明确疑问，这些形成了判决的框架，也抵消了陪审团判决未说明理由所带来的影响[*R. v. Belgium*(dec.)，*Zarouali v. Belgium*(dec.)，*Planka v. Austria*(dec.)；*Papon v. France*(dec.)]。当巡回法庭拒绝对每一个被告就不断恶化的情况提出不同的问题时，陪审团就无法对每一个被告的个人刑事责任进行判决，本法院认为这违反了第6条第1款(*Goktepe v. Belgium*，§28)。

116. 在贝勒林·拉加尔诉西班牙案[*Bellerín Lagares v. Spain*(dec.)]中，根据判决所附的陪审团讨论记录，本法院发现受质疑的判决包括了一系列陪审团判定申诉人有罪的事实依据，对这些事实的分析，以及为了量刑的目的而提及目前的情况，都会影响本案申诉人承担责任的程度。因此，本法院认为有充分理由判断该判决符合第6条第1款的要求。

117. 任何上诉渠道都必须向被告开放(*Taxquet v. Belgium*[GC]，§92)。在该案中，只有四个问题和申诉人有关，而这四个问题与询问其他共同被告的措辞相同，使他无法确定自己被定罪的事实依据或法律依据，于是申诉人无法理解为何被判有罪，这就属于不公正的审判(同上，§100)。

118. 在贾奇诉英国案[*Judge v. the United Kingdom*(dec.)]中，本法院认为，虽然苏格兰陪审团的判决未说明理由，但该判决的基本框架足以使被告理解自己为何被定罪。

另外,苏格兰法律规定的上诉权也足以纠正陪审团的任何不恰当判决。在可适用的上诉法律中,上诉法院享有自由裁量权,可以审查并撤销因审判不公导致的定罪。

(三)保持沉默以及不自证其罪的权利

1. 确认以及适用范围

119. 任何受到刑事指控的人都有保持沉默以及不自证其罪的权利(*Funke v. France*, § 44; *O'Halloran and Francis v. the United Kingdom*[GC], § 45; *Saunders v. the United Kingdom*, § 60)。尽管第6条没有特别提及,但保持沉默以及不自证其罪的权利是国际通认的,也是第6款正当程序概念的核心。上述豁免权保护被告免受当局不合理的压迫,也有助于防止错判,维护第6条的目标(*John Murray v. the United Kingdom*, § 45)。

120. 从各类最简单的刑事诉讼到最复杂的刑事诉讼,不自证其罪的权利始终贯穿其中(*Saunders v. the United Kingdom*, § 74)。

121. 从被警方询问开始,被告即享有保持沉默的权利(*John Murray v. the United Kingdom*, § 45)。

2. 范围

122. 不自证其罪的权利意味着刑事案件的控方在设法证明其指控内容时,不得通过强迫或压制被告违背其个人意愿的手段来获得证据(*Saunders v. the United Kingdom*, § 68; *Bykov v. Russia*[GC], § 92)。

123. 然而,不自证其罪的权利不适用于下列情况:尽管物证是通过强制力从被告处获得,但其存在独立于嫌疑人的意愿,例如,依据搜查证获取的文件、呼吸、血尿样本,以及为进行 DNA 鉴定而获得的体表组织(*Saunders v. the United Kingdom*, § 69; *O'Halloran and Francis v. the United Kingdom*[GC] § 47)。

124. 能否尽快获得律师帮助,是本法院在审查某程序中是否存在不自证其罪的权利时特别关注的一点。为了保证第6条第1款获得公正审判的权利"实用并且有效",嫌疑人在第一次被警方询问时就应当有权获得律师帮助,这应当作为一项规则,除非证明在某个案子的特别情形下有不可抗拒的理由限制该权利(*Salduz v. Turkey*[GC], §§ 54-55)。

125. 被警方拘留的人享有不自证其罪、保持沉默以及在被质询时获得律师帮助的权利。这些权利彼此独立:放弃其中一项不意味着放弃其余权利。不过,这些权利是相互补充的,因为被警方拘留的人如果没有事先被告知保持沉默的权利,就更应该获得律师帮助了(*Navone and Others v. Monaco*,§ 74;*Brusco v. France*,§ 54)。告知嫌疑人保持沉默的权利的重要性在于,即使已经被告知他的陈述可能会作为不利证据,嫌疑人仍然有可能愿意向警方做出陈述,但如果嫌疑人没有被明确告知自己有保持沉默的权利,或者他的决定是在没有法律顾问的情况下做出的,那么就不能认为嫌疑人的选择是在被充分告知权利的前提下做出的(*Navone and Others v. Monaco*,§ 74;*Stojkovic v. France and Belgium*,§ 54)。

126. 保持沉默并且不自证其罪的权利主要是为了保护嫌疑人在受到警方询问时有选择说或不说的自由。在下面这一案件中,这种自由遭受了严重的损害:嫌疑人在被质询时选择保持沉默,当局采用诡计诱导出嫌疑人的供词或者其他使其入罪的表述,这类供述是无法通过质询获得的(在这个案件中,嫌疑人向同一个牢房的卧底犯人坦白),或者该口供是在审判的物证环节获得(*Allan v. the United Kingdom*,§ 50)。

127. 相反,在贝科夫诉俄罗斯案(*Bykov v. Russia*[GC])中,申诉人没有受到任何压力或胁迫,也没有被拘留,可以自由选择是否去见卧底犯人。而且,该对话记录在审判时未被用于判定有罪的核心,其在国内法院审查的大量复杂证据中只起了有限的作用(同上,§§ 102 – 103)。

3. 相对的权利

128. 保持沉默的权利并不是绝对的(*John Murray vthe United Kingdom*,§ 47)。

129. 在审查某一程序是否损害了不自证其罪的权利时,本法院特别关注以下要素:

- 强迫的性质和程度;
- 程序中是否存在任何相关的保护措施;
- 物证如何使用(*Jalloh v. Germany*[GC],§ 101;*O'Halloran and Francis v. the United Kingdom*[GC],§ 55;*Bykov v. Russia*[GC],§ 104)。

130. 一方面,不能仅仅因为被告沉默或是拒绝回答问题、拒绝提供证据就对其定罪。另一方面,如果明显需要嫌疑人做出解释,在国内法院衡量控方证据的说服力时,保持沉默的权利就并不意味着不能将被告的沉默纳入考量。因此,也不能说刑事程序中被告保持沉默的决定不会有任何影响。

131. 任何从被告的沉默而得的不利推论,判断其是否违反了第6条时,需要考虑整个案子的所有情况,特别要关注国内法院在审核证据和胁迫程度时,对这些不利推论的依赖程度(*John Murray v. the United Kingdom*,§ 47)。

132. 另外,调查中涉及的公共利益和对特定犯罪行为的惩罚也必须纳入考虑范围,并且要对通过合法手段收集的不利于被告的证据进行衡量。但是考虑公共利益并不意味着剥夺申诉人的辩护权(包括不自证其罪的权利)是合法的,(*Jalloh v. Germany*[GC],§ 97)。采取强制手段在非司法性调查中获得答案,并在审判中利用该答案指控被告,这种行为不能以公共利益为借口进行正当化(*Heaney and McGuinness v. Ireland*,§ 57)。

(四)使用通过非法手段或侵害公约权利而获得的证据

133. 尽管第6条保证了获得公平听证的权利,但并没有制定证据准入方面的规则,这主要由各国法律自行制定(*Schenk v. Switzerland*,§§ 45-46;*Heglas v. the Czech Republic*,§ 84)。

134. 原则上判断某种特定类型的证据(如以违反国内法的手段获得的证据)是否可用并不属于本法院的职责。但本法院必须判断整个程序(包括获得证据的手段)是否公平,这需要考察被诉的不法行为,在公约权利受到侵害的情况中,则需要考察侵害行为的性质(*Khan v. the United Kingdom*,§ 34;*P. G. and J. H. v. the United Kingdom*,§ 76;*Allan v. the United Kingdom*,§ 42)。

135. 在判断程序整体是否公平时,必须关注辩方权利是否得到尊重。特别要考察的是,申诉人是否有机会质疑证据的真实性并反对其适用。另外,也必须考虑证据的质量,必须考虑影响证据获取的所有情节以及这些情节是否会令人对证据的可靠性和真实性产生怀疑。尽管当获得的证据没有其他物证佐证时,未必会产生公平的问题,但值得一提的是,当证据十分有力、没有不可靠的风险时,对附属支持证据的需要也就相应减少(*Bykov v. Russia*[GC],§ 89;*Jalloh v. Germany*[GC],§ 96)。在这一点上,本法院也特别关注受到质疑的证据对刑事结果是否起决定作用(*Gäfgen v. Germany*)。

136. 在考察违反公约的行为的性质时,要考虑的问题是,以违反公约第8条所获得的信息作为证据,是否会导致整个审判的不公,与之相反,第6条必须考虑案件中所有情节,特别是申诉人的辩护权利是否得到尊重,以及证据的质量和重要性(*Gäfgen v. Germany*[GC],§ 165)。

137. 然而,在使用违反公约第3条获得的证据时要特别注意,这些证据都是通过侵犯公约所保护的核心且绝对的权利而获取的,即便这些证据对定罪没有决定性作用,但使用这些证据就总是会招致对审判公正性的质疑,(*Jalloh v. Germany*[GC],§§ 99

and 105；*Harutyunyan v. Armenia*，§ 63）。

138. 因此，在刑事程序中通过违反公约第 3 条而获得的供述，不论是通过酷刑，还是非人道的或有损人格的待遇，都会因为触犯了第 6 条而自动使得整个审判不公（*El Haski v. Belgium*；*Gäfgen v. Germany*[GC]，§ 166）。这也同样适用于通过酷刑而直接获得的真实证据（*Jalloh v. Germany*[GC]，§ 105；*Gäfgen v. Germany*[GC]，§ 167）。但是，使用通过违反第 3 条、施加不人道但还未达到酷刑的行为获得的证据，只有在会对被告的定罪量刑有影响时，才会认为违反了第 6 条（*El Haski v. Belgium*，§ 85；*Gäfgen v. Germany*[GC]，§ 178）。

139. 这些原则不仅适用于受害者作为被告的情况，也适用于涉及第三方的情况（*El Haski v. Belgium*，§ 85）。特别是本法院认为使用通过酷刑获得的证据等同于公然的司法不公，即使该酷刑针对的是第三方[*Othman（Abu Qatada）v. the United Kingdom*，§§ 263 and 267]。

（五）诱捕

1. 一般规定

140. 本法院注意到有关部门需要使用特殊的调查手段，特别是在涉及有组织的犯罪和贪污腐败案件时。在这一点上，本法院认为使用特殊调查手段，特别是秘密技术，本身并不损害获得公正审判的权利。不过为了防止这些技术所带来的警方教唆的风险，必须对这些手段的使用加以明确的限制（*Ramanauskas v. Lithuania*[GC]，§ 51）。

141. 尽管有组织犯罪的不断增加促使国家采取合理的手段，获得公正审判的权利（公正司法的要求也是从中推断而来）依然适用于所有类型的刑事犯罪——从最简单的到最复杂的。获得公正司法的权利在民主社会中占有重要地位，不能为了方便调查而牺牲这一权利（同上，§ 53）。在这一点上，本法院强调警方可以秘密行动但不能引诱（*Khudobin v. Russia*，§ 128）。

142. 此外，尽管在初步调查阶段或者犯罪性质所允许的情况下，公约并不反对匿名情报的使用，但审判法院随后使用这类消息定罪就是另外一回事了（*Teixeira de Castro v. Portugal*，§ 35）。只有具备了适当且充分的防止滥用的保护措施，特别是具备了清楚、可预见的程序用来批准、执行、监管相应的调查手段时，才可以允许使用匿名情报（*Ramanauskas v. Lithuania*[GC]，§ 51）。本法院也考虑到，当局在进行秘密行动时，尽管司法监督可能是最合适的,但是如果具备了恰当的程序和保护措施,也可以使用其他手段,如检察官的监督(*Bannikova v. Russia*, § 50)。

143. 尽管使用有明确限制和防护措施的卧底也是允许的,但公共利益不能成为使用警方诱捕所获证据的合法性借口,这会使得被告可能在一开始就被剥夺获得公正审判的权利(*Ramanauskas v. Lithuania*[GC], § 54)。

144. 因此,在涉及使用卧底的案件中,为了确认是否侵犯了获得公正审判的权利,本法院第一步要考察是否存在诱捕("教唆的实质检验"),如果存在,接下来要考察申诉人是否能够在国内法院针对诱捕进行抗辩(*Bannikova v. Russia*, §§ 37 和 51)。不论卧底是国家雇佣的还是协助国家机关的私人雇佣的,如果他的行为构成了诱捕,并且由此获得的证据在刑事案件中用于指控当事人,本法院就会认为这违反了公约第 6 条第 1 款(*Ramanauskas v. Lithuania*[GC], § 73)的规定。

2. 教唆的实质检验

145. 本法院定义的诱捕不同于合法的卧底调查,是指涉及的工作人员(无论是安全部门的成员还是依照其指令行事的人员)并没有以一种被动的方式调查犯罪活动,而是对引诱本不会发生的犯罪行为施加了影响,使之可能构成犯罪,并依此提供证据进行起诉(*Ramanauskas v. Lithuania*[GC], § 55)。

146. 在确认调查是否是"被动"时,本法院会审查当局进行秘密行动的理由。特别是审查是否有客观理由怀疑申诉人参与了犯罪活动或有可能实施犯罪(*Bannikova v. Russia*, § 38)。

147. 在审查中,本法院会考察许多因素。例如,在较早的具有里程碑意义的案件——特谢拉·德·卡斯特罗诉葡萄牙案(*Teixeira de Castro v. Portugal*, §§ 37-38)中,除了别的因素以外,本法院还考察了申诉人没有犯罪记录、此前没有受到过调查、警方对他一无所知、在他的家里没有找到毒品以及在逮捕过程中搜到的毒品数量不超过卧底所要求的数量等事实。本法院认为该卧底的行为越界了,他们引诱了这起犯罪,而且没有任何证据可以证明,如果没有警方的参与,这起犯罪也会发生(同上,§§ 37-38)。

148. 之前的犯罪记录并不表明罪犯更有可能犯罪(*Constantin and Stoian v. Romania*, § 55)。但是如果申诉人熟知当下毒品的价格,并且能在短时间内获得毒品,尽管有很多机会退出毒品交易但他未能退出,这些都会使本法院考察其先前的犯罪活动和意图[*Shannon v. the United Kingdom*(dec.)]。

149. 另一个需要考察的因素是申诉人是否被强迫实施犯罪。在没有任何客观证据怀疑申请人参与了刑事犯罪或很有可能犯罪的情况下，联系申诉人(*Burak Hun v. Turkey*, § 44)，不顾申诉人最初的拒绝、坚持引诱、反复报价(*Ramanauskas v. Lithuania* [GC], § 67)、提供高于市场价的价格(*Malininas v. Lithuania*, § 37)、提起戒毒过程中出现的症状博取申诉人的同情(*Vanyan v. Russia*, §§ 11 and 49)，这些行为被本法院认为是向申诉人施加压力促使其犯罪——无论该卧底是安全部门的成员还是按照其指示工作的个人。

150. 还有一个重要的问题是国家卧底是否被认定为"参与"或是"渗入"而非"发起"刑事犯罪。被认定为"参与"或"渗入"的案件中，受质疑的行动没有超出卧底工作的界限。在米利涅内诉立陶宛案(*Milinienė v. Lithuania*)中，本法院认为，尽管警方影响了案件，特别是为某个人提供设备来记录对话，并且资助其引诱申诉人，但由于是该个人主动实施犯罪，因此警方的这些行为被认定是"参与"而非"发起"刑事犯罪。被认定为"发起"刑事犯罪的案件中，有人向警方投诉称申诉人向警方行贿以获取有利的结果，但必须是在副检察长审查并批准该申诉之后[相类似的，*Sequieira v. Portugal*(dec.)；*Eurofinacom v. France*(dec.)]。

151. 审查申请人是否遭受陷害时，卧底警察行动的开展和执行方式也是需要考察的因素。缺乏清晰可预见的程序来批准、实施、监督受质疑的调查手段，将会使本法院更倾向于认为受质疑的行为构成诱捕：例如，在特谢拉·德·卡斯特罗诉葡萄牙案(*Teixeira de Castro v. Portugal*, § 38)中，本法院注意到卧底的介入不属于受法官监督的官方打击毒品的行动；在拉曼诺斯卡斯诉立陶宛案(*Ramanauskas v. Lithuania* [GC], § 64)中，本法院认为没有理由或个人动机能够表明卧底接近申诉人是出于个人意愿而没有向上级报告(§ 64)；在万扬诉俄罗斯案(*Vanyan v. Russia*, §§ 46-47)中，本法院注意到警方的行动由负责机构的一个简单的行政决定授权，并且这项决定中关于这次行动测试的原因和目的的内容很少，也没有任何司法机关或独立的监督机构对该行动进行监督。在这一点上，俄罗斯当局使用的"行动测试"一词在维斯洛夫等人诉俄罗斯案(*Veselov and Others v. Russia*)中受到详细审查，本法院认为受到质疑的程序有缺陷，使申诉人遭受了警方的专横行为，损害了刑事程序的正义。本法院还认为，国内法院未能充分审查申诉人遭受诱捕的抗辩，特别是没有审核这次测试行动的理由和警方及线人的行为(§127)。

3. 有关诱捕抗辩的司法观点

152. 在有关诱捕的案件中,只有当申诉人在审判中能够以反对或其他手段有效地提出对诱捕的控诉时,公约第6条才能适用。法院认为,仅仅有通常的保护措施(如平等手段原则或辩方的权利)是不够的(*Ramanauskas v. Lithuania* [GC],§69)。对于这类案子,本法院指出,如果被告的主张未必全部属实,那么就应当由控方证明不存在诱捕。

153. 如果申诉人提出了诱捕抗辩,也有确定的表面证据,司法机关必须审查案件事实,采取必要措施调查真相,以确定是否存在诱捕。如果确实存在,司法机关必须依据公约做出判断(*Ramanauskas v. Lithuania* [GC],§70)。仅仅有申诉人对刑事指控的认罪也不能免除法院对诱捕的指控进行审查的职责(*Ramanauskas v. Lithuania* [GC],§72)。

154. 在这一点上,本法院审查有指控诱捕的表面证据是否在国内法上构成实质辩护,或者为排除证据提供理由,或其他类似结果(*Bannikova v. Russia*,§54)。尽管面对诱捕抗辩时,是由国内当局决定何种程序适当,但是本法院要求受质疑的程序必须是对抗式的、充分的、完整的,并且在诱捕问题上有确定的答案(*Bannikova v. Russia*,§57)。而且,在调查当局不披露相关信息的情况下,本法院将会尤其关注是否符合对抗式程序以及平等手段原则(*Bannikova v. Russia*,§58)。

155. 当被告坚称自己受引诱而犯罪,刑事法院必须仔细审查证据,因为根据公约第6条第1款公正审判的含义,所有因为警方诱捕而获得的证据必须排除。当警方行动缺乏充分的法律依据和保护措施时,尤其应当如此(*Ramanauskas v. Lithuania* [GC],§60)。

156. 如果已有的信息无法使本法院确定申请人是否遭受了诱捕,关于诱捕抗辩的司法审查就成为决定性作用(*Edwards and Lewis v. the United Kingdom* [GC],§46;*Ali v. Romania*,§101;见 *Khudobin v. Russia*,国内法院无法通过分析相关的事实和法律要素区分诱捕和合法的调查活动;*V. v. Finland*,申请人无法对诱捕提出抗辩;以及 *Shannon v. the United Kingdom*,此案中国内法院对卧底的手段进行了仔细审查,发现申诉人关于诱捕的主张是没有实质根据的)。

(六)放弃获得公正审判的保障

157. 无论是公约第 6 条的字面意思还是其暗含精神,都没有禁止个人以明示或暗示的方式放弃他的自由意志或公正审判的权利。然而,如果要实现公约的目标,他必须以明确的方式表示,并得到相应的最低限度的保护措施,这样的放弃才是有效的。另外,也不能与任何重要的公众利益相冲突(*Hermi v. Italy* [GC], § 73; *Sejdovic v. Italy* [GC], § 86)。

158. 只有证明被告能够合理地预见他行为的后果,他才可以通过其行为以默示的方式放弃公约第 6 条所规定的重要权利(*Hermi v. Italy* [GC], § 74; *Sejdovic v. Italy* [GC], § 87)。

二、公开审讯

> **第 6 条第 1 款**
>
> "在决定……对某人确定任何刑事罪名时,任何人有权……受到……审判机构的……公开的审讯。判决应当公开宣布。但是,基于对民主社会中的道德、公共秩序或者国家安全的利益,以及对民主社会中的少年的利益或者是保护当事人的私生活权利的考虑,或者是法院认为,在特殊情况下,如果公开审讯将损害公平利益的话,可以拒绝记者和公众参与旁听全部或者部分审讯。"

(一)公开性原则

159. 审讯程序的公开特征保护当事人在没有公开审查的情况下免受司法机关的暗箱操作,这也是维持法院公信力的方式之一。司法运作的可见性和公开性有助于实现公约第 6 条第 1 款的目标,即公正审判,保障审判的公正也是民主社会的一项基本原则(*Riepan v. Austria*, § 27; *Krestovskiy v. Russia*, § 24; *Sutter v. Switzerland*, § 26)。

160. 法院程序的公开性原则包括两个方面:举行公开审讯以及公开宣布判决(*Tierce and Others v. San Marino*, § 93; *Sutter v. Switzerland*, § 27)。

(二)获得口头审讯以及出席审判的权利

161. 第 6 条第 1 款"公开审讯"的权利必然意味着获得"口头审讯"的权利(*Döry v.*

Sweden, § 37)。

162. 在刑事案件中,口头公开审讯的原则尤为重要,当某人受到刑事指控时,他必须能够在一审中出席审讯(*Tierce and Others v. San Marino*, § 94; *Jussila v. Finland* [GC], § 40)。

163. 很难想象受指控的人在不出庭的情况下如何行使第6条第3款第c、d、e项列举的权利,即"为自己辩护""询问证人"和"如果不懂或不会讲法院所使用的工作语言可以请求免费翻译"的权利。因此,保护刑事诉讼中的被告在法院出席的权利是第6条最关键的要求之一(*Hermi v. Italy* [GC], §§ 58 - 59; *Sejdovic v. Italy* [GC], §§ 81 and 84)。

164. 尽管在被告缺席的情况下开展的审讯本身不违背公约第6条,但如果某人在缺席时被定罪,之后也不能请求法院重新审查指控的法律和事实依据而且没有理由认为其放弃了出席为自己辩护的权利或者试图逃脱审判,那么就可以认为存在司法不公(*Sejdovic v. Italy* [GC], § 82)。

165. 进行审讯的义务并非在所有案件中都绝对属于第6条的刑事部分。根据更宽泛的关于"刑事指控"的定义,对于那些传统上不属于刑法范畴的案件(例如,行政处罚、海关法和税收滞纳金)有不同的考量。公平审讯的要求是刑法核心中最严格的,第6条对于刑法方面的保障并不一定适用于上述其他类型的案件,也没有任何程度上的特征(*Jussila v. Finland* [GC], §§ 41 - 43)。

166. 合法取消口头审讯情形的特征与管辖法院处理案件的性质有关,特别是那些实质上基于案件文件资料无法充分解决的事实或法律上的问题。当对事实没有争议、对可靠性没有质疑时,不需要口头展示证据、交叉询问证人,或使被告有充分的机会以书面方式提出控告并质疑对其不利的证据,此时口头审讯并不是必须的(*Jussila v. Finland* [GC], §§ 41 - 42, 47 - 48)。在这一点上,国内法院考虑到效率和经济上的要求取消口头审讯是合法的(*Jussila v. Finland* [GC], §§ 41 - 43, 47 - 48,有关税收滞纳金诉讼; *Suhadolc v. Slovenia* (dec.),有关道路交通违法的简易程序)。

(三)申诉程序

167. 和初审不同,被告在申诉审讯中是否出席并不那么重要。在上诉法院期间第6条的适用取决于所涉程序的特征,同时也必须考虑到国内法律秩序的整个程序和之后上诉法院所起的作用(*Hermi v. Italy* [GC], § 60)。

168. 和对事实的质疑不同，如果一审已经进行了公开审讯，即使上诉法院不能亲自审问申诉人，上诉许可程序和对法律质疑的程序也有可能符合第 6 条的要求（关于上诉许可：*Monnell and Morris v. the United Kingdom*，§ 58；关于上诉法院：*Sutter v. Switzerland*，§ 30）。

169. 即使上诉法院有权从事实和法律两方面重审案件，第 6 条也并不总是要求公开审讯，更不必说要求亲自出席（*Fejde v. Sweden*，§ 31）。为了确定这个问题，必须关注程序的特征以及在上诉程序中对申诉人利益的保护方式，特别是要考虑待确定的争议点的性质（*Seliwiak v. Poland*，§ 54；*Sibgatullin v. Russia*，§ 36）。

170. 然而，当上诉法院必须从事实和法律两方面审查案件，并对有罪与否做出全面的审查时，如果没有直接审查被告为了证明自己没有犯所控罪名而亲自提交的证据，那么上诉法院就不能做出有罪与否的判决（*Popovici v. Moldova*，§ 68；*Lacadena Calero v. Spain*，§ 38）。审讯应当公开的原则包含了被告亲自向上诉法院提交证据的权利。从这方面看，公开原则有利于实现保护被告辩护权利的目标（*Tierce and Others v. San Marino*，§ 95）。

（四）公开性原则的例外

171. 举行公开审讯原则有例外。从第 6 条第 1 款的字面含义来看，它包含了以下条款："……出于对未成年人利益或当事人私生活的保护，或者是在特殊情况下，法院认为公开审讯会损害公正利益，则可以拒绝媒体和公众旁听全部或部分审讯。"不论是全部还是部分审讯，上述情形必须严格适用非公开形式（*Welke and Białek v. Poland*，§ 74；*Martinie v. France* [GC]，§ 40）。

172. 如果有理由适用其中一种或多种例外情形，当局认为此种限制是有正当理由的，那么就有权（而非有义务）命令审讯以非公开形式进行 [*Toeva v. Bulgaria*（dec.）]。

173. 尽管刑事程序要求高度公开性，第 6 条有时也限制程序的公开，例如，为了保护证人的安全或隐私，或是为了追求正义而促进信息观点的自由交换（*B. and P. v. the United Kingdom*，§ 37）。

174. 安全问题是许多刑事案件的共同特点，但是仅仅基于安全问题就能合法地排除公众旁听审判的案件仍然是很少见的（*Riepan v. Austria*，§ 34）。安全措施应当谨慎地适用并符合必要性原则。司法机关应该考虑所有可能的替代手段来保证法庭的安全，当能达到同样目的时，优先适用最不苛刻的手段（*Krestovskiy v. Russia*，§ 29）。

175. 出于公共秩序和安全的考虑,在对已定罪的犯人的监狱纪律处分程序中可以不适用公开性原则(Campbell and Fell v. the United Kingdom,§ 87)。

176. 在监狱举行一场普通刑事程序的审判并不一定意味着审判是非公开的。然而,为了应对不在常规的法庭审理所面对的障碍,国家有义务采取补偿措施以保证公众和媒体按时获知审讯的地点并能有效进入(Riepan v. Austria,§§ 28-29)。

177. 在没有衡量公开性和国家安全的情况下,案件档案中存在保密材料并不自动暗示着审判必须对公众保密。在拒绝公众旁听刑事程序之前,法院必须确认不公开对于保护必要的国家利益是必须的,而且保密的程度必须限制在保护此种利益的范围内(Belashev v. Russia,§ 83;Welke and Białek v. Poland,§ 77)。

(五)判决的公开宣布

178. 本法院没有局限于采用"公开宣布"的文义解释(Sutter v. Switzerland,§ 33;Campbell and Fell v. the United Kingdom,§ 91)。

179. 除了该条字面含义所要求的在法庭上公开宣读的方式,其他公开宣布判决的方式也符合第6条第1款。通常,作为应诉国,其国内法律关于公开判决的形式必须依据程序特征并参考第6条第1款追求的目标进行审查,也就是为了保护获得公正审判的权利而保证对司法程序的审查。在审查时,必须考虑整个诉讼程序(Welke and Białek v. Poland,§ 83,此案中对判决的执行部分采用非公开形式并没有违反第6条)。

180. 完全向公众隐瞒判决是不合理的。可以采用某些手段解决关于安全的担忧,例如,仅对披露后会损害国家安全或其他人安全的判决内容进行保密(Raza v. Bulgaria,§ 53;Fazliyski v. Bulgaria,§§ 67-68)。

三、合理的时间

> 第6条第1款
> "在决定……对某人确定任何刑事罪名时,任何人有权……受到……审判机构的公平的……的审讯。……"

(一)诉讼程序期间的终止

181. 刑事案件中,第6条第1款规定任何人都有在合理的时间内获得公正诉讼的权利,这一规定的目标是保证被告无须因指控持续时间过长而撒谎,并保证对指控做出明确判决(Wemhoff v Germany, § 18; Kart v. Turkey[GC], § 68)。

1. 期间的起始时间

182. 期间自被告人受指控之日起算(Neumeister v. Austria, § 18)。

183. "合理时间"可能开始于案件提交审判法院之前(Deweer v. Belgium, § 42),如自逮捕之日起(Wemhoff v. Germany, § 19)、自提出指控之日起(Neumeister v. Austria, § 18)或者初步调查之日起(Ringeisen v. Austria, § 110)。

184. 根据第 6 条第 1 款的目标,"指控"应该被定义成"当局对于某人就其犯下的刑事违法行为而给予的官方通告"(Deweer v. Belgium, § 46),该定义也与考察嫌疑人的处境是否被"实质影响"相呼应(Deweer v. Belgium, § 46; Neumeister v. Austria, § 13; Eckle v. Germany, § 73; McFarlane v. Ireland[GC], § 143)。

2. 期间的终止

185. 本法院认为第 6 条规定的期间适用于刑事案件的所有程序(König v. Germany, § 98),包括上诉程序(Delcourt v. Belgium, §§ 25–26; König v. Germany, § 98; V. v. the United Kingdom[GC], § 109)。而且,第 6 条第 1 款表明期间终止于对指控做出判决之时,也可以是上诉法院对指控的实质内容做出决定之时(Neumeister v. Austria, § 19)。

186. 期间被认为直至判决无罪或有罪时终止,即使涉及上诉裁判。没有理由认为针对刑事程序延期的保护应当在第一次审判时终止:对无理由的延期或审判法院的过度延期应当产生担忧(Wemhoff v. Germany, § 18)。

187. 如果已经定罪,但只要处刑并非绝对确定,就不存在第 6 条第 1 款规定的"确定……刑事指控"(Eckle v. Germany, § 77; Ringeisen v. Austria, § 110; V. v. the United Kingdom[GC], § 109)。

188. 出于第 6 条的目标,任何法院判决的执行必须被看作是审判的一部分(Assanidze v. Georgia[GC], § 181)。如果缔约国的国内法律或行政系统允许一个宣告无罪的有约束力的最终的司法判决对宣告无罪的人是无效的,公约第 6 条提供的保障就会变成泡影。刑事程序是一个整体,第 6 条提供的担保不会随着宣告无罪的判决而停止(同上,§ 182)。如果国家行政机关拒绝或未能履行或者延迟履行宣告被告无罪的判决,刑事程序中被告享有的第 6 条的保障就是部分形同虚设的(同上,§ 183)。

(二)合理时间的审查

1. 原则

189. 诉讼程序期间长短的合理性由案件的具体情况决定,需要进行全面的审查(*Boddaert v. Belgium*, § 36)。诉讼程序中的不同阶段需要以合理的速度推进,但是诉讼程序的总期间不能超过"合理的时间"(*Dobbertin v. France*, § 44)。

190. 第6条要求司法程序迅速而有效率,但也制定了更为概括的适当司法行政原则。这项基本要求在不同方面需要保持平衡(*Boddaert v. Belgium*, § 39)。

2. 标准

191. 在确定刑事程序期间是否合理时,本法院会考虑诸如案件的复杂程度、申请人的行为以及相关行政部门和司法部门的行为等因素(*König v. Germany*, § 99; *Neumeister v. Austria*, § 21; *Ringeisen v. Austria*, § 110; *Pélissier and Sassi v. France* [GC], § 67; *Pedersen and Baadsgaard v. Denmark*, § 45)。

192. 案件的复杂性可能来自于以下因素:指控的数量、案件中涉及的人数如被告和证人的数量,或者案件的国际化程度(*Neumeister v. Austria*, § 20,此案中涉及的交易在许多不同国家都有衍生,需要国际刑警组织的帮助以及履行法律互助协议,涉及22个人,其中有些人在国外)。如果案件涉及"白领"犯罪,也会特别复杂——大面积的诈骗牵涉数个国家,为了逃避调查机构的审查而需要设计复杂的交易,并且需要大量的会计和金融专业知识(*C. P. and Others v. France*, § 30)。

193. 即使案件非常复杂,本法院也不能将案件中没有解释的无作为期间视为"合理"(*Adiletta v. Italy*, § 17,本案中,审理期限长达13年5个月,包括将案件提交给调查法官和质询被告及证人之间延迟的5年,以及将案件返还给调查法官和重新将申诉人收押待审之间延迟的1年9个月)。

194. 申诉人的行为:第6条并不要求申诉人和司法机关积极合作。申诉人也不能因为充分利用国内法提供的救济措施而受惩罚。不过,他们的行为属于客观事实,不能归因于应诉国一方,在判断审讯期间是否合理时也必须纳入考量(*Eckle v. Germany*, § 82,本案中申诉人使用越来越多的类似延长诉讼程序的救济措施,如有计划地要求法官回避;有些行为可以看作是故意的干扰)。

195. 有一种情况是申诉人试图延长调查,这种行为必须纳入考虑范围,这从案件材料上可以明显看出(*I. A. v. France*, § 121,本案中的申诉人在要求一系列额外的调查手续之前,等待被告知需要立即将案件材料转交给公诉人)。

196. 申诉人逃避本国法律制裁的时间不能计入合理时间内。如果被告逃避本国依照法律实施的制裁,可以假定他无权控诉诉讼程序的延长,除非他能提供充分的理由推翻该假定(*Vayiç v. Turkey*, § 44)。

197. 相关机构的行为:第 6 条第 1 款要求缔约国在构建司法体系时应当设立符合公约标准的法院(*Abdoella v. the Netherlands*, § 24;*Dobbertin v. France*, § 44)。

198. 如果缔约国及时采取救济措施处理例外情形,那么缔约国就无需因暂时积压案件而负责(*Milasi v. Italy*, § 18;*Baggetta v. Italy*, § 23),但是本法院很少将机构繁重的工作量以及各种救济措施视作有决定性的影响力(*Eckle v. Germany*, § 92)。

199. 在审查诉讼期间的合理性时,应当考虑与申诉人利害相关的因素。例如,当某人处于审前羁押时,需要考虑该指控是否会在合理期限内判决(*Abdoella v. the Netherlands*, § 24:本案持续时间为 4 年 4 个月,其中两次要求将文件上交给最高法院的时间总和就超过了 1 年 9 个月。本法院认为如此长的无作为期间是不可接受的,特别是此时被告仍处于羁押之中)。

(三) 几个例子

1. 超过合理期限

- 9 年 7 个月:不考虑有关部门在暴乱时期处理法院的某些特殊案件所采取的措施,除了涉及人数为 35 人外,没有其他特别的复杂之处(*Milasi v. Italy*, §§ 14 – 20)。
- 13 年 4 个月:地区政治动乱,法院工作量过多,多年后国家才开始设法改善法院的工作条件(*Baggetta v. Italy*, §§ 20 – 25)。
- 5 年 5 个月 18 天:其中,从做出判决直到负责法官写出完整的判决历经 2 年 9 个月,在此期间没有采取任何恰当的惩戒措施(*B. v. Austria*, §§ 48 – 55)。
- 5 年 11 个月:在这一严重渎职案中,被质询的人数众多,审查文件的技术性强,因此案件比较复杂,但这并不是调查行动持续五年零两个月的正当理由;而且有关部门在很长一段时间内无作为。因此,尽管审判期限看起来很合理,但是并不能说进行了尽职调查(*Rouille v. France*, § 29)。
- 12 年 7 个月 10 天:没有复杂情况,被告也没有使用任何手段来延长期限,但自行政法院提交申请直到税务部门收到最初的请求,之间相隔时间长达 2 年 9 个月多(*Clinique Mozart SARL v. France*,§§ 34-36)。

2.没有超过合理期限

- 5年2个月:案件非常复杂,涉及诈骗和破产欺诈,除了要求释放之外,申诉人还提出其他大量的请求和申诉,包括质疑大部分相关法官并请求将该诉讼转移至其他法院审理(*Ringeisen v. Austria*,§ 110)。
- 7年4个月:提出指控之后过了7年仍然没有对被告做出有罪或无罪判决,这是特别长的一段时间,在大多数案件中被视作超过了合理期限;而且,在其中长达1年3个月的时间内,法官没有质询人数众多的共同被告或证人中的任何一人,也没有履行其他职责;不过,这起案件特别复杂,涉及诸多罪名,牵涉人数众多,涉外因素也造成了请求国外司法协助的困难,因此,认为没有超过合理期限(*Neumeister v. Austria*,§ 21)。

第五节 具体保障

一、第6条第2款:无罪推定

> **第6条第2款**
> "凡受刑事指控者在未经依法证明为有罪之前,应当推定为无罪。"

(一)证明责任

200. 无罪推定原则尤其要求法庭成员在履行职责时不能先入为主地认为被告已犯所控罪行;控方负有证明责任,而且任何疑点都应采取有利于被告的解释。控方告知被告本案将会对他起诉,以使被告可以相应地准备并辩护,同时控方要提出足以使其定罪的证据(*Barberà, Messegué and Jabardo v. Spain*,§ 77;*Janosevic v. Sweden*,§ 97)。如果将证明责任从控方转移到辩方,就违反了无罪推定原则(*Telfner v. Austria*,§ 15)。在诉讼程序终止后的赔偿环节,证明责任不能倒置(*Capeau v. Belgium*,§ 25)。

201. 刑事上免责不排除基于相同事实但承担更轻证明责任的民事赔偿责任

[*Ringvold v. Norway*, § 38; *Y v. Norway*, § 41; *Lundkvist v. Sweden*(dec.)]。

(二)事实推定和法律推定

202. 在刑事案件中,被告被推定为无罪并要求控方承担证明责任的权利不是绝对的,因为所有刑事系统都会采用事实推定和法律推定,公约也没有禁止这两种推定方式[*Falk v. the Netherlands*(dec.),此案涉及交通违法,涉案车辆登记的车主并非实际驾驶人,但是对其施加了罚款]。在某些情形下,缔约国无需考虑行为人是出于刑事犯罪目的还是出于过失,可以对诸如此类的简单或客观事实施加处罚(*Salabiaku v. France*, § 27,对于从毒品持有者处走私的,推定承担刑事责任; *Janosevic v. Sweden*, § 100,基于客观理由,在法院判决前科以税收滞纳金)。不过第6条第2款要求各国对推定要有合理的限制,应当考虑相关利益的重要性,同时要保证辩方权利(*Salabiaku v. France*, § 28; *Radio France and Others v. France*, § 24,推定一位在广播节目中进行诽谤的出版主任应承担刑事责任; *Klouvi v. France*, § 41,根据法律推定,对因缺乏证据而被宣告无罪的被告提起指控的做法是错误的,因此不能对恶意起诉进行辩护)。

203. 在刑法中适用推定时,缔约国要在所涉利益的重要性和辩方权利之间保持平衡;换句话说,为实现立法目的而采取的手段必须合乎比例[*Janosevic v. Sweden*, § 101; *Falk v. the Netherlands*(dec.)]。

(三)第6条第2款的适用范围

1. 刑事诉讼

204. 第6条第2款适用于整个刑事诉讼,不论控诉结果如何,也不仅仅适用于案件的实质审查(*Poncelet v. Belgium*, § 50; *Minelli v. Switzerland*, § 30; *Garycki v. Poland*, § 68)。

205. 当一审判决被告有罪,被告提起上诉时,无罪推定原则仍然继续适用(*Konstas v. Greece*, § 36)。

206. 一旦被告被证明有罪,在量刑环节,第6条第2款不能适用于有关被告性格和行为的主张,除非此种主张的性质和程度足以构成一项新的"指控"(*Phillips v. the United Kingdom*, § 35; *Böhmer v. Germany*, § 55; *Geerings v. the Netherlands*, §43)。

207. 不过无罪推定原则及辩方承担证明责任,属于公约第6条第1款规定的公正审判权利一般概念的一部分,在量刑环节仍然适用(*Phillips v. the United Kingdom*,

§§ 39 – 40;Grayson and Barnham v. the United Kingdom,§§ 37 and 39)。

2. 后续程序

208. 无罪推定原则可以保护被宣告无罪的被告或者继续进行的诉讼中的被告免于被政府官员或机构当作实际有罪而对待。如果没有保护措施来保证对无罪或诉讼终止结果的尊重,第6条第2款提供的保障将有形同虚设之嫌。一旦刑事程序终结,当事人的名誉以及大众的评价也会受到影响(Allen v. the United Kingdom[GC],§ 94)。

209. 在后续程序中,关于第6条第2款能否适用的问题,申请人必须证明已终结的程序和后续程序之间的联系。这种联系是有可能呈现的,例如,后续程序要求审查之前刑事程序的结果,特别是要求法院分析判决;参与刑事文档中证据的重审和评估;审查申诉人在刑事指控所指向的部分或全部事件中的参与度;评估关于申诉人可能有罪的暗示和迹象(Allen v. the United Kingdom[GC],§ 104)。

210. 本法院认为,在下列情形中,第6条第2款可以适用于在刑事诉讼终结后做出的司法决定:

- 由被告承担法庭和控方诉讼费用;
- 被告针对还押期间的拘留及刑事诉讼带来的其他不便请求赔偿;
- 被告请求控方承担辩护费用;
- 被告针对调查或控诉中的不当行为造成的损害请求赔偿;
- 承担向受害人赔偿的民事责任;
- 拒绝申诉人针对保险人提起的民事索赔;
- 在控方决定不针对家长虐待儿童进行起诉后,仍然保持照顾儿童命令的效力;
- 处分或开除;
- 撤销申诉人享有保障性住房的权利(见 Allen v. the United Kingdom[GC],§ 98,之后被大量的案件引用)。

(四)不利声明

211. 第6条第2款旨在防止和诉讼有关的不利声明损害刑事诉讼的公正性。当这样的诉讼根本不存在或尚未存在时,导致刑事或其他应受谴责行为的声明会引起公约第6条和第8条所规定权利的有关争议,这类声明与针对诽谤的保护措施以及基于民事权利向法院提起诉讼的权利密切相关[Zollmann v. the United Kingdom(dec.),

Ismoilov and Others v. Russia，§ 160］。

212. 一份仅是怀疑某人犯罪的声明和一份在没有最终定罪的情况下明确宣称某人犯罪的声明之间有根本的区别（*Ismoilov and Others v. Russia*，§ 166；*Nešťák v. Slovakia*，§ 89）。后者违反了无罪推定原则，而前者在多种情况下被本法院视作是不客观的（*Garycki v. Poland*，§ 67）。

213. 在判断法官或其他政府官员做出的声明是否违反了无罪推定原则时，必须考虑做出该抨击声明时的具体情况（*Daktaras v. Lithuania*，§ 42；*A. L. v. Germany*，§ 31）。

214. 比起其他调查机关，法官做出的声明要接受更严格的审查（*Pandy v. Belgium*，§ 43）。

215. 只要刑事诉讼的结果并未对指控实质内容下定论，那么表达对被告的怀疑就是可以接受的（*Sekanina v. Austria*，§ 30）。然而，一旦最终决定是判定无罪，任何怀疑有罪的表达就不符合无罪推定原则（*Rushiti v. Austria*，§ 31；*O. v. Norway*，§ 39；*Geerings v. the Netherlands*，§ 49；*Paraponiaris v. Greece*，§ 32）。

（五）司法机关的声明

216. 如果司法决定在依法证明某人有罪之前就假设其有罪，就违反了无罪推定原则。即使没有任何正式的证据，但只要有理由说明法院将被告当作有罪对待就足够（*Minelli v. Switzerland*，§ 37；*Nerattini v. Greece*，§ 23；*Didu v. Romania*，§ 41）。法庭表达如此不成熟的观点本身就不可避免地与无罪推定相冲突（*Nešťák v. Slovakia*，§ 88；*Garycki v. Poland*，§ 66）。

217. 在适用第 6 条第 2 款时，重要的是声明的真实内容而非字面形式（*Lavents v. Latvia*，§ 126）。

218. 即使申诉人最终被定罪，这也不能剥夺他在依法被证明有罪之前被推定无罪的权利。（*Matijašević v. Serbia*，§ 49；*Nešťák v. Slovakia*，§ 90，有关延长申请人在押候审期限的决定）。

（六）政府官员的声明

219. 除了法官或法院，其他政府官员也有可能违反无罪推定原则（*Allenet de Ribemont v. France*，§ 36；*Daktaras v. Lithuania*，§ 42；*Petyo Petkov v. Bulgaria*，§ 91）。第 6 条第 2 款禁止政府官员在刑事调查尚在进行时发布声明引导大众认为被告有罪，影响司法机关的审查（*Ismoilov and Others v. Russia*，§ 161；*Butkevicius v. Lithuania*，§ 53）。

220. 无罪推定原则并不禁止当局向公众告知刑事程序的进展,但必须在尊重无罪推定的基础上谨慎告知(*Fatullayev v. Azerbaijan*,§ 159;*Allenet de Ribemont v. France*,§ 38;*Garycki v. Poland*,§ 69)。

221. 本法院强调,政府官员在某人被判定有罪之前做出声明时应当谨慎选择措辞[*Daktaras v. Lithuania*,§ 41;*Arrigo and Vella v. Malta*(dec.),§ 94]。

(七)负面新闻活动

222. 在民主社会中,媒体针对有关公共利益的案件进行激烈讨论有时是不可避免的[*Viorel Burzo v. Romania*,§ 160;*Akay v. Turkey*(dec.)]。

223. 然而,恶意的新闻活动会影响公众舆论,从而影响负责判定被告有罪或无罪的陪审员,因此不利于审判的公正性(*Kuzmin v Russia*,§ 62)。真正起决定性作用的不是审判法院在主观上对嫌疑人没有偏见,而是在案件的特定情形下,嫌疑人的恐惧可以被认为是客观合理的[*Włoch v. Poland*(dec.),*Daktaras v. Lithuania*(dec.),*Priebke v. Italy*(dec.);以及 *Mustafa Kamal Mustafa(Abu Hamza)(no.1)v. the United Kingdom*(dec.),§§ 37-40,有关媒体报道对审判法院的公正性的影响]。

224. 不同于陪审团的成员,国内法院由职业法官组成,他们通常具有丰富的经验,并且接受了足够的训练,很难受外界影响[*Craxi v. Italy*(no.1),§ 104;*Mircea v. Romania*,§ 75]。

225. 发布嫌疑人的照片本身并不违反无罪推定(*Y. B. and Others v. Turkey*,§ 47)。在某些情况下,在电视上发布嫌疑人的照片可能会引起与第6条第2款规定有关的争议[*Rupa v. Romania*(no.1),§ 232]。

(八)对于不提供信息的行为的制裁

226. 无罪推定原则和不得自证其罪紧密相连(*Heaney and McGuinness v. Ireland*,§ 40)。

227. 要求车主辨认出交通违法行为发生时的实际驾驶员,这符合公约第6条的规定(*O'Halloran and Francis v. the United Kingdom*[GC])。

228. 要求驾驶员进行呼吸测试或血液检测并不违反无罪推定[*Tirado Ortiz and Lozano Martin v. Spain*(dec.)]。

二、第 6 条第 3 款:辩方的权利

> **第 6 条第 3 款**
>
> "凡受刑事罪指控者具有下列最低限度的权利:
>
> a. 以他所了解的语言立即详细地通知他被指控罪名的性质以及被指控的原因;
>
> b. 应当有适当的时间和便利条件为辩护作准备;
>
> c. 由他本人或者由他自己选择的律师协助自己辩护,或者如果他无力支付法律协助费用的,则基于公平利益的考虑,应当免除他的有关费用;
>
> d. 询问不利于他的证人,并在与不利于他的证人具有相同的条件下,让有利于他的证人出庭接受询问;
>
> e. 如果他不懂或者不会讲法院所使用的工作语言,可以请求免费的译员协助翻译。"

229. 第 6 条第 3 款关于辩方权利的要求可以看作是公约第 6 条第 1 款保障的获得公正审判权利的特别方面(*Sakhnovskiy v. Russia*[GC],§ 94;*Gäfgen v. Germany*[GC],§ 169)。

230. 第 6 条第 3 款规定的具体保障措施针对刑事案件中的典型程序情形,举例说明了公平审判的概念,但这些措施的本质目标是保证或是有助于保证刑事诉讼整体的公平。因此,第 6 条第 3 款规定的保护措施并不仅限于其本身的含义,必须针对相关程序的具体情形解释其相应的作用(*Mayzit v. Russia*,§ 77;*Can v. Austria*,§ 48)。

(一)第 6 条第 3 款第 a 项:有关指控性质和原因的信息

> **第 6 条第 3 款第 a 项**
>
> "凡受刑事罪指控者具有下列最低限度的权利:
>
> a. 以他所了解的语言立即详细地通知他被指控罪名的性质以及被指控的原因;"

1. 一般规定

231. 必须依据公约第 6 条第 1 款规定的获得公正审判的权利,对第 6 条第 3 款的适用范围进行审查。在刑事案件中,提供全面详细的指控信息使得法院能够采用该法律表述,是保证诉讼公正的必要前提(*Pélissier and Sassi v. France*[GC],§ 52;*Sejdovic v. Italy*[GC],§ 90)。

232. 第 6 条第 3 款的第 a 项与第 b 项是相互联系的,因为在审查被告知指控信息的权利时,必须结合被告所享有的准备辩护的权利来考察(*Pélissier and Sassi v. France*[GC],§ 54,§ 47)。

2. 有关指控的信息

233. 第 6 条第 3 款 a 项指出需要特别注意通知被告其被起诉。犯罪事实在刑事程序中起关键作用,因为正是在收到书面通知时,嫌疑人被告知其所受指控的事实依据和法律依据(*Kamasinski v. Austria*,§ 79;*Pélissier and Sassi v. France*[GC],§ 51)。

234. 第 6 条第 3 款 a 项赋予被告的权利不仅包括得知指控的"原因"(即指控所依据的他所实施的犯罪行为),也包括罪名的"性质"(即对这些行为的法律表述)(*Mattoccia v. Italy*,§ 59;*Penev v. Bulgaria*,§§ 33 and 42)。

235. 这些信息不一定需要提及指控所依据的证据[*X. v. Belgium*(dec.);*Collozza and Rubinat v. Italy*]。

236. 第 6 条第 3 款第 a 项对通知被告所指控罪名的性质和原因没有特殊的形式上的要求(*Pélissier and Sassi v. France*[GC],§ 53;*Drassich v. Italy*,§ 34;*Giosakis v. Greece*(no.3),§ 29)。

237. 控方应当承担通知被指控者的义务,并且不能只是消极地公开消息,即不以引起辩方注意的方式通知(*Mattoccia v. Italy*,§ 65;*Chichlian and Ekindjian v. France*,§ 71)。

238. 被指控者必须确实收到了指控信息;仅仅有法律推定的接收是不够的[*C. v. Italy*(dec.)]。

239. 如果被申诉的情形是被指控者自身行为造成的,那么被指控者没有资格主张其辩护权利受到侵犯[*Erdogan v. Turkey*(dec.);*Campbell and Fell v. the United Kingdom*,§ 96]。

240. 被指控者患有精神疾病,当局被要求采取额外措施使其能够得知被指控罪名的性质和原因(*Vaudelle v. France*,§ 65)

3. 指控的重新归类

241. 被指控者必须能够及时充分得知被指控的罪名及原因的任何变化,而且必须有适当的时间和便利条件予以回应,并基于新的信息或主张准备辩护[Mattoccia v. Italy, § 61; Bäckström and Andersson v. Sweden(dec.)]

242. 有关指控的信息(包括法院可能会适用的法律定性)必须在审判前的起诉书中提交,或者至少在审判过程中通过其他诸如正式的或暗示的指控延伸方式提出。仅提及法院可能就犯罪成立条件得出与控方不一样的结论是明显不够的(I. H. and Others v. Austria, § 34)。

243. 在诉讼程序中对事实进行重新归类时,必须保证被指控者能够及时有效地行使辩护权(Pélissier and Sassi v. France[GC], § 62; Block v. Hungary, § 24)。

244. 如果罪名的重新归类涉及到指控的某一本质要素,那么对被告而言就应当是可以充分预见的[De Salvador Torres v. Spain, § 33; Sadak and Others v. Turkey(no. 1), §§ 52 and 56; Juha Nuutinen v. Finland, § 32]。

245. 如果被告有机会就新指控向上级法院提起上诉,并依据所有相关的法律和事实进行辩护,那么指控罪名通知的缺陷就可以在上诉阶段得以修正(Dallos v. Hungary, §§ 49 – 52; Sipavičius v. Lithuania, §§ 30 – 33; Zhupnik v. Ukraine, §§ 39 – 43; I. H. and Others v. Austria, §§ 36 – 38)。

4."详细"

246. 尽管信息的"详细"程度依据案件不同情况而定,但被指控者至少要有足够的信息以充分理解对其指控的罪名,准备恰当的辩护。

247. 必须依据第 6 条第 3 款第 b 项以及第 6 条第 1 款,考察信息的充分程度(第 6 条第 3 款第 b 项规定给予被指控者适当的时间和便利条件准备辩护,第 6 条第 1 款规定的是获得公正审判的权利)[Mattoccia v. Italy, § 60; Bäckström and Andersson v. Sweden(dec.)]。

5."及时"

248. 信息必须及时传递给被告供其准备辩护,这也是第 6 条第 3 款第 a 项的目的暗含的原则[C. v. Italy(dec.), 此案中,本法院认为在审判前四个月通知申诉人是可以接受的;相反在博里索瓦诉保加利亚案(Borisova v. Bulgaria, §§ 43 – 45)中,在没有律师的情况下,申诉人只有几个小时时间准备辩护]。

249. 在审查是否符合第 6 条第 3 款第 a 项时,本法院会考虑"被指控"以及"刑事指控"的含义,并依据客观内容而非形式方面进行解释[*Padin Gestoso v. Spain*(dec.);*Casse v. Luxembourg*, § 71]。

6."语言"

250. 如果有理由相信被告对提供信息所使用的语言不了解,当局必须为他提供翻译[*Brozicek v. Italy*, § 41;*Tabaï v. France*(dec.)]。

251. 尽管第 6 条第 3 款第 a 项没有具体要求相关信息必须以书面形式或是翻译成书面形式提供给外国被告人,但如果被告没有获得以他所能理解的语言翻译的书面起诉书,而他又不熟悉法院所使用的语言,可能实际会处于不利位置(*Hermi v. Italy* [GC], § 68;*Kamasinski v. Austria*, § 79)。

252. 但是如果被告能够准备辩护,那么关于指控的详细信息也可以通过口头翻译起诉书的方式提供[*Kamasinski v. Austria*, § 81;*Husain v. Italy*(dec.)]。

253. 本条款没有规定被告获得法院所有文件翻译的权利(*X. v. Austria*, Commission decision)。

254. 依据第 6 条第 3 款第 e 项规定的获得免费翻译的权利,指控的翻译费用由国家承担(*Luedicke, Belkacem and Koç v. Germany*, § 45)。

(二)第 6 条第 3 款第 b 项:准备辩护

> **第 6 条第 2 款第 b 项**
> "凡受刑事罪指控者具有下列最低限度的权利:b. 应当有适当的时间和便利条件为辩护作准备;"

1. 一般性考虑因素

255. 公约第 6 条第 3 款第 b 项规定了恰当辩护的两个要素,即便利条件和时间。该条款意味着被告的实质辩护活动包含了任何对准备审判而言"必要"的要件。被告必须有机会以恰当的方式准备辩护,不受任何其在审判中提交辩护依据从而影响诉讼结果的限制(*Can v. Austria*, § 53;*Gregačević v. Croatia*, § 51)。

256. 被告获得的适当时间和便利条件依据不同案件的具体情形而定(*Iglin v.*

Ukraine,§ 65;Galstyan v. Armenia,§ 84)。

2. 适当的时间

257. 公约第 6 条第 3 款第 b 项保护被告不受轻率的审判;[Kröcher and Möller v. Switzerland(dec.);Bonzi v. Switzerland(dec.)]。尽管诉讼应及时进行,但不能以牺牲某方的程序权利为代价(OAO Neftyanaya Kompaniya Yukos v. Russia,§ 540)。

258. 在审查被告是否有充分的时间准备辩护时,要特别关注诉讼的性质,以及案件的复杂程度和进展阶段(Gregačević v. Croatia,§ 51)。此外,也要考虑律师的通常工作负担;然而,如果案件有特殊紧急情况,要求辩护律师改变工作重点也是合理的[Mattick v. Germany(dec.)]。

259. 公约第 6 条第 3 款第 b 项不要求审判的准备在第一次听证前完成。审判过程不可能全部提前计划,可能会显现出之前没有预见的要素,需要各方做进一步准备[Mattick v. Germany(dec.)]。

260. 诉讼过程中发生特定情形时,必须给予辩方额外的时间以调整定位、准备请求、提起上诉(Miminoshvili v. Russia,§ 141)。这类"情形"包括起诉书的变更(Pélissier and Sassi v. France[GC],§ 62)、控方提出新证据(G. B. v. France,§§ 60 - 62),或者审判中专家意见突然发生重大改变(G. B. v. France,§§ 69 - 70)。

261. 如果发现与时间相关的问题,被告有望请求审讯休庭或延期[Campbell and Fell v. the United Kingdom,§ 98;Bäckström and Andersson v. Sweden(dec.);Craxi v. Italy(no.1),§ 72)],除非有特殊情形(Goddi v. Italy,§ 31)或者国内法律及实践中没有这类权利的依据(Galstyan v. Armenia,§ 85)。

262. 在特定情形下,法院可以主动决定休庭以给予辩方充足的时间做准备(Sadak and Others v. Turkey(no.1),§ 57;Sakhnovskiy v. Russia[GC],§§ 103 and 106)。

263. 为了使被告能够充分行使上诉权,国内法院必须明确指出判决的依据(Hadjianastassiou v. Greece,§ 33)。如果在上诉期限届满前无法做出论理充分的判决,就必须给予被告足够的信息以便其能够上诉(Zoon v. the Netherlands,§§ 40 - 50;Baucher v. France,§§ 46 - 51)。

264. 国家必须保证每一个受到刑事指控的人得到第 6 条第 3 款的保障。要求上诉人证明已确定的期间何时开始或届满,这和"尽职"一词含义不符——缔约国必须做到"尽职"来保证公约第 6 条的权利得以有效行使(Vacher v. France,§ 28)。

3. 适当的便利条件

(1) 获取证据。

265. 任何受刑事指控的人都应该获得的便利条件包括了解调查结果以便准备辩护的机会（*Huseyn and Others v. Azerbaijan*, § 175；*OAO Neftyanaya Kompaniya Yukos v. Russia*, § 538）。

266. 当某人被拘留候审时，"便利条件"包括能够专心阅读和书写的环境（*Mayzit v. Russia*, § 81；*Moiseyev v. Russia*, § 221）。保证被告及其辩护律师能够参与诉讼并提交意见而无须受过分的疲累之苦也非常重要（*Makhfi v. France*, § 40；*Barberà, Messegué and Jabardo v. Spain*, § 70）。

267. 被告应享有的便利条件仅限于在准备辩护过程中帮助或可能帮助被告的条件 [*Padin Gestoso v. Spain*(dec.)；*Mayzit v. Russia*, § 79]。

268. 无须保证被告直接获取案件材料，由他的代理人告知就足够了（*Kremzow v. Austria*, § 52）。然而，被告获取案件材料权利的有限性并不能阻止被告在审判前获得证据，被告也有机会通过律师的口头意见发表评论（*Öcalan v. Turkey*[GC], § 140）。

269. 当被告被允许自行辩护，否认其获取案件材料的权利等同于侵犯其辩护权（*Foucher v. France*, §§ 33-36）。

270. 为了便于辩护，被告可以获取相关案件材料的复印件，并汇编、使用其笔记（*Rasmussen v. Poland*, §§ 48-49；*Moiseyev v. Russia*, §§ 213-218；*Matyjek v. Poland*, § 59；*Seleznev v. Russia*, §§ 64-69）。

271. 获取案件材料的权利并不是绝对的。在某些案件中，为了保护其他人的基本权利，或是为了维护如国家安全之类的公共利益，或是出于保护证人的需要，或是为了保障警方的犯罪调查手段，有必要将某些证据排除在被告可获取的范围之外。然而，这些限制辩方权利的措施只有在十分必要的情形中才是第6条第1款所允许的。本法院将会严格审查决策程序以保证其符合对抗制诉讼、平等手段原则的要求，并保证其保护被告利益的手段是恰当的（*Natunen v. Finland*, §§ 40-41；§§ 42-43；*Mirilashvili v. Russia*, §§ 203-209）。

272. 不向辩方出示可能使其脱罪或减刑的证据，这可能会被认为是拒绝为被告准备辩护提供必要的便利条件，因此侵犯了公约第6条第3款第b项所保障的权利。不过，被告应该给出请求的详细理由，而且国内法院有权审查这些理由的效力 [*Natunen v.*

Finland, § 43; *C. G. P. v. the Netherlands*(dec.)]。

（2）向律师咨询。

273. 向被告提供的"便利条件"包括向律师咨询（*Campbell and Fell v. the United Kingdom*, § 99; *Goddi v. Italy*, § 31）。咨询辩护律师的机会对于被告准备辩护来说至关重要[*Bonzi v. Switzerland*(dec.); *Can v. Austria*, § 52]。

274. 第6条第3款第b项和第6条第3款第c项都规定了获取法律协助的权利（例如，*Lanz v. Austria*, §§ 5053; *Öcalan v. Turkey*[GC], § 148; *Trepashkin v. Russia*(no. 2), §§ 159-168）。

（三）第6条第3款第c项：本人亲自辩护或者获取法律协助的权利

> **第6条第3款第c项**
> "凡受刑事罪指控者具有下列最低限度的权利：
> c. 由他本人或者由他自己选择的律师协助自己辩护，如果他无力支付法律协助费用，则基于公正利益考虑，应当免除他的有关费用；"

275. 第6条第3款第c项规定的是第6条第1款获得公正审判权利的特殊方面[*Correia de Matos v. Portugal*(dec.); *Foucher v. France*, § 30]。该项保证了针对被告的诉讼不会在辩方没有充分辩护的情况下发生（*Pakelli v. Germany*, § 84）。这包含了三项权利：亲自为自己辩护的权利，自己选择律师协助辩护的权利，以及在特殊情况下免费获得法律协助的权利（*Pakelli v. Germany*, § 31）。

1. 适用范围

276. 任何受到刑事指控的人在诉讼程序的任何阶段都受到第6条第3款第c项的保护（*Imbrioscia v. Switzerland*, § 37）。甚至在案件送至法院之前，只要审判可能会因为不符合第6条的规定而有严重偏见，该保护就可以适用（*Imbrioscia v. Switzerland*, § 36; *Öcalan v. Turkey*[GC], § 131; *Magee v. the United Kingdom*, § 41）。

277. 第6条第3款第b项与案件审判准备中的获取法律协助的权利相关，而第6条第3款第c项规定的是一项更为概括的、在整个诉讼过程中获得律师帮助的权利（*Can v. Austria*, § 54）。

278. 在审前阶段即初步调查阶段，第6条第3款第c项的适用方式取决于程序的特征以及案件的具体情况（Brennan v. the United Kingdom, § 45; Berlinski v. Poland, § 75）。第 6 条通常要求被告在被警方询问的初步阶段就能得到律师的帮助（John Murray v. the United Kingdom, § 63; Öcalan v. Turkey [GC], § 131; Salduz v. Turkey [GC], § 54; Averill v. the United Kingdom, § 59; Brennan v. the United Kingdom, § 45; Dayanan v. Turkey, § 31）。然而,这个权利有可能因正当理由而受限制（Magee v. the United Kingdom, § 41; John Murray v. the United Kingdom, § 63）。案件的问题在于,从诉讼的整个过程来看,该限制是否剥夺了被告获得公正审判的权利（John Murray v. the United Kingdom, § 63; Brennan v. the United Kingdom, § 45）。即使在例外情况下,存在强有力的理由拒绝律师的介入,所施加的限制也不能不当损害第 6 条规定的被告权利（Salduz v. Turkey [GC], § 55）。

279. 第 6 条第 3 款第 c 项在上诉法庭的适用方式取决于所涉程序的特征（Pakelli v. Germany, § 29; Meftah and Others v. France [GC], § 41）。必须考虑在国内法律秩序中进行的整个诉讼过程以及上诉法院在其中扮演的角色（Monnell and Morris v. the United Kingdom, § 56; Meftah and Others v. France [GC], § 41）。也有必要考虑上诉许可程序的性质及其在整个刑事诉讼中的重要性,上诉法院的权力范围,以及上诉法院呈现并保护申诉人利益的具体形式（Monnell and Morris v. the United Kingdom, § 56）。

2. 亲自辩护

280. 公约第 6 条的对象和目标整体上体现了受到刑事指控者参与审讯的权利（Zana v. Turkey [GC], § 68; Monnell and Morris v. the United Kingdom, § 58）。与此紧紧相连的第 6 条第 3 款第 c 项为被告提供了为自己辩护的可能性。因此,被告依照个人意愿亲自为自己辩护通常不会违反第 6 条的要求,除非为了实现正义而要受制于其他要求（Galstyan v. Armenia, § 91）。

281. 由本人亲自辩护的权利并不是绝对的。是允许由被告本人辩护还是为其指派律师,属于缔约国的自由裁量范围,比起本法院,缔约国能够更好地选择国内司法系统中恰当的方式保障被告的权利 [Correia de Matos v. Portugal (dec.)]。因此国内法院有权出于对正义的考虑要求指派律师（Croissant v. Germany, § 27; Lagerblom v. Sweden, § 50）。保证被告为自己辩护的权利,是保护被告利益的一种方式 [Correia de Matos v. Portugal (dec.)]。

282. 此外,第 6 条第 3 款第 c 项并没有提供无限制使用任何辩护理由的权利。当被告选择由自己辩护时,他也就放弃了由律师协助的权利,并有责任用心地进行辩护(*Melin v. France*, § 25)。受刑事指控者在行使辩护权利时,有意地引起对于刑事案件中证人或其他人的行为错误怀疑,这种怀疑可能会导致对相关人员的惩罚,而被指控者却被认为不会因此受到控告,这就滥用了辩护权的概念(*Brandstetter v. Austria*, § 52)。仅因为被告接下来出于辩护存在被控告的可能性并不能认为是侵犯了第6条第3款第c项的权利。如果依据国内法律或实践产生的后果过于严重,后续控告的危险会使得被告无法自由行使辩护权,那情况又另当别论(*Brandstetter v. Austria*, § 53)。

3. 法律协助

283. 受到刑事指控的人有权得到律师的有效辩护是公正审判的基本特征之一(*Salduz v. Turkey*[GC], § 51)。作为规则,嫌疑人自被警方拘留或审前羁押时起就应得到法律协助(*Dayanan v. Turkey*, § 31)。通常,被告有效参与刑事审判的权利不仅包括出席审判的权利,也包括必要情况下接受法律协助的权利(*Lagerblom v. Sweden*, § 49; *Galstyan v. Armenia*, § 89)。同样,只有申诉人的律师出席不足以代替被告的出席(*Zana v. Turkey*[GC], § 72)。

284. 法律代理的权利不依赖于被告是否出席(*Van Geyseghem v. Belgium*[GC], § 34; *Campbell and Fell v. the United Kingdom*, § 99; *Poitrimol v. France*, § 34)。不论是否被正式传唤,即使没有缺席理由,被告没有出席也不代表可以合法地剥夺其由律师辩护的权利(*Van Geyseghem v. Belgium*[GC], § 34; *Pelladoah v. the Netherlands*, § 40; *Krombach v. France*, § 89, *Galstyan v. Armenia*, § 89)。

285. 任何受刑事指控者都可以由自己选择的律师辩护的权利不是绝对的(*Meftah and Others v. France*[GC], § 45; *Pakelli v. Germany*, § 31)。尽管通常应该尊重被告对律师的选择(*Lagerblom v. Sweden*, § 54),但如果有充分的理由认为为了公正利益有必要如此,国内法院可能驳回被告的选择(*Meftah and Others v. France*[GC], § 45; *Croissant v. Germany*, § 29)。举个例子,从整体上考虑,诉讼的特殊性质可能会使专业律师在做口头陈述时有垄断优势(*Meftah and Others v. France*[GC], § 47)。

286. 为了使获取法律协助的权利有效且实用,而不只是停留在理论上,行使该权利时不能依赖于满足形式上的条件,应该由法院来保证审判公正,相应地,应保证为被告辩护的律师有机会在审判中获得公正(*Van Geyseghem v. Belgium*[GC], § 33; *Pelladoah v. the Netherlands*, § 41)。

287. 和其他公正审判权利一样,被告也有可能放弃获取法律协助的权利(*Pishchalnikov v. Russia*, § 77)。然而,在被告通过其行为暗示放弃第 6 条规定的如此重要的权利之前,必须表明他能够合理地预见行为的后果。当被告要求配备律师的时候,额外的保障措施也是必要的,因为如果被告没有律师,他被告知自己权利的机会也就越小,从而其权利受到尊重的可能性也就越小(*Pishchalnikov v. Russia*, § 78)。

4. 法律援助

288. 第 6 条第 3 款第 c 项包含的第三项即最后一项权利——法律援助,在适用时应满足两个条件。

289. 首先,被告必须证明无法支付法律协助费用。然而,他不需要证明"排除所有怀疑",只要证明存在"某些迹象"就足够了,换言之,可以认定"不存在相反情况"就足够了(*Pakelli v. Germany*, § 34)。

290. 其次,只有"当为了实现公正利益的要求时",缔约国才有义务提供法律援助。这必须依据案件的整体事实来判断,不仅包括做出法律援助决定时的情形,也包括国内法院依据案件的不同情况做出裁决时的情形(*Granger v. the United Kingdom*, § 46)。

291. 在判断司法利益是否要求向被告提供免费的法律代理时,本法院会考虑多个标准,包括犯罪行为的严重程度以及惩罚的严苛程度。原则上,当很有可能剥夺个人自由时,出于正义的考虑应当提供法律代理(*Benham v. the United Kingdom*[GC], § 61;*Quaranta v. Switzerland*, § 33;*Zdravko Stanev v. Bulgaria*, § 38)。

292. 关于是否属于"公正利益所要求"的考量,另外两个标准是案件的复杂程度(*Quaranta v. Switzerland*, § 34;*Pham Hoang v. France*, § 40;*Twalib v. Greece*, § 53)和被告的个人情况(*Zdravko Stanev v. Bulgaria*, § 38)。后者尤其关注被告在没有获得法律援助的情况下自行抗辩的能力,例如,在其不熟悉法院或司法系统所使用的语言的情形下(*Quaranta v. Switzerland*, § 35;*Twalib v. Greece*, § 53)。

293. 在采用"司法利益"检验时,不是考察缺乏法律援助是否对辩护造成了"实际损害",而是考察另一个较为宽松的方面:律师进行协助是否会被认为"在特定情形下似乎是合理的"(*Artico v. Italy*, § 34 - 35;*Alimena v. Italy*, § 20)。

294. 尽管律师和客户之间的信任非常重要,但是当涉及免费法律援助时,"自己选择"辩护律师的权利必然受到一定限制。例如,法院在指定辩护律师时必须考虑被告的意愿,但当有充分的理由时可以为了司法利益的需要予以否决(*Croissant v. Germany*,

§ 29；*Lagerblom v. Sweden*，§ 54）。类似地，第6条第3款第 c 项不能被解释为保护替换公共辩护律师的权利（*Lagerblom v. Sweden*，§ 55）。此外，已被一审程序公正审判定罪的人，即使在客观上没有胜诉的可能，但仍然希望上诉，此时不能以司法利益为由自动提供法律援助（*Monnell and Morris v. the United Kingdom*，§ 67）。

5. 实用而有效的法律援助

295. 第6条第3款第 c 项直接规定了有权获得"实用有效"的法律援助，仅仅指派了法律援助律师并不能保证有效的帮助，因为他可能会死亡、重病，或是由于期限过长而不恰当履行职责（*Artico v. Italy*，§ 33）。

296. 得到有效法律援助的权利包括私下和律师交流的权利。只有在特殊情形下，国家可以限制已拘留的嫌疑人和其辩护律师的秘密交流（*Sakhnovskiy v. Russia*［GC］，§ 102）。如果律师无法会见当事人，并且不能在没有监视的情况下获得秘密指示，他的帮助作用就很小（*S. v. Switzerland*，§ 48；*Brennan v. the United Kingdom*，§ 58）。任何对律师与当事人之间关系的限制，无论是明示或暗示，都不能阻碍被告享有有效的法律援助（*Sakhnovskiy v. Russia*［GC］，§ 102）。监听律师和被告的电话（*Zagaria v. Italy*，§ 36）以及过度限制律师会见被告的次数和时长（*Öcalan v. Turkey*［GC］，§ 135）都可能违反保证提供有效帮助的要求。

297. 然而，缔约国无须为法律援助指派的或被告选定的律师的每一个缺点负责（*Lagerblom v. Sweden*，§ 56；*Kamasinski v. Austria*，§ 65）。由于法律职业的独立性，辩护行为实质上是被告和其法律代理人之间的事务；只有在律师明显无法提供有效代理时，才要求国家介入（*Kamasinski v. Austria*，§ 65；*Imbrioscia v. Switzerland*，§ 41；*Daud v. Portugal*，§ 38）。当律师无法为被告辩护（*Artico v. Italy*，§§ 33，36）或没有符合关键的程序要求时，国家就应当承担责任，其中，不符合程序要求不能简单地等同于不当的辩护或纯粹的论据瑕疵（*Czekalla v. Portugal*，§§ 65，71）。

（四）第6条第3款第 d 项：质询证人

> **第6条第3款第 d 项**
>
> "凡受刑事罪指控者具有下列最低限度的权利：……
>
> d. 询问不利于他的证人，并在与不利于他的证人具有相同的条件下，让有利于他的证人出庭接受询问；"

1."证人"的自身含义

298. 不论国内法如何分类,"证人"在公约体系中有其自身的含义(*Damir Sibgatullin v. Russia*,§45;*S. N. v. Sweden*,§45)。如果证词足以作为定罪的基础,就属于控方证据,公约第6条第1款和第3款第d项规定的保护措施就得以适用(*Kaste and Mathisen v. Norway*,§53;*Lucà v. Italy*,§41)。

299. 该用语包括了共同被告(*Trofimov v. Russia*,§37)、受害人(*Vladimir Romanov v. Russia*,§97)和专家证人(*Doorson v. the Netherlands*,§§81-82)。

300. 第6条第3款第d项也适用于书面证据(*Mirilashvili v. Russia*,§§158-159)。

2.质询证人的权利

(1)一般原则。

301. 第6条第3款第d项规定了一项原则:在被告被定罪之前,所有对其不利的证据必须在公开的审讯中正式进行对抗抗辩。该原则可能有例外,但不能侵害辩护权,被告应该有充分且适当的机会质询对其不利的证人,不论是在证人陈述时还是在之后的诉讼阶段(*Hümmer v. Germany*,§38;*Lucà v. Italy*,§39;*Solakov v. the Former Yugoslav Republic of Macedonia*,§57)。

302. 上述一般原则有两个要求。首先,证人若不出席必须要有正当理由。其次,如果定罪纯粹或主要依据为未经被告质询过的证人证词,不论是在调查还是审判阶段,辩护权都受到了一定程度的限制,从而有悖第6条的保障措施(所谓的"唯一或决定性规则")(*Al-Khawaja and Tahery v. the United Kingdom*[GC],§119)。

303. 考虑到民主社会中公正司法的权利,只有在极其必要时才可采取限制辩护权的措施。如果有更轻程度的措施可以达到同样效果,应该采取程度更轻的措施(*Van Mechelen and Others v. the Netherlands*,§58)。

304. 被告有机会在法官面前和证人对质是公正审判的重要内容(*Tarău v. Romania*,§74;*Graviano v. Italy*,§38)。

(2)尽力保证证人出席的义务。

305. 在确定证据是否唯一或具有决定性之前,必须先审查证人不出席的正当理由。如果证人没有出庭作证,就有义务调查其缺席是否有正当理由(*Al-Khawaja and Tahery v. the United Kingdom*[GC],§120;*Gabrielyan v. Armenia*,§§78,81-84)。

306. 公约第 6 条第 1 款和第 3 款要求缔约国积极采取行动使被告能够质询对其不利的证人(*Trofimov v. Russia*, §33;*Sadak and Others v. Turkey*(no.1), §67)。

307. 由于证人失踪而无法质询的,当局应当尽力保证他们出庭(*Karpenko v. Russia*, §62;*Damir Sibgatullin v. Russia*, §51;*Pello v. Estonia*, §35;*Bonev v. Bulgaria*, §43)。

308. 然而,任何人都不能被强迫做自己无法做的事,如果当局不会因为未能给予被告向证人质询的机会而被起诉,证人缺席就并不意味着要中止诉讼[*Gossa v. Poland*, §55;*Haas v. Germany*(dec.);*Calabrò v. Italy and Germany*(dec.);*Ubach Mortes v. Andorra*(dec.)]。

(3)说明拒绝证人作证理由的义务。

309. 尽管对证据的相关性表达观点不是本法院的职责,但不能合法说明拒绝检验或传召证人的理由就等同于限制辩护权,这与公正审判的保障措施相违背(参见 *Popov v. Russia*, §188;*Bocos-Cuesta v. the Netherlands*, §72;*Wierzbicki v. Poland*, §45;*Vidal v. Belgium*, §34)。

(4)依赖不在法庭上做出的证人证言。

310. 在某些情况下,可能需要引用调查阶段的证言(*Lucà v. Italy*, §40),例如,证人死亡(*Mika v. Sweden*(dec.), §37;*Ferrantelli and Santangelo v. Italy*, §52),证人行使保持沉默的权利[*Vidgen v. the Netherlands*, §47;*Sofri and Others v. Italy*(dec.);*Craxi v. Italy*(no.1), §86],或者当局试图保证证人出席的努力以失败告终(*Mirilashvili v. Russia*, §217)。

311. 鉴于证人缺席对辩护权的影响程度,如果证人没有在之前的任何诉讼阶段被质询过,允许提交证人证言代替出庭作证是最后的手段(*Al-Khawaja and Tahery v. the United Kingdom*[GC], §125)。

312. 处理证人在无法保证公约所要求的辩护权的情况下得到的证据时,需要特别注意(*S. N. v. Sweden*, §53;*Doorson v. the Netherlands*, §76)。

313. 当证人有正当理由不能出席对抗式质询时,如果其证言能够被其他证据佐证,那么国内法院就可以将审前程序中证人所做的证言纳入考量范围[*Mirilashvili v. Russia*, §217;*Scheper v. the Netherlands*(dec.);*Calabrò v. Italy and Germany*(dec.);*Ferrantelli and Santangelo v. Italy*, §52]。

314. 第 6 条第 3 款第 d 项只规定了当证人证言不是在审判阶段做出并且其在定罪中起主要或决定作用时，交叉质询证人的可能性[参见 *Kok v. the Netherlands*(dec.);*Krasniki v. the Czech Republic*,§ 79]。

315. 即使传闻证据是针对被告的唯一或决定性证据，将其列为证据也不一定会违反第 6 条第 1 款。然而，如果定罪完全或很大程度上取决于缺席证人的陈述，那这将是非常重要的考量因素，并且要求其他充分的平衡因素，包括强有力的程序保障措施。每个案件都要考虑是否存在足够的平衡因素，如审查证据可靠性的公正合理的措施。由于证据在案件中的重要性，只有当证据足够可靠时才允许在此基础上定罪(*Al-Khawaja and Tahery v. the United Kingdom*[GC],§ 147)。

（5）匿名证人。

316. 尽管匿名证人和缺席证人产生的问题并不完全相同，但从原则上来看两者的情形并无区别，因为都有可能对被告不利。处理该问题的基本原则为刑事案件中的被告应当有实际的机会质询对其不利的证人(*Al-Khawaja and Tahery v. the United Kingdom*[GC],§ 127)。

317. 依据匿名证人的证言定罪并非在所有情况下都违反公约的规定(*Doorson v. the Netherlands*,§ 69;*Van Mechelen and Others v. the Netherlands*,§ 52;*Krasniki v. the Czech Republic*,§ 76)。

318. 尽管公约第 6 条并没有明确要求考虑证人的利益，但是他们的生命、自由或人身安全可能属于公约第 8 条保护的利益。缔约国应当确保刑事诉讼的安排不会损害他们的利益。因此公正审判原则要求平衡辩方利益和证人利益(*Doorson v. the Netherlands*,§ 70;*Van Mechelen and Others v. the Netherlands*,§ 53)。

319. 国内当局必须提出充分的相关理由确保特定证人的身份得到保密[*Doorson v. the Netherlands*,§ 71;*Visser v. the Netherlands*,§ 47;*Sapunarescu v. Germany*(dec.);*Dzelili v. Germany*(dec.)]。

320. 如果控方证人保持匿名，辩方将会面临刑事程序通常不会涉及的困难。在这类案件中，司法机关必须通过程序解决辩方面临的障碍[*Doorson v. the Netherlands*,§ 72;*Van Mechelen and Others v. the Netherlands*,§ 54;*Haas v. Germany*(dec.)]。

321. 不能阻止申诉人审查匿名证人的可靠性(§ 29;*Van Mechelen and Others v. the Netherlands*,§§ 59 和 62;*Kostovski v. the Netherlands*,§ 42)。

322. 另外,当审查质询匿名证人的程序是否足以解决对辩方造成的困难时,必须考虑匿名证言对定罪的决定性程度。如果从任何方面来看证言都不具有决定性,那么辩方面临的困难程度则降低[*Kok v. the Netherlands*(dec.); *Krasniki v. the Czech Republic*, § 79]。

(6)性侵犯案件中的证人。

323. 涉及性侵的刑事诉讼程序常被认为是对受害人的折磨,特别是当受害人不愿意面对被告的时候。涉及未成年人的案件更是如此。在审查此类诉讼中被告是否受到公正审判时,必须考虑受害人的私生活权利。因此,在涉及性侵的刑事案件中,为了保护受害人,必须采取一定的措施,为了保证辩方充分有效行使权利,这类措施可能会做出一些让步。为了保证辩方的权利,司法机关可能需要采取一定措施消除辩方人员遇到的障碍[*Aigner v. Austria*, § 37; *D. v. Finland*, § 43; *F. and M. v. Finland*, § 58; *Accardi and Others v. Italy*(dec.); *S. N. v. Sweden*, § 47; *Vronchenko v. Estonia*, § 56]。

324. 考虑到涉及性侵的刑事案件的特征,第6条第3款第d项不能被解释为所有案件中被告或其辩护律师都有权通过交叉询问或其他方式直接质询证人(*S. N. v. Sweden*, § 55)。

325. 被告必须能够观察被质询证人的行为并质疑其证言和可信度[*Bocos-Cuesta v. the Netherlands*, § 71; *P. S. v. Germany*, § 26; *Accardi and Others v. Italy*(dec.); *S. N. v. Sweden*, § 52]。

326. 如果被告没有机会质询证人,仅观看证人陈述的视频记录不足以保障辩方权利(*D. v. Finland*, § 50; *A. L. v. Finland*, § 41)。

(7)向证人提供有利条件以换取证言。

327. 以豁免其罪或其他有利条件换取证人证言,是国内当局打击重大犯罪的重要手段。然而,采用此类证言可能有损诉讼程序的公正性,也可能会导致一些微妙的问题,如可能会出现操纵证言的情况,证人可能会纯粹为了交换有利条件或出于私人报复的目的而编造证言。这类证词有时十分模糊,而且可能会出现基于未经证实的未必公正的主张而起诉某人,这些问题都是不容低估的。不过,使用这类证言本身并不足以导致诉讼不公[*Cornelis v. the Netherlands*(dec.)]。

(8)传闻证据。

328. 公约第6条第1款和第3款第d项暗含了推定不得在刑事诉讼中使用对被告

不利的传闻证据。当传闻证据被认为对辩方有利,排除此类证据也是合法的[*Thomas v. United Kingdom*(dec.)]。

(9)传唤辩方证人的权利。

329. 通常而言,国内法院审核已提交的证据以及辩方试图出示的证据的相关性。同样,第6条第3款第d项规定由国内法院审核是否应该传唤证人。这并不要求所有辩方证人都要出席并接受询问,正如"在同等条件下"的用语所表现出来的那样,其真正目的是充分体现"平等手段原则"(*Perna v. Italy*[GC],§29;*Solakov v. the Former Yugoslav Republic of Macedonia*,§57)。

330. 辩方仅主张他未被允许质询特定证人是不够的;为了支持他的请求,辩方还应解释质询证人的理由,而且该证据必须是对于还原事件真相和保护辩方权利来说必不可少的(*Perna v. Italy*[GC],§29;*Bacanu and SC《R》S. A. v. Romania*,§75)。

331. 如果辩方要求质询证人的请求不是无理取闹而是有充分理由的,并与控告相关,可能有利于辩方,甚至可能导致被告无罪,国内当局必须提出相关理由才能驳回请求(*Topić v. Croatia*,§42;*Polyakov v. Russia*,§§34-35)。

332. 第6条并没有赋予原告要求证人出席法庭的无限制的权利。通常是由国内法院决定质询证人是否必要或可行[*S. N. v. Sweden*,§44;*Accardi and Others v. Italy*(dec.)]。

333. 可能存在例外情形使得本法院认为无法质询证人违反了第6条(*Dorokhov v. Russia*,§65;*Popov v. Russia*,§188;*Bricmont v. Belgium*,§89)。

(五)第6条第3款第e项:翻译

> **第6条第3款第e项**
>
> "凡受刑事罪指控者具有下列最低限度的权利:
>
> e. 如果他听不懂或者不会讲法院所使用的工作语言,可以请求免费的译员协助翻译。"

1. 如果被告"听不懂或不会讲法院所使用的工作语言"

334. 免费获得翻译帮助的权利只有在被告听不懂或不会讲法院所使用的工作语言时才适用[*K. v. France*(dec.)]。被告理解该语言的,不能坚持要求翻译帮助他用另一种语言进行辩护,包括他所属的少数民族的语言[K. v. France (dec.) ; Bideault v. France ; Lagerblom v. Sweden , § 62] 。

335. 通常来说,当被告由律师代理时,只有律师理解法院所使用的语言而被告不理解,这是不够的。诉讼程序要求获得公正审判权利,该要求包括参与审讯的权利,要求被告能够理解诉讼程序从而告知律师辩护要点(Kamasinski v. Austria , § 74 ; Cuscani v. the United kingdom , § 38)。

336. 第6条第3款第e项不适用于被告和律师之间的关系,只适用于被告和法官之间(X. v. Austria)。

337. 被告可以放弃获得翻译帮助的权利,但这必须由被告而非律师决定(Kamasinski v. Austria , § 80)。

2. 刑事诉讼中的保护要素

338. 第6条第3款第e项保证了被告在诉讼中有权请求翻译免费翻译文件或陈述,这对于被告理解法院所使用的语言从而获得公正审判来说是必要的(Luedicke, Belkacem and Koç v. Germany , § 48 ; Ucak v. the United Kingdom(dec.) ; Hermi v. Italy [GC] , § 69 ; Lagerblom v. Sweden , § 61)。

339. 第6条第3款第e项不仅适用于审讯阶段的口头陈述,也适用于书面材料和审前程序(Kamasinski v. Austria , § 74 ; Hermi v. Italy[GC] , § 70)。

340. 然而,也没必要翻译诉讼中所有的纸质证据或官方文件(Kamasinski v. Austria , § 74)。例如,没有纸质翻译的判决书本身并不违反第6条第3款第e项(Kamasinski v. Austria , § 85)。第6条第3款第e项指向的是"口译"而非"笔译",这意味着口译足以满足公约要求(Husain v. Italy(dec.) ; Hermi v. Italy[GC] , § 70)。

341. 总而言之,翻译的帮助必须足以使得被告理解案件从而为自己辩护,特别是能够在法庭上表达自己对案件的看法[Kamasinski v. Austria , § 74 ; Hermi v. Italy[GC] , § 70 ; Güngör v. Germany(dec.) ; Protopapa v. Turkey , § 80]。

3. "免费"协助

342. 提供免费协助的义务不依赖于被告的收入;为被告提供翻译是国家刑事司法公正体系提供的便利条件之一。然而,被告可能要为在他未能参加的审讯中提供工作的翻译付费[Fedele v. Germany(dec.)]。

343. 不能在之后向被告索取翻译费用(Luedicke, Belkacem and Koç v. Germany,

§ 46)。第 6 条第 3 款第 e 项意味着国内法院让已定罪之人承担费用等同于限制了公约所提供的保障(*Luedicke，Belkacem and Koç v. Germany*，§ 42；*Işyar v. Bulgaria*，§ 45；*Öztürk v. Germany*，§ 58)。

4. 翻译的条件

344. 在第 6 条第 3 款第 e 项中规定翻译协助被告的具体条件是不合适的。翻译不属于第 6 条第 1 款规定的法院或审判庭的一员，对其独立和公正性也没有正式的要求。翻译向被告提供的帮助必须有效地帮助其进行辩护，不能损害诉讼公正(*Ucak v. the United Kingdom*)。

5. 积极的义务

345. 法官应当询问申诉人，确认其是否确实需要翻译，尤其是在律师已经向法官反映过和申诉人沟通困难的情况下。法官必须保证翻译的缺席不会影响申诉人充分参与对其至关重要的事件(*Cuscani v. the United Kingdom*，§ 38)。

346. 辩护行为实质上是被告和其律师之间的事务(*Kamasinski v. Austria*，§ 65，*Stanford v. the United Kingdom*，§ 28)，诉讼公正(也包括有可能不为外籍被告提供翻译的情况)的最终守卫者是国内法院(*Cuscani v. the United Kingdom*，§ 39；*Hermi v. Italy*[GC]，§ 72；*Katritsch v. France*，§ 44)。

347. 被告的语言能力非常重要，为了判断要理解法院所使用的语言对于被告而言是否太过困难，法院也必须审查被告被指控的罪名性质以及国内当局向被告传达的所有通知[*Hermi v. Italy*[GC]，§ 71；*Katritsch v. France*，§ 41；*Şaman v. Turkey*，§ 30；*Güngör v. Germany*(dec.)]。

348. 鉴于保证第 6 条第 3 款第 e 项规定的权利为实用有效的需要，当局的义务不仅限于任命翻译，也包括在特定情形下保证翻译的妥当性(*Kamasinski v. Austria*，§ 74；*Hermi v. Italy*[GC]，§ 70；*Protopapa v. Turkey*，§ 80)。

第六节 第 6 条的域外效力

349. 公约不要求缔约国在第三方国家或地区适用他们的标准(*Drozd and Janousek v. France and Spain*，§ 110)。缔约国没有义务审查第三方国家进行的包含引渡在内的审判是否符合第 6 条的所有要求。

一、公然违背公正

350. 根据本法院的判例法,在某些被引渡或驱逐的情形下,个人可能无法获得公正审判,也就是被请求国公然违背公正,此时可能会产生与第 6 条有关的问题。该原则首先在索林诉英国案(*Soering v. the United Kingdom*,§ 113)中得以确立,之后在许多案件中得到本法院的确认(*Mamatkulov and Askarov v. Turkey*[GC],§§ 90 – 91;*Al-Saadoon and Mufdhi v. the United Kingdom*,§ 149;*Ahorugeze v. Sweden*,§ 115;*Othman（Abu Qatada）v. the United Kingdom*,§ 258)。

351. "公然违背公正"被认为等同于明显违反第 6 条或其所体现原则的审判(*Sejdovic v. Italy*[GC],§ 84;*Stoichkov v. Bulgaria*,§ 56;*Drozd and Janousek v. France and Spain*,§ 110)。尽管还没有更精准的定义,本法院仍然认为特定的几类不公正的形式等同于公然违背公正,包括:

- 缺席判决,并且之后没有依据案件事实重新判决的可能性(*Einhorn v. France*（dec.）,§ 33;*Sejdovic v. Italy*[GC],§ 84;*Stoichkov v. Bulgaria*,§ 56);
- 审判本质上是简易程序,完全忽略了辩方权利(*Bader and Kanbor v. Sweden*,§ 47);
- 拘留的合法性没有受到公正独立的审判庭审查[*Al-Moayad v. Germany*（dec.）,§ 101];
- 有计划地故意拒绝律师介入,特别是针对在国外被拘留的公民[*Al-Moayad v. Germany*（dec.）];
- 违反第 3 条,在刑事诉讼中使用通过虐待嫌疑人或第三人的方式得到的供述[*Othman（Abu Qatada）v. the United Kingdom*,§ 267;*El Haski v. Belgium*,§ 85]。

352. 自索林诉英国案(*Soering v. the United Kingdom*)后 20 年,也就是 2012 年,本法院在奥斯曼诉英国案[*Othman（Abu Qatada）v. the United Kingdom*]中首次判决引渡或驱逐事实上违反了第 6 条。如前述,这表明判断是否"公然违背公正"的标准很严格,它不仅要求缔约国违反公约第 6 条,不遵守规则或缺少保障措施,还要求对于公约第 6 条保障的公正审判的基本权利的违反达到了废弃或损毁第 6 条保障的权利实质的程度[*Ahorugeze v. Sweden*,§ 115;*Othman（Abu Qatada）v. the United Kingdom*,§ 260]。

二、"真实的风险":审查标准和证明责任

353. 在审查引渡或驱逐是否公然违背公正时,本法院认为应当适用第3条对引渡或驱逐的审查标准。因此,应当由申诉人提出充足的理由证明,如果被缔约国驱逐,他将会遭受公然违背公正的真实风险。在申诉人提出这类证据后,由政府负责排除怀疑(*Ahorugeze v. Sweden*, § 116; *Othman (Abu Qatada) v. the United Kingdom*, §§ 272 – 280; *El Haski v. Belgium*, § 86; *Saadi v. Italy*[GC], § 129)。

354. 为了确定是否存在公然违背公正的真实风险,本法院必须考虑整体情形以及个人情况,审查遣送申诉人返回其国家的可预见后果(*Al-Saadoon and Mufdhi v. the United Kingdom*, § 125; *Saadi v. Italy*[GC], § 130)。缔约国必须在驱逐时就已知或应知的事实审查风险的存在(*Al-Saadoon and Mufdhi v. the United Kingdom*, § 125; *Saadi v. Italy*[GC], § 133)。不过,如果驱逐或转移行为在审查案件之日前就已经发生,本法院应知道随后披露的消息(*Al-Saadoon and Mufdhi v. the United Kingdom*, § 149; *Mamatkulov and Askarov v. Turkey*[GC], § 69)。

援引案例一览

本指南援引的判例法涉及欧洲人权法院的判决或裁定以及欧洲人权委员会的决定或报告。

除非另行指明,所有参考皆是本法院审判庭依法作出的判决。缩写"(dec.)"是指该处援引为本法院裁定,"[GC]"是指该案件由大审判庭审判。

本指南电子版中援引案例的超链接直接跳转 HUDOC 数据库〈http://hudoc.echr.coe.int〉。该数据库提供本法院(包括大审判庭、审判庭和委员会的判决、裁定和相关案例、咨询意见以及案例法信息注解中的法律总结)、委员会(决定和报告)和部长委员会(决议)的判例法。

本法院以英语和/或法语这两种官方语言发布判决和裁定。HUDOC 也包含许多重要案例的近30种非官方言语的翻译,以及由第三方制作的大约100个在线案例汇总的链接。

(注:为了避免重复,本章所附的相关案例索引没有在中文部分进行翻译,读者可在对应的英文部分阅读。)

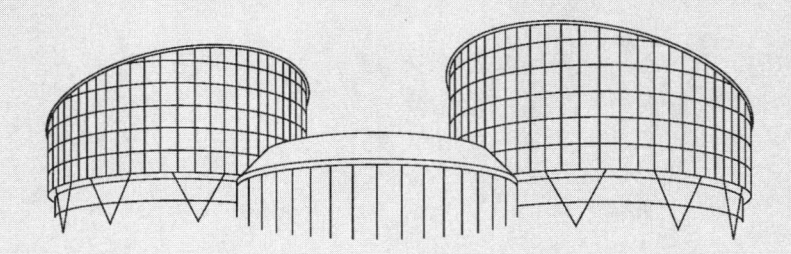

EUROPEAN COURT OF HUMAN RIGHTS
COUR EUROPÉENNE DES DROITS DE L'HOMME

Chapter IV Guide on Article 6 of the European Convention on Human Rights Right to A Fair Trial

(Criminal Limb)

COUNCIL OF EUROPE
CONSEIL DE L'EUROPE

Publishers or organisations wishing to reproduce this document (or a translation thereof) in print or online are asked to contact publishing@echr.coe.int for further instructions.

This Guide has been prepared by the Research and Library Division, within the Directorate of the Jurisconsult, and does not bind the Court. The text was finalised on 31 December 2013; it may be subject to editorial revision.

The document is available for downloading at ⟨www.echr.coe.int⟩ (Case-Law-Case-Law Analysis-Case-Law Guides).

For publication updates please follow the Court's Twitter account at ⟨https:/twitter.com/echrpublication⟩.

©Council of Europe/European Court of Human Rights, 2014

Note to readers

This Guide is part of the series of Case-Law Guides published by the European Court of Human Rights (hereafter "the Court", "the European Court" or "the Strasbourg Court") to inform legal practitioners about the fundamental judgments delivered by the Strasbourg Court. This particular Guide analyses and sums up the case-law on Article 6 (criminal limb) of the European Convention on Human Rights (hereafter "the Convention" or "the European Convention") until 31 December 2013. Readers will find the key principles in this area and the relevant precedents.

The case-law cited has been selected among the leading, major, and/or recent judgments and decisions. *

The Court's judgments serve not only to decide those cases brought before the Court but, more generally, to elucidate, safeguard and develop the rules instituted by the Convention, thereby contributing to the observance by the States of the engagements undertaken by them as Contracting Parties (*Ireland v. the United Kingdom*, 18 January 1978, § 154, Series A no. 25.). The mission of the system set up by the Convention is thus to determine, in the general interest, issues of public policy, thereby raising the standards of protection of human rights and extending human rights jurisprudence throughout the community of the Convention States (*Konstantin Markin v. Russia* [GC], no. 30078/06, § 89, ECHR 2012).

---

* The case-law cited may be in either or both of the official languages (English and French) of the Court and the European Commission of Human Rights. Unless otherwise indicated, all references are to a judgment on the merits delivered by a Chamber of the Court. The abbreviation "(dec.)" indicates that the citation is of a decision of the Court and "[GC]" that the case was heard by the Grand Chamber.

Article 6 of the Convention-Right to a fair trial

"1. In the determination of his civil rights and obligations or of any criminal charge against him, everyone is entitled to a fair and public hearing within a reasonable time by an independent and impartial tribunal established by law. Judgment shall be pronounced publicly but the press and public may be excluded from all or part of the trial in the interests of morals, public order or national security in a democratic society, where the interests of juveniles or the protection of the private life of the parties so require, or to the extent strictly necessary in the opinion of the court in special circumstances where publicity would prejudice the interests of justice.

2. Everyone charged with a criminal offence shall be presumed innocent until proved guilty according to law.

3. Everyone charged with a criminal offence has the following minimum rights:

(a) to be informed promptly, in a language which he understands and in detail, of the nature and cause of the accusation against him;

(b) to have adequate time and facilities for the preparation of his defence;

(c) to defend himself in person or through legal assistance of his own choosing or, if he has not sufficient means to pay for legal assistance, to be given it free when the interests of justice so require;

(d) to examine or have examined witnesses against him and to obtain the attendance and examination of witnesses on his behalf under the same conditions as witnesses against him;

(e) to have the free assistance of an interpreter if he cannot understand or speak the language used in court."

I. Scope: the notion of "criminal charge"

> **Article 6 § 1 of the Convention**
> "1. In the determination of... any criminal charge against him, everyone is entitled to a fair... hearing... by [a] tribunal..."

A. General principles

1. The concept of a "criminal charge" has an "autonomous" meaning, independent of the categorisations employed by the national legal systems of the member States (*Adolf v. Austria*, § 30).

2. The concept of "charge" has to be understood within the meaning of the Convention. It may thus be defined as "the official notification given to an individual by the competent authority of an allegation that he has committed a criminal offence", a definition that also corresponds to the test whether "the situation of the [suspect] has been substantially affected" (*Deweer v. Belgium*, §§ 42 and 46; *Eckle v. Germany*, § 73). The Court has also held that a person in police custody who was required to swear an oath before being questioned as a witness was already the subject of a "criminal charge" and had the right to remain silent (*Brusco v. France*, §§ 46–50).

3. As regards the autonomous notion of "criminal", the Convention is not opposed to the moves towards "decriminalisation" among the Contracting States. However, offences classified as "regulatory" following decriminalisation may come under the autonomous notion of a "criminal" offence. Leaving States the discretion to exclude these offences might lead to results incompatible with the object and purpose of the Convention (*Öztürk v. Germany*, § 49).

4. The starting-point for the assessment of the applicability of the criminal aspect of

Article 6 of the Convention is based on the criteria outlined in *Engel and Others v. the Netherlands*, §§ 82 – 83:

 a. classification in domestic law;

 b. nature of the offence;

 c. severity of the penalty that the person concerned risks incurring.

5. The first criterion is of relative weight and serves only as a starting-point. If domestic law classifies an offence as criminal, then this will be decisive. Otherwise the Court will look behind the national classification and examine the substantive reality of the procedure in question.

6. In evaluating the second criterion, which is considered more important (*Jussila v. Finland* [GC], § 38), the following factors can be taken into consideration:

- whether the legal rule in question is directed solely at a specific group or is of a generally binding character (*Bendenoun v. France*, § 47);
- whether the proceedings are instituted by a public body with statutory powers of enforcement (*Benham v. the United Kingdom*, § 56);
- whether the legal rule has a punitive or deterrent purpose (*Öztürk v. Germany*, § 53; *Bendenoun v. France*, § 47);
- whether the imposition of any penalty is dependent upon a finding of guilt (*Benham v. the United Kingdom*, § 56);
- how comparable procedures are classified in other Council of Europe member States (*Öztürk v. Germany*, § 53).

7. The third criterion is determined by reference to the maximum potential penalty for which the relevant law provides (*Campbell and Fell v. the United Kingdom*, § 72; *Demicoli v. Malta*, § 34).

8. The second and third criteria laid down in *Engel and Others v. the Netherlands* are alternative and not necessarily cumulative; for Article 6 to be held to be applicable, it suffices that the offence in question should by its nature be regarded as "criminal" from the point of view of the Convention, or that the offence rendered the person liable to a sanction which, by its nature and degree of severity, belongs in general to the "criminal" sphere

(*Lutz v. Germany*, § 55; *Öztürk v. Germany*, § 54). The fact that an offence is not punishable by imprisonment is not in itself decisive, since the relative lack of seriousness of the penalty at stake cannot divest an offence of its inherently criminal character (ibid., § 53; *Nicoleta Gheorghe v. Romania*, § 26).

A cumulative approach may, however, be adopted where separate analysis of each criterion does not make it possible to reach a clear conclusion as to the existence of a criminal charge(*Bendenoun v. France*, § 47).

9. In using the terms "criminal charge" and "charged with a criminal offence" the three paragraphs of Article 6 refer to identical situations. Therefore, the test of applicability of Article 6 under its criminal head will be the same for the three paragraphs.

B. Application of the general principles

1. Disciplinary proceedings

10. Offences against military discipline, carrying a penalty of committal to a disciplinary unit for a period of several months, fall within the ambit of the criminal head of Article 6 of the Convention (*Engel and Others v. the Netherlands*, § 85). On the contrary, strict arrest for two days has been held to be of too short a duration to belong to the "criminal law" sphere (ibid.).

11. With regard to professional disciplinary proceedings, the question remains open since the Court has considered it unnecessary to give a ruling on the matter, having concluded that the proceedings fell within the civil sphere (*Albert and Le Compte v. Belgium*, § 30). In the case of disciplinary proceedings resulting in the compulsory retirement of a civil servant, the Court has found that such proceedings were not "criminal" within the meaning of Article 6, inasmuch as the domestic authorities managed to keep their decision within a purely administrative sphere [*Moullet v. France* (dec.)]. It has also excluded from the criminal head of Article 6 a dispute concerning the discharge of an army officer for breaches of discipline [*Suküt v. Turkey* (dec.)].

12. While making "due allowance" for the prison context and for a special prison disciplinary regime, Article 6 may apply to offences against prison discipline, on account of

the nature of the charges and the nature and severity of the penalties (forty and seven additional days' custody respectively in *Ezeh and Connors v. the United Kingdom* [GC], § 82; conversely, see *Štitić v. Croatia*, §§ 51–63). However, proceedings concerning the prison system as such do not in principle fall within the ambit of the criminal head of Article 6 (*Boulois v. Luxembourg* [GC], § 85). Thus, for example, a prisoner's placement in a high-supervision unit does not concern a criminal charge; access to a court to challenge such a measure and the restrictions liable to accompany it should be examined under the civil head of Article 6 § 1 (*Enea v. Italy* [GC], § 98).

13. Measures ordered by a court under rules concerning disorderly conduct in proceedings before it (contempt of court) are considered to fall outside the ambit of Article 6, because they are akin to the exercise of disciplinary powers (*Ravnsborg v. Sweden*, § 34; *Putz v. Austria*, §§ 33–37). However, the nature and severity of the penalty can make Article 6 applicable to a conviction for contempt of court classified in domestic law as a criminal offence (*Kyprianou v. Cyprus* [GC], §§ 61–64, concerning a penalty of five days' imprisonment).

14. With regard to contempt of Parliament, the Court distinguishes between the powers of a legislature to regulate its own proceedings for breach of privilege applying to its members, on the one hand, and an extended jurisdiction to punish non-members for acts occurring elsewhere, on the other hand. The former might be considered disciplinary in nature, whereas the Court regards the latter as criminal, taking into account the general application and the severity of the potential penalty which could have been imposed (imprisonment for up to sixty days and a fine in *Demicoli v. Malta*, § 32).

2. Administrative, tax, customs, financial and competition-law proceedings

15. The following administrative offences may fall within the ambit of the criminal head of Article 6:

- road-traffic offences punishable by fines or driving restrictions, such as penalty points or disqualifications (*Lutz v. Germany*, § 182; *Schmautzer v. Austria*; *Malige v. France*);
- minor offences of causing a nuisance or a breach of the peace (*Lauko v. Slovakia*; *Nicoleta Gheorghe v. Romania*, §§ 25–26);

- offences against social-security legislation (*Hüseyin Turan v. Turkey*, §§ 18 – 21, for a failure to declare employment, despite the modest nature of the fine imposed);

- administrative offence of promoting and distributing material promoting ethnic hatred, punishable by an administrative warning and the confiscation of the publication in question (*Balsytė-Lideikienė v. Lithuania*, § 61).

16. Article 6 has been held to apply to tax surcharges proceedings, on the basis of the following elements:

- the law setting out the penalties covered all citizens in their capacity as taxpayers;
- the surcharge was not intended as pecuniary compensation for damage but essentially as a punishment to deter reoffending;
- the surchargewas imposed under a general rule with both a deterrent and a punitive purpose;
- the surcharge was substantial [*Bendenoun v. France*; conversely, see the interest for late payment in *Mieg de Boofzheim v. France* (dec.)].

The criminal nature of the offence may suffice to render Article 6 applicable, notwithstanding the low amount of the tax surcharge (10% of the reassessed tax liability in *Jussila v. Finland* [GC], § 38).

17. Article 6 under its criminal head has been held to apply to customs law (*Salabiaku v. France*), to penalties imposed by a court with jurisdiction in budgetary and financial matters (*Guisset v. France*), and to certain administrative authorities with powers in the spheres of economic, financial and competition law (*Lilly France S. A. v. France* (dec.); *Dubus S. A. v. France*; *A. Menarini Diagnostics S. r. l. v. Italy*).

3. Political issues

18. Article 6 has been held not to apply in its criminal aspect to proceedings concerning electoral sanctions (*Pierre-Bloch v. France*, §§ 53 – 60); the dissolution of political parties [*Refah Partisi (the Welfare Party) and Others v. Turkey* (dec.)]; parliamentary commissions of inquiry [*Montera v. Italy* (dec.)]; and to impeachment proceedings against a country's President for a gross violation of the Constitution (*Paksas v. Lithuania* [GC], §§ 66 – 67).

19. With regard to lustration proceedings, the Court has held that the predominance of aspects with criminal connotations (nature of the offence-untrue lustration declaration-and nature and severity of the penalty-prohibition on practising certain professions for a lengthy period) could bring those proceedings within the ambit of the criminal head of Article 6 of the Convention [*Matyjek v. Poland* (dec.); conversely, see *Sidabras and Džiautas v. Lithuania* (dec.)].

4. Expulsion and extradition

20. Procedures for the expulsion of aliens do not fall under the criminal head of Article 6, notwithstanding the fact that they may be brought in the context of criminal proceedings (*Maaouia v. France* [GC], § 39). The same exclusionary approach applies to extradition proceedings [*Peñafiel Salgado v. Spain* (dec.)] or proceedings relating to the European arrest warrant [*Monedero Angora v. Spain* (dec.)].

21. Conversely, however, the replacement of a prison sentence by deportation and exclusion from national territory for ten years may be treated as a penalty on the same basis as the one imposed at the time of the initial conviction (*Gurguchiani v. Spain*, §§ 40 and 47–48).

5. Different stages of criminal proceedings, ancillary proceedings and subsequent remedies

22. Measures adopted for the prevention of disorder or crime are not covered by the guarantees in Article 6 (*Raimondo v. Italy*, § 43, for special supervision by the police; *R. v. the United Kingdom* (dec.), for or a warning given by the police to a juvenile who had committed indecent assaults on girls from his school).

23. As regards the pre-trial stage (inquiry, investigation), the Court considers criminal proceedings as a whole. Therefore, some requirements of Article 6, such as the reasonable-time requirement or the right of defence, may also be relevant at this stage of proceedings in so far as the fairness of the trial is likely to be seriously prejudiced by an initial failure to comply with them (*Imbrioscia v. Switzerland*, § 36). Although investigating judges do not determine a "criminal charge", the steps taken by them have a direct influence on the conduct and fairness of the subsequent proceedings, including the actual trial. Accordingly,

Article 6 § 1 may be held to be applicable to the investigation procedure conducted by an investigating judge, although some of the procedural safeguards envisaged by Article 6 § 1 might not apply (*Vera Fernández-Huidobro v. Spain*, §§ 108 – 114).

24. Article 6 § 1 is applicable throughout the entirety of proceedings for the determination of any "criminal charge", including the sentencing process (for instance, confiscation proceedings enabling the national courts to assess the amount at which a confiscation order should be set, in *Phillips v. the United Kingdom*, § 39). Article 6 may also be applicable under its criminal limb to proceedings resulting in the demolition of a house built without planning permission, as the demolition could be considered a "penalty" (*Hamer v. Belgium*, § 60). However, it is not applicable to proceedings for bringing an initial sentence into conformity with the more favourable provisions of the new Criminal Code (*Nurmagomedov v. Russia*, § 50).

25. Proceedings concerning the execution of sentences-such as proceedings for the application of an amnesty [*Montcornet de Caumont v. France* (dec.)], parole proceedings (*A. v. Austria*, Commission decision), transfer proceedings under the Convention on the Transfer of Sentenced Persons (*Szabó v. Sweden* (dec.), but see, for a converse finding, *Buijen v. Germany*, §§ 40 – 45)-and *exequatur* proceedings relating to the enforcement of a forfeiture order made by a foreign court [*Saccoccia v. Austria* (dec.)] do not fall within the ambit of the criminal head of Article 6.

26. In principle, forfeiture measures adversely affecting the property rights of third parties in the absence of any threat of criminal proceedings against them do not amount to the "determination of a criminal charge" (seizure of an aircraft in *Air Canada v. the United Kingdom*, § 54; forfeiture of gold coins in *AGOSI v. the United Kingdom*, §§ 65 – 66). Such measures instead fall under the civil head of Article 6 (*Silickienė v. Lithuania*, §§ 45 – 46).

27. The Article 6 guarantees apply in principle to appeals on points of law (*Meftah and Others v. France* [GC], § 40), and to constitutional proceedings [*Gast and Popp v. Germany*, §§ 65 – 66; *Caldas Ramírez de Arrellano v. Spain* (dec.)] where such proceedings are a further stage of the relevant criminal proceedings and their results may be decisive for the convicted persons.

28. Lastly, Article 6 does not apply to proceedings for the reopening of a case because a person whose sentence has become final and who applies for his case to be reopened is not "charged with a criminal offence" within the meaning of that Article [*Fischer v. Austria* (dec.)]. Only the new proceedings, after the request for reopening has been granted, can be regarded as concerning the determination of a criminal charge (*Löffler v. Austria*, §§ 18 – 19). Similarly, Article 6 does not apply to a request for the reopening of criminal proceedings following the Court's finding of a violation [*Öcalan v. Turkey* (dec.)]. However, supervisory review proceedings resulting in the amendment of a final judgment do fall under the criminal head of Article 6 (*Vanyan v. Russia*, § 58).

II. Right of access to a court

> Article 6 § 1 of the Convention
> "1. In the determination of... any criminal charge against him, everyone is entitled to a... hearing ... by [a] tribunal ... "

29. The "right to a court" is no more absolute in criminal than in civil matters. It is subject to implied limitations (*Deweer v. Belgium*, § 49; *Kart v. Turkey* [GC], § 67).

30. However, these limitations must not restrict the exercise of the right in such a way or to such an extent that the very essence of the right is impaired. They must pursue a legitimate aim and there must be a reasonable proportionality between the means employed and the aim sought to be achieved (*Guérin v. France* [GC], § 37; *Omar v. France* [GC], § 34, citing references to civil cases).

A. Limitations

31. Limitations on the right of access to a court may result from:

1. Parliamentary immunity

32. The guarantees offered by both types of parliamentary immunity (non-liability and inviolability) serve the same need-that of ensuring the independence of Parliament in the performance of its task. Without a doubt, inviolability helps to achieve the full independence of Parliament by preventing any possibility of politically motivated criminal proceedings and thereby protecting the opposition from pressure or abuse on the part of the majority (*Kart v. Turkey* [GC], § 90, citing references to civil cases). Furthermore, bringing proceedings against members of parliament may affect the very functioning of the assembly to which they belong and disrupt Parliament's work. This system of immunity, constituting an exception to the ordinary law, can therefore be regarded as pursuing a legitimate aim (ibid., § 91).

33. However, without considering the circumstances of the case no conclusions can be drawn as to the compatibility with the Convention of this finding of the legitimacy of parliamentary immunity. It must be ascertained whether parliamentary immunity has restricted the right of access to a court in such a way that the very essence of that right is impaired. Reviewing the proportionality of such a measure means taking into account the fair balance which has to be struck between the general interest in preserving Parliament's integrity and the applicant's individual interest in having his parliamentary immunity lifted in order to answer the criminal charges against him in court. In examining the issue of proportionality, the Court must pay particular attention to the scope of the immunity in the case before it (ibid., §§ 92 – 93). The less the protective measure serves to preserve the integrity of Parliament, the more compelling its justification must be (ibid., § 95). Thus, for example, the Court has held that the inability of a member of parliament to waive his immunity did not infringe his right to a court, since the immunity was simply a temporary procedural obstacle to the criminal proceedings, being limited to the duration of his term of parliamentary office (ibid., §§ 111 – 113).

2. Procedural rules

34. These are, for example, the admissibility requirements for an appeal.

35. However, although the right of appeal may of course be subject to statutory

requirements, when applying procedural rules the courts must avoid excessive formalism that would infringe the fairness of the proceedings (*Walchli v. France*, § 29). The particularly strict application of a procedural rule may sometimes impair the very essence of the right of access to a court (*Labergère v. France*, § 23), particularly in view of the importance of the appeal and what is at stake in the proceedings for an applicant who has been sentenced to a long term of imprisonment (ibid., § 20).

36. The right of access to a court is also fundamentally impaired by a procedural irregularity, for example where a prosecution service official responsible for verifying the admissibility of appeals against fines or applications for exemptions acted *ultra vires* by ruling on the merits of an appeal himself, thus depriving the applicants of the opportunity to have the "charge" in question determined by a community judge (*Josseaume v. France*, § 32).

37. The same applies where a decision declaring an appeal inadmissible on erroneous grounds led to the retention of the deposit equivalent to the amount of the standard fine, with the result that the fine was considered to have been paid and the prosecution was discontinued, making it impossible for the applicant, once he had paid the fine, to contest before a "tribunal" the road-traffic offence of which he was accused (*Célice v. France*, § 34).

38. A further example: the applicant suffered an excessive restriction of his right of access to a court where his appeal on points of law was declared inadmissible for failure to comply with the statutory time-limits, when this failure was due to the defective manner in which the authorities had discharged their obligation to serve the lower court's decision on the applicant, who was in detention and could therefore have been located (*Davran v. Turkey*, §§ 40-47).

3. Requirement of enforcement of a previous decision

39. As regards the automatic inadmissibility of appeals on points of law lodged by appellants who have failed to surrender to custody although warrants have been issued for their arrest:

- where an appeal on points of law is declared inadmissible on grounds connected with the applicant's having absconded, this amounts to a disproportionate sanction, having regard to the signal importance of the rights of the defence and of the principle of the rule of law in a democratic society (*Poitrimol v. France*, § 38; *Guérin v. France*, § 45; *Omar v. France*, § 42);

- where an appeal on points of law is declared inadmissible solely because the appellant has not surrendered to custody pursuant to the judicial decision challenged in the appeal, this ruling compels the appellant to subject himself in advance to the deprivation of liberty resulting from the impugned decision, although that decision cannot be considered final until the appeal has been decided or the time-limit for lodging an appeal has expired. This imposes a disproportionate burden on the appellant, thus upsetting the fair balance that must be struck between the legitimate concern to ensure that judicial decisions are enforced, on the one hand, and the right of access to the Court of Cassation and the exercise of the rights of the defence on the other (ibid., §§ 40–41; *Guérin v. France*, § 43).

40. The same applies where the right to appeal on points of law is forfeited because of failure to comply with the obligation to surrender to custody (*Khalfaoui v. France*, § 46; *Papon v. France* (no. 2), § 100).

41. However, the requirement to lodge a deposit before appealing against a speeding fine-the aim of this requirement being to prevent dilatory or vexatious appeals in the sphere of road-traffic offences-may constitute a legitimate and proportionate restriction on the right of access to a court [*Schneider v. France* (dec.)].

4. Other restrictions in breach of the right of access to a court

42. They may occur, for example, where an accused person is persuaded by the authorities to withdraw an appeal on the basis of a false promise of remission of the sentence imposed by the first-instance court (*Marpa Zeeland B. V. and Metal Welding B. V. v. the Netherlands*, §§ 46–51); or where a court of appeal has failed to inform an accused person of a fresh time-limit for lodging an appeal on points of law following the refusal of his officially assigned counsel to assist him (*Kulikowski v. Poland*, § 70).

III. General guarantees: institutional requirements

> Article 6 § 1 of the Convention
> "1. In the determination of... any criminal charge against him, everyone is entitled to a... hearing... by an independent and impartial tribunal established by law...."

A. The notion of a "tribunal"

43. A disciplinary or administrative body can have the characteristics of a "tribunal" within the autonomous meaning of Article 6, even if it is not termed a "tribunal" or "court" in the domestic system. In the Court's case law a tribunal is characterised in the substantive sense of the term by its judicial function, that is to say, determining matters within its competence on the basis of rules of law and after proceedings conducted in a prescribed manner. It must also satisfy a series of further requirements-independence, in particular of the executive; impartiality; duration of its members' terms of office; guarantees afforded by its procedure-several of which appear in the text of Article 6 § 1 itself (*Belilos v. Switzerland*, § 64; *Coëme and Others v. Belgium*, § 99; *Richert v. Poland*, § 43).

44. Conferring the prosecution and punishment of minor "criminal" offences on administrative authorities is not inconsistent with the Convention provided that the person concerned is enabled to take any decision thus made against him before a tribunal that does offer the guarantees of Article 6 (*Öztürk v. Germany*, § 56; *A. Menarini Diagnostics S. R. L. v. Italy*). Therefore, decisions taken by administrative authorities which do not themselves satisfy the requirements of Article 6 § 1 of the Convention must be subject to subsequent review by a "judicial body that has full jurisdiction". The defining characteristics of such a body include the power to quash in all respects, on questions of

fact and law, the decision of the body below (ibid., § 59; *Schmautzer v. Austria*, § 36; *Gradinger v. Austria*, § 44): for instance, administrative courts carrying out a judicial review that went beyond a "formal" review of legality and included a detailed analysis of the appropriateness and proportionality of the penalty imposed by the administrative authority (*A. Menarini Diagnostics S. R. L. v. Italy*, §§ 63 – 67, in respect of a fine imposed by an independent regulatory authority in charge of competition). Similarly, a judicial review may satisfy Article 6 requirements even if it is the law itself which determines the sanction in accordance with the seriousness of the offence (*Malige v. France*, §§ 46 – 51, in respect of the deduction of points from a driving licence).

45. The power to give a binding decision which may not be altered by a non-judicial authority is inherent in the very notion of "tribunal" (*Findlay v. the United Kingdom*, § 77).

B. Tribunal established by law

46. Under Article 6 § 1 of the Convention, a tribunal must always be "established by law". This expression reflects the principle of the rule of law, which is inherent in the system of protection established by the Convention and its Protocols (*Jorgic v. Germany*, § 64; *Richert v. Poland*, § 41). Indeed, an organ not established according to the legislation would be deprived of the legitimacy required, in a democratic society, to hear individual complaints (*Lavents v. Latvia*, § 114; *Gorgiladze v. Georgia*, § 67; *Kontalexis v. Greece*, § 38).

47. "Law", within the meaning of Article 6 § 1, comprises in particular the legislation on the establishment and competence of judicial organs (*Lavents v. Latvia*, § 114; *Richert v. Poland*, § 41; *Jorgic v. Germany*, § 64) but also any other provision of domestic law which, if breached, would render the participation of one or more judges in the examination of a case unlawful (*Pandjikidze and Others v. Georgia*, § 104; *Gorgiladze v. Georgia*, § 68). The phrase "established by law" covers not only the legal basis for the very existence of a tribunal, but also compliance by the tribunal with the particular rules that govern it (ibid.), and the composition of the bench in each case

(*Posokhov v. Russia*, § 39; *Fatullayev v. Azerbaijan*, § 144; *Kontalexis v. Greece*, § 42).

48. Accordingly, if a tribunal does not have jurisdiction to try a defendant in accordance with the provisions applicable under domestic law, it is not "established by law" within the meaning of Article 6 § 1 (*Richert v. Poland*, § 41; *Jorgic v. Germany*, § 64).

49. The object of the term "established by law" in Article 6 "is to ensure that the judicial organisation in a democratic society does not depend on the discretion of the executive, but that it is regulated by law emanating from Parliament" (*Richert v. Poland*, § 42; *Coëme and Others v. Belgium*, § 98). Nor, in countries where the law is codified, can the organisation of the judicial system be left to the discretion of the judicial authorities, although this does not mean that the courts do not have some latitude to interpret relevant domestic legislation (ibid.; *Gorgiladze v. Georgia*, § 69).

50. In principle, a violation of the domestic legal provisions on the establishment and competence of judicial organs by a tribunal gives rise to a violation of Article 6 § 1. The Court is therefore competent to examine whether the national law has been complied with in this respect. However, having regard to the general principle that it is in the first place for the national courts themselves to interpret the provisions of domestic law, the Court may not question their interpretation unless there has been a flagrant violation of domestic law (*Coëme and Others v. Belgium*, § 98 *in fine*; *Lavents v. Latvia*, § 114). The Court's task is therefore limited to examining whether reasonable grounds existed for the authorities to establish jurisdiction (*Jorgic v. Germany*, § 65).

51. Examples where the Court found that the body in question was not "a tribunal established by law":

- the Court of Cassation which tried co-defendants other than ministers for offences connected with those for which ministers were standing trial, since the connection rule was not established by law (*Coëme and Others v. Belgium*, §§ 107-108);
- a court composed of two lay judges elected to sit in a particular case in breach of the statutory requirement of drawing of lots and the maximum period of two weeks' service per year (*Posokhov v. Russia*, § 43);

- a court composed of lay judges who continued to decide cases in accordance with established tradition, although the law on lay judgeshad been repealed and no new law had been enacted (*Pandjikidze and Others v. Georgia*, §§ 108 – 111);
- a court whose composition was not in accordance with the law, since two of the judges were disqualified by law from sitting in the case (*Lavents v. Latvia*, § 115).

52. The Court found that the tribunal was "established by law" in the following cases:
- a German court trying a person for acts of genocide committed in Bosnia (*Jorgic v. Germany*, §§ 66 –71);
- a special court established to try corruption and organised crime (*Fruni v. Slovakia*, § 140).

C. Independence and impartiality

53. The right to a fair trial in Article 6 § 1 requires that a case be heard by an "independent and impartial tribunal" established by law. There is a close link between the concepts of independence and objective impartiality. For this reason the Court commonly considers the two requirements together (*Findlay v. the United Kingdom*, § 73).

The principles applicable when determining whether a tribunal can be considered "independent and impartial" apply equally to professional judges, lay judges and jurors (*Holm v. Sweden*, § 30).

1. Independent tribunal

a. General principles

54. Article 6 § 1 of the Convention requires independence from the other branches of power-that is, the executive and the legislature-and also from the parties [*Ninn-Hansen v. Denmark* (dec.)].

55. Although the notion of the separation of powers between the political organs of government and the judiciary has assumed growing importance in the Court's case-law, neither Article 6 nor any other provision of the Convention requires States to comply with any theoretical constitutional concepts regarding the permissible limits of the powers'

interaction. The question is always whether, in a given case, the requirements of the Convention are met (*Henryk Urban and Ryszard Urban v. Poland*, § 46).

b. Criteria for assessing independence

56. In determining whether a body can be considered to be "independent" the Court has had regard to the following criteria (*Findlay v. the United Kingdom*, § 73):

i. the manner of appointment of its members and

ii. the duration of their term of office;

iii. the existence of guarantees against outside pressures;

iv. whether the body presents an appearance of independence.

i. Manner of appointment of a body's members

57. The mere appointment of judges by Parliament cannot be seen to cast doubt on their independence [*Filippini v. San Marino* (dec.); *Ninn-Hansen v. Denmark* (dec.)]

58. Similarly, appointment of judges by the executive is permissible, provided that appointees are free from influence or pressure when carrying out their adjudicatory role (*Henryk Urban and Ryszard Urban v. Poland*, § 49; *Campbell and Fell v. the United Kingdom*, § 79).

59. Although the assignment of a case to a particular judge or court falls within the margin of appreciation enjoyed by the domestic authorities in such matters, the Court must be satisfied that this was compatible with Article 6 § 1, and, in particular, with its requirements of independence and impartiality (*Moiseyev v. Russia*, § 176).

ii. Duration of appointment of a body's members

60. No particular term of office has been specified as a necessary minimum. Irremovability of judges during their term of office must in general be considered a corollary of their independence. However, the absence of formal recognition of this irremovability in the law does not in itself imply lack of independence provided that it is recognised in fact and that other necessary guarantees are present (*Campbell and Fell v. the United Kingdom*, § 80).

iii. Guarantees against outsidepressure

61. Judicial independence demands that individual judges be free from undue influences

outside the judiciary, and from within. Internal judicial independence requires that they be free from directives or pressures from fellow judges or those who have administrative responsibilities in the court, such as the president of the court or the president of a division in the court. The absence of sufficient safeguards securing the independence of judges within the judiciary, in particular vis-à-vis their judicial superiors, may lead the Court to conclude that an applicant's doubts as to the independence and impartiality of a court may be said to have been objectively justified (*Parlov-Tkalčić v. Croatia*, § 86; *Daktaras v. Lithuania*, § 36; *Moiseyev v. Russia*, § 184).

iv. Appearance of independence

62. In order to determine whether a tribunal can be considered to be "independent" as required by Article 6 § 1, appearances may also be of importance. What is at stake is the confidence which the courts in a democratic society must inspire in the public and above all, as far as criminal proceedings are concerned, in the accused (*Şahiner v. Turkey*, § 44).

63. In deciding whether there is a legitimate reason to fear that a particular court lacks independence or impartiality, the standpoint of the accused is important but not decisive. What is decisive is whether his doubts can be held to be objectively justified (*Incal v. Turkey*, § 71). No problem arises as regards independence when the Court is of the view that an "objective observer" would have no cause for concern about this matter in the circumstances of the case at hand [*Clarke v. the United Kingdom* (dec.)].

64. Where a tribunal's members include persons who are in a subordinate position, in terms of their duties and the organisation of their service, *vis-à-vis* one of the parties, the accused may entertain a legitimate doubt about those persons' independence (*Şahiner v. Turkey*, § 45).

2. Impartial tribunal

65. Article 6 § 1 of the Convention requires a tribunal falling within its scope to be "impartial". Impartiality normally denotes the absence of prejudice or bias and its existence or otherwise can be tested in various ways (*Kyprianou v. Cyprus* [GC], § 118; *Micallef v. Malta* [GC], § 93).

a. Criteria for assessing impartiality

66. The Court has distinguished between:

i. a *subjective approach*, that is, endeavouring to ascertain the personal conviction or interest of a given judge in a particular case;

ii. an *objective approach*, that is, determining whether he or she offered sufficient guarantees to exclude any legitimate doubt in this respect (*Kyprianou v. Cyprus* [GC], § 118; *Piersack v. Belgium*, § 30; *Grieves v. the United Kingdom* [GC], § 69).

67. However, there is no watertight division between the two notions since the conduct of a judge may not only prompt objectively held misgivings as to impartiality from the point of view of the external observer (objective test) but may also go to the issue of his or her personal conviction (subjective test). Therefore, whether a case falls to be dealt with under one test or the other, or both, will depend on the particular facts of the contested conduct (*Kyprianou v. Cyprus* [GC], §§ 119 and 121).

i. Subjective approach

68. In applying the subjective test, the Court has consistently held that the personal impartiality of a judge must be presumed until there is proof to the contrary (*Kyprianou v. Cyprus* [GC], § 119; *Hauschildt v. Denmark*, § 47).

69. As regards the type of proof required, the Court has, for example, sought to ascertain whether a judge has displayed hostility or ill will or has arranged to have a case assigned to himself for personal reasons (*De Cubber v. Belgium*, § 25).

70. Although in some cases it may be difficult to procure evidence with which to rebut the presumption of the judge's subjective impartiality, the requirement of objective impartiality provides a further important guarantee. The Court has indeed recognised the difficulty of establishing a breach of Article 6 on account of subjective partiality and has therefore in the vast majority of cases focused on the objective test (*Kyprianou v. Cyprus* [GC], § 119).

ii. Objective approach

71. Under the objective test, when applied to a body sitting as a bench, it must be determined whether, quite apart from the personal conduct of any of the members of that

body, there are ascertainable facts which may raise doubts as to its impartiality (*Castillo Algar v. Spain*, § 45).

72. In deciding whether in a given case there is a legitimate reason to fear that a particular body lacks impartiality, the standpoint of those claiming that it is not impartial is important but not decisive. What is decisive is whether the fear can be held to be objectively justified (*Ferrantelli and Santangelo v. Italy*, § 58; *Padovani v. Italy*, § 27).

73. The objective test mostly concerns hierarchical or other links between the judge and other persons involved in the proceedings which objectively justify misgivings as to the impartiality of the tribunal, and thus fail to meet the Convention standard under the objective test (*Micallef v. Malta* [GC], § 97). It must therefore be decided in each individual case whether the relationship in question is of such a nature and degree as to indicate a lack of impartiality on the part of the tribunal (*Pullar v. the United Kingdom*, § 38).

74. In this respect even appearances may be of a certain importance. What is at stake is the confidence which the courts in a democratic society must inspire in the public, including the accused. Thus, any judge in respect of whom there is a legitimate reason to fear a lack of impartiality must withdraw (*Castillo Algar v. Spain*, § 45).

75. Account must also be taken of questions of internal organisation [*Piersack v. Belgium*, § 30 (d)]. The existence of national procedures for ensuring impartiality, namely rules regulating the withdrawal of judges, is a relevant factor. Such rules manifest the national legislature's concern to remove all reasonable doubts as to the impartiality of the judge or court concerned and constitute an attempt to ensure impartiality by eliminating the causes of such concerns. In addition to ensuring the absence of actual bias, they are directed at removing any appearance of partiality and so serve to promote the confidence which the courts in a democratic society must inspire in the public (see *Micallef v. Malta* [GC], § 99; *Mežnarić v. Croatia*, § 27; *Harabin v. Slovakia*, § 132). The Court will take such rules into account when making its own assessment as to whether a "tribunal" was impartial and, in particular, whether the applicant's fears can be held to be objectively justified (*Pfeifer and Plankl v. Austria*, § 6; *Oberschlick v. Austria* (no. 1), § 50; *Pescador Valero v. Spain*, §§ 24-29).

b. Situations in which the question of a lack of judicial impartiality may arise

76. There are two possible situations in which the question of a lack of judicial impartiality arises (*Kyprianou v. Cyprus* [GC], § 121):

i. the first is *functional in nature* and concerns, for instance, the exercise of different functions within the judicial process by the same person, or hierarchical or other links with another person involved in the proceedings;

ii. the second is *of a personal character* and derives from the *conduct of the judges* in a given case.

i. Situations of a functional nature

α. *The exercise of different judicial functions*

77. The mere fact that a judge in a criminal court has also made pre-trial decisions in the case, including decisions concerning detention on remand, cannot be taken in itself as justifying fears as to his lack of impartiality; what matters is the extent and nature of these decisions (*Fey v. Austria*, § 30; *Sainte-Marie v. France*, § 32; *Nortier v. the Netherlands*, § 33). When decisions extending detention on remand required "a very high degree of clarity" as to the question of guilt, the Court found that the impartiality of the tribunals concerned was capable of appearing open to doubt and that the applicant's fears in this regard could be considered objectively justified (*Hauschildt v. Denmark*, §§ 49–52).

78. The fact that a judge was once a member of the public prosecutor's department is not a reason for fearing that he lacks impartiality; nevertheless, if an individual, after holding in that department an office whose nature is such that he may have to deal with a given matter in the course of his duties, subsequently sits in the same case as a judge, the public are entitled to fear that he does not offer sufficient guarantees of impartiality [*Piersack v. Belgium*, § 30 (b) and (d)].

79. The successive exercise of the functions of investigating judge and trial judge by one and the same person in the same case has also led the Court to find that the impartiality of the trial court was capable of appearing to the applicant to be open to doubt (*De Cubber v. Belgium*, §§ 27–30).

However, where the trial judge's participation in the investigation had been limited in time and consisted in questioning two witnesses and had not entailed any assessment of the evidence or required him to reach a conclusion, the Court found that the applicant's fear that the competent national court lacked impartiality could not be regarded as objectively justified (*Bulut v. Austria*, §§ 33 – 34).

80. No question of a lack of judicial impartiality arises when a judge has already delivered purely formal and procedural decisions in other stages of the proceedings; however, problems with impartiality may emerge if, in other phases of the proceedings, a judge has already expressed an opinion on the guilt of the accused (*Gómez de Liaño y Botella v. Spain*, §§ 67 – 72).

81. The mere fact that a judge has already ruled on similar but unrelated criminal charges or that he or she has already tried a co-accused in separate criminal proceedings is not in itself sufficient to cast doubt on that judge's impartiality in a subsequent case (*Kriegisch v. Germany* (dec.); *Khodorkovskiy and Lebedev v. Russia*, § 544). It is, however, a different matter if the earlier judgments contain findings that actually prejudge the question of the guilt of an accused in such subsequent proceedings (*Poppe v. the Netherlands*, § 26; *Schwarzenberger v. Germany*, § 42; *Ferrantelli and Santangelo v. Italy*, § 59).

82. The obligation to be impartial cannot be construed so as to impose an obligation on a superior court which sets aside an administrative or judicial decision to send the case back to a different jurisdictional authority or to a differently composed branch of that authority [*Thomann v. Switzerland*, § 33; *Stow and Gai v. Portugal* (dec.)].

β. *Hierarchical or other links with another participant in the proceedings*

• *Hierarchical links*

83. The determination by military service tribunals of criminal charges against military service personnel is not in principle incompatible with the provisions of Article 6 (*Cooper v. the United Kingdom* [GC], § 110). However, where all the members of the court martial were subordinate in rank to the convening officer and fell within his chain of command, the applicant's doubts about the tribunal's independence and impartiality could be objectively justified (*Findlay v. the United Kingdom*, § 76; *Miller and Others v. the United Kingdom*, §§ 30 – 31).

84. The trial of civilians by a court composed in part of members of the armed forces can give rise to a legitimate fear that the court might allow itself to be unduly influenced by partial considerations (*Incal v. Turkey*, § 72; *Iprahim Ülger v. Turkey*, § 26). Even when a military judge has participated only in an interlocutory decision in proceedings against a civilian that continues to remain in effect, the whole proceedings are deprived of the appearance of having been conducted by an independent and impartial court (*Öcalan v. Turkey* [GC], § 115).

85. Situations in which a military court has jurisdiction to try a civilian for acts against the armed forces may give rise to reasonable doubts about such a court's objective impartiality. A judicial system in which a military court is empowered to try a person who is not a member of the armed forces may easily be perceived as reducing to nothing the distance which should exist between the court and the parties to criminal proceedings, even if there are sufficient safeguards to guarantee that court's independence (*Ergin v. Turkey* (no.6), § 49).

86. The determination of criminal charges against civilians in military courts could be held to be compatible with Article 6 only in very exceptional circumstances (*Martin v. the United Kingdom*, § 44).

- *Other links*

87. Objectively justified doubts as to the impartiality of the trial court presiding judge were found to exist when her husband was the head of the team of investigators dealing with the applicants' case (*Dorozhko and Pozharskiy v. Estonia*, §§ 56–58).

88. The fact that a member of a tribunal has some personal knowledge of one of the witnesses in a case does not necessarily mean that he will be prejudiced in favour of that person's testimony. In each individual case it must be decided whether the familiarity in question is of such a nature and degree as to indicate a lack of impartiality on the part of the tribunal (*Pullar v. the United Kingdom*, § 38, concerning the presence in the jury of an employee of one of the two key prosecution witnesses; *Hanif and Khan v. the United Kingdom*, § 141, concerning the presence of a police officer in the jury).

ii. Situations of a personal nature

89. The judicial authorities are required to exercise maximum discretion with regard to

the cases with which they deal in order to preserve their image as impartial judges. That discretion should dissuade them from making use of the press, even when provoked. It is the higher demands of justice and the elevated nature of judicial office which impose that duty (*Lavents v. Latvia*, § 118; *Buscemi v. Italy*, § 67). Thus, where a court president publicly used expressions which implied that he had already formed an unfavourable view of the applicant's case before presiding over the court that had to decide it, his statements were such as to justify objectively the accused's fears as to his impartiality (ibid., § 68; see also *Lavents v. Latvia*, § 119, where a judge engaged in public criticism of the defence and publicly expressed surprise that the accused had pleaded not guilty).

90. No violation of Article 6 was found in relation to statements made to the press by a number of members of the national legal service and a paper published by the National Association of judges and prosecutors criticising the political climate in which the trial had taken place, the legislative reforms proposed by the Government and the defence strategy, but not making any pronouncement as to the applicant's guilt. Moreover, the court hearing the applicant's case had been made up entirely of professional judges whose experience and training enabled them to rise above external influence (*Previti v. Italy* (dec.), § 253).

IV. General guarantees: procedural requirements

A. Fairness

Article 6 § 1 of the Convention

"1. In the determination of... any criminal charge against him, everyone is entitled to a fair... hearing... by [a] tribunal ..."

1. Equality of arms and adversarial proceedings

91. Equality of arms is an inherent feature of a fair trial. It requires that each party be

given a reasonable opportunity to present his case under conditions that do not place him at a substantial disadvantage *vis-à-vis* his opponent (*Foucher v. France*, § 34; *Bulut v. Austria*; *Bobek v. Poland*, § 56; *Klimentyev v. Russia*, § 95). Equality of arms requires that a fair balance be struck between the parties, and applies equally to criminal and civil cases.

92. The right to an adversarial hearing means in principle the opportunity for the parties to have knowledge of and comment on all evidence adduced or observations filed with a view to influencing the court's decision. The right to an adversarial trial is closely related to equality of arms and indeed in some cases the Court finds a violation of Article 6 § 1 looking at the two concepts together.

93. There has been a considerable evolution in the Court's case-law, notably in respect of the importance attached to appearances and to the increased sensitivity of the public to the fair administration of justice (*Borgers v. Belgium*, § 24).

94. In criminal cases Article 6 § 1 overlaps with the specific guarantees of Article 6 § 3, although it is not confined to the minimum rights set out therein. Indeed, the guarantees contained in Article 6 § 3 are constituent elements, amongst others, of the concept of a fair trial set forth in Article 6 § 1.

a. Equality of arms

95. A restriction on the rights of the defence was found in *Borgers v. Belgium*, where the applicant was prevented from replying to submissions made by the *avocat général* before the Court of Cassation and had not been given a copy of the submissions beforehand. The inequality was exacerbated by the *avocat général*'s participation, in an advisory capacity, in the court's deliberations.

96. The Court has found a violation of Article 6 § 1 combined with Article 6 § 3 in criminal proceedings where a defence lawyer was made to wait for fifteen hours before finally being given a chance to plead his case in the early hours of the morning (*Makhfi v. France*). Equally, the Court found a violation of the principle of equality of arms in connection with a Supreme Court ruling in a criminal case. The applicant, who had been convicted on appeal and had requested to be present, had been excluded from a preliminary hearing held in camera (*Zhuk v. Ukraine*, § 35).

97. In contrast, a complaint concerning equality of arms was declared inadmissible as being manifestly ill-founded where the applicant complained that the prosecutor had stood on a raised platform in relation to the parties. The accused had not been placed at a disadvantage regarding the defence of his interests (*Diriöz v. Turkey*, § 25).

98. The failure to lay down rules of criminal procedure in legislation may breach equality of arms, since their purpose is to protect the defendant against any abuse of authority and it is therefore the defence which is the most likely to suffer from omissions and lack of clarity in such rules (*Coëme and Others v. Belgium*, § 102).

99. Witnesses for the prosecution and the defence must be treated equally; however, whether a violation is found depends on whether the witness in fact enjoyed a privileged role (*Bonisch v. Austria*, § 32; conversely, see *Brandstetter v. Austria*, § 45).

100. Non-disclosure of evidence to the defence may breach equality of arms (as well as the right to an adversarial hearing) (*Kuopila v. Finland*, § 38, where the defence was not given an opportunity to comment on a supplementary police report).

101. Equality of arms may also be breached when the accused has limited access to his case file or other documents on public-interest grounds (*Matyjek v. Poland*, § 65).

b. Adversarial hearing

102. It is a fundamental aspect of the right to a fair trial that criminal proceedings, including the elements of such proceedings which relate to procedure, should be adversarial and that there should be equality of arms between the prosecution and defence. The right to an adversarial trial means, in a criminal case, that both prosecution and defence must be given the opportunity to have knowledge of and comment on the observations filed and the evidence adduced by the other party. In addition Article 6 § 1 requires that the prosecution authorities disclose to the defence all material evidence in their possession for or against the accused (*Rowe and Davis v. the United Kingdom* [GC], § 60).

103. In a criminal trial, Article 6 § 1 usually overlaps with the defence rights under Article 6 § 3, such as the right to question witnesses.

104. In cases where evidence has been withheld from the defence on public-interest grounds the Court will not itself review whether or not an order permitting non-disclosure

was justified in a particular case. Rather, it examines the decision-making procedure to ensure that it complied, as far as possible, with the requirements of adversarial proceedings and equality of arms and incorporated adequate safeguards to protect the interests of the accused.

105. In *Rowe and Davis v. the United Kingdom* [GC], the Court found a violation of Article 6 § 1 on account of the prosecution's failure to lay the evidence in question before the trial judge and to permit him to rule on the question of disclosure, thereby depriving the applicants of a fair trial. However, in *Jasper v. the United Kingdom* [GC] (§ 58), the Court found no violation of Article 6 § 1, relying on the fact that the material which was not disclosed formed no part of the prosecution case whatever, and was never put to the jury.

106. However, the entitlement to disclosure of relevant evidence is not an absolute right. In criminal proceedings there may be competing interests, such as national security or the need to protect witnesses who are at risk of reprisals or to keep secret the methods used by the police to investigate crime, which must be weighed against the rights of the accused. In some cases it may be necessary to withhold certain evidence from the defence so as to preserve the fundamental rights of another individual or to safeguard an important public interest. However, only such measures restricting the rights of the defence which are strictly necessary are permissible under Article 6 § 1 (*Van Mechelen and Others v. the Netherlands*, § 58). Moreover, in order to ensure that the accused receives a fair trial, any difficulties caused to the defence by a limitation on its rights must be sufficiently counterbalanced by the procedures followed by the judicial authorities (ibid., § 54; *Doorson v. the Netherlands*, § 72).

107. In *Edwards and Lewis v. the United Kingdom* [GC], the applicants were denied access to the evidence, and hence it was not possible for their representatives to argue the case on entrapment in full before the judge. The Court accordingly found a violation of Article 6 § 1 because the procedure employed to determine the issues of disclosure of evidence and entrapment did not comply with the requirements to provide adversarial proceedings and equality of arms, nor did it incorporate adequate safeguards to protect the interests of the accused.

108. A breach of the right to an adversarial trial has also been found where the parties had not received the reporting judge's report before the hearing, whereas the advocate-general had, nor had they had an opportunity to reply to the advocate-general's submissions (*Reinhardt and Slimane-Kaïd v. France*, §§ 105-106).

2. Reasoning of judicial decisions

109. According to established case-law reflecting a principle linked to the proper administration of justice, judgments of courts and tribunals should adequately state the reasons on which they are based [*Papon v. France* (dec.)].

110. Reasoned decisions serve the purpose of demonstrating to the parties that they have been heard, thereby contributing to a more willing acceptance of the decision on their part. In addition, they oblige judges to base their reasoning on objective arguments, and also preserve the rights of the defence. However, the extent of the duty to give reasons varies according to the nature of the decision and must be determined in the light of the circumstances of the case (*Ruiz Torija v. Spain*, § 29).

111. While courts are not obliged to give a detailed answer to every argument raised (*Van de Hurk v. the Netherlands*, § 61), it must be clear from the decision that the essential issues of the case have been addressed (*Boldea v. Romania*, § 30).

112. National courts should indicate with sufficient clarity the grounds on which they base their decision so as to allow a litigant usefully to exercise any available right of appeal (ibid.; *Hadjianastassiou v. Greece*).

Reasons for decisions given by juries

113. Juries in criminal cases rarely give reasoned verdicts and the relevance of this to fairness has been touched upon in a number of cases, first by the Commission and latterly by the Court.

114. The Convention does not require jurors to give reasons for their decision and Article 6 does not preclude a defendant from being tried by a lay jury even where reasons are not given for the verdict [*Saric v. Denmark* (dec.)]. Nevertheless, for the requirements of a fair trial to be satisfied, the accused, and indeed the public, must be able to understand the verdict that has been given; this is a vital safeguard against arbitrariness (*Taxquet v. Belgium* [GC], § 92; *Legillon v. France*, § 53).

115. In the case of assize courts sitting with a lay jury, any special procedural features must be accommodated, seeing that the jurors are usually not required-or not permitted-to give reasons for their personal convictions. In these circumstances, Article 6 requires an assessment of whether sufficient safeguards were in place to avoid any risk of arbitrariness and to enable the accused to understand the reasons for his conviction. Such procedural safeguards may include, for example, directions or guidance provided by the presiding judge to the jurors on the legal issues arising or the evidence adduced and precise, unequivocal questions put to the jury by the judge, forming a framework on which the verdict is based or sufficiently offsetting the fact that no reasons are given for the jury's answers [*R. v. Belgium*, Commission decision; *Zarouali v. Belgium*, Commission decision; *Planka v. Austria*, Commission decision; *Papon v. France* (dec.)]. Where an assize court refuses to put distinct questions in respect of each defendant as to the existence of aggravating circumstances, thereby denying the jury the possibility of determining the applicant's individual criminal responsibility the Court has found a violation of Article 6 § 1 (*Goktepe v. Belgium*, § 28).

116. In *Bellerín Lagares v. Spain* (dec.) the Court observed that the impugned judgment-to which a record of the jury's deliberations had been attached-contained a list of the facts which the jury had held to be established in finding the applicant guilty, a legal analysis of those facts and, for sentencing purposes, a reference to the circumstances found to have had an influence on the applicant's degree of responsibility in the case at hand. It therefore found that the judgment in question had contained sufficient reasons for the purposes of Article 6 § 1 of the Convention.

117. Regard must be had to any avenues of appeal open to the accused (*Taxquet v. Belgium* [GC], § 92). In this case only four questions were put as regards the applicant; they were worded in identical terms to the questions concerning the other co-accused and did not allow him to determine the factual or legal basis on which he was convicted. Thus, his inability to understand why he was found guilty led to an unfair trial (ibid., § 100).

118. In *Judge v. the United Kingdom* (dec.), the Court found that the framework surrounding a Scottish jury's unreasoned verdict was sufficient for the accused to understand

his verdict. Moreover, the Court was also satisfied that the appeal rights available under Scots law would have been sufficient to remedy any improper verdict by the jury. Under the applicable legislation, the Appeal Court enjoyed wide powers of review and was empowered to quash any conviction which amounts to a miscarriage of justice.

3. Right to remain silent and not to incriminate oneself

a. Affirmation and sphere of application

119. Anyone accused of a criminal offence has the right to remain silent and not to contribute to incriminating himself (*Funke v. France*, § 44; *O'Halloran and Francis v. the United Kingdom* [GC], § 45; *Saunders v. the United Kingdom*, § 60). Although not specifically mentioned in Article 6, the right to remain silent and the privilege against self-incrimination are generally recognised international standards which lie at the heart of the notion of a fair procedure under Article 6. By providing the accused with protection against improper compulsion by the authorities these immunities contribute to avoiding miscarriages of justice and to securing the aims of Article 6 (*John Murray v. the United Kingdom*, § 45).

120. The right not to incriminate oneself applies to criminal proceedings in respect of all types of criminal offences, from the most simple to the most complex (*Saunders v. the United Kingdom*, § 74).

121. The right to remain silent applies from the point at which the suspect is questioned by the police (*John Murray v. the United Kingdom*, § 45).

b. Scope

122. The right not to incriminate oneself presupposes that the prosecution in a criminal case seek to prove their case against the accused without recourse to evidence obtained through methods of coercion or oppression in defiance of the will of the accused (*Saunders v. the United Kingdom*, § 68; *Bykov v. Russia* [GC], § 92).

123. However, the privilege against self-incrimination does not extend to the use in criminal proceedings of material which may be obtained from the accused through recourse to compulsory powers but which has an existence independent of the will of the suspect, such as documents acquired pursuant to a warrant, breath, blood and urine samples, and

bodily tissue for the purpose of DNA testing (*Saunders v. the United Kingdom*, § 69; *O'Halloran and Francis v. the United Kingdom* [GC], § 47).

124. Early access to a lawyer is part of the procedural safeguards to which the Court will have particular regard when examining whether a procedure has extinguished the very essence of the privilege against self-incrimination. In order for the right to a fair trial under Article 6 § 1 to remain sufficiently "practical and effective", access to a lawyer should, as a rule, be provided from the first time a suspect is questioned by the police, unless it is demonstrated in the light of the particular circumstances of each case that there are compelling reasons to restrict this right (*Salduz v. Turkey* [GC], §§ 54 – 55).

125. Persons in police custody enjoy both the right not to incriminate themselves and to remain silent and the right to be assisted by a lawyer whenever they are questioned. These rights are quite distinct: a waiver of one of them does not entail a waiver of the other. Nevertheless, these rights are complementary, since persons in police custody must *a fortiori* be granted the assistance of a lawyer when they have not previously been informed by the authorities of their right to remain silent (*Brusco v. France*, § 54; *Navone and Others v. Monaco*, § 74). The importance of informing a suspect of the right to remain silent is such that, even where a person willingly agrees to give statements to the police after being informed that his words may be used in evidence against him, this cannot be regarded as a fully informed choice if he has not been expressly notified of his right to remain silent and if his decision has been taken without the assistance of counsel (ibid.; *Stojkovic v. France and Belgium*, § 54).

126. The right to remain silent and the privilege against self-incrimination serve in principle to protect the freedom of a suspect to choose whether to speak or to remain silent when questioned by the police. Such freedom of choice is effectively undermined in a case in which the suspect has elected to remain silent during questioning and the authorities use subterfuge to elicit confessions or other statements of an incriminatory nature from the suspect which they were unable to obtain during such questioning (in this particular case, a confession made to a police informer sharing the applicant's cell), and where the confessions or statements thereby obtained are adduced in evidence at trial (*Allan v. the United Kingdom*, § 50).

127. Conversely, in the case of *Bykov v. Russia* [GC] (§§ 102 – 103), the applicant had not been placed under any pressure or duress and was not in detention but was free to see a police informer and talk to him, or to refuse to do so. Furthermore, at the trial the recording of the conversation had not been treated as a plain confession capable of lying at the core of a finding of guilt; it had played a limited role in a complex body of evidence assessed by the court.

c. A relative right

128. The right to remain silent is not absolute (*John Murray v. the United Kingdom*, § 47).

129. In examining whether a procedure has extinguished the very essence of the privilege against self-incrimination, the Court will have regard, in particular, to the following elements:

- the nature and degree of compulsion;
- the existence of any relevant safeguards in the procedure;
- the use to which any material so obtained is put (*Jalloh v. Germany* [GC], § 101; *O'Halloran and Francis v. the United Kingdom* [GC], § 55; *Bykov v. Russia* [GC], § 104).

130. On the one hand, a conviction must not be solely or mainly based on the accused's silence or on a refusal to answer questions or to give evidence himself. On the other hand, the right to remain silent cannot prevent the accused's silence-in situations which clearly call for an explanation from him-from being taken into account in assessing the persuasiveness of the evidence adduced by the prosecution. It cannot therefore be said that an accused's decision to remain silent throughout criminal proceedings should necessarily have no implications.

131. Whether the drawing of adverse inferences from an accused's silence infringes Article 6 is a matter to be determined in the light of all the circumstances of the case, having particular regard to the weight attached to such inferences by the national courts in their assessment of the evidence and the degree of compulsion inherent in the situation (*John Murray v. the United Kingdom*, § 47).

132. Furthermore, the weight of the public interest in the investigation and punishment of the particular offence in issue may be taken into consideration and weighed against the individual's interest in having the evidence against him gathered lawfully. However, public-interest concerns cannot justify measures which extinguish the very essence of an applicant's defence rights, including the privilege against self-incrimination (*Jalloh v. Germany* [GC], § 97). The public interest cannot be relied on to justify the use of answers compulsorily obtained in a non-judicial investigation to incriminate the accused during the trial proceedings (*Heaney and McGuinness v. Ireland*, § 57).

4. Use of evidence obtained unlawfully or in breach of Convention rights

133. While Article 6 guarantees the right to a fair hearing, it does not lay down any rules on the admissibility of evidence as such, which is primarily a matter for regulation under national law (*Schenk v. Switzerland*, §§ 45 – 46; *Heglas v. the Czech Republic*, § 84).

134. It is not, therefore, the role of the Court to determine, as a matter of principle, whether particular types of evidence-for example, evidence obtained unlawfully in terms of domestic law-may be admissible. The question which must be answered is whether the proceedings as a whole, including the way in which the evidence was obtained, were fair. This involves an examination of the alleged unlawfulness in question and, where the violation of another Convention right is concerned, the nature of the violation found (*Khan v. the United Kingdom*, § 34; *P. G. and J. H. v. the United Kingdom*, § 76; *Allan v. the United Kingdom*, § 42).

135. In determining whether the proceedings as a whole were fair, regard must also be had to whether the rights of the defence have been respected. In particular, it must be examined whether the applicant was given an opportunity to challenge the authenticity of the evidence and to oppose its use. In addition, the quality of the evidence must be taken into consideration, as must the circumstances in which it was obtained and whether these circumstances cast doubt on its reliability or accuracy. While no problem of fairness necessarily arises where the evidence obtained was unsupported by other material, it may be noted that where the evidence is very strong and there is no risk of its being unreliable, the

need for supporting evidence is correspondingly weaker (*Bykov v. Russia* [GC], § 89; *Jalloh v. Germany* [GC], § 96). In this connection, the Court also attaches weight to whether the evidence in question was or was not decisive for the outcome of the criminal proceedings (*Gäfgen v. Germany* [GC]).

136. As to the examination of the nature of the Convention violation found, the question whether the use as evidence of information obtained in violation of Article 8 rendered a trial as a whole unfair contrary to Article 6 has to be determined with regard to all the circumstances of the case, and in particular to the question of respect for the applicant's defence rights and the quality and importance of the evidence in question (ibid., § 165).

137. However, particular considerations apply in respect of the use in criminal proceedings of evidence obtained in breach of Article 3. The use of such evidence, secured as a result of a violation of one of the core and absolute rights guaranteed by the Convention, always raises serious issues as to the fairness of the proceedings, even if the admission of such evidence was not decisive in securing a conviction (*Jalloh v. Germany* [GC], §§ 99 and 105; *Harutyunyan v. Armenia*, § 63).

138. Therefore, the use in criminal proceedings of statements obtained as a result of a violation of Article 3-irrespective of the classification of the treatment as torture, inhuman or degrading treatment-renders the proceedings as a whole automatically unfair, in breach of Article 6 (*El Haski v. Belgium*; *Gäfgen v. Germany* [GC], § 166). This also holds true for the use of real evidence obtained as a direct result of acts of torture (ibid., § 167; *Jalloh v. Germany* [GC], § 105). The admission of such evidence obtained as a result of an act classified as inhuman treatment in breach of Article 3, but falling short of torture, will only breach Article 6 if it has been shown that the breach of Article 3 had a bearing on the outcome of the proceedings against the defendant, that is, had an impact on his or her conviction or sentence (*El Haski v. Belgium*, § 85; *Gäfgen v. Germany* [GC], § 178).

139. These principles apply not only where the victim of the treatment contrary to Article 3 is the actual defendant but also where third parties are concerned (*El Haski v.*

Belgium, § 85). In particular, the Court has found that the use in a trial of evidence obtained by torture would amount to a flagrant denial of justice even where the person from whom the evidence had thus been extracted was a third party (*Othman (Abu Qatada) v. the United Kingdom*, §§ 263 and 267).

5. Entrapment

a. General considerations

140. The Court has recognised the need for the authorities to have recourse to special investigative methods, notably in organised crime and corruption cases. It has held, in this connection, that the use of special investigative methods-in particular, undercover techniques-does not in itself infringe the right to a fair trial. However, on account of the risk of police incitement entailed by such techniques, their use must be kept within clear limits (*Ramanauskas v. Lithuania* [GC], § 51).

141. While the rise of organised crime requires the States to take appropriate measures, the right to a fair trial, from which the requirement of the proper administration of justice is to be inferred, nevertheless applies to all types of criminal offence, from the most straightforward to the most complex. The right to the fair administration of justice holds so prominent a place in a democratic society that it cannot be sacrificed for the sake of expedience (ibid., § 53). In this connection, the Court has emphasised that the police may act undercover but not incite (*Khudobin v. Russia*, § 128).

142. Moreover, while the Convention does not preclude reliance, at the preliminary investigation stage and where this may be warranted by the nature of the offence, on sources such as anonymous informants, the subsequent use of such sources by the trial court to found a conviction is a different matter (*Teixeira de Castro v. Portugal*, § 35). Such a use can be acceptable only if adequate and sufficient safeguards against abuse are in place, in particular a clear and foreseeable procedure for authorising, implementing and supervising the investigative measures in question (*Ramanauskas v. Lithuania* [GC], § 51). As to the authority exercising control over undercover operations, the Court has considered that, while judicial supervision would be the most appropriate means, other means may be used provided that adequate procedures and safeguards are in place, such as supervision by a prosecutor (*Bannikova v. Russia*, § 50).

143. While the use of undercover agents may be tolerated provided that it is subject to clear restrictions and safeguards, the public interest cannot justify the use of evidence obtained as a result of police incitement, as this would expose the accused to the risk of being definitely deprived of a fair trial from the outset (*Ramanauskas v. Lithuania* [GC], § 54).

144. Consequently, in order to ascertain whether the right to a fair trial was respected in a case involving the use of undercover agents the Court examines, first, whether there was entrapment (the "substantive test of incitement") and, if so, whether the applicant was able to make an entrapment defence before the domestic courts (*Bannikova v. Russia*, §§ 37 and 51). If the actions of the agent, irrespective of whether he or she was employed by the State or a private person assisting the authorities, constituted entrapment and the evidence obtained as a result was used against the applicant in the criminal proceedings brought against him, the Court will find a violation of Article 6 § 1 of the Convention (*Ramanauskas v. Lithuania* [GC], § 73).

b. The substantive test of incitement

145. The Court has defined entrapment,[①] as opposed to a legitimate undercover investigation, as a situation where the officers involved whether members of the security forces or persons acting on their instructions-do not confine themselves to investigating criminal activity in an essentially passive manner, but exert such an influence on the subject as to incite the commission of an offence that would otherwise not have been committed, in order to make it possible to establish the offence, that is to provide evidence and institute a prosecution (*Ramanauskas v. Lithuania* [GC], § 55).

146. In deciding whether the investigation was "essentially passive" the Court examines the reasons underlying the covert operation and the conduct of the authorities carrying it out. In particular, it will determine whether there were objective suspicions that the applicant had been involved in criminal activity or was predisposed to commit a criminal offence (*Bannikova v. Russia*, § 38).

[①] The terms entrapment, police incitement and *agent provocateurs* are used in the Court's case-law interchangeably.

147. In its assessment the Court takes into account a number of factors. For example, in the early landmark case of *Teixeira de Castro v. Portugal* (§§ 37–38) the Court took into account, *inter alia*, the fact that the applicant had no criminal record, that no investigation concerning him had been opened, that he was unknown to the police officers, that no drugs were found in his home and that the amount of drugs found on him during arrest was not more than the amount requested by the undercover agents. It found that the agents' actions had gone beyond those of undercover agents because they had instigated the offence and there was nothing to suggest that without their intervention the offence in question would have been committed.

148. A previous criminal record is not by itself indicative of a predisposition to commit a criminal offence (*Constantin and Stoian v. Romania*, § 55). However, the applicant's familiarity with the current price of drugs and his ability to obtain drugs at short notice, combined with his failure to withdraw from the deal despite a number of opportunities to do so, have been considered by the Court to be indicative of pre-existing criminal activity or intent [*Shannon v. the United Kingdom* (dec.)].

149. Another factor to be taken into account is whether the applicant was pressured into committing the offence in question. Taking the initiative in contacting the applicant in the absence of any objective suspicions that the applicant had been involved in criminal activity or was predisposed to commit a criminal offence (*Burak Hun v. Turkey*, § 44), reiterating the offer despite the applicant's initial refusal, insistent prompting (*Ramanauskas v. Lithuania* [GC], § 67), raising the price beyond average (*Malininas v. Lithuania*, § 37) and appealing to the applicant's compassion by mentioning withdrawal symptoms (*Vanyan v. Russia*, §§ 11 and 49) have been regarded by the Court as conduct which can be deemed to have pressured the applicant into committing the offence in question, irrespective of whether the agent in question was a member of the security forces or a private individual acting on their instructions.

150. A further question of importance is whether the State agents can be deemed to have "joined" or "infiltrated" the criminal activity rather than to have initiated it. In the

former case the action in question remains within the bounds of undercover work. In *Miliniene v. Lithuania* (§§ 37 – 38) the Court considered that, although the police had influenced the course of events, notably by giving technical equipment to the private individual to record conversations and supporting the offer of financial inducements to the applicant, their actions were treated as having "joined" the criminal activity rather than as having initiated it as the initiative in the case had been taken by a private individual. The latter had complained to the police that the applicant would require a bribe to reach a favourable outcome in his case, and only after this complaint was the operation authorised and supervised by the Deputy Prosecutor General, with a view to verifying the complaint [for similar reasoning, see *Sequieira v. Portugal* (dec.); *Eurofinacom v. France* (dec.)].

151. The manner in which the undercover police operation was launched and carried out is relevant in assessing whether the applicant was subjected to entrapment. The absence of clear and foreseeable procedures for authorising, implementing and supervising the investigative measure in question tips the balance in favour of finding that the acts in question constitute entrapment: see, for example, *Teixeira de Castro v. Portugal*, § 38, where the Court noted the fact that the undercover agents' intervention had not taken place as part of an official anti-drug-trafficking operation supervised by a judge; *Ramanauskas v. Lithuania* [GC], § 64, where there was no indication of what reasons or personal motives had led the undercover agent to approach the applicant on his own initiative without bringing the matter to the attention of his superiors; *Vanyan v. Russia*, §§ 46 – 47, where the Court noted that the police operation had been authorised by a simple administrative decision by the body which later carried out the operation, that the decision contained very little information as to the reasons for and purposes of the planned test purchase, and that the operation was not subject to judicial review or any other independent supervision. In this connection, the "test purchase" technique used by the Russian authorities was closely scrutinised in the case of *Veselov and Others v. Russia*, where the Court held that the procedure in question was deficient and that it exposed the applicants to arbitrary action by

the police and undermined the fairness of the criminal proceedings against them. It further found that the domestic courts had also failed to adequately examine the applicants' plea of entrapment, and in particular to review the reasons for the test purchase and the conduct of the police and their informants *vis-à-vis* the applicants (ibid., § 127).

c. Judicial review of the entrapment defence

152. In cases raising issues of entrapment, Article 6 of the Convention will be complied with only if the applicant was effectively able to raise the issue of incitement during his trial, whether by means of an objection or otherwise. The mere fact that general safeguards, such as equality of arms or the rights of the defence, have been observed is not sufficient (*Ramanauskas v. Lithuania* [GC], § 69). In such cases the Court has indicated that it falls to the prosecution to prove that there was no incitement, provided that the defendant's allegations are not wholly improbable.

153. If a plea of entrapment is made and there is certain prima facie evidence of entrapment, the judicial authorities must examine the facts of the case and take the necessary steps to uncover the truth in order to determine whether there was any incitement. Should they find that there was, they must draw inferences in accordance with the Convention (ibid., § 70). The mere fact that the applicant pleaded guilty to the criminal charges does not dispense the trial court from the duty to examine allegations of entrapment (ibid., § 72).

154. In this connection the Court verifies whether a prima facie complaint of entrapment constitutes a substantive defence under domestic law or gives grounds for the exclusion of evidence or leads to similar consequences (*Bannikova v. Russia*, § 54). Although it is up to the domestic authorities to decide what procedure is appropriate when faced with a plea of incitement, the Court requires the procedure in question to be adversarial, thorough, comprehensive and conclusive on the issue of entrapment (ibid., § 57). Moreover, in the context of non-disclosure of information by the investigative authorities, the Court attaches particular weight to compliance with the principles of adversarial proceedings and equality of arms (ibid., § 58).

155. Where an accused asserts that he was incited to commit an offence, the criminal courts must carry out a careful examination of the material in the file, since for the trial to be fair within the meaning of Article 6 § 1 of the Convention, all evidence obtained as a result of police incitement must be excluded. This is especially true where the police operation took place without a sufficient legal framework or adequate safeguards (*Ramanauskas v. Lithuania* [GC], § 60).

156. If the available information does not enable the Court to conclude whether the applicant was subjected to entrapment, the judicial review of the entrapment plea becomes decisive (*Edwards and Lewis v. the United Kingdom* [GC], § 46; *Ali v. Romania*, § 101; see also, *Khudobin v. Russia*, where the domestic courts failed to analyse the relevant factual and legal elements to distinguish entrapment from a legitimate form of investigative activity; *V. v. Finland*, where it was impossible for the applicant to raise the defence of entrapment; and *Shannon v. the United Kingdom* (dec.), where the subterfuge used by a private individual was the subject of careful examination by domestic courts, which found the allegation of entrapment unsubstantiated).

6. Waiver of the guarantees of a fair trial

157. Neither the letter nor the spirit of Article 6 of the Convention prevents a person from waiving of his own free will, either expressly or tacitly, the entitlement to the guarantees of a fair trial. However, such a waiver must, if it is to be effective for Convention purposes, be established in an unequivocal manner and be attended by minimum safeguards commensurate with its importance. In addition, it must not run counter to any important public interest (*Hermi v. Italy* [GC], § 73; *Sejdovic v. Italy* [GC], § 86).

158. Before an accused can be said to have implicitly, through his conduct, waived an important right under Article 6 of the Convention it must be shown that he could reasonably have foreseen what the consequences of his conduct would be (*Hermi v. Italy* [GC], § 74; *Sejdovic v. Italy* [GC], § 87).

B. Public hearing

> Article 6 § 1 of the Convention
>
> "1. In the determination of... any criminal charge against him, everyone is entitled to a... public hearing... by [a] tribunal.... Judgment shall be pronounced publicly but the press and public may be excluded from all or part of the trial in the interests of morals, public order or national security in a democratic society, where the interests of juveniles or the protection of the private life of the parties so require, or to the extent strictly necessary in the opinion of the court in special circumstances where publicity would prejudice the interests of justice."

1. The principle of publicity

159. The public character of proceedings protects litigants against the administration of justice in secret with no public scrutiny; it is also one of the means whereby confidence in the courts can be maintained. By rendering the administration of justice visible, publicity contributes to the achievement of the aim of Article 6 § 1, namely a fair trial, the guarantee of which is one of the fundamental principles of any democratic society (*Riepan v. Austria*, § 27; *Krestovskiy v. Russia*, § 24; *Sutter v. Switzerland*, § 26).

160. The principle of the public nature of court proceedings entails two aspects: the holding of public hearings and the public delivery of judgments (ibid., § 27; *Tierce and Others v. San Marino*, § 93).

2. The right to an oral hearing and presence at trial

161. The entitlement to a "public hearing" in Article 6 § 1 necessarily implies a right to an "oral hearing" (*Döry v. Sweden*, § 37).

162. The principle of an oral and public hearing is particularly important in the criminal context, where a person charged with a criminal offence must generally be able to attend a hearing at first instance (*Tierce and Others v. San Marino*, § 94; *Jussila v. Finland* [GC], § 40).

163. Without being present, it is difficult to see how that person could exercise the specific rights set out in sub-paragraphs (c), (d) and (e) of paragraph 3 of Article 6, i. e. the right to "defend himself in person", "to examine or have examined witnesses" and "to have the free assistance of an interpreter if he cannot understand or speak the language used in court". The duty to guarantee the right of a criminal defendant to be present in the courtroom ranks therefore as one of the essential requirements of Article 6 (*Hermi v. Italy* [GC], §§ 58-59; *Sejdovic v. Italy* [GC], §§ 81 and 84).

164. Although proceedings that take place in the accused's absence are not of themselves incompatible with Article 6 of the Convention, a denial of justice nevertheless occurs where a person convicted *in absentia* is unable subsequently to obtain from a court which has heard him a fresh determination of the merits of the charge, in respect of both law and fact, where it has not been established that he has waived his right to appear and to defend himself or that he intended to escape trial (ibid., § 82).

165. The obligation to hold a hearing is, however, not absolute in all cases falling under the criminal head of Article 6. In the light of the broadening of the notion of a "criminal charge" to cases not belonging to the traditional categories of criminal law (such as administrative penalties, customs law and tax surcharges), there are "criminal charges" of differing weights. While the requirements of a fair hearing are the strictest concerning the hard core of criminal law, the criminal-head guarantees of Article 6 do not necessarily apply with their full stringency to other categories of cases falling under that head and not carrying any significant degree of stigma (*Jussila v. Finland* [GC], §§ 41-43).

166. The character of the circumstances which may justify dispensing with an oral hearing essentially comes down to the nature of the issues to be dealt with by the competent court-in particular, whether these raise any question of fact or law which could not be adequately resolved on the basis of the case file. An oral hearing may not be required where there are no issues of credibility or contested facts which necessitate an oral presentation of evidence or cross-examination of witnesses and where the accused was given an adequate opportunity to put forward his case in writing and to challenge the evidence against him (ibid., §§ 41-42 and 47-48). In this connection, it is legitimate for the national

authorities to have regard to the demands of efficiency and economy (ibid., §§ 41 – 43 and 47 – 48, concerning tax-surcharge proceedings; *Suhadolc v. Slovenia* (dec.), concerning a summary procedure for road traffic offences).

3. Appeal proceedings

167. The personal attendance of the defendant does not take on the same crucial significance for an appeal hearing as it does for a trial hearing. The manner in which Article 6 is applied to proceedings before courts of appeal depends on the special features of the proceedings involved, and account must be taken of the entirety of the proceedings in the domestic legal order and of the role of the appellate court therein (*Hermi v. Italy* [GC], § 60).

168. Leave-to-appeal proceedings and proceedings involving only questions of law, as opposed to questions of fact, may comply with the requirements of Article 6, despite the fact that the appellant is not given the opportunity to be heard in person by the appeal or cassation court, provided that a public hearing is held at first instance (*Monnell and Morris v. the United Kingdom*, § 58, as regards the issue of leave to appeal; *Sutter v. Switzerland*, § 30, as regards the court of cassation).

169. Even where the court of appeal has jurisdiction to review the case both as to the facts and as to the law, Article 6 does not always require a right to a public hearing, still less a right to appear in person (*Fejde v. Sweden*, § 31). In order to decide this question, regard must be had to the specific features of the proceedings in question and to the manner in which the applicant's interests were actually presented and protected before the appellate court, particularly in the light of the nature of the issues to be decided by it (*Seliwiak v. Poland*, § 54; *Sibgatullin v. Russia*, § 36).

170. However, where an appellate court has to examine a case as to the facts and the law and make a full assessment of the issue of guilt or innocence, it cannot determine the issue without a direct assessment of the evidence given in person by the accused for the purpose of proving that he did not commit the act allegedly constituting a criminal offence (*Popovici v. Moldova*, § 68; *Lacadena Calero v. Spain*, § 38). The principle that hearings should be held in public entails the right for the accused to give evidence in person

to an appellate court. From that perspective, the principle of publicity pursues the aim of guaranteeing the accused's defence rights (*Tierce and Others v. San Marino*, § 95).

4. Exceptions to the rule of publicity

171. The requirement to hold a public hearing is subject to exceptions. This is apparent from the text of Article 6 § 1 itself, which contains the proviso that "the press and public may be excluded from all or part of the trial ... where the interests of juveniles or the private life of the parties so require, or to the extent strictly necessary in the opinion of the court in special circumstances where publicity would prejudice the interests of justice". Holding proceedings, whether wholly or partly, in camera must be strictly required by the circumstances of the case (*Welke and Białek v. Poland*, § 74; *Martinie v. France* [GC], § 40).

172. If there are grounds to apply one or more of these exceptions, the authorities are not obliged, but have the right, to order hearings to be held in camera if they consider that such a restriction is warranted [*Toeva v. Bulgaria* (dec.)].

173. Although in criminal proceedings there is a high expectation of publicity, it may on occasion be necessary under Article 6 to limit the open and public nature of proceedings in order, for example, to protect the safety or privacy of witnesses or to promote the free exchange of information and opinion in the pursuit of justice (*B. and P. v. the United Kingdom*, § 37).

174. Security problems are a common feature of many criminal proceedings, but cases in which security concerns alone justify excluding the public from a trial are nevertheless rare (*Riepan v. Austria*, § 34). Security measures should be narrowly tailored and comply with the principle of necessity. The judicial authorities should consider all possible alternatives to ensure safety and security in the courtroom and give preference to a less strict measure over a stricter one when it can achieve the same purpose (*Krestovskiy v. Russia*, § 29).

175. Considerations of public order and security problems may justify the exclusion of the public in prison disciplinary proceedings against convicted prisoners (*Campbell and Fell v. the United Kingdom*, § 87).

176. The holding of a trial in ordinary criminal proceedings in a prison does not

necessarily mean that it is not public. However, in order to counter the obstacles involved in having a trial outside a regular courtroom, the State is under an obligation to take compensatory measures so as to ensure that the public and the media are duly informed about the place of the hearing and are granted effective access (*Riepan v. Austria*, §§ 28 – 29).

177. The mere presence of classified information in the case file does not automatically imply a need to close a trial to the public, without balancing openness with national-security concerns. Before excluding the public from criminal proceedings, courts must make specific findings that closure is necessary to protect a compelling governmental interest, and must limit secrecy to the extent necessary to preserve such an interest (*Belashev v. Russia*, § 83; *Welke and Białek v. Poland*, § 77).

5. Public pronouncement of judgments

178. The Court has not felt bound to adopt a literal interpretation of the words "pronounced publicly" (*Sutter v. Switzerland*, § 33; *Campbell and Fell v. the United Kingdom*, § 91).

179. Despite the wording, which would seem to suggest that reading out in open court is required, other means of rendering a judgment public may be compatible with Article 6 § 1. As a general rule, the form of publication of the "judgment" under the domestic law of the respondent State must be assessed in the light of the special features of the proceedings in question and by reference to the object pursued by Article 6 § 1 in this context, namely to ensure scrutiny of the judiciary by the public with a view to safeguarding the right to a fair trial. In making this assessment, account must be taken of the entirety of the proceedings (*Welke and Białek v. Poland*, § 83, where limiting the public pronouncement to the operative part of the judgments in proceedings held in camera did not contravene Article 6).

180. Complete concealment from the public of the entirety of a judicial decision cannot be justified. Legitimate security concerns can be accommodated through certain techniques, such as classification of only those parts of the judicial decisions whose disclosure would compromise national security or the safety of others (*Raza v. Bulgaria*, § 53; *Fazliyski v.*

Bulgaria, §§ 67-68).

C. Reasonable time

> **Article 6 § 1 of the Convention**
> "1. In the determination of... any criminal charge against him, everyone is entitled to a... hearing within a reasonable time..."

1. Determination of the length of proceedings

181. In criminal matters, the aim of Article 6 § 1, by which everyone has the right to a hearing within a reasonable time, is to ensure that accused persons do not have to lie under a charge for too long and that the charge is determined (*Wemhoff v. Germany*, § 18; *Kart v. Turkey* [GC], § 68).

a. Starting-point of the period to be taken into consideration

182. The period to be taken into consideration begins on the day on which a person is charged (*Neumeister v. Austria*, § 18).

183. The "reasonable time" may begin to run prior to the case coming before the trial court (*Deweer v. Belgium*, § 42), for example from the time of arrest (*Wemhoff v. Germany*, § 19), the time at which a person is charged (*Neumeister v. Austria*, § 18) or the institution of the preliminary investigation (*Ringeisen v. Austria*, § 110).

184. "Charge", for the purposes of Article 6 § 1, may be defined as "the official notification given to an individual by the competent authority of an allegation that he has committed a criminal offence" (*Deweer v. Belgium*, § 46), a definition that also corresponds to the test whether the situation of the suspect has been "substantially affected" (ibid.; *Neumeister v. Austria*, § 13; *Eckle v. Germany*, § 73; *McFarlane v. Ireland* [GC], § 143).

b. End of the period

185. The Court has held that in criminal matters the period to which Article 6 is applicable covers the whole of the proceedings in question (*König v. Germany*, § 98),

including appeal proceedings (*Delcourt v. Belgium*, §§ 25 – 26; *König v. Germany*, § 98; *V. v. the United Kingdom* [GC], § 109). Article 6 § 1, furthermore, indicates as the final point the judgment determining the charge; this may be a decision given by an appeal court when such a court pronounces upon the merits of the charge (*Neumeister v. Austria*, § 19).

186. The period to be taken into consideration lasts at least until acquittal or conviction, even if that decision is reached on appeal. There is furthermore no reason why the protection afforded to those concerned against delays in judicial proceedings should end at the first hearing in a trial: unwarranted adjournments or excessive delays on the part of trial courts are also to be feared (*Wemhoff v. Germany*, § 18).

187. In the event of conviction, there is no "determination... of any criminal charge", within the meaning of Article 6 § 1, as long as the sentence is not definitively fixed (*Eckle v. Germany*, § 77; *Ringeisen v. Austria*, § 110; *V. v. the United Kingdom* [GC], § 109).

188. The execution of a judgment given by any court must be regarded as an integral part of the trial for the purposes of Article 6 (*Assanidze v. Georgia* [GC], § 181). The guarantees afforded by Article 6 of the Convention would be illusory if a Contracting State's domestic legal or administrative system allowed a final, binding judicial decision to acquit to remain inoperative to the detriment of the person acquitted. Criminal proceedings form an entity and the protection afforded by Article 6 does not cease with the decision to acquit (ibid., § 182). If the State administrative authorities could refuse or fail to comply with a judgment acquitting a defendant, or even delay in doing so, the Article 6 guarantees previously enjoyed by the defendant during the judicial phase of the proceedings would become partly illusory (ibid., § 183).

2. Assessment of a reasonable time

a. Principles

189. The reasonableness of the length of proceedings is to be determined in the light of the circumstances of the case, which call for an overall assessment (*Boddaert v. Belgium*, § 36). Where certain stages of the proceedings are in themselves conducted at an

acceptable speed, the total length of the proceedings may nevertheless exceed a "reasonable time" (*Dobbertin v. France*, § 44).

190. Article 6 requires judicial proceedings to be expeditious, but it also lays down the more general principle of the proper administration of justice. A fair balance has to be struck between the various aspects of this fundamental requirement (*Boddaert v. Belgium*, § 39).

b. Criteria

191. When determining whether the duration of criminal proceedings has been reasonable, the Court has had regard to factors such as the complexity of the case, the applicant's conduct and the conduct of the relevant administrative and judicial authorities (*König v. Germany*, § 99; *Neumeister v. Austria*, § 21; *Ringeisen v. Austria*, § 110; *Pélissier and Sassi v. France* [GC], § 67; *Pedersen and Baadsgaard v. Denmark*, § 45).

192. *The complexity of a case*: it may stem, for example, from the number of charges, the number of people involved in the proceedings, such as defendants and witnesses, or the international dimension of the case (*Neumeister v. Austria*, § 20, where the transactions in issue had ramifications in various countries, requiring the assistance of Interpol and the implementation of treaties on mutual legal assistance, and 22 persons were concerned, some of whom were based abroad). A case may also be extremely complex where the suspicions relate to "white-collar" crime, that is to say, large-scale fraud involving several companies and complex transactions designed to escape the scrutiny of the investigative authorities, and requiring substantial accounting and financial expertise (*C. P. and Others v. France*, § 30).

193. Even though a case may be of some complexity, the Court cannot regard lengthy periods of unexplained inactivity as "reasonable" (*Adiletta v. Italy*, § 17, where there was an overall period of thirteen years and five months, including a delay of five years between the referral of the case to the investigating judge and the questioning of the accused and witnesses, and a delay of one year and nine months between the time at which the case was returned to the investigating judge and the fresh committal of the applicants for trial).

194. *The applicant's conduct*: Article 6 does not require applicants to cooperate actively with the judicial authorities. Nor can they be blamed for making full use of the remedies available to them under domestic law. However, their conduct constitutes an objective fact which cannot be attributed to the respondent State and which must be taken into account in determining whether or not the length of the proceedings exceeds what is reasonable (*Eckle v. Germany*, § 82, where the applicants increasingly resorted to actions likely to delay the proceedings, such as systematically challenging judges; some of these actions could even suggest deliberate obstruction).

195. One example of conduct that must be taken into account is the applicant's intention to delay the investigation, where this is evident from the case file (*I. A. v. France*, § 121, where the applicant, among other things, waited to be informed that the transmission of the file to the public prosecutor was imminent before requesting a number of additional investigative measures).

196. An applicant cannot rely on a period spent as a fugitive, during which he sought to avoid being brought to justice in his own country. When an accused person flees from a State which adheres to the principle of the rule of law, it may be presumed that he is not entitled to complain of the unreasonable duration of proceedings after he has fled, unless he can provide sufficient reasons to rebut this presumption (*Vayiç v. Turkey*, § 44).

197. *The conduct of the relevant authorities*: Article 6 § 1 imposes on the Contracting States the duty to organise their judicial systems in such a way that their courts can meet each of its requirements (*Abdoella v. the Netherlands*, § 24; *Dobbertin v. France*, § 44).

198. Although a temporary backlog of business does not involve liability on the part of the Contracting States provided that they take remedial action, with the requisite promptness, to deal with an exceptional situation of this kind (*Milasi v. Italy*, § 18; *Baggetta v. Italy*, § 23), the heavy workload referred to by the authorities and the various measures taken to redress matters are rarely accorded decisive weight by the Court (*Eckle v. Germany*, § 92).

199. What is at stake for the applicant must be taken into account in assessing the

reasonableness of the length of proceedings. For example, where a person is held in pre-trial detention, this is a factor to be considered in assessing whether the charge has been determined within a reasonable time (*Abdoella v. the Netherlands*, § 24, where, the time required to forward documents to the Supreme Court on two occasions amounted to more than 21 months of the 52 months taken to deal with the case. The Court found such protracted periods of inactivity unacceptable, especially as the accused was in detention).

3. Several examples

a. Reasonable time exceeded

- 9 years and 7 months, without any particular complexity other than the number of people involved (35), despite the measures taken by the authorities to deal with the court's exceptional workload following a period of rioting (*Milasi v. Italy*, §§ 14 – 20).
- 13 years and 4 months, political troubles in the region and excessive workload for the courts, efforts by the State to improve the courts' working conditions not having begun until years later (*Baggetta v. Italy*, §§ 20 – 25).
- 5 years, 5 months and 18 days, including 33 months between delivery of the judgment and production of the full written version by the judge responsible, without any adequate disciplinary measures being taken (*B. v. Austria*, §§ 48 – 55).
- 5 years and 11 months, complexity of case on account of the number of people to be questioned and the technical nature of the documents for examination in a case of aggravated misappropriation, although this could not justify an investigation that had taken five years and two months; also, a number of periods of inactivity attributable to the authorities. Thus, while the length of the trial phase appeared reasonable, the investigation could not be said to have been conducted diligently (*Rouille v. France*, § 29).
- 12 years, 7 months and 10 days, without any particular complexity or any tactics by the applicant to delay the proceedings, but including a period of two years and more than nine months between the lodging of the application with the

administrative court and the receipt of the tax authorities' initial pleadings (*Clinique Mozart SARL v. France*, §§ 34–36).

b. Reasonable time not exceeded

- 5 years and 2 months, complexity of connected cases of fraud and fraudulent bankruptcy, with innumerable requests and appeals by the applicant not merely for his release, but also challenging most of the judges concerned and seeking the transfer of the proceedings to different jurisdictions (*Ringeisen v. Austria*, § 110).

- 7 years and 4 months: the fact that more than seven years had already elapsed since the laying of charges without their having been determined in a judgment convicting or acquitting the accused certainly indicated an exceptionally long period which in most cases should be regarded as in excess of what was reasonable; moreover, for 15 months the judge had not questioned any of the numerous co-accused or any witnesses or carried out any other duties; however, the case had been especially complex (number of charges and persons involved, international dimension entailing particular difficulties in enforcing requests for judicial assistance abroad etc.) (*Neumeister v. Austria*, § 21).

V. Specific guarantees

A. The presumption of innocence (Article 6 § 2)

Article 6 § 2 of the Convention

"2. Everyone charged with a criminal offence shall be presumed innocent until proved guilty according to law."

1. Burden of proof

200. The principle of the presumption of innocence requires, *inter alia*, that when carrying out their duties, the members of a court should not start with the preconceived idea that the accused has committed the offence charged; the burden of proof is on the prosecution, and any doubt should benefit the accused. It is for the prosecution to inform the accused of the case that will be made against him, so that he may prepare and present his defence accordingly, and to adduce evidence sufficient to convict him (*Barberà, Messegué and Jabardo v. Spain*, § 77; *Janosevic v. Sweden*, § 97). The presumption of innocence will be infringed where the burden of proof is shifted from the prosecution to the defence (*Telfner v. Austria*, § 15). The burden of proof cannot be reversed in compensation proceedings brought following a final decision to discontinue proceedings (*Capeau v. Belgium*, § 25).

201. Exoneration from criminal liability does not preclude the establishment of civil liability to pay compensation arising out of the same facts on the basis of a less strict burden of proof [*Ringvold v. Norway*, § 38; *Y v. Norway*, § 41; *Lundkvist v. Sweden* (dec.)].

2. Presumptions of fact and of law

202. A person's right in a criminal case to be presumed innocent and to require the prosecution to bear the onus of proving the allegations against him or her is not absolute, since presumptions of fact or of law operate in every criminal-law system and are not prohibited in principle by the Convention (*Falk v. the Netherlands* (dec.), concerning the imposition of a fine on a registered car owner who had not been the actual driver at the time of the traffic offence). In particular, the Contracting States may, under certain conditions, penalise a simple or objective fact as such, irrespective of whether it results from criminal intent or from negligence (*Salabiaku v. France*, § 27, concerning a presumption of criminal liability for smuggling inferred from possession of narcotics; *Janosevic v. Sweden*, § 100, concerning the imposition of tax surcharges on the basis of objective grounds and enforcement thereof prior to a court determination). However, Article 6 § 2 requires States to confine these presumptions within reasonable limits which take into account the importance of what is at stake and maintain the rights of the defence (*Salabiaku v. France*,

§ 28; *Radio France and Others v. France*, § 24, concerning the presumption of criminal liability of a publishing director for defamatory statements made in radio programmes; *Klouvi v. France*, § 41, regarding the inability to defend a charge of malicious prosecution owing to a statutory presumption that an accusation against a defendant acquitted for lack of evidence was false).

203. In employing presumptions in criminal law, the Contracting States are required to strike a balance between the importance of what is at stake and the rights of the defence; in other words, the means employed have to be reasonably proportionate to the legitimate aim sought to be achieved [*Janosevic v. Sweden*, § 101; *Falk v. the Netherlands* (dec.)].

3. Scope of Article 6 § 2

a. Criminal proceedings

204. Article 6 § 2 governs criminal proceedings in their entirety, irrespective of the outcome of the prosecution, and not solely the examination of the merits of the charge (see, among many authorities, *Poncelet v. Belgium*, § 50; *Minelli v. Switzerland*, § 30; *Garycki v. Poland*, § 68).

205. The presumption of innocence does not cease to apply solely because the first-instance proceedings resulted in the defendant's conviction when the proceedings are continuing on appeal (*Konstas v. Greece*, § 36).

206. Once an accused has properly been proved guilty, Article 6 § 2 can have no application in relation to allegations made about the accused's character and conduct as part of the sentencing process, unless such accusations are of such a nature and degree as to amount to the bringing of a new "charge" within the autonomous Convention meaning (*Böhmer v. Germany*, § 55; *Geerings v. the Netherlands*, § 43; *Phillips v. the United Kingdom*, § 35).

207. Nevertheless, a person's right to be presumed innocent and to require the prosecution to bear the onus of proving the allegations against him or her forms part of the general notion of a fair hearing under Article 6 § 1 of the Convention which applies to a sentencing procedure (ibid., §§ 39–40; *Grayson and Barnham v. the United Kingdom*, §§ 37 and 39).

b. Subsequent proceedings

208. The presumption of innocence also protects individuals who have been acquitted of a criminal charge, or in respect of whom criminal proceedings have been continued, from being treated by public officials and authorities as though they are in fact guilty of the offence with which they have been charged. Without protection to ensure respect for the acquittal or the discontinuation decision in any other proceedings, the guarantees of Article 6 § 2 could risk becoming theoretical and illusory. What is also at stake once the criminal proceedings have concluded is the person's reputation and the way in which that person is perceived by the public (*Allen v. the United Kingdom* [GC], § 94).

209. Whenever the question of the applicability of Article 6 § 2 arises in the context of subsequent proceedings, the applicant must demonstrate the existence of a link between the concluded criminal proceedings and the subsequent proceedings. Such a link is likely to be present, for example, where the subsequent proceedings require an examination of the outcome of the prior criminal proceedings and, in particular, where they oblige the court to analyse the criminal judgment; to engage in a review or evaluation of the evidence in the criminal file; to assess the applicant's participation in some or all of the events leading to the criminal charge; or to comment on the subsisting indications of the applicant's possible guilt (ibid., § 104).

210. The Court has considered the applicability of Article 6 § 2 to judicial decisions taken following the conclusion of criminal proceedings concerning *inter alia*:

- a former accused's obligation to bear court costs and prosecution costs;
- a former accused's request for compensation for detention on remand or other inconvenience caused by the criminal proceedings;
- a former accused's request for defence costs;
- a former accused's request for compensation for damage caused by an unlawful or wrongful investigation or prosecution;
- the imposition of civil liability to pay compensation to the victim;
- the refusal of civil claims lodged by the applicant against insurers;
- the maintenance in force of a child care order, after the prosecution decided not to

bring charges against the parent for child abuse;
- disciplinary or dismissal issues; and
- the revocation of the applicant's right to social housing (see *Allen v. the United Kingdom* [GC], § 98 with numerous further references).

4. Prejudicial statements

211. Article 6 § 2 is aimed at preventing the undermining of a fair criminal trial by prejudicial statements made in close connection with those proceedings. Where no such proceedings are or have been in existence, statements attributing criminal or other reprehensible conduct are more relevant to considerations of protection against defamation and adequate access to court to determine civil rights, raising potential issues under Articles 8 and 6 of the Convention (*Zollmann v. the United Kingdom* (dec.); *Ismoilov and Others v. Russia*, § 160).

212. A fundamental distinction must be made between a statement that someone is merely suspected of having committed a crime and a clear declaration, in the absence of a final conviction, that an individual has committed the crime in question (ibid., § 166; *Nešťák v. Slovakia*, § 89). The latter infringes the presumption of innocence, whereas the former has been regarded as unobjectionable in various situations examined by the Court (*Garycki v. Poland*, § 67).

213. Whether a statement by a judge or other public authority is in breach of the principle of the presumption of innocence must be determined in the context of the particular circumstances in which the impugned statement was made (*Daktaras v. Lithuania*, § 42; *A. L. v. Germany*, § 31).

214. Statements by judges are subject to stricter scrutiny than those by investigative authorities (*Pandy v. Belgium*, § 43).

215. The voicing of suspicions regarding an accused's innocence is conceivable as long as the conclusion of criminal proceedings has not resulted in a decision on the merits of the accusation (*Sekanina v. Austria*, § 30). However, once an acquittal has become final, the voicing of any suspicions of guilt is incompatible with the presumption of innocence (*Rushiti v. Austria*, § 31; *O. v. Norway*, § 39; *Geerings v. the Netherlands*, § 49; *Paraponiaris v. Greece*, § 32).

5. Statements by judicial authorities

216. The presumption of innocence will be violated if a judicial decision concerning a person charged with a criminal offence reflects an opinion that he is guilty before he has been proved guilty according to law. It suffices, even in the absence of any formal finding, that there is some reasoning suggesting that the court regards the accused as guilty (see, as the leading authority, *Minelli v. Switzerland*, § 37; and, more recently, *Nerattini v. Greece*, § 23; *Didu v. Romania*, § 41). A premature expression of such an opinion by the tribunal itself will inevitably fall foul of this presumption (*Nešťák v. Slovakia*, § 88; *Garycki v. Poland*, § 66).

217. What is important in the application of the provision of Article 6 § 2 is the true meaning of the statements in question, not their literal form (*Lavents v. Latvia*, § 126).

218. The fact that the applicant was ultimately found guilty cannot vacate his initial right to be presumed innocent until proved guilty according to law (*Matijašević v. Serbia*, § 49; *Nešťák v. Slovakia*, § 90, concerning decisions prolonging the applicants' detention on remand).

6. Statements by public officials

219. The presumption of innocence may be infringed not only by a judge or court but also by other public authorities (*Allenet de Ribemont v. France*, § 36; *Daktaras v. Lithuania*, § 42; *Petyo Petkov v. Bulgaria*, § 91). Article 6 § 2 prohibits statements by public officials about pending criminal investigations which encourage the public to believe the suspect guilty and prejudge the assessment of the facts by the competent judicial authority (*Ismoilov and Others v. Russia*, § 161; *Butkevičius v. Lithuania*, § 53).

220. The principle of presumption of innocence does not prevent the authorities from informing the public about criminal investigations in progress, but it requires that they do so with all the discretion and circumspection necessary if the presumption of innocence is to be respected (*Fatullayev v. Azerbaijan*, § 159; *Allenet de Ribemont v. France*, § 38; *Garycki v. Poland*, § 69).

221. The Court has emphasised the importance of the choice of words by public officials in their statements before a person has been tried and found guilty of an offence

(*Daktaras v. Lithuania*, § 41; *Arrigo and Vella v. Malta* (dec.); *Khuzhin and Others v. Russia*, § 94).

7. Adverse press campaign

222. In a democratic society, severe comments by the press are sometimes inevitable in cases concerning public interest [*Viorel Burzo v. Romania*, § 160; *Akay v. Turkey* (dec.)].

223. A virulent press campaign can, however, adversely affect the fairness of a trial by influencing public opinion and, consequently, jurors called upon to decide the guilt of an accused (*Kuzmin v Russia*, § 62). What is decisive is not the subjective apprehensions of the suspect concerning the absence of prejudice required of the trial courts, however understandable, but whether, in the particular circumstances of the case, his fears can be held to be objectively justified (*Włoch v. Poland* (dec.); *Daktaras v. Lithuania* (dec.); *Priebke v. Italy* (dec.); *Mustafa (Abu Hamza) v. the United Kingdom* (dec.), §§ 37 – 40, concerning the effect of press coverage on the impartiality of the trial court).

224. National courts which are entirely composed of professional judges generally possess, unlike members of a jury, appropriate experience and training enabling them to resist any outside influence (*Craxi v. Italy* (no.1), § 104; *Mircea v. Romania*, § 75).

225. The publication of photographs of suspects does not in itself breach the presumption of innocence (*Y. B. and Others v. Turkey*, § 47). Broadcasting of the suspect's images on television may in certain circumstances raise an issue under Article 6 § 2 (*Rupa v. Romania* (no.1), § 232).

8. Sanctions for failure to provide information

226. The presumption of innocence is closely linked to the right not to incriminate oneself (*Heaney and McGuinness v. Ireland*, § 40).

227. The requirement for car owners to identify the driver at the time of a suspected traffic offence is not incompatible with Article 6 of the Convention (*O'Halloran and Francis v. the United Kingdom* [GC]).

228. Obliging drivers to submit to a breathalyser or blood test is not contrary to the principle of presumption of innocence [*Tirado Ortiz and Lozano Martin v. Spain* (dec.)].

B. The rights of the defence (Article 6 § 3)

> Article 6 § 3 of the Convention
>
> "3. Everyone charged with a criminal offence has the following minimum rights:
>
> (a) to be informed promptly, in a language which he understands and in detail, of the nature and cause of the accusation against him;
>
> (b) to have adequate time and facilities for the preparation of his defence;
>
> (c) to defend himself in person or through legal assistance of his own choosing or, if he has not sufficient means to pay for legal assistance, to be given it free when the interests of justice so require;
>
> (d) to examine or have examined witnesses against him and to obtain the attendance and examination of witnesses on his behalf under the same conditions as witnesses against him;
>
> (e) to have the free assistance of an interpreter if he cannot understand or speak the language used in court."

229. The requirements of Article 6 § 3 concerning the rights of the defence are to be seen as particular aspects of the right to a fair trial guaranteed by Article 6 § 1 of the Convention (*Sakhnovskiy v. Russia* [GC], § 94; *Gäfgen v. Germany* [GC], § 169).

230. The specific guarantees laid down in Article 6 § 3 exemplify the notion of fair trial in respect of typical procedural situations which arise in criminal cases, but their intrinsic aim is always to ensure, or to contribute to ensuring, the fairness of the criminal proceedings as a whole. The guarantees enshrined in Article 6 § 3 are therefore not an end in themselves, and they must accordingly be interpreted in the light of the function which they have in the overall context of the proceedings (*Mayzit v. Russia*, § 77; *Can v. Austria*, Commission report, § 48).

1. Information on the nature and cause of the accusation [Article 6 § 3 (a)]

> Article 6 § 3 (a) of the Convention
> "3. Everyone charged with a criminal offence has the following minimum rights:
> (a) to be informed promptly, in a language which he understands and in detail, of the nature and cause of the accusation against him;"

a. General

231. The scope of Article 6 § 3 (a) must be assessed in the light of the more general right to a fair hearing guaranteed by Article 6 § 1 of the Convention. In criminal matters the provision of full, detailed information concerning the charges against a defendant, and consequently the legal characterisation that the court might adopt in the matter, is an essential prerequisite for ensuring that the proceedings are fair (*Pélissier and Sassi v. France* [GC], § 52; *Sejdovic v. Italy* [GC], § 90).

232. Sub-paragraphs (a) and (b) of Article 6 § 3 are connected in that the right to be informed of the nature and the cause of the accusation must be considered in the light of the accused's right to prepare his defence (*Pélissier and Sassi v. France* [GC], § 54; *Dallos v. Hungary*, § 47).

b. Information about the charge

233. Article 6 § 3 (a) points to the need for special attention to be paid to the notification of the "accusation" to the defendant. Particulars of the offence play a crucial role in the criminal process, in that it is from the moment of their service that the suspect is formally put on written notice of the factual and legal basis of the charges against him (*Kamasinski v. Austria*, § 79; *Pélissier and Sassi v. France* [GC], § 51).

234. Article 6 § 3 (a) affords the defendant the right to be informed not only of the "cause" of the accusation, that is to say, the acts he is alleged to have committed and on which the accusation is based, but also of the "nature" of the accusation, that is, the legal characterisation given to those acts (*Mattoccia v. Italy*, § 59; *Penev v. Bulgaria*, §§ 33 and 42).

235. The information need not necessarily mention the evidence on which the charge is based (*X. v. Belgium*, Commission decision; *Collozza and Rubinat v. Italy*, Commission report).

236. Article 6 § 3 (a) does not impose any special formal requirement as to the manner in which the accused is to be informed of the nature and cause of the accusation against him (*Pélissier and Sassi v. France* [GC], § 53; *Drassich v. Italy*, § 34; *Giosakis v. Greece* (no. 3), § 29).

237. The duty to inform the accused rests entirely on the prosecution and cannot be complied with passively by making information available without bringing it to the attention of the defence (*Mattoccia v. Italy*, § 65; *Chichlian and Ekindjian v. France*, Commission report, § 71).

238. Information must actually be received by the accused; a legal presumption of receipt is not sufficient (*C. v. Italy*, Commission decision).

239. If the situation complained of is attributable to the accused's own conduct, the latter is not in a position to allege a violation of the rights of the defence (*Erdogan v. Turkey*, Commission decision; *Campbell and Fell v. the United Kingdom*, § 96).

240. In the case of a person with mental difficulties, the authorities are required to take additional steps to enable the person to be informed in detail of the nature and cause of the accusation against him (*Vaudelle v. France*, § 65).

c. Reclassification of the charge

241. The accused must be duly and fully informed of any changes in the accusation, including changes in its "cause", and must be provided with adequate time and facilities to react to them and organise his defence on the basis of any new information or allegation [*Mattoccia v. Italy*, § 61; *Bäckström and Andersson v. Sweden* (dec.)].

242. Information concerning the charges made, including the legal characterisation that the court might adopt in the matter, must either be given before the trial in the bill of indictment or at least in the course of the trial by other means such as formal or implicit extension of the charges. Mere reference to the abstract possibility that a court might arrive at a different conclusion from the prosecution as regards the qualification of an offence is clearly not sufficient (*I. H. and Others v. Austria*, § 34).

243. In the case of reclassification of facts during the course of the proceedings, the accused must be afforded the possibility of exercising his defence rights in a practical and effective manner, and in good time (*Pélissier and Sassi v. France* [GC], § 62; *Block v. Hungary*, § 24).

244. A reclassification of the offence is considered to be sufficiently foreseeable to the accused if it concerns an element which is intrinsic to the accusation (*De Salvador Torres v. Spain*, § 33; *Sadak and Others v. Turkey* (no. 1), §§ 52 and 56; *Juha Nuutinen v. Finland*, § 32).

245. Defects in the notification of the charge could be cured in the appeal proceedings if the accused has the opportunity to advance before the higher courts his defence in respect of the reformulated charge and to contest his conviction in respect of all relevant legal and factual aspects (ibid., § 33; *Dallos v. Hungary*, §§ 49 – 52; *Sipavičius v. Lithuania*, §§ 30 – 33; *Zhupnik v. Ukraine*, §§ 39 – 43; *I. H. and Others v. Austria*, §§ 36 – 38).

d. "In detail"

246. While the extent of the "detailed" information varies depending on the particular circumstances of each case, the accused must at least be provided with sufficient information to understand fully the extent of the charges against him, in order to prepare an adequate defence.

247. In this connection, the adequacy of the information must be assessed in relation to Article 6 § 3 (b), which confers on everyone the right to have adequate time and facilities for the preparation of their defence, and in the light of the more general right to a fair hearing enshrined in Article 6 § 1 [*Mattoccia v. Italy*, § 60; *Bäckström and Andersson v. Sweden* (dec.)].

e. "Promptly"

248. The information must be submitted to the accused in good time for the preparation of his defence, which is the principal underlying purpose of Article 6 § 3 (a) (*C. v. Italy*, Commission decision, where the notification of charges to the applicant four months before his trial was deemed acceptable; see, by contrast, *Borisova v. Bulgaria*, §§ 43 – 45, where the applicant had only a couple of hours to prepare her defence without a

lawyer).

249. In examining compliance with Article 6 § 3 (a), the Court has regard to the autonomous meaning of the words "charged" and "criminal charge", which must be interpreted with reference to the objective rather than the formal situation (*Padin Gestoso v. Spain* (dec.); *Casse v. Luxembourg*, § 71).

f. "Language"

250. If it is shown or there are reasons to believe that the accused has insufficient knowledge of the language in which the information is given, the authorities must provide him with a translation [*Brozicek v. Italy*, § 41; *Tabaï v. France* (dec.)].

251. Whilst Article 6 § 3 (a) does not specify that the relevant information should be given in writing or translated in written form for a foreign defendant, a defendant not familiar with the language used by the court may be at a practical disadvantage if he is not also provided with a written translation of the indictment into a language which he understands (*Hermi v. Italy* [GC], § 68; *Kamasinski v. Austria*, § 79).

252. However, sufficient information on the charges may also be provided through an oral translation of the indictment if this allows the accused to prepare his defence [ibid., § 81; *Husain v. Italy* (dec.)].

253. There is no right under this provision for the accused to have a full translation of the court files (*X. v. Austria*, Commission decision).

254. The cost incurred by the interpretation of the accusation must be borne by the State in accordance with Article 6 § 3 (e), which guarantees the right to the free assistance of an interpreter (*Luedicke, Belkacem and Koç v. Germany*, § 45).

2. Preparation of the defence [Article 6 § 3 (b)]

Article 6 § 3 (b) of the Convention

"3. Everyone charged with a criminal offence has the following minimum rights:

...

(b) to have adequate time and facilities for the preparation of his defence;"

a. General considerations

255. Article 6 § 3 (b) of the Convention concerns two elements of a proper defence, namely the question of facilities and that of time. This provision implies that the substantive defence activity on the accused's behalf may comprise everything which is "necessary" to prepare the trial. The accused must have the opportunity to organise his defence in an appropriate way and without restriction as to the ability to put all relevant defence arguments before the trial court and thus to influence the outcome of the proceedings (*Can v. Austria*, Commission report, § 53; *Gregačević v. Croatia*, § 51).

256. The issue of adequacy of the time and facilities afforded to an accused must be assessed in the light of the circumstances of each particular case (*Iglin v. Ukraine*, § 65; *Galstyan v. Armenia*, § 84).

b. Adequate time

257. Article 6 § 3 (b) protects the accused against a hasty trial (*Kröcher and Möller v. Switzerland*, Commission decision; *Bonzi v. Switzerland*, Commission decision). Although it is important to conduct proceedings at good speed, this should not be done at the expense of the procedural rights of one of the parties (*OAO Neftyanaya Kompaniya Yukos v. Russia*, § 540).

258. When assessing whether the accused had adequate time for the preparation of his defence, particular regard has to be had to the nature of the proceedings, as well as the complexity of the case and the stage of the proceedings (*Gregačević v. Croatia*, § 51). Account must be taken also of the usual workload of legal counsel; however, it is not unreasonable to require a defence lawyer to arrange for at least some shift in the emphasis of his work if this is necessary in view of the special urgency of a particular case [*Mattick v. Germany* (dec.)].

259. Article 6 § 3 (b) of the Convention does not require the preparation of a trial lasting over a certain period of time to be completed before the first hearing. The course of trials cannot be fully charted in advance and may reveal elements which have not hitherto come to light and which require further preparation by the parties (ibid.).

260. The defence must be given additional time after certain occurrences in the

proceedings in order to adjust its position, prepare a request, lodge an appeal, etc. (*Miminoshvili v. Russia*, § 141). Such "occurrences" may include changes in the indictment (*Pélissier and Sassi v. France* [GC], § 62), introduction of new evidence by the prosecution (*G. B. v. France*, §§ 60 – 62), or a sudden and drastic change in the opinion of an expert during the trial (ibid., §§ 69 – 70).

261. An accused is expected to seek an adjournment or postponement of a hearing if there is a perceived problem with the time allowed (*Campbell and Fell v. the United Kingdom*, § 98; *Bäckström and Andersson v. Sweden* (dec.); *Craxi v. Italy* (no. 1), § 72), save in exceptional circumstances (*Goddi v. Italy*, § 31) or where there is no basis for such a right in domestic law and practice (*Galstyan v. Armenia*, § 85).

262. In certain circumstances a court may be required to adjourn a hearing of its own motion in order to give the defence sufficient time (*Sadak and Others v. Turkey* (no. 1), § 57; *Sakhnovskiy v. Russia* [GC], §§ 103 and 106).

263. In order for the accused to exercise effectively the right of appeal available to him, the national courts must indicate with sufficient clarity the grounds on which they based their decision (*Hadjianastassiou v. Greece*, § 33). When a fully reasoned judgment is not available before the expiry of the time-limit for lodging an appeal, the accused must be given sufficient information in order to be able to make an informed appeal (*Zoon v. the Netherlands*, §§ 40 – 50; *Baucher v. France*, §§ 46 – 51).

264. States must ensure that everyone charged with a criminal offence has the benefit of the safeguards of Article 6 § 3. Putting the onus on convicted appellants to find out when an allotted period of time starts to run or expires is not compatible with the "diligence" which the Contracting States must exercise to ensure that the rights guaranteed by Article 6 are enjoyed in an effective manner (*Vacher v. France*, § 28).

c. Adequate facilities

i. Access to evidence

265. The "facilities" which everyone charged with a criminal offence should enjoy include the opportunity to acquaint himself, for the purposes of preparing his defence, with the results of investigations carried out throughout the proceedings (*Huseyn and Others v. Azerbaijan*, § 175; *OAO Neftyanaya Kompaniya Yukos v. Russia*, § 538).

266. Where a person is detained pending trial, the notion of "facilities" may include such conditions of detention that permit the person to read and write with a reasonable degree of concentration (*Mayzit v. Russia*, § 81; *Moiseyev v. Russia*, § 221). It is crucial that both the accused and his defence counsel should be able to participate in the proceedings and make submissions without suffering from excessive tiredness (*Makhfi v. France*, § 40; *Barberà, Messegué and Jabardo v. Spain*, § 70).

267. The facilities which must be granted to the accused are restricted to those which assist or may assist him in the preparation of his defence (*Padin Gestoso v. Spain* (dec.); *Mayzit v. Russia*, § 79).

268. An accused does not have to be given direct access to the case file, it being sufficient for him to be informed of the material in the file by his representatives (*Kremzow v. Austria*, § 52). However, an accused's limited access to the court file must not prevent the evidence being made available to the accused before the trial and the accused being given an opportunity to comment on it through his lawyer in oral submissions (*Öcalan v. Turkey* [GC], § 140).

269. When an accused has been allowed to conduct his own defence, denying him access to the case file amounts to an infringement of the rights of the defence (*Foucher v. France*, §§ 33–36).

270. In order to facilitate the conduct of the defence, the accused must not be hindered in obtaining copies of relevant documents from the case file and compiling and using any notes taken (*Rasmussen v. Poland*, §§ 48–49; *Moiseyev v. Russia*, §§ 213–218; *Matyjek v. Poland*, § 59; *Seleznev v. Russia*, §§ 64–69).

271. The right of access to the case file is not absolute. In some cases it may be necessary to withhold certain evidence from the defence so as to preserve the fundamental rights of another individual or to safeguard an important public interest such as national security or the need to protect witnesses or safeguard police methods of investigation of crime. However, only such measures restricting the rights of the defence which are strictly necessary are permissible under Article 6 § 1. The Court will scrutinise the decision-making procedure to ensure that it complied with the requirements to provide adversarial proceedings

and equality of arms and incorporated adequate safeguards to protect the interests of the accused (*Natunen v. Finland*, §§ 40 – 41; *Dowsett v. the United Kingdom*, §§ 42 – 43; *Mirilashvili v. Russia*, §§ 203 – 209).

272. Failure to disclose to the defence material evidence containing items that could enable the accused to exonerate himself or have his sentence reduced may constitute a refusal of the facilities necessary for the preparation of the defence, and therefore a violation of the right guaranteed in Article 6 § 3 (b) of the Convention. The accused may, however, be expected to give specific reasons for his request and the domestic courts are entitled to examine the validity of these reasons (*Natunen v. Finland*, § 43; *C. G. P. v. the Netherlands*, Commission decision).

ii. Consultation with a lawyer

273. "Facilities" provided to an accused include consultation with his lawyer (*Campbell and Fell v. the United Kingdom*, § 99; *Goddi v. Italy*, § 31). The opportunity for an accused to confer with his defence counsel is fundamental to the preparation of his defence (*Bonzi v. Switzerland*, Commission decision; *Can v. Austria*, Commission report, § 52).

274. Article 6 § 3 (b) overlaps with a right to legal assistance in Article 6 § 3 (c) of the Convention (*Lanz v. Austria*, §§ 50 – 53; *Öcalan v. Turkey* [GC], § 148; *Trepashkin v. Russia* (no. 2), §§ 159 – 168).

3. Right to defend oneself in person or through legal assistance [Article 6 § 3 (c)]

> Article 6 § 3 (c) of the Convention
>
> "3. Everyone charged with a criminal offence has the following minimum rights:
>
> ...
>
> (c) to defend himself in person or through legal assistance of his own choosing or, if he has not sufficient means to pay for legal assistance, to be given it free when the interests of justice so require;"

275. Article 6 § 3 (c) encompasses particular aspects of the right to a fair trial within the meaning of Article 6 § 1 (*Correia de Matos v. Portugal* (dec.); *Foucher v. France*, § 30). This sub-paragraph guarantees that the proceedings against an accused person will not take place without adequate representation of the case for the defence (*Pakelli v. Germany*, Commission report, § 84). It comprises three separate rights: to defend oneself in person, to defend oneself through legal assistance of one's own choosing and, subject to certain conditions, to be given legal assistance free (ibid., § 31).

a. Scope of application

276. Any person subject to a criminal charge must be protected by Article 6 § 3 (c) at every stage of the proceedings (*Imbrioscia v. Switzerland*, § 37). This protection may thus become relevant even before a case is sent for trial if and so far as the fairness of the trial is likely to be seriously prejudiced by an initial failure to comply with the provisions of Article 6 (ibid., § 36; *Öcalan v. Turkey* [GC], § 131; *Magee v. the United Kingdom*, § 41).

277. While Article 6 § 3 (b) is tied to considerations relating to the preparation of the trial, Article 6 § 3 (c) gives the accused a more general right to assistance and support by a lawyer throughout the whole proceedings (*Can v. Austria*, Commission report, § 54).

278. The manner in which Article 6 § 3 (c) is to be applied in the pre-trial phase, i. e. during the preliminary investigation, depends on the special features of the proceedings involved and on the circumstances of the case (*Brennan v. the United Kingdom*, § 45; *Berliński v. Poland*, § 75). Article 6 will normally require that the accused be allowed to benefit from the assistance of a lawyer from the initial stages of police questioning (*John Murray v. the United Kingdom*, § 63; *Öcalan v. Turkey* [GC], § 131; *Salduz v. Turkey* [GC], § 54; *Averill v. the United Kingdom*, § 59; *Brennan v. the United Kingdom*, § 45; *Dayanan v. Turkey*, § 31). This right may, however, be subject to restriction for good cause (*Magee v. the United Kingdom*, § 41; *John Murray v. the United Kingdom*, § 63). The question in each case is whether the restriction, in the light of the entirety of the proceedings, has deprived the accused of a fair hearing (ibid.; *Brennan v. the United Kingdom*, § 45). Even where compelling reasons may exceptionally justify denial of

access to a lawyer, such a restriction must not unduly prejudice the rights of the accused under Article 6 (*Salduz v. Turkey* [GC], § 55).

279. Similarly, the manner in which Article 6 § 3 (c) is to be applied in relation to appellate or cassation courts depends upon the special features of the proceedings involved (*Pakelli v. Germany*, Commission report, § 29; *Meftah and Others v. France* [GC], § 41). Account must be taken of the entirety of the proceedings conducted in the domestic legal order and of the role of the appellate or cassation court therein (ibid.; *Monnell and Morris v. the United Kingdom*, § 56). It is necessary to consider matters such as the nature of the leave-to-appeal procedure and its significance in the context of the criminal proceedings as a whole, the scope of the powers of the court of appeal, and the manner in which the applicant's interests were actually presented and protected before the court of appeal (ibid.).

b. Defence in person

280. The object and purpose of Article 6 of the Convention taken as a whole show that a person charged with a criminal offence is entitled to take part in the hearing (*Zana v. Turkey* [GC], § 68; *Monnell and Morris v. the United Kingdom*, § 58). Closely linked with this right Article 6 § 3 (c) offers the accused the possibility of defending himself in person. It will therefore normally not be contrary to the requirements of Article 6 if an accused is self-represented in accordance with his own will, unless the interests of justice require otherwise (*Galstyan v. Armenia*, § 91).

281. Yet the right to defend oneself in person is not guaranteed in absolute terms. Whether to allow an accused to defend himself in person or to assign him a lawyer falls within the margin of appreciation of the Contracting States, which are better placed than the Court to choose the appropriate means within their judicial system to guarantee the rights of the defence [*Correia de Matos v. Portugal* (dec.)]. The domestic courts are therefore entitled to consider that the interests of justice require the compulsory appointment of a lawyer (*Croissant v. Germany*, § 27; *Lagerblom v. Sweden*, § 50). It is a measure in the interests of the accused designed to ensure the proper defence of his interests [*Correia de Matos v. Portugal* (dec.)].

282. Furthermore, Article 6 § 3 (c) does not provide for an unlimited right to use any defence arguments. Where the accused chooses to defend himself, he deliberately waives his right to be assisted by a lawyer and is considered to be under a duty to show diligence in the manner in which he conducts his defence (*Melin v. France*, § 25). It would overstrain the concept of the right of defence of those charged with a criminal offence if it were to be assumed that they could not be prosecuted when, in exercising that right, they intentionally aroused false suspicions of punishable behaviour concerning a witness or any other person involved in the criminal proceedings (*Brandstetter v. Austria*, § 52). The mere possibility of an accused being subsequently prosecuted on account of allegations made in his defence cannot be deemed to infringe his rights under Article 6 § 3 (c). The position might be different if, as a consequence of national law or practice in this respect being unduly severe, the risk of subsequent prosecution is such that the defendant is genuinely inhibited from freely exercising his defence rights (ibid., § 53).

c. Legal assistance

283. The right of everyone charged with a criminal offence to be effectively defended by a lawyer is one of the fundamental features of a fair trial (*Salduz v. Turkey* [GC], § 51). As a rule, a suspect should be granted access to legal assistance from the moment he is taken into police custody or pre-trial detention (*Dayanan v. Turkey*, § 31).

The right of an accused to participate effectively in a criminal trial includes, in general, not only the right to be present, but also the right to receive legal assistance, if necessary (*Lagerblom v. Sweden*, § 49; *Galstyan v. Armenia*, § 89). By the same token, the mere presence of the applicant's lawyer cannot compensate for the absence of the accused (*Zana v. Turkey* [GC], § 72).

284. The right to legal representation is not dependent upon the accused's presence (*Van Geyseghem v. Belgium* [GC], § 34; *Campbell and Fell v. the United Kingdom*, § 99; *Poitrimol v. France*, § 34). The fact that the defendant, despite having been properly summoned, does not appear, cannot-even in the absence of an excuse-justify depriving him of his right to be defended by counsel (*Van Geyseghem v. Belgium* [GC], § 34; *Pelladoah v. the Netherlands*, § 40; *Krombach v. France*, § 89; *Galstyan v. Armenia*, § 89).

285. The right of everyone charged with a criminal offence to be defended by counsel of his own choosing is not absolute (*Meftah and Others v. France* [GC], § 45; *Pakelli v. Germany*, Commission report, § 31). Although, as a general rule, the accused's choice of lawyer should be respected (*Lagerblom v. Sweden*, § 54), the national courts may override that person's choice when there are relevant and sufficient grounds for holding that this is necessary in the interests of justice (*Meftah and Others v. France* [GC], § 45; *Croissant v. Germany*, § 29). For instance, the special nature of the proceedings, considered as a whole, may justify specialist lawyers being reserved a monopoly on making oral representations (*Meftah and Others v. France* [GC], § 47).

286. For the right to legal assistance to be practical and effective, and not merely theoretical, its exercise should not be made dependent on the fulfilment of unduly formalistic conditions: it is for the courts to ensure that a trial is fair and, accordingly, that counsel who attends trial for the apparent purpose of defending the accused in his absence, is given the opportunity to do so (*Van Geyseghem v. Belgium* [GC], § 33; *Pelladoah v. the Netherlands*, § 41).

287. As with other fair-trial rights it is possible for an accused to waive his right to legal assistance (*Pishchalnikov v. Russia*, § 77). However, before an accused can be said to have implicitly, through his conduct, waived such an important right under Article 6, it must be shown that he could reasonably have foreseen what the consequences of his conduct would be. Additional safeguards are necessary when the accused asks for counsel because if an accused has no lawyer, he has less chance of being informed of his rights and, as a consequence, there is less chance that they will be respected (ibid., § 78).

d. Legal aid

288. The third and final right encompassed in Article 6 § 3 (c), the right to legal aid, is subject to two conditions.

289. First, the accused must show that he lacks sufficient means to pay for legal assistance. He need not, however, do so "beyond all doubt"; it is sufficient that there are "some indications" that this is so or, in other words, that a "lack of clear indications to the contrary" can be established (*Pakelli v. Germany*, Commission report, § 34).

290. Second, the Contracting States are under an obligation to provide legal aid only "where the interests of justice so require". This is to be judged by taking account of the facts of the case as a whole, including not only the situation obtaining at the time the decision on the application for legal aid is handed down but also that obtaining at the time the national court decides on the merits of the case (*Granger v. the United Kingdom*, § 46).

291. In determining whether the interests of justice require an accused to be provided with free legal representation the Court has regard to various criteria, including the seriousness of the offence and the severity of the penalty at stake. In principle, where deprivation of liberty is at stake, the interests of justice call for legal representation (*Benham v. the United Kingdom* [GC], § 61; *Quaranta v. Switzerland*, § 33; *Zdravko Stanev v. Bulgaria*, § 38).

292. As a further condition of the "required by the interests of justice" test the Court considers the complexity of the case (*Quaranta v. Switzerland*, § 34; *Pham Hoang v. France*, § 40; *Twalib v. Greece*, § 53) as well as the personal situation of the accused (*Zdravko Stanev v. Bulgaria*, § 38). The latter requirement is looked at especially with regard to the capacity of the particular accused to present his case-for example, on account of unfamiliarity with the language used at court and/or the particular legal system-were he not granted legal assistance (*Quaranta v. Switzerland*, § 35; *Twalib v. Greece*, § 53).

293. When applying the "interests of justice" requirement the test is not whether the absence of legal aid has caused "actual damage" to the presentation of the defence but a less stringent one: whether it appears "plausible in the particular circumstances" that the lawyer would be of assistance (*Artico v. Italy*, §§ 34-35; *Alimena v. Italy*, § 20).

294. Notwithstanding the importance of a relationship of confidence between lawyer and client, the right to be defended by counsel "of one's own choosing" is necessarily subject to certain limitations where free legal aid is concerned. For example, when appointing defence counsel the courts must have regard to the accused's wishes but these can be overridden when there are relevant and sufficient grounds for holding that this is necessary in the interests of justice (*Croissant v. Germany*, § 29; *Lagerblom v. Sweden*,

§ 54). Similarly, Article 6 § 3 (c) cannot be interpreted as securing a right to have public defence counsel replaced (ibid., § 55). Furthermore, the interests of justice cannot be taken to require an automatic grant of legal aid whenever a convicted person, with no objective likelihood of success, wishes to appeal after having received a fair trial at first instance in accordance with Article 6 (*Monnell and Morris v. the United Kingdom*, § 67).

e. Practical and effective legal assistance

295. Article 6 § 3 (c) enshrines the right to "practical and effective" legal assistance Bluntly, the mere appointment of a legal-aid lawyer does not ensure effective assistance since the lawyer appointed may die, fall seriously ill, be prevented for a protracted period from acting or shirk his duties (*Artico v. Italy*, § 33).

296. The right to effective legal assistance includes, *inter alia*, the accused's right to communicate with his lawyer in private. Only in exceptional circumstances may the State restrict confidential contact between a person in detention and his defence counsel (*Sakhnovskiy v. Russia* [GC], § 102). If a lawyer is unable to confer with his client and receive confidential instructions from him without surveillance, his assistance loses much of its usefulness (*S. v. Switzerland*, § 48; *Brennan v. the United Kingdom*, § 58). Any limitation on relations between clients and lawyers, whether inherent or express, should not thwart the effective legal assistance to which a defendant is entitled (*Sakhnovskiy v. Russia* [GC], § 102). To tap telephone conversations between an accused and his lawyer (*Zagaria v. Italy*, § 36) and to obsessively limit the number and length of lawyers' visits to the accused (*Öcalan v. Turkey* [GC], § 135) represent further possible breaches of the requirement to ensure effective assistance.

297. However, a Contracting State cannot be held responsible for every shortcoming on the part of a lawyer appointed for legal-aid purposes or chosen by the accused (*Lagerblom v. Sweden*, § 56; *Kamasinski v. Austria*, § 65). Owing to the legal profession's independence, the conduct of the defence is essentially a matter between the defendant and his representative; the Contracting States are required to intervene only if a failure by counsel to provide effective representation is manifest or is sufficiently brought to their

attention (ibid. ; *Imbrioscia v. Switzerland*, § 41; *Daud v. Portugal*, § 38). State liability may arise where a lawyer simply fails to act for the accused (*Artico v. Italy*, §§ 33 and 36) or where he fails to comply with a crucial procedural requirement that cannot simply be equated with an injudicious line of defence or a mere defect of argumentation (*Czekalla v. Portugal*, §§ 65 and 71).

4. Examination of witnesses [Article 6 § 3 (d)]

> Article 6 § 3 (d) of the Convention
> "3. Everyone charged with a criminal offence has the following minimum rights:
> ...
> (d) to examine or have examined witnesses against him and to obtain the attendance and examination of witnesses on his behalf under the same conditions as witnesses against him;"

a. Autonomous meaning of the term "witness"

298. The term "witness" has an autonomous meaning in the Convention system, regardless of classifications under national law (*Damir Sibgatullin v. Russia*, § 45; *S. N. v. Sweden*, § 45) Where a deposition may serve to a material degree as the basis for a conviction, it constitutes evidence for the prosecution to which the guarantees provided by Article 6 §§ 1 and 3 (d) of the Convention apply (*Kaste and Mathisen v. Norway*, § 53; *Lucà v. Italy*, § 41).

299. The term includes a co-accused (*Trofimov v. Russia*, § 37), victims (*Vladimir Romanov v. Russia*, § 97) and expert witnesses (*Doorson v. the Netherlands*, §§ 81 – 82).

300. Article 6 § 3 (d) may also be applied to documentary evidence (*Mirilashvili v. Russia*, §§ 158 – 159).

b. Right to examine or have examined witnesses

i. General principles

301. Article 6 § 3 (d) enshrines the principle that, before an accused can be

convicted, all evidence against him must normally be produced in his presence at a public hearing with a view to adversarial argument. Exceptions to this principle are possible but must not infringe the rights of the defence, which, as a rule, require that the accused should be given an adequate and proper opportunity to challenge and question a witness against him, either when that witness makes his statement or at a later stage of proceedings (*Hümmer v. Germany*, § 38; *Lucà v. Italy*, § 39; *Solakov v. the former Yugoslav Republic of Macedonia*, § 57).

302. There are two requirements which follow from the above general principle. First, there must be a good reason for the non-attendance of a witness. Second, when a conviction is based solely or to a decisive degree on depositions that have been made by a person whom the accused has had no opportunity to examine or to have examined, whether during the investigation or at the trial, the rights of the defence may be restricted to an extent that is incompatible with the guarantees provided by Article 6 (the so-called "sole or decisive rule") (*Al-Khawaja and Tahery v. the United Kingdom* [GC], § 119).

303. Having regard to the place that the right to a fair administration of justice holds in a democratic society, any measures restricting the rights of the defence should be strictly necessary. If a less restrictive measure can suffice then that measure should be applied (*Van Mechelen and Others v. the Netherlands*, § 58).

304. The possibility for the accused to confront a material witness in the presence of a judge is an important element of a fair trial (*Tarău v. Romania*, § 74; *Graviano v. Italy*, § 38).

ii. Duty to make a reasonable effort in securing attendance of a witness

305. The requirement that there be a good reason for the non-attendance of a witness is a preliminary question which must be examined before any consideration is given as to whether that evidence was sole or decisive. When witnesses do not attend to give live evidence, there is a duty to enquire whether their absence is justified (*Al-Khawaja and Tahery v. the United Kingdom* [GC], § 120; *Gabrielyan v. Armenia*, §§ 78, 8184).

306. Article 6 § 1 taken together with § 3 requires the Contracting States to take positive steps to enable the accused to examine or have examined witnesses against him (*Trofimov v. Russia*, § 33; *Sadak and Others v. Turkey* (no. 1), § 67).

307. In the event that the impossibility of examining the witnesses or having them examined is due to the fact that they are missing, the authorities must make a reasonable effort to secure their presence (*Karpenko v. Russia*, § 62; *Damir Sibgatullin v. Russia*, § 51; *Pello v. Estonia*, § 35; *Bonev v. Bulgaria*, § 43).

308. However, *impossibilium nulla est obligatio*; provided that the authorities cannot be accused of a lack of diligence in their efforts to afford the defendant an opportunity to examine the witnesses in question, the witnesses' unavailability as such does not make it necessary to discontinue the prosecution [*Gossa v. Poland*, § 55; *Haas v. Germany* (dec.); *Calabrò v. Italy and Germany* (dec.); *Ubach Mortes v. Andorra* (dec.)].

iii. Duty to give reasons for refusal to hear a witness

309. Although it is not the Court's function to express an opinion on the relevance of the evidence produced, failure to justify a refusal to examine or call a witness can amount to a limitation of defence rights that is incompatible with the guarantees of a fair trial (*Popov v. Russia*, § 188; *Bocos-Cuesta v. the Netherlands*, § 72; *Wierzbicki v. Poland*, § 45; *Vidal v. Belgium*, § 34).

iv. Reliance on witness testimony not adduced in court

310. It may prove necessary in certain circumstances to refer to depositions made during the investigative stage (*Lucà v. Italy*, § 40), for example, when a witness has died (*Mika v. Sweden* (dec.), § 37; *Ferrantelli and Santangelo v. Italy*, § 52) or has exercised the right to remain silent (*Vidgen v. the Netherlands*, § 47; *Sofri and Others v. Italy* (dec.); *Craxi v. Italy* (no.1), § 86), or when reasonable efforts by the authorities to secure the attendance of a witness have failed (*Mirilashvili v. Russia*, § 217).

311. Given the extent to which the absence of a witness adversely affects the rights of the defence, when a witness has not been examined at any prior stage of the proceedings, allowing the admission of a witness statement in lieu of live evidence at trial must be a measure of last resort (*Al-Khawaja and Tahery v. the United Kingdom* [GC], § 125).

312. Evidence obtained from a witness under conditions in which the rights of the defence cannot be secured to the extent normally required by the Convention should be

treated with extreme care (*S. N. v. Sweden*, § 53; *Doorson v. the Netherlands*, § 76).

313. If a witness was unavailable for adversarial examination for good reason, it is open to a domestic court to have regard to the statements made by the witness at the pre-trial stage, if these statements are corroborated by other evidence (*Mirilashvili v. Russia*, § 217; *Scheper v. the Netherlands* (dec.); *Calabrò v. Italy and Germany* (dec.); *Ferrantelli and Santangelo v. Italy*, § 52).

314. Article 6 § 3 (d) only requires the possibility of cross-examining witnesses whose testimony was not adduced before the trial court in situations where this testimony played a main or decisive role in securing the conviction (*Kok v. the Netherlands* (dec.); *Krasniki v. the Czech Republic*, § 79)

315. Even where a hearsay statement is the sole or decisive evidence against a defendant, its admission as evidence will not automatically result in a breach of Article 6 § 1. However, the fact that a conviction is based solely or to a decisive extent on the statement of an absent witness would constitute a very important factor to weigh in the scales and one which would require sufficient counterbalancing factors, including the existence of strong procedural safeguards. The question in each case is whether there are sufficient counterbalancing factors in place, including measures that permit a fair and proper assessment of the reliability of that evidence to take place. This would permit a conviction to be based on such evidence only if it is sufficiently reliable given its importance in the case (*Al-Khawaja and Tahery v. the United Kingdom* [GC], § 147).

v. Anonymous witnesses

316. While the problems raised by anonymous and absent witnesses are not identical, the two situations are not different in principle, since each results in a potential disadvantage for the defendant. The underlying principle is that the defendant in a criminal trial should have an effective opportunity to challenge the evidence against him (*Al-Khawaja and Tahery v. the United Kingdom* [GC], § 127).

317. The use of statements made by anonymous witnesses to found a conviction is not under all circumstances incompatible with the Convention (*Doorson v. the Netherlands*,

§ 69; *Van Mechelen and Others v. the Netherlands*, § 52; *Krasniki v. the Czech Republic*, § 76).

318. While Article 6 does not explicitly require the interests of witnesses to be taken into consideration, their life, liberty or security of person may be at stake, as may interests coming generally within the ambit of Article 8 of the Convention. Contracting States should organise their criminal proceedings in such a way that those interests are not unjustifiably imperilled. The principles of a fair trial therefore require that in appropriate cases the interests of the defence are balanced against those of witnesses or victims called upon to testify (*Doorson v. the Netherlands*, § 70; *Van Mechelen and Others v. the Netherlands*, § 53).

319. The national authorities must have adduced relevant and sufficient reasons to keep secret the identity of certain witnesses [*Doorson v. the Netherlands*, § 71; *Visser v. the Netherlands*, § 47; *Sapunarescu v. Germany* (dec.); *Dzelili v. Germany* (dec.)].

320. If the anonymity of prosecution witnesses is maintained, the defence will be faced with difficulties which criminal proceedings should not normally involve. In such cases, the handicaps under which the defence labours must be sufficiently counterbalanced by the procedures followed by the judicial authorities [*Doorson v. the Netherlands*, § 72; *Van Mechelen and Others v. the Netherlands*, § 54; *Haas v. Germany* (dec.)].

321. In particular, an applicant should not be prevented from testing the anonymous witness's reliability (*Birutis and Others v. Lithuania*, § 29; *Van Mechelen and Others v. the Netherlands*, §§ 59 and 62; *Kostovski v. the Netherlands*, § 42).

322. In addition, when assessing whether the procedures followed in the questioning of an anonymous witness was sufficient to counterbalance the difficulties caused to the defence, due weight has to be given to the extent to which the anonymous testimony was decisive in convicting the applicant. If this testimony was not in any respect decisive, the defence was handicapped to a much lesser degree [*Kok v. the Netherlands* (dec.); *Krasniki v. the Czech Republic*, § 79].

vi. Witnesses in sexual abuse cases

323. Criminal proceedings concerning sexual offences are often conceived of as an

ordeal by the victim, in particular when the latter is unwillingly confronted with the defendant. These features are even more prominent in a case involving a minor. In the assessment of the question whether or not in such proceedings an accused received a fair trial, the right to respect for the private life of the alleged victim must be taken into account. Therefore, in criminal proceedings concerning sexual abuse, certain measures may be taken for the purpose of protecting the victim, provided that such measures can be reconciled with the adequate and effective exercise of the rights of the defence. In securing the rights of the defence, the judicial authorities may be required to take measures which counterbalance the handicaps under which the defence labours (*Aigner v. Austria*, § 37; *D. v. Finland*, § 43; *F and M v. Finland*, § 58; *Accardi and Others v. Italy* (dec.); *S. N. v. Sweden*, § 47; *Vronchenko v. Estonia*, § 56).

324. Having regard to the special features of criminal proceedings concerning sexual offences, Article 6 § 3 (d) cannot be interpreted as requiring in all cases that questions be put directly by the accused or his or her defence counsel, through cross-examination or by other means (*S. N. v. Sweden*, § 52; *W. S. v. Poland*, § 55).

325. The accused must be able to observe the demeanour of the witnesses under questioning and to challenge their statements and credibility (*Bocos-Cuesta v. the Netherlands*, § 71; *P. S. v. Germany*, § 26; *Accardi and Others v. Italy* (dec.); *S. N. v. Sweden*, § 52).

326. The viewing of a video recording of a witness account cannot be regarded alone as sufficiently safeguarding the rights of the defence where no opportunity to put questions to a person giving the account has been afforded by the authorities (*D. v. Finland*, § 50; *A. L. v. Finland*, § 41).

vii. Advantages offered to witnesses in exchange for their statements

327. The use of statements made by witnesses in exchange for immunity or other advantages forms an important tool in the domestic authorities' fight against serious crime. However, the use of such statements may put in question the fairness of the proceedings against the accused and is capable of raising delicate issues as, by their very nature, such statements are open to manipulation and may be made purely in order to obtain the

advantages offered in exchange, or for personal revenge. The sometimes ambiguous nature of such statements and the risk that a person might be accused and tried on the basis of unverified allegations that are not necessarily disinterested must not, therefore, be underestimated. However, the use of these kinds of statements does not in itself suffice to render the proceedings unfair [*Cornelis v. the Netherlands* (dec.), with further references].

viii. Hearsay

328. Article 6 §§ 1 and 3 (d) of the Convention contain a presumption against the use of hearsay evidence against a defendant in criminal proceedings. Exclusion of the use of hearsay evidence is also justified when that evidence may be considered to assist the defence [*Thomas v. the United Kingdom* (dec.)].

ix. Right to call witnesses for the defence

329. As a general rule, it is for the national courts to assess the evidence before them as well as the relevance of the evidence which defendants seek to adduce. Article 6 § 3 (d) leaves it to them, again as a general rule, to assess whether it is appropriate to call witnesses. It does not require the attendance and examination of every witness on the accused's behalf; its essential aim, as is indicated by the words "under the same conditions", is full "equality of arms" in the matter (*Perna v. Italy* [GC], § 29; *Solakov v. the former Yugoslav Republic of Macedonia*, § 57).

330. It is accordingly not sufficient for a defendant to complain that he has not been allowed to question certain witnesses; he must, in addition, support his request by explaining why it is important for the witnesses concerned to be heard, and their evidence must be necessary for the establishment of the truth and the rights of the defence (*Perna v. Italy* [GC], § 29; *Băcanu and SC 'R' S.A. v. Romania*, § 75).

331. When a request by a defendant to examine witnesses is not vexatious, is sufficiently reasoned, is relevant to the subject matter of the accusation and could arguably have strengthened the position of the defence or even led to his acquittal, the domestic authorities must provide relevant reasons for dismissing such a request (*Topić v. Croatia*, § 42; *Polyakov v. Russia*, §§ 34 – 35).

332. Article 6 does not grant the accused an unlimited right to secure the appearance of witnesses in court. It is normally for the national courts to decide whether it is necessary or advisable to examine a witness [*S. N. v. Sweden*, § 44; *Accardi and Others v. Italy* (dec.)].

333. There might be exceptional circumstances which could prompt the Court to conclude that the failure to examine a person as a witness was incompatible with Article 6 (*Dorokhov v. Russia*, § 65; *Popov v. Russia*, § 188; *Bricmont v. Belgium*, § 89).

5. Interpretation [Article 6 § 3 (e)]

> Article 6 § 3 (e) of the Convention
>
> "3. Everyone charged with a criminal offence has the following minimum rights:
>
> ...
>
> (e) to have the free assistance of an interpreter if he cannot understand or speak the language used in court."

a. If the accused "cannot understand or speak the language used in court"

334. The right to free assistance of an interpreter applies exclusively in situations where the accused cannot understand or speak the language used in court (*K. v. France*, Commission decision). An accused who understands that language cannot insist upon the services of an interpreter to allow him to conduct his defence in another language, including a language of an ethnic minority of which he is a member (ibid.; *Bideault v. France*, Commission decision; *Lagerblom v. Sweden*, § 62).

335. Where the accused is represented by a lawyer, it will generally not be sufficient that the accused's lawyer, but not the accused, knows the language used in court. Interpretation of the proceedings is required as the right to a fair trial, which includes the right to participate in the hearing, requires that the accused be able to understand the proceedings and to inform his lawyer of any point that should be made in his defence (*Kamasinski v. Austria*, § 74; *Cuscani v. the United Kingdom*, § 38).

336. Article 6 § 3 (e) does not cover the relations between the accused and his

counsel but only applies to the relations between the accused and the judge (*X. v. Austria*, Commission decision).

337. The right to an interpreter may be waived, but this must be a decision of the accused, not of his lawyer (*Kamasinski v. Austria*, § 80).

b. Protected elements of the criminal proceedings

338. Article 6 § 3 (e) guarantees the right to the free assistance of an interpreter for translation or interpretation of all documents or statements in the proceedings which it is necessary for the accused to understand or to have rendered into the court's language in order to have the benefit of a fair trial (*Luedicke, Belkacem and Koç v. Germany*, § 48; *Ucak v. the United Kingdom* (dec.); *Hermi v. Italy* [GC], § 69; *Lagerblom v. Sweden*, § 61).

339. Article 6 § 3 (e) applies not only to oral statements made at the trial hearing but also to documentary material and the pre-trial proceedings (*Kamasinski v. Austria*, § 74; *Hermi v. Italy* [GC], § 70).

340. However, it does not go so far as to require a written translation of all items of written evidence or official documents in the proceedings (*Kamasinski v. Austria*, § 74). For example, the absence of a written translation of a judgment does not in itself entail a violation of Article 6 § 3 (e) (ibid., § 85). The text of Article 6 § 3 (e) refers to an "interpreter", not a "translator". This suggests that oral linguistic assistance may satisfy the requirements of the Convention (*Husain v. Italy* (dec.); *Hermi v. Italy* [GC], § 70).

341. In sum, the interpretation assistance provided should be such as to enable the defendant to have knowledge of the case against him and to defend himself, notably by being able to put before the court his or her version of the events (ibid.; *Kamasinski v. Austria*, § 74; *Güngör v. Germany* (dec.); *Protopapa v. Turkey*, § 80).

c. "Free" assistance

342. The obligation to provide "free" assistance is not dependent upon the accused's means; the services of an interpreter for the accused are instead a part of the facilities required of a State in organising its system of criminal justice. However, an accused may

be charged for an interpreter provided for him at a hearing that he fails to attend [*Fedele v. Germany* (dec.)].

343. The costs of interpretation cannot be subsequently claimed back from the accused (*Luedicke, Belkacem and Koç v. Germany*, § 46). To read Article 6 § 3 (e) as allowing the domestic courts to make a convicted person bear these costs would amount to limiting in time the benefit of the Article (ibid. , § 42; *Işyar v. Bulgaria*, § 45; *Öztürk v. Germany*, § 58).

d. Conditions of interpretation

344. It is not appropriate to lay down any detailed conditions under Article 6 § 3 (e) concerning the method by which interpreters may be provided to assist accused persons. An interpreter is not part of the court or tribunal within the meaning of Article 6 § 1 and there is no formal requirement of independence or impartiality as such. The services of the interpreter must provide the accused with effective assistance in conducting his defence and the interpreter's conduct must not be of such a nature as to impinge on the fairness of the proceedings [*Ucak v. the United Kingdom* (dec.)].

e. Positive obligations

345. The verification of the applicant's need for interpretation facilities is a matter for the judge to determine in consultation with the applicant, especially if he has been alerted to counsel's difficulties in communicating with the applicant. The judge has to reassure himself that the absence of an interpreter would not prejudice the applicant's full involvement in a matter of crucial importance for him (*Cuscani v. the United Kingdom*, § 38).

346. While it is true that the conduct of the defence is essentially a matter between the defendant and his counsel (*Kamasinski v. Austria*, § 65; *Stanford v. the United Kingdom*, § 28), the ultimate guardians of the fairness of the proceedings-encompassing, among other aspects, the possible absence of translation or interpretation for a non-national defendant-are the domestic courts (*Cuscani v. the United Kingdom*, § 39; *Hermi v. Italy* [GC], § 72; *Katritsch v. France*, § 44).

347. The defendant's linguistic knowledge is vital and the court must also examine the nature of the offence with which the defendant is charged and any communications

addressed to him by the domestic authorities, in order to assess whether they are sufficiently complex to require a detailed knowledge of the language used in court [*Hermi v. Italy* [GC], § 71; *Katritsch v. France*, § 41; *Şaman v. Turkey*, § 30; *Güngör v. Germany* (dec.)].

348. In view of the need for the right guaranteed by Article 6 § 3(e) to be practical and effective, the obligation of the competent authorities is not limited to the appointment of an interpreter but, if they are put on notice in the particular circumstances, may also extend to a degree of subsequent control over the adequacy of the interpretation provided (*Kamasinski v. Austria*, § 74; *Hermi v. Italy* [GC], § 70; *Protopapa v. Turkey*, § 80).

VI. Extra-territorial effect of Article 6

349. The Convention does not require the Contracting Parties to impose its standards on third States or territories (*Drozd and Janousek v. France and Spain*, § 110). The Contracting Parties are not obliged to verify whether a trial to be held in a third State following extradition, for example, would be compatible with all the requirements of Article 6.

A. Flagrant denial of justice

350. According to the Court's case-law, however, an issue might exceptionally arise under Article 6 as a result of an extradition or expulsion decision in circumstances where the individual would risk suffering a flagrant denial of a fair trial, i.e. a flagrant denial of justice, in the requesting country. This principle was first set out in *Soering v. the United Kingdom* (§ 113) and has subsequently been confirmed by the Court in a number of cases (*Mamatkulov and Askarov v. Turkey* [GC], §§ 90-91; *Al-Saadoon and Mufdhi v. the United Kingdom*, § 149; *Ahorugeze v. Sweden*, § 115; *Othman (Abu Qatada) v. the United Kingdom*, § 258).

351. The term "flagrant denial of justice" has been considered synonymous with a trial

which is manifestly contrary to the provisions of Article 6 or the principles embodied therein (*Sejdovic v. Italy* [GC], § 84; *Stoichkov v. Bulgaria*, § 56; *Drozd and Janousek v. France and Spain*, § 110). Although it has not yet been required to define the term in more precise terms, the Court has nonetheless indicated that certain forms of unfairness could amount to a flagrant denial of justice. These have included:

- conviction *in absentia* with no subsequent possibility of a fresh determination of the merits of the charge (*Einhorn v. France* (dec.), § 33; *Sejdovic v. Italy* [GC], § 84; *Stoichkov v. Bulgaria*, § 56);
- a trial which is summary in nature and conducted with a total disregard for the rights of the defence (*Bader and Kanbor v. Sweden*, § 47);
- detention without any access to an independent and impartial tribunal to have the legality of the detention reviewed (*Al-Moayad v. Germany* (dec.), § 101);
- deliberate and systematic refusal of access to a lawyer, especially for an individual detained in a foreign country (ibid.);
- use in criminal proceedings of statements obtained as a result of a suspect's or another person's treatment in breach of Article 3 (*Othman (Abu Qatada) v. the United Kingdom*, § 267; *El Haski v. Belgium*, § 85).

352. It took over twenty years from the *Soering v. the United Kingdom* judgment-that is, until the Court's 2012 ruling in the case of *Othman (Abu Qatada) v. the United Kingdom*-for the Court to find for the first time that an extradition or expulsion would in fact violate Article 6. This indicates, as is also demonstrated by the examples given in the preceding paragraph, that the "flagrant denial of justice" test is a stringent one. A flagrant denial of justice goes beyond mere irregularities or lack of safeguards in the trial proceedings such as might result in a breach of Article 6 if occurring within the Contracting State itself. What is required is a breach of the principles of a fair trial guaranteed by Article 6 which is so fundamental as to amount to a nullification, or destruction of the very essence, of the right guaranteed by that Article (*Ahorugeze v. Sweden*, § 115; *Othman (Abu Qatada) v. the United Kingdom*, § 260).

B. The "real risk": standard and burden of proof

353. When examining whether an extradition or expulsion would amount to a flagrant denial of justice, the Court considers that the same standard and burden of proof should apply as in the examination of extraditions and expulsions under Article 3. Accordingly, it is for the applicant to adduce evidence capable of proving that there are substantial grounds for believing that, if removed from a Contracting State, he would be exposed to a real risk of being subjected to a flagrant denial of justice. Where such evidence is adduced, it is for the Government to dispel any doubts about it (*Ahorugeze v. Sweden*, § 116; *Othman (Abu Qatada) v. the United Kingdom*, §§ 272 – 280; *El Haski v. Belgium*, § 86; *Saadi v. Italy* [GC], § 129).

354. In order to determine whether there is a risk of a flagrant denial of justice, the Court must examine the foreseeable consequences of sending the applicant to the receiving country, bearing in mind the general situation there and his personal circumstances (*Al-Saadoon and Mufdhi v. the United Kingdom*, § 125; *Saadi v. Italy* [GC], § 130). The existence of the risk must be assessed primarily with reference to those facts which were known or ought to have been known to the Contracting State at the time of expulsion (*Al-Saadoon and Mufdhi v. the United Kingdom*, § 125; *Saadi v. Italy* [GC], § 133). Where the expulsion or transfer has already taken place by the date on which it examines the case, however, the Court is not precluded from having regard to information which comes to light subsequently (*Al-Saadoon and Mufdhi v. the United Kingdom*, § 149; *Mamatkulov and Askarov v. Turkey* [GC], § 69).

List of cited cases

The case-law cited in this Guide refers to judgments or decisions delivered by the Court and to decisions or reports of the European Commission of Human Rights ("the Commission").

Unless otherwise indicated, all references are to a judgment on the merits delivered by a Chamber of the Court. The abbreviation "(dec.)" indicates that the citation is of a decision of the Court and "[GC]" that the case was heard by the Grand Chamber.

Thehyperlinks to the cases cited in the electronic version of the Guide are directed to the HUDOC database (〈http://hudoc.echr.coe.int〉) which provides access to the case-law of the Court (Grand Chamber, Chamber and Committee judgments and decisions, communicated cases, advisory opinions and legal summaries from the Case-Law Information Note) and of the Commission (decisions and reports), and to the resolutions of the Committee of Ministers.

The Court delivers its judgments and decisions in English and/or French, its two official languages. HUDOC also contains translations of many important cases into more than thirty non-official languages, and links to around one hundred online case-law collections produced by third parties.

— A —

A. v. Austria, no. 16266/90, Commission decision of 7 May 1990, Decisions and Reports 65

A. Menarini Diagnostics S. R. L. v. Italy, no. 43509/08, 27 September 2011

A. L. v. Finland, no. 23220/04, 27 January 2009

A. L. v. Germany, no. 72758/01, 28 April 2005

Abdoella v. the Netherlands, 25 November 1992, Series A no. 248 – A

Accardiand Others v. Italy (dec.), no. 30598/02, ECHR 2005 – II

Adilettaand Others v. Italy, 19 February 1991, Series A no. 197 – E

Adolf v. Austria, 26 March 1982, series A no. 49

AGOSI v. the United Kingdom, 24 October 1986, Series A no. 108

Ahorugeze v. Sweden, no. 37075/09, 27 October 2011

Aigner v. Austria, no. 28328/03, 10 May 2012

Air Canada v. the United Kingdom, 5 May 1995, Series A no. 316 – A

Akay v. Turkey (dec.), no. 34501/97, 19 February 2002

Al-Khawaja and Tahery v. the United Kingdom [GC], nos. 26766/05 and 22228/06, ECHR 2011

Al-Moayad v. Germany (dec.), no. 35865/03, 20 February 2007

Al-Saadoon and Mufdhi v. the United Kingdom, no. 61498/08, ECHR 2010

Albert and Le Compte v. Belgium, 10 February 1983, Series A no. 58

Ali v. Romania, no. 20307/02, 9 November 2010

Alimena v. Italy, 19 February 1991, Series A no. 195 – D

Allan v. the United Kingdom, no. 48539/99, ECHR 2002 – IX

Allen v. the United Kingdom [GC], no. 25424/09, ECHR 2013

Allenet de Ribemont v. France, 10 February 1995, Series A no. 308

Arrigo and Vella v. Malta (dec.), no. 6569/04, 10 May 2005

Artico v. Italy, 13 May 1980, Series A no. 37

Assanidze v. Georgia [GC], no. 71503/01, ECHR 2004 – II

Averill v. the United Kingdom, no. 36408/97, ECHR 2000 – VI

— B —

B. v. Austria, 28 March 1990, Series A no. 175

B. and P. v. the United Kingdom, nos. 36337/97 and 35974/97, ECHR 2001 – III

Băcanu and SC 《 R 》 S. A. v. Romania, no. 4411/04, 3 March 2009

Bäckström and Andersson v. Sweden (dec.), no. 67930/01, 5 September 2006

Bader and Kanbor v. Sweden, no. 13284/04, ECHR 2005 – XI

Baggetta v. Italy, 25 June 1987, Series A no. 119

Balsyte-Lideikiene v. Lithuania, no. 72596/01, 4 November 2008

Bannikova v. Russia, no. 18757/06, 4 November 2010

Barberà, Messegué and Jabardo v. Spain, 6 December 1988, Series A no. 146

Baucher v. France, no. 53640/00, 24 July 2007

Belashev v. Russia, no. 28617/03, 4 December 2008

Belilos v. Switzerland, 29 April 1988, Series A no. 132

Bellerín Lagares v. Spain (dec.), no. 31548/02, 4 November 2003

Bendenoun v. France, 24 February 1994, Series A no. 284

Benham v. the United Kingdom, 10 June 1996, Reports of Judgments and Decisions 1996 – Ⅲ

Berliński v. Poland, nos. 27715/95 and 30209/96, 20 June 2002

Bideault v. France, no. 11261/84, Commission decision of 9 December 1987, Decisions and Reports 48

Birutisand Others v. Lithuania, nos. 47698/99 and 48115/99, 28 March 2002

Block v. Hungary, no. 56282/09, 25 January 2011

Bobek v. Poland, no. 68761/01, 17 July 2007

Bocos-Cuesta v. the Netherlands, no. 54789/00, 10 November 2005

Boddaert v. Belgium, 12 October 1992, Series A no. 235 – D

Böhmer v. Germany, no. 37568/97, 3 October 2002

Boldea v. Romania, no. 19997/02, 15 February 2007

Bonev v. Bulgaria, no. 60018/00, 8 June 2006

Bonisch v. Austria, 6 May 1985, Series A no. 92

Bonzi v. Switzerland, no. 7854/77, Commission decision of 12 July 1978, Decisions and Reports 12

Boulois v. Luxembourg [GC], no. 37575/04, ECHR 2012

Borisova v. Bulgaria, no. 56891/00, 21 December 2006

Borgers v. Belgium, 30 October 1991, Series A no. 214 – B

Brandstetter v. Austria, 28 August 1991, Series A no. 211

Brennan v. the UnitedKingdom, no. 39846/98, ECHR 2001 – X

Bricmont v. Belgium, 7 July 1989, Series A no. 158

Brozicek v. Italy, 19 December 1989, Series A no. 167

Brusco v. France, no. 1466/07, 14 October 2010

Buijen v. Germany, no. 27804/05, 1 April 2010

Bulut v. Austria, 22 February 1996, Reports of Judgments and Decisions 1996 – II

Burak Hun v. Turkey, no. 17570/04, 15 December 2009

Buscemi v. Italy, no. 29569/95, ECHR 1999 – VI

Butkevičius v. Lithuania, no. 48297/99, ECHR 2002 – II (extracts)

Bykov v. Russia [GC], no. 4378/02, 10 March 2009

— C —

C. v. Italy, no. 10889/84, Commission decision of 11 May 1988, Decisions and Reports 56

C. G. P. v. the Netherlands, no. 29835/96, Commission decision of 15 January 1997

C. P. and Others v. France, no. 36009/97, 1 August 2000

Campbell and Fell v. the United Kingdom, 28 June 1984, Series A no. 80

Calabrò v. Italy and Germany (dec.), no. 59895/00, ECHR 2002 – V

Caldas Ramírez de Arrellano v. Spain (dec.), no. 68874/01, ECHR 2003 – I (extracts)

Can v. Austria, no. 9300/81, Commission report of 12 July 1984

Capeau v. Belgium, no. 42914/98, ECHR 2005 – I

Casse v. Luxembourg, no. 40327/02, 27 April 2006

Castillo Algar v. Spain, 28 October 1998, Reports of Judgments and Decisions 1998 – VIII

Célice v. France, no. 14166/09, 8 March 2012

Chichlian and Ekindjian v. France, no. 10959/84, Commission report of 16 March 1989

Clarke v. the United Kingdom (dec.), no. 23695/02, 25 August 2005

Clinique Mozart SARL v. France, no. 46098/99, 8 June 2004

Coëme and Others v. Belgium, nos. 32492/96 and 4 others, ECHR 2000 – VII

Collozza and Rubinat v. Italy, no. 9024/80, Commission report of 5 May 1983, Series A no. 89

Constantin and Stoian v. Romania, nos. 23782/06 and 46629/06, 29 September 2009

Cooper v. the United Kingdom [GC], no. 48843/99, 16 December 2003

Cornelis v. the Netherlands (dec.), no. 994/03, ECHR 2004 – V (extracts)

Correia de Matos v. Portugal (dec.), no. 48188/99, ECHR 2001 – XII

Craxi v. Italy (no. 1), no. 34896/97, 5 December 2002

Croissant v. Germany, 25 September 1992, Series A no. 237 – B

Cuscani v. the United Kingdom, no. 32771/96, 24 September 2002

Czekalla v. Portugal, no. 38830/97, ECHR 2002 – VIII

— D —

D. v. Finland, no. 30542/04, 7 July 2009

Daktaras v. Lithuania (dec.), no. 42095/98, 11 January 2000

Daktaras v. Lithuania, no. 42095/98, ECHR 2000 – X

Dallos v. Hungary, no. 29082/95, ECHR 2001 – II

Damir Sibgatullin v. Russia, no. 1413/05, 24 April 2012

Daud v. Portugal, 21 April 1998, Reports of Judgments and Decisions 1998 – II

Davran v. Turkey, no. 18342/03, 3 November 2009

Dayanan v. Turkey, no. 7377/03, 13 October 2009

De Cubber v. Belgium, 26 October 1984, Series A no. 86

De Salvador Torres v. Spain, 24 October 1996, Reports of Judgments and Decisions 1996 – V

Delcourt v. Belgium, 17 January 1970, Series A no. 11

Demicoli v. Malta, 27 August 1991, Series A no. 210

Deweer v. Belgium, 27 February 1980, Series A no. 35

Didu v. Romania, no. 34814/02, 14 April 2009

Diriöz v. Turkey, no. 38560/04, 31 May 2012

Dobbertin v. France, 25 February 1993, Series A no. 256 – D

Doorson v. the Netherlands, 26 March 1996, Reports of Judgments and Decisions 1996 – II

Dorokhov v. Russia, no. 66802/01, 14 February 2008

Dorozhko and Pozharskiy v. Estonia, nos. 14659/04 and 16855/04, 24 April 2008

Döry v. Sweden, no. 28394/95, 12 November 2002

Dowsett v. the United Kingdom, no. 39482/98, ECHR 2003 – Ⅶ

Drassich v. Italy, no. 25575/04, 11 December 2007

Drozd and Janousek v. France and Spain, 26 June 1992, Series A no. 240

Dubus S. A. v. France, no. 5242/04, 11 June 2009

Dzelili v. Germany (dec.), no. 15065/05, 29 September 2009

— E —

Eckle v. Germany, 15 July 1982, series A no. 51

Edwards and Lewis v. the United Kingdom [GC], nos. 39647/98 and 40461/98, ECHR 2004 – Ⅹ

Einhorn v. France (dec.), no. 71555/01, ECHR 2001 – Ⅺ

El Haski v. Belgium, no. 649/08, 25 September 2012

Enea v. Italy [GC], no. 74912/01, ECHR 2009

Engeland Others v. the Netherlands, 8 June 1976, Series A no. 22

Erdogan v. Turkey, no. 14723/89, Commission decision of 9 July 1992, Decisions and Reports 73

Ergin v. Turkey (no. 6), no. 47533/99, ECHR 2006 – Ⅵ (extracts)

Eurofinacom v. France (dec.), no. 58753/00, ECHR 2004 – Ⅶ

Ezeh and Connors v. the United Kingdom [GC], nos. 39665/98 and 40086/98, 9 October 2003, ECHR 2003Ⅹ

— F —

F and M v. Finland, no. 22508/02, 17 July 2007

Falk v. the Netherlands (dec.), no. 66273/01, ECHR 2004 – Ⅺ

Fatullayev v. Azerbaijan, no. 40984/07, 22 April 2010

Fazliyski v. Bulgaria, no. 40908/05, 16 April 2013

Fedele v. Germany (dec.), no. 11311/84, 9 December 1987

Fejde v. Sweden, 29 October 1991, Series A no. 212 – C

Ferrantelli and Santangelo v. Italy, 7 August 1996, Reports of Judgments and Decisions 1996 – Ⅲ

Fey v. Austria, 24 February 1993, Series A no. 255 – A

Filippini v. San Marino (dec.), no. 10526/02, 28 August 2003

Findlay v. the United Kingdom, 25 February 1997, Reports of Judgments and Decisions 1997 – I

Fischer v. Austria (dec.), no. 27569/02, ECHR 2003 – VI

Foucher v. France, 18 March 1997, Reports of Judgments and Decisions 1997 – II

Fruni v. Slovakia, no. 8014/07, 21 June 2011

Funke v. France, 25 February 1993, Series A no. 256 – A

— G —

G. B. v. France, no. 44069/98, ECHR 2001 – X

Gabrielyan v. Armenia, no. 8088/05, 10 April 2012

Gäfgen v. Germany [GC], no. 22978/05, ECHR 2010

Galstyan v. Armenia, no. 26986/03, 15 November 2007

Garycki v. Poland, no. 14348/02, 6 February 2007

Gast and Popp v. Germany, no. 29357/95, ECHR 2000 – II

Geerings v. the Netherlands, no. 30810/03, ECHR 2007 – III

Giosakis v. Greece (no. 3), no. 5689/08, 3 May 2011

Goddi v. Italy, 9 April 1984, Series A no. 76

Goktepe v. Belgium, no. 50372/99, 2 June 2005

Gorgiladze v. Georgia, no. 4313/04, 20 October 2009

Gossa v. Poland, no. 47986/99, 9 January 2007

Gómez de Liaño y Botella v. Spain, no. 21369/04, 22 July 2008

Gradinger v. Austria, 23 October 1995, Series A no. 328 – C

Granger v. the United Kingdom, 28 March 1990, Series A no. 174

Graviano v. Italy, no. 10075/02, 10 February 2005

Grayson and Barnham v. the United Kingdom, nos. 19955/05 and 15085/06, 23 September 2008

Gregačević v. Croatia, no. 58331/09, 10 July 2012

Grieves v. the United Kingdom [GC], no. 57067/00, ECHR 2003 – XII (extracts)

Guérin v. France, 29 July 1998, Reports of Judgments and Decisions 1998 – V

Guisset v. France, no. 33933/96, ECHR 2000 – IX

Güngör v. Germany (dec.), no. 31540/96, 24 January 2002

Gurguchiani v. Spain, no. 16012/06, 15 December 2009

— H —

Haas v. Germany (dec.), no. 73047/01, 17 November 2005

Hadjianastassiou v. Greece, 16 December 1992, Series A no. 252

Hamer v. Belgium, no. 21861/03, ECHR 2007 – V (extracts)

Hanif and Khan v. the United Kingdom, nos. 52999/08 and 61779/08, 20 December 2011

Harabin v. Slovakia, no. 58688/11, 20 November 2012

Harutyunyan v. Armenia, no. 36549/03, ECHR 2007 – III

Hauschildt v. Denmark, 24 May 1989, Series A no. 154

Heaney and McGuinness v. Ireland, no. 34720/97, ECHR 2000 – XII

Heglas v. the Czech Republic, no. 5935/02, 1 March 2007

Henryk Urban and Ryszard Urban v. Poland, no. 23614/08, 30 November 2010

Hermi v. Italy [GC], no. 18114/02, ECHR 2006 – XII

Holm v. Sweden, 25 November 1993, Series A no. 279 – A

Hümmer v. Germany, no. 26171/07, 19 July 2012

Husain v. Italy (dec.), no. 18913/03, ECHR 2005 – III

Hüseyin Turan v. Turkey, no. 11529/02, 4 March 2008

Huseyn and Others v. Azerbaijan, nos. 35485/05 and 3 others, 26 July 2011

— I —

I. A. v. France, 23 September 1998, Reports of Judgments and Decisions 1998 – VII

I. H. and Others v. Austria, no. 42780/98, 20 April 2006

Iglin v. Ukraine, no. 39908/05, 12 January 2012

Imbrioscia v. Switzerland, 24 November 1993, Series A no. 275

Incal v. Turkey, 9 June 1998, Reports of Judgments and Decisions 1998 – IV

Iprahim Ülger v. Turkey, no. 57250/00, 29 July 2004

Ismoilovand Others v. Russia, no. 2947/06, 24 April 2008

Işyar v. Bulgaria, no. 391/03, 20 November 2008

— J —

Jalloh v. Germany [GC], no. 54810/00, ECHR 2006 – IX

Janosevic v. Sweden, no. 34619/97, ECHR 2002 – VII

Jasper v. the United Kingdom [GC], no. 27052/95, 16 February 2000

John Murray v. the United Kingdom, 8 February 1996, Reports of Judgments and Decisions 1996 – I

Jorgic v. Germany, no. 74613/01, ECHR 2007 – III

Josseaume v. France, no. 39243/10, 8 March 2012

Judge v. the United Kingdom (dec.), no. 35863/10, 8 February 2011

Juha Nuutinen v. Finland, no. 45830/99, 24 April 2007

Jussila v. Finland [GC], no. 73053/01, ECHR 2006 – XIV

— K —

K. v. France, no. 10210/82, Commission decision of 7 December 1983, Decisions and Reports 35

Kamasinski v. Austria, 19 December 1989, Series A no. 168

Karpenko v. Russia, no. 5605/04, 13 March 2012

Kaste and Mathisen v. Norway, nos. 18885/04 and 21166/04, ECHR 2006 – XIII

Kart v. Turkey [GC], no. 8917/05, ECHR 2009 (extracts)

Katritsch v. France, no. 22575/08, 4 November 2010

Khalfaoui v. France, no. 34791/97, ECHR 1999 – IX

Khan v. the United Kingdom, no. 35394/97, ECHR 2000 – V

Khodorkovskiy and Lebedev v. Russia, nos. 11082/06 and 13772/05, 25 July 2013

Khudobin v. Russia, no. 59696/00, ECHR 2006 – XII (extracts)

Khuzhinand Others v. Russia, no. 13470/02, 23 October 2008

Klimentyev v. Russia, no. 46503/99, 16 November 2006

Klouvi v. France, no. 30754/03, 30 June 2011

Kok v. the Netherlands (dec.), no. 43149/98, ECHR 2000 – VI

König v. Germany, 28 June 1978, Series A no. 27

Konstas v. Greece, no. 53466/07, 24 May 2011

Kontalexis v. Greece, no. 59000/08, 31 May 2011

Kostovski v. the Netherlands, 20 November 1989, Series A no. 166

Krasniki v. the Czech Republic, no. 51277/99, 28 February 2006

Kremzow v. Austria, 21 September 1993, Series A no. 268 – B

Krestovskiy v. Russia, no. 14040/03, 28 October 2010

Kriegisch v. Germany (dec.), no. 21698/06, 23 November 2010

Kröcher and Möller v. Switzerland, no. 8463/78, Commission decision of 9 July 1981, Decisions and Reports 26

Krombach v. France, no. 29731/96, ECHR 2001 – II

Kulikowski v. Poland, no. 18353/03, 19 May 2009

Kuopila v. Finland, no. 27752/95, 27 April 2000

Kuzmin v. Russia, no. 58939/00, 18 March 2010

Kyprianou v. Cyprus [GC], no. 73797/01, ECHR 2005 – XIII

— L —

Labergere v. France, no. 16846/02, 26 September 2006

Lacadena Calero v. Spain, no. 23002/07, 22 November 2011

Lagerblom v. Sweden, no. 26891/95, 14 January 2003

Lanz v. Austria, no. 24430/94, 31 January 2002

Lauko v. Slovakia, 2 September 1998, Reports of Judgments and Decisions 1998 – VI

Lavents v. Latvia, no. 58442/00, 28 November 2002

Legillon v. France, no. 53406/10, 10 January 2013

Lilly v. France (dec.), no. 53892/00, 3 December 2002

Löffler v. Austria, no. 30546/96, 3 October 2000

Lucà v. Italy, no. 33354/96, ECHR 2001 – II

Luedicke, Belkacem and Koç v. Germany, 28 November 1978, Series A no. 29

Lundkvist v. Sweden (dec.), no. 48518/99, ECHR 2003 – XI

Lutz v. Germany, 25 August 1987, Series A no. 123

— M —

Maaouia v. France [GC], no. 39652/98, ECHR 2000 – X

Magee v. the United Kingdom, no. 28135/95, ECHR 2000 – VI

Makhfi v. France, no. 59335/00, 19 October 2004

Malige v. France, 23 September 1998, Reports of Judgments and Decisions 1998 – VII

Malininas v. Lithuania, no. 10071/04, 1 July 2008

Mamatkulov and Askarov v. Turkey [GC], nos. 46827/99 and 46951/99, ECHR 2005 – I

Marpa Zeeland B. V. and Metal Welding B. V. v. the Netherlands, no. 46300/99, ECHR 2004X (extracts)

Martin v. the United Kingdom, no. 40426/98, 24 October 2006

Martinie v. France [GC], no. 58675/00, ECHR 2006 – VI

Matijašević v. Serbia, no. 23037/04, 19 September 2006

Mattick v. Germany (dec.), no. 62116/00, ECHR 2005 – VII

Mattoccia v. Italy, no. 23969/94, ECHR 2000 – IX

Matyjek v. Poland, no. 38184/03, 24 April 2007

Mayzit v. Russia, no. 63378/00, 20 January 2005

McFarlane v. Ireland [GC], no. 31333/06, 10 September 2010

Meftah and Others v. France [GC], nos. 32911/96 and 2 others, ECHR 2002 – VII

Melin v. France, 22 June 1993, Series A no. 261 – A

Micallef v. Malta [GC], no. 17056/06, ECHR 2009

Mieg de Boofzheim v. France (dec.), no. 52938/99, ECHR 2002 – X

Mika v. Sweden (dec.), no. 31243/06, 27 January 2009

Milasi v. Italy, 25 June 1987, Series A no. 119

Milinienė v. Lithuania, no. 74355/01, 24 June 2008

Miller and Others v. the United Kingdom, nos. 45825/99 and 2 others, 26 October 2004

Miminoshvili v. Russia, no. 20197/03, 28 June 2011

Minelli v. Switzerland, 25 March 1983, Series A no. 62

Mircea v. Romania, no. 41250/02, 29 March 2007

Mirilashvili v. Russia, no. 6293/04, 11 December 2008

Monedero Angora v. Spain (dec.), no. 41138/05, ECHR 2008

Monnell and Morris v. the United Kingdom, 2 March 1987; Series A no. 115

Montcornet de Caumont v. France (dec.), no. 59290/00, ECHR 2003 – VII

Montera v. Italy (dec.), no. 64713/01, 9 July 2002

Moiseyev v. Russia, no. 62936/00, 9 October 2008

Moullet v. France (dec.), no. 27521/04, 13 September 2007

Mežnarić v. Croatia, no. 71615/01, 15 July 2005

Mustafa (Abu Hamza) v. the United Kingdom (dec.), no. 31411/07, 18 January 2011

— N —

Natunen v. Finland, no. 21022/04, 31 March 2009

Navoneand Others v. Monaco, nos. 62880/11 and 2 others, 24 October 2013

Nerattini v. Greece, no. 43529/07, 18 December 2008

Nešt'ák v. Slovakia, no. 65559/01, 27 February 2007

Neumeister v. Austria, 27 June 1968, Series A no. 8

Nicoleta Gheorghe v. Romania, no. 23470/05, 3 April 2012

Ninn-Hansen v. Denmark (dec.), no. 28972/75, ECHR 1999 – V

Nortier v. the Netherlands, 24 August 1993, Series A no. 267

Nurmagomedov v. Russia, no. 30138/02, 7 June 2007

— O —

O. v. Norway, no. 29327/95, ECHR 2003 – II

O'Halloran and Francis v. the United Kingdom [GC], nos. 15809/02 and 25624/02, ECHR 2007 – VIII

OAO Neftyanaya Kompaniya Yukos v. Russia, no. 14902/04, 20 September 2011

Oberschlick v. Austria (no. 1), 23 May 1991, Series A no. 204

Öcalan v. Turkey [GC], no. 46221/99, ECHR 2005 – IV

Öcalan v. Turkey (dec.), no. 5980/07, 6 July 2010

Omar v. France, 29 July 1998, Reports of Judgments and Decisions 1998 – V

Othman (Abu Qatada) v. the United Kingdom, no. 8139/09, ECHR 2012

Öztürk v. Germany, 21 February 1984, Series A no. 73

— P —

P. G. and J. H. v. the United Kingdom, no. 44787/98, ECHR 2001 – IX

P. S. v. Germany, no. 33900/96, 20 December 2001

Padin Gestoso v. Spain (dec.), no. 39519/98, ECHR 1999 – II (extracts)

Padovani v. Italy, 26 February 1993, Series A no. 257 – B

Pakelli v. Germany, no. 8398/78, Commission report of 12 December 1981

Paksas v. Lithuania [GC], no. 34932/04, ECHR 2011 (extracts)

Pandjikidze and Others v. Georgia, no. 30323/02, 27 October 2009

Pandy v. Belgium, no. 13583/02, 21 September 2006

Papon v. France (dec.), no. 54210/00, ECHR 2001 – XII

Papon v. France (no. 2), no. 54210/00, ECHR 2002 – VII

Paraponiaris v. Greece, no. 42132/06, 25 September 2008

Parlov-Tkalčić v. Croatia, no. 24810/06, 22 December 2009

Pedersen and Baadsgaard v. Denmark, no. 49017/99, 19 June 2003

Pélissier and Sassi v. France [GC], no. 25444/94, ECHR 1999 – II

Pelladoah v. the Netherlands, 22 September 1994, Series A no. 297 – B

Pello v. Estonia, no. 11423/03, 12 April 2007

Penev v. Bulgaria, 20494/04, 7 January 2010

Peñafiel Salgado v. Spain (dec.), no. 65964/01, 16 April 2002

Perna v. Italy [GC], no. 48898/99, ECHR 2003 – V

Pescador Valero v. Spain, no. 62435/00, ECHR 2003 – VII

Petyo Petkov v. Bulgaria, no. 32130/03, 7 January 2010

Pfeifer and Plankl v. Austria, 25 February 1992, Series A no. 227

Pham Hoang v. France, 25 September 1992, Series A no. 243

Phillips v. the United Kingdom, no. 41087/98, ECHR 2001 – VII

Pierre-Bloch v. France, 21 October 1997, Reports of Judgments and Decisions

1997 – VI

    Piersack v. Belgium, 1 October 1982, Series A no. 53

    Pishchalnikov v. Russia, no. 7025/04, 24 September 2009

    Planka v. Austria, no. 25852/94, Commission decision of 15 May 1996

    Poitrimol v. France, 23 November 1993, Series A no. 277 – A

    Polyakov v. Russia, no. 77018/01, 29 January 2009

    Poncelet v. Belgium, no. 44418/07, 30 March 2010

    Popov v. Russia, no. 26853/04, 13 July 2006

    Popovici v. Moldova, nos. 289/04 and 41194/04, 27 November 2007

    Poppe v. the Netherlands, no. 32271/04, 24 March 2009

    Posokhov v. Russia, no. 63486/00, ECHR 2003 – IV

    Previti v. Italy (dec.), no. 45291/06, 8 December 2009

    Priebke v. Italy (dec.), no. 48799/99, 5 April 2001

    Protopapa v. Turkey, no. 16084/90, 24 February 2009

    Pullar v. the United Kingdom, 10 June 1996, Reports of Judgments and Decisions 1996 – III

    Putz v. Austria, 22 February 1996, Reports of Judgments and Decisions 1996 – I

— Q —

    Quaranta v. Switzerland, 24 May 1991, Series A no. 205

— R —

    R. v. Belgium, no. 15957/90, Commission decision of 30 March 1992, Decisions and Reports 72

    R. v. the United Kingdom (dec.), no. 33506/05, 4 January 2007

    Radio Franceand Others v. France, no. 53984/00, ECHR 2004 – II

    Raimondo v. Italy, 22 February 1994, Series A no. 281 – A

    Ramanauskas v. Lithuania [GC], no. 74420/01, ECHR 2008

    Rasmussen v. Poland, no. 38886/05, 28 April 2009

    Ravnsborg v. Sweden, 23 March 1994, Series A no. 283 – B

    Raza v. Bulgaria, no. 31465/08, 11 February 2010

Refah Partisi（the Welfare Party）and Others v. Turkey（dec.）, nos. 41340/98 and 3 others, 3 October 2000

Reinhardt and Slimane-Kaïd v. France, 31 March 1998, Reports of Judgments and Decisions 1998 – II

Richert v. Poland, no. 54809/07, 25 October 2011

Riepan v. Austria, no. 35115/97, ECHR 2000 – XII

Ringeisen v. Austria, 16 July 1971, Series A no. 13

Ringvold v. Norway, no. 34964/97, ECHR 2003 – II

Rouille v. France, no. 50268/99, 6 January 2004

Rowe and Davis v. the United Kingdom [GC], no. 28901/95, ECHR 2000 – II

Ruiz Torija v. Spain, 9 December 1994, Series A no. 303 – A

Rupa v. Romania（no. 1）, no. 58478/00, 16 December 2008

Rushiti v. Austria, no. 28389/95, 21 March 2000

— S —

S. v. Switzerland, 28 November 1991, Series A no. 220

S. N. v. Sweden, no. 34209/96, ECHR 2002 – V

Saadi v. Italy [GC], no. 37201/06, ECHR 2008

Saccoccia v Austria（dec.）, no. 69917/01, 5 July 2007

Sadakand Others v. Turkey（no. 1）, nos. 29900/96 and 3 others, ECHR 2001 – VIII

Şahiner v. Turkey, no. 29279/95, 25 September 2001

Sainte-Marie v. France, 16 December 1992, Series A no. 253 – A

Sakhnovskiy v. Russia [GC], no. 21272/03, 2 November 2010

Salabiaku v. France, 7 October 1988, Series A no. 141 – A

Salduz v. Turkey [GC], no. 36391/02, ECHR 2008

Şaman v. Turkey, no. 35292/05, 5 April 2011

Sapunarescu v. Germany（dec.）, no. 22007/03, 11 September 2006

Saric v. Denmark（dec.）, no. 31913/96, 2 February 1999

Saunders v. the United Kingdom, 17 December 1996, Reports of Judgments and Decisions 1996 – VI

Schenk v. Switzerland, 12 July 1988, Series A no. 140

Scheper v. the Netherlands (dec.), no. 39209/02, 5 April 2005

Schmautzer v. Austria, 23 October 1995, Series A no. 328 – A

Schneider v. France (dec.), no. 49852/06, 30 June 2009

Schwarzenberger v. Germany, no. 75737/01, 10 August 2006

Sejdovic v. Italy [GC], no. 56581/00, ECHR 2006 – II

Sekanina v. Austria, 25 August 1993, Series A no. 266 – A

Seleznev v. Russia, no. 15591/03, 26 June 2008

Seliwiak v. Poland, no. 3818/04, 21 July 2009

Sequieira v. Portugal (dec.), no. 73557/01, ECHR 2003 – VI

Shannon v. the United Kingdom (dec.), no. 67537/01, ECHR 2004 – IV

Sibgatullin v. Russia, no. 32165/02, 23 April 2009

Sidabras and Diautas v. Lithuania (dec.), nos. 55480/00 and 59330/00, 1 July 2003

Silickienė v. Lithuania, no. 20496/02, 10 April 2012

Sipavičius v. Lithuania, no. 49093/99, 21 February 2002

Soering v. the United Kingdom, 7 July 1989, Series A no. 161

Solakov v. the former Yugoslav Republic of Macedonia, no. 47023/99, ECHR 2001 – X

Sofriand Others v. Italy (dec.), no. 37235/97, ECHR 2003 – VIII

Stanford v. the United Kingdom, 23 February 1994, Series A no. 282 – A

Stitic v. Croatia, no. 29660/03, 8 November 2007

Stoichkov v. Bulgaria, no. 9808/02, 24 March 2005

Stojkovic v. France and Belgium, no. 25303/08, 27 October 2011

Stow and Gai v. Portugal (dec.), no. 18306/04, 4 October 2005

Suhadolc v. Slovenia (dec.), no. 57655/08, 17 May 2011

Suküt v. Turkey (dec.), no. 59773/00, 11 September 2007

Sutter v. Switzerland, 22 February 1984, Series A no. 74

Szabó v. Sweden (dec.), no. 28578/03, 27 June 2006

— T —

Tabaï v. France (dec.), no. 73805/01, 17 February 2004

Tarău v. Romania, no. 3584/02, 24 February 2009

Taxquet v. Belgium [GC], no. 926/05, ECHR 2010

Teixeira de Castro v. Portugal, 9 June 1998, Reports of Judgments and Decisions 1998 – IV

Telfner v. Austria, no. 33501/96, 20 March 2001

Thomann v. Switzerland, 10 June 1996, Reports of Judgments and Decisions 1996 – III

Thomas v. the United Kingdom (dec.), no. 19354/02, 10 May 2005

Tierceand Others v. San Marino, nos. 24954/94 and 2 others, ECHR 2000 – IX

Tirado Ortiz and Lozano Martin v. Spain (dec.), no. 43486/98, ECHR 1999 – V

Toeva v. Bulgaria (dec.), no. 53329/99, 9 September 2004

Topic v. Croatia, no. 51355/10, 10 October 2013

Trepashkin v. Russia (no. 2), no. 14248/05, 16 December 2010

Trofimov v. Russia, no. 1111/02, 4 December 2008

Twalib v. Greece, 9 June 1998, Reports of Judgments and Decisions 1998 – IV

— U —

Ubach Mortes v. Andorra (dec.), no. 46253/99, ECHR 2000 – V

Ucak v. the United Kingdom (dec.), no. 44234/98, 24 January 2002

— V —

V. v. Finland, no. 40412/98, 24 April 2007

V. v. the United Kingdom [GC], no. 24888/94, ECHR 1999 – IX

Vacher v. France, 17 December 1996, Reports of Judgments and Decisions 1996 – VI

Van de Hurk v. the Netherlands, 19 April 1994, Series A no. 288

Van Geyseghem v. Belgium [GC], no. 26103/95, ECHR 1999 – I

Van Mechelen and Others v. the Netherlands, 23 April 1997, Reports of Judgments and Decisions 1997 – III

Vanyan v. Russia, no. 53203/99, 15 December 2005

Vaudelle v. France, no. 35683/97, ECHR 2001 – I

Vayiç v. Turkey, no. 18078/02, ECHR 2006 – VIII (extracts)

Vera Fernández-Huidobro v. Spain, no. 74181/01, 6 January 2010

Veselov and Others v. Russia, nos. 23200/10 and 2 others, 11 September 2012

Vidal v. Belgium, 22 April 1992, Series A no. 235 – B

Vidgen v. the Netherlands, no. 29353/06, 10 July 2012

Viorel Burzo v. Romania, nos. 75109/01 and 12639/02, 30 June 2009

Visser v. the Netherlands, no. 26668/95, 14 February 2002

Vladimir Romanov v. Russia, no. 41461/02, 24 July 2008

Vronchenko v. Estonia, no. 59632/09, 18 July 2013

— W —

W. S. v. Poland, no. 21508/02, 19 June 2007

Walchli v. France, no. 35787/03, 26 July 2007

Welke and Białek v. Poland, no. 15924/05, 1 March 2011

Wemhoff v. Germany, 27 June 1968, Series A no. 7

Wierzbicki v. Poland, no. 24541/94, 18 June 2002

Włoch v. Poland (dec.), no. 27785/95, 30 March 2000

— X —

X. v. Austria, no. 6185/73, Commission decision of 29 May 1975, Decisions and Reports 2

X. v. Belgium, no. 7628/73, Commission decision of 9 May 1977, Decisions and Reports 9

— Y —

Y v. Norway, no. 56568/00, ECHR 200 – 3 II (extracts)

Y. B. and Others v. Turkey, nos. 48173/99 and 48319/99, 28 October 2004

— Z —

Zagaria v. Italy, no. 58295/00, 27 November 2007

Zana v. Turkey, 25 November 1997, Reports of Judgments and Decisions 1997 – VII

Zarouali v. Belgium, no. 20664/92, Commission decision of 29 June 1994, Decisions and Reports 78

Zdravko Stanev v. Bulgaria, no. 32238/04, 6 November 2012

Zhuk v. Ukraine, no. 45783/05, 21 October 2010

Zhupnik v. Ukraine, no. 20792/05, 9 December 2010

Zollmann v. the United Kingdom (dec.), no. 62902/00, ECHR 2003 – XII

Zoon v. the Netherlands, no. 29202/95, ECHR 2000 – XII

中国人民大学食品安全治理协同创新中心丛书

欧洲人权法院
判例指南（下卷）

Case-law Guides
of the European Court of Human Rights

陆海娜 | 主编

目 录
Contents

下 卷

第五章 《欧洲人权公约》第 7 条适用指南　法无明文规定不得处罚：罪刑法定原则 / 497

读者须知 / 499

第一节　引言 / 500

第二节　范围 / 500

　一、"认定有罪"的概念 / 500

　二、"刑事犯罪"的概念 / 501

　三、"法律"的概念 / 501

　四、"刑罚"的概念 / 502

第三节　罪刑法定原则 / 506

　一、可获得性 / 508

　二、可预见性 / 508

第四节　刑法的法不溯及既往原则 / 513

　一、总体考量 / 513

　二、持续犯 / 515

　三、累犯 / 515

第五节　较轻刑罚的溯及原则 / 516

第六节　第 7 条第 2 款：文明国家所认可的一般法律原则 / 517

第七节 欧洲人权法院在违反公约第 7 条的案件中所指示的措施 / 518

援引案例一览 / 519

Chapter Ⅴ　Guide on Article 7 of the European Convention on Human Rights No Punishment Without Law: the Principle that Only the Law Can Define A Crime and Prescribe A Penalty / 521

Note to readers / 523

Ⅰ. Introduction / 524

Ⅱ. Scope / 525

 A. The concept of "finding of guilt" / 525

 B. The concept of "criminal offence" / 525

 C. The concept of "law" / 526

 D. The concept of a "penalty" / 527

Ⅲ. Principle that only the law can define a crime and prescribe a penalty / 533

 A. Accessibility / 535

 B. Foreseeability / 535

Ⅳ. Principle of non-retroactivity of criminal law / 543

 A. General considerations / 543

 B. Continuing offences / 545

 C. Recidivism / 546

Ⅴ. Principe of the retroactivity of the lighter penalty / 547

Ⅵ. Article 7 § 2: the general principles of law recognised by civilised nations / 548

Ⅶ. Measures indicated by the Court in cases of violation of Article 7 of the Convention / 549

List of cited cases / 551

第六章　《欧洲人权公约》第 9 条适用指南　思想、良心和宗教自由 / 557

读者须知 / 559

第一节　引言 / 560

第二节　基本原则及其适用 / 562

　　一、第 9 条在民主社会的重要性以及在宗教团体的法定地位 / 562

　　二、第 9 条保护的信仰 / 562

　　三、有信仰的权利以及表达信仰的权利 / 566

　　四、国家的消极和积极义务 / 571

　　五、第 9 条与公约其他条款规定的重叠之处 / 575

第三节　第 9 条保护的行为 / 577

　　一、消极方面 / 577

　　二、积极方面 / 582

　　三、宗教自由和迁徙自由 / 601

第四节　国家作为宗教自由保卫者的义务 / 604

　　一、消极义务：不妨碍宗教组织正常运作的义务 / 604

　　二、消极义务：尊重宗教组织的自治权 / 622

　　三、积极义务 / 633

援引案例一览 / 643

Chapter VI　Guide to Article 9 Freedom of Thought, Conscience and Religion / 645

Notice to readers / 647

Ⅰ. Introduction / 648

Ⅱ. General principles and applicability / 651

　　1. The importance of Article 9 of the convention in a democratic society and the locus standi of religious bodies / 651

　　2. Convictions protected under Article 9 / 652

　　3. The right to hold a belief and the right to manifest it / 656

　　4. Negative and positive obligations on the State / 663

　　5. Overlaps between the safeguards of Article 9 and the other convention provisions / 669

Ⅲ. Actions protected under article 9 / 672

1. Negative aspect / 672

　　2. Positive aspect / 680

　　3. Freedom of religion and immigration / 708

Ⅳ. The state's obligations as garantor of freedom of religion / 713

　　1. Negative obligations: obligation not to impede the normal functioning of religious organisations / 713

　　2. Negative obligations: respect for the autonomy of religious organisations / 740

　　3. Positive obligations / 758

Index of cited cases / 772

第七章　《欧洲人权公约》第 15 条适用指南　紧急状态下的克减 / 789

读者须知 / 791

第一节　基本原则 / 792

第二节　第 15 条第 1 款：缔约国何时能正当克减 / 793

　一、"战时或者其他威胁国家生存的公共紧急状态" / 793

　二、"情况的紧急性所严格要求的范围内" / 795

　三、"只要上述措施不与其根据国际法的规定所应当履行的其他义务相抵触" / 797

第三节　第 15 条第 2 款：不可克减的权利 / 798

第四节　第 15 条第 3 款：告知的要求 / 799

援引案例一览 / 801

Chapter Ⅶ　Guide on Article 15 of the European Convention on Human Rights　Derogation in Time of Emergency / 803

Note to readers / 805

Ⅰ. General principles / 806

Ⅱ. Article 15 § 1: when a State may validly derogate / 807

　　A. "... war or other public emergency threatening the life of the nation..." / 808

　　B. "... measures ... strictly required by the exigencies of the situation..." / 810

C. "... provided that such measures are not inconsistent with [the High Contracting Party's] other obligations under international law" / 812

Ⅲ. Article 15 § 2: non-derogable rights / 813

Ⅳ. Article 15 § 3: the notification requirements / 815

List of cited cases / 817

第八章 《欧洲人权公约》第一议定书第2条适用指南 受教育权 / 819

读者须知 / 821

第一节 基本原则 / 822

一、第一议定书第2条的结构 / 822

二、第一议定书第2条的含义和适用范围 / 822

三、解释的原则 / 823

第二节 受教育权 / 824

一、受教育权的原则 / 824

二、受教育权的限制 / 825

三、教育方面的歧视 / 828

第三节 尊重家长的权利 / 831

一、适用范围 / 831

二、免修课程的可能性 / 832

三、明显的宗教标志 / 833

援引案例一览 / 835

Chapter Ⅷ Guide on Article 2 of Protocol No. 1 to the European Convention on Human Rights Right to Education / 837

Note to readers / 839

Ⅰ. General principles / 840

A. Structure of Article 2 of Protocol No. 1 / 840

B. Meaning and scope of Article 2 of Protocol No. 1 / 840

C. Principles of interpretation ／ 841
　Ⅱ. Right to education ／ 842
　　　A. Principle of the right to education ／ 842
　　　B. Restrictions on access to education ／ 844
　　　C. Discrimination in access to education ／ 848
　Ⅲ. Respect for parental rights ／ 852
　　　A. Scope ／ 852
　　　B. Possibility of exemption ／ 853
　　　C. Conspicuous religious symbols ／ 856
List of cited cases ／ 858

第九章　《欧洲人权公约》第一议定书第3条适用指南　自由选举权 ／ 863

读者须知 ／ 865
第一节　基本原则 ／ 866
　一、含义和范围 ／ 866
　二、解释原则 ／ 867
第二节　积极方面：选举权 ／ 869
　一、公民权的丧失 ／ 869
　二、关于囚犯的特定案件 ／ 870
　三、居住与选举权的关系 ／ 872
第三节　消极方面：被选举权 ／ 875
　一、被选举权的剥夺和民主秩序 ／ 876
　二、历史环境的重要性 ／ 877
　三、组织选举 ／ 878
　四、其他的合法性目的 ／ 882
　五、"从竞选活动……" ／ 883
　六、"……到行使职权" ／ 885
第四节　选举争议 ／ 886
援引案例一览 ／ 889

Chapter IX Guide on Article 3 of Protocol No. 1 to the European Convention on Human Rights Right to Free Elections / 891

Note to readers / 893

Ⅰ. General principles / 894

　　A. Meaning and scope / 894

　　B. Principles of interpretation / 896

Ⅱ. Active aspect: the right to vote / 898

　　A. Loss of civil rights / 899

　　B. Specific case of prisoners / 900

　　C. Residence, condition of access to voting rights / 903

Ⅲ. Passive aspect: the right to stand for election / 907

　　A. Inability to stand for election and the democratic order / 909

　　B. Importance of historical context / 910

　　C. Organisation of elections / 912

　　D. Other legitimate aims / 917

　　E. From the election campaign... / 920

　　F. ... to the exercise of office / 921

Ⅳ. Electoral disputes / 924

List of cited cases / 928

第十章 《欧洲人权公约》第四议定书第4条适用指南 禁止集体驱逐外国人 / 935

读者须知 / 937

第一节 第4条的起源与宗旨 / 938

第二节 "集体驱逐"的定义 / 938

第三节 属人范围的适用:"外国人"的定义 / 939

第四节 属地规则的适用及管辖问题 / 939

第五节　集体驱逐的案例 / 940

第六节　不属于集体驱逐的情况 / 942

第七节　与公约第 13 条的关系 / 943

援引案例一览 / 945

Chapter X　Guide on Article 4 of Protocol No. 4 to the European Convention on Human Rights Prohibition of Collective Expulsions of Aliens / 947

Note to readers / 949

Ⅰ. Origins and purpose of the Article / 950

Ⅱ. The definition of "collective expulsion" / 950

Ⅲ. The personal scope of application: the definition of "aliens" / 952

Ⅳ. Questions of territorial applicability and jurisdiction / 952

Ⅴ. Examples of collective expulsions / 954

Ⅵ. Examples of measures not amounting to collective expulsions / 956

Ⅶ. Relationship with Article 13 of the Convention / 958

List of cited cases / 960

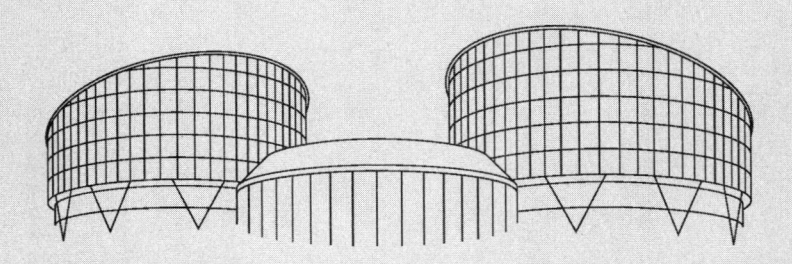

EUROPEAN COURT OF HUMAN RIGHTS
COUR EUROPÉENNE DES DROITS DE L'HOMME

第五章　《欧洲人权公约》第7条适用指南
法无明文规定不得处罚：
罪刑法定原则

读者须知

本指南是欧洲人权法院(以下简称、本法院、欧洲法院、斯特拉斯堡法院)出版的公约指南系列的一部分,旨在让执业律师了解斯特拉斯堡法院做出的基本判决。本指南分析和汇总了截至 2016 年 1 月 31 日的关于《欧洲人权公约》(以下简称公约、欧洲公约)第 7 条的判例法。读者可以从中发现本领域的基本原则和相关判例。

援引的判例法选取了具有指导性的、重要的以及最新的判决。

本法院的判例不仅用于审判呈交至本法院的案件,而且从更为一般的意义上用于阐释、捍卫和发展公约创立的各项规则,并以此促使各缔约国对之加以遵守(*Ireland v. the United Kingdom*, 1978 年 1 月 18 日, §154, Series A no. 25.)。因此,从普遍意义来说,公约确立此机制的任务便是通过决定公共政策的各种问题来提升人权保护的标准,并在缔约国范围内推广人权法学(*Konstantin Markin v. Russia*[GC], 30078/06, §89, ECHR 2012)。

第一节　引言

> **第 7 条　法无明文规定不得处罚**
>
> "(1) 任何人作为或不作为的行为,在其发生时根据国内法或国际法不构成刑事犯罪的,不得认定其有罪。所处刑罚不得重于犯罪时所适用的刑罚。
>
> (2) 如果根据文明国家所认可的一般法律原则,该作为或者不作为在其发生时构成刑事犯罪行为,则本条不得妨碍对该人的作为或者不作为进行审判或者予以惩罚。"

1. 第 7 条提供的保障是法治的重要组成部分,而且根据第 15 条关于战时和公共危机的规定,不得克减第 7 条规定的义务,可见第 7 条在公约的保护体系中居于主导地位。该条应根据其对象和目的加以解释、适用,从而有效防止任意的起诉、定罪和处罚行为(*S. W. v. the United Kingdom*, § 34; *C. R. v. United Kingdom*, § 32; *Del Río Prada v. Spain* [GC], § 77; *Vasiliauskas v. Lithuania* [GC], § 153)。

2. 第 7 条不仅限于禁止刑法上不利于当事人的溯及既往,同时还表明,只有法律可以定义犯罪并规定相应的处罚(*nullum crimen, nulla poena sine lege*),此外,刑法还禁止不利于被告的解释,如类推解释(*Kokkinakis v. Greece*, § 52, *Vasiliauskas v. Lithuania* [GC], § 154)。

第二节　范围

一、"认定有罪"的概念

3. 第 7 条仅适用于当事人"被认定构成"刑事"犯罪"的情况。这不仅包括正在进行的起诉(*Lukanov v. Bulgaria*, 委员会决定),或者引渡个人的决定(*X v. Netherlands*, 委员会决定);从公约的目的来看,除非根据法律认为行为违法,否则不能"定罪"(*Varvara v. Italy*,§69)。

4. 未被"认定有罪"而受到"处罚"的情况,违反了公约第 7 条的规定。这是因为,对经审判未被定罪者进行处罚与该条确立的法律原则相矛盾(*Varvara v. Italy*,§§ 61 and 72-73)。"刑罚"和"处罚"的理论以及英文中"有罪"的概念和法语中与之对应的"有罪之人"的概念,支撑了对于第 7 条的解释:必须由国内法院认定被指控者有罪,才能将违法行为归因于犯罪者,并对犯罪者施加相应的处罚(*Varvara v. Italy*,§71;关于违法行为中对犯罪者犯罪意图的要求,参见 *Sud Fondi srl and Others v. Italy*,§116)。

二、"刑事犯罪"的概念

5. 和公约第 6 条中的"刑事指控"概念一样,"刑事犯罪"(法语版对应词为"*infraction*")的概念也有自治的意思。① 恩格尔等人诉荷兰案(*Engel and Others v. Netherlands*,§82)确立了 3 项标准(之后在 *Jussila v. Finland*[GC],§30 中再次得以重申),用于判断一项指控是否属于第 6 条规定的"刑事"指控,这些标准同样应当适用于第 7 条[*Brown v. United Kingdom*(dec.)]:

- 国内法上的分类;
- 犯罪行为的性质(最重要的标准,*Jussila v. Finland*[GC],§38);
- 相关行为人可能遭受的处罚的严重程度。

6. 在适用这些标准时,本法院认为,根据第 6 条与第 7 条的立法目的,违反军纪不属于"犯罪"的范围[*Çelikateş and Others v. Turkey*(dec.)]。同样的情形还包括:解雇、限制雇佣前苏联保安部门代理人[*Sidabras and Džiautas v. Lithuania*(dec.)]、学生在学校违纪[*Monaco v. Italy*(dec.),§§ 40 and 68-69],以及对共和国总统明显违反宪法的弹劾程序(*Paksas v. Lithuania*[GC],§§ 64-69)。本法院认为,缺少"违反刑法"这一要件的控诉不符合公约规定的属事管辖权。

三、"法律"的概念

7. 第 7 条所使用的"法律"(法语对应词为"*droit*")的概念与公约其他条文中所确

---

① 关于第 6 条(犯罪方面)的范围和"刑事指控"的概念,参见第 6 条(犯罪方面)指南第 6 到 10 页,可以通过法院官网获取(〈www.echr.coe.int〉-Case-law)。

立的这一概念一致,既包括国内立法和判例法,也包括对于法律性质上的要求,尤其是可获得性和可预见性(*S. W. v. United Kingdom*, § 35, *Del Río Prada v. Spain* [GC], § 91)。法律不仅包括制定的法律(*S. W. v. United Kingdom* §§ 36 and 41 – 43),同时也包括法规和位阶低于法规的法令(如监狱规则,见 *Kafkaris v. Cyprus* [GC], §§ 145 – 146)。本法院必须把国内法视作整体并将其运用于诉讼期间(*Kafkaris v. Cyprus*, § 145;*Del Río Prada v. Spain* [GC], § 90)。

8. 另一方面,与现行的成文法规定相矛盾的国家实践以及本应是立法依据但却缺乏实质内容的"法律",不属于第 7 条所指的"法律"[德意志民主共和国实施边界警戒的做法,明显违反其自身的法律体系和基本权利,参见 *Streletz, Kessler and Krenz v. Germany* [GC], §§ 67 – 87;还有明显违反前捷克斯洛伐克的相关立法和宪法而进行审判,之后施行死刑,从而消除共产党政权的对手的做法,参见 *Polednová v. Czech Republic* (dec.)]。

9. 第 7 条第 1 款中"国际法"的概念是指相关国家签署的国际条约(*Streletz, Kessler and Krenz v. Germany* [GC], §§ 90 – 106),以及国际法惯例(关于国际法以及战争惯例,参见 *Kononov v. Latvia* [GC], §§ 186, 213, 227, 237 and 244;关于"反人道罪"的概念,参见 *Korbely v. Hungary* [GC], §§ 78 – 85;关于"种族灭绝"的概念,参见 *Vasiliauskas v. Lithuania* [GC], §§ 171 – 175 和 178),以及相关的尚未正式公布的法律(*Kononov v. Latvia* [GC], § 237)。

四、"刑罚"的概念

(一)整体考量

10. 公约第 7 条第 1 款确立的"刑罚"的概念在范围上具有自主性。为了确保此条所确立的保护机制的效力,本法院必须能够透过表象,自主判定一项具体措施是否实际构成第 7 条第 1 款意义上的"刑罚"。要判断某项争议措施是否构成"刑罚",第一步是要查明该措施是否是在认定行为人构成"刑事犯罪"的基础上而采取的。其他的因素也可能与这方面有关:争议措施的性质和目的(尤其是其惩罚性目的)、国内法上的分类、其所采用和实行相关的程序以及措施的严厉程度。(*Welch v. the United Kingdom*, § 28, *Del Río Prada v. Spain* [GC], § 82)。但是措施的严厉程度本身并不具有决定性,因为许多预防性的非刑罚措施也会对相关人产生实质性的影响[*Del Río Prada v. Spain* [GC];*Van der Velden v. Netherlands* (dec.)]。

11. 在适用这些标准时,本法院特别指出,以下措施应当视作"刑罚":
- 根据认定有罪之后的刑事诉讼程序而颁布的没收令,鉴于其惩罚性目的及其预防性和赔偿性,应当视作"刑罚"(*Welch v. the United Kingdom*,§§ 29–35,毒品走私诉讼程序中进行的没收);
- 因违约而采取羁押措施,从而确保那些不能证明自己破产的债务人履行支付罚金的义务,这种羁押措施应当视作"刑罚"(*Jamil v. France*,§ 32);
- 在一件关于城市发展的案件中,对违章建筑施加了与其等值的罚金,具有惩罚性和预防性功能,应当视作"刑罚"[*Valico SLR v. Italy*(dec.)];
- 刑事法院在宣告无罪后没收建有违法建筑的土地,具有惩罚性目的,同时旨在防止违法行为再次发生,因此属于预防性和惩罚性措施,应当视作"刑罚"[*Sud Fondi srl and Others v. Italy*(dec.);*Varvara v. Italy*,§§ 22 and 51,根据法规的限制性规定做出中止的决定后发布的没收令];
- 因严重违法而定罪之后,审判庭采取的预防性拘留措施。考虑到其预防性和惩罚性,而且是在普通监狱里执行,还没有期限限制,应当视作"刑罚"(*M. v. Germany*,§§ 123–133;*Jendrowiak v. Germany*,§ 47;*Glien v. Germany*,§§ 120–130;反例参见 *Bergmann v. Germany*,§§ 153–182,考虑到原告正在专家中心接受治疗,对其进行预防性拘留);
- 用驱逐以及为期 10 年的禁止居住措施替代有期徒刑,应当视作"刑罚"(*Gurguchiani v. Spain*,§ 40);
- 国内法院命令永久性禁止从事相关职业,作为二次处罚,这种禁止命令应当视作"刑罚"(*Gouarré Patte v. Andorra*,§ 30)。

12. 反之,以下情形被排除在"刑罚"的概念之外:
- 对没有刑事责任的人施加的预防性措施(包括强制性的收容治疗)(*Berland v. France*,§§ 39–47);
- 出于预防和羁押的目的,对性犯罪或暴力犯罪者进行的治安登记或司法登记[*Adamson v. the United Kingdom*(dec.);*Gardel v. France*,§§ 39–47];
- 当局对已定罪之人进行的 DNA 鉴定[*Van der Velden v. Netherlands*(dec.)];
- 为防止个人参与非法活动而进行的拘留(*Lawless v. Ireland*(no.3),§ 19);
- 刑事定罪后禁止居住(在监禁刑之外另行实施),这项禁止令相当于公共命令措施(*Renna v. France*, Commission decision；在第 6 条第 1 款的刑事部分中，*Maaouia v. France*[GC]，§ 39)(细节略有变更)；

- 行政性的驱逐令或禁止居住[*Vikulov and Others v. Latvia* (dec.)；*C. G. and Others v. Bulgaria* (dec.)]；

- 根据欧洲委员会《被判刑人移管公约》附加议定书将被判刑的人员移交至其他国家,该项措施旨在帮助被判刑人更好地重新融入其原籍国社会[*Szabó v. Sweden* (dec.)；被判刑人根据有关欧盟逮捕令的欧盟框架决定进行的自首以及成员国之间的自首程序，*Giza v. Poland* (dec.)，§ 30]；

- 针对涉嫌黑社会性质的组织实施的预防性财产没收令,不以刑法上的定罪为先决条件(*M. v. Italy*, Commission decision)；

- 旨在防止刑事违法犯罪,针对危险人物实施的警察监督或者监视居住(*Mucci v. Italy*, Commission decision；*Raimondo v. Italy*，§ 43，关于第 6 条第 1 款的刑事部分)；

- 在刑事诉讼中针对第三方的没收令[*Yildirim v. Italy* (dec.)；*Bowler International Unit v. France*，§§ 65–68]；

- 撤回议员的议会授权以及因政党的解散而宣告议员失去被选举资格[*Sobacı v. Turkey* (dec.)]；

- 因总统严重违反宪法而按照弹劾程序对其进行弹劾,并宣告其不能胜任总统(*Paksas v. Lithuania* [GC]，§§ 65–68)；

- 依照纪律性程序暂停公务员领取养老金的权利[*Haioun v. France* (dec.)]；

- 单独关押三个星期(*A. v. Spain*；*Payet v. France*，§§ 94–100,在第 6 条的刑事部分中)；

- 由于申诉人是监狱唯一的犯人,导致了犯人的社会隔离。本法院认为这项措施过于特殊,因此不能合理期待国家提供相关立法细节[*Öcalan v. Turkey* (no.2)，§ 187]。

(二)刑法实体法与程序法的区别

13. 本法院指出,公约第 7 条有关溯及力的规则只适用于关于违法行为及相关惩罚的规定。原则上,这些规则并不适用于程序法,但本法院认为,如果在程序法中直接适用这些规则不违背法不溯及既往原则,那么也是可取的。(*Scoppola v. Italy* (no. 2)

[GC]，§110，参考与公约第6条相关的案件：例如，*Bosti v. Italy*（dec.），§55，与目击者陈述的使用相关的规则，被称为"程序性规则"），不过这种适用也不能任意而为[*Morabito v. Italy*（dec.）]。如果一项规定在国内法上被划分为程序性规定会影响施加刑罚的严厉程度，那么本法院就会将这项规定划分为"刑事实体法"，对其可适用第7条第1款最后一句的规定（*Scoppola v. Italy*（no.2）[GC]，§§110-113，涉及刑事诉讼法典中关于简易程序中施加刑罚的严厉程度的规定）。

14. 关于法令的特殊限制，本法院认为，第7条并不禁止在正在进行的诉讼过程中直接适用延长限制期限的规则，这一情形下所指称的违法行为并不受到限制（*Coëme and Others v. Belgium*，§149），而且在这一情形下也不存在任意专断[（*Previti v. Italy*（dec.），§§80-85]。因此本法院将有关期限限制的规则划分为程序法，因为这些规则并没有规定违法和犯罪，而且可以解释为为审查案件提供了简单的前提。[*Previti v. Italy*（dec.），§80；*Borcea v. Romania*（dec.），§64]。另外，在国际法框架下，个人被指控的犯罪具有可罚性时，可适用的诉讼时效必须在相关国际法实际生效的期限内（*Kononov v. Latvia*[GC]，§§229-233，本法院认为，相关的生效国际法在生效期间并没有指定战争罪的诉讼时效，因此针对申诉人的起诉并没有超过诉讼时效。对比 *Kolk and Kislyiy v. Estonia*（dec.）与 *Penart v. Estonia*（dec.），本法院认为反人类的犯罪并不受条文的限制）。

（三）必须区别"刑罚"与刑罚的执行

15. 本法院在构成"刑罚"的措施与实施"与"执行"刑罚相关的措施之间进行了区分。如果采取的措施在性质和目的上涉及判刑的减轻或者假释程序的变更，那么该项措施就不属于第7条意义上的"刑罚"不可分割的一部分（关于同意减刑，参见 *Grava v. Italy*，§49，以及 *Kafkaris v. Cyprus*[GC]），§151；关于假释条件的立法修正案，参见 *Hogben v. United Kingdom*，Commission decision，以及 *Uttley v. the United Kingdom*（dec.）；各类不同的移管被判刑人案件中，假释的相关规定不同，*Ciok v. Poland*（dec.），§§33-34）。与释放政策、其实施的方式以及所依据的理由等相关的问题，属于成员国自行决定其刑法政策的权力范围（*Kafkaris v. Cyprus*[GC]，§151）。对于在第7条范围内定罪已经成为最终判决的也不能适用特赦法[*Montcornet de Caumont v. France*（dec.）]。

16. 然而，在实践中，构成"刑罚"的措施与有关刑罚"执行"的措施之间的区别并不总是明显的。例如，本法院认为，针对所涉刑罚，对关于加强判刑的监狱规章进行解释和实施的方式明显超出了执行的范围，因此实际上已经属于判刑的范畴（*Kafkaris v. Cyprus*[GC]，§148，关于无期徒刑）。同样，刑罚执行法院依据在申诉人犯下罪行后才生效的法律，延长预防性拘留的时间，构成了"额外的刑罚"，因此并不只涉及刑罚的执行（*M. v. Germany* §135）。

17. 在这方面，本法院强调，第7条第1款第2句中使用的"施加"一词，不能解释为被排除在宣判刑罚后采取措施的范围之外（*Del Río Prada v. Spain*[GC]，§88）。因此，如果立法机关、行政机关或法院在刑罚已经实施完毕或正在实施之时所采取的措施导致初审法院施加的"惩罚"的范围被重新定义或修改，那么这些措施应当属于公约第7条第1款刑罚溯及既往有关规定的范围（*Del Río Prada v. Spain*[GC]，§89）。为了确定在执行刑罚时采取的措施是否只涉及刑罚执行的方式，还是同时也影响了刑罚的范围，本法院必须在每一个案中考察在现行的国内法中施加的"刑罚"所实际包含的内容，换言之，考虑其内在的本质是什么（*Del Río Prada v. Spain*[GC]，§90）。本法院认为新的减刑体系的适用方法已经导致刑罚范围被重新定义，因为新的适用方法对更改被判刑人的处罚产生了影响（*Del Río Prada v. Spain*[GC]，§§109–110 and 117，根据判例法中的撤销制度，对于三十年的有期徒刑，无法针对已经拘留的部分进行减刑）。

（四）与公约的其他条文以及议定书的联系

18. 公约第7条的目的为"惩罚"，除与第6条第1款的刑事部分和"刑事指控"概念具有明显联系之外（参见上文第5段；同时参见 *Bowler International Unit*，§§66–67），也与第七议定书第4条确立的一事不再理原则的适用有关（*Sergueï Zolotoukhine v. Russia*[GC]，§§52–57，关于刑事诉讼的概念）。关于什么构成"刑罚"，在公约不同条文之间不应有所差别（*Göktan v. France*，§48；同时参见公约第6条的刑事部分与第七议定书第2条中提到的"刑事犯罪"概念之间的关系，*Zaicevs v. Latvia*，§53）。

第三节 罪刑法定原则

19. 公约第7条要求判刑或者施加刑罚要有法律依据。因此，本法院必须确认，当被告实施导致他被诉并被定罪的行为时，应当具有现行法律规定该行为可罚，同时施加的惩罚不得超过该法律规定的限度(*Coëme and Others v. Belgium*, § 145; *Del Río Prada v. Spain* [GC], § 80)。

20. 鉴于公约体系的附属性质,处理国内法院认定事实或适用法律的错误不属于本法院的职能,除非该错误侵犯了公约保护的权利和自由。(*Streletz, Kessler and Krenz v. Germany* [GC], § 49; *Vasiliauskas v. Lithuania* [GC], § 160),或者国内法院做出的判定明显是任意专断的(*Kononov v. Latvia* [GC], § 189)。即使不要求本法院对罪行的法律分类或申诉人的个人刑事责任进行规制,这也是国内法院审查案件首先需要考虑的问题(*Kononov v. Latvia* [GC], § 187; *Rohlena v. the Czech Republic* [GC], § 51),第7条第1款要求本法院审查对申诉人定罪是否具有现行法上的依据,而且国内法院达成的结果应符合公约第7条的规定。减弱本法院的审查权力,将会违背公约第7条的目的(*Rohlena v. the Czech Republic* [GC], § 52; *Kononov v. Latvia* [GC], § 198; *Vasiliauskas v. Lithuania* [GC], § 161)。

21. 此外,罪刑法定原则排除了对被告人实施比他所犯罪行更重的刑罚。因此,考虑到申诉人所遭受的刑罚属于由国内法院评估的可以减轻的情形,本法院可以认为,国内法院在确定刑罚的严重程度时出现的错误违反了第7条(*Gabarri Moreno v. Spain*, §§ 22–34)。通过类推施加刑罚,也违反了第7条规定的"法无明文规定不得处罚"原则(*Başkaya and Okçuoğlu v. Turkey* [GC], §§ 42–43,根据适用于主编的规定,对出版商施加刑罚)。

22. 罪刑法定原则要求犯罪和相应的刑罚由法律明确规定(参见上文第7至第9段关于"法律"的概念)。"法律"的概念在第7条中的含义与在公约其他条款(如第8~11条)中一样,提出了性质上的要求,特别是可获得性和可预见性(*Cantoni v. France*, § 29; *Kafkaris v. Cyprus* [GC], § 140; *Del Río Prada v. Spain* [GC], § 91; *Perinçek v. Switzerland* [GC], § 134)。不论是违法行为的定义(*Jorgic v. Germany*, §§ 103–114),还是违法行为必须受到的惩罚或其范围,都必须满足这些性质上的要求(*Kafkaris v. Cyprus* [GC], § 150; *Camilleri v. Malta*, §§ 39–45,适用的量刑标准的可预见性,完全取决于检察官对于审判法院的选择,而不是根据法律所规定的标准)。如果涉及违法行为的定义以及适用的刑罚的"法律质量"不达标,就会构成对公约第7条的违反(*Kafkaris v. Cyprus* [GC], §§ 150 and 152)。

一、可获得性

23. 关于可获得性,本法院应查明定罪所依据的刑事法律对于申诉人来说能否获得,即该法律是否已经公开[解释部分法律的国内判例法的可获得性,Kokkinakis v. Greece,§40,以及 G. v. France,§25;"执行令"的可获得性,Custers, Deveaux and Turk v. Denmark(dec.),§82]。如果定罪纯粹是以应诉国签署的国际条约为依据,那么本法院就需要确认该条约是否被吸收进国内法之中,还要确认是否发表在官方出版物上。(关于《日内瓦公约》,参见 Korbely v. Hungary[GC],§§74 – 75)。本法院也可以依据国际惯例,来评估犯罪定义的可获得性(在 1948 年通过的《防止及惩治灭绝种族罪公约》生效之前,联合国大会谴责灭绝种族罪的决议,Vasiliauskas v. Lithuania[GC],§§167 – 168;依据有关战争的国际法和国际惯例——这些国际法和国际惯例并没有发表在官方出版物上——同时对犯罪定义的可获得性和可预测性进行考察,Kononov v. Latvia[GC],§§234 – 239 and 244)。

二、可预见性

(一)总体考量

24. 任何个人必须能够从相关条款的措辞以及在必要情况下通过法院的解释和适当的法律建议,来得知何种作为或不作为会让他承担刑事责任,以及会相应地受到何种处罚(Cantoni v. France,§29;Kafkaris v. Cyprus[GC],§140;Del Río Prada v. Spain[GC],§79)。"适当的建议"意指获得法律建议的可能性(Chauvy and Others v. France(dec.);Jorgic v. Germany,§113)。

25. 由于法条具有一般性,其措辞不是绝对精确的。为了避免法条过度刚性,确保法条的内涵与社会环境的变化保持同步,很多法律都会不可避免地有着或多或少的模糊性,这些规定的解释和适用都取决于实践的需要(Kokkinakis v. Greece,§40,"改信宗教"的违法行为的定义;Cantoni v. France,§31,"医学产品"的法律定义)。在使用分类立法技术时,对法律概念的定义经常会存在灰色地带。如果能证明边缘事实在大多数情况下足够清楚,那么其不确定性本身并不会使得条文规定与公约第 7 条不一致(Cantoni v. France,§32)。另外,在解释法律规定时,使用过于模糊的概念和准则,会使得规定本身不符合清晰度和可预见性的要求(Liivik v. Estonia,§§96 – 104)。

26. 可预见性概念的范围在很大程度上取决于所涉法律文书的内容、计划涵盖的领域以及目标对象的数量和地位(Kononov v. Latvia [GC], § 235; Cantoni v. France, § 35)。即使在一定情形下相关人会通过适当的法律咨询去评估一个特定行为可能带来的后果,法律仍然有可能满足可预见性的要求(Cantoni v. France)。这一点对于那些从事专业性活动的人来说尤为突出,他们在进行自己的职业活动时保持着高度谨慎,因此在评估这些活动所带来的风险时,就需要特别注意(Cantoni v. France; Pessino v. France, § 33; Kononov v. Latvia [GC], § 235)。例如,本法院认为,超市经理能够获得适当的法律建议,应该认识到非法销售药物产品有被起诉的风险(Cantoni v. France § 35)。对于下列有关个人的定罪,本法院也持类似观点:一家香烟销售公司的经理在香烟盒上印上了违法的短语[Delbos and Others v. France(dec.)];一家视听公司的发行经理,通过一份"在发布给公众之前已经确定的"声明公开诽谤一名公务员(Radio France and Others v. France, § 20);一家销售食品补充剂公司的经理销售的产品含有法律禁止的添加剂[Ooms v. France (dec.)];一本书的作者和出版商进行公开诽谤[Chauvy and Others v. France (dec.),出版社的专业地位要求它应该提醒作者被起诉的风险];律师在没有授权的情况下作为被领养儿童的中间人进行代理[Stoica v. France (dec.),该人是家庭法律师];绿色和平组织积极分子非法进入格陵兰岛的军事防御区[Custers, Deveaux and Turk v. Denmark (dec.), §§ 95 - 96];那些曾因主使东德谋杀案(这些被害者于1979年至1989年间试图穿过两德边界逃离东德)被定罪的政客们,之后在东德的国家机关位居高职(Streletz, Kessler and Krenz v. Germany [GC], § 78);1972年,东德边境警卫杀害了一名试图穿过两德边界的人,尽管他是在执行上级命令(K.-H. W. v. Germany [GC], §§ 68 - 81);苏联军队的一名指挥官带领一支"红色游击队"讨伐"二战"的奸细,其中的风险本应该被精细评估(Kononov v. Latvia [GC], §§ 235 - 239)。至于士兵个人的刑事责任,本法院认为,对于那些不仅公然违反国内法,还公然侵犯国际公认的人权(特别是生命权,即人权在国际层面的最高价值体现)的命令,士兵不能全盘地、盲目地服从(Kononov v. Latvia [GC], § 236; K.-H. W. v. Germany [GC], § 75)。

27. 可预见性必须从被定罪之人在犯下被指控之罪时的角度来评价(很有可能是在被定罪之人获得了法律建议之后)(Del Río Prada v. Spain [GC], §§ 112 and 117,申诉人被定罪时,即实施犯罪行为后,所施加处罚的范围发生变更的可预见性)。

28. 如果定罪完全基于国际法或者国际法原则,本法院会根据诉讼期间国际法适用的标准,来评估定罪的可预见性,所依据的国际法包括国际条约(在涉及有关东德的问题时适用《公民政治及国际权利公约》,*Streletz, Kessler and Krenz v. Germany* [GC], §§ 90 - 106;1948 年的《防止及惩治灭绝种族罪公约》,*Jorgic v. Germany*, § 106),和国际惯例(1953 年,国际惯例关于灭绝种族罪的定义,*Vasiliauskas v. Lithuania* [GC], §§ 171 - 175;1944 年的《战争法律和惯例》,*Kononov v. Latvia* [GC], §§ 205 - 227;禁止在国际冲突中使用芥子气的国际惯例,*Van Anraat v. Netherlands* (dec.), §§ 86 - 97)。

(二)司法解释:关于法律规则的说明

29. 在任何法律体系中,无论法律规定有多么明确,都需要进行司法解释。国内法院的裁判角色就是解决这种解释中存在的疑惑(*Kafkaris v. Cyprus* [GC], § 141)。通过司法立法来推动刑法的发展,是公约缔约国的法律传统中固有的、必要的一部分。公约第 7 条不能被解读为禁止通过个案中的司法解释来逐步明确刑事责任规则,因为对于法律内容的司法解释与法律对于犯罪的规定在本质上具有一致性,并且能够合理预见(*S. W. v. the United Kingdom*, § 36;*Streletz, Kessler and Krenz v. Germany* [GC], § 50;*Kononov v. Latvia* [GC], § 185)。

30. 司法解释的可预见性与犯罪构成(*Pessino v. France*, §§ 35 - 36,*Dragotoniu and Militaru-Pidhorni v. Romania*, §§ 43 - 47)和适用刑罚都有关(*Alimuçaj v. Albania*, §§ 154 - 162;*Del Río Prada v. Spain* [GC], §§ 111 - 117)。如果本法院认为定罪或犯罪缺乏可预见性,就不能再去评判施加的刑罚是否符合第 7 条所要求的由法律规定(*Plechkov v. Romania*, § 75)。严格程序事项的解释对犯罪的预见性没有影响,因此不会涉及有关第 7 条的问题(主张在起诉原告时遇到了程序上的困难,*Khodorkovskiy and Lebedev v. Russia*, §§ 788 - 790)。

31. 关于国内司法解释与犯罪本质的相容性,本法院必须通过上下文确定解释是否与所涉刑事法律规定的措辞相一致,以及是否合理(关于灭绝种族罪,*Jorgic v. Germany*, §§ 104 - 108)。

32. 关于司法解释的合理预见性,本法院必须评估申诉人当时是否可以——如有必要,在律师的协助下——合理地预见被指控和定罪并受到相应处罚的风险(*Jorgic v. Germany*, §§ 109 - 113)。本法院必须确定刑事司法解释是否只是延续可预见的判例法的发展(*S. W. v. the United Kingdom* 以及 *C. R. v. the United Kingdom*,两名妇女,分别遭到丈夫强奸和强奸未遂。本法院指出,强奸对被害人人格的贬损性显而易见,因此英国法院的决定是可预见并且符合公约的基本目标的,"公约最核心的内容就是尊重人的尊严和自由"),或者国内法院是否采取了一种申诉人无法预见的新的方式(*Pessino v. France*,§ 36;*Dragotoniu and Militaru-Pidhorni v. Romania*,§ 44;*Del Río Prada v. Spain*,§§ 111 – 117)。评价一项司法解释的可预见性时,缺乏可比较适用的先例对于判断结果并不具有决定性(*K. A. and A. D. v. Belgium*,§§ 55 – 58,本法院认为因施虐导致实际身体伤害罪是极不正常的暴力行为;*Soros v. France*,§ 58)。当国内法院首次解释某一刑法规定时,如果对罪行范围的解释与该罪的本质一致,就应当将其视作一项规则,认为其具有可预见性(*Jorgic v. Germany*,§ 109,申诉人是第一个依据刑法典被认定犯灭绝种族罪的人)。如果根据国内法规定以及行为的本质,对于现行犯罪行为范围的新解释是合理的,那么这一解释就符合第 7 条目的所要求的可预见性(对于"逃税"这一概念的新解释,见 *Khodorkovskiy* 以及 *Lebedev v. Russia*,§§ 791 – 821,本法院认为,刑法中关于税收的规定可以足够灵活,以适应新的情况,并具有可预见性)。

33. 尽管本法院会考虑关键时刻对于法律的原则性解释——尤其是当这一解释与司法解释相一致时(*K. A. and A. D. v. Belgium*,§ 59;*Alimuçaj v. Albania*,§§ 158 – 160),即使立法者已经解释过条文,也不能代替判例法(*Dragotoniu and Militaru-Pidhorni v. Romania*,§§ 26 and 43)。

34. 尽管在一定的情形下,长期容忍某种行为可能会使得这些行为在某些案例中实际上去刑事化——这些行为本来是可能受到刑事处罚的,不能仅因为其他人没有被起诉或定罪,就免除被判刑申诉人的刑事责任,也不能因此认为定罪不符合公约第 7 条目的所要求的可预见性(*Khodorkovskiy and Lebedev v. Russia*,§§ 816 – 820)。

35. 在解释基于公开的国际法制定的法律条文时,国内法院必须确定在国内法中适用哪种解释,这一解释应当与违法行为的实质相一致,并在诉讼期间具有可预见性(德国法院对于灭绝种族罪采取了一个较为宽泛的解释,之后这一解释就被其他国际法院所否决,如联合国国际法院,*Jorgic v. Germany*,§§ 103 – 116)。

36. 本法院认为,(恶意地)对刑法做出不利于被告的扩张性解释,根据不可预见的判例法的撤销做出解释(*Dragotoniu and Militaru-Pidhorni v. Romania*,§§ 39 – 48),以及通过类推做出与犯罪行为实质不一致的解释(*Vasiliauskas v. Lithuania* [GC],§§ 179 – 186,灭绝种族罪的定罪),都不符合可预见性的要求。这也有可能会与国家依据犯罪之后新增的判例法对犯罪行为定罪相违背[从外部协助及教唆黑社会性质组织犯罪,*Contrada v. Italy* (no.3),§§ 64-76]。

37. 陪审团负责考虑案件、适用刑法,这并不意味着法律的效力不符合第 7 条的目的所要求的可预见性[*Jobe v. the United Kingdom* (dec.)]。如果足够明确地规定自由裁量权的范围及其行使方式,充分保护个体免于任意性的专断,那么授予陪审团关于具体案件法律适用的自由裁量权并不违背公约的要求[*O'Carroll v. the United Kingdom* (dec.),陪审团对于猥亵的构成要件的认定]。

(三)国家继承的特殊情况

38. 司法解释的概念适用于民主法治国家判例法的逐步发展,在国家继承的情况下也同样有效。本法院认为,在一国领土上国家主权变更或国家政体变更的事件中,一个法治国家对那些在前一政体统治期间犯罪的人提起刑事诉讼是合法的;同样,这种由新政权取代旧政权的国家中的法院,根据法治国家所遵循的法律原则,在诉讼期间对现行法律规定进行应用和解释是不应该被批判的(*Streletz, Kessler and Krenz v. Germany* [GC],§§ 79-83;*Vasiliauskas v. Lithuania* [GC],§ 159)。特别是当存在争议的问题涉及生命权时,这一权利是公约和人权在国际层面的最高价值体现,缔约方对其具有首要的保护义务(*Kononov v. Latvia* [GC],§ 241)。一国容忍或鼓励被国内法或国际法视为刑事犯罪的行为,使得犯罪之人认为其可以免受处罚,这并不妨碍他们接受审判和惩罚(*Vasiliauskas v. Lithuania* [GC],§ 158;*Streletz, Kessler and Krenz v. Germany* [GC],§§ 74 and 77-79)。本法院认为,对杀害1979年至1989年间试图穿过两德边界逃离东德的人的东德政治领袖和边境警卫的定罪是可预见的,这一定罪已经由重新统一后的德国的法院基于德意志民主共和国的立法做出宣判(*Streletz, Kessler and Krenz v. Germany* [GC],§§ 77-89;*K.-H. W. v. Germany* [GC],§§ 68-91)。关于"二战"期间苏军指挥官战争罪行的认定,也可以得出一致的结论,在拉脱维亚于1990年和1991年宣告独立后,拉脱维亚法院对其罪行做出了宣判(*Kononov v. Latvia* [GC],§§ 240-241)。

39. 本法院还认为,尽管在诉讼期间立陶宛还没有被认可为一个独立的国家,但根据重新恢复独立的立陶宛共和国的法律进行定罪是可充分预见的,并且符合公约第 7 条的规定(*Kuolelis, Bartosevicius and Burokevicius v. Lithuania*,§§116-122,对在1991年1月参与颠覆与反政府活动的苏联共产党立陶宛分支领导人进行定罪)。

（四）国家普遍刑事管辖权的特殊情况及可适用的国内法

40. 以一国国内法为依据进行定罪，可能涉及犯罪嫌疑人在另一国的犯罪行为 [*Jorgic v. Germany*; *Van Anraat v. Netherlands* (dec.)]。一国国内法院的域外或普遍管辖权问题并不属于第 7 条所规定的范围 [*Ould Dah v. France* (dec.)]，而属于如公约第 6 条第 1 款及第 5 条第 1 款第 a 项所规定的依法设立的国内法院或审判庭的权利（"由有管辖权的法院判决后对被定罪之人进行的合法拘留"）(*Jorgic v. Germany*, §§ 64-72，对在波黑发生的灭绝种族行为的定罪）。

41. 一国的国内法院基于普遍刑事管辖权判决一个人有罪时，可根据公约第 7 条审查国内法的适用是否损害了罪行发生地所在国的法律。例如，在一个由法国法院（基于《联合国反酷刑公约》）对在毛里塔尼亚实施酷刑和暴行的毛里塔尼亚官员进行定罪的案件中，本法院认为，适用法国刑法对毛里塔尼亚特赦法的损害（已在所有的刑事程序前颁布）并不违背罪刑法定原则 [*Ould Dah v. France* (dec.)]。在这方面，本法院认为，"如果国家只能行使司法管辖权而不能适用法律，那么禁止酷刑和起诉违反普遍规则之人的绝对必要性以及缔约国基于《联合国反酷刑公约》所具有的普遍管辖权，将丧失其本质。为了维护犯罪发生地所在国为保护其公民而通过的决定或特殊法案，而认为行使普遍管辖权的国家法律不能适用，或者是受到犯罪者直接或间接的影响，为了使其免罪而适用行使普遍管辖权的国家的法律，这些毫无疑问都会使普遍管辖权的行使机制趋于瘫痪，同时也违反《联合国反酷刑公约》所追求的目标。"本法院重申禁止酷刑在所有有关人权保护的国际文书中处于很重要的地位，同时也是民主社会的基本价值观。

第四节　刑法的法不溯及既往原则

一、总体考量

42. 第 7 条无条件禁止刑法不利于被告的溯及既往的适用（*Del Río Prada v. Spain* [GC], § 116; *Kokkinakis v. Greece*, § 52）。刑法的法不溯及既往原则不仅适用于对违法行为的定义（*Vasiliauskas v. Lithuania* [GC], §§ 165-166），同时也适用于犯罪行为

带来的刑事处罚(*Jamil v. France*, §§ 34 – 36; *M. v. Germany*, §§ 123 and 135 – 137; *Gurguchiani v. Spain*, §§ 32 – 44)。甚至是在已经判处最终刑罚之后或正在执行刑罚之时,法不溯及既往的规定也排除立法机关、行政机关和国内法院对所判处的刑罚做出不利于被告的重新定义或修改(*Del Río Prada v. Spain* [GC], § 89,根据判例法撤销一个 30 年监禁的判决,对于已拘留的刑期不能有效适用减刑,而当申诉人犯下罪行时,最高法定刑被视为一个新的、独立的判决,此时可以对已拘留的刑期适用减刑)。

43. 对在相关规定生效之前发生的行为适用该规定,违背了法不溯及既往原则,该原则禁止将现有的罪行范围扩大到以前未被规定为刑事犯罪的行为。然而,如果根据当时可适用的刑法典,该行为就已具有可罚性,则不违反第 7 条的规定——即使他们只是作为一个加重情节具有可罚性,而不是一个独立的违法行为——[*Ould Dah v. France*(dec.),只要所判处的刑罚不超过该刑法规定的最高刑]或者是基于当时可适用的国际法对申诉人定罪(*Vasiliauskas v. Lithuania*[GC], §§ 165 – 166,国内法院根据 1953 年生效的国际法对申诉人定罪,本法院处理这一问题时指出,国内法院溯及既往地适用了 2003 年立陶宛法律关于种族灭绝的规定; *Šimšić v. Bosnia and Herzegovina* (dec.),1992 年实施的反人类罪)。在后一种情况下,尽管相对于国际法,国内法上往往会采取一种更加广泛的定义(参见上文第 35 段),他们无法在重新定义之前行为的基础上,溯及既往地适用刑罚(*Vasiliauskas v. Lithuania*[GC], § 181,根据 2003 年刑法典对灭绝种族的行为进行定罪,该刑法典涉及的是 1953 年针对政治组织成员实施的行为)。

44. 关于刑罚的严重程度,本法院对犯罪判处的刑罚有所限制,不能比犯罪时可适用的刑罚更重。有关处罚适当性的问题不属于公约第 7 条讨论的范围。决定监禁的期限以及对于特定违法行为施加刑罚的类型并不是本法院的职能(*Hummatov v. Azerbaijan* (dec.); *Hakkar v. France* (dec.); *Vinter and Others v. the United Kingdom* [GC], § 105)。然而,可以根据公约第 3 条考察刑罚的合比例性问题(*Vinter and Others v. the United Kingdom* [GC], § 102,"明显不合比例的惩罚"的概念)。

45. 关于刑罚的严重或严厉程度,本法院已经规定,判处终身监禁并不比死刑更严重,然而后者可以在行为人实施犯罪时适用,但随后已被废除并被终身监禁取代 [*Hummatov v. Azerbaijan* (dec.); *Stepanenko and Ososkalo v. Ukraine* (dec.); *Öcalan v. Turkey* (no.2), § 177]。

46. 在确定是否存在任何不利于被告的溯及既往的刑罚适用时,必须注意在每部刑法典中可适用的量刑标准(法定最高刑和最低刑)。例如,即使对申诉人判处的刑罚同时处于两部可适用的刑法典的范围内,如果原本可根据其中一部刑法典所规定的更轻的法定最低刑做出一个更轻的判决,而国内法院并没有依此对被告判处更轻的刑罚,那么就已经违反了第 7 条的规定(*Maktouf and Damjanović v. Bosnia and Herzegovina*[GC],§§ 65 – 76)。

二、持续犯

47. 对于"持续"或"继续"的罪行(涉及一段时间内持续的行为),本法院认为,根据法律确定性原则,应在起诉书中明确导致个人承担刑事责任的犯罪行为的要素。此外,国内法院做出的决定也必须明确,对被告人的定罪和判决是基于在起诉中已经确立"持续性"行为的构成要件 *Ecer and Zeyrek v. Turkey*,§ 33)。最近,本法院认为,国内法院根据修改后的刑法典对个人的违法行为定罪,同时对在修改生效之前实施的并且被国内法认定为"持续性的"犯罪行为进行定罪,这并不属于不利于被告的溯及既往的刑法适用(*Rohlena v. the Czech Republic*[GC],§§ 57 – 64,对同居者实施的虐待行为)。本法院指出,在所涉及的国内法中,"持续"的罪行被认为构成了一个单一的行为,由于在旧法施行期间实施的行为在旧法中也具有可罚性,因此在对该罪行进行刑法上的分类时,必须根据在犯罪行为最后一次发生并完成时有效的法律加以考察。此外,由于在原告实施第一次行为之前,持续犯的概念已被引入刑事法典,因此国内法院根据国内法对持续犯概念加以适用也就具有可预见性(*Rohlena v. the Czech Republic*[GC],§§ 60 – 64)。本法院还认为,根据"持续"犯罪的分类对申诉人判处的刑罚,不会比在对申诉人立法修改之前及之后实施的行为分别进行评价时可能判处的刑罚更加严重(同上,§§ 65 – 69)。

48. 相反地,如果依据当时有效的国内法,对持续犯定罪是不可预见的,而且还导致加重了对申诉人判处的刑罚,那么本法院会认定为刑法被溯及既往地适用且不利于申诉人[*Veeber v. Estonia*(no.2),§§ 30 – 39;*Puhk v. Estonia*,§§ 24 – 34]。

三、累犯

49. 申诉人之前在刑法上的身份在之后被审判庭和上诉法院纳入考虑范围,这是由于其在 1984 年的定罪被保存在犯罪记录中,鉴于被起诉和惩罚的犯罪行为是在新法生效后发生,这一新法中延长了可能构成累犯的期限,本法院认为,审判庭和上诉法庭的做法并不违反第7条的规定(Achour v. France [GC], §§ 44-61,国内法院直接适用了新的刑法,新的刑法规定在10年的期限内均有可能构成累犯,而在申诉人实施第一次违法行为时,有效的旧法典规定的期限是5年,根据申诉人的主张,在5年期满时,他便享有"被遗忘"的权利)。这种溯及既往的方法不同于严格意义上的溯及既往的概念。

第五节 较轻刑罚的溯及原则

50. 尽管公约第7条第1款并未明确提及较轻刑罚的溯及原则(不同于《联合国公民权利和政治权利公约》第15条第1款及《美洲人权公约》第9条做出的详细规定),但本法院认为,第7条第1款不仅能保障更严厉的刑法不溯及既往的原则,也含蓄地表明,溯及适用更宽松的刑法的原则。这一原则体现为,当犯罪行为实施时有效的法律与行为发生之后、最终判决做出之前制定生效的法律之间存在差别时,国内法院必须适用对被告人最有利的法律规定(Scoppola v. Italy (no.2) [GC], §§ 103-109,判处30年的监禁而非死刑)。本法院认为,"仅因为依据在实施犯罪时法律已规定的刑罚而判处较重的刑罚,意味着适用不利于被告的刑法在时间上的延续性的规则。此外,这相当于无视任何有利于被告的、可能发生在定罪之前的立法变化,并继续施加处罚,而国家及其所代表的共同体现在会觉得这些刑罚过于严重"(Scoppola v. Italy (no.2) [GC], § 108)。本法院指出,在欧洲和国际上逐渐出现了一个共识,认为应适用提供了更宽松处罚的刑法——甚至于这一刑法是在违法行为实施之后才颁布,这已成为刑法的基本原则(Scoppola v. Italy (no.2) [GC], § 106)。

51. 即使在斯科珀拉诉意大利案(Scoppola v. Italy (no.2) [GC])中,本法院并没有明确支持任何有利于被定罪之人的立法变化的溯及力效果,但本法院确实对定罪之人适用了更轻刑罚的溯及力原则,因为国内法律明文要求,当之后的法律减轻了适用于犯罪行为的处罚时,国内法院应当审查因职权判处的刑罚(Gouarré Patte v. Andorra, §§ 28-36)。本法院认为,如果国家在其法律中明文规定更为有利的法律的溯及力原则,就必须允许其公民在与公约一致的范围内行使该权利(Gouarré Patte v. Andorra, § 35)。

第六节　第7条第2款：文明国家所认可的一般法律原则

> **第7条第2款**
> "如果根据文明国家所认可的一般法律原则，该作为或者不作为在其发生时构成刑事犯罪行为，则本条不得妨碍对该人的作为或者不作为进行审判或者予以惩罚。"

52. 从公约的筹备文件中可以看出，第7条第1款可以被视为有关法不溯及既往的一般原则，而第7条第2款则只是对该原则责任部分的阐明，因此确保在"二战"后起诉"二战"期间罪行的有效性是毋庸置疑的（*Kononov v. Latvia*［GC］，§186；*Maktouf and Damjanović v. Bosnia and Herzegovina*［GC］，§72）。这也表明，公约的订立者并非允许法不溯及既往原则的一般例外。事实上，本法院在一些案件中指出，第7条的两款条文之间存在内在联系，并且应当结合起来解释（*Tess v. Latvia*（dec.）；*Kononov v. Latvia*［GC］，§186）。

53. 根据这些原则，在对1992年和1993年发生于波斯尼亚的战争行为进行定罪时（*Maktouf and Damjanović v. Bosnia and Herzegovina*［GC］，§72，其中，政府主张，根据"文明国家认可的一般法律原则"，被指责的行为属于犯罪，不能适用禁止溯及既往的原则），以及在对1953年实施的灭绝种族行为进行定罪时（*Vasiliauskas v. Lithuania*［GC］，§§187-190），本法院排除了第7条第2款的适用。关于对"二战"期间实施的战争行为的定罪，本法院认为，考虑到申诉人的行为从第7条第1款的意义上来说构成了"国际法"上的犯罪，因此没必要根据第7条第2款来对这些罪行进行评价（*Kononov v. Latvia*［GC］，§§244-246，参考了国际惯例，尤其是战争法律和惯例）。

第七节　欧洲人权法院在违反公约第7条的案件中所指示的措施

54. 根据公约第46条的规定,在任何情况下,缔约国都应遵守本法院的最终判决,并由部长委员会监督执行。本法院认为被诉国违反本公约或其议定书时,被诉国不仅应通过满足条件的方式向相关人支付款项(公约第41条),同时也要在部长委员会的监督下,在其国内法律秩序中采取普遍性措施或个别性措施(如果恰当)来杜绝本法院所认定的违反公约的行为,并尽可能地修正其影响。此外,应诉国仍然可以自由选择其履行第46条所规定义务的方式,只要履行方式与本法院判决得出的结论相一致即可(*Scozzari and Giunta v. Italy*［GC］,§249)。

55. 然而,在某些特定情况下,为了帮助被诉国履行第46条所规定的义务,本法院可能会对用以杜绝违反公约行为的个别性措施或普遍性措施做出一些指示。在违反第7条的案件中,出现例外情形时,本法院有时会对可行的个别性措施做出指示:根据申诉人的要求重新启动国内诉讼程序(*Dragotoniu and Militaru-Pidhorni v. Romania*,§55,在个人被指控违反公约第6条时适用了同样的规则);在尽可能早的日期释放申诉人(*Del Río Prada v. Spain*［GC］,§139,实施中的第3号规定,被认为违反了公约第7条以及第5条第1款);或要求应诉国根据较轻刑罚的溯及力原则,用不超过30年的有期徒刑取代申诉人的无期徒刑(*Scoppola v. Italy*(no.2)［GC］,§154,执行中的第6条第a款规定)。

援引案例一览

本指南援引的判例法涉及欧洲人权法院的判决或裁定以及欧洲人权委员会的决定或报告。

除非另行指明,所有参考皆是本法院审判庭依法做出的判决。缩写"(dec.)"是指该处援引为本法院裁定,"[GC]"是指该案件由大审判庭审判。

本指南电子版中援引案例的超链接直接跳转 HUDOC 数据库〈http://hudoc.echr.coe.int〉。该数据库提供本法院(包括大审判庭、审判庭和委员会的判决、裁定和相关案例、咨询意见以及案例法信息注解中的法律总结)、委员会(决定和报告)和部长委员会(决议)的判例法。

本法院以英语和/或法语这两种官方语言发布判决和裁定。HUDOC 也包含许多重要案例的近 30 种非官方言语的翻译,以及由第三方制作的大约 100 个在线案例汇总的链接。

(注:为了避免重复,本章所附的相关案例索引没有在中文部分进行翻译,读者可在对应的英文部分阅读。)

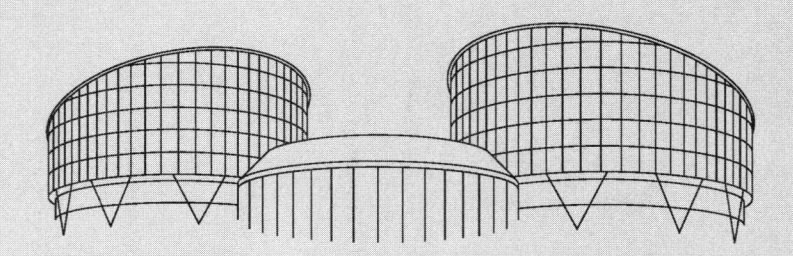

EUROPEAN COURT OF HUMAN RIGHTS
COUR EUROPÉENNE DES DROITS DE L'HOMME

Chapter V   Guide on Article 7 of the European Convention on Human Rights
No Punishment Without Law:
the Principle that Only the Law Can Define A Crime and Prescribe A Penalty

COUNCIL OF EUROPE
CONSEIL DE L'EUROPE

Publishers or organisations wishing to translate and/or reproduce all or part of this report in the form of a printed or electronic publication are invited to contact publishing@echr.coe.int for information on the authorisation procedure.

This guide was prepared by the Research and Library Division, within the Directorate of the Jurisconsult, and does not bind the Court. The text was finalised on 31 January 2016; it may be subject to editorial revision.

The document is available for downloading at ⟨www.echr.coe.int⟩ (Case-Law-Case-Law Analysis-Case-Law Guides).

For publication updates please follow the Court's Twitter account at ⟨https:/twitter.com/echrpublication⟩.

© Council of Europe/European Court of Human Rights, 2016

Note to readers

This Guide is part of the series of Case-Law Guides published by the European Court of Human Rights (hereafter "the Court", "the European Court" or "the Strasbourg Court") to inform legal practitioners about the fundamental judgments delivered by the Strasbourg Court. This particular Guide analyses and sums up the case-law under Article 7 of the European Convention on Human Rights (hereafter "the Convention" or "the European Convention") until 31 January 2016. Readers will find the key principles in this area and the relevant precedents.

The case-law cited has been selected among the leading, major, and/or recent judgments and decisions. *

The Court's judgments serve not only to decide those cases brought before the Court but, more generally, to elucidate, safeguard and develop the rules instituted by the Convention, thereby contributing to the observance by the States of the engagements undertaken by them as Contracting Parties (*Ireland v. the United Kingdom*, § 154, 18 January 1978, Series A no. 25.). The mission of the system set up by the Convention is thus to determine, in the general interest, issues of public policy, thereby raising the standards of protection of human rights and extending human rights jurisprudence throughout the community of the Convention States (*Konstantin Markin v. Russia* [GC], § 89, no. 30078/06, ECHR 2012).

---

* The case-law cited may be in either or both of the official languages (English and French) of the Court and the European Commission of Human Rights. Unless otherwise indicated, all references are to a judgment on the merits delivered by a Chamber of the Court. The abbreviation "(dec.)" indicates that the citation is of a decision of the Court and "[GC]" that the case was heard by the Grand Chamber.

I. Introduction

> Article 7 of the Convention-No punishment without law
>
> "1. No one shall be held guilty of any criminal offence on account of any act or omission which did not constitute a criminal offence under national or international law at the time when it was committed. Nor shall a heavier penalty be imposed than the one that was applicable at the time the criminal offence was committed.
>
> 2. This article shall not prejudice the trial and punishment of any person for any act or omission which, at the time when it was committed, was criminal according to the general principles of law recognised by civilised nations."

1. The guarantee enshrined in Article 7, which is an essential element of the rule of law, occupies a prominent place in the Convention system of protection, as is underlined by the fact that no derogation from it is permissible under Article 15 in time of war or other public emergency. It should be construed and applied, as follows from its object and purpose, in such a way as to provide effective safeguards against arbitrary prosecution, conviction and punishment (*S. W. v. the United Kingdom*, § 34; *C. R. v. the United Kingdom*, § 32; *Del Río Prada v. Spain* [GC], § 77; *Vasiliauskas v. Lithuania* [GC], § 153).

2. Article 7 of the Convention is not confined to prohibiting the retrospective application of criminal law to an accused's disadvantage. It also embodies, more generally, the principles that only the law can define a crime and prescribe a penalty (*nullum crimen, nulla poena sine lege*) and that the criminal law must not be extensively construed to an accused person's disadvantage, for instance by analogy (ibid., § 154; *Kokkinakis v. Greece*, § 52).

II. Scope

A. The concept of "finding of guilt"

3. Article 7 only applies where the person has been "found guilty" of committing a criminal offence. It does not cover mere ongoing prosecutions, for example (*Lukanov v. Bulgaria*, Commission decision), or a decision to extradite an individual (*X v. the Netherlands*, Commission decision). For the purposes of the Convention, there can be no "conviction" unless it has been established in accordance with the law that there has been an offence (*Varvara v. Italy*, § 69).

4. Nevertheless, the imposition of a "penalty" without a "finding of guilt" can sometimes fall within the scope of Article 7 of the Convention and give rise to a violation of the latter, inasmuch as punishing an accused whose trial did not lead to a finding of guilt is irreconcilable with the legality principle guaranteed by that Article (*Varvara v. Italy*, §§ 61 and 72 – 73). The "penalty" and "punishment" rationale and the "guilty" concept and the corresponding notion of "*personne coupable*" (in the French version) support an interpretation of Article 7 as requiring, in order to implement punishment, a finding of liability by the national courts enabling the offence to be attributed to and the penalty to be imposed on its perpetrator (ibid., § 71; see also, as regards the requirement of *mens rea* in the perpetrator of the offence, *Sud Fondi srl and Others v. Italy*, § 116).

B. The concept of "criminal offence"

5. The "criminal offence" concept ("*infraction*" in the French version) has an autonomous meaning, like "criminal charge" in Article 6 of the Convention.① The three criteria set out in the case of *Engel and Others v. the Netherlands*, § 82 (as more recently

---

① For the scope of Article 6 (criminal aspect) and the concept of a "criminal charge", see pages 7 to 11 of the Guide on Article 6 (criminal limb), available on the Court website (⟨www.echr.coe.int⟩-Case-law).

reaffirmed in *Jussila v. Finland* [GC], §30) for assessing whether a charge is "criminal" within the meaning of Article 6 must also be applied to Article 7 [*Brown v. the United Kingdom* (dec.)]:

- classification in domestic law;
- the very nature of the offence (the most important criterion, see *Jussila v. Finland* [GC], §38);
- the degree of severity of the penalty that the person concerned risks incurring.

6. In applying those criteria, the Court held that a breach of military discipline did not fall within the "criminal" sphere for the purposes of either Article 6 or Article 7 [*Çelikateş and Others v. Turkey* (dec.)]. The same applies to dismissals and restrictions on employment of former KGB agents [*Sidabras and Džiautas v. Lithuania* (dec.)], a disciplinary offence committed by a student on university premises (*Monaco v. Italy* (dec.), §§ 40 and 68 – 69) and impeachment proceedings against the President of the Republic for gross violations of the Constitution (*Paksas v. Lithuania* [GC], §§ 64 – 69). In the absence of a "criminal offence" the Court found that the complaint was incompatible *ratione materiae* with the provisions of the Convention relied upon.

C. The concept of "law"

7. The concept of "law" ("*droit*" in the French version) as used in Article 7 corresponds to that set out in other Convention articles, covering both domestic legislation and case-law, and comprises qualitative requirements, notably those of accessibility and foreseeability (*Del Río Prada v. Spain* [GC], § 91; *S. W. v. the United Kingdom*, § 35). It obviously also embraces not only judicial law-making (ibid., §§ 36 and 41 – 43) but also statutes and enactments of lower rank than statutes (prison rules in *Kafkaris v. Cyprus* [GC], §§ 145 – 146). The Court must have regard to the domestic law "as a whole" and to the way it was applied at the material time (ibid., § 145; *Del Río Prada v. Spain* [GC], § 90).

8. On the other hand, State practice incompatible with the rules of the written law in force and which emptied of its substance the legislation on which it was supposed to be

based cannot be considered as "law" within the meaning of Article 7 [the border-policing practice of the German Democratic Republic (GDR) in flagrant breach of its own legal system and the fundamental rights, in *Streletz, Kessler and Krenz v. Germany* [GC], §§ 67 – 87; also the practice of eliminating opponents of the communist regime by means of death penalties imposed after trials conducted in flagrant breach of the legislation and constitution of former Czechoslovakia, in *Polednová v. the Czech Republic* (dec.)].

9. The concept of "international law" set out in Article 7 § 1 refers to the international treaties ratified by the State in question (*Streletz, Kessler and Krenz v. Germany* [GC], §§ 90 – 106), as well as customary international law (for the international laws and customs of war see *Kononov v. Latvia* [GC], §§ 186, 213, 227, 237 and 244; for the concept of "crime against humanity" see *Korbely v. Hungary* [GC], §§ 78 – 85; and for the concept of "genocide" see *Vasiliauskas v. Lithuania* [GC], §§ 171 – 175 and 178), even where the corresponding law has never been formally published (*Kononov v. Latvia* [GC], § 237).

D. The concept of a "penalty"

1. General considerations

10. The concept of "penalty" set out in Article 7 § 1 of the Convention is also autonomous in scope. In order to ensure the efficacy of the protection secured under this article, the Court must be free to go beyond appearances and autonomously assess whether a specific measure is, substantively, a "penalty" within the meaning of Article 7 § 1. The starting point for any assessment of the existence of a "penalty" is to ascertain whether the measure in question was ordered following a conviction for a "criminal offence". Other factors may be deemed relevant in this respect: the nature and aim of the measure in question (particularly its punitive aim), its classification under domestic law, the procedures linked to its adoption and execution and its severity (*Welch v. the United Kingdom*, § 28; *Del Río Prada v. Spain* [GC], § 82). However, the severity of the measure is not decisive in itself, because many non-criminal measures of a preventive nature can have a substantial impact on the person concerned [ibid.; *Van der Velden v. the Netherlands* (dec)].

11. In applying these criteria the Court has, in particular, pinpointed the following measures as "penalties":
- a confiscation order in respect of the proceedings of a criminal offence following a finding of guilt, in view of its punitive purpose, in addition to its preventive and compensatory nature (*Welch v. the United Kingdom*, §§ 29 – 35, concerning the confiscation of the proceedings of drug-trafficking);
- a measure involving imprisonment in default geared to guaranteeingpayment of a fine by enforcement directed at the person of a debtor who has not demonstrated his insolvency (*Jamil v. France*, § 32);
- an administrative fine imposed in an urban development case equivalent to 100% of the value of the wrongfully erected building, which fine had both a preventive and a punitive function [*Valico SLR v. Italy* (dec.)];
- confiscationof land on the grounds of unlawful construction ordered by a criminal court following an acquittal, with a primarily punitive aim geared to preventing recurrent breaches of the law and therefore constituting a preventive and punitive measure (*Sud Fondi srl and Others v. Italy* (dec.); *Varvara v. Italy*, §§ 22 and 51, concerning a confiscation order issued following a discontinuance decision on the grounds of statute limitation);
- preventive detention ordered by a trial court following a conviction for serious offences, having regard to its preventive and also punitive nature, the mode of its enforcement in an ordinary prison, and its unlimited duration (*M. v. Germany*, §§ 123 – 133; *Jendrowiak v. Germany*, § 47; *Glien v. Germany*, §§ 120 – 130; *a contrario*, *Bergmann v. Germany*, §§ 153 – 182, concerning preventive detention imposed on the applicant with a view to his undergoing therapy in a specialist centre);
- replacement of a prison sentence with expulsion and a ten-year prohibition of residence (*Gurguchiani v. Spain*, § 40);
- permanent prohibition on engaging in an occupation ordered by a trial court as a secondary penalty (*Gouarré Patte v. Andorra*, § 30).

12. Conversely, the following are excluded from the concept of "penalty":
- preventive measures (including mandatory hospitalisation) imposed on a person lacking criminal responsibility (*Berland v. France*, §§ 39-47);
- inclusion of an individual on a police or judicial register of sex or violent offenders for preventive and deterrent purposes (*Adamson v. the United Kingdom* (dec); *Gardel v. France*, §§ 39-47);
- DNA profiling of convicted persons by the authorities [*Van der Velden v. the Netherlands* (dec.)];
- detention geared to preventing an individual from engaging in unlawful activities, in view of its preventive nature (*Lawless v. Ireland* (no.3), § 19);
- prohibition of residence (imposed in addition to a prison sentence) following a criminal conviction, the ban being treated as equivalent to a public-order measure (*Renna v. France*, Commission decision; see, *mutatis mutandis*, under the criminal head of Article 6 § 1, *Maaouia v. France* [GC], § 39);
- anadministrative expulsion order or prohibition of residence [*Vikulov and Others v. Latvia* (dec.); *C. G. and Others v. Bulgaria* (dec.)];
- transfer of a sentenced person to another country under the Additional Protocol to the Council of Europe Convention on the Transfer of Sentenced Persons, which measure is geared to promoting the person's social reintegration into his country of origin (*Szabó v. Sweden* (dec.); *Giza v. Poland* (dec.), § 30, as regards the surrender of a sentenced person under the EU Framework Decision on the European Arrest Warrant and the procedure for surrenders between Member States);
- a preventive property confiscation order based on suspected belonging to mafia-type organisations, which order was not conditional upon any prior criminal conviction (*M. v. Italy*, Commission decision);
- special police surveillance or house arrest of a dangerous person designed to prevent the perpetration of criminal offences (*Mucci v. Italy*, Commission decision; *Raimondo v. Italy*, § 43, as regards the criminal aspect of Article 6 § 1);
- a confiscation order imposed in the framework of criminal proceedings against third

parties (*Yildirim v. Italy* (dec.); *Bowler International Unit v. France*, §§ 65–68);

- revocation of an MP's parliamentary mandate and declaration that he had become ineligible following the dissolution of a political party [*Sobacı v. Turkey* (dec.)];
- impeachment and declaration of ineligibility against a President following impeachment proceedings for serious violation of the Constitution (*Paksas v. Lithuania* [GC], §§ 65–68);
- suspensionof a civil servant's pension rights following disciplinary proceedings [*Haioun v. France* (dec.)];
- three weekends in solitary confinement (*A. v. Spain*, Commission decision; *Payet v. France*, §§ 94–100, under the criminal aspect of Article 6);
- socialisolation of a prisoner owing to the fact that the applicant was the only inmate of the prison, in respect of which the Court found that this was such an extraordinary measure that a State could not be reasonably expected to provide details in its legislation on the regime to be applied in such cases [*Öcalan v. Turkey* (no.2), § 187].

2. Distinction between substantive criminal law and procedural law

13. The Court has specified that the rules on retroactivity set out in Article 7 of the Convention only apply to the provisions defining the offences and the corresponding penalties. In principle, they do not apply to procedural laws, the immediate application of which in conformity with the *tempus regit actum* principle was deemed reasonable by the Court (*Scoppola v. Italy* (no. 2) [GC], § 110, with the references therein to cases concerning Article 6 of the Convention: see, for example, the rules concerning the use of witness statements, referred to as "procedural rules", in *Bosti v. Italy* (dec.), § 55), subject to the absence of arbitrariness [*Morabito v. Italy* (dec.)]. However, where a provision classified as procedural in domestic law influences the severity of the penalty to be imposed, the Court classifies that provision as "substantive criminal law" to which the last sentence of Article 7 § 1 is applicable (*Scoppola v. Italy* (no.2) [GC], §§ 110–113,

in connection with a provision of the Code of Criminal Procedure concerning the severity of the penalty to be imposed in proceedings using the simplified procedure).

14. As regards statutory limitation in particular, the Court has held that Article 7 does not impede the immediate application to live proceedings of laws extending limitation periods, where the alleged offences have never become subject to limitation (*Coëme and Others v. Belgium*, § 149), and where there is no arbitrariness (*Previti v. Italy* (dec.), §§ 80 – 85). The Court has thus classified rules on limitation periods as procedural laws, inasmuch as they do not define offences and penalties and can be construed as laying down a simple precondition for the assessment of the case (ibid., § 80; *Borcea v. Romania* (dec.), § 64). Furthermore, where the crimes for which an individual was convicted were punishable under international law, the issue of the applicable limitation period must be decided in the light of the relevant international law in force at the material time (*Kononov v. Latvia* [GC], §§ 229 – 233, where the Court found that the relevant international law in force at the material time had not specified any limitation period for war crimes and therefore held that the proceedings against the applicant had never become statute-barred; compare *Kolk and Kislyiy v. Estonia* (dec.) and *Penart v. Estonia* (dec.), where the Court held that crimes against humanity were not subject to statutory limitations).

3. A distinction must be drawn between the "penalty" and its enforcement

15. The Court has drawn a distinction between measures constituting a "penalty" and measures relating to the "enforcement" or "implementation" of that penalty. Where the nature and purpose of a given measure concern remission of sentence or a change in the procedure for conditional release, that measure is not an integral part of the "punishment" within the meaning of Article 7 (for the granting of sentence remission, see *Grava v. Italy*, § 49; and *Kafkaris v. Cyprus* [GC], § 151; for a legislative amendment on the conditions for release on parole, see *Hogben v. the United Kingdom*, Commission decision; and *Uttley v. the United Kingdom* (dec.); for differences between the regulations on release on parole in various cases of transfer of sentenced persons, see *Ciok v. Poland* (dec.), §§ 33 – 34). Issues relating to release policies, the manner of their

implementation and the reasoning behind them fall within the power of the member States to determine their own criminal policy (*Kafkaris v. Cyprus* [GC], § 151). Nor does a failure to apply amnesty legislation to a conviction which has already become final fall within the ambit of Article 7 [*Montcornet de Caumont v. France* (dec.)].

16. In practice, however, the distinction between a measure that constitutes a "penalty" and one that relates to the "enforcement" of a penalty is not always clear. For instance, the Court has accepted that the manner in which a set of prison regulations on the method of enforcing sentences had been construed and implemented *vis-à-vis* the penalty in question went beyond straightforward enforcement and thereby covered the actual scope of the sentence (*Kafkaris v. Cyprus* [GC], § 148, relating to a life sentence). Similarly, the extension of preventive detention by the sentence enforcement courts under legislation which had come into force after the applicant had committed the offence amounted to an "additional penalty" and therefore did not exclusively concern the enforcement of the penalty (*M. v. Germany*, § 135).

17. In that regard, the Court has emphasised that the term "imposed", used in the second sentence of Article 7 § 1, cannot be interpreted as excluding from the scope of that provision all measures introduced after the pronouncement of the sentence (*Del Río Prada v. Spain* [GC], § 88). Consequently, when measures taken by the legislature, the administrative authorities or the courts after the final sentence has been imposed or while the sentence is being served result in the redefinition or modification of the scope of the "penalty" imposed by the trial court, those measures should fall within the scope of the prohibition of the retroactive application of penalties enshrined in Article 7 § 1 *in fine* of the Convention (ibid., § 89). In order to determine whether a measure taken during the execution of a sentence concerns only the manner of execution of the sentence or, on the contrary, also affects its scope, the Court must examine in each case what the "penalty" imposed actually entailed under the domestic law in force at the material time or, in other words, what its intrinsic nature was (ibid., § 90). For example, the Court considered the application of a new approach to the system of remissions of sentence as having led to the redefinition of the scope of the penalty, inasmuch as the new approach had had the effect of

modifying the scope of the penalty imposed to the sentenced person's disadvantage (ibid., §§ 109 – 110 and 117, concerning a thirty-year prison sentence to which, under a case-law reversal, no remissions of sentence for work done in detention would effectively be applied).

4. Links with other provisions of the Convention and the Protocols thereto

18. In addition to the obvious links with the criminal aspect of Article 6 § 1 and the concept of "criminal charge" (see paragraph 5 above and *Bowler International Unit*, §§ 66 – 67), the classification as a "penalty" for the purposes of Article 7 of the Convention is also relevant in determining the applicability of the *non bis in idem* rule as enshrined in Article 4 of Protocol no. 7 (*Serguei̇̈ Zolotoukhine v. Russia* [GC], §§ 52 – 57, as regards the concept of criminal procedure). The notion of what constitutes a "penalty" cannot vary from one Convention provision to another (*Göktan v. France*, § 48; *Zaicevs v. Latvia*, § 53, as regards the relationship between the criminal aspect of Article 6 § 1 of the Convention and the concept of "criminal offence" mentioned in Article 2 of Protocol no. 7).

III. Principle that only the law can define a crime and prescribe a penalty

19. Article 7 of the Convention requires the existence of a legal basis in order to impose a sentence or a penalty. The Court must therefore verify that at the time when an accused person performed the act which led to his being prosecuted and convicted there was in force a legal provision which made that act punishable, and that the punishment imposed did not exceed the limits fixed by that provision (*Coëme and Others v. Belgium*, § 145; *Del Río Prada v. Spain* [GC], § 80).

20. Given the subsidiary nature of the Convention system, it is not the Court's function to deal with errors of fact or law allegedly committed by a national court unless and in so far as they may have infringed rights and freedoms protected by the Convention (*Streletz,*

Kessler and Krenz v. Germany [GC], § 49; *Vasiliauskas v. Lithuania* [GC], § 160), and unless the assessment conducted by the domestic courts is manifestly arbitrary (*Kononov v. Latvia* [GC], § 189). Even though the Court is not called upon to rule on the legal classification of the offence or the applicant's individual criminal responsibility, that being primarily a matter for assessment by the domestic courts (ibid., § 187; *Rohlena v. the Czech Republic* [GC], § 51), Article 7 § 1 requires the Court to examine whether there was a contemporaneous legal basis for the applicant's conviction and, in particular, it must satisfy itself that the result reached by the relevant domestic courts was compatible with Article 7 of the Convention. To accord a lesser power of review to the Court would render Article 7 devoid of purpose (ibid., § 52; *Kononov v. Latvia* [GC], § 198; *Vasiliauskas v. Lithuania* [GC], § 161).

21. Moreover, the principle of legality precludes the imposition on an accused person of a penalty heavier than that carried by the offence of which he was found guilty. Therefore, the Court can find a violation of Article 7 in the case of an error committed by the domestic courts in determining the severity of the sentence passed, having regard to the penalty incurred by the applicant pursuant to the mitigating circumstances as assessed by those courts (*Gabarri Moreno v. Spain*, §§ 22–34). The imposition of a penalty by analogy can also violate the "*nulla poena sine lege*" principle enshrined in Article 7 (*Başkaya and Okçuoğlu v. Turkey* [GC], §§ 42–43, concerning a prison sentence imposed on a publisher under a provision applicable to editors-in-chief).

22. The principle of legality requires the offences and corresponding penalties to be clearly defined by law (see paragraphs 7–9 above, with regard to the concept of "law"). The concept of "law" within the meaning of Article 7, as in other Convention articles (for instance Articles 8 to 11), comprises qualitative requirements, in particular those of accessibility and foreseeability (*Cantoni v. France*, § 29; *Kafkaris v. Cyprus* [GC], § 140; *Del Río Prada v. Spain* [GC], § 91; *Perinçek v. Switzerland* [GC], § 134). These qualitative requirements must be satisfied as regards both the definition of an offence (*Jorgic v. Germany*, §§ 103–114) and the penalty the offence in question carries or its scope (*Kafkaris v. Cyprus* [GC], § 150; *Camilleri v. Malta*, §§ 39–45, concerning

the foreseeability of the applicable sentencing standards, which depended entirely on the choice of trial court by the prosecutor rather than on criteria established by law). Insufficient "quality of law" concerning the definition of the offence and the applicable penalty constitutes a breach of Article 7 of the Convention (*Kafkaris v. Cyprus* [GC], § § 150 and 152).

A. Accessibility

23. As regards accessibility, the Court verifies whether the criminal "law" on which the impugned conviction was based was sufficiently accessible to the applicant, that is to say whether it had been made public (as regards the accessibility of domestic case-law interpreting a section of a law, see *Kokkinakis v. Greece*, § 40; and *G. v. France*, § 25; on the accessibility of an "executive order", see *Custers, Deveaux and Turk v. Denmark* (dec.), § 82). Where a conviction is exclusively based on an international treaty ratified by the respondent State, the Court can verify whether that treaty has been incorporated into domestic law and whether it appears in an official publication (as regards the Geneva Conventions, see *Korbely v. Hungary* [GC], § § 74 – 75). The Court may also consider the accessibility of the definition of the crime at issue in the light of the applicable customary international law (as regards a Resolution of the United Nations General Assembly condemning genocide even before the entry into force of the 1948 Convention on Genocide, see *Vasiliauskas v. Lithuania* [GC], § § 167 – 168; for a joint consideration of the accessibility and foreseeability of the definition of war crimes in the light of the international laws and customs of war-which had not appeared in any official publication-, see *Kononov v. Latvia* [GC], § § 234 – 239 and 244).

B. Foreseeability

1. General considerations

24. An individual must know from the wording of the relevant provision and, if need be, with the assistance of the courts' interpretation of it and after taking appropriate legal advice, what acts and/or omissions will make him criminally liable and what penalty will

be imposed for the act committed and/or omission (*Cantoni v. France*, § 29; *Kafkaris v. Cyprus* [GC], § 140; *Del Río Prada v. Spain* [GC], § 79). The concept of "appropriate advice" refers to the possibility of taking legal advice (*Chauvy and Others v. France* (dec.); *Jorgic v. Germany*, § 113).

25. Owing to their general nature of statutes, their wording cannot be absolutely precise. The need to avoid excessive rigidity and to keep pace with changing circumstances means that many laws are inevitably couched in terms which, to a greater or lesser extent, are vague, and the interpretation and application of such enactments depend on practice (*Kokkinakis v. Greece*, § 40, as regards the definition of the offence of "proselytism"; *Cantoni v. France*, § 31, as regards the legal definition of "medicinal product"). When the legislative technique of categorisation is used, there will often be grey areas at the fringes of the definition. This penumbra of doubt in relation to borderline facts does not in itself make a provision incompatible with Article 7, provided that it proves to be sufficiently clear in the large majority of cases (ibid., § 32). On the other hand, the use of overly vague concepts and criteria in interpreting a legislative provision can render the provision itself incompatible with the requirements of clarity and foreseeability as to its effects (*Liivik v. Estonia*, §§ 96 – 104).

26. The scope of the concept of foreseeability depends to a considerable degree on the content of the instrument in issue, the field it is designed to cover and the number and status of those to whom it is addressed (*Kononov v. Latvia* [GC], § 235; *Cantoni v. France*, § 35). A law may still satisfy the requirement of foreseeability even if the person concerned has to take appropriate legal advice to assess, to a degree that is reasonable in the circumstances, the consequences which a given action may entail (ibid.). This is particularly true in the case of persons carrying on a professional activity, who are used to having to proceed with a high degree of caution when pursuing their occupation. They can on this account be expected to take special care in assessing the risks that such activity entails (ibid.; *Pessino v. France*, § 33; *Kononov v. Latvia* [GC], § 235). For example, the Court held that a manager of a supermarket, with the benefit of appropriate legal advice, should have appreciated that he ran a real risk of prosecution for the unlawful

sale of medicinal products (*Cantoni v. France*, § 35). The Court reached a similar conclusion on the convictions of the following individuals: directors of a cigarette distribution company for printing on its cigarette packets a phrase which was not prescribed by law [*Delbos and Others v. France* (dec.)]; the director of publication of an audiovisual company for public defamation of a civil servant via a statement "fixed prior to being communicated to the public" (*Radio France and Others v. France*, § 20); the manager of a company selling food supplements for commercialising a product containing a prohibited additive [*Ooms v. France* (dec.)]; the author and publisher of a book for the offence of public defamation (*Chauvy and Others v. France* (dec.), having regard to the professional status of the publisher, which should have alerted the author to the risk of prosecution); a lawyer for acting, without authorisation, as a go-between for the adoption of children [*Stoica v. France* (dec.), given her status as a lawyer specialising in family law]; Greenpeace activists for illegally entering a military defence area in Greenland [*Custers, Deveaux and Turk v. Denmark* (dec.), §§ 95–96]; politicians holding high office in the GDR state apparatus who had been convicted as the masterminds of the murders of East Germans who had attempted to leave the GDR between 1971 and 1989 by crossing the border between the two German States (*Streletz, Kessler and Krenz v. Germany* [GC], § 78); a GDR border guard for murdering an individual who had attempted to cross the border between the two German States in 1972, even though he was acting on the orders of his superior officers (*K.-H. W. v. Germany* [GC], §§ 68–81); and a commanding officer in the Soviet army for having led a unit of "Red Partisans" in a punitive expedition against alleged collaborators during the Second World War, whereby the risks should have been meticulously assessed (*Kononov v. Latvia* [GC], §§ 235–239). As regards the individual criminal responsibility of private soldiers, the Court found that such soldiers could not show total, blind obedience to orders which flagrantly infringed not only domestic law but also internationally recognised human rights, in particular the right to life, a supreme value in the international hierarchy of human rights (ibid., § 236; *K.-H. W. v. Germany* [GC], § 75).

27. Foreseeability must be appraised from the angle of the convicted person (possibly

after the latter has taken appropriate legal advice) at the time of the commission of the offence charged (see, however, *Del Río Prada v. Spain* [GC], §§ 112 and 117, concerning the foreseeability of the change in the scope of the penalty imposed at the time of the applicant's conviction, that is to say *after* the commission of the offences).

28. Where a conviction is based exclusively on international law or refers to the principles of international law, the Court assesses the foreseeability of the conviction in the light of the standards of international law applicable at the material time, including international treaty law (the International Covenant on Civil and Political Rights as regards the GDR in *Streletz, Kessler and Krenz v. Germany* [GC], §§ 90 – 106; or the 1948 Convention for the Prevention and Suppression of the Crime of Genocide in the case of Germany in *Jorgic v. Germany*, § 106), and/or customary international law (see the definition of genocide in customary international law in 1953 in *Vasiliauskas v. Lithuania* [GC], §§ 171 – 175; the Laws and Customs of War in 1944 in *Kononov v. Latvia* [GC], §§ 205 – 227; and customary international law prohibiting the use of mustard gas in international conflicts in *Van Anraat v. the Netherlands* (dec.), §§ 86 – 97).

2. Judicial interpretation: clarification of legal rules

29. However clearly drafted a legal provision may be, in any system of law, there is an inevitable element of judicial interpretation. The role of adjudication vested in the courts is precisely to dissipate such interpretational doubts as remain (*Kafkaris v. Cyprus* [GC], § 141). The progressive development of the criminal law through judicial law-making is a well-entrenched and necessary part of legal tradition in the States Parties to the Convention. Article 7 of the Convention cannot be read as outlawing the gradual clarification of the rules of criminal liability through judicial interpretation from case to case, provided that the resultant development is consistent with the essence of the offence and could reasonably be foreseen (*S. W. v. the United Kingdom*, § 36; *Streletz, Kessler and Krenz v. Germany* [GC], § 50; *Kononov v. Latvia* [GC], § 185).

30. The foreseeability of judicial interpretation relates both to the elements of the offence (*Pessino v. France*, §§ 35 – 36, *Dragotoniu and Militaru-Pidhorni v. Romania*, §§ 43 – 47) and to the applicable penalty (*Alimuçaj v. Albania*, §§ 154 – 162; *Del Río*

Prada v. Spain [GC], §§ 111 – 117). A finding by the Court that a conviction/offence lacks foreseeability dispenses it from assessing whether the penalty imposed was in itself prescribed by law within the meaning of Article 7 (*Plechkov v. Romania*, § 75). The interpretation of strictly procedural matters has no impact on the foreseeability of the offence and therefore raises no issues under Article 7 (*Khodorkovskiy and Lebedev v. Russia*, §§ 788 – 790, as regards alleged procedural obstacles to charging the applicants).

31. As regards the compatibility of the domestic judicial interpretation with the essence of the offence, the Court must determine whether that interpretation was in line with the wording of the provision of the criminal legislation in question as read in its context, and whether or not it was unreasonable (see, among many other authorities, *Jorgic v. Germany*, §§ 104 – 108, as regards the crime of genocide).

32. As regards the reasonable foreseeability of the judicial interpretation, the Court must assess whether the applicant could reasonably have foreseen at the material time, if necessary with the assistance of a lawyer, that he risked being charged with and convicted of the crime in question (*Jorgic v. Germany*, §§ 109 – 113), and that he would incur the penalty which that offence carried. The Court must ascertain whether the judicial interpretation of the criminal law merely continued a perceptible line of case-law development (*S. W. v. the United Kingdom* and *C. R. v. the United Kingdom*, concerning rape and attempted rape of two women by their husbands, in which the Court noted that the essentially debasing character of rape is so manifest that the decisions of the British courts should be deemed foreseeable and in conformity with the fundamental objectives of the Convention, "the very essence of which is respect for human dignity and human freedom"), or whether the courts had adopted a new approach which the applicant could not have foreseen (*Pessino v. France*, § 36; *Dragotoniu and Militaru-Pidhorni v. Romania*, § 44; *Del Río Prada v. Spain*, §§ 111 – 117). In assessing the foreseeability of a judicial interpretation, no decisive importance should be attached to a lack of comparable precedents (*K. A. and A. D. v. Belgium*, §§ 55 – 58, concerning sadomasochistic practices which led to a conviction for actual bodily harm, the unusual violence of which was underscored by the Court; see also *Soros v. France*, § 58). Where

the domestic courts are called on to interpret a provision of criminal law for the first time, an interpretation of the scope of the offence which was consistent with the essence of that offence must, as a rule, be considered as foreseeable (*Jorgic v. Germany*, § 109, where the applicant was the first person to be convicted of genocide under a provision of the Criminal Code). Even a new interpretation of the scope of an existing offence may be reasonably foreseeable for the purposes of Article 7, provided that it is reasonable in terms of domestic law and consistent with the essence of the offence (see, as regards a new interpretation of the concept of tax evasion, *Khodorkovskiy and Lebedev v. Russia*, §§ 791–821, where the Court found that criminal law on taxation could be sufficiently flexible to adapt to new situations, without, however, becoming unpredictable).

33. Even though the Court can have regard to the doctrinal interpretation of the law at the material time, particularly where it tallies with the judicial interpretation (*K. A. and A. D. v. Belgium*, § 59; *Alimuçaj v. Albania*, §§ 158–160), the fact that writers have freely interpreted a statute cannot replace the existence of a body of case-law (*Dragotoniu and Militaru-Pidhorni v. Romania*, §§ 26 and 43).

34. Although under certain circumstances a long-lasting toleration of certain types of conduct, otherwise punishable under the criminal law, may grow into a *de facto* decriminalisation of such conduct in certain cases, the mere fact that other individuals were not prosecuted or convicted cannot absolve the sentenced applicant from criminal liability or render his conviction unforeseeable for the purposes of Article 7 (*Khodorkovskiy and Lebedev v. Russia*, §§ 816–820).

35. Where the domestic courts interpret legal provisions based on public international law, they must decide which interpretation to adopt in domestic law, provided that the interpretation is consistent with the essence of the offence and reasonably foreseeable at the material time (see, for example, the broader concept of genocide adopted by the German courts and subsequently rejected by other international courts such as the International Court of Justice, in *Jorgic v. Germany*, §§ 103–116).

36. The Court has found that the foreseeability requirement was not met in cases of extensive interpretations of criminal law to the accused's disadvantage (*in malam partem*), both where that interpretation stems from an unforeseeable case-law reversal (*Dragotoniu*

and Militaru-Pidhorni v. Romania, §§ 39 – 48) and in cases of an interpretation by analogy which is incompatible with the essence of the offence (for example, the conviction for genocide in *Vasiliauskas v. Lithuania* [GC], §§ 179 – 186). It may also find against a State on the grounds of a conviction for an offence resulting from case-law development consolidated after the commission of that offence (for example, the offence of aiding and abetting a mafia-type organisation from the outside in *Contrada v. Italy* (no. 3), §§ 64 – 76).

37. The fact that a jury is responsible for considering a case and applying the criminal law to it does not mean that the effect of the law is unforeseeable for the purposes of Article 7 [*Jobe v. the United Kingdom* (dec.)]. Conferring a discretion on a jury to apply the law to a particular case is not in itself inconsistent with the requirements of the Convention, provided that the scope of the discretion and the manner of its exercise are indicated with sufficient clarity, to give the individual adequate protection against arbitrariness [*O'Carroll v. the United Kingdom* (dec.), concerning a jury assessment of what constitutes indecency].

3. The special case of State succession

38. The concept of judicial interpretation applies to the gradual development of case-law in a given State subject to the rule of law and under a democratic regime, but it remains just as valid in the case of State succession. In the event of a change of State sovereignty over a territory or a change of political regime on a national territory, the Court has held that it is legitimate for a State governed by the rule of law to bring criminal proceedings against those who have committed crimes under a former regime; similarly, the courts of such a State, having taken the place of those which existed previously, cannot be criticised for applying and interpreting the legal provisions in force at the material time in the light of the principles governing a State subject to the rule of law (*Streletz, Kessler and Krenz v. Germany* [GC], §§ 79 – 83; *Vasiliauskas v. Lithuania* [GC], § 159). It is especially the case when the matter at issue concerns the right to life, a supreme value in the Convention and international hierarchy of human rights and which right Contracting Parties have a primary Convention obligation to protect (*Kononov v. Latvia* [GC], § 241). A State practice of tolerating or encouraging certain acts that have been deemed criminal

offences under national or international legal instruments and the sense of impunity which such a practice instils in the perpetrators of such acts does not prevent their being brought to justice and punished (*Vasiliauskas v. Lithuania* [GC], § 158; *Streletz, Kessler and Krenz v. Germany* [GC], §§ 74 and 77–79). Thus the Court found foreseeable the convictions of GDR political leaders and a border guard for the murders of East Germans who had attempted to leave the GDR between 1971 and 1989 by crossing the border between the two German States, which convictions had been pronounced by the German courts after reunification on the basis of GDR legislation (ibid., §§ 77–89; *K.-H. W. v. Germany* [GC], §§ 68–91). It came to the same conclusion regarding the conviction of a commanding officer of the Soviet army for war crimes committed during the Second World War, as pronounced by the Latvian courts after Latvia's declarations of independence of 1990 and 1991 (*Kononov v. Latvia* [GC], §§ 240–241).

39. The Court also held that a conviction based on the legislation of the restored Republic of Lithuania was sufficiently foreseeable and therefore in conformity with Article 7 of the Convention, despite the fact that Lithuania had not yet been recognised as an independent State at the material time (*Kuolelis, Bartosevicius and Burokevicius v. Lithuania*, §§ 116–122, concerning the conviction of the leaders of the Lithuanian branch of the USSR Communist Party for their involvement in subversive and anti-State activities in January 1991).

4. The special case of a State's universal criminal jurisdiction and the applicable national legislation

40. A conviction by the national courts of a given State on the basis of that State's domestic law may concern acts committed by the individual in question in another State [*Jorgic v. Germany*; *Van Anraat v. the Netherlands* (dec.)]. The issue of the extraterritorial or universal jurisdiction of a State's national courts falls within the ambit not of Article 7 [*Ould Dah v. France* (dec.)] but of the right to a tribunal or court established by law as enshrined in Article 6 § 1 and Article 5 § 1 (a) of the Convention ("lawful detention of a person after conviction by a competent court") (*Jorgic v. Germany*, §§ 64–72, concerning a conviction for acts of genocide committed in Bosnia and Herzegovina).

41. However, when a State's national courts convict a person under universal criminal

jurisdiction, the application of domestic law to the detriment of the law of the State in which the acts were committed can be examined under Article 7. For instance, in a case involving the conviction of a Mauritanian officer by the French courts for acts of torture and barbarity committed in Mauritania (on the basis of the United Nations Convention against Torture), the Court held that the application of French criminal law to the detriment of a Mauritanian amnesty law (which had been enacted before any criminal proceedings) was not incompatible with the principle of legality [*Ould Dah v. France* (dec.)]. In that regard, it held that "the absolute necessity of prohibiting torture and prosecuting anyone who violates that universal rule, and the exercise by a signatory State of the universal jurisdiction provided for in the United Nations Convention against Torture, would be deprived of their very essence if States could exercise only their jurisdictional competence and not apply their legislation. There is no doubt that were the law of the State exercising its universal jurisdiction to be deemed inapplicable in favour of decisions or special Acts passed by the State of the place in which the offence was committed, in an effort to protect its own citizens or, where applicable, under the direct or indirect influence of the perpetrators of such an offence with a view to exonerating them, this would have the effect of paralysing any exercise of universal jurisdiction and defeat the aim pursued by the United Nations Convention against Torture". The Court reiterated that the prohibition of torture occupies a prominent place in all international instruments relating to the protection of human rights and enshrines one of the basic values of democratic societies.

IV. Principle of non-retroactivity of criminal law

A. General considerations

42. Article 7 unconditionally prohibits the retrospective application of the criminal law where it is to an accused's disadvantage (*Del Río Prada v. Spain* [GC], § 116; *Kokkinakis v. Greece*, § 52). The principle of non-retroactivity of criminal law applies

both to the provisions defining the offence (*Vasiliauskas v. Lithuania* [GC], §§ 165 – 166) and to those setting the penalties incurred (*Jamil v. France*, §§ 34 – 36; *M. v. Germany*, §§ 123 and 135 – 137; *Gurguchiani v. Spain*, §§ 32 – 44). Even after the final sentence has been imposed or while the sentence is being served, the prohibition of retroactivity of penalties prevents the legislature, the administrative authorities and the courts from redefining or modifying the scope of the penalty imposed to the sentenced person's disadvantage (*Del Río Prada v. Spain* [GC], § 89, concerning a thirty-year prison sentence to which, under a case-law reversal, no remissions of sentence for work done in detention could effectively be applied, whereas at the time the applicant had committed the offences the maximum legal term of imprisonment was treated as a new, independent sentence to which remission of sentence for work done in detention should be applied).

43. The principle of non-retroactivity is infringed in cases of retroactive application of legislative provisions to offences committed before those provisions came into force. It is prohibited to extend the scope of existing offences to acts which previously were not criminal offences. However, there is no violation of Article 7 where the acts in question were already punishable under the Criminal Code applicable at the material time-even if they were only punishable as an aggravating circumstance rather than an independent offence- (*Ould Dah v. France* (dec.), provided that the penalty imposed does not exceed the maximum laid down in that Criminal Code) or where the applicant's conviction was based on the international law applicable at the material time (*Vasiliauskas v. Lithuania* [GC], §§ 165 – 166, where the Court dealt with the applicant's conviction in the light of the international law in force in 1953, having noted that the provisions of the 2003 Lithuanian law on genocide had been applied retroactively; *Šimšić v. Bosnia and Herzegovina* (dec.), concerning crimes against humanity committed in 1992). In the latter case, although the domestic authorities can always adopt a broader definition of an offence than that set out in international law (§ 35 above), they cannot impose *retroactive* sentences on the basis of that new definition in respect of acts committed previously (*Vasiliauskas v. Lithuania* [GC], § 181, concerning a conviction for genocide based on a 2003 Criminal

Code, relating to acts committed against members of political group in 1953).

44. As regards the severity of the penalty, the Court confines itself to satisfying itself that no heavier penalty is imposed than that which was applicable at the time of commission of the offence. Issues relating to the appropriateness of a penalty do not fall within the scope of Article 7 of the Convention. It is not the Court's role to decide the length of the prison sentence or the type of penalty which is suited to any given offence (*Hummatov v. Azerbaijan* (dec.); *Hakkar v. France* (dec.); *Vinter and Others v. the United Kingdom* [GC], § 105). Issues relating to the proportionality of a penalty may, however, be assessed under Article 3 of the Convention (ibid., § 102, concerning the concept of a "clearly disproportionate penalty").

45. As regards penalty severity/heaviness, the Court has, for example, ruled that a life sentence is not heavier that the death penalty, whereby the latter had been applicable at the time the offence was committed but had subsequently been abolished and replaced by life imprisonment (*Hummatov v. Azerbaijan* (dec.); *Stepanenko and Ososkalo v. Ukraine* (dec.); *Öcalan v. Turkey* (no.2), § 177).

46. In determining whether there has been any retroactive application of a penalty to an accused person's disadvantage regard must be had to the sentencing standards (minimum and maximum sentence) applicable under each criminal code. For example, even if the sentence imposed on the applicant was within the compass of two potentially applicable criminal codes, the mere possibility that a lighter sentence could have been imposed applying a lighter minimum sentence under a criminal code is sufficient for a finding of a violation of Article 7 (*Maktouf and Damjanović v. Bosnia and Herzegovina* [GC], §§ 65–76).

B. Continuing offences

47. In cases of "continuing" or "continuous" offences (concerning acts extending over a period of time), the Court has specified that the principle of legal certainty requires the elements of the offence incurring the person's criminal liability to be clearly set out in the indictment. Furthermore, the decision rendered by the domestic court must also make it clear that the accused's conviction and sentence result from a finding that the ingredients of

a "continuing" offence have been made out by the prosecution (*Ecer and Zeyrek v. Turkey*, § 33). The Court recently held that the fact that the domestic courts had convicted a person of an offence introduced under a reform of the Criminal Code, *inter alia* for acts committed prior to the entry into force of that reform, classified as a "continuing" offence in domestic law, did not amount to retroactive application of a criminal law to the accused's disadvantage (*Rohlena v. the Czech Republic* [GC], §§ 57-64, concerning the offence of abusing a person living under the same roof). The Court noted that under the domestic law in question, a "continuing" offence was considered to constitute a single act, whose classification in criminal law had to be assessed under the law in force at the time of completion of the last occurrence of the offence, provided that the acts committed under any previous law would also have been punishable under the older law. Moreover, the application by the domestic courts of the concept of continuing offence as introduced into the Criminal Code before the first act committed by the applicant had been sufficiently foreseeable in the light of domestic law (ibid., §§ 60-64). The Court also ascertained that the penalty imposed on the applicant under the "continuing" offence classification was not more severe that the penalty which would have been imposed if the acts which he had committed before the legislative reform had been assessed separately from those committed afterwards (ibid., §§ 65-69).

48. Conversely, where a conviction for a continuing offence was not foreseeable under the domestic law applicable at the material time and it had the consequence of increasing the sentence imposed on the applicant, the Court found that criminal law had been applied retroactively to the latter's disadvantage (*Veeber v. Estonia* (no. 2), §§ 30-39; *Puhk v. Estonia*, §§ 24-34).

C. Recidivism

49. The Court held that the fact that the applicant's previous criminal status was subsequently taken into account by the trial and appeal courts, a possibility resulting from the fact that his 1984 conviction remained in his criminal record, was not in breach of the provisions of Article 7, seeing that the offence for which he was prosecuted and punished

took place after the entry into force of a new law extending the time during which recidivism was possible (*Achour v. France* [GC], §§ 44–61, concerning the immediate application of a new criminal code laying down a ten-year period during which recidivism was possible, whereas the old code which had been in force at the time of commission of the first offence stipulated a five-year period, on whose expiry, according to the applicant, he would have benefited from a "right to oblivion"). Such a retrospective approach is distinct from the concept of retroactivity in the strict sense.

V. Principe of the retroactivity of the lighter penalty

50. Even though Article 7 § 1 of the Convention does not expressly mention the principle of the retroactivity of the lighter penalty (unlike Article 15 § 1 *in fine* of the United Nations Covenant on Civil and Political Rights and Article 9 of the American Convention on Human Rights), the Court held that Article 7 § 1 guarantees not only the principle of non-retroactivity of more stringent criminal laws but also, and implicitly, the principle of retrospectiveness of the more lenient criminal law. That principle is embodied in the rule that where there are differences between the criminal law in force at the time of the commission of the offence and subsequent criminal laws enacted before a final judgment is rendered, the courts must apply the law whose provisions are most favourable to the defendant (*Scoppola v. Italy* (no. 2) [GC], §§ 103–109, concerning a thirty-year prison sentence instead of a life sentence). The Court considered that "inflicting a heavier penalty for the sole reason that it was prescribed at the time of the commission of the offence would mean applying to the defendant's detriment the rules governing the succession of criminal laws in time. In addition, it would amount to disregarding any legislative change favourable to the accused which might have come in before the conviction and continuing to impose penalties which the State-and the community it represents-now consider excessive" (ibid., § 108). The Court noted that a consensus had gradually emerged in Europe and internationally around the view that application of a criminal law

providing for a more lenient penalty, even one enacted after the commission of the offence, had become a fundamental principle of criminal law (ibid., § 106).

51. Even though in *Scoppola v. Italy* (no. 2) [GC] the Court did not explicitly come down in favour of any retrospective effect of legislative changes in favour of convicted persons, it did recently apply the principle of the retroactivity of the lighter penalty to a convicted person, inasmuch as domestic law expressly required the domestic courts to review a sentence ruling *ex officio* where a subsequent law had reduced the penalty applicable to an offence (*Gouarré Patte v. Andorra*, §§ 28 – 36). The Court held that where a State expressly provided in its legislation for the principle of the retroactivity of the more favourable law, it had to allow its citizens to use that right in accordance with the guarantees of the Convention (ibid., § 35).

VI. Article 7 § 2: the general principles of law recognised by civilised nations

> Article 7 § 2 of the Convention
>
> "...
>
> 2. This Article shall not prejudice the trial and punishment of any person for any action or omission which, at the time when it was committed, was criminal according to the general principles of law recognised by civilised nations."

52. It transpires from the *travaux préparatoires* to the Convention that Article 7 § 1 can be considered to contain the general rule of non-retroactivity and that Article 7 § 2 is only a contextual clarification of the liability limb of that rule, included so as to ensure that there was no doubt about the validity of prosecutions after the Second World War in respect of the crimes committed during that war (*Kononov v. Latvia* [GC], § 186; *Maktouf and Damjanović v. Bosnia and Herzegovina* [GC], § 72). This makes it clear that the

authors of the Convention did not intend to allow for a general exception to the non-retroactivity rule. In fact, the Court has pointed out in several cases that the two paragraphs of Article 7 are interlinked and are to be interpreted in a concordant manner (*Tess v. Latvia* (dec.); *Kononov v. Latvia* [GC], § 186).

53. In the light of these principles, the Court excluded the application of Article 7 § 2 to a conviction for war crimes committed in Bosnia in 1992 and 93 (*Maktouf and Damjanović v. Bosnia and Herzegovina* [GC], §§ 72, in which the Government had contended that the impugned acts had been criminal under the "general principles of law recognised by civilised nations" and that the non-retroactivity of penalties should not apply), and to a conviction for genocide committed in 1953 (*Vasiliauskas v. Lithuania* [GC], §§ 187–190). As regards a conviction for war crimes committed during the Second World War, the Court considered it unnecessary to assess it under Article 7 § 2 given that the applicant's acts constituted an offence under "international law" within the meaning of Article 7 § 1 (*Kononov v. Latvia* [GC], §§ 244–246, understood as referring to customary international law, in particular the Laws and Customs of War).

VII. Measures indicated by the Court in cases of violation of Article 7 of the Convention

54. Under Article 46 of the Convention the Contracting Parties undertook to abide by the final judgment of the Court in any case to which they are parties, execution being supervised by the Committee of Ministers. A respondent State which is found to have violated the Convention or the Protocols thereto is required not just to pay those concerned the sums awarded by way of just satisfaction (Article 41 of the Convention) but also to choose, subject to supervision by the Committee of Ministers, the general and/or, if appropriate, individual measures to be adopted in their domestic legal order to put an end to the violation found by the Court and to redress so far as possible the effects. Furthermore, it is understood that the respondent State remains free to choose the means by which it will

discharge its legal obligation under Article 46 of the Convention, provided that such means are compatible with the conclusions set out in the Court's judgment (*Scozzari and Giunta v. Italy* [GC], § 249).

55. However, in some specific situations, in order to help the respondent State to discharge its obligations under Article 46, the Court may seek to indicate the of individual and/or general measures which might be taken to put an end to the situation giving rise to the finding of a violation. In the event of violation of Article 7, the Court has sometimes, on an exceptional basis, indicated practical individual measures: reopening the domestic proceedings at the applicant's request (*Dragotoniu and Militaru-Pidhorni v. Romania*, § 55, applying the same principle as where an individual has been convicted in breach of Article 6 of the Convention); releasing the applicant at the earliest possible date (*Del Río Prada v. Spain* [GC], § 139 and operative provision no. 3, having found a violation of Article 7 and Article 5 § 1 of the Convention); or requiring the respondent State to ensure that the applicant's sentence of life imprisonment is replaced by a sentence not exceeding thirty years' imprisonment, pursuant to the principle of the retroactivity of the lighter penalty (*Scoppola v. Italy* (no. 2) [GC], § 154 and operative provision no. 6 [a]).

List of cited cases

The case-law cited in this Guide refers to judgments or decisions delivered by the Court and to decisions or reports of the European Commission of Human Rights ("the Commission").

Unless otherwise indicated, all references are to a judgment on the merits delivered by a Chamber of the Court. The abbreviation "(dec.)" indicates that the citation is of a decision of the Court and "[GC]" that the case was heard by the Grand Chamber.

The hyperlinks to the cases cited in the electronic version of the Guide are directed to the HUDOC database (⟨http://hudoc.echr.coe.int⟩) which provides access to the case-law of the Court (Grand Chamber, Chamber and Committee judgments and decisions, communicated cases, advisory opinions and legal summaries from the Case-Law Information Note) and of the Commission (decisions and reports), and to the resolutions of the Committee of Ministers. Some decisions from the European Commission are not in HUDOC database; they are only available in paper version in the relevant Yearbooks of the European Convention on Human Rights.

The Court delivers its judgments and decisions in English and/or French, its two official languages. HUDOC also contains translations of many important cases into more than thirty non-official languages, and links to around one hundred online case-law collections produced by third parties.

— A —

A. v. Spain, no. 11885/85, Commission decision of 13 October 1986

Achour v. France [GC], no. 67335/01, ECHR 2006 – Ⅳ

Adamson v. the United Kingdom (dec.), no. 42293/98, 26 January 1999

Alimuçaj v. Albania, no. 20134/05, 7 February 2012

— B —

Başkaya and Okçuoğlu v. Turkey [GC], nos. 23536/94 and 24408/94, ECHR

1999 – IV

 Bergmann v. Germany, no. 23279/14, 7 January 2016

 Berland v. France, no. 42875/10, 3 September 2015

 Borcea v. Romania (dec.), no. 55959/14, 22 September 2015

 Bosti v. Italy (dec.), no. 43952/09, 13 November 2014

 Bowler International Unit v. France, no. 1946/06, 23 July 2009

 Brown v. the United Kingdom (dec.), no. 38644/97, 24 November 1998

— C —

 C. G. and Others v. Bulgaria (dec.), no. 1365/07, 13 March 2007

 C. R. v. the United Kingdom, 22 November 1995, Series A no. 335 – C

 Camilleri v. Malta, no. 42931/10, 22 January 2013

 Cantoni v. France, 15 November 1996, Reports of Judgments and Decisions 1996 – V

 Çelikateş and Others v. Turkey (dec.), no. 45824/99, 7 November 2000

 Chauvy and Others v. France (dec.), no. 64915/01, 23 September 2003

 Ciok v. Poland (dec.), no. 498/10, 23 October 2012

 Coëme and Others v. Belgium, nos. 32492/96 and 4 others, ECHR 2000 – VII

 Contrada v. Italy (no. 3), no. 66655/13, 14 April 2015

 Custers, Deveaux and Turk v. Denmark (dec.), nos. 11843/03 and 2 others, 9 May 2006

— D —

 Del Río Prada v. Spain [GC], no. 42750/09, ECHR 2013

 Delbos and Others v. France (dec.), no. 60819/00, ECHR 2004 – IX

 Dragotoniu and Militaru-Pidhorni v. Romania, nos. 77193/01 and 77196/01, 24 May 2007

— E —

 Ecer and Zeyrek v. Turkey, nos. 29295/95 and 29363/95, ECHR 2001 – II

 Engel and Others v. the Netherlands, 8 June 1976, Series A no. 22

— G —

 G. v. France, 27 September 1995, Series A no. 325 – B

Gabarri Moreno v. Spain, no. 68066/01, 22 July 2003

Gardel v. France, no. 16428/05, ECHR 2009

Giza v. Poland, no. 48242/06, 13 July 2010

Glien v. Germany, no. 7345/12, 28 November 2013

Göktan v. France, no. 33402/96, ECHR 2002 – V

Gouarré Patte v. Andorra, no. 33427/10, 12 January 2016

Grava v. Italy, no. 43522/98, 10 July 2003

Gurguchiani v. Spain, no. 16012/06, 15 December 2009

— H —

Haioun v. France (dec.), no. 70749/01, 7 September 2004

Hakkar v. France (dec.), no. 43580/04, 7 April 2009

Hogben v. the United Kingdom, no. 11653/85, Commission decision of 3 March 1986, Decisions and Reports 46

Hummatov v. Azerbaijan (dec.), nos. 9852/03 and 13413/04, 18 May 2006

— J —

Jamil v. France, 8 June 1995, Series A no. 317 – B

Jendrowiak v. Germany, no. 30060/04, 14 April 2011

Jobe v. the United Kingdom (dec.), no. 48278/09, 14 June 2011

Jorgic v. Germany, no. 74613/01, ECHR 2007 – III

Jussila v. Finland [GC], no. 73053/01, ECHR 2006 – XIV

— K —

K.-H. W. v. Germany [GC], no. 37201/97, ECHR 2001 II (extracts)

K. A. and A. D. v. Belgium, nos. 42758/98 and 45558/99, 17 February 2005

Kafkaris v. Cyprus [GC], no. 21906/04, ECHR 2008

Khodorkovskiy and Lebedev v. Russia, nos. 11082/06 and 13772/05, 25 July 2013

Kokkinakis v. Greece, 25 May 1993, Series A no. 260 – A

Kolk and Kislyiy v. Estonia (dec.), nos. 23052/04 and 24018/04, 17 January 2006

Kononov v. Latvia [GC], no. 36376/04, ECHR 2010

Korbely v. Hungary [GC], no. 9174/02, ECHR 2008

Kuolelis, Bartosevicius and Burokevicius v. Lithuania, nos. 74357/01 and 2 others, 19 February 2008

— L —

Lawless v. Ireland ($n°$ 3), 1 July 1961, Series A no. 3

Liivik v. Estonia, no. 12157/05, 25 June 2009

Lukanov v. Bulgaria, no. 21915/93, Commission decision of 12 January 1995, Decisions and Reports 80 – A

— M —

M. v. Germany, no. 19359/04, ECHR 2009

M. v. Italy, no. 12386/86, Commission decision of 15 April 1991, Decisions and Reports 70

Maaouia v. France [GC], no. 39652/98, ECHR 2000 – X

Maktouf and Damjanović v. Bosnia and Herzegovina [GC], nos. 2312/08 and 34179/08, ECHR 2013 (extracts)

Monaco v. Italy (dec.), no. 34376/13, 8 December 2015

Montcornet de Caumont v. France (dec.), no. 59290/00, ECHR 2003 – Ⅶ

Morabito v. Italy (dec.), no. 58572/00, 7 June 2005

Mucci v. Italy, no. 33632/96, Commission decision of 4 March 1998

— O —

O'Carroll v. the United Kingdom, no. 35557/03, 15 March 2005

Öcalan v. Turkey (no. 2), no. 19681/92, 5 June 2001

Ooms v. France (dec.), no. 38126/06, 25 September 2009

Ould Dah v. France (dec.), no. 13113/03, ECHR 2009

— P —

Paksas v. Lithuania [GC], no. 34932/04, ECHR 2011 (extracts)

Payet v. France, no. 19606/08, 20 January 2011

Penart v. Estonia (dec.), no. 14685/04, 24 January 2016

Perinçek v. Switzerland [GC], no. 27510/08, ECHR 2015 (extracts)

Pessino v. France, no. 40403/02, 10 October 2006

Plechkov v. Romania, no. 1660/03, 16 September 2014

Polednová v. the Czech Republic, no. 2615/10, 21 June 2011

Previti v. Italy (dec.), no. 1845/08, 12 February 2013

Puhk v. Estonia, no. 55103/00, 10 February 2004

— R —

Radio France and Others v. France, no. 53984/00, ECHR 2004 – II

Raimondo v. Italy, 22 February 1994, Series A no. 281 – A

Renna v. France, no. 32809/96, Commission decision of 26 February 1997

Rohlena v. the Czech Republic [GC], no. 59552/08, ECHR 2015

— S —

S. W. v. the United Kingdom, 22 November 1995, Series A no. 335 – B

Sergueï Zolotoukhine v. Russia [GC], no. 14939/03, ECHR 2009

Scoppola v. Italy (no. 2) [GC], no. 10249/03, 17 September 2009

Scozzari and Giunta v. Italy [GC], nos. 39221/98 and 41963/98, ECHR 2000 – VIII

Sidabras and Džiautas v. Lithuania (dec.), nos. 55480/00 and 59330/00, 1 July 2003

Šimšić v. Bosnia and Herzegovina (dec.), no. 51552/10, 10 April 2012

Sobacı v. Turkey, no. 26733/02, 29 November 2007

Soros v. France, no. 50425/06, 6 October 2011

Stepanenko and Ososkalo v. Ukraine (dec.), nos. 31430/09 and 29104/11, 14 January 2014

Stoica v. France (dec.), no. 46535/08, 20 April 2010

Streletz, Kessler and Krenz v. Germany [GC], nos. 34044/96 and 2 others, ECHR 2001 – II

Sud Fondi srl and Others v. Italy (dec.), no. 75909/01, 30 August 2007

Sud Fondi srl and Others v. Italy, no. 75909/01, 20 January 2009

Szabó v. Sweden (dec.), no. 28578/03, ECHR 2006 VIII

— T —

Tess v. Latvia (dec.), no. 19363/05, 4 January 2008

— U —

Uttley v. the United Kingdom (dec.), no. 36946/03, 29 November 2005

— V —

Valico SRL v. Italy (dec.), no. 70074/01, 21 March 2006

VanAnraat v. the Netherlands (dec.), no. 65389/09, 6 July 2006

Van der Velden v. the Netherlands (dec.), no. 29514/05, ECHR 200-6 XV

Varvara v. Italy, no. 17475/09, 29 October 2013

Vasiliauskas v. Lithuania [GC], no. 35343/05, ECHR 2015

Veeber v. Estonia (no. 2), no. 45771/99, ECHR 2003 - I

Vikulov and Others v. Latvia (dec.), no. 16870/03, 23 March 2004

Vinter and Others v. the United Kingdom [GC], nos. 66069/09 and 2 others, ECHR 2013 (extracts)

— W —

Welch v. the United Kingdom, 9 February 1995, Series A no. 307 - A

— X —

X v. the Netherlands, no. 7512/76, Commission decision of 6 July 1976, Decisions and Reports 6

— Y —

Yildirim v. Italy (dec.), no. 38602/02, ECHR 2003 - IV

— Z —

Zaicevs v. Latvia, no. 65022/01, 31 July 2007

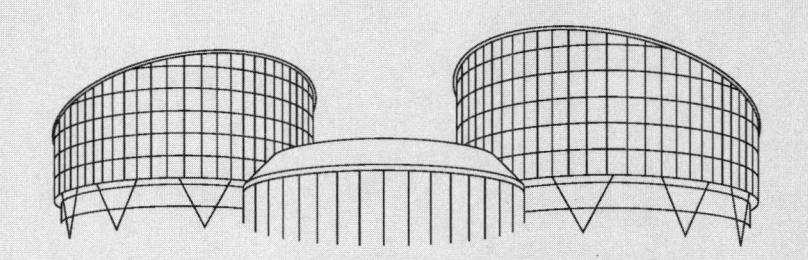

EUROPEAN COURT OF HUMAN RIGHTS
COUR EUROPÉENNE DES DROITS DE L'HOMME

第六章 《欧洲人权公约》第9条适用指南
思想、良心和宗教自由

COUNCIL OF EUROPE

CONSEIL DE L'EUROPE

读者须知

本指南是公约机构对关于《欧洲人权公约》第 9 条的判例法解释（欧洲人权法院的判决和裁定以及欧洲人权委员会的决定）。涵盖时间自 1957 年至 2015 年 9 月 1 日。

然而,本报告并未涉及以下情形:

- 涉及第 9 条,但最后被剔除或者基于正式理由（例如,未用尽国内救济手段,不符合 6 个月的规定或时间不相符）被裁定不予受理的案件;
- 重复的案件（例如,包括卡拉茨案在内的多个案件中针对土耳其的裁定）;
- 已被明确推翻并不能再适用的判例（例如,在巴亚泰安诉亚美尼亚一案判决之前所处理的出于良心反对服兵役的案件）。

本指南将使用以下缩写:

- "委员会":欧洲人权委员会,根据 1998 年 11 月 1 日的《欧洲人权公约》第十一议定书,已被废除;
- "年鉴":欧洲人权公约年鉴;
- "DR":委员会报告和决定。

> **第 9 条**
> （1）人人有权享有思想、良心和宗教自由。此项权利包括改变其宗教信仰以及单独地或者同他人一起，公开地或者私下地，通过礼拜、传教、仪式以及对教规的遵守表示其宗教或者信仰的自由。
> （2）表示个人宗教或者信仰的自由仅受到法律规定的限制，以及基于在民主社会中出于公共安全的利益考虑，为了保护公共秩序、健康或者道德，为了保护他人的权利与自由而施加的必需的限制。

第一节　引言

1. 思想、良心和宗教自由是一项基本权利，该权利不仅见于《欧洲人权公约》（以下简称公约），还见于许多国家、国际以及欧洲的文书中。

2. 公约第 9 条规定，

"1. 人人有权享有思想、良心和宗教自由。此项权利包括改变其宗教信仰以及单独地或者同他人在一起时，公开地或者私下地，通过礼拜、传教、仪式以及对教规的遵守表示其宗教或者信仰的自由。

2. 表达个人宗教或者信仰的自由仅受到法律规定的限制，以及基于在民主社会中出于公共安全的利益考虑，为了保护公共秩序、健康或者道德，为了保护他人的权利与自由而施加的必需的限制。"

3. 公约第一议定书第 2 条涉及宗教自由的一个特殊方面，即父母有权确保其孩子所受教育与其宗教信仰相符：

"任何人不得被剥夺受教育的权利。国家在行使其任何有关教育和教学的职能时，应当尊重父母确保这种教育或教学符合其宗教或哲学信仰的权利。"

4. 第 9 条也经常和公约第 14 条结合使用，第 14 条规定了禁止基于宗教信仰和观点的歧视：

"对本公约所规定的任何权利和自由的享有应当得到保障，不应因任何理由，如性别、种族、肤色、语言、宗教、政治或其他观点，民族或社会出身、与某一少数民族的联系、财产、出生或其他情况等而受到歧视。"

5. 思想、良心和宗教自由不仅是公约规定的基本权利,也是联合国的一项主要的基本权利。例如,根据《公民权利和政治权利国际公约》第 18 条的规定,人人有权享受思想、良心和宗教自由;此项权利包括个人维持或改变其宗教或信仰的自由,以及单独或集体、公开或私下地以礼拜、戒律、实践和教义来表明他的宗教或信仰的自由。任何人不得遭受足以损害他维持或改变他的宗教或信仰自由的强迫。表达自己的宗教或信仰的自由,仅受法律规定的限制以及为保障公共安全、秩序、卫生、道德或他人的基本权利和自由所必需的限制。此外,该公约第 18 条最后还规定该公约各缔约国应当尊重父母和(如适用时)法定监护人保证他们的子女能按照他们自己的信仰接受宗教和道德教育的自由。该公约第 26 条规定了非歧视原则,该原则也包括不得基于宗教信仰歧视他人。

6. 宗教自由的原则在其他文件中也有出现,如《儿童权利公约》第 14 条就做了明确规定。类似地,《美洲人权公约》第 12 条规定了每个人享有良心和宗教自由。该权利包括维持或者改变其宗教或信仰的自由,以及单独或集体、公开或私下表明或传播其宗教或信仰的自由。任何人不得遭受可能损害其维持或改变自己宗教或信仰自由的限制。表达个人的宗教或信仰的自由,仅受法律所规定的为保障公共安全、秩序、卫生、道德或他人的基本权利和自由所必需的限制。最后,《美洲人权公约》第 12 条规定父母或监护人在特定情况下有权根据他们自身的信仰对其子女或被监护人进行宗教和道德教育。

7.《欧洲联盟基本权利宪章》(以下简称《宪章》)也通过和公约相同的方式保障思想、良心和宗教自由(《宪章》第 10 条)。它也规定了父母的权利,即"父母确保其孩子受到的教育和教学符合其自身的宗教、哲学和教育信仰的权利,应受到规制该权利行使的相关国内法的保障"(第 14 条第 3 款)。

8. 欧洲人权法院(以下简称本法院)在多个场合强调了思想、良心和宗教自由的重要性。一般来说,思想、良心和宗教自由被认为是民主社会的基础之一;具体来说,欧洲法官认为宗教自由是形成信仰者身份及生活理念的重要因素。事实上,本法院将宗教信仰自由上升到了公约实体权利的地位,这种地位的提升最开始是通过间接方式,后来转为更加直接的方式。

9. 应当注意的是在过去的 15 年间,欧洲人权法院审理的涉及公约第 9 条的案件不断增多,该趋势可解释为宗教及其相关事宜在社会政治生活中越来越重要。

第二节　基本原则及其适用

一、第 9 条在民主社会的重要性以及在宗教团体的法定地位

10. 从公约的意义上来说,第 9 条规定的思想、良心和宗教自由是"民主社会"的基础之一。从宗教的角度来说,它是构成信仰者身份及其生活理念的最重要因素之一,也是无神论者、不可知论者、怀疑论者以及不关心者的宝贵财富。与民主社会息息相关的多元论近几个世纪以来赢得了巨大的成功,有赖于思想、良心和宗教自由。尤其是这项自由包括有或没有宗教信仰的自由以及信仰或不信仰某一宗教的自由(*Kokkinakis v. Greece*,§ 31;*Buscarini and Others v. San Marino*[GC],§ 34)。

11. 同样地,一个教会或宗教团体可以代表其信众行使公约第 9 条的权利(*Cha'are Shalom Ve Tsedek v. France*[GC],§ 72;*Leela Förderkreis e. V. and Others v. Germany*,§ 79)。这意味着如果教堂或者宗教组织提起一项诉讼,主张其信众集体的宗教信仰自由受到了侵害,根据属人管辖原则,该诉求符合公约规定,而且根据公约第 34 条的规定,该教堂或组织可以称自己为侵害行为的"受害者"。

12. 另一方面,如果一个已被认可的宗教团体被拒绝进行重新注册,由于该团体有行为能力向欧洲人权法院提出申诉,所以个人申诉人不能宣称自己为国内机构拒绝行为的受害者,因为该行为只影响申诉人团体。因此,根据属人管辖原则,他们根据第 9 条提出的诉求不符合公约规定(*Jehovah's Witnesses of Moscow and Others v. Russia*,§ 168)。

13. 法人可以主张自己是思想和宗教自由受到侵害的受害者,但它不能行使良心自由(*Kontakt-Information-Therapie*(*KIT*) *and Hagen v. Austria*)。

二、第 9 条保护的信仰

14. 公约第 9 条和欧洲人权法院的判例法都没有对"宗教"进行定义。这种遗漏非常合理,因为这种定义需足够灵活以便能囊括全球所有宗教(主流的或少数的,老的或新的,有神论的或无神论的),同时也需足够特定以便能在个案中适用,而兼顾前述两个

方面是异常困难甚至实际上是不可能的。一方面,第 9 条的范围非常广泛,它保护宗教的和非宗教的观点和信仰。另一方面,并不是所有的观点或信仰必然会落在条款规定的范围内,而且第 9 条第 1 款中使用的"实践"一词并不包括每一个受宗教或信仰驱使或影响的行为(*Pretty v. the United Kingdom*,§ 82)。

15. 个人或集体信仰若想享有"思想、良心和宗教自由"的权利,其必须有一定的说服力、严肃性、凝聚力和重要性。如果满足上述条件,则国家中立和公正的义务不允许国家拥有任何审查宗教信仰或者这些信仰的表达方式的合法性的权力(*Eweida and Others v. the United Kingdom*,§ 81)。因此,欧洲人权法院的任务不是确定某个宗教的核心是何种原则或信仰,也不是就宗教问题给予任何其他类型的解释[*Kovaļkovs v. Latvia*(dec.),§ 60]。

16. 公约机构已经通过明示或暗示的方式确认公约第 9 条第 1 款适用于下列情况:
(1) 已经存在上千年或几个世纪的世界"主要的"或"古老的"宗教,例如,

- 阿拉维派(*Sinan Işık v. Turkey*;*Cumhuriyetçi Eğitim ve Kültür Merkezi Vakfı v. Turkey*);
- 佛教(*Jakóbski v. Poland*);
- 基督教不同教派(*Sviato-Mykhaïlivska Parafiya v. Ukraine*;*Savez crkava Riječ života and Others v. Croatia*);
- 印度教的各类形式[*Kovaļkovs v. Latvia*(dec.)];
- 伊斯兰教(*Hassan and Tchaouch v. Bulgaria*[GC];*Leyla Şahin v. Turkey*[GC]);
- 犹太教(*Cha'are Shalom Ve Tsedek v. France*[GC];*Francesco Sessa v. Italy*);
- 锡克教[*Phull v. France*(dec.);*Jasvir Singh v. France*(dec.)];
- 道教[*X. v. the United Kingdom*(dec.)];

(2) 新的或相对较新的宗教,例如,

- 马达罗唯心教(*Association des Chevaliers du Lotus d'Or v. France*);
- 薄伽梵·室利·拉杰尼希运动,也称奥修教(*Leela Förderkreis e. V. and Others v. Germany*);
- 教士文鲜明统一教(*Nolan and K. v. Russia*;*Boychev and Others v. Bulgaria*);
- 摩门教,又称耶稣基督后期圣徒教会(*The Church of Jesus Christ of Latter-day*

Saints v. the United Kingdom);
- 雷尔利安运动[F. L. v. France (dec.)];
- 新异教[Ásatrúarfélagið v. Iceland (dec.)];
- "胜坨丹"宗教仪式,包括使用叫做"死藤水"(Santo Daime)的迷幻药[Fränklin-Beentjes and CEFLU-Luz da Floresta v. the Netherlands (dec.)];
- 耶和华见证会(Religionsgemeinschaft der Zeugen Jehovas and Others v. Austria;Jehovah's Witnesses of Moscow and Others v. Russia);

(3)各类长期且虔诚的哲学信仰,例如,
- 反战主义(Arrowsmith v. the United Kingdom,§69);
- 有原则地反对服兵役(Bayatyan v. Armenia [GC]);
- 素食主义以及反对加工动物类产品或进行动物实验[W. v. the United Kingdom (dec.)];
- 反对堕胎[Knudsen v. Norway (dec.),no.11045/84,委员会1985年3月8日决定,DR 42,p.258;Van Schijndel and Others v. the Netherlands,(dec.)];
- 医生有关替代药的观点,构成医学哲学的一种表现形式[Nyyssönen v. Finland (dec.)];
- 认为婚姻是男女一生结合的观念以及反对同性结合(Eweida and Others v. the United Kingdom)。

17. 同样,我们可以说目前尚不能完全确定一个全部或部分基于信仰或哲学理念但完全为了谋取利益的行为是否可以受到第9条的保护。委员会认为,商业有限责任公司作为一个谋利团体,即使由哲学团体管理,也不能享有或依赖第9条所保障的权利[Company X. v. Switzerland (dec.);Kustannus OY Vapaa Ajattelija AB and Others v. Finland (dec.)]。同样地,委员会认为第9条不保护那些名义上是宗教信仰,实则为宗教团体通过纯商业的广告方式来销售"观点"的言论。在此方面,委员会区分了仅是"信息性"或"描述性"的广告和售卖物品的商业广告。一旦广告属于后者,即使该广告是关于某宗教物品,且该物品用于满足某宗教特定需求,该广告中就宗教内容的表述依然会被认为是以营销商品获取利益为目的,而不是为了表达信仰。在委员会审理的这类案件中,委员会拒绝将第9条的保护扩展至被消费保护机构惩处的"E米"和"哈伯德静电计"的广告中[Church of Scientology and Others v. Sweden (dec.)]。

18. 然而,近年来的案件中,对于第9条是否适用于宗教组织的营利活动的问题,委员会和本法院似乎持开放态度[该问题在 *Cumhuriyetçi Eğitim ve Kültür Merkezi Vakfi v. Turkey* 案件中被提出;瑜伽课不免费案,*Association Sivananda de Yoga Vedanta v. France*(dec.)]。

19. 在这种情况下,将山达基教归类为"宗教"在缔约国之间是一个主要争论点。委员会并没有明确地处理过该问题,因为涉及该问题的所有申诉都已经因为其他理由而被裁定不予受理[*X. and Church of Scientology v. Sweden*,(dec.);*Church of Scientology and Others v. Sweden*(dec.);*Scientology Kirche Deutschland e. V. v. Germany*(dec.)]。然而,至少在前三个引用案件中的第一个和第三个案件中,委员会似乎暗示其已接受山达基教是一个"宗教团体"。

20. 欧洲人权法院曾直接处理过山达基教的问题,但就这部分问题遵从了应诉国当局的判决。在一起涉及俄罗斯政府拒绝将山达基教注册为法人的案件中,本法院表示,在理论上确定一个信仰实体及其相关活动是否属于第9条意义上的"宗教"并不是需要其判定的内容。在本案中,一个地方山达基教中心开始被登记为非宗教团体,最后被解散,理由是其活动是"宗教性质的"。包括国内法院在内的国家当局一直认为山达基教本质上是宗教。在这种情况下,欧洲人权法院认为公约第9条适用于向其提交的案件(*Kimlya and Others v. Russia*,§§ 79 – 81;*Church of Scientology of Moscow v. Russia*,§ 64)。在另一个案件中,涉案团体受到了同样的干预,其理由却是部分基于某宗教研究得出的结论:涉案团体的活动在本质上不属于宗教性质的。然而,欧洲人权法院认为该干预是根据只适用于宗教组织的法律条款而实施的,因此第9条是完全可以适用的(*Church of Scientology of St Petersburg and Others v. Russia*,§ 32)。

21. 至于无神论,委员会考虑了无神论者根据第9条提起的诉求[*Angeleni v. Sweden*(dec.)]。在一个略有不同的情境下,委员会表示无神论思潮只表达了一种关于人的形而上学概念,这种概念限定了他对世界的感知,并证明了他的行为是正当的,因而不能有效地区别于传统意义上的宗教教派。因此,国家赋予其与其他宗教教派截然不同的法律地位的行为是不正当的(*Union des Athées v. France*,§ 79)。此外,欧洲人权法院已经明确表示思想、良心和宗教自由是"无神论者、不可知论者、怀疑论者以及不关心者的宝贵财富"(*Kokkinakis v. Greece*,§ 31)。

22. 欧洲人权法院目前还未对第9条是否适用于共济会做出裁判;这一问题被默认

予以保留(N. F. v. Italy, §§ 35-40)。

三、有信仰的权利以及表达信仰的权利

23. 公约第9条第1款包括两个方面,一个是有信仰的权利,另一个是表达该信仰的权利:

(1)完全有任何信仰(不论是宗教的还是非宗教的)以及改变个人宗教或信仰的权利。本权利是绝对的和无条件的;国家不能进行干涉,例如,不能命令某人持何种信仰或强制要求他改变信仰(Ivanova v. Bulgaria);

(2)独自私下表达自己信仰以及与他人一起公开实践信仰的权利。此项权利不是绝对的:因为个人对其宗教信仰的表达可能对他人产生影响,公约起草者将宗教自由的这部分内容规定在第9条第2款中。第2款规定表示加诸于个人宗教或者信仰自由的限制必须由法律规定,且是在民主社会中为实现法律所规定的一个或多个合理目的所必需的[Eweida and Others v. the United Kingdom, § 80)]。也就是说,第9条第2款的规定仅是对表达个人宗教或信仰自由的限制,而无关有宗教信仰的权利(Ivanova v. Bulgaria, § 79)。

24. 第9条第1款确保"公开地或私下地表达(个人)宗教或信仰……的自由"。然而,"公开地或私下地",这可供选择的两部分并不意味着相互排斥或给予政府当局选择的权利;该表述只是为了指出宗教信仰可以通过两者之中任一方式进行(X. v. the United Kingdom)。

25. 即使涉案信仰在说服力和重要程度上达到了法定水平,也不能认为任何受到该信仰启发、激励或影响的行为都构成了对该信仰的"表达"。因此,例如,没有直接表达所涉信仰或者仅与信仰有很小关联的作为或不作为不受到第9条第1款的保护。涉案行为必须与宗教或信仰有紧密联系,才属于第9条规定的"表达"行为。膜拜或虔诚的行为可能是一个例子,这种行为是实施宗教或信仰行为的一部分,而且是被普遍承认的形式。然而,表达宗教或信仰并不限于此类行为;必须根据每个案件的事实来确定在行为和其背后的信仰之间存在着足够密切和直接的联系。特别是,如果申诉人宣称某一行为属于表达其宗教或信仰的自由,其并不需要证明自己的行为是为了履行该宗教所要求的义务[Eweida and Others v. the United Kingdom, § 82,以及 S. A. S. v. France [GC], § 55]。

26. 因此,作为一般原则,如果没有可靠的、有说服力的证据予以支持,国内当局对个人所宣称的对信仰的虔诚表示质疑是不正当的。因此,本法院驳回应诉国政府的下述辩解:

- 法国政府辩解:申诉人宣称信仰穆斯林并希望在公开场合戴全脸面纱,但并未表明其确为伊斯兰教信徒以及其希望戴面纱是出于宗教理由。此外,欧洲人权法院认为只有一小部分穆斯林女性如此作为的情况并不影响其法律特征(*S. A. S. v. France*﹝GC﹞,§ 56);
- 拉脱维亚政府主张囚犯申诉人并不是毗湿奴派(印度教的毗湿奴变体)的信徒,理由是他曾进行圣经远程学习,并没有正式加入国际奎师那意识协会在当地的分支﹝*Kovaļkovs v. Latvia*(dec.),§ 57﹞;罗马尼亚政府提出了非常相似的主张,即申诉人可能声称自己是佛教徒,以便在狱中获得更好的食物﹝*Vartic v. Romania*(no. 2),§ 46﹞。

27. 然而,公约机构在一些特殊情况下接受质疑个人对所宣称的宗教的虔诚度的可能性。当然,正如上文所指出的,欧洲人权法院的职责并不是评估宗教主张的合法性,也不是质疑某一特定方面的信仰或实践的有效性或解释的相对合理之处。个人信仰的性质和重要性是无法深入讨论的,因为一个人认为神圣的宗教可能对另一个人来说是荒谬的或令人反感的,而且没有一种法律或逻辑论据可以挑战信徒的主张,即某一特定信仰或实践是其宗教义务的重要组成部分。然而,这不妨碍欧洲人权法院通过发现事实来确定申诉人是否真实虔诚地持有宗教信仰﹝*Skugar and Others v. Russia*(dec.)﹞。

28. 例如,公约机构拒绝承认申诉人对所宣称的宗教信仰的虔诚:

(1)本案中,囚犯希望在监狱内登记为"威卡"教的信徒。委员会认为,这类登记将使该囚犯享受特定的权利和设施以便其信仰该宗教,因此要求囚犯证明其所宣称的宗教客观存在是合理的;然而,申诉人没有提供任何信息来确认该宗教是客观存在的﹝*X. v. the United Kingdom*(dec)﹞。

(2)本案中,申诉人是国有电力公司的雇员并宣称自己为穆斯林,因在一年内两次缺勤以庆祝伊斯兰教节日而受到纪律处分。国内法院承认相关法律准许信仰伊斯兰教的公民在宗教节日时离岗;但在申诉人的案件中,他对伊斯兰教的虔诚度是值得怀疑的,因为他不了解该宗教的基本教义,而且他曾经经常庆祝基督教节日。因此,国内法院认为申诉人宣称自己为穆斯林只是为了获得额外的休假天数。欧洲人权法院认为,法律规定给予一个宗教团体的成员一项特权或特别豁免时——特别是在涉及雇佣时，要求相关人员在一定程度上证明其属于该社团因而能够享受前述特别待遇的做法是不违反第9条的（*Kosteski v. the former Yugoslav Republic of Macedonia*，§39）。

29. 公约机构拒绝为下述情形提供第9条第1款所赋予的保护（这并不意味着在恰当的情形下，该诉求不能依据公约其他条款审理）：

- 语言自由，包括接受教育时或与政府交流时选择所使用语言的权利[*Vingt-trois habitants d'Alsemberg et de Beersel v. Belgium*；*Inhabitants of Leeuw-St. Pierre v. Belgium*①（dec.），no. 2333/64，委员会1965年7月15日的裁定，*Yearbook* 8，p. 105]；

- 在一个强制参选的国家，拒绝在一般选举或总统选举中投票[*X. v. Austria*（dec.），no. 1718/62，委员会1965年4月22日的裁定，*Yearbook* 8，p. 169②，*X. v. Austria*（dec.）]；

- 申诉人要求取消其洗礼和坚信礼[*X. v. Iceland*（dec.）]；

- 一名男性拒绝根据民法规定的程序与其伴侣缔结婚姻，但却要求国家承认他们的结合为有效婚姻[*X. v. Germany*（dec.）]；

- 一个信仰佛教的囚犯希望通过佛教杂志出版文章，而申诉人并未证明信仰该宗教需要出版此类文章[*X. v. the United Kingdom*（dec.）]；

- 分发宗教类手册，尽管基于和平主义思想，但却煽动士兵擅离职守、违反军队纪律[*Arrowsmith v. the United Kingdom*，§§74-75；*Le Cour Grandmaison and Fritz v. France*（dec.）]；

- 申诉人希望将其骨灰撒于其财产上以免被埋葬在被基督教标志包围的墓地里[*X. v. Germany*（dec.）]；

- 囚犯希望被认定为"政治囚犯"，并拒绝在监狱内劳作，拒绝穿狱服以及打扫其牢房[*McFeeley and Others v. the United Kingdom*（dec.）；*X. v. the United Kingdom*（dec.）]；

- 信仰犹太教的人在离婚后拒绝移交"断绝关系函"，因此使其能够以宗教仪式再婚[*D. v. France*（dec.）]；

---

① 裁定只有书面文本，请见欧洲人权法院图书馆《欧洲人权公约年鉴》。
② 裁定只有书面文本，请见欧洲人权法院图书馆《欧洲人权公约年鉴》。

- 医生拒绝认购专业养老保险计划[*V. v. the Netherlands*(dec.)];
- 一个社团,出于理想主义,希望给囚犯提供法律建议并保障他们的利益[*Vereniging Rechtswinkels Utrecht v. the Netherlands*(dec.)];
- 一名宗教牧师为了抗议法律放宽堕胎规定而拒绝在州立教堂履行行政职责,因此被解雇[*Knudsen v. Norway*(dec.)];
- 一名男性希望与一名女孩结婚并发生性关系,但该女孩未达到允许进行性行为的法定年龄,该男性的理由是这样的婚姻在伊斯兰教法律下是有效的[*Khan v. the United Kingdom*(dec.)];
- 申诉人希望离婚(*Johnston and Others v. Ireland*,§ 63);
- 电力消费者希望规避其自愿签订的合同中的义务并拒绝支付全部电费,理由是相应电费金额中一定比例被分配融资给核电站[*K. and V. v. the Netherlands*(dec.)];
- 父亲希望体罚其孩子(*Abrahamsson v. Sweden*);
- 两名建筑师拒绝加入建筑家协会,这一做法违反法律规定[*Revert and Legallais v. France*(dec.)];
- 希望在火车站展开写有政治口号的横幅[*K. v. the Netherlands*(dec.)];
- 在一个私人宴会中举行的有关历史政治讨论的内容[*F. P. v. Germany*(dec)];
- 申诉人希望能自由选择医生并使用其健康保险基金报销非签约医生的费用[*B. C. v. Switzerland*(dec.);*Marty v. Switzerland*(dec.)];
- 申诉人基于其基督教信仰希望在堕胎诊所附近分发堕胎抗议书[*Van den Dungen v. the Netherlands*(dec.)];
- 一名男性控诉其需要支付给其前妻和孩子的抚养费所产生的经济负担使其无法参拜佛教寺庙,而最近的一座寺庙距离其家上百英里[*Logan v. the United Kingdom*(dec.)];
- 一名父亲因其未达法定年龄的女儿改变宗教信仰而拒绝支付抚养费[*Karakuzey v. Germany*(dec.)];
- 拥有土耳其空军上校军衔的军事法官,因"其行为显示其采纳了非法的原教旨主义者的观点"而被要求退休,在本案中,被责难的内容并不是申请人的宗教观点和信仰或是他履行宗教职责的方式,而是他的行为违反了军事纪律和政教分

离原则(Kalaç v. Turkey);

- 家长在没有任何宗教动机的情况下,希望给其孩子取特别的名字[Salonen v. Finland(dec.)];
- 家长希望逃避国内立法所规定的给孩子接种疫苗的义务[Boffa and Others v. San Marino(dec.)];
- 律师断然拒绝开展正式分配给其的工作——代理还押候审人员[Mignot v. France(dec.)];
- 驾驶员在驾驶摩托车时拒绝系安全带,以表明他有权选择保护其身体和精神完整性的方式[Viel v. France(dec.)];
- 一名在"伊斯兰拯救阵线"中非常活跃的阿尔及利亚人控诉瑞士政府的一项有关收缴其为政治宣传而使用的通信媒介的裁定[Zaoui v. Switzerland(dec.)];
- 一家药店的联名业主拒绝出售避孕药[Pichon and Sajous v. France(dec.)];
- 出于个人自主原则的信念,希望协助自杀(Pretty v. the United Kingdom, § 82);
- 申诉人希望继续由其已经死亡的丈夫或父亲提起的反对任命穆夫提的司法程序[Sadik Amet and Others v. Greece(dec.)];
- 一名学生因为有胡子而被拒绝进入大学校园,尽管他从未宣称此举受到任何宗教的或其他的特定观念或信仰的鼓舞[Tiğ v. Turkey(dec.)];
- 希望将有死者照片的纪念石放在家庭墓碑上[Jones v. the United Kingdom(dec.)];
- 被定罪为恐怖组织成员[Gündüz v. Turkey(dec.); Kenar v. Turkey(dec.)];
- 法官因认为自己带有偏见而拒绝审理案件,因此受到责难[Cserjés v. Hungary(dec.)],受雇于公共卫生保险部门的医生因拒绝为一名见习医生体检而被解雇,其拒绝的原因是担心"可能存在偏见",且如果将来他不得不和见习医生一起工作,这种偏见可能会带来问题[Blumberg v. Germany(dec.)];
- 修女在祈祷时大声说话而导致宗教仪式发生骚乱,因此被判处罚金[Bulgaru v. Romania(dec.)];
- 一位靠失业救济金生活的父亲控诉市政当局拒绝退还圣诞树和花环的费用[Jenik v. Austria(dec.);根据公约第35条第3款第a项的规定,该申请因滥用诉讼权利而被驳回];

- 一位已经在法律上和其妻子分开的父亲反对其未到法定年龄的女儿(其母享有监护权)在罗马天主教中长大,即使母亲只是根据国内法院判决,基于女儿的自由选择而做出决定[*Rupprecht v. Spain*(dec.)];
- 两个犹太教团体要求乌克兰法院修复在乌克兰多个城镇中的陈旧的犹太公墓(已经被遗弃了70多年)的边界并禁止在其上开展建筑工作[参见 *Representation of the Union of Councils for Jews in the Former Soviet Union and the Union of Jewish Religious Organisations of Ukraine*(dec.)];
- 申诉人希望在公众场合裸体行走,因为他相信这种行为在社会上是可以被接受的(*Gough v. the United Kingdom*,§§ 185 – 188)。

四、国家的消极和积极义务

(一)对受保护权利的行使进行干涉及其正当性

30. 根据公约第9条第2款的规定,基于下列合法目的干涉个人表达其宗教或信仰是正当的:公共安全、保护公共秩序、健康和道德或者保护他人的权利与自由。对合法目的的列举是完全穷尽的,对目的的定义需要严格限制;只有当所追求的目的与该条款列举的某一情况有关联时,对该自由的限制才符合公约的规定(*Sviato-Mykhaïlivska Parafiya v. Ukraine*,§§ 132 and137;*S. A. S. v. France*[GC],§ 113)。

31. 与公约第8条第2款、第10条第2款、第11条第2款以及第四议定书第2条第3款不同,"国家安全"不在第9条第2款列举的目的之中。这种遗漏并非偶然;相反,公约起草者拒绝将该理由纳入合法干预理由,这反映出"作为民主社会基石"的宗教多样性的至关重要性以及国家不能命令个人持某种信仰或采取强制措施要求个人改变其信仰的至关重要性(*Nolan and K. v. Russia*,§ 73)。这意味着国家不能将保护国家安全的需要作为限制一个人或一群人行使宗教表达自由的权利的唯一依据。

32. 此外,应当注意的是公约第15条允许国家"在情况的紧急性所严格要求的范围内"克减第9条所规定的义务,但"该等措施不得与其根据国际法的规定所应当履行的其他义务相抵触",公约还在第15条第3款进一步规定了国家需要满足的程序要求。

33. 对行使公约第9条的权利进行干预时可采取如下形式:
- 因为行使了所提及的权利而施以刑事或行政处罚或者开除(*Kokkinakis v.*

Greece；*Ivanova v. Bulgaria*；*Masaev v. Moldova*）；

- 对个人行使第 9 条权利设置物理障碍，如由警察中断会议（*Boychev and Others v. Bulgaria*）；

- 解散宗教组织［*Jehovah's Witnesses of Moscow and Others v. Russia*，§§ 99 - 103；*Biblical Centre of the Chuvash Republic v. Russia*，§ 52；这与旧委员会判例法不同，旧委员会判例法认为解散以及禁止宗教组织不侵犯个人宗教自由，*X. v. Austria*，（dec.）］；

- 拒绝旨在便于行使所述权利的授权、承认或许可（*Metropolitan Church of Bessarabia and Others v. Moldova*；*Vergos v. Greece*）；

- 颁布一项表面中立的法律，而该法律允许国家直接干预宗教内部纠纷（*Holy Synod of the Bulgarian Orthodox Church*（*Metropolitan Inokentiy*）*and Others v. Bulgaria*，§ 157）；

- 在官方文件中使用贬损宗教群体的表述，且该类表述可能会对宗教自由的行使产生消极影响（*Leela Förderkreis e. V. and Others v. Germany*，§ 84）。

34. 另一方面，作为一般规定，第 9 条所保障权利的行使在立法中不受干预，因为立法的实施是由公约规定的，且在不影响第 9 条保障的自由的情况下普遍中立地适用于公共领域［*C. v. the United Kingdom*，（dec.）；*Skugar and Others v. Russia*（dec.）］。

35. 当申诉人控诉国内法对于他们意图采取的行为施加处罚并主张自己有权利获得第 9 条的保护时，如果他们被要求改变其行为或者有被起诉的风险，或者他们是直接受涉案法律影响的那类人中的成员，那么他们可以声称自己为公约第 34 条意义上的"受害者"。因此，本法院承认，出于宗教原因希望公开戴着全脸面纱的穆斯林女性只有在这种行为会被法律惩罚（并处或单处罚金或强制性公民课程）的情况下才可以宣称自己是"受害者"。因此在这种情况下，申诉人处于两难境地：要么遵从该禁令，不按照其信仰宗教的方式来穿着；要么拒绝遵守而面临被诉（*S. A. S. v. France* ［GC］，§ 57）。

36. 国家有权确定那些形式上追求宗教目的的运动或协会开展的活动是否有害于公众或公共秩序（*Manoussakis and Others v. Greece*，§ 40；*Metropolitan Church of Bessarabia and Others v. Moldova*，§ 105）。在一些案件中，国家可以采取预防措施来保护他人的基本权利；国家的这种预防性干预的权利完全符合公约第 1 条规定的国家积极义务，即缔约国必须"保证在它们管辖之下的每个人都享有本公约……所确定的权利和自由"(*Leela Förderkreis e. V. and Others v. Germany*, §99)。

37. 在民主社会,数个宗教能够在同一人群中共存,为了调和各个团体的利益并确保每个人的信仰得到尊重,可能需要对该项自由进行限制。然而,在对该领域以及各类宗教、教派和信仰之间的关系行使规制权时,国家有义务保持中立和公正。这里的关键是保障多元主义以及民主的正常运行(*Metropolitan Church of Bessarabia and Others v. Moldova*, §§115-116)。

38. 本法院的任务是确定在国内采取的措施是否在原则上是正当的以及合比例的(*Leyla Şahin v. Turkey* [GC], §110)。这意味着没有其他方式可以实现相同目的,同时对所涉基本权利造成的侵害更小;在这一点上,当局负有义务证明已经不存在其他该类措施((*Biblical Centre of the Chuvash Republic v. Russia*, §58)。公约第9条第2款暗示着任何干预必须出于"紧迫的社会需要";因此,"必需"的表述不如其他诸如"有用""希望"等表述那样可以变通(*Sviato-Mykhaïlivska Parafiya v. Ukraine*, §116)。

39. 在判断干预行为是否合比例时,本法院允许缔约国在评估干预的存在以及必要性程度方面有一定自由裁量权。应谨记公约机制的角色从根本上来说是起补充作用的。原则上,国家当局比国际法院能更好地评估本地区的需求和情况,因此在涉及民主社会中可能存在合理差别的一般政策时,尤其是当涉及国家和宗教教派之间的关系问题时,需要特别重视国内政策制定者的角色。至于公约第9条,原则上,在确定对表达个人宗教或信仰的权利的限制是否是"必需"的以及在何种程度上是"必需"的问题上,国家应当有较大的自由裁量权。然而,在确定具体个案中自由裁量的程度时,欧洲人权法院必须考虑案件中的具体问题以及第9条涵盖的一般问题,即保障真正的宗教多样性(任何民主社会得以存在的重要因素)的需要。在确定干预是否如第9条第1款所规定的为"社会所需要"以及是否"与所追求的合法目的相适应"时,应当重点注意干预的必要性。显然,该自由裁量权与欧洲监管体制相适应,即应同时考虑法律以及适用法律的决定,甚至包括独立的国内法院做出的判决。据此,在适当的情况下,欧洲人权法院亦可以考虑缔约国在实践中形成的任何共识和共同价值(*Bayatyan v. Armenia* [GC], §§121-122; *S. A. S. v. France* [GC], §129)。

40. 此外,在审查国内措施是否与公约第9条第2款的规定一致时,欧洲人权法院必须考虑涉案宗教的教义、仪式、组织等历史背景和特点(有关该问题的两个实际案例, *Cha'are Shalom Ve Tsedek v. France* [GC], §§13-19; *Miroļubovs and Others v.*

Latvia，§§ 8-16）。这是根据作为第 9 条基础的一般原则所推导出的逻辑结果，即公开或私下信仰宗教的自由、宗教团体的内部自治以及尊重宗教多元性。考虑到公约所建立的保护个人权利的机制是辅助性的，国内当局需要承担起相同的义务，即在处理其与各类宗教的关系时做出有约束力的决定（Miroļubovs and Others v. Latvia，§ 81）。在这一点上，欧洲人权法院经常参考与公约第 14 条（禁止歧视）有关的判例法。根据这些判例法，如果国家在一些情况下没有给予情况显著不同的人群不同的待遇，则构成对该条的违反（Thlimmenos v. Greece ［GC］，§ 44）。

41. 如果国内法规定行使宗教或宗教其中一个方面的自由的权利受制于前置审批系统，那么对已被承认的教会机构的授权程序，尤其是对一个属于不同教派、层级或派别机构的授权程序，与第 9 条第 2 款的要求不符（Metropolitan Church of Bessarabia and Others v. Moldova，§ 117；Vergos v. Greece，§ 34；经适当修正后，Pentidis and Others v. Greece）。

42. 最后，欧洲人权法院在行使监管职责时，必须基于案卷整体情况来审查被控诉的干预（Metropolitan Church of Bessarabia and Others v. Moldova，§ 119）。如若必要，还应当审查案件的所有事实并从整体上考虑事件的先后顺序，而不是割裂各个事件进行考察（Ivanova v. Bulgaria，§ 83）。此外，欧洲人权法院必须确保国家当局就宗教自由做出的决定是基于对相关事实的合理评估（Svyato-Mykhaïlivska Parafiya v. Ukraine，§ 138）。

（二）缔约国的积极义务

43. 根据公约第 1 条的规定，缔约国必须"保证在它们管辖之下的每个人都享有本公约……所确定的权利和自由"。因此，在某些情况下，尤其是当被控诉的行为是私人机构实施的而不直接归咎于应诉国时，国家不得干预第 9 条权利的消极义务可能需要结合这些权利内含的积极义务来一并考虑。因此，这些义务有时可能会要求国家采取必要措施保障影响个人人际关系结构的宗教自由（Siebenhaar v. Germany，§ 38）。尽管公约规定的国家积极义务和消极义务之间没有一个明确的边界，但适用的原则是类似的。在两种情况下，都必须平衡个人利益和社会整体利益；而且国家在两种情况下都享有一定的自由裁量权。此外，即使涉及的是公约第 9 条第 1 款规定的积极义务，第 2 款规定的目的也可能有一定的相关性（Jakóbski v. Poland，§ 47；Eweida and Others v. the United Kingdom，§ 84）。

44. 就条款本身来说,第9条没有规定从保护宗教自由的预防性措施中获益的权利[Hernandez Sanchez v. Spain (dec.)]。

五、第9条与公约其他条款规定的重叠之处

45. 就其本质来说,公约第9条的实质内容有时可能与公约其他条款的内容重叠;也就是说,向欧洲人权法院提交的同一个控诉有时可能涉及不止一个条款。在这些情况下,欧洲人权法院通常只选择其认为与案件具体情形更相关的一个条款来审理诉求;然而,欧洲人权法院同时也不会忽视其他条款,会在解释其选择的那一条款时考虑其他条款。对于同一事实或诉求,那些最有可能与第9条关联的条款如下。

(1)公约第6条第1款(获得公正审判的权利,特别是诉诸法庭的权利)。希腊上诉法院拒绝承认克利特罗马天主教教区大教堂的法人地位,从而否认其保护自身财产的诉讼资格,欧洲人权法院决定仅根据公约第6条第1款而非第9条审理申诉人机构提出的控诉(Canea Catholic Church v. Greece, §§ 33 and 50)。类似地,国内法院最终判决承认教区及其成员可以根据他们特殊的仪式在地方墓地埋葬其身体的权利,申诉人控诉该判决没有得到执行,欧洲人权法院决定仅根据第6条第1款审查该控诉[Greek Catholic Parish of Pesceana v. Romania (dec.), § 43];

(2)公约第8条(私生活和家庭生活受到尊重的权利)。欧洲人权法院曾在审查某些申诉时仅依据公约第8条或连同公约第14条一并审理。例如,国内法院裁定一名未达法定年龄的儿童与父母一方居住,主要原因是另一方是耶和华见证会的教徒(Hoffmann v. Austria; Palau-Martinez v. France; Ismailova v. Russia)。欧洲人权法院指出,国内法院确定的父母对孩子行使亲权的实际安排本身不能侵犯申诉人表达其宗教的自由[Deschomets v. France (dec.)];

(3)第10条(表达自由)。欧洲人权法院只审查依据第10条审理的申诉——例如,国家有权机构禁止一家独立电台播放一则具有宗教性质的付费广告(Murphy v. Ireland),或者有权机构拒绝给一家播放基督教节目的电台颁发许可证(Glas Nadejda EOOD and Anatoli Elenkov v. Bulgaria)。当申诉人控诉国家机关干涉其通过广播信息表达信仰和观点时,第10条属于第9条的特别法,因此就没有必要再单独考虑第9条了[Balsytė-Lideikienė v. Lithuania (dec.)]。

(4)第11条(集会和结社自由)。欧洲人权法院在审理下列申诉时依据了第11条:

- 根据第 11 条解释第 9 条——例如,国家干预在同一宗教团体内的两个对立团体的纠纷(Hassan and Tchaouch v. Bulgaria [GC],§ 65)、宗教组织的解散(Jehovah's Witnesses of Moscow and Others v. Russia,§§ 102 - 103),以及长期拒绝承认一个宗教团体的法人地位(Religionsgemeinschaft der Zeugen Jehovas and Others v. Austria,§ 60);

- 根据第 11 条和第 6 条第 1 款解释第 9 条——例如,国内当局拒绝登记宗教组织对章程中有关批准变更组织教派的规定的修改(Svyato-Mykhaïlivska Parafiya v. Ukraine,§ 152);

- 根据第 9 条解释第 11 条(结社自由)——例如,拒绝续展宗教组织的登记(Moscow Branch of the Salvation Army v. Russia,§§ 74 - 75);

- 根据第 9 条解释第 11 条(集会自由)——例如,不允许新德鲁伊教团体在巨石阵历史遗迹区庆祝夏至[Pendragon v. the United Kingdom (dec.)];相反情况,见[Chappell v. the United Kingdom (dec.)];

(5)第一议定书第 1 条(财产保护)。欧洲人权法院选择只依据第一议定书第 1 条审理案件——例如,反对狩猎的土地所有者对在其土地上的狩猎行为有容忍的义务(Chassagnou and Others v. France [GC];Herrmann v. Germany [GC]);

(6)第一议定书第 2 条(父母确保其孩子受到的教育与自己的宗教和哲学信仰相符的权利)。欧洲人权法院在审理下列案件时选择依据此条:

- 仅依据第一议定书第 2 条——例如,公立学校对宗教文化和德育必修课的管理(Hasan and Eylem Zengin v. Turkey),或者教育机构拒绝同意儿童免修基督教必修课(Folgerø and Others v. Norway [GC]);

- 分别单独依据第一议定书第 2 条和公约第 9 条,欧洲人权法院基于详细的论证判定不违反前一条款,并通过简单引述前述论证而判定不违反后一条款(Kjeldsen, Busk Madsen and Pedersen v. Denmark);

- 根据第 9 条解释第一议定书第 2 条——例如,在公立学校的教室内强制安放十字架(Lautsi and Others v. Italy [GC]);

- 针对父母依据第一议定书第 2 条,针对孩子依据公约第 9 条——校长对拒绝参加学校游行的小学生进行处罚(Valsamis v. Greece)。

46. 在涉及教育和教学时,第一议定书第 2 条基本上是公约第 9 条的特别法。如同本案一样,这一点至少应适用于下述案件:案件的核心争论点是缔约国根据第一议定书第 2 条第 2 句所负有的义务,即缔约国在行使其任何有关教育和教学的职能时,应当尊重父母确保这种教育或教学符合其宗教和哲学信仰的权利(*Lautsi and Others v. Italy* [GC],§ 59)。

第三节 第 9 条保护的行为

一、消极方面

(一)不信仰宗教或不披露个人信仰的权利

47. 宗教自由也涉及消极权利,即不信仰宗教的权利(*Alexandridis v. Greece*,§ 32)。这意味着国家不能要求个人实施可能被视为宣誓效忠某一宗教的行为。例如,欧洲人权法院认为,法律上要求申诉人向福音书宣誓放弃其议会席位违反了公约第 9 条(*Buscarini and Others v. San Marino* [GC],§§ 34 and 39)。

48. 表达自己宗教信仰自由的消极方面还意味着不得要求个人披露其宗教派系或信仰;也不能强制个人实施能够推测出其持有或不持有某种信仰的行为。国家当局不得通过询问个人的宗教信仰或强迫个人表露自己的信仰,来肆意干涉其良心自由(*Alexandridis v. Greece*,§ 38;*Dimitras and Others v. Greece*,§ 78)。

49. 此外,这类干涉可能是间接的;例如,如果国家签发的官方文件(身份证、学校报告等)有宗教一栏,在该栏留白就不可避免地具有特殊隐含意味。在一起涉及身份证的案件中,欧洲人权法院判决,在这类证件上表明宗教——无论是强制的还是可选择的,都违反了公约第 9 条的规定(*Sinan Işık v. Turkey*,§§ 51-52 and 60)。第 9 条也不保障在个人身份证上记录宗教的权利,即使个人是自愿记录的[*Sofianopoulos and Others v. Greece* (dec.)]。欧洲人权法院也拒绝同意出于人口统计的目的而在民事登记册上或身份证上写明宗教,因为这必然涉及在法律上规定强制个人披露宗教信仰(*Sinan Işık v. Turkey*,§ 44)。另一方面,雇员事先告知其雇主其所信仰宗教的要求,以便获得特定权利——例如,为了去清真寺有权每周五缺勤,这种需要不能与"披露个人宗教信仰的义务"相提并论[*X. v. the United Kingdom* (dec.)]。

50. 在下列案件中,欧洲人权法院判定违反公约第 9 条(单独考虑第 9 条或连同第 14 条有关禁止歧视的规定一并考虑):

- 将法院组织宣誓程序作为法律执业的前提,而该程序是基于所涉人员为正统基督教徒且愿意做出宗教宣誓而进行的;但为了被允许进行庄严的宣誓而非宗教宣誓,申诉人不得不披露他不是正统基督教徒(Alexandridis v. Greece, §§ 36–41);
- 在阿里山缀迪斯案(Alexandridis)中存在着相同问题,只不过有关人员是参加刑事诉讼的证人、控诉人或嫌疑人[Dimitras and Others v. Greece; Dimitras and Others v. Greece (no.2); Dimitras and Others v. Greece (no.3)]。
- 由于缺少申诉人可能参加的伦理替代课程,一名小学生免于参加宗教课程,而随后,在其所有的学校报告以及小学学位证书上,"宗教/伦理"一栏上都只有"–"(横线);即使在该栏中所显示的标记并不能表明涉案小学生是否参加过宗教或伦理课程,但没有成绩很明显表明他没有上过这类课程,而这会导致他遭受侮辱的风险[Grzelak v. Poland; cf. 公约机构基于明显无根据而判定类似诉求不予受理的两个案件, C. J., J. J. and E. J. v. Poland (dec.); Saniewski v. Poland, (dec.)]。

51. 相反,在申诉人个人所得税证件上的信息栏中标明"– –"(两条横线),以表明其不属于需要缴纳教会税的教会或宗教团体,欧洲人权法院认为这不违反第 9 条。欧洲人权法院认为,保留在雇主和税收机关处的涉案文件并不是出于公共使用的目的,因而应当限缩受到责难的干预的范围(Wasmuth v. Germany, §§ 58–59)。

(二)出于良心而反对兵役:不实施违背个人良心或信仰的行为的权利

52. 第 9 条并没有明确提出出于良心而反对在军队服兵役或进行公民服务的权利。然而,欧洲人权法院判定,第 9 条提供的保障原则上适用于反对兵役——当这种反对是由于强制兵役和个人良心或其虔诚信仰的宗教或其他信仰间存在严重且不可调和的冲突时。反对服兵役是否以及在多大程度上适用第 9 条因各个案件的具体情况而有所不同。例如,申诉人是耶和华见证会(该宗教团体的信仰包括反对为军队提供服务,即使该种服务是非武力服务)的信徒,其因逃避服兵役而被定罪,但法律并没有规定其他可替代的公民服务,欧洲人权法院认为对其定罪的做法违反了公约第 9 条(Bayatyan v. Armenia, § 110)。

53. 随后,欧洲人权法院在一系列与巴亚天(Bayatyan)非常类似的案件中判定亚美尼亚(*Bukharatyan v. Armenia*；*Tsaturyan v. Armenia*)和土耳其(*Erçep v. Turkey*；*Feti Demirtaş v. Turkey*；*Buldu and Others v. Turkey*)违反公约第 9 条。特别是在菲迪黛米塔斯(*Feti Demirtaş*)案中,申诉人被多次定罪,虽然最终因为医学报告指出他患有适应障碍而让他退伍,但是欧洲人权法院认为这并不能改变任何情况,而且也不影响申诉人"受害者"的地位;恰恰相反,申诉人的心理障碍是在服兵役期间爆发的,这进一步加重了应诉国的责任(*Feti Demirtaş v. Turkey*, §§ 73 – 77 and 113 – 114)。

54. 上述所有案件中,出于良心而反对兵役者都是耶和华见证会教徒。然而,在两件涉及没有宗教信仰的和平主义者的案件中,欧洲人权法院也认为违反了第 9 条。在这些案件中,欧洲人权法院着重考虑了国家的积极义务,认为土耳其法律体系内没有可利用的有效程序以确认申诉人是否是出于良心而反对兵役者的地位,因而违反公约(*Savda v. Turkey*；*Tarhan v. Turkey*)。在此前一起控诉罗马尼亚的案件中,申诉人声称国内当局拒绝将其登记为出于良心而反对兵役者,对其构成歧视,因为在国内法中,只有出于宗教原因而反对的人能主张该地位,而他只是一个和平主义者。然而,考虑到申诉人从未被定罪或起诉,且罗马尼亚已经取消了在和平时期强制服兵役的规定,欧洲人权法院认为申诉人不能成为所主张的违反公约行为的"受害者"[*Butan v. Romania* (dec.)]。

55. 欧洲人权法院在三起案件中确认违反第 14 条(禁止歧视)以及第 9 条的规定,在这三起案件中,奥地利耶和华见证会的牧师控诉国家拒绝他们免于服兵役以及替代的公民服务的申请,因为此类豁免权利只有那些"被承认的宗教组织"的牧师才能享有,而耶和华见证会这类"已登记"的宗教组织的牧师,尽管其与其他任何一个宗教的牧师的职能类似,但在当时却不能享有该项权利(*Löffelmann v. Austria*；*Gütl v. Austria*；*Lang v. Austria*)。此外,欧洲人权法院认为,一个福音派传教士要求完全豁免军队兵役或公民服务的申请被拒,这并不违反第 14 条以及第 9 条的规定。在本案中,欧洲人权法院注意到,申诉人并没有申请"被承认的宗教团体"地位,因而他的情况不能与此类组织中牧师的地位相比(*Koppi v. Austria*)。

56. 有关过去处理过的个人出于良心而反对兵役的权利遭到侵犯而需要赔偿的情况,欧洲人权法院认为,基督复临安息日会的一个教徒提出的申诉明显无根据。该教徒曾在共产主义时期被征召,并且因拒绝宣誓和拒绝参加星期六的武器展示而构成"违令",并被判处监禁。随着民主制度的建立,法律规定为在旧制度中受到政治迫害的受害者提供更高的退休金以及其他利益,而这些利益他并没有享受到,因为根据国内判例法,不论基于何种理由被判处军队违令罪,都不能被认为是"政治迫害"。根据第 14 条及第 9 条,申诉人控诉国内法院拒绝考虑其是由于宗教信仰而被定罪的事实。欧洲人权法院判定,尽管第 14 条规定的积极义务要求国家消除判处军队违令罪给出于良心而反对兵役者带来的任何消极后果,但这绝不是指通过对其提供仅为其他类别人员提供的经济利益这种积极方式来对定罪进行价值补偿。在此情况下,被责难的判例法有客观合理的依据,而且符合国家一般的自由裁量[*Baciu v. Romania* (dec.)]。

57. 至于学校方面,欧洲人权法院曾经审理这样一起案件:两名年轻的耶和华见证会信徒在希腊国立中学上学,他们因为拒绝参加学校关于纪念意大利法西斯与希腊间战争爆发周年日的游行,而被下令禁止上学一至两天,欧洲人权法院认为这一做法没有违反公约第 9 条。申诉人分别告知了他们各自的校长:他们的宗教信仰禁止他们通过参与游行活动加入到有关战争的纪念活动中——无论是在民间机构,还是教堂或者军事机构中,这种游行活动通常会与官方相关联,而且与阅兵仪式在同一天。欧洲人权法院在有关父母确保其子女所接受的教育与其宗教信仰一致(第一议定书第 2 条)的问题上,没有找到违反公约的地方,因此欧洲人权法院在涉及其女儿本身的宗教信仰自由权时,也得出了相同的结论。欧洲人权法院注意到,她们免受宗教教育和避开东正教信徒的请求已经得到满足。至于强制参加学校游行方面,欧洲人权法院认为,无论是从游行的目的,还是从学校游行的安排上看,该游行活动本身并没有侵犯女孩们的反战信仰。而且从活动方式看,这种国家活动层面的纪念是符合和平的目的与公共利益的(*Valsamis v. Greece*;*Efstratiou v. Greece*)。

58. 在平民方面,一般而言,个人可以依据自己的意志表达其宗教信仰,但当涉及公共利益,需要顾忌社会整体利益时,该信仰的表达会受到严格限制。这一限制在同性恋伴侣问题上尤其突出(*Eweida and Others v. the United Kingdom*,§ 105)。委员会也接受在涉及职业需要的时候,在实施良心条款(如律师的良心条款)时所表达的信仰原则上也可能受到第 9 条的保护。因此,尽管会带有职业本身的需求,但考虑到其特殊性,这样的条款可能会和律师的个人信仰相混淆。通常而言,律师的个人信仰只涉及其个人而与其职业能力无关[*Mignot v. France*,(dec.)]。

59. 在下列案件中,欧洲人权法院认为没有违反第 9 条(单独或者连同公约第 14 条禁止歧视条款):

- 一名当地机构的基督徒雇员因为拒绝为一个同性恋民间联盟进行登记手续,而受到纪律处分并被免职(*Eweida and Others v. the United Kingdom*, nos. 48420/10, 59842/10, 51671/10 and 36516/10, §§ 102 – 106, ECHR 2013);
- 私人公司的一名员工因为拒绝为同性恋伴侣提供性心理学治疗,而受到纪律处分并被免职(*Eweida and Others v. the United Kingdom*)。

60. 公约机构也否认了一些基于良心的目的而行使的信仰行为,因而在下列案件中,认为违反了公约第9条:

- 一名和平主义的贵格会教徒,除非国家保证不会将他的钱用于军事机构,否则拒绝交税[*C. v. the United Kingdom*(dec.),*H. and B. v. the United Kingdom*(dec.)的情况与此相同。另外,法国一名反对堕胎的纳税人拒绝缴纳税款,以免被用于资助堕胎(*Bouessel du Bourg v. France*(dec.)]。在所有的这些案件中,欧洲人权法院认为属于通常义务的纳税并不涉及对个人良心的影响,因为纳税的义务是中立的,纳税人无法影响税收的分配或者在被收缴后决定税收的分配;
- 一名律师因为正式拒绝了依据法律分派给他的任务而受到了纪律处分。该任务要求其代理被拘留人员,处分的理由是他违反了相关的法律。虽然律师职业良心条款可能会受到公约第9条的保护,但是委员会注意到申诉人基本没有质疑与其良心相悖的法律,没有抱怨这项要求其出现在与其良心相违背的场合的法律。而这些质疑可以在某种程度使其得以依据律师职业良心条款进行申诉[*Mignot v. France*(dec.)];
- 本案中的申诉人是一家制药企业的共同所有人,他们基于宗教信仰的原因拒绝销售避孕药[*Pichon and Sajous v. France*(dec.)]。

61. 本法院还拒绝受理如下申诉:

- 一项由失业者提起的申诉——他声称自己不属于任何特定的宗教,其失业补贴被暂时取消,取消的原因是他拒绝在当地新教教堂的会议和讨论中心做接待员。欧洲人权法院注意到接待员涉及的工作仅仅是为来客提供帮助,也就是说这份工作实质上与任何宗教信仰都无关,此外也没有宣称这份工作会侵犯申诉人不信仰某个宗教的自由[*Dautaj v. Switzerland*(dec.)];
- 一名受雇于公共健康保险部门的医生提起的申诉。他因为拒绝在一名实习医生身上进行医学实验而被解雇。他之所以拒绝是因为他害怕产生"可能的偏见",如果在今后,他不得不与那名实习医生一起工作,那么这一偏见可能会为他带来麻烦。欧洲人权法院注意到,申诉人的态度并没有清晰地表达其在根本问题上的观点,而且他没有解释希望避免的道德困境。因此,就第9条的目的而言,该行为并没有涉及"表达个人信仰"的问题[Blumberg v. Germany(dec.)];

- 几个俄罗斯人提起申诉,抱怨相关的法律将个人的"纳税人号码"分配给所有纳税人。他们认为该行为是反对基督徒的前兆。欧洲人权法院注意到,这一措施是在公共领域内中立且普遍适用,申诉人也并没有被要求申请或使用纳税人号码,因为法律官方文件明文许可大多数纳税人可以不使用该号码,而且,欧洲人权法院重申,官方文件或数据库的内容不能由列于其中的个人的意愿所决定。因此,该措施并没有侵犯公约第9条所保障的权利[Skugar and Others v. Russia(dec.)]。

二、积极方面

(一)一般原则

62. 虽然宗教自由主要是个人良心的问题,但它同时也暗示了"表达个人宗教信仰"的自由。该自由的表达不限于特定的场合,可能是独自一人的时候,可能是与他人一起时,也可能是在公众场合或是在具有同一信仰的场合。第9条列举了表达个人宗教信仰的形式,如做礼拜、教育、仪式以及对教规的遵守(Metropolitan Church of Bessarabia and Others v. Moldova,§114)。

63. 除非常特殊的案件,公约所保障的宗教自由的权利与一个国家衡量宗教信仰或者信仰表达方式合法性的权力不同(Hassan and Tchaouch v. Bulgaria[GC],§76;Leyla Şahin v. Turkey[GC],§107)。因此,国家在这一问题上的自由裁量权较小,而且,在干预个人依据自己宗教信仰标准做出的选择时,国家必须给出严谨的、有说服力的理由。当个人的选择与公约的核心原则不符时,一项干预就可以根据第9条第2款得以合法化,例如,一夫多妻和未达到法定结婚年龄的婚姻或者是对性别平等的公然违反,或者被强迫信仰(Jehovah's Witnesses of Moscow and Others v. Russia)。

64. 第9条并不保护任何因为宗教或信仰导致的行为，并且不总是保护因个人的宗教或信仰在公共场合做出相关行为的权利（Kalaç v. Turkey）。同样，作为一项一般规则，它确实并未在宗教信仰的基础上赋予个人拒绝遵守根据公约制定并公正普遍实施的法律的权利［Fränklin-Beentjes and CEFLU-Luz da Floresta v. the Netherlands (dec.)］。如果一个行为被宗教或者一系列的信仰所激励、鼓动或影响，那么该行为将会被视为第9条中的有关宗教或信仰的"表示"，因而该行为会与所涉宗教或信仰紧密相连。一个典型的例子是通常意义上被认为属于宗教或信仰的一部分的礼拜或祈祷。然而，宗教或信仰的"表示"并不局限于这些行为；需要依据每个案例的事实决定是否存在行为与潜在信仰之间的紧密而直接的联系。特别是，申诉人在声称一个行为涉及他们宗教与信仰的表达自由时，并不需要去证实他们的行为实际上履行了所涉宗教的义务（S. A. S. v. France［GC］，§55）。

65. 有时，在行使宗教表达自由时，个人需要考虑他们特定的职业或者契约性的场合［X. v. the United Kingdom (dec.); and Kalaç v. Turkey, §27］。例如，欧洲人权法院曾宣布申诉人的一项诉求明显缺乏依据。该申诉人之前开办了一个私人安保机构，但由于之后加入了一个少数教派，而依据瑞士法律，这使得他不再符合所要求的"荣誉"的标准，因而其开办机构的权利被国内法院取消。国内法院认为该教派的领导者是一个危险人物，其教文涉及世界末日逼近的言论，因此应该为诱使其成员犯罪或实施暴力负责。在这种情况下，如果让这家保障机构继续运营将会对公共利益与秩序构成威胁。因此，欧洲人权法院支持国内法院的判决，认为该案中被质疑的干预符合公约第9条第2款的规定［C. R. v. Switzerland (dec.)］。

66. 纵观欧洲人权法院的一系列判例，都涉及了对宗教自由不同的解读。这些宗教自由涉及范围广泛，从最私人的内容（如健康问题）到最公共的内容（如关于集体礼拜的自由以及设立礼拜场所的权利）。

（二）宗教自由以及健康问题自由

67. 欧洲人权法院认为，从原则上来说，耶和华见证会拒绝输血是属于私人自治范围的事务，因此受到公约第8条和第9条的保护。在这种情况下，欧洲人权法院首先注意到，由于耶和华见证会信徒并不普遍拒绝接受医学治疗，所以拒绝输血不能被视为自杀行为；输血是他们基于宗教原因唯一拒绝接受的医疗程序。根据被认可的医学观点，某些输血行为对于拯救病人生命或者避免对其健康造成不可弥补的损害而言是至关重要的,即使患者拒绝接受这种输血,欧洲人权法院仍然认为根据个人选择的方式处置自己身体的自由包括进行那些公认的对当事人身体有危害或具有危险性质的活动的自由。在医疗救助方面,即使患者拒绝接受一项特定的治疗可能会带来致命的危害,但医护人员如果在没得到一个具有行为能力的成年患者同意的情况下对其实施该治疗,将会干预他或者她保持身体完整性的权利以及公约第 8 条所保护的权利。然而,要使这种自由得以实现,那么患者必须能够依据其意见和价值观做出选择——即使这些选择在他人看起来是不合理、不明智或是鲁莽的。考虑到相关的国内立法,欧洲人权法院认为这使得成年患者的自由选择以及未成年人的客观利益(通过授权法院否决父母对可能拯救孩子生命的医疗措施的反对意见)都能得到充分的保护。最终,欧洲人权法院判决耶和华见证会拒绝输血的规定不能作为解散该组织及禁止其活动的正当理由 (*Jehovah's Witnesses of Moscow and Others v. Russia*, §§ 131 – 144)。

(三)对饮食教规的遵守

68. 宗教或者哲学体系所要求的对饮食教规的遵守属于宗教"仪式"活动,受到公约第 9 条第 1 款的保护(*Cha'are Shalom Ve Tsedek v. France* [GC], §§ 73 – 74; *Jakóbski v. Poland*)。在两个案例中,欧洲人权法院认为违反了公约第 9 条。这两个案例中,在有能力负担的情况下,监狱机关拒绝为申诉人——信仰佛教的囚犯,提供不含肉的食物[*Jakóbski v. Poland* ; *Vartic v. Romania* (no.2)];尤其在第二个案例中,申诉人只能得到提供给患病囚犯的食物,而这种食物中也是含肉的。欧洲人权法院注意到,申诉人只能在极小的范围内接受与其宗教相符合的食物,尤其是在司法部长禁止邮递食物包裹之后[*Vartic v. Romania* (no.2), §§ 47 – 50]。

69. 相反,对于这一申诉,委员会宣布不予受理:申诉人是一名正在服刑的正统派犹太教信徒,抱怨国家没有向其定期提供犹太食物。委员会注意到,国家已经为申诉人提供了符合犹太食物要求的素食,还咨询了首席拉比的意见,他同意当局出于尊重申诉人宗教权利的目的而采取的措施[*X v. the United Kingdom* (dec.)]。

70. 在一个案例中,法国极正统派犹太教的一个礼拜协会的成员要求有权享用符合比犹太教标准教规更严格的规定的屠宰动物"格拉特"肉,并抱怨国家机关拒绝授权允许其屠夫依据其要求的标准进行屠宰。然而,在巴黎,一个大多数法国犹太人所在的犹太协会所提出的这种要求却得到了许可。在该案中,无论是单独看第 9 条,还是结合公约第 14 条(反歧视)的规定,欧洲人权法院都认为国家的拒绝行为没有违反公约规定。

欧洲人权法院注意到,申诉人协会在比利时可以轻易获得他们所需要的"格拉特"食物,并且很多肉店在该协会的控制下为犹太人提供符合标准的"格拉特"食物。因此,欧洲人权法院判决当局的拒绝没有损害申诉人协会表达其宗教自由的权利。欧洲人权法院详述道,因为申诉人所在协会及其成员能够获得有关食物,其受公约第9条所保障的宗教自由的权利不能扩大到个人亲自参与屠宰仪式并参与后续的认证过程(Cha'are Shalom Ve Tsedek v. France [GC], §82)。

(四)宗教服饰及标志

71. 一个健全的民主社会需要容忍并支持宗教信仰的多元化和多样性,而且原则上应该允许将宗教视为生活信条的个人享有向他人传播其信仰的权利,如穿戴有宗教标志或物件的服饰(Eweida and Others v. the United Kingdom, §94)。因为依个人的宗教信仰和意愿穿戴此类服饰是属于通过礼拜、仪式或对教规的遵守表达宗教信仰,因此这种行为受到公约第9条第1款的保护(Eweida and Others v. the United Kingdom, §89)。然而,穿戴有宗教标志或者物件的服饰的权利并不是绝对的,必须与其他自然人和法人的法定利益相平衡。欧洲人权法院目前在该领域的判例法覆盖了三个不同的领域:(1)公共领域;(2)办公场所;(3)学校和大学。

72. 首先,关于在公众领域穿戴有宗教标志或者物件的服饰,土耳其立法禁止在非宗教仪式的公共场合穿戴某些类型的宗教服饰,根据这一立法规定,几名"Aczimendi tarikatı"宗教组织成员被刑事定罪,欧洲人权法院认为这违反了公约第9条。在该案中,所涉及的服饰是黑色的头巾、黑色的裤子以及带有棒子的黑色祭袍。考虑到该案的事实、国内法院的具体判决,以及宗教分离原则对土耳其民主制度的重要性,欧洲人权法院认为由于所涉的干预是为了使其符合世俗和民主原则,因而该项禁止行为所追求的是公约第9条第2款中所列举的几个合法性目的,如保护公共安全、公共秩序及他人的权利与自由。然而,欧洲人权法院认为,对于实现其目标,实施该项措施并不满足必要性条件。欧洲人权法院认为,当局的禁止措施并非针对被要求在其行使义务的时候行使裁量权的公务员,而是针对普通公民,并且针对的不是特定的公共场合而是所有公共场合。其次,从案卷来看,申诉人在清真寺外穿着宗教服装聚集在一起,只是为了参加宗教仪式,这种通过特定类型的服饰来表达其信仰的方式,并不能表明已经构成了危害公共秩序、对他人施加压力的情形或对构成这种情形负有责任。最后,对于土耳其政府关于申诉人有可能参加了改变信仰活动的说法,欧洲人权法院认为,案卷中并没有证据表明他们为了宣扬自己的教义曾试图给街上和公众场合路人施加不当的压力(*Ahmet Arslan and Others v. Turkey*)。

73. 相反,法国颁布的一项法律规定,如果在公共场合穿戴试图遮脸的服饰(因此包括布尔卡和尼卡伯),将会受到处罚,欧洲人权法院认为这一规定并不违反第9条。该法律规定的责任承担方式是罚金及/或强制性公民课程。欧洲人权法院认为,本案和阿米特·阿斯兰等人诉土耳其案(*Ahmet Arslan and Others v. Turkey*)明显不同,因为面纱是遮住全部的脸,仅仅只可能露出眼睛。由此类推,本案中法国的禁止并未明确针对服饰的宗教内涵。欧洲人权法院认可应诉国政府论据的合法性,即由于脸在人类交往中起到了重要作用,因此人们在公众场合或许不希望看到此类行为对开放的人际交往造成障碍,而开放的人际交往被公认为法国社会生活不可或缺的一部分。因此,欧洲人权法院认为,面纱将脸部遮挡,对他人造成了障碍,构成了应诉国家所认为的使生活更融洽的社交场合中其他人的权利的侵犯;换言之,国家可能认为个人间的交往很重要,可以认为在公众场合戴面纱的行为影响了人际交往。而对于另外一些质疑,如通过全部禁止(考虑到只涉及少部分女性)的方式解决社会融洽问题的必要性以及对所涉女性造成的消极影响,如认为自己被孤立。欧洲人权法院认为应诉国没有超越自由裁量的范围,尤其是在宽大量刑的问题上(*S. A. S. v. France* [GC])。

74. 公约机构一直拒绝受理涉及暂时禁止穿戴相关宗教服饰的强制性要求的申诉。例如,他们曾拒绝受理以下申诉:

- 一名锡克教徒因为骑乘摩托车时没有戴头盔而被罚款;申诉人认为其宗教要求他一直戴着包头巾,因而她无法佩戴头盔[*X. v. the United Kingdom* (dec.)];
- 要求一名锡克教徒在通过候机厅的安检通道时取下头巾[*Phull v. France* (dec.)];
- 申诉人在摩洛哥的法国总领事馆申领签证,需要取下面纱进行身份确认;由于拒绝摘下面纱,申诉人被禁止进入领事馆因而无法获得签证。申诉人称她只能在女人面前摘下面纱,欧洲人权法院对这一理由不予支持;欧洲人权法院认为,法国领事当局没有安排女性工作人员核实身份并不超越裁量范围[*El Morsli v. France* (dec.)];
- 在官方文件上要求使用免冠证件照,更具体地说,要求穆斯林学生提供免冠证件照以获取大学毕业文凭[*Karaduman v. Turkey* (dec.); *Araç v. Turkey*

- 在官方文件上要求使用免冠证件照,更具体地说,当局拒绝接受一名锡克教徒戴着头巾的照片[*Mann Singh v. France*(dec.)]。

75. 在工作场合,为了表达特定的商业形象,一家商业公司可以对员工要求符合一定的着装标准,该标准有时可能会限制穿戴宗教服饰(*Eweida and Others v. the United Kingdom*,§94)。同样,出于对患者及医务人员健康及安全的考虑,医院在这方面也有一定的自由裁量权(*Eweida and Others v. the United Kingdom*,§99)。但是,这些利益尽管合法,也不是绝对的,总是需要与个人表达宗教的自由相权衡。

76. 例如,一家私营企业因为员工拒绝取下基督徒十字架而将其停职,却允许穿戴其他宗教的某些服饰(包头纱或面巾),欧洲人权法院认为这种做法违反了第9条(*Eweida and Others v. the United Kingdom*,§§94-95)。

77. 另外,老年病房的一名护士拒绝取下脖子上的十字架将其作为胸针穿戴或者塞进高领衣服内,因此被医院调出老年病房。在国内法院,申诉人的管理者认为精神失常的患者可能会去扯链子而伤到自己或者申诉人,又或者十字架会向前摇晃而触碰到患者裸露的伤口(*Eweida and Others v. the United Kingdom*,§§98-100)。

78. 最后,关于在国家教育机构穿戴宗教服饰,欧洲人权法院一直强调一国在该领域享有非常大的自由裁量权。在全欧洲很难找到关于宗教重要性的统一概念,而且公开表达宗教信仰的意义及影响也随着时间和社会环境的变化而有所不同。根据不同国家的传统和基于保护他人权利和自由以及维持公共秩序的自由的需要,有关这方面的规定在各国之间有所不同。因此,关于此类规定的程度及形式的选择问题,无疑需要在一定程度上留给所涉国家基于国内具体情况自主决定的权利(*Leyla Şahin v. Turkey*[GC],§109)。欧洲人权法院从这一角度出发审理的案件,基于申诉人是老师还是学生,可以分为两类。

79. 如果申诉人是老师,欧洲人权法院会权衡老师表达其宗教信仰的权利、尊重教育中立性及保障学生在宗教和谐环境下学习的合法利益之间的关系。尽管国家可以要求公务员基于职权有义务避免在公众场合宣扬宗教,但是公务员也属于个人,因而属于公约第9条的保护范围。因此,欧洲人权法院需要根据每个案件的具体情形,判断一国在两项利益即个人宗教自由的利益与民主国家为了实现公约第9条第2款中所列的合法公共服务目的的合法利益的权衡上,是否进行了公平、合理的判断[*Kurtulmuş v.*

Turkey（dec.）]。在这方面,需要考虑到学校老师特殊的职业要求,老师既是一个教育机构活动的参与者和孩子们眼中国家的代表人,也是一个可能因为自己的穿着具有改变他人宗教信仰的影响的人。此外,学生的年龄也是需要考虑的重要因素,因为比起年纪较长的学生,较为年轻的学生会对许多事物更加好奇,也更容易受到影响[*Dahlab v. Switzerland*（dec.）]。

80. 在这样的逻辑下,欧洲人权法院认为一个国家有较大的裁量权,并且认为下面这些申诉缺乏足够的依据：

- 禁止一名小学老师在教书时穿戴伊斯兰头巾,该老师所教学生年龄偏小(4 到 8 岁)。欧洲人权法院认为在民主社会中,老师应当向学生传递诸如包容、尊重他人以及平等、非歧视等信息,而伊斯兰头巾是一种"强有力的外部标志",很难与前述所要传递的信息相容。此外,欧洲人权法院否定了申诉人关于该措施构成了性别歧视(公约第 14 条)的主张,因为在类似的情况下,这项规定也适用于一名穿戴着不同信仰服饰的男子[*Dahlab v. Switzerland*（dec.）]；

- 申诉人是土耳其一所国立大学的助理教授,她在教书时穿戴了伊斯兰头巾,被认为违反了有关公务员穿着的规定,从而被处以纪律处罚。欧洲人权法院认为一个民主国家有权要求公务员遵守宪法原则,而政教分离是土耳其的一项重要原则,因此申诉人作为一名教育机构工作者以及自愿成为国家公务员的人,应当遵守不在公开场合明显表达其宗教信仰自由的规定。欧洲人权法院也否定了申诉人关于该措施同时构成性别歧视和宗教歧视(公约第 14 条)的主张,因为男性工作人员也需要遵守类似的规定[*Kurtulmuş v. Turkey*（dec.）；在一个暂停伊玛目哈提普中学一名初中女教师职务的案例中也是如此,*Karaduman v. Turkey*（dec.）]。

81. 在学生方面,欧洲人权法院在下列案例中认为没有违反公约第 9 条,或者认为申诉没有足够的依据：

- 禁止土耳其一所国立大学的一名医科学生在班上穿戴伊斯兰头巾。考虑到土耳其特定的历史和宪法体系,欧洲人权法院认为国家当局为了维持其政教分离的原则所采取的措施具有合法性,该原则被土耳其宪法法院解释为一项基本原则,欧洲人权法院认为该项原则应当与公约体现的价值相一致,并且与法治、人权及民主价值相一致。欧洲人权法院考虑到下列因素,认为该措施并没有违反

第 9 条：土耳其宪法体系强调性别平等，这是公约的一项基本原则，也是欧洲委员会成员国所追求的目标之一；将伊斯兰头巾问题放在土耳其的特殊背景下进行考察的时候，不能不考虑这些表现出或被认为是强制性宗教义务的标志对其他人可能造成的影响；根据土耳其法院的观点，穿戴头巾在该国具有政治意义；土耳其存在极端主义运动，试图向社会强行推行他们的宗教标志和建立在宗教意义上的社会概念。在这样一种背景下，土耳其的措施符合之前提到的合法目的，因而有利于保护大学的多元性（*Leyla Şahin v. Turkey*［GC］）；

- 禁止伊玛目哈提普中学（土耳其国家资助的宗教中学）的学生在《可兰经》课外穿戴头巾，并且禁止穿戴头巾的学生来上课。欧洲人权法院认为相关的土耳其法律规定所有的中学学生上学时需要穿制服并且露出额头；在伊玛目哈提普中学，有一个例外，即女孩可以在《可兰经》的课堂上遮住她们的头。因此，该项争议的规定属于不考虑宗教信仰的普遍适用的规则，这些规定旨在确保避免学生承受压力和风险的中学教育中立的合法目的［*Köse and Others v. Turkey*（dec.）］；

- 法国国立中学拒绝让穿戴头巾的学生上体育课，并在之后以他们没有参与必修课程为由将他们开除。欧洲人权法院承认法国的非宗教模式与公约价值的相容性。国内法表明穿戴宗教标志并不必然与学校多元化原则不相容，但是根据具体情形以及穿戴这种标志可能造成的后果，则有可能与多元化原则相冲突。欧洲人权法院同意，认为穿戴如伊斯兰头巾之类的面纱从健康的安全的角度而言不便于运动的观点是合理的。它特别指出，针对申诉人的纪律处分程序已经完全满足了平衡各种利益的义务。因此，应诉国没有超越其自由裁量权（*Dogru v. France*；*Kervanci v. France*）；

- 法国禁止该国小学及初中的学生穿戴"明显表达其宗教的标志或服饰"，该规定并不局限于体育课，并且之后学校开除了在校内穿戴伊斯兰头巾、锡克头巾或者"小头巾"的学生。欧洲人权法院认为，上述措施具有符合公约价值的保护宪法确定的政教分离原则的目的，具有正当理由。此外，欧洲人权法院认为校长的决定，即禁止穆斯林学生穿戴头巾，并禁止他们进入教室，或者用不含有宗教意义的帽子或手帕取代头巾，或者允许锡克教徒用"小头巾"取代他们的头巾，没有违反公约第 9 条，因为这属于国家的自由裁量权［*Gamaleddyn v. France* (dec.); *Aktas v. France* (dec.); *Ranjit Singh v. France* (dec.); *Jasvir Singh v. France* (dec.)]。

(五)宗教自由、家庭及孩子的教育

82. 第9条并不试图调整任何宗教意义上的婚姻,应该由每个特定的教派去决定其宗教婚姻的形式,尤其是在是否以及在哪种程度上允许同性结合的问题上,完全取决于每个宗教的规定[*Parry v. the United Kingdom* (dec.)]。例如,委员会拒绝将公约第9条的保护扩展到一个因为和不满16岁的女孩(法定有能力同意性交的年龄)进行性交而处以监禁的人,即使在伊斯兰法下他们已经缔结婚姻;委员会同时认为该行为并没有违反公约第12条(结婚权)的规定[*Khan v. the United Kingdom* (dec.)]。委员会还拒绝了这样一项申诉:一名男子拒绝依据民事法的程序与其伴侣缔结婚姻,但是要求其所在国家承认其婚姻缔结的合法效力——他声称他们在第一次发生性关系之前已经正式结婚,因为他们已经依据宗教的规定朗读了旧约段落[*X. v. Germany* (dec.)]。

83. 第9条并没有保障离婚的权利(*Johnston and Others v. Ireland*, §63)。同样,委员会宣布根据公约第9条对一名犹太教徒提起的申诉不予受理。该申诉人在离婚后拒绝将断绝关系信交给其妻,这样自己就可以以宗教仪式再婚,他因此被民事法庭判决向其妻进行赔偿。在本案中,申诉人解释称他希望通过这种方式保留与妻子复婚的可能性,因为他属于科恩团体,摩西法典禁止其娶一个离婚的女人——即使是他的前妻。委员会认为申诉人拒绝给信的行为本身不属于第9条意义上的"宗教的表达",特别是申诉人拒绝给信的行为已经被犹太法庭追诉,很明显他的拒绝行为与他所声称的宗教观念不相符合[*D. v. France* (dec.)]。

84. 众所周知,宗教的生活方式要求信教者遵守宗教规则并且献身于宗教事业,而这会占据信教者很大一部分时间,有时甚至会使信教者以修道士的极端形式出现,这对于很多基督徒,或者在更小范围内,对于佛教和印度教徒是很普遍的。这种生活方式的选择大多出于成年人的自由意志,即使有时会因为这种选择与不同意该项选择的其他家庭成员发生冲突,但这种选择是完全受到公约第9条保护的(*Jehovah's Witnesses of Moscow and Others v. Russia*, §111)。

85. 根据公约第一议定书第2条,委员会认为父母确保其孩子接受的教育与他们的宗教与哲学信仰一致的权利属于亲权的一种,因此那些已经被司法判决撤销监护权的人不能行使该权利[*X. v. Sweden* (dec.)]。

86. 根据这些原则,委员会宣布对以下申请不予受理:

- 申诉人是波兰人,住在德国,他的前妻和未成年儿子住在瑞典。申诉人诉称瑞典法院不允许他探望孩子,他还诉称孩子是在路德教环境中长大的,这与他接受的罗马天主教堂的教义不一样;他的前妻没有遵守她在结婚时的承诺,即按照罗马天主教堂教会法的要求,在罗马天主教环境中将孩子抚养长大。委员会认为这与公约的属人管辖不一致,因而驳回了申诉。因为受质疑的行为并不归因于应诉国,而是仅仅归因于申诉人的前妻,她是孩子唯一的监护权人,因而有权利和义务保证他的教育[*X. v. Sweden*(dec.)①, no. 172/56;同时参见申诉人提出的其他申诉;*X. v. Sweden*(dec.), no. 911/60②,因为实质上和第一个案件相同而被拒绝受理];

- 苏联中亚地区的一名政治难民诉称他的侄女和侄子因为在一个罗马天主教机构长大而远离了伊斯兰信仰。暂不考虑申诉人是否能够代表孩子或者作为间接"受害人"进行申诉,委员会指出该案中并不存在对宗教自由的破坏,尤其是,在国内法院做出判决的时候,该案中的侄子和侄女已经分别到了20岁和21岁的年龄[*X. v. Germany*(dec.)];

- 一对犹太教父母诉称瑞典的社会保障机构决定将他们的几个未成年女儿安置在了一个新教徒家庭而不是一个犹太家庭,他们认为这一行为侵犯了他们确保子女受到的教育与他们的宗教信仰相一致的权利。结合公约第9条与第一议定书第2条,委员会认为该机构实际上在当地拉比的帮助下,已经花费极大的功夫去积极寻找犹太家庭,同时也一直保持向他们的父母告知有关进度,并听取了他们的意见;然而,保障机构最终还是没能在当地找到一个犹太家庭[*Tennenbaum v. Sweden*(dec.)];

- 申诉人是一名离异的穆斯林男子,他由于拒绝支付女儿的生活费而被判处监禁,他声称这么做是因为女儿的母亲让其接受了罗马天主教堂的洗礼从而改变了女儿的宗教。根据申诉人的说法,一个孩子,如果不再信仰伊斯兰(即使是在其母亲的影响下)只能被视为"不存在",因此,要求一个信仰伊斯兰教的父亲支付生活费将会违反宗教自由。委员会认为,支付生活费给一个监护权已经被授

---

① 裁定只有书面文本,请见欧洲人权法院图书馆《欧洲人权公约年鉴》。
② 裁定只有书面文本,请见欧洲人权法院图书馆《欧洲人权公约年鉴》。

予另一半的孩子的义务是普遍适用的,并且行为本身没有直接的有关宗教或良知的内涵,因此并没有干涉申诉人的宗教自由[*Karakuzey v. Germany* (dec.)]。

87. 本法院

- 宣布对一项由一些父母依据公约第8条(尊重私生活和家庭生活的权利)和其他几条规定提起的申诉不予受理。这些父母的成年孩子加入了马其顿东正教的修道院,申诉人诉称,该教派建立修道院并允许他们的孩子进入其中的行为侵犯了他们的权利。这些权利包括与他们的孩子保持联系,在年老或疾病的时候得到子女帮助,以及拥有孙子女;因此国家应该反对该教派的行为,保护他们的权利。欧洲人权法院认为孩子有权自己选择生活方式,父母与已长大成人的孩子之间的联系、尊重及互相的感情是严格的私人领域,国家对此没有积极义务,而且公约不保障成为祖父母的权利[*Şijakova and Others v. the former Yugoslav Republic of Macedonia* (dec.)];

- 宣布对一项由一名母亲提起的申诉不予受理。该母亲是雷尔运动中的一员,并已与其配偶离异,但是共同实施亲权。该案涉及一项法院命令,该命令禁止她使孩子与雷尔教派信徒(除她自己和她的新配偶以外)产生联系,并禁止她带他们参加雷尔教的会议。欧洲人权法院认为,这项由法律规定的旨在追求一个合法目的(保护孩子和他们的父亲的权利)的干预是"民主社会所必需的"。申诉人能够继续不受限制地信仰其宗教,并且可以在子女面前信仰该宗教,只要他们未使子女与雷尔运动的其他成员产生联系。欧洲人权法院同时强调应当优先考虑孩子们的最佳利益,协调父母双方的教育选择,试图平衡父母双方的想法,排除任何价值判断,并且在必要的时候,制定有关个人宗教实践的最低限度的规则。基于同样的理由,欧洲人权法院认为不存在违反第14条所禁止的歧视现象[*F. L. v. France* (dec.)];

- 认为俄罗斯法院对于解散耶和华见证人的地方分支机构以及禁止他们的活动的做法所提出的论据不具有说服力,欧洲人权法院认为该宗教团体为了使支持者与其家庭分离并摧毁家庭,而向他们施加"心理压力",因此认为该措施违反了第9条。首先,欧洲人权法院认为耶和华见证人信徒完全投身宗教生活的决定是自由的、非强制的,并且与全球主要的"传统"宗教采取的方式非常相似;其次,提供的数据不可信,因为仅涉及了 6 个与耶和华见证人家庭冲突有关的案例,本可以采取合适的方法去比较在非宗教信仰者中、在该国主要宗教的支持者中以及在耶和华见证人信徒中的家庭分裂的频率(*Jehovah's Witnesses of Moscow and Others v. Russia*,§§109-104);

- 由于不符合公约的属事管辖,宣布对一项申诉不予受理。该申诉由一名父亲提起,他反对未成年女儿(监护权判给了她的母亲)受罗马天主教洗礼并参加其教义讲授课堂。他诉称西班牙法院拒绝下令将任何有关他女儿宗教教育的决定推迟到他女儿成年后,也拒绝下令确认他在这方面是唯一一个对其女儿教育负责的人。欧洲人权法院认为拥有监护权的母亲尊重了其女儿的愿望,因此合理保障了他女儿的最佳利益[*Rupprecht v. Spain* (dec.);根据公约第一议定书第 2 条,本法院对一个类似的案子进行了审查,见 X. 诉荷兰案 *X. v. the Netherlands*,(dec.)]。

88. 关于学校教育,第 9 条保护个人免受国家的宗教教化[*Angeleni v. Sweden* (dec.); *C. J., J. J. and E. J. v. Poland* (dec.)]。此外,一些强制入学的案例或许会和家庭的宗教信仰产生矛盾。例如,公约机构驳回了下列申诉:

- 一项涉及瑞典国家学校董事会拒绝同意国立学校一名学生申诉人免修宗教课程的申诉。该名学生声称自己是无神论者,她诉称这样的教学要求她接受基督教的思维模式,还主张这是违反公约第 14 条的歧视行为,因为在当时生效的瑞典法律允许归属于"宗教团体"并从中接受宗教教育的学生免修此类宗教课程,而这条规定不适用于无神论者。委员会认为本案中的女孩已经在很大程度上得以免修了包含礼拜内容的课程(如唱赞美歌)。其余部分,欧洲人权法院同意瑞典政府的观点,即教学包含了所涉及的宗教,但不仅限于某一特定宗教——即使主要集中在基督教。因此,申诉人并没有接受宗教教化,也没有被强制参加任何特定类型的礼拜(*Angeleni v. Sweden* (dec.);相反地,参见 *Folgerø and Others v. Norway* [GC]);

- 一项由声称受到歧视的父母提起的申诉。该申诉基于这样一个事实:根据卢森堡的法律,学生免修宗教和道德的课程或者道德和社会教育的课程的唯一合法理由是信奉宗教,但是这对父母希望基于哲学信仰使他们的孩子免修。委员会认为,在没有任何宗教或者其他教化的情况下,孩子们参加道德和社会教育课堂的义务不等同于干涉思想或良心自由的行使。在本案中,处理方式的差别追求的是合法的目标(减少学生的旷课,使所有的年轻人接受道德教育),而且对于实现该目标来说是合比例的,因为相关的立法规定这些课程应当特别包括人权的学习,并且以一种保障观点多元化的方式组织起来[Bernard and Others v. Luxembourg (dec.)];

- 一项由一对基督复临安息日会信徒夫妇提起的申诉。该申诉称卢森堡市政当局拒绝允许他们的儿子在周六即该宗教团体的休息日免于参加义务教育。欧洲人权法院认为,所质疑的干预具有合法性,因为保障孩子的受教育权优先于父母的宗教信仰,并且在所涉案件中,遵守了合理的比例关系[Martins Casimiro and Cerveira Ferreira v. Luxembourg (dec.)]。

(六)布道及改变信仰

89. 表达宗教的自由原则上应包括试图通过"布道"的方式使他人信仰某宗教以及改变他人宗教信仰的权利,否则,第9条所规定的"改变他人宗教或信仰的自由"将形同虚设(Kokkinakis v. Greece,§31)。另外,第9条并不保护不恰当地改变信仰的行为,如提供物质或社会利益,或者通过施加不当压力的方式增加教会成员(Larissis and Others v. Greece,§45)。

90. 例如,欧洲人权法院认为下面这一案件中的行为违反了公约第9条的规定。申诉人是一名耶和华见证人信徒,他前往当地东正教教堂一名领唱者妻子家里,并与其讨论宗教的本质问题,因此被逮捕并被刑事法庭定罪(Kokkinakis v. Greece)。然而,在另一起希腊的案件中,欧洲人权法院采取了有细微差别的处理方法。在这一案件中,申诉人在当时是一名空军官员,军事法庭以其改变了几名级别较低的空军和平民的宗教信仰为由将其定罪。关于试图改变空军成员信仰的问题,欧洲人权法院认为在这方面对其定罪的做法没有违反第9条。空军的特征是等级结构,这体现在军队成员关系的各个方面,下级很难拒绝上级军官的接近或者退出由他发起的谈话。因此,对普通人而言非常自然地接受或者拒绝的聊天行为,在军事生活的背景下看,会被视为骚扰或者滥用权力施压。并不是所有不平等级别的个人之间的宗教或其他敏感问题都属于这种类型。但是,在某些必要的场合,国家会采取特殊措施保护下级军官的权利与自由,这种做法是正当的。另外,关于改变平民信仰的问题,欧洲人权法院认为在这方面对其定罪的做法违反了公约第9条,因为申诉人没有对平民施加压力或强制措施,在民主社会来说,对其定罪是不必要的(Larissis and Others v. Greece)。

(七)宗教礼拜的自由

91. 宗教自由意味着表达信仰的自由,不仅包括私下单独表达信仰的自由,也包括与他人一同在公众场合或具有同样信仰的社区内表达信仰的自由。换言之,无论是独自还是与他人一起,是公开还是私下,每个人都能自由表达自己的信仰。公约第9条列举了宗教或信仰的多种表达方式,如礼拜、教授、实践及遵守(Güler and Uğur v. Turkey,§35)。这意味着第9条保障信仰者以其宗教规定的方式和平地做礼拜的权利(The Church of Jesus Christ of Latter-day Saints v. the United Kingdom; Cumhuriyetçi Eğitim ve Kültür Merkezi Vakfi v. Turkey,§41)。然而,第9条本身或者结合公约第11条(集会自由),并没有授权申诉人在任何他们希望的地方展开集会以表达他们的宗教信仰[Pavlides and Georgakis v. Turkey (dec.),§29]。

92. 例如,欧洲人权法院认为以下案件违反了宗教自由:

- 在"北塞浦路斯土耳其共和国",实行措施规制希腊塞浦路斯东正教的信仰,禁止他们离开自己的村庄去其他礼拜场所参加宗教仪式或者参观寺院(Cyprus v. Turkey [GC],§§243-246);

- 俄罗斯警察驱散了参加在国家职业中学大礼堂举办的周末活动的耶和华见证人信徒。该活动中,耶和华见证人组织基于合法订立的租赁合同租下了该场所。即使从国内法角度看,警察的措施也是明显非法滥用权力(Kuznetsov and Others v. Russia)。在另一个类似案件中,欧洲人权法院认为相关措施违反了公约,因为驱散的耶和华见证人年度庆祝活动是在依据国内法租赁的农业学术大厅举行的。有许多警察参与实施了驱散措施,包括一个武装特警部队小组;申诉人被逮捕并且被拘禁数小时。暂且不论干预行为本身的合法性问题,欧洲人权法院认为,很显然该措施"在民主社会是不必要的"(Krupko and Others v. Russia);

- 摩尔多瓦警察驱散了一群穆斯林在私人家中举办的祈祷仪式,同时,因为"进行与不被国家认可的宗教有关的行为",对申诉人处以行政罚款(Masaev v. Moldova);

- 教士文鲜明创办的统一教的多名信徒在一名信徒家中进行集会,保加利亚警察闯入破坏了集会,随后依据检察官的许可搜查了公寓,最后没收了书籍、录音以及其他物件,实施这些措施的理由是该宗教团体没有在国家登记注册。该案中涉及的措施明显缺乏相应的国内法依据。此外,关于未注册的宗教组织开展宗教集会的可能性,国内法没有明确规定;当时,国内法有一些支持该政府行为的判例,认为这样的集会非法(Boychev and Others v. Bulgaria);

- 传唤申诉人去当地的警察局并质问她的宗教信仰,随后搜查她的家,并没收其书籍和录音,最后警告命令她停止在家中进行她所属的福音派的集会。欧洲人权法院认为这样的干预没有法律依据,因为该措施是在没有进行刑事调查的情况下实施的,这是明显违反国内法的行为(Dimitrova v. Bulgaria);

- 申诉人因为参加了在一个政治党派的办公场所举行的穆斯林宗教仪式活动而被监禁,该政治党派是为了纪念被安保人员杀害的三名非法机构的成员而成立。欧洲人权法院认为,仅依据集会是在具有恐怖组织标志的政治党派办公场所举办的事实,不能剥夺公约第9条所保护的参与人员的权利。在本案中,所施加的惩罚没有满足明确性和可预见性的要求,因为无法预见纯粹参加宗教活动的行为会被归入防止恐怖主义法所规制的范围之内(Güler and Uğur v. Turkey)。

93. 相反在以下案件中,公约机构没有发现有违反第9条的行为或者宣布相关的申诉缺乏足够的依据:

- 英国当局决定在夏至日关闭巨石阵的场所,并且不允许德鲁伊教徒前往举行他们的夏至庆祝活动。委员会认为,即使假设存在干预第9条权利的行为,那也是为了保护公众安全,并且可以第9条第2款作为正当依据,特别是因为当局提前已经做了极大的努力来满足与巨石阵有关的个人及组织的需要[Chappell v. the United Kingdom(dec.);同时参见 Pendragon v. the United Kingdom(dec.)];

- 几个人因为进入一个堕胎诊所抗议堕胎并在过道内跪地祈祷,打扰了诊所内安静的环境而被处以罚款,该惩罚被暂停。委员会认为这几个人的行为属于第9条所规定的范围,但是根据第9条第2款,所涉嫌的干预是正当的[Van Schijndel and Others v. the Netherlands(dec.)];

- 申诉人是一名居住在岛屿南部的塞浦路斯人,无法前往位于北部的即在"北塞浦路斯土耳其共和国"的教堂及修道院。欧洲人权法院注意到,申诉人与岛屿北部的唯一联系是其从父母那里继承的耕地,而且没有任何因素阻止他在南塞浦路斯行使第 9 条所保护的权利[*Josephides v. Turkey*（dec.）]；

- 一群东正教信徒在没有获得事先许可的情况下，在位于"北塞浦路斯土耳其共和国"领土上的一所修道院（现在是一间博物馆）举办集会，警察中断了该集会。欧洲人权法院认为该案中存在误解，因为申诉人善意地相信他们已经获得了许可，但是负责管理文化遗产的当局认为该集会是未经授权的非法集会。虽然有鉴于所有相关情况，如没有采用不合比例的措施，在北塞浦路斯特定的政治环境下避免矛盾的需要等，欧洲人权法院仍认为该干预行为是合乎比例的[*Pavlides and Georgakis v. Turkey*（dec.）]。

94. 欧洲人权法院宣布对以下申请不予受理，因为相比于申诉人遵守宗教规定仪式的利益而言，第 9 条规定的合法利益明显具有优先性：

- 一项市政规定禁止罗马天主教区教堂的钟声在早上七点半之前超过一定分贝。欧洲人权法院认为这项干预旨在保护其他人的合法权利——在本案中即当地居民的休息权，而且该措施对于达到该目的是合比例的。实际上，减小音量也可以敲响钟声；在一天中的其他时间没有对音量进行限制[*Schilder v. the Netherlands*（dec.）]；

- 在"胜坨丹宗教"仪式中服用死藤水——一种含有迷幻药成分的物质，有权机关将死藤水没收。欧洲人权法院认为，根据与毒品有关的法律所采取的为了保护健康的措施，"在民主社会是必要的"。申诉人诉称，与基督教相比，自己受到了歧视，因为基督教徒在他们的仪式上可以饮酒（圣餐酒）。欧洲人权法院认为，这两种情形不具有可比性：首先，红酒不属于毒品法律规制的对象；其次，基督徒的仪式不包括为了喝醉而使用影响心智的物质[*Fränklin-Beentjes and CEFLU-Luz da Floresta v. the Netherlands*（dec.）]。

95. 欧洲人权法院宣布不予受理一项由希腊东正教修道院提起的申诉。申诉人称在其附近所建立的通信、电台和电视天线侵犯了进行礼拜的自由。欧洲人权法院认为相关措施并没有干预第 9 条所保障的权利，因为尽管早就有这些天线，但修道院也一直开放，并且已经在该片土地上办理了续租[*Iera Moni Profitou Iliou Thiras v. Greece*（dec.）]。

96. 礼拜自由也适用于埋葬逝者的行为，因为它构成了宗教实践的一个重要部分[*Johannische Kirche and Peters v. Germany*（dec.）]。然而，在一个案件中，申诉人称他们的女儿在医院死亡,但是当局将尸体归还给他们时已经超过了恰当的时间,这导致他们在数月内无法以宗教的方式将她埋葬或在她的坟前祈祷。欧洲人权法院决定依据公约第 8 条(尊重私人的和家庭生活)对这一申诉进行审查。因为被申诉的行为并不涉及当局对第 9 条权利的直接干预,只是基于延迟造成的结果,而欧洲人权法院认为这一结果是可以依据第 8 条进行审查的[*Johannische Kirche and Peters v. Germany* (dec.)]。

(八)礼拜的场所及建筑

97. 公约第 9 条原则上保护提供、开设以及维护用于宗教礼拜的场所或建筑的权利。因此,在特定情况下,宗教建筑能够对宗教群体表达自己的宗教信仰产生影响(*The Church of Jesus Christ of Latter-day Saints v. the United Kingdom*, §30; *Cumhuriyetçi Eğitim ve Kültür Merkezi Vakfi v. Turkey*, §41)。同样的原则也适用于墓地的设计布局,因为它构成了宗教实践的一个极其重要的部分[*Johannische Kirche and Peters v. Germany* (dec.)]。

98. 第 9 条并没有授予宗教社区从公共机关处获取礼拜场所的权利[*Griechische Kirchengemeinde München und Bayern e. V. v. Germany* (dec.)]。公共机构多年来容忍为了宗教目的而持续使用国有建筑的行为,但是只有这一事实不足以使这些机构负有积极义务[*Juma Mosque Congregation and Others v. Azerbaijan* (dec.), §60]。

99. 公约条款也没有暗示国家有义务授予礼拜场所任何特殊地位。但是,如果国家在公约所规定的义务之外,对其授予了特殊地位,它就不能否认这一特定宗教团体的优势地位,这种否认是歧视性的,违反公约第 14 条的规定(*Cumhuriyetçi Eğitim ve Kültür Merkezi Vakfi v. Turkey*, §§ 48–49)。

100. 通常而言,在当今社会,规划立法被认为是避免不受控制的发展的必要措施,所以缔约国在城市规划的问题上有较大的自由裁量权。如果国家机关在平衡不同的规划设想时充分考虑了宗教自由,那么宗教组织不能利用第 9 条所保障的权利去规避现行的规划立法[*ISKCON and Others v. the United Kingdom* (dec.)]。

101. 例如,在以下这一案件中,欧洲人权法院认为侵犯了宗教自由:申诉人租用了一个私人房间作为耶和华见证人礼拜场所并实际使用了该房间,而在此之前其没有得到"被认可的基督教权威者"(如当地的希腊东正教主教)以及教育和宗教事务部的许可,因此被处以监禁和罚金。欧洲人权法院认为,国内法相关的条文在这方面赋予当局极大的自由裁量权,这一权力事实上用来限制主导的东正教之外的其他宗教的活动(*Manoussakis and Others v. Greece*;同时参见委员会在 *Pentidis and Others v. Greece* 案中的建议,该建议使得该案被否定)。

102. 另外,在以下案件中,欧洲人权法院认为没有违反公约第 9 条(或者宣布申诉明显缺乏充分依据):

- 希腊当局颁布一项决定,命令一名希腊东正教信徒移动其父亲的墓地以便利道路的拓宽工作。委员会注意到,在相同的情况下,东正教的其他信徒自愿移动了他们家人的墓地,而且申诉人联系了希腊东正教权威者,该权威者拒绝介入支持申诉人。此外,申诉人没有解释为何移动墓地会阻止他履行其信仰所要求的义务,也没有解释为何履行义务需要使墓地处于原处 [*Daratsakis v. Greece* (dec.)];

- 当地规划局对国际奎师那意识协会送达的通知。该通知是关于该学会所购买庄园的使用问题,并下命令限制其只能在购买时被允许的范围内使用(当地的神学院及礼拜场所,每天最多容纳 1000 名游客);事实上,为了宗教目的,该庄园的使用范围在不断扩大,吸引了大量的人群,受到了周边民众的诸多抱怨。欧洲人权法院承认确实存在对申诉团体行使宗教自由的干预,但是依据第 9 条第 2 款,这种干预是正当的;欧洲人权法院尤其认为,当局一直在努力对该问题达成和解,而且国内决策程序适当地考虑了申诉团体特定的宗教利益 [*ISKCON and Others v. the United Kingdom* (dec.)];

- 澳大利亚法院指定的管理者的行为。该管理者负责管理塞尔维亚东正教团体的财产,该团体在贝尔格莱德主教统治下出现分裂状态,因此其在世俗法领域内进行活动的权利被法律所暂停:管理者已经与塞尔维亚主教指定的两名牧师签订了租约。即使假设存在干预申诉人行使第 9 条权利的行为,这一干预行为对于保护其他人的权利也是必要的,而且对于达成该目的来说也是合比例的,因为所争议的措施被限制在一定的范围之内,而且只有当分裂状态持续存在时,租约才具有效力 [*Serbisch-griechisch-orientalische Kirchengemeinde zum Heiligen Sava in Wien v. Austria* (dec.)];

- 德国当局拒绝对一个宗教组织授予许可令许可其在未开发的保护区建一个墓地。欧洲人权法院认为所争议的措施符合第 9 条第 2 款的规定,因为该措施是依据有关规划、环境保护以及公共设施建设的法律规定而采取的,而且在所涉及的区域内没有其他建筑[*Johannische Kirche and Peters v. Germany* (dec.)];

- 希腊地方当局拒绝了申诉人有关修改当地发展规划的请求。申诉人希望通过修改当地发展规划使其能够在其所拥有的土地上建一座房屋进行"真正正统的基督教徒"(希腊旧历法)的祈祷;当局拒绝的理由是因为所涉的宗教团体在该市的成员人数不足,修改规划缺乏"社会需要"。欧洲人权法院认为与马努萨基斯案(Manoussakis)不同,这个案件涉及的是一般的空间规划法,从表面上来看是中立的。希腊最高法院适用的定量标准不能被认为是任意专断的,因为只有出于"公共利益"的需要才能许可修改当地发展规划。在这一假定下,考虑宗教团体的客观需要是合理的,但与合理的空间规划有关的公共利益不能被个人的宗教利益所取代,更何况周边的城镇有一个用于祈祷的房屋能够满足该区域的"真正正统的基督教徒"的需要,因此,国家是在自由裁量权范围内行使权力(*Vergos v. Greece*);

- 申诉人将他们购买的私人公寓用作礼拜场所,事先没有办理土耳其法律所规定的手续,尤其是缺少应楼房的所有共同所有人签订的强制性事先协定。这几名土耳其新教成员申诉人受到了罚款。欧洲人权法院认为,本案与马努萨基斯案不同,该案中所需要办理的手续不涉及任何宗教的认可或行使问题,因而不能被视为等同于先前授权;他们只是与保护他人权利以及维持公共秩序有关。欧洲人权法院还注意到,国家当局已经在对所涉手续的遵守与宗教自由的要求之间进行了权衡,如首先请求申诉人遵守这些手续。因此,该干预可以被视为是正当的、合比例的。最后,欧洲人权法院认为,没有什么地方表明国内当局是以歧视性的方式对申诉人适用了相关立法,因而也就没有违反公约第14条 [*Tanyar and Others v. Turkey* (dec.)];

- 根据最终判决,将穆斯林集会从一栋被列为历史遗迹的老式清真寺建筑中驱逐;尽管申诉团体使用该建筑的期限已经超过了10年,但是该团体对建筑物并不享有所有权,也没有租赁该建筑物(不同于马努萨基斯案中的情况)。尤其是,申诉团体没有辩称他们不能在其他地方自由设立礼拜场所[*Juma Mosque Congregation and Others v. Azerbaijan* (dec.)]。

103. 欧洲人权法院还审查了一项基于第14条和第9条提起的个人申诉。该项申诉涉及一项禁止建造宣礼塔的命令,这一禁令通过全民公投被加入瑞士联邦宪法中。欧洲人权法院认为,申诉人没有受到所争议的措施的直接影响,并且没有声明其希望建造一座带有宣礼塔的清真寺,因此不能声称自己是所主张的侵犯行为的"受害者"[参见 *Ouardiri v. Switzerland*(dec.)]。

104. 委员会宣布对一项依据第9条提起的申诉不予受理。法国神父所是一个基于宗教法设立在土耳其的罗马天主教组织,受到1923年的《洛桑条约》保护。国内当局以充国库的名义取消了法国神父所的财产契据以及在所涉财产上进行的登记。这一行为切断了该组织的主要财产来源,使得它无法提供宗教服务,也无法维持教会的生存。[*Institute of French Priests and Others v. Turkey*(dec.)]。在法庭的诉讼程序中,该案以友好和解的方式结案[*Institute of French Priests and Others v. Turkey*(friendly settlement)]。

三、宗教自由和迁徙自由

(一)外国人在一国领土上的居住、工作以及宗教自由

105. 公约没有保证非本国公民进入或居住在某国的权利。根据一项被公认的国际法原则,缔约国有权控制非本国公民进入、居住或离开其领土(*Perry v. Latvia*,§51)。因此,第9条并没有保证外国人在相应国家居留的权利。驱逐不属于对受保护权利的干预,除非可以证实该项驱逐命令旨在制止该权利的行使并且遏制了申诉人及其跟随者的宗教或哲学的传播[*Omkarananda and the Divine Light Zentrum v. Switzerland*(dec.)]。

106. 例如,在以下案件中,欧洲人权法院认为违反了第9条:

- 申诉人是一名美国福音派牧师,国家有权机关首先拒绝延长其居留证,之后发给他另一类型的许可证,并给出了一个半官方的解释,即他不再有权进行公开宗教活动;该项限制并没有国内法依据(*Perry v. Latvia*);
- 申诉人是教士文鲜明统一教的一名美籍活跃分子,俄罗斯当局将他遣返,撤销了他的签证,并禁止他进入俄罗斯,即使他已经在此合法居住多年,而且其未成年的儿子也居住在俄罗斯;该措施很明显是由申诉人在俄罗斯的宗教活动所引起的。应诉国政府提交意见称申诉人危及了国民安全——第9条第2款的规定并没有包括这一理由,但并没有证实此项意见(*Nolan and K. v. Russia*)。

107. 对于下列申诉,欧洲人权法院认为没有违反第9条,宣布不予受理:

- 申诉人是一名被保加利亚的大穆夫提所认证的巴勒斯坦牧师及伊斯兰教老师,国内当局取消了他的永久居留证,并且将其驱逐,理由是他的宗教活动强行灌输伊斯兰原教旨主义并且表明其与一个极端组织"穆斯林兄弟会"有联系[*Al-Nashif v. Bulgaria*(dec.)]。欧洲人权法院认为,国内当局的行为违反了公约第8条(尊重家庭生活的权利),同时认为没有必要审查申诉人声称的其他侵犯其宗教自由的行为(*Al-Nashif v. Bulgaria*, §§ 139 – 142);

- 申诉人是一对耶和华见证人信徒夫妇,由于他们在保加利亚的宗教活动,而被当局取消了永久居留证[参见 *Lotter v. Bulgaria*(dec.)]。该案以友好和解的方式结案[*Lotter and Lotter v. Bulgaria*(friendly settlement)]。

108. 另外,由于明显缺乏依据,委员会宣布对一项申诉不予受理。该项申诉是关于一项针对印度僧侣及哲学家的驱逐命令。申诉人因为危及社会公共秩序而被定罪,因为他持续性地扰乱当地安宁;这一命令并没有被实施,因为申诉人在此期间因为一系列的刑事指控被定罪并被判处14年的监禁,并被驱逐出瑞典15年[*Omkarananda and the Divine Light Zentrum v. Switzerland*(dec.)]。

109. 此外,公约第9条并不赋予外国人以在缔约国工作为目的获得居留证的权利,即使该雇主是一个宗教团体(*Hüsnü Öz v. Germany*(dec.);*Perry v. Latvia*;*El Majjaoui and Stichting Touba Moskee v. the Netherlands*(striking out)[GC],§ 32)。依据该原则,委员会驳回了一项申诉,申诉人是一名信仰伊斯兰教的牧师,同时是土耳其国籍的宗教老师(伊玛目),他诉称其与当地伊斯兰协会的工作合同到期后,表达了继续作为伊玛目留在德国为最初邀请他过来的组织之外的另一组织工作的意愿,并申请延长暂时居留证,但是没有得到许可[*Hüsnü Öz v. Germany*(dec.)]。

110. 近期,欧洲人权法院宣布受理一项申诉。该申诉是关于荷兰政府拒绝对一个摩洛哥国籍的人授予居留证,而申诉人需要凭借该居留证作为伊玛目在一个宗教基金会工作。政府拒绝的理由是基金会没有做出足够的努力在国内或者欧洲劳动力市场寻找其他候选人,也没有试图从在荷兰受过训练的人中招募伊玛目[*El Majjaoui and Stichting Touba Moskee v. the Netherlands*(dec.)]。然而,在基金会的一项最新请求之后,申诉人最终获得了在荷兰的临时工作许可证及居留证;因此,欧洲人权法院认为该争端已经被解决,并依据公约第37条第1款第b项将该申诉从列表中撤出(*El Majjaoui*

and Stichting Touba Moskee v. the Netherlands（striking out）[GC]，§32）。

111. 在以下这一案件中，欧洲人权法院认为违反了第9条和第14条（禁止歧视）。奥地利当局拒绝将耶和华见证人团体从《外国人就业法案》中豁免，即要求允许将居留证授予一对夫妇，夫妇二人都是菲律宾国籍的牧师，申诉团体希望在奥地利雇佣夫妇二人。事实上，依据国内法，这种豁免只能授予"被认可的宗教组织"，而不能授予如本案中的"登记注册"的宗教组织（*Jehovas Zeugen in Österreich v. Austria*）。

（二）违反宗教自由被驱逐到另一国的行为

112. 如果第三国会极大地阻碍个人行使宗教自由，那么缔约国可以将外国人驱逐到该国吗？一般认为，如果缔约国的驱逐行为使得个人的权利在其管辖领域外有被侵犯的危险，缔约国可能会承担间接责任。当存在违反第2条（生命权）和第3条（禁止酷刑）的情况时，欧洲人权法院会认为存在该种责任。欧洲人权法院在此方面的判例是基于这些条款的重要意义，因为他们所规定的保障在实践中应当是有效的，禁止酷刑具有绝对性，而且这些判例包含了国际普遍接受的标准；欧洲人权法院还强调了遭受危险的严重性及不可挽回性。之后，欧洲人权法院在某些情形下发展了这一原则，将其涵盖内容扩大至第6条（获得公正审判的权利）和第5条（自由权及禁止随意拘禁）。但是，这些重要的考虑并不是自动适用于公约其他条款的。从纯实用主义的角度出发，不能要求缔约国只能将外国人驱逐到一个完全符合公约规定、使得被驱逐人的权利能够得到充分有效保护的国家。即使第9条规定的权利构成了"民主社会的基石之一"，这也是第一个基于民主、法治和人权在缔约国之间适用的标准。当然，根据前面提及的判例法，如果申诉人能够证明他们可能会遭受基于宗教等原因的迫害或者将处于死亡或严重虐待的风险之中，或者可能因为宗教关系（以及其他其他原因）被公然拒绝获得公正审判或者被任意拘留，那么其权利就应该得到保护。如果个人声称返回自己的国家会被以尚未达到禁止程度的方式阻碍其进行宗教礼拜，那么仅依据第9条只能获得有限的帮助。相反，缔约国将有义务积极作为，间接保障被驱逐人在其他国家的礼拜自由。如果一个在公约庇护外的国家将禁止一个宗教，但是不施加任何迫害、控诉、剥夺自由或虐待的措施，那么是否能将公约理解为可以要求缔约国向被禁止的信徒提供在其自己国家的领土上行使宗教自由的可能性，这一问题尚且存疑 [*Z. and T. v. the United Kingdom*（dec.）]。

113. 但是，欧洲人权法院并不否认，如果申诉人在接收国面临明显侵犯第9条所保障权利的风险,那么驱逐个人的国家就可能需要承担基于该条规定而产生的责任;然而,欧洲人权法院认为,难以设想一个明显违反公约第9条的行为不同时包括违反公约第3条的情形[Z. and T. v. the United Kingdom (dec.)]。

114. 根据上文的论述,欧洲人权法院认为,一项由具有巴基斯坦国籍的两个基督徒提起的申诉明显缺乏依据。他们诉称,如果将他们驱逐到巴基斯坦,他们将不能行使宗教自由。欧洲人权法院指出,申诉人没有列举可能基于宗教原因受到迫害的情形,也没有证实公约第2条或者第3条所保护的权利将受到侵犯,而且申诉人也没有遭受身体攻击或者被禁止信仰其宗教。通过审查巴基斯坦的相关情况,欧洲人权法院认为尽管最近有针对教堂和基督徒的攻击行为,但是基督教在巴基斯坦并没有受到任何官方的限制,他们有自己的议会成员代表,而且巴基斯坦执法及司法部门都分别采取措施保护教堂及学校,同时,也逮捕、起诉及惩罚了袭击者。在这些情况下,欧洲人权法院认为,申诉人并没有表明他们本人正处于这种风险之中,或者属于这种易受攻击的群体或受到威胁的群体的一员,或作为基督徒处于危险的地位以至于可能会受到违反公约第9条的行为的侵害[Z. and T. v. the United Kingdom (dec.);同时参见 Razaghi v. Sweden (dec.)]。

第四节　国家作为宗教自由保卫者的义务

一、消极义务:不妨碍宗教组织正常运作的义务

(一)缔约国宗教组织的法定地位

115. 在欧洲,国家和宗教团体之间的关系没有一个固定的模式;相反,欧洲有各种各样的宪法模式管理这种关系(Sindicatul 'Păstorul cel Bun' v. Romania [GC], § 138)。现行制度可分为三类:(1)存在国家教会;(2)国家与所有宗教组织完全分离;(3)协约型关系(这是欧洲国家的主要模式)。欧洲人权法院认为,三种类型的制度都符合公约第9条。

116. 某些欧洲国家拥有国家教会(或官方教会),其具有特殊宪法地位。这种制度本身并不违反公约第9条;实际上,在制定公约或这些国家成为公约缔约国时,这种制度已经生效。此外,欧洲人权法院认为,国家在宗教事务中的中立义务不能被认为可能

削弱与某一国家人口在历史、文化上相联系的信仰或教会的角色(*Members of the Gldani Congregation of the Jehovah's Witnesses and Others v. Georgia*,§132)。法律可以认可此种教会的法人资格[*Holy Synod of the Bulgarian Orthodox Church（Metropolitan Inokentiy）and Others v. Bulgaria*,§157]。原则上来说,不论在何种情况下,是否延续这些传统都属于应诉国的自由裁量权范围内。此外,欧洲人权法院必须考虑欧洲各成员国的多样性——特别是在文化和历史发展领域。然而,考虑传统并不能豁免缔约国尊重公约及其议定书所载权利和自由的义务(*Lautsi and Others v. Italy*,[GC],§68)。要满足第 9 条的要求,国家教会制度就必须具体地保障个人的宗教自由。尤其是任何人都不得被迫加入或被禁止退出特定国家教会[*Ásatrúarfélagið v. Iceland*（dec.）,§27;亦可参见委员会对案件的意见,*Darby v. Sweden*,§45]。

117. 此外,即使在存在国家教会的国家,该教会在其所负责的领域所做出的决定也不会导致国家承担公约责任。例如,委员会审议了瑞典教会(当时的国家教会)的芬兰语教区提起的一项申诉,教会大会做出决定,禁止其使用芬兰福音派路德教的祷告文,并强制其使用翻译成芬兰语的瑞典祷告文。委员会认为,教会及其教区是"非政府组织",国家不应对申诉人所称的教会大会的决定造成的侵害负责。考虑到申诉教区不会被禁止退出瑞典教会,国家并没有不履行保护教区宗教自由的义务[*Finska Församlingen i Stockholm and Hautaniemi v. Sweden*（dec.）]。

118. 在其他国家,宪法模式以世俗主义原则为基础,国家和所有宗教群体完全分离。欧洲人权法院认为此种模式也与公约价值相符(*Leyla Şahin v. Turkey*[GC],§108; *Dogru v. France*,§72)。

119. 最后,在其宪法模式允许的情况下,国家可以与某一个(或某几个)特定教会达成合作协议,在有客观且合理的正当理由的前提下,为教会提供特殊地位(税务或其他),进行区别对待,其他希望如此的教会也可以与国家订立相似的协议[*Alujer Fernández and Caballero Garcia v. Spain*（dec.）;*Savez crkava 'Riječ života' and Others v. Croatia*,§85]。国家还可用不同于其他宗教组织的特别制度来规制某一宗教组织,免除其强制登记义务或宣布并承认其法人资格[*Holy Synod of the Bulgarian Orthodox Church（Metropolitan Inokentiy）and Others v. Bulgaria*]。然而,如果一个国家设立制度框架,赋予某一宗教团体法人资格以及特定地位,所有有意向的宗教团体必须有公平的机会申请这一地位,而且所确定的标准必须以非歧视性的方式适用

(*Religionsgemeinschaft der Zeugen Jehovas and Others v. Austria*)。宗教自由绝不意味着宗教团体或宗教信徒必须获得与其他现存宗教团体不同的特定法律地位；但是，如果这种地位已经建立，则必须以非歧视的方式被授予（*Cumhuriyetçi Eğitim ve Kültür Merkezi Vakfi v. Turkey*，§45）。

120. 国家还可以将具体的公共任务和职能委派给一个或多个宗教组织，这些任务和职能的委派及资助方式均由国家自由裁量[*Bruno v. Sweden*（dec.）；*Lundberg v. Sweden*（dec.）]。

121. 最后，须铭记的是，在确定宗教与国家关系的这一复杂领域，国家原则上享有较大的自由裁量权（*Cha'are Shalom Ve Tsedek v. France*[GC]，§84）。

（二）承认、注册以及解散宗教组织

122. 干涉集体宗教自由的最激进的形式之一是解散现有的宗教组织。这种激进的措施需要有非常严重的理由，以证明"在民主社会中是必要的"（*Biblical Centre of the Chuvash Republic v. Russia*，§54）。

123. 例如，在下列案件中，欧洲人权法院认为违反了公约第9条（结合第11条）：

- 根据检察官的请求，俄罗斯法院下令解散耶和华见证人教会的一个地方分支，并禁止其活动。在审查国内法院的所有调查结果（其被指控对信徒家属施压，恐吓消灭信徒；干扰信徒的私生活以及他们选择职业的权利；侵犯未加入耶和华见证人教会的父母的亲权；"洗脑"和"心理控制"；煽动自杀或拒绝医疗，包括禁止输血；诱使未成年人进入该组织；煽动不服兵役、不尊重国家标志和拒绝参加国家庆祝活动）。欧洲人权法院认为所有这些指控或是没有得到具体证据的支持，或是涉及相当正常的宗教自由表达方式，这些表达方式是由信徒在第9条规定的个人自主权的框架内自由选择的。此外，这些表达方式与世界各地的主要"传统"宗教的做法（禁食、禁欲主义、私人生活中的限制性戒律等）非常相似。因此，该组织的解体显然不符合公约所要求的合法目标，特别是因为在这一案件中适用的立法极其僵化，不允许对宗教团体可能做出的不当行为处以比任何解散更轻的惩罚（*Jehovah's Witnesses of Moscow and Others v. Russia*）；

- 俄罗斯法院下令解散一个新教（圣灵降临教）圣经中心，理由是它开设的儿童主日学校和成人圣经学院（在学业完成时颁发结业证书或"文凭"）不具备法人资格。解散的原因在于:首先,圣经学院在未经事先许可的情况下开放;其次,这两个机构未能遵守有关立法所规定的健康和安全要求。欧洲人权法院注意到,当局没有向申诉组织发出任何要求其遵守任何法律或法规要求的事先警告。此外,申诉组织不能合理地预见其行为的后果,因为俄罗斯法院某些判例相互矛盾,有些判决表明,诸如本案所涉及的主日学校的学习中心不需要特别许可(*Biblical Centre of the Chuvash Republic v. Russia*)。

124. 还有其他与解散相类似的干涉形式。宗教社会传统上普遍地以有组织的实体形式存在。因此,根据公约第11条来解释第9条,欧洲人权法院裁决,为保证在宗教领域集体行动的能力而设立一个受国家承认的法人的可能性,是宗教自由最重要的方面之一,缺乏这种可能性,宗教自由便毫无意义。因此,拒绝承认宗教团体的法人资格或拒绝赋予其法人资格,妨碍了团体本身以及其成员行使第9条所保护的权利(*Metropolitan Church of Bessarabia and Others v. Moldova*,§105;*Religionsgemeinschaft der Zeugen Jehovas and Others v. Austria*,§62)。事实上,根据第11条,欧洲人权法院认为,设立法人以便在共同关心的领域集体行动的能力是结社自由的最重要方面之一,缺乏这种能力,结社自由将形同虚设。国内当局拒绝赋予宗教或其他个人团体以法人地位,这等同于干涉个人的结社自由。从这方面来说,当局拒绝登记某一团体的行为,不仅影响到该团体本身,同时还影响到其管理层、创始人及其他成员(*Kimlya and Others v. Russia*,§84)。

125. 如果只有认可一个宗教组织才能赋予有关人员权利,那么国家当局单纯容许一个未被承认的宗教组织的宗教活动的行为,不能代替国家对宗教组织的认可(*Metropolitan Church of Bessarabia and Others v. Moldova*,§129)。如果国内为具有法人资格的注册组织保留了宗教活动所必需的全部一系列权利,那么即使立法明确授权未经注册的宗教团体可以运营,这也是不充分的(*Sviato-Mykhaïlivska Parafiya v. Ukraine*,§122)。上述权利包括拥有或租赁财产,维持银行账户,雇用雇员,确保对社区、成员及其资产的司法保护,设立礼拜场所,在公众可接触的地方开展宗教服务,制作、获取和分发宗教文学作品,创建教育机构,以及与国际交流和会议保持联系(*Kimlya and Others v. Russia*,§§85-86)。此外,特别是对于宗教团体而言,行使集体宗教自由权的方式之一是尽可能对团体、成员及其资产提供司法保护,如此一来,第9条不仅可以根据第11条进行解释,还可以根据第6条第1款关于获得公正审判和诉诸法庭的权利的规定进行解释(*Sviato-Mykhaïlivska Parafiya v. Ukraine*,§152;*Religionsgemeinschaft der*

Zeugen Jehovas and Others v. Austria，§ 63）。

126. 同理,不具有法人资格的宗教团体,通过运营附属机构得到部分补偿,但这并不具有决定性作用,也不能解决问题（Religionsgemeinschaft der Zeugen Jehovas and Others v. Austria，§ 67）。

127. 关于宗教团体的承认和登记问题,各国有权核查一个运动或组织是否出于表面上的宗教目的而进行危害群众或公共安全的活动。由于一个组织可能通过其所宣称的目标和意图,来隐藏与之不同的目标和意图,因而为了证明它并未这样做,可能需要将其所规划的内容与其所组织的行动和其所保卫的立场相比较（Metropolitan Church of Bessarabia and Others v. Moldova，§§ 105 and 125）。特别是当以没有向当局提供有关宗教的基本戒律的说明为由,拒绝对宗教组织进行登记时,这一拒绝行为可以以确定该组织是否会对民主社会和第9条第2款承认的基本利益构成任何危险作为正当依据〔Cârmuirea Spirituală a Musulmanilor din Republica Moldova v. Moldova（dec.）；Church of Scientology of Moscow v. Russia，§ 93；Lajda and Others v. Czech Republic（dec.）〕。尽管如此,虽然各国确实有权审查宗教团体的目标和活动是否符合立法规定的规则,但是它们必须谨慎地使用这些权力,其方式应符合其根据公约所应履行的义务,并且属于公约机构所规定的权限范围内（Jehovah's Witnesses of Moscow and Others v. Russia，§ 100）。

128. 当局用于考虑上述承认或登记申请以及审查合规性的等待时间,必须是合理的短时间（Religionsgemeinschaft der Zeugen Jehovas and Others v. Austria，§ 79）。同样,如果一个国家的法律制度包括与其他组织相比享有特权（如具有法人地位）的宗教组织,国家可以例外地规定更长的等待和核查期,特别是对于新设立的和未知的宗教团体。但是,对于主管当局所熟悉的早期设立且在国内长期存在的宗教团体,很难有理由将过长的等待时间正当化（Religionsgemeinschaft der Zeugen Jehovas and Others v. Austria，§§ 97 – 98）。

129. 例如,在下列案件中,欧洲人权法院认为违反了公约第9条（单独和/或结合第14条）：

- 摩尔多瓦当局以给予承认会侵犯已被政府承认的受莫斯科主教（俄罗斯东正教教堂）管辖的摩尔多瓦大都会教会的利益为由,拒绝授予受布加勒斯特主教（罗马尼亚东正教）管辖的自治东正教教会比萨拉比亚大都会教会以法人资格。缺乏法人资格，申诉人教会无法从事其活动；其牧师不能进行礼拜，其成员不能践行宗教信仰，而且由于缺乏法人资格，它无权获得对其资产的司法保护，也无权保证自己免受恐吓。由于以申诉教会只是东正教内的一个"分裂团体"为由拒绝承认其法人资格，因而摩尔多瓦政府没有履行其中立和公正的职责。此外，政府提交的指控申诉教会危害国家领土完整和社会稳定的陈述显然缺乏依据（*Metropolitan Church of Bessarabia and Others v. Moldova*）；

- 与上述案件情况相同，地方当局拒绝向申诉人发放其所需的用于注册贝萨拉比亚大都会教堂的证书，因为摩尔多瓦大都会教会已经注册并在该区域运营；欧洲人权法院认为，这种被指控的干预不是"法律所规定的"（*Fusu Arcadie and Others v. The Republic of Moldova*）；

- 尽管有判决命令它进行登记，主管行政当局仍拒绝对申诉教会进行登记；在这种情况下，欧洲人权法院认为，被指控的干预不是"法律所规定的"（*Biserica Adevărat Ortodoxă din Moldova and Others v. Moldova*）；

- 从向奥地利当局提交耶和华见证人会的法律认可申请，直至当局做出最终授予其"已登记"宗教组织地位的决定，这之间时隔20年。国内当局以申诉团体没有作为未经"登记"的组织在奥地利至少运营10年为由，拒绝授予其"被认可的宗教团体"地位——这一地位包括法律人格和国内法规定的一系列特权，欧洲人权法院认为这一拒绝行为构成歧视，违反了第14条。应诉国政府没有表明存在任何客观和合理的正当理由来支持这种差别对待，特别是因为"10年"的要求没有适用于与耶和华见证人情况相似的另一宗教团体（*Religionsgemeinschaft der Zeugen Jehovas and Others v. Austria*）；

- 俄罗斯当局拒绝将山达基教的两个地方分支机构注册为"宗教组织"——这一注册会自动赋予其法人地位，理由是他们没有作为"宗教团体"（没有法律人格）在俄罗斯至少运营15年。欧洲人权法院注意到应诉国政府没有提到任何有力的社会需要来支持该限制或任何相关和足够的理由来将如此长的等待期正当化，根据第11条来进行解释，可以认为违反了第9条；特别是没有证据表明申诉人——不论是团体还是团体中的个人，曾经进行或曾意图进行任何非法活动或追求宗教礼拜、教学、实践和遵守教规以外的目标。拒绝登记的原因是纯粹形式上的原因，且与所涉团体的运营无关，申诉人被认定有罪的唯一"罪行"是他们在该地区未能存续15年却打算申请登记作为"宗教性质"的组织，（Kimlya and Others v. Russia）。在另一个非常类似的案件中，拒绝登记申请的理由之一是地方市政委员会没有权力颁发该等证书。与前述案件不同的是，欧洲人权法院认为这种限制不是"法律规定的"，因此没有必要考虑合比例性的问题（Church of Scientology of St Petersburg and Others v. Russia）；

- 克罗地亚政府任意和歧视性地拒绝与几名改革派教会申诉人缔结一项公共利益领域的合作协议，该合作协议能使这些教会得以在公立学校提供宗教教育，并保证承认其牧师主持的婚姻的民事效果。在本案中，由于申诉人没有单独或共同地满足政府指令中规定的缔结此类协定的标准，因此政府有正当理由拒绝缔结此类协定。然而，其他几个团体已被免除数值标准，而对于历史标准（"欧洲文化圈的历史宗教团体"），政府没有解释为什么属于新教改革主义传统的申诉教会不满足该项标准。因此，欧洲人权法院认为违反了公约第14条（Savez crkava《Riječ života》and Others v. Croatia）。

130. 另一方面，欧洲人权法院分别判定捷克共和国和保加利亚的文鲜明统一教会提起的申诉明显缺乏依据：

- 第一个案件是由欧洲人权法院结合第11条和第9条进行审查的，申诉人诉称捷克当局拒绝将其组织作为具有法人资格的教会注册，原因有两个：其一，申诉人拒绝向当局提供解释其教义的背景文件；其二，他们违反了关于向"接受教会教义的人"收集签名的一般规定。在进行补充核查后，当局否定了所收集的部分签名，认为他们只是同情者而不是与教会存在神学联系的信仰者；欧洲人权法院认为这种对法律的解释是合理且非任意的。剩余的签名数量低于法律要求登记教堂所需的总数10 000。虽然欧洲人权法院接受这个数字在表面上似乎不成比例，但也指出，同时颁布的新法律已将要求的总数减少到300，因此申诉人提出的登记其教会的新请求并不存在障碍[Lajda and Others v. Czech Republic（dec.）]；

- 第二个案件是由欧洲人权法院根据第9条进行审查的，申诉人诉称保加利亚政府默示拒绝登记其组织。欧洲人权法院注意到，申诉人没有收到拒绝登记的正式通知；他们收到了政府的一封信，请他们补充和解释所提交的文件，但申诉人决定不遵守这些指示。鉴于该案件的情况，欧洲人权法院的结论是，政府的态度既不属于拖延手段,也不属于任何默示拒绝(*Boychev and Others v. Bulgaria*)。

131. 关于拒绝继续登记一个已经得到国家承认的宗教组织——剥夺其法人资格或将其归为较低的法律地位,欧洲人权法院倾向于根据公约第 11 条(结社自由)并结合公约第 9 条来考虑这种情况。例如,在下列案件中,欧洲人权法院认为违反了第 11 条:

- 俄罗斯当局拒绝为当地救世军分支机构进行继续登记,从而剥夺了其法人资格,欧洲人权法院认为其所提出的理由缺乏国内法依据或者是任意且不合理的(申诉人的"外国出身";申诉人宗教信仰方面的数据不足;申诉人的"准军事"性质;申诉人意图违反俄罗斯法律等)(*Moscow Branch of the Salvation Army v. Russia*, §§ 74 – 75);
- 俄罗斯当局拒绝为山达基教地方分支机构进行继续登记,并以相互矛盾的理由任意拒绝了至少 11 份继续登记的申请(声称文件不完整,却没有指出哪些文件丢失;在无法律规定的情况下,要求提交原件而不是副本)(*Church of Scientology of Moscow v. Russia*)。在另一个非常类似的案件中,欧洲人权法院认为拒绝继续登记耶和华见证人地方分支机构的行为违反了第 11 条(*Jehovah's Witnesses of Moscow and Others v. Russia*)。
- 由于立法改革,以前在匈牙利被认为是"教会"的一些宗教组织被降级为在法律地位、权利和特权方面与教会相比均处在劣势的"协会"(*Magyar Keresztény Mennonita Egyház and Others v. Hungary*)。

132. 公约第 9 条第 1 款没有要求缔约国给予宗教婚姻与民事婚姻平等的法律地位和相同的法律效果[*X. v. Germany* (dec.);*Khan v. the United Kingdom* (dec.);*Spetz and Others v. Sweden* (dec.);*Serif v. Greece*, § 50;*Şerife Yiğit v. Turkey* (GC), § 102]。此外,由于宗教婚姻的形式完全由每个特定宗教自行决定,因此第 9 条没有规定宗教婚姻的形式,特别是由每个宗教自己决定是否以及在多大程度上允许同性婚姻的问题[*Parry v. the United Kingdom* (dec.)]。如果国家要求根据民法规定发布结婚公告,并在与就业问题有关的框架内拒绝承认宗教发布的结婚公告的有效性,这也不违反第 9 条[*Von Pelser v. Italy* (dec.)]。

133. 委员会驳回了比利时一国民提起的申诉,申诉涉及的事实是比利时出于税收目的而合并配偶收入的制度不利于已婚夫妇;申诉人认为,对于有些夫妇的宗教而言,婚姻是神圣的,他们无法通过同居避免结婚的消极税收后果。委员会认为,无论从专业还是道德的角度来看,该行为都没有侵犯申诉人的宗教自由,因为申诉人仅就所得税领域将已婚夫妇的情况与同居夫妇的情况进行比较是武断的,这忽视了配偶双方因婚姻而产生的其他权利和义务[*Hubaux v. Belgium*(dec.)]。

134. 国家无须承认宗教法院根据国家法律制度做出的决定(*Serif v. Greece*, §50)。

135. 此外,与"教学"有关的宗教权利并未扩张至要求国家允许公立学校进行宗教教育(*Savez crkava 'Riječ života' and Others v. Croatia*, §57)。然而,如果国家决定赋予某些宗教群体这一特权,那么就属于第9条的讨论范围,并且应当适用公约第14条关于禁止歧视的规定(*Savez crkava 'Riječ života' and Others v. Croatia*, §58)。

136. 另外,如果根据国内法,某些宗教的牧师被授权主持在民法中具有法律效力的婚姻,或裁定某些民事纠纷(如家庭和继承问题),那么国家就有合法理由采取特别的措施以防止某些法律关系可能受宗教牧师影响的人被欺骗(*Serif v. Greece*, §5)。

(三)国家对宗教团体使用贬义词语的后果

137. 在官方文件中使用针对宗教团体的贬义词语可能会侵犯公约第9条保障的权利,因为这会对宗教自由的行使产生消极后果(*Leela Förderkreis e. V. and Others v. Germany*, §84)。

138. 委员会宣布不予受理的申诉包括下列情况:

- 国内法院驳回了申诉协会要求德国联邦政府停止在名为"德意志联邦共和国所谓的青年派和精神团体"的政府出版物中提到该协会。委员会指出,申诉人协会表达其宗教的结社自由并没有受到侵犯,因为被质疑的出版物对该权利的行使没有任何直接的影响。据国内法院所言,出版物的制作仅是为了告知并警醒公众关于申诉协会的活动——如倡导以宗教信仰取代医疗,因此具有正当理由[*Universelles Leben e. V. v. Germany*(dec.)];

- 巴伐利亚教育部为警告学生山达基教的危险性,在教育杂志上发表了有关的文章,而国内法院拒绝对该文章的出版发布临时禁令。委员会认为,被抨击的文章将山达基教认定为世界范围的活动,而非申诉人个人行为。虽然申诉人申诉其邻居和当地媒体对他们持否定态度,却没有迹象表明被抨击的文章与这些事实之间存在因果关系;不论何种情况,该文章对申诉人根据公约第9条享有的权利不产生直接影响;因此,该申诉不符合公约的属人管辖[*Keller v. Germany* (dec.)]。

139. 欧洲人权法院认为,即使致力于奥修(Bhagwan Shree Rajneesh)教学的申诉协会诉称德国联邦政府及其成员在官方信函中重复使用了诸如"教派""青年派""心理学派""伪宗教""破坏性宗教运动""操纵其成员的运动"等词,但德国联邦政府及其成员并不存在违反公约第9条的情况。德国联邦宪法法院已经认定政府有权使用大部分该等争议的词语;此外,使用"伪宗教""破坏性宗教运动"和对操纵的指控违反了宪法。即使假设这些词语干预了公约第9条所保障的权利,欧洲人权法院也认为这一干预是为了追求合法目标(公共安全和维护公共秩序以及他人的权利和自由)。实际上,联邦当局在向公众通报与公共利益相关的问题时,只是想提请公民注意其认为需警觉的现象,即许多新的宗教运动的出现以及他们对年轻人的吸引力。当局所追求的唯一目的是使人们在必要时能充分了解事实并避免仅因为无知而陷入困境。此外,政府的行为并不阻止申诉协会行使公约第9条赋予的权利;并且,德国当局最终依照专家报告中提出的建议停止使用存在争议的词语(*Leela Förderkreis e. V. and Others v. Germany*)。

140. 欧洲人权法院还宣布对一项由耶和华见证人团体提起的关于侵犯他们宗教自由的申诉不予受理,因为法国政府授予"家庭和个人保护协会全国联合会"(National Union of Associations for the Defence of Families and the Individual)以公共利益的地位,而其目的是打击"破坏性教派""侵犯人权和基本自由"的行为,并公开反对申诉人的宗教团体。欧洲人权法院认为,国家根据该组织的章程而授予其公共利益地位,但不能对该组织的所有行动负责。授予此等地位的事实并不影响任何公共权力的转移,而公共权力的转移是公约赋予国家唯一的责任。因此,虽然申诉人认为"家庭和个人保护协会全国联合会"的行动侵犯了他们的权利,但这些指控应由国内法院根据相应的补救办法处理。欧洲人权法院最终决定,申诉人不能声称其是所称侵权行为的"受害者",而且他们的申诉不符合欧洲人权法院的属人管辖(*Gluchowski and Others v. France*)。

(四)财务和税务措施

141. 教会或宗教团体的融资和税务问题在欧洲没有统一标准,因为这些事项与每个国家的历史和传统密切相关。因此,国家在这方面拥有较大的自由裁量权(*Alujer Fernández and Caballero Garcia v. Spain*)。

142. 宗教组织不能依据公约第9条以宗教自由为借口来要求特别税收地位

(*Association Sivananda de Yoga Vedanta v. France*)。在这种情况下,宗教自由不能赋予教会或其成员与其他纳税人不同的税收地位[*Alujer Fernández and Caballero García v. Spain*(dec.)]。此外,第9条不能被解释为以用于礼拜为由而免税[*Iglesia Bautista 'El Salvador' and Ortega Moratilla v. Spain* (dec.)]。然而,针对一个宗教组织所采取的经济、财务或财政措施有时可能会妨碍公约第9条规定的权利的行使,因为这些措施有时可能对行使该权利造成实际和严重的障碍。特别是,在某些情况下,与维护和使用宗教建筑物有关的事项,包括由于这些建筑物的税收而产生的费用,可能对宗教团体成员表达宗教信仰的权利产生重大影响(*The Church of Jesus Christ of Latter-day Saints v. the United Kingdom*,§ 30;*Cumhuriyetçi Eğitim ve Kültür Merkezi Vakfı v. Turkey*,§ 41)。

143. 例如,在下列案件中,欧洲人权法院认为违反了第9条:

- 对法国耶和华见证人(*Association des Témoins de Jéhovah de France*)收到的个人捐款进行征税,并收取违约利息和滞纳金,并对申诉团体适用一般团体的标准税制,使其不能享有为某些其他团体(包括宗教团体)保留的税收优惠。被质疑措施的实施对象涵盖了申诉团体收到的所有个人捐款,这占据其收入来源的90%,因此产生了切断该团体收入来源的后果,因而妨碍该团体保障其信徒践行宗教信仰的自由。欧洲人权法院认为,由于所适用的一般税务法条款用语模糊,所申诉的干预行为并不满足合法性要求(*Association Les Témoins de Jéhovah v. France*);对于非常类似的情况所做出的相同判决,参见 *Église Évangélique Missionnaire et Salaûn v. France*;

- 对两个为奥米斯特社区和为在曼达姆修道院(Mandarom monastery)修建寺庙而接受个人捐款的团体征税。在税务调整之前,两个团体决定解散并将所有资产转交给目的相似的团体,以便继续有关教派的公共活动;税务机关随后向主管法院提起诉讼,取消了财产转移。欧洲人权法院认为,由于该措施针对有关宗教的庆祝和礼拜场所,因此妨碍了公约第9条所保护的权利的行使;欧洲人权法院以与法国耶和华见证人(*Association Les Témoins de Jéhovah*)案相同的理由裁定违反了公约(*Association Cultuelle du Temple Pyramide v. France*,和 *Association des Chevaliers du Lotus d'Or v. France*)。

144. 此外,欧洲人权法院对一项与上一案件类似的申诉宣布不予受理,虽然申诉团体的运营是部分依靠个人捐款,但对个人捐款征税并未产生切断团体重要收入来源或阻碍其宗教活动的后果（*Sukyo Mahikari France v. France*，§ 20）。

145. 在下列案件中，欧洲人权法院认为违反了公约第 9 条和第 14 条（禁止歧视）：
- 拒绝豁免耶和华见证人团体支付继承税和赠与税的责任，理由是根据国内法，这种豁免只能授予"被认可的宗教社团"，而不是如申诉团体这种"登记的宗教组织"（*Jehovas Zeugen in Österreich v. Austria*）；
- 土耳其宗教事务局为清真寺、基督教礼拜堂和犹太教堂支付电费，但拒绝以同样的方式为建造朝圣场所的阿列维（Alevi）宗教中心支付电费，因为土耳其当局拒绝将阿列维视为一个单独的宗教，而是将其作为伊斯兰的一个分支看待，因此不将其所建设的朝圣场所认定为"礼拜场所"。欧洲人权法院认为，这种差别待遇没有客观和合理的理由（*Cumhuriyetçi Eğitim ve Kültür Merkezi Vakfı v. Turkey*）。

146. 另一方面，关于英国当局拒绝批准对摩门圣殿（不向公众开放，只有持有现行的"推荐书"的摩门教徒才能进入）完全免除特定纳税义务，欧洲人权法院认为不违反第 9 条和第 14 条，尽管当局同时对向公众开放的摩门教堂和"教区中心"豁免税收。欧洲人权法院对这一争议是否适用第 9 条的规定表示怀疑。然而，即使假定该条款可以适用，所谓的差别待遇确实有客观和合理的理由，因为公众接触宗教仪式有利于整个社会，它可以消除怀疑，并有助于打破多信仰社会中的偏见。此外，摩门教没有被与其他宗教团体区别对待，包括官方的英国国教会，其私人教堂与摩门圣殿适用同一税法。此外，作为礼拜场所的圣殿还可享受 80% 的降税率（*The Church of Jesus Christ of Latter-day Saints v. the United Kingdom*）。

147. 同样地，公约机构驳回了对下列情况的申诉：
- 西班牙税务机关拒绝豁免福音新教教会与其礼拜场所有关的土地税，尽管罗马天主教会确实受益于这种豁免。委员会认为在这种情况下没有出现歧视，因为罗马天主教会享有的免税是由应诉国和罗马教廷缔结的协议规定的，这项协议对双方施加了相互的义务。鉴于申诉团体从未要求与该国缔结类似的协议，它并不承担与罗马天主教会相同的义务（*Iglesia Bautista 'El Salvador' and Ortega Moratilla v. Spain*）；
- 对进行瑜伽教学的申诉团体征收企业税，理由是它以营利为目的提供瑜伽课程。此外，申诉协会认为与其他团体的宗教活动相比，尤其是与罗马天主教会

（其非营利的地位受到了国家认可）的活动相比,自己受到了歧视,委员会否定了这一主张。申诉团体不具有宗教团体地位,与宗教团体不存在相似的,甚至是不存在可比较的情况(*Association Sivananda de Yoga Vedanta v. France*);

- 德国当局和国内法院决定将前德意志民主共和国统治下的民主社会主义党向申诉人——伊斯兰协会提供的捐赠,交由信托代理机构管理,并没收相应的资产。欧洲人权法院指出,被质疑的措施是在与德国重新统一有关的特殊情况下命令实施的;具体而言,该措施是根据重新统一前在德意志民主共和国提出的一般管理规则而实施的,目的是检查政党和相关组织的资产来源。在发现被质疑的干预行为符合第一议定书第1条(保护财产)的规定后,欧洲人权法院就第9条得出了同样的结论。它对存在干涉行使宗教自由的行为表示怀疑,因为被质疑的措施既不涉及申诉团体的内部组织,也不涉及国家的官方认可。无论如何,上述措施都是由法律规定的,追求的是保护公共道德及他人权利和自由的合法目的,而且措施对于所追求的目的来说是合比例的(*Islamische Religionsgemeinschaft in Berlin e. V. v. Germany*)。

148. 一些欧洲国家设有宗教税(教会税、宗派税等),要么由国家征收然后将其转让给特定宗教组织,要么由宗教组织直接征收,宗教组织可以通过国内法院的诉讼程序强制其支付。在其他国家,纳税人可以合法地将一定比例的所得税分配给特定的宗教组织。这种宗教税的存在本身并不会引起任何与公约第9条有关的问题,因为国家征税的权利是第9条第2款承认的"合法目的"之一(*Wasmuth v. Germany*, § 55)。此外,关于保护财产的第一议定书第1条明确授予国家征税权(*C. v. the United Kingdom*)。然而,在教会税收问题上赋予各国广泛的自由裁量权并不意味着在这个领域中不会出现宗教自由的问题。相反,欧洲人权法院认为,在某些情况下,如果与教会税收制度相关的干预很严重,以及如果涉及相互冲突的利益之间的平衡,则可能导致其认为构成了对公约的违反(*Wasmuth v. Allemagne*, § 61)。

149. 教会在国家帮助下征收其成员缴纳的会费,不会干预第9条第1款所列的活动(礼拜、教学、践行和庆祝)。一个宗教组织的成员在这方面的情况与向自己所属的私人协会出资的义务相当,第9条不能解释为赋予个人保留教会成员身份的权利,但仍然有权根据有关教会的自治条例免除这种作为成员所产生的法律义务,特别是金钱义务(*E. and G. R. v. Austria*)。

150. 显然,即使国家可以为教会征收教会税或类似的款项,这种方式只能涵盖教会成员——除非在特殊情况下,教会也履行某些非宗教的公共服务职能,并且所涉税款仅用于资助前述非宗教职能。

- 在以下这一案件中,委员会认为违反了公约第 9 条:申诉人在瑞典工作,具有合法的瑞典"居民"身份,被要求支付瑞典教会税(在当时具有国家教会地位的路德教会),他并未加入该教会,没有任何豁免的可能(参见委员会于 *Darby v. Sweden*,§§ 57–60 中的意见)。但是,欧洲人权法院在审理这一案件时,决定根据公约第 14 条而不是第 9 条,结合第一议定书第 1 条(对于居民与非居民之间行使财产保护权的歧视),认为存在违反的情况(*Darby v. Sweden*,§§ 34–35)。

- 欧洲人权法院宣布一项由一个瑞典国民提起的申诉明显缺乏依据,该国民不是瑞典教会的成员,但是必须支付相当于标准教会税 25% 的"异议税"。欧洲人权法院注意到,在本案中,向申诉人所要求的出资是用于资助瑞典教会为了全体人民的利益而进行的非宗教工作,例如,组织葬礼、照顾年老者以及管理国家建筑遗产;此外,25% 的数字不是任意的,而是根据此类活动的成本所占教会整体财务的百分比计算的 [*Bruno v. Sweden*(dec.);*Lundberg v. Sweden*(dec.)]。

151. 上述所有案件均涉及自然人。然而,一家完全属于营利性质的商业公司也不能依据第 9 条被豁免支付依法适用于所有商业公司的教会税,即使该公司是由哲学组织成立和经营的 [*Company X. v. Switzerland*(dec.);*Kustannus OY Vapaa Ajattelija AB and Others v. Finland*(dec.)]。

152. 因此,如果国内法允许公民在自愿的前提下自由退出教会,则教会税本身不违背宗教自由。然而,关于个人离开宗教教会决定的有效性的条件,国内当局有较大的自由裁量权去确定;因此,他们可以要求个人清晰明确地表达其在此方面的意愿 [*Gottesmann v. Switzerland*(dec.)]。

153. 在下列案件中,公约机构认为没有违反第 9 条(单独或结合禁止歧视的第 14 条):

- 奥地利教会制度要求一对罗马天主教夫妇申诉人定期向罗马天主教会缴费;如果不付款,教会有权对他们提起民事诉讼要求支付有关款项。委员会指出,一方面,通过立法明确规定申诉人离开教会后可以免除所涉及的义务,国家已采取了充分保障申诉人行使宗教自由的措施;另一方面,申诉人不能从公约第9条中得出任何保留罗马天主教会成员资格的"权利",同时也免除后者规定的义务。此外,国家使得教会得以基于与任何其他团体或个人相同的理由请求民事法庭来确保义务的履行,这一事实不会产生与第一议定书第1条所规定的保护财产的权利有关的问题(E. and G. R. v. Austria);

- 申诉人曾经是罗马天主教会的成员,因此瑞士当局溯及既往地要求他们履行支付教会税义务,但他们在申诉意见中表示,他们此时已不再是该教会的成员。事实上,只有从他们每个人明确和清楚地表示他们希望不再属于教会时起,国家当局才承认他们退出教会,因此,仅仅将报税表上宗教详情的部分划去,不足以达到退出教会目的(Gottesmann v. Switzerland);

- 申诉人——一群西班牙福音派新教徒被要求将所得税的一部分用于财政以支持罗马天主教会或者其他符合公共利益的活动,但是不能交给自己的教会。欧洲人权法院指出,申诉人所属的宗教团体没有试图与西班牙国家缔结协议以使他们能够按照自己的意愿使用税款——尽管国内法允许做出这种选择。赋予罗马天主教会的特别财政优待是基于应诉国和教廷达成的协议,对双方施加了相互的义务,例如,要求教会允许整个西班牙社会能够接触其历史、艺术和文献遗产[Alujer Fernández and Caballero Garcia v. Spain (dec.)];

- 意大利纳税人向国家、罗马天主教会或代表其他五种宗教(这些宗教同意与国家缔结特殊协议,接受这种分配)的机构之一分配了他们所得税的8‰。与申诉人的论点相反,欧洲人权法院认为,法律还给予了纳税人不做出任何这样的选择的权利,因此被质疑的条款不包括表明自己的宗教信仰的义务[Spampinato v. Italy (dec.)];

- 国家立法,授权法律承认的所有宗教团体的成员向其各自的社区分配一部分税款,但也从国家预算中给予国家教会(冰岛路德教会)特定年度数额,国家教会的牧师具有公务员地位[Ásatrúarfélagið v. Iceland (dec.)]。

154. 应当注意的是,前面提到的案件或是涉及特定的教会税,或是涉及纳税人自愿分配的向纳税机关缴纳的一般税款中的特定比例。然而,在面对国家的一般财政预算政策时,特定款项的交付与其之后的用途之间没有直接的、可追溯的联系,此种情况下公约第 9 条并不赋予纳税人任何权利。因此,委员会驳回了一名和平贵格会信徒的申诉:申诉人拒绝支付其税款的一定比例,除非他能够确保该款项不会被用于资助军事部门。委员会认为缴税义务是一种一般性义务,不会对出于良心反对服兵役的权利产生特定影响;其中立性表现为纳税人不得影响其税款的分配或者在税款已被征收之后决定此种分配[*C. v. the United Kingdom*(dec.),在 *H. and B. v. the United Kingdom*(dec.)一案中得到确认]。委员会在下述案中得出了同样的结论,一名法国律师反对堕胎并要求行使其拒绝缴纳用于资助堕胎的额定比例的税款的权利[*Bouessel du Bourg v. France*(dec.)]。

155. 委员会之后确定,即使国家将通过一般税收获得的预算拨款用于资助特定的宗教团体或其宗教活动,也不会侵犯宗教自由(参见 *Darby v. Sweden*, § 56, Comission's opion)。

156. 关于强制保险和社会保险,委员会在 20 世纪 60 年代处理了几项由荷兰归正教会教徒提起的申诉,申诉人依据第 9 条,要求享有不参加多种强制保险以及不附属于国立机构组织的权利。他们的论据如下:首先,上帝赐予人类以福祸,因此禁止试图提前阻止或限制可能发生的不幸。其次,在圣经中,上帝命令所有基督教徒向老者和弱者提供食物,在这种情况下,当局通过接管这一事务并建立养老制度,违背了上帝的明确命令,申诉人拒绝同此项罪孽联系起来。在这类案件中,欧洲人权法院驳回了下列申诉:

- 一名奶粉经销商提起的申诉。申诉人拒绝参加健康保险计划,而这是从事畜牧业的法定前提条件,申诉人因此被处罚;即使假设存在对第 9 条权利的干预,出于保护"公共健康"的目的——其目标理应包括防止畜禽疾病,这一干预也是"民主社会所必要的"(*X. v. the Netherlands*[①]);
- 归正教会及其两名代表提起的申诉。尽管他们没有反对所有形式的保险,但是希望能免除缴纳养老保险计划的义务。委员会注意到,荷兰法律豁免了出于良心反对服兵役者直接缴纳该保险计划的义务,同时以同等数额的税款的方式进行替代。因此,国内法律充分考虑了归正教会的特定利益,在本案中没有违反第 9 条(参见 *Reformed Church X. and Others v. the Netherlands*[②]);

---

① 裁定只有书面文本,请见欧洲人权法院图书馆《欧洲人权公约年鉴》。
② 裁定只有书面文本,请见欧洲人权法院图书馆《欧洲人权公约年鉴》。

- 一名男子提起的申诉。他声称自己受到了歧视,因为荷兰法律只对那些因宗教原因严格反对所有形式保险的人豁免强制缴纳养老保险计划的义务,而不对申诉人适用[*X. v. the Netherlands*(dec.)];

- 一名店主提起的申诉。申诉人反对所有形式的保险,因为其在没有缴纳强制民事责任保险的情况下驾驶职业用车而被处以罚款,并被没收车辆。申诉人承认他是可以获得法定豁免的,但是由于无论如何都要缴纳相同数额的税款,他认为这种选择从道德上来说是令人无法接受的。委员会认为,为了保护"其他人的权利",也就是容易成为潜在交通事故受害人的第三人的权利,所申诉的干预"在民主社会是必要的"[*X. v. the Netherlands*(dec.)]。

157. 最近,委员会还驳回了一名荷兰医生提起的类似申诉,他是一名主张人智说原则的全科医生,要求享有不参加法定专业养老金计划的权利。委员会认为,加入养老金计划的义务是完全中立地适用于所有全科医生,不能说与申诉人的宗教或信仰有任何关系[*V. v. the Netherlands*(dec.)]。

158. 欧洲人权法院认为,一项健康保险基金要求"致力于通过艺术和美实现人类的全面发展"的基督教团体的领导人参与一般社会保障体系,这并不违反第14条(禁止歧视)和第9条,理由是所有相关费用全由团体支付,从法律术语上看活动是"有偿的",而不是"自愿的"。申诉团体认为,与不需要参与一般社会保障体系的宗教教派牧师相比,以及与申诉协会所属联邦的其他志愿工作人员相比,它受到了歧视待遇。欧洲人权法院认为,根据法国法律,僧侣和尼姑受制于一般社会保障体系,同时保留参加特定计划的可能性;然而,当参加与其宗教训练无关的活动时,他们需要参与一般社会保障体系[*Office Culturel de Cluny v. France*(dec.)]。

(五)针对由宗教驱动的政治党派所采取的措施

159. 第9条既不禁止政党资助,也不授予作为政党参加选举的权利[*X., Y. and Z. v. Germany*(dec.)]。

160. 欧洲人权法院从来不认为设立一个受到宗教假定启发的政党是公约第9条所保护的"信仰表达形式"。另外,它涉及由该类政党提起的有关国家针对他们采取的措施的申诉。在这方面,欧洲人权法院发现,在以下两个条件下,一个政党可以促进法律的变化或者国家法律和宪法结构的改变:第一,为此目的使用的手段必须是合法和民主的;第二,所提出的改变本身必须符合基本的民主原则。基于此可得出的结论是,如果一个政党的领导人煽动暴力或者提出不尊重民主或旨在破坏民主和蔑视民主中承认的权利和自由的政策,那么这个政党就不能要求公约保护他们免除基于上述理由的处罚。只要满足前述的两个条件,一个受到宗教所奉行的道德价值启发的政党就不能被视为对公约所规定的基本民主原则是必然有害的[Refah Partisi (the Welfare Party) and Others v. Turkey [GC]; Staatkundig Gereformeerde Partij v. the Netherlands (dec.), § 71]。此外,任何缔约国可以为了实现公约目的而合法阻止在其司法管辖范围内适用有损于公共秩序和民主价值的宗教灵感的私法规则[Refah Partisi (the Welfare Party) and Others v. Turkey [GC], § 128]。

161. 例如,欧洲人权法院认为:

- 解散一个土耳其政党,以及禁止其领导人在任何其他政党中担任类似职务的临时禁令没有违反公约第 11 条(结社自由)。欧洲人权法院注意到,所涉政党正在努力建立一个基于伊斯兰教法的政治制度(不符合民主要求),并建立多个允许针对有关各方的性别歧视的法律制度,例如,一夫多妻制以及男性在离婚与继承方面的特权(这与公约保护的基本价值之一的性别平等相违背)[Refah Partisi (the Welfare Party) and Others v. Turkey [GC], § 128];

- "全球伊斯兰政党"控告相关德国当局禁止其在德国活动的申诉是不可被受理的,因为该申诉不符合公约的属事管辖。欧洲人权法院认为,由于它要求暴力破坏以色列国,并要求驱逐和杀害其居民,因此根据第 17 条(禁止滥用基本权利)的规定,该政党不能主张公约第 9 条、第 10 条和第 11 条的保护[Hizb Ut-Tahrir and Others v. Germany (dec.)];

- 荷兰归正教党派针对荷兰最高法院的一项判决提起的申诉因明显缺乏依据而不被受理,该判决大意为,国家应该采取(未指明的)行动终止荷兰归正教党派不接纳妇女进入理事机构或其选举候选人名单的做法,这种做法是基于对圣经某些段落的虔诚信仰。欧洲人权法院不加区别地根据公约第 9、10 和 11 条审查了该项申诉。暂且不考虑在国家对申诉党采取任何具体行动之前申诉方是否可以认为自己是"受害者"的问题,欧洲人权法院宣布该党就妇女的政治角色的立场公然违反了公约的基本价值。虽然没有一个妇女曾表示希望成为申诉党的候选人,但欧洲人权法院认为这一事实并不具有决定性[Staatkundig Gereformeerde Partij v. the Netherlands (dec.)]。

二、消极义务：尊重宗教组织的自治权

(一)宗教组织自治原则

162. 宗教团体传统上普遍以有组织结构的形式存在。在涉及有关宗教团体组织方式的案件中,公约第9条必须根据第11条解释,第11条保护组织体生活免受国家不合理的干涉。从这个角度来看,信徒的宗教自由权包括了宗教团体被允许和平运作、不受国家任意干预的期望。宗教团体的自主存在对于民主社会的多元主义来说是不可或缺的,因此是第9条保护的核心问题。它不仅直接关系到宗教团体本身的组织,而且也关系到其所有活跃成员能否有效享有宗教自由权。如果宗教团体的组织生活不受公约第9条的保护,个人宗教自由的所有其他方面都将变得脆弱不堪(*Hassan and Tchaouch v. Bulgaria* [GC], §§ 62 and 91; *Fernández Martínez v. Spain* [GC], § 127)。宗教组织的内部结构和关于其成员的条例必须被视为这种组织能够表达其信仰和维护其宗教传统的一种手段(*Sviato-Mykhaïlivska Parafiya v. Ukraine*, § 150)。

163. 上述自治原则意味着国家不能要求某宗教团体接纳新成员或驱逐现有成员。宗教组织必须有权完全自由地决定接纳新成员和驱逐现有成员的方式(*Sviato-Mykhaïlivska Parafiya v. Ukraine*, §§ 146 and 150)。

164. 在开展活动时,宗教团体遵守常被追随者视为神圣起源的规则。当宗教仪式由为此目的被授权的领袖主持进行并符合宗教规则时,宗教仪式对信徒而言就有其意义和神圣的价值。毫无疑问,宗教领袖的性格对宗教团体的每个成员都很重要。因此,参与宗教生活是个人信仰的一种特定表达,受到公约第9条的保护(*Hassan and Tchaouch v. Bulgaria* [GC], § 62; *Miroļubovs and Others v. Latvia*, § 80)。

165. 例如,欧洲人权法院认为,"北塞浦路斯土耳其共和国"当局规制其境内信奉东正教的塞浦路斯人的宗教生活的措施是违反第9条的:尽管当地整个地区仅剩一名牧师,其也没有批准在该地区任命牧师(*Cyprus v. Turkey* [GC], §§ 243–246)。

166. 仅因为担任一个愿意跟随他的团体的宗教领袖(尽管这一事实没有得到国家认可)而惩罚一个人,这难以被认为与民主社会中的宗教多元化的要求相一致(*Serif v. Greece*, § 51)。欧洲人权法院认为,申诉人——一名希腊穆斯林神学家因为"篡夺'知名宗教'领袖的职能",且"在无权情况下公开穿戴该领袖服饰"而被定罪,这种做法是

违反第9条的。事实上,申诉人已经被穆斯林选为罗多彼穆夫提,但没有得到国家认可,国家已任命其他人为穆夫提。申诉人实际上参加了一系列的宗教庆祝活动,但从未试图履行国家立法规定的穆夫提和其他"被认可宗教"的领袖应当履行的司法和行政职能(*Serif v. Greece*)。在另一类似的关于被选为克桑西的穆夫提的案件中,欧洲人权法院也得出了同样的结论,指出两个穆夫提共存可能导致当地居民之间关系紧张的理论可能性不足以使国家对宗教组织的干预正当化,因为正是国家当局有义务确保对立团体之间的相互容忍[*Serif v. Greece*(no.2);see also *Agga v. Greece*(no.3);*Agga v. Greece*(no.4)]。

167. 关于救世军,其内部结构以类似于军队的等级制度和制服的穿着为基础,欧洲人权法院认为,这种情况可被视为该组织宗教信仰的合法表达。因此,不能认为这意味着救世军侵犯了国家的统一或安全(*Moscow Branch of the Salvation Army v. Russia*,§92)。

(二)国家对国内宗教间或宗教内部冲突的干预

168. 多元主义、包容和心胸豁达是"民主社会"的标志。虽然个人利益有时必须服从于群体利益,但民主并不意味着多数人的意见必须总是占上风,必须实现平衡,确保公平合理地对待少数群体,避免滥用主导地位(*Leyla Şahin v. Turkey*[GC],§108)。多元主义和民主还必须建立在对话和妥协精神的基础上,必须要求个人或个人团体做出各种让步,以维持和促进民主社会的理想和价值(*S. A. S. v. France*[GC],§128)。在一个民主社会中,有若干宗教在同一群人中共存,可能有必要限制这种自由,以调和各群体的利益,确保每个人的信仰得到尊重。但是,在行使其在这一领域的监管权力时,以及在其与各种宗教、宗派和信仰的关系中,国家有义务保持中立和公正。这里的核心问题是要维护多元主义和民主的合理运作(*Metropolitan Church of Bessarabia and Others v. Moldova*,§§115-116)。

169. 从这个角度来看,欧洲人权法院经常强调国家作为行使各种宗教、信念和信仰的中立和公正的组织者的作用,强调这种作用有利于民主社会的公共秩序、宗教和谐以及包容(*Bayatyan v. Armenia*[GC],§120;*S. A. S. v. France*[GC],§127)。这既适用于信徒与非信徒之间的关系,也适用于各种宗教、信念和信仰的信徒之间的关系(*Lautsi and Others v. Italy*[GC],§60)。

170. 如果某一特定国家的人口在历史上和文化上与某信仰或某教会相关联,上述国家中立的义务不能被认为可能削弱该信仰或该教会扮演的角色(Members of the Gldani Congregation of the Jehovah's Witnesses and Others v. Georgia,§132)。事实上,决定是否延续传统原则上属于被告国的自由裁量范围。欧洲人权法院还必须考虑到欧洲的组成国之间存在巨大差异,尤其是在文化和历史发展领域。然而,对传统的参考不能免除缔约国尊重公约及其各项议定书所载权利和自由的义务(Lautsi and Others v. Italy [GC],§68)。

171. 国家中立和公正的义务与任何国家决定宗教信仰或用来表达这种信仰的手段是否合法的自由裁量权是不相容的(Manoussakis and Others v. Greece,§47;Bayatyan v. Armenia [GC],§120)。同样,如果国内法律规定行使宗教自由权或其一方面的权利受制于前置审批制度,则对已被承认的教会机构的授权程序,尤其对一个属于不同宗派、层级或宗教的教会机构的授权程序进行干预,与第9条第2款的要求是不相符的(Metropolitan Church of Bessarabia and Others v. Moldova,§117;Vergos v. Greece,§34)。

172. 中立的义务防止国家决定个人或团体的宗教归属问题,宗教归属仅由有关宗教团体的最高精神权威决定(Miroļubovs and Others v. Latvia,§§89-90)。换言之,国家不能违背个人或团体的意愿任意"强加"或"重新归类"其宗教归属。例如,在下列案件中,欧洲人权法院认为违反了第9条:

- 申诉人无法确保在身份证上用"阿勒维"一词代替"伊斯兰"条目,因为负责伊斯兰教有关事务的国家当局认为阿勒维宗教只是伊斯兰教的一个分支(Sinan Işık v. Turkey,§§45-46);
- 拉脱维亚宗教事务局在当地的老东正教团体(俄罗斯老东正教会的信徒)的激烈争端背景下做出的决定;这项决定是根据专家(这些专家都不属于老东正教)提供的两项意见做出的,决定认为通过与俄罗斯东正教教士交往,申诉人事实上改变了其宗派。执行该决定导致申诉人被驱逐出礼拜场所(Miroļubovs and Others v. Latvia,§§33-36 and 88-89)。

173. 如果国家的行为有利于一个分裂的宗教团体中的某个领导人,或者旨在迫使分裂的宗教团体违背其自身意愿结合在一起并接受统一领导,则同样构成对宗教自由的干预。在民主社会中,国家不需要采取措施推行一种宗教解释形式而损害其他解释形式,或迫使分裂的宗教团体或其中一部分在统一领导下合并(Hassan and Tchaouch v.

Bulgaria［GC］,§78;*Metropolitan Church of Bessarabia and Others v. Moldova*,§117)。当一群信仰者和/或宗教领袖脱离了他们以前所属的宗教组织,或者甚至决定改变宗派时,这种行为是集体行使"改变宗教或信仰的自由"的一个实例,这种自由受到公约第9条第1款的明确保障(*Miroļubovs and Others v. Latvia*,§93)。国家当局的作用不是通过消除多元化来消除紧张局势的根源,而是确保竞争的群体相互容忍,即使它们都来自同一群体(*Metropolitan Church of Bessarabia and Others v. Moldova*,§123)。

174. 国家作为宗教多元主义的最终保证者的作用有时可能要求它在对立方之间进行调解;中立的调解在原则上不会构成国家对公约第9条规定的信徒权利的干预——虽然国家当局在这个特别脆弱的区域确实必须谨慎行动(*Supreme Holy Council of the Muslim Community v. Bulgaria*,§80)。无论如何,国家当局在这一领域所做的任何决定都必须基于对有关事实的令人接受的审查(*Sviato-Mykhaïlivska Parafiya v. Ukraine*,§138)。

175. 在下列案件中,欧洲人权法院认为违反了公约第9条:

- 摩尔多瓦当局拒绝给予巴萨拉比亚大都会教堂法律承认,该教堂是布加勒斯特主教(罗马尼亚东正教)管辖下的一座自治教堂,当局拒绝的理由是这种承认会危及摩尔多瓦大都会教会的利益,它属于莫斯科主教(俄罗斯东正教教会)管辖,并已被政府承认。以申诉人教会相对于俄罗斯教会只是一个"分裂"团体为由拒绝承认其地位,并宣布申诉人教会的信徒可以在国家承认的其他东正教教会中表现其信仰,摩尔多瓦政府的这种行为没有履行中立和公正的义务(*Metropolitan Church of Bessarabia and Others v. Moldova*);

- 乌克兰当局任意拒绝承认和登记某东正教教区成员全体会议通过的对该东正教教区章程的修改,根据该修改,教区的管辖权从俄罗斯东正教(莫斯科宗主教)转移到乌克兰东正教(基辅的主教)。在本案中所指出的任意性的主要方面之一是,乌克兰当局和国内法院完全忽视了教会章程所界定的教区的内部组织,将没有教区居民身份的人视为"教区居民",并认为由于这些人没有参加全体会议所以全体会议是非法的。由于国内法院未能纠正行政当局的任意行为,欧洲人权法院认为违反了公约第9条以及第6条第1款和第11条(*Sviato-Mykhaïlivska Parafiya v. Ukraine*)。

176. 米洛卢博夫斯等人案(*Miroļubovs and Others*)涉及国家干预分裂有关宗教团

体的争端。然而,有时国家可能发现自己参与了其本身直接帮助创造的宗派内部争端。在这方面,我们应该提到 3 个针对保加利亚的类似案件的法院判决。所有这些情况必须考虑到这个国家特有的历史和政治环境,即在 1989 年,该国从共产主义极权政权迅速过渡到民主制度。1989 年以后,保加利亚国家推行了一项政策,用以干预该国最大的两个宗教团体即东正教会和穆斯林的内部运作。政府首先试图替换掉两个宗教组织的领导人,因为据称他们与旧的共产主义政权合作;该政策立即导致了组织中每个宗教社区的分裂。随后,在连续的大选后,每个新政府都采取措施,试图将两个团体置于在政治上忠于执政党的宗教领袖的统一领导之下,同时将与执政党对立的团体领导人边缘化。此外,根据保加利亚当局的标准行政做法,关于宗教教派的法律被解释为禁止属于同一教派的两个平行组织的运作,并要求每个教派仅有一个被国家所认可的领导[情况概述,参见 Holy Synod of the Bulgarian Orthodox Church (Metropolitan Inokentiy) and Others v. Bulgaria,§§ 68 and 127]。

177. 在此背景下,欧洲人权法院认为以下 3 种情况都违反了公约第 9 条:

- 保加利亚政府在未提供任何理由或解释的情况下,通过承认申诉人的对立教派领导人为整个宗教的唯一合法代表,来干预伊斯兰教领导人的选择。虽然保加利亚最高法院裁定要求部长理事会审查第一申诉人提交的登记请求,但政府拒绝遵守这一裁定。欧洲人权法院认为,被质疑的干预不是"法律规定的",因为它是任意的,并且是基于允许行政部门享有不受约束的自由裁量权的法律规定(Hassan and Tchaouch v. Bulgaria [GC]);

- 国家当局组织了一次保加利亚穆斯林统一会议,以结束上述分裂局面,并非常积极地参与会议的筹备和举行——特别是在甄选与会者时。本案中的申诉人是穆斯林共同体最高神圣理事会,代表反对哈桑先生和肖什先生的一方,拒绝承认有关会议的合法性。在这种情况下,保加利亚当局对分裂的穆斯林团体施加压力,迫使它接受一个领导,而不是仅指出统一努力的失败,而且如有必要,继续本着对话的精神作为双方的调解人。欧洲人权法院认为,被质疑的干预是"法律规定的",并且追求合法的目的,但所采取的措施相对于这一目标来说不合比例(Supreme Holy Council of the Muslim Community v. Bulgaria);

- 国家干预一场分裂保加利亚东正教会的争端,而且政府在 1992 年直接煽动该争端,宣布选举牧师马克西姆领导教会的行为是无效的,并改为任命临时领导

(称为"替代大会")。考虑到案件的特殊情况,欧洲人权法院驳回了政府的论据,即"替代大会"的成员及其信徒可以自由地与由牧师马克西姆领导的教会一起创建和登记自己的教会。实际上,争端不是关于拒绝承认一个宗教组织,而是关于国家干预一个宗教内两个层级之间的内部事务,每个层级都基于表面上看来既非捏造又非不合理的理由认为另一个是非权威的。保加利亚国家通过帮助争端当事方之一获得对整个东正教宗教事务的代表权和控制权的专有权力,迫使对立方退出,并派遣执法机构帮助将申诉人大会的信徒们从他们所占据的礼拜场所驱逐出去,国家的这种行为没有履行中立义务[Holy Synod of the Bulgarian Orthodox Church (Metropolitan Inokentiy) and Others v. Bulgaria;同时参见 Sotirov and Others v. Bulgaria (dec.)]。

178. 在前东正教牧师和部分教区居民已皈依希腊天主教会并因此改变了教派的情况下,当局未能执行允许希腊天主教教区中的居民进入它与东正教教区共享的墓地的最终判决,欧洲人权法院认为,从表面上来看,没有任何违反第 9 条(单独或结合公约第 14 条)的情况。欧洲人权法院注意到,当局已采取适当和合理的措施来平息争端(包括分配资金建立一个新的希腊天主教堂和建立一个新的公墓)。关于被质疑的判决,申诉教区没有表现出必要的勤勉以确保判决的适当执行[Greek Catholic Parish Pesceana and Others v. Romania (dec.), § 43]。

179. 国家对宗教之间或宗教内部争端的干预必须与国家当局在没有自己帮助创造和支持某一方的情况下从先前存在的宗教争端中得出不可避免的世俗结论中区分开来[Griechische Kirchengemeinde München und Bayern e. V. v. Germany (dec.); Serbisch-griechisch-orientalische Kirchengemeinde zum Heiligen Sava in Wien v. Austria (dec.)]。例如,希腊东正教宗教国被国家强制要求返还一幢已由其占有 150 多年的教堂,提起申诉,欧洲人权法院认为明显缺乏依据,宣布不予受理。1828 年,巴伐利亚国王路德维希一世将建筑提供给"希腊宗教团体,国家保留所有权"。然而,在 20 世纪 70 年代,该团体已经断绝了与以前所属的君士坦丁堡主教区的地方大都会的关系,并转移到"真正的东正教"的管辖下。根据巴伐利亚州提起的一系列诉讼,德国法院决定,从 1828 年起,建筑的贷款应被视为撤销,并且应将教堂返还给国家,并随后转移到大都会。国内法院认为,申诉团体使用建筑物的方式与原来的捐赠者(国王路德维希一世)的意图不符,他希望教堂真正代表当地希腊东正教群体并与希腊东正教会和君士坦丁堡主教会进行交流;然而,申诉团体已不再满足这些条件。考虑到国内法院提出的论据,欧洲人权法院认为不存在国家当局对宗教内部纠纷的干预,也不存在违反国家中立原则的情况 [*Griechische Kirchengemeinde München und Bayern e. V. v. Germany* (dec.)]。

180. 使用宗教建筑物的权利也是米洛路博夫斯等人案(*Miroļubovs and Others*)的核心问题。在该案中,申诉人是拉脱维亚老东正教会的信徒,他们对教堂的使用权被转移给了其对立教派。宗教事务局长官认为他们事实上改变了宗派,不能再合法地代表所涉宗教团体。欧洲人权法院认为,宗教事务局的行为违反了公约第9条,其谨慎地区分了本案与 *Griechische Kirchengemeinde München und Bayern e. V* 案;欧洲人权法院强调,拉脱维亚当局切实干预了宗教争端,而不是局限于在世俗层面从中得出法律结论(*Miroļubovs and Others v. Latvia*, § 94)。

(三)宗教组织与其成员(信徒和宗教牧师)之间的争议

181. 各国没有义务要求宗教团体在其管辖范围内确保信徒和宗教领袖的宗教信仰自由和言论自由[*X. v. Denmark* (dec.)]。许多宗教的一个共同特征是,他们决定教徒们在私生活中必须遵守的行为标准(*Jehovah's Witnesses of Moscow and Others v. Russia*, § 118)。因此,公约第9条没有确保在宗教组织内拥有异见的权利。尊重国家承认的宗教群体的自主权尤其意味着,国家应该接受这种群体根据自己的规则和利益对其中出现的任何可能对他们的凝聚力、形象或团结构成威胁的异议运动做出反应的权利。因此,国家当局的任务不是作为宗教组织和其中存在或可能出现的各种异议派别之间的仲裁者(*Sindicatul 'Păstorul cel Bun' v. Romania* [GC], § 165; *Fernández Martínez v. Spain* [GC], § 128)。同样,第9条不保证信徒有权选择其教区的宗教领袖或反对宗教组织关于选举或任命领袖的决定[*Kohn v. Germany* (dec.); *Sotirov and Others v. Bulgaria* (dec.)]。在宗教团体与其成员之间存在教义或组织分歧的情况下,宗教团体成员的宗教自由是通过离开有关团体的自由来实现的[*X. v. Denmark* (dec.); *Miroļubovs and Others v. Latvia*, § 80]。

182. 然而,第9条第1款不能解释为授予个人任何"权利"强制教会"取消"他或她在童年时受到的洗礼或坚信礼[*X. v. Iceland* (dec.)]。

183. 对于下列案件,公约机构宣布不予受理:

- 丹麦教会部决定对丹麦国家(路德)教会的一位牧师启动纪律程序,因为该牧师在儿童洗礼时额外附加了教会所没有要求的条件[*X. v. Denmark* (dec.)];

- 瑞典国家(路德)教会教区主教的决定,经政府确认,声明申诉人不符合牧师职位的资格,因为他反对妇女的任职,且未表明与女教士合作的意愿[*Karlsson v. Sweden*(dec.)];
- 申诉人是英国教会的牧师,他反对教会大会任命妇女的决定[*Williamson v. the United Kingdom*(dec.)];
- 五旬节运动婚姻委员会决定撤销申诉人举行经国家承认的婚礼的权利,理由是申请人不再属于五旬节运动[*Spetz and Others v. Sweden*(dec.)];
- 汉诺威犹太社区行政理事会的前成员控告德国法院执行德意志中央犹太人宗教法院仲裁庭的决定,该决定声称他已丧失其职位,并命令将他驱逐出该团体处所;在这种情况下,国家没有干预,因为德国法院仅执行被起诉的决定,而没有核实其实体事实,因此尊重了该犹太团体的内部自治[*Kohn v. Germany*(dec.)]。

(四)宗教组织与其雇员之间的争议

184. 由于有自治权,宗教团体可以向为他们工作或代表他们的人要求一定程度的忠诚。许多宗教的一个共同特征是,他们决定教徒们在私生活中必须遵守的行为标准(*Jehovah's Witnesses of Moscow and Others v. Russia*,§118)。这些人担任的职位的性质是在审查有关国家或有关宗教组织采取的限制措施的相称性时应考虑的一个重要因素。特别是,分配给一个宗教组织中的有关个人的具体任务是确定该人是否应承担更高忠诚义务的相关考虑因素(*Fernández Martínez v. Spain*[GC],§131)。在这样做时,应特别重视申诉人的活动与所涉宗教组织所声称的任务之间的接近度(*Schüth v. Germany*,§69)。

185. 在一个有关宗教教育教师的案件中,教会或宗教团体期待教师如教会代表一样对教会特别忠诚,这种期待是合理的。如果教师公开积极反对那些必须被传授给学生的想法,那么这些想法和教师的个人信念之间的差异可能会引起可信度的问题。可以被合理接受的是,为了保持可信,宗教必须由这样一个人来教授:其生活方式和公开声明不与所涉宗教公然不同,尤其是当该宗教应管理其教徒的私人生活和个人信仰的时候(*Fernández Martínez v. Spain*[GC],§§137-138)。

186. 此外,宗教团体仅声称某雇员与其权利存在冲突,会对其自治造成实际或潜在威胁是不够的,这不足以作为教会干预其雇员权利的正当理由,雇员的权利也受到公约保护(特别是公约第8、9、10和11条)。此外,就每个个别案件的不同情形,有关宗教团体还必须表明其所指称的风险是可能的和具有实质性的,而且被质疑的对他人私人生活权利的干预不能超过消除这种风险的必要程度,也不具有与行使宗教团体自治权无关的其他目的,同时也不影响所涉权利的实质内容。因此,当欧洲人权法院被请求裁定宗教团体的自治权与另一个人所享有的同样受公约保护的权利之间的冲突时,国内法院必须对案件的情况进行深入审查,彻底平衡相互竞争的利益。国家须保障这两项权利,如果对一方的保护导致对另一方的干预,则必须选择适当的手段使这种干预与所追求的目标相称。国家在这类问题上有较大的自由裁量权(*Fernández Martínez v. Spain* [GC],§§ 123 and 132)。

187. 在进行上述平衡工作时,这两种权利应被视为值得同等考虑:申诉的结果原则上不会因为由宗教组织根据第9条声称其自治权受到侵犯而向欧洲人权法院提起申诉或由另一方根据其他条款来保护其权利而向欧洲人权法院提起申诉而有所区别(*Sindicatul 'Păstorul cel Bun' v. Romania* [GC],§ 160)。

188. 根据公约,如果雇主的道德意识是基于宗教或哲学信仰之上的,那么他就可以对雇员要求履行忠诚的特定职责。然而,雇主基于自主权因雇员违反上述特定忠诚义务而将其解雇的决定,不能仅受到有关国内就业法庭有限的司法审查,却不考虑有关职位的性质,也缺乏根据相称性原则对所涉及的利益进行适当平衡(*Schüth v. Germany*,§ 69)。

189. 此外,在上述对冲突利益的平衡中,被教会雇主解雇的雇员能找到另一份工作的机会是十分有限的,这一事实特别重要,尤其是当雇主在某一特定行业中占据主导地位并且享有某些普通法律义务的克减时,或者被解雇的雇员有特定的资质而难以(即使不是不可能)在受雇教会以外找到一份新的工作时,正如在舒特诉德国案(*Schüth v. Germany*)中发生的那样(*Fernández Martínez v. Spain* [GC],§ 144;*Schüth v. Germany*,§ 73)。

190. 例如,德国天主教教区的一名风琴演奏者和唱诗班指挥家因为离开其妻子,与另一个女子保持婚外关系并使其怀孕,违反了对天主教会的忠诚义务,被视为通奸并且违反婚姻永续性,因而被解雇(已尽到适当通知的义务),欧洲人权法院认为教会解雇他违反了公约第8条(尊重私生活的权利)规定的应诉国应承担的积极义务。德国法院做出了对申诉人不利的判决,欧洲人权法院没有谴责该判决的实质内容,但批判了其得出结论的方式。德国法院没有充分解释教会雇主的利益远远超过申诉人的利益的原因，而且未能以符合公约的方式平衡申诉人和雇主的权利。特别是，教会的利益没有与申诉人享有的要求尊重其私人和家庭生活的权利相平衡，而是仅与申诉人保留其职位的利益相平衡；没有适当考虑申诉人的活动与教会宣称的使命之间的关系，也没有考虑根据申诉人的资质能否找到另一个职位；国内法院没有适当审查下面这一事实：申诉人并没有反对天主教会所采取的立场，而仅是没有在实践中遵守这些立场。此外，欧洲人权法院认为，申诉人在签署雇佣合同同时接受对天主教会的忠诚义务不能被视为明确的个人承诺，即承诺其在分居或离婚的情况下过禁欲的生活(*Schüth v. Germany*)。

191. 在下列案件中，欧洲人权法院认为没有违反第8条：

- 在德国耶稣基督后期圣徒教会（摩门教会）公共关系部的欧洲主任向上司透露他与别人保持婚外关系之后，上司在没有适当通知的情况下解雇了他。不同于舒特案(*Schüth*)，欧洲人权法院接受了劳动法庭的论据，认为他们充分地证明了，鉴于摩门教会教义中通奸的严重性以及申诉人在教会中所担当的重要公共职务，为了保护摩门教会的可信度，对申诉人施加的忠诚义务是可以接受的。德国法院也提供了充分的解释，说明为什么不是首先要求雇主施加更宽松的惩罚，如警告(*Obst v. Germany*)；

- 不与申诉人续签雇佣合同。申诉人是一名还俗的天主教神父并已经结婚，教廷将其从独身身份中分离开来，之前曾在国立中学被聘为天主教的宗教和伦理教师，这项决定是根据地方教区的一份备忘录提出的，备忘录中提到，对于他的家庭状况和他属于"选择独身运动"的新闻报道造成了教会法中的"丑闻"。欧洲人权法院首先指出，对于申诉人而言，限制较弱的措施当然不会在维持教会的可信度方面具有同样的效力；另外，决定不续约其合同的后果在本案的特殊情况下并不过分，特别是考虑到申诉人明知而将自己置于完全违反教会规则的情况中(*Fernández Martínez v. Spain*［GC］)。

192. 关于公约第9条保护的雇员的权利，欧洲人权法院认为，在下面这一案件中，对教师的解雇行为没有违反从公约第9条所衍生出来的积极义务：一名教师受雇于德国新教教会运营的幼儿教育中心，在没有得到正式通知的情况下被解雇，理由是她同时是一个被称为"普世教会/人类兄弟会"的团体的活跃成员，该团体的教义被新教教会认为绝对违背自己的教义。国内法院对案件的情况进行了深入审查，并仔细平衡了相互冲突的利益。申诉人保留其职位的利益必须服从于新教教会维持其在公众眼中和将孩子送到该中心的家长眼中可信度的利益，以防止这些孩子受到任何来自一位自身是某个宗教团体（其教义与教会规则相矛盾）成员的教师的影响，这是完全合理的（Siebenhaar v. Germany）。

193. 关于公约第 10 条保护的受宗教组织雇用的个人的言论自由，委员会宣布对德国天主教医院雇用的一名医生提起的申诉不予受理，该医生签署了一份在媒体上发表的公开信，在堕胎的问题上表达了与天主教会的立场相矛盾的意见，因此被医院解雇。虽然委员会承认，仅有申诉人接受在天主教医院就业这一事实并不意味着放弃了他的言论自由，但同时指出，他已自愿接受对教会的忠诚义务，这就使得他的言论自由被限制在某种程度之内。申诉人曾为了保护其言论自由寻求国内法院的救济，该法院的判例法确认教会对其雇员施加其观点的权利不是无限的，过分的要求是不可接受的。事实上，天主教医院的医生的职位涉及行使教会的一项基本使命，鉴于教会对堕胎问题的极度重视，禁止教会医生发表与教会关于堕胎的立场相矛盾的声明并不过分 [Rommelfanger v. Germany（dec.）]。

194. 罗马教廷天主教教育公理会拒绝与圣心米兰天主教大学的一名法哲学教授续签订工作合同，理由是该教授的一些立场"明显与天主教教义不相符"，但是公理会未能说明是哪些立场，欧洲人权法院认为天主教教育公理会的行为违反了第 10 条。欧洲人权法院指出，国家当局没有义务审查公理会决定的实质内容。但是，申诉人没有收到就其非正统意见提出指控的通知，国内法院将对该决定的合法性的审查局限于法学院委员会已经注意到存在拒绝同意这一事实。然而，通知这些事实绝不会使得司法当局有必要对申诉人的立场与天主教教义之间的相容性做出决定；另外，它将使申诉人能够认识到并因此质疑所述意见与他作为天主教大学教师的活动之间的所谓不相容性。大学提供基于天主教教义的教学的利益重要性不能侵犯申诉人根据公约第 10 条享有的程序性保障的实质内容（Lombardi Vallauri v. Italy）。

195. 关于神职人员和其他宗教领袖可能享有的结社自由，欧洲人权法院必须首先确定有关人员是否在"雇佣关系"的框架内为公约第 11 条的目的执行任务。如果是这样，国内法院的任务是确保结社自由和宗教团体的自治权都可以依据可适用的法律（包括公约）在这些团体内得到遵守。在涉及干预结社自由的情况下，根据公约第 9 条，宗教团体有权就其成员进行的任何可能损害其自治权的集体活动提出自己的意见，而且这一意见原则上必须受国家当局尊重。然而,宗教团体仅声称其自治权受到实际或潜在的威胁,不足以使其对成员工会权利的干预符合公约第 11 条规定。它还必须根据个别案件的情况表明所称的风险是真实和实质性的,对结社自由的干预不会超出消除这种风险所必需的限度,并且不能服务于任何其他与宗教社团自治权的行使无关的目的(Sindicatul 'Păstorul cel Bun' v. Romania [GC], § 159)。

196. 罗马尼亚当局拒绝承认和登记由罗马尼亚东正教的一群神职人员和雇员组成的工会,因为大主教没有给予其同意和祝福,根据前面提到的原则,欧洲人权法院认为,罗马尼亚当局的做法没有违反公约第 11 条。拒绝的决定基于经政府法令批准并纳入国内法的教会法和教会规约做出。鉴于所有证据,欧洲人权法院认为,尽管罗马尼亚东正教的神职人员有特殊的情况和精神使命,但他们履行使命时是在"雇佣关系"的背景下进行的,因此原则上可以根据第 11 条要求享有结社自由的权利,特别是因为罗马尼亚法院已经明确承认东正教神职人员和雇员的工会权利。此外,欧洲人权法院认为,应诉国当局的干预行为可以被认为与所追求的合法目标相称,因此符合公约第 11 条第 2 款的要求。在拒绝登记申诉工会时,国家只是拒绝参与罗马尼亚东正教的组织和运作,从而遵守其中的义务。工会登记申请不符合教会规约的要求,因为其成员没有遵守设立这种协会的特别程序。此外,没有其他因素阻止申诉工会成员利用公约第 11 条规定的权利,组建一个追求与教会规约相符的目的的协会,又不至于给教会的传统等级结构和决策程序带来问题(Sindicatul 'Păstorul cel Bun' v. Romania [GC], § 159)。

197. 关于公约第 6 条第 1 款所保障的寻求法院救济的权利,欧洲人权法院宣布对一项由两名捷克斯洛伐克胡斯教会的前神父提起的申诉不予受理,他们被教区委员会决定解雇,他们请求法院判决确认上述决定的非法性并要求教会支付拖欠工资。捷克法院支持了他们的第二点诉请(支付拖欠工资),但驳回了第一点诉请(决定的非法性),因为国内法院拒绝审查上述决定的实体事实——教会因其自治地位而对该项决定享有唯一的管辖权。欧洲人权法院认为,申诉人提起的诉讼没有涉及国内法承认的可争辩的"权利",因此,这一申诉不符合欧洲人权法院的属事管辖 [Dudová and Duda v. Czech Republic (dec.)]。

三、积极义务

(一)保护教会免遭第三人的人身、口头或象征性的攻击

198. 选择行使表达宗教自由的个人不能合理地期望在这样做时免受任何批评。相

反,宗教团体的成员必须容忍和接受他人否定他们的宗教信仰,甚至传播与他们信仰敌对的教义[Dubowska and Skup v. Poland (dec.)]。然而,如果对宗教信仰进行反对或拒绝的方式是禁止拥有这种信仰的人行使其拥有或表达其自由的权利,那么国家就有责任介入。在这种情况下,国家应确保信徒和平地享有第9条所保障的权利[Church of Scientology and Others v. Sweden (dec.);Begheluri v. Georgia,§160]。事实上,一国在有效尊重公约第9条所保障的权利方面可能存在某些积极义务,这可能涉及采取某些旨在确保尊重宗教自由的措施,甚至是在个人之间关系的领域。在某些情况下,这些措施可以是一种确保个人进行礼拜时不会受到他人的活动干扰的法律手段[Dubowska and Skup v. Poland (dec.)]。

199. 当一群人组织一场游行示威活动以表明反对某一特定宗教群体的信仰或习俗时,两种基本权利会发生冲突:游行示威者的言论与和平集会自由(公约第10条和第11条),以及宗教团体在没有不公正的外部干涉的条件下和平表达其信仰的权利。所有这些权利都受到公约的平等保护;两者都不是绝对的,它们的行使可能受上述条款第二段规定的限制。公约没有预先在这些权利之间建立任何等级:原则上,它们应得到平等尊重。因此,它们必须相互平衡,以便尊重它们在多元化、包容和心胸豁达的社会中的重要性。在这样做时,国家必须遵守以下三个原则:

(1)在尽可能合理的范围内,国家必须确保两项相互冲突的权利受到保护;这一义务对国家当局来说是义不容辞的,即使可能妨碍自由行使其中任一权利的行为是由私人发起的;

(2)国家必须确保建立适当的法律框架——特别是为了保护上述权利免受第三方的侵害,并且必须采取有效行动,确保权利在实践中得到尊重;

(3)欧洲人权法院在行使欧洲审查权时,有义务根据整个案件核实国家当局是否在公约所载的各种相互冲突的权利之间实现了公正的平衡。在这样做时,欧洲人权法院不应以事后的利益行事,也不应该简单地以自身意见代替国家当局的意见。在任何特定情况下,国家当局都处于更好的立场评估在何处实现适当的平衡,以及如何最好地实现这种平衡。对于警察必须在实践中达到这种平衡的情况,尤为如此。考虑到监管现代社会的困难,警察或其他当局的积极义务必须以不对他们施加不可能或不成比例的负担的方式进行解释(Karaahmed v. Bulgaria,§§91-96)。

200. 根据同一推理方法,在下列案件中,欧洲人权法院认为违反了公约:

- 违反了第 9 条,同时违反了公约第 14 条(禁止歧视):一名被免去圣职的东正教牧师领导一群人对正在和平集会的耶和华见证人信徒进行人身攻击,申诉人遭到猛烈的暴力殴打和侮辱,他们的宗教文学作品在其眼前被烧毁。警察拒绝立即当场进行干预以保护申诉人,随后,申诉人遭到了有关当局的漠视,因为有关当局对耶和华见证人充满敌意,拒绝执行可适用的法律或对他们的诉求采取任何行动(*Members of the Gldani Congregation of the Jehovah's Witnesses and Others v. Georgia*;也参见 *Begheluri v. Georgia*);

- 单独违反第 9 条,但不违反第 14 条:游行示威已转变为暴力——但该游行之前已被宣布符合法律规定因此是合法的,而且是由一个政党的成员组织的抗议星期五祈祷的活动,在保加利亚首都索非亚的清真寺内外举行(威胁喊叫和手势;扔鸡蛋;在清真寺屋顶上放置扬声器以淹没祈祷召唤的声音;试图焚烧祈祷垫;游行示威者强迫集会成员进入清真寺并对成员进行人身攻击等)。在这种情况下,保加利亚当局没有做出任何符合合理期望的、确保双方行使其各自权利自由的措施。在已经意识到有关当事方对伊斯兰和土耳其人秉持非常消极立场的情况下,当局完全可以通过将示威者安排在与清真寺保持安全距离的地方以尽量减少暴力的风险,但他们未能做到。此外,现场的警察人数显然不足以控制这种情况,他们的行为十分被动,无法保护集会成员。最后,当局在事件发生后进行的调查不符合必要的有效性标准(*Karaahmed v. Bulgaria*)。

201. 此外,第 9 条(与第 10 条和第 11 条一样)不能被解释为授权不同意宗教组织某一观点的个人中断或干扰仪式。欧洲人权法院宣布一项由一名罗马尼亚东正教修女提起的申诉明显缺乏依据,该名修女积极参与谴责其教会等级结构中的弊端,并在罗马尼亚东正教牧师举行的仪式上造成骚乱,喊叫:(或大声说)"他不值得祷告",因此被判处罚款。罚款的目的是惩罚其造成公众骚乱,而不是惩罚其表达意见,因此,欧洲人权法院认为,当局在这类事项上的正常自由裁量权范围内做出了回应[*Bulgaru v. Romania* (dec.)]。

202. 此外,欧洲人权法院认为,对宗教崇拜物品的挑衅性描绘在某些情况下可能违反第 9 条规定的信徒的权利(*Otto-Preminger-Institut v. Austria*,§ 47)。然而,欧洲人权法院迄今为止几乎总是按照公约第 10 条(言论自由)审理这种类型的案件,对因违反对信徒情感的必要尊重而被制裁的人提起的申诉进行判决[*Otto-Preminger-Institut v.*

Austria；*Wingrove v. the United Kingdom*；*I. A. v. Turkey*；*Giniewski v. France*；*Klein v. Slovakia*；也参见 *X. Ltd. and Y. v. the United Kingdom*（dec.）]。

203. 公约机构迄今为止一直驳回宗教情感受到侵犯的人根据第 9 条提起的申诉。特别是第 9 条所保障的免受干预的权利并不一定在任何情况下都意味着有权对通过作者身份或出版物侵犯一个人或一群人情感的行为提起任何特定形式的诉讼[*Dubowska and Skup v. Poland*（dec.）]。在下列案件中，公约机构驳回了这类申诉：

- 神学教授在演讲过程中发表了对于山达基教会的具有敌意的评论，随后在当地报纸上出版，山达基教会就此要求获得损害赔偿，但因为科学教会对损害赔偿缺乏诉讼资格，但它没有证明有关评论阻碍了申诉人行使第 9 条规定的权利，因此欧洲人权法院以缺乏诉讼资格为由驳回该申诉[*Church of Scientology and Others v. Sweden*（dec.）]；

- 萨尔曼·鲁西迪和出版商分别撰写和出版了小说《撒旦诗篇》，从伊斯兰教角度看，这本书是亵渎神灵的，英国当局拒绝对二者提起刑事诉讼[*Choudhury v. the United Kingdom*（dec.）]；

- 波兰公共检察官办公室决定终止针对一本周刊杂志的主编提起有关公开侮辱宗教情感的刑事诉讼，该主编在杂志封面用防毒面具取代了琴斯托霍瓦处女和儿童的脸，而琴斯托霍瓦处女和儿童的标志在波兰全境深得崇敬。控方认为，该图像是用来说明波兰的空气污染状况，并没有刻意冒犯宗教情感。委员会注意到，申诉人已经就其遭受侮辱的宗教情感获得了国内法院的救济，他们也信赖该项救济。检察官在对案件的所有情况和相互冲突的利益进行认真的审查之后，驳回了该案。在这种情况下，申诉人没有被阻止行使第 9 条规定的权利，而且当局最终认为，没有犯下任何罪行本身不能被视为未能保护由该条款保障的权利。出于同样的原因，委员会认为不存在第 14 条禁止的歧视[*Dubowska and Skup v. Poland*（dec.）；*Kubalska and Kubalska-Holuj v. Poland*（dec.）]；

- 生活在摩洛哥的一个摩洛哥国民以及在该国建立和运作的两个摩洛哥协会针对丹麦提起的申诉，控诉丹麦当局拒绝禁止和惩罚涉及伊斯兰教先知穆罕默德的一系列漫画的出版。欧洲人权法院指出，根据公约第 1 条的目的，从管辖权方面来看，申诉人和丹麦之间没有联系，甚至也不存在"域外行为"的情况[*Ben El Mahi and Others v. Denmark*（dec.）]。

(二)工作场所、军队和法院的宗教

204. 关于武装部队成员在履行职责过程中表现其宗教的权利,欧洲人权法院裁决,各国可以对其军队采取规定禁止特定类型行为的方式,特别是针对某种有害于兵役要求的既定秩序的行为。例如,欧洲人权法院认为,法官支持在土耳其空军部队中约束空军上校的等级,这种做法没有干预宗教自由,理由是"他的行为和态度表明他已采纳了非法的原教旨主义观点"。欧洲人权法院指出,在选择从事军事职业时,申诉人自己接受了一种军事纪律制度,其本质上意味着有可能对武装部队成员的某些权利和自由施加那些不可能施加于平民的限制。申诉人在军事生活要求的限制范围内,能够履行其宗教所规定的宗教义务;该案中采取的措施并不是基于他的宗教观点和信仰或者他履行宗教职责的方式,而是基于他的行为和态度,因为他的行为和态度违反了军事纪律和世俗主义原则[*Kalaç v. Turkey*;类似案例参见 *Çinar v. Turkey*(dec.);*Acarca v. Turkey*(dec.);*Sert v. Turkey*(dec.)]。

205. 在其他土耳其案件中,公约机构指出,在土耳其的特殊情况下,兵役的限制可能包括军事人员负有不得参加穆斯林原教旨主义运动的义务——该运动的目的和方案是确保宗教规则的优先权[*Yanaşık v. Turkey*(dec.);*Tepeli and Others v. Turkey*(dec.)]。特别是,土耳其军事学院禁止那些自由选择了军事职业并能在军事生活范围内履行其宗教义务的学员加入伊斯兰原教旨主义运动,这并不构成对宗教和良心自由的干预[*Yanaşık v. Turkey*(dec.)]。

206. 欧洲人权法院在一名俄罗斯法官的案件中遵循了类似的逻辑,该名法官因为没有履行司法机关的义务并损害了司法机关的权威而被解雇。本案中的申诉人利用其法官职位来促进其宗教团体的利益,并威胁她的诉讼当事人(例如,她在法庭听证期间公开祷告,向某些诉讼当事人许诺如果他们加入教会就给予他们有利结果,并从基督教角度公开批评某些当事人的道德)。因此,申诉人不是因她属于教会或具有任何其他"地位"而被解雇,而是因为她的具体活动,因为其具体活动与司法职位的要求不符,违反了法治原则。因此,欧洲人权法院认为,在申诉人行使其根据第10条和第9条所享有的权利时受到了干预,但这种干预与所追求的合法目的相称[*Pitkevich v. Russia*(dec.)]。

207. 在此之前,委员会驳回了一名律师提起的申诉,该律师也是一名被授以圣职的天主教神父(虽然他从未履行过神父职务)。他(根据单独的第9条并结合第14条)控诉比利时司法部长拒绝其对于替代法官职位的申请,而根据比利时法律规定,法官职位与教会职位不可兼得。委员会首先认为,申诉人在行使其宗教权利包括他的神父职责方面没有受到阻碍;其次,公约本身并没有确保其申请司法职位的权利[*Demeester v. Belgium*(dec.);但是,根据第一议定书第 3 条,参见 *Seyidzade v. Azerbaijan*]。

208. 在公共部门的雇佣关系框架内,保加利亚国家职业学校的一名游泳池管理员是新教会成员,鉴于其反对该教区的政治/媒体运动的社会背景被解雇,欧洲人权法院认为这违反了第 9 条。即使上述解雇行为符合劳动立法,并且上述解雇是由于岗位资格标准发生变化而申诉人没有达到新标准,但欧洲人权法院对案件的整体事实进行了分析,得出结论,认为采取该措施的真正原因是申诉人的宗教信仰。此外,政府没有提供任何证据证明申诉人曾在学校传教或犯有任何专业错误(*Ivanova v. Bulgaria*)。

209. 某些宗教的仪式规则(不要与上文第 52－61 段提及的道德规范相混淆)有时会与其信徒的专业义务相冲突,因此他们要求其雇主(无论是公共的还是私人的)采用具体措施以接纳他们。但是,欧洲人权法院认为,根据第 9 条,其没有在特定宗教庆祝日离开工作岗位的权利(*Kosteski v. the former Yugoslav Republic of Macedonia*,§ 45)。

210. 在以这个角度审查的案件中,委员会总是拒绝向申诉人提供公约第 9 条第 1 款的保护,因为对他们采取的行动不是基于他们的宗教信仰,而是基于他们与雇主之间具体的合同义务。在下列案件中,委员会以这种方式进行了裁决:

- 英国教育当局拒绝准许申诉人——一名信仰伊斯兰教的国立学校教师,离开工作岗位去清真寺参加星期五祷告。他被迫辞职,然后再次以较低工资的兼职方式被雇用。委员会拒绝详细审查伊斯兰教是否和在多大程度上要求在清真寺参加星期五祷告的问题;它简单地指出,申诉人自愿接受合同规定的教学义务,因而使其不能同时在周五进行教育机构工作和参加星期五祷告。此外,在他为学校服务的前六年,申诉人没有在星期五离开工作岗位或者通知他的雇主他可能需要在正常上课时间休息,以便在清真寺祷告。此外,鉴于组织教育制度的紧迫性,委员会没有被要求代替国家当局审查何为教育领域最好的政策[*X. v. the United Kingdom*(dec.)];

- 芬兰国家铁路公司的一名雇员是基督复临安息日会的成员,而该会禁止其成员在星期五日落后工作,该雇员因未能遵守正常工作时间被芬兰国家铁路公司解雇。委员会认为不存在宗教歧视(公约第 14 条),因为国家立法规定,星期日是

平常的每周休息日[*Konttinen v. Finland*(déc.)];
- 私人部门雇主(一家旅行社)因其雇员拒绝在星期日工作解雇了该雇员[*Stedman v. Royaume Uni*(dec.)]。

211. 马其顿电力公司(一家公共事业公司)对申诉人——该公司的一名雇员,实行纪律处分(暂时减薪),欧洲人权法院同样认为没有违反公约第9条。该雇员宣称他是一个穆斯林,在一年的时间里,两次因为伊斯兰宗教节日而离开工作岗位。国内法院承认,法律允许穆斯林公民在其宗教节日上享有带薪假的权利。然而,从申诉人的具体情况来看,他自称属于上述宗教的可信度是值得怀疑的,因为他不了解该宗教的基本教义,而且以前他一直庆祝基督教节日。因此,国内法院认为,申诉人声称其为穆斯林仅仅是为了从额外的休假中受益。欧洲人权法院认为,如果法律规定特定宗教团体的成员享有特权或特别豁免(特别是在就业领域),则要求有关人员对其属于某宗教提供某种程度的证据是不违反第9条规定的(根据与出于良心反对服兵役的情况相同的逻辑,申诉人原则上必须能够证明他的信念的可信度)。因此,欧洲人权法院对案件是否涉及申诉人所称宗教的"表达"表示怀疑,在第9条第2款的意义上,认为被控诉的干预是为了保护他人权利而在"民主社会所必要的"。欧洲人权法院还认为,不存在任何第14条意义上的歧视(*Kosteski v. the former Yugoslav Republic of Macedonia*)。

212. 关于司法程序当事人的宗教自由:
- 委员会宣布对两名奥地利犹太教人士提起的申诉不予受理,申诉人是民事诉讼中的被告,他们控诉法院拒绝对在犹太盛节期间举行的听证会予以延期。委员会主要根据第6条第1款(获得公正审判的权利)对案件进行了审查,发现缺少了对申诉人的调查,因为申诉人花了太长时间提醒法院关于时间的不相容性。委员会还单独根据第9条以及结合第14条(禁止歧视)驳回了申诉人的申诉[*S. H. and H. V. v. Austria*(dec.)];
- 刑事案件中两名原告之一的犹太宗教律师申请延期开庭,因为开庭日期正好是犹太教假期,司法当局拒绝了其请求,欧洲人权法院认为这没有违反公约第9条。申诉人没有出席听证会,因此听证会在其缺席的情况下进行。欧洲人权法院认为,根据现行法律规定,申诉人应该预料到他的请求将被拒绝,而且他可以安排他人代替他参加有关的听证会(*Francesco Sessa v. Italy*)。

(三) 囚犯的宗教自由

213. 国家当局必须尊重囚犯的宗教自由，避免任何不正当干预行使公约第 9 条规定的权利的行为，并且考虑到监狱环境的特殊要求，在必要时应采取积极行动，为这些权利的自由行使提供便利条件。特别是，在监狱中祈祷、阅读宗教书籍和在其他囚犯面前冥想难免有所不便，但这并不违反表达自己宗教的自由的本质 [*Kovaļkovs v. Latvia* (dec.)]。此外，作为一般规则，第 9 条没有给予囚犯在被拘押的机构中传教的权利，也没有给予其在该机构以外表达宗教的权利 [*J. L. v. Finland* (dec.)]。

214. 同样，第 9 条并没有赋予囚犯不被认为是具有与其他囚犯不同的特殊地位的"政治犯"的权利，也没有赋予其免受管理监禁生活的一般规则约束的权利，例如，参加劳动、穿戴监狱制服和打扫他们的监室 [*McFeeley and Others v. the United Kingdom* (dec.); *X. v. the United Kingdom* (dec.)]。委员会还认为，第 9 条没有规定缔约国有任何一般义务向囚犯提供其认为为践行宗教或发展其生活哲学所必需的设施 (参见 *X. v. Austria*, no. 1753/63①)。

215. 在下列案件中，欧洲人权法院认为违反了公约第 9 条：

- 被判处死刑但刑罚随后被减刑至终身监禁的人不能接受牧师的探视 (*Poltoratski v. Ukraine*, §§ 163 – 171, ECHR 2003 – V; *Kuznetsov v. Ukraine*, §§ 143 – 151);
- 相关法官拒绝批准已被还押的申诉人参加在监狱牧师工作处举行的宗教庆祝活动，这种拒绝行为缺乏国内法依据 (*Igors Dmitrijevs v. Latvia*);
- 监狱管理部门拒绝向申诉人——一名佛教徒，提供无肉餐，尽管这样的安排不会对监狱造成过重的负担 (*Jakóbski v. Poland*)。

216. 在下列案件中，公约机构认为没有违反第 9 条：

- 禁止佛教囚犯蓄留山羊胡 (理由是需要避免妨碍他的身份认定)，拒绝返还他的佛珠——佛珠在他入狱时已被安全保管。委员会认为，这些限制符合第 9 条第 2 款，因为它们旨在维护公共秩序 (参见 *X. v. Austria*, no. 1753/63②);
- 一名被关押在德国的英国国民声称无法参加英国圣公会服务或接受英国圣公

---

① 裁定只有书面文本，请见欧洲人权法院图书馆《欧洲人权公约年鉴》。
② 裁定只有书面文本，请见欧洲人权法院图书馆《欧洲人权公约年鉴》。

会牧师的探视。委员会认为申诉人事实上已能接触到新教徒和新教牧师[X. v. Germany（dec.）]；

- 禁止佛教囚犯投送文章在佛教杂志上出版，尽管申诉人没有解释为什么遵守他的宗教规则涉及或要求出版这些文章[X. v. the United Kingdom（dec.）]；另一案件中是拒绝准许佛教囚犯订阅罗马天主教杂志，尽管后者显然与他的宗教没有任何联系（参见 X. v. Austria，no. 1753/63①）；

- 一名东正教犹太人针对其关押条件提起申诉，但是他被提供犹太素食，还被允许在监狱牧师的协助下接受犹太人的探视，大拉比也同意了当局为了保障申诉人宗教权利所采取的这些措施[X v. the United Kingdom（dec.）]；

- 监狱管理部门拦截了一名道教囚犯订阅的哲学/宗教书籍，理由是书中包含了一章关于武术的带有插图的内容；这种干预对于保护"他人的权利和自由"是必要的[X. v. the United Kingdom（dec.）]；

- 监狱主任拒绝将申诉人作为威卡教信徒记入监狱登记册。委员会认为，如果这种登记涉及囚犯实践其宗教的某些特权和便利，则对于所宣称的宗教是可以辨认的这一要求是合理的；然而，申诉人没有提供任何证据证明这种宗教的客观存在[X. v. the United Kingdom（dec.）]。在类似的情况下，委员会驳回了一名声称是"光明的信徒"的囚犯的申诉，该囚犯没有解释他如何实践其宗教或当局如何阻碍他实践宗教[X. v. Germany（dec.）]；

- 对申诉人拒绝穿制服和进行清洁牢房的一系列惩罚。申诉人称，作为锡克教徒，他拒绝承认在他自己和上帝之间有其他权威的存在，特别是因为他认为他是一个"政治犯"（因此他拒绝穿制服）。此外，由于他是高级种姓，他"在文化上不能接受"清洁地板的任务（因此他拒绝清洁他的牢房）。委员会宣布第一项申诉（关于制服）与公约不符（部分属事管辖和部分属人管辖），第二项申诉明显缺乏依据：即使假定存在对申诉人宗教自由的干预，这种干预也是为了保护健康所必要的，而且从第9条第2款的意义上来说是正当的[X. v. the United Kingdom（dec.）]；

- 由于囚犯拒绝在印刷店工作而对其施加纪律处分。该囚犯拒绝工作的理由是，作为素食主义者，他认为在道德上不能接受据称曾在动物身上进行测试的产品

---

① 裁定只有书面文本，请见欧洲人权法院图书馆《欧洲人权公约年鉴》。

（染料）。即使假设存在对申诉人第9条权利的干预，这种干预也是符合第9条第2款的。一方面，委员会接受了应诉国政府的论据，即有必要建立一个被认为是公平的、没有偏袒的工作分配制度；另一方面，委员会也注意到了处罚的宽容性[*W. v. the United Kingdom*（dec.）]；

- 拒绝批准申诉人参加弥撒——申诉人被认为具有危险性并受到特别高度安全的拘留，但是申诉人能够从他的牢房看到弥撒，而且他从来没有声称被阻止接受牧师的探视[*Indelicato v. Italy*（dec.）；类似的案例参见 *Natoli v. Italy*（dec.）]；

- 申诉人是一名印度克里西纳派教徒，监狱管理部门拒绝批准给予他一个单独的房间以便他阅读、祈祷、冥想和阅读宗教材料，并没收他的香火棒，理由是需要尊重其他囚犯的权利[*Kovaļkovs v. Latvia*（dec.）]。

217. 欧洲人权法院还驳回了一名犯有一系列非常严重罪行的申诉人提起的申诉。该申诉人曾被强行关押在精神病医院。由于申诉人说他是耶和华见证人，医院允许他与该宗教组织保持联系；然而，他因为向其他病人和医院工作人员布道和散发传单而受到警告。欧洲人权法院认为，为了维持医院秩序和保护其他病人的利益，这项措施是必要的。对于其余措施，欧洲人权法院认为，申诉人根据第9条所享有的权利已经得到了尊重[*J. L. v. Finland*（dec.）]。

援引案例一览

本指南援引的判例法涉及欧洲人权法院的判决或裁定以及欧洲人权委员会的决定或报告。

除非另行指明，所有参考皆是欧洲人权法院审判庭依法作出的判决。缩写"(dec.)"是指该处援引为欧洲人权法院裁定，"[GC]"是指该案件由大审判庭审判。

本指南电子版中援引案例的超链接直接跳转 HUDOC 数据库(http://hudoc.echr.coe.int)。该数据库提供欧洲人权法院(包括大审判庭、审判庭和委员会的判决、裁定和相关案例、咨询意见以及案例法信息注解中的法律总结)、委员会(决定和报告)和部长委员会(决议)的判例法。

欧洲人权法院以英语和/或法语这两种官方语言发布判决和裁定。HUDOC 也包含许多重要案例的近 30 种非官方言语的翻译，以及由第三方制作的大约 100 个在线案例汇总的链接。

（注：为了避免重复，本章所附的相关案例索引没有在中文部分进行翻译，读者可在对应的英文部分阅读。）

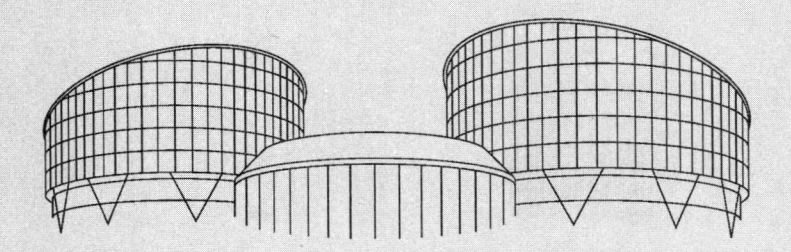

EUROPEAN COURT OF HUMAN RIGHTS
COUR EUROPÉENNE DES DROITS DE L'HOMME

Chapter VI   Guide to Article 9
Freedom of Thought, Conscience and Religion

COUNCIL OF EUROPE

CONSEIL DE L'EUROPE

Publishers or organisations wishing to translate and/or reproduce all or part of this report in the form of a printed or electronic publication are invited to contact publishing@echr.coe.int for information on the authorisation procedure.

©Council of Europe/ European Court of Human Rights, 2015

This document can be downloaded at the following address: www.echr.coe.int (Case-law-Case-law analysis-Case-law guide).

The present document was prepared by the Research and Library Division, within the Directorate of the Jurisconsult and is not binding on the Court. The text was completed on 1 September 2015; it may be subject to editorial revision.

Notice to readers

This guide constitutes an explanation of the case-law of the organs of the Convention (judgments and decisions of the European Court of Human Rights, and decisions and reports of the European Commission of Human Rights) concerning Article 9 of the Convention. It covers the period from 1957 to 1 September 2015.

However, the following are not mentioned in the report:

- cases concerning Article 9 which ended with striking out or an inadmissibility decision on formal grounds (such as non-exhaustion of domestic remedies, non-compliance with the six-month rule or incompatibility *ratione temporis*);
- straightforward repetitive cases (for example, decisions against Turkey in cases such as *Kalaç*);
- case-law which has become irrelevant following a clear and unequivocal reversal of case-law (for example, cases relating to conscientious objection *vis-à-vis* military service dealt with prior to the *Bayatyan v. Armenia* judgment).

The following abbreviations will be used:

- "the Commission"-the European Commission of Human Rights, abolished under Protocol No. 11 to the Convention on 1 November 1998;
- "*Yearbook*"-the *Yearbook of the European Convention of Human Rights*;
- "DR"-Reports and Decisions of the Commission.

> **Article 9**
>
> "1. *Everyone has the right to freedom of thought, conscience and religion; this right includes freedom to change his religion or belief and freedom, either alone or in community with others and in public or private, to manifest his religion or belief, in worship, teaching, practice and observance.*
>
> *2. Freedom to manifest one's religion or beliefs shall be subject only to such limitations as are prescribed by law and are necessary in a democratic society in the interests of public safety, for the protection of public order, health or morals, or for the protection of the rights and freedoms of others.*"

I. Introduction

1. Freedom of thought, conscience and religion is a fundamental right which is enshrined not only in the European Convention on Human Rights (hereafter "the Convention") but also in a wide range of national, international and European texts.

2. Under the terms of Article 9 of the Convention,

"1. Everyone has the right to freedom of thought, conscience and religion; this right includes freedom to change his religion or belief and freedom, either alone or in community with others and in public or private, to manifest his religion or belief, in worship, teaching, practice and observance.

2. Freedom to manifest one's religion or beliefs shall be subject only to such limitations as are prescribed by law and are necessary in a democratic society in the interests of public safety, for the protection of public order, health or morals, or for the protection of the rights and freedoms of others."

3. Article 2 of Protocol No. 1 to the Convention concerns one specific aspect of freedom of religion, namely the right of parents to ensure the education of their children in accordance with their religious convictions:

"No person shall be denied the right to education. In the exercise of any functions which it assumes in relation to education and to teaching, the State shall respect the right of parents to ensure such education and teaching for their children in conformity with their own religious and philosophical convictions. "

4. Article 9 is often relied upon in conjunction with Article 14 of the Convention, which prohibits discrimination based on, among other things, religion and opinions:

"The enjoyment of the rights and freedoms set forth in [the] Convention shall be secured without discrimination on any ground such as sex, race, colour, language, **religion**, political or **other opinion**, national or social origin, association with a national minority, property, birth or other status. "

5. Beyond the Convention, freedom of thought, conscience and religion is quite obviously also one of the United Nations' main fondamental rights. For instance, under the terms of Article 18 of the International Covenant on Civil and Political Rights, everyone has the right to freedom of thought, conscience and religion; this right includes freedom to have or to adopt a religion or belief of one's choice, and freedom, either individually or in community with others and in public or private, to manifest one's religion or belief in worship, observance, practice and teaching. No one may be subject to coercion which would impair his freedom to have or to adopt a religion or belief of his choice. Freedom to manifest one's religion or beliefs may be subject only to such limitations as are prescribed by law and are necessary to protect public safety, order, health, or morals or the fundamental rights and freedoms of others. Furthermore, Article 18 *in fine* specifies that the States Parties to the Covenant undertake to have respect for the liberty of parents and, when applicable, legal guardians to ensure the religious and moral education of their children in conformity with their own convictions. Article 26 of the Covenant sets forth a general non-discrimination principle, which also covers religion.

6. The principle of freedom of religion also appears in a number of other texts, including the International Convention on the Rights of the Child, Article 14 of which sets it out very clearly. Similary, Article 12 of the American Convention on Human Rights states

that everyone has the right to freedom of conscience and religion. This right includes the freedom to maintain or to change one's religion or beliefs, as well as the freedom to profess or disseminate one's religion or beliefs, either individually or together with others, in public or in private. No one may be subject to restrictions that might impair his freedom to maintain or to change his religion or beliefs. Freedom to manifest one's religion and beliefs may be subject only to the limitations prescribed by law that are necessary to protect public safety, order, health, or morals, or the rights or freedoms of others. Lastly, Article 12 of the American Convention provides that parents or guardians, as the case may be, have the right to provide for the religious and moral education of their children or wards that is in accord with their own convictions.

7. The European Union Charter of Fundamental RIghts also protects freedom of thought, conscience and religion in the same way as the Convention (Article 10 of the Charte). It also lays down parents' right to "ensure the education and teaching of their children in conformity with their religious, philosophical and pedagogical convictions shall be respected, in accordance with the national laws governing the exercise of such … right" (Article 14 § 3).

8. The importance of freedom of thought, conscience and religion has been emphasised on several occasions by the European Court of Human Rights (hereafter "the Court"). Broadly speaking, freedom of thought, conscience and religion is considered as one of the foundations of democratic society; more specifically, the European judges regards religious freedom as a vital factor in forming the identity of believers and their conception of life. In fact, the Court raised freedom of religion to the rank of a substantive right under the Convention, at first indirectly and, later on, more directly.

9. It should be noted that over the last fifteen years the number of cases examined by the Court under Article 9 has been constantly increasing; this trend can be explained by the increasing importance of religion and related matters in socio-political discourse.

II. General principles and applicability

1. The importance of Article 9 of the convention in a democratic society and the locus standi of religious bodies

10. Freedom of thought, conscience and religion as enshrined in Article 9 of the Convention represents one of the foundations of a "democratic society" within the meaning of the Convention. It is, in its religious dimension, one of the most vital elements that go to make up the identity of believers and their conception of life, but it is also a precious asset for atheists, agnostics, sceptics and the unconcerned. The pluralism indissociable from a democratic society, which has been dearly won over the centuries, depends on it. That freedom entails, *inter alia*, freedom to hold or not to hold religious beliefs and to practise or not to practise a religion (*Kokkinakis v. Greece*, § 31; *Buscarini and Others v. San Marino* [GC], § 34).

11. An ecclesiastical or religious body may, as such, exercise on behalf of its adherents the rights guaranteed by Article 9 of the Convention (*Cha'are Shalom Ve Tsedek v. France* [GC], § 72; *Leela Förderkreis e. V. and Others v. Germany*, § 79). That means that a complaint lodged by a church or a religious organisation alleging a violation of the collective aspect of its adherents' freedom of religion is compatible *ratione personae* with the Convention, and the church or organisation may claim to be the "victim" of that violation within the meaning of Article 34 of the Convention.

12. On the other hand, in a case of denial of re-registration of an already recognised religious community, since that community had retained legal capacity to lodge an application with the Strasbourg Court, individual applicants could not themselves claim to be victims of a violation resulting from the domestic authorities' denial of re-registration, which affected only the applicant community as such. Their complaint under Article 9 was therefore incompatible *ratione personae* with the Convention (*Jehovah's Witnesses of Moscow and Others v. Russia*, § 168).

13. Although a **legal entity** can claim to be a victim of a violation of its freedom of *thought and religion*, it cannot exercise, as such, freedom of *conscience* [*Kontakt-Information-Therapie* (*KIT*) *and Hagen v. Austria*].

2. Convictions protected under Article 9

14. The word "religion" is defined neither by the text of Article 9 nor in the Court's case-law. This omission is quite logical, because such a definition would have to be both flexible enough to embrace the whole range of religions worldwide (major and minor, old and new, theistic and non-theistic) and specific enough to be applicable to individual cases-an extremely difficult, indeed impossible undertaking. On the one hand, the scope of Article 9 is very wide, as it protects both religious and non-religious opinions and convictions. On the other hand, **not all opinions or convictions necessarily fall within the scope of the provision, and the term "practice" as employed in Article 9 § 1 does not cover each act which is motivated or influenced by a religion or belief** (*Pretty v. the United Kingdom*, § 82).

15. If a personal or collective conviction is to benefit from the right to "freedom of thought, conscience and religion" it must attain a **certain level of cogency, seriousness, cohesion and importance.** Provided this condition is satisfied, the State's duty of neutrality and impartiality is incompatible with any power on the State's part to assess the legitimacy of religious beliefs or the ways in which those beliefs are expressed (*Eweida and Others v. the United Kingdom*, § 81). Therefore, it is not the Court's task to determine what principles and beliefs are to be considered central to any given religion or to enter into any other sort of interpretation of religious questions [*Kovaļkovs v. Latvia* (dec.), § 60].

16. The organs of the Convention have explicitly or implicitly acknowledged that the safeguards of Article 9 § 1 of the Convention apply to:

(a) the "major" or "ancient" world religions which have existed for millennia or for several centuries, such as:

- Alevism (*Sinan Işık v. Turkey*; *Cumhuriyetçi Eğitim ve Kültür Merkezi Vakfi v. Turkey*);

- Buddhism (*Jakóbski v. Poland*);
- the different Christian denominations (among many other authorities, *Sviato-Mykhaïlivska Parafiya v. Ukraine*; *Savez crkava 'Riječ života' and Others v. Croatia*);
- the various forms of Hinduism [*Kovaļkovs v. Latvia* (dec.)];
- Islam (*Hassan and Tchaouch v. Bulgaria* [GC]; *Leyla Şahin v. Turkey* [GC]);
- Judaism (*Cha'are Shalom Ve Tsedek v. France* [GC]; *Francesco Sessa v. Italy*,);
- Sikhism [*Phull v. France* (dec.); *Jasvir Singh v. France* (dec.)];
- Taoism [*X. v. the United Kingdom* (dec.)];

(b) new or relatively new religions such as:

- Aumism of Mandarom (*Association des Chevaliers du Lotus d'Or v. France*);
- the Bhagwan Shree Rajneesh movement, known as Osho (*Leela Förderkreis e.V. and Others v. Germany*);
- the Reverend Sun Myung Moon's Unification Church (*Nolan and K. v. Russia*; *Boychev and Others v. Bulgaria*);
- Mormonism, or the Church of Jesus Christ of Latter-Day Saints (*The Church of Jesus Christ of Latter-day Saints v. the United Kingdom*);
- the Raëlian Movement [*F.L. v. France* (dec.)];
- Neo-Paganism [*Ásatrúarfélagið v. Iceland* (dec.)];
- the "Santo Daime" religion, whose rituals include the use of a hallucinogenic substance known as "*ayahuasca*" [*Fränklin-Beentjes and CEFLU-Luz da Floresta v. the Netherlands* (dec.)];
- the Jehovah's Witnesses (*Religionsgemeinschaft der Zeugen Jehovas and Others v. Austria*; *Jehovah's Witnesses of Moscow and Others v. Russia*);

(c) various coherent and sincerely-held philosophical convictions, such as:

- pacifism (*Arrowsmith v. the United Kingdom*, § 69);
- principled opposition to military service (*Bayatyan v. Armenia* [GC]);

- veganism and opposition to the manipulation of products of animal origin or tested on animals [W. v. the United Kingdom (dec.)];
- opposition to abortion [Knudsen v. Norway (dec.), No. 11045/84, Commission decision of 8 March 1985, DR 42, p. 258; Van Schijndel and Others v. the Netherlands, (dec.)];
- a doctor's opinions on alternative medicine, constituting a form of manifestation of medical philosophy [Nyyssönen v. Finland (dec.)];
- the conviction that marriage is a lifelong union between a man and a woman and rejection of homosexual unions (Eweida and Others v. the United Kingdom).

17. By the same token, we might say that the answer to the question whether an activity which is wholly or partly based on a belief or a philosophy but which is **entirely profit-making** is eligible for protection under Article 9 is not yet completely clear. The Commission decided that a commercial limited-liability *company*, as a profit-making corporation-albeit one managed by a philosophical association-could neither benefit from nor rely upon the rights secured under Article 9 [Company X. v. Switzerland (dec.); Kustannus OY Vapaa Ajattelija AB and Others v. Finland (dec.)]. Similarly, the Commission decided that Article 9 did not protect statements of purported religious belief which appear as selling "arguments" in advertisements of a purely commercial nature by a religious group. In this connection the Commission drew a distinction between advertisements which were merely "informational" or "descriptive" in character and commercial advertisements offering objects for sale. Once an advertisement enters into the latter category, even if it concerns religious objects central to a particular need, statements of religious content represent the manifestation of a desire to market goods for profit rather than the manifestation of a belief in practice. In the case which they considered, the Commission refused to extend the protection of Article 9 to an advertisement for an "E-meter" or "Hubbard Electrometer", sanctioned by the consumer protection authorities [Church of Scientology and Others v. Sweden (dec.)].

18. In more recent cases, however, the Commission and the Court would appear to leave it open whether Article 9 applies to a profit-making *activity* conducted by a religious

organisation [the question arose in *Cumhuriyetçi Eğitim ve Kültür Merkezi Vakfi v. Turkey*; for yoga courses which were not free of charge, *Association Sivananda de Yoga Vedanta v. France* (dec.)].

19. In that context, the classification of **Scientology** as a "religion" is a bone of contention among the Contracting States. The Commission did not explicitly address this issue because the applications in question were in any case inadmissible for other reasons [*X. and Church of Scientology v. Sweden*, (dec.); *Church of Scientology and Others v. Sweden* (dec.); *Scientology Kirche Deutschland e. V. v. Germany* (dec.)]. Nevertheless, at least in the first and third of the three cases cited above, the Commission would seem implicitly to have accepted that the Church of Scientology was a "religious group".

20. The Court, which has directly tackled the Scientology issue, has, for its part, deferred to the judgment of the authorities in the respondent State. In a case concerning a refusal by the Russian authorities to register the Church of Scientology as a legal entity, the Court stated that it was not its task to decide *in abstracto* whether a body of beliefs and related practices could be considered a "religion" within the meaning of Article 9. In the instant case the local Centre of Scientology, which had initially been registered as a non-religious entity, was eventually dissolved on the ground that its activities were "religious in nature". The national authorities, including the courts, had consistently expressed the view that Scientology groups were religious in nature. Under those circumstances the Court considered that Article 9 of the Convention was applicable to the case before it (*Kimlya and Others v. Russia*, §§ 79 – 81; see also *Church of Scientology of Moscow v. Russia*, § 64). In another case, the same type of interference had been partly based on a religious study which had concluded that the activities of the group in question were not religious in nature. However, the Court noted that the interference had taken place in pursuance of a legislative provision which applied exclusively to religious organisations, and that Article 9 was therefore well and truly applicable (*Church of Scientology of St Petersburg and Others v. Russia*, § 32).

21. As regards **atheism**, the Commission considered complaints lodged by atheists

under Article 9 [*Angeleni v. Sweden* (dec.)]. In a slightly different context it stated that this current of thought only expressed a certain metaphysical conception of man which conditioned his perception of the world and justified his action and therefore could not be validly distinguished from a religious denomination in the traditional sense; therefore, the State was not justified in assigning it a legal status radically different from that of other religious denominations (*Union des Athées v. France*, § 79). Moreover, the Court has made it clear that freedom of thought, conscience and religion is "a precious asset for atheists, agnostics, sceptics and the unconcerned" (*Kokkinakis v. Greece*, § 31).

22. The Court has not yet issued a ruling on the applicability of Article 9 to **Freemasonry**; this question has been tacitly left open (*N. F. v. Italy*, §§ 35–40).

3. The right to hold a belief and the right to manifest it

23. Article 9 § 1 of the Convention contains two strands, one on the right to *hold* a belief and the other on the right to *manifest* that belief:

(a) the right to deeply **hold** any belief (whether religious or not) and to change one's religion or beliefs. This right is **absolute and unconditional**; the State cannot interfere with it, for instance by dictating what a person believes or taking coercive steps to make him change his beliefs (*Ivanova v. Bulgaria*);

(b) the right to **manifest** one's beliefs alone and in private, but also to practice them in company with others and in public. This right is not absolute: since the manifestation by one person of his or her religious belief may have an impact on others, the drafters of the Convention qualified this aspect of freedom of religion in the manner set out in Article 9 § 2. This second paragraph provides that any limitation placed on a person's freedom to manifest religion or belief must be prescribed by law and necessary in a democratic society in pursuit of one or more of the legitimate aims set out therein (*Eweida and Others v. the United Kingdom*, § 80). In other words, the limitations set out in Article 9 § 2 only relate to the freedom to *manifest* one's religion or belief and not to the right to *have* a religion or belief (*Ivanova v. Bulgaria*, § 79).

24. Article 9 § 1 guarantees "freedom ... in public or private, to manifest (one's)

religion or belief". However, the two parts of the alternative "in public or private" cannot be seen a mutually exclusive or as leaving the public authorities a choice; the wording merely points to the fact that religion may be practised in either way [X. v. the United Kingdom (dec.)].

25. Even where the belief in question attains the required level of cogency and importance, it cannot be said that every act which is in any way inspired, motivated or influenced by that belief constitutes a "manifestation" of it. **Thus, for example, acts or omissions which do not directly express the belief concerned or which are only distantly connected to a precept of faith fall outside the protection of Article 9 § 1. In order to count as a "manifestation" within the meaning of Article 9, the act in question must be intimately linked to the religion or belief.** One example might be an act of worship or devotion which forms part of the practice of a religion or belief in a generally recognised form. However, the manifestation of religion or belief is not limited to such acts; the existence of a sufficiently close and direct nexus between the act and the underlying belief must be determined on the facts of each case. In particular, applicants claiming that an act falls within their freedom to manifest their religion or beliefs are not required to establish that they acted in fulfilment of a duty mandated by the religion in question (*Eweida and Others v. the United Kingdom*, § 82, and *S. A. S. v. France* [GC], § 55).

26. Accordingly, as a general rule, the domestic authorities are not justified in casting doubt on the **sincerity of the beliefs** which an individual claims to hold without supporting their position with solid, cogent evidence. The Court thus dismissed the following objections raised by respondent Governments:

- the French Government had argued that an applicant, who claimed to be a practising Muslim and wished to wear the full-face veil in public, had not shown that she was an adherent of Islam and that she wished to wear the veil for religious reasons. Moreover, the Court took the view that the fact that this was a minority practice among Muslim women did not affect its legal characterisation (*S. A. S. v. France* [GC], § 56);
- the Latvian Government had submitted that an applicant, a prisoner, was not a

follower of *Vaishnavism* (the Vishnuite variant of Hinduism) on the grounds that he had taken a distance-learning Bible study course and that he did not formally belong to the local branch of the International Krishna Consciousness Society [*Kovaļkovs v. Latvia* (dec.), § 57]; the Romanian Government put forward the very similar allegation to the effect that an applicant had probably claimed to be a Buddhist in order to obtain better food in prison [*Vartic v. Romania* (no. 2), § 46].

27. Nevertheless, the organs of the Convention have accepted the **possibility of questioning the sincerity of an individual's alleged religion** in exceptional cases. Certainly, as already pointed out above, it is not the Court's task to evaluate the legitimacy of religious claims or to question the validity or relative merits of interpretation of particular aspects of beliefs or practices. It is ill-equipped to delve into discussion about the nature and importance of individual beliefs, for what one person holds as sacred may be absurd or anathema to another and no legal or logical argument can be invoked to challenge a believer's assertion that a particular belief or practice is an important element of his religious duty. Nevertheless, this does not prevent the Court from making factual findings as to whether an applicant's religious claims are genuine and sincerely held [*Skugar and Others v. Russia* (dec.)].

28. For instance, the organs of the Convention refused to acknowledge the sincerity of the applicants' alleged religious beliefs:

- in the case of a prisoner who wished to be entered in the prison registers as an adherent of the "*Wicca*" religion. The Commission held that where such a register entry entails specific privileges and facilities to enable the person concerned to practice his religion it was reasonable to require the declared religion to be identifiable; however, the applicant had provided no information to ascertain the objective existence of such a religion [see *X. v. the United Kingdom* (dec)].

- in a case of disciplinary sanctions imposed on an applicant, an employee of the national Electricity Company who had declared himself Muslim, for absence from work on two occasions during the same year to celebrate Muslim religious holidays. The domestic courts had acknowledged that the relevant law entitled citizens of Muslim faith to paid leave on the dates of the religious holidays; in the applicant's case however, the sincerity of his adherence to Islam was doubtful because he was ignorant of the basic tenets of that religion and because he had previously always celebrated Christian holidays. The domestic courts had therefore found that the applicant had claimed to be a Muslim solely in order to benefit from additional days of leave. The Court accepted that where the law established a privilege or special exemption for members of a given religious community-especially in the employment field-it was not incompatible with Article 9 to require the person concerned to provide some level of substantiation of his belonging to that community in order to be eligible for the said special treatment (*Kosteski v. the former Yugoslav Republic of Macedonia*, § 39).

29. The organs of the Convention have **refused to grant the protection of Article 9 § 1** (which does not mean that the same complaints could not, where appropriate, be examined under other provisions of the Convention) to:

- language freedom, including the right to use the language of one's choice in education and in contacts with the authorities [*Vingt-trois habitants d'Alsemberg et de Beersel v. Belgium* (dec.); *Inhabitants of Leeuw-St. Pierre v. Belgium*[①] (dec.), no. 2333/64, Commission decision of 15 July 1965, *Yearbook* 8, p. 105];

- a refusal to vote in general or presidential elections in a country in which turnout is compulsory [*X. v. Austria* (dec.), No. 1718/62, Commission decision of 22 April 1965, *Yearbook* 8, p. 169[②]; *X. v. Austria* (dec.)];

- an applicant's demand to have his christening and confirmation cancelled [*X. v. Iceland* (dec.)];

[①] Decision available in paper copy only in the **Yearbooks of the European Convention on Human Rights at the Court library**.

[②] Decision available in paper copy only in the **Yearbooks of the European Convention on Human Rights at the Court library**.

- a man who refused to enter into marriage with his partner in accordance with the procedure prescribed by civil law, while demanding that the State recognise their union as a valid marriage [*X. v. Germany* (dec.)];
- a Buddhist prisoner's desire to send articles for publication in a Buddhist magazine, whereas the applicant had not shown how practising his religion required the publication of such articles [*X. v. the United Kingdom* (dec.)];
- the distribution of tracts which, although based on pacifistic ideas, incited soldiers to be absent without leave and to infringe army discipline [*Arrowsmith v. the United Kingdom*, §§ 74 – 75; *Le Cour Grandmaison and Fritz v. France* (dec.)];
- an applicant's wish to have his ashes scattered on his property in order to avoid being buried in a cemetery amidst Christian symbols [*X. v. Germany* (dec.)];
- a prisoner's wish to be recognised as a "political prisoner" and his refusal to work in prison, to wear prison uniform and to clean his cell [*McFeeley and Others v. the United Kingdom* (dec.); *X. v. the United Kingdom* (dec.)];
- a practising Jew's refusal to hand over the *get* (letter of repudiation) after the civil divorce, thus allowing him to remarry under a religious ceremony [*D. v. France* (dec.)];
- a doctor's refusal to subscribe to a professional old-age insurance scheme [*V. v. the Netherlands* (dec.)];
- an association's wish to provide prisoners with legal advice and safeguard their interests for idealistic reasons [*Vereniging Rechtswinkels Utrecht v. the Netherlands* (dec.)];
- a minister of religion who had been dismissed for refusing to discharge his administrative duties in a State Church in protest at a law relaxing the rules on abortion [*Knudsen v. Norway* (dec.)];
- a man's wish to marry and have sexual relations with a girl under the legal age of sexual consent on the grounds that such a marriage was valid under Islamic law [*Khan v. the United Kingdom* (dec.)];

- the applicant's wish to divorce (*Johnston and Others v. Ireland*, § 63);
- the desire of electricity consumers to avoid contractual obligations into which they had freely entered and their refusal to pay an electricity bill in full on the ground that a percentage of the corresponding amount would be allocated to financing a nuclear power station [*K. and V. v. the Netherlands* (dec.)];
- a father's wish to inflict corporal punishment on his child (*Abrahamsson v. Sweden*);
- the refusal of two architects to subscribe to the Architects Association in breach of legal requirements [*Revert and Legallais v. France* (dec.)];
- the wish to unfurl a banner bearing a political slogan in a railway station [*K. v. the Netherlands* (dec.)];
- the content of an historical-political discussion held during a private party [*F. P. v. Germany* (dec)];
- an applicant's wish to have a free choice of doctor and to force his health insurance fund to refund a non-contracted doctor's fees [*B. C. v. Switzerland* (dec.); *Marty v. Switzerland* (dec.)];
- an applicant's wish, albeit motivated by his Christian faith, to hand out tracts against abortion nearby an abortion clinic [*Van den Dungen v. the Netherlands* (dec.)];
- a man who complained that the financial burden of the maintenance which he had to pay to his former wife and children prevented him from visiting Buddhist monasteries, the nearest one being located hundreds of miles from his home [*Logan v. the United Kingdom* (dec.)];
- a father's refusals to pay maintenance to his under-age daughter on the grounds that she had changed her religion [*Karakuzey v. Germany* (dec.)];
- a military judge, a Turkish air force colonel who had been retired on the grounds that "his behaviour and actions showed that he had adopted unlawful fundamentalist opinions"; in the instant case the impugned measure was based not on the applicant's religious opinions and beliefs or the manner in which he

discharged his religious duties, but on his behaviour and actions, which infringed military discipline and the principle of secularism (*Kalaç v. Turkey*);

- a wish on the part of parents to give their child a particular forename without mentioning any religious motivation [*Salonen v. Finland* (dec.)];
- a wish on the part of parents to evade the obligation set out in domestic legislation to have their children vaccinated [*Boffa and Others v. San Marino* (dec.)];
- a blunt refusal by a lawyer to take part in assignments to which he was officially assigned in order to represent persons remanded in police custody [*Mignot v. France* (dec.)];
- a refusal by a driver to fasten his seatbelt while driving a motor car in order to express the view that he should be allowed to choose his own means of protecting his physical and mental integrity [*Viel v. France* (dec.)];
- an Algerian national active in the Islamic Salvation Front who complained of a decision by the Swiss authorities to seize his communication media which he had been using for purposes of political propaganda [*Zaoui v. Switzerland* (dec.)];
- a refusal by the joint owners of a pharmacy to sell the contraceptive pill [*Pichon and Sajous v. France* (dec.)];
- a desire to commit assisted suicide motivated by commitment to the principle of personal autonomy (*Pretty v. the United Kingdom*, § 82);
- the applicants' wish to continue judicial proceedings instigated by their husband/father, who had since died, against the appointment of a mufti [*Sadik Amet and Others v. Greece* (dec.)];
- a student who had been denied access to a university campus on the ground that he had a beard, although he had never claimed to be inspired by any specific ideas or beliefs, whether religious or otherwise [*Tiğ v. Turkey* (dec.)];
- the desire to place a memorial stone on a family member's grave incorporating a photograph of the deceased [*Jones v. the United Kingdom* (dec.)];
- persons convicted of membership of organisations considered as terrorist [see, among many other authorities, *Gündüz v. Turkey* (dec.); *Kenar v. Turkey* (dec.)];

- a judge who had been reprimanded for refusing to consider cases because he felt biased [*Cserjés v. Hungary* (dec.)], and a doctor employed by a public health insurance department who had been dismissed for refusing to conduct a medical examination of an apprentice, because he feared a "possible bias" which could lead to difficulties if he had to work with the apprentice in the future [*Blumberg v. Germany* (dec.)];
- a nun sentenced to a fine for causing a disturbance during a religious ceremony by making loud statements during prayers [*Bulgaru v. Romania* (dec.)];
- a father living on unemployment benefit who complained of the municipal authorities' refusal to refund the cost of a Christmas tree and an Advent wreath [*Jenik v. Austria* (dec.); application dismissed as abusive within the meaning of Article 35 § 3 a) of the Convention];
- a father who had been judicially separated from his wife and who objected to his under-age daughter (custody of whom had been entrusted to the mother) being raised in the Roman Catholic religion, even though, according to the domestic courts, the mother had merely been acting in accordance with the daughter's freely-expressed choice [*Rupprecht v. Spain* (dec.)];
- two Jewish organisations which had asked the Ukrainian courts to restore the former boundaries of several old Jewish cemeteries in various towns in Ukraine (which had been abandoned for over seventy years) and to prohibit building work on them [see *Representation of the Union of Councils for Jews in the Former Soviet Union and the Union of Jewish Religious Organisations of Ukraine* (dec.)];
- an applicant's wish to walk naked in public on the basis of his belief that such behaviour was socially acceptable (*Gough v. the United Kingdom*, §§ 185 – 188).

4. Negative and positive obligations on the State

(a) Interference in the exercise of protected rights and justification thereof

30. Under the terms of Article 9 § 2 of the Convention, the legitimate aims liable to

justify interference in an individual's manifestation of his religion or beliefs are **public safety, the protection of public order, health and morals, or the protection of the rights and freedoms of others**. This enumeration of legitimate aims is strictly exhaustive and the definition of the aims is necessarily restrictive; if a limitation of this freedom is to be compatible with the Convention it must, in particular, pursue an aim that can be linked to one of those listed in this provision (*Sviato-Mykhaïlivska Parafiya v. Ukraine*, §§ 132 and 137; *S. A. S. v. France* [GC], § 113).

31. In contrast to Articles 8 § 2, 10 § 2 and 11 § 2 of the Convention and Article 2 § 3 of Protocol No. 4, "**national security**" is not included among the aims listed in Article 9 § 2. This omission is by no means accidental; on the contrary, the refusal by the drafters of the Convention to include this specific ground among the legitimate grounds of interference reflects the fundamental importance of religious pluralism as "one of the foundations of a democratic society" and of the fact that the State cannot dictate what a person believes or take coercive steps to make him change his beliefs (*Nolan and K. v. Russia*, § 73). This means that the State cannot use the need to protect national security as the sole basis for restricting the exercise of the right of a person or a group of persons to manifest their religion.

32. Moreover, it should be noted that **Article 15** of the Convention authorises States to derogate from their obligations under Article 9 "to the extent strictly required by the exigencies of the situation, provided that such measures are not inconsistent with (their) other obligations under international law", with the further proviso that the procedural formalities set out in Article 15 § 3 are complied with.

33. **Interference** in the exercise of the rights secured under Article 9 of the Convention may, for instance, take the form of:

- a criminal or administrative penalty or a dismissal for having exercised the rights in question (*Kokkinakis v. Greece*; *Ivanova v. Bulgaria*; *Masaev v. Moldova*);
- a physical obstacle to the persons exercising their rights under Article 9, such as the interruption of a meeting by the police (*Boychev and Others v. Bulgaria*);
- the dissolution of a religious organisation [*Jehovah's Witnesses of Moscow and*

Others v. Russia, §§ 99 – 103; *Biblical Centre of the Chuvash Republic v. Russia*, § 52; this contrasts with older Commission case-law to the effect that the dissolution and prohibition of a religious association did not infringe the freedom of religion of an individual, namely *X. v. Austria*, (dec.)];

- denial of authorisation, recognition or approval designed to facilitate the exercise of the said rights (*Metropolitan Church of Bessarabia and Others v. Moldova*; *Vergos v. Greece*);

- enactment of an ostensibly neutral law which has the effect of allowing the State to interfere directly in an intra-denominational dispute [*Holy Synod of the Bulgarian Orthodox Church (Metropolitan Inokentiy) and Others v. Bulgaria*, § 157];

- the use in official documents of pejorative expressions against a religious community, insofar as it may lead to negative consequences for the exercise of freedom of religion (*Leela Förderkreis e. V. and Others v. Germany*, § 84).

34. On the other hand, as a general rule, there is no interference with the exercise of the rights secured under Article 9 in the case of legislation the operation of which is provided for by the Convention and which is generally and neutrally applicable in the public sphere, without impinging on the freedoms guaranteed by Article 9 [*C. v. the United Kingdom*, (dec.); *Skugar and Others v. Russia* (dec.)].

35. Where applicants complain of the **existence in domestic law of a penalty imposed for an action which they intend to take** and where they lay claim to the protection afforded by Article 9, they can claim to be "victims", within the meaning of Article 34 of the Convention, if they are required either to modify their conduct or risk being prosecuted, or if they are members of a category of persons who risk being directly affected by the legislation in question. Thus, for instance, the Court acknowledged that a Muslim woman wishing to wear the full-face veil in public for religious reasons could claim to be a "victim" solely because such conduct was punishable by law, by means of a fine accompanied or replaced by a compulsory citizenship course. The applicant was thus confronted with a dilemma: either she complied with the ban and refrained from dressing in accordance with her approach to religion; or she refused to comply and faced prosecution (*S. A. S. v. France* [GC], § 57).

36. States are entitled to verify whether a movement or association carries on, ostensibly in pursuit of religious aims, activities which are harmful to the population or to public order (*Manoussakis and Others v. Greece*, § 40; *Metropolitan Church of Bessarabia and Others v. Moldova*, § 105). In some cases the State can take preventive action to protect the fundamental rights of others; such a power of preventive intervention on the State's part is fully consistent with the positive obligation under Article 1 of the Convention to the effect that the Contracting States must "secure to everyone within their jurisdiction the rights and freedoms defined in … [the] Convention" (*Leela Förderkreis e. V. and Others v. Germany*, § 99).

37. In a democratic society, in which several religions coexist within one and the same population, it may be necessary to place restrictions on this freedom in order to reconcile the interests of the various groups and ensure that everyone's beliefs are respected. However, in exercising its regulatory power in this sphere and in its relations with the various religions, denominations and beliefs, the State has a duty to remain neutral and impartial. What is at stake here is the preservation of pluralism and the proper functioning of democracy (*Metropolitan Church of Bessarabia and Others v. Moldova*, §§ 115 – 116).

38. The Court's task is to determine whether the measures taken at national level are justified in principle and proportionate (*Leyla Şahin v. Turkey* [GC], § 110). That means that **there must be no other means of achieving the same end that would interfere less seriously with the fundamental right concerned**; on that point, the burden is on the authorities to show that no such measures were available (*Biblical Centre of the Chuvash Republic v. Russia*, § 58). It is implicit in Article 9 § 2 of the Convention that any interference must correspond to a "pressing social need"; thus the notion "necessary" does not have the flexibility of such expressions as "useful" or "desirable" (*Sviato-Mykhaïlivska Parafiya v. Ukraine*, § 116).

39. When assessing whether or not an interference is proportionate the Court grants the States Parties to the Convention a certain **margin of appreciation** in evaluating the existence and extent of the need for that interference. We should remember that the role of the

Convention mechanism is fundamentally subsidiary. The national authorities are, in principle, better placed than an international court to evaluate local needs and conditions and, as a result, in matters of general policy, on which opinions within a democratic society may reasonably differ, the role of the domestic policy-maker should be given special weight-particularly where such matters concern relations between the State and religious denominations. As regards Article 9 of the Convention, in principle, the State should be granted a wide margin of appreciation in deciding whether and to what extent a restriction on the right to manifest one's religion or beliefs is "necessary". Nevertheless, in determining the extent of the margin of appreciation in a given case, the Court must also take account of both the specific issue at stake in that case and the general issue covered by Article 9, namely the need to preserve genuine religious pluralism, which is vital for the survival of any democratic society. Major importance should be attached to the necessity of the interference where it must be determined, as required by Article 9 § 1, whether the interference meets an "overriding social need" and is "proportionate to the legitimate aim pursued". Clearly, this margin of appreciation goes hand in hand with European supervision embracing both the law and the decisions applying it, even where they are issued by an independent domestic court. In this connection the Court may also, if appropriate, have regard to any consensus and common values emerging from the practices of the States Parties to the Convention (*Bayatyan v. Armenia* [GC], §§ 121 – 122; *S. A. S. v. France* [GC], § 129).

40. Furthermore, in assessing the conformity of a domestic measure with Article 9 § 2 of the Convention, the Court must take account of the historical background and special features of the religion in question, covering dogma, observance, organisation and so on (for two practical examples of this approach, see *Cha'are Shalom Ve Tsedek v. France* [GC], §§ 13 – 19; *Miroļubovs and Others v. Latvia*, §§ 8 – 16). This is a logical consequence of the general principles underpinning Article 9, that is to say freedom to practice a religion in public or private, the internal autonomy of religious communities and respect for religious pluralism. In view of the subsidiary nature of the mechanism for protecting individual rights established by the Convention, the same obligation may also be

incumbent on the national authorities in taking binding decisions in their relations with various religions (*Miroļubovs and Others v. Latvia*, § 81). In this regard, the Court usually refers to its case-law under Article 14 of the Convention (prohibition of discrimination), according to which this provision may, under certain circumstances, be violated when States fail to treat differently persons whose situations are significantly different (*Thlimmenos v. Greece* [GC], § 44).

41. Where domestic law makes the exercise of the right to freedom of religion or of one of its aspects subject to a system of prior authorisation, the involvement in the procedure for granting authorisation of a recognised ecclesiastical authority-particularly an authority belonging to a different denomination, hierarchy or persuasion-cannot be reconciled with the requirements of paragraph 2 of Article 9 (*Metropolitan Church of Bessarabia and Others v. Moldova*, § 117; *Vergos v. Greece*, § 34; and, *mutatis mutandis*, *Pentidis and Others v. Greece*).

42. Lastly, in exercising its supervision, the Court must consider the interference complained of on the basis of the file as a whole (*Metropolitan Church of Bessarabia and Others v. Moldova*, § 119). It must, if need be, assess all the facts of the case and consider the sequence of events in their entirety, rather than as separate and distinct incidents (*Ivanova v. Bulgaria*, § 83). Moreover, the Court must always satisfy itself that decisions taken by the State authorities in the field of freedom of religion are based on an acceptable assessment of the relevant facts (*Svyato-Mykhaïlivska Parafiya v. Ukraine*, § 138).

(b) Positive obligations on Contracting States

43. Under the terms of Article 1 of the Convention, the Contracting States must "secure to everyone within their jurisdiction the rights and freedoms defined in … [the] Convention". Therefore, the rather negative obligation on a State to refrain from interfering in the rights guaranteed by Article 9 may be combined with the **positive obligations** inherent in those rights-*inter* alia where the impugned acts were committed by private agents and are thus not directly attributable to the respondent State. Therefore, these obligations can sometimes necessitate measures to ensure respect for freedom of religion affecting the very

fabric of **individuals' interpersonal relations** (*Siebenhaar v. Germany*, § 38). Although the boundary between the State's positive and negative obligations under the Convention is not susceptible to an exact definition, the applicable principles are nonetheless comparable. In both contexts regard must be had to the fair balance to be struck between the competing interests of the individual and of the community as a whole; and in both contexts the State enjoys a certain **margin of appreciation**. Furthermore, even in relation to the positive obligations flowing from the first paragraph of Article 9, the aims mentioned in the second paragraph may be of a certain relevance (*Jakóbski v. Poland*, § 47; *Eweida and Others v. the United Kingdom*, § 84).

44. Article 9 does not guarantee, as such, the right to benefit from **preventive measures** to protect freedom of religion [*Hernandez Sanchez v. Spain* (dec.)].

5. Overlaps between the safeguards of Article 9 and the other convention provisions

45. By its very nature, the substantive content of Article 9 of the Convention may sometimes overlap with the content of other provisions of the Convention; in other words, one and the same complaint submitted to the Court can sometimes come under more than one article. In such cases the Court usually opts for assessing the complaint under only one article, which it considers more relevant in the light of the specific circumstances of the case; however, in so doing, it also bears the other article(s) in mind and interprets the article which it had opted to consider in the light of the latter. The articles most likely to be involved alongside Article 9 for the same facts and the same complaints are as follows:

(a) **Article 6 § 1 of the Convention** (right to a fair trial, particularly the right of access to a tribunal). In a case concerning a refusal by the Greek Court of Cassation to recognise the legal personality of the Cathedral of the Roman Catholic diocese of Crete, thereby denying it *locus standi* to protect its property, the Court decided to assess the applicant body's complaints solely under Article 6 § 1 of the Convention rather than under Article 9 (*Canea Catholic Church v. Greece*, §§ 33 and 50). Similarly, in a case of an alleged failure to enforce a final judgment acknowledging the right of a parish and its members to bury their dead in the local cemetery in accordance with their specific rites, the

Court decided to consider the complaint solely under Article 6 § 1 [*Greek Catholic Parish of Pesceana v. Romania* (dec.), § 43];

(b) **Article 8 of the Convention** (right to respect for private and/or family life). The Court has considered applications:

- solely under Article 8, on its own or in conjunction with Article 14 for example, as regards a decision by the domestic courts to establish the under-age children's residence with one of the parents essentially because the other parent was a Jehovah's Witness (*Hoffmann v. Austria*; *Palau-Martinez v. France*; *Ismailova v. Russia*). The Court pointed out that the practical arrangements for exercising parental authority over children defined by the domestic courts could not, as such, infringe an applicant's freedom to manifest his or her religion [*Deschomets v. France* (dec.)];

(c) **Article 10** (freedom of expression). The Court has considered applications solely under Article 10 – for example, as regards a prohibition imposed by the competent State body on an independent radio station broadcasting a paid advertisement of a religious nature (*Murphy v. Ireland*), or the refusal by the competent body to grant a broadcasting licence for a radio station with Christian religious programming (*Glas Nadejda EOOD and Anatoli Elenkov v. Bulgaria*). Thus, in so far as the applicant complains of interference with the expression of his beliefs and opinions by broadcasting information, Article 10 constitutes a *lex specialis* in relation to Article 9, so that a separate assessment under the latter is unnecessary [*Balsytė-Lideikienė v. Lithuania* (dec.)];

(d) **Article 11** (freedom of assembly and association). The Court has considered applications:

- under Article 9 as interpreted in the light of Article 11 for example as regards State interference in a dispute between two rival groups within the same religious community (*Hassan and Tchaouch v. Bulgaria* [GC], § 65), the dissolution of a religious organisation (*Jehovah's Witnesses of Moscow and Others v. Russia*, §§ 102 – 103), or the protracted refusal to recognise the legal personality of a religious community (*Religionsgemeinschaft der Zeugen Jehovas and Others v. Austria*, § 60);

- under Article 9 as interpreted in the light of Articles 11 and 6 § 1 for example as regards a refusal by the domestic authorities to register changes to the statutes of a religious organisation geared to ratifying the organisation's change of denomination (*Svyato-Mykhaïlivska Parafiya v. Ukraine*, § 152);

- under Article 11 (freedom of association) as interpreted in the light of Article 9 – for example as regards a refusal to renew the registration of a religious organisation (*Moscow Branch of the Salvation Army v. Russia*, §§ 74 – 75);

- under Article 11 (freedom of assembly) as interpreted in the light of Article 9 for example as regards a denial of access for a group practising Neo-Druidism to the historic site of Stonehenge to celebrate the summer solstice [*Pendragon v. the United Kingdom* (dec.); to converse effect, see also *Chappell v. the United Kingdom* (dec.)];

(e) **Article 1 of Protocol No. 1** (protection of property). The Court has chosen to consider cases solely under Article 1 of Protocol No. 1 for example as regards the obligation on landowners who are personally opposed to hunting to tolerate it on their land (*Chassagnou and Others v. France* [GC]; *Herrmann v. Germany* [GC]);

(f) **Article 2 of Protocol No. 1** (right of parents to respect for their religious and philosophical convictions in the framework of their children's education). The Court has chosen to consider cases:

- solely under Article 2 of Protocol No. 1 for example as regards the administration of compulsory classes in religious culture and moral instruction in State schools (*Hasan and Eylem Zengin v. Turkey*), or a refusal by educational authorities to grant children complete exemption from compulsory classes on Christianity (*Folgerø and Others v. Norway* [GC]);

- under Article 2 of Protocol No. 1 and Article 9 of the Convention taken alone, finding no violation of the former on the basis of an elaborate argumentation and no violation of the latter with simple reference to that argumentation (*Kjeldsen, Busk Madsen and Pedersen v. Denmark*);

- under Article 2 of Protocol No. 1 as interpreted in the light of Article 9 for example as regards the compulsory presence of crucifixes in classrooms in State schools (*Lautsi and Others v. Italy* [GC]);
- under Article 2 of Protocol No. 1 for the parents and Article 9 of the Convention for the child-as regards punishment inflicted by a head teacher on a pupil for refusing to take part in a school parade (*Valsamis v. Greece*).

46. In the field of education and teaching, Article 2 of Protocol No. 1 is basically a *lex specialis* in relation to Article 9 of the Convention. This applies at least where, as in the present case, the issue at stake is the obligation on the Contracting States-as set out in the second sentence of this article to respect, in the exercise of any functions which they assume in relation to education and teaching, the right of parents to ensure such education and teaching in conformity with their own religious and philosophical convictions (*Lautsi and Others v. Italy* [GC], § 59).

III. Actions protected under article 9

1. Negative aspect

(a) The right not to practice a religion or to reveal one's beliefs

47. Freedom of religion also involves negative rights, that is to say the freedom not to belong to a religion and not to practice it (*Alexandridis v. Greece*, § 32). **That means that the State cannot require a person to conduct an act which might reasonably be seen as swearing allegiance to a given religion.** For instance, the Court found that there had been a violation of Article 9 of the Convention as a result of a legal requirement on the applicants to take the oath on the Gospels on pain of forfeiting their parliamentary seats (*Buscarini and Others v. San Marino* [GC], §§ 34 and 39).

48. The negative aspect of freedom to manifest one's religious beliefs also means that **individuals cannot be required to reveal their religious affiliation or beliefs**; nor can

they be forced to adopt behaviour from which it might be inferred that they hold-or do not hold-such beliefs. State authorities are not free to interfere in individuals' freedom of conscience by asking them about their religious beliefs or forcing them to express those beliefs (*Alexandridis v. Greece*, § 38; *Dimitras and Others v. Greece*, § 78).

49. Moreover, such interference can be indirect; for example, when an official document issued by the State (identity card, school report, etc.) has a religion box, leaving that box blank inevitably has a specific connotation. In the particular case of identity cards, the Court has ruled that the indication-whether obligatory or optional-of religion on such cards is contrary to Article 9 of the Convention (*Sinan Işık v. Turkey*, § 51 – 52 and 60). Nor does Article 9 secure a right to record one's religion on one's identity card, even on a voluntary basis [*Sofianopoulos and Others v. Greece* (dec.)]. The Court has also refused to recognise the need to mention religion in civil registers or on identity cards for demographic purposes, as that would necessarily involve legislation making it mandatory to declare one's religious beliefs (*Sinan Işık v. Turkey*, § 44). On the other hand, the need for an employee to inform his employer in advance of requirements dictated by his religion on which he wishes to rely in order to request a privilege-for example the right to be absent from work every Friday in order to attend Mosque-cannot be equated with an "obligation to reveal one's religious beliefs" [*X. v. the United Kingdom* (dec.)].

50. The Court has found a violation of Article 9 of the Convention (taken alone or in conjunction with Article 14 prohibiting discrimination):

- as a result of the organisation of a swearing-in procedure in court as a precondition for exercising the legal profession, which procedure was based on the presumption that the person in question was an Orthodox Christian and wished to take the religieux oath; in order to be allowed to make a solemn declaration instead of a religious oath, the applicant had had to reveal that he was not an Orthodox Christian (*Alexandridis v. Greece*, §§ 36 – 41);
- in connection with the same issue as in *Alexandridis*, albeit in relation to individuals participating in criminal proceedings as witnesses, complainants or

suspects [*Dimitras and Others v. Greece*; *Dimitras and Others v. Greece* (no. 2); *Dimitras and Others v. Greece* (no. 3)];

- owing to the absence of an alternative course in ethics which might have been taken by the applicant, a pupil who had been dispensed from courses in religion, subsequently to which all his school reports and his primary school diploma had a dash ("-") in the space reserved for "*Religion/Ethics*"; even if the mark entered in this space did not show whether the pupil in question had taken a course in religion or ethics, the total absence of a mark clearly showed that he had taken neither type of course, thus exposing him to a risk of stigmatisation [*Grzelak v. Poland*; cf. two cases in which the organs of the Convention had declared similar complaints inadmissible as manifestly ill-founded, *C. J. , J. J. and E. J. v. Poland* (dec.); *Saniewski v. Poland*, (dec.)].

51. Conversely, the Court found no violation of Article 9 in the case of the indication "--" (two dashes) in the corresponding space on the applicant's income tax card, showing that he belonged to none of the Churches or religious organisations for which the State levied a church tax. The Court found that the document in question, which was reserved for the employer and the tax authorities, was not designed for public use, thus limiting the scope of the impugned interference (*Wasmuth v. Germany*, §§ 58–59).

(b) Conscientious objection: the right not to act contrary to one's conscience and convictions

52. Article 9 does not explicitly mention the right to conscientious objection, whether in the military or civilian sphere. Nevertheless, the Court has ruled that the safeguards of Article 9 apply, in principle, to opposition to **military** service, when it is motivated by a serious, insuperable conflict between compulsory service in the army and an individual's conscience or his or her sincere and deeply-held religious or other convictions. The answer to the question whether and to what extent objection to service military falls within the ambit of Article 9 will vary according to the specific circumstances of each case. For example, the Court concluded that there had been a violation of Article 9 resulting from the conviction of the applicant, a Jehovah's Witness (a religious group whose beliefs include the

conviction that service, even unarmed, within the military is to be opposed), for having evaded compulsory military service, whereas no alternative civilian service was provided for by law (*Bayatyan v. Armenia* [GC], § 110).

53. The Court has subsequently found violations of Article 9 in a series of cases bearing a strong resemblance to the case of *Bayatyan*, directed against Armenia (*Bukharatyan v. Armenia*; *Tsaturyan v. Armenia*) and Turkey (*Erçep v. Turkey*; *Feti Demirtaş v. Turkey*; *Buldu and Others v. Turkey*). In the case of *Feti Demirtaş* in particular, the Court ruled that the fact that the applicant, who had been convicted several times, had finally been demobilised on the basis of a medical report stating that he was suffering from adjustment disorder had changed nothing and did not detract from his "victim" status; quite the contrary-it was during his military service that his psychological disorder had emerged, further exacerbating the respondent State's responsibility (*Feti Demirtaş v. Turkey*, §§ 73 – 77 and 113 – 114).

54. All the aforementioned cases concerned conscientious objectors who were Jehovah's Witnesses. However, the Court also found violations of Article 9 in two cases of pacifists who mentioned no religious beliefs. In those cases the Court concentrated on the State's positive obligations, finding a violation as a result of the lack of an effective and accessible procedure under the Turkish legal system whereby the applicants might have ascertained whether they could claim conscientious objector status (*Savda v. Turkey*; *Tarhan v. Turkey*). Previously, in a case against Romania, the applicant had complained that he had been a victim of discrimination as a result of the national authorities' refusal to register him as a conscientious objector, because under domestic law only objectors who put forward religious reasons could lay claim to such status, whereas he himself was quite simply a pacifist. Nevertheless, as the applicant had never been convicted or prosecuted and compulsory military service in peacetime had meanwhile been abolished in Romania, the Court considered that he could no longer claim to be a "victim" of the alleged violation [*Butan v. Romania* (dec.)].

55. The Court found a violation of Article 14 (prohibition of discrimination) in conjunction with Article 9 in three cases in which ministers of the Jehovah's Witnesses in

Austria complained that they had been denied complete exemption from military service *and* alternative civilian service, as such an exemption was reserved for ministers of "recognised religious associations", and was unavailable for such "registered" religious organisations as the Jehovah's Witnesses at the time-despite the similarity of the functions exercised by all religious ministers (*Löffelmann v. Austria*; *Gütl v. Austria*; *Lang v. Austria*). On the other hand, the Court found no violation of Article 14 in conjunction with Article 9 in the case of an evangelical preacher who had been denied complete exemption from military and civilian service. In that case the Court noted that the applicant had never applied for "recognised religious association" status; his situation was therefore not comparable to that of ministers leading worship in such associations (*Koppi v. Austria*).

56. As regards compensation for persons having suffered a violation of the right to conscientious objection in the past, the Court declared manifestly ill-founded an application lodged by a Seventh-Day Adventist who had been conscripted during the Communist era and been sentenced to imprisonment for the "insubordination" of having refused to take the oath and attend the symbolic presentation of his weapon on a Saturday. After the collapse of Communism and the establishment of the democratic regime he had not been afforded a higher pension and other advantages granted by law to the victims of political persecution under the old regime, on the basis of domestic case-law to the effect that convictions for military insubordination-on whatever grounds-were not considered as "political persecution". Under Article 14 in conjunction with Article 9, the applicant complained of the domestic courts' refusal to take account of the fact that his conviction had been motivated by his religious beliefs. The Court ruled that although the positive obligations flowing from Article 14 could force the State to eliminate the negative consequences for conscientious objectors of any convictions for military insubordination, they in no way involved valorising the said convictions in a positive manner by granting financial advantages reserved for other categories of persons. In this case the impugned case-law had had an objective and reasonable justification consonant with the State's normal margin of appreciation [*Baciu v. Romania* (dec.)].

57. As regards schools, the Court found no violation of Article 9 in the cases of two

young Jehovah's Witnesses attending State secondary schools in Greece, who had been punished with one or two days' suspension from school for refusing to take part in a school parade commemorating the anniversary of the outbreak of war between Fascist Italy and Greece. The applicants had informed the headmasters of their respective schools that their religious beliefs forbade them joining in the commemoration of a war by taking part, in front of the civil, Church and military authorities, in a school parade that would follow an official Mass and would be held on the same day as a military parade. Having found no violation, in respect of the parents, of the right to ensure their daughters' education and teaching in conformity with their own philosophical convictions (Article 2 of Protocol No. 1), the Court reached the same conclusion as regards the right to freedom of religion in respect of the daughters themselves. It noted that they had been exempted from religious education and Orthodox Mass as requested. As regards the compulsory participation in the school parade, the Court held that neither the purpose of the parade nor the arrangements for it could have offended either girl's pacifist convictions, and that such commemorations of national events served, in their way, both pacifist objectives and the public interest (*Valsamis v. Greece*; *Efstratiou v. Greece*).

58. In the civilian field, an applicant's interest in not having to act contrary to his conscience may be seriously restricted by the public interest in ensuring equal treatment for all users, particularly as regards the treatment of same-sex couples (*Eweida and Others v. the United Kingdom*, § 105). The Commission also accepted that the convictions expressed in exercising the conscience clause in a professional context-for instance a lawyer's conscience clause-may, in principle, fall within the scope of Article 9. Thus, in view of its specificity and notwithstanding its professional nature, such a clause might become confused with the personal convictions of the lawyer in his capacity not as an officer of the court but as a private individual [*Mignot v. France*, (dec.)].

59. The Court found no violation of Article 9 (alone or in conjunction with Article 14 of the Convention on prohibition of discrimination) in the following cases:
- disciplinary proceedings against a Christian employee of a local authority for refusing to work on registering homosexual civil unions, and her dismissal

(*Eweida and Others v. the United Kingdom*, nos. 48420/10, 59842/10, 51671/10 and 36516/10, §§ 102–106, ECHR 2013);

- disciplinary proceedings against a private company employee for refusing to provide psycho-sexual therapy for same-sex couples, and his dismissal following those proceedings (*Eweida and Others v. the United Kingdom*).

60. The organs of the Convention also refused to recognise the right to conscientious objection, and therefore to find any violation of Article 9 of the Convention, in the following cases:

- the refusal of a pacifistic Quaker to pay a certain percentage of his tax unless he could be sure it would not be allocated to financing the military sector (*C. v. the United Kingdom* (dec.); this approach was confirmed in *H. and B. v. the United Kingdom* (dec.), and the refusal of a French taxpayer who was opposed to abortion to pay a percentage of the tax used for funding abortions [*Bouessel du Bourg v. France* (dec.)]. In all these cases the Court held that the general obligation to pay tax had, in itself, no specific impact in terms of the individual conscience, because the neutrality of the obligation was illustrated by the fact that individual taxpayers could not influence the allocation of taxes or decide such allocation once the taxes had been levied;

- a disciplinary penalty imposed on a lawyer for formally refusing to conduct tasks to which he had been officially assigned in accordance with law, representing persons held in police custody, on the grounds that he was opposed in principle to the law in question. While accepting that the lawyers professional conscience clause could fall within the scope of Article 9, the Commission noted that the applicant had merely contested the legal system in question, without ever having complained about being required to appear in an actual case which had offended his conscience, which might have allowed him to rely on the said clause [*Mignot v. France* (dec.)];

- a case in which the applicants, the joint owners of a pharmacy, had refused to sell the contraceptive pill in their pharmacy on the grounds of their religious beliefs [*Pichon and Sajous v. France* (dec.)].

61. The Court also dismissed the following applications:

- an application lodged by an unemployed person-who stated that he belonged to no particular religion-whose unemployment benefit had been temporarily suspended after he had refused a job as a receptionist in a conference and seminar centre belonging to the local protestant church. The Court noted that the job in question merely involved assisting customers, that by definition the work was unrelated to any kind of religious beliefs, and that it had not been demonstrated that the job would have infringed the applicant's freedom not to adhere to a religion [*Dautaj v. Switzerland* (dec.)];

- an application lodged by a doctor employed by a public health insurance department who had been dismissed for refusing to conduct a medical examination of an apprentice because he feared a "possible bias" which could lead to difficulties if he had to work with the apprentice in the future. The Court noted that the applicant's attitude did not constitute an expression of a coherent view on a fundamental problem and that he had not explained the moral dilemma which he had wished to obviate. Therefore, there was no "manifestation of personal beliefs" for the purposes of Article 9 [*Blumberg v. Germany* (dec.)];

- an application lodged by several Russian nationals complaining about legislation which assigned individual "taxpayer numbers" to all taxpayers and which they considered as a forerunner of the Sign of the Antichrist. The Court noted that this measure applied neutrally and generally in the public sphere, and that the applicants had not been required to apply for, or to make use of, the taxpayers' numbers, as the law explicitly authorised most taxpayers not to use it in official documents. Moreover, the Court reiterated that the contents of official documents or databases could not be determined by the wishes of the individuals listed therein. There had consequently been no interference in the rights secured under Article 9 [*Skugar and Others v. Russia* (dec.)].

2. Positive aspect

(a) General principles

62. While freedom of religion is primarily a matter of individual conscience, it also implies, *inter alia*, freedom to "manifest [one's] religion" alone and in private or in community with others, in public and within the circle of those whose faith one shares. Article 9 lists a number of forms which manifestation of one's religion or belief may take, namely worship, teaching, practice and observance (*Metropolitan Church of Bessarabia and Others v. Moldova*, § 114).

63. Save in very exceptional cases, the right to freedom of religion as secured by the Convention is incompatible with any power on the State's part to assess the legitimacy of religious beliefs or the ways in which those beliefs are expressed (*Hassan and Tchaouch v. Bulgaria* [GC], § 76; *Leyla Şahin v. Turkey* [GC], § 107). Accordingly, the State has a narrow margin of appreciation and must advance serious and compelling reasons for an interference with the choices that people may make in pursuance of the religious standard of behaviour within the sphere of their personal autonomy. An interference may be justified in the light of paragraph 2 of Article 9 if their choices are incompatible with the key principles underlying the Convention, such as, for example, polygamous or underage marriage or a flagrant breach of gender equality, or if they are imposed on the believers by force or coercion (*Jehovah's Witnesses of Moscow and Others v. Russia*).

64. Article 9 does not protect every act motivated or inspired by a religion or belief and does not always secure the right to behave in the public sphere in a manner dictated or inspired by one's religion or beliefs (*Kalaç v. Turkey*). Similarly, as a general rule, it does does not confer a right to refuse, on the basis of religious convictions, to abide by legislation the operation of which is provided for by the Convention and which applies neutrally and generally [*Fränklin-Beentjes and CEFLU-Luz da Floresta v. the Netherlands* (dec.)]. If an act which is inspired, motivated or influenced by a religion or set of beliefs is to count as a "manifestation" of the latter within the meaning of Article 9, it must be intimately linked to the religion or beliefs in question. One example might be an act of

worship or devotion which forms part of the practice of a religion or beliefs in a generally recognised form. However, the "manifestation" of religion or belief is not limited to such acts; the existence of a sufficiently close and direct nexus between the act and the underlying belief must be determined on the facts of each case. In particular, applicants claiming that a given act falls within their freedom to manifest their religion or beliefs are not required to establish that they acted in fulfilment of a duty mandated by the religion in question (*S. A. S. v. France* [GC], § 55).

65. Sometimes, in exercising their freedom to manifest their religion, individuals may need to take account of their specific professional or contractual situation [*X. v. the United Kingdom* (dec.); and *Kalaç v. Turkey*, § 27]. For example, the Court declared manifestly ill-founded a complaint submitted by an applicant whose authorisation to operate a private security agency had been cancelled on the ground that he had become a member of the Aumist Community of Mandarom and therefore no longer satisfied the "honourability" criterion required under Swiss law for the granting of such authorisation. The domestic courts had found that the leader of that Community was a dangerous person, that his teaching concerned the imminence of the Apocalypse, that he was liable to induce his followers to commit suicide or violence, and lastly, that to leave the possibilities inherent in operating a security agency in the hands of an adherent of such an organisation could well pose a risk to public order and security. The Court, in substance, supported the findings of the domestic courts, and concluded that the impugned interference was in conformity with Article 9 § 2 of the Convention [*C. R. v. Switzerland* (dec.)].

66. The ensuing overview of the Court's case-law covers the various manifestations of freedom of religion, ranging from the most personal and intimate forms (relating health issues) to the most communal and public expressions (concerning freedom of collective worship and the right to open places of worship).

(b) Freedom of religious and health issues

67. The Court has ruled that the refusal of **blood transfusions** freely consented by Jehovah's Witnesses is, in principle, a matter for the individual's personal autonomy and as such is protected by Articles 8 and 9 of the Convention. In this context, the Court firstly

noted that refusing a transfusion could not be equated with suicide because the Jehovah's Witnesses did not refuse medical treatment in general; transfusion was the only medical procedure which they rejected on religious grounds. Even if the patient refuses a transfusion which, according to considered medical opinion, is absolutely essential in order to save his life or to prevent irreparable damage to his health, the Court has held that the freedom to conduct one's life in a manner of one's own choosing includes freedom to pursue activities perceived to be of a physically harmful or dangerous nature for the individual concerned. In the sphere of medical assistance, even where refusal to accept a particular treatment might have a fatal outcome, the imposition of medical treatment without the consent of a mentally competent adult patient would interfere with his or her right to physical integrity and impinge on the rights protected under Article 8. However, if such personal freedom is to be genuine patients must be able to make choices in line with their own opinions and values-even if those choices seem irrational, ill-advised or rash to others. Having considered the relevant domestic legislation, the Court found that it provided sufficient protection for both the freedom of choice of adult patients and the objective interests of minors (by empowering the courts to overrule the parents' opposition to medical treatment likely to save the child's life). Consequently, the prohibition of blood transfusions in the teaching of the Jehovah's Witnesses cannot serve as justification for dissolving the organisation and prohibiting its activities (*Jehovah's Witnesses of Moscow and Others v. Russia*, §§ 131–144).

(c) Observance of dietary laws

68. The observance of dietary laws dictated by a religion or a philosophical system is a "practice" which is protected by Article 9 § 1 of the Convention (*Cha'are Shalom Ve Tsedek v. France* [GC], §§ 73–74; *Jakóbski v. Poland*). In two cases the Court found a violation of Article 9 owing to a prison administration's refusal to provide the applicants, prisoners of Buddhist faith, with meat-free meals, even though such an arrangement would not have been an excessive burden on the prisons in question [*Jakóbski v. Poland*; *Vartic v. Romania* (no.2)]. In the latter case, in particular, the applicant had only been able to obtain a diet for sick prisoners which contained meat. The Court noted that the applicant

had very little scope for receiving food which complied with his religion, especially after the Minister of Justice prohibited food parcels being received by post [*Vartic v. Romania* (no. 2), §§ 47 – 50].

69. Conversely, the Commission declared inadmissible an application in which the applicant, an Orthodox Jew serving a prison sentence, complained that he had not been regularly provided with kosher food. The Commission noted that the applicant had been offered a vegetarian kosher diet, that the Chief Rabbi had been consulted on the matter and that he had approved the measures taken by the authorities in order to respect the applicant's religious rights [*X v. the United Kingdom* (dec.)].

70. The Court also found no violation of Article 9, taken alone or in combination with Article 14 of the Convention (prohibition of discrimination) in a case in which the applicant association, a French ultra-orthodox Jewish liturgical association whose members had demanded the right to eat "*glatt*" meat from animals slaughtered in accordance with stricter prescriptions than the standard kashrut, complained of the national authorities' refusal to grant it the requisite approval to authorise its own slaughterers to perform the requisite ritual slaughter, even though it had granted such approval to the Jewish Consistorial Association of Paris, to which the great majority of Jews in France belong. Noting that the applicant association could easily obtain supplies of "*glatt*" meat in Belgium and that a number of butcher's shops operating under the control of the Consistorial Association made duly certified "*glatt*" meat available to Jews, the Court ruled that the denial of approval complained of did not constitute an interference with the applicant association's right to freedom to manifest its religion. It specified that since the applicant association and its members were able to procure the meat in question, the right to freedom of religion guaranteed by Article 9 of the Convention could not extend to the right to participate personally in the performance of ritual slaughter and the subsequent certification process (*Cha'are Shalom Ve Tsedek v. France* [GC], § 82).

(d) Wearing of religious clothing and symbols

71. A healthy democratic society needs to tolerate and sustain pluralism and diversity in the religious sphere. Moreover, an individual who has made religion a central tenet of his

or her life must, in principle, be able to communicate that belief to others, *inter alia* by wearing religious symbols and items of clothing (*Eweida and Others v. the United Kingdom*, § 94). Wearing such a symbol or item of clothing as motivated by the person's faith and his or her desire to bear witness to that faith constitutes a manifestation of his or her religious belief, in the form of worship, practice and observance; it is therefore an action protected by Article 9 § 1 (*Eweida and Others v. the United Kingdom*, § 89). However, the right to wear religious clothing and symbols is not absolute and must be balanced with the legitimate interests of other natural and legal persons. The Court's current case-law in this field covers three different areas: a) the public space; b) the workplace; and c) schools and universities.

72. Firstly, as regards the first hypothesis of wearing religieux clothing and symbols in the **public space**, the Court found a violation of Article 9 arising from the criminal conviction of applicants who were members of a religious group called "*Aczimendi tarikatı*", on the basis of Turkish legislation banning the wearing of certain types of religious costumes in public places open to all, outside of religious ceremonies. In this case the costume in question comprised a black turban, black sirwal trousers and a black tunic, accompanied by a baton. Having regard to the circumstances of the case and the wording of the decisions given by the domestic courts, and taking into account the importance of the principle of secularism to the democratic system in Turkey, the Court accepted that inasmuch as the interference in question had been geared to ensuring compliance with secular and democratic principles, it had pursued several of the legitimate aims listed in Article 9 § 2, i.e. the protection of public security, public order and the rights and freedoms of others. The Court did, however, consider that the necessity of the measure *vis-à-vis* such aims had not been established. It noted that the prohibition had been directed not at public servants who are required to show discretion in exercising their duties, but at ordinary citizens, and that it had targeted clothing worn not in specific public establishments but throughout the public space. Furthermore, it did not transpire from the case file that the manner in which the applicants-who had gathered outside a mosque wearing the costume in question with the sole aim of taking part in a religieux ceremony had manifested their beliefs by means of a

specific type of clothing had constituted or been liable to constitute a threat to public order or a means of exerting pressure on others. Lastly, in reply to the Turkish Government's argument that the applicants might have been engaging in proselytism, the Court found no evidence in the case-file to show that they had attempted to exert wrongful pressure on passers-by in the streets and public areas in order to promote their religious beliefs (*Ahmet Arslan and Others v. Turkey*).

73. Conversely, the Court found no violation of Article 9 in a case against France concerning the enactment of a law penalising the wearing in the public space of an item of clothing intended to conceal the face (therefore including the burqa and the niqab). Such an act was punishable with a fine and/or a compulsory course in citizenship. The Court considered that this case differed significantly from the case of *Ahmet Arslan and Others v. Turkey* because the full-face Islamic veil had the particularity of entirely concealing the face, with the possible exception of the eyes. By the same token, the prohibition in the French case had not been explicitly based on the religious connotation of the item of clothing in question. The Court acknowledged the legitimacy of the respondent Government's argument that the face played an important role in human interaction and that individuals who were present in places open to all might not wish to see practices or attitudes developing there which fundamentally called into question the possibility of open interpersonal relationships, which, by virtue of an established consensus, formed an indispensable element of community life within the society in question. The Court therefore accepted that the barrier raised against others by a veil concealing the face was perceived by the respondent State as breaching the right of others to live in a space of socialisation which made living together easier; in other words, the State might find it essential to give particular weight in this connection to the interaction between individuals and could consider this to be adversely affected by the fact that some concealed their faces in public places. While voicing some doubt as to the need to tackle the challenge in question by means of a blanket ban (given the small number of women involved) and expressing its concerns about the risk of a negative impact on the social situation of the women in question, who might find themselves isolated, the Court found that the respondent State had not overstepped its

margin of appreciation, particularly in view of the leniency of the penalties incurred (*S. A. S. v. France* [GC]).

74. The organs of the Convention have always refused to acknowledge the merits of complaints concerning compulsory temporary removal for **security reasons** of an item of clothing associated with a religion. For example, they have dismissed applications concerning:

- the fining of a practising Sikh for breaches of the obligation on motorcyclists to wear a crash helmet; the applicant submitted that his religion required him to wear a turban at all times, which made it impossible to wear a helmet [*X. v. the United Kingdom* (dec.)];
- the obligation on a practising Sikh to remove his turban when passing the walk-through scanner before entering the airport departure lounge [*Phull v. France* (dec.)];
- an obligation imposed on an applicant, who had gone to the Consulate-General of France in Morocco in order to request a visa, to remove her veil for an identity check; having refused to do so, she was prevented from entering the Consulate premises and was unable to obtain her visa. The Court rejected the applicant's argument that she would have been prepared to remove her veil, but only in the presence of a woman; it considered that the fact that the French consular authorities did not assign a female officer to carry out the identification of the applicant does not exceed the State's margin of appreciation in these matters [*El Morsli v. France* (dec.)];
- the obligation to appear bare-headed in identity photographs for official documents and, more specifically, the obligation imposed on a Muslim student to provide an identity photograph showing her bare-headed in order to obtain her university diploma [*Karaduman v. Turkey* (dec.); *Araç v. Turkey* (dec.)];
- the obligation to be bare-headed in identity photographs for official documents and, more specifically, the authorities' refusal to accept photographs showing the applicant, a Sikh, wearing a turban [*Mann Singh v. France* (dec.)].

75. As regards the second hypothesis-**the workplace**-a commercial company may legitimately impose a dress code on its employees in order to project a specific commercial image; implementing this code can sometimes lead to restrictions on the wearing of religious symbols (*Eweida and Others v. the United Kingdom*, § 94). Similarly, hospitals have a wide margin of discretion in laying down their rules on clothing geared to protecting the health and safety of their patients and medical staff (*Eweida and Others v. the United Kingdom*, § 99). Nevertheless, these interests, however legitimate, are not absolute and must always be weighed up against the individual's right to manifest his or her religion.

76. For example, the Court found a violation of Article 9 in a case where a private company had suspended an employee for refusing to conceal the Christian cross which she wore, while certain symbols of other religions (turban or hijab) were authorised (*Eweida and Others v. the United Kingdom*, §§ 94-95).

77. On the other hand, the Court found no violation of Article 9 in a case where a nurse working in a geriatric ward was transferred for refusing to remove the cross she wore on a chain round her neck, to wear it as a brooch or tucked under a high-necked top. In the domestic court the applicants' managers had explained that there was a risk that a disturbed patient might seize and pull the chain, thereby injuring herself or the applicant, or that the cross might swing forward and could, for example, come into contact with an open wound (*Eweida and Others v. the United Kingdom*, §§ 98-100).

78. Finally, as regards the third hypothesis of wearing religious symbols and clothing in **State educational institutions**, the Court has always emphasised that States enjoy a very extensive margin of appreciation in this field. It is not possible to discern throughout Europe a uniform conception of the significance of religion in society, and the meaning or impact of the public expression of a religious belief will differ according to time and context. Rules in this sphere will consequently vary from one country to another according to national traditions and the requirements imposed by the need to protect the rights and freedoms of others and to maintain public order. Accordingly, the choice of the extent and form such regulations should take must inevitably be left, up to a point, to the State concerned, as it

will depend on the specific domestic context (*Leyla Şahin v. Turkey* [GC], § 109). The cases which have been assessed by the Court from this point of view break down into two different categories based on whether the applicant demanding the right to wear religious clothing was a teacher or a student (or pupil).

79. As regards **teachers**, the Court has balanced the teacher's right to manifest his or her religion against respect for the neutrality of State education and the protection of the students' legitimate interests by ensuring inter-faith harmony. Although it is legitimate for a State to impose on public servants, on account of their status, a duty to refrain from any ostentation in the expression of their religious beliefs in public, public servants are individuals and, as such, qualify for the protection of Article 9 of the Convention. It therefore falls to the Court, having regard to the circumstances of each case, to determine whether a fair balance has been struck between the fundamental right of the individual to freedom of religion and the legitimate interest of a democratic State in ensuring that its public service properly furthers the purposes enumerated in Article 9 § 2 [*Kurtulmuş v. Turkey* (dec.)]. In that regard, account should be taken of the very nature of the profession of State school teachers, who are both participants in the exercise of educational authority and representatives of the State in the eyes of their pupils, and of the possible proselytising effect which wearing the clothing or symbols in question might have on them. Moreover, the pupils' age is a further important factor to be taken into consideration, since younger children wonder about many things and are also more easily influenced than older pupils [*Dahlab v. Switzerland* (dec.)].

80. In line with this logic, the Court acknowledges that the State has a wide margin of appreciation, and has found manifestly ill-founded applications concerning:

- a prohibition on a State primary school teacher responsible for a class of small children (aged between four and eight) wearing an Islamic headscarf in the performance of her teaching duties. The Court attached particular importance to the fact that wearing the Islamic headscarf, a "powerful external symbol", was difficult to reconcile with the message of tolerance, respect for others and, above all, equality and non-discrimination that all teachers in a democratic society must convey to their pupils. Furthermore, the Court rejected the applicant's allegation that the impugned measure constituted discrimination on the ground of sex (Article 14 of the Convention), as it could also be applied to a man who, in similar circumstances, wore clothing that clearly identified him as a member of a different faith [*Dahlab v. Switzerland* (dec.)];

- a disciplinary sanction imposed on an applicant, an associate professor at a State university in Turkey, for wearing the Islamic headscarf in the performance of her teaching duties in breach of the rules on dress for public servants. The Court observed that a democratic State was entitled to require its public servants to be loyal to the constitutional principles on which it is founded; the principle of secularism is one of the fundamental principles of the Turkish State; therefore, the applicant, a person in authority at the university and a representative of the State who had assumed the status of a public servant of her own free will, could have been expected to comply with the rules requiring her not to express her religious beliefs in public in an ostentatious manner. The Court also dismissed the applicant's allegation that the impugned measure amounted to discrimination on the grounds of both sex and religious affiliation (Article 14 of the Convention), as male members of staff were also subject to analogous rules requiring them not to express their religious beliefs in an ostentatious manner [*Kurtulmuş v. Turkey* (dec.); for a similar case concerning the suspension of a female teacher from an "*imam-Hatip*" secondary school, see *Karaduman v. Turkey* (dec.)].

81. As regards **pupils and students**, the Court found no violation of Article 9 or manifest ill-foundedness *vis-à-vis* the complaints raised in the following cases:

- a prohibition on a medical student in a Turkish State university wearing the Islamic headscarf in class. In view of the specific history of Turkey and its particular constitutional system, the Court recognised the legitimacy of the efforts expended by the national authorities to maintain the principle of secularism, one of the fundamental principles of the Turkish State as interpreted by the Turkish Constitutional Court. The Court considered this notion of secularism to be consistent with the values underpinning the Convention and compatible with the rule of law and respect for human rights and democracy. In finding no violation of Article 9, the Court drew on the following considerations: the Turkish constitutional system emphasised gender equality, one of the fundamental principles underpinning the Convention and one of the goals pursued by the member States of the Council of Europe; the issue of the Islamic headscarf could not be assessed in the context of Turkey without considering the potential impact of this symbol, presented or perceived as a mandatory religious duty, on those who did not wear it; according to the Turkish courts wearing the headscarf had taken on a political meaning in the country; Turkey had extremist movements endeavouring to impose on society as a whole their religious symbols and conception of a society founded on religious precepts. Against such a background, the impugned regulations constituted a measure geared to attaining the aforementioned legitimate aims and thereby preserving pluralism in the university (*Leyla Şahin v. Turkey* [GC]);

- a prohibition on pupils at "*imam-Hatip*" secondary schools (Turkish State-funded religious secondary schools) wearing the Islamic headscarf outside of Koran classes and a ban on class attendance by pupils wearing the headscarf. The Court noted that the relevant Turkish regulations required all secondary school pupils to wear a uniform and to attend school bare-headed; in the "*imam-Hatip*" schools there was one exception, to the effect that girls could cover their heads during Koran lessons. Consequently, the impugned regulations comprised provisions of a general nature applicable to all pupils regardless of their religious beliefs; the provisions pursued the legitimate aim of preserving the neutrality of secondary education for teenagers liable to be exposed to a risk of pressure [*Köse and Others v. Turkey* (dec.)];
- the refusal by French State secondary schools to admit pupils wearing headscarves to physical education and sports classes and their subsequent exclusion from school for non-compliance with compulsory school attendance. While acknowledging the compatibility of the French secular model with the values underpinning the

Convention, the Court took account of domestic case-law from which it transpired that the wearing of religious signs was not inherently incompatible with the principle of secularism in schools, but became so according to the conditions in which they were worn and the possible consequences of wearing such a sign. The Court acknowledged that it was not unreasonable to consider that wearing a veil such as the Islamic headscarf was incompatible on health and safety grounds with practising a sport. It noted in particular that the disciplinary proceedings against the applicants had fully satisfied the obligation to balance all the interests at stake. The respondent State had therefore not overstepped its margin of appreciation (*Dogru v. France*; *Kervanci v. France*);

- a prohibition on pupils at State primary and secondary schools in France wearing "signs or clothing ostentatiously manifesting their religious affiliation", which prohibition was general and not confined solely to physical education and sports classes, and the subsequent exclusion of pupils for wearing an Islamic headscarf or a Sikh turban or "*keski*" ("mini-turban") on the school premises. The Court considered that the aim of protecting the constitutional principle of secularism in conformity with the values underpinning the Convention was sufficient to justify the impugned measure. Moreover, the Court held that the head teacher's decision to refuse to authorise Muslim pupils to wear their headscarves and then remove them on entering the classroom, or to replace them with a cap or a bandana devoid of any religious connotations, or to authorise Sikh pupils to replace their turbans with *keskis*, was not contrary to Article 9 of the Convention because it fell well within the State's margin of appreciation [*Gamaleddyn v. France* (dec.); *Aktas v. France* (dec.); *Ranjit Singh v. France* (dec.); *Jasvir Singh v. France* (dec.)].

(e) Religious freedom, family and education of children

82. Article 9 does not purport to regulate marriage in any religious sense and it depends on each particular religion to decide on the modalities of religious marriage. In particular, it is up to each religion to decide whether and to what extent they permit same-sex unions

[*Parry v. the United Kingdom* (dec.)]. For instance, the Commission refused to extend the protection of Article 9 to a man sentenced to prison for having had sexual intercourse with a girl under the age of sixteen (the legal age of consent) although he was married to her under Islamic law; the Commission also concluded that there had been no appearance of a violation of Article 12 of the Convention (the right to marriage) [*Khan v. the United Kingdom* (dec.)]. The Commission also dismissed an application from a man who refused to enter into marriage with his partner in accordance with the procedure prescribed by civil law, while demanding that the State recognise their union, which he claimed had been made official by the reading out of a passage from the Old Testament before their first sexual intercourse, as a legally valid marriage [*X. v. Germany* (dec.)].

83. Article 9 does not secure the right to **divorce** (*Johnston and Others v. Ireland*, § 63). Similarly, the Commission declared inadmissible a complaint under Article 9 submitted by a practising Jew who had been sentenced by a civil court to pay his ex-wife damages for refusing to hand over the *get* (letter of repudiation) after the civil divorce, thus allowing him to remarry under a religious ceremony. In this case the applicant explained that he had hoped in this way to retain a possibility of remarrying her because he belonged to the *Cohen* group and the law of Moses prohibited him from marrying a divorced woman, even his own ex-wife. The Commission noted that the refusal to hand over the *get* was not a "manifestation of religion" within the meaning of Article 9, especially since the applicant, who had been prosecuted by the Rabbinical Tribunal for that refusal, was apparently opposed to the religious precepts which he invoked [*D. v. France* (dec.)].

84. It is a known fact that a religious way of life requires of its followers both abidance by religious rules and self-dedication to religious work that can take up a significant portion of the believer's time and sometimes assume such extreme forms as monasticism, which is common to many Christian denominations and, to a lesser extent, also to Buddhism and Hinduism. In so far as the adoption of such a way of life is the result of a free and independent decision by an adult, it is fully covered by the safeguards of Article 9 of the Convention, even if it may lead to conflict with family members who disapprove of that choice (*Jehovah's Witnesses of Moscow and Others v. Russia*, § 111).

85. Under Article 2 of Protocol No. 1, the Commission decided that the right of parents to ensure the education of their children in conformity with their own religious and philosophical convictions was one of the attributes of parental authority, so that it could not be exercised by the parent from whom that custody has been withdrawn by judicial decision [X. v. Sweden (dec.)].

86. In pursuance of these principles the Commission declared inadmissible:

- an application from a Polish national living in Germany whose ex-wife was living in Sweden with their under-age son. In addition to the refusal by the Swedish courts to grant him the right to visit his child, the applicant complained that the child was being raised in the Lutheran religion contrary to the teachings of the Roman Catholic Church in which he had been baptised; his ex-wife had not honoured the solemn undertaking which she made on their marriage to bring the child up in the Roman Catholic religion, as required by the canon law of the Roman Catholic Church. The Commission dismissed this complaint as incompatible with the Convention *ratione personae*, as the impugned acts were attributable only to the applicant's ex-wife, who had sole custody of the child and had the right and duty to ensure his education, and not to the respondent State [X. v. Sweden (dec.)①, No. 172/56; see also the applications lodged by the same applicant; X. v. Sweden (dec.); X v. Sweden (dec.), no. 911/60②], rejecting similar complaints as being substantially the same as in the first case);

- an application from a political refugee from Soviet Central Asia who complained that his niece and nephew were estranged from their Muslim faith by being brought up in a Roman Catholic institution. Leaving aside the question whether the applicant could act on the children's behalf or claim to be an indirect "victim" of the alleged violation, the Commission noted the absence of any infringement of freedom of

---

① Decision available in paper copy only in the **Yearbooks of the European Convention on Human Rights at the** Court library.

② Decision available in paper copy only in the **Yearbooks of the European Convention on Human Rights at the** Court library.

religion, especially since at the time of the court decision the niece and nephew had been aged twenty and twenty-one respectively [*X. v. Germany* (dec.)];

- a complaint submitted by Jewish parents concerning a decision by the Swedish social welfare authorities to place their under-age daughters in a protestant foster family rather than a Jewish one, which they claimed violated their right to educate their children in conformity with their own religious convictions. Under Article 9 of the Convention taken in conjunction with Article 2 of Protocol No. 1, the Commission noted that in fact the authorities had expended considerable efforts to actively seek out a Jewish foster family with the assistance of the local rabbi, while keeping the parents informed of their moves and inviting them to express their opinion; however, the authorities had been unable to find a Jewish foster family in the region [*Tennenbaum v. Sweden* (dec.)];

- an application lodged by a divorced Muslim man who had been sentenced to prison for refusing to pay maintenance for his under-age daughter on the ground that she had changed religion, as her mother had had her baptised in the Roman Catholic Church. According to the applicant, a child who had left the Muslim faith (even under its mother's influence) had to be considered "non-existent"; consequently, to require its Muslim father to pay maintenance would be contrary to freedom of religion. The Commission found that there had been no interference in the applicant's freedom of religion, as the obligation to pay maintenance for a child, custody of whom had been granted to the other parent, was generally applicable and had no direct implications *per se* for the sphere of religion or conscience [*Karakuzey v. Germany* (dec.)].

87. As regards the Court,

- it declared inadmissible an application under Article 8 (right to respect for private and family life) and several other Convention articles lodged by a group of parents whose adult children had entered the monastic order of the Macedonian Orthodox Church. The applicants complained that by founding a monastic order and admitting their children the Church had infringed their rights, including those to remain in contact with their children, to be helped by them in old age or illness, and to have grandchildren; the State should therefore have acted against the Church to protect those rights. The Court noted that the children's choice of way of life had been free, that contact, respect and mutual affection between parents and their grown-up children were matters strictly for the private sphere and could give rise to no kind of positive obligation on the part of the State, and lastly, that the Convention did not guarantee the right to become a grandparent [*Şijakova and Others v. the former Yugoslav Republic of Macedonia* (dec.)];

- it declared inadmissible as manifestly ill-founded a complaint from a mother, who was a member of the Raëlian Movement and was separated from her partner but exercised joint parental authority, concerning a court order prohibiting her from bringing her children into contact with Raëlians (apart from herself and her new partner) and taking them to Raëlian meetings. The Court considered that such interference, which was prescribed by law and pursued a legitimate aim (protection of the rights of the children and their father), was also "necessary in a democratic society". The applicant was able to continue to practise her religion personally and without restriction, and could even do so in her children's presence provided that they were not brought into contact with other members of the Raëlian Movement. The Court also emphasised the priority aim of taking account of the best interests of children, which involved reconciling the educational choices of each parent and attempting to strike a satisfactory balance between the parents' individual conceptions, precluding any value judgments and, where necessary, laying down minimum rules on personal religious practices. On very similar grounds the Court found no appearance of discrimination as prohibited by Article 14 [*F. L. v. France* (dec.)];

- finding a violation of Article 9, the Court declared unconvincing the argument advanced by the Russian courts in order to dissolve the local branch of the Jehovah's Witnesses and to prohibit its activities, contending that that religious community exerted "psychological pressure" in order to separate adherents from their families and to destroy the latter. The Court held, first of all, that the Jehovah's Witnesses' decision to devote themselves fully to their religious life had been taken freely, without coercion and in a very similar manner to the major "traditional" religions worldwide, and secondly, that the statistical data provided were not credible because they concerned only six cases of disputes in the families of Jehovah's Witnesses, whereas the proper approach could have been to compare the frequency of family break-ups among non-believers, among adherents of the majority religion in the country and among the Jehovah's Witnesses (*Jehovah's Witnesses of Moscow and Others v. Russia*, § 109 – 104);

- it declared inadmissible for incompatibility *ratione materiae* with the Convention a complaint from a father who objected to his under-age daughter (custody of whom had been entrusted to the mother) being baptised and taking Roman Catholic catechism classes and who complained of the Spanish courts' refusal to order that any decision concerning his daughter's religious education should be postponed until she came of age, and that in the meantime he should take sole responsibility for his daughter's education in that regard. The courts had found that the mother, who held custody, had simply complied with the girl's wishes, thus appropriately guaranteeing the latter's best interests [*Rupprecht v. Spain* (dec.); for a fairly similar case assessed under Article 2 of Protocol No. 1, see *X. v. the Netherlands*, (dec.)].

88. As regards **schooling**, Article 9 protects persons against religious indoctrination by the State [*Angeleni v. Sweden* (dec.); *C. J., J. J. and E. J. v. Poland* (dec.)]. Furthermore, in some cases **compulsory school attendance** may come into conflict with a family's religious beliefs. For example, the organs of the Convention dismissed:

- an application concerning a refusal by the Swedish National School Board to exempt the applicant, a State school pupil who claimed to be an atheist, from the teaching of religious knowledge; she argued that such teaching required her to adopt a Christian mode of thought. The applicant also alleged discrimination contrary to Article 14 inasmuch as the Swedish legislation in force at the material time provided for exempting pupils from such religious knowledge classes provided that they belonged to a "religious congregation" and that they were receiving religious education from the latter; that did not apply to atheists. The Commission noted that the girl had already been largely exempted from the classes in question whenever they comprised elements of worship (hymn-singing, etc.). For the remainder the Court agreed with the Swedish Government that the teaching provided concerned *religions*, and not the teaching of *one specific religion*-even if it concentrated more on Christianity. The applicant was therefore not being subjected to religious indoctrination or being forced to take part in any particular type of worship (*Angeleni v. Sweden* (dec.); see, conversely, *Folgerø and Others v. Norway* [GC]);

- an application from parents who alleged discrimination owing to the fact that under Luxembourg legislation the only valid ground for exempting a pupil from religious and moralor moral and social education classes was adherence to religious belief, whereas they wanted their children to be exempted on the grounds of philosophical convictions. The Commission considered that in the absence of any allegation of religious or other indoctrination, the obligation on children taking moral and social education classes did not amount to interference in the exercise of freedom of thought or conscience. The difference in treatment complained of in this case had pursued a legitimate aim (reducing pupil absenteeism in order to provide all young people with moral education) and had been proportionate to that aim inasmuch as the relevant legislation stated that the classes in question had to specifically cover study of human rights and be organised in such a way as to guarantee diversity of opinion [*Bernard and Others v. Luxembourg* (dec.)];

- an application from a Seventh-Day Adventist couple complaining of the Luxembourg municipal authorities' refusal to grant their son a general exemption from compulsory school on Saturdays, a day of absolute rest in this religious community. The Court decided that the impugned interference had been justified because of the need to guarantee the child's right to education, which had to take precedence over his parents' religious beliefs, and that a reasonable relationship of proportionality had been observed in the case in question [*Martins Casimiro and Cerveira Ferreira v. Luxembourg* (dec.)].

(f) Preaching and proselytism

89. Freedom to manifest one's religion comprises, in principle, **the right to attempt to convince and convert other people**, for example through "teaching", failing which, moreover, "freedom to change [one's] religion or belief", enshrined in Article 9 of the Convention, would be likely to remain a dead letter (*Kokkinakis v. Greece*, § 31). On the other hand, Article 9 does not protect improper proselytism, such as the offering of material or social advantage or the application of improper pressure with a view to gaining new members for a Church (*Larissis and Others v. Greece*, § 45).

90. For example, the Court found a violation of Article 9 in a case where the applicant, a Jehovah's Witness, had been arrested and criminally convicted of going to the home of the wife of the local Orthodox Church cantor and holding a discussion of a religious nature with her (*Kokkinakis v. Greece*). However, it adopted a more nuanced approach in another Greek case where the applicants, who had been air force officers at the material time, had been convicted by the military courts of proselytising several lower-ranking airmen and civilians. As regards attempts to convert *members of the armed forces*, the Court found that the impugned conviction did not infringe Article 9. It noted that the hierarchical structures which were a feature of life in the armed forces could colour every aspect of the relations between military personnel, making it difficult for a subordinate to rebuff the approaches of an individual of superior rank or to withdraw from a conversation initiated by him. Thus, what would in the civilian world be seen as an innocuous exchange of ideas which the recipient was free to accept or reject, could, within the confines of military life, be viewed as a form of harassment or the application of undue pressure in abuse of power. Not every discussion about religion or other sensitive matters between individuals of unequal rank would fall into this category. Nonetheless, where the circumstances so required, States might be justified in taking special measures to protect the

rights and freedoms of subordinate members of the armed forces. Moreover, the Court found that the applicants' conviction for proselytising *civilians*, on whom they had exerted no pressure or coercion, had not been necessary in a democratic society and was therefore in violation of Article 9 of the Convention (*Larissis and Others v. Greece*).

(g) Freedom of religious worship

91. Freedom of religion implies freedom to manifest one's religion not only alone and in private but also in community with others, in public and within the circle of those whose faith one shares. In other words, whether alone or **in community with others**, in public or in private, everyone is free to manifest his or her beliefs. Article 9 of the Convention list various forms which the manifestation of a religion or belief can take, namely worship, teaching, practice and observance (*Güler and Uğur v. Turkey*, § 35). This means that Article 9 protects the right of believers to meet peacefully in order to worship in the manner prescribed by their religion (*The Church of Jesus Christ of Latter-day Saints v. the United Kingdom*; *Cumhuriyetçi Eğitim ve Kültür Merkezi Vakfı v. Turkey*, § 41). However, Article 9, taken alone or conjunction with Article 11 of the Convention (freedom of assembly), does not bestow a right at large for applicants to gather to manifest their religious beliefs wherever they wish [*Pavlides and Georgakis v. Turkey* (dec.), § 29].

92. For example, the Court found a violation of freedom of religion in the following cases:

- measures regulating the religious life of Greek Cypriots of Orthodox faith enclaved in the "Turkish Republic of Northern Cyprus", preventing them from leaving their villages to attend religious ceremonies in places of worship elsewhere or to visit a monastery (*Cyprus v. Turkey* [GC], §§ 243–246);
- the dispersal by the Russian police of a Sunday service held by Jehovah's Witnesses in the assembly hall of a State vocational secondary school, which the national Jehovah's Witnesses organisation rented on the basis of a lawfully concluded lease agreement. The police measure had been clearly unlawful and arbitrary, even in the light of domestic law (*Kuznetsov and Others v. Russia*). In another similar case the Court found a violation because of the dispersal of an annual Jehovah's

Witnesses celebration held in the Agricultural Academy assembly hall, which had also been rented in conformity with domestic law. The impugned operation had been conducted by a large number of police officers, including an armed unit of the Special Police Force; the applicants were arrested and remanded in custody for several hours. Leaving aside the issue of the lawfulness of the interference, the Court found that it had clearly not been "necessary in a democratic society" (*Krupko and Others v. Russia*);

- the dispersal by the Moldovan police of a prayer meeting held by a group of Muslims in a private house and the imposition on the applicant of an administrative fine for "practising a religion not recognised by the State" (*Masaev v. Moldova*);

- the break-up by the Bulgarian police of a gathering of adherents of the Reverend Moon's Unification Church in an adherent's home, followed by a search of the apartment with the public prosecutor's authorisation, and finally, the seizure of books, recordings and other items, all because the religious community had not been registered by the State. The impugned measures had manifestly lacked any legal basis in domestic law. Furthermore, the domestic legislation had been unclear as regards the possibility of holding religious gatherings where the organisation in question had not been registered; at the material time there had been an administrative practice, supported by some domestic precedents, of declaring such gatherings unlawful (*Boychev and Others v. Bulgaria*);

- the summonsing of an applicant to attend the local police station and her questioning on the subject of her religious beliefs, followed by a search of her home, accompanied by seizure of books and recordings, and lastly, a police warning ordering the applicant to discontinue the meetings in her home of the evangelical congregation to which she belonged. The Court concluded that there had been no statutory basis for the interference as the impugned measures had been implemented in the absence of any criminal investigation, in flagrant breach of domestic law (*Dimitrova v. Bulgaria*);

- a prison sentence passed on the applicants for having taken part in a Muslim religious ceremony (*mevlüt*) held on the premises of a political party in remembrance of three members of an illegal organisation who had been killed by the security forces. The Court took the view that the mere fact that the ceremony in question had been organised on the premises of a political party in which symbols of a terrorist organisation were displayed did not deprive the participants of the protection guaranteed by Article 9. In this case the penalty had not met the requirements of clarity and foreseeability since it would have been impossible to foresee that mere participation in a religious service would fall within the scope of the Law on the prevention of terrorism (*Güler and Uğur v. Turkey*).

93. Conversely, the organs of the Convention found no violation of Article 9 or declared the corresponding complaints manifestly ill-founded in the following cases:

- a decision by the UK authorities to close the Stonehenge site over the immediate period of the midsummer solstice and not to allow a group of Druids to celebrate their solstice ceremony there. The Commission considered that even assuming there had been an interference with the exercise of rights under Article 9, it had been aimed at protecting public safety and been justified within the meaning or Article 9 § 2, particularly because the authorities had previously expended considerable efforts to satisfy the interests of individuals and organisations interested in Stonehenge [*Chappell v. the United Kingdom* (dec.) ; see also *Pendragon v. the United Kingdom* (dec.)];

- the sentencing to payment of a fine, suspended, for breach of the peace in respect of several persons opposing abortion who had entered the premises of an abortion clinic and prayed on their knees in one of the corridors. The Commission acknowledged that the activities in question fell within the scope of Article 9, but held that the interference complained of had been clearly justified in the light of Article 9 § 2 [*Van Schijndel and Others v. the Netherlands* (dec.)];

- the inability of an applicant, who was a Cypriot national who had always lived in the southern part of the island, to visit churches and monasteries located in the northern area, i. e. in the territory of the "Turkish Republic of Northern Cyprus".

The Court noted that the applicant's only link with the north of the island consisted of arable land which he had inherited from his parents and that there was nothing to prevent him from exercising his rights under Article 9 in southern Cyprus [*Josephides v. Turkey* (dec.)];

- the interruption by the police of an Orthodox mass held without prior authorisation in a monastery, now used as a museum, located in the territory of the "Turkish Republic of Northern Cyprus". The Court acknowledged that there had been a mistake in this case because the applicants had believed in good faith that they had been given authorisation, whereas to the authorities responsible for the cultural heritage the gathering in question had not been authorised and was unlawful. Nevertheless, in the light of all the relevant circumstances-no use of disproportionate force, the need to prevent conflicts in the specific political context of Northern Cyprus, etc. -the Court found that the impugned interference had not been disproportionate [*Pavlides and Georgakis v. Turkey* (dec.)].

94. The Court declared the following applications inadmissible on the grounds that the legitimate interests mentioned in Article 9 § 2 clearly took precedence over the applicants' interest in observing certain rites prescribed by their religions:

- a municipal ban on a Roman Catholic parish ringing the church bell above a certain volume before 7.30 a.m. The Court decided that the interference had pursued the legitimate aim of protecting the rights of others-in this case the local residents' night rest-and was proportionate to that aim. In fact, the bell could still be rung provided the volume was reduced; no limit was imposed on the volume of ringing for the rest of the day [*Schilder v. the Netherlands* (dec.)];

- the seizure and confiscation of a quantity of *ayahuasca*, an hallucinogenic substance which is consumed during ceremonies in the religion known as the "Santo Daime Church". The Court decided that the impugned measure, taken under drugs legislation, had been "necessary in a democratic society" for the protection of health. Inasmuch as the applicants had claimed to be victims of discrimination as compared with the Christian churches, which used alcohol (communion wine) in their ceremonies, the Court considered that the two situations were not comparable: first of all, wine was not subject to drugs legislation, and secondly, the rites of the Christian churches did not include the use of psychoactive substances for the purposes of intoxication [*Fränklin-Beentjes and CEFLU-Luz da Floresta v. the Netherlands* (dec.)].

95. The Court also declared inadmissible an application from a Greek Orthodox monastery complaining that the installation of telecommunications, radio and television aerials in the environs of the monastery infringed its freedom of worship. The Court found no interference with the rights secured under Article 9 because the monastery had long operated despite the presence of the aerials and had itself renewed the lease of the land on which they had been installed [*Iera Moni Profitou Iliou Thiras v. Greece* (dec.)].

96. Freedom of worship also applies to **the manner of burying the dead** inasmuch as it constitutes an essential aspect of religious practice [*Johannische Kirche and Peters v. Germany* (dec.)]. however, in a case where the applicants complained of the time-lapse before the authorities had returned to them the body of their daughter who had died in hospital, as a result of which they had for many months been unable to give her a religious burial or pray on her tomb, the Court decided to assess the complaint exclusively under Article 8 of the Convention (respect for private and family life) on the ground that the act complained of had not involved a direct interference by the authorities with the rights guaranteed by Article 9 but was only a consequence of the delay caused, which the Court considered was susceptible to consideration under Article 8 [*Pannulo and Forte v. France* (dec.)].

(h) Places and buildings of worship

97. Article 9 of the Convention protects, in principle, the right to provide, open and maintain places or buildings devoted to religious worship. Accordingly, under certain circumstances the operation of religious buildings is capable of having an impact on the exercise of the right of members of religious groups to manifest religious belief (*The Church of Jesus Christ of Latter-day Saints v. the United Kingdom*, § 30; *Cumhuriyetçi Eğitim ve Kültür Merkezi Vakfı v. Turkey*, § 41). The same principle applies to **cemetery**

layout, inasmuch as it constitutes an essential aspect of religious practice [*Johannische Kirche and Peters v. Germany* (dec.)].

98. Article 9 does not grant a religious community the right to obtain a place of worship from the public authorities [*Griechische Kirchengemeinde München und Bayern e. V. v. Germany* (dec.)]. The mere fact that the public authorities have tolerated the continued use of a State-owned building for religious purposes for a number of years gives rise to no kind of positive obligation on the part of those authorities [*Juma Mosque Congregation and Others v. Azerbaijan* (dec.), § 60].

99. Nor do the provisions of the Convention imply any obligation on the State to grant special status to places of worship. Nevertheless, if the State itself offers special privileged status to places of worship-above and beyond its obligations under the Convention-it cannot deny this advantage to specified religious groups in a discriminatory manner contrary to Article 14 (*Cumhuriyetçi Eğitim ve Kültür Merkezi Vakfı v. Turkey*, §§ 48–49).

100. As a general rule, the Contracting States have a wide margin of appreciation in matters of urban planning, in that planning legislation is generally accepted as necessary in modern society to prevent uncontrolled development. If the national authorities have given adequate weight to freedom of religion in balancing the various planning considerations, a religious organisation cannot use the rights secured under Article 9 to circumvent existing planning legislation [*ISKCON and Others v. the United Kingdom* (dec.)].

101. For instance, the Court found a violation of freedom of religion in the case of the sentencing of applicants to a prison term and a fine for having used a private room which they had rented to serve as a place of worship for the Jehovah's Witnesses, without having obtained prior authorisation from the "recognised ecclesiastical authority" (i.e. the local Greek Orthodox bishop) and the Ministry of Education and Religious Affairs. The Court found that the relevant provisions of domestic law conferred an exorbitant discretionary power on the authorities in this sphere, which power they used in practice to restrict the activities of denominations other than the dominant Orthodox Church (*Manoussakis and Others v. Greece*; see also the Commission's opinion the case of *Pentidis and Others v. Greece*, which led to the case being struck off).

102. On the other hand, the Court found no violation of Article 9 (or declared the application manifestly ill-founded) in the following cases:

- a decision by the Greek authorities ordering an adherent of the Greek Orthodox Church to move his father's grave in order to facilitate road widening works. The Commission noted that other individuals of Orthodox religion in the same situation had voluntarily moved their family graves and that the Greek Orthodox Church authorities contacted by the applicant had refused to intervene in his favour. Moreover, the applicant had not demonstrated how the fact of moving the grave would prevent him from discharging the duties prescribed by his beliefs or how the discharging of those duties could require the grave to remain in its original place [*Daratsakis v. Greece* (dec.)];

- notice served by a local planning authority on the International Society for Krishna Consciousness Ltd. concerning the use of a manor purchased by that society and ordering it to restrict its use to that which had been authorised at the time of purchase (residential theological college and place of worship accommodating a maximum of one thousand visitors per day); in fact, the actual use of the manor for religious purposes had since greatly expanded, attracting large crowds and leading to numerous complaints from neighbours. The Court acknowledged that there had been an interference in the applicant society's exercise of freedom of religion, but that such interference had been justified under Article 9 § 2; it found in particular that the local authorities had made constant efforts to reach a friendly settlement of the problem and that the applicant society's particular religious interest had been adequately taken into account in the domestic decision-making process [*ISKCON and Others v. the United Kingdom* (dec.)];

- the behaviour of the curator appointed by the Austrian courts to manage the property of a SerbianOrthodox community whose power to act in the sphere of secular law had been suspended by law owing to the community's schismatic situation *vis-à-vis* the Belgrade Patriarchate: the curator had concluded tenancy contracts with two priests appointed by the Serbian Patriarch and the competent bishop. Even supposing that there had been an interference in the exercise by the applicant of its rights under Article 9, the interference had been necessary for the protection of the rights of others and had been proportionate to that aim, because the impugned measure had been limited in scope and the tenancy contracts would only remain valid as long as the schismatic situation lasted [*Serbisch-griechisch-orientalische Kirchengemeinde zum Heiligen Sava in Wien v. Austria* (dec.)];

- the German authorities' refusal to grant a religious organisation a permit to install a cemetery in an undeveloped protected zone. The Court held that the impugned interference, which had been based on legal provisions relating to planning, environmental conservation and installation of public services, and had in particular been motivated by the fact that there were no other constructions in the zone in question, was in conformity with Article 9 § 2 [*Johannische Kirche and Peters v. Germany* (dec.)];

- the Greek local authorities' dismissal of an applicant's request to amend the local development plan in order to enable him to build a house of prayer for the "True Orthodox Christians" (Greek Old Calendarists, or "*Paleoimerologites*") on a plot of land which he owned; the reason given for this refusal was that there was no "social need" to amend the development plan because the municipality included insufficient numbers of members of the religious community in question. The Court found that in contrast to the *Manoussakis* case, this case concerned the application of a general spatial planning law which was, on the face of it, neutral. The quantitative criterion applied by the Greek Supreme Court could not be described as arbitrary, because authorisation to amend the local development could only be granted for the construction of a building "in the public interest". In such an hypothesis it was reasonable to take account of the objective needs of the religious community since the public interest in rational spatial planning could not be supplanted by the religious needs of one single person, whereas a neighbouring town comprised a house of prayer catering for the needs of the "True Orthodox

Christians" in the region. The State had therefore acted within the limits of its margin of appreciation (*Vergos v. Greece*);

- the fining of the applicants, who were members of a Turkish protestant church, for having used as a place of worship a private apartmentwhich they had purchased, without having complied with the requisite formalities under Turkish law, especially the mandatory prior agreement of all the joint owners of the building. The Court found that unlike in the case of *Manoussakis*, the formalities did not concern the recognition or the exercise of any religion and could not, therefore, be regarded as equivalent to prior authorisation; they were geared solely to protecting the rights and freedoms of others and public order. The Court also noted that the national authorities had balanced compliance with the formalities in question with the requirements of freedom of religion by first of all inviting the applicants to comply with those formalities. That being the case, the impugned interference could be seen as having been justified and proportionate. Lastly, the Court noted nothing to suggest that the relevant legislation had been applied to the applicants in a discriminatory manner in breach of Article 14 of the Convention [*Tanyar and Others v. Turkey* (dec.)];

- the expulsion of a Muslim congregation from an old Mosque building listed as an historic monument, in pursuance of a final judgment; despite the fact that the applicant congregation had been using the building for more than ten years, it neither owned nor rented it (contrasting with the situation in *Manoussakis and Others*). In particular, the applicant congregation had not argued that it could not freely set up a place of worship elsewhere [*Juma Mosque Congregation and Others v. Azerbaijan* (dec.)].

103. The Court also considered an application from an individual under Articles 14 and 9 of the Convention concerning a ban on building minarets which had been added to the Swiss Federal Constitution by referendum. It decided that as the applicant was not directly affected by the impugned measure and had never voiced any wish himself to build a mosque

with a minaret, he could not claim to be a "victim" of the alleged violation [see *Ouardiri v. Switzerland* (dec.)].

104. The Commission declared admissible a complaint under Article 9 that the annulment of the property deeds of the *Institut de Prêtres français*, a Roman Catholic institute established under canon law and located in Turkey, protected by the 1923 Treaty of Lausanne, and the registration of the property in question in the name of the Treasury, had had the effect of cutting the institute off from its vital resources and rendering it incapable of providing religious services and ensuring the survival of the Church [*Institute of French Priests and Others v. Turkey* (dec.)]. In proceedings before the Court this case ended with a friendly settlement [*Institute of French Priests and Others v. Turkey* (friendly settlement)].

3. Freedom of religion and immigration

(a) Residence and employment of foreigners in the national territory and freedom of religion

105. The Convention does not guarantee as such the right to enter or reside in a State of which one is not a national. Under a well-established principle of international law the Contracting States are entitled to control the entry, stay and removal of non-nationals (*Perry v. Latvia*, § 51). Accordingly, Article 9 of the Convention **does not guarantee as such the right of a foreigner to remain in a given country**. Expulsion is therefore not, as such, an interference in the exercise of the rights secured under this provision, unless it can be established that the expulsion order was designed to repress the exercise of such rights and stifle the spreading of the religion or philosophy of the applicant and his followers [*Omkarananda and the Divine Light Zentrum v. Switzerland* (dec.)].

106. For example, the Court found a violation of Article 9 in the following cases:
- the initial refusal of the competent national authority to extend the residence permit of an applicant, an American evangelical pastor, followed by the issue of a different type of permit accompanied by a semi-informal explanation that he was no longer entitled to engage in public religious activities; that restriction had no basis in domestic law (*Perry v. Latvia*);

- the *refoulement* of an applicant, an American national active in the Church of Reverend Moon's Unification Church, cancelling his visa and preventing him from entering Russia, even though he had lawfully resided there for years and his underage son was living in the country; that measure had very clearly been triggered by the applicant's religious activities in Russia. The respondent Government submitted that the applicant jeopardised national security-a ground which is not provided for in Article 9 § 2 of the Convention-without substantiating that submission (*Nolan and K. v. Russia*).

107. The Court also declared admissible the following complaints, without subsequently finding a violation of Article 9:
- the cancellation of the permanent residence permit of the applicant, an ethnic Palestinian preacher and teacher of Islamic religion, certified by the Grand Mufti of Bulgaria, and his expulsion from the national territory on the ground that his religious activities had been geared to imposing the fundamentalist version of Islam and showed that he was linked to the "Muslim Brothers", an extremist organisation [*Al-Nashif v. Bulgaria* (dec.)]. Finding a violation of Article 8 of the Convention (right to respect for family life), the Court did not consider it necessary to assess the applicant's other allegation of violation of his freedom of religion (*Al-Nashif v. Bulgaria*, §§ 139-142);
- the cancellation of the residence permits of two applicants, a Jehovah's Witness couple of Austrian nationality, because of their alleged religious activities in Bulgaria [see *Lotter v. Bulgaria* (dec.)]. This case ended with a friendly settlement [*Lotter and Lotter v. Bulgaria* (friendly settlement)].

108. On the other hand, the Commission declared inadmissible as manifestly ill-founded an application concerning an expulsion order against an Indian monk and philosopher who had been found guilty of endangering public order because of persistent breaches of the peace in his local neighbourhood; this order had not been enforced because the applicant had in the meantime been found guilty of a series of criminal offences and

sentenced to fourteen year's imprisonment and expulsion from Switzerland for fifteen years [*Omkarananda and the Divine Light Zentrum v. Switzerland* (dec.)].

109. Furthermore, Article 9 of the Convention does not grant foreign nationals the right to obtain a residence permit for the purposes of taking up **employment** in a Contracting State, even where the employer is a religious association (*Hüsnü Öz v. Germany* (dec.); *Perry v. Latvia*; *El Majjaoui and Stichting Touba Moskee v. the Netherlands* (striking out) [GC], § 32). Pursuant to this principle the Commission dismissed an application complaining of the failure to renew a temporary residence permit issued to a Muslim minister of religion and religious teacher (imam) of Turkish nationality whose employment contract with the local Islamic association had terminated and who wished to remain in Germany in order to work-still as an imam-for an association other than the one which had originally invited him there [*Hüsnü Öz v. Germany* (dec.)].

110. More recently, the Court declared admissible an application concerning a refusal by the Netherlands authorities to issue a Moroccan national with the residence permit which he needed in order to take up employment as an imam by a religious foundation, on the ground, in particular, that the foundation had not made sufficient efforts to find other candidates on the national and European labour market and that it had not begun by attempting to recruit its imam from among those trained in the Netherlands [*El Majjaoui and Stichting Touba Moskee v. the Netherlands* (dec.)]. However, following a fresh request from the foundation, the applicant finally obtained a temporary work permit and residence permit in the Netherlands; the Court therefore considered that the dispute had been settled and struck the application out of its list, in conformity with Article 37 § 1 b) of the Convention [*El Majjaoui and Stichting Touba Moskee v. the Netherlands* (striking out) [GC], § 32].

111. The Court found a violation of Article 14 (prohibition of discrimination) in conjunction with Article 9 in a case where the Austrian authorities had refused to exempt the Jehovah's Witness community from the Employment of Aliens Act, which would have allowed a residence permit to be issued to a couple who were both preachers holding Philippines nationality and whom the applicant community wished to employ in Austria. In

fact, under domestic law such an exemption was only allowed for "recognised religious associations" but not for "registered" religious organisations such as the applicant community (*Jehovas Zeugen in Österreich v. Austria*).

(b) Expulsion to a country which violates freedom of religion

112. Can a Contracting State **expel** foreign nationals to a third country in which they are likely to be considerably impeded in the exercise of their freedom of religion? Admittedly a Contracting State's responsibility can be incurred indirectly if it imposes on individuals a genuine risk of violation of their rights in a country outside its jurisdiction. The Court has acknowledged such responsibility in cases of risks of violation of Articles 2 (right to life) and 3 (prohibition of torture). The Court's case-law on this point is based on the fundamental importance of those articles, as the safeguards which they lay down must needs be rendered effective in practice, as well as on the absolute nature of the prohibition of torture and the fact that it encapsulated an internationally accepted standard; the Court also emphasised the serious and irreparable nature of the suffering risked. Later on the Court extended the same principle, under certain conditions, to the guarantees of Articles 6 (right to a fair trial) and 5 (right to liberty and prohibition of arbitrary detention). Nevertheless, these overriding considerations are not automatically applicable under the other provisions of the Convention. On a purely pragmatic basis, it cannot be required that an expelling Contracting State only return an alien to a country where the conditions are in full and effective accord with each of the safeguards of the rights and freedoms set out in the Convention. Even if the rights secured under Article 9 constitute "one of the foundations of a democratic society", this is first and foremost the standard applied within the Contracting States, which are committed to democratic ideals, the rule of law and human rights. Of course, under the above-mentioned case-law, protection is offered to those who have a substantiated claim that they will either suffer persecution for, *inter alia*, religious reasons or will be at real risk of death or serious ill-treatment, and possibly flagrant denial of a fair trial or arbitrary detention, because of their religious affiliation (as for any other reason). Where an individual claims that on return to his own country he would be impeded in his religious worship in a manner which falls short of those

proscribed levels, very limited assistance, if any, can be derived from Article 9 by itself. Otherwise it would be imposing an obligation on Contracting States effectively to act as indirect guarantors of freedom of worship for the rest of world. If, for example, a country outside the umbrella of the Convention were to ban a religion but not impose any measure of persecution, prosecution, deprivation of liberty or ill-treatment, it is doubtful whether the Convention could be interpreted as requiring a Contracting State to provide the adherents of that banned sect with the possibility of pursuing that religion freely and openly on their own territories [Z. and T. v. the United Kingdom (dec.)].

113. Nevertheless, the Court has not dismissed the possibility that the responsibility of a State expelling an individual can exceptionally be incurred under Article 9 of the Convention if the applicant runs a real risk of a flagrant violation of this article in the receiving country; however, according to the Court, it is difficult to visualise a case in which a sufficiently flagrant violation of Article 9 would not also involve treatment in violation of Article 3 of the Convention [Z. and T. v. the United Kingdom (dec.)].

114. In the light of the foregoing, the Court declared manifestly ill-founded an application lodged by two Christians of Pakistani nationality who had submitted that if they were expelled to Pakistan they would not be able fully to exercise their right to freedom of religion. The Court noted that the applicants had failed to make out a case of persecution on religious grounds or to substantiate that they were at risk of a violation of Articles 2 or 3. Neither applicant had herself been subject to any physical attack or prevented from adhering to her faith. Assessing the general situation in Pakistan, the Court noted that despite recent attacks on churches and Christians, the Christian community in Pakistan was under no official bar, they had their own parliamentary representatives, and the Pakistani law enforcement and judicial bodies respectively were taking steps to protect churches and schools and to arrest, prosecute and punish those who carried out attacks. In those circumstances, the Court found that the applicants had not shown that they were personally at such risk or were members of such a vulnerable or threatened group or in such a precarious position as Christians as might disclose any appearance of a flagrant violation of Article 9 of the Convention [Z. and T. v. the United Kingdom (dec.); see also *Razaghi v. Sweden* (dec.)].

IV. The state's obligations as garantor of freedom of religion

1. Negative obligations: obligation not to impede the normal functioning of religious organisations

(a) Legal status of religious organisations in the contracting States

115. In Europe there is no one model for relations between the State and the religious communities; quite the contrary: Europe has a wide variety of constitutional models governing such relations (*Sindicatul 'Păstorul cel Bun' v. Romania* [GC], § 138). The current systems can be divided into three categories: a) existence of a State Church; b) complete separation between the State and all religious organisations; and c) concordat-type relations (the latter is the predominant model in European countries). The Court has acknowledged that all three types of system are, as such, compatible with Article 9 of the Convention.

116. Some European States have a **State Church** (or Official Church) endowed with a special constitutional status. Such a system is not *per se* contrary to Article 9 of the Convention; in fact, it was already in force in the aforementioned States when the Convention was drawn up and those States became Parties to it. Moreover, the Court has ruled that the State's duty of neutrality in religious matters cannot be conceived as being likely to diminish the role of a faith or a Church with which the population of a specific country has historically and culturally been associated (*Members of the Gldani Congregation of the Jehovah's Witnesses and Others v. Georgia*, § 132). The legal personality of such a Church may be recognised by law [*Holy Synod of the Bulgarian Orthodox Church (Metropolitan Inokentiy) and Others v. Bulgaria*, § 157]. At all events the decision whether or not to perpetuate a tradition falls, in principle, within the margin of appreciation of the respondent State. The Court must, moreover, take account of the great diversity in Europe among its component States, particularly in the sphere of cultural and

historical development. However, the reference to a tradition cannot relieve a Contracting State of its obligation to respect the rights and freedoms enshrined in the Convention and its Protocols (*Lautsi and Others v. Italy* [GC], § 68). If a State Church system is to satisfy the requirements of Article 9, it must include specific safeguards for the individual's freedom of religion. In particular, no one may be forced to enter, or be prohibited from leaving, a State Church [*Ásatrúarfélagið v. Iceland* (dec.), § 27; see also the Commission's opinion in the case of *Darby v. Sweden*, § 45].

117. Furthermore, even in States which have a State Church, a decision taken by that Church in fields for which it is responsible does not incur the State's responsibility under the Convention. For example, the Commission considered a complaint lodged by a Finnish-speaking parish of the Church of Sweden-a State Church at the time-concerning a decision taken by the Assembly of the Church prohibiting it from using the liturgy of the Finnish Lutheran-Evangelical Church and imposing the use of the Swedish liturgy translated into Finnish. The Commission held that the Church and its parishes were "non-governmental organisations" and that the State could not be held responsible for an alleged violation resulting from a decision by the Assembly of the Church. Given that the applicant parish would not be prevented from leaving the Church of Sweden, the State had in no way failed in its obligation to protect the parish's freedom of religion [*Finska Församlingen i Stockholm and Hautaniemi v. Sweden* (dec.)].

118. In other States the constitutional model is based on the principle of **secularism**, which involves complete separation of State and all religious communities. The Court has declared that such a model is also compatible with the values underpinning the Convention (*Leyla Şahin v. Turkey* [GC], § 108; *Dogru v. France*, § 72).

119. Finally, States whose constitutional model so permits can conclude a **cooperation agreement** with a specific Church (or several Churches) providing for special (tax or other) status for the latter, provided that there is an objective and reasonable justification for the difference in treatment and that similar agreements may be entered into by other Churches wishing to do so [*Alujer Fernández and Caballero Garcia v. Spain* (dec.); *Savez crkava 'Riječ života' and Others v. Croatia*, § 85]. The State can also make a

religious organisation subject to a special regime different from the others by exempting it from compulsory registration or declaration and recognising its legal personality *ex lege* [*Holy Synod of the Bulgarian Orthodox Church (Metropolitan Inokentiy) and Others v. Bulgaria*]. However, if a State sets up a framework for conferring legal personality on religious groups together with a specific status, all religious groups which so wish must have a fair opportunity to apply for this status and the criteria established must be applied in a non-discriminatory manner (*Religionsgemeinschaft der Zeugen Jehovas and Others v. Austria*). Freedom of religion in no way implies that religious groups or adherents of a religion must be granted a specific legal status different from that of other existing bodies; if, however, such a status has been set up, it must be granted in a non-discriminatory manner (*Cumhuriyetçi Eğitim ve Kültür Merkezi Vakfi v. Turkey*, § 45).

120. The State may also **delegate specific public tasks and functions to one or more religious organisations**, whereby the delegation of such tasks and functions and their mode of financing are matters for the State's margin of appreciation [*Bruno v. Sweden* (dec.); *Lundberg v. Sweden* (dec.)].

121. Lastly, it should be remembered that in this difficult sphere of establishing relations between religions and the State, the latter benefits, in principle, from a wide margin of appreciation (*Cha'are Shalom Ve Tsedek v. France* [GC], § 84).

(b) Recognition, registration and dissolution of religious organisations

122. One of the most radical forms of interference with the collective aspect of freedom of religion is the **dissolution** of an existing religious organisation. Such a drastic measure requires very serious reasons by way of justification in order to be recognised as "necessary in a democratic society" (*Biblical Centre of the Chuvash Republic v. Russia*, § 54).

123. For example, the Court found a violation of Article 9, read in conjunction with Article 11 of the Convention, in the following cases:
- the dissolution of a local branch of the Jehovah's Witnesses and the prohibition of its activities, as ordered by the Russian courts at the prosecutor's request. Having examined all the findings of the domestic courts (alleged pressure on adherents' families geared to destroying them; alleged interference with adherents' private life

and with their right to choose their occupations; alleged violations of the parental rights of parents not belonging to the Jehovah's Witnesses; allegations of "brainwashing" and "mind control"; alleged incitement to suicide or refusal of medical treatment, including prohibition of blood transfusions; alleged luring of minors into the organisation; incitement not to serve in the army, to disrespect State emblems and refuse to take part in national celebrations), the Court found that all the allegations either had not been supported by concrete evidence or had concerned quite normal manifestations of freedom of religion freely chosen by the adherents in the framework of their personal autonomy as protected by Article 9. Moreover, these manifestations were very similar to the practices of the major "traditional" religions worldwide (fasting, asceticism, restrictive precepts in private life, etc.). the dissolution of the organisation had therefore been manifestly disproportionate to the legitimate aims pursued, especially since the legislation applied in this case had been extremely rigid and did not allow for possible wrongdoing by a religious community to be punished with any sanction less drastic than dissolution (*Jehovah's Witnesses of Moscow and Others v. Russia*);

- the dissolution by the Russian courts of a protestant (Pentecostal) biblical centre on the ground that it ran a Sunday school for children and a Biblical College for adults (issuing certificates or "diplomas" on completion of studies) which lacked legal-entity status. The reasons for the dissolution were, first of all, the fact that the Biblical College had been opened without prior authorisation, and secondly, the fact that the two bodies in question had failed to comply with the health and safety requirements set out in the relevant legislation. The Court noted that the authorities had not given the applicant organisation any prior warning, which would have enabled it to comply with any legal or statutory requirements. Furthermore, the applicant organisation could not reasonably have foreseen the consequences of its acts because of the Russian courts' contradictory case-law, with some judgments declaring that a study centre such as the Sunday school at issue did not require special authorisation (*Biblical Centre of the Chuvash Republic v. Russia*).

124. There are also other forms of interference which may be placed in the same category as dissolution. Religious societies have traditionally and universally existed in the form of organised bodies. Accordingly, interpreting Article 9 in the light of Article 11 of the Convention, the Court has ruled that the ability to set up a legal entity recognised by the State in order to guarantee the capacity for collective action in the religious sphere is one of the most important aspects of freedom of religion, without which that freedom would be meaningless. Consequently, the refusal to recognise the **legal personality** of a religious community or to grant it such personality constitutes interference with the exercise of the rights secured under Article 9, in their external and collective dimension, in respect of the community itself but also of its members (*Metropolitan Church of Bessarabia and Others v. Moldova*, § 105; *Religionsgemeinschaft der Zeugen Jehovas and Others v. Austria*, § 62). Indeed, under Article 11, the Court has found that the ability to establish a legal entity in order to act collectively in a field of mutual interest is one of the most important aspects of freedom of association, without which that right would be deprived of any meaning. A refusal by the domestic authorities to grant legal-entity status to an association, religious or otherwise, of individuals amounts to an interference with the exercise of the right to freedom of association. In this regard, the authorities' refusal to register a group directly affects both the group itself and its presidents, founders or individual members (*Kimlya and Others v. Russia*, § 84).

125. Mere tolerance by the national authorities of the activities of a non-recognised religious organisation is no substitute for recognition if recognition alone is capable of conferring rights on those concerned (*Metropolitan Church of Bessarabia and Others v. Moldova*, § 129). Even where legislation expressly authorises the operation of unregistered religious groups, that is insufficient if domestic law reserves a whole series of rights essential for conducting religious activities for registered organisations with legal personality (*Sviato-Mykhaïlivska Parafiya v. Ukraine*, § 122). Those rights include those to own or rent property, to maintain bank accounts, to hire employees, to ensure judicial

protection of the community, its members and its assets, to establish places of worship, to hold religious services in places accessible to the public, to produce, obtain and distribute religious literature, to create educational institutions, and to maintain contacts for international exchanges and conferences (*Kimlya and Others v. Russia*, §§ 85 - 86). Moreover, one of the means of exercising the right to manifest one's religion, especially for a religious community, in its collective dimension, is the possibility of guaranteeing the judicial protection of the community, its members and its assets, so that Article 9 must be seen not only in the light of Article 11, but also in the light of Article 6 § 1 of the Convention on the right to a fair trial and to access to a tribunal (*Sviato-Mykhaïlivska Parafiya v. Ukraine*, § 152; *Religionsgemeinschaft der Zeugen Jehovas and Others v. Austria*, § 63).

126. By the same reasoning, the fact that the religious community's lack of legal personality may be compensated in part by running auxiliary associations is not decisive and does not solve the problem (*Religionsgemeinschaft der Zeugen Jehovas and Others v. Austria*, § 67).

127. As regards the recognition and registration of religious communities, States are empowered to verify whether a movement or association is conducting, for ostensibly religious purposes, activities harmful to the population or endangering public security. Since it cannot be ruled out that an organisation's programme might conceal objectives and intentions different from the ones it proclaims, to verify that it does not the content of the programme might be compared with the organisation's actions and the positions it defends (*Metropolitan Church of Bessarabia and Others v. Moldova*, §§ 105 and 125). In particular, the refusal to register a religious organisation on the ground that it has not provided the authorities with a description of the fundamental precepts of the religion in question may be justified by the need to establish whether that organisation presents any danger for a democratic society and the fundamental interests recognised by Article 9 § 2 [*Cârmuirea Spirituală a Musulmanilor din Republica Moldova v. Moldova* (dec.); *Church of Scientology of Moscow v. Russia*, § 93; *Lajda and Others v. Czech Republic* (dec.)]. Nevertheless, although States do have a right of scrutiny concerning the

conformity of the objectives and activities of a religious association with the rules established by legislation, they must use it sparingly, in a manner compatible with their obligations under the Convention and subject to the purview of the organs of the Convention (*Jehovah's Witnesses of Moscow and Others v. Russia*, § 100).

128. The **waiting time** for the authorities to consider an application for recognition or registration and scrutinise conformity as mentioned above must be reasonably short (*Religionsgemeinschaft der Zeugen Jehovas and Others v. Austria*, § 79). Similarly, where a State's legal system comprises religious organisations which are specially privileged as compared with others (holding, for example, legal-entity status), the State may exceptionally impose a longer waiting and verification period, particularly in the case of newly established and unknown religious groups. But it hardly appears justified in respect of religious groups with a long-standing existence internationally which are also long established in the country and therefore familiar to the competent authorities (*Religionsgemeinschaft der Zeugen Jehovas and Others v. Austria*, §§ 97–98).

129. For example, the Court found a violation of Article 9 of the Convention (taken alone and/or in conjunction with Article 14) in the following cases:
- the Moldovan authorities' refusal to grant legal recognition to the Metropolitan Church of Bessarabia, an autonomous Orthodox Church operating under the authority of the Patriarchate of Bucharest (the Romanian Orthodox Church), on the ground that such recognition would infringe the interests of the Metropolitan Church of Moldova, which comes under the Patriarchate of Moscow (the Russian Orthodox Church), which is already recognised by the Government. Lacking legal recognition, the applicant church was unable to engage in its activities; its priests could not conduct divine service, its members could not meet to practise their religion and, moreover, lacking legal personality, it was not entitled to judicial protection of its assets or allowed to defend itself against acts of intimidation. By denying recognition on the ground that the applicant church was only a "schismatic group" within the Orthodox Church, the Moldovan Government had failed in their duty of neutrality and impartiality. For the remainder, the Government's

- submissions accusing the applicant church of jeopardising the country's territorial integrity and social stability were manifestly ill-founded (*Metropolitan Church of Bessarabia and Others v. Moldova*);
- in the same context as the foregoing case: a refusal by a local authority to issue the applicants with a certificate which they needed in order to register the Metropolitan Church of Bessarabia, on the ground that the Metropolitan Church of Moldova was already registered and operated in the area in question; the Court found that the impugned interference was not "prescribed by law" (*Fusu Arcadie and Others v. The Republic of Moldova*);
- a refusal by the competent administrative authority to register the applicant Church despite a judgment ordering it to do so; in this case the Court found that the impugned interference was not "prescribed by law" (*Biserica Adevărat Ortodoxă din Moldova and Others v. Moldova*);
- a time-lapse of twenty years between the lodging with the Austrian authorities of an application for legal recognition by a Jehovah's Witnesses congregation and the authorities' decision finally to grant it "registered" religious organisation status. The Court also found that there had been discrimination in breach of Article 14 as a result of the refusal to grant the applicant community "recognised religious society" status, which embraced legal personality and bestowed a whole series of privileges under domestic law, on the ground that it had not operated as a "registered" organisation in Austria for a minimum of ten years. The respondent Government had not demonstrated the existence of any objective and reasonable justification for this difference in treatment, especially since the "ten-year" requirement had not been applied to another religious community in a similar situation to that of the Jehovah's Witnesses (*Religionsgemeinschaft der Zeugen Jehovas and Others v. Austria*);
- the Russian authorities' refusal to register two local branches of the Church of Scientology as "religious organisations", which would have automatically given them legal entity status, on the ground that they had not been operating in Russia

as "religious groups" (without legal personality) for at least fifteen years. Finding a violation of Article 9 interpreted in the light of Article 11, the Court noted that the respondent Government had not mentioned any overriding social need in support of the impugned restriction or any relevant and sufficient reason justifying such a long waiting period; in particular, it had never been contended that the applicants-as a group or as individuals had conducted or intended to conduct any unlawful activities or had pursued aims other than those of religious worship, teaching, practice and observance. The reason for the denial of registration had been purely formal, unrelated to the operation of the groups in question, and the only "offence" of which the applicants had been found guilty was their intention to apply for the registration of an association of a "religious nature" which had not existed in the region for a minimum of fifteen years (*Kimlya and Others v. Russia*). In another very similar case, one of the reasons given for rejecting the application for registration was the fact that the local municipal council had no competence to issue such a certificate. In contrast to the *Kimlya* case, the Court found that the interference had not been "prescribed by law" and that it was therefore unnecessary to consider the issue of its proportionality (*Church of Scientology of St Petersburg and Others v. Russia*);

- the Croatian Government's arbitrary and discriminatory refusal to conclude with the applicants, several Reformist Churches, a cooperation agreement in public-interest fields enabling these Churches to provide religious education in State schools and guarantee recognition of the civil effects of marriages celebrated by their ministers. In this case the Government had justified its refusal by the fact that the applicants had not satisfied, either individually or jointly, the criteria set forth in a governmental instruction for the purposes of concluding such agreements. Nevertheless, several other communities had been exempted from the numerical criterion, and as to the historical criterion ("historic religious communities of European cultural circle"), the Government had not explained why the applicant Churches, of the Protestant reformist tradition, failed to satisfy it. The Court therefore found a violation of Article 14 of the Convention (*Savez crkava 'Riječ života' and Others v. Croatia*).

130. On the other hand, the Court declared manifestly ill-founded complaints lodged by two groups of adherents of Sun Myung Moon's Church of Unification in the Czech Republic and Bulgaria respectively:

- in the first case, which the Court considered under Article 11 read in conjunction with Article 9, the applicants complained about the Czech authorities' refusal to register their organisation as a church with legal personality on two different grounds: firstly, the applicants' refusal to provide the authorities with a background document explaining their teachings, and secondly the fact that they had infringed the general regulations on the collection of signatures from "persons embracing the doctrine of the Church". Having carried out additional verifications, the authorities had rejected many of the signatures collected on the ground that they were mere sympathisers rather than believers with a theological link to the Church; the Court accepted this interpretation of the law as reasonable and non-arbitrary. However, the number of signatures remaining was below the total of 10,000 required by law in order to register a church. While accepting that this figure might seem disproportionate on the face of it, the Court noted that the new law enacted in the meantime had reduced it to 300 and that there was nothing to prevent the applicants from lodging a fresh request for the registration of their church [*Lajda and Others v. Czech Republic* (dec.)];

- in the second case, which the Court considered under Article 9, the applicants complained of an alleged implicit refusal by the Bulgarian Government to register their organisation. The Court noted that the applicants had received no formal denial of registration; they had received a letter from the Government inviting them to complement and explain the documents submitted, but had decided not to follow these instructions. In view of the circumstances of the case, the Court concluded that the Government's attitude had pointed neither to delaying tactics nor to any implicit refusal (*Boychev and Others v. Bulgaria*).

131. As regards **refusals to re-register** a religious organisation already recognised by the State-either depriving it of legal personality or relegating it to a lower legal status-the Court prefers to consider this kind of case under Article 11 of the Convention (freedom of association) read in conjunction with Article 9. For instance, the Court found a violation of Article 11 in the following cases:

- the Russian authorities' refusal to re-register the local branch of the Salvation Army, thus depriving it of legal personality, on grounds which the Court deemed either devoid of any legal basis in domestic law or arbitrary and unreasonable (the applicant's "foreign origin"; the alleged insufficiency of the data on its religious affiliation; the applicant's alleged "paramilitary" nature; its alleged intention to infringe Russian legislation, etc.) (*Moscow Branch of the Salvation Army v. Russia*, §§ 74–75);
- the Russian authorities' refusal to re-register the local branch of the Church of Scientology, rejecting at least eleven applications for re-registration on mutually contradictory and arbitrary grounds (allegedly incomplete files, with no indication of which documents were missing; request to submit originals rather than copies even though this was not a legal requirement, etc.) (*Church of Scientology of Moscow v. Russia*). In another very similar case the Court found a violation of Article 11 as a result of a refusal to re-register a local branch of the Jehovah's Witnesses (*Jehovah's Witnesses of Moscow and Others v. Russia*);
- a legislative change under which some of the religious organisations previously recognised in Hungary as "churches" were relegated to the status of "associations", a much lower status affording far fewer advantages in terms of rights and privileges (*Magyar Keresztény Mennonita Egyház and Others v. Hungary*);

132. Article 9 § 1 of the Convention does not go so far as to require Contracting States to grant **religious marriages** equal status and equal legal consequences to civil marriage [*X. v. Germany* (dec.); *Khan v. the United Kingdom* (dec.); *Spetz and Others v. Sweden* (dec.); *Serif v. Greece*, § 50; *Şerife Yiğit v. Turkey* [GC], § 102]. Moreover,

Article 9 does not cover the modalities of religious marriage, in the sense that it depends entirely on each particular religion to decide on such modalities. In particular, it is up to each religion to decide whether and the extent to which they permit same-sex unions [*Parry v. the United Kingdom* (dec.)]. Nor is it contrary to Article 9 if the State requires the banns to be published under civil law and refuses to recognise the validity of religious publication of the banns in the framework of an employment-related problem [*Von Pelser v. Italy* (dec.)].

133. The Commission dismissed a complaint from a Belgian national concerning the fact that the Belgian system of combining the spouses' incomes for tax purposes worked to the disadvantage of married couples; according to the applicant, couples under whose religion marriage was a holy sacrament were unable to evade the negative tax consequences of marriage by cohabiting. The Commission found no infringement of the applicant's freedom of religion, considering that it was artificial to compare the situation of a married couple with that of a cohabiting couple by concentrating solely, as the applicant was doing, on the field of income tax and thus overlooking the other rights and obligations arising out of marriage for the spouses, whether in professional or moral terms [*Hubaux v. Belgium* (dec.)].

134. The State is not required to recognise decisions taken by religious courts under the national legal system (*Serif v. Greece*, § 50).

135. Furthermore, the right to manifest religion in "teaching" does not go so far as to entail an obligation on States to allow religious education in public schools (*Savez crkava 'Riječ života' and Others v. Croatia*, § 57). Nevertheless, if the State decides to grant this kind of privilege to certain religious communities, the special rights and privileges fall within the scope of Article 9, such that the prohibition of discrimination enshrined in Article 14 of the Convention becomes applicable (*Savez crkava 'Riječ života' and Others v. Croatia*, § 58).

136. Moreover, if, under domestic law, the ministers of certain denominations are authorised to perform marriages having legal effects in civil law or to adjudicate on certain civil-law dispute (for example in family and inheritance matters), the State has a legitimate

interest in taking special measures to protect from deceit those whose legal relationships can be affected by the acts of religious ministers (*Serif v. Greece*, § 50).

(c) Use by the State of derogatory terms against a religious community

137. The use in official documents of pejorative expressions against a religious community can amount to interference with the rights secured under Article 9 inasmuch as it is liable to have negative consequences for the exercise of freedom of religion (*Leela Förderkreis e. V. and Others v. Germany*, § 84).

138. The Commission declared inadmissible applications concerning the following situations:

- the competent domestic court's dismissal of a request from the applicant association to prohibit the German Federal Government from mentioning it in a governmental publication entitled "So-called youth sects and psycho-groups in the Federal Republic of Germany". The Commission noted that the applicant association's right to manifest its religion had not been infringed because the impugned publication had not had any direct repercussions on the exercise of that right. The publication had been produced for the sole purpose of informing the general public, especially since, according to the domestic courts some of the applicant association's activities-for instance the fact of advocating the replacement of medical treatment by religious belief-justified warning the public about them [*Universelles Leben e. V. v. Germany* (dec.)];

- an article published by the Bavarian Ministry of Education in an educational magazine for the purpose of warning pupils of the alleged dangers of scientology, and the courts' refusal to grant an interim injunction against the distribution of the article. The Commission took the view that the impugned article had targeted scientology in general as a movement operating at world level, not individual adherents of that movement such as the applicants. In so far as the applicants complained of their neighbours' and the local press's negative attitude to them, there was no indication of a causal link between the impugned article and these facts; in any case, the effects of the article were too indirect and remote to have had any effect on their rights under Article 9; the complaint was therefore incompatible *ratione personae* with the Convention [*Keller v. Germany* (dec.)].

139. The Court found no violation of Article 9 in a case in which the applicant associations devoted to the teachings of Bhagwan Shree Rajneesh (Osho) complained of the repeated use in specified official communications from the German Federal Government and its members, of the terms "sect" "youth sect", "psycho-sect", "pseudo-religion", "destructive religious movement", "movement manipulating its members", etc., with reference to those teachings. The German Federal Constitutional Court had decided that the Government was entitled to use most of the terms in issue; on the other hand, the use of the expressions "pseudo-religion" and "destructive religious movement" and the allegation of manipulation were contrary to the Constitution. Drawing on the assumption that there had been interference in the rights guaranteed by Article 9, the European Court of Human Rights held that the interference had pursued legitimate aims (public safety and the protection of public order and the rights and freedoms of others) and had been proportionate to those aims. Indeed, in the exercise of their obligation to inform the public about public-interest issues, the Federal authorities had only intended to draw citizens' attention to a phenomenon which they considered alarming, that is to say the emergence of a multitude of new religious movements and their attractiveness to young people. The only aim pursued by the authorities had been to enable people where necessary to act with full knowledge of the facts and to avoid ending up in difficulties solely because of ignorance. Furthermore, the Government's conduct had in no way prevented the applicant associations from exercising their rights as secured under Article 9 of the Convention; moreover, the German authorities had finally ceased using the impugned terms in pursuance of the recommendations set out in an expert report (*Leela Förderkreis e. V. and Others v. Germany*).

140. The Court also declared inadmissible an application lodged by a group of Jehovah's Witnesses complaining that the French Government had infringed their right to freedom of religion by granting public-interest status to an association known as the "National Union of Associations for the Defence of Families and the Individual" (UNADFI), which pursues the aim of "combating infringements of human rights and fundamental freedoms" committed by

"destructive sects", which association the applicants accused of being openly hostile to their religious community. The Court considered that the State could not be held responsible for all the actions of associations to which, having regard to their statutes, it had granted public-interest status. The fact of granting such status did not effect any transfer of public power, for which transfer the Convention ascribes sole responsibility to the State. Although the applicants considered that the actions of the UNADFI had infringed their rights, such allegations should have been dealt with under the corresponding remedies before the competent domestic courts. The Court ultimately decided that the applicants could not claim to be "victims" of the alleged violation and that their complaints fell outside its jurisdiction *ratione personae* [*Gluchowski and Others v. France* (dec.)].

(d) Financial and tax measures

141. There is no joint standard at the European level in the field of financing and taxing churches or religious communities, as such matters are closely linked to the history and traditions of each individual country. States therefore benefit from a particularly wide margin of appreciation in this sphere [*Alujer Fernández and Caballero Garcia v. Spain* (dec.)].

142. A religious organisation cannot rely on Article 9 of the Convention in order to demand special tax status on the pretext of religious freedom [*Association Sivananda de Yoga Vedanta v. France* (dec.)]. That being the case, freedom of religion does not entail churches or their members being given a different tax status to that of other taxpayers [*Alujer Fernández and Caballero Garcia v. Spain* (dec.)]. Furthermore, Article 9 cannot be interpreted as granting a right to tax exemption in respect of used for worship [*Iglesia Bautista 'El Salvador' and Ortega Moratilla v. Spain* (dec.)]. However, an economic, financial or fiscal measure taken against a religious organisation can sometimes constitute an interference with the exercise of rights secured under Article 9 of the Convention inasmuch as it is demonstrate that it creates a real and serious obstacle to the exercise of those rights. In particular, under certain circumstances, matters relating to the upkeep and use of religious buildings, including expenses incurred owing to the taxation status of those buildings, are liable to have major repercussions on the exercise of the right of members of

religious groups to manifest their religious beliefs (*The Church of Jesus Christ of Latter-day Saints v. the United Kingdom*, § 30; *Cumhuriyetçi Eğitim ve Kültür Merkezi Vakfı v. Turkey*, § 41).

143. For example, the Court found a violation of Article 9 in the following cases:

- taxation of individual donations received by the *Association des Témoins de Jéhovah de France*, accompanied by default interest and surcharges, making the applicant association subject to the standard tax system for associations and excluding it from the tax benefits reserved for certain other associations, including religious ones. The impugned measure, which covered all the individual donations received by the applicant association, totalling 90% of its resources, had the effect of cutting off the association's vital resources, thus preventing it from guaranteeing its adherents' freedom to exercise their religious beliefs. The Court did not consider that the interference complained of met the legality requirement because of the very vague wording of the Article of the General Taxation Code which had been applied [*Association Les Témoins de Jéhovah v. France* (*merits*); for a very similar case with the same outcome, see *Église Évangélique Missionnaire et Salaûn v. France*];

- taxation of individual donations received by two associations intended for the Aumist community and the building of temples in the Mandarom monastery. Prior to the tax adjustment the two association had decided to disband and to transmit all their assets to an association pursuing very similar aims so that it could continue the public activities of the sect in question; the tax authorities then instituted proceedings with the competent court and obtained the cancellation of the financial transfer. The Court acknowledged that since the impugned measure targeted the observance and the place of worship of the religion in question, it amounted to an interference with the exercise of the rights protected by Article 9 of the Convention; the Court found a violation on the same grounds as in the case of *Association Les Témoins de Jéhovah*, (*Association Cultuelle du Temple Pyramide v. France*, and *Association des Chevaliers du Lotus d'Or v. France*).

144. On the other hand, the Court declared inadmissible an application which was similar to those mentioned above apart from the fact that, although the applicant association operated partly on the basis of individual donations, the taxation of the latter had not had the effect of cutting off the association's vital resources or of impeding its religious activities [Sukyo Mahikari France v. France (dec.), § 20].

145. The Court found a violation of Article 14 of the Convention (prohibition of discrimination) in conjunction with Article 9 in the following cases:
- a refusal to exempt the Jehovah's Witnesses community from payment of inheritance and gift tax on the ground that under domestic law such exemption could only be granted to "recognised religious society" and not to "registered religious organisations" such as the applicant community (Jehovas Zeugen in Österreich v. Austria);
- a refusal by the Turkish Directorate of Religious Affairs to pay the electricity bills for an Alevi religious centre housing a *cemevi* (an Alevi place of worship) in the same way as it paid energy bills for mosques, churches and synagogues. This refusal was based on the non-recognition of a *cemevi* as a "place of worship", which was in turn the result of the Turkish authorities' refusal to consider Alevism as a separate religion rather than as a branch of Islam. The Court held that this differential treatment had no objective and reasonable justification (Cumhuriyetçi Eğitim ve Kültür Merkezi Vakfı v. Turkey).

146. On the other hand, the Court found no violation of Article 14 in conjunction with Article 9 as regards a refusal by the United Kingdom authorities to grant a Mormon Temple (which is closed to the public and accessible only to Mormons who hold a current "recommend") total exemption from specified taxes, even though they grant such exemption to Mormon chapels and "stake centres", which are open to the public. The Court voiced doubts as to whether the dispute fell within the ambit of Article 9. However, even supposing that that provision was applicable, the alleged differential treatment did have an objective and reasonable justification: it was based on the idea that access by the general public to religious ceremonies was beneficial to society as a whole because it could dispel

suspicions and help break down prejudice in a multi-faith society. Furthermore, the Mormon Church was not treated any differently from the other religious communities, including the official Anglican Church, whose private chapels were subject to the same tax law as Mormon Temples. Moreover, as a place of worship the Temple in question nonetheless benefited from an 80 % reduction in rates (*The Church of Jesus Christ of Latter-day Saints v. the United Kingdom*).

147. By the same token the organs of the Convention dismissed complaints concerning the following situations:

- a refusal by the Spanish tax authorities to exempt an evangelical protestant church from land tax appertaining to its place of worship, even though the Roman Catholic Church did benefit from such exemption. The Commission found no appearance of discrimination in this case, because the tax exemptions enjoyed by the Roman Catholic Church had been provided for by the agreements concluded by the respondent State and the Holy See, which imposed mutual obligations on both parties. On the other hand, given that the applicant community had never requested the conclusion of such an agreement with the State, it did not have the same obligations as the Roman Catholic Church *vis-à-vis* the latter [*Iglesia Bautista 'El Salvador' and Ortega Moratilla v. Spain* (dec.)];

- the fact of imposing corporate tax on the applicant association, which was involved in the teaching of yoga, on the ground that it provided yoga lessons on a profit-making basis. Furthermore, the Commission rejected the applicant association's allegation that it had suffered discrimination as compared with the religious activities of other communities, particularly those of the Roman Catholic Church, whose non-profit status was recognised by the State. Lacking religious association status the applicant association was not in an analogous or even a comparable situation to that of religious associations [*Association Sivananda de Yoga Vedanta v. France*, (dec.)];

- a decision by the German authorities and courts to place the donation which had been given to the applicant, an Islamic association, by the Party of Democratic

Socialism under the regime of the former German Democratic Republic (GDR), under the administration of the Trust Agency, and the seizure of the corresponding assets. The Court noted that the impugned measure had been ordered under exceptional circumstances related to German reunification; more specifically, the measure had been implemented under the general regulations introduced in the GDR during the pre-reunification period with a view to checking the provenance of assets belonging to political parties and related organisations. Having found that the impugned interference was in conformity with Article 1 of Protocol No. 1 (protection of property), the Court reached the same conclusion as regards Article 9. It voiced doubts as to the existence of an interference with the exercise of freedom of religion because the impugned measure had concerned neither the internal organisation of the applicant association nor its official recognition by the State. In any case the said measure had been prescribed by law, had pursued the legitimate aims of protecting public morals and the rights and liberties of others, and had not been disproportionate to those aims [*Islamische Religionsgemeinschaft in Berlin e. V. v. Germany* (dec.)].

148. Some European States have a **religious tax** (church tax, denominational tax, etc.), levied either by the State, which then transfers it to specific religious organisations, or directly by religious organisations, which can enforce payment under proceedings in the national courts. In other States taxpayers may legally allocate a certain proportion of their income tax to a specified religious organisation. The existence of such a religious tax does not in itself raise any issues under Article 9 of the Convention, as the State's right to levy such a tax is one of the "legitimate aims" mentioned in Article 9 § 2 (*Wasmuth v. Germany*, § 55). Moreover, Article 1 of Protocol No. 1 on the protection of property explicitly empowers the State to levy taxes [*C. v. the United Kingdom* (dec.)]. Nevertheless, the wide margin of appreciation granted to States in matters of church tax does not mean that no freedom of religion issues can ever arise in this sphere. On the contrary, the Court has stated that there may be situations in which an interference linked to

the church tax system is significant and where the exercise of balancing the competing interests may lead it to find a violation (*Wasmuth v. Allemagne*, § 61).

149. The levying by a Church, with State assistance, of contributions payable by its members does not, as such, interfere with the activities listed in Article 9 § 1 ("worship, teaching, practice and observance"). The situation of the members of a religious organisation in this connection is comparable to the obligation to contribute to a private association of which one is a member, and Article 9 cannot be interpreted as conferring on the individual the right to remain a member of a Church and yet to be exempted from the legal, and particularly the financial, obligations stemming from such membership in accordance with the autonomous regulations of the Church in question [*E. and G. R. v. Austria* (dec.)].

150. Clearly, even though the State may levy a church tax or a similar contribution for a Church, such measure **can only cover the latter's *membership*** -save in exceptional cases where the Church in question also performs certain public-service functions which are by nature non-religious and where the tax in question is used only for financing said non-religious functions:

- the Commission found a violation of Article 9 of the Convention in a case where the applicant, who worked in Sweden but who did hold legal Swedish "resident" status, had been required to pay church tax for the Church of Sweden (a Lutheran church which held State Church status at the time) to which he did not belong, without any possibility of exemption (see the Commission's opinion in the case of *Darby v. Sweden*, §§ 57-60). However, when the case reached the Court, the latter decided to consider it in the light not of Article 9 but of Article 14 of the Convention, taken in conjunction with Article 1 of Protocol No. 1 (discrimination between residents and non-residents in the exercise of their right to protection of property), of which it found a violation (*Darby v. Sweden*, §§ 34-35);
- the Court declared manifestly ill-founded a complaint lodged by a Swedish national who was not a member of the Church of Sweden but nonetheless had to pay it a "dissenting tax" corresponding to 25% of the standard church tax. The Court

noted that the contribution demanded of the applicant in this case was intended to fund non-religious work carried out by the Church of Sweden in the interests of the whole population, such as organising funerals, looking after elderly persons and managing the national architectural heritage; furthermore, the figure of 25% was not arbitrary but had been calculated on the basis of the percentage of the cost of such activities within the Church's overall economy [*Bruno v. Sweden* (dec.); *Lundberg v. Sweden* (dec.)].

151. All the cases cited above concerned *natural persons*. However, an exclusively profit-making *commercial company* cannot, even if it has been set up and is run by a philosophical association, cannot rely upon Article 9 in order to avoid paying the church tax levied on the basis of a law applicable to all commercial companies [*Company X. v. Switzerland* (dec.); *Kustannus OY Vapaa Ajattelija AB and Others v. Finland* (dec.)].

152. Therefore, church tax is not in itself contrary to freedom of religion where domestic law allows the individual to **leave the church concerned** if he so wishes. Nevertheless, the domestic authorities have a wide discretion to decide on what conditions an individual may validly be regarded as having decided to leave a religious denomination; they can therefore demand a clear, unequivocal expression of the person's wishes in that regard [*Gottesmann v. Switzerland* (dec.)].

153. The organs of the Convention found no appearance of a violation of Article 9 (alone or in conjunction with Article 14 prohibiting discrimination) in the following cases:
- the implementation in respect of the applicants, a Roman Catholic couple, of the Austrian system of church contributions requiring them pay regular contributions to the Roman Catholic Church; in the event of non-payment that Church was entitled to institute civil proceedings against them for payment of the amounts in question. The Commission noted that the obligation in issue could be obviated it the applicants left the Church; by explicitly providing for such a possibility in legislation the State had created sufficient safeguards to guarantee the applicants' exercise of their freedom of religion; on the other hand the applicants could not derive from Article 9 of the Convention any "right" to retain their membership of

the Roman Catholic Church while also being exempted from the obligations imposed by the latter. Furthermore, the fact that the State places its civil courts at the disposal of the Churches, on the same basis as any other entity or person, to secure the enforcement of an obligation does raise no issues as regards the right to protection of property secured under Article 1 of Protocol No. 1 [*E. and G. R. v. Austria* (dec.)];

- the obligation imposed on the applicants by the Swiss authorities to pay retroactively a church tax liable by dint of their belonging to the Roman Catholic Church for a period when, in their submission, they had no longer been members of that Church. In fact the national authorities had only recognised their withdrawal from the Church from the time each of them had explicitly and clearly expressed their wish no longer to belong to it, arguing that the mere fact of crossing out the space for religious details on their tax returns was insufficient for the purpose [*Gottesmann v. Switzerland* (dec.)];

- the choice given to the applicants, a group of Spanish evangelical protestants, between allocating a certain proportion of their income tax either to financially supporting the Roman Catholic Church or to other activities in the public interest, but not to their own Church. The Court noted that the religious community to which the applicants belonged had not attempted to conclude an agreement with the Spanish State enabling the tax to be used as they wished, despite the fact that domestic law allowed for that option. The special fiscal advantages granted to the Roman Catholic Church was based on agreements entered into by the respondent State and the Holy See, which imposed mutual obligations on both parties, for instance requiring the Church to place its historic, artistic and documentary heritage at the service of Spanish society as a whole [*Alujer Fernández and Caballero Garcia v. Spain* (dec.)];

- the facility for Italian taxpayers to allocate eight thousandths of their income tax to the State, the Roman Catholic Church or one of the institutions representing the other five religions which had agreed to accept such a subsidy on concluding a special agreement with the State. Contrary to the applicant's contentions, the Court found that the law also gave taxpayers the option of refraining from making any such choice, such that the impugned provision did not entail an obligation to manifest one's religious beliefs [*Spampinato v. Italy* (dec.)];

- national legislation which entitled the members of *all* legally recognised religious communities to allocate a proportion of their tax to their respective community, but also granted specified annual amounts from the State budget exclusively to the national Church (the Lutheran Church of Iceland), whose ministers hold civil servant status [*Ásatrúarfélagið v. Iceland* (dec.)].

154. It should be noted that the aforementioned cases concerned either a specific church tax or the voluntary allocation by taxpayers of a specific proportion of the general tax which they paid to the tax authorities. However, Article 9 of the Convention does not grant the taxpayer any rights *vis-à-*vis the **State's general fiscal and budgetary** policy where there is no direct, traceable link between the payment of a specified amount and its subsequent utilisation. Consequently, the Commission dismissed a complaint from a pacifist Quaker who had refused to pay a certain percentage of his tax unless he could be sure it would not be allocated to financing the military sector. The Commission took the view that the obligation to pay tax was an obligation of a general nature which had no specific impact as such in terms of conscientious objection; its neutrality was illustrated by the fact that taxpayers could not influence the allocation of their taxes or decide on such allocation once the taxes had been levied [*C. v. the United Kingdom* (dec.), as confirmed in *H. and B. v. the United Kingdom* (dec.)]. The Commission reached the same conclusion in the case of a French lawyer who was opposed to abortion and who demanded the right not to pay a specific proportion of tax which was used to fund abortions [*Bouessel du Bourg v. France* (dec.)].

155. The Commission subsequently specified that that there was no appearance of an infringement of freedom of religion even where a State used the budgetary appropriations obtained through general taxation to support specific religious communities or their religious activities (see the Commission's opinion in *Darby v. Sweden*, § 56).

156. As regards compulsory insurance and social security, in the 1960s the Commission dealt with several applications from Dutch reformed Protestants who were demanding the

right, relying on Article 9, not to take out various types of compulsory insurance and not to be affiliated to certain bodies or mechanisms set up by the State. They argued as follows: first of all, God sends both prosperity and adversity to mankind and it is therefore forbidden to attempt to prevent or limit in advance the effects of possible misfortune. Secondly, in the Bible God orders all Christians to provide sustenance to the elderly and infirm; that being the case, by taking over this matter and setting up a State old-age pension system, the authorities had breached God's express commandment, and the applicants refused to be associated with this sin. In this category of cases the Commission dismissed the following complaints:

- a complaint from a milk dealer concerning penalties imposed on him owing to his refusal to join the health insurance scheme, which is a legal precondition for stockbreeding; even supposing that there had been an interference with the exercise of the rights secured under Article 9, it had been "necessary in a democratic society" for the purposes of protecting "public health", which aim could reasonably include the prevention of livestock diseases (see *X. v. the Netherlands*①);

- a complaint from a Reformed Church and two of its representatives who, although they were not opposed to all forms of insurance, nonetheless wished to be exempted from the obligation to contribute to the old-age pension scheme. The Commission noted that Netherlands law exempted conscientious objectors from contributing directly to the scheme, replacing such contributions with equivalent payments in the form of taxes. The national legislature had therefore taken sufficient account of the specific interests of the Reformed Church and there had been no appearance of a violation of Article 9 in that case (see *Reformed Church X. and Others v. the Netherlands*②);

- a complaint from a man alleging discrimination because Netherlands legislation

---

① Decision available in paper copy only in the **Yearbooks of the European Convention on Human Rights at the** Court.

② Decision available in paper copy only in the **Yearbooks of the European Convention on Human Rights at the** Court library.

only exempted from compulsory contribution to the old-age pension scheme (while requiring those concerned to pay equivalent amounts in the form of taxes) persons who, for religiousreasons, were strictly opposed to all forms of insurance, which did not apply to the applicant [X. v. the Netherlands (dec.)];

- a complaint from a shopkeeper opposed to all forms of insurance who had been sentenced to a fine and the confiscation of his professional vehicle for driving it without the compulsory civil-liability insurance. The applicant acknowledged that he was eligible for the exemption prescribed by law, but since he would in any case be paying equivalent sums in the form of taxes, he considered this option as morally unacceptable. The Commission found that the interference complained of was "necessary in a democratic society" for the protection "of the rights of others", that is to say of third persons liable to the victims of potential accidents [X. v. the Netherlands (dec.)].

157. Somewhat more recently, the Commission also dismissed a similar application lodged by a Dutch doctor, who was a general medical practitioner following anthroposophical principles, demanding the right not to be affiliated to a professional pension scheme as required by law. The Commission found that the obligation of affiliation to a pension scheme applied to all general practitioners on a completely neutral basis and could not be said to be closely linked in any way with the applicant's religion or beliefs [V. v. the Netherlands (dec.)].

158. The Court found that there was no appearance of a violation of Article 14 (prohibition of discrimination) taken in conjunction with Article 9 in a case where the a health insurance fund required the leaders of a Christian-based association "geared to working towards full human self-development through art and beauty" to subscribe to the general social security system on the grounds that their activities, for which the association defrayed all the relevant costs, were "paid" rather than "voluntary", in legal terms. The applicant association considered that it had suffered discriminatory treatment as compared with the ministers of religious denominations whose religious activities did not come under the general social security system, and also as compared with other voluntary workers in the

federation to which the applicant association belonged. The Court found that under French law monks and nuns were subject to the general social security system, while retaining the possibility of being admitted to a special scheme; however, when taking part in activities extraneous to their religious training they were subject to the general social security system [*Office Culturel de Cluny v. France* (dec.)].

(e) Measures taken against religiously inspired political parties

159. Article 9 neither prohibits the subsidising of political parties nor confers the right to stand in elections as a political party [*X., Y. and Z. v. Germany* (dec.)].

160. The Court has never held that the setting up of a **political party inspired by the postulates of a religion** is a form of "manifestation of religion" protected by Article 9 of the Convention. On the other hand, it has dealt with applications lodged by such parties complaining of measures taken against them by States. In this regard the Court has found that a political party can promote a change in the law or the legal and constitutional structures of the State on two conditions: firstly, the means used to that end must be legal and democratic; secondly, the change proposed must itself be compatible with fundamental democratic principles. It necessarily follows that a political party whose leaders incite to violence or put forward a policy which fails to respect democracy or which is aimed at the destruction of democracy and the flouting of the rights and freedoms recognised in a democracy cannot lay claim to the Convention's protection against penalties imposed on those grounds. Provided that it satisfies these conditions, a political party animated by the moral values imposed by a religion cannot be regarded as intrinsically inimical to the fundamental principles of democracy, as set forth in the Convention [*Refah Partisi (the Welfare Party) and Others v. Turkey* [GC]; *Staatkundig Gereformeerde Partij v. the Netherlands* (dec.), § 71]. On the other hand, any Contracting State may legitimately prevent the application within its jurisdiction of private-law rules of religious inspiration prejudicial to public order and the values of democracy for Convention purposes (*Refah Partisi (the Welfare Party) and Others v. Turkey* [GC], § 128).

161. For example, the Court found:

- no violation of Article 11 of the Convention (freedom of association) in a case of the dissolution of a Turkish political party and the temporary prohibition banning leaders from holding similar office in any other political party. The Court noted that the party in question was endeavouring to establish a political system based on Islamic law (sharia) (which would be incompatible with democracy) and a plurality of legal systems permitting discrimination based on the gender of the parties concerned, as in polygamy and privileges for the male sex in matters of divorce and succession (which would be contrary to sex equality, one of the fundamental values protected by the Convention) [*Refah Partisi (the Welfare Party) and Others v. Turkey* [GC], § 128];

- the inadmissibility on grounds of incompatibility *ratione materiae* with the Convention of an application lodged by a "global Islamic political party" complaining of the prohibition by the relevant German authorities of its activities in Germany. The Court considered that since it called for the violent destruction of the State of Israel and for the banishment and killing of its inhabitants, this party could not rely on the protection of Articles 9, 10 and 11, in pursuance of Article 17 of the Convention (prohibition of abuse of fundamental rights) [*Hizb Ut-Tahrir and Others v. Germany* (dec.)];

- the inadmissibility as manifestly ill-founded of an application lodged by the Dutch Reformed Protestant Party complaining about a judgment delivered by the Netherlands Supreme Court to the effect that the State should take (unspecified) action to terminate the said party's practice of not admitting women to its governing bodies or on to its lists of candidates for elections, that practice being motivated by a sincere belief based on certain passages of the Bible. The Court considered the application under Articles 9, 10 and 11 of the Convention without distinction. Leaving aside the question whether the applicant party could consider itself as a "victim" before any specific action had been taken against it, the Court declared that the party's position on the role of women in politics blatantly contradicted the fundamental values of the Convention. The Court did not consider decisive the fact that no woman had ever expressed a wish to stand as a candidate for the applicant party [*Staatkundig Gereformeerde Partij v. the Netherlands* (dec.)].

2. Negative obligations: respect for the autonomy of religious organisations

(a) Principle of the autonomy of religious organisations

162. Religious communities have traditionally and universally existed in the form of organised structures. In cases concerning the mode of organisation of the religious community in question, Article 9 of the Convention must be interpreted in the light of Article 11, which safeguards associative life against unjustified State interference. Regarded from this angle, the believers' right to freedom of religion encompasses the expectation that the community will be allowed to function peacefully, free from arbitrary State intervention. The **autonomous existence of religious communities** is indispensable for pluralism in a democratic society and is therefore an issue at the very heart of the protection which Article 9 affords. It directly concerns not only the organisation of the community as such but also the effective enjoyment of the right to freedom of religion by all its active members. Were the organisational life of the community not protected by Article 9 of the Convention, all other aspects of the individual's freedom of religion would become vulnerable (*Hassan and Tchaouch v. Bulgaria* [GC], §§ 62 and 91; *Fernández Martínez v. Spain* [GC], § 127). The **internal structure** of a religious organisation and the regulations governing its membership must be seen as a means by which such organisations are able to express their beliefs and maintain their religious traditions (*Sviato-Mykhaïlivska Parafiya v. Ukraine*, § 150).

163. The above-mentioned autonomy principle means that the State cannot oblige a religious community to admit new members or exclude existing members. Religious associations must be completely free to determine at their own discretion the manner in which new members are admitted and existing members excluded (*Sviato-Mykhaïlivska Parafiya v. Ukraine*, §§ 146 and 150).

164. When conducting their activities, religious communities abide by rules which are often seen by followers as being of a divine origin. Religious ceremonies have their meaning and sacred value for the believers if they have been conducted by ministers empowered for that purpose in compliance with these rules. The personality of the religious

ministers is undoubtedly of importance to every member of the community. Participation in the life of the community is thus a particular manifestation of one's religion, protected by Article 9 of the Convention (*Hassan and Tchaouch v. Bulgaria* [GC], § 62; *Miroḷubovs and Others v. Latvia*, § 80).

165. For example, the Court found a violation of Article 9 as a result of measures regulating the religious life of Greek Cypriots of Orthodox faith enclaved in the "Turkish Republic of Northern Cyprus": the authorities of the latter had not approved the appointment of priests in the region even though there was only one priest left to cover the whole region (*Cyprus v. Turkey* [GC], §§ 243 – 246).

166. Punishing a person merely for acting as the religious leader of a group that willingly followed him-even if that fact was not recognised by the State-can hardly be considered compatible with the demands of religious pluralism in a democratic society (*Serif v. Greece*, § 51). The Court found that there had been a violation of Article 9 on the grounds that the applicant, a Greek Muslim theologian, had been convicted for having "usurped the functions of a minister of a 'known religion'" and for having "publicly worn the dress of such a minister without having the right to do so". In fact the applicant had been elected Mufti of Rodopi by fellow Muslims without recognition by the State, which had appointed someone else to the post of Mufti. He had indeed taken part in a series of religious celebrations as Mufti but had never attempted to exercise the judicial and administrative functions laid down in the State legislation on muftis and other ministers of "recognised religions" (*Serif v. Greece*). In a similar case, this time concerning the person elected as Mufti of Xanthi, the Court reached the same conclusion, pointing out that the theoretical possibility that the coexistence of two muftis might cause tension among the local residents was insufficient to legitimise the impugned interference, because, precisely, it was incumbent on the State authorities to ensure mutual tolerance between opposing groups [*Agga v. Greece* (no. 2); see also *Agga v. Greece* (no. 3); *Agga v. Greece* (no. 4)].

167. In connection with the Salvation Army, whose internal structure is based on a system of ranks similar to those of the army and on the wearing of a uniform, the Court

held that this situation could be seen as a legitimate manifestation of that organisation's religious beliefs. Accordingly, it could not be seriously claimed that this meant that the Salvation Army infringed the integrity or the security of the State (*Moscow Branch of the Salvation Army v. Russia*, § 92).

(b) State interference in intra-or inter-denominational conflicts

168. Pluralism, tolerance and broadmindedness are hallmarks of a "democratic society". Although individual interests must on occasion be subordinated to those of a group, democracy does not simply mean that the views of a majority must always prevail: a balance must be achieved which ensures the fair and proper treatment of people from minorities and avoids any abuse of a dominant position (*Leyla Şahin v. Turkey* [GC], § 108). Pluralism and democracy must also be based on dialogue and a spirit of compromise necessarily entailing various concessions on the part of individuals or groups of individuals which are justified in order to maintain and promote the ideals and values of a democratic society (*S. A. S. v. France* [GC], § 128). In a democratic society, in which several religions coexist within one and the same population, it may be necessary to place restrictions on this freedom in order to reconcile the interests of the various groups and ensure that everyone's beliefs are respected. However, in exercising its regulatory power in this sphere and in its relations with the various religions, denominations and beliefs, the State has a duty to remain neutral and impartial. What is at stake here is the preservation of pluralism and the proper functioning of democracy (*Metropolitan Church of Bessarabia and Others v. Moldova*, §§ 115 – 116).

169. From that angle, the Court has frequently emphasised the State's role as the neutral and impartial organiser of the exercise of various religions, faiths and beliefs, emphasising that this role is conducive to public order, religious harmony and tolerance in a democratic society (*Bayatyan v. Armenia* [GC], § 120; *S. A. S. v. France* [GC], § 127). That applies both to relations between believers and non-believers and to relations between the adherents of various religions, faiths and beliefs (*Lautsi and Others v. Italy* [GC], § 60).

170. This duty of neutrality cannot be conceived as being likely to diminish the role of

a faith or a Church with which the population of a specific country has historically and culturally been associated (*Members of the Gldani Congregation of the Jehovah's Witnesses and Others v. Georgia*, § 132). Indeed, the decision whether or not to perpetuate a tradition falls, in principle, within the margin of appreciation of the respondent State. The Court must also take into account the fact that Europe is marked by a great diversity between its component States, particularly in the sphere of cultural and historical development. However, the reference to tradition cannot relieve a Contracting State of its obligation to respect the rights and freedoms enshrined in the Convention and its Protocols (*Lautsi and Others v. Italy* [GC], § 68).

171. The State's duty of neutrality and impartiality is incompatible with any discretion on the part of the State to determine whether religious beliefs or the means used to express such beliefs are legitimate (*Manoussakis and Others v. Greece*, § 47; *Bayatyan v. Armenia* [GC], § 120). Similarly, where domestic law makes the exercise of the right to freedom of religion or of one of its aspects subject to a system of prior authorisation, interfering in the procedure for granting authorisation of a recognised ecclesiastical authority-especially one belonging to a different denomination, hierarchy or religion-cannot be reconciled with the requirements of Article 9 § 2 (*Metropolitan Church of Bessarabia and Others v. Moldova*, § 117; *Vergos v. Greece*, § 34).

172. The duty of neutrality prevents the State from deciding the question of the **religious belonging** of an individual or group, which is the sole responsibility of the supreme spiritual authorities of the religious community in question (*Miroļubovs and Others v. Latvia*, §§ 89 – 90). In other words, the State cannot arbitrarily "impose" or "reclassify" the religious belonging of individuals or groups against their will. For example, the Court found a violation of Article 9 in the following cases:

- the applicant's inability to secure the replacement of the "Islam" entry on his identity card with the word "Alevi", because the State authority responsible for matters relating to the Muslim religion considered that the Alevi religion was only a branch of Islam (*Sinan Işık v. Turkey*, §§ 45 –46);
- a decision taken by the Latvian Directorate of Religious Affairs in the framework of

a bitter dispute in the local Old-Orthodox community (adherents of the Russian Old-Orthodox Church); the decision, which had been adopted on the basis of two opinions provided by experts, none of whom belonged to the Old-Orthodox religion, stated that by taking communion with a priest of the Russian Orthodox Church the applicants had *ipso facto* changed denomination. The implementation of that decision led to the applicants' expulsion from their place of worship (*Miroļubovs and Others v. Latvia*, §§ 33 – 36 and 88 – 89).

173. State action favouring one leader of a divided religious community or undertaken with the purpose of forcing the community to **come together under a single leadership** against its own wishes would likewise constitute an interference with freedom of religion. In democratic societies the State does not need to take measures to promote one interpretation of religion to the detriment of others or to force a divided religious community or a part thereof to merge under a unified leadership (*Hassan and Tchaouch v. Bulgaria* [GC], § 78; *Metropolitan Church of Bessarabia and Others v. Moldova*, § 117). When a group of adherents and/or ministers of religion splits off from the community to which they previously belonged, or even decides to change denomination, such an act is an instance of collective exercise of the "freedom to change religion or belief", which is expressly guaranteed by Article 9 § 1 of the Convention (*Miroļubovs and Others v. Latvia*, § 93). The role of the State authorities is not to remove the cause of tension by eliminating pluralism, but to ensure that the competing groups tolerate each other, even where both they originated from the same group (*Metropolitan Church of Bessarabia and Others v. Moldova*, § 123).

174. The State's role as the ultimate guarantor of religious pluralism may sometimes require it to **mediate** between opposing parties; neutral mediation between groups of believers would not, in principle, amount to State interference with the believers' rights under Article 9 of the Convention, although the State authorities must exercise caution in this particularly delicate area (*Supreme Holy Council of the Muslim Community v. Bulgaria*, § 80). At all events, any decision taken by the State authorities in this sphere

must be based on an acceptable assessment of the relevant facts (*Sviato-Mykhaïlivska Parafiya v. Ukraine*, § 138).

175. For example, the Court found a violation of Article 9 of the Convention in the following cases:

- a refusal by the Moldovan authorities to grant legal recognition to the Metropolitan Church of Bessarabia, an autonomous Orthodox Churchoperating under the authority of the Patriarchate of Bucharest (Romanian Orthodox Church), on the ground that such recognition would jeopardise the interests of the Metropolitan Church of Moldova, which comes under the Patriarchate of Moscow (Russian Orthodox Church) and which was already recognised by the Government. By denying recognition on the ground that the applicant Church was only a "schismatic group" *vis-à-vis* the Russian Church and declaring that the adherents of the applicant Church could manifest their religion in the other Orthodox Church recognised by the State, the Moldovan Government had failed in its duty of neutrality and impartiality (*Metropolitan Church of Bessarabia and Others v. Moldova*);

- an arbitrary refusal by the Ukrainian authorities to recognise and register changes to the statutes of an Orthodox parish as adopted by the plenary assembly of its membership, pursuant to which the parish transferred from the jurisdiction of the Russian Orthodox Church (Patriarchate of Moscow) to that of the Ukrainian Orthodox Church (Patriarchate of Kyiv). One of the main aspects of the arbitrariness noted in this case lay in the fact that the Ukrainian authorities and courts had completely ignored the internal organisation of the parish as defined in its statutes, considered as "parishioners" persons who did not hold parishioner status according to the statutes, and concluded that the plenary assembly in question was illegitimate because those persons had not attended. As the domestic courts had failed to remedy the arbitrary action of the administrative authorities, the Court found a violation of Article 9 of the Convention in conjunction with Articles 6 § 1 and 11 (*Sviato-Mykhaïlivska Parafiya v. Ukraine*).

176. The case of *Miroļubovs and Others* concerned State interference in a dispute which had been tearing the religious community in question apart. However, the State can sometimes find itself involved in intra-denominational dispute which it has itself directly helped to create. In this regard we should mention three Court judgments in three similar cases against Bulgaria. All these cases must be seen in the peculiar historical and political context of this country, which had in 1989 instigated a rapid transition from the communist totalitarian regime to democracy. After 1989 the Bulgarian State pursued a policy of interfering in the internal functioning of the two largest religious communities in the country, namely the Orthodox Church and the Muslims. The Government first of all attempted to secure the replacement of the leaders of both religious organisations because of their alleged collaboration with the old communist regime; that policy immediately caused a split in each of the religious communities in question. Subsequently, after successive general elections, every new government adopted measures to try to bring together each of the two communities under the sole leadership of religious dignitaries deemed politically loyal to the ruling party, while sidelining opposing group leaders. Furthermore, under the standard administrative practice of the Bulgarian authorities, the Law on religious denominations was interpreted as prohibiting the operation of two parallel organisations belonging to the same denomination and requiring a single leadership for each denomination, such leadership being the only one recognised by the State [for a general summary of the situation, see *Holy Synod of the Bulgarian Orthodox Church (Metropolitan Inokentiy) and Others v. Bulgaria*, §§ 68 and 127].

177. In this context, the Court found a violation of Article 9 of the Convention in all three cases, as follows:

- the Bulgarian Government's interference in the choice of leaders of the Muslim community by recognising, without providing any reasons or explanations, the leaders of the party opposing the applicants as the sole legitimate representatives of the entire community. Although the Bulgarian Supreme Court had ruled that the Council of Ministers was required to consider the request for registration submitted by the first applicant, the Government had refused to comply with this injunction.

The Court found that the impugned interference had not been "prescribed by law" in that it had been arbitrary and based on legal provisions which allowed an unfettered discretion to the executive (*Hassan and Tchaouch v. Bulgaria* [GC]);

- the fact that the national authorities had organised a Bulgarian Muslim Unification Conference in order to put an end to the aforementioned split and interfere very actively in the preparation and running of the conference, particularly where the selection of participants was concerned. The applicant in this case was the Supreme Holy Council of the Muslim Community, representing the side opposed to that of Mr Hasan and Mr Chaush and refusing to recognise the legitimacy of the conference in question. In this case the Bulgarian authorities had exerted pressure on the split Muslim community with a view to forcing it to accept a single leadership, instead of just noting the failure of the efforts at reunification and, if necessary, continuing to act as mediators for both parties in a spirit of dialogue. The Court found that the impugned interference was "prescribed by law" and pursued a legitimate aim but was disproportionate to that aim (*Supreme Holy Council of the Muslim Community v. Bulgaria*);

- State interference in a dispute which was tearing the Bulgarian Orthodox Church apart and which the Government had itself directly fomented in 1992 by declaring invalid the election of Patriarch Maxim to lead the Church and instead appointing a temporary leadership (referred to as the "alternative Synod"). Having regard to the particular circumstances of the case the Court rejected the Government's argument that the members of the "alternative Synod" and their adherents had been free to create and register their own Church alongside the Church led by Patriarch Maxim. The dispute had in fact concerned not the refusal to recognise a religious organisation but the interference by the State in the internal affairs of a community torn between two hierarchies, each of which considered the other as non-canonical on the basis of arguments which were, on the face of it, neither fabricated nor unreasonable. By helping one of the parties to the dispute to obtain exclusive power of representation and control over the affairs of the entire Orthodox community, sidelining the adverse party and sending in the law enforcement agencies to help expel the adherents of the applicant Synod from the places of worship which they were occupying, the Bulgarian State had failed in its obligation of neutrality [*Holy Synod of the Bulgarian Orthodox Church (Metropolitan Inokentiy) and Others v. Bulgaria*; see also *Sotirov and Others v. Bulgaria* (dec.)].

178. On the other hand, the Court found a lack of any appearance of violation of Article 9 (alone or in conjunction with Article 14 of the Convention) in a case of alleged failure to enforce a final judgment granting the Greek Catholic parish access to the cemetery which it shared with the Orthodox parish, in the context of the change of denomination effected by the former Orthodox priest and some of the parishioners, who had been converted to the Greek Catholic Church. The Court noted that the authorities had taken appropriate and reasonable measures to quell the dispute (including allocating funds to build a new Greek Catholic Church and creating a new cemetery). As regards the impugned judgment, the applicant parish had not shown the requisite diligence in ensuring its proper enforcement [*Greek Catholic Parish Pesceana and Others v. Romania* (dec.), § 43].

179. State interference in an inter-or intra-denominational dispute must be distinguished from the mere fact of the national authorities **drawing the inevitable secular conclusions** from a pre-existing religious dispute when they themselves did not help create and in which they have not taken sides [*Griechische Kirchengemeinde München und Bayern e. V. v. Germany* (dec.); see also *Serbisch-griechisch-orientalische Kirchengemeinde zum Heiligen Sava in Wien v. Austria* (dec.)]. For instance, the Court declared inadmissible as manifestly ill-founded a complaint from a Greek Orthodox community concerning the compulsory return to the State of a church which had been placed at its disposal for over 150 years. In 1828 King Ludwig I of Bavaria had made the building available to the "Greek religious community, subject to State ownership". In the 1970s, however, the community had broken off relations with the local Metropolis of the Patriarchate of Constantinople, to which it had previously belonged, and transferred to the jurisdiction of the "True Orthodox Church". Following a series of suits brought by the State of Bavaria, the German courts

decided that the loan of the building dating from 1828 should be considered revoked and that the church building should revert to the State for subsequent transfer to the Metropolis. The courts held that the use of the building at issue by the applicant community had become incompatible with the intentions of the original donator (King Ludwig I), who had wished to make over the church to a group genuinely representative of the local Greek Orthodox community and in communion with the Greek Orthodox Church and the Patriarchate of Constantinople; however, the applicant community had no longer satisfied those conditions. Having regard to the arguments put forward by the domestic courts, the Court found no appearance of an interference by the national authorities in an intra-religious dispute and or of an infringement of the principle of State neutrality [*Griechische Kirchengemeinde München und Bayern e. V. v. Germany* (dec.)].

180. The **right to use a religious building** was also central to the case of *Miroļubovs and Others*, in which the applicants, adherents of the Old-Orthodox Church of Latvia, had lost the use of their church to the adverse group, the Directorate of Religious Affairs having decided that they had changed denomination *de facto* and could no longer legitimately represent the religious community in question. Finding a violation of Article 9 of the Convention, the Court was careful to draw a distinction between this case and that of *Griechische Kirchengemeinde München und Bayern e. V*; it emphasised that the Latvian authorities had genuinely interfered in the religious dispute instead of confining themselves to drawing the legal conclusions from it at the secular level (*Miroļubovs and Others v. Latvia*, § 94).

(c) Disputes between religious organisations and their members (adherents and ministers of religion)

181. States are not obliged to require religious communities coming under their jurisdiction to ensure freedom of religion and expression for the adherents and ministers of the religion in question [*X. v. Denmark* (dec.)]. It is a common feature of many religions that they determine doctrinal standards of behaviour by which their followers must abide in their private lives (*Jehovah's Witnesses of Moscow and Others v. Russia*, § 118). Consequently, Article 9 of the Convention does not secure any right to dissent within

a religious organisation. Respect for the autonomy of religious communities recognised by the State implies, in particular, that the State should accept the right of such communities to react, in accordance with their own rules and interests, to any dissident movements emerging within them that might pose a threat to their cohesion, image or unity. It is therefore not the task of the national authorities to act as the arbiter between religious organisations and the various dissident factions that exist or may emerge within them (*Sindicatul 'Păstorul cel Bun' v. Romania* [GC], § 165; *Fernández Martínez v. Spain* [GC], § 128). Similarly, Article 9 does not guarantee to believers a right to choose the religious leaders of their community or to oppose decisions by the religious organisation regarding the election or appointment of ministers [*Kohn v. Germany* (dec.); *Sotirov and Others v. Bulgaria* (dec.)]. In the event of doctrinal or organisational disagreement between a religious community and one of its members, the latter's freedom of religion is exercised by his freedom to leave the community in question [*X. v. Denmark* (dec.);, *Miroļubovs and Others v. Latvia*, § 80].

182. Nevertheless, Article 9 § 1 cannot be interpreted as granting an individual any "right" to oblige the Church to "annul" a baptism or confirmation which he or she received in childhood [*X. v. Iceland* (dec.)].

183. The organs of the Convention declared inadmissible the applications concerning the following cases:

- adecision by the Danish Church Ministry to instigate disciplinary proceedings against a clergyman of the Danish National (Lutheran) Church for having made the christening of children subject to an additional condition which was not required by the Church [*X. v. Denmark* (dec.)];
- adecision by the diocesan chapter of the Swedish National (Lutheran) Church of the time, as confirmed by the Government, to declare the applicant unqualified for the post of vicar because he was opposed to the ordination of women and had failed to state his willingness to cooperate with women priests [*Karlsson v. Sweden* (dec.)];
- an applicant, a priest in the Church of England, who objected to a decision by the

Synod of the Church to ordain women [*Williamson v. the United Kingdom* (dec.)];

- a decision by the Marriage Board of the Pentecostal Movement to revoke the applicants' right to conduct marriage ceremonies recognised by the State on the ground that they no longer belonged to the Movement in question [*Spetz and Others v. Sweden* (dec.)];
- a former member of the Administrative Council of the Hanover Jewish community who complained about the enforcement by the German courts of a decision given by the arbitration tribunal of the Central Jewish Consistory of Germany, stating that he had forfeited his post and ordering his expulsion from the premises of the said community; in this case there had been no interference by the State because the latter had confined itself to enforcing the impugned decision, without verifying its merits, thus respecting the internal autonomy of the Jewish community [*Kohn v. Germany* (dec.)].

(d) Disputes between religious organisations and their employees

184. As a consequence of their autonomy, religious communities can demand a certain degree of loyalty from those working for them or representing them. It is a common feature of many religions that they determine doctrinal standards of behaviour by which their followers must abide in their private lives (*Jehovah's Witnesses of Moscow and Others v. Russia*, § 118). The nature of the post occupied by those persons is an important element to be taken into account when assessing the proportionality of a restrictive measure taken by the State or the religious organisation concerned. In particular, the **specific mission** assigned to the person concerned in a religious organisation is a relevant consideration in determining whether that person should be subject to a **heightened duty of loyalty** (*Fernández Martínez v. Spain* [GC], § 131). In so doing, particular importance should be attached to the proximity between the applicant's activity and the proclamatory mission of the religious organisation in question (*Schüth v. Germany*, § 69).

185. In the specific case of **religious education teachers**, it is not unreasonable for a church or a religious community to expect particular loyalty of them in so far as they may

be regarded as its representatives. The existence of a discrepancy between the ideas that have to be taught and the teacher's personal beliefs may raise an issue of credibility if the teacher actively and publicly campaigns against the ideas in question. It can reasonably be accepted that in order to remain credible, religion must be taught by a person whose way of life and public statements are not flagrantly at odds with the religion in question, especially where the religion is supposed to govern the private life and personal beliefs of its followers (*Fernández Martínez v. Spain* [GC], §§ 137–138).

186. Moreover, a mere allegation by a religious community that there is an actual or potential threat to its autonomy is not sufficient to justify any interference with its employees' competing rights, which are also protected by the Convention (particularly under Articles 8, 9, 10 and 11). In addition, the religious community in question must also show, in the light of the circumstances of the individual case, that the alleged risk is probable and substantial and that the impugned interference with the right to respect for private life does not go beyond what is necessary to eliminate that risk and serves no other purpose unrelated to the exercise of the religious community's autonomy. Neither should it affect the substance of the right in question. Accordingly, when the Court is called upon to adjudicate a conflict between a religious community's right to autonomy and another person's competing right which is also protected by the Convention, the national courts must conduct an in-depth examination of the circumstances of the case and a thorough balancing exercise between the competing interests at stake. The State is called upon to guarantee both rights, and if the protection of one leads to an interference with the other, to choose adequate means to make this interference proportionate to the aim pursued. The State has a wide margin of appreciation in such matters (*Fernández Martínez v. Spain* [GC], §§ 123 and 132).

187. When conducting the aforementioned balancing exercise, both rights should be treated as deserving equal consideration: the outcome of the application should not, in principle, vary according to whether it was lodged with the Court under Article 9 by the religious organisation claiming to be a victim of infringement of its right to autonomy or under another article securing a competing right for another party to the dispute (*Sindicatul 'Păstorul cel Bun' v. Romania* [GC], § 160).

188. Under the Convention, an employer whose ethos is based on religion or on a philosophical belief may impose specific duties of loyalty on its employees. However, a dismissal decision based on a breach of such duty cannot only be subjected, on the basis of the employer's right of autonomy, to a limited judicial scrutiny exercised by the relevant domestic employment tribunal without having regard to the nature of the post in question and without properly balancing the interests involved in accordance with the principle of proportionality (*Schüth v. Germany*, § 69).

189. Furthermore, in the above-mentioned exercise of balancing the competing interests, the fact that an employee who has been dismissed by an ecclesiastical employer will have limited opportunities of finding another job is particularly important. This is especially true where the employer has a predominant position in a given sector of activity and enjoys certain derogations from the ordinary law, or where the dismissed employee has specific qualifications that make it difficult, if not impossible, to find a new job outside the employing church, as was the case in *Schüth v. Germany* (*Fernández Martínez v. Spain* [GC], § 144); *Schüth v. Germany*, § 73).

190. For instance, the Court found a violation of the positive obligations incumbent on the respondent State under **Article 8** of the Convention (right to respect for private life) in the case of an organist and choirmaster of a German Catholic parish who had been dismissed (with due notice) on the ground that by leaving his wife and having an extramarital relationship with another woman, who was expecting his child, he had breached his obligation of loyalty to the Catholic Church, which considers such a situation as adultery and a violation of the indissolubility of marriage. The German courts having found against the applicant, the Court did not attack the substance of their decision but criticised the manner in which they had reached their conclusion. The courts had insufficiently explained why the interests of the employing Church far outweighed those of the applicant and had failed to balance the applicant's and the employer's rights in a manner compatible with the Convention. In particular, the interests of the Church had not been balanced with the applicant's right to respect for his private and family life, but exclusively with his interest in retaining his post; the matter of the proximity of the applicant's activity and the Church's

proclamatory mission had not been duly considered, nor had his ability to find another post corresponding to his qualifications; the domestic courts had not duly examined the fact that the applicant had not combated the positions adopted by the Catholic Church but had rather failed to respect them in practice. Furthermore, the Court found that the applicant's acceptance of the duty of loyalty to the Catholic Church when he had signed his contract of employment could not be regarded as an unequivocal personal undertaking to live a life of abstinence in the event of separation or divorce (*Schüth v. Germany*).

191. On the other hand, the Court found no violation of Article 8 in the following cases:

- the dismissal (without due notice) of the EuropeDirector of the Public Relations Department of the Church of Jesus Christ of Latter-Day Saints (the Mormon Church) in Germany, after his disclosure to his superior that he was involved in an extramarital relationship. Unlike in *Schüth*, the Court accepted the labour courts' arguments, finding that they had sufficiently demonstrated that the obligations of loyalty imposed on the applicant were acceptable as they were designed to protect the credibility of the Mormon Church in view of the seriousness of adultery in its teachings and the important public position which the applicant held in it. The German courts had also provided sufficient explanations as to why the employer had not been required first of all to impose a more lenient penalty such as a warning (*Obst v. Germany*);

- the non-renewal of the employment contract of the applicant, a secularised Catholic priest who had been dispensed from celibacy by the Holy See and was married, and who had previously been employed as a teacher of Catholic religion and ethics in a state secondary school; this decision had been based on a memorandum from the local diocese mentioning that press coverage of his family situation and his belonging to the "Movement for Optional Celibacy" for priests had caused a "scandal" within the meaning of canon law. The Court first of all noted that a less restrictive measure for the applicant would certainly not have had the same effectiveness in terms of preserving the credibility of the Church, and secondly, that the consequences of the decision not to renew his contract did not appear to have been excessive in the circumstances of the case, having regard in particular to the fact that the applicant had knowingly placed himself in a situation that was completely in opposition to the Church's precepts (*Fernández Martínez v. Spain* [GC]).

192. As regards the competing rights of an employee as secured under **Article 9** of the Convention, the Court found no violation of the positive obligations flowing from this provision in the case of a teacher who had been employed at a day-care centre run by the German Protestant Church and had been dismissed without due notice on the ground that she was simultaneously an active member of a community known as the "Universal Church/ Brotherhood of Man", whose teachings were considered by the Protestant Church as absolutely incompatible with its own doctrine. The domestic courts had conducted an in-depth assessment of the circumstances of the case and carried out a detailed exercise of balancing the competing interests at stake. It was in no way unreasonable for the applicant's interest in retaining her post to have to give way to that of the Protestant Church in retaining its credibility in the eyes of the general public and the parents of the children attending the kindergarten and preventing any risk of the children being influenced by a teacher who was a member of a religious community whose teachings contradicted the precepts of the Church in question (*Siebenhaar v. Germany*).

193. As regards the **freedom of expression** of individuals employed by religious organisations, as protected by **Article 10 of the** Convention, the Commission declared inadmissible an application from a doctor employed by a German Catholic hospital who had been dismissed for signing an open letter published in the press expressing an opinion on abortion contradicting the position of the Catholic Church. While acknowledging that the applicant had not waived his freedom of expression by the mere fact of accepting employment in a Catholic hospital, the Commission noted that he had freely accepted a duty of loyalty towards the Church, which had limited his freedom of expression to a certain extent. The applicant had had access, in order to protect that freedom, to the domestic courts, whose case-law had affirmed that the Churches' right to impose their views on their

employees was not unlimited and that excessive demands were unacceptable. Indeed, it was not unreasonable to suggest that the post of physician in a Catholic hospital involved exercising one of the fundamental missions of the Church and that the obligation to refrain from issuing statements on abortion which contradicted the Church's position was not excessive in view of the cardinal importance which the Church attached to that issue [*Rommelfanger v. Germany* (dec.)].

194. On the other hand, the Court found a violation of Article 10 as regards the non-renewal of the work contract of a professor of legal philosophy at the Milan Catholic University of the Sacred Heart, the Holy See's Congregation for Catholic Education having denied him its approval on the ground that some of his positions "were clearly incompatible with Catholic doctrine" although they failed to specify those positions. The Court noted that it was not incumbent on the State authorities to assess the substance of the Congregation's decision. However, the applicant had not been notified of the allegations of unorthodox opinions which had been levelled against him and the domestic courts had confined their assessment of the legitimacy of the impugned decision to the fact that the Law Faculty Council had noted the existence of the denial of approval. However, communicating those facts would in no way have entailed a judgment on the part of the judicial authorities regarding the compatibility between the applicant's positions and Catholic doctrine; on the other hand it would have enabled the applicant to have cognisance of and therefore to challenge the alleged incompatibility between the said opinions and his activities as a teacher at the Catholic University. The importance attached to the University's interest in providing teaching based on Catholic Doctrine could not go so far as to impinge on the very substance of the procedural guarantees which must be provided to the applicant under Article 10 of the Convention (*Lombardi Vallauri v. Italy*).

195. As regards possible **freedom of association** for the clergy and other ministers of religion, the Court must first of all establish whether the persons concerned are carrying out their mission in the framework of an "employment relationship" for the purposes of **Article 11** of the Convention. If so, it is the domestic courts' task to ensure that both freedom of association and the autonomy of religious communities can be observed within such

communities in accordance with the applicable law, including the Convention. Where interferences with the right to freedom of association are concerned, it follows from Article 9 of the Convention that religious communities are entitled to their own opinion on any collective activities conducted by their members that might undermine their autonomy and that this opinion must in principle be respected by the national authorities. However, a mere allegation by a religious community that there is an actual or potential threat to its autonomy is not sufficient to render any interference with its members' trade-union rights compatible with the requirements of Article 11 of the Convention. It must also show, in the light of the circumstances of the individual case, that the risk alleged is real and substantial and that the impugned interference with freedom of association does not go beyond what is necessary to eliminate that risk and does not serve any other purpose unrelated to the exercise of the religious community's autonomy (*Sindicatul 'Păstorul cel Bun' v. Romania* [GC], § 159).

196. In accordance with these principles, the Court found no violation of Article 11 of the Convention in the case of a refusal by the Romanian authorities to recognise and register a trade union set up by a group of priests and lay employees of the Romanian Orthodox Church because the archbishop had not given his consent and blessing. The refusal was based on the canon law and the Church's Statute which had been approved by governmental decree and incorporated into domestic law. In the light of all the evidence before it, the Court considered that notwithstanding any special features inherent in their situation and their spiritual mission, members of the clergy of the Romanian Orthodox Church fulfilled their mission in the context of an "employment relationship", and could therefore, in principle, lay claim to freedom of association within the meaning of Article 11, especially since the Romanian courts had already expressly recognised the trade union rights of members of the clergy and lay employees of the Orthodox Church. On the other hand, the Court found that the impugned interference could be deemed proportionate to the legitimate aims pursued and therefore compatible with the requirements of Article 11 § 2 of the Convention. In refusing to register the applicant union, the State was simply declining to become involved in the organisation and operation of the Romanian Orthodox Church,

thereby observing its duty of neutrality. The application for registration of the trade union did not satisfy the requirements of the Church's Statute because its members had not complied with the special procedure in place for setting up such an association. Furthermore, there was nothing to stop the applicant union's members from availing themselves of their right under Article 11 of the Convention by forming an association of this kind that pursued aims compatible with the Church's Statute and did not call into question the Church's traditional hierarchical structure and decision-making procedures (*Sindicatul 'Păstorul cel Bun' v. Romania* [GC]).

197. As regards the **right of access to courts** as secured under **Article 6 § 1** of the Convention, the Court declared inadmissible an application lodged by two former priests of the Czechoslovak Hussite Church who had been dismissed by decision of their diocesan council and had applied to the courts to secure recognition of the unlawfulness of the aforementioned decision and the payment of salary arrears. The Czech courts found in their favour as regards the second point (salary arrears) but not on the first (unlawfulness of decision), because the courts declined jurisdiction for reviewing the merits of a decision for which the Church held sole jurisdiction thanks to its autonomous status. The Court found that the proceedings brought by the applicants did not concern an arguable "right" recognised under domestic law, and that the complaint was therefore incompatible *ratione materiae* [*Dudová and Duda v. Czech Republic* (dec.)].

3. Positive obligations

(a) Protection against physical, verbal or symbolic attacks by third persons

198. Individuals who choose to exercise freedom to manifest their religion cannot reasonably expect to be shielded from any criticism while doing so. On the contrary, members of a religious community must tolerate and accept the denial by others of their religious beliefs and even the propagation by others of doctrines hostile to their faith [*Dubowska and Skup v. Poland* (dec.)]. Nevertheless, the responsibility of the State may be engaged where religious beliefs are opposed or denied in a manner which inhibits those who hold such beliefs from exercising their freedom to hold or express them. In such

cases the State may be called upon to ensure the peaceful enjoyment of the rights guaranteed under Article 9 to the holders of those beliefs [*Church of Scientology and Others v. Sweden* (dec.) ; *Begheluri v. Georgia*, § 160]. Indeed, there may be certain positive obligations on the part of a State inherent in an effective respect for rights guaranteed under Article 9 (Art. 9) of the Convention, which may involve the adoption of measures designed to secure respect for freedom of religion even in the sphere of the relations of individuals between themselves. Such measures may, in certain circumstances, constitute a legal means of ensuring that an individual will not be disturbed in his worship by the activities of others [*Dubowska and Skup v. Poland* (dec.)].

199. When a group of individuals organises a public demonstration intended to demonstrate their opposition to the beliefs or practices of a given religious community, two fundamental rights come into conflict: the demonstrators' right to freedom of expression and of peaceful assembly (Articles 10 and 11 of the Convention) , and the right of the religious community peacefully to manifest its faith without unjustified outside interference. All these rights benefit from equal protection under the Convention; none of them is absolute, and their exercise may be subject to the restrictions set out in the second paragraphs of the above-mentioned articles. The Convention does not create any hierarchy among these rights *a priori*: in principle, they deserve equal respect. Consequently, they must be balanced against each other in such a way as to respect their importance in a society based on pluralism, tolerance and broadmindedness. In so doing the State must comply with the following three principles:

(a) as far as is reasonably possible, the State must ensure that the two competing rights are protected; this obligation is incumbent on the national authorities even where the acts liable to impede the free exercise of either right are instigated by private individuals;

(b) accordingly, the State must ensure that an appropriate legal framework is established-particularly in order to protect the aforementioned rights against attacks by third parties-and must take effective action to ensure that the rights are respected in practice;

(c) it is incumbent on the Court, in exercising its power of European review, to verify, in the light of the case as a whole, whether the national authorities have struck a fair balance among the various competing rights enshrined in the Convention. In doing so, the Court should not act with the benefit of hindsight. Nor should it simply substitute its view for that of the national authorities who, in any given case, are much better placed to assess where the appropriate balance lay and how best to achieve that balance. That is particularly true where it is the police who must in practice strike that balance. Having regard to the difficulties in policing modern societies, the positive obligations on the police or on other authorities must be interpreted in a way which does not impose an impossible or disproportionate burden on them (*Karaahmed v. Bulgaria*, §§ 91 – 96).

200. In the same line of reasoning the Court found a violation:

- of Article 9, alone and in conjunction with Article 14 of the Convention (prohibition of discrimination), in the case of a physical assault on a peaceful meeting of Jehovah's Witnesses by a groupof individuals led by a defrocked Orthodox priest, during which the applicants had been violently beaten and humiliated; their religious literature had been burnt before their eyes. The police had refused to intervene promptly *in situ* in order to protect the applicants; subsequently, the applicants had been faced with total indifference on the part of the relevant authorities, which, out of hostility towards the Jehovah's Witness religion, had refused to implement the applicable law or take any action on their complaints (*Members of the Gldani Congregation of the Jehovah's Witnesses and Others v. Georgia*; see also *Begheluri v. Georgia*);

- of Article 9 alone (but not Article 14), in the case of a demonstration which had turned violent-but had been lawful because it had previously been declared in conformity with the law-andwhich had been organised by members of a political party in protest against Friday prayers held inside and outside the Mosque in Sofia, the Bulgarian capital (threatening shouts and gestures; egg-throwing; loudspeakers placed on the Mosque roof in order to drown out the call to prayer; attempted burning of prayer mats; physical assaults on members of the congregation by demonstrators having forced their way into the Mosque, etc.). In this case the Bulgarian authorities had not done all that could reasonably have been expected of them to ensure the freedom of both sides to exercise their respective rights. Being aware of the highly negative position adopted by the party in question *vis-à-vis* Islam and the Turks, the authorities could have minimised the risk of violence by allocating the demonstrators specific areas at a safe distance from the Mosque, but they had failed to do so. Furthermore, the number of police officers present on the spot was clearly insufficient to control the situation, and they behaved too passively to protect the members of the congregation. Lastly, the investigation instigated by the authorities after the events did not satisfy the requisite effectiveness criteria (*Karaahmed v. Bulgaria*).

201. Furthermore, Article 9 (like Articles 10 and 11) cannot be interpreted as authorising an individual who disagrees with a religious organisation on a given point to interrupt or cause a disturbance during a ceremony. The Court declared manifestly ill-founded a complaint from a Romanian Orthodox nun, who was actively involved in denouncing alleged abuse in the hierarchy of her Church and had been sentenced to a fine for causing a disturbance during a ceremony conducted by the Romanian Orthodox Patriarch and shouting (or saying loudly) that he "did not deserve to be prayed for". Since the fine imposed had been geared to punishing the public disturbance rather than the expression of an opinion, the Court held that the authorities had reacted within the framework of their normal margin of appreciation in such matters [*Bulgaru v. Romania* (dec.)].

202. Moreover, the Court has held that the **provocative portrayals of objects of religious veneration** can in some cases violate the rights of believers under Article 9 (*Otto-Preminger-Institut v. Austria*, § 47). However, the Court has hitherto almost invariably examined this type of case under Article 10 of the Convention (freedom of expression), adjudicating on complaints from persons who have been sanctioned for violating the necessary respect for believers' feelings [*Otto-Preminger-Institut v. Austria*; *Wingrove v. the United Kingdom*; *I. A. v. Turkey*; *Giniewski v. France*; *Klein v. Slovakia*; see also *X. Ltd. and Y. v. the United Kingdom* (dec.)].

203. On the other hand, the organs of the Convention have hitherto invariably dismissed complaints submitted under Article 9 by persons whose religious sensibilities have

been offended. In particular, the right to freedom from interference with the rights guaranteed by Article 9 does not necessarily and in all circumstances imply a right to bring any specific form of proceedings against those who, by authorship or publication, offend the sensitivities of an individual or of a group of individuals [*Dubowska and Skup v. Poland* (dec.)]. The organs of the Convention rejected this kind of complaint in the following cases:

- dismissal for lack of *locus standi* of a claim by the Church of Scientology for damages in relation to hostile comments on Scientology proffered by a professor of theology in the course of a lecture and subsequently published in a local newspaper, because it had not been established that the comments in question had prevented the applicants from exercising their rights under Article 9 [*Church of Scientology and Others v. Sweden* (dec.)];
- a refusal by the United Kingdom authorities to bring criminal proceedings against Salman Rushdie and a publisher for having written and published, respectively, the novel "The Satanic Verses", which is considered blasphemous from the Islamic point of view [*Choudhury v. the United Kingdom* (dec.)];
- a decision by the Polish public prosecutor's office to discontinue criminal proceedings on the ground of public insult to religious feelings against the editor-in-chief of a weekly magazine for publishing, on its cover, an image of the Częstochowa Virgin and Child-an icon which is deeply venerated throughout Poland-replacing both their faces with gas-masks. The prosecution found that the image had been used to illustrate information on air pollution in Poland and had not been deliberately intended to offend religious sensibilities. The Commission noted that the applicants had had a domestic remedy against the insult to their religious feelings, which remedy they had relied on. It had been dismissed by the prosecutor following meticulous assessment of all the circumstances of the case and of the competing interests. That being the case, the applicants had not been deterred from exercising their rights under Article 9, and the mere fact that the authorities had ultimately found that no offence had been committed could not, in itself, be

regarded as a failure to protect the rights guaranteed by that provision. For the same reason the Commission found that there had been no discrimination as prohibited by Article 14 [*Dubowska and Skup v. Poland* (dec.); *Kubalska and Kubalska-Holuj v. Poland* (dec.)];

- an application against Denmark lodged by a Moroccan national living in Morocco and two Moroccan associations established and operating in that country, complaining about the Danish authorities' refusal to prohibit and punish the publication of a series of caricatures of the Prophet of Islam, Mohammed. The Court noted that there was no link in terms of jurisdiction, for the purposes of Article 1 of the Convention, between the applicants and Denmark, even under any "extraterritorial act" [*Ben El Mahi and Others v. Denmark* (dec.)].

(b) Religion at the workplace, in the army and in court

204. As regards, first of all, the right of **members of the armed forces** to manifest their religion in the course of their duties, the Court has ruled that States can adopt disciplinary regulations for their armies prohibiting specific types of behaviour, particularly attitudes inimical to an established order reflecting the requirements of military service. For example, the Court found that there had been no interference with the freedom of religion of a judge advocate holding the rank of group captain in the Turkish air force, on the ground that "his conduct and attitude revealed that he had adopted unlawful fundamentalist opinions". The Court pointed out that in choosing to pursue a military career the applicant had accepted of his own accord a system of military discipline that by its very nature implied the possibility of placing on certain of the rights and freedoms of members of the armed forces limitations incapable of being imposed on civilians. The applicant, within the limits imposed by the requirements of military life, had been able to fulfil the religious obligations imposed by his religion; as regards the impugned measure, it had been based not on his religious opinions and beliefs or the way he had performed his religious duties but on his conduct and attitude, thus breaching military discipline and infringing the principle of secularism [*Kalaç v. Turkey*; for similar cases see *Çinar v. Turkey* (dec.); *Acarca v. Turkey* (dec.); *Sert v. Turkey* (dec.)].

205. In other Turkish cases the organs of the Convention have pointed out that in the particular context of Turkey, the limitations specific to military service may include a duty for military personnel to refrain from participating in the Muslim fundamentalist movement, whose aim and programme is to ensure the pre-eminence of religious rules [*Yanaşık v. Turkey* (dec.); *Tepeli and Others v. Turkey* (dec.)]. In particular, the fact that a Turkish Military Academy prohibits cadets who have freely chosen a military career and who can fulfil their religious obligations within the limits imposed by military life from joining an Islamic fundamentalist movement does not constitute an interference with freedom of religion and conscience [*Yanaşık v. Turkey* (dec.)].

206. The Court followed similar logic in the case of a Russian **judge** who had been dismissed from her post for failing in the obligations inherent in the judiciary and undermining the latter's authority. The applicant in this case had used her position as a judge to promote the interests of her religious community and to intimidate parties to proceedings before her (for example she had prayed publicly during court hearings, had promised certain parties to proceedings a favourable outcome to their cases if they joined her Church, and had publicly criticised the morality of certain parties from the Christian angle). Consequently, the applicant had not been dismissed on the basis of her belonging to the Church or having any other "status", but by reason of her specific activities, which had been incompatible with the requirements for judicial office and infringed the principle of the rule of law. The Court therefore decided that there had been an interference in the applicant's exercise of her rights under Articles 10 and 9 but that that interference had been proportionate to the legitimate aims pursued [*Pitkevich v. Russia* (dec.)].

207. Further back in time, the Commission rejected an application lodged by a lawyer who wasalso an ordained Catholic priest (although he had never carried out pastoral duties), complaining (under Article 9 alone and in conjunction with Article 14) about the rejection by the Belgian Minister of Justice of his application for a post as substitute judge, the office of judge being incompatible with an ecclesiastical status under Belgian law. The Commission considered, first of all, that the applicant had in no way been impeded in the exercise of his religion, including his priestly duties, and secondly, that the Convention did

not secure *per se* a right to apply for a judicial post [*Demeester v. Belgium* (dec.); see, however, under Article 3 of Protocol No. 1, *Seyidzade v. Azerbaijan*].

208. In the framework of employment **relations in the public sector**, the Court found a violation of Article 9 of the Convention in a case involving the dismissal of an applicant, a swimming pool manager at a State vocational school in Bulgaria, because of her membership of a protestant evangelical community, against the general background of a political/media campaign against that community. Even though the impugned dismissal had complied with labour legislation and been formally based on a change in the qualification criteria for her post and the introduction of new criteria which the applicant did not meet, an analysis of the overall facts of the case led the Court to the conclusion that the real reason for the measure had indeed been the applicant's religious affiliation and beliefs. Furthermore, the Government had provided no evidence that there had ever been any credible accusations that the applicant had proselytised at the school or committed any professional fault (*Ivanova v. Bulgaria*).

209. The ***ritual* precepts** of certain religions (not to be confused with the *ethical* precepts mentioned in §§ 52 – 61 above) can sometimes clash with their professional obligations of their adherents, who therefore demand that their employer (whether public or private) adopt specific measures to **accommodate** them. However, the Court found that there was no right as such under Article 9 to have leave from work for particular religious holidays (*Kosteski v. the former Yugoslav Republic of Macedonia*, § 45).

210. The Commission, in cases which it examined from this angle, always refused to afford applicants the protection of Article 9 § 1 of the Convention on the basis that the action taken against them had been motivated not by their religious beliefs but by specific contractual obligations between them and their employers. The Commission adjudicated in this way in the following cases:

- a refusal by the UK educational authorities to grant the applicant, a State school teacher of Muslim faith, leave of absence to attend Friday prayers at the mosque. He had been forced to resign and was then taken on again on a part-time basis with a lower salary. The Commission refused to examine in detail the question whether and to what extent Islam required attendance at congressional Friday prayers at the mosque; it simply noted that the applicant had, of his own free will, accepted teaching obligations under his contract, thus making himself unable both to work with the education authority and to attend Friday prayers. Moreover, for his first six years of service in the school the applicant had not taken leave of absence on Friday or informed his employer that he might require time off during normal school hours in order to attend prayers at the mosque. Moreover, in view of the exigencies of organising an educational system, Commission was not called upon to substitute for the assessment by the national authorities of what might be the best policy in this field [X. v. the United Kingdom (dec.)];

- dismissal of an employee of the Finnish State Railways for failing to observe normal working hours on the grounds that the Seventh-Day Adventist Church, to which he belonged, prohibited its members from working after sunset on Fridays. Furthermore, the Commission found no appearance of religious discrimination (Article 14 of the Convention) because national legislation provided that Sunday was the usual weekly day of rest [Konttinen v. Finland (déc.)];

- dismissal of an employee by a private sector employer (a travel agency) following her refusal to work on Sundays [Stedman v. Royaume Uni (dec.)].

211. Similarly, the Court found no violation of Article 9 of the Convention in the case of disciplinary sanctions (in the form of temporary wage cuts) imposed on an applicant, an employee of the Electricity Company of Macedonia, a public utility company, who had declared that he was a Muslim, for having taken time off work on two occasions in the space of a year on the occasion of Muslim religious festivals. The domestic courts had acknowledged that the law granted citizens of Muslim faith the right to paid leave on their religious feast days. In the specific case of the applicant, however, the sincerity of his professed belonging to that religion was doubtful because he was ignorant of the basic tenets of that religion and because previously he had always celebrated Christian holidays. The domestic courts had therefore found that the applicant had claimed to be a Muslim solely in order to benefit from additional days of leave. The Court accepted that where the law

established a privilege or special exemption for members of a given religious community-especially in the employment field-it was not incompatible with Article 9 to require the person concerned to provide some level of substantiation of his belonging to that community (in line with the same logic as in cases of conscientious objection, where the applicant must in principle be able to prove the sincerity of his convictions). Accordingly, while expressing doubts as to whether the case concerned a "manifestation" of the applicant's alleged religion, the Court found that the interference complained of had been "necessary in a democratic society" for the protection of the rights of others, within the meaning of Article 9 § 2. It also found that there had been no discrimination within the meaning of Article 14 (*Kosteski v. the former Yugoslav Republic of Macedonia*).

212. As regards the religious freedom of parties to judicial proceedings:
- the Commission declared inadmissible an application lodged by two Austrian nationals of Jewish religion, who had been defendants in civil proceedings, complaining about the court's refusal to adjourn the hearing to be held during the Jewish Feast of Tabernacles (*Sukkot*). Examining the case chiefly under Article 6 § 1 (right to a fair trial), the Commission found an absence of expedition on the part of the applicants, as they had taken an excessively long time to alert the court to the incompatibility. It also rejected the applicants' complaints under Article 9 alone and in conjunction with Article 14 (prohibition of discrimination) [*S. H. and H. V. v. Austria* (dec.)];
- the Court found no violation of Article 9 of the Convention in the case of a refusal by a judicial authority to adjourn a hearing which the applicant, a lawyer of Jewish religion, was to attend as representative of one of the two plaintiffs in a criminal case; the date of the hearing coincided with a Jewish religious holiday. The applicant did not attend the hearing, which went ahead in his absence. The Court held that the applicant should have expected his request to be rejected in pursuance of the legal provisions in force, and that he could have arranged to be replaced at the hearing in question (*Francesco Sessa v. Italy*).

(c) Religious freedom for prisoners

213. The national authorities are required to respect prisoners' freedom of religion by

refraining from any unjustified interference with the exercise of the rights laid down in Article 9 of the Convention and, if necessary, taking positive action to facilitate the free exercise of those rights, having regard to the particular requirements of the prison environment. In particular, the fact of being required to pray, read religious books and meditate in the presence of other prisoners is an inconvenience which is virtually unavoidable in prison, but which does not go against the very essence of the freedom to manifest one's religion [*Kovaļkovs v. Latvia* (dec.)]. On the other hand, as a general rule, Article 9 grants prisoners neither the right to proselytise in the institution where they are being held nor the right to manifest their religion outside that institution [*J. L. v. Finland* (dec.)].

214. Similarly, Article 9 affords prisoners neither the right to be recognised as a "political prisoner" with a special status different from other prisoners, nor the right to be exempted from the general rules governing prison life such as the obligation to work, wear prison uniform and clean their cells [*McFeeley and Others v. the United Kingdom* (dec.); *X. v. the United Kingdom* (dec.)]. The Commission also decided that Article 9 did not impose on States any general obligation to provide prisoners with installations which the latter considered necessary for exercising their religion or developing their life philosophy (see *X. v. Austria*, No. 1753/63①).

215. The Court found a violation of Article 9 of the Convention in the following cases:
- the inability of persons who had been sentenced to death but whose sentence had subsequently been commuted to life imprisonment to receive visits from a priest (*Poltoratski v. Ukraine*, §§ 163 – 171, ECHR 2003 V; *Kuznetsov v. Ukraine*, §§ 143 – 151);
- a refusal by the relevant judge to authorise the applicant, who had been remanded in custody, to take part in religious celebrations held at the prison chaplaincy, which refusal had lacked any basis in domestic law (*Igors Dmitrijevs v. Latvia*);
- a refusal by the prison administration to provide the applicant, a Buddhist, with

---

① Decision available in paper copy only in the **Yearbooks of the European Convention on Human Rights at the Court library**.

meat-free meals, even though such an arrangement would not have been an excessive burden on the prison (*Jakóbski v. Poland*).

216. On the other hand, the organs of the Convention found that there had been no appearance of a violation of Article 9 in the following cases:

- a prohibition on a Buddhist prisoner growing a goatee beard (the reason given being the need to avoid hampering his identification) and a refusal to return to him his prayer beads, which had been placed in safe custody on his committal to prison. The Commission considered that those restrictions had been in conformity with Article 9 § 2 inasmuch as they had been intended to protect public order (see *X. v. Austria*, No. 1753/63①);

- the alleged inability of a United Kingdom national imprisoned in Germany to attend Anglican service or receive visits from an Anglican priest. The Commission found that the applicant had in fact had access to protestant worship and protestant pastors [*X. v. Germany* (dec.)];

- the prohibition on a Buddhist prisoner sending articles for publication in a Buddhist magazine, even though the applicant had not explained why the observance of his religion involved or required the publication of such articles [*X. v. the United Kingdom* (dec.)], and a refusal to authorise another Buddhist prisoner to subscribe to a Roman Catholic magazine, although the latter was very clearly devoid of any link with his religion (see *X. v. Austria*, No. 1753/63②);

- the conditions of detention of an Orthodox Jew who had been offered kosher vegetarian meals and who had been allowed to receive visits from a lay Jewish visitor assisted by the prison chaplain, whereby the Chief Rabbi had approved the authorities' efforts to safeguard the applicant's religious rights [*X v. the United Kingdom* (dec.)];

---

① Decision available in paper copy only in the **Yearbooks of the European Convention on Human Rights at the** Court library.

② Decision available in paper copy only in the **Yearbooks of the European Convention on Human Rights at the** Court library.

- the retention by the prison administration of a philosophical/religious book ordered by a Taoist prisoner on the grounds that it contained a chapter, with illustrations, on the martial arts; this interference had been necessary for the protection of the "rights and liberties of others" [X. v. the United Kingdom (dec.)];

- a refusal by a prison director to enter the applicant in the prison registers as an adherent of the "*Wicca*" religion. The Commission held that where such an entry involved certain privileges and facilities for the prisoner to practice his religion, it was reasonable to require the declared religion to be identifiable; however, the applicant had provided no evidence to enable the objective existence of such a religion to be established [X. v. the United Kingdom (dec.)]. In a similar case the Commission rejected an application from a prisoner who claimed to be a "worshipper of the light" ("*Lichtanbeter*") but who had not explained how his religion was practised or how the authorities had impeded such practice [X. v. Germany (dec.)];

- a series of disciplinary penalties imposed on an applicant for refusing to wear prison uniform and to clean his cell. The applicant stated that as a Sikh he recognised no authority between himself and his God, particularly since he maintained that he was a "political prisoner" (whence his refusal to wear uniform); moreover, since he was of high caste, it was "culturally unacceptable" for him to clean floors (whence his refusal to clean his cell). The Commission declared the first complaint (concerning uniform) incompatible with the Convention (partly *ratione materiae* and partly *ratione personae*) and the second manifestly ill-founded: even supposing there had been an interference in the applicant's freedom of religion, it had been necessary for the protection of health and justified within the meaning of Article 9 § 2 [X. v. the United Kingdom (dec.)];

- a disciplinary penalty imposed on a prisoner for refusing to work in a print shop on the ground that as an adherent of veganism he found it morally unacceptable to work with products which had allegedly been tested on animals (dyes). Even assuming that there had been an interference with the applicant's rights under

Article 9, it had been in conformity with Article 9 § 2. On the one hand, the Commission accepted the respondent Government's argument that it was necessary to have a system of allocation of work which is perceived to be fair and without favouritism, and on the other it noted the leniency of the penalty [W. v. the United Kingdom (dec.)];

- a refusal to authorise an applicant, who was considered dangerous and was subject to a special high-security detention regime, to attend Mass, although he was able to watch Mass from his cell and he had never claimed to have been prevented from receiving visits from a chaplain [Indelicato v. Italy (dec.); for a similar case, Natoli v. Italy (dec.)];

- a refusal by the prison administration to grant an applicant, an adherent of the Hare Krishna movement, a separate room where he could read, pray, meditate and read religious material, as well as the confiscation of his incense sticks, the latter on grounds of the need to respect the rights of other prisoners [Kovaļkovs v. Latvia (dec.)].

217. The Court also dismissed the complaints of an applicant who had committed a series of very serious crimes and had been forcibly interned in a psychiatric hospital. As the applicant had stated that he was a Jehovah's Witness, the hospital had allowed him to keep in touch with that religious organisation; he had however, been admonished for preaching and distributing leaflets to other patients and hospital staff. The Court considered that that measure had been necessary in order to maintain order in the hospital and to protect the interests of other patients. For the remainder the Court found that the applicant's rights under Article 9 had been respected [J. L. v. Finland (dec.)].

Index of cited cases

The case-law cited in this Guide refers to judgments or decisions delivered by the European Court of Human Rights and to decisions or reports of the European Commission of Human Rights.

Unless otherwise indicated, all references are to a judgment on the merits delivered by a Chamber of the Court. The abbreviation "(dec.)" indicates that the citation is of a decision of the Court and "[GC]" that the case was heard by the Grand Chamber.

The hyperlinks to the cases cited in the electronic version of the Guide are directed to the HUDOC database (http://hudoc.echr.coe.int) which provides access to the case-law of the Court (Grand Chamber, Chamber and Committee judgments, decisions, communicated cases, advisory opinions and legal summaries from the Case-Law Information Note), the Commission (decisions and reports) and the Committee of Ministers (resolutions).

The Court delivers its judgments and decisions in English and/or French, its two official languages. HUDOC also contains translations of many important cases into nearly thirty non-official languages, and links to around one hundred online case-law collections produced by third parties.

— A —

Abrahamsson v. Sweden, no. 12154/86, 5 October 1987

Acarca v. Turkey (dec.), no. 45823/99, 3 October 2002

Agga v. Greece (no. 2), nos. 50776/99 and 52912/99, 17 October 2002

Agga v. Greece (no. 3), no. 32186/02, 13 July 2006

Agga v. Greece (no. 4), no. 33331/02, 13 July 2006

Ahmet Arslan and Others v. Turkey, no. 41135/98, 23 February 2010

Aktas v. France (dec.), no. 43563/08, 30 June 2009

Al-Nashif v. Bulgaria (dec.), no. 50963/99, 25 January 2001

Al-Nashif v. Bulgaria, no. 50963/99, 20 June 2002

Alexandridis v. Greece, no. 19516/06, 21 February 2008

Alujer Fernández and Caballero Garcia v. Spain (dec.), no. 53072/99, 14 June 2001

Angeleni v. Sweden (dec.), no. 10491/83, Commission decision of 3 December 1986, DR 51, p. 41

Araç v. Turkey (dec.), no. 9907/02, 19 September 2006

Arrowsmith v. the United Kingdom, no. 7050/75, rapport de la Commission du 12 October 1978, DR 19

Ásatrúarfélagið v. Iceland (dec.), no. 22897/08, 18 September 2012

Association Cultuelle du Temple Pyramide v. France, no. 50471/07, 31 January 2013

Association des Chevaliers du Lotus d'Or v. France, no. 50615/07, 31 January 2013

Association Les Témoins de Jéhovah v. France, no. 8916/05, 30 June 2011

Association Sivananda de Yoga Vedanta v. France (dec.), no. 30260/96, Commission decision of 16 April 1998

— B —

B. C. v. Switzerland (dec.), no. 19898/92, Commission (Plenary), 30 August 1993, DR 75, p. 223

Baciu v. Romania (dec.), no. 76146/12, 17 September 2013

Balsytė-Lideikienė v. Lithuania (dec.), no. 72596/01; 24 November 2005

Bayatyan v. Armenia [GC], no. 23459/03, ECHR 2011

Begheluri v. Georgia, no. 28490/02, 7 October 2014

Ben El Mahi and Others v. Denmark (dec.), no. 5853/06, ECHR 2006 – XV

Bernard and Others v. Luxembourg (dec.), no. 17187/90, Commission decision of 8 September 1993, DR 75, p. 57

Biblical Centre of the Chuvash Republic v. Russia, no. 33203/08, 12 June 2014

Biserica Adevărat Ortodoxă din Moldova and Others v. Moldova, no. 952/03, 27 February 2007

Blumberg v. Germany (dec.), no. 14618/03, 18 March 2008

Boffa and Others v. San Marino（dec.），no. 26536/95，Commission decision of 15 January 1998，DR 95，p. 27

Boychev and Others v. Bulgaria，no. 77185/01，27 January 2011

Bouessel du Bourg v. France（dec.），no. 20747/92，Commission decision of 18 February 1993

Bruno v. Sweden（dec.），no. 32196/96，28 August 2001

Bukharatyan v. Armenia，no. 37819/03，10 January 2012

Buldu and Others v. Turkey，no. 14017/08，3 June 2014

Bulgaru v. Romania（dec.），no. 22707/05，15 May 2012

Buscarini and Others v. San Marino [GC]，no. 24645/94，ECHR 1999 – I

Butan v. Romania（dec.），no. 34644/02，5 January 2010

— C —

C. v. the United Kingdom（dec.），no. 10358/83，Commission decision of 15 December 1983

C. J., J. J. and E. J. v. Poland（dec.），no. 23380/94，16 January 1996

C. R. v. Switzerland（dec.），no. 40130/98，14 October 1999

Canea Catholic Church v. Greece，16 December 1997，*Reports of Judgments and Decisions* 1997 – VIII

Cârmuirea Spirituală a Musulmanilor din Republica Moldova v. Moldova（dec.），no. 12282/02，14 June 2005

Cha'are Shalom Ve Tsedek v. France [GC]，no. 27417/95，ECHR 2000 – VII

Chappell v. the United Kingdom（dec.），no. 12587/86，Commission decision of 14 July 1987

Chassagnou and Others v. France [GC]，nos. 25088/94，28331/95 and 28443/95，ECHR 1999 – III

Choudhury v. the United Kingdom（dec.），no. 17439/90，Commission decision of 5 March 1991

Church of Scientology and Others v. Sweden（dec.），no. 8282/78，Commission decision of 14 July 1980，DR 21，p. 109

Church of Scientology of Moscow v. Russia, no. 18147/02, 5 April 2007

Church of Scientology of St Petersburg and Others v. Russia, no. 47191/06, 2 October 2014

Çinar v. Turkey (dec.), no. 39334/98, 9 July 2002

Company X. v. Switzerland (dec.), no. 7865/77, Commission decision of 27 February 1979, DR 16, p. 85

Cserjés v. Hungary (dec.), no. 45599/99, 5 April 2001

Cumhuriyetçi Eğitim ve Kültür Merkezi Vakfi v. Turkey, no. 32093/10, 2 December 2014

Cyprus v. Turkey [GC], no. 25781/94, ECHR 2001 – IV

— D —

D. v. France (dec.), no. 10180/82, Commission decision of 6 December 1983, DR 35, p. 199

Dahlab v. Switzerland (dec.), no. 42393/98, ECHR 2001 – V

Daratsakis v. Greece, no. 12902/87, Commission decision of 7 October 1987

Darby v. Sweden, no. 11581/85, 23 October 1990, Series A no. 187, pp. 17 – 18

Dautaj v. Switzerland (dec.), no. 32166/05, 20 September 2007

Demeester v. Belgium (dec.), no. 8493/79, Commission decision of 8 October 1981

Deschomets v. France (dec.), no. 31956/02, 16 May 2006

Dimitras and Others v. Greece, nos. 42837/06, 3237/07, 3269/07, 35793/07 and 6099/08, 3 June 2010

Dimitras and Others v. Greece (no. 2), nos. 34207/08 and 6365/09, 3 November 2011

Dimitras and Others v. Greece (no. 3), nos. 44077/09, 15369/10 and 41345/10, 8 January 2013

Dimitrova v. Bulgaria, no. 15452/07, 10 February 2015

Dogru v. France, no. 27058/05, 4 December 2008

Dubowska and Skup v. Poland (dec.), nos. 33490/96 and 34055/96, Commission decision of 18 April 1997, DR 89, p. 156

Dudová and Duda v. Czech Republic (dec.), no. 40224/98, 30 January 2001

— E —

E. and G. R. v. Austria (dec.), no. 9781/82, Commission decision of 14 May 1984, DR 37, p. 42

Efstratiou v. Greece, 18 December 1996, *Reports of Judgments and Decisions* 1996 – VI

Église Évangélique Missionnaire et Salaûn v. France, no. 25502/07, 31 January 2013

Église Réformée de X. and Others v. the Netherlands (dec.), no. 1497/62, Commission decision of 14 December 1962, *Year book* 5, p. 286)[①]

El Majjaoui and Stichting Touba Moskee v. the Netherlands (strike out) [GC], no. 25525/03, 20 December 2007

El Majjaoui and Stichting Touba Moskee v. the Netherlands (dec.), no. 25525/03, 14 February 2006

El Morsli v. France (dec.), no. 15585/06, 4 March 2008

Erçep v. Turkey, no. 43965/04, 22 November 2011

Eweida and Others v. the United Kingdom, nos. 48420/10, 59842/10, 51671/10 and 36516/10, ECHR 2013 (extracts)

— F —

F. L. v. France (dec.), no. 61162/00, 3 November 2005

F. P. v. Germany (dec.), no. 19459/92, Commission decision of 29 March 1993

Fernández Martínez v. Spain [GC], no. 56030/07, ECHR 2014 (extracts)

Feti Demirtaş v. Turkey, no. 5260/07, 17 January 2012

Finska Församlingen i Stockholm and Hautaniemi v. Sweden (dec.), no. 24019/94, Commission decision of 11 April 1996, DR 85, p. 94

Folgerø and Others v. Norway [GC], no. 15472/02, ECHR 2007 – III

Francesco Sessa v. Italy, no. 28790/08, ECHR 2012 (extracts)

Fränklin-Beentjes and CEFLU-Luz da Floresta v. the Netherlands, (dec.), no. 28167/07, 6 May 2014

Fusu Arcadie and Others v. The Republic of Moldova, no. 22218/06, 17 July 2012

[①] Decision available in paper copy only in the **Yearbooks of the European Convention on Human Rights at the Court library.**

— G —

Gamaleddyn v. France (dec.), no. 18527/08, 30 June 2009

Giniewski v. France, no. 64016/00, ECHR 2006 - I

Glas Nadejda EOOD and Anatoli Elenkov v. Bulgaria, no. 14134/02, 11 October 2007

Gluchowski and Others v. France (dec.), no. 44789/98, 14 December 1999

Gottesmann v. Switzerland (dec.), no. 10616/83, Commission decision of 4 December 1984, DR 40, p. 284

Gough v. the United Kingdom, no. 49327/11, 28 October 2014

Greek Catholic Parish Pesceana and Others v. Romania (dec.), no. 35839/07, 14 April 2015

Griechische Kirchengemeinde München und Bayern e. V. v. Germany (dec.), no. 52336/99, 18 September 2007

Grzelak v. Poland, no. 7710/02, 15 June 2010

Güler and Uğur v. Turkey, nos. 31706/10 and 33088/10, 2 December 2014

Gündüz v. Turkey (dec.), no. 59997/00, 9 November 2004

Gütl v. Austria, no. 49686/99, 12 March 2009

— H —

H. and B. v. the United Kingdom (dec.), no. 11991/86, Commission decision of 18 July 1986

Habitants de Leeuw-St.-Pierre v. Belgium[①] (dec.), no. 2333/64, Commission decision of 15 July 1965, *Year book* 8, p. 105

Hasan and Eylem Zengin v. Turkey, no. 1448/04, 9 October 2007

Hassan and Tchaouch v. Bulgaria [GC], no. 30985/96, ECHR 2000 - XI

Hernandez Sanchez v. Spain (dec.), no. 30479/96, Commission decision of 4 September 1996

Herrmann v. Germany [GC], no. 9300/07, 26 June 2012

[①] Decision available in paper copy only in the **Yearbooks of the European Convention on Human Rights at the Court library.**

Hizb Ut-Tahrir and Others v. Germany (dec.), no. 31098/08, 12 June 2012

Hoffmann v. Austria, 23 June 1993, Series A no. 255 – C

Holy Synod of the Bulgarian Orthodox Church (Metropolitan Inokentiy) and Others v. Bulgaria, nos. 412/03 and 35677/04, 22 January 2009

Hubaux v. Belgium (dec.), no. 11088/84, Commission decision of 9 May 1988

Hüsnü Öz v. Germany (dec.), no. 32168/96, Commission decision of 3 December 1996

— I —

I. A. v. Turkey, no. 42571/98, ECHR 2005 – VIII

Iera Moni Profitou Iliou Thiras v. Greece (dec.), no. 32259/02, 21 November 2002

Iglesia Bautista 《El Salvador》 and Ortega Moratilla v. Spain (dec.), no. 17522/90, Commission decision of 11 January 1992, DR 72, p. 256

Igors Dmitrijevs v. Latvia, no. 61638/00, 30 November 2006

Indelicato v. Italy (dec.), no. 31143/96, 6 July 2000

Institute of French Priests and Others v. Turkey (dec.), no. 26308/95, Commission decision of 19 January 1998, DR 92, p. 15

Institute of French Priests and Others v. Turkey (friendly settlement), no. 26308/95, 14 December 2000

ISKCON and Others v. the United Kingdom (dec.), no. 20490/92, Commission decision of 8 March 1994, DR 76, p. 90

Islamische Religionsgemeinschaft in Berlin e. V. v. Germany (dec.), no. 53871/00, ECHR 2002 – X

Ismailova v. Russia, no. 37614/02, 29 November 2007

Ivanova v. Bulgaria, no. 52435/99, 12 April 2007

— J —

J. L. v. Finland (dec.), no. 32526/96, 16 November 2000

Jakóbski v. Poland, no. 18429/06, 7 December 2010

Jasvir Singh v. France (dec.), no. 25463/08, 30 June 2009

Jehovah's Witnesses of Moscow and Others v. Russia, no. 302/02, 10 June 2010

Jehovas Zeugen in Österreich v. Austria, no. 27540/05, 25 September 2012

Jenik v. Austria (dec.), nos. 37794/07, 11568/08, 23036/08, 23044/08, 23047/08, 23053/08, 23054/08 and 48865/08, 20 November 2012

Johannische Kirche and Peters v. Germany (dec.), no. 41754/98, ECHR 2001 – VIII

Johnston and Others v. Ireland, 18 December 1986, Series A no. 112

Jones v. the United Kingdom (dec.), no. 42639/04, 13 September 2005

Josephides v. Turkey (dec.), no. 21887/93, 24 August 1999

Juma Mosque Congregation and Others v. Azerbaijan (dec.), no. 15405/04, 8 January 2013

— K —

K. v. the Netherlands (dec.), no. 15928/89, Commission decision of 13 May 1992

K. and V. v. the Netherlands (dec.), no. 11086/84, Commission decision of 16 July 1987

Karaahmed v. Bulgaria, no. 30587/13, 24 February 2015

Kalaç v. Turkey, 1er July 1997, *Reports of Judgments and Decisions* 1997 – IV

Karaduman v. Turkey (dec.), no. 16278/90, Commission decision of 3 May 1993, DR 74, p. 93

Karaduman v. Turkey (dec.), no. 41296/04, 3 April 2007

Karakuzey v. Germany (dec.), no. 26568/95, Commission decision of 16 October 1996

Karlsson v. Sweden (dec.), no. 12356/86, Commission decision of 8 September 1988, DR 57, p. 172

Keller v. Germany (dec.), no. 36283/97, Commission decision of 4 March 1998

Kenar v. Turkey (dec.), no. 67215/01, 1 December 2005

Kervanci v. France, no. 31645/04, 4 December 2008

Khan v. the United Kingdom (dec.), no. 11579/85, Commission decision of 7 July 1986, DR 48, p. 253

Kimlya and Others v. Russia, nos. 76836/01 and 32782/03, ECHR 2009

Kjeldsen, Busk Madsen and Pedersen v. Denmark, 7 December 1976, Series A no. 23

Klein v. Slovakia, no. 72208/01, 31 October 2006

Knudsen v. Norway (dec.), no. 11045/84, Commission decision of 8 March 1985, DR 42, p. 258

Kohn v. Germany (dec.), no. 47021/99, 23 March 2000

Kokkinakis v. Greece, 25 May 1993, Series A no. 260 – A

Kontakt-Information-Therapie (KIT) and Hagen v. Austria (dec.), no. 11921/86, Commission decision of 12 October 1988, DR 57, p. 81

Konttinen v. Finland (dec.), no. 24949/94, 3 December 1996, DR 87, p. 69

Köse and Others v. Turkey (dec.), no. 26625/02, ECHR 2006 – II

Kosteski v. theformer Yugoslav Republic of Macedonia, no. 55170/00, 13 April 2006

Koppi v. Austria, no. 33001/03, 10 December 2009

Kouznetsov v. Ukraine, no. 39042/97, 29 April 2003

Kuznetsov and Others v. Russia, no. 184/02, 11 January 2007

Kovaļkovs v. Latvia (dec.), no. 35021/05, 31 January 2012

Krupko and Others v. Russia, no. 26587/07, 26 June 2014

Kubalska and Kubalska-Holuj v. Poland (dec.), no. 35579/97, Commission decision of 22 October 1997

Kurtulmuş v. Turkey (dec.), no. 65500/01, ECHR 2006 – II

Kustannus OY Vapaa Ajattelija AB and Others v. Finland (dec.), Commission decision of 15 April 1996, DR 85, p. 29

Kuznetsov v. Ukraine, no. 39042/97, 29 April 2003

— L —

Lajda and Others v. Czech Republic (dec.), no. 20984/05, 3 March 2009

Lang v. Austria, no. 28648/03, 19 March 2009

Larissis and Others v. Greece, 24 February 1998, *Reports of Judgments and Decisions* 1998 – I

Lautsi and Others v. Italy [GC], no. 30814/06, ECHR 2011 (extracts)

Le Cour Grandmaison and Fritz v. France (dec.), nos. 11567/85 and 11568/85, Commission decision of 6 July 1987, DR 53, p. 150

Leela Förderkreis e. V. and Others v. Germany, no. 58911/00, 6 November 2008

Leyla Şahin v. Turkey [GC], no. 44774/98, ECHR 2005 – XI

Löffelmann v. Austria, no. 42967/98, 12 March 2009

Logan v. the United Kingdom (dec.), no. 24875/94, Commission decision of 6 September 1996, DR 86, p. 74

Lombardi Vallauri v. Italy, no. 39128/05, 20 October 2009

Lotter v. Bulgaria (dec.), no. 39015/97, 6 February 2003

Lotter and Lotter v. Bulgaria (friendly settlement), no. 39015/97, 19 May 2004

Lundberg v. Sweden (dec.), no. 36846/97, 28 August 2001

— M —

Magyar Keresztény Mennonita Egyház and Others v. Hungary, nos. 70945/11, 23611/12, 26998/12, 41150/12, 41155/12, 41463/12, 41553/12, 54977/12 and 56581/12, ECHR 2014 (extracts)

Mann Singh v. France (dec.), no. 24479/07, 13 November 2008

Manoussakis and Others v. Greece, 26 September 1996, *Reports of Judgments and Decisions* 1996 – IV

Martins Casimiro and Cerveira Ferreira v. Luxembourg (dec.), no. 44888/98, 27 April 1999

Marty v. Switzerland (dec.), no. 21566/93, Commission decision of 30 August 1993

Masaev v. Moldova, no. 6303/05, 12 May 2009

McFeeley and Others v. the United Kingdom (dec.), no. 8317/78, Commission decision of 15 May 1980, DR 20, p. 44

Members of the Gldani Congregation of the Jehovah's Witnesses and Others v. Georgia, no. 71156/01, 3 May 2007

Metropolitan Church of Bessarabia and Others v. Moldova, no. 45701/99, ECHR 2001 – XII

Mignot v. France (dec.), no. 37489/97, Commission decision of 21 October 1998

Miroļubovs and Others v. Latvia, no. 798/05, 15 September 2009

Moscow Branch of the Salvation Army v. Russia, no. 72881/01, ECHR 2006 – XI

Murphy v. Ireland, no. 44179/98, ECHR 2003 – IX (extracts)

— N —

N. F. v. Italy, no. 37119/97, ECHR 2001 – IX

Natoli v. Italy (dec.), no. 26161/95, Commission decision of 18 May 1998

Nolan and K. v. Russia, no. 2512/04, 12 February 2009

Nyyssönen v. Finland (dec.), no. 30406/96, Commission decision of 15 January 1998

— O —

Obst v. Germany, no. 425/03, 23 September 2010

Office Culturel de Cluny v. France (dec.), no. 1002/02, 22 March 2005

Omkarananda and the Divine Light Zentrum v. Switzerland (dec.), no. 8118/77, Commission decision of 19 March 1981, DR 25, p. 118

Otto-Preminger-Institut v. Austria, 20 September 1994, Series A no. 295 – A

Ouardiri v. Switzerland (dec.), no. 65840/09, 28 June 2011

— P —

Palau-Martinez v. France, no. 64927/01, ECHR 2003 – XII

Pannulo and Forte v. France (dec.), no. 37794/97, 23 November 1999

Parry v. the United Kingdom (dec.), no. 42971/05, ECHR 2006 – XV

Pavlides and Georgakis v. Turkey (dec.), nos. 9130/09 and 9143/09, 2 July 2013

Pendragon v. the United Kingdom (dec.), no. 31496/98, Commission decision of 19 October 1998

Pentidis and Others v. Greece, 9 June 1997, *Reports of Judgments and Decisions* 1997 – III

Perry v. Latvia, no. 30273/03, 8 November 2007

Phull v. France (dec.), no. 35753/03, ECHR 2005 – I

Pichon and Sajous v. France (dec.), no. 49853/99, ECHR 2001 – X

Pitkevich v. Russia (dec.), no. 47936/99, 8 February 2001

Poltoratski v. Ukraine, no. 38812/97, ECHR 2003 – V

Pretty v. the United Kingdom, no. 2346/02, ECHR 2002 – III

— Q —

— R —

Ranjit Singh v. France (dec.), no. 27561/08, 30 June 2009

Razaghi v. Sweden (dec.), no. 64599/01, 11 March 2003

Refah Partisi (the Welfare Party) and Others v. Turkey [GC], nos. 41340/98, 41342/98, 41343/98 and 41344/98, ECHR 2003 - II

Religionsgemeinschaft der Zeugen Jehovas and Others v. Austria, no. 40825/98, 31 July 2008

Representation of the Union of Councils for Jews in the Former Soviet Union and the Union of Jewish Religious organisations of Ukraine v. Ukraine (dec.), no. 13276/05, 1er April 2014

Revert and Legallais v. France (dec.), nos. 14431/88 and 14432/88, Commission decision of 8 September 1989, DR 62, p. 309

Rommelfanger v. Germany (dec.), no. 12242/86, Commission decision of 6 September 1989, DR 62, p. 151

Rupprecht v. Spain (dec.), no. 38471/10, 19 February 2013

— S —

S. A. S. v. France [GC], no. 43835/11, ECHR 2014 (extracts)

S. H. and H. V. v. Austria (dec.), no. 19860/91, Commission decision of 13 January 1993

Sadik Amet and Others v. Greece (dec.), no. 64756/01, 10 October 2002

Salonen v. Finland (dec.), no. 27868/95, Commission decision of 2 July 1997, DR 90, p. 60

Saniewski v. Poland, (dec.), no. 40319/98, 26 June 2001

Savda v. Turkey, no. 42730/05, 12 June 2012

Savez crkava 'Riječ života' and Others v. Croatia, no. 7798/08, 9 December 2010

Schüth v. Germany, no. 1620/03, ECHR 2010

Schilder v. the Netherlands (dec.), no. 2158/12, 16 October 2012

Scientology Kirche Deutschland e. V. v. Germany (dec.), Commission decision of 7 April 1997, DR 89, p. 163

Serbisch-griechisch-orientalische Kirchengemeinde zum Heiligen Sava in Wien v. Austria (dec.), no. 20966/92, Commission decision of 30 November 1994

Serif v. Greece, no. 38178/97, ECHR 1999 – IX

Şerife Yiğit v. Turkey [GC], no. 3976/05, 2 November 2010

Sert v. Turkey (dec.), no. 47491/99, 8 July 2004

Seyidzade v. Azerbaijan, no. 37700/05, 3 december 2009

Siebenhaar v. Germany, no. 18136/02, 3 February 2011

Şijakova andOthers v. the former Yugoslav Republic of Macedonia (dec.), no. 67914/01, 6 March 2003

Sinan Işık v. Turkey, no. 21924/05, ECHR 2010

Sindicatul 《Păstorul cel Bun》 v. Romania [GC], no. 2330/09, ECHR 2013 (extracts)

Skugar and Others v. Russia (dec.), no. 40010/04, 3 december 2009

Sofianopoulos and Others v. Greece (dec.), nos. 1977/02, 1988/02 and 1997/02, ECHR 2002 – X

Sotirov and Others v. Bulgaria (dec.), no. 13999/05, 5 July 2011

Spampinato v. Italy (dec.), no. 23123/04, 29 March 2007

Spetz and Others v. Sweden (dec.), no. 20402/92, Commission decision of 12 October 1994

Staatkundig Gereformeerde Partij v. the Netherlands (dec.), no. 58369/10, 10 July 2012

Stedman v. Royaume Uni (dec.), no. 29107/95, Commission decision of 9 April 1997, DR 89, p. 104

Sukyo Mahikari France v. France (dec.), no. 41729/09, 8 January 2013

Supreme Holy Council of the Muslim Community v. Bulgaria, no. 39023/97, 16 December 2004

Svyato-Mykhaïlivska Parafiya v. Ukraine, no. 77703/01, 14 June 2007

— T —

Tanyar and Others v. Turkey (dec.), no. 74242/01, 7 June 2005

Tarhan v. Turkey, no. 9078/06, 17 July 2012

Tennenbaum v. Sweden (dec.), no. 16031/90, Commission decision of 3 May 1993

Tepeli and Others v. Turkey (dec.), no. 31876/96, 11 September 2001

The Church of Jesus Christ of Latter-day Saints v. the United Kingdom, no. 7552/09, 4 March 2014

Thlimmenos v. Greece [GC], no. 34369/97, ECHR 2000 – IV

Tiğ v. Turkey (dec.), no. 8165/03, 24 May 2005

Tsaturyan v. Armenia, no. 37821/03, 10 January 2012

— U —

Union des Athées v. France, no. 14635/89, Commission's report of 6 July 1994

Universelles Leben e. V. v. Germany (dec.), no. 29745/96, Commission decision of 27 November 1996

— V —

V. v. the United Kingdom (dec.), no. 10358/83, Commission decision of 15 December 1983, DR 37, p. 148

V. v. the Netherlands (dec.), no. 10678/83, Commission decision of 5 July 1984, DR 39, p. 267

V. J., J. J. and E. J. v. Poland (dec.), no. 23380/94, Commission decision of 16 January 1996

Valsamis v. Greece, 18 December 1996, *Reports of Judgments and Decisions* 1996 – VI

Van den Dungen v. the Netherlands (dec.), no. 22838/93, Commission decision of 22 February 1995, DR 80, p. 147

Vartic v. Romania (no. 2), no. 14150/08, 17 December 2013

Van Schijndel and Others v. the Netherlands (dec.), no. 30936/96, Commission decision of 10 September 1997

Vereniging Rechtswinkels Utrecht v. the Netherlands (dec.), no. 11308/84, Commission decision of 13 March 1986, DR 46, p. 203

Vergos v. Greece, no. 65501/01, 24 June 2004

Viel v. France (dec.), no. 41781/98, 14 December 1999

Vingt-trois habitants d'Alsemberget de Beersel v. Belgium (dec.), no. 1474/62,

Commission decision of 26 July 1963

 Von Pelser v. Italy (dec.), no. 14254/88, Commission decision of 9 November 1990

— W —

 W. v. the United Kingdom (dec.), no. 18187/91, Commission decision of 10 February 1993

 Wasmuth v. Germany, no. 12884/03, 17 February 2011

 Williamson v. the United Kingdom (dec.), no. 27008/95, Commission decision of 17 May 1995

 Wingrove v. the United Kingdom, 25 November 1996, Reports of Judgments and Decisions 1996 – V

— X —

 X. v. Germany (dec.), no. 2413/65, Commission decision of 16 December 1966, Collection 23, p. 1

 X. v. Germany (dec.), no. 3110/67, Commission decision of 19 July 1968, Year book 11, p. 495

 X. v. Germany (dec.), no. 4445/70, Commission decision of 1er April 1970, Collection 37, p. 119

 X. v. Germany (dec.), no. 6167/73, Commission decision of 18 December 1974, DR 1, p. 64

 X. v. Germany (dec.), no. 8741/79, Commission decision of 10 March 1981, DR 24, p. 137

 X. v. Austria (dec.), no. 1718/62, Commission decision of 22 April 1965, Year book 8, p. 169[①]

 X. v. Austria (dec.), no. 1753/63, Commission decision of 15 February 1965, Year book 8, p. 175[②]

 X. v. Austria (dec.), no. 4982/71, Commission decision of 22 March 1972, Year

---

[①] Decision available in paper copy only in the **Yearbooks of the European Convention on Human Rights at the Court library.**

[②] Decision available in paper copy only in the **Yearbooks of the European Convention on Human Rights at the Court library.**

book 15, p. 469

X. v. Austria (dec.), no. 8652/79, Commission decision of 15 October 1981, DR 26, p. 89

X. v. Denmark (dec.), no. 7374/76, Commission decision of 8 March 1976, DR 5, p. 157

X. v. Iceland (dec.), no. 2525/65, Commission decision of 6 February 1967, *Collection* 22, p. 33

X. v. the Netherlands (dec.), no. 1068/61, Commission decision of 14 December 1962, *Year book* 5, p. 278)①

X. v. the Netherlands (dec.), no. 2065/63, Commission decision of 14 December 1965, *Year book* 8, p. 267

X. v. the Netherlands (dec.), no. 2648/65, Commission decision of 6 February 1968, *Year book* 11, p. 355

X. v. the Netherlands (dec.), no. 2988/66, Commission decision of 31 May 1967, *Year book* 10, p. 473

X. v. the United Kingdom (dec.), no. 5442/72, Commission decision of 20 December 1974, DR 1, p. 41

X v. the United Kingdom (dec.), no. 5947/72, Commission decision of 5 March 1976, DR 5, p. 8

X. v. the United Kingdom (dec.), no. 6886/75, Commission decision of 18 May 1976, DR 5, p. 100

X. v. the United Kingdom (dec.), no. 7291/75, Commission decision of 4 October 1977, DR 11, p. 55

X. v. the United Kingdom (dec.), no. 7992/77, Commission decision of 12 July 1978, DR 14, p. 234

X. v. the United Kingdom (dec.), no. 8160/78, Commission decision of 12 March 1981, DR 22, p. 27

X. v. the United Kingdom (dec.), no. 8231/78, Commission decision of 6 March

---

① Decision available in paper copy only in the **Yearbooks of the European Convention on Human Rights at the Court library.**

1982, DR 28, p. 5

X. v. Sweden (dec.), no. 172/56, Commission decision of 20 December 1957, Yearbook 1, p. 211①

X. v. Sweden (dec.), no. 434/58, Commission decision of 30 June 1959, Yearbook 3, p. 355

X. v. Sweden (dec.), no. 7911/77, Commission decision of 12 December 1977, DR 12, p. 192

X. v. the United Kingdom (dec.), no. 7291/75, Commission decision of 4 October 1977

X. and Church of Scientology v. Sweden (dec.), no. 7805/77, Commission decision of 5 May 1979, DR 16, p. 68

X. Ltd. and Y. v. the United Kingdom (dec.), no. 8710/79, Commission decision of 7 May 1982, DR 28, p. 77

X., Y. and Z. v. Germany (dec.), no. 6850/74, Commission decision of 18 May 1976, DR 5, p. 90

— Y —

Yanaşık v. Turkey (dec.), no. 14524/89, Commission decision of 6 January 1993, DR 74, p. 14

— Z —

Z. and T. v. the United Kingdom (dec.), no. 27034/05, ECHR 2006 - Ⅲ

Zaoui v. Switzerland (dec.), no. 41615/98, 18 January 2001

v. Sweden (dec.), no. 911/60, Commission decision of 10 April 1961, Yearbook 4②

---

① Decision available in paper copy only in the **Yearbooks of the European Convention on Human Rights at the Court library.**

② Decision available in paper copy only in the **Yearbooks of the European Convention on Human Rights at the Court library.**

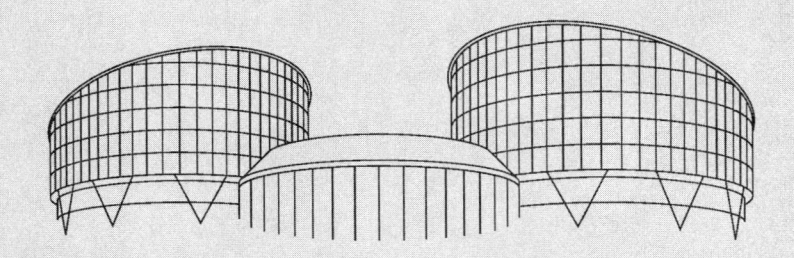

EUROPEAN COURT OF HUMAN RIGHTS
COUR EUROPÉENNE DES DROITS DE L'HOMME

第七章 《欧洲人权公约》第15条适用指南

紧急状态下的克减

COUNCIL OF EUROPE
CONSEIL DE L'EUROPE

读者须知

本指南是欧洲人权法院（以下简称法院、欧洲法院、斯特拉斯堡法院）公布的"公约指南"系列的一部分，用于向法律从业者介绍斯特拉斯堡法院。本指南分析并总结了《欧洲人权公约》第 15 条（以下简称公约或欧洲公约）的判例法，直至 2016 年 8 月 31 日。读者将找到这方面的关键原则及相关先例。

所引用的判例选自重要、主要和/或最近的判决和决定。*

法院的判决不仅用于裁决提交法院的案件，而且更一般地阐明、保障和制定公约规定的规则，从而有助于各国遵守它们作为缔约方所做的承诺（*Ireland v. the United Kingdom*, 18 January 1978, § 154, Series A no. 25.）。因此，公约建立的机制的任务是从普遍利益出发，确定公共政策问题，从而提高保护人权的标准，并在公约缔约国共同体内扩大人权法判例（*Konstantin Markin v. Russia* [GC], no. 30078/06, § 89, ECHR 2012）。

---

* 指南电子版引用的案例的超链接是指法院做出的判决或裁决的英文或法文原文（法院的两种官方语言），以及欧洲人权委员会的决定或报告（以下简称"委员会"）。除非另有说明，所有的引用都是对法院审判庭的案情的判决。缩写"（dec.）"表示引用是法院的决定，"[GC]"案由大审判庭审理。

第一节　基本原则

> **公约第 15 条　紧急状态下的克减**
>
> "(1)在战时或者其他威胁国家生存的公共紧急状态时期,任何缔约国有权在情况的紧急性所严格要求的范围内采取减弱其根据本公约所应当履行的义务的措施。但是,上述措施不得与其根据国际法的规定所应当履行的其他义务相抵触。
>
> (2)除了因战争行为引起的死亡之外,不得因上述规定而削弱对公约第 2 条所规定的权利的保护,也不得削弱对公约第 3 条、第 4 条(第 1 款)以及第 7 条所规定的权利的保护。
>
> (3)任何采取上述克减权利措施的缔约国,都应当向欧洲委员会秘书长全面报告它所采取的措施以及采取该措施的理由。缔约国应当在已经停止实施上述措施并且正在重新执行本公约的规定时,通知欧洲委员会秘书长。"

1. 第 15 条是一个克减条款。在例外情况下,它给予缔约国在监督下有限地减损其根据公约保障某些权利和自由的义务的可能性。

2. 第 15 条的内容是根据《联合国人权公约》草案第 4 条制定的,后者后来成为《公民权利和政治权利国际公约》(International Covenant on Civil and Political Rights,简称"ICCPR")第 4 条[①]。

3. 第 15 条由三个部分组成。第 15 条第 1 款规定了缔约国可以有效地克减其公约义务的情形,也限制了在任何克减过程中可能采取的措施。第 15 条第 2 款保护公约的某些基本权利免受任何克减。第 15 条第 3 款规定了任何实施克减措施的缔约国都必须遵守的程序要求。

[①] 参见关于第 15 条的准备工作文件(document DH (56) 4)第 10 页和附件 1,可在法院图书馆的网站〈www.echr.coe.int/Library〉上查阅。《美洲人权公约》也包含一个克减条款(第 27 条)。《非洲人权和人民权利宪章》中没有这样的条款。

4. 做出克减不一定意味着缔约国承认无法保障公约所规定的权利。事实上,缔约国提出克减是声明它所采取的措施"可能"涉及对公约的克减。因此,当申诉人主张其人权在克减时期受到侵犯时,本法院会首先审查当局所采取的措施是否符合公约的实体规定;只有当认定采取该措施不合理时,本法院才会继续审查该克减是否正当[*A. and Others v. the United Kingdom* [GC],§161;*Lawless v. Ireland* (no.3),§15]。

第二节 第15条第1款:缔约国何时能正当克减

> **第15条第1款**
> "在战时或者其他威胁国家生存的公共紧急状态时期,任何缔约国有权在情况的紧急性所严格要求的范围内采取减弱其根据本公约所应当履行的义务的措施。但是,上述措施不得与其根据国际法的规定所应当履行的其他义务相抵触。……"

5. 第15条第1款规定了正当克减应满足的三个条件:
(1) 必须在战争期间或者其他危及国家生存的其他公共紧急状态时期;
(2) 针对该战争或公共紧急状态所采取的措施不能超过该紧急情况所严格要求的程度;
(3) 该措施不得与其根据国际法的规定所应当履行的其他义务相抵触。

一、"战时或者其他威胁国家生存的公共紧急状态"

6. 本法院未被要求解释第15条第1款中"战争"的含义;在任何情况下,任何重大暴力或突发骚乱都可能属于第15条第1款中的第二分支,即"威胁国家生存的公共紧急状态"的范围。

7. "威胁国家生存的公共紧急状态"在自然和习惯上的含义是清晰的,是指"波及整个人口,并且威胁到该国家的社区群体生命安全的特殊危机或紧急情况"[*Lawless v. Ireland* (no.3),§28]。

8. 该紧急情况须是实际的或紧迫的;一个只涉及缔约国的某个特定地区的危机可被视为一种危及"国家生存"的公共紧急状态(Ireland v. the United Kingdom,§ 205,北爱尔兰的克减,Aksoy v. Turkey,§ 70,土耳其东南部的克减);该危机或危险必须是很特殊的,以至于公约所允许的用于维持公共安全、公共健康和公共秩序的正常措施或限制明显不够[Denmark,Norway,Sweden and the Netherlands v. Greece(the "Greek case"),Commission Report,§ 153]。

9. 到目前为止,本法院的判例法未明确地规定紧急状态须是暂时的,事实上,案例反而表明第 15 条含义中的"公共紧急状态"有可能持续很多年(参见北爱尔兰的安全情势:Ireland v. the United Kingdom,Brannigan and McBride v. the United Kingdom,Marshall v. the United Kingdom(dec.);以及基地组织袭击美国后该地的安全情势:A. and Others v. the United Kingdom[GC],§ 178)。

10. 通常情况下,公约机构会将是否存在特殊情势交由国内当局判定。正如本法院在爱尔兰诉英国案(Ireland v. the United Kingdom,§ 207)中所提出的:"首先应由缔约国来决定某个'公共紧急状态'是否危及其生存,这属于缔约国对自己的生存所应负起的责任"。

11. 北爱尔兰的恐怖主义符合公共紧急状态的标准,因为数年来,它对"英国的领土完整、(北爱尔兰的)6 个郡的制度和该省居民的生活带来了特别深远和严重的危险"[Ireland v. the United Kingdom,§§ 205 and 212;Brannigan and McBride v. the United Kingdom,§ 48;Marshall v. the United Kingdom(dec.)]。土耳其东南部的库尔德工人党恐怖活动(Aksoy v. Turkey,§ 70)以及 2001 年 9 月 11 日之后在英国发生的严重恐怖主义袭击(A. and Others v. the United Kingdom[GC],§ 181)也符合这个标准。然而,对于迫切性的要求不能狭义地解释为只有在灾害发生时国家才能采取措施(A. and Others v. the United Kingdom[GC],§ 177)。

12. 尽管这一事项交由缔约国判定,但也应受到一定限制:例如,在 1967 年针对"上校"政变针对希腊提起的"希腊案"中(委员会报告,第 159 至 165 段以及第 207 段),委员会认为,根据其获得的证据,没有任何公共紧急情况可以作为克减的理由。应当注意的是,在上述关于北爱尔兰和土耳其东南部局势的案件中,"公共紧急状态"的存在没有争议,而在"希腊案"中,关于希腊军政府试图采取的克减,这一点在细节上显然有争议。

13. 由于第 15 条的目的是允许各国采取克减措施,保护其人民免受未来的风险,因此必须首先根据在克减时期的已知事实来评估国家生存是否受到威胁。但是,本法院不排除考虑这之后出现的情况(*A. and Others v. the United Kingdom* [GC],§ 177)。

14. 但是公约不允许在适用克减的领土之外采取措施,在这种情况下,有关政府不能依据克减的规定来证明措施的正当性(*Sakık and Others v. Turkey*,§ 39;*Sadak v. Turkey*,§§ 56;*Yurttas v. Turkey*,§ 58;*Abdülsamet Yaman v. Turkey*,§ 69)。

15. 关于公约的域外适用问题,本法院认为:"自公约订立以来,虽然有一些缔约国在域外进行军事活动,但没有任何国家根据公约第 15 条就这些活动克减公约义务。……克减应当基于缔约国内部冲突或恐怖主义威胁的原因而做出(*Hassan v. the United Kingdom* [GC],§ 101)。

二、"情况的紧急性所严格要求的范围内"

16. 本法院认为,在涉及第 15 条的情形中,对本法院审查权力的限制是"特别明显"的(*Ireland v. the United Kingdom*,§ 207):

"每个缔约国对"国家的生存"都负有责任,因此首先应由缔约国来确定其生存是否受到"公共紧急状态"的威胁;若确实存在,则需要确定应该怎样应对紧急情况。由于他们直接和持续地面临当前需求,原则上来说,国内当局比国际法官更有立场决定是否存在这种紧急情况,以及为应对这种紧急情况所必须采取的克减措施的性质和范围。在这方面,第 15 条第 1 款赋予了国内当局很大的自由裁量权。"

17. 然而,各国在此方面并非享有无限的权力:本法院有权裁决这些国家是否超出了危机的"紧急性所严格要求的范围"(同上)。

18. 在确定一国是否超出了严格要求的范围时,本法院将适当考虑诸如受克减影响的权利的性质、引发的情况以及紧急情况的持续时间等因素(*Brannigan and McBride v. the United Kingdom*,§ 43;*A. and Others v. the United Kingdom* [GC],§ 173)。

19. 本法院会考虑以下事项:

- 普通法律是否足以应付公共紧急情况造成的危险[*Lawless v. Ireland* (no. 3),§ 36;*Ireland v. the United Kingdom*,§ 212];
- 这些措施是否确实被用于应对紧急情况(*Brannigan and McBride v. the United*

Kingdom, § 51);

- 这些措施是否用于其获批准时的目的[Lawless v. Ireland (no.3), § 38];
- 克减的范围和支持理由是否受到限制(Brannigan and McBride v. the United Kingdom, § 66);
- 克减的需求是否受过审查(Brannigan and McBride v. the United Kingdom, § 54);
- 施加的措施中的任何减弱因素(Ireland v. the United Kingdom, § 220);
- 这些措施是否受到保障[Ireland v. the United Kingdom, §§ 216-219; Lawless v. Ireland (no.3), § 37; Brannigan and McBride v. the United Kingdom, §§ 61-65; Aksoy v. Turkey, §§ 79-84];
- 所涉权利的重要性,以及对该权利进行司法控制的更为广泛的目的(Aksoy v. Turkey, § 76);
- 这些措施的司法控制是否切实可行(同上, § 78①; Brannigan and McBride v. the United Kingdom, § 59);
- 措施的相称性以及是否涉及任何不合理的歧视(A. and Others v. the United Kingdom [GC], § 190);
- 审理了这个问题的国内法院的意见:如果缔约国的国内最高法院得出的结论是,这些措施并不是严格需要的,那么只有在确定国内法院误解或误用了第15条及本法院的相关判例,或者得出的结论明显不合理的情况下,本法院才可以合理地得出相反的结论(同上, § 174)。

20. 本法院通常会根据"最初采取和随后适用这些措施时的条件和情况"考虑以上因素,这并非溯及既往(Ireland v. the United Kingdom, § 214)。但是,如同判定是否存在公共紧急状况一样,本法院也不排除考虑随后出现的信息(A. and Others v. the United Kingdom [GC], § 177,本法院参考了2005年7月在伦敦发生的爆炸和爆炸未遂事件,这些事件就发生在2001年宣布克减的几年之后)。

---

① 同样可参见"后阿克索伊案":Demir and Others v. Turkey, §§ 49-58; Nuray Şen v. Turkey, §§ 25-29; Elçi and Others v. Turkey, § 684; Bilen v. Turkey, §§ 44-50。

三、"只要上述措施不与其根据国际法的规定所应当履行的其他义务相抵触"

21. 如有必要,本法院将自行考虑第 15 条第 1 款的这一限制[*Lawless v. Ireland* (no. 3), §40],即使发现该国的克减行为与其根据国际法所应履行的义务之间没有任何不一致。

22. 在布兰尼根和麦克布莱德诉英国案(*Brannigan and McBride v. the United Kingdom*)中,申诉人认为正式宣告是《公民权利和政治权利国际公约》第 4 条①所规定的有效克减的一项要求,缺乏这种宣告意味着英国的克减违背其国际法义务,本法院驳回了这一意见。本法院认为,权威地界定《公民权利和政治权利国际公约》第 4 条中"正式宣告"一词的含义不是本法院的职责。然而,本法院必须审查申诉人是否有合理的依据。它发现,内政大臣对下议院做出的关于克减的声明"完全符合正式宣告的概念"(§§ 67 – 73)。②

23. 在马歇尔诉英国案[*Marshall v. the United Kingdom*(dec.)]中,申诉人依据联合国人权事务委员会的意见,认为北爱尔兰的紧急条款是"过度"的,且应当撤消根据《公民权利和政治权利国际公约》第 4 条做出的克减。本法院认为,这些意见并没有表明英国政府在 1995 年之后维持其克减状态的做法应被视为违背《公民权利和政治权利国际公约》规定的义务。因此,申诉人不能继续主张克减的依然生效违背了当局的国际法义务。

24. 在哈桑诉英国案(*Hassan v. the United Kingdom*[GC])中,本法院须决定,若在国际冲突的情况下没有做出克减,是否仍可以根据国际(人道主义)法律的原则重新解释公约的规定。本法院的结论是肯定的。虽然根据第 5 条规定,缔约国不能通过拘留来剥夺他人自由,但缔约国不必通过对第 5 条规定的义务做出克减来拘留战俘和在冲突情形下威胁国家安全的平民。因为该条可以根据国际人道法(即《日内瓦第三公约》和《日内瓦第四公约》)的原则加以解释和适用。

---

① 《公民权利和政治权利国际公约》第 4 条第 1 款在相关部分中规定:"在威胁国家生命并且官方宣布存在的公共紧急情况时……"。

② 参见委员会对塞浦路斯诉土耳其案(*Cyprus v. Turkey*,委员会 1976 年 7 月 10 日报告,第 527 段)的结论,该结论认为第 15 条要求:"某种正式和公开的克减行为,例如,宣布戒严或紧急状态,如果有关缔约国没有宣布此种行为,尽管该国并非处在不能这样做的情形中,第 15 条也不能适用。"

第三节　第 15 条第 2 款：不可克减的权利

> **第 15 条第 2 款**
> "除了因战争行为引起的死亡之外,不得因上述规定而削弱对公约第 2 条所规定的权利的保护,也不得削弱对公约第 3 条、第 4 条(第 1 款)以及第 7 条所规定的权利的保护。……"

25. 第 15 条第 2 款保护某些权利免受克减。根据第 15 条第 2 款的规定,这些权利条款是:第 2 条(生命权),但由于合法的战争行为造成的死亡除外;第 3 条(禁止酷刑和其他形式的虐待);第 4 条第 1 款(禁止蓄奴);和第 7 条(法无规定不得处罚)。

26. 公约的 3 个附加议定书也包括了禁止减损某些权利的条款,分别是第六议定书(在和平时期废除死刑和在战时限制死刑),第七议定书(仅指该议定书第 4 条所规定的一事不再理原则)和第十三议定书(完全废除死刑)。[①]

27. 第 15 条第 2 款(以及第 6、第 7 和第十三议定书中相应的不可克减条款)的效力是,在战时或公共紧急状态时期等任何时候,不论缔约国是否做出任何克减,这些条款所提及的权利都会继续受到保护。

28. 至于公约第 2 条和第 7 条,这些条款中已经规定的例外也将继续适用。

29. 因此,关于第 2 条,如果剥夺生命的行为是在第 2 条第 2 款第 a 项至 c 项规定的情况下使用武力且没有超过绝对必要的(即捍卫任何人免受非法暴力,进行合法逮捕或防止合法拘留的人逃脱,为了镇压暴动或动乱而合法采取的行动),则不会违反该条。第 15 条第 2 款增加了另一个例外,即如果死亡是由合法的战争行为造成的,生命权不会受到侵犯。

30. 同样,关于第 7 条,法无规定不得处罚的原则受到第 7 条第 2 款的约束,即如果根据文明国家所认可的一般法律原则,该作为或者不作为在其发生时构成刑事犯罪行为,则本条不得妨碍对该人的作为或者不作为进行审判或者予以惩罚。

[①] 分别为第六议定书第 3 条、第七议定书第 4 条第 3 款和第十三议定书第 2 条。

第四节　第15条第3款：告知的要求

第 15 条第 3 款

"任何采取上述克减权利措施的缔约国，都应当向欧洲委员会秘书长全面报告它所采取的措施以及采取该措施的理由。缔约国应当在已经停止实施上述措施并且正在重新执行本公约的规定时，通知欧洲委员会秘书长。"

31. 告知秘书长的首要目的是使克减得以公开。另一个目的是，公约是一个集体执行机制，须通过秘书长通知其他缔约国与克减有关的情况：根据部长委员会第 56(16) 号决议，任何根据第 15 条第 3 款提交给秘书长的信息，秘书长必须尽快通知其他缔约国(*Greece v. the United Kingdom*, Commission report, § 158)。

32. 在没有正式和公开通知克减的情况下，第 15 条不适用于被诉国所采取的措施(*Cyprus v. Turkey*, Commission report of 4 October 1983, §§ 66–68)。

33. 通知秘书长采取的措施和理由通常是通过写信并附上将采取紧急措施的法律文本副本，以及解释其目的[*Lawless v. Ireland* (no.3), § 47]的方式进行的。如果没有提供所有相关措施的副本，则不符合要求[the "*Greek case*", Commission report, § 81(1) and (2)]。

34. 在希腊诉英国案(*Greece v. the United Kingdom*)中，委员会认为，从第 15 条第 3 款的措词可以明确地看出，通知不需要在采取有关措施之前做出，而且本条款的措辞也没有指明必须做出通知的时间以及向秘书长告知信息的范围和程度。委员会认为，有关国家应在没有任何不可避免的拖延的情况下告知所采取的措施，并充分提供有关这些措施的资料，使其他缔约国足以了解克减的性质和程度。在该案中，采取克减措施和告知秘书长之间的时间间隔长达 3 个月，而且该紧急情况造成的行政拖延也不构成正当理由。同样地，"希腊案"中是采取措施 4 个月后才通知，这也是不被接受的[Commission report, § 81(3)]。相反地，本法院认为在措施生效 12 天后通知是适当的[*Lawless v. Ireland* (no.3), § 47]。

35. 即使其他当事方没有任何质疑,本法院也将自行审查一个国家的通知是否符合第 15 条第 3 款的形式要求(*Aksoy v. Turkey*,§§ 85 – 86)。

36. 本法院还认为,第 15 条第 3 款要求对紧急措施的必要性进行常设性审查(*Brannigan and McBride v. the United Kingdom*,§ 54)。

37. 最后,(根据第 15 条第 3 款的最后一句)克减撤销后,对于任何有关在克减撤销后采取措施的案件,本法院将在申诉所依据的条款完全适用的基础上来进行审查。但是,这不排除适当考虑案件的背景情况。应由本法院确定这些情况的重要性,并根据其具体措辞和条款的总体目标和宗旨,确定该情形是否符合有关条款的可适用规定(*Brogan and Others v. the United Kingdom*,§ 48,涉及第 5 条)。

援引案例一览

本指南援引的判例法涉及欧洲人权法院的判决或裁定以及欧洲人权委员会的决定或报告。

除非另行指明,所有参考皆是本法院审判庭依法做出的判决。缩写"(dec.)"是指该处援引为本法院裁定,"[GC]"是指该案件由大审判庭审判。

本指南电子版中援引案例的超链接直接跳转 HUDOC 数据库〈http://hudoc.echr.coe.int〉。该数据库提供本法院(包括大审判庭、审判庭和委员会的判决、裁定和相关案例、咨询意见以及案例法信息注解中的法律总结)、委员会(决定和报告)和部长委员会(决议)的判例法。

本法院以英语和/或法语这两种官方语言发布判决和裁定。HUDOC 也包含许多重要案例的近 30 种非官方言语的翻译,以及由第三方制作的大约 100 个在线案例汇总的链接。

(注:为了避免重复,本章所附的相关案例索引没有在中文部分进行翻译,读者可在对应的英文部分阅读。)

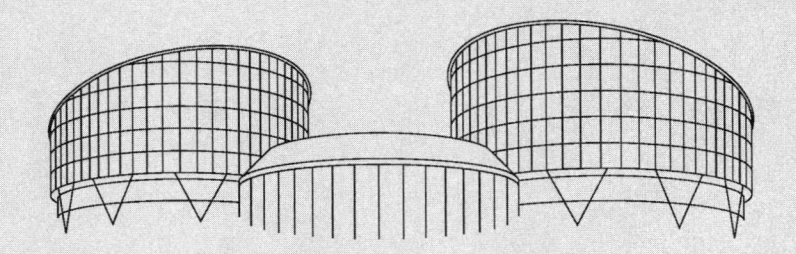

EUROPEAN COURT OF HUMAN RIGHTS
COUR EUROPÉENNE DES DROITS DE L'HOMME

Chapter VII   Guide on Article 15 of the European Convention on Human Rights Derogation in Time of Emergency

COUNCIL OF EUROPE
CONSEIL DE L'EUROPE

Publishers or organisations wishing to reproduce this report (or a translation thereof) in print or online are asked to contactpublishing@echr.coe.int for further instructions.

This Guide has been prepared by the Research and Library Division, within the Directorate of the Jurisconsult, and does not bind the Court. The text was finalised on 31 August 2016; it may be subject to editorial revision.

The document is available for downloading at ⟨www.echr.coe.int⟩ (Case-Law-Case-Law Analysis-Case-Law Guides).

For publication updates please follow the Court's Twitter account at ⟨https:/twitter.com/echrpublication⟩.

©Council of Europe/European Court of Human Rights, 2016

Chapter VII Guide on Article 15 of the European Convention on Human Rights Derogation in Time of Emergency

Note to readers

This Guide is part of the series of Case-Law Guides published by the European Court of Human Rights (hereafter "the Court", "the European Court" or "the Strasbourg Court") to inform legal practitioners about the fundamental judgments delivered by the Strasbourg Court. This particular Guide analyses and sums up the case-law on Article 15 of the European Convention on Human Rights (hereafter "the Convention" or "the European Convention") until 31 August 2016. Readers will find the key principles in this area and the relevant precedents.

The case-law cited has been selected among the leading, major, and/or recent judgments and decisions. *

The Court's judgments serve not only to decide those cases broughtbefore the Court but, more generally, to elucidate, safeguard and develop the rules instituted by the Convention, thereby contributing to the observance by the States of the engagements undertaken by them as Contracting Parties (*Ireland v. the United Kingdom*, 18 January 1978, § 154, Series A no. 25.). The mission of the system set up by the Convention is thus to determine, in the general interest, issues of public policy, thereby raising the standards of protection of human rights and extending human rights jurisprudence throughout the community of the Convention States (*Konstantin Markin v. Russia* [GC], no. 30078/06, § 89, ECHR 2012).

---

* The case-law cited may be in either or both of the official languages (English and French) of the Court and the European Commission of Human Rights. Unless otherwise indicated, all references are to a judgment on the merits delivered by a Chamber of the Court. The abbreviation "(dec.)" indicates that the citation is of a decision of the Court and "[GC]" that the case was heard by the Grand Chamber.

I. General principles

> **Article 15 of the Convention-Derogation in time of emergency**
>
> "1. In time of war or other public emergency threatening the life of the nation any High Contracting Party may take measures derogating from its obligations under [the] Convention to the extent strictly required by the exigencies of the situation, provided that such measures are not inconsistent with its other obligations under international law.
>
> 2. No derogation from Article 2, except in respect of deaths resulting from lawful acts of war, or from Articles 3, 4 (§ 1) and 7 shall be made under this provision.
>
> 3. Any High Contracting Party availing itself of this right of derogation shall keep the Secretary General of the Council of Europe fully informed of the measures which it has taken and the reasons therefore. It shall also inform the Secretary General of the Council of Europe when such measures have ceased to operate and the provisions of the Convention are again being fully executed."

1. Article 15 is a derogation clause. It affords to Contracting States, in exceptional circumstances, the possibility of derogating, in a limited and supervised manner, from their obligations to secure certain rights and freedoms under the Convention.

2. The text of Article 15 is based on the draft Article 4 of the United Nations draft Covenant on Human Rights, which later became Article 4 of the International Covenant on Civil and Political Rights (ICCPR).[①]

3. Article 15 has three parts. Article 15 § 1 defines the circumstances in which Contracting States can validly derogate from their obligations under the Convention. It also

---

[①] See p. 10 of, and Appendix I to, the *Travaux préparatoires* on Article 15 (document DH (56) 4 available on the Court's Library website at 〈www.echr.coe.int/Library〉). The American Convention on Human Rights also contains a derogation clause (Article 27). There is no such clause in the African Charter on Human and Peoples' Rights.

limits the measures they may take in the course of any derogation. Article 15 § 2 protects certain fundamental rights in the Convention from any derogation. Article 15 § 3 sets out the procedural requirements that any State making a derogation must follow.

4. The making of a derogation need not be a concession that the State will not be able to guarantee the rights contained in the Convention. Indeed, the practice when lodging a derogation has been for the Contracting State to state that the measures it is taking "may" involve a derogation from the Convention. For this reason, in any case where an applicant complains that his Convention rights were violated during a period of derogation, the Court will first examine whether the measures taken can be justified under the substantive articles of the Convention; it is only if it cannot be so justified that the Court will go on to determine whether the derogation was valid [for instance, *A. and Others v. the United Kingdom* [GC], § 161; *Lawless v. Ireland* (no. 3), § 15].

II. Article 15 § 1: when a State may validly derogate

> Article 15 § 1 of the Convention
>
> "1. In time of war or other public emergency threatening the life of the nation any High Contracting Party may take measures derogating from its obligations under [the] Convention to the extent strictly required by the exigencies of the situation, provided that such measures are not inconsistent with its other obligations under international law.
> ..."

5. Article 15 § 1 sets out three conditions for a valid derogation:

i. it must be in time of war or other public emergency threatening the life of the nation;

ii. the measures taken in response to that war or public emergency must not go beyond the extent strictly required by the exigencies of the situation; and

iii. the measures must not be inconsistent with the State's other obligations under international law.

A. "…war or other public emergency threatening the life of the nation…"

6. The Court has not been required to interpret the meaning of "war" in Article 15 § 1; in any case, any substantial violence or unrest short of war is likely to fall within the scope of the second limb of Article 15 § 1, a "public emergency threatening the life of the nation".

7. The natural and customary meaning of "public emergency threatening the life of the nation" is clear and refers to "an exceptional situation of crisis or emergency which affects the whole population and constitutes a threat to the organised life of the community of which the State is composed" [*Lawless v. Ireland* (no. 3), § 28].

8. The emergency should be actual or imminent; a crisis which concerns only a particular region of the State can amount to a public emergency threatening "the life of the nation" (see, for instance, derogations in respect of Northern Ireland in *Ireland v. the United Kingdom*, § 205, and in respect of South-East Turkey in *Aksoy v. Turkey*, § 70); and the crisis or danger should be exceptional in that the normal measures or restrictions permitted by the Convention for the maintenance of public safety, health and order are plainly inadequate [*Denmark, Norway, Sweden and the Netherlands v. Greece* (the "*Greek case*"), Commission report, § 153].

9. The Court's case-law has never, to date, explicitly incorporated the requirement that the emergency be temporary and, indeed, the cases demonstrate that it is possible for a "public emergency" within the meaning of Article 15 to continue for many years [see the security situation in Northern Ireland: *Ireland v. the United Kingdom*, *Brannigan and McBride v. the United Kingdom*, *Marshall v. the United Kingdom* (dec.); and the security situation in place in the aftermath of the al-Qaeda attacks in the United States: *A. and Others v. the United Kingdom* [GC], § 178].

10. Generally the Convention organs have deferred to the national authorities' assessment as to whether such an exceptional situation exists. As the Court stated in *Ireland v. the United Kingdom* (§ 207): "it falls in the first place to each Contracting State, with

its responsibility for 'the life of [its] nation', to determine whether that life is threatened by a 'public emergency'".

11. Terrorism in Northern Ireland met the standard of a public emergency, since for a number of years it represented a "particularly far-reaching and acute danger for the territorial integrity of the United Kingdom, the institutions of the six counties [of Northern Ireland] and the lives of the province's inhabitants" [ibid., §§ 205 and 212; *Brannigan and McBride v. the United Kingdom*, § 48; *Marshall v. the United Kingdom* (dec.)]. So, too, did PKK terrorist activity in South-East Turkey (*Aksoy v. Turkey*, § 70) and the imminent threat of serious terrorist attacks in the United Kingdom after 11 September 2001 (*A. and Others v. the United Kingdom* [GC], § 181). The requirement of imminence is not, however, to be interpreted so narrowly as to require a State to wait for disaster to strike before taking measures to deal with it (ibid., § 177).

12. Notwithstanding this general approach of deference towards the national authorities' assessment, it is not unlimited: for instance, in the "*Greek case*" [Commission report, §§ 159 – 165 and 207)], the case brought against Greece in response to the "colonels" coup in 1967, the Commission found that, on the evidence before it, there was no public emergency which justified the derogation made. It should be noted that the existence of a "public emergency" was not disputed in the above-noted cases concerning the situation in Northern Ireland and south-east Turkey, whereas this was clearly disputed in some detail in the "*Greek case*" as regards the attempted derogation by the military government in Greece.

13. Since the purpose of Article 15 is to permit States to take derogating measures to protect their populations from future risks, the existence of the threat to the life of the nation must be assessed primarily with reference to those facts which were known at the time of the derogation. The Court is not precluded, however, from having regard to information which comes to light subsequently (*A. and Others v. the United Kingdom* [GC], § 177).

14. However, if measures are taken outside the territory to which the derogation applies, the derogation will not apply and the Government concerned will not be able to rely

on it to justify the measures (*Sakık and Others v. Turkey*, § 39; *Sadak v. Turkey*, §§ 56; *Yurttas v. Turkey*, § 58; *Abdülsamet Yaman v. Turkey*, § 69).

15. As to the extraterritorial application of the Convention, the Court has acknowledged that "although there have been a number of military missions involving Contracting States acting extra-territorially since their ratification of the Convention, no State has ever made a derogation pursuant to Article 15 of the Convention in respect of these activities. The derogations (...) have been rendered necessary as a result of internal conflicts or terrorist threats to the Contracting State" (*Hassan v. the United Kingdom* [GC], § 101).

B. "... measures ... strictly required by the exigencies of the situation..."

16. The Court has said that the limits on its powers of review are "particularly apparent" where Article 15 is concerned (*Ireland v. the United Kingdom*, § 207):

"It falls in the first place to each Contracting State, with its responsibility for 'the life of [its] nation', to determine whether that life is threatened by a 'public emergency' and, if so, how far it is necessary to go in attempting to overcome the emergency. By reason of their direct and continuous contact with the pressing needs of the moment, the national authorities are in principle in a better position than the international judge to decide both on the presence of such an emergency and on the nature and scope of derogations necessary to avert it. In this matter Article 15 § 1 (...) leaves those authorities a wide margin of appreciation."

17. Nevertheless, the States do not enjoy an unlimited power in this respect: the Court is empowered to rule on whether the States have gone beyond the "extent strictly required by the exigencies" of the crisis (ibid.).

18. In determining whether a State has gone beyond what is strictly required, the Court will give appropriate weight to factors such as the nature of the rights affected by the derogation, the circumstances leading to, and the duration of, the emergency situation (*Brannigan and McBride v. the United Kingdom*, § 43; *A. and Others v. the United Kingdom* [GC], § 173).

19. This involves the Court considering matters such as:

- whether ordinary laws would have been sufficient to meet the danger caused by the public emergency (*Lawless v. Ireland* (no. 3), § 36; *Ireland v. the United Kingdom*, § 212);
- whether the measures are a genuine response to an emergency situation (*Brannigan and McBride v. the United Kingdom*, § 51);
- whether the measures were used for the purpose for which they were granted [*Lawless v. Ireland* (no. 3), § 38];
- whether the derogation is limited in scope and the reasons advanced in support of it (*Brannigan and McBride v. the United Kingdom*, § 66);
- whether the need for the derogation was kept under review (ibid., § 54);
- any attenuation in the measures imposed (*Ireland v. the United Kingdom*, § 220);
- whether the measures were subject to safeguards (ibid., §§ 216 – 219; *Lawless v. Ireland* (no. 3), § 37; *Brannigan and McBride v. the United Kingdom*, §§ 61 – 65; *Aksoy v. Turkey*, §§ 79 – 84);
- the importance of the right at stake, and the broader purpose of judicial control over interferences with that right (ibid., § 76);
- whether judicial control of the measures was practicable (ibid., § 78;[1] *Brannigan and McBride v. the United Kingdom*, § 59);
- the proportionality of the measures and whether they involved any unjustifiable discrimination (*A. and Others v. the United Kingdom* [GC], § 190); and
- the views of any national courts which have considered the question: if the highest domestic court in a Contracting State has reached the conclusion that the measures were not strictly required, the Court will be justified in reaching a contrary conclusion only if satisfied that the national court had misinterpreted or misapplied Article 15 or the Court's jurisprudence under that Article, or reached a conclusion which was manifestly unreasonable (ibid., § 174).

---

[1] See also the post-*Aksoy* cases: *Demir and Others v. Turkey*, §§ 49 – 58; *Nuray Şen v. Turkey*, §§ 25 – 29; *Elçi and Others v. Turkey*, § 684; *Bilen v. Turkey*, §§ 44 – 50.

20. These factors will normally be assessed, not retrospectively, but on the basis of the "conditions and circumstances reigning when [the measures] were originally taken and subsequently applied" (*Ireland v. the United Kingdom*, § 214). However, it may be that, as with the assessment of whether there is a public emergency, the Court is not precluded from having regard to information which comes to light subsequently (*A. and Others v. the United Kingdom* [GC], § 177, where the Court took note of the bombings and attempted bombings in London in July 2005, which took place therefore years after the notification of the derogation in 2001).

C. "... provided that such measures are not inconsistent with [the High Contracting Party's] other obligations under international law"

21. The Court will consider this limb of Article 15 § 1 of its own motion if necessary [*Lawless v. Ireland* (no. 3), § 40], even if only to observe that it has not found any inconsistency between the derogation and a State's other obligations under international law.

22. In *Brannigan and McBride v. the United Kingdom*, the Court considered the applicants' submission that official proclamation was a requirement for a valid derogation under Article 4 of the International Convenant on Civil and Political Rights[①] and the absence of such proclamation meant the United Kingdom's derogation was not consistent with its obligations under international law. The Court rejected that submission. It found that it was not its role to seek to define authoritatively the meaning of the terms "officially proclaimed" in Article 4 of the ICCPR. Nevertheless, it had to examine whether there was any plausible basis for the applicants' submission. It found that the Home Secretary's statement to the House of Commons on the derogation was "well in keeping with the notion of an official proclamation" (ibid. §§ 67 – 73).[②]

[①] Article 4 § 1 of the ICCPR providing, in relevant part: "In time of public emergency which threatens the life of the nation and the existence of which is officially proclaimed...".

[②] Cf. the Commission's conclusion in the case of *Cyprus v. Turkey* (Commission report of 10 July 1976, § 527): "Article 15 requires some formal and public act of derogation, such as a declaration of martial law or state of emergency, and that, where no such act has been proclaimed by the High Contracting Party concerned, although it was not in the circumstances prevented from doing so, Article 15 cannot apply."

23. In *Marshall v. the United Kingdom* (dec.), the applicant relied on the observation of the United Nations Human Rights Committee that the emergency provisions in Northern Ireland were "excessive" and that withdrawal of the derogation made under Article 4 of the ICCPR should be envisaged. The Court stated that it found nothing in these references to suggest that the Government must be considered in breach of their obligations under the ICCPR by maintaining their derogation after 1995. On that account, the applicant could not maintain that the continuance in force of the derogation was incompatible with the authorities' obligations under international law.

24. In *Hassan v. the United Kingdom* [GC], the Court had to decide whether, in the absence of a derogation in an international conflict context, the Court could nevertheless re-interpret a Convention provision in accordance with the principles of international (humanitarian) law. The Court replied in the affirmative, accepting that, although internment was not a permitted ground for the deprivation of liberty under the text of Article 5, the Contracting Party was not required to derogate from its obligations under Article 5 in order to allow for the internment of prisoners of war and civilians posing a threat to security in a conflict context because that Article could be interpreted and applied in accordance with the principles of international humanitarian law namely, (the Third and Fourth Geneva Conventions).

III. Article 15 § 2: non-derogable rights

> Article 15 § 2 of the Convention
>
> "...
>
> 2. No derogation from Article 2, except in respect of deaths resulting from lawful acts of war, or from Articles 3, 4 (§ 1) and 7 shall be made under this provision.
>
> ..."

25. Article 15 § 2 protects certain rights from a derogation. According to the text of Article 15 § 2, these are: Article 2 (the right to life), except in respect of deaths resulting from lawful acts of war; Article 3 (the prohibition of torture and other forms of ill-treatment); Article 4 § 1 (the prohibition of slavery or servitude); and Article 7 (no punishment without law).

26. Three of the additional protocols to the Convention also contain clauses which prohibit derogation from certain of the rights contained in them. These are Protocol No. 6 (the abolition of the death penalty in time of peace and limiting the death penalty in time of war), Protocol No. 7 (the *ne bis in idem* principle only, as contained in Article 4 of that protocol) and Protocol No. 13 (the complete abolition of the death penalty).①

27. The effect of Article 15 § 2 (and the corresponding non-derogation clauses in Protocol Nos. 6, 7 and 13) is that the rights to which they refer continue to apply during any time of war or public emergency, irrespective of any derogation made by a Contracting State.

28. In respect of Articles 2 and 7 of the Convention, the exceptions already contained in those rights will also continue to apply.

29. Thus as regards Article 2, any deprivation of life will not be in contravention of the article if it results from the use of force which is no more than absolutely necessary in the circumstances set out in Article 2 § 2 (a)-(c) (the defence of any person from unlawful violence, to effect a lawful arrest or prevent escape of a person lawfully detained, action lawfully taken for the purpose of quelling a riot or insurrection). Article 15 § 2 adds the additional exception that the right to life will not be violated if the death results from a lawful act of war.

30. Equally, as regards Article 7, the prohibition on no punishment without law is subject to the provisions of Article 7 § 2, namely that the article shall not prejudice the trial and punishment of any person for any act or omission which, at the time when it was committed, was criminal according to the general principles of law recognised by civilized nations.

---

① Article 3 of Protocol No. 6, Article 4 § 3 of Protocol No. 7, and Article 2 of Protocol No. 13.

IV. Article 15 § 3: the notification requirements

> Article 15 § 3 of the Convention
>
> "...
>
> 3. Any High Contracting Party availing itself of this right of derogation shall keep the Secretary General of the Council of Europe fully informed of the measures which it has taken and the reasons therefore. It shall also inform the Secretary General of the Council of Europe when such measures have ceased to operate and the provisions of the Convention are again being fully executed."

31. The primary purpose of informing the Secretary General is that the derogation becomes public. A further purpose is that the Convention is a system of collective enforcement and it is through the Secretary General that the other Contracting States are informed of the derogation: by Resolution 56(16) of the Committee of Ministers, any information transmitted to the Secretary General in pursuance of Article 15 § 3 must be communicated by him as soon as possible to the other Contracting States (*Greece v. the United Kingdom*, Commission report, § 158)

32. In the absence of an official and public notice of derogation, Article 15 does not apply to the measures taken by the respondent State (*Cyprus v. Turkey*, Commission report of 4 October 1983, §§ 66–68).

33. The requirement to notify the Secretary General of the measures taken and the reasons therefor is usually met by writing a letter and attaching copies of the legal texts under which the emergency measures will be taken, with an explanation of their purpose [*Lawless v. Ireland* (no.3), § 47]. If copies of all relevant measures are not provided, the requirement will not be met [the "*Greek case*", Commission report, § 81(1) and (2)].

34. In the case of *Greece v. the United Kingdom*, the Commission found that it was clear from the wording of Article 15 § 3 that the notification did not need to be made before the measure in question had been introduced but also that the wording of this provision did not give guidance either as to the time within which the notification must be made or as to the extent of the information to be furnished to the Secretary General. The Commission considered that it was for the State concerned to notify the measures in question without any unavoidable delay together with sufficient information concerning them to enable the other High Contracting Parties to appreciate the nature and extent of the derogation which the measures involved. In that case, the three-month period between the taking of the derogating measure and its notification had been too long and could not be justified by administrative delays resulting from the alleged emergency. The same was true for the notification of certain measures four months after they were taken in the "*Greek case*" [Commission report, § 81(3)]. On the contrary, the Court found that notification twelve days after the measures entered into force was sufficient [*Lawless v. Ireland* (no. 3), § 47].

35. The question of whether a notification by a State complies with the formal requirements provided by Article 15 § 3 will be examined by the Court *motu proprio* even if it has not been contested by any of the other parties (*Aksoy v. Turkey*, §§ 85–86).

36. The Court has also found that Article 15 § 3 implies a requirement of permanent review of the need for emergency measures (*Brannigan and McBride v. the United Kingdom*, § 54).

37. Finally, when the derogation is withdrawn (in compliance with the last sentence of Article 15 § 3), in any case concerning measures taken after the withdrawal of the derogation, the Court will examine the case on the basis that the relevant articles of the Convention in respect of which complaints have been made are fully applicable. This does not, however, preclude proper account being taken of the background circumstances of the case. It is for the Court to determine the significance to be attached to those circumstances and to ascertain whether the balance struck complied with the applicable provisions of the relevant article, in the light of their particular wording and the article's overall object and purpose (*Brogan and Others v. the United Kingdom*, § 48, in respect of Article 5).

Chapter Ⅶ Guide on Article 15 of the European Convention on Human Rights Derogation in Time of Emergency

List of cited cases

The case-law cited in this Guide refers to judgments or decisions delivered by the Court and to decisions or reports of the European Commission of Human Rights ("the Commission").

Unless otherwise indicated, all references are to a judgment on the merits delivered by a Chamber of the Court. The abbreviation "(dec.)" indicates that the citation is of a decision of the Court and "[GC]" that the case was heard by the Grand Chamber.

The hyperlinks to the cases cited in the electronic version of the Guide are directed to the HUDOC database (〈http://hudoc.echr.coe.int〉) which provides access to the case-law of the Court (Grand Chamber, Chamber and Committee judgments and decisions, communicated cases, advisory opinions and legal summaries from the Case-Law Information Note) and of the Commission (decisions and reports), and to the resolutions of the Committee of Ministers.

The Court delivers its judgments and decisions in English and/or French, its two official languages. HUDOC also contains translations of many important cases into more than thirty non-official languages, and links to around one hundred online case-law collections produced by third parties.

— A —

A. and Others v. the United Kingdom [GC], no. 3455/05, ECHR 2009

Abdülsamet Yaman v. Turkey, no. 32446/96, 2 November 2004

Aksoy v. Turkey, 18 December 1996, Reports of Judgments and Decisions 1996 – Ⅵ

— B —

Bilen v. Turkey, no. 34482/97, 21 February 2006

Brannigan and McBride v. the United Kingdom, 26 May 1993, Series A no. 258 – B

Brogan and Others v. the United Kingdom, 29 November 1988, Series A no. 145 – B

— C —

Cyprus v. Turkey, nos. 6780/74 and 6950/75, Commission report of 10 July 1976

Cyprus v. Turkey, no. 8007/77, Commission report of 6 October 1983

— D —

Demir and Others v. Turkey, 23 September 1998, Reports of Judgments and Decisions 1998 – VI

Denmark, Norway, Sweden and the Netherlands v. Greece (the "*Greek case*"), nos. 3321/67 and 3 others, Commission report of 5 November 1969, Yearbook 12

— E —

Elçi and Others v. Turkey, nos. 23145/93 and 25091/94, 13 November 2003

— G —

Greece v. the United Kingdom, no. 176/56, Commission report of 26 September 1958

— H —

Hassan v. the United Kingdom [GC], no. 29750/09, ECHR 2014

— I —

Ireland v. the United Kingdom, 18 January 1978, Series A no. 25

— L —

Lawless v. Ireland (no. 3), 1 July 1961, Series A no. 3

— M —

Marshall v. the United Kingdom (dec.), no. 41571/98, 10 July 2001

— N —

Nuray Şen v. Turkey, no. 41478/98, 17 June 2003

— S —

Sadak v. Turkey, nos. 25142/94 and 27099/95, 8 April 2004

Sakık and Others v. Turkey, 26 November 1997, Reports of Judgments and Decisions 1997 – VII

— Y —

Yurttas v. Turkey, nos. 25143/94 and 27098/95, 27 May 2004

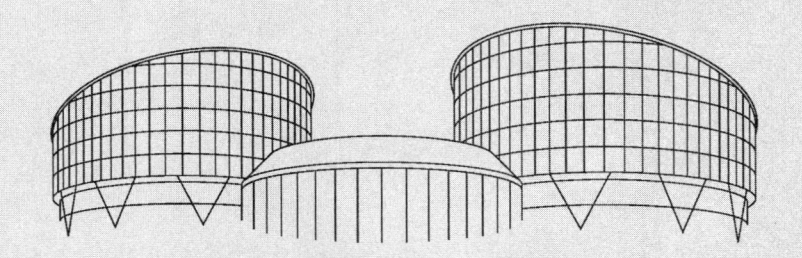

EUROPEAN COURT OF HUMAN RIGHTS
COUR EUROPÉENNE DES DROITS DE L'HOMME

第八章 《欧洲人权公约》
第一议定书第2条适用指南
受教育权

COUNCIL OF EUROPE

CONSEIL DE L'EUROPE

读者须知

本指南是欧洲人权法院(以下简称本法院、欧洲法院、斯特拉斯堡法院)出版的公约指南系列的一部分,旨在让执业律师了解斯特拉斯堡法院做出的基本判决。本指南分析和汇总了截至 2015 年 12 月 31 日的关于《欧洲人权公约》(以下简称公约、欧洲公约)第一议定书第 2 条的判例法。读者可以从中发现本领域的基本原则和相关判例。

援引的判例法选取了具有指导性的、重要的以及最新的判决。

本法院的判例不仅用于审判呈交至本法院的案件,而且从更为一般的意义上用于阐释、捍卫和发展公约创立的各项规则,并以此促使各缔约国对其加以遵守(*Ireland v. the United Kingdom*,1978 年 1 月 18 日,§ 154,Series A no. 25.)。因此,从普遍意义来说,公约确立的此机制的任务便是通过决定公共政策的各种问题来提升人权保护的标准,并在缔约国范围内推广人权法学(*Konstantin Markin v. Russia* [GC],30078/06,§ 89,ECHR 2012)。

第一节 基本原则

> **第一议定书第 2 条 受教育权**
>
> 任何人不得被剥夺受教育的权利。国家在行使其任何有关教育和教学的职能时,应当尊重父母确保这种教育或教学符合其宗教或哲学信仰的权利。

一、第一议定书第 2 条的结构

1. 第一议定书第 2 条的第一句保障了个人受教育的权利,第二句保障了父母确保他们的孩子接受符合其宗教和哲学信仰的教育的权利。

2. 第一议定书第 2 条构成了以第一句为主干、第二句为基本教育权补充的整体(*Campbell and Cosans v. the United Kingdom*,§ 40)。

二、第一议定书第 2 条的含义和适用范围

3. 第一议定书第 2 条的特点在于其使用的否定式用语①,这意味着缔约国并不需要将这一权利看作是要求其通过提供资金或补贴,来进行某种特定类别或特定水平的教育[Case "relating to certain aspects of the laws on the use of languages in education in Belgium("比利时语言案"),§ 3, p. 31]。因此,国家并没有义务建立公立教育体系或资助私人学校。这些领域内,国家进行自由处理。

4. 不能将该条理解为国家仅承担避免干涉的消极义务,而无积极义务来确保此项权利的实现。这项规定当然涉及一项实质权利及其产生的义务,因此国家不能否认其建立或授权的教育机构进行教育的权利。

5. 受教育权并不是绝对的,因为它可能包括隐含的限制,同时"它本质上是要求国

---

① 这一点在准备工作文件中得到确认[参见 Doc. CM/WP VI (51) 7, p. 4, and AS/JA (3) 13, p. 4]。在驳回欧洲委员会于 1950 年 8 月通过的"积极公式"时,缔约国显然不想让第一议定书第 2 条的第一句话被解释为缔约国有义务采取有效措施确保个人能够接受其选择的教育或创立教育机构,抑或是资助私人教育。

家进行规制的"(Case "relating to certain aspects of the laws on the use of languages in education in Belgium", § 5, p. 32; *Golder v. the United Kingdom*, § 38; *Fayed v. the United Kingdom*, § 65)。因此,虽然是由本法院最终确定是否遵守公约的要求,但是国内当局在这一事项上享有一定的自由裁量权。为了确保所施加的限制不会削弱该权利以至于损害其本质、剥夺其效力,本法院必须确保,对于相关人员来说,这些限制是可预见的,并且目的具有合法性(*Leyla Şahin v. Turkey* [GC], § 154)。

6. 与公约第8条至第11条不同,对该权利的限制不仅限于第一议定书第2条所列举的"合法目的"。而且,只有当所采取的手段与寻求实现的目标之间存在合理的比例关系,所施加的限制才符合第一议定书第2条的规定(*Leyla Şahin v. Turkey* [GC],第154段及之后)。

7. 原则上来说,在教育和教学领域,第一议定书第2条属于特别法(*Lautsi and Others v. Italy* [GC], § 59)。

三、解释的原则

8. 在民主社会中,受教育权对于促进其他人权发展有着不可或缺的作用,因此对第一议定书第2条第一句进行限制性解释不符合该条的宗旨或目的(*Leyla Şahin v. Turkey* [GC], § 137; *Timishev v. Russia*, § 64)。

9. 第一议定书第2条的两个句子不仅必须作为整体来解读,更应联系公约第8条、第9条和第10条来进行理解。公约第8条、第9条和第10条规定包括父母和子女在内的每个人都应享有"私人生活和家庭生活受到尊重的权利""思想、良心和宗教自由"以及"接收和传达信息及思想的自由"(*Kjeldsen, Busk Madsen and Pedersen v. Denmark*, § 52)。此外,第一议定书第2条也与公约第14条以及禁止歧视的规定密切相关。

10. 为了解释第一议定书第2条的相关概念,法院参照了有关国际文书的判例法,例如《世界人权宣言》(1948年),《反对教育歧视公约》(1960年),《公民权利和政治权利国际公约》(1966年),《经济、社会及文化权利国际公约》(1966年),《联合国儿童权利公约》(1989)(*Catan and Others v. the Republic of Moldova and Russia* [GC], §§ 77-81),《欧洲地区高等教育相关资格认可公约》(*Leyla Şahin v. Turkey* [GC], § 66),以及修订后的《欧洲社会宪章》(*Ponomaryovi v. Bulgaria*)。

第二节 受教育权

> **第一议定书第 2 条第 1 句 受教育权**
> "任何人不得被剥夺受教育的权利……"

一、受教育权的原则

11. 受教育权包括了在特定时间接受教育的权利(Belgian linguistic case, § 4, p. 31)、传播知识和智力发展的权利(Campbell and Cosans v. the United Kingdom, § 33),还包括从所接受的教育中获益的可能性,也就是说,根据每个国家的现行规定,以某种形式获得对已完成学业的官方认可的权利(Belgian linguistic case, §§ 3 – 5, pp. 30 – 32),如学历资质。然而,以没有满足所要求的条件为由,拒绝认可在国外修完的医学专业课程,不构成违反第一议定书第 2 条的情形(Kök v. Turkey, § 60)。

12. 第一议定书第 2 条涉及小学[Sulak v. Turkey(dec.)]、中学(Cyprus v. Turkey [GC], § 278)、高等教育(Leyla Şahin v. Turkey [GC], § 141;Mürsel Eren v. Turkey, § 41)和职业教育。因此,第一议定书第 2 条保障的权利人包括儿童,也包括成年人。更准确地说,包括所有希望从受教育权中受益的人(Velyo Velev v. Bulgaria)。

13. 国家应对公立和私立学校负责(Kjeldsen, Busk Madsen and Pedersen v. Denmark)。同时,国家不能将其确保受教育权的义务委派给私人机构或个人。第一议定书第 2 条保障开设和经营私立学校的权利,但国家没有积极义务对特定的教学提供补贴[Verein Gemeinsam Lernen v. Austria(dec.)]。最后,国家有保护小学生免受公立和私立学校虐待的积极义务(O'Keeffe v. Ireland [GC], §§ 144 – 152)。

14. 第一议定书第 2 条第一句规定的受教育权本身就需要国家规制,在不同时间、不同地点,根据社区和个人需求及资源的不同,这种规制也可能有所不同。这种规制不得损害受教育权的实质内容,也不得与公约规定的其他权利相冲突。因此,公约要寻求保护共同体的普遍利益和尊重基本人权之间的公正平衡(Belgian linguistic case，§ 5，p. 32)。

二、受教育权的限制

15. 尽管在第一议定书第 2 条中没有明确表述,但对受教育权的限制确实存在,但任何权利限制都不得损害该权利的本质和剥夺其效力。尽管第一议定书第 2 条并未穷尽列举"合法目的",但这些限制必须是可预见的,并且是为了追求"合法目的"(Leyla Şahin v. Turkey，§ 154)。

16. 因此,受教育权并不排除纪律处分措施,特别是那些因欺诈[Sulak v. Turkey (dec.)]或不当行为[Whitman v. the United Kingdom (dec.)]而被教育机构临时或永久开除的情况。

(一)语言

17. 第一议定书第 2 条没有特别规定为尊重受教育权而必须使用的教育语言。但是,如果受教育权不包括以本国语言或某种国内语言接受教育的权利,就无法使权利人受益,那么受教育权将失去意义(Belgian linguistic case，§ 3, p. 31)。

18. 因此,在卡坦等人诉摩尔多瓦共和国和俄罗斯案(Catan and Others v. the Republic of Moldova and Russia [GC])中,主张分离主义的当局施行语言政策强制关闭学校,并在学校重新开放后进行骚扰,这违反了受教育权的规定。没有任何迹象表明这些措施追求的是合法目的。大审判庭认为,小学和中学教育对每个儿童的个人发展和未来成功至关重要,并重申人们有权用本国语言接受教育。在一定时期内实际掌控相关行政机构的政府,尽管没有直接或间接干预该机构的语言政策,仍应为受教育权受到侵犯承担责任。

19. 将要求以库尔德语开设选修课的学生们临时开除的行为,也属于违反该条的情形(Irfan Temel and Others v. Turkey)。

(二)录取标准和入学考试

20. 国家拒绝保证入学机会可能会侵犯受教育权(Campbell and Cosans v. the United Kingdom)。

21. 但是,本法院允许对受教育权进行适当的限制。

1. 录取标准

22. 国家可以规定教育机构的录取标准。然而,毫无预兆地对大学录取规则进行修改,并且缺乏过渡性的补救措施,可能会违反公约第 14 条和第一议定书第 2 条(*Altınay v. Turkey*,§§ 56 – 61)。申诉人无法预见到高等教育录取规则的修改内容,同时还缺乏可适用的补救措施,其受到的差别待遇减损了申诉人享有受教育权的效力,限制了申诉人的受教育权,因此与该权利所追求的目的相悖。

23. 对于那些满足大多数课程所要求的学术水平的学生而言,限制其学术研究不被视为对受教育权的剥夺(*X. v. the United Kingdom*, Commission decision)。在该案件中,申诉人没有通过第一年的考试,并且没有修满所有的必修课程。校方认为他没有足够的水平复读第一年的学科,但这并没有剥夺他修读其他学科的可能性。

24. 此外,国家有权规定大学学习的最长期限。在委员会关于 X 诉奥地利案(*X. v. Austria*)的裁定中,奥地利政府将医学学习的最长期限定为 7 年,由于申诉人没有在规定时间内通过考试,奥地利政府便拒绝其进入任何医学院校。

2. 法定强制性入学考试

25. 立法规定进入(公共和私营部门)医学和牙科大学需要进行入学考试,这并不构成对受教育权的侵犯(*Tarantino and Others v. Italy*)。设定入学考试是一项合理的措施,即通过考试评估候选人,筛选出最优秀的生源,以确保大学的最低教育水平。此外,考虑到大学的容纳人数和资源,以及社会对特定专业的需求,入学限制体系具有正当性。

3. 取消入学考试中的合格成绩。

26. 由于候选人前几年的成绩不佳,而取消其在大学入学考试中的合格成绩,构成对受教育权的侵犯(*Mürsel Eren v. Turkey*)。该行为缺乏法律或理性基础,因此是任意而为。

(三)学费

27. 国家可以依据合法理由在一定程度上对急需的公共教育服务资源限制使用,但必须有所节制。国家在这一领域的自由裁量权随着教育水平的提高而增加,与教育对相关人员和整个社会的重要性成反比。中等教育对于个人发展以及个人的社会化和专业化发挥着越来越大的作用。任何对接受中等教育的限制都不得构成公约第 14 条禁止的歧视性制度(*Ponomaryovi v. Bulgaria*,§ 41 以下)。

(四)国籍

28. 受教育权并不能赋予一个外国人进入或居留于特定国家的权利(*Foreign

Students v. the United Kingdom，Commission decision，§ 4）。由于保障的权利主要涉及初等教育，所以原则上来说，开除外国学生不会侵犯他的受教育权。

29. 另外，只有在特别慎重考虑之后，本法院才可能认定基于国籍的差别待遇不违反公约。受教育权受公约的直接保护，它涉及一种非常具体的公共服务，不仅使受教育者受益，更使整个社会受益，从民主维度来看，后者应包括少数群体（*Ponomaryovi v. Bulgaria*）。

30. 此外，在蒂米舍夫诉俄罗斯案（*Timishev v. Russia*）中，申诉人的孩子们在过去两年一直就读的学校拒绝他们入学。入学被拒的真正原因是申诉人已上交了他的移民卡，从而丧失了在该城镇以居民身份注册的资格。然而，俄罗斯法律不允许将父母在居住地登记作为儿童行使受教育权的前提条件。因此，本法院认为，申诉人的子女被剥夺了国内法规定的受教育权。

（五）教育资格认证的最低年龄要求

31. 申诉人反对持有小学毕业证书才能加入古兰经学习班的限制要求，本法院认为该申诉明显缺乏依据，裁定不予受理［*Çiftçi v. Turkey*（dec.）］。该限制旨在确保那些希望在古兰经学习班接受宗教教育的儿童已通过小学教育达到一定的"成熟"状态。该法定要求实际上是为了防止未成年人在最具好奇心的年龄受到思想灌输，更进一步而言，在这个年龄他们可能很容易受到古兰经学习班的影响。

（六）法律问题

1. 监狱

32. 被依法羁押的囚犯继续享有公约保障的除自由权以外的其他所有基本权利和自由。因此，他们享有第一议定书第 2 条所保障的受教育权。拒绝囚犯进入现有监狱学校的行为违反该条款的规定（*Velyo Velev v. Bulgaria*）。但是，囚犯无权援引第一议定书第 2 条的规定，要求国家在监狱中组织特定类型的教育或培训。

33. 被法院定罪之后，申诉人在羁押期间无法继续学习其大学课程，该情形没有违反第一议定书第 2 条的规定［*Georgiou v. Greece*（dec.）；*Durmaz and Others v. Turkey*（dec.）；*Arslan v. Turkey*（dec.）］。此外，申诉人提出在服刑期间无法完成中学最后一年的学业，本法院认为他的申诉明显缺乏依据，因此裁定不予受理（*Epistatu v. Romania*）。

2. 犯罪调查

34. 在艾力诉英国案(Ali v. the United Kingdom)中，本法院认为，在对校园事件进行刑事调查时，在符合比例原则的前提下，可以将学生长时间排除在中学之外，这不构成对受教育权的剥夺。对申诉人的排除仅限于刑事调查期间。此外，在排除期间，向申诉人提供了替代教育，虽然没有涵盖全部国家课程，但考虑到排除期在任何时候都被认为是刑事调查结束前的临时措施，因而这一做法是合理的。然而，如果将处在义务教育阶段的学生永久排除在一所学校之外，而后其又无法在另一所学校接受全部国家课程的全日制教育，情况可能会有所不同。

3. 驱逐措施

35. 由于被驱逐出境而中断教育不被视为违反第一议定书第 2 条的情形。如果驱逐措施阻止某人在某一国家继续接受教育，那么该措施本身不能被视为干涉此人基于本条所享有的受教育权(Sorabjee v. the United Kingdom; Jaramillo v. the United Kingdom; Dabhi v. the United Kingdom, Commission decision)。

36. 在家附近上学的吉普赛申诉人被驱逐出境，不违反第一议定书第 2 条的规定。该申诉人没有证实他的申诉，即没有证实该驱逐措施确实剥夺了其孙子女的受教育权(Lee v. the United Kingdom [GC])。

三、教育方面的歧视

37. 如果缔约国在履行第一议定书第 2 条规定的义务时采取差别待遇，则可能会导致出现与公约第 14 条有关的问题。

> **公约第 14 条　禁止歧视**
>
> 享有公约所规定的权利和自由时不应受到任何歧视，如性别、种族、肤色、语言、宗教、政治或其他见解、国籍或社会来源、与少数民族的联系、财产、出身或其他状态等。

38. 差别待遇必须是为了追求合法目的才不会被认定为歧视。在比利时语言案中，法院讨论了这样一种情况：生活在荷语区以法语为母语的儿童无法以法语上课，而居住在法语区以荷语为母语的儿童却可以用荷语上课。本法院认为，这项措施并不是为了学校的利益,也不是基于行政或财政原因而实施的,而仅仅是基于语言的考虑(*Belgian linguistic case*, §32, p.70),因此,违反了第一议定书第2条以及公约第14条的规定。

39. 若想符合第14条的规定,仅具有合法目的是不够的,差别待遇也必须是适当的。因此,在审查了大学入学制度的修改内容后,即使这些修改内容是为了快速提高高等教育的质量,本法院也认为这种做法违反了公约第14条和第一议定书第2条。本法院认为,由于缺乏可预见性并且没有任何补正措施,相对于所希望达成的目的来说,新制度的实施是不符合比例原则的(*Altınay v. Turkey*, §60)。

(一)残疾人

40. 涉及残疾人的案件在本法院比较少见。根据第一议定书第2条,前委员会发现,越来越多的人认为,只要有可能,残疾儿童就应与其他同龄儿童一同成长。然而,这项政策不能适用于所有残疾儿童,必须赋予有关当局较大的自由裁量权,以便充分利用可用资源,保障整个残疾儿童群体的利益。不能认为第2条第2句要求的是将一个有严重听力障碍的儿童安置在常规学校中(要么需要额外聘请特殊教员,要么会损害其他学生的利益),而不将其安置在特殊学校中(*Klerks v. the Netherlands*, Commission decision)。关于公共基金和资源的支配,未能在小学安装电梯以便利患有肌营养不良症的学生,无论是否同时考虑公约第14条,都不违反第一议定书第2条(*McIntyre v. the United Kingdom*)。

(二)行政身份和国籍

41. 在波诺马廖夫诉保加利亚案(*Ponomaryovi v. Bulgaria*)中,本法院对两名与母亲共同居住在比利时但没有永久居留权的俄罗斯籍学生的情况进行了审查。在保加利亚,中学教育是免费的,但是这两名学生却因他们的移民身份而需要缴纳学费。申诉人并不是非法抵达该国然后要求使用包括免费教育在内的公共服务。即使申诉人发现自己缺乏永久居留许可(有时并非有意为之),当局也没有对他们留在保加利亚提出实质性的反对意见,而且显然从未有任何将他们驱逐出境的明显意图。保加利亚当局并没有考虑到这种情况。但无论如何,立法并没有规定可以收取学费的例外情况。因此,鉴于中学教育的重要性,本法院认为,这两名学生由于他们的国籍和移民身份而被要求为中学教育支付费用,构成了对公约第14条和第一议定书第2条的违反。

(三)种族

42. 本法院在许多案件中提出了关于欧洲许多国家中罗马儿童教育问题的困境(*D. H. and Others v. the Czech Republic* [GC], §205)。由于他们动荡的历史和不断的迁徙,罗马社群已成为一个落后而脆弱的特定少数群体。因此,他们需要特殊保护,并且这种保护应延伸到教育领域(*D. H. and Others v. the Czech Republic* [GC], §182)。

43. 鉴于罗马社群的脆弱性,为了纠正不平等现象,应当采取差别待遇,各国有必要特别注意他们的需求,主管部门也应当为罗马儿童入学提供便利条件,即使有些必要的行政文件已经丢失(*Sampanis and Others v. Greece*, §86)。

44. 然而,仅仅招收罗马儿童入学不足以同时满足第一议定书第2条和公约第14条的要求。在这方面,本法院的主要依据为欧洲反对种族偏见委员会(ECRI)的报告(*Oršuš and Others v. Croatia* [GC]; *D. H. and Others v. the Czech Republic* [GC])。同时国家还必须提供一个良好的就读环境。本法院认可缔约国为照顾有特殊教育需求的儿童而决定保留特殊学校制度的做法(*D. H. and Others v. the Czech Republic* [GC], §198)。此外,以儿童未充分掌握语言为由,将其临时安置在一个单独的班级中,这并不当然违反公约第14条的规定(*Oršuš and Others v. Croatia* [GC], §157)。然而,罗马儿童被错误安排在特殊学校的情况,在整个欧洲都有着悠久的历史(*Horváth and Kiss v. Hungary*, §115)。因此,必须为罗马儿童的入学安排提供保障措施,确保国家考虑到了他们的特殊需要(*D. H. and Others v. the Czech Republic* [GC], §207; *Sampanis and Others v. Greece*, §103)。该决定必须是透明的,必须基于明确规定的标准,而不仅仅是基于种族原因(*Sampanis and Others v. Greece*, §89; *Oršuš and Others v. Croatia* [GC], §182)。最后,如果这些措施使得罗马儿童接受教育更加困难,阻碍了他们今后的个人发展,而不能解决他们的实际问题或帮助他们融入普通学校,不能帮助他们发展技能从而融入大多数人的生活,那么这些措施将被视为不合理、不适当的(*D. H. and Others v. the Czech Republic*, §207)。仅没有歧视的意图是不够的,各国有积极的义务采取有效措施防止种族隔离现象(*Lavida and Others v. Greece*, §73)。

第三节　尊重家长的权利

> **第一议定书第 2 条第 2 句：受教育权**
> "……国家在行使其任何有关教育和教学的职能时，应当尊重父母确保这种教育或教学符合其宗教或哲学信仰的权利。"

一、适用范围

45. 家长的宗教和哲学信仰得到尊重的权利基于受教育权这一基本权利而存在，因此，家长不得以其信念为由拒绝让儿童接受教育［*Konrad and Others v. Germany*（dec.）］。

46. 本法院对本条中的"父母"进行了扩大解释，它不仅限于父亲和母亲，至少还可能包括祖父母、外祖父母（*Lee v. the United Kingdom*［GC］）。接受教育的儿童不能主张自己是第一议定书第 2 条第 2 句所保障的家长权利受到侵害的受害者（*Eriksson v. Sweden*，§ 93）。

47. "尊重"一词不仅仅是"承认"或"考虑到"，除了消极保障外，它还指国家应当承担某些积极的义务（*Campbell and Cosans v. the United Kingdom*，§ 37）。关于"信念"这个词，它本身并不同于"意见"或"想法"，它表示具有一定程度的说服力、严肃性、凝聚力和重要性的观点（*Valsamis v. Greece*，§§ 25 and 27）。因此，家长反对学校体罚孩子，也属于"哲学信念"的一种（*Campbell and Cosans v. the United Kingdom*，§ 36）。

48. 第一议定书第 2 条适用于所有科目，而不仅适用于宗教教学。因此，性教育和伦理教育也属于第一议定书第 2 条的范围［*Jimenez Alonso and Jimenez Merino v. Spain*；*Dojan and Others v. Germany*（dec.）；*Appel-Irrgang and Others v. Germany*，§ 53 以下］。

49. 此外，该条既适用于教学内容，也适用于教学方式。因此，第一议定书第 2 条也适用于节假日期间要求学生在学校范围外游行的情形。学校以暂时停学为惩罚手段，要求学生们参加上述活动,虽然暂时停学的时间较短,本法院还是对此感到十分震惊。然而,本法院认为,这种纪念国家事件的活动,以追求和平为目标并服务于公共利益,虽然有些游行队伍中会出现军事代表,但并不改变这些游行本身的性质。此外,要求学生参加游行并没有剥夺家长教导孩子、向孩子提供建议,或者按照自己的宗教或哲学信念引导孩子的权利(*Efstratiou v. Greece*,§32;*Valsamis v. Greece*,§31)。

50. 课程的制定和规划原则上属于缔约国的职权范围(*Valsamis v. Greece*,§28),公约没有理由禁止课程包含宗教或哲学性质的信息或知识(*Kjeldsen, Busk Madsen and Pedersen v. Denmark*,§53)。

二、免修课程的可能性

51. 某些情况下,家长会基于宗教信仰自由得到尊重的权利,要求在家给孩子提供教育。在这一方面,本法院认为,对于强制上小学的问题,各缔约国意见没有达成一致。有些国家允许家庭教育,而其他国家强制规定学生必须在国立或私立学校接受教育。因此,本法院最终认为缔约国可以自由裁量是否依据以下观点适用本条规定:小学教育的重要目标不仅是获得知识,还包括融入社会以及初次经历社会;家庭教育或许可以使孩子获得与学校教育相同的知识水平,但是无法实现上述目的。在本案中,本法院认为,国内法院一方面强调社会的总体利益,避免出现有着独立哲学信念的平行社会,另一方面考虑了少数人融入社会的重要性,该论证依据符合本法院判例法中有关多元主义对于民主的重要性的相关规定。因此,裁定驳回申诉人对当局不允许父母在家里教育子女的控诉[*Konrad and Others v. Germany*(dec.)]。

52. 某些情况下,出于尊重家长哲学信念的考虑,如有必要,可以允许学生免修某些课程。在福尔杰等人诉挪威案(*Folgerø and Others v. Norway*[GC],§§95-100)中,国立小学拒绝了申诉人为其子女申请完全免修"基督教、宗教和哲学"课程的请求,这违反了第一议定书第2条。与其他宗教和哲学相比,基督教的教学不仅仅存在数量的差异,甚至存在性质的差异。不可否认,有可能存在部分免修的情形,但它关乎活动本身,而不关乎通过活动传播的知识。活动和知识之间的这种区分不仅在实践中很复杂,而且似乎大大削弱了部分免修权的效力。部分免修制度会使父母承受巨大压力,有可能不适当地暴露其私生活,而且潜在的冲突可能阻碍他们提出这种要求。

53. 然而,缔约国不必系统地提供免修的途径。在多杰等人诉德国案[*Dojan and*

Others v. Germany（dec.）]中,小学课程的内容包含了性教育必修课程。学校决定定期举办戏剧讲习班,作为强制性活动,以提高对儿童性虐待问题的认识。学校的另外一个传统是每年组织一次嘉年华活动,但是如果有学生不想参加,也会给他们准备替代的活动。申诉人因阻止其子女参加上述全部或部分活动而被罚款,申诉人拒绝缴纳罚款,于是被关进监狱。本法院指出,这些性别教育课程是对生育、避孕、怀孕和分娩知识的中立性传播,设立的依据是现行法律规定和课程指导规范,后者也是基于科学标准和教育标准制定,戏剧讲习班符合多元主义和客观性的原则,嘉年华活动也没有伴随任何宗教活动,而且孩子们都可以选择参加替代活动,因此,在家长认为这些课程和活动不符合其宗教信念并申请免修时,拒绝这类免修申请并不违反第一议定书第 2 条。同理,本法院认为,在设置没有任何免修可能性的伦理类必修课程时,缔约国可以对第一议定书第 2 条的适用进行自由裁量（*Appel-Irrgang and Others v. Germany*）。

54. 虽然个人利益有时必须服从群体利益,但务必要确保公平和适当地对待少数人,防止滥用支配地位（*Valsamis v. Greece*,§27）。例如,本法院认为,土耳其学校课程的设置倾向于伊斯兰教多数教派,而不是伊斯兰教少数教派或其他宗教和哲学信仰,这种情况本身不应视为不尊重多元化和客观性,而可能被解释为教化。然而,鉴于阿拉维派与逊尼派伊斯兰教教义的特殊关系,一些父母可以合法地认为,教授"宗教文化和伦理知识"课程的方式可能会给他们的子女带来学校教育和自身价值观之间的冲突。此时,有必要允许适当免修（*Mansur Yalçın and Others v. Turkey*,§§71-75）。在这种情况下,如果父母被强制要求告知学校其宗教或哲学信念,就是以不恰当的方式保证尊重其信仰自由;更糟糕的是,在没有任何明文规定的情况下,学校总是可以拒绝这类请求（*Hasan and Eylem Zengin v. Turkey*,§§75-76）。

三、明显的宗教标志

55. 第一议定书第 2 条第 2 句禁止各国实行可能被认为不尊重父母的宗教和哲学信念的教育,即思想控制（*Kjeldsen, Busk Madsen and Pedersen v. Denmark*,§53）。然而,本法院也认为,在公立学校教室中摆放十字架,并不违反第一议定书第 2 条。本法院认为,虽然法律允许基督教的标志(即十字架)出现在校园,赋予了该主体宗教在学校环境中的主导性,但这本身不足以表明应诉国在实施思想控制。墙上的十字架实质上是一个被动的象征,不应被认为足以对学生产生等同于言语说教或参与宗教活动的影响。应当正确看待十字架对学校中基督教存在性的影响,因为它与基督教的强制传教没有联系,而且国家的教学环境也对其他宗教开放(*Lautsi and Others v. Italy* [GC], §§ 71–76)。

56. 最后,国家有责任做一个中立的仲裁者,在允许学生在校园表达他们的宗教信仰时,要注意确保其表达形式不会过于夸张从而导致压力和排斥。因此,禁止戴面纱的年轻女孩上学并不违反第一议定书第 2 条,因为该措施是可预见且合理的,并且没有侵犯父母按照自己的宗教或哲学信念引导孩子的权利(*Köse and Others v. Turkey*)。在高等教育中,情况也是如此(*Leyla Şahin v. Turkey* [GC])。

援引案例一览

本指南援引的判例法涉及欧洲人权法院的判决或裁定以及欧洲人权委员会的决定或报告。

除非另行指明,所有参考皆是本法院审判庭依法作出的判决。缩写"(dec.)"是指该处援引为本法院裁定,"[GC]"是指该案件由大审判庭审判。

本指南电子版中援引案例的超链接直接跳转 HUDOC 数据库〈http://hudoc.echr.coe.int〉。该数据库提供本法院(包括大审判庭、审判庭和委员会的判决、裁定和相关案例、咨询意见以及案例法信息注解中的法律总结)、委员会(决定和报告)和部长委员会(决议)的判例法。

本法院以英语和/或法语这两种官方语言发布判决和裁定。HUDOC 也包含许多重要案例的近 30 种非官方言语的翻译,以及由第三方制作的大约 100 个在线案例汇总的链接。

(注:为了避免重复,本章所附的相关案例索引没有在中文部分进行翻译,读者可在对应的英文部分阅读。)

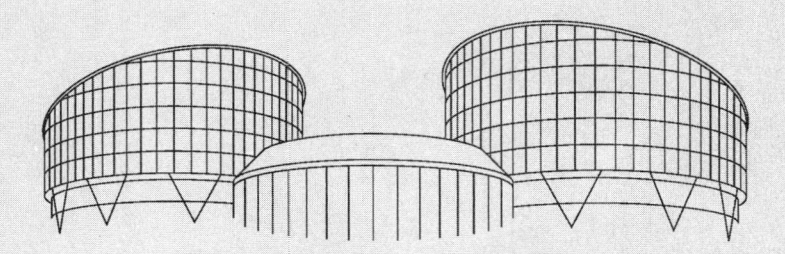

EUROPEAN COURT OF HUMAN RIGHTS
COUR EUROPÉENNE DES DROITS DE L'HOMME

Chapter VIII Guide on Article 2 of Protocol No.1 to the European Convention on Human Rights Right to Education

Publishers or organisations wishing to reproduce this report (or a translation thereof) in print or online are asked to contactpublishing@echr.coe.int for further instructions.

This guide has been prepared by the Research and Library Division within the Directorate of the Jurisconsult and does not bind the Court. The manuscript was finalised in December 2015; it may be subject to editorial revision.

The document is available for downloading at ⟨www.echr.coe.int⟩ (Case-Law-Case-Law Analysis-Case-Law Guides).

For publication updates please follow the Court's Twitter account at ⟨https:/twitter.com/echrpublication⟩.

©Council of Europe/European Court of Human Rights, 2015

Note to readers

This guide is part of the series of Case-Law Guides published by the European Court of Human Rights (hereafter "the Court", "the European Court" or "the Strasbourg Court") to inform legal practitioners about the fundamental judgments delivered by the Strasbourg Court. This particular guide analyses and sums up the case-law on Article 2 of Protocol No. 1 to the European Convention on Human Rights (hereafter "the Convention" or "the European Convention") until 31 December 2015. Readers will find the key principles in this area and the relevant precedents.

The case-law cited has been selected among the leading, major, and/or recent judgments and decisions. *

The Court's judgments serve not only to decide those cases brought before the Court but, more generally, to elucidate, safeguard and develop the rules instituted by the Convention, thereby contributing to the observance by the States of the engagements undertaken by them as Contracting Parties (*Ireland v. the United Kingdom*, 18 January 1978, § 154, Series A no. 25.). The mission of the system set up by the Convention is thus to determine, in the general interest, issues of public policy, thereby raising the standards of protection of human rights and extending human rights jurisprudence throughout the community of the Convention States (*Konstantin Markin v. Russia* [GC], 30078/06, § 89, ECHR 2012).

---

* The case-law cited may be in either or both of the official languages (English and French) of the Court and the European Commission of Human Rights. Unless otherwise indicated, all references are to a judgment on the merits delivered by a Chamber of the Court. The abbreviation "(dec.)" indicates that the citation is of a decision of the Court and "[GC]" that the case was heard by the Grand Chamber.

Ⅰ. General principles

> Article 2 of Protocol No. 1 – Right to education
> "No person shall be denied the right to education. In the exercise of any functions which it assumes in relation to education and to teaching, the State shall respect the right of parents to ensure such education and teaching in conformity with their own religious and philosophical convictions."

A. Structure of Article 2 of Protocol No. 1

1. The first sentence of Article 2 of Protocol No. 1 guarantees an individual right to education. The second guarantees the right of parents to have their children educated in conformity with their religious and philosophical convictions.

2. Article 2 of Protocol No. 1 constitutes a whole that is dominated by its first sentence, the right set out in the second sentence being an adjunct of the fundamental right to education (*Campbell and Cosans v. the United Kingdom*, § 40).

B. Meaning and scope of Article 2 of Protocol No. 1

3. Article 2 of Protocol No. 1 is distinguished by its negative wording which means[①] that the Contracting Parties do not recognise such a right to education as would require them to establish at their own expense, or to subsidise, education of any particular type or at any particular level [*Case "relating to certain aspects of the laws on the use of languages in*

[①] This is confirmed by the *travaux préparatoires* (see in particular Doc. CM/WP Ⅵ (51) 7, p. 4, and AS/JA (3) 13, p. 4). In dismissing the "positive formula" adopted by the Council of Europe Assembly in August 1950, the signatory States apparently did not want the first sentence of Article 2 of Protocol No. 1 to become interpreted as an obligation for the States to take effective measures so that individuals could receive the education of their choosing and to create education themselves, or to subsidise private education.

education in Belgium" ("*the Belgian linguistic case*"), § 3, p. 31]. Thus there is no positive obligation for States to create a public education system or to subsidise private schools. These areas are left to their discretion.

4. It cannot, however, be inferred that the State only has obligations to refrain from interference and no positive obligation to ensure respect for this right, as protected by Article 2 of Protocol No. 1. The provision certainly concerns a right with a certain substance and obligations arising from it. States cannot therefore deny the right to education for the educational institutions they have chosen to set up or authorise.

5. The right to education is not absolute, however, as it may give rise to implicitly accepted limitations, bearing in mind that "it by its very nature calls for regulation by the State" (ibid., § 5, p. 32; see also, *mutatis mutandis*, *Golder v. the United Kingdom*, § 38; *Fayed v. the United Kingdom*, § 65). Consequently, the domestic authorities enjoy in such matters a certain margin of appreciation, although the final decision as to the observance of the Convention's requirements rests with the Court. In order to ensure that the restrictions that are imposed do not curtail the right in question to such an extent as to impair its very essence and deprive it of its effectiveness, the Court must satisfy itself that they are foreseeable for those concerned and pursue a legitimate aim (*Leyla Şahin v. Turkey* [GC], § 154).

6. Unlike the position with respect to Articles 8 to 11 of the Convention, the permitted restrictions are not bound by an exhaustive list of "legitimate aims" under Article 2 of Protocol No. 1. Furthermore, a limitation will only be compatible with Article 2 of Protocol No. 1 if there is a reasonable relationship of proportionality between the means employed and the aim sought to be achieved (ibid., §§ 154 et seq.).

7. In the area of education and teaching Article 2 of Protocol No. 1 is in principle the *lex specialis* (*Lautsi and Others v. Italy* [GC], § 59).

C. Principles of interpretation

8. In a democratic society, the right to education, which is indispensable to the furtherance of human rights, plays such a fundamental role that a restrictive interpretation of the first

sentence of Article 2 of Protocol No. 1 would not be consistent with the aim or purpose of that provision (*Leyla Şahin v. Turkey* [GC], § 137; *Timishev v. Russia*, § 64).

9. The two sentences of Article 2 of Protocol No. 1 must be read not only in the light of each other but also, in particular, of Articles 8, 9 and 10 of the Convention, which proclaim the right of everyone, including parents and children, "to respect for his private and family life", to "freedom of thought, conscience and religion", and to "freedom... to receive and impart information and ideas" (*Kjeldsen, Busk Madsen and Pedersen v. Denmark*, § 52). In addition, Article 2 of Protocol No. 1 is also closely linked to Article 14 of the Convention and to the prohibition of discrimination.

10. To interpret the notions contained in Article 2 of Protocol No. 1, the Court has already relied in its case-law on international instruments such as the Universal Declaration of Human Rights (1948), the Convention against Discrimination in Education (1960), the International Covenant on Civil and Political Rights (1966), the International Covenant on Economic, Social and Cultural Rights (1966), the UN Convention on the Rights of the Child (1989) (*Catan and Others v. the Republic of Moldova and Russia* [GC], §§ 77 – 81), the Convention on the Recognition of Qualifications concerning Higher Education in the European Region (*Leyla Şahin v. Turkey* [GC], § 66), and the revised European Social Charter (*Ponomaryovi v. Bulgaria*).

II. Right to education

> Article 2, first sentence, of Protocol No. 1 – Right to education
> "No person shall be denied the right to education. ..."

A. Principle of the right to education

11. The right to education covers a right of access to educational institutions existing at a given time (*Belgian linguistic case*, § 4, p. 31), transmission of knowledge and

intellectual development (*Campbell and Cosans v. the United Kingdom*, § 33) but also the possibility of drawing profit from the education received, that is to say, the right to obtain, in conformity with the rules in force in each State, and in one form or another, official recognition of the studies which have been completed (*Belgian linguistic case*, §§ 3 – 5, pp. 30 – 32), for example by means of a qualification. But a refusal to recognise a specialised medical course followed abroad, because the required conditions were not satisfied, did not constitute a violation of Article 2 of Protocol No. 1 (*Kök v. Turkey*, § 60).

12. Article 2 of Protocol No. 1 concerns elementary schooling (*Sulak v. Turkey* (dec.) but also secondary education (*Cyprus v. Turkey* [GC], § 278), higher education (*Leyla Şahin v. Turkey* [GC], § 141; *Mürsel Eren v. Turkey*, § 41) and specialised courses. Thus the holders of the right guaranteed in Article 2 of Protocol No. 1 are children, but also adults, or indeed any person wishing to benefit from the right to education (*Velyo Velev v. Bulgaria*).

13. Furthermore, the State is responsible for public but also private schools (*Kjeldsen, Busk Madsen and Pedersen v. Denmark*). In addition, the State cannot delegate to private institutions or individuals its obligations to secure the right to education for all. Article 2 of Protocol No. 1 guarantees the right to open and run a private school, but the States do not have a positive obligation to subsidise a particular form of teaching [*Verein Gemeinsam Lernen v. Austria* (dec.)]. Lastly, the State has a positive obligation to protect pupils from both State and private schools from ill-treatment (*O'Keeffe v. Ireland* [GC], §§ 144 – 152).

14. The right to education guaranteed by the first sentence of Article 2 of Protocol no. 1 by its very nature calls for regulation by the State, regulation which may vary in time and place according to the needs and resources of the community and of individuals. Such regulation must never injure the substance of the right to education nor conflict with other rights enshrined in the Convention. The Convention therefore implies a just balance between the protection of the general interest of the Community and the respect due to fundamental human rights (*Belgian linguistic case*, § 5, p. 32).

B. Restrictions on access to education

15. Restrictions on the right to education do exist even though no express restriction can be found in Article 2 of Protocol No. 1. However, any restrictions must not curtail the right in question to such an extent as to impair its very essence and deprive it of its effectiveness. They must be foreseeable for those concerned and pursue a legitimate aim, although there is no exhaustive list of "legitimate aims" under Article 2 of Protocol No. 1 (*Leyla Şahin v. Turkey*, § 154).

16. Thus the right to education does not rule out disciplinary measures, in particular temporary or permanent expulsion from an educational institution for fraud [*Sulak v. Turkey* (dec.)] or for misbehaviour [*Whitman v. the United Kingdom* (dec.)].

1. Language

17. Article 2 of Protocol No. 1 does not specify the language in which education must be conducted in order that the right to education should be respected. However the right to education would be meaningless if it did not imply in favour of its beneficiaries, the right to be educated in the national language or in one of the national languages, as the case may be (*Belgian linguistic case*, § 3, p. 31).

18. Thus the case of *Catan and Others v. the Republic of Moldova and Russia* [GC] concerned a violation of the right to education owing to the forced closure of schools in connection with the language policy of separatist authorities and the measures of harassment that followed their reopening. There was nothing to suggest that such measures pursued a legitimate aim. The Grand Chamber emphasised the fundamental importance of primary and secondary education for each child's personal development and future success. It reiterated that there was a right to receive education in a national language. The State which exercised effective control during the period in question over the relevant administration, regardless of the fact that it intervened neither directly nor indirectly in that administration's language policy, engaged its responsibility as regards the interference with the right to education.

19. The temporary expulsion of students who had asked the university administration to introduce optional classes in the Kurdish language also constituted a violation (*Irfan Temel and Others v. Turkey*).

2. Admission criteria and entrance examinations

20. The refusal by a State to guarantee access to a school may constitute a violation of the right to education (*Campbell and Cosans v. the United Kingdom*).

21. The Court, however, recognises the proportionality of certain restrictions with the right of access to education.

a. Admission criteria

22. A State may impose criteria for admission to an educational institution. However, the fact of changing the rules governing access to university unforeseeably and without transitional corrective measures may constitute a violation of Article 14 of the Convention taken together with Article 2 of Protocol No. 1 (*Altınay v. Turkey*, §§ 56 – 61). Thus, in view of a lack of foreseeability to an applicant of changes to rules on access to higher education and the lack of any corrective measures applicable to his case, the impugned difference in treatment had restricted the applicant's right of access to higher education by depriving it of effectiveness and it was not, therefore, reasonably proportionate to the aim pursued.

23. It was not regarded as a denial of the right to education to limit access to academic studies to student candidates who had attained the academic level required to most benefit from the courses offered (*X. v. the United Kingdom*, Commission decision). In that case the applicant had failed his first-year exams and had not been attending all his obligatory tutorials. The university had considered that he did not have a sufficient level to repeat his first year of studies, but it did not exclude the possibility that he pursue a different subject.

24. In addition, a State is entitled to fix a maximum duration for university studies. In the Commission decision of *X. v. Austria*, the Austrian Government had set at seven years the maximum length of medical studies and had refused the applicant access to any medical school as he had not passed his exams within the allotted time.

b. Compulsory entrance examination with numerus clausus

25. Legislation imposing an entrance examination with *numerus clausus* for university studies in medicine and dentistry (public and private sectors) did not constitute a violation of the right to education (*Tarantino and Others v. Italy*). In relation to the entrance

examination, assessing candidates through relevant tests in order to identify the most meritorious students was a proportionate measure designed to ensure a minimum and adequate education level in the universities. As to the *numerus clausus* system, the capacity and resource considerations of universities, together with society's need for a particular profession, justified its existence.

c. Annulment of a positive result in the entrance examination

26. The fact of annulling a candidate's positive result in a university entrance examination, in view of his poor results in previous years, entailed a violation of his right to education (*Mürsel Eren v. Turkey*). The decision had no legal or rational basis and was therefore arbitrary.

3. School fees

27. States may have legitimate reasons for curtailing the use of resource-hungry public services up to a point in the field of education, but not unreservedly. The State's margin of appreciation in this domain increases with the level of education, in inverse proportion to the importance of that education for those concerned and for society at large. Secondary education plays an ever-increasing role in successful personal development and in the social and professional integration of the individuals concerned. Any restrictions on access to it must not, in particular, have the effect of creating a discriminatory system in breach of Article 14 of the Convention (*Ponomaryovi v. Bulgaria*-see § 41 below).

4. Nationality

28. The right to education does not grant a right for an alien to enter or stay in a given country (*Foreign Students v. the United Kingdom*, Commission decision, § 4). As the right guaranteed was concerned primarily with elementary education, the expulsion of a foreign student did not, in principle, interfere with his right to education.

29. Otherwise, only very strong considerations may lead the Court to find compatible with the Convention a difference in treatment exclusively based on nationality. The right to education is directly protected by the Convention and it concerns a public service of a very specific nature which benefits not only users but more broadly society as a whole, whose democratic dimension involves the integration of minorities (*Ponomaryovi v. Bulgaria*).

30. In addition, in the case of *Timishev v. Russia*, the applicants' children had been refused admission to the school that they had been attending for the past two years. The true reason for the refusal had been that the applicant had surrendered his migrant's card and had thereby forfeited his registration as a resident in the relevant town. However, Russian law did not allow the exercise of the right to education by children to be made conditional on the registration of their parents' place of residence. The Court thus found that the applicant's children had been denied the right to education provided for by domestic law.

5. Minimum age requirement by means of an education certificate

31. The Court found inadmissible as manifestly ill-founded an application challenging the obligation to hold a primary-school leaving certificate in order to enrol in Koranic study classes [*Çiftçi v. Turkey* (dec.)]. The restriction in question was intended to ensure that children who wished to receive religious instruction in Koranic study classes had attained a certain "maturity" through the education provided at primary school. The statutory requirement was in fact designed to limit the possible indoctrination of minors at an age when they wondered about many things and, moreover, when they might be easily influenced by Koranic study classes.

6. Legal questions

a. Prisons

32. Prisoners legally detained continue to enjoy all the fundamental rights and freedoms guaranteed by the Convention, with the exception of the right to liberty. They thus have the right to education guaranteed by Article 2 of Protocol No. 1. The refusal to enrol a prisoner in an existing prison school constituted a violation of that provision (*Velyo Velev v. Bulgaria*). However, prisoners are not entitled to invoke Article 2 of Protocol No. 1 to impose on the State an obligation to organise a particular type of education or training in prison.

33. The fact that an applicant had been prevented, during the period corresponding to his detention after being convicted by a court, from continuing his university course, was not interpreted as a deprivation of the right to education within the meaning of Article 2 of Protocol No. 1 [*Georgiou v. Greece* (dec.); *Durmaz and Others v. Turkey* (dec.); *Arslan v. Turkey* (dec.)]. In addition, the Court declared inadmissible as manifestly ill-

founded an application concerning the applicant's inability to finish his last year of secondary school while serving a prison sentence (*Epistatu v. Romania*).

b. Criminal investigation

34. In the case of *Ali v. the United Kingdom*, the Court found that a pupil could be excluded from a secondary school for a lengthy period pending a criminal investigation into an incident in the school without this amounting to a denial of the right to education, provided the proportionality principle was upheld. The applicant was only excluded until the termination of the criminal investigation. Moreover, the applicant was offered alternative education during the period of exclusion, and although the alternative did not cover the full national curriculum, it was adequate in view of the fact that the period of exclusion was at all times considered temporary pending the outcome of the criminal investigation. However, the situation might well have been different if a pupil of compulsory school age were to be permanently excluded from one school and were not able to subsequently secure full-time education in line with the national curriculum at another school.

c. Removal and eviction measures

35. The discontinuance of education as a result of deportation has not been regarded as a breach of Article 2 of Protocol No. 1. If a removal measure prevents someone from continuing their education in a given country, that measure cannot *per se* be seen as an interference with the person's right to education under that Article (see the Commission decisions in *Sorabjee v. the United Kingdom*; *Jaramillo v. the United Kingdom*; *Dabhi v. the United Kingdom*).

36. Furthermore, the eviction of a gypsy applicant from his land, when his grandchildren were going to a school next to their home on that land, did not constitute a violation of Article 2 of Protocol No. 1. The applicant had failed to substantiate his complaints that his grandchildren had effectively been denied the right to education as a result of the planning measures complained of (*Lee v. the United Kingdom* [GC]).

C. Discrimination in access to education

37. Where a State applies different treatment in the implementation of its obligations under Article 2 of Protocol No. 1, an issue may arise under Article 14 of the Convention.

> Article 14 of the Convention-Prohibition of discrimination
>
> "The enjoyment of the rights and freedoms set forth in [the] Convention shall be secured without discrimination on any ground such as sex, race, colour, language, religion, political or other opinion, national or social origin, association with a national minority, property, birth or other status."

38. For a difference in treatment not to be regarded as discriminatory, it must pursue a legitimate aim. In the *Belgian linguistic case* the Court had occasion to address the question of the inability for children with French as their mother tongue, living in a Dutch-speaking region, to follow classes in French whereas Dutch-speaking children living in the French-language region could follow classes in Dutch. It found that the measure in question was not imposed in the interest of schools, for administrative or financial reasons, but proceeded solely from considerations relating to language (§ 32, p. 70). There had thus been a violation of Article 2 of Protocol No. 1 taken together with Article 14 of the Convention.

39. In order to comply with Article 14, the existence of a legitimate aim is insufficient. The difference in treatment must also be proportionate. Thus, where the Court examined changes to a system of access to university, it found a violation of Article 14 taken together with Article 2 of Protocol No. 1, even though the aim of those changes was the rapid improvement of the quality of higher education. It took the view that on account of the unforeseeability of its application and in the lack of any corrective measures, the implementation of the new system was not reasonably proportionate to that aim (*Altınay v. Turkey*, § 60).

1. Persons with disabilities

40. The specific case of persons with disabilities has only rarely been raised before the Court. Under Article 2 of Protocol No. 1 taken alone, the former Commission took the view that there was an increasing body of opinion which held that, whenever possible, disabled children should be brought up with other children of their own age. That policy could not,

however, apply to all handicapped children. A wide measure of discretion had to be left to the appropriate authorities as to how to make the best use possible of the resources available to them in the interests of disabled children generally. It could not be said that the second sentence of Article 2 required the placing of a child with a serious hearing impairment in a regular school (either with the expense of additional teaching staff which would be needed or to the detriment of the other pupils) rather than in an available place in a special school (*Klerks v. the Netherlands*, Commission decision). The use of public funds and resources also led to the conclusion that the failure to install a lift at a primary school for the benefit of a pupil suffering from muscular dystrophy did not entail a violation Article 2 of Protocol No. 1, whether taken alone or together with Article 14 of the Convention (*McIntyre v. the United Kingdom*).

2. Administrative status and nationality

41. In the case of *Ponomaryovi v. Bulgaria*, the Court addressed the case of two pupils of Russian nationality living in Belgium with their mother but not having permanent residence permits. Whereas secondary education was free in Bulgaria, these two pupils, on account of their administrative status, had been charged school fees. The applicants were not in the position of individuals arriving in the country unlawfully and then laying claim to the use of its public services, including free schooling. Even when the applicants found themselves, somewhat inadvertently, in the situation of aliens lacking permanent residence permits, the authorities had no substantive objection to their remaining in Bulgaria and apparently never had any serious intention of deporting them. The Bulgarian authorities had not taken this situation into account. In any event, the legislation did not provide for any exemption from school fees. Consequently, and in view of the importance of secondary education, the Court found that the requirement for the two pupils to pay fees for their secondary education on account of their nationality and immigration status constituted a violation of Article 14 of the Convention read in conjunction with Article 2 of Protocol No. 1.

3. Ethnic origin

42. The Court has addressed in many cases the difficulties relating to the education of Roma children in a number of European States (*D. H. and Others v. the Czech Republic*

[GC], § 205). As a result of their turbulent history and constant uprooting the Roma have become a specific type of disadvantaged and vulnerable minority. They therefore require special protection and this protection extends to the sphere of education (ibid., § 182).

43. Given the Roma community's vulnerability, a difference of treatment in order to correct inequality made it necessary for States to pay particular attention to their needs, and for the competent authorities to facilitate the enrolment of Roma children, even if some of the requisite administrative documents were missing (*Sampanis and Others v. Greece*, § 86).

44. However, the mere enrolment in schools of Roma children does not suffice for a finding of compliance with Article 14 of the Convention taken together with Article 2 of Protocol No. 1. In this connection, the Court has relied extensively on reports by the European Commission against Racism and Intolerance (ECRI) (*Oršuš and Others v. Croatia* [GC]; *D. H. and Others v. the Czech Republic* [GC]). The enrolment must also take place in satisfactory conditions. The Court accepted that a State's decision to retain the special-school system was motivated by the desire to find a solution for children with special educational needs (ibid., § 198). Similarly, temporary placement of children in a separate class on the ground that they lack an adequate command of the language is not, as such, automatically in breach of Article 14 (*Oršuš and Others v. Croatia* [GC], § 157). However, the misplacement of Roma children in special schools has a long history across Europe (*Horváth and Kiss v. Hungary*, § 115). Consequently, schooling arrangements for Roma children must be attended by safeguards that ensure that the State takes into account their special needs (*D. H. and Others v. the Czech Republic* [GC], § 207; *Sampanis and Others v. Greece*, § 103). The decision must be transparent and based on clearly defined criteria, not only ethnic origin (ibid., § 89; *Oršuš and Others v. Croatia* [GC], § 182). Lastly, such measures cannot be regarded as reasonable and proportionate where they result in an education which compounds the difficulties of Roma children and compromises their subsequent personal development instead of tackling their real problems or helping them to integrate into the ordinary schools and develop the skills that would

facilitate life among the majority population (*D. H. and Others v. the Czech Republic*, § 207). A lack of discriminatory intent is not sufficient. The States are under a positive obligation to take positive effective measures against segregation (*Lavida and Others v. Greece*, § 73).

III. Respect for parental rights

> Article 2, second sentence, of Protocol No. 1 – Right to education
>
> "... In the exercise of any functions which it assumes in relation to education and to teaching, the State shall respect the right of parents to ensure such education and teaching in conformity with their own religious and philosophical convictions."

A. Scope

45. It is onto the fundamental right to education that is grafted the right of parents to respect for their religious and philosophical convictions. Consequently, parents may not refuse a child's right to education on the basis of their convictions [*Konrad and Others v. Germany* (dec.)].

46. The term "parents" seems to be interpreted widely by the Court; it is not confined to fathers and mothers but may include, at least, grandparents (*Lee v. the United Kingdom* [GC]). Conversely, a child receiving education cannot claim to be a victim of the rights guaranteed to the parents by the second sentence of Article 2 of Protocol No. 1 (*Eriksson v. Sweden*, § 93).

47. The word "respect" means more than "acknowledge" or "taken into account"; in addition to a primarily negative undertaking, it implies some positive obligation on the part of the State (*Campbell and Cosans v. the United Kingdom*, § 37). As to the word "convictions", taken on its own, it is not synonymous with the terms "opinions" and

"ideas". It denotes views that attain a certain level of cogency, seriousness, cohesion and importance (*Valsamis v. Greece*, §§ 25 and 27). The refusal of parents to accept corporal punishment at their child's school was thus covered by their philosophical convictions (*Campbell and Cosans v. the United Kingdom*, § 36).

48. Article 2 of Protocol No. 1 applies to all subjects and not only religious instruction. Sexual education and ethics thus fall within the scope of Article 2 of Protocol No. 1 [*Jimenez Alonso and Jimenez Merino v. Spain*; *Dojan and Others v. Germany* (dec.); *Appel-Irrgang and Others v. Germany*-see § 53 below].

49. Moreover, the provision applies to both the content of the teaching and the manner of its provision. Article 2 of Protocol No. 1 thus also applied to an obligation to parade outside the school precincts on a holiday. The Court was surprised that pupils could be required to take part in such an event on pain of suspension from school-even if only for a limited time. However, it found that such commemorations of national events served, in their way, both pacifist objectives and the public interest, and that the presence of military representatives at some of the parades did not in itself alter the nature of those parades. Furthermore, the obligation on the pupil did not deprive her parents of their right to enlighten and advise their children, or to guide their children on a path in line with the parents' own religious or philosophical convictions (*Efstratiou v. Greece*, § 32; *Valsamis v. Greece*, § 31).

50. The setting and planning of the curriculum fall in principle within the competence of the Contracting States (ibid., § 28) and there is nothing to prevent it containing information or knowledge of a religious or philosophical nature (*Kjeldsen, Busk Madsen and Pedersen v. Denmark*, § 53).

B. Possibility of exemption

51. Parents sometimes invoke the right to respect for their religious convictions to justify a decision to educate their children at home. The Court has noted in this connection that there appears to be no consensus among the Contracting States with regard to compulsory attendance at primary school. While some countries permit home education,

others provide for compulsory attendance at State or private schools. As a result, the Court has accepted as falling within the State's margin of appreciation the view that not only the acquisition of knowledge but also integration into, and first experiences of, society are important goals in primary-school education and that those objectives cannot be met to the same extent by home education, even if it allows children to acquire the same standard of knowledge provided by primary-school education. In the same case, the Court further regarded as being in accordance with its own case-law on the importance of pluralism for democracy the domestic courts' reasoning stressing both the general interest of society in avoiding the emergence of parallel societies based on separate philosophical convictions and the importance of integrating minorities into society. It therefore rejected a complaint concerning a refusal to allow the parents to educate their children at home as manifestly ill-founded [*Konrad and Others v. Germany* (dec.)].

52. It is sometimes necessary, if the parents' philosophical convictions are to be respected, for pupils to have the possibility of being exempted from certain classes. In the case of *Folgerø and Others v. Norway* [GC] (§§ 95 – 100), a refusal to grant the applicant parents full exemption from "Christianity, religion and philosophy" classes for their children in State primary schools gave rise to a violation of Article 2 of Protocol No. 1. Not only quantitative but even qualitative differences applied to the teaching of Christianity as compared to that of other religions and philosophies. There was admittedly the possibility of partial exemption but it related to the activity as such, not to the knowledge to be transmitted through the activity concerned. This distinction between activity and knowledge must not only have been complicated to operate in practice but also seems likely to have substantially diminished the effectiveness of the right to a partial exemption as such. The system of partial exemption was capable of subjecting the parents concerned to a heavy burden with a risk of undue exposure of their private life and the potential for conflict was likely to deter them from making such requests.

53. However, the possibility of an exemption does not have to be offered systematically. In the case of *Dojan and Others v. Germany* (dec.), compulsory sexual education classes were on the curriculum of primary school pupils. The school had decided

that a theatre workshop would be organised at regular intervals as a mandatory event for the purpose of raising awareness of the problem of sexual abuse of children. In addition, it was a school tradition to organise an annual carnival celebration, but there was an alternative activity for children who did not wish to attend. The applicants prevented their children from taking part in all or some of the above-mentioned activities and were consequently fined. When two of the parents refused to pay they were imprisoned. The Court observed that the sex-education classes at issue aimed at the neutral transmission of knowledge regarding procreation, contraception, pregnancy and child birth in accordance with the underlying legal provisions and the ensuing guidelines and the curriculum, which were based on current scientific and educational standards. The theatre workshop was consonant with the principles of pluralism and objectivity. As to the carnival celebrations at issue, these were not accompanied by any religious activities and in any event the children had the possibility of attending alternative events. Consequently, the refusal to exempt the children from classes and activities that were regarded by their parents as incompatible with their religious convictions was not in breach of Article 2 of Protocol No. 1. In the same vein, the Court took the view that the inclusion of compulsory secular ethics classes without any possibility of exemption fell within the margin of appreciation afforded to States under Article 2 of Protocol No. 1 (*Appel-Irrgang and Others v. Germany*).

54. Although individual interests must on occasion be subordinated to those of a group, a balance must be achieved which ensures the fair and proper treatment of minorities and avoids any abuse of a dominant position (*Valsamis v. Greece*, § 27). The Court has, for example, found that the fact that a school curriculum gave more prominence to Islam as practised and interpreted by the majority of the population in Turkey than to the various minority interpretations of Islam or other religions and philosophies could not in itself be regarded as failing to respect the principles of pluralism and objectivity that might be analysed as indoctrination. However, in view of the specificities of the Alevi faith in relation to the Sunni conception of Islam, the parents concerned could legitimately take the view that the way in which "religious culture and ethical knowledge" classes were taught

might entail for their children a conflict of allegiance between the school and their own values. In those circumstances an appropriate exemption was thus crucial (*Mansur Yalçın and Others v. Turkey*, §§ 71 – 75). Where parents were obliged, in this connection, to inform the school authorities of their religious or philosophical convictions, this was an inappropriate means of ensuring respect for their freedom of conviction, especially as, in the absence of any clear text, the school authorities always had the option of refusing such requests (*Hasan and Eylem Zengin v. Turkey*, §§ 75 – 76).

C. Conspicuous religious symbols

55. The second sentence of Article 2 of Protocol No. 1 prevents States from pursuing an aim of indoctrination that might be considered as not respecting parents' religious and philosophical convictions (*Kjeldsen, Busk Madsen and Pedersen v. Denmark*, § 53). However, the Court has also taken the view that the presence of crucifixes in State-school classrooms did not entail a violation of Article 2 of Protocol No. 1. In the Court's view, while it was true that by prescribing the presence of crucifixes-a sign which undoubtedly referred to Christianity-the regulations conferred on the country's majority religion preponderant visibility in the school environment, that was not in itself sufficient to denote a process of indoctrination on the respondent State's part. A crucifix on a wall was an essentially passive symbol and it could not be deemed to have an influence on pupils comparable to that of didactic speech or participation in religious activities. The effects of the greater visibility which the presence of the crucifix gave to Christianity in schools needed to be further placed in perspective, as it was not associated with compulsory teaching about Christianity and as the State opened up the school environment in parallel to other religions (*Lautsi and Others v. Italy*[GC], §§ 71 – 76).

56. Lastly, a State has a role as a neutral arbiter and must be very careful to ensure that when they permit students to manifest their religious beliefs on school premises, such manifestation does not become ostentatious and thus a source of pressure and exclusion. Consequently, the fact of refusing access to school to young girls wearing the veil did not

constitute a violation of Article 2 of Protocol No. 1 since it did not deprive the parents of their right to guide their children on a path in line with the parents' own religious or philosophical convictions, and provided the refusal was foreseeable and proportionate (*Köse and Others v. Turkey*). The same was true in the context of higher education (*Leyla Şahin v. Turkey* [GC]).

List of cited cases

The case-law cited in this Guide refers to judgments or decisions delivered by the Court and to decisions or reports of the European Commission of Human Rights ("the Commission").

Unless otherwise indicated, all references are to a judgment on the merits delivered by a Chamber of the Court. The abbreviation "(dec.)" indicates that the citation is of a decision of the Court and "[GC]" that the case was heard by the Grand Chamber.

The hyperlinks to the cases cited in the electronic version of the Guide are directed to the HUDOC database (〈http://hudoc.echr.coe.int〉) which provides access to the case-law of the Court (Grand Chamber, Chamber and Committee judgments and decisions, communicated cases, advisory opinions and legal summaries from the Case-Law Information Note) and of the Commission (decisions and reports), and to the resolutions of the Committee of Ministers.

The Court delivers its judgments and decisions in English and/or French, its two official languages. HUDOC also contains translations of many important cases into more than thirty non-official languages, and links to around one hundred online case-law collections produced by third parties.

— A —

Ali v. the United Kingdom, no. 40385/06, 11 January 2011

Altınay v. Turkey, no. 37222/04, 9 July 2013

Appel-Irrgang and Others v. Germany (dec.), no. 45216/07, ECHR 2009

Arslan v. Turkey (dec.), no. 31320/02, 1 June 2006

— C —

Campbell and Cosans v. the United Kingdom, 25 February 1982, Series A no. 48

Case "relating to certain aspects of the laws on the use of languages in education in Belgium" ("the *Belgian linguistic case*") (merits), 23 July 1968, Series A no. 6

Catan and Others v. the Republic of Moldova and Russia [GC], nos. 43370/04 and 2 others, ECHR 2012 (extracts)

Çiftçi v. Turkey (dec.), no. 71860/01, ECHR 2004 – VI

Cyprus v. Turkey [GC], no. 25781/94, ECHR 2001 – IV

— D —

D. H. and Others v. the Czech Republic [GC], no. 57325/00, ECHR 2007 – IV

Dahbi v. the United Kingdom, no. 28627/95, Commission decision of 17 January 1997

Dojan and Others v. Germany (dec.), nos. 319/08 and 4 others, 13 September 2011

Durmaz and Others v. Turkey (dec.), nos. 46506/99 and 3 others, 4 September 2001

— E —

Efstratiou v. Greece, 18 December 1996, Reports of Judgments and Decisions 1996 – VI

Epistatu v. Romania, no. 29343/10, 24 September 2013

Eriksson v. Sweden, 22 June 1989, Series A no. 156

— F —

Fayed v. the United Kingdom, 21 September 1994, Series A no. 294 – B

Foreign Students v. the United Kingdom, nos. 7671/76 and 14 others, Commission decision of 19 May 1977, Decisions and Reports 9

— G —

Georgiou v. Greece (dec.), no. 45138/98, 13 January 2000

Golder v. the United Kingdom, 21 February 1975, Series A no. 18

— H —

Hasan and Eylem Zengin v. Turkey, no. 1448/04, 9 October 2007

Horváth and Kiss v. Hungary, no. 11146/11, 29 January 2013

— I —

Irfan Temel and Others v. Turkey, no. 36458/02, 3 March 2009

— J —

Jaramillo v. the United Kingdom, no. 24865/94, Commission decision of 23 October 1995

Jiménez Alonso and Jiménez Merino v. Spain (dec.), no. 51188/99, ECHR 2000 – VI

— K —

Kjeldsen, Busk Madsen and Pedersen v. Denmark, 7 December 1976, Series A no. 23

Klerks v. the Netherlands, no. 25212/94, Commission decision of 4 July 1995, Decisions and Reports 82 – A

Kök v. Turkey, no. 1855/02, 19 October 2006

Köse and Others v. Turkey (dec.), no. 26625/02, ECHR 2006 – II

Konrad v. Germany (dec.), no. 35504/03, ECHR 2006 – XIII

— L —

Lautsi and Others v. Italy [GC], no. 30814/06, ECHR 2011

Lavida and Others v. Greece, no. 7973/10, 30 May 2013

Lee v. the United Kingdom [GC], no. 25289/94, 18 January 2001

Leyla Şahin v. Turkey [GC], no. 44774/98, ECHR 2005 – XI

— M —

Mansur Yalçın and Others v. Turkey, no. 21163/11, 16 September 2014

McIntyre v. the United Kingdom, no. 29046/95, Commission decision of 21 October 1998

Mürsel Eren v. Turkey, no. 60856/00, ECHR 2006 – II

— O —

O'Keeffe v. Ireland [GC], no. 35810/09, ECHR 2014 (extracts)

Oršuš and Others v. Croatia [GC], no. 15766/03, ECHR 2010

— P —

Ponomaryovi v. Bulgaria, no. 5335/05, ECHR 2011

— S —

Sampanis and Others v. Greece, no. 32526/05, 5 June 2008

Sorabjee v. the United Kingdom, no. 23938/94, Commission decision of 23 October 1995

Sulak v. Turkey, no. 24515/94, Commission decision of 17 January 1996, Decisions and Reports 84 – A

— T —

Tarantino and Others v. Italy, nos. 25851/09 and 2 others, ECHR 2013 (extracts)

Timishev v. Russia, nos. 55762/00 and 55974/00, ECHR 2005 – XII

— V —

Valsamis v. Greece, 18 December 1996, Reports of Judgments and Decisions 1996 – VI

Velyo Velev v. Bulgaria, no. 16032/07, ECHR 2014 (extracts)

Verein Gemeinsam Lernen v. Austria, no. 23419/94, Commission decision of 6 September 1995, Decisions and Reports 82 – A

— W —

Whitman v. the United Kingdom, no. 13477/87, Commission decision of 4 October 1989

— X —

X. v. Austria, no. 5492/72, Commission decision of 16 July 1973

X. v. the United Kingdom, no. 8844/80, Commission decision of 9 December 1980, Decisions and Reports 23

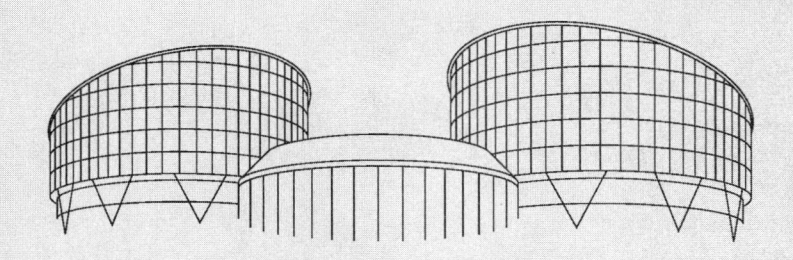

EUROPEAN COURT OF HUMAN RIGHTS
COUR EUROPÉENNE DES DROITS DE L'HOMME

第九章 《欧洲人权公约》第一议定书第3条适用指南
自由选举权

COUNCIL OF EUROPE

CONSEIL DE L'EUROPE

读者须知

本指南是欧洲人权法院(以下简称本法院、欧洲法院、斯特拉斯堡法院)出版的公约指南系列的一部分,旨在让执业律师了解斯特拉斯堡法院做出的基本判决。本指南分析和汇总了截至2016年5月31日的关于《欧洲人权公约》(以下简称公约、欧洲公约)第一议定书第3条的判例法。读者可以从中发现本领域的基本原则和相关判例。

援引的判例法选取了具有指导性的、重要的以及最新的判决。

本法院的判例不仅用于审判呈交至本法院的案件,而且从更为一般的意义上用于阐释、捍卫和发展公约创立的各项规则,并以此促使各缔约国对之加以遵守(*Ireland v. the United Kingdom*,1978年1月18日,§ 154,Series A no. 25.)。因此,从普遍意义来说,公约确立的此机制的任务便是通过决定公共政策的各种问题来提升人权保护的标准,并在缔约国范围内推广人权法学(*Konstantin Markin v. Russia* [GC],30078/06,§ 89,ECHR 2012)。

第一节 基本原则

> **公约第一议定书第3条自由选举权**
>
> "各缔约国保证以合理的周期通过秘密投票的方式举行自由选举,保障公民在选举立法机关成员时的表达自由。"

一、含义和范围

1. "根据公约序言,通过'有效的政治民主',才能最好地维持基本人权和自由。第一议定书第3条在公约体系中至关重要,因为它包含了典型的民主原则"(*Mathieu-Mohin and Clerfayt v. Belgium*,§47)。

2. 第一议定书第3条只涉及立法机关成员的选举。但是,这里所说的立法机关并不限于国家议会。必须对案件所涉及国家的宪法机制进行审查(*Timke v. Germany*,Commission decision)。一般来说,第一议定书第3条的范围不涵盖地方性选举,包括市级(*Xuereb v. Malta*;*Salleras Llinares v. Spain*)和区级(*Malarde v. France*)。虽然立法权并不一定仅限于国家议会[*Mółka v. Poland*(dec.)],但是本法院发现,制定法规、条例的权力和第一议定书第3条规定的立法权被区别开来,许多国家将前者授予地方当局。

关于总统选举,本法院认为,国家首脑的权力不能解释为第一议定书第3条意义上的"立法机关"的一种形式。但是,这并不排除将第一议定书第3条适用于总统选举的可能性。如果所涉及国家首脑享有提案和通过法律的权力或者享有控制法律通过或对主要立法机关进行审查的权力,那么国家首脑就可以被视为第一议定书第3条意义上的"立法机关"[*Boškoski v. the former Yugoslav Republic of Macedonia*(dec.);*Brito Da Silva Guerra and Sousa Magno v. Portugal*(dec.)]。然而,在随后的案例中(*Paksas v. Lithuania*[GC];*Anchugov and Gladkov v. Russia*,§§55–56),这种可能性并没有被采用过,甚至没有被提及。

3. 在许多情况下,本法院认为,欧洲议会构成了第一议定书第 3 条意义上的"立法机关"的一部分[Matthews v. the United Kingdom [GC],§§ 45 - 54; Occhetto v. Italy (dec.),§ 42]。

4. 关于选举的实质性特征,第一议定书第 3 条的文本只说明了选举自由和秘密投票,委员会和本法院也在之后对此不断重申(X. v. the United Kingdom, Commission decision of 6 October 1976)。该条款还规定必须以合理的周期举行选举,各国就此事项享有较大的自由裁量权,但是判例法对此提供了以下指导:

"委员会认为应该依据议会选举目的来判断选举周期是否合理。选举的目的是确保主流舆论的重大变化能够在民众代表的意见中得以反映。原则上,议会必须以发展和执行其立法意图为立场——包括长期的立法规划。如果选举的周期太短,可能会妨碍执行民意的政治规划;如果选举的周期太长,可能导致议会政治集团僵化,进而使得议会无法表达主流民意。"(Timke v. Germany, Commission decision)

5. 本法院判例法一直在推广普选权的要求,现已成为基本原则(X. v. Germany, Commission decision; Hirst v. the United Kingdom (no. 2) [GC],§§ 59 and 62; Mathieu-Mohin and Clerfayt v. Belgium,§ 51)。尽管第一议定书第 3 条规定了公民平等行使投票权的原则,但并不意味着在计算选举结果时所有选票所占比重必须相同。因此,不存在能够杜绝"废票"的选举机制[Mathieu-Mohin and Clerfayt v. Belgium,§ 54; Partija "Jaunie Demokrāti" and Partija "Mūsu Zeme" v. Latvia (dec.)]。

6. 每位选民的选票都必须具有影响立法机关组成的可能性。否则,选举权、选举程序乃至民主秩序本身都将失去意义(Riza and Others v. Bulgaria,§ 148)。因此,各国对于组织投票享有较大的自由裁量权。只要公民自由意志得以准确反映,那么导致各选区人口不等的选举边界检查就不违反第一议定书第 3 条的规定[Bompard v. France (dec.)]。最后,关于选举机制的选择,只要在选举立法机关成员的过程中,民意得以自由表达,那么各国可以自由裁量决定采用比例代表制、多票胜选制或是其他选举机制(Matthews v. the United Kingdom [GC],§ 64)。

二、解释原则

7. 第一议定书第 3 条不同于公约及议定书中的其他实质性规定,它通过规定各缔约国举行选举的义务来保证民意得以自由表达,而非就此规定一项特定的权利或自由。

但是，根据第一议定书第 3 条的准备文件以及公约体系中条款的解释，本法院确认该条款也暗含个人权利，包括选举权（"积极"方面）和被选举权（"消极"方面）（*Mathieu-Mohin and Clerfayt v. Belgium*，§§ 48 – 51；*Ždanoka v. Latvia*［GC］，§ 102）。

8. 上述权利并非是绝对的，存在着"内在限制"，并且各缔约国应当享有较大的自由裁量权。在判断限制权利的目的是否具有相关性时，第一议定书第 3 条意义上的"内在限制"的概念具有重要意义。第 3 条不受某一特定系列的"合法目的"的限制，如第 8 条到第 11 条所列举的"合法目的"，因此，只要在个案的特定情形中该目的符合法治原则并且与公约的一般性目标相一致，那么各缔约国就可以依据该系列之外的某一目的来证明其对权利进行限制的合法性。

9. "内在限制"的概念同样意味着本法院不适用"必要"或者"紧迫的社会需要"等传统的检验标准，第 8 条到第 11 条规定的就是这些检验标准。在检验是否符合第一议定书第 3 条时，本法院主要依据两个标准：第一，是否存在任意性或者缺乏合理性；第二，该限制是否妨碍了民意的自由表达。此外，"内在限制"还强调需要根据国家政治演变情况来评估选举立法，也就是说，在某一机制内让人难以接受的事项可能在另一机制内就变得有理可依（*Mathieu-Mohin and Clerfayt v. Belgium*，§ 52；*Ždanoka v. Latvia*［GC］，§§ 103 – 104 and 115）。

10. 被选举（"消极"方面）为议员的资格比选举（"积极"方面）资格具有更严格的要求。实际上，本法院对于第一议定书第 3 条中"积极"方面的检验通常包括更为广泛地审查剥夺个人或群体选举权的法定条款的合比例性，而对于"消极"方面的检验，在很大程度上仅限于确认剥夺被选举权的国内程序是否存在任意性（*Ždanoka v. Latvia*［GC］,115；*Melnitchenko v. Ukraine*，§ 57）。

11. 关于有权主张权利"消极"方面被侵害的主体，本法院认为，如果选举法或者国家当局限制党派人士以个人名义竞选，那么政党可以独立主张其候选人的权利受到侵害（*Georgian Labour Party v. Georgia*，§§ 72 – 74；*Riza and Others v. Bulgaria*，§ 142）。

12. 最后，不论是积极方面还是消极方面，本法院在检验一个国家的选举机制时，会考虑各个国家不同的历史背景。这些不同的历史背景可能促使本法院接受国与国之间选举机制的差异，这也解释了不同历史发展阶段的相应要求的变化。

第二节 积极方面:选举权

13. "积极"方面是受到限制的。此处,如第一议定书第3条规定的其他方面一样,缔约国享有一定的自由裁量权,可以根据自身的历史背景做出调整。例如,可以对选民的最低年龄做出规定,以此确保选民的意志足够成熟[*Hirst v. the United Kingdom*(no. 2)[GC],§62]。

14. 但是,在对于这些限制的合比例性进行的广泛审查中也存在着监督。缔约国不能利用自由裁量权来禁止特定个人或群体参与本国政治生活,特别是通过任免立法机关人员的方式来禁止(*Aziz v. Cyprus*,§28;*Tănase v. Moldova*[GC],§158)。在阿齐兹诉塞浦路斯案(*Aziz v. Cyprus*)中,本法院对土耳其裔塞浦路斯社区是否有权参与立法机关成员的选举争议做出判决。本法院认为,考虑到塞浦路斯自1963年以来存在的特殊情况以及立法真空的状态,作为居住于塞浦路斯共和国土耳其裔塞浦路斯社区的一员,申诉人被完全剥夺了在众议院议员选举中表达个人观点的机会,申诉人的选举权因此受到实质性损害。本法院还发现,在土耳其裔塞浦路斯社区和希腊裔塞浦路斯社区成员间,就上述权利的享有方面存在明显不平等,因此违反了公约第14条以及第一议定书第3条。

15. 同样需要注意的是,对于不属于第一议定书第3条适用范围内的选举,在恰当的情况下也有可能根据公约的其他条款提出申诉。例如,在莫尔卡诉波兰案(*Mółka v. Poland*)中,申诉人无法在市议会、区议会和地方议会选举中行使投票权。坐轮椅的残障人士不能在投票站投票,不在本区域内的人员也不能领取选票。本法院认为,如果国家当局无法为希望积极参与政治生活的申诉人提供良好的投票渠道,可能会引起申诉人关于自主能力乃至私人生活质量方面的羞耻感和忧虑感。因此,本法院认为,在此种情况下,第8条得以适用。

一、公民权的丧失

16. 法院尤为关注个人或群体选举权被剥夺的问题。剥夺选举权必须出于合法性目的,同时需要经过更为严格的合比例性审查。因此,本法院审查了许多在刑事犯罪调查中剥夺选举权的案件。拉比塔诉意大利案(*Labita v. Italy*, [GC])是关于涉嫌作为黑手党成员的个人的公民权利的自动短期丧失的问题。本法院认可这一措施是出于合法性目的,但是,考虑到该限制措施只在申诉人被宣判无罪后加以适用,本法院认为,因为缺乏实质性证据认定申诉人是黑手党成员,因此该措施并不合理。在维托·桑特·桑托洛诉意大利案(*Vito Sante Santoro v. Italy*)中,申诉人因为居所受到警方监视而被暂时剥夺选举权。但是,从他被下令接受监视到被从选举名单中除名之间相隔了9个多月。结果是申诉人在两场选举中都丧失了投票权,如果限制措施得以立即执行,就不会发生这样的情况。政府对于这一时间延迟没有提供任何正当性理由。因此,本法院认为此处违反了第一议定书第3条的规定。

17. 公民权的丧失问题不仅发生在刑事犯罪领域。阿尔巴内斯诉意大利案(*Albanese v. Italy*)是在申诉人的破产诉讼期间暂停其选举权。本法院指出,破产诉讼属于民事而非刑事法律范围,因此就破产人而言不存在任何欺诈成分。所以,对其选举权进行限制的目的在于施加必要的惩罚。因此,除了贬低破产者之外,该措施毫无作用——不考虑破产者是否有违法行为,仅因为其破产便加以谴责。因此,此种限制并非出于第一议定书第3条所规定的合法性目的。

18. 本法院还审查了由于受部分监护而丧失选举权的情况(*Alajos Kiss v. Hungary*)。本法院认为,此种措施可能出于合法性目的,也就是确保参与公共事务的公民有能力评估自己行为的后果并做出审慎而明智的决定。但是,上述对选举权的禁令被自动地、全面地运用,而不考虑被监护人的实际行为能力,同时也不区分部分监护和完全监护。本法院进一步指出,把具有智力或者精神缺陷的人群简单地同等对待是值得怀疑的,同时对于他们权利的缩减需要接受更为严格的审查。因此,相对于其所追求的目的来说,缺乏个体性的公正评估而不加区分地剥夺选举权的做法并不具有合理性。

二、关于囚犯的特定案件

19. 一般来说,除了公约第5条规定的在合法监禁期间内可以剥夺人身自由之外,囚犯仍然享有公约保障的所有基本权利和自由[*Hirst v. the United Kingdom* (no. 2) [GC],§69],第一议定书第3条所保障的权利也不例外。因此,毫无疑问,囚犯只有在定罪后被监禁时才会丧失其公约权利。但是,这并不妨碍采取措施以保护社会免受试图摧毁公约权利和自由的活动之危害。

20. 因此,如果个人严重滥用公职或者其行为对法治原则或民主基础造成威胁,那么第一议定书第3条就不排除对其选举权进行限制。但是,必须慎重采取剥夺公民选举权的严厉措施,同时,合比例性原则也要求制裁与个体行为及个人状况之间具有明显且充分的联系[*Hirst v. the United Kingdom* (no.2) [GC], § 71]。

21. 因此,剥夺囚犯的政治权利应当出于预防犯罪和提高公民责任的合法性目的,同时尊重法治并确保民主政体的良好运作和维持。但是,这样的限制措施不能自动适用,否则将会违反合比例性要求。

22. 各缔约国可以选择由其国内法院确定限制有罪囚犯选举权的措施是否合比例,或者在本国法律纳入相关条款,确定该限制措施适用的情形。在后面这种情况下,将由立法机关自身来平衡各方利益,以防止普遍、自动或者不加区分的限制。相应地,在缺乏特定司法判决的情况下,选举权禁令的适用本身并不违反第一议定书第3条[*Scoppola v. Italy* (no.3) [GC], § 102]。

23. 在赫斯特诉英国案[*Hirst v. the United Kingdom* (no.2) [GC]]中,因为上述选举权禁令是一个全面性禁令,被自动适用于所有服监禁刑的囚犯,所以本法院认为违反了第一议定书第3条。该禁令影响到48 000名囚犯——这是一个很大的数字,涉及所有种类的监禁刑——从监禁一天到终身监禁,并且关乎各种违法行为——从最轻微的到最严重的。此外,在个人违法行为与剥夺个人选举权之间不存在直接联系。在索依乐诉土耳其案(*Söyler v. Turkey*)中,本法院同样认为违反了第一议定书第3条。在该案中,对罪犯选举权的限制范围和影响过大,甚至限制未被监禁或者监禁刑期届满之人的选举权。在弗洛都诉奥地利案(*Frodl v. Austria*)中,剥夺选举权没有系统地影响所有囚犯,只涉及因故意违法行为而被判处一年以上监禁的罪犯,不过,在限制措施的自动适用和个人违法行为或案件相关情况之间没有联系。因此,本法院认为该选举权禁令相对于所追求的目的而言并不具有相称性。

24. 但是,在斯科波拉诉意大利案[*Scoppola v. Italy* (no.3) [GC]]中,本法院审查了一项选举权禁令,这一禁令只适用于为特定违法行为或者监禁超过法定期间的罪犯。此案中,立法机关根据个案的特殊情况以及所施加的刑罚,间接而言也就是根据刑罚的严重性,谨慎地调整过禁令存续期间,许多罪犯仍然可以在立法选举中投票。此外,该机制使得被永久剥夺选举权的罪犯可能重获选举权。如此一来,意大利的这一机制被标记为并非过分严格。因此,本法院认为没有违反第一议定书第3条。

25. 但必须注意的是，囚犯必须证明他们确实被剥夺选举权，本法院才可能认定禁令违反第一议定书第 3 条。仅以被监禁的状态为依据还不够，因为诸如提前释放或者移送精神病院等情况可能于上述选举日之前发生，这样的申诉会因为明显缺乏根据而不被受理 [Dunn and Others v. the United Kingdom（dec.）]。

26. 而且本法院绝不会指示缔约国应当采取何种必要措施杜绝因囚犯选举权禁令而造成的侵犯公约的情形，至多会提出一个时间表（Greens and M. T. v. the United Kingdom，§ 120）。但是，各缔约国不能以修改侵犯公约的法律太复杂作为借口。在安储科夫和格拉德科夫诉俄罗斯案（Anchugov and Gladkov v. Russia）中，被诉国的辩论依据是，禁令是依据宪法的一项规定做出的，但是议会无权修改该宪法规定，只能通过制订新宪法对其进行修改，因此程序特别复杂。但是，本法院认为，在部长委员会的监督下，当局有必要选择恰当的方式使国内立法与公约协调统一。各国政府可以自由探索各种可能的方式以符合第一议定书第 3 条规定的要求，包括政治程序的形式或者以符合公约的方式解释宪法（Anchugov and Gladkov v. Russia，§ 111）。

三、居住与选举权的关系

（一）侨民的选举权

27. 自 1961 开始的一系列案例中，委员会以明显缺乏根据为由，拒绝受理针对依据居住标准提起的选举权限制的申诉 [Commission decisions：X. and Others v. Belgium；X. v. the United Kingdom（11 December 1976）；X. v. the United Kingdom（28 February 1979）；X. v. the United Kingdom（13 May 1982）；Polacco and Garofalo v. Italy；Luksch v. Germany]。

28. 本法院随后重申了第一议定书第 3 条在居住标准问题上的适用性。依据居住标准做出的选举权限制具有许多正当性理由：第一，我们可以推定非本国居民并不那么直接或持续地受到本国日常问题的影响，并且对这些问题了解得更少；第二，竞选议会的候选人难以向侨居国外的公民展示选举议题，这些侨民对于候选人的选举或者竞选宣言的起草也缺乏影响力；第三，议会选举中的投票权与胜选的政治组织的活动对其的直接影响密切相关；第四，出于合法要求，立法机关可能限制侨居国外的公民在选举中的影响力，因为这些选举涉及的问题主要影响在于国内的居民。

29. 即使相关人员并没有切断所有与他或她的原籍国的联系，并且上述的理由可能无法对其适用,法律也无法顾及每个个案,而只能制定一般性规范[*Hilbe v. Liechtenstein*(dec.);*Doyle v. the United Kingdom*(dec.);*Shindler v. the United Kingdom*,§105]。

30. 因此,本法院认为离开原籍国的侨民的申诉的理由不充分[*Hilbe v. Liechtenstein*(dec.)]。在接下来的两个案例中,本法院特别考虑到了这一事实:非本国居民的公民可以在他们移居国外之后的最初15年参与国家选举,而且如果他们返回原籍国居住,他们的选举权自返回居住时起可以恢复。因此,本法院认为此种情况下的限制措施并无不妥[*Doyle v. the United Kingdom*(dec.);*Shindler v. the United Kingdom*,§108]。在最后提到的这个案例里,本法院还认为其与以下事实相关:英国议会多次权衡各方利益,并且就非本国居民的公民选举权问题进行过深入的讨论;议会中的意见变化反映在自非本国居民的公民首次获得投票权开始的各个限期修正案中。

31. 在辛德勒诉英国案(*Shindler v. the United Kingdom*)中,本法院注意到,就欧洲来看,对于因移民引发的关于在原籍国和居住国的政治参与问题的关注正在上升。但是,正如法律规定的那样,不可能强制各缔约国保证非本国居民的公民毫无限制地获得选举权。在成员国的法律和实践中,允许非本国居民的公民投票的趋势很明显,并且很大一部分成员国支持选举权不受限制,但是即便如此,也不足以建立任何实质性的共同方法或者共识来赋予非本国居民的公民不受限制的选举权。因此,本法院认为,尽管此事有待进一步商榷,但是缔约国依然保有较大的自由裁量权(*Shindler v. the United Kingdom*,§§109-115)。

(二)某些地区的具体案例

32. 在派诉法国案(*Py v. France*)中,本法院重申了待定选民与相关地区之间应当存在密切联系的意见。一位来自法国大陆的法国公民被拒绝参与新喀里多尼亚议会的选举的权利,理由是他无法证明自己在该地区居住10年以上。本法院认为居住期长短的分界点所解决的问题是投票必须反映"相关"人员的意愿,并且选举结果不能受到该地区新来者的影响,因为他们与该地区之间尚未形成密切联系。而且,选举权限制是建立新喀里多尼亚公民身份的直接且必然的结果。新喀里多尼亚政治机构的活动并不会对申诉人造成与当地居民同等程度的影响。如此一来,居住方面所要求的条件就是正当的,同时也是出于合法性目的。新喀里多尼亚的历史和现状——处于获得完全主权和自治前的过渡时期——可以被视为"当地的要求",与10年居住期同样重要的限制性条件也得以正当化,这些限制性条件在缓解当地血腥冲突方面也具有重要作用。

33. 在瑟温格诉荷兰案(*Sevinger v. the Netherlands*)中,享有一定自治权的阿鲁巴岛的居民在荷兰议会选举中不具有投票权,但是他们有权投票选举阿鲁巴岛议会,该议会有权向荷兰议会派遣特别代表。因此,本法院认为,居住在阿鲁巴岛上的荷兰公民能够对荷兰下议院的决定产生一定影响,而且荷兰议会的活动并不会对阿鲁巴岛居民造成与荷兰本土居民同等程度的影响。本法院也拒绝受理基于公约第14条和第一议定书第3条提起的申诉,认为只有居住于阿鲁巴岛的荷兰公民有权选举阿鲁巴岛议会,因此他们的情况和荷兰本土公民的情况并不相同。

34. 关于相关国家范围内区域性的投票组织,本法院认可这些组织将选民从某一选区名单中删除并加入另一选区名单的义务是出于合法性目的,即确保选民名册是在时间和监督都充分的情况下进行编纂的,以此使得相关投票活动得以合理组织并且避免欺诈。在法定期限内完成这些法定程序,属于缔约国自由裁量权的范围(*Benkaddour v. France*)。

(三)为侨民组织境外选举

35. 第一议定书第3条没有要求各缔约国创设一种机制来确保非本国居民的公民享有选举权。在斯塔洛普洛斯和基亚寇莫普洛斯诉希腊案(*Sitaropoulos and Giakoumopoulos v. Greece*[GC])中,申诉人指出,由于缺乏这方面的规范,他们作为侨民在侨居国(法国)不享有选举权——尽管他们的原籍国(希腊)的宪法提供了该种可能性。本法院认为,从实质性损害选举权这点来看,申诉人的经济、家庭和职业生活因往返希腊而受到的影响是合理的,因而在此并没有违反第一议定书第3条。

36. 但是,当国内法律确实建立了这样一种机制的时候,特定的义务便会随之产生,特别是必要时在国外另行组织选举的义务。在利扎等人诉保加利亚案(*Riza and Others v. Bulgaria*)中,本法院认为,在另一个主权国家另行组织选举,即使只设置少数的投票站,也将面临重大的外交和组织障碍,同时需要支出额外费用。但是,本法院发现,于投票站另行组织选举,在选举委员会看来是非常不可思议的,但是它符合取消选举结果的合法性目的,也就是说,选举过程的合法性的保留包括选举权和被选举入议会的权利。

37. 在奥兰诉土耳其案(*Oran v. Turkey*)中,侨居国外的土耳其选民无权在海关投票站为独立的无党派候选人投票,在此条件下只能对政治党派进行投票。这样的限制是正当的,因为为侨居选民分派选区是不可能的。本法院认为,在审查这一限制时,需要考虑到普遍认可的对侨民选举权的限制,特别是,出于合法要求,立法机关可能会限制侨居国外的公民在选举中的影响力,因为这些选举涉及的问题主要影响居于国内的居民。本法院同时还强调政党扮演的角色,政党是唯一的执政主体,它们能够影响整个国家体制。此外,这一限制还出于另外两个合法性目的:提高民主多元化的同时防止候选人资格过度分散和失衡,从而加强立法机关选举中的民意表达。如此一来,这一限制便符合立法机关对于确保国家政治稳定以及在选举之后领导政坛的新政府稳定的合法要求。因此,此处没有违反第一议定书第3条。

第三节 消极方面:被选举权

38. "消极"方面,顾名思义就是被选举权,它和"积极"方面一样,在案例法中得以发展,因此本法院认为被选举权是"真正的民主政体内涵中所固有的内容"(*Podkolzina v. Latvia*, §35)。相较于对选举权限制的审查,本法院对第一议定书第3条消极方面限制的审查要更为严谨,合比例性检验标准也更为狭窄。因此,各缔约国就"消极"方面享有更大的自由裁量权(*Etxeberria and Others v. Spain*, §50)。

39. 公约第14条规定的禁止歧视同样适用。在这种情况下,即使缔约国就被选举权享有较大的自由裁量权,如果差别对待是基于人种、肤色或者族裔做出的,那么关于客观合理的理由的概念必须被尽可能严格地解释(*Sejdić and Finci v. Bosnia-Herzegovina* [GC], §44)。

40. 在塞基迪克和芬奇诉波斯尼亚和黑塞哥维那案(*Sejdić and Finci v. Bosnia-Herzegovina* [GC])中,本法院审查了一项排除性规则,该规则规定只有宣布与"选民"建立友好关系的人才有权竞选众议院(国家议会的第二级议院),拒绝做出此宣言的候选人则无权竞选。本法院注意到,这一排除性规则至少在一个目的上与公约的一般性目标大体契合,即恢复和平。当这些令人质疑的宪法条款落实到位后,事实上已经达成了一个很脆弱的停火协议。这些条款是为结束如种族灭绝和种族清洗这样典型的血腥冲突而制定的,这些冲突的性质意味着条款需要"选民"(波斯尼亚人、克罗地亚人和塞尔维亚人)的认可才能确保和平的实现。无须过多论证,这一点可以解释在和平谈判中其他团体(比如当地的罗马和犹太团体)代表的缺席,以及在冲突后的社会中,与会者对于"选民"之间实质平等的关注。但是,岱顿协定(Dayton Agreement)签署后,波斯尼亚和黑塞哥维那的关系取得了较大的积极进展。此外,通过毫无保留地签署公约以及相关议定书,应诉国自愿同意达到相关标准。因此,本法院判定,长期剥夺(罗马或犹太裔的)申诉人的被选举权缺乏客观合理的依据,违反了公约第14条及第一议定书第3条的规定。

41. 在佐尼克诉波斯尼亚和黑塞哥维那案(Zornić v. Bosnia-Herzegovina)中,出于同样的原因,本法院判决,基于与上述案件同样的理由而剥夺申诉人竞选众议院议员和总统的权利的做法,违反了第一议定书第3条。鉴于塞基迪克和芬奇诉波斯尼亚和黑塞哥维那案中判决的执行被严重拖延从而违反公约的情况,本法院根据公约第46条做出裁决。在波斯尼亚和黑塞哥维那灾难性冲突18年后,本法院发现,随着时间的推移,这个国家采用的政治机制能够不分种族地保障本国所有公民竞选众议院议员和总统的权利(Zornić v. Bosnia-Herzegovina,§ 43)。

42. 在塔纳斯诉摩尔多瓦案(Tănase v. Moldova[GC])中,本法院仅依据第一议定书第3条对双重国籍的问题做出了裁决。本法院认为,允许多重国籍的存在是共识,持有多国国籍不能成为丧失竞选议员的权利的原因,而且在种族多元化的国家中多重国籍议员的数量可能很多。

一、被选举权的剥夺和民主秩序

43. 关于对被选举权的限制,维护民主秩序是与法治原则和公约一般性目标相一致的目的之一。

44. 为了符合公约的规定,剥夺被选举权首先必须是合法的:特别是要依据法律的规定。在迪克莱和萨达克诉土耳其案(Dicle and Sadak v. Turkey)中,议员们所在的政党被解散,他们也因为加入非法组织而被判处严重的监禁刑。在欧洲人权法院判决之后他们获得了重审。但是,他们却因为服刑未满而被剥夺被选举为议员的权利。在根据公约第6条第2款对其进行审查时,本法院认为,从土耳其国内判决来看,遵从本法院判决对案件进行重审时,要视为初审一样进行审判。本法院判定,维持申诉人的初次定罪并剥夺其被选举权缺乏法律依据,因此违反了第一议定书第3条。

45. 在艾特克斯贝里亚等人诉西班牙案(Etxeberria and Others v. Spain)中,申诉人因从事与3个政党相关的活动而被剥夺被选举权,这3个政党因为支持暴力以及恐怖组织埃塔的活动而被宣布违法并被解散。本法院发现,西班牙当局掌握足够的证据确定上述选举团体想要继续进行哪些政党的活动。西班牙最高法院基于这些团体的声明之外的因素做出推论,西班牙当局决定剥夺他们个人的被选举权。在对抗性程序的审查之后——对抗程序期间这些团体可以提交观察报告,西班牙国内法院发现它们和那些被宣布非法的政党之间存在明确联系。最后,在当时的西班牙,政府机构中的一些自治团体和政党(尤其是巴斯克地区)要求独立,这一政局证明这一令人疑虑的限制措施并不属于禁止独立性言论的政策。因此,本法院认为这一限制与其追求的合法性目的相符合。

46. 尽管相对于第一议定书第3条规定的积极方面而言,本法院对于消极方面的审查较为宽松,但是并不意味着本法院对其不进行审查。尽管合比例性的检验相对灵活,但也是切实进行的。本法院已经发现了许多由于所施加的惩罚不合比例从而违反第一议定书第3条的情况:议员所属政党因为破坏领土完整和国家统一或者保留政治机制的非宗教性而被解散,在此之后,对议员施加了不合比例的惩罚(参见下文,第82至84段)。

47. 值得注意的是,因政党宣言与民主原则相冲突而取缔政党的案例通常依据公约第11条(集会结社自由)进行审查。第一议定书第3条只在不引起其他问题的情况下作为依据,并不作为首选依据(*Refah Partisi（the Welfare Party）and Others v. Turkey*[GC]; *Linkov v. the Czech Republic*; *Parti nationaliste basque-Organisation régionale d'Iparralde v. France*)。

二、历史环境的重要性

48. 尽管在确保选举独立和选民自由方面具有相同渊源,不同国家的选任标准却因历史和政治因素不同而存在差别。在这一方面,国情的多样性在欧洲委员会许多成员国的宪法和选举立法中表现为多种多样的选任方法。因此,要想适用第一议定书第3条,必须根据相关国家的政治进程审查其选举立法(*Mathieu-Mohin and Clerfayt v. Belgium*, § 54; *Podkolzina v. Latvia*, § 33; *Ždanoka v. Latvia* [GC], § 106)。

49. 在茨塔洛卡诉拉脱维亚案(*Ždanoka v. Latvia* [GC])中,申诉人是一名政党成员,该党曾经在1991年试图发动政变。该政党在试图发动政变后继续存在,由于曾参与上述政党的活动,她被多次剥夺被选举权。本法院认为,考虑到申诉人之前在该政党的职位以及她在1991年事件中的立场,剥夺其竞选国家议会议员的权利是正当的。在一个已经建立起几十年或者几个世纪的民主制度体系的国家,这一措施可能被认为是难以接受的,但是,鉴于拉脱维亚的历史政治环境——曾经导致这一措施的适用并对新的民主秩序构成威胁,这一措施是可以被接受的。然而,本法院注意到,拉脱维亚议会有义务定期审查法定限制,以期尽早结束限制措施。就拉脱维亚现在更稳定的社会环境而言,这一判定显得更为正当,尤其是拉脱维亚已经完全欧化。因此,拉脱维亚立法机关在这方面的任何失败措施都可能导致本法院做出不同的判决(*Ždanoka v. Latvia* [GC],§132-135)。

50. 本法院随后再一次强调有关肃清法案的通过时间和重新审查的重要性。在阿丹颂斯诉拉脱维亚案(*Ādamsons v. Latvia*)中,申诉人是拉脱维亚前总理,其基于曾是苏联国家安全委员会的"官员"的原因而被剥夺被选举权。本法院根据拉脱维亚的历史环境维持了这一判决。但是,本法院补充道,已过去多年时间,仅出于对一群人普遍的怀疑不足以继续作为采取限制措施的理由,拉脱维亚当局必须基于额外的论据和证据来使这一限制措施正当化。在此案中,法律的适用涉及苏联国家安全委员会"官员"。鉴于苏联国家安全委员会义务的多样性,这一范围未免太广。在这些情况下,仅仅证明相关人员隶属于某一个特定组织不再足以作为采取限制措施的理由。上述组织划定得太过笼统,在对其成员选举权进行限制时,应该考虑他们各自的实际行为,并据此采取特定的方法。随着时间的推移,我们越来越需要这样一种具体问题具体分析的方法。申诉人从来没有因为直接或者间接地参与集权主义政权恶行而被控告,也没有做出任何对恢复拉脱维亚独立和民主秩序表现反对或者敌意的行为。而且,申诉人在复苏的拉脱维亚历经10年出色的军旅和政治生涯之后,一直被官方认定为无任选资格。在这些情况下,只有最令人信服的理由才能够使剥夺申诉人被选举权的行为正当化。此外,可以对苏联国家安全委员会曾任官员适用10年的限制措施的期限在其他立法文件中又被延长了10年,对此拉脱维亚议会和政府没有给出任何理由。因此,本法院认为,这种延期对申诉人而言显然是任意专断的。

三、组织选举

51. 组织选举是一个复杂的事项,也对制定和修改法律有所要求。在被要求审查这一事项时,本法院没有忽视其中的复杂性和各缔约国的特定国情。因此,在这一事项上,各缔约国享有较大的自由裁量权。

52. 本法院尤其认为对选民名册的合理管理是自由公正投票的前提条件。毫无疑问,被选举权是否具有效力取决于选举权是否能够公正行使。对选民名单的管理不善将会削弱候选人平等公正竞选的机会(*Georgian Labour Party v. Georgia*,§§ 82 - 83)。在某一个案例中,选民名单的编纂规则在选举前一个月突然被更改,本法院承认新的选民登记机制并不完美,但是更重视国内当局不遗余力地使新的投票机制更加公平的事实。尤其是当局还面临着在"后革命"的政治格局中于短期内弥补选民名单明显缺陷的挑战,因此,期望国家当局拿出一个理想的解决方案,将会是一个过分且不切实际的负担。应当由选民核实其登记情况并在必要时要求更正。本法院认为这属于缔约国自由裁量的范围(*Georgian Labour Party v. Georgia*)。

(一)捍卫被选举权的严肃性:保证金要求

53. 许多缔约国的选举法规定候选人需要交纳保证金,以此打消那些视选举为儿戏的候选人的念头。这样的举措提高了竞选人的责任感,并将选举限于那些认真参选的候选人之间,同时避免了公款的不合理支出。因此,是出于保证民意被有效且合理代表的合法性的目的(*Sukhovetskyy v. Ukraine*,§§ 61 - 62)。

54. 不过,保证金数额必须合理,这个数额标准应当既能阻退轻率的候选人,又能保证严肃的候选人得以登记。因此,本法院考虑了因国家举行的选举活动和其他组织选举而产生的繁重花销的数额总和,这项保证金也许可以用来贴补支出。

55. 要想符合合比例性检验标准,规定的保证金不能过高或者对决定参选的候选人造成行政或经济障碍,更不能阻碍具有代表性的政治潮流的出现,同时不能影响多元化原则(*Sukhovetskyy v. Ukraine*,§§ 72 - 73)。考虑到缔约国在这一事项所享有的自由裁量权,要求支付保证金以及规定只有在政党获得一定比例选票时才能退还保证金或者竞选费用,都是为了充分促进具有代表性的政治思潮的发展,因此相对于第一议定书第3条所追求的目的来说是合理的(*Russian Conservative Party of Entrepreneurs and Others v. Russia*,§ 94)。即使保证金不予归还,上述判定依然成立(*Sukhovetskyy v. Ukraine*)。

但是,是否归还保证金可能会引发与第一议定书第1条有关的问题。在俄罗斯企业家保守党等诉俄罗斯案(*Russian Conservative Party of Entrepreneurs and Others v.*

Russia)中,本法院认为俄罗斯国内程序违反了法律的确定性原则,在这一程序中,因为某些候选人提供的信息有误,而取消了某一政党全体成员的被选举权。提出申诉的政党已交纳选举保证金。鉴于依据第一议定书第 3 条做出的裁决,本法院认为俄罗斯拒绝返还该党保证金以及其他费用的做法违反了第一议定书第 1 条。

(二)避免政治局势过度分裂

56. 要求公布候选人名单中的签名数量的条件并不损害选民在选举立法机关时的表达自由[*Asensio Serqueda v. Spain*(dec.);*Federación nacionalista Canaria v. Spain*(dec.);*Brito Da Silva Guerra and Sousa Magno v. Portugal*(dec.);*Mihaela Mihai Neagu v. Romania*(dec.),§ 31]。

57. 但是,这样的限制措施必须出于合法性目的,如为了确定代表人并排除不合格的候选人而在候选人之间进行合理筛选,同时相对于此目的来说必须合比例。10 万个签名代表已占登记在选民名单上的全体公民的 0.55%,符合第一议定书第 3 条的规定。

58. 本法院同样认为,在要求签名的同时要求签名者证明其已登记在选民名单上,是出于合法性目的,即确保签名者拥有选举权以及每个人只能支持一名候选人。因此,排除不满足上述形式要件的候选人的做法是合比例的[*Brito Da Silva Guerra and Sousa Magno v. Portugal*(dec.)]。

59. 但是,签名数量的最低要求及其核实必须符合法治原则,维护选举公平。在泰罗夫诉阿塞拜疆案(*Tahirov v. Azerbaijan*)中,阿塞拜疆选举委员会否认了申诉人的被选举权,该决定的保障措施不够充分——尤其是在关于委任专家决定签名是否有效的问题上。此外,申诉人无法参加选举委员会会议,也无法提交个人意见,选举委员会对这两个事项都没有进行审查,因此,声称申诉人提供的签名无效从而剥夺其被选举权的做法是专断的。基于欧洲安全与合作委员会的一项报告,本法院注意到这些弊端对整个选举的不良影响以及基于这些弊端而被剥夺被选举权的案件数量。本法院认为,政府单方面的宣告不足以保障对人权的尊重,因而将该决定推翻并根据具体案情进行审查。

60. 本法院同样接受与根据选举结果进行的席位分配相关的准入标准。有时候,选举机制试图实现的目标之间难以相容:一方面要公平公正地反映民意,另一方面要引导政治思潮以此促进足够明确清晰的政治意愿的出现。因此,第一议定书第 3 条并不意味着所有选票对选举结果来说都必须具有同等分量,也并不意味着所有的候选人都拥有同等的获胜机会,能够杜绝"废票"的选举机制是不存在的[*Partija "Jaunie Demokrāti" and Partija "Mūsu Zeme" v. Latvia*(dec.)]。

61. 在不同国家,选举门槛产生的效果各异,不同的选举机制可能致力于实现不同的、甚至是相反的政治目标。某一选举机制可能更加关注议会中政党代表的公平性,而另一机制也许意在避免政治体制的分裂以及促使议会多数党执政的形成。本法院认为这些目标本身都是合理的。而且,准入门槛所扮演的角色依据设置标准和每个国家政党体制的差异而有所不同。较低的门槛只排除较少数群体,这样会导致难以形成稳定的大多数,然而在一些政党体制严重分裂的案例中,较高的门槛剥夺了许多选民的代表权,种类繁多的情况表明了潜在选择的多样性。因此,在没有考虑选举机制的情况下,本法院不能对作为选举机制一部分的某一特定门槛做出评估(*Yumak and Sadak v. Turkey*[GC],§§ 131 - 132)。

62. 例如,关于满足两个条件之一的要求——要么获得一个独立小岛选区30%以上的有效选票,要么获得整个自治社区6%以上的有效选票,本法院认为这样的选举机制远不足以对被选举权构成妨碍,反而对较小的政治群体进行了很好的保护[*Federación nacionalista Canaria v. Spain*(dec.)]。为了能够入选并参与议会席位的分配,候选人同样需要获得5%的选票,本法院认为,这一门槛符合第一议定书第3条的规定,因为这一要求充分鼓舞了具有代表性的思潮并且有助于避免议会的过度分裂[*Partija "Jaunie Demokrāti" and Partija "Mūsu Zeme" v. Latvia*(dec.)]。

63. 相反,在豫马科和萨达克诉土耳其案(*Yumak and Sadak v. Turkey*[GC])中,本法院认为,通常来说,10%的选票门槛太高,这一门槛和欧洲委员会的机构相同,欧洲委员会建议降低这一门槛。这一门槛迫使政党使用无益于保证选举程序透明的计谋。但是,在根据选举所处的具体政治背景进行审查时,通过纠正的方式和其他保障措施——如和其他政党组成选举联盟或者宪法法院发挥作用(宪法法院在实践中效用并不明显),本法院并不认为10%的选票门槛会对第一议定书第3条赋予申诉人的权利造成实质性损害。

64. 最后,计票规则发生突然和不可预见的更改可能会违反第一议定书第3条的规定。特别最高法院对现有的关于计票规则的判例法做出不可预见的改变,从而剥夺议员的席位,本法院认为这一做法违反了第一议定书第3条。本法院特别考虑到,在选举之后,该判例法的更改改变了空白选票的意义和分量并因此会改变那些投空白选票的选民民意,这也会造成新选任议员与现任议员在被选任方式上存在差异(*Paschalidis, Koutmeridis and Zaharakis v. Greece*)。

四、其他的合法性目的

65. 正如公约第 8 至 11 条一样,合法性目的不受条款列举的限制,本法院也可能接受其他使限制选举权的做法正当化的合法性目的。

66. 本法院在忠于国家和忠于政府之间进行了区分。如果出于忠于国家的需要可以使对选举权的限制正当化,那么这就不是出于对政府的忠诚(*Tănase v. Moldova* [GC],§ 166)。要求足够熟悉官方语言也同样可以出于合法性目的(*Podkolzina v. Latvia*)。本法院同时还认为,在议会选举中要求候选人提交准确的职业信息和党籍有助于选民在了解其职业和政治背景的基础上做出选择,因而属于合法性目的(*Krasnov and Skuratov v. Russia*)。相反,仅因为候选人提交的文件存在所谓的形式缺陷而剥夺其选举权的做法,并非出于合法性目的(*Krasnov and Skuratov v. Russia*, §§ 65 – 66)。

67. 本法院也可能对要求某一非常传统的新教政党接纳女性作为候选人的申诉裁定不予受理。本法院认为,缔约国在性别平等方面的发展有助于避免女性作用次于男性的理念[*Staatkundig Gereformeerde Partij v. the Netherlands* (dec.)]。

68. 此外,在梅尔尼琛科诉乌克兰案(*Melnitchenko v. Ukraine*)中,申诉人以难民身份居住于美国,政府以其提供虚假的居住信息为由而剥夺其被选举权。根据现行法律,他提供的信息来源于他仍然持有的国内护照,该信息显示他居住于乌克兰。本法院认为就候选人登记设置居住条件的做法是可以接受的。但是,本法院指出,申诉人遵守的乌克兰国内法并没有要求其持续居住该国。此外,申诉人还处于这样一种境地,他要么居留乌克兰但同时可能面临人身伤害的威胁,这使得他根本不可能行使政治权利,要么就离开乌克兰但是丧失被选举权。因此,本法院认为该规定违反了第一议定书第 3 条。

69. 最后,在安东恩科诉俄罗斯案[*Antonenko v. Russia* (dec.)]中,俄罗斯一法院以申诉人财务违规及竞选活动不公为由,在投票前一天禁止申诉人竞选议会议员。申诉人申诉的内容并非其候选人资格被取消,而是该取消决定在投票即将开始前突然做出。本法院认为做出该决定的时间符合俄罗斯国内法的规定,并且不影响申诉人可能进行的上诉——尽管申诉人并没有就此决定提起上诉。

70. 在很多时候,本法院也认可潜在候选人因为所居职位而被取消候选人资格的做法。在吉托纳斯等人诉希腊案(*Gitonas and Others v. Greece*)中,希腊法律排除了某些类别的公职人员——包括授薪公务员以及政府机构和公共事业单位的人员——参加竞选的权利以及在选举前3年内已经任职3个月以上的选区被选举的权利:不同于某些其他类别的公务员,现任这些类别公职的候选人即使事先辞职,以上限制依然成立。本法院认为该限制措施出于双重目的:确保拥有不同政治信仰的候选人拥有发挥同样影响力的方式以及保护选民免受公职人员的压力。次年,本法院重申,对于当地政府的有效政治民主来说,限制当地政府特定类别公务员参与政治活动的权利是出于保护其他诸如议员和选民等人权利的合法性目的。只有当申诉人在担任这些限制性政治职位时,才会对他们施加这些限制性措施,因此,这些措施是合比例的(*Ahmed and Others v. the United Kingdom*)。在布黎克诉拉脱维亚案(*Brike v. Latvia*)中,本法院补充道,对于保证公务员部门独立性的要求来说,对公务员进行限制的做法是合比例的,对于法官而言尤其如此,对法官进行限制是出于保护公约第6条所赋予的公民权利的目的。因此,法院认为该限制措施没有对公约保障的权利造成实质性损害,因为若法官希望竞选的话可以选择辞职。

71. 但是,即使是出于合法性目的,对被选举权的限制也一定不能导致权利失效——要么因为限制性条件适用得太晚或太突然,要么因为这些条件不够明确。在黎考勒佐斯诉希腊案(*Lykourezos v. Greece*)中,使得职业活动与议员职责相冲突的法律突然被适用于现存立法机关,即使在被选举前议员并没有被告知这些冲突,他们也不得不放弃自己的议会席位。并没有紧迫的必要性可以使得这种限制措施的突然适用正当化。本法院首次适用合法性期待原则,判决该措施违反第一议定书第3条。在艾克格拉斯诺斯特诉保加利亚案(*Ekoglasnost v. Bulgaria*)中,本法院再次适用了该原则。保加利亚在选举立法中新设立的3个条件本身没有引起任何问题,但是因为设立得太晚,申诉人只有1个月时间来遵守。本法院认为,施加于政治团体的竞选条件属于基本选举规则的一部分,因此,这些条件应该和选举机制中的其他基本因素具有同样的稳定性。本法院还认为,关于剥夺曾任神职人员的候选人资格的条款过于模糊,因而是无法预见的。因此,在适用这些限制措施时,选举机构被赋予了过大的自由裁量权和过多的任意空间(*Seyidzade v. Azerbaijan*)。

五、"从竞选活动……"

72. 为了维护第一议定书第3条所保障的权利的有效性,对于它们的保护不能限定于候选资格本身,竞选活动同样也应受到该条款的调整。

73. 早在关于公约第 10 条的诸多案例中,本法院就已经强调了自由选举权和表达自由之间的密切关系。本法院认为这些权利,特别是政治辩论自由,共同组成了民主体制的基石。这两种权利相互关联、相辅相成:例如,表达自由是"确保选民在选举立法机关成员时意愿得以自由表达"的必要"条件"之一。因此,在选举前的阶段,各种观点和信息自由流通显得尤为重要(Bowman v. the United Kingdom, § 42)。

74. 因为这些权利相互依存,所以大量关于竞选活动的案例都根据公约第 10 条进行审查。例如,挪威某一电视频道播放了一个小政党的广告,违反了该国禁止政党在电视上播放广告的法律规定,因而被处以罚款,本法院判处该法律违反了第 10 条(TV Vest AS and Rogaland Pensjonistparti v. Norway)。在另一个案例中,乌克兰某一女政客因为在电视直播中把竞选对手描述为小偷而遭到警告,本法院同样判决其违反公约第 10 条。法院判决赋予了另一(女性)候选人应诉的权利(Vitrenko and Others v. Ukraine)。

75. 关于预选活动期间播放时间的分配可能引发与第一议定书第 3 条相关的问题。在某一关于赋予各候选人平等的播放时间的案例中,本法院认为,第一议定书第 3 条高度重视公民在行使选举权时一律得到平等对待的原则,但是就其本身而言,并没有保证政党在预选活动期间获得广播或电视播放时间的任何权利。不过,在某些例外的情况下,问题的确会产生。例如,在竞选过程中,某一政党被拒绝给予广播宣传而其他政党却获得了一定的播放时间[Partija "Jaunie Demokrāti" and Partija "Mūsu Zeme" v. Latvia(dec.)]。

76. 在俄罗斯共产党等诉俄罗斯案(Communist Party of Russia and Others v. Russia)中,本法院就政府根据第一议定书第 3 条是否应当负有积极义务来保证正规媒体的报道是客观的并且不违背"自由选举"的精神(即使没有直接的证据证明存在故意操纵)这一问题做出处理。本法院认为,现存的选举救济机制足以满足国家的程序性积极义务。关于国家的实体性义务以及关于国家应该确保视听媒体的中立性的主张,本法院认为政府已经采取了实质性措施保证竞争党派和竞争候选人在电视上具有一定的曝光度,也保证了报纸社论的独立性和媒体的中立性。这些措施可能无法确保实质平等,但不能因此认为政府在该领域没有尽到积极义务,从而违反了第一议定书第 3 条的规定。

77. 最后,在奥兰诉土耳其案中,作为独立候选人的申诉人因为无法像政党候选人一样从土耳其广播电视在全国范围内的竞选宣传受益而提出申诉。本法院认为,不同于政党候选人,申诉人作为独立的候选人只能在其代表选区进行选举。此外,申诉人没有被阻止使用其他任何可能的竞选方式,所有的无党派独立候选人在相关时期都能够获得这一保证。因此本法院判决没有违反第一议定书第3条。

六、"……到行使职权"

78. 从1984年起,委员会一直声明个人拥有被选举权还不够,他还必须在被人民选中时有权拥有席位、成为其中的一名成员,否则将导致被选举权失去意义(*M. v. the United Kingdom*, Commission decision)。但是,在同一案例中,委员会认为如果胜选议员无法拥有席位是因为其已经是国外立法机关成员,则不违反第一议定书第3条。

79. 在3起诉土耳其的案例中,本法院就议员所属政党被解散的结果进行了审查。在萨达克等人诉土耳其案[*Sadak and Others v. Turkey* (no. 2)]中,某一政党因破坏领土完整和国家统一而被解散,该政党议员自动丧失议会席位。本法院认为对反对派议员表达自由的干预需要经过特别严格的审查。申诉人议会席位的丧失是自动的,而且与他们以个人名义从事的政治活动无关。因此,土耳其当局采取的是极端严厉的措施,对于所提及的任何合法性目的而言都是不合比例的。

80. 在卡瓦克次诉土耳其案(*Kavakçl v. Turkey*)中,申诉人因其所属政党最终解散而被暂时限制政治权利。本法院认为采取该措施是为了维持土耳其政体的长期特色,而且,考虑到该原则对于土耳其民主政体的重要性,本法院认为该限制措施是出于防止秩序混乱以及保护其他人权利和自由的合法性目的。但是,关于制裁的合比例性问题,土耳其现行宪法在关于政党解散的问题上规定涵盖范围相当广泛。党员的一切行动和言论都可归结于政党,土耳其当局会将政党视为反宪法活动的中心并决定将其解散。在这些遭受质疑的活动中,不会对各成员的参与程度进行区分。另外,某些与申诉人处境相似的政党成员,特别是总统和副总统,则没有受到相似的处罚。因此,本法院认为该制裁不合比例,违反了第一议定书第3条的规定。

81. 另一个诉土耳其的案例是关于一名来自同一政党的议员也丧失了议会席位的情况,本法院再次判决土耳其当局违反第一议定书第3条,但是同时指出,宪法修正案的通过强化了议员身份,同时也可能使得基于此原因剥夺议员席位的做法越来越少(*Sobacı v. Turkey*)。

82. 在黎考勒佐斯诉希腊案(*Paunović and Milivojević v. Serbia*)中,本法院发现关于现任议员职业与议员身份不相符的新规定在选举前并没有予以通告,该新规定让申诉人和投票给他的选民都大为惊讶。本法院认为，国内法官在根据希腊2003年开始生效的新的宪法条款对申诉人的选举进行审查时，没有考虑到他在此之前的选举活动是完全合法的，无视合法性期待原则，剥夺了申诉人的代表席位，也使得那些自由民主地选举其作为4年代表的选民失去了其代表候选人。同样地，在帕斯卡里迪斯、库特梅里迪斯和扎哈拉其斯诉希腊案（*Paschalidis, Koutmeridis and Zaharakis v. Greece*）中，在选举之后，采用了一种从未有过且无法预见的方式计算当选票额，导致一些当选议员被排除资格，本法院认为，这一做法违反了第一议定书第3条。

83. 在波诺维克和米力沃杰维克诉塞尔维亚案（*Paunović and Milivojević v. Serbia*）中，某些政党要求党内议员成员在就职之前签署没有标明日期的辞职信，如此一来这些政党就可以违背这些成员的意愿随时解雇他们，本法院在此案中对该做法做出了判决。本法院认为，即使辞职信是由政党提出的，但仍然只有议会有权剥夺议员席位。因此，最终应当是塞尔维亚当局通过接受辞职信的方式剥夺议员的席位。因此，根据属人原则，本法院可以受理一名失去议席的议员提出的申诉。本法院认为，这一遭受争议的做法与塞尔维亚国内法不符，该法规定议员辞职需要本人提交，因此该做法违反了第一议定书第3条。欧克托诉意大利案［*Occhetto v. Italy*（dec）］是关于放弃欧洲议会席位的问题。因为和同一政治运动的共同发起人达成协议，申诉人签署了放弃席位的文件，但是事后反悔。然而，仅次于申诉人的候选人早已占据了上述议会席位。本法院认为，选举之后，候选人有权在立法机关占据席位，但是没有这样做的义务。任何候选人都可以出于政治或者个人原因宣布放弃就任其当选的职位，就此进行登记的决定也不能被视为与普选原则相悖。本法院补充道，拒绝接受申诉人弃权的撤销是出于合法性目的，即维护选举程序法律的确定性以及保障他人权利，特别是在申诉人弃权之后当选该席位的候选人的权利。申诉人的意愿是以明确的书面方式表达的，而且他当初也表明其放弃是最终的决定。最后，与欧盟法相符合的意大利国内程序允许申诉人提交他认为有用的辩护论据。因此，本法院认为没有违反第一议定书第3条。

第四节 选举争议

84. 有很多案例是与选举争议有关，但这个问题不能根据公约第6条进行审查，因为本法院认为该条无法在此进行适用。本法院认为，申诉人在法国国民议会的被选举权以及拥有议席的权利是一项政治权利,而非第6条第1款规定的"民事"权利,因此,有关该项权利行使的争议不属于第一议定书第3条所讨论的范围(Pierre-Bloch v. France,§50)。第6条涉及的刑事部分也不能视为因违反选举规则而施加的惩罚(Pierre-Bloch v. France,§61)。在格拉圭恩·科尔贺德·帕特咖玛沃拉坎·阿库姆布诉亚美尼亚案(Geraguyn Khorhurd Patgamavorakan Akumb v. Armenia)中,提出申诉的非政府组织是议会选举中的观察评论者,随后因为该组织没有传达一些文件而发生了争议。本法院认为,上述程序结果对该非政府组织的权利不具有决定性影响,因此不属于公约第6条第1款的规制范围之内。

85. 但是在某些时候,本法院会根据公约第13条对选举过程中有效救济的缺失进行审查。本法院指出,在选举事项中,只有那些能够确保民主程序正常运作的救济才可能被视为有效(Petkov and Others v. Bulgaria)。在佩特科夫等人诉保加利亚案(Petkov and Others v. Bulgaria)中,在选举日前10天时,申诉人被从候选人名单中删去,做出该决定所依据的法律也是不到3个月前才通过的。这些除名决定随后被宣布无效,但是由于选举当局并没有恢复申诉人的候选人身份,他们因此无法竞选。保加利亚的选举救济方式只有经济赔偿,本法院认为,根据公约第13条,该救济不能被视为有效。在格洛萨鲁诉罗马尼亚案(Grosaru v. Romania)中,本法院认为,在议会选举中败选的申诉人无法就受到质疑的选举立法的解释获得司法审查,因此认为违反了公约第13条和第一议定书第3条。

86. 即使存在救济,根据第一议定书第3条,本法院仍然可能发现很多不足。当这些不足之处挑战了选举过程的完整性时,就可能构成对该条款的违反。关于剥夺选举权或者选举结果争议的决策过程必须得到最低限度的保障以防止专断,尤其是,上述决定必须由能够保证最低程度公正的机关做出。同样地,相关机关享有的自由裁量权不能过大:国内法规定必须对其进行足够精确的限制。最后,决策程序必须足以保证得出一个公平、客观和足够合理的决定,并且足以防止相关当局权力的滥用(Podkolzina v. Latvia,§35;Kovatch v. Ukraine,§54-55;Kerimova v. Azerbaijan,§§44-45;Riza and Others v. Bulgaria,§144)。但是,本法院在对此进行审查时,主要是判断国内机关做出的决定是否专断或者明显不合理(Riza and Others v. Bulgaria,§144;Kerimli and Alibeyli v. Azerbaijan,§§38-42)。

87. 使选举无效的决定必须反映真正的无法与民意相连的事实。在克利莫娃诉阿塞拜疆案(*Kerimova v. Azerbaijan*)中，本法院发现两名选举官员实施的篡改行为没有改变最终的选举结果，申诉人赢得了选举。不过，阿塞拜疆当局没有考虑篡改行为造成的影响的有限性，而宣布该违反国内选举法的选举结果无效。如此一来，阿塞拜疆当局实际上相当于帮助了那两个官员妨碍选举。这一决定剥夺了申诉人被选入议会的权利，任意地侵犯了她的选举权。而且阿塞拜疆当局对选举程序的完整性和有效性缺乏关注，这与自由选举权的精神不符。国内法院的角色不是改变民意。因此，在两个案例中[*I. Z. v. Greece*, Commission decision; *Babenko v. Ukraine*（dec.）]，公约机构对声称选举程序不公平的败选候选人提出的申诉进行审查，但是因为该程序对选举结果没有造成实质性破坏，所以他们的申诉被驳回。在利扎等人诉保加利亚案(*Riza and Others v. Bulgaria*)中，保加利亚设立于境外的23个投票站的投票结果因所谓的不规范被宣布无效，并且因此剥夺了一名议员的席位。本法院同时审查了对101名选民投票权和该名议员的被选举权的干预情形以及他所代表的政党。本法院发现，关于宣布许多投票站选举无效的理由纯粹是官方的。此外，保加利亚法院做出选举无效的判决所依据的客观情况在国内法中没有足够明确和可预见的规定，并且这些客观情况的出现并不代表他们可以改变选民的选择或者歪曲选举结果。而且，选举法没有规定在这些被宣布结果无效的选举站重新选举的可能性——与《威尼斯委员会选举事务良好实践守则》（Venice Commission's Code of Good Practice in Electoral Matters）相悖——其本可以通过取消选举结果来实现合法性目的，也就是说维持选举过程的合法性，包括选民的选举权和候选人入选议会的权利。因此，本法院认为此处违反了第一议定书第3条。使选举无效的决定必须建立在真正的无法与民意相连的事实基础之上。

88. 但是，缔约国必须确保个人提出的关于选举不规范的、存在争议的申诉得以有效解决，并且确保国内就此做出的判决足够合理。主要得益于《威尼斯委员会选举事务良好实践守则》，本法院才得以发现缔约国当局为了避免就选举事项受到实质性审查而提供了过于形式主义的理由。在确定这些不规范情况对整个选举结果的影响之前，候选人得票的悬殊并不影响对这些选举不规范的情况进行独立审查(*Namat Aliyev v. Azerbaijan*)。

援引案例一览

本指南援引的判例法涉及欧洲人权法院的判决或裁定以及欧洲人权委员会的决定或报告。

除非另行指明,所有参考皆是本法院审判庭依法做出的判决。缩写"(dec.)"是指该处援引为本法院裁定,"[GC]"是指该案件由大审判庭审判。

本指南电子版中援引案例的超链接直接跳转 HUDOC 数据库(http://hudoc.echr.coe.int)。该数据库提供本法院(包括大审判庭、审判庭和委员会的判决、裁定和相关案例、咨询意见以及案例法信息注解中的法律总结)、委员会(决定和报告)和部长委员会(决议)的判例法。

本法院以英语和/或法语这两种官方语言发布判决和裁定。HUDOC 也包含许多重要案例的近 30 种非官方言语的翻译,以及由第三方制作的大约 100 个在线案例汇总的链接。

(注:为了避免重复,本章所附的相关案例索引没有在中文部分进行翻译,读者可在对应的英文部分阅读。)

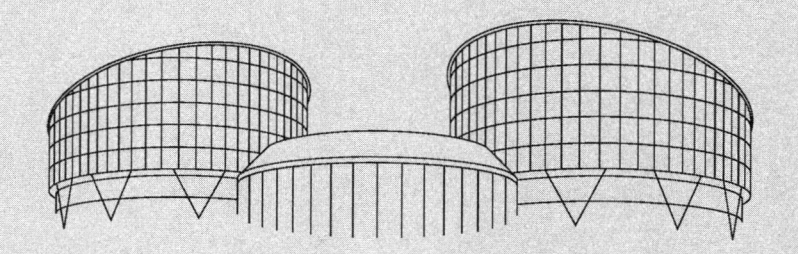

EUROPEAN COURT OF HUMAN RIGHTS
COUR EUROPÉENNE DES DROITS DE L'HOMME

Chapter IX   Guide on Article 3 of Protocol No.1 to the European Convention on Human Rights Right to Free Elections

COUNCIL OF EUROPE
CONSEIL DE L'EUROPE

Publishers or organisations wishing to reproduce this report (or a translation thereof) in print or online are asked to contact publishing@echr.coe.int for further instructions.

This Guide has been prepared by the Case-Law Information and Publications Division, within the Directorate of the Jurisconsult, and does not bind the Court. The text was finalised on 31 May 2016; it may be subject to editorial revision.

The document is available for downloading at ⟨www.echr.coe.int⟩ (Case-Law-Case-Law Analysis-Case-Law Guides).

For publication updates please follow the Court's Twitter account at ⟨https:/twitter.com/echrpublication⟩.

©Council of Europe/European Court of Human Rights, 2016

Note to readers

This Guide is part of the series of Guides on the Convention published by the European Court of Human Rights (hereafter "the Court", "the European Court" or "the Strasbourg Court") to inform legal practitioners about the fundamental judgments delivered by the Strasbourg Court. This particular Guide analyses and sums up the case-law on Article 3 of Protocol No. 1 to the European Convention on Human Rights (hereafter "the Convention" or "the European Convention") until 31 May 2016. Readers will find the key principles in this area and the relevant precedents.

The case-law cited has been selected among the leading, major, and/or recent judgments and decisions. *

The Court's judgments serve not only to decide those cases brought before the Court but, more generally, to elucidate, safeguard and develop the rules instituted by the Convention, thereby contributing to the observance by the States of the engagements undertaken by them as Contracting Parties (*Ireland v. the United Kingdom*, 18 January 1978, § 154, Series A no. 25.). The mission of the system set up by the Convention is thus to determine, in the general interest, issues of public policy, thereby raising the standards of protection of human rights and extending human rights jurisprudence throughout the community of the Convention States (*Konstantin Markin v. Russia* [GC], 30078/06, § 89, ECHR 2012).

---

* The case-law cited may be in either or both of the official languages (English and French) of the Court and the European Commission of Human Rights. Unless otherwise indicated, all references are to a judgment on the merits delivered by a Chamber of the Court. The abbreviation "(dec.)" indicates that the citation is of a decision of the Court and "[GC]" that the case was heard by the Grand Chamber.

I. General principles

> Article 3 of Protocol No. 1 – Right to free elections
>
> "The High Contracting Parties undertake to hold free elections at reasonable intervals by secret ballot, under conditions which will ensure the free expression of the opinion of the people in the choice of the legislature."

A. Meaning and scope

1. "According to the Preamble to the Convention, fundamental human rights and freedoms are best maintained by 'an effective political democracy'. Since it enshrines a characteristic principle of democracy, Article 3 of Protocol No. 1 is accordingly of prime importance in the Convention system" (*Mathieu-Mohin and Clerfayt v. Belgium*, § 47).

2. Article 3 of Protocol No. 1 concerns only the choice of the legislature. This expression is not, however, confined to the national parliament. The constitutional structure of the State in question has to be examined (*Timke v. Germany*, Commission decision). Generally speaking, the scope of Article 3 of Protocol No. 1 does not cover local elections, whether municipal (*Xuereb v. Malta*; *Salleras Llinares v. Spain*) or regional (*Malarde v. France*). The Court has found that the power to make regulations and by-laws, which is conferred on the local authorities in many countries, is to be distinguished from legislative power, which is referred to in Article 3 of Protocol No. 1, even though legislative power may not be restricted to the national parliament alone [*Mółka v. Poland* (dec.)].

As regards presidential elections, the Court has taken the view that the powers of the Head of State cannot as such be construed as a form of "legislature" within the meaning of Article 3 of Protocol No. 1. It does not exclude, however, the possibility of applying Article 3 of Protocol No. 1 to presidential elections. Should it be established that the office of the Head of State in question had been given the power to initiate and adopt legislation or enjoyed wide powers to control the passage of legislation or the power to censure the principal legislation-setting authorities, then it could arguably be considered to be a "legislature" within the meaning of Article 3 of Protocol No 1 [*Boškoski v. the former Yugoslav Republic of Macedonia* (dec); *Brito Da Silva Guerra and Sousa Magno v. Portugal* (dec.)]. This possibility has never be used, however, and has not even been mentioned in subsequent cases (*Paksas v. Lithuania* [GC]; *Anchugov and Gladkov v. Russia*, §§ 55 –56).

3. The Court has, on a number of occasions, taken the view that the European Parliament forms part of the "legislature" within the meaning of Article 3 of Protocol No. 1 [*Matthews v. the United Kingdom* [GC], §§ 45 – 54; *Occhetto v. Italy* (dec.), § 42].

4. As to the actual features of elections, the text of Article 3 of Protocol No. 1 provides only that they should be free and by secret ballot, as the Commission and then the Court have constantly reiterated (*X. v. the United Kingdom*, Commission decision of 6 October 1976). The provision further makes it clear that elections must be held at reasonable intervals. The States have a broad margin of appreciation in such matters. The case-law nevertheless provides the following guidelines:

"The Commission finds that the question whether elections are held at reasonable intervals must be determined by reference to the purpose of parliamentary elections. That purpose is to ensure that fundamental changes in prevailing public opinion are reflected in the opinions of the representatives of the people. Parliament must in principle be in a position to develop and execute its legislative intentions-including longer term legislative plans. Too short an interval between elections may impede political planning for the implementation of the will of the electorate; too long an interval can lead to the petrification of political groupings in Parliament which may no longer bear any resemblance to the prevailing will of the electorate." (*Timke v. Germany*, Commission decision)

5. The Court's case-law has continued to develop the requirement of universal suffrage, which is now the benchmark principle (*X. v. Germany*, Commission decision; *Hirst v. the*

United Kingdom (no. 2) [GC], §§ 59 and 62; *Mathieu-Mohin and Clerfayt v. Belgium*, § 51). However, while Article 3 of Protocol No. 1 includes the principle of equality of treatment of all citizens in the exercise of their right to vote, it does not follow, however, that all votes must necessarily carry equal weight as regards the outcome of the election. Thus no electoral system can eliminate "wasted votes" [ibid., § 54; *Partija "Jaunie Demokrāti" and Partija "Mūsu Zeme" v. Latvia* (dec.)].

6. However, the vote of each elector must have the possibility of affecting the composition of the legislature, otherwise the right to vote, the electoral process and, ultimately, the democratic order itself, would be devoid of substance (*Riza and Others v. Bulgaria*, § 148). States thus enjoy a broad margin of appreciation in the organisation of the ballot. An electoral boundary review giving rise to constituencies of unequal population does not breach Article 3 of Protocol No. 1 provided that the free will of the people is accurately reflected [*Bompard v. France* (dec.)]. Lastly, the choice of electoral system by which the free expression of the opinion of the people in the choice of the legislature is ensured-whether it be based on proportional representation, the "first-past-the-post" system or some other arrangement-is a matter in which the State enjoys a wide margin of appreciation (*Matthews v. the United Kingdom* [GC], § 64).

B. Principles of interpretation

7. Article 3 of Protocol No. 1 differs from the other substantive provisions of the Convention and the Protocols as it is phrased in terms of the obligation of the High Contracting Party to hold elections which ensure the free expression of the opinion of the people rather than in terms of a particular right or freedom. However, having regard to the preparatory work in respect of Article 3 of Protocol No. 1 and the interpretation of the provision in the context of the Convention as a whole, the Court has established that this provision also implies individual rights, comprising the right to vote (the "active" aspect) and to stand for election (the "passive" aspect) (*Mathieu-Mohin and Clerfayt v. Belgium*, §§ 48 – 51; *Ždanoka v. Latvia* [GC], § 102).

8. The rights in question are not absolute. There is room for "implied limitations",

and the Contracting States must be given a wide margin of appreciation in this sphere. The concept of "implied limitations" under Article 3 of Protocol No. 1 is of major importance for the determination of the relevance of the aims pursued by the restrictions on the rights guaranteed by this provision. Given that Article 3 is not limited by a specific list of "legitimate aims" such as those enumerated in Articles 8 to 11, the Contracting States are therefore free to rely on an aim not contained in that list to justify a restriction, provided that the compatibility of that aim with the principle of the rule of law and the general objectives of the Convention is proved in the particular circumstances of a given case.

9. The concept of "implied limitations" also means that the Court does not apply the traditional tests of "necessity" or "pressing social need" which are used in the context of Articles 8 to 11. In examining compliance with Article 3 of Protocol No. 1, the Court has focused mainly on two criteria: whether there has been arbitrariness or a lack of proportionality, and whether the restriction has interfered with the free expression of the opinion of the people. In addition, it underlines the need to assess any electoral legislation in the light of the political evolution of the country concerned, which means that unacceptable features in one system may be justified in another (*Mathieu-Mohin and Clerfayt v. Belgium*, § 52; *Ždanoka v. Latvia* [GC], §§ 103–104 and 115).

10. Stricter requirements may be imposed on eligibility to stand for election to Parliament (the "passive" aspect) than is the case for eligibility to vote (the "active" aspect). In fact, while the test relating to the "active" aspect of Article 3 of Protocol No. 1 has usually included a wider assessment of the proportionality of the statutory provisions disqualifying a person or a group of persons from the right to vote, the Court's test in relation to the "passive" aspect has been limited largely to verification of the absence of arbitrariness in the domestic procedures leading to disqualification of an individual from standing as a candidate (ibid., § 115; *Melnitchenko v. Ukraine*, § 57).

11. As to the question of who is entitled to rely on an alleged violation of the "passive" aspect of the right, the Court has admitted that, where electoral law or national authorities restrict the right of candidates individually to stand for election on a party's list, the party concerned may, in that capacity, claim to be a victim of such a violation

independently of its candidates (*Georgian Labour Party v. Georgia*, §§ 72 – 74; *Riza and Others v. Bulgaria*, § 142).

12. Lastly, when it subjects a country's electoral system to its examination-whether it concerns the active or the passive aspect-, the Court takes account of the diversity of the States' historical contexts. Those different contexts may thus lead the Court to accepting divergences in electoral rules from one country to another but also to explaining any evolution in the level of requirement depending on the period under consideration.

II. Active aspect: the right to vote

13. The "active" aspect is subject to limitations. Here, as in any other area under Article 3 of Protocol No. 1, the member States enjoy a certain margin of appreciation which varies depending on the context. It is, for example, possible to fix a minimum age to ensure that individuals taking part in the electoral process are sufficiently mature (*Hirst v. the United Kingdom* (no. 2) [GC], § 62).

14. However, the supervision exercised consists in a relatively comprehensive review of proportionality. The margin of appreciation afforded to States cannot have the effect of prohibiting certain individuals or groups from taking part in the political life of the country, especially through the appointment of members of the legislature (*Aziz v. Cyprus*, § 28; *Tănase v. Moldova* [GC], § 158). In the case of *Aziz v. Cyprus*, the Court ruled on the inability for members of the Turkish-Cypriot community to vote in legislative elections. It took the view that, on account of the abnormal situation existing in Cyprus since 1963 and the legislative vacuum, the applicant, as a member of the Turkish-Cypriot community living in the Republic of Cyprus, was completely deprived of any opportunity to express his opinion in the choice of the members of the House of Representatives. The very essence of the applicant's right to vote was thus impaired. The Court also found a clear inequality of treatment in the enjoyment of the right in question, between the members of the Turkish-Cypriot community and those of the Greek-Cypriot community. There had accordingly

been a violation of Article 14 of the Convention in conjunction with Article 3 of Protocol No. 1.

15. It should also be noted that complaints concerning elections not falling under Article 3 of Protocol No. 1 may, if appropriate, be raised under other Articles of the Convention. Thus, in the case of *Mółka v. Poland*, the applicant was unable to vote in elections to municipal councils, district councils and regional assemblies. The polling station was not accessible to individuals in wheelchairs and it was not permitted to take ballot papers outside the premises. The Court took the view that it could not be excluded that the authorities' failure to provide appropriate access to the polling station for the applicant, who wished to lead an active life, might have aroused feelings of humiliation and distress capable of impinging on his personal autonomy, and thereby on the quality of his private life. The Court thus accepted the idea that, in such circumstances, Article 8 was engaged.

A. Loss of civil rights

16. When an individual or group has been deprived of the right to vote, the Court is particularly attentive. Deprivation of the right to vote must then pursue a legitimate aim but also pass a more stringent proportionality test. The Court has thus had occasion to examine a number of cases in which the deprivation of voting rights was part of a criminal investigation. The case of *Labita v. Italy* [GC] concerned the automatic temporary loss of civil rights imposed on an individual suspected of belonging to the mafia. The Court agreed that the measure pursued a legitimate aim. However, taking into account the fact that the measure had only been applied after the applicant's acquittal, it found that it had been disproportionate as there was no actual basis on which to suspect him of belonging to the mafia. In the case of *Vito Sante Santoro v. Italy*, the applicant had also been deprived of his right to vote for a limited period on account of his placement under police surveillance. However, more than nine months had passed between the order placing him under surveillance and the deletion of his name from the electoral roll. As a result, the applicant had been prevented from voting in two elections, which would not have been the case if the measure had been applied immediately. The Government had not provided any reason to

justify that time lapse. The Court thus found that there had been a violation of Article 3 of Protocol No. 1.

17. The question of the loss of civil rights does not only arise in a criminal context. The case of *Albanese v. Italy* concerned the suspension of the applicant's electoral rights for the duration of bankruptcy proceedings against him. The Court pointed out that bankruptcy proceedings came within the ambit of civil rather than criminal law and therefore did not imply any deceit or fraud on the part of the bankrupt person. The aim of the restrictions on the person's electoral rights was therefore essentially punitive. The measure thus served no purpose other than to belittle persons who had been declared bankrupt, reprimanding them simply for having been declared insolvent irrespective of whether they had committed an offence. It did not therefore pursue a legitimate aim for the purposes of Article 3 of Protocol No. 1.

18. The Court also examined the loss of voting rights on account of placement under partial guardianship (*Alajos Kiss v. Hungary*). It took the view that such a measure could pursue a legitimate aim, namely to ensure that only citizens capable of assessing the consequences of their decisions and making conscious and judicious decisions should participate in public affairs. However, the voting ban in question had been imposed as an automatic, blanket restriction, regardless of the protected person's actual faculties and without any distinction being made between full and partial guardianship. The Court further considered that the treatment as a single class of those with intellectual or mental disabilities was a questionable classification, and the curtailment of their rights must be subject to strict scrutiny. It therefore concluded that an indiscriminate removal of voting rights, without an individualised judicial evaluation, could not be considered proportionate to the aim pursued.

B. Specific case of prisoners

19. Prisoners in general continue to enjoy all the fundamental rights and freedoms secured by the Convention, except for the right to liberty where lawful detention falls expressly within the scope of Article 5 of the Convention (*Hirst v. the United Kingdom* (no. 2) [GC], § 69). The rights guaranteed by Article 3 of Protocol No. 1 are no

exception. There is no question, therefore, that a prisoner should forfeit his rights under the Convention merely because of his status as a person detained following conviction. That does not preclude the taking of steps to protect society against activities intended to destroy the Convention rights and freedoms.

20. Article 3 of Protocol No. 1 does not therefore exclude that restrictions on electoral rights could be imposed on an individual who has, for example, seriously abused a public position or whose conduct threatens to undermine the rule of law or democratic foundations. The severe measure of disenfranchisement must not, however, be resorted to lightly and the principle of proportionality requires a discernible and sufficient link between the sanction and the conduct and circumstances of the individual concerned (ibid., § 71).

21. To deprive a prisoner of his political rights may thus meet the legitimate aims of preventing crime and enhancing civic responsibility, together with respect for the rule of law and ensuring the proper functioning and preservation of the democratic regime. However, such a measure cannot be imposed automatically or it would not meet the proportionality requirement.

22. The States may decide either to leave it to the courts to determine the proportionality of a measure restricting convicted prisoners' voting rights, or to incorporate provisions into their laws defining the circumstances in which such a measure should be applied. In this latter case, it will be for the legislature itself to balance the competing interests in order to avoid any general, automatic and indiscriminate restriction. Accordingly, the application of a voting ban in the absence of a specific judicial decision will not in itself entail a violation of Article 3 of Protocol No. 1 (*Scoppola v. Italy* (no. 3) [GC], § 102).

23. In the case of *Hirst v. the United Kingdom* (no. 2) [GC], the Court found a violation of Article 3 of Protocol No. 1 because the voting ban in question had been a blanket ban applied automatically to anyone serving a custodial sentence. It affected 48,000 prisoners, which was a high number, and concerned all sorts of prison sentences, ranging from one day to life, and for various types of offences from the most minor to the most serious. In addition, there was no direct link between the offence committed by an

individual and the withdrawal of his voting rights. The Court also found a violation of Article 3 of Protocol No. 1 in the case of *Söyler v. Turkey*, where restrictions imposed on the voting rights of convicted persons had an even broader scope and impact because they even applied to those who were not, or no longer, serving time in prison. In the case of *Frodl v. Austria*, the deprivation of voting rights did not systematically affect all prisoners, but only those who had been sentenced to prison for more than a year for an offence committed voluntarily. Nevertheless, there was no link between the automatic imposition of the measure and the conduct of the individual or the circumstances of the case. The Court thus found that the voting ban was not proportionate to the aims pursued.

24. In the case of *Scoppola v. Italy* (no. 3) [GC], however, the Court examined a voting ban which applied only to persons convicted of certain well-determined offences or to a custodial sentence exceeding a statutory threshold. The legislature had been careful to adjust the duration of this measure according to the specific features of each case. It had also adjusted the duration of the ban depending on the sentence imposed and therefore, indirectly, on the gravity of the sentence. Many of the convicted prisoners had retained the possibility of voting in legislative elections. In addition, this system had been complemented by the possibility for convicts affected by a permanent ban to recover their voting rights. The Italian system was not therefore marked by excessive rigidity. The Court thus held that there had been no violation of Article 3 of Protocol No. 1.

25. It must nevertheless be noted that for a violation of Article 3 of Protocol No. 1 to be found, prisoners must show that they have actually been prevented from voting. It is not sufficient for them to rely on their state of detention alone, because events such as early release or admission to a psychiatric institution, etc., may take place before the date of the elections in question. Such applications are thus declared inadmissible as manifestly ill-founded [*Dunn and Others v. the United Kingdom* (dec.)].

26. Moreover, the Court has never found it appropriate to indicate to States the necessary measures to be taken in order to put an end to violations caused by a prisoner voting ban. At best it has set out a timetable (*Greens and M. T. v. the United Kingdom*, § 120). However, States cannot rely on the complexity of making changes to the law

which led to the violation. In the case of *Anchugov and Gladkov v. Russia*, the Court took note of the argument that the prohibition had been imposed by a provision of the Constitution which could not be amended by Parliament and could only be revised by adopting a new Constitution, thus implying a particularly complex procedure. However, it pointed out that it was essentially for the authorities to choose, under the supervision of the Committee of Ministers, the means to be used to bring the legislation into conformity with the Convention. It is open to governments to explore all possible avenues to ensure compliance with Article 3 of Protocol No. 1, including by a form of political process or by interpreting the Constitution in conformity with the Convention (ibid., § 111).

C. Residence, condition of access to voting rights

1. Right of citizens residing abroad to vote

27. In a series of cases beginning in 1961, the Commission declared inadmissible, as manifestly ill-founded, complaints about restrictions on voting rights based on a residence criterion [see the Commission decisions: *X. and Others v. Belgium*; *X. v. the United Kingdom* (11 December 1976); *X. v. the United Kingdom* (28 February 1979); *X. v. the United Kingdom* (13 May 1982); *Polacco and Garofalo v. Italy*; *Luksch v. Germany*].

28. The Court subsequently reiterated the compatibility with Article 3 of Protocol No. 1 of the residence criterion. Such a restriction can be justified for a number of reasons: first, the presumption that non-resident citizens are less directly or less continuously concerned by their country's day-to-day problems and have less knowledge of them; second, the fact that candidates standing for election to parliament cannot so easily present the election issues to citizens living abroad, who will also have less influence on the selection of candidates or on the drafting of their manifestos; third, the close connection between the right to vote in parliamentary elections and the fact of being directly affected by the acts of the political bodies thus elected; and, fourth, the legitimate concern the legislature may have to limit the influence of citizens living abroad in elections concerning issues which, while fundamental, primarily affect those living in the country.

29. Even if the person concerned has not severed all ties with his or her country of

origin and some of the above-mentioned factors perhaps do not apply to that person, the law cannot always take account of every individual case but must lay down a general rule [*Hilbe v. Liechtenstein* (dec.); *Doyle v. the United Kingdom* (dec.); *Shindler v. the United Kingdom*, § 105].

30. The Court thus considered ill-founded the applications of nationals who had left their country of origin [*Hilbe v. Liechtenstein* (dec.)]. In two cases it particularly took account of the fact that non-residents could vote in national elections for the first fifteen years following their emigration and that their right was, in any event, restored if and when they returned to live in their country of origin, thus finding that the measure was not disproportionate [*Doyle v. the United Kingdom* (dec.); *Shindler v. the United Kingdom*, § 108]. In the last-mentioned case, the Court also found it pertinent that Parliament had sought, more than once, to weigh up the competing interests, and had debated in detail the question of the voting rights of non-residents; the evolution of opinions in Parliament were reflected in the amendments to the cut-off period since non-resident citizens had first been allowed to vote.

31. In the case of *Shindler v. the United Kingdom* the Court noted that there was a growing awareness at European level of the problems posed by migration in terms of political participation in the countries of origin and residence. However, none of the material examined formed a basis for concluding that, as the law currently stood, States were under an obligation to grant non-residents unrestricted access to the franchise. While there was a clear trend, in the law and practice of the member States, to allow non-residents to vote, and a significant majority of States were in favour of an unrestricted right of access, this was not sufficient to establish the existence of any common approach or consensus in favour of unrestricted voting rights for non-residents. The Court thus concluded that, although the matter might need to be kept under review, the margin of appreciation enjoyed by the State in this area remained a wide one (ibid., §§ 109–115).

2. Particular case of certain territories

32. In the case of *Py v. France* the Court referred back to the idea of a sufficiently

strong tie between the potential voter and the territory concerned. A French national from mainland France was refused the right to vote in elections to the Congress of New Caledonia on the ground that he could not prove at least 10 years of residence in the territory. The Court took the view that cut-off points as to length of residence addressed the concern that ballots should reflect the will of the population "concerned" and that their results should not be affected by mass voting by recent arrivals in the territory who did not have strong ties with it. Furthermore, the restriction on the right to vote was the direct and necessary consequence of establishing New Caledonian citizenship. The applicant was not affected by the acts of political institutions in New Caledonia to the same extent as resident citizens. Consequently, the residence condition was justified and pursued a legitimate aim. The history and status of New Caledonia-a transitional phase prior to the acquisition of full sovereignty and part of a process of self-determination-could be regarded as constituting "local requirements" warranting a restriction as important as the ten-year residence requirement, a condition which had also been instrumental in alleviating the bloody conflict.

33. The case of *Sevinger v. the Netherlands* concerned the inability of the residents of the island of Aruba, which enjoyed a certain autonomy, to vote in elections to the Dutch Parliament. They were able, however, to vote in elections to the Parliament of Aruba, which was entitled to send special delegates to the Dutch Parliament. The Court took the view that Dutch nationals residing in Aruba were thus able to influence decisions taken by the Lower House of the Dutch Parliament and that they were not affected by the acts of that Parliament to the same extent as Dutch nationals residing in the Netherlands. It also rejected the complaint under Article 14 taken together with Article 3 of Protocol No. 1. It found that it was only those Dutch nationals residing in Aruba who were entitled to vote for members of the Parliament of Aruba and that therefore their situation was not relevantly similar to that of other Dutch nationals.

34. As regards the geographical and territorial organisation of the ballot within the relevant State, the Court acknowledged that the obligation to seek the deletion of one's name from one electoral roll and its addition to another pursued legitimate aims: to ensure

the compilation of electoral rolls in satisfactory conditions of time and supervision, to enable the proper organisation of ballot-related operations and to avoid fraud. The obligation to comply with those formalities within the statutory deadline fell within the exercise of the State's broad margin of appreciation in such matters (*Benkaddour v. France*).

3. Organisation of elections abroad for non-resident nationals

35. Article 3 of Protocol No. 1 does not oblige States to introduce a system that ensures the exercise of the right to vote for their non-resident citizens. In the case of *Sitaropoulos and Giakoumopoulos v. Greece* [GC] the applicants complained that, in the absence of regulation on that point, they could not exercise their voting right in the country where they lived as expatriates (France) even though the constitution of their country of origin (Greece) provided for that possibility. The Court found that there had been no violation of Article 3 of Protocol No. 1 as the disruption to the applicants' financial, family and professional lives that would have been caused had they had to travel to Greece would not have been disproportionate to the point of impairing the very essence of their voting rights.

36. However, where national law does provide for such a system, specific obligations may arise as a result, in particular the obligation to hold fresh elections in the foreign country if necessary. In the case of *Riza and Others v. Bulgaria* the Court stated that it did not overlook the fact that the organisation of fresh elections in another sovereign country, even in only a limited number of polling stations, might face major diplomatic or organisational obstacles and entail additional costs. It found, however, that the holding of fresh elections, in a polling station where there had been serious anomalies in the voting process on the part of the electoral board on the day of the election, would have reconciled the legitimate aim behind the annulment of the election results, namely the preservation of the legality of the electoral process, with the rights of the voters and the candidates standing for election to Parliament.

37. The case of *Oran v. Turkey* concerned the inability for Turkish voters living abroad to vote for independent non-party candidates in polling stations set up in customs posts. Votes cast in those conditions could only be for political parties. That limitation was

justified by the fact that it was impossible to assign expatriated voters to a constituency. The Court found that the limitation had to be assessed taking account of generally agreed restrictions on the exercise of voting rights by expatriates and, in particular, the legitimate concern the legislature might have to limit the influence of citizens resident abroad in elections on issues which primarily affect persons living in the country. It also emphasised the role played by political parties, the only bodies which could come to power and have the capacity to influence the whole national regime. Furthermore, the limitation also pursued two further legitimate aims: enhancing democratic pluralism while preventing the excessive and dysfunctional fragmentation of candidatures, thereby strengthening the expression of the opinion of the people in the choice of the legislature. Consequently, the restriction met the legislature's legitimate concern to ensure the political stability of the country and of the government which would be responsible for leading it after the elections. There had not therefore been a violation of Article 3 of Protocol No. 1.

III. Passive aspect: the right to stand for election

38. Like the "active" aspect, the "passive" aspect, namely the right to stand as a candidate for election, has been developed in the case-law. The Court has thus stated that the right to stand for election is "inherent in the concept of a truly democratic regime" (*Podkolzina v. Latvia*, § 35). It has been even more cautious in its assessment of restrictions under this aspect of Article 3 of Protocol No. 1 than when it has been called upon to examine restrictions on the right to vote; the proportionality test is more limited. The States thus enjoy a broader margin of appreciation in respect of the "passive" aspect (*Etxeberria and Others v. Spain*, § 50).

39. However, the prohibition of discrimination, under Article 14 of the Convention, is equally applicable. In this context, even though the margin of appreciation usually afforded to States as regards the right to stand for election is a broad one, where a difference in treatment is based on race, colour or ethnicity, the notion of objective and reasonable

justification must be interpreted as strictly as possible (*Sejdić and Finci v. Bosnia-Herzegovina* [GC], § 44).

40. In the case of *Sejdić and Finci v. Bosnia-Herzegovina* [GC] the Court examined an exclusion rule to the effect that only persons declaring affiliation with a "constituent people" were entitled to run for the House of Peoples (second chamber of the State Parliament). Potential candidates who refused to declare such an affiliation could not therefore stand. The Court noted that this exclusion rule pursued at least one aim which was broadly compatible with the general objectives of the Convention, namely the restoration of peace. When the impugned constitutional provisions were put in place a very fragile ceasefire was in effect on the ground. The provisions were designed to end a brutal conflict marked by genocide and ethnic cleansing. The nature of the conflict was such that the approval of the "constituent peoples" (namely, the Bosniacs, Croats and Serbs) was necessary to ensure peace. This could explain, without necessarily justifying, the absence of representatives of the other communities (such as local Roma and Jewish communities) at the peace negotiations and the participants' preoccupation with effective equality between the "constituent peoples" in the post-conflict society. However, there had been significant positive developments in Bosnia and Herzegovina since the Dayton Agreement. In addition, by ratifying the Convention and the Protocols thereto without reservations, the respondent State had voluntarily agreed to meet the relevant standards. The Court thus concluded that the applicants' continued ineligibility (being of Roma or Jewish origin) to stand for election lacked an objective and reasonable justification and had therefore breached Article 14 in conjunction with Article 3 of Protocol No. 1.

41. In the case of *Zornić v. Bosnia-Herzegovina* the Court found, for the same reasons, a violation of Article 3 of Protocol No. 1 as regards the applicant's ineligibility, for the same reason, to stand for election to the House of Peoples and to the Presidency. Observing that there had been excessive delay in executing its judgment in *Sejdić and Finci v. Bosnia-Herzegovina* [GC] and that the violation complained of was the direct result of that delay, the Court made a ruling under Article 46 of the Convention. It found that, eighteen years after the tragic conflict in Bosnia-Herzegovina, the time had come to adopt a

political system capable of affording all citizens of that country the right to stand for election to the House of Peoples and to the presidency without any distinction as to ethnic origin (*Zornić v. Bosnia-Herzegovina*, § 43).

42. In the case of *Tănase v. Moldova* [GC] the Court ruled on the question of dual nationality, albeit under Article 3 of Protocol No. 1 alone. It found that there was a consensus that where multiple nationalities were permitted, the holding of more than one nationality should not be a ground for ineligibility to sit as an MP, even where the population is ethnically diverse and the number of MPs with multiple nationalities may be high.

A. Inability to stand for election and the democratic order

43. As regards limitations on the right to stand for election, the protection of the democratic order is one of the aims compatible with the principle of the rule of law and the general objectives of the Convention.

44. However, in order to be compatible with the Convention, the rejection of a candidature must in the first place be legal: in particular it must be prescribed by law. In the case of *Dicle and Sadak v. Turkey* the applicants, MPs from a political party that had been dissolved, had been sentenced to heavy prison sentences for membership of an illegal organisation. They were given a retrial after a judgment of the European Court of Human Rights. However, their candidatures for the parliamentary elections were rejected on the ground that they had not served their sentences in full. In its examination under Article 6 § 2 of the Convention, the Court noted that it was clear from the national decisions that, following the decision to hold a retrial, the case had to be heard as if the applicants were standing trial for the first time. It concluded that the maintaining of the initial conviction on the applicants' criminal record and the subsequent refusal of their candidature was not prescribed by law and that there had thus been a violation of Article 3 of Protocol No. 1.

45. In the case of *Etxeberria and Others v. Spain* the applicants' candidatures had been annulled on the grounds that they were pursuing the activities of the three political parties which had been declared illegal and dissolved on account of their support for violence and

for the activities of the ETA, a terrorist organisation. The Court found that the national authorities had had considerable evidence enabling them to conclude that the electoral groupings in question wished to continue the activities of the political parties concerned. The Supreme Court had based its reasoning on elements external to the manifestos of the disputed groupings and the authorities had taken decisions to bar individual candidates. After an examination in adversarial proceedings, during which the groupings had been able to submit observations, the domestic courts had found an unequivocal link with the political parties that had been declared illegal. Lastly, the political context in Spain, namely the presence in the government bodies of certain autonomous communities, and in particular in the Basque country, of political parties calling for independence, proved that the impugned measure was not part of a policy to ban any expression of separatist views. The Court thus found that the restriction had been proportionate to the legitimate aim pursued.

46. However, whilst it is less stringent than when it concerns the active aspect of Article 3 of Protocol No.1, the Court's scrutiny-of the passive aspect-is not absent. In particular, the proportionality test, although relatively flexible, is a real one. The Court has, in particular, found a number of violations of Article 3 of Protocol No.1 on account of the disproportionate nature of sanctions imposed on MPs after their parties had been dissolved for undermining territorial integrity and the unity of the State, or to preserve the secular nature of the political system (see below, paragraphs 82 – 84).

47. It is noteworthy that cases concerning the banning of political parties on account of the incompatibility of their manifestos with democratic principles are usually examined under Article 11 (freedom of assembly and association) of the Convention. Article 3 of Protocol No.1 is then regarded only as secondary and as not raising a separate issue [*Refah Partisi (the Welfare Party) and Others v. Turkey* [GC]; *Linkov v. the Czech Republic*; *Parti nationaliste basque-Organisation régionale d'Iparralde v. France*].

B. Importance of historical context

48. Although they have a common origin in the need to ensure both the independence of elected representatives and the freedom of choice of electors, the eligibility criteria vary

in accordance with the historical and political factors specific to each State. The multiplicity of situations provided for in the constitutions and electoral legislation of numerous member States of the Council of Europe shows the diversity of possible approaches in this area. Therefore, for the purposes of applying Article 3 of Protocol No. 1, any electoral legislation must be assessed in the light of the political evolution of the country concerned (*Mathieu-Mohin and Clerfayt v. Belgium*, § 54; *Podkolzina v. Latvia*, § 33; *Ždanoka v. Latvia* [GC], § 106).

49. In the case of *Ždanoka v. Latvia* [GC] the applicant had been a member of a party which had attempted to bring about a *coup d'état* in 1991. Her candidature for elections was subsequently rejected a number of times on account of her activities in the party in question, continued after the attempted *coup d'état*. The Court took the view that the applicant's former position in that party, coupled with her stance during the events of 1991, still warranted her exclusion from standing as a candidate to the national parliament. While such a measure might scarcely be considered acceptable, for example, in a country which had an established framework of democratic institutions going back many decades or centuries, it might nonetheless be considered acceptable in Latvia in view of the historical and political context which had led to its adoption and given the threat to the new democratic order. The Court nevertheless found that the Latvian parliament had a duty to keep the statutory restriction under constant review, with a view to bringing it to an early end. Such a conclusion was all the more justified in view of the greater stability which Latvia now enjoyed, *inter alia*, by reason of its full European integration. Hence, any failure by the Latvian legislature to take active steps in that connection might result in a different finding by the Court (ibid., §§ 132–135).

50. The Court subsequently emphasised once again the importance of the passage of time and the need to reassess legislation concerning lustration laws. In *Ādamsons v. Latvia* the applicant, a former Prime Minister, had had his candidature refused on the ground that he had been a KGB "official". The Court confirmed its findings on the country's historical context. It added, however, that over the years a mere general suspicion about a group of individuals was no longer sufficient and that the authorities had to justify such a measure on

the basis of additional arguments and evidence. The law applied in this case concerned former KGB "officials". In view of the diversity of duties which had existed in that service, the scope was too broad. In those circumstances, it was no longer sufficient merely to find that the person concerned belonged to a particular group. The group in question having been defined too generally, any restriction on the electoral rights of its members should have followed an individualised approach, taking into account their actual conduct. The need for such a case-by-case approach had becoming increasingly important with the passage of time. The applicant had never been accused of being directly or indirectly involved in the misdeeds of the totalitarian regime, or in any act capable of showing opposition or hostility to the restoration of Latvia's independence and democratic order. Moreover, he had only very belatedly been officially recognised as ineligible, after ten years of an outstanding military and political career in the restored Latvia. Only the most compelling reasons could justify the applicant's ineligibility in those circumstances. In addition, the ten-year time-frame during which former KGB officials could be subjected to the restrictions provided for in other legislative instruments had been extended by ten additional years, without any reasons having been given by Parliament or the Government. The Court thus found that this prolongation had been manifestly arbitrary in respect of the applicant.

C. Organisation of elections

51. The practical organisation of elections is a complex subject, requiring as it does the introduction and occasionally the amendment of elaborate legislation. When called upon to examine this subject, the Court does not overlook the complexity or the features specific to each State. As a result, a broad margin of appreciation is also afforded to States in this connection.

52. The Court has taken the view, in particular, that the proper management of electoral rolls is a pre-condition for a free and fair ballot. The effectiveness of the right to stand for election is undoubtedly contingent upon the fair exercise of the right to vote. The mismanagement of an electoral roll could diminish the candidates' chances of standing

equally and fairly for election (*Georgian Labour Party v. Georgia*, §§ 82 – 83). In a case where the rules for the compilation of electoral rolls had been changed unexpectedly just one month before the election, the Court accepted that the new system of registration was not perfect but attached greater importance to the fact that the authorities had not spared any effort to make the new ballot fairer. In particular, the electoral authorities had had the challenge of remedying manifest shortcomings in the electoral rolls within very tight deadlines, in a "post-revolutionary" political situation, and it would thus have been an excessive and impracticable burden to expect an ideal solution from the authorities. It was up to the electors to verify that they were registered and to request any correction if necessary. The Court found that this fell within the State's margin of appreciation (ibid.).

1. Guaranteeing serious candidatures: the deposit requirement

53. The electoral laws of a number of States provide for the payment of a deposit by candidates to discourage frivolous candidatures. Such measures enhance the responsibility of those standing for election and confine elections to serious candidates, whilst avoiding any unreasonable outlay of public funds. They may therefore pursue the legitimate aim of guaranteeing the right to effective, streamlined representation (*Sukhovetskyy v. Ukraine*, §§ 61 –62).

54. The amount of the deposit must nevertheless remain proportionate, such that it strikes a balance between, on the one hand, deterring frivolous candidates, and, on the other, allowing the registration of serious candidates. The Court thus takes into account the amount of the sum involved, the electoral campaign services provided by the State and the other burdensome costs of organising elections which such deposits may help to allay.

55. For the proportionality test to be satisfied, the deposit required cannot be considered to have been excessive or to constitute an insurmountable administrative or financial barrier for a determined candidate wishing to enter the electoral race, and even less an obstacle to the emergence of sufficiently representative political currents or an interference with the principle of pluralism (ibid., §§ 72 –73). The requirement to pay an election deposit, and provisions making reimbursement of the deposit and/or campaigning expenses conditional on the party's having obtained a certain percentage of

votes, serve to promote sufficiently representative currents of thought and are justified and proportionate under Article 3 of Protocol No. 1, having regard to the wide margin of appreciation afforded to the Contracting States in this matter (*Russian Conservative Party of Entrepreneurs and Others v. Russia*, § 94). This remains true even where the deposit cannot be refunded (*Sukhovetskyy v. Ukraine*).

However, the question whether or not a deposit can be refunded may raise questions under Article 1 of Protocol No. 1. In the case of *Russian Conservative Party of Entrepreneurs and Others v. Russia*, the Court found that the domestic procedure whereby the entire list of a party had been annulled on account of incorrect information having been given by certain candidates had breached the principle of legal certainty. The applicant party had already paid the election deposit. In view of its finding under Article 3 of Protocol No. 1, the Court took the view that a refusal to return that sum breached Article 1 of Protocol No. 1.

2. Avoiding excessive fragmentation of the political landscape

56. Conditions concerning the number of signatures required for the presentation of a list of candidates do not constitute an impediment to the expression of the opinion of the people in the choice of the legislature [*Asensio Serqueda v. Spain*, Commission decision; *Federación nacionalista Canaria v. Spain* (dec.); *Brito Da Silva Guerra and Sousa Magno v. Portugal* (dec.); *Mihaela Mihai Neagu v. Romania* (dec.), § 31].

57. However, such measures must pursue a legitimate aim, such as that of a reasonable selection among the candidates in order to ensure their representative character and to exclude any improper candidatures, and must be proportionate to that aim. Thus, a threshold of 100,000 signatures, representing 0.55% of all citizens registered on the electoral rolls, was found to be compliant with Article 3 of Protocol No. 1 (ibid.).

58. Similarly, the Court took the view that a requirement for such signatures to be accompanied by certificates showing that the signatories were registered on the electoral rolls pursued the legitimate aim of ensuring that the signatories had voting rights and that each of them was supporting only one candidature. It was not therefore disproportionate to reject a candidature which did not satisfy the formalities in question [*Brito Da Silva Guerra and Sousa Magno v. Portugal* (dec.)].

59. However, the imposition of a minimum number of signatures and their verification must comply with the rule of law and protect the integrity of the elections. In the case of *Tahirov v. Azerbaijan* the safeguards provided by the Electoral Board, which had rejected the applicant's candidature, were not sufficient, in particular concerning the appointment of the experts who decided on the validity of the signatures. In addition, the applicant had not been able to attend the Board's meetings or submit his arguments, none of which had been examined by the Board. The rejection of the applicant's candidature on account of the alleged invalidity of the signatures he had provided was thus arbitrary. Based on a report by the OSCE, the Court noted the systemic nature of these shortcomings and the number of candidatures arbitrarily rejected on those grounds. It concluded that the Government's unilateral declaration did not suffice to guarantee respect for human rights, rejected it and pursued its examination on the merits.

60. Such threshold criteria have also been accepted by the Court in connection with the allocation of seats according to the results of the elections. Electoral systems seek to fulfil objectives which are sometimes scarcely compatible with each other: on the one hand to reflect fairly faithfully the opinions of the people, and, on the other, to channel currents of thought so as to promote the emergence of a sufficiently clear and coherent political will. Article 3 of Protocol No. 1 thus does not imply that all votes must necessarily have equal weight as regards the outcome of the election or that all candidates must have equal chances of winning, and no electoral system can eliminate "wasted votes" [*Partija* "*Jaunie Demokrāti*" *and Partija* "*Mūsu Zeme*" *v. Latvia* (dec.)].

61. The effects of an electoral threshold can differ from one country to another and the various systems can pursue different, sometimes even opposing, political aims. One system might concentrate more on a fair representation of the parties in Parliament, while another one might aim to avoid a fragmentation of the party system and encourage the formation of a governing majority of one party in Parliament. The Court has taken the view that none of these aims can be considered unreasonable in itself. Moreover, the role played by thresholds varies in accordance with the level at which they are set and the party system in each country. A low threshold excludes only very small groupings, which makes it more

difficult to form stable majorities, whereas in cases where the party system is highly fragmented a high threshold deprives many voters of representation. This large variety of situations shows the diversity of the possible options. The Court cannot therefore assess any particular threshold without taking into account the electoral system of which it forms a part (*Yumak and Sadak v. Turkey* [GC], §§ 131–132).

62. As regards, for example, the requirement to fulfil two alternative conditions-to obtain either at least 30% of valid votes cast in an individual island constituency, or at least 6% of valid votes cast in an entire autonomous community-the Court took the view that such a system, far from constituting a hindrance to electoral candidatures, granted a certain protection to smaller political formations [*Federación nacionalista Canaria v. Spain* (dec.)]. Similarly, the Court concluded that the threshold of 5% of votes that had to be attained by a list of candidates in order to be considered elected and to participate in the allotment of seats was compliant with Article 3 of Protocol No. 1, in that it encouraged sufficiently representative currents of thought and helped to avoid an excessive fragmentation of Parliament [*Partija "Jaunie Demokrāti" and Partija "Mūsu Zeme" v. Latvia* (dec.)].

63. In the case of *Yumak and Sadak v. Turkey* [GC], by contrast, the Court found that, in general, a 10% electoral threshold appeared excessive, and concurred with the organs of the Council of Europe, which had recommended that it be lowered. The threshold compelled political parties to make use of stratagems which did not contribute to the transparency of the electoral process. However, the Court was not persuaded that, when assessed in the light of the specific political context of the elections in question, and attended as it was by correctives and other guarantees-such as the possibility of forming an electoral coalition with other political parties or the role of the Constitutional Court-which had limited its effects in practice, the 10% threshold had had the effect of impairing in their essence the rights secured to the applicants by Article 3 of Protocol No. 1

64. Finally, a sudden and unforeseeable change in the rules for calculating votes might infringe Article 3 of Protocol No. 1. The Court found a violation of that Article as regards MPs deprived of their seats following an unpredictable departure by the Special Supreme

Court from its settled case-law concerning the calculation of the electoral quotient. In particular, it took account of the fact that the change in case-law, after the elections, had changed the meaning and weight given to blank ballot papers and that it had therefore been liable to alter the will of the electorate as expressed in the ballot box. It had also created a disparity in the manner in which sitting MPs had been elected (*Paschalidis, Koutmeridis and Zaharakis v. Greece*).

D. Other legitimate aims

65. Not being limited by an exhaustive list, as in the context of Articles 8 to 11 of the Convention, a number of other legitimate aims may be accepted by the Court as justifying a restriction on the right to stand for election.

66. The Court has thus made a distinction between loyalty towards the State and loyalty towards the government. While the need to ensure loyalty towards the State may constitute a legitimate aim justifying restrictions of electoral rights, that is not the case for loyalty towards the government (*Tănase v. Moldova* [GC], § 166). Similarly, the obligation to have sufficient knowledge of the official language may pursue a legitimate aim (*Podkolzina v. Latvia*). The Court has also found that the obligation imposed on candidates in a parliamentary election to submit accurate information on their employment and party membership served to enable voters to make an informed choice with regard to the candidate's professional and political background and thus constituted a legitimate aim (*Krasnov and Skuratov v. Russia*). By contrast, a candidate's ineligibility founded solely on an allegedly defective form of a document provided by him was not proportionate to the legitimate aim pursued (ibid., §§ 65 – 66).

67. The Court also declared inadmissible an application complaining about an obligation for a very traditional Protestant party to open its lists of candidates to women. It found that the progression towards gender equality in the member States precluded the State from supporting the idea that the woman's role was secondary to that of the man [*Staatkundig Gereformeerde Partij v. the Netherlands* (dec.)].

68. Moreover, in the case of *Melnitchenko v. Ukraine*, the applicant, who had refugee

status in the USA, had had his candidature refused on the ground that he had provided false information about his residence. In accordance with the legislation in force, he had given information from his internal passport, which he still possessed, showing that he lived in Ukraine. The Court agreed that it could be acceptable to impose a residence condition for the registration of candidatures. However, it noted that the applicant had complied with domestic law, which did not require continuous residence in the country. In addition, he was in a situation where he could either stay in Ukraine and face a threat of bodily harm, which would have made it impossible for him to exercise his political rights, or leave the country and no longer qualify to stand for election. The Court thus found there had been a violation of Article 3 of Protocol No. 1.

69. Lastly, in the case of *Antonenko v. Russia* (dec.), a court had banned the applicant from standing in the parliamentary elections the day before the ballot on the grounds that there had been financial irregularities and that the election campaign had been unfair. The applicant did not complain about the actual annulment of his candidature, but about the fact that it had been decided shortly before the polling stations opened. The Court found that the timing in question was compliant with domestic law and had no consequence for a possible appeal, as no further appeal lay against the decision.

70. The Court has also accepted, on a number of occasions, that potential candidates may be excluded on account of the positions held by them. In the case of *Gitonas and Others v. Greece*, legislation precluded certain categories of holders of public office-including salaried public servants and members of staff of public-law entities and public undertakings-from standing for election and being elected in any constituency where they had performed their duties for more than three months in the three years preceding the elections: the disqualification would moreover stand notwithstanding a candidate's prior resignation, unlike the position with certain other categories of public servant. The Court found that this measure served a dual purpose: to ensure that candidates of different political persuasions enjoyed equal means of influence and to protect the electorate from pressure from public officials. The following year, the Court reiterated that restrictions on the participation of specific categories of local government officers in forms of political activity

pursued the legitimate aim of protecting the rights of others, council members and the electorate alike, to effective political democracy at the local level. Having regard to the fact that they only operated for as long as the applicants occupied politically restricted posts, the measures remained proportionate (*Ahmed and Others v. the United Kingdom*). In the case of *Brike v. Latvia* the Court added that as the ineligibility of civil servants constituted a proportionate response to the requirement that the civil service be independent, this was all the more true for the ineligibility of judges, the purpose of which was to secure to citizens the rights protected by Article 6 of the Convention. It thus concluded that there had been no impairment of the very essence of the guaranteed rights, as the judge could have resigned from her post in order to stand for election.

71. However, restrictions on the right to stand for election, even if they pursue a legitimate aim, must not have the result of rendering that right ineffective, either because the conditions are introduced too late or too suddenly, or because they are not clear enough. In the case of *Lykourezos v. Greece* legislation making all professional activity incompatible with the duties of a member of parliament was applied immediately to the current legislature and MPs had to forfeit their seats even though that incompatibility had not been announced prior to their election. There were no grounds of pressing importance that could have justified the immediate application of the absolute disqualification. For the first time the Court relied on the principle of legitimate expectation and thus found a violation of Article 3 of Protocol No. 1. It applied that principle again in *Ekoglasnost v. Bulgaria*. While none of the three new conditions introduced in the electoral legislation raised a problem in itself, on account of their belated introduction the applicant had only had one month to comply. The Court took the view that the conditions of participation in elections imposed on political groups were part of the basic electoral rules. Those conditions should thus have the same stability in time as the other basic elements of the electoral system. The Court has also found that the provisions on the basis of which a former member of the clergy had had his candidature refused were too imprecise and therefore unforeseeable. Consequently, they gave the electoral bodies an excessive margin of appreciation and left too much room for arbitrariness in the application of that restriction (*Seyidzade v. Azerbaijan*).

E. From the election campaign...

72. In order for the rights guaranteed by Article 3 of Protocol No. 1 to be effective, their protection cannot remain confined to the candidature itself. The election campaign thus also falls within the scope of the provision.

73. Already in a number of cases concerning Article 10 of the Convention, the Court had emphasised the close relationship between the right to free elections and freedom of expression. It has found that these rights, particularly freedom of political debate, together form the bedrock of any democratic system. The two rights are inter-related and operate to reinforce each other: for example, freedom of expression is one of the "conditions" necessary to "ensure the free expression of the opinion of the people in the choice of the legislature". For this reason, it is particularly important in the period preceding an election for opinions and information of all kinds to be permitted to circulate freely (*Bowman v. the United Kingdom*, § 42).

74. As these rights are inter-dependent, numerous cases concerning election campaigns are examined under Article 10. The Court, for example, found a violation of Article 10 on account of a fine imposed on a television channel for broadcasting an advertisement for a small political party, in breach of legislation prohibiting any political advertising on television (*TV Vest AS and Rogaland Pensjonistparti v. Norway*). A violation of Article 10 was also found in a case where a warning had been issued to a female politician for describing a rival candidate as a thief on live television in the run up to the election. A court decision had granted the other (female) candidate a right to reply to the accusation (*Vitrenko and Others v. Ukraine*).

75. However, cases concerning, in particular, the distribution of airtime during the pre-election campaigning period may raise issues under Article 3 of Protocol No. 1. In a case concerning the equality of airtime granted to the various candidates, the Court stated that, while Article 3 of Protocol No. 1 enshrined the principle of equal treatment of all citizens in the exercise of their electoral rights, it did not guarantee, as such, any right for a political party to be granted airtime on radio or television during the pre-election

campaign. However, an issue may indeed arise in exceptional circumstances, for example, if in the run up to an election one party were denied any kind of party political broadcast whilst other parties were granted slots for that purpose [*Partija "Jaunie Demokrāti" and Partija "Mūsu Zeme" v. Latvia* (dec.)].

76. In the case of *Communist Party of Russia and Others v. Russia*, the Court addressed the question whether the State had a positive obligation under Article 3 of Protocol No. 1 to ensure that coverage by regulated media was objective and compatible with the spirit of "free elections", even in the absence of direct evidence of deliberate manipulation. It found that the existing system of electoral remedies was sufficient to satisfy the State's positive obligation of a procedural nature. As to the substantive aspect of the obligation and the allegation that the State should have ensured neutrality of the audio-visual media, it took the view that certain steps had been taken to guarantee some visibility to opposition parties and candidates on TV and to secure the editorial independence and neutrality of the media. These arrangements had probably not secured *de facto* equality, but it could not be considered established that the State had failed to meet its positive obligations in this area to such an extent as to amount to a violation of Article 3 of Protocol No. 1.

77. Lastly, in the case of *Oran v. Turkey*, the applicant had complained that, as an independent candidate, he had not been able to benefit from nationwide electoral broadcasting on Turkish radio and television, unlike political parties. The Court took the view that, unlike political parties, the applicant, as an independent candidate, had only to address the constituency in which he was standing. In addition, he had not been prevented from using all the other available methods of electioneering, which were accessible to all the unaffiliated independent candidates at the relevant time. The Court thus found that there had been no violation of Article 3 of Protocol No. 1.

F. ...to the exercise of office

78. From 1984 onwards the Commission stated that it was not enough that an individual had the right to stand for election; he must also have a right to sit as a member once he has been elected by the people. To take the opposite view would render the right to stand for

election meaningless (*M. v. the United Kingdom*, Commission decision). In that same case, however, it took the view that the inability for an elected MP to take up his seat on the grounds that he was already a member of a foreign legislature was a restriction compatible with Article 3 of Protocol No. 1.

79. In three cases against Turkey the Court examined the consequences for MPs of the dissolution of the political parties to which they belonged. In the case of *Sadak and Others v. Turkey* (no. 2) a political party was dissolved for breaching the territorial integrity and unity of the State. The MPs belonging to that party automatically forfeited their seats. The Court took the view that interference with the freedom of expression of an opposition MP required particularly stringent scrutiny. The loss by the applicants of their seats in Parliament was automatic and independent of their political activities in which they engaged on a personal basis. It had thus been an extremely severe measure and one that was disproportionate to any legitimate aim invoked.

80. In the case of *Kavakçl v. Turkey* temporary limitations had been imposed on the applicant's political rights on account of the final dissolution of the party to which she belonged. The Court took the view that those measures had the purpose of preserving the secular character of the Turkish political regime and that, having regard to the importance of that principle for the democratic regime in Turkey, the measure pursued the legitimate aims of preventing disorder and protecting the rights and freedoms of others. As to the proportionality of the sanction, however, the constitutional provisions concerning the dissolution of a political party, as then in force, had a very broad scope. All the acts and remarks of party members could be imputable to the party in finding it to be a centre of anti-constitutional activity and deciding on its dissolution. No distinction was made between the various degrees of involvement of members in the impugned activities. In addition, certain party members who were in a comparable situation to that of the applicant, especially the President and Vice-President, had not been penalised. Consequently, the Court found that the sanction was not proportionate and that there had been a violation of Article 3 of Protocol No. 1.

81. In another case concerning an MP from the same party who had also lost his seat,

the Court again found a violation of Article 3 of Protocol No. 1 but noted with interest the adoption of a constitutional amendment reinforcing the status of MPs and probably having the effect of making the disqualification of MPs on such grounds less frequent (*Sobacı v. Turkey*).

82. In the case of *Lykourezos v. Greece* the Court had found that the new professional incompatibility applicable to MPs had not been announced prior to the elections and had surprised both the applicant and those who had voted for him, during his term of office. It took the view that in assessing the applicant's election under the new Article of the Constitution which entered into force in 2003, without taking account of the fact that his election had taken place beforehand perfectly legally, the judge had stripped the applicant of his seat and deprived his voters of the candidate whom they had freely and democratically chosen to represent them for four years, in disregard of the principle of legitimate expectation. Similarly, in the case of *Paschalidis, Koutmeridis and Zaharakis v. Greece*, the Court had found that an unforeseeable departure from precedent, after the elections, concerning the calculation of the electoral quotient, with the effect of disqualifying a number of elected MPs, had entailed a violation of Article 3 of Protocol No. 1.

83. In the case of *Paunović and Milivojević v. Serbia* the Court had occasion to rule on the practice of political parties consisting of using undated resignation letters signed, before taking up office, by their members who are elected to Parliament; the party is thus able to remove those members from office at any time and against their will. The Court began by taking the view that, even though the resignation letter would be presented by the party, only Parliament was entitled to withdraw a seat. It was therefore the State which deprived the MP of his or her seat by accepting the resignation. The application of an MP who had lost his seat was thus admissible *ratione personae*. The Court then found that the impugned practice was at odds with domestic law, which required such resignations to be submitted by the MP in person. There had thus been a violation of Article 3 of Protocol No. 1. The case of *Occhetto v. Italy* (dec) concerned the relinquishment of a seat in the European Parliament. After signing a document relinquishing his seat, as a result of an agreement with the co-founder of the political movement to which he belonged, the applicant had

changed his mind. However, the candidate next on the list had already taken up the seat in question. The Court found that, following an election, a candidate was entitled to take up a seat in a legislature, but had no obligation to do so. Any candidate could renounce, for political or personal reasons, the office to which he or she was elected, and the decision to register such a renouncement could not be regarded as contrary to the principle of universal suffrage. It added that the refusal to accept the withdrawal of the applicant's relinquishment had pursued the legitimate aims of legal certainty in the electoral process and the protection of the rights of others, in particular the rights of the person who had been declared elected to the seat which could otherwise have been occupied by the applicant. The applicant's wish had been expressed in writing and in unequivocal terms, and he had stipulated that his relinquishment was final. Lastly, the domestic proceedings-in compliance with EU law-had enabled him to submit the arguments that he deemed useful for his defence. The Court thus found that there had been no violation of Article 3 of Protocol No. 1.

Ⅳ. Electoral disputes

84. Cases concerning election-related disputes have been numerous. This issue cannot, however, be examined under Article 6 of the Convention, which the Court has found inapplicable. It took the view that an applicant's right to stand for election to the French National Assembly and to keep his seat was a political one and not a "civil" one within the meaning of Article 6 § 1, such that disputes relating to the arrangements for the exercise of that right lay outside the scope of Article 3 of Protocol No. 1 (*Pierre-Bloch v. France*, § 50). Nor was the criminal limb of Article 6 engaged as regards penalties imposed for non-compliance with electoral rules (ibid., § 61). In the case of *Geraguyn Khorhurd Patgamavorakan Akumb v. Armenia*, the applicant NGO had been an observer during parliamentary elections. There was a subsequent dispute as to its failure to transmit various documents. The Court took the view that the outcome of the proceedings in question had not been decisive of the NGO's rights and that it did not therefore fall within the scope of

Article 6 § 1 of the Convention.

85. However, on several occasions, the lack of an effective remedy in the context of the electoral process has been examined under Article 13 of the Convention. The Court has indicated that in electoral matters only those remedies which are capable of ensuring the proper functioning of the democratic process may be regarded as effective (*Petkov and Others v. Bulgaria*). In the case of *Petkov and Others v. Bulgaria*, the applicants' names had been struck out of the lists of candidates only ten days before the election day, and on the basis of legislation passed less than three months earlier. Those strike-out decisions were subsequently declared null and void but, as the electoral authorities had not reinstated the applicants as candidates, they were unable to stand for election. The Court took the view that, since the remedy available in the context of the elections offered only pecuniary redress, it could not be regarded as effective under Article 13 of the Convention. In *Grosaru v. Romania* the Court noted that the applicant, who was an unsuccessful candidate in legislative elections, had not been able to obtain any judicial review of the interpretation of the impugned electoral legislation and it found a violation of Article 13 taken together with Article 3 of Protocol No. 1.

86. Where a remedy does exist, any deficiencies may be raised before the Court under Article 3 of Protocol No. 1. Such deficiencies may constitute a violation of that Article when they call into question the integrity of the electoral process. The decision-making process concerning ineligibility or a dispute as to election results must be surrounded by certain minimum safeguards against arbitrariness. In particular, the findings in question must be reached by a body which can provide minimum guarantees of its impartiality. Similarly, the discretion enjoyed by the body concerned must not be exorbitantly wide: it must be circumscribed, with sufficient precision, by the provisions of domestic law. Lastly, the procedure must be such as to guarantee a fair, objective and sufficiently reasoned decision and prevent any abuse of power on the part of the relevant authority (*Podkolzina v. Latvia*, § 35;, *Kovatch v. Ukraine*, §§ 54 – 55; *Kerimova v. Azerbaijan*, §§ 44 – 45; *Riza and Others v. Bulgaria*, § 144). Where it engages in such an examination, the Court confines itself, however, to ascertaining whether the decision

rendered by the domestic body was arbitrary or manifestly unreasonable in nature (ibid., § 144; *Kerimli and Alibeyli v. Azerbaijan*, §§ 38–42).

87. Decisions to invalidate an election must reflect a genuine inability to establish the wishes of the electors (*Kovatch v. Ukraine*). In *Kerimova v. Azerbaijan* the Court found that tampering by two election officials had not succeeded in altering the final result of the election, in which the applicant had been successful. The national authorities had, nevertheless, invalidated the results in breach of domestic electoral law and without taking into account the limited impact of the effects of the tampering. By doing so, the authorities had essentially helped the officials to obstruct the election. This decision had arbitrarily infringed the applicant's electoral rights by depriving her of the benefit of election to Parliament. It had also shown a lack of concern for the integrity and effectiveness of the electoral process which could not be considered compatible with the spirit of the right to free elections. The role of the courts is not to modify the expression of the people. Thus in two cases [*I. Z. v. Greece*, Commission decision; *Babenko v. Ukraine* (dec.)] the Convention organs examined complaints by unsuccessful candidates who alleged that the electoral processes had been unfair, but dismissed them for lack of any real damage with regard to the outcome of the election. In *Riza and Others v. Bulgaria* the results of 23 polling stations set up abroad had been invalidated on account of alleged anomalies, depriving an MP of his seat. The Court examined both the interference with the voting rights of 101 electors and the right to stand for election of the MP and the party he represented. It found that only purely formal grounds had been given to invalidate the election in a number of polling stations. In addition, the circumstances relied on by the court to justify its decision were not provided for, in a sufficiently clear and foreseeable manner, in the domestic law, and it had not been shown that they would have altered the choice of the voters or distorted the result of the election. In addition, electoral law did not provide for the possibility of organising fresh elections in the polling stations where the ballot had been invalidated-contrary to the Venice Commission's Code of Good Practice in Electoral Matters-which would have reconciled the legitimate aim pursued by the annulment of the election results, namely the preservation of the legality of the election process, with

the subjective rights of the electors and the candidates in parliamentary elections. Consequently, the Court found that there had been a violation of Article 3 of Protocol No. 1. Decisions to invalidate a ballot must therefore be based on a genuine inability to establish the wishes of the electors.

88. Nevertheless, States must ensure that arguable complaints by individuals concerning election irregularities are effectively addressed and that domestic decisions are sufficiently reasoned. Relying in particular on the Venice Commission's Code of Good Practice in Electoral Matters, the Court has had occasion to find that national authorities had given excessively formalistic reasons to avoid examining the substance of electoral complaints. The fact that there was a wide difference in votes between candidates did not matter when it came to examining, independently, the extent of the irregularities, before determining their effects on the overall result of the election (*Namat Aliyev v. Azerbaijan*).

List of cited cases

The case-law cited in this Guide refers to judgments or decisions delivered by the Court and to decisions or reports of the European Commission of Human Rights ("the Commission").

Unless otherwise indicated, all references are to a judgment on the merits delivered by a Chamber of the Court. The abbreviation "(dec.)" indicates that the citation is of a decision of the Court and "[GC]" that the case was heard by the Grand Chamber.

The hyperlinks to the cases cited in the electronic version of the Guide are directed to the HUDOC database (http://hudoc.echr.coe.int) which provides access to the case-law of the Court (Grand Chamber, Chamber and Committee judgments and decisions, communicated cases, advisory opinions and legal summaries from the Case-Law Information Note) and of the Commission (decisions and reports), and to the resolutions of the Committee of Ministers.

The Court delivers its judgments and decisions in English and/or French, its two official languages. HUDOC also contains translations of many important cases into more than thirty non-official languages, and links to around one hundred online case-law collections produced by third parties.

— A —

Ādamsons v. Latvia, no. 3669/03, 24 June 2008

Ahmed and Others v. the United Kingdom, 2 September 1998, Reports of Judgments and Decisions 1998 – Ⅵ

Alajos Kiss v. Hungary, no. 38832/06, 20 May 2010

Albanese v. Italy, no. 77924/01, 23 March 2006

Anchugov and Gladkov v. Russia, nos. 11157/04 and 15162/05, 4 July 2013

Antonenkov. Russia (dec.), no. 42482/02, 23 May 2006

Asensio Serqueda v. Spain (dec.), no. 23151/94, Commission decision of 9 May 1994, Decisions and Reports 77 – B

Azizv. Cyprus, no. 69949/01, ECHR 2004 – V

— B —

Babenkov. Ukraine (dec.), no. 43476/98, 4 May 1999

Benkaddourv. France (dec.), no. 51685/99, 10 November 2003

Bompardv. France (dec.), no. 44081/02, ECHR 2006 – IV

Boškoski v. the former Yugoslav Republic of Macedonia (dec.), no. 11676/04, ECHR 2004 – VI

Bowman v. the United Kingdom, 19 February 1998, Reports of Judgments and Decisions 1998 – I

Brikev. Latvia (dec.), no. 47135/99, 29 June 2000

Brito Da Silva Guerraand Sousa Magno v. Portugal (dec.), nos. 26712/06 and 26720/06, 17 June 2008

— C —

Communist Party of Russia and Others v. Russia, no. 29400/05, 19 June 2012

— D —

Dicleand Sadak v. Turkey, no. 48621/07, 16 June 2015

Doylev. the United Kingdom (dec.), no. 30158/06, 6 February 2007

Dunnand Others v. the United Kingdom (dec.), nos. 566/10 and 130 others, 13 May 2014

— E —

Ekoglasnostv. Bulgaria, no. 30386/05, 6 November 2012

Etxeberriaand Others v. Spain, nos. 35579/03 and 3 others, 30 June 2009

— F —

Federación nacionalista Canariav. Spain (dec.), no. 56618/00, ECHR 2001 – VI

Frodlv. Austria, no. 20201/04, 8 April 2010

— G —

Georgian Labour Party v. Georgia, no. 9103/04, ECHR 2008

Geraguyn Khorhurd Patgamavorakan Akumbv. Armenia (dec.), no. 11721/04, 14 April 2009

Gitonasand Others v. Greece, 1 June 1997, Reports of Judgments and Decisions 1997 – Ⅳ

Greensand M. T. v. the United Kingdom, nos. 60041/08 and 60054/08, ECHR 2010 (extracts)

Grosaruv. Romania, no. 78039/01, ECHR 2010

— H —

Hilbev. Liechtenstein (dec.), no. 31981/96, ECHR 1999 – Ⅵ

Hirst v. the United Kingdom (no. 2) [GC], no. 74025/01, ECHR 2005 – Ⅸ

— I —

I. Z. v. Greece, no. 18997/91, Commission decision of 28 February 1994, Decisions and Reports 76 – A

— K —

Kavakçl v. Turkey, no. 71907/01, 5 April 2007

Kerimliand Alibeyli v. Azerbaijan, nos. 18475/06 and 22444/06, 10 January 2012

Kerimovav. Azerbaijan, no. 20799/06, 30 September 2010

Kovatchv. Ukraine, no. 39424/02, ECHR 2008

Krasnovand Skuratov v. Russia, nos. 17864/04 and 21396/04, 19 July 2007

— L —

Labitav. Italy [GC], no. 26772/95, ECHR 2000 – Ⅳ

Linkovv. the Czech Republic, no. 10504/03, 7 December 2006

Lukschv. Germany, no. 35385/97, Commission decision of 21 May 1997

Lykourezosv. Greece, no. 33554/03, ECHR 2006 – Ⅷ

— M —

M. v. the United Kingdom, no. 10316/83, Commission decision of 7 March 1984, Decisions and Reports 37

Malardev. France (dec.), no. 46813/99, 5 September 2000

Mathieu-Mohinand Clerfayt v. Belgium, 2 March 1987, Series A no. 113

Matthewsv. the United Kingdom [GC], no. 24833/94, ECHR 1999 – Ⅰ

Melnitchenkov. Ukraine, no. 17707/02, ECHR 2004 – Ⅹ

Mihaela Mihai Neaguv. Romania (dec.), no. 66345/09, 6 March 1994

Mółka v. Poland (dec.), no. 56550/00, ECHR 2006 – IV

— N —

Namat Aliyevv. Azerbaijan, no. 18705/06, 8 April 2010

— O —

Occhettov. Italy (dec.), no. 14507/07, 12 November 2013

Oranv. Turkey, nos. 28881/07 and 37920/07, 15 April 2014

— P —

Paksasv. Lithuania [GC], no. 34932/04, ECHR 2011 (extracts)

Partija "Jaunie Demokrāti" and Partija "Mūsu Zeme" v. Latvia (dec.), nos. 10547/07 and 34049/07, 29 November 2007

Parti nationaliste basque-Organisation régionale d'Iparralde v. France, no. 71251/01, ECHR 2007 – II

Paschalidis, Koutmeridisand Zaharakis v. Greece, nos. 27863/05 and 2 others, 10 April 2008

Paunović and Milivojević v. Serbia, no. 41683/06, 24 May 2016

Petkovand Others v. Bulgaria, nos. 77568/01 and 2 others, 11 June 2009

Pierre-Blochv. France, no. 24194/94, 21 October 1997

Podkolzinav. Latvia, no. 46726/99, ECHR 2002 – II

Polacco and Garofalo v. Italy, no. 23450/94, Commission decision of 15 September 1997

Py v. France, no. 66289/01, ECHR 2005 – I (extracts)

— R —

Refah Partisi (the Welfare Party) and Others v. Turkey [GC], nos. 41340/98 and 3 others, ECHR 2003 – II

Riza and Others v. Bulgaria, nos. 48555/10 and 48377/10, 13 October 2015

Russian Conservative Party of Entrepreneurs and Others v. Russia, nos. 55066/00 and 55638/00, 11 January 2007

— S —

Sadak and Others v. Turkey (no. 2), nos. 25144/94 and 8 others, ECHR 2002 – IV

Salleras Llinares v. Spain (dec.), no. 52226/99, ECHR 2000 - XI

Scoppola v. Italy (no. 3) [GC], no. 126/05, 22 May 2012

Sejdić and Finci v. Bosnia-Herzegovina [GC], nos. 27996/06 and 34836/06, ECHR 2009

Sevinger v. the Netherlands (dec.), nos. 17173/07 and 17180/07, 6 September 2007

Seyidzade v. Azerbaijan, no. 37700/05, 3 December 2009

Shindler v. the United Kingdom, no. 19840/09, 7 May 2013

Sitaropoulos and Giakoumopoulos v. Greece [GC], no. 42202/07, ECHR 2012

Sobacl v. Turkey, no. 26733/02, 29 November 2007

Socialist Party and Others v. Turkey, 25 May 1998, Reports of Judgments and Decisions 1998 - III

Sukhovetskyy v. Ukraine, no. 13716/02, ECHR 2006 - VI

Söyler v. Turkey, no. 29411/07, 17 September 2013

Staatkundig Gereformeerde Partij v. the Netherlands (dec.), no. 58369/10, 10 July 2012

— T —

Tahirovv. Azerbaijan, no. 31953/11, 11 June 2015

Tănase v. Moldova [GC], no. 7/08, ECHR 2010

Timkev. Germany, no. 27311/95, Commission decision of 11 September 1995

TV Vest AS and Rogaland Pensjonistparti v. Norway, no. 21132/05, ECHR 2008

— V —

Vito Sante Santorov. Italy, no. 36681/97, ECHR 2004 - VI

Vitrenko and Others v. Ukraine, no. 23510/02, 16 December 2008

— U —

United Communist Party of Turkey and Others v. Turkey, 30 January 1998, Reports of Judgments and Decisions 1998 - I

— X —

X. v. Germany, no. 2728/66, Commission decision of 6 October 1967, Collection 25

X. v. the United Kingdom, no. 7140/75, Commission decision of 6 October 1976,

Decisions and Reports 7

X. v. the United Kingdom, no. 7566/76, Commission decision of 11 December 1976, Decisions and Reports 9

X. v. the United Kingdom, no. 7730/76, Commission decision of 28 February 1979, Decisions and Reports 15

X. v. the United Kingdom, no. 8873/80, Commission decision of 13 May 1982, Decisions and Reports 28

X. and Others v. Belgium, no. 6837/74, Commission decision of 2 October 1975, Decisions and Reports 3

Xuereb v. Malta, no. 52492/99, 15 June 2000

— Y —

Yumak and Sadak v. Turkey [GC], no. 10226/03, ECHR 2008

— Z —

Ždanoka v. Latvia [GC], no. 58278/00, ECHR 2006 – IV

Zornić v. Bosnia-Herzegovina, no. 3681/06, 15 July 2014

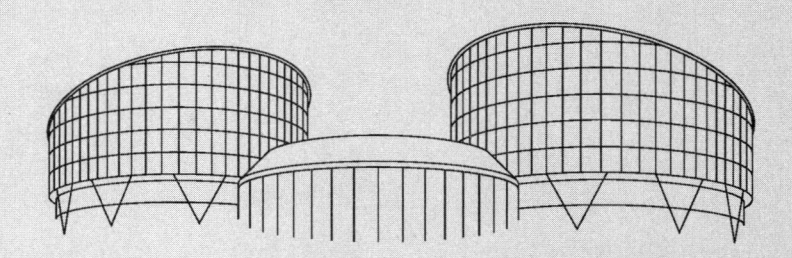

EUROPEAN COURT OF HUMAN RIGHTS
COUR EUROPÉENNE DES DROITS DE L'HOMME

第十章 《欧洲人权公约》第四议定书第4条适用指南

禁止集体驱逐外国人

COUNCIL OF EUROPE

CONSEIL DE L'EUROPE

读者须知

本指南是欧洲人权法院（以下简称本法院、欧洲法院、斯特拉斯堡法院）出版的公约指南系列的一部分，旨在让执业律师了解斯特拉斯堡法院做出的基本判决。本指南分析和汇总了截至 2016 年 4 月 30 日的关于《欧洲人权公约》（以下简称公约、欧洲公约）第四议定书第 4 条的判例法。读者可以从中发现本领域的基本原则和相关判例。

援引的判例法选取了具有指导性的、重要的以及最新的判决。

本法院的判例不仅用于审判呈交至本法院的案件，而且从更为一般的意义上用于阐释、捍卫和发展公约创立的各项规则，并以此促使各缔约国对之加以遵守（*Ireland v. the United Kingdom*, 1978 年 1 月 18 日, § 154, Series A no. 25.）。因此，从普遍意义来说，公约确立的此机制的任务便是通过决定公共政策的各种问题来提升人权保护的标准，并在缔约国范围内推广人权法学（*Konstantin Markin v. Russia* [GC], 30078/06, § 89, ECHR 2012）。

> **第四议定书第 4 条　禁止集体驱逐外国人**
> "禁止集体驱逐外国人。"

第一节　第 4 条的起源与宗旨

1. 第四议定书起草于 1963 年,是第一个旨在解决集体驱逐问题的国际条约。其解释报告表明第 4 条的宗旨是正式禁止"近代以来集体驱逐外国人的现象"。因而,"虽然同意适用公约第 4 条及第 3 条第 1 款(禁止驱逐公民),但这并不能被解为过去发生的集体驱逐行为得以合法化、正当化"(*Hirsi Jamaa and Others v. Italy* [GC], § 174)。

2. 本条的核心宗旨是防止国家未审查外国人的个人具体情况便将其驱逐出境,从而使外国人无法对采取措施的有关机构提起抗辩(同上,§ 177)。

第二节　"集体驱逐"的定义

3. "集体驱逐"较为完整的定义是"有关部门将外国人作为一个群体强行驱逐出境的所有措施,除非该措施是在对该群体的每一名成员的具体情况进行了合理且客观的评估之后采取的。"[*Andric v. Sweden* (dec.); *Čonka v. Belgium*, § 59; *Sultani v. France*, § 81; *the Comission decisions Becker v. Denmark*; *K. G. v. the Federal Republic of Germany*; *O. and Others v. Luxembourg*; *Alibaks and Others v. the Netherlands*; *Tahiri v. Sweden*, the Commission decisions]。如果每一个相关个人已被给予机会单独就驱逐决定向有关部门提出抗辩,则若干外国人收到相似决定这一事实不能得出存在"集体驱逐"的结论[*Alibaks and Others v. The Netherlands*, Commission decision; *Andric v. Sweden* (dec.); *Sultani v. France*, § 81]。然而,这并不意味着,如果已经对每一个当事人的个人情况进行了合理且客观的评估,"在认定该情形是否符合第四议定书第 4 条的规定时,便不再需要考虑驱逐令实施时的客观情况"(*Čonka v. Belgium*, § 59)。

4. 如果国家基于申诉人自己应受谴责的行为而未做出驱逐决定,那么将不会认为其违反了第四议定书第 4 条[*Berisha and Haljiti v. the former Yugoslav Republic of Macedonia*(dec.),本案中申诉人已经寻求过集体庇护并收到了一般决定;*Dritsas v. Italy*(dec.),本案中申诉人曾拒绝向警察出示身份证明,因此警方无法以申诉人的名字起草相关的驱逐命令]。

5. "驱逐"可以使用该议定书第 3 条(禁止驱逐公民)中的含义:根据第四议定书起草者的解释,"驱逐"一词应该被解释为"在当下使用的通用含义(即驱逐出某个地方)"(*Hirsi Jamaa and Others v. Italy*[GC],§174,参考第四议定书的准备文件)。

第三节 属人范围的适用:"外国人"的定义

6. 第四议定书第 4 条中的"外国人"不仅指在一国领域内合法居住的外国人,也指"那些并不拥有与国籍相关联的一切权利的人,无论他们是仅路过某国还是居住于此,无论他们是难民还是未经允许进入某国的人,也无论他们是无国籍人还是拥有另一国籍的人"(*Hirsi Jamaa and Others v. Italy*[GC],§174,第四议定书的准备文件;*Georgia v. Russia*(I)[GC],§168)。第四议定书第 4 条的措辞不同于议定书第 2 条("在一国领域内合法地"迁徙的自由),也不同于第七议定书第 1 条(驱逐"合法居住在一国领域内的"外国人的有关程序保障),它的适用与个人的法律地位无关。

7. 根据以上解释,本法院认为,第四议定书第 4 条适用的主体是基于各种原因居住在一国领土内的人(*Čonka v. Belgium* and *Sultani v. France*,这两起案件涉及寻求庇护者;*Georgia v. Russia*(I)[GC],§170,本案涉及移民,不考虑他们是否合法居住在被诉国),或在公海上被悬挂有被诉国国旗的船只拦截并遣送回国籍国的人(*Hirsi Jamaa and Others v. Italy*[GC])。

第四节 属地规则的适用及管辖问题

8. 公约机构依据第四议定书第 4 条处理的案件中,大部分案件涉及的外国人已经处于被诉国领土内[*K. G. v. Germany*, Commission decision;*Andric v. Sweden*(dec.);

Čonka v. Belgium]。因此,不涉及属地规则的适用问题。然而,在丹麦驻前德意志民主共和国大使馆人员被驱逐的案件中,本法院没有适用第四议定书第4条,因为本法院认为大使馆不属于丹麦领土的一部分(M. v. Denmark,此案中判定这一申诉不符合属地原则)。

9. 在希尔西·贾马等人诉意大利案(Hirsi Jamaa and Others v. Italy [GC])中,意大利当局在公海上对非法移民采取驱逐措施并将他们移交给利比亚。本法院需要考虑的是当驱逐发生在一国领土之外即公海上时,第四议定书第4条是否适用的问题。本法院认为无论是公约文本还是公约的准备文件都没有排除该条的域外适用。并且,如果第四议定书第4条仅适用于公约缔约国领土范围内集体驱逐的情况,就无法处理当下大量的移民问题。而且那些冒着生命危险,试图到达某国边境的海上移民,在被驱逐前,不像陆上移民那样可以享有被审查个人情况的权利。和"管辖权"的概念一样,驱逐的概念也主要是就领土的意义而言。然而,在某些例外情况下,如果某国在其领土外行使了管辖权,本法院有可能会认为该国进行域外管辖的行为也属于集体驱逐。本法院重申,海洋环境的特殊性并不代表它可以成为法外之地。因此得出结论:如果某国当局出于阻止移民入境的目的甚至出于将移民从该国遣送回他国的目的,在公海上行使主权,对外国人拦截驱逐,那么这一在公海上的驱逐行为可以被视为国家行使管辖权的行为,而这一管辖权的行使使得国家有可能承担第四议定书第4条所带来的责任(Hirsi Jamaa and Others v. Italy[GC],§§ 169 – 182)。

10. 在边境警察拦截并立即驱逐秘密入境移民的案件中,本法院采用了相同的方法,驳回了政府的反对意见——政府认为在拒绝外国人非法进入本国领土的案件中,不适用第四议定书第4条的属地管辖(Sharifi and Others v. Italy and Greece,§§ 210 – 213,此案涉及一项将移民遣送至希腊的驱逐命令。该案中,这群移民秘密乘船至意大利并在意大利安科纳港下船)。本法院认为没有必要考虑申诉人是在到达意大利领土之前还是之后被遣回,因为第四议定书第4条在这两种情况下都可以适用。

第五节 集体驱逐的案例

11. 本法院仅在4个案例中发现了违反第四议定书第4条的情形。其中的两个案件中(Čonka v. Belgium and Georgia v. Russia (I) [GC]),这些被驱逐的群体有着相同的出身(分别是来自斯洛伐克的罗马家庭和格鲁吉亚公民)。而在另外两个案件中(*Hirsi Jamaa and Others v. Italy* [GC] and *Sharifi and Others v. Italy and Greece*),被诉国在未适当审查群体个人身份的前提下遣返一整个群体(移民和寻求庇护者)。

12. 在贡加诉比利时案(*Čonka v. Belgium*)中,申诉人被遣送仅因为其在比利时的停留时间超过了3个月,而且驱逐命令并未提及申诉人的庇护申请或者对相关决定的申请。在这些情况下,考虑到与本案申诉人具有类似遭遇的大量人群,本法院认为,当局所采取的程序措施不能完全消除其对于该驱逐属于集体驱逐的怀疑。以下这些因素更进一步增强了这一怀疑:第一,在申诉人被遣送前,警方声明将会有此类措施并指示相关部门执行;第二,有关外国人被要求同时到达警察局;第三,警方下达的命令要求他们离开领土,对他们的逮捕令也采用了同样的措辞;第四,外国人联系律师非常困难;第五,庇护程序没有完成。总之,从外国人收到通知去警察局到他们被遣送这段时间,相关程序没有提供足够的保障证明当局已切实考虑过所涉外国人群体的个人情况。因而,本法院认为这违反了第四议定书第4条(*Čonka v. Belgium*, §§ 59 – 63)。

13. 在希尔西等人诉意大利案(*Hirsi Jamaa and Others v. Italy* [GC])中,当局未审查个人情况便将申诉人(索马里和厄立特里亚公民)移送到利比亚。在此期间,意大利当局没有进行过任何身份审查,仅让他们上船并将他们留在利比亚。而且,军用船只的工作人员没有接受过有关个人面谈的培训,也没有翻译或法律人员辅助他们进行工作。综上所述,本法院认为当局将申诉人遣送的行为具备集体性质,违反了第四议定书第4条(*Hirsi Jamaa and Others v. Italy* [GC], §§ 185 – 186)。

14. 在佐治亚诉俄罗斯案(*Georgia v. Russia* (*I*) [GC])中,俄罗斯法院命令驱逐数千名格鲁吉亚公民。本法院注意到,即使俄罗斯法院的决定是针对案件中每一个格鲁吉亚公民做出的,但是由于该驱逐行为发生在一段特殊时期(2006年9月至2007年1月),而且被驱逐的格鲁吉亚公民的人数较多,这就使得当局难以合理客观地审查每个人的情况。此外,俄罗斯已经实施了一项关于逮捕、拘留及驱逐格鲁吉亚公民的配套政策。即使本法院认可国家有权制定自己的移民政策,但国家不得以管制移民浪潮中面临的问题为正当理由,实施不符合公约的措施。综上,本法院认为,由于俄罗斯在颁布驱逐令之前,未针对个人具体情况进行合理且客观的审查,该行为违反了第四议定书第4条[*Georgia v. Russia* (*I*) [GC], §§ 171 – 178]。

15. 在沙里夫等人诉意大利和希腊案(*Sharifi and Others v. Italy and Greece*)中,意

大利当局主张,在都柏林体系中(该体系用于决定哪个欧盟成员国有义务审查第三国家公民在某一成员国的庇护申请),只有希腊有权就庇护申请做出决定,于是将一群人(阿富汗公民)集体遣送到希腊。然而,本法院认为意大利当局应该分析每个申诉人的具体情况,以确定在该问题上,希腊是否确实有管辖权,而不是草率地将他们全部驱逐。任何形式的不加区分的集体驱逐都不能通过引用都柏林体系得以合法化,驱逐行为在任何情况下都应当以符合公约的形式进行。同时,本法院还注意到了第三方或其他国际机构提交的一些报告。这些报告描述了意大利当局在亚得里亚海港以不加区分的方式将外国人遣送至希腊,并剥夺了他们的实体及程序权利的事实。根据这些资料,只有凭借边境警察的善意,被拦截的没有身份证明的人才能和翻译或者官方人员接触,而这些人能够向他们提供最低限度的有关庇护权的程序信息。他们经常会被立即送交至相关承运负责人手中以遣送到希腊。综上所述,本法院认为,申诉人被立即遣送的情况等同于不加区分的集体驱逐,违反了第四议定书第4条(同上,§§ 214 – 225)。

第六节　不属于集体驱逐的情况

16. 在苏坦尼诉法国案(*Sultani v. France*)中,本法院认为国内当局在执行驱逐的时候,已经对申诉人的情况进行了审查,申诉人可以对驱逐进行抗辩,而且国内当局不仅考虑了阿富汗的整体局势,还考虑了申诉人的个人情况以及遣送回阿富汗时他将面临的风险[*Sultani v. France*, § 83,由于根据《欧洲人权法院工作规则》第 39 条采取了临时措施,当局便没有执行将申诉人"集体遣送"回阿富汗的驱逐令;*Ghulami v. France* (dec.),在这起有关强制驱逐出境至阿富汗的案例中,也采用了与前案相同的措施;同时,还有其他不被认定为集体驱逐出境的案例,*Andric v. Sweden* (dec.);*Tahiri v. Sweden*, Commission decision]。

17. 如果当局在驱逐前对相关人员的具体情况进行了审查,那么即使之后将他们带到了警察局,并且将其中的一部分人集体驱逐,但当局下发的驱逐令及相关文件都是以正式的形式书写的,即采用了相同的措辞,并且在庇护程序中未特别参考之前的决定,那么本法院便不会认为当局违反了公约(*M. A. v. Cyprus*, §§ 252 – 255,该案中申诉人声称被连同一群叙利亚库尔德人一起受到集体驱逐;与该案中的情况形成对比的案

例是 *Čonka v. Belgium*，§ 10)。如果当局在所涉人员的个人情况方面做出了错误决定（尤其是申诉人，因为当他的庇护程序仍在进行时，驱逐出境的命令已经发出了），这一事实本身不能表明存在集体驱逐行为(*M. A. v. Cyprus*，§§ 134 and 254)。

18. 在克莱菲雅等人诉意大利案(*Khlaifia and Others v. Italy* [GC])中，法院认为第四议定书第 4 条在任何情况下都不保证个别审查的权利；当外国人可能真实且有效地对他或她被驱逐的意见表示反对，并且这些意见获得被告国当局适当的审查时(同上，§ 248)便符合了本条款的规定。本案涉及的申请人经历了两次身份验证。在这一过程中，他们的国籍得到了确认，同时如果他们愿意，便一直拥有对被驱逐的意见提出反对的真实且有效的可能性。虽然拒绝入境令在起草时使用了相似的术语(仅在移民的个人信息方面存在差别)，并且在同一时间来自同一个国家(突尼斯)的大量移民被驱逐出境，但本法院认为拒绝入境令相对简单和格式化性质可以通过下列事实被解释清楚：申请人没有任何有效的旅行证件，且没有声称他们受到了虐待，或者他们被驱逐的决定存在任何法律问题。因此，这些命令相对简单和格式化，其本身是合理的。在该案的具体情况下，同时驱逐三名申请人不能得出他们被集体驱逐的结论。

第七节 与公约第 13 条的关系

19. 公约第 13 条中有效救济的概念要求救济可以阻止当局执行那些不符合公约规定且执行后果通常无法挽回的措施。因此，在审查采取的措施是否符合公约之前，国内当局若执行了此类措施，那么该行为将是不符合公约第 13 条规定的(*Čonka v. Belgium*，§ 79)。这意味着一项救济如果要符合公约第 13 条和第四议定书第 4 条的要求，那么该救济必须具有中止的效力(*Čonka v. Belgium*，§§ 77 - 85，本案涉及在最高行政法院面前的有效救济方式)。然而，应当注意的是，当申请人不主张其目的国存在违背公约第 2 条和第 3 条所保障的权利的真实风险时(*Khlaifia and Others v. Italy* [GC]，§281)，驱逐决定缺乏中止效力本身并不违背第 13 条和第四议定书第 4 条的规定。在这种情况下，公约没有对国家施加绝对义务，要求其具备自动中止救济，但是要求相关个人拥有对驱逐决定提出质疑的有效可能性，并由独立和公正的国内审判机构来对其申诉进行充分的全面审查(同上，§279)。

20. 国内程序缺失,导致潜在的寻求庇护者无法基于公约(公约第 3 条——禁止酷刑和不人道或有辱人格的待遇,以及第四议定书第 4 条)向有关当局提起诉讼,而且其请求无法在其被驱逐前得到全面、严格的评估,此时就有可能违反公约第 13 条(*Hirsi Jamaa v. Italy* [GC],§§ 201 - 207; *Sharifi and Others v. Italy and Greece*,§§ 240 - 243)。在某些情况下,执行集体驱逐措施会阻碍涉案人员申请庇护或者寻求符合第 13 条要求的其他国内救济(*Sharifi and Others v. Italy and Greece*,§ 242)。

21. 不过,国内是否缺乏有效、可行的救济这一问题本身也在第四议定书第 4 条的审查范围之内,因此本法院认为在个案中没有必要再另行依据公约第 13 条进行审查(*Georgia v. Russia* (I) [GC],§ 212)。

援引案例一览

本指南援引的判例法涉及欧洲人权法院的判决或裁定以及欧洲人权委员会的决定或报告。

除非另行指明,所有参考皆是本法院审判庭依法做出的判决。缩写"(dec.)"是指该处援引为本法院裁定,"[GC]"是指该案件由大审判庭审判。

本指南电子版中援引案例的超链接直接跳转 HUDOC 数据库⟨http://hudoc.echr.coe.int⟩。该数据库提供本法院(包括大审判庭、审判庭和委员会的判决、裁定和相关案例、咨询意见以及案例法信息注解中的法律总结)、委员会(决定和报告)和部长委员会(决议)的判例法。欧洲委员会的某些决定不在 HUDOC 数据库中;它们仅在相关欧洲人权法院年鉴的纸质版中可以找到。

本法院以英语和/或法语这两种官方语言发布判决和裁定。HUDOC 也包含许多重要案例的近 30 种非官方言语的翻译,以及由第三方制作的大约 100 个在线案例汇总的链接。

(注:为了避免重复,本章所附的相关案例索引没有在中文部分进行翻译,读者可在对应的英文部分阅读。)

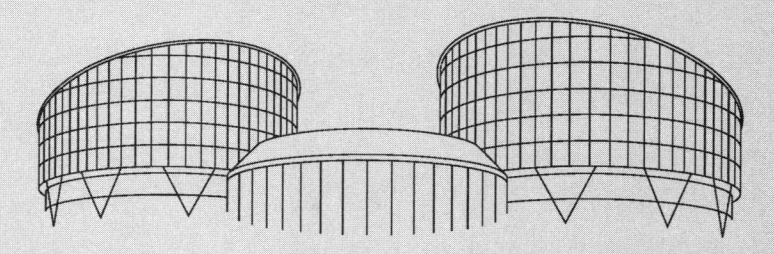

EUROPEAN COURT OF HUMAN RIGHTS
COUR EUROPÉENNE DES DROITS DE L'HOMME

Chapter X   Guide on Article 4 of Protocol No.4 to the European Convention on Human Rights Prohibition of Collective Expulsions of Aliens

Updated on 15 December 2016

COUNCIL OF EUROPE

CONSEIL DE L'EUROPE

Publishers or organisations wishing to reproduce this report (or a translation thereof) in print or online are asked to contact publishing@echr.coe.int for further instructions.

This Guide has been prepared by the Research and Library Division, within the Directorate of the Jurisconsult, and does not bind the Court. The text was finalised on 30 April 2016 and updated on 15 December 2016; it may be subject to editorial revision.

The document is available for downloading at ⟨www.echr.coe.int⟩ (Case-Law-Case-Law Analysis-Case-Law Guides).

For publication updates please follow the Court's Twitter account at ⟨https:/twitter.com/echrpublication⟩.

©Council of Europe/European Court of Human Rights,2017

Note to readers

This Guide is part of the series of Case-Law Guides published by the European Court of Human Rights (hereafter "the Court", "the European Court" or "the Strasbourg Court") to inform legal practitioners about the fundamental judgments delivered by the Strasbourg Court. This particular Guide analyses and sums up the case-law on Article 4 of Protocol No. 4 to the European Convention on Human Rights (hereafter "the Convention" or "the European Convention") until 15 December 2016. Readers will find the key principles in this area and the relevant precedents.

The case-law cited has been selected among the leading, major, and/or recent judgments and decisions. *

The Court's judgments serve not only to decide those cases brought before the Court but, more generally, to elucidate, safeguard and develop the rules instituted by the Convention, thereby contributing to the observance by the States of the engagements undertaken by them as Contracting Parties (*Ireland v. the United Kingdom*, 18 January 1978, § 154, Series A no. 25.). The mission of the system set up by the Convention is thus to determine, in the general interest, issues of public policy, thereby raising the standards of protection of human rights and extending human rights jurisprudence throughout the community of the Convention States (*Konstantin Markin v. Russia* [GC], no. 30078/06, § 89, ECHR 2012).

---

* The case-law cited may be in either or both of the official languages (English and French) of the Court and the European Commission of Human Rights. Unless otherwise indicated, all references are to a judgment on the merits delivered by a Chamber of the Court. The abbreviation "(dec.)" indicates that the citation is of a decision of the Court and "[GC]" that the case was heard by the Grand Chamber.

> Article 4 of Protocol No. 4 – Prohibition of collective expulsion of aliens
> "Collective expulsion of aliens is prohibited."

I . Origins and purpose of the Article

1. When Protocol No. 4 was drafted in 1963, it was the first international treaty to address collective expulsion. Its explanatory report reveals that the purpose of Article 4 was to formally prohibit "collective expulsions of aliens of the kind which was a matter of recent history". Thus, it was "agreed that the adoption of [Article 4] and paragraph 1 of Article 3 (prohibition of expulsion of nationals) could in no way be interpreted as in any way justifying measures of collective expulsion which may have been taken in the past" (*Hirsi Jamaa and Others v. Italy* [GC], § 174).

2. The core purpose of the Article is to prevent States from being able to remove a certain number of aliens without examining their personal circumstances and, consequently, without enabling them to put forward their arguments against the measure taken by the relevant authority (ibid., § 177).

II . The definition of "collective expulsion"

3. The well-established definition of "collective expulsion" is "any measure of the competent authorities compelling aliens as a group to leave the country, except where such a measure is taken after and on the basis of a reasonable and objective examination of the particular cases of each individual alien of the group" [*Andric v. Sweden* (dec.); *Čonka v. Belgium*, § 59; *Sultani v. France*, § 81; and the Commission decisions *Becker v. Denmark*; *K. G. v. Germany*; *O. and Others v. Luxembourg*; *Alibaks and Others v. the Netherlands*; *Tahiri v. Sweden*]. The fact that a number of aliens receive similar decisions

does not lead to the conclusion that there is a "collective expulsion" when each person concerned has been given the opportunity to put arguments against his expulsion to the competent authorities on an individual basis [*Alibaks and Others v. the Netherlands*, Commission decision; *Andric v. Sweden* (dec.); *Sultani v. France*, § 81]. That does not mean, however, that where there has been a reasonable and objective examination of the particular case of each individual "the background to the execution of the expulsion orders plays no further role in determining whether there has been compliance with Article 4 of Protocol No. 4" (*Čonka v. Belgium*, § 59).

4. Furthermore, there will be no violation of Article 4 of Protocol No. 4 if the lack of an expulsion decision made on an individual basis is the consequence of an applicant's own culpable conduct (*Berisha and Haljiti v. the former Yugoslav Republic of Macedonia* (dec.), where the applicants had pursued a joint asylum procedure and thus received a single common decision; *Dritsas v. Italy* (dec.), where the applicants had refused to show their identity papers to the police and thus the latter had been unable to draw up expulsion orders in the applicants' names).

5. "Expulsion" can be taken to have the same meaning as it has under Article 3 of the Protocol (prohibition of expulsion of nationals): according to the drafters of Protocol No. 4, the word "expulsion" should be interpreted "in the generic meaning, in current use (to drive away from a place)" (*Hirsi Jamaa and Others v. Italy* [GC], § 174, with references to the *travaux préparatoires* of Protocol No. 4). In *Khlaifia and Others v. Italy* [GC], the Italian Government emphasised that the procedure which the applicants had been subjected to was classified in domestic law as a "refusal of entry with removal" and not as an "expulsion". The Court, however, saw no reason to depart from its earlier established definition and noted that there was no doubt that the applicants, who had been on Italian territory (in a reception centre on the island of Lampedusa and later transferred to ships moored in Palermo harbor), were removed from that State and returned to Tunisia against their will, thus constituting an "expulsion" within the meaning of Article 4 of Protocol No. 4 (ibid., §§ 243–244).

III. The personal scope of application: the definition of "aliens"

6. The "aliens" to whom Article 4 of Protocol No. 4 refers are not only those lawfully residing within the territory, but also "all those who have no actual right to nationality in a State, whether they are merely passing through a country or reside or are domiciled in it, whether they are refugees or entered the country on their own initiative, or whether they are stateless or possess another nationality" [Hirsi Jamaa and Others v. Italy [GC], § 174, with references to the *travaux préparatoires* of Protocol No. 4; Georgia v. Russia (I) [GC], § 168]. The wording of Article 4 of Protocol No. 4 does not refer to the legal situation of the persons concerned, unlike Article 2 of the Protocol (freedom of movement of persons "lawfully within the territory of a State") and Article 1 of Protocol No. 7 (procedural safeguards relating to expulsion of aliens "lawfully resident in the territory of a State").

7. In accordance with that interpretation, in the cases that have been brought before it the Court has applied Article 4 of Protocol No. 4 to persons who, for various reasons, were residing within the territory of a State (asylum-seekers in *Čonka v. Belgium* and *Sultani v. France*; migrants in *Georgia v. Russia* (I) [GC], § 170, irrespective of whether they were lawfully resident in the respondent State or not) or were intercepted on the high seas by ships flying the flag of the respondent State and returned to the originating State (*Hirsi Jamaa and Others v. Italy* [GC]).

IV. Questions of territorial applicability and jurisdiction

8. The majority of the cases brought before the Convention organs under Article 4 of Protocol No. 4 involved aliens who were already on the territory of the respondent State [*K. G. v. Germany*, Commission decision; *Andric v. Sweden* (dec.); *Čonka v. Belgium*].

Therefore, no question of territorial applicability arose. However, Article 4 of Protocol No. 4 was held not to apply to an incident involving individuals expelled from the Danish embassy in the former German Democratic Republic, as the embassy premises were not part of Danish territory (*M. v. Denmark*, Commission decision declaring this complaint incompatible *ratione materiae*).

9. *Hirsi Jamaa and Others v. Italy* [GC] concerned push-back operations on the high seas and transfer of irregular migrants to Libya by the Italian authorities. The Court had to consider whether Article 4 of Protocol No. 4 applied when the removal took place outside national territory, namely on the high seas. The Court observed that neither the text nor the *travaux préparatoires* of the Convention precluded the extraterritorial application of that provision. Furthermore, if Article 4 of Protocol No. 4 were to apply only to collective expulsions from the national territory of the States Parties to the Convention, a significant component of contemporary migratory patterns would not fall within the ambit of that provision and migrants having taken to the sea, often risking their lives, and not having managed to reach the borders of a State, would not be entitled to an examination of their personal circumstances before being expelled, unlike those travelling by land. The notion of expulsion, like the concept of "jurisdiction", was clearly principally territorial. Where, however, the Court found that a State had, exceptionally, exercised its jurisdiction outside its national territory, it could accept that the exercise of extraterritorial jurisdiction by that State had taken the form of collective expulsion. The Court also reiterated that the special nature of the maritime environment did not make it an area outside the law. It therefore concluded that the removal of aliens carried out in the context of interception on the high seas by the authorities of a State in the exercise of their sovereign authority, the effect of which is to prevent migrants from reaching the borders of the State or even to push them back to another State, constitutes an exercise of jurisdiction which engages the responsibility of the State in question under Article 4 of Protocol No. 4 (ibid., §§ 169–182).

10. The Court followed the same approach regarding the interception and immediate deportation by the border police of migrants who had arrived clandestinely, therefore rejecting the Government's objection that Article 4 of Protocol No. 4 was not applicable

ratione materiae to cases of refusal to allow entry to the national territory to persons who arrived illegally (*Sharifi and Others v. Italy and Greece*, §§ 210 – 213, concerning deportation to Greece of migrants who had clandestinely boarded vessels for Italy and arrived in the Italian port of Ancona). The Court did not consider it necessary to determine whether the applicants had been returned after reaching the Italian territory or before, since Article 4 of Protocol No. 4 was in any event applicable to both situations.

V. Examples of collective expulsions

11. The Court has found a violation of Article 4 of Protocol No. 4 only in four cases. In two of them (*Čonka v. Belgium* and *Georgia v. Russia* (*I*) [GC]), the individuals targeted for expulsion had the same origin (Roma families from Slovakia and Georgian nationals, respectively). In the other two cases (*Hirsi Jamaa and Others v. Italy* [GC] and *Sharifi and Others v. Italy and Greece*), the violation found involved the return of an entire group of people (migrants and asylum-seekers) without adequate verification of the individual identities of the group members.

12. In *Čonka v. Belgium* the applicants were deported solely on the basis that their stay in Belgium had exceeded three months and the orders made no reference to their application for asylum or to the decisions on that issue. In those circumstances and in view of the large number of persons of the same origin who had suffered the same fate as the applicants, the Court considered that the procedure followed did not enable it to eliminate all doubt that the expulsion might have been collective. That doubt was reinforced by a series of factors: *firstly*, prior to the applicants' deportation, the political authorities concerned had announced that there would be operations of that kind and given instructions to the relevant authority for their implementation; *secondly*, all the aliens concerned had been required to attend the police station at the same time; *thirdly*, the orders served on them requiring them to leave the territory and for their arrest had been couched in identical terms; *fourthly*, it had been very difficult for the aliens to contact a lawyer; *lastly*, the asylum procedure had

not been completed. In short, at no stage during the period between the service of the notice on the aliens to attend the police station and their expulsion had the procedure afforded sufficient guarantees demonstrating that the personal circumstances of each of those concerned had been genuinely and individually taken into account. In conclusion, there had been a violation of Article 4 of Protocol No 4 (ibid., §§ 59–63).

13. In *Hirsi Jamaa and Others v. Italy* [GC] the transfer of the applicants (Somali and Eritrean nationals) to Libya had been carried out without any examination of each individual situation. No identification procedure had been carried out by the Italian authorities, who had merely embarked the applicants and then disembarked them in Libya. Moreover, the personnel aboard the military ships were not trained to conduct individual interviews and were not assisted by interpreters or legal advisers. The Court concluded that the removal of the applicants had been of a collective nature, in breach of Article 4 of Protocol No. 4 (ibid., §§ 185–186).

14. *Georgia v. Russia (I)* [GC] concerned Russian courts' orders to expel thousands of Georgian nationals. The Court noted that, even though a court decision had been made in respect of each Georgian national, the conduct of the expulsion procedures during that period (September 2006 January 2007) and the number of Georgian nationals expelled made it impossible to carry out a reasonable and objective examination of the particular case of each individual. Furthermore, Russia had implemented a coordinated policy of arresting, detaining and expelling Georgian nationals. Even though the Court did not call into question the right of States to establish their own immigration policies, problems with managing migratory flows could not justify recourse to practices not compatible with the Convention. The Court concluded that the expulsions of Georgian nationals had not been carried out on the basis of a reasonable and objective examination of the particular case of each individual and that this had amounted to an administrative practice in breach of Article 4 of Protocol No. 4 (ibid., §§ 171–178).

15. In *Sharifi and Others v. Italy and Greece*, Italy had deported certain individuals (Afghan nationals) to Greece, while claiming that only Greece had jurisdiction under the Dublin system (which serves to determine which European Union Member State is

responsible for examining an asylum application lodged in one of the Member States by a third-country national) to rule on the possible asylum requests. The Court, however, considered that the Italian authorities ought to have carried out an individualised analysis of the situation of each applicant in order to establish whether Greece did indeed have jurisdiction on this point, rather than deporting them all. No form of collective and indiscriminate returns could be justified by reference to the Dublin system, which had, in all cases, to be applied in a manner compatible with the Convention. Furthermore, the Court took note of the concurring reports submitted by the intervening third parties or obtained from other international sources, which described episodes of indiscriminate return to Greece by the Italian border authorities in the ports of the Adriatic Sea, depriving the persons concerned of any substantive and procedural rights. According to these sources, it was only through the goodwill of the border police that intercepted persons without papers were put in contact with an interpreter and officials capable of providing them with the minimum information concerning the procedures relating to the right of asylum. More often than not, they were immediately handed over to the captains of ferries for return to Greece. In the light of all these elements, the Court concluded that the immediate returns to which the applicants had been subjected amounted to collective and indiscriminate expulsions in breach of Article 4 of Protocol No. 4 (ibid., §§ 214–225).

VI. Examples of measures not amounting to collective expulsions

16. In *Sultani v. France*, the Court found that the applicant's situation had been examined individually. He had been able to set out the arguments against his expulsion and the domestic authorities had taken account, not only of the overall context in Afghanistan, but also of the applicant's statements concerning his personal situation and the risks he would allegedly run in the event of a return to his country of origin (ibid., § 83, where the deportation of the applicant on a "collective flight" to Afghanistan had not been

enforced due to the interim measure indicated by the Court on the basis of Rule 39 of its Rules of Court; *Ghulami v. France* (dec.), where the same approach was followed concerning an enforced deportation to Afghanistan; see also, for no appearance of a collective expulsion, *Andric v. Sweden* (dec.); *Tahiri v. Sweden*, Commission decision).

17. Where the persons concerned have had an individual examination of their personal circumstances, no violation will be found, even if they had been taken together to police headquarters, some had been deported in groups and the deportation orders and the corresponding letters had been couched in formulaic and, therefore, identical terms and had not specifically referred to the earlier decisions regarding the asylum procedure (*M. A. v. Cyprus*, §§ 252 –255, concerning an individual who claimed to have been subjected to a collective expulsion operation with a group of Syrian Kurds; compare the circumstances in *Čonka v. Belgium*, § 10). The mere fact that a mistake had been made in relation to the status of some of the persons concerned (in particular the applicant, since the deportation order had been issued when his asylum proceedings were still pending) could not be taken as showing that there had been a collective expulsion (*M. A. v. Cyprus*, §§ 134 and 254).

18. In *Khlaifia and Others v. Italy* [GC], the Court clarified that Article 4 of Protocol No. 4 does not guarantee the right to an individual interview in all circumstances; the requirements of this provision may be satisfied where each alien has a genuine and effective possibility of submitting arguments against his or her expulsion, and where those arguments are examined in an appropriate manner by the authorities of the respondent State (ibid., § 248). The applicants had undergone identification on two occasions, their nationality had been established and they had at all times had a genuine and effective possibility of submitting arguments against their expulsion had they wished to do so. Although the refusal-of-entry orders had been drafted in comparable terms-only differing as to the personal data of each migrant-and despite the fact that a large number of migrants from the same country (Tunisia) had been expelled at the relevant time, the Court found that the relatively simple and standardised nature of the orders could be explained by the fact that the

applicants did not have any valid travel documents and had not alleged either that they feared ill-treatment in the event of their return or that there were any other legal impediments to their expulsion. It was therefore not unreasonable in itself for those orders to have been relatively simple and standardized. In the particular circumstances of the case, it followed that the virtually simultaneous removal of the three applicants did not lead to the conclusion that their expulsion was collective (ibid., §§ 249 – 254).

VII. Relationship with Article 13 of the Convention

19. The notion of an effective remedy under Article 13 of the Convention requires that the remedy may prevent the execution of measures that are contrary to the Convention and whose effects are potentially irreversible. Consequently, it is inconsistent with Article 13 for such measures to be executed before the national authorities have examined whether they are compatible with the Convention (*Čonka v. Belgium*, § 79). This means that a remedy must have a suspensive effect to meet the requirements of Article 13 of the Convention taken in conjunction with Article 4 of Protocol No. 4 (ibid., §§ 77 – 85, concerning the effectiveness of the remedies before the *Conseil d'État*). However, it should be noted that the lack of suspensive effect of a removal decision does not in itself constitute a violation of Article 13 taken together with Article 4 of Protocol No. 4, where an applicant does not allege that there is a real risk of a violation of the rights guaranteed by Articles 2 or 3 in the destination country (*Khlaifia and Others v. Italy* [GC], § 281). In such situation the Convention does not impose an absolute obligation on a State to guarantee an automatically suspensive remedy, but merely requires that the person concerned should have an effective possibility of challenging the expulsion decision by having a sufficiently thorough examination of his or her complaints carried out by an independent and impartial domestic forum (ibid., § 279).

20. The absence of any domestic procedure to enable potential asylum-seekers to lodge their Convention-based complaints (under Article 3 of the Convention-prohibition of torture

and inhuman or degrading treatment-and Article 4 of Protocol No. 4) with a competent authority and to obtain a thorough and rigorous assessment of their requests before the enforcement of the removal may also lead to a violation of Article 13 of the Convention (*Hirsi Jamaa v. Italy* [GC], §§ 201 – 207; *Sharifi and Others v. Italy and Greece*, §§ 240 – 243). In some circumstances, there is a clear link between the enforcement of collective expulsions and the fact that the persons concerned were effectively prevented from applying for asylum or from having access to any other domestic procedure which met the requirements of Article 13 (ibid., § 242).

21. However, since the lack of effective and accessible remedies is also examined under Article 4 of Protocol No. 4 on its own, the Court may also consider that in a particular case there is no need to examine this aspect separately under Article 13 of the Convention (*Georgia v. Russia (I)* [GC], § 212).

List of cited cases

The case-law cited in this Guide refers to judgments or decisions delivered by the Court and to decisions or reports of the European Commission of Human Rights ("the Commission").

Unless otherwise indicated, all references are to a judgment on the merits delivered by a Chamber of the Court. The abbreviation "(dec.)" indicates that the citation is of a decision of the Court and "[GC]" that the case was heard by the Grand Chamber.

The hyperlinks to the cases cited in the electronic version of the Guide are directed to theHUDOC database (⟨http://hudoc.echr.coe.int⟩) which provides access to the case-law of the Court (Grand Chamber, Chamber and Committee judgments and decisions, communicated cases, advisory opinions and legal summaries from the Case-Law Information Note) and of the Commission (decisions and reports), and to the resolutions of the Committee of Ministers.

The Court delivers its judgments and decisions in English and/or French, its two official languages. HUDOC also contains translations of many important cases intomore than thirty non-official languages, and links to around one hundred online case-law collections produced by third parties.

— A —

Alibaks and Others v. the Netherlands, no. 14209/88, Commission decision of 16 December, Decisions and Reports 59

Andric v. Sweden (dec.), no. 45917/99, 23 February 1999

— B —

Becker v. Denmark, no. 7011/75, Commission decision of 3 October 1975, Decisions and Reports 4

Berisha and Haljiti v. the former Yugoslav Republic of Macedonia (dec.), no. 18670/03, ECHR 2005 – VIII (extracts)

— C —

Čonka v. Belgium, no. 51564/99, ECHR 2002 - I

— D —

Dritsas v. Italy (dec), no. 2344/02, 1 February 2011

— G —

Georgia v. Russia (I) [GC], no. 13255/07, ECHR 2014 (extracts)

Ghulami v. France (dec.), no. 45302/05, 7 April 2009

— H —

Hirsi Jamaa and Others v. Italy [GC], no. 27765/09, ECHR 2012

— K —

K. G. v. Germany, 7704/76, Commission decision of 1 March 1977

Khlaifia and Others v. Italy [GC], no. 16483/12, ECHR 2016 (extracts)

— M —

M. v. Denmark, no. 17392/90, Commission decision of 14 October 1992

M. A. v. Cyprus, no. 41872/10, ECHR 2013 (extracts)

— O —

O. and Others v. Luxembourg, no. 7757/77, Commission decision of 3 March 1978

— S —

Sharifi and Others v. Italy and Greece, no. 16643/09, 21 October 2014

Sultani v. France, no. 45223/05, ECHR 2007 - IV (extracts)

— T —

Tahiri v. Sweden, no. 25129/94, Commission decision of 11 January 1995